M000284242

JOHNSON'S DICTIONARY

An Anthology

JOHNSON'S DICTIONARY
An Anthology

Selected, edited and with an Introduction by

DAVID CRYSTAL

PENGUIN BOOKS

ALLEN LANE
THE PENGUIN PRESS

Published by the Penguin Group
Penguin Books Ltd, 80 Strand, London WC2R ORL, England
Penguin Group (USA) Inc., 375 Hudson Street, New York, New York 10014, USA
Penguin Group (Canada), 10 Alcorn Avenue, Toronto, Ontario, Canada M4V 3B2
(a division of Pearson Penguin Canada Inc.)
Penguin Ireland, 25 St Stephen's Green, Dublin 2, Ireland (a division of Penguin Books Ltd)
Penguin Group (Australia), 250 Camberwell Road, Camberwell, Victoria 3124, Australia
(a division of Pearson Australia Group Pty Ltd)
Penguin Books India Pvt Ltd, 11 Community Centre, Panchsheel Park, New Delhi – 110 017, India
Penguin Group (NZ), cnr Airborne and Rosedale Roads, Albany, Auckland 1310, New Zealand
(a division of Pearson New Zealand Ltd)
Penguin Books (South Africa) (Pty) Ltd, 24 Sturdee Avenue, Rosebank 2196, South Africa

Penguin Books Ltd, Registered Offices: 80 Strand, London WC2R ORL, England

www.penguin.com

This selection first published 2005
1

Set in 9.75/12.25 pt PostScript Minion
Typeset by Rowland Phototypesetting Ltd, Bury St Edmunds, Suffolk
Printed in England by Clays Ltd, St Ives plc

ISBN 0-713-99887-3

Contents

Introduction

The concept of an anthology is routine with reference to such genres as poetry and the short story, but it is unusual, to say the least, in relation to a dictionary. For a dictionary is a tool, compiled to solve a problem of the moment – to check a spelling, a pronunciation, a meaning, a point of usage. It is not there for browsing. Who, apart from lexicographers suffering from withdrawal symptoms, would ever want to read for pleasure a selection of entries from – a dictionary? For such an exercise to succeed, the source work would have to be of very special historical significance, and its compiler a person whose literary or linguistic standing was sufficiently pre-eminent to demand respect, and sufficiently idiosyncratic to evoke curiosity. There would probably also need to be a special occasion.

All three criteria are satisfied in the case of Samuel Johnson's *Dictionary of the English Language*. It was written at a critical time in English linguistic history, at the very beginning of a period which would introduce prescriptive principles into English language study, and when the demand for a standard language was at its strongest. It was written – as James Boswell claims in the final sentence of his biography – by a man 'whose talents, acquirements, and virtues, were so extraordinary, that the more his character is considered, the more he will be regarded by the present age, and by posterity, with admiration and reverence', a judgement with which few would quarrel. Who else, after all, has been given the sobriquet of a genre in the way that 'Dictionary Johnson' was? And the first edition of the *Dictionary* was published in 1755 – thus motivating those who believe in the significance of round numbers to treat 2005 as a year of special memorial consequence.

So, how does one anthologize a lexicographer? I believe, in the same way that one would a poet. The editor has to look for works (entries, in the lexicographer's case) that are acknowledged to be the writer's best, or which illustrate special features of style, or points of biographical interest, such as upbringing, milieu, beliefs – or, indeed, eccentricities. There will be a concern to be genuinely representative of the oeuvre as a whole. Some works (entries) might be chosen because they illustrate a stage in the author's career, or a particular stage in literary – or, in this case, linguistic – history. And some will be there because, quite simply, the editor likes them. Background information about the writer's intentions will also be useful: just as the Preface to the *Lyrical Ballads* was invaluable in informing our thinking about William Wordsworth and Samuel Taylor Coleridge, so Johnson's Plan and Preface, as well as the relevant parts of Boswell's biography, provide an indispensable perspective for reading the *Dictionary* entries (which is why they are included in this book).

Applying these criteria to the present case, several types of entry in the *Dictionary* immediately clamour for inclusion, and some of them have to be regretfully declined. Within the latter category I would place the kinds of lengthy entry which indeed live up to Johnson's characterization of his task as 'drudgery' (see the entry at *lexicographer*, and also *dull* sense 8). Every lexicographer knows what these are – the need to handle with precision the grammatical words of the language (such as *what*, *as*, *of*, *but*), the everyday words (*one*, *two*, *three*, *January*, *December*), the remarkable number of words beginning with such prefixes as *un-* and *self-*, or those 'light verbs' – verbs of 'vague and indeterminate' use, as he puts it in his Preface – which play an important part in English idiom, such as *make* and *do*. In Johnson's case, the longest entry is for *take*, whose 134 uses (including phrasal verbs) take up 11 full columns of print; but a special mention should be made of the verbs *set* (88 uses), *put* (80), *stand* (69), *go* and *run* (both 68). Such mammoth entries were unprecedented in English dictionaries, and they are remarkable in their attention to semantic nuance, but they can hardly be illustrated in a small anthology, which therefore loses in representativeness what it gains in interest by focusing on shorter entries. However, I have included a few of Johnson's medium-length entries – such as *clear*, *foot* and *manner* – to convey something of the flavour of his more ambitious treatments, and I have included a sprinkling of the shorter grammatical entries (such as *he*, *that* and *the*).

THE INDIVIDUALIST

But how to select among the thousands of remaining entries?[1] There are of course a number which have to be included because they have achieved a certain degree of notoriety due to the personal opinions expressed in their definitions. Characterizing them as instances of 'capricious and humourous indulgence' (p. xlii), Boswell lists *Tory*, *Whig*, *pension*, *oats*, *excise*, 'and a few more' – by which he means such entries as *lexicographer*, *patron*, *leader* (sense 4), *reformation* and *reformer*, *aleconner*, *palmistry* and *stockjobber*. As a characteristic of Johnson's lexicography, their fame far exceeds their significance; some routinely appear in books of quotations. There are less than twenty of them in the whole work, and the most famous one of all – *oats* defined as 'grain, which in England is generally given to horses, but in Scotland supports the people' – was almost certainly one of those in-jokes that lexicographers love to bury in their books. It would have been no more than a friendly dig at his amanuenses, five of whom, as Boswell points out (p. xxxiii) were from Scotland, and whose influence is reflected in dozens of allusions to Scottish English throughout the *Dictionary*. A similar sympathy pervades his famous definition of *lexicographer*: I have never met one of these individuals who did not delight in the characterization of their profession as that of a 'harmless drudge'.[2]

These entries illustrate Johnson's authorial fingerprints on a genre which in later times is notable for the absence of personality traits. But they are far outnumbered by other signs of individualism. He repeatedly cites his own limitations. 'Of this word I know not the meaning', he says of *dogbolt*, and similar sentiments are to be found in several entries, such as *etch*, *minnock*, *skilt* and *stammel* (though he had tracked down a meaning for this last item by the fourth edition). The derivation of *tatterdemalion* is described as '*tatter* and I know not what'. Of deciding between *tricker* and *trigger*, he comments 'I know not which is right'. Of *plication* all he can say is that it is 'used somewhere in [Samuel Richardson's] *Clarissa*'. Such honesty is endearing, and it is conscious honesty, for he repeatedly acknowledges his limitations in his Preface. At the same time, we have sometimes to take his self-dismissal with a pinch of salt. Of the verb *bear*, for example, he says, 'This is a word used with such latitude, that it is not easily explained.' He then goes on to distinguish, with impressive precision, thirty-eight uses – too many to illustrate in the present selection.

He does not shirk to acknowledge other people's limitations too. If he feels that someone uses a word carelessly, he says so: of *hyper* as a noun, he comments drily, Matthew Prior (whom he quotes using it) 'did not know the meaning of the word'. He is especially scathing about some of his etymological sources. Of *scamble*, he says, 'This word, which is scarcely in use, has much exercised the etymological sagacity of *Meric Casaubon*; but, as is usual, to no purpose' (see also the etymological note at *spruce*). Of *quaff*, he says, '*Junius*, with his usual idleness of conjecture, derives it from the Greek.' He is severe in his judgements about individual words, and his linguistic temperament permeates the dictionary: *dissever* 'ought to be ejected from our language'; *finesse* is 'an unnecessary word'; *twittletwattle* is 'A vile word'; *opiniatry* is a word 'not yet received, nor is it wanted'; *shab* gets three barrels – 'a low barbarous cant word'; and of *precarious* he asserts 'No word is more unskilfully used.' There are words he favours too – *impartible*, for example, 'is elegant, though used by few writers' – but his recorded dislikes seriously exceed his likes.

He is quite open about his preferences. Foreign loan words, in particular, have to be kept under control, as he asserts in his Preface:

> The words which our authours have introduced by their knowledge of foreign languages, or ignorance of their own, by vanity or wantonness, by compliance with fashion, or lust of innovation, I have registred as they occurred, though commonly only to censure them, and warn others against the folly of naturalizing useless foreigners to the injury of the natives.

And censure he does. Thus of *souvenance* he comments: 'A French word which with many more is now happily disused.' He is suspicious of noun-to-verb conversion too: *to proselyte* is 'A bad word'; *to proverb* is 'Not a good word' (notwithstanding the quotations accompanying it from Milton and Shakespeare). He is ready to defer to custom when the evidence starts to pile up against him, as can be seen by his comments at *friend* sense 3, *outragious* and *strew*. But the two principles are contradictory, and the tension between them can be sensed throughout the *Dictionary*.

THE OBSERVER

Alongside Johnson the opinionator, there is Johnson the observer, and his observations include far more than what is strictly linguistic. Although he distances himself in his Preface from proper names (p. 26), he is very much an encyclopedist by temperament, and the *Dictionary* contains a great deal of real-world (what he calls 'extradictionary') information. 'I have determined to consult the best writers for explanations real as well as verbal', he says in his Plan, and some of his quotations are indeed extensive, especially in the domain of science: we find a 750-word explanation for *comet*, and a 400-word one on *ammoniac*; he lists 84 species at *pear*, 27 at *plant* and 34 at *vine*. These entries are too large for inclusion in this anthology, but a hint of his encyclopedic interests can be seen in the items I have included relating to manufactured products (such as *cardmatch*, *rocket*), social structure, both secular and religious (*Bilingsgate*, *board-wages*, *cardinal*, *stocah*), and contemporary beliefs and practices (*all fours*, *plenist*, *vacuist*, *tarantula*, *toad*, *electricity*, *scarify*, *parlour*). A good example of a straightforward encyclopedic entry is *Doomsday-book*.

But Johnson is above all a linguistic observer; and as most readers of this anthology will be language enthusiasts too, it seemed appropriate to include all the entries where he makes a point of linguistic interest, such as *many-languaged*, *nominative*, *solecism*, *style*, *syncopist* and *verb*. I have included all his letter-openers (*A*, *B*, etc.), because of the information they contain about contemporary spelling.[3] And I have also included most of the entries which make an observation about regional usage. There are not many of them, but they fall into three main types: words from his home town and county, Lichfield and Staffordshire (*gnarled*, *goldfinch*, *moreland*, *orrery*, *shaw*), occasional observations about other English dialects (*amper*, *atter*, *haver*, *onset*), and above all usages from Scottish English (*mow*, *scambler*, *sponk*), which are common enough to suggest that his amanuenses were being used for far more than their copy-writing skills.

The verbal dimension of his enquiry into the best writers raises a problem. Johnson is quite clear about the range of coverage of his work, as he points out in his Plan:

> Of antiquated or obsolete words, none will be inserted but such as are to be found in authors who wrote since the accession of Elizabeth, from which we date the golden age of our language;[4] and of these many might be omitted, but that the reader may require, with an appearance of reason, that no difficulty should be left unresolved in books which he finds himself invited to read, as confessed and established models of stile.

It is certainly a sensible aim to include words which readers of great literature are likely to encounter: 'Obsolete words are admitted, when they are found in authours not obsolete, or when they have any force or beauty that may deserve revival' (Preface). But this period of coverage, from Edmund Spenser to his own time, is some two hundred years, and a great deal of lexical change had taken place during that period. Although Johnson does often say that a word is 'not in use' (*accourt*, *diswitted*, *morbosity*, *reverb*), he is by no means systematic in his observations, and the idiosyncratic use of many of Shakespeare's coinages, for example, are not given any comment (though see the long note at *intrenchant*). A good example is *cousin*, which is given in its Shakespearian senses, and largely illustrated from the bard. Was this still in use when Johnson was compiling? Judging by the *Oxford English Dictionary*,[5] the general sense of *cousin* had died out – its last citation was 1748 – but there is no suggestion of this in the entry. *Sevennight*, by contrast, is given a helpful usage note about its continuing usage. Another type of instance is the Latinate 'hard word'; examples are encountered on most pages of the *Dictionary*. How many of these scholarly ('inkhorn') coinages (*deambulation*, *misacceptation*) were still in use? They are often unillustrated, or given a reference simply to a preceding dictionary.[6]

To a modern reader, a great deal of the interest of the *Dictionary* is the information it provides about eighteenth-century usage. For example, some prefixes (such as *circum-* and *ob-*) were evidently much more commonly used then than they are today. Hundreds of entries show the way the language has changed between then and now, demonstrating the wisdom of Johnson's famously revised opinion. In his Plan, he had been unequivocal:

one great end of this undertaking is to fix the English language.

In his Preface he is more realistic:

Those who have been persuaded to think well of my design, require that it should fix our language, and put a stop to those alterations which time and chance have hitherto been suffered to make in it without opposition. With this consequence I will confess that I flattered myself for a while; but now begin to fear that I have indulged expectation which neither reason nor experience can justify. When we see men grow old and die at a certain time one after another, from century to century, we laugh at the elixir that promises to prolong life to a thousand years; and with equal justice may the lexicographer be derided, who being able to produce no example of a nation that has preserved their words and phrases from mutability, shall imagine that his dictionary can embalm his language, and secure it from corruption and decay . . .

Notions of corruption and decay make no sense at all when studying lexical change, as the changes move in all kinds of semantic directions. New words and senses are continually entering the language, and old words and senses are disappearing, all at different rates. Johnson is better at drawing our attention to the arrivals than the departures, as any lexicographer would be, because the birth of a word is something readily noticeable, whereas the death of a word usually goes unremarked until long after it has happened. Examples of innovations noted can be found at *methodist*, *tea* and *verdant*. He does quite often suggest that a word is out of use, but the comment is sometimes misleading. Among those words said to be no longer used are *chivalrous*, *expropriate*, *ignore*, *jeopardy*, *missive* (sense 1), *remediate* – all still in the language today. Among those which have definitely died are the following, many of which continue to fascinate wordsmiths because of their different semantic perspective:

airling, armisonous, compotation, curtain-lecture, fopdoodle, fribble, horrisonous, merrythought, nappiness, nidget, nidorous, noctuary, novercal, nullibiety, optimity, orbity, oscitancy, pandect, pandiculation, perpotation, pugil, querimonious, rhabarbarate, shapesmith, smellfeast, sternutation, stirious, suggilate, suppedaneous, tepefaction, traveltainted, vaticide, vitellary, worldling

Anyone who encounters *merrythought*, for example, is unlikely to think of a wishbone in exactly the same way thereafter. And if nothing else, such words show how difficult it is for anyone to state confidently that 'there has never been such a word in English'.

Most words disappear because there is no longer a need for them, or because an alternative word becomes the norm, as in the case of *chirurgeon* (*surgeon*). An example is *toothdrawer*, which was leaving the language while Johnson was writing. Its replacement, *dentist*, has its first recorded usage in 1759, and the quotation in the *Oxford English Dictionary* shows that it was being seen as an innovation:

Dentist figures it now in our newspapers, and may do well enough for a French puffer; but we fancy Rutter is content with being called a *tooth-drawer*.

Johnson does not include *dentist*, one of many surprising omissions in his coverage. Several words also lack senses which would have been strong in the eighteenth century: *sentence*, for example, lacks linguistic definition; *towel* lacks an ecclesiastical sense; *degree* is missing its sense of academic proficiency.

It remains one of the great mysteries of historical lexicology why some words stay in the language and others disappear. Words are often in competition with each other, and it is never possible to predict the ones that are going to be successful. An interesting feature of the *Dictionary* is to see several such pairs of words evidently in competition at the time: examples include *appliable* and *applicable*, *difficil* and *difficult*, *preconceit* and *preconception*, *primeval* and *primevous*, *promulgate* and *promulge*, *rivality* and *rivalry*, *schemer* and *schematist*, *subtile* and *subtle*. An example of a three-way competition is *momentany*, *momentaneous* and *momentary*. A more complex example, because of the overlaps of meaning involved, is *review*, *revisal*, *revise* and *revision*. The winners of the competitions, of course, we now know.

Comparing Johnson's definitions with those we find in a modern dictionary, there are many interesting points of comparison. Some words have lost senses (*fluster* its drunkenness sense, *saucer* its sauce sense (sense 1), *humanist* and *humanity* their philological sense); some have gained them (*overture* a musical sense, *romantick* an amatory sense, *temperature* a scientific sense, *titillation* a sexual sense). Some words have reduced in force: *bloody-minded* is no longer just 'inclined to bloodshed', *worry* no longer 'mangle' or 'persecute brutally'. Some words have narrowed in meaning (*cabaret* no longer refers to a location, *police* no longer refers to general regulation, *tomboy* no longer applies to both sexes); some have broadened (*ethnick* 'Heathen', *novel* 'A small tale, generally of love', *paraphernalia* 'Goods in the wife's disposal', *salesman* 'One who sells cloaths ready made', *veterinarian* 'One skilled in the diseases of cattle'). Some have changed their domain of application: *aftermath* from agriculture, *attitude* from art forms, *technical* from the arts in general, *handkerchief* from the neck, *urinator* from diving. Several words have lost their negative associations: *sophistication* ('adulteration'), *storyteller* (its usage note says: 'In contempt'), *strapping* ('Used of large men or women in contempt'), *sturdy* ('always used of men with some disagreeable idea of coarseness or rudeness'). Some of the older definitions can still cause a frisson of surprise (*lunch* 'As much food as one's hand can hold', *scavenger* 'A petty magistrate, whose province is to keep the streets clean'). Of particular interest are the idioms which have now gone out of use: *at rovers, to serve one the same sauce* (see *sauce*), *to stave and tail* (see *stave*), *to be in the suds, to be on the tenters, to weather a point.*

VARIATION IN USAGE

There are several other aspects of eighteenth-century usage represented in the *Dictionary* which an anthology ought to reflect. A number of entries provide information about contemporary pronunciation or the way it was changing: *chagrin, fault, heronry, medicine, medicinal, mesh, quoit* (in the entry on letter Q), *seraglio, toll.* Most headwords show the location of the primary stress, with a mark placed after the first vowel of the stressed syllable (an innovation introduced earlier in the century by the lexicographer Nathan Bailey). The location of this stress in a polysyllabic word seems to have varied as much then as it does today (examples such as *avenue, revenue* and *sojourn* correspond to modern variation in *research, dispute* and *controversy*), the issue being heightened by the way poets varied the words to meet different metrical constraints. And Johnson seems to have a phonetician's ear, if entries such as *pence* are anything to go by:

The plural of *penny*; formed from *pennies*, by a contraction usual in the rapidity of colloquial speech.

His phonetic observations are not frequent, but I have included them when they occur.

Many words show the distance that English spelling had to travel before it reached the present-day standard (*fewel*, *raindeer*, *villany*). Some words were printed solid which today would be given spaces (*anotherguess*, *brownstudy*, *illnature*, *welldone*, *wellmet*, *whitewine*). Words ending in *-c* were routinely spelled *-ck* (*acrostick*, *antick*, *comick*): 'The English never use *c* at the end of a word' says the opening entry at letter *K*. The choice between final *-l* and *-ll* was still in flux: *downfal* but *pitfall*, *petrol* but *comptroll*. So was the choice between *-or* and *-our*: *confessor* and *inheritor* alongside *oratour* and *possessour*. Johnson often comments on the variation. He acknowledges that there are problems with certain endings: *resistance* or *resistence*, *sailer* or *sailor*. And he points out in the Preface: 'Some combinations of letters having the same power are used indifferently without any discoverable reason of choice, as in *choak*, *choke*; *soap*, *sope*; *fewel*, *fuel*, and many others; which I have sometimes inserted twice, that those who search for them under either form, may not search in vain.' Other examples are *shrug* and *shrugg*, *choir* and *quire*, *summersault* and *somersault*, *evesdropper* and *eavesdrop*, and *hearse* and *herse* – though it should be noted that Johnson does not always draw attention to the connection, and judging by the inconsistencies of treatment between entries he may not always have noticed it (with *hearse/herse*, a connection is pointed out only in the fourth edition). Such pairs as *sicamore* and *sycamore* or *screen* and *skreen* appear to have been composed independently, with similar definitions but different quotations. His own spellings reflect the uncertain spelling of the time. He sometimes changes his mind: the spelling of *sciomachy* alters between first and fourth editions, as does his treatment of *dependant* (see note to *dependent*). He sometimes gets into a tangle: *sizers* is cross-referred to *scissars* (which is indeed his usual spelling – see its use at *snip*, for example), but there is no such item in the dictionary; the entry on this object is found at *scissor*. At other times, well aware of the problems posed by a pair of overlapping spellings, he recommends a solution, which in the case of *travel* and *travail* was the one eventually adopted.

Stylistic variation is another important dimension of language, so I have included many of the entries which contain an observation about eighteenth-century usage – or, at least, Johnson's opinion about contemporary usage.

The stylistic range of the *Dictionary* is in fact very wide. At one extreme we find highly formal words of classical origin (*adumbrate*, *prognostication*, *sagacity*); at the other we find colloquial interjections (*ay*, *foh*, *hist*, *look*, *right*, *tush*, *tut*). We find social locutions (*howd'ye*), terms of address (*servant*) and gender differences ('women's words', such as *frightfully* and *horrid*). Johnson is well aware of the modern difference between semantics and pragmatics, as his entry on *surely* illustrates:

Certainly; undoubtedly; without doubt. It is often used rather to intend and strengthen the meaning of the sentence, than with any distinct and explicable meaning.

At the same time, being part of the spirit of his age, he routinely draws attention to words he considers improper, using such terms as 'bad', 'low', 'vulgar', 'cant', 'barbarous', 'ludicrous' and 'corrupt' to describe such words as *alamode*, *budge*, *cajole*, *coax*, *nowise*, *plaguy* and *sconce* (sense 2). We can sense his concern to warn his readers about words which it might be dangerous to use in 'polite' society. However, we should not exaggerate his attitudes: terms such as 'low' and 'vulgar' may have been intended to convey no more than the labels used by modern lexicographers, such as 'informal'.

A critical consideration for Johnson was to ensure that a word is of good breeding, by having a demonstrable etymology from Classical or Germanic sources:

By tracing in this manner every word to its original, and not admitting, but with great caution, any of which no original can be found, we shall secure our language from being over-run with *cant*, from being crouded with low terms, the spawn of folly or affectation, which arise from no just principles of speech, and of which therefore no legitimate derivation can be shown. (Plan)

Tiff and *traipse*, for example, are considered 'low' words, so he supposes they will have no etymology. He is firm in his belief that spelling should reflect etymology, as we can see from his remarks at *hoop*, *strew*, *tong*, or his explanation at *sithe* (i.e. *scythe*) 'I have chosen the orthography which is at once most simple and most agreeable to etymology.' His etymological notes are often quite extensive (*agast/aghast*, *sleeveless* – the longest is at *loord*), and he readily criticizes writers who are 'inattentive' to etymology (as at *kindly*). Ironically, it is in this domain that his own work has been most strongly criticized. Even Boswell was circumspect: 'The etymologies, though they exhibit learning and judgement, are not, I think, entitled to the first praise amongst the various parts of this immense work' (p. xli).

They do indeed need to be read with extreme caution. His explanations are often wrong, and he continually cites analogues in a few languages (especially Welsh) that are often irrelevant (*looby, mug, trice*). *Stallion* illustrates his reasoning:

ysdalwyn, an old Welch word: the one is derived from the other; but which from which I cannot certainly tell.

But we must be fair. Johnson warns us about his etymologies himself, and here there is no false modesty: 'the orthography which I recommend is still controvertible, the etymology which I adopt is uncertain, and perhaps frequently erroneous'. And we must remember that this work was carried out in the 1750s. It would not be until 1785 that Sir William Jones would make his statement about the common origins of cognate words, and launch the science of comparative philology.

TREATMENT

Of the two major dimensions in any dictionary – coverage (which items to include) and treatment (how to deal with them) – Johnson is in no doubt that treatment is the greater problem. As he says in his Plan, after talking about issues to do with selection and identification: 'The great labour is yet to come, the labour of interpreting these words and phrases with brevity, fulness and perspicuity.' It was indeed a huge labour, and when we look at a sequence of Johnsonian definitions today, it is obvious how much thought must have gone into them. They are the dictionary's primary strength, and its chief claim to fame. Anyone can get a sense of the problem by trying to formulate for themselves appropriate definitions for such words as *effect*, *may*, *nature*, *relation* and *sign*, and comparing their attempt with Johnson's entries. The plural, 'definitions', is important: most words in a language have more than one sense. Some, as we have seen, have dozens. Abstract words pose particular problems, but all words require definitions that are clear, succinct, well-sequenced and contrastive (with words of related meaning), and Johnson's achievement can be seen on virtually any page. For clarity and succinctness, see *acquiescence*, *dovetail*, *falsifier*, *heresiarch* (with its cheeky alliteration), *message*, *preparation*, *proximate*, *rear*. His definitions are often elegant (*history*: 'A narration of events and facts delivered with dignity'), thoughtful (such as his additional note to *sorrow*: 'Sorrow is not commonly understood as the effect of present evil, but of lost good'), and perceptive, such as his definition of *sorry*:

Grieved for something past. It is generally used of slight or casual miscarriages or vexations, but sometimes of greater things. It does not imply any long continuance of grief.

There are many illustrations of the care he takes to sequence his definitions in a semantically related way, and to provide a balance between definition and associated quotation: illustrative are *fierceness*, *flesh*, *knowledge*, *ring* (noun), *shade* and *taste*. His concern to relate words to other words can be seen in his synonym lists, as at *careless*, *chafe* and *flatter*. Most lexicographers would be satisfied with just two or three synonyms: Johnson's *careless*, for example, gives twelve. And the way in which he draws attention to contrasts in meaning can be seen in such entries as *amend* (distinguished from *improve*), *ancient* (vs. *old*), *bowl* (vs. *cup*), *staff* sense 3 (vs. *club*), *tempest* (vs. *breeze*, *gale*, *gust*, *storm*) and *sore* (vs. *wound*, *tumour*, *bruise*) – a feature which is particularly noticeable in the second half of the *Dictionary*. 'It is necessary likewise to explain many words by their opposition to others; for contraries are best seen when they stand together', he commented in his Plan. In this respect he anticipates twentieth-century structural semantics.

'A large work is difficult because it is large', Johnson remarked in his Preface; so it is not surprising to find definitions that are weak by his own exacting standards. *Volcano* could have been better defined than 'burning mountain', and there is more to *warren* than 'A kind of park for rabbits', delightful though this last characterization is. Sometimes the definition strays into an anecdote (as in *dilemma*). Sometimes he lets his sources do the job for him: *holly* is defined as 'A plant', with the detail left to a quotation from Philip Miller; and the complexity of *spectrum* is left to a quotation from Isaac Newton. (Cases where a quotation replaces a definition are shown in this anthology by leaving the quotation in roman type.) Sometimes Johnson simply gives up: *drayplough* ('A plough of a particular kind'), *sonata* ('A tune'), *surprise* sense 2 ('A dish, I suppose, which has nothing in it'). This is reminiscent of the approach of earlier English lexicographers.

Johnson has often been criticized for the 'difficulty' of his definitions, in such cases as *cough* ('A convulsion of the lungs, vellicated by some sharp serosity') and *network* ('Any thing reticulated or decussated, at equal distances, with interstices between the intersections'). The importance of the point has been exaggerated, for there are not many like these. But here, as in so many other ways, he anticipated his critics:

sometimes easier words are changed into harder, as *burial* into *sepulture* or *interment*, *drier* into *desiccative*, *dryness* into *siccity* or *aridity*, *fit* into *paroxysm*;

for the easiest word, whatever it be, can never be translated into one more easy. But easiness and difficulty are merely relative, and if the present prevalence of our language should invite foreigners to this dictionary, many will be assisted by those words which now seem only to increase or produce obscurity. (Preface)

To modern eyes, such definitions do often seem lexically abstruse, but they have to be seen in the context of his time, which was a period when 'hard words' were much more routine than today. The definitions would have been challenging, but not obscure, to his contemporaries. And the frequency with which some of the hard words were used makes them more palatable, even to the modern reader: *reticulated* is one of several words in the dictionary beginning with *reti-*; *interstice* turns up in a number of entries (*dense*, *imporous*, *mesh*, *net*), both in definitions and quotations, and also has a entry of its own.

An analysis of Johnson's use of quotations – over 113,000 in the first edition (including some duplications), and a further 3,000 in the fourth – would take an essay in itself. Though his approach has several continental forerunners, this is the first English dictionary to use quotations in such an integrated and extensive way (only a few specialist dictionaries had used examples previously), and its influence on later lexicography was unparalleled, both in following his practice as well as reacting against it. Shakespeare, John Dryden, Joseph Addison and Francis Bacon provide over a third of the quotations, but there are over 500 authors used in all. It has often been pointed out that his selection was only partly based on linguistic considerations. Many quotes are there because they represent a moral point of view in which he strongly believed, such as the frequent quotations from conservative Anglican theologians and the absence of quotations from the freethinking Thomas Hobbes. As he states in his Plan:

In citing authorities, on which the credit of every part of this work must depend, it will be proper to observe some obvious rules, such as of preferring writers of the first reputation to those of an inferior rank; of noting the quotations with accuracy; and of selecting, when it can be conveniently done, such sentences, as, besides their immediate use, may give pleasure or instruction by conveying some elegance of language, or some precept of prudence, or piety.

Many illustrations are also there for educational reasons, providing encyclopedic information and informing readers about the current state of knowledge: see his mini-essay on *electricity*, for example. This is a big difference with later lexicographic uses of quotation (such as in the *Oxford English*

Dictionary), where the illustration is chosen to show the historical evolution of a word rather than its encyclopedic status or literary excellence. But he is actually very good at finding quotations which illustrate linguistic issues, as in his quotation at *arrant*, which shows both comparative and superlative forms. (His illustration at *twister* needs no comment.) His quotations policy is often serendipitous. It is obvious that he had a copy of a work by Abraham Cowley to hand when he was preparing the entries on *that* and *the*: nine of the twenty-eight quotations for the former, and five of the eleven quotations for the latter, are from that author. And sometimes he just didn't know how to stop. There is no space to include in this anthology the seriously over-quoted entries, such as the 27 quotations attached to *for* in the sense of 'because of', the 38 quotations for the adverbial use of *new*, or the 55 quotations for the adverbial use of *ill*. But *fault* sense 1 is an example of an entry which does not really need all the quotations it receives.

LINGUIST

Johnson is by temperament – and also as a result of his working experience – a descriptive linguist who found himself living in a prescriptive age. From Boswell's accounts we know he rejoiced in linguistic diversity, and he repeatedly demonstrates his interest in linguistic minutiae. He is surprisingly modern in some of his usage notes, taking into account points of grammatical or semantic importance: he notes the use of *that* with *notwithstanding*, the way *alone* usually goes with (collocates with) *let*, and the collocations of *amicable* and *ail* (sense 4). His account of *ought* and *this/that* would not seem out of place in a modern grammar. Alongside this, he reflects the emerging prescriptive spirit of his age, with its disparagement of lower-class usage and its emphasis on logical analysis and etymological priorities. Thus he worries about the 'illogic' of such verbs as *unloose*, and will not allow a word like *extreme* to be given a superlative use because of its already superlative meaning. And while acknowledging the role of custom, for the use of some words, he does not hesitate to impose his own critical judgement upon the use of others.

There is a profound and unresolved contradiction in what he was trying to do. On the one hand, his Plan promises to show that 'every word will have its history'; on the other, he intends to restrict his search to 'the pure sources of genuine diction'. On the one hand, he intends to 'discover and promulgate the decrees of custom'; on the other, he is ready 'to interpose my own judgment . . . to support what appears to me most consonant to grammar and reason'. He wants to present the whole of a word's history, but does not go back further than Spenser and ignores writers of whom he disapproves. It is, of course, not possible to have it both ways. On the whole, as we have already seen, the descriptive linguist in him carried the day. 'All change is of itself an evil', he said in his Plan. By the time the *Dictionary* appeared he had already revised his view (see p. xii), recognizing the inevitability of change and trying to describe it. But there is an unevenness of application of this fresh vision throughout the work.

In summarizing the development of a historical frame of reference in early dictionary-writing, US lexicographer Allan Walker Read had this to say:

> It was necessary that the lexicographer should present the evidence of actual usage, that he should trust it in determining the treatment of words, and that he should extend the scope both as to time and as to the variety of the writers drawn upon. Samuel Johnson assumes the most important place in this development . . .[7]

Notwithstanding the various European models on which Johnson drew, his *Dictionary* contains an unprecedented amount of innovation in lexicographical method, especially in its application to English, such as his sophisticated analysis of senses (as seen in the original dictionary with *take* and *come*), his usage essays, the complementary roles of definition and quotation, and the inclusion of phrasal verbs (*come in*, *come off*, etc.) – more than just a detail, for such verbs are a major characteristic of the English language. The sociolinguistic impact of his work on English dictionary-making was immense, reaching across the Atlantic (where his *Dictionary* became the standard reference for over fifty years), and extending into the end of the nineteenth century, when James Murray's 'New' English dictionary bowed respectfully in its direction. Johnson's contribution to lexicography continues to be assessed and revised, as more information becomes known about his working methods, but his place in the history of this subject remains unchallenged, and he will continue to be a focus of study as lexicography itself develops as an academic subject. Expect a great deal more to be published in the next few years. With the arrival of an electronic version of the *Dictionary*,[8] and with the increasing availability of his sources online, we seem to be at the beginning of a new investigative era.

THE PRESENT ANTHOLOGY

It remains only to summarize my editorial approach and the conventions I have used in compiling this anthology. I have tried to reflect Johnson's balance of treatment through the alphabet, giving proportionately more space to those letters he treats in greater depth. Much has been said about a supposed imbalance in his *Dictionary*, due to his devoting too much attention to the opening letters of the alphabet; but in fact in this respect his practice is not very different from that of modern lexicographers. His letter C ends at p. 477[9] (out of 2,261 pages – 21%); the *New Oxford Dictionary of English* (1998) has its letter C ending at p. 460 (out of 2,152 – 21%); the *Longman Dictionary of the English Language* (1984) has its letter C ending at p. 366 (out of 1,760 – 21%). If there is a bias, it is one shared by all lexicographers.

I have not interfered with Johnson's alphabetical ordering of entries, which is a mixture of principles. It is generally letter-by-letter, as is usual in modern dictionaries, but it is sometimes word by word (*common* precedes *common law* which precedes *commonage*), sometimes word-class by word-class (*moderns* (noun) precedes *modernism* (noun) which precedes *modernise* (verb)), sometimes based on morphology (with the base form first, as when *hypercritick* precedes *hypercritical*), and sometimes based on semantics (as when *deter* is followed by *determent* which precedes *deterge* and *detergent*). A detail about ordering is to note that I/J and U/V are conflated: for example, *ejectment* precedes *eigh* and *avast* precedes *auction*.

Once I had selected an entry, I used all of it, not excluding any quotation or sense. I have left the information in the entries as it is, and not made editorial changes to content, even in cases where there are clearly errors in a source or in an etymology. Where there are spelling variations, in his definitions or sources, I have retained them. So, for example, we find both *Antony* and *Anthony* along with *Cleopatra*, *Friar* alongside *Fryar*, and *Cornwal* as well as *Cornwall*. The only name I have altered is that of *Ben Jonson* (always spelled *Johnson* by Samuel), where I have used the modern spelling to avoid confusion in cases where a quote is assigned simply to *Johnson*. Similarly, I have retained Johnson's variants in describing his sources – for example, sometimes referring to PARADISE LOST and sometimes to MILTON'S PARADISE LOST. However, I have expanded the abbreviations used in identifying the authors of quotations, whose names were often arbitrarily and sometimes heavily truncated to make them fit into the printed line. *Shakespeare*, for example, is often abbreviated to *Shakesp*, *Shak*, *Sh* and even *S* in the *Dictionary*, but in the interests of clarity the name is given in full in this anthology. Similarly, abbreviated words in titles of sources have also been expanded.

Punctuation and spelling in all entries (as well as in the Plan and Preface) are as in the original work, with just one exception. In the case of 'Saxon' words in etymologies, I have replaced Old English letters *wynn* and *yogh* by *w* and *g* respectively. I have kept his long dash (——) to show a switch between characters in a quotation from a play. I have silently corrected a few obvious typographical errors of spacing and punctuation, such as *Thosepeople* in *antipodes*, and incorporated any such changes when these were made in the fourth edition of 1773. I have retained Johnson's use of italic capitals in headwords to mark a word he considers foreign (Plan), but not distinguished between headwords printed in large vs. small capitals.

It has often been said that Johnson's *Dictionary* is not one dictionary but two, for many additions, deletions, and alterations were made in preparing the fourth edition. I have therefore systematically included all fourth-edition changes made to the selection of entries included in this anthology, and these are described in the Notes. For a full appreciation of Johnson's method it is important to read them, for they illustrate his continued interest in the *Dictionary* and his obsessive search for the perfection that he knew would ever evade him.

Notes

1. There are 42,733 entries in the first edition and 43,279 in the fourth.
2. Only two of his personal definitions seem to have caused Johnson any trouble. The story of *excise* is told by Boswell (see note 11 to p. xlii). And Johnson's view of a *pension* as 'pay given to a state hireling for treason to his country' was the source of much merriment, some quite vindictive, when he accepted just such a pension (of £300) from the king in 1762. All quotations from Boswell's *The Life of Samuel Johnson, LL.D.*, 4 vols. (1826).
3. Of special interest is *X*, where he says there are no words in the language beginning with this letter. In fact there are over thirty words recorded in the *Oxford English Dictionary* as having occurred in English before Johnson's time, several of which were in use in his century. They are mainly technical – such as *xebec*, *xenodochium*, *xerasia*, *xerophagy*, *xiphias*, *xoanon*, *xyphoid*, *xystus* – apart from *Xmas*.

4. In fact there are a few references to Middle English, as in the references to Chaucer at *braid*, *drotchel* and *glitterand*.

5. On the '*OED*', as it is popularly known, see p. xxviii.

6. The source for many entries is given simply as *Dict.* (=Dictionaries), which most often seems to mean Nathan Bailey's *Universal Etymological English Dictionary*, first published in 1723. There were many later editions, including a 1736 revision which was the one Johnson used.

7. Alan Walker Read, 'The history of lexicography', in *Lexicography: an emerging international profession*, ed. Robert Ilson (Manchester University Press, 1986), p. 44. For a mid-twentieth-century assessment, see the bicentenary essays in J. H. Sledd and G. J. Kolb (eds), *Dr Johnson's Dictionary: Essays in the Biography of a Book* (University of Chicago, 1955).

8. The first and fourth editions are available on CD-ROM, in an edition prepared by Anne McDermott and published by Cambridge University Press in 1996 – an invaluable aid in the preparation of the present anthology.

9. This is my numeration: the pages of the *Dictionary* are not numbered sequentially.

Samuel Johnson

Samuel Johnson was born at Lichfield, in Staffordshire, on the 18th of September, N. S.[1] 1709; and his initiation into the Christian church was not delayed; for his baptism is recorded, in the register of St. Mary's parish in that city, to have been performed on the day of his birth . . .

Thus James Boswell opens his account of the life of Johnson, one of the most dominant literary figures of the eighteenth century. The son of a provincial bookseller and stationer, he was one of two children: there was a younger brother Nathanael, who died at the age of twenty-five. A physical condition early affected him, as Boswell goes on to report:

Young Johnson had the misfortune to be much afflicted with the scrophula,[2] or king's evil, which disfigured a countenance naturally well formed, and hurt his visual nerves so much, that he did not see at all with one of his eyes, though its appearance was little different from that of the other. There is amongst his prayers one inscribed "*When my* EYE *was restored to its use*," which ascertains a defect that many of his friends knew he had, though I never perceived it.

He attended school in Lichfield until he was fifteen, spent a year at a school in Stourbridge, then stayed at home for two years. Boswell, in his opening chapter, takes up the story:

The two years which he spent at home, after his return from Stourbridge, he passed in what he thought idleness, and was scolded by his father for his want of steady application. He had no settled plan of life, nor looked forward at all, but merely lived from day to day. Yet he read a great deal in a desultory manner, without any scheme of study; as chance threw books in his way, and inclination directed him through them.

There is an illustration:

He used to mention one curious instance of his casual reading, when but a boy. Having imagined that his brother had hid some apples behind a large folio upon an upper shelf in his father's shop, he climbed up to search for them. There were no apples; but the large folio proved to be Petrarch, whom he had seen mentioned, in some preface, as one of the restorers of learning. His curiosity having been thus excited, he sat down with avidity, and read a great part of the book.

This was evidently not the only occasion:

> What he read during these two years, he told me, was not works of mere amusement, "not voyages and travels, but all literature, Sir, all ancient writers, all manly: though but little Greek, only some of Anacreon and Hesiod: but in this irregular manner (added he) I had looked into a great many books, which were not commonly known at the Universities, where they seldom read any books but what are put into their hands by their tutors; so that when I came to Oxford, Dr. Adams, now master of Pembroke College, told me, I was the best qualified for the University that he had ever known come there."

Dr Percy, the Bishop of Dromore, told Boswell another story:

> [W]hen a boy he was immoderately fond of reading romances of chivalry, and he retained his fondness for them through life; so that (adds his lordship) spending part of a summer at my parsonage-house in the country, he chose for his regular reading the old Spanish romance of FELIXMARTE OF HIRCANIA, in folio, which he read quite through. Yet I have heard him attribute to these extravagant fictions that unsettled turn of mind which prevented his ever fixing in any profession.

There are several anecdotes concerning his prodigious memory:

> He was uncommonly inquisitive; and his memory was so tenacious, that he never forgot any thing that he either heard or read. Mr. Hector remembers having recited to him eighteen verses, which, after a little pause, he repeated verbatim, varying only one epithet, by which he improved the line.

Johnson went up to Pembroke College, Oxford, when he was nineteen, in October 1728, but was unable to complete his degree. Although his father had earlier been successful in his business, he lost most of his wealth after a failed venture in the manufacture of parchment, and was no longer able to support his son. Johnson was forced to leave Oxford in 1731, and the next year obtained employment as usher in the school at Market Bosworth, in Leicestershire. However, according to Boswell, he found the repetitive daily routine of the school 'painful drudgery', and left after a few months. He then spent some time with Thomas Warren, the first bookseller to be established in Birmingham. Warren found the young man a great help, both for his knowledge of literature and for his writing ability, and Johnson was able to contribute items to Warren's newspaper.

Johnson returned home in 1734. He married a much older woman – a widow, Elisabeth Porter – then set up a private academy at Edial, near Lichfield, where one of his pupils was David Garrick, later a Shakespearian actor. But within two years he had decided to move to London. There he began to write for the *Gentleman's Magazine*, and regular contributions to it became his main source of income. He also worked on the book catalogue for the Earl of Oxford's Harleian Library. Copyright problems prevented him from proceeding with an edition of Shakespeare, so he turned instead to lexicography. He was already familiar with dictionary-writing, having helped his friend Robert James compile his *Medicinal Dictionary* (1743–5). He also knew the work of Denis Diderot and the French encyclopedists, who were compiling their *Encyclopédie* at the time.

He produced a 'Short Scheme for compiling a new Dictionary of the English Language' on 30 April 1746, and on 18 June signed a contract with a consortium of booksellers (see p. xxx). Work began immediately: the first of his amanuenses, Francis Stewart, was paid an advance of three guineas, and began work on midsummer day. An elaborated plan of the dictionary appeared the following year (see 'Plan', pp. 3–19). Johnson approached Lord Chesterfield, secretary of state, as a patron, but received little support from him, so when Chesterfield sent two eulogistic but condescending papers to the *World*[3] at the end of 1754, a few months before the *Dictionary*'s publication, Johnson responded with a letter which has become renowned for its scornful rejection of their content (pp. xxxvii–xxxviii).

The work had occupied seven years, with little financial support other than the booksellers' advance. It took Johnson some three years to read his source works and mark the citations to be used. He underlined the word to be illustrated and wrote its initial letter as a capital in the margin. The beginning and end of the extract were identified using vertical strokes. These were then copied by his amanuenses on to slips of paper and filed alphabetically. Only after all slips were collated did he begin to draft definitions. Definitions and quotations were then pasted on to large sheets of paper, and these were sent for printing.

The first seventy sheets (*A* to *Carry*) were printed by the end of 1750, and further sections were slowly printed over the next three years. He was perhaps surprised by the amount of space the entries took: letter A comprises 137 folio pages (40 × 25 cm), and by the end of letter C the book had reached 477 pages – 43 per cent of the first volume.[4] At that rate the whole dictionary would have made three or four folio volumes. Later letters show greater economy in coverage and treatment. Even so, the two volumes together comprise 2,261 pages, exclusive of the 51 pages of preliminary matter (the Preface, an outline History of the English Language and an outline Grammar).

The work was complete by 1754, and an edition of 2,000 copies appeared on 15 April 1755, priced £4. 10s. A few weeks later there was a second edition, published in 165 weekly sections at sixpence each. A third edition of 1,024 copies was published in 1765, to coincide with Johnson's edition of Shakespeare. And in 1771 he began a major revision of the work, which was published as the fourth edition in 1773. Other editions followed after his death. The work dominated British lexicography for over a century, continuing to be reprinted until the 1880s. It only began to lose its authority with the arrival of the 'new' English dictionary, edited by James Murray, the first part published in 1884, and the forerunner of the present-day *Oxford English Dictionary*.

Although the *Dictionary* took up an enormous amount of time and energy, Johnson nonetheless managed to continue with his literary work. Indeed, creative writing proved a welcome relief. In 1750, as Boswell put it, 'he came forth in the character for which he was eminently qualified, a majestick teacher of moral and religious wisdom', introducing a periodical which he named *The Rambler*. He published it without interruption every Tuesday and Saturday for two years, until it closed, on Saturday 17 March 1752. It was the day which also saw the death of his wife.

After the *Dictionary* was published, Johnson continued as a literary journalist, and received financial security from a pension granted by George III. He met his biographer, James Boswell, in 1763, and in 1764 founded the Literary Club, where many of his famous conversations took place. Later major works include the eight-volume edition of Shakespeare's plays and a ten-volume *Lives of the Most Eminent English Poets*.

In June 1783 he suffered a stroke, which temporarily robbed him of his speech but left him able to write. A letter he wrote to Harriet Thrale three days later (19 June) reports the event, incidentally including a typically Johnsonian procedure:

> On Monday, the 16th, I sat for my picture, and walked a considerable way with little inconvenience. In the afternoon and evening I felt myself light and easy, and began to plan schemes of life. Thus I went to bed, and in a short time waked and sat up, as has long been my custom, when I felt a confusion and indistinctness in my head, which lasted, I suppose, about half a minute. I was alarmed, and prayed GOD, that however he might afflict my body, he would spare my understanding.

This prayer, that I might try the integrity of my faculties, I made in Latin verse. The lines were not very good, but I knew them not to be very good: I made them easily, and concluded myself to be unimpaired in my faculties.

He died on 13 December 1784, and was buried a week later in Westminster Abbey.

He had received a master of arts degree from Oxford in 1754, and was granted an honorary doctorate by Trinity College Dublin in 1765, and another doctorate by Oxford in 1775. Thus he received the title by which he has come to be most widely known: Dr Johnson. But perhaps, for the present book, it is more fitting to refer to him by the other name which he received at the time: Dictionary Johnson.

Notes

1. N.S. is 'New Style', according to the Gregorian Calendar, adopted 1752.
2. Scrofula, in its modern spelling, is a tuberculous skin disease affecting the lymph nodes of the neck and certain other parts of the body, causing inflammation and sores which can leave scars.
3. The *World* was a weekly periodical, published between 1753 and 1757, devoted to satirizing fashionable society.
4. But see the comparative figures on p. xxii.

James Boswell's account of the *Dictionary* project

1747[1]

But the year 1747 is distinguished as the epoch, when Johnson's arduous and important work, his DICTIONARY OF THE ENGLISH LANGUAGE, was announced to the world, by the publication of its Plan or *Prospectus*.

How long this immense undertaking had been the object of his contemplation, I do not know. I once asked him by what means he had attained to that astonishing knowledge of our language, by which he was enabled to realise a design of such extent and accumulated difficulty. He told me, that "it was not the effect of particular study; but that it had grown up in his mind insensibly." I have been informed by Mr. James Dodsley, that several years before this period, when Johnson was one day sitting in his brother Robert's shop, he heard his brother suggest to him that a Dictionary of the English Language would be a work that would be well received by the publick; that Johnson seemed at first to catch at the proposition, but, after a pause, said, in his abrupt decisive manner, "I believe I shall not undertake it." That he, however, had bestowed much thought upon the subject, before he published his "Plan," is evident from the enlarged, clear, and accurate views which it exhibits; and we find him mentioning in that tract, that many of the writers whose testimonies were to be produced as authorities, were selected by Pope; which proves that he had been furnished, probably by Mr. Robert Dodsley, with whatever hints that eminent poet had contributed towards a great literary project, that had been the subject of important consideration in a former reign.

The booksellers who contracted with Johnson, single and unaided, for the execution of a work, which in other countries has not been effected but by the co-operating exertions of many, were Mr. Robert Dodsley, Mr. Charles Hitch, Mr. Andrew Millar, the two Messieurs Longman, and the two Messieurs Knapton. The price stipulated was 1575*l.*

The "Plan" was addressed to Philip Dormer, Earl of Chesterfield, then one of his Majesty's Principal Secretaries of State; a nobleman who was very ambitious of literary distinction, and who, upon being informed of the design, had expressed himself in terms very favourable to its success. There is, perhaps, in every thing of any consequence, a secret history which it would be amusing to know, could we have it authentically communicated. Johnson told me, "Sir, the way in which the plan of my Dictionary came to be inscribed to Lord Chesterfield, was this: I had neglected to write it by the time appointed. Dodsley suggested a desire to have it addressed to Lord Chesterfield. I laid hold of this as a pretext for delay, that it might be better done, and let Dodsley have his desire. I said to my friend, Dr. Bathurst, 'Now if any good comes of my addressing to Lord Chesterfield, it will be ascribed to deep policy, when, in fact, it was only a casual excuse for laziness.'"

It is worthy of observation, that the "Plan" has not only the substantial merit of comprehension, perspicuity, and precision, but that the language of it is unexceptionably excellent; it being altogether free from that inflation of style, and those uncommon but apt and energetick words, which in some of his writings have been censured, with more petulance than justice; and never was there a more dignified strain of compliment than that in which he courts the attention of one who, he had been persuaded to believe would be a respectable patron.

"With regard to questions of purity or propriety (says he), I was once in doubt whether I should not attribute to myself too much in attempting to decide them, and whether my province was to extend beyond the proposition of the question, and the display of the suffrages on each side; but I have been since determined by your Lordship's opinion, to interpose my own judgement, and shall therefore endeavour to support what appears to me most consonant to grammar and reason. Ausonius thought that modesty forbad him to plead inability for a task to which Cæsar had judged him equal:

Cur me posse negem, posse quod ille putat?[2]

And I may hope, my Lord, that since you, whose authority in our language is so generally acknowledged, have commissioned me to declare my own opinion, I shall be considered as exercising a kind of vicarious jurisdiction; and that the power which might have been denied to my own claim, will be readily allowed me as the delegate of your Lordship."

This passage proves, that Johnson's addressing his "Plan" to Lord Chesterfield was not merely in consequence of the result of a report by means of Dodsley, that the Earl favoured the design; but that there had been a particular communication with his Lordship concerning it. Dr. Taylor told me, that Johnson sent his "Plan" to him in manuscript for his perusal: and that when it was lying upon his table, Mr. William Whitehead happened to pay him a visit, and being shewn it, was highly pleased with such parts of it as he had time to read, and begged to take it home with him, which he was allowed to do; that from him it got into the hands of a noble Lord, who carried it to Lord Chesterfield. When Taylor observed this might be an advantage, Johnson replied, "No, Sir, it would have come out with more bloom, if it had not been seen before by any body."

The opinion conceived of it by another noble authour, appears from the following extract of a letter from the Earl of Orrery to Dr. Birch:

"Caledon, Dec. 30, 1747.

> "I HAVE just now seen the specimen of Mr. Johnson's Dictionary, addressed to Lord Chesterfield. I am much pleased with the plan, and I think the specimen is one of the best that I have ever read. Most specimens disgust, rather than prejudice us in favour of the work to follow; but the language of Mr. Johnson's is good, and the arguments are properly and modestly expressed. However, some expressions may be cavilled at, but they are trifles. I'll mention one: the *barren* laurel. The laurel is not barren, in any sense whatever; it bears fruits and flowers. *Sed hæ sunt nugæ*,[3] and I have great expectations from the performance."

1748

That he was fully aware of the arduous nature of the undertaking, he acknowledges; and shews himself perfectly sensible of it in the conclusion of his "Plan;" but he had a noble consciousness of his own abilities, which enabled him to go on with undaunted spirit.

Dr. Adams found him one day busy at his Dictionary, when the following dialogue ensued. "ADAMS: This is a great work, Sir. How are you to get all the etymologies? JOHNSON: Why, Sir, here is a shelf with Junius, and Skinner, and others; and there is a Welsh gentleman who has published a collection of Welsh proverbs, who will help me with the Welsh. ADAMS: But, Sir, how can you do this in three years? JOHNSON: Sir, I have no doubt that I can do it in three years. ADAMS: But the French Academy, which consists of forty members, took forty years to compile their Dictionary. JOHNSON: Sir, thus it is. This is the proportion. Let me see; forty times forty is sixteen hundred. As three to sixteen hundred, so is the proportion of an Englishman to a Frenchman." With so much ease and pleasantry could he talk of that prodigious labour which he had undertaken to execute.[4]

The publick has had, from another pen, a long detail of what had been done in this country by prior Lexicographers; and no doubt Johnson was wise to avail himself of them, so far as they went; but the learned, yet judicious research of etymology, the various, yet accurate display of definition, and the rich collection of authorities, were reserved for the superiour mind of our great philologist. For the mechanical part he employed, as he told me, six amanuenses; and let it be remembered by the natives of North Britain, to whom he is supposed to have been so hostile, that five of them were of that country. There were two Messieurs Macbean; Mr. Shiels, who we shall hereafter see partly wrote the Lives of the Poets to which the name of [Colley] Cibber is affixed; Mr. Stewart, son of Mr. George Stewart, bookseller at Edinburgh; and a Mr. Maitland. The sixth of these humble assistants was Mr. Peyton, who, I believe, taught French, and published some elementary tracts.

To all these painful labourers, Johnson shewed a never-ceasing kindness, so far as they stood in need of it. The elder Mr. Macbean had afterwards the honour of being Librarian to Archibald, Duke of Argyle, for many years, but was left without a shilling. Johnson wrote for him a Preface to, "A System of Ancient Geography;" and, by the favour of Lord Thurlow, got him admitted a poor brother of the Charter-house. For Shiels, who died of a consumption, he had much tenderness; and it has been thought that some choice sentences in the Lives of the Poets were supplied by him. Peyton, when reduced to penury, had frequent aid from the bounty of Johnson, who at last was at the expense of burying him and his wife.

While the Dictionary was going forward, Johnson lived part of the time in Holborn, part in Gough-square, Fleet-street; and he had an upper room fitted up like a counting-house for the purpose, in which he gave to the copyists their several tasks. The words, partly taken from other dictionaries, and partly supplied by himself, having been first written down with spaces left between them, he delivered in writing their etymologies, definitions, and various significations. The authorities were copied from the books themselves, in which he had marked the passages with a black-lead pencil, the traces of which could easily be effaced. I have seen several of them, in which that trouble had not been taken; so that they were just as when used by the copyists. It is remarkable, that he was so attentive in the choice of the passages in which words are authorized, that one may read page after page of his Dictionary with improvement and pleasure; and it should not pass unobserved, that he has quoted no authour whose writings had a tendency to hurt sound religion and morality.

The necessary expense of preparing a work of such magnitude for the press, must have been a considerable deduction from the price stipulated to be paid for the copyright. I understand that nothing was allowed by the booksellers on that account; and I remember his telling me, that a large portion of it having, by mistake, been written upon both sides of the paper, so as to be inconvenient for the compositor, it cost him twenty pounds to have it transcribed upon one side only.

He is now to be considered as "tugging at his oar," as engaged in a steady continued course of occupation, sufficient to employ all his time for some years; and which was the best preventive of that constitutional melancholy which was ever lurking about him, ready to trouble his quiet. But his enlarged and lively mind could not be satisfied without more diversity of employment, and the pleasure of animated relaxation. He therefore not only exerted his talents in occasional composition, very different from Lexicography, but formed a club in Ivy-lane, Paternoster-row, with a view to enjoy literary discussion, and amuse his evening hours . . .

1754

The Dictionary, we may believe, afforded Johnson full occupation this year. As it approached to its conclusion, he probably worked with redoubled vigour, as seamen increase their exertion and alacrity when they have a near prospect of their haven.

Lord Chesterfield, to whom Johnson had paid the high compliment of addressing to his Lordship the Plan of his Dictionary, had behaved to him in such a manner as to excite his contempt and indignation. The world has been for many years amused with a story confidently told, and as confidently repeated with additional circumstances, that a sudden disgust was taken by Johnson upon occasion of his having been one day kept long in waiting in his Lordship's antechamber, for which the reason assigned was, that he had company with him; and that at last, when the door opened, out walked Colley Cibber; and that Johnson was so violently provoked when he found for whom he had been so long excluded, that he went away in a passion, and never would return. I remember having mentioned this story to George Lord Lyttelton, who told me, he was very intimate with Lord Chesterfield; and holding it as a well-known truth, defended Lord Chesterfield by saying, that "Cibber, who had been introduced familiarly by the back-stairs, had probably not been there above ten minutes." It may seem strange even to entertain a doubt concerning a story so long and so widely current, and thus implicitly adopted, if not sanctioned, by the authority which I have mentioned; but Johnson himself assured me, that there was not the least foundation for it. He told me, that there never was any particular incident which produced a quarrel between Lord Chesterfield and him; but that his Lordship's continued neglect was the reason why he resolved to have no connexion with him. When the Dictionary was upon the eve of publication, Lord Chesterfield, who, it is said, had flattered himself with expectations that Johnson would dedicate the work to him, attempted, in a courtly manner, to soothe and insinuate himself with the Sage, conscious, as it should seem, of the cold indifference with which he had treated its learned authour; and farther attempted to conciliate him, by writing two papers in "The World," in recommendation of the work; and it must be confessed, that they contain some studied compliments, so finely turned, that if there had been no previous offence, it is probable that Johnson would have been highly delighted. Praise, in general, was pleasing to him; but by praise from a man of rank and elegant accomplishments, he was peculiarly gratified.

His lordship says, "I think the publick in general, and the republick of letters in particular, are greatly obliged to Mr. Johnson, for having undertaken, and executed so great and desirable a work. Perfection is not to be expected from man; but if we are to judge by the various works of Johnson already published, we have good reason to believe, that be will bring this as near to perfection as any man could do. The Plan of it, which he published some years ago, seems to me to be a proof of it. Nothing can be more rationally imagined, or more accurately and elegantly expressed. I therefore recommend the previous perusal of it to all those who intend to buy the Dictionary, and who, I suppose, are all those who can afford it."

* * * *

"It must be owned, that our language is, at present, in a state of anarchy, and hitherto, perhaps, it may not have been the worse for it. During our free and open trade, many words and expressions have been imported, adopted, and naturalized from other languages, which have greatly enriched our own. Let it still preserve what real strength and beauty it may have borrowed from others; but let it not, like the Tarpeian maid, be overwhelmed and crushed by unnecessary ornaments. The time for discrimination seems to be now come. Toleration, adoption, and naturalization have run their lengths. Good order and authority are now necessary. But where shall we find them, and, at the same time, the obedience due to them? We must have recourse to the old Roman expedient in times of confusion, and choose a dictator. Upon this principle, I give my vote for Mr. Johnson to fill that great and arduous post. And I hereby declare, that

I make a total surrender of all my rights and privileges in the English language, as a free-born British subject, to the said Mr. Johnson, during the term of his dictatorship. Nay more, I will not only obey him like an old Roman, as my dictator, but, like a modern Roman, I will implicitly believe in him as my Pope, and hold him to be infallible while in the chair, but no longer. More than this he cannot well require; for, I presume, that obedience can never be expected, where there is neither terrour to enforce, nor interest to invite it."

* * * *

"But a Grammar, a Dictionary, and a History of our Language through its several stages, were still wanting at home, and importunately called for from abroad. Mr. Johnson's labours will now, I dare say, very fully supply that want, and greatly contribute to the farther spreading of our language in other countries. Learners were discouraged, by finding no standard to resort to; and, consequently, thought it incapable of any. They will now be undeceived and encouraged."

This courtly device failed of its effect. Johnson, who thought that "all was false and hollow," despised the honeyed words, and was even indignant that Lord Chesterfield should, for a moment, imagine, that he could be the dupe of such an artifice. His expression to me concerning Lord Chesterfield, upon this occasion, was, "Sir, after making great professions, he had, for many years, taken no notice of me; but when my Dictionary was coming out, he fell a scribbling in 'The World' about it. Upon which, I wrote him a letter expressed in civil terms, but such as might shew him that I did not mind what he said or wrote, and that I had done with him."

This is that celebrated letter of which so much has been said, and about which curiosity has been so long excited, without being gratified. I for many years solicited Johnson to favour me with a copy of it, that so excellent a composition might not be lost to posterity. He delayed from time to time to give it me;[5] till at last in 1781, when we were on a visit at Mr. Dilly's, at Southill in Bedfordshire, he was pleased to dictate it to me from memory. He afterwards found among his papers a copy of it, which he had dictated to Mr. Baretti, with its title and corrections, in his own hand-writing. This he gave to Mr. Langton; adding, that if it were to come into print, he wished it to be from that copy. By Mr. Langton's kindness, I am enabled to enrich my work with a perfect transcript of what the world has so eagerly desired to see.

"TO THE RIGHT HONOURABLE THE EARL OF CHESTERFIELD.

February 7, 1755.

"MY LORD,

"I HAVE been lately informed, by the proprietor of the World, that two papers, in which my Dictionary is recommended to the publick, were written by your Lordship. To be so distinguished, is an honour, which, being very little accustomed to favours from the great, I know not well how to receive, or in what terms to acknowledge.

"When, upon some slight encouragement, I first visited your Lordship, I was overpowered, like the rest of mankind, by the enchantment of your address, and could not forbear to wish that I might boast myself *Le vainqueur du vainqueur de la terre;*[6]—that I might obtain that regard for which I saw the world contending; but I found my attendance so little encouraged, that neither pride nor modesty would suffer me to continue it. When I had once addressed your Lordship in publick, I had exhausted all the art of pleasing which a retired and uncourtly scholar can possess. I had done all that I could; and no man is well pleased to have his all neglected, be it ever so little.

"Seven years, my Lord, have now past, since I waited in your outward rooms, or was repulsed from your door; during which time I have been pushing on my work through difficulties, of which it is useless to complain, and have brought it, at last, to the verge of publication, without one act of assistance,[7] one word of encouragement, or one smile of favour. Such treatment I did not expect, for I never had a Patron before.

"The shepherd in Virgil[8] grew at last acquainted with Love, and found him a native of the rocks.

"Is not a Patron, my Lord, one who looks with unconcern on a man struggling for life in the water, and, when he has reached ground, encumbers him with help? The notice which you have been pleased to take of my labours, had it been early, had been kind; but it has been delayed till I am indifferent, and cannot enjoy it; till I am solitary, and cannot impart it; till I am known, and do not want it. I hope it is no very cynical asperity not to confess obligations where no benefit has been received, or to be unwilling that the publick should consider me as owing that to a Patron, which Providence has enabled me to do for myself.

"Having carried on my work thus far with so little obligation to any favourer of learning, I shall not be disappointed though I should conclude it, if less be possible, with less; for I have been long wakened from that dream of hope, in which I once boasted myself with so much exultation, my Lord,

"Your Lordship's most humble
"Most obedient servant,
"SAM. JOHNSON."

"While this was the talk of the town (says Dr. Adams, in a letter to me), I happened to visit Dr. Warburton, who finding that I was acquainted with Johnson, desired me earnestly to carry his compliments to him, and to tell him, that he honoured him for his manly behaviour in rejecting these condescensions of Lord Chesterfield, and for resenting the treatment he had received from him with a proper spirit. Johnson was visibly pleased with this compliment, for he had always a high opinion of Warburton." Indeed, the force of mind which appeared in this letter, was congenial with that which Warburton himself amply possessed.

There is a curious minute circumstance which struck me, in comparing the various editions of Johnson's Imitations of Juvenal. In the tenth Satire one of the couplets upon the vanity of wishes even for literary distinction stood thus:

"Yet think what ills the scholar's life assail,
Toil, envy, want, the *garret*, and the jail."

But after experiencing the uneasiness which Lord Chesterfield's fallacious patronage made him feel, he dismissed the word *garret* from the sad group, and in all the subsequent editions the line stands,

"Toil, envy, want, the *Patron*, and the jail."

That Lord Chesterfield must have been mortified by the lofty contempt, and polite, yet keen, satire with which Johnson exhibited him to himself in this letter, it is impossible to doubt. He, however, with that glossy duplicity which was his constant study, affected to be quite unconcerned. Dr. Adams mentioned to Mr. Robert Dodsley that he was sorry Johnson had written his letter to Lord Chesterfield. Dodsley, with the true feelings of trade, said "he was very sorry too; for that he had a property in the Dictionary, to which his Lordship's patronage might have been of consequence." He then told Dr. Adams, that Lord Chesterfield had shewn him the letter. "I should have imagined (replied Dr. Adams) that Lord Chesterfield would have concealed it." "Poh! (said Dodsley) do you think a letter from Johnson could hurt Lord Chesterfield? Not at all, Sir. It lay upon his table, where any body might see it. He read it to me; said, 'this man has great powers,' pointed out the severest passages, and observed how well they were expressed." This air of indifference, which imposed upon the worthy Dodsley, was certainly nothing but a specimen of that dissimulation which Lord Chesterfield inculcated as one of the most essential lessons for the conduct of life. His Lordship endeavoured to justify himself to Dodsley from the charges brought against him by Johnson; but we may judge of the flimsiness of his defence, from his having excused his neglect of Johnson, by saying, "that he had heard he had changed his lodgings, and did not know where he lived;" as if there could have been the smallest difficulty to inform himself of that circumstance, by inquiring in the literary circle with which his Lordship was well acquainted, and was, indeed, himself, one of its ornaments.

Dr. Adams expostulated with Johnson, and suggested, that his not being admitted when he called on him, was probably not to be imputed to Lord Chesterfield; for his Lordship had declared to Dodsley, that "he would have turned off the best servant he ever had if he had known that he denied him to a man who would have been always more than welcome;" and in confirmation of this, he insisted on Lord Chesterfield's general affability and easiness of access, especially to literary men. "Sir (said Johnson), that is not Lord Chesterfield; he is the proudest man this day existing." "No (said Dr. Adams), there is one person, at least, as proud; I think, by your own account you are the prouder man of the two." "But mine (replied Johnson instantly) was *defensive* pride." This, as Dr. Adams well observed, was one of those happy turns for which he was so remarkably ready.

Johnson having now explicitly avowed his opinion of Lord Chesterfield, did not refrain from expressing himself concerning that nobleman with pointed freedom: "This man (said he) I thought had been a Lord among wits; but, I find, he is only a wit among Lords." And when his Letters to his natural son were published, he observed, that "they teach the morals of a whore, and the manners of a dancing-master."

The character of a "respectable Hottentot," in Lord Chesterfield's letters, has been generally understood to be meant for Johnson, and I have no doubt that it was. But I remember when the *Literary Property* of those letters were contested in the Court of Session in Scotland, and Mr. Henry Dundas, one of the counsel for the proprietors, read this character as an exhibition of Johnson, Sir David Dalrymple, Lord Hailes, one of the judges, maintained, with some warmth, that it was not intended as a portrait of Johnson, but of a late noble Lord, distinguished for abstruse science. I have heard Johnson himself talk of the character, and say that it was meant for George Lord Lyttelton, in which I could by no means agree; for his Lordship had nothing of that violence which is a conspicuous feature in the composition. Finding that my illustrious friend could bear to have it supposed that it might be meant for him, I said, laughingly, that there was one trait which unquestionably did not belong to him; "he throws his meat any where but down his throat." "Sir (said he), Lord Chesterfield never saw me eat in his life." . . .

1755

The Dictionary, with a Grammar and History of the English Language, being now at length published, in two volumes folio, the world contemplated with wonder so stupendous a work achieved by one man, while other countries had thought such undertakings fit only for whole academies. Vast as his powers were, I cannot but think that his imagination deceived him, when he supposed that by constant application he might have performed the task in three years. Let the Preface be attentively perused, in which is given, in a clear, strong, and glowing style, a comprehensive, yet particular view of what he had done; and it will be evident, that the time he employed upon it was comparatively short. I am unwilling to swell my book with long quotations from what is in every body's hands, and I believe there are few prose compositions in the English language that are read with more delight, or are more impressed upon the memory, than that preliminary discourse. One of its excellencies has always struck me with peculiar admiration; I mean the perspicuity with which he has expressed abstract scientifick notions. As an instance of this, I shall quote the following sentence: "When the radical idea branches out into parallel ramifications, how can a consecutive series be formed of senses in their own nature collateral?" We have here an example of what has been often said, and I believe with justice, that there is for every thought a certain nice adaptation of words which none other could equal, and which when a man has been so fortunate as to hit, he has attained, in that particular case, the perfection of language.

The extensive reading which was absolutely necessary for the accumulation of authorities, and which alone may account for Johnson's retentive mind being enriched with a very large and various store of knowledge and imagery, must have occupied several years. The Preface furnishes an eminent instance of a double talent, of which Johnson was fully conscious. Sir Joshua

Reynolds[9] heard him say, "There are two things which I am confident I can do very well: one is an introduction to any literary work, stating what it is to contain, and how it should be executed in the most perfect manner; the other is a conclusion, shewing from various causes why the execution has not been equal to what the authour promised to himself and to the publick."

How should puny scribblers be abashed and disappointed, when they find him displaying a perfect theory of lexicographical excellence, yet at the same time candidly and modestly allowing that he "had not satisfied his own expectations." Here was a fair occasion for the exercise of Johnson's modesty, when he was called upon to compare his own arduous performance, not with those of other individuals (in which case his inflexible regard to truth would have been violated had he affected diffidence), but with speculative perfection; as he, who can outstrip all his competitors in the race, may yet be sensible of his deficiency when he runs against time. Well might he say, that "the English Dictionary was written with little assistance of the learned;" for he told me, that the only aid which he received was a paper containing twenty etymologies, sent to him by a person then unknown, who he was afterwards informed was Dr. Pearce, Bishop of Rochester. The etymologies, though they exhibit learning and judgement, are not, I think, entitled to the first praise amongst the various parts of this immense work. The definitions have always appeared to me such astonishing proofs of acuteness of intellect and precision of language, as indicate a genius of the highest rank. This it is which marks the superiour excellence of Johnson's Dictionary over others equally or even more voluminous, and must have made it a work of much greater mental labour than mere Lexicons, or *Word-Books*, as the Dutch call them. They, who will make the experiment of trying how they can define a few words of whatever nature, will soon be satisfied of the unquestionable justice of this observation, which I can assure my readers is founded upon much study, and upon communication with more minds than my own.

A few of his definitions must be admitted to be erroneous. Thus, *Windward* and *Leeward*, though directly of opposite meaning, are defined identically the same way,[10] as to which inconsiderable specks it is enough to observe, that his Preface announces that he was aware there might be many such in so immense a work; nor was he at all disconcerted when an instance was pointed out to him. A lady once asked him how he came to define *Pastern* the *knee* of a horse: instead of making an elaborate defence, as she expected, he at once answered, "Ignorance, Madam, pure ignorance." His definition of *Network* has been often quoted with sportive malignity, as obscuring a thing in itself very plain. But to these frivolous censures no other answer is necessary than that with which we are furnished by his own Preface. "To explain, requires the use of terms less abstruse than that which is to be explained, and such terms cannot always be found. For as nothing can be proved but by supposing something intuitively known, and evident without proof, so nothing can be defined but by the use of words too plain to admit of definition. Sometimes easier words are changed into harder; as, *burial*, into *sepulture* or *interment; dry*, into *desiccative; dryness*, into *siccity*, or *aridity; fit*, into *paroxysm;* for, the *easiest* word, whatever it be, can never be translated into one more easy."

His introducing his own opinions, and even prejudices, under general definitions of words, while at the same time the original meaning of the words is not explained, as his *Tory, Whig, Pension, Oats, Excise*,[11] and a few more, cannot be fully defended, and must be placed to the account of capricious and humourous indulgence. Talking to me upon this subject when we were at Ashbourne in 1777, he mentioned a still stronger instance of the predominance of his private feelings in the composition of this work, than any now to be found in it. "You know, Sir, Lord Gower forsook the old Jacobite interest. When I came to the word *Renegado*, after telling that it meant 'one who deserts to the enemy, a revolter,' I added, *Sometimes we say a* GOWER. Thus it went to the press: but the printer had more wit than I, and struck it out."

Let it, however, be remembered, that this indulgence does not display itself only in sarcasm towards others, but sometimes in playful allusion to the notions commonly entertained of his own laborious task. Thus; "*Grub-street*, the name of a street in London, much inhabited by writers of small histories, *dictionaries*, and temporary poems; whence any mean production is called *Grub-street*."—"*Lexicographer*, a writer of dictionaries, a *harmless drudge*."

At the time when he was concluding his very eloquent Preface, Johnson's mind appears to have been in such a state of depression, that we cannot contemplate without wonder the vigorous and splendid thoughts which so highly distinguish that performance. "I (says he) may surely be contented without the praise of perfection, which if I could obtain in this gloom of solitude, what would it avail me? I have protracted my work till most of those whom I wished to please have sunk into the grave; and success and miscarriage are empty sounds. I therefore dismiss it with frigid tranquillity, having little to fear or hope from censure or from praise." That this indifference was rather a temporary than an habitual feeling, appears, I think, from his letters to Mr. Warton; and however he may have been affected for the moment, certain it is that the honours which his great work procured him, both at home and abroad, were very grateful to him. His friend the Earl of Corke and Orrery, being at Florence, presented it to the *Academia della Crusca*. That Academy sent Johnson their *Vocabulario*, and the French Academy sent him their *Dictionnaire*, which Mr. Langton had the pleasure to convey to him.

It must undoubtedly seem strange, that the conclusion of his Preface should be expressed in terms so desponding, when it is considered that the authour was then only in his forty-sixth year. But we must ascribe its gloom to that miserable dejection of spirits to which he was constitutionally subject, and which was aggravated by the death of his wife two years before. I have heard it ingeniously observed by a lady of rank and elegance, that "his melancholy was then at its meridian." It pleased God to grant him almost thirty years of life after this time; and once when he was in a placid frame of mind, he was obliged to own to me that he had enjoyed happier days, and had many more friends, since that gloomy hour, than before . . .

1756

In 1756 Johnson found that the great fame of his Dictionary had not set him above the necessity of "making provision for the day that was passing over him." No royal or noble patron extended a munificent hand to give independence to the man who had conferred stability on the language of his country. We may feel indignant that there should have been such unworthy neglect; but we must, at the same time, congratulate ourselves, when we consider, that to this very neglect, operating to rouse the natural indolence of his constitution, we owe many valuable productions, which otherwise, perhaps, might never have appeared.

He had spent, during the progress of the work, the money for which he had contracted to write his Dictionary. We have seen that the reward of his labour was only fifteen hundred and seventy-five pounds; and when the expense of amanuenses and paper, and other articles, are deducted, his clear profit was very inconsiderable. I once said to him, "I am sorry, Sir, you did not get more for your Dictionary." His answer was, "I am sorry too. But it was very well. The booksellers are generous liberal-minded men." He, upon all occasions, did ample justice to their character in this respect. He considered them as the patrons of literature; and, indeed, although they have eventually been considerable gainers by his Dictionary, it is to them that we owe its having been undertaken and carried through at the risk of great expense, for they were not absolutely sure of being indemnified.

Notes

1. These extracts are taken from Boswell's *Life of Johnson*, for the stated years.
2. 'Why should I deny possession of that which he believes me to possess?' (Ausonius, *Praefatiunculae*, sect. 1).
3. But these are trifles.
4. David Garrick later wrote a complimentary epigram 'On Johnson's Dictionary':

   Talk of war with a Briton, he'll boldly advance,
   That one English soldier will beat ten of France;
   Would we alter the boast from the sword to the pen,
   Our odds are still greater, still greater our men;
   In the deep mines of science though Frenchmen may toil,
   Can their strength be compar'd to Locke, Newton, and Boyle?
   Let them rally their heroes, send forth all their pow'rs,
   Their verse-men and prose-men, then match them with ours!
   First Shakspeare and Milton, like Gods in the fight,
   Have put their whole drama and epick to flight;
   In satires, epistles, and odes, would they cope,
   Their numbers retreat before Dryden and Pope;
   And Johnson, well-arm'd like a hero of yore,
   Has beat forty French, and will beat forty more!

5. Boswell's footnote at this point:

   Dr. Johnson appeared to have had a remarkable delicacy with respect to the circulation of this letter; for Dr. Douglas, Bishop of Salisbury, informs me, that having many years ago pressed him to be allowed to read it to the second Lord Hardwicke, who was very desirous to hear it (promising at the same time, that no copy of it should be taken), Johnson seemed much pleased that it had attracted the attention of a nobleman of such a respectable character; but, after pausing some time, declined to comply with the request, saying, with a smile, "No, Sir; I have hurt the dog too much already;" or words to that purpose.

6. The conqueror of the conqueror of the world.
7. Boswell's footnote:

   The following note is subjoined by Mr. Langton. "Dr. Johnson, when he gave me this copy of his letter, desired that I would annex to it his information to me, that whereas it is said in the letter that 'no assistance has been received,' he did once receive from Lord Chesterfield the sum of 10*l.*, but as that was so inconsiderable a sum, he thought the mention of it could not properly find a place in a letter of the kind that this was."

8. Virgil, *Eclogues.*

9. The leading portrait painter of the later eighteenth century.

10. Boswell adds a remark from the music historian Charles Burney: 'He owns in his Preface the deficiency of the technical part of his work; and he said, he should be much obliged to me for definitions of musical terms for his next edition, which he did not live to superintend.'

11. Boswell's footnote:

> He thus defines Excise—"A hateful tax levied upon commodities, and adjudged not by the common judges of property, but wretches hired by those to whom Excise is paid." The Commissioners of Excise being offended by this severe reflection, consulted Mr. Murray, then Attorney-General, to know whether redress could be legally obtained. I wished to have procured for my readers a copy of the opinion which he gave, and which may now be justly considered as history: but the mysterious secrecy of office it seems would not permit it. I am, however, informed by very good authority, that its import was, that the passage might be considered as actionable; but that it would be more prudent in the board not to prosecute. Johnson never made the smallest alteration in this passage. We find he still retained his early prejudice against Excise; for in "The Idler, No. 65," there is the following very extraordinary paragraph: "The authenticity of *Clarendon's* history, though printed with the sanction of one of the first Universities of the world, had not an unexpected manuscript been happily discovered, would, with the help of factious credulity, have been brought into question, by the two lowest of all human beings, a Scribbler for a party, and a Commissioner of Excise." The persons to whom he alludes were Mr. John Oldmixon, and George Ducket, Esq.

The Plan of *A Dictionary of the English Language*

Addressed to
the Right Honourable PHILIP DORMER Earl of *CHESTERFIELD*;
One of His MAJESTY's Principal Secretaries of State.

(LONDON: Printed for J. and P. KNAPTON, T. LONGMAN
and T. SHEWELL, C. HITCH, A. MILLAR, and R. DODSLEY.
MDCCXLVII.)

MY LORD,

WHEN first I undertook to write an English Dictionary, I had no expectation of any higher patronage than that of the proprietors of the copy, nor prospect of any other advantage than the price of my labour; I knew, that the work in which I engaged is generally considered as drudgery for the blind, as the proper toil of artless industry; a task that requires neither the light of learning, nor the activity of genius, but may be successfully performed without any higher quality than that of bearing burdens with dull patience, and beating the track of the alphabet with sluggish resolution.

Whether this opinion, so long transmitted and so widely propagated, had its beginning from truth and nature, or from accident and prejudice, whether it be decreed by the authority of reason, or the tyranny of ignorance, that of all the candidates for literary praise, the unhappy lexicographer holds the lowest place, neither vanity nor interest incited me to inquire. It appeared that the province allotted me was of all the regions of learning generally confessed to be the least delightful, that it was believed to produce neither fruits nor flowers, and that after a long and laborious cultivation, not even the barren laurel had been found upon it.

Yet on this province, my Lord, I enter'd with the pleasing hope, that as it was low, it likewise would be safe. I was drawn forward with the prospect of employment, which, tho' not splendid, would be useful; and which tho' it could not make my life envied, would keep it innocent; which would awaken no passion, engage me in no contention, nor throw in my way any temptation to disturb the quiet of others by censure, or my own by flattery.

I had read indeed of times, in which princes and statesmen thought it part of their honour to promote the improvement of their native tongues, and in which dictionaries were written under the protection of greatness.

To the patrons of such undertakings, I willingly paid the homage of believing that they, who were thus solicitous for the perpetuity of their language, had reason to expect that their actions would be celebrated by posterity, and that the eloquence which they promoted would be employed in their praise. But I considered such acts of beneficence as prodigies, recorded rather to raise wonder than expectation; and content with the terms that I had stipulated, had not suffer'd my imagination to flatter me with any other encouragement, when I found that my design had been thought by your Lordship of importance sufficient to attract your favour.

How far this unexpected distinction can be rated among the happy incidents of life, I am not yet able to determine. Its first effect has been to make me anxious lest it should fix the attention of the public[1] too much upon me, and as it once happened to an epic poet of France, by raising the reputation of the attempt, obstruct the reception of the work. I imagine what the world will expect from a scheme, prosecuted under your Lordship's influence, and I know that expectation, when her wings are once expanded, easily reaches heights which performance never will attain, and when she has mounted the summit of perfection, derides her follower, who dies in the pursuit.

Not therefore, to raise expectation, but to repress it, I here lay before your Lordship the plan of my undertaking, that more may not be demanded than I intend; and that before it is too far advanced to be thrown into a new method, I may be advertised of its defects or superfluities. Such informations I may justly hope from the emulation with which those who desire the praise of elegance or discernment must contend in the promotion of a design that you, my Lord, have not thought unworthy to share your attention with treaties and with wars.

In the first attempt to methodise my ideas, I found a difficulty which extended itself to the whole work. It was not easy to determine by what rule of distinction the words of this dictionary were to be chosen. The chief intent of it is to preserve the purity and ascertain the meaning of our English idiom; and this seems to require nothing more than that our language be considered so far as it is our own; that the words and phrases used in the general intercourse of life, or found in the works of those whom we commonly stile polite writers, be selected, without including the terms of particular professions, since, with the arts to which they relate, they are generally derived from other nations, and are very often the same in all the languages of this part of the world. This is perhaps the exact and pure idea of a grammatical dictionary; but in lexicography, as in other arts, naked science is too delicate for the purposes of life. The value of a work must be estimated by its use; it is not enough that a dictionary delights the critic, unless at the same time it instructs the learner; as it is to little purpose, that an engine amuses the philosopher by the subtilty of its mechanism, if it requires so much knowledge in its application as to be of no advantage to the common workman.

The title which I prefix to my work has long conveyed a very miscellaneous idea, and they that take a dictionary into their hands have been accustomed to expect from it, a solution of almost every difficulty. If foreign words therefore were rejected, it could be little regarded, except by critics, or those who aspire to criticism; and however it might enlighten those that write, would be all darkness to them that only read. The unlearned much oftener consult their dictionaries, for the meaning of words, than for their structures or formations; and the words that most want explanation, are generally terms of art, which therefore experience has taught my predecessors to spread with a kind of pompous luxuriance over their productions.

The academicians of France, indeed, rejected terms of science in their first essay, but found afterwards a necessity of relaxing the rigour of their determination; and, tho' they would not naturalize them at once by a single act, permitted them by degrees to settle themselves among the natives, with little opposition, and it would surely be no proof of judgment to imitate them in an error which they have now retracted, and deprive the book of its chief use by scrupulous distinctions.

Of such words however, all are not equally to be considered as parts of our language; for some of them are naturalized and incorporated, but others still continue aliens, and are rather auxiliaries than subjects. This naturalization is produced either by an admission into common speech in some metaphorical signification, which is the acquisition of a kind of property among us; as we say the *zenith* of advancement, the *meridian* of life, the †*cynosure* of neighbouring eyes; or it is the consequence of long intermixture and frequent use, by which the ear is accustomed to the sound of words till their original is forgotten, as in *equator, satellites*; or of the change of a foreign to an English termination, and a conformity to the laws of the speech into which they are adopted, as in *category, cachexy, peripneumony.*

Of those which still continue in the state of aliens, and have made no approaches towards assimilation, some seem necessary to be retained,

† *Milton*

because the purchasers of the dictionary will expect to find them. Such are many words in the common law, as *capias*, *habeas corpus*, *præmunire*, *nisi prius*: such are some terms of controversial divinity, as *hypostasis*; and of physick, as the names of diseases; and in general all terms which can be found in books not written professedly upon particular arts, or can be supposed necessary to those who do not regularly study them. Thus when a reader not skilled in physick happens in Milton upon this line,

– – – – pining atrophy,
Marasmus, and wide-wasting pestilence.

he will with equal expectation look into his dictionary for the word *marasmus*, as for *atrophy*, or *pestilence*; and will have reason to complain if he does not find it.

It seems necessary to the completion of a dictionary design'd not merely for critics but for popular use, that it should comprise, in some degree, the peculiar words of every profession; that the terms of war and navigation should be inserted so far as they can be required by readers of travels, and of history; and those of law, merchandise and mechanical trades, so far as they can be supposed useful in the occurrences of common life.

But there ought, however, to be some distinction made between the different classes of words, and therefore it will be proper to print those which are incorporated into the language in the usual character, and those which are still to be considered as foreign, in the Italick letter.

Another question may arise, with regard to appellatives, or the names of species. It seems of no great use to set down the words *horse*, *dog*, *cat*, *willow*, *alder*, *dasy*,[2] *rose*, and a thousand others, of which it will be hard to give an explanation not more obscure than the word itself. Yet it is to be considered, that, if the names of animals be inserted, we must admit those which are more known, as well as those with which we are, by accident, less acquainted; and if they are all rejected, how will the reader be relieved from difficulties produced by allusions to the crocodile, the camæleon,[3] the ichneumon, and the hyæna? If no plants are to be mentioned, the most pleasing part of nature will be excluded, and many beautiful epithets be unexplained. If only those which are less known are to be mentioned, who shall fix the limits of the reader's learning? The importance of such explications appears from the mistakes which the want of them has occasioned. Had Shakespeare had a dictionary of this kind, he had not made the *woodbine* entwine the *honeysuckle*; nor would Milton, with such assistance, have disposed so improperly of his *ellops* and his *scorpion*.

Besides, as such words, like others, require that their accents should be settled, their sounds ascertained, and their etymologies deduced, they cannot be properly omitted in the dictionary. And though the explanations of some may be censured as trivial, because they are almost universally understood, and those of others as unnecessary, because they will seldom occur, yet it seems not proper to omit them; since it is rather to be wished that many readers should find more than they expect, than that one should miss what he might hope to find.

When all the words are selected and arranged, the first part of the work to be considered is the ORTHOGRAPHY, which was long vague and uncertain, which at last, when its fluctuation ceased, was in many cases settled but by accident, and in which, according to your Lordship's observation, there is still great uncertainty among the best critics; nor is it easy to state a rule by which we may decide between custom and reason, or between the equiponderant authorities of writers alike eminent for judgment and accuracy.

The great orthographical contest has long subsisted between etymology and pronunciation. It has been demanded, on one hand, that men should write as they speak; but as it has been shewn that this conformity never was attained in any language, and that it is not more easy to perswade men to agree exactly in speaking than in writing, it may be asked with equal propriety, why men do not rather speak as they write. In France, where this controversy was at its greatest height, neither party, however ardent, durst adhere steadily to their own rule; the etymologist was often forced to spell with the people; and the advocate for the authority of pronunciation, found it sometimes deviating so capriciously from the received use of writing, that he was constrained to comply with the rule of his adversaries, lest he should lose the end by the means, and be left alone by following the croud.

When a question of orthography is dubious, that practice has, in my opinion, a claim to preference, which preserves the greatest number of radical letters, or seems most to comply with the general custom of our language. But the chief rule which I propose to follow, is to make no innovation, without a reason sufficient to balance the inconvenience of change; and such reasons I do not expect often to find. All change is of itself an evil, which ought not to be hazarded but for evident advantage; and as inconstancy is in every case a mark of weakness, it will add nothing to the reputation of our tongue. There are, indeed, some who despise the inconveniencies of confusion, who seem to take pleasure in departing from custom, and to think alteration desirable for its own sake; and the reformation of our orthography, which these writers have attempted, should not pass without its due honours, but that I suppose they hold singularity its own reward, or may dread the fascination of lavish praise.

The present usage of spelling, where the present usage can be distinguished, will therefore in this work be generally followed, yet there will be often occasion to observe, that it is in itself inaccurate, and tolerated rather than chosen; particularly, when by the change of one letter, or more, the meaning of a word is obscured, as in *farrier* for *ferrier*, as it was formerly written, from *ferrum* or *fer*; in *gibberish* for *gebrish*, the jargon of Geber and his chymical followers, understood by none but their own tribe. It will be likewise sometimes proper to trace back the orthography of different ages, and shew by what gradations the word departed from its original.

Closely connected with orthography is PRONUNCIATION, the stability of which is of great importance to the duration of a language, because the first change will naturally begin by corruptions in the living speech. The want of certain rules for the pronunciation of former ages, has made us wholly ignorant of the metrical art of our ancient poets; and since those who study their sentiments regret the loss of their numbers, it is surely time to provide that the harmony of the moderns may be more permanent.

A NEW pronunciation will make almost a new speech, and therefore since one great end of this undertaking is to fix the English language, care will be taken to determine the accentuation of all polysyllables by proper authorities, as it is one of those capricious phænomena which cannot be easily reduced to rules. Thus there is no antecedent reason for difference of accent in the two words *dolorous* and *sonorous*; yet of the one Milton gives the sound in this line,

> He pass'd o'er many a region *dolorous*,

and that of the other in this,

> *Sonorous* metal blowing martial sounds.

It may be likewise proper to remark metrical licences, such as contractions *generous*, *gen'rous*; *reverend*, *rev'rend*; and coalitions, as *region*, *question*.

But it is still more necessary to fix the pronunciation of monosyllables, by placing with them words of correspondent sound, that one may guard the other against the danger of that variation, which to some of the most common, has already happened, so that the words *wound*, and *wind*, as they are now frequently pronounced, will not rhyme to *sound*, and *mind*. It is to be remarked that many words written alike are differently pronounced, as *flow*, and *brow*, which may be thus registered *flow*, *woe*, *brow*, *now*, or of which the exemplification may be generally given by a distich. Thus the words *tear* or lacerate, and *tear* the water of the eye, have the same letters, but may be distinguished thus, *tear*, *dare*; *tear*, *peer*.

Some words have two sounds, which may be equally admitted, as being equally defensible by authority. Thus *great* is differently used.

> For Swift and him despis'd the farce of state,
> The sober follies of the wise and *great*. POPE.
>
> As if misfortune made the throne her seat,
> And none could be unhappy but the *great*. ROWE.

The care of such minute particulars may be censured as trifling, but these particulars have not been thought unworthy of attention in more polished languages.

The accuracy of the French, in stating the sounds of their letters, is well known; and, among the Italians, Crescembeni has not thought it unnecessary to inform his countrymen of the words, which, in compliance with different rhymes, are allowed to be differently spelt, and of which the number is now so fix'd, that no modern poet is suffered to encrease it.

When the orthography and pronunciation are adjusted, the ETYMOLOGY or DERIVATION is next to be considered, and the words are to be distinguished according to the different classes, whether simple, as *day*, *light*, or compound as *day-light*; whether primitive, as, to *act*, or derivative, as *action*, *actionable*; *active*, *activity*. This will much facilitate the attainment of our language, which now stands in our dictionaries a confused heap of words without dependence, and without relation.

When this part of the work is performed, it will be necessary to inquire how our primitives are to be deduced from foreign languages, which may be often very successfully performed by the assistance of our own etymologists. This search will give occasion to many curious disquisitions, and sometimes perhaps to conjectures, which, to readers unacquainted with this kind of study, cannot but appear improbable and capricious. But it may be reasonably imagined, that what is so much in the power of men as language, will very often be capriciously conducted. Nor are these disquisitions and conjectures to be considered altogether as wanton sports of wit, or vain shews of learning; our language is well known not to be primitive or self-originated, but to have adopted words of every generation, and either for the supply of its necessities, or the encrease of its copiousness, to have received additions from very distant regions; so that in search of the progenitors of our speech, we may wander from the tropic to the frozen zone, and find some in the vallies of Palestine and some upon the rocks of Norway.

Beside the derivation of particular words, there is likewise an etymology of phrases. Expressions are often taken from other languages, some apparently, as to *run a risque, courir un risque*; and some even when we do not seem to borrow their words; thus, to *bring about* or accomplish, appears an English phrase, but in reality our native word *about* has no such import, and it is only a French expression, of which we have an example in the common phrase, *venir à bout d'une affaire.*

In exhibiting the descent of our language, our etymologists seem to have been too lavish of their learning, having traced almost every word through various tongues, only to shew what was shewn sufficiently by the first derivation. This practice is of great use in synoptical lexicons, where mutilated and doubtful languages are explained by their affinity to others more certain and extensive, but is generally superfluous in English etymologies. When the word is easily deduced from a Saxon original, I shall not often enquire further, since we know not the parent of the Saxon dialect, but when it is borrowed from the French, I shall shew whence the French is apparently derived. Where a Saxon root cannot be found, the defect may be supplied from kindred languages, which will be generally furnished with much liberality by the writers of our glossaries; writers who deserve often the highest praise, both of judgment and industry, and may expect at least to be mentioned with honour by me, whom they have freed from the greatest part of a very laborious work, and on whom they have imposed, at worst, only the easy task of rejecting superfluities.

By tracing in this manner every word to its original, and not admitting, but with great caution, any of which no original can be found, we shall secure our language from being over-run with *cant*, from being crouded with low terms, the spawn of folly or affectation, which arise from no just principles of speech, and of which therefore no legitimate derivation can be shown.

When the etymology is thus adjusted, the ANALOGY of our language is next to be considered; when we have discovered whence our words are derived, we are to examine by what rules they are governed, and how they are inflected through their various terminations. The terminations of the English are few, but those few have hitherto remained unregarded by the writers of our dictionaries. Our substantives are declined only by the plural termination, our adjectives admit no variation but in the degrees of comparison, and our verbs are conjugated by auxiliary words, and are only changed in the preter tense.

To our language may be with great justness applied the observation of *Quintilian*, that speech was not formed by an analogy sent from heaven. It did not descend to us in a state of uniformity and perfection, but was produced by necessity and enlarged by accident, and is therefore composed of dissimilar parts, thrown together by negligence, by affectation, by learning, or by ignorance.

Our inflections therefore are by no means constant, but admit of numberless irregularities, which in this dictionary will be diligently noted. Thus *fox* makes in the plural *foxes*, but *ox* makes *oxen*. *Sheep* is the same in both numbers. Adjectives are sometimes compared by changing the last syllable, as *proud, prouder, proudest*; and sometimes by particles prefixed, as *ambitious*, *more* ambitious, *most* ambitious. The forms of our verbs are subject to great variety; some end their preter tense in *ed*, as I *love*, I *loved*, I have *loved*, which may be called the regular form, and is followed by most of our verbs of southern original. But many depart from this rule, without agreeing in any other, as I *shake*, I *shook*, I have *shaken*, or *shook*, as it is sometimes written in poetry; I *make*, I *made*, I have *made*; I *bring*, I *brought*; I *wring*, I *wrung*; and many others, which, as they cannot be reduced to rules, must be learned from the dictionary rather than the grammar.

The verbs are likewise to be distinguished according to their qualities, as actives from neuters; the neglect of which has already introduced some barbarities in our conversation, which, if not obviated by just animadversions, may in time creep into our writings.

Thus, my Lord, will our language be laid down, distinct in its minutest subdivisions, and resolved into its elemental principles. And who upon this survey can forbear to wish, that these fundamental atoms of our speech might obtain the firmness and immutability of the primogenial and constituent particles of matter, that they might retain their substance while they alter their appearance, and be varied and compounded, yet not destroyed.

But this is a privilege which words are scarcely to expect; for, like their author, when they are not gaining strength, they are generally losing it. Though art may sometimes prolong their duration, it will rarely give them perpetuity; and their changes will be almost always informing us, that language is the work of man, of a being from whom permanence and stability cannot be derived.

Words having been hitherto considered as separate and unconnected, are now to be likewise examined as they are ranged in their various relations to others by the rules of SYNTAX or construction, to which I do not know that any regard has been yet shewn in English dictionaries, and in which the grammarians can give little assistance. The syntax of this language is too inconstant to be reduced to rules, and can be only learned by the distinct consideration of particular words as they are used by the best authors. Thus, we say, according to the present modes of speech, the soldier died *of* his wounds, and the sailor perished *with* hunger; and every man acquainted with our language would be offended by a change of these particles, which yet seem originally assigned by chance, there being no reason to be drawn from grammar why a man may not, with equal propriety, be said to dye *with* a wound, or perish *of* hunger.

Our syntax therefore is not to be taught by general rules, but by special precedents; and in examining whether Addison has been with justice accused of a solecism in this passage,

> The poor inhabitant—
> Starves in the midst of nature's bounty curst,
> And in the loaden vineyard *dies for thirst*—

it is not in our power to have recourse to any established laws of speech, but we must remark how the writers of former ages have used the same word, and consider whether he can be acquitted of impropriety, upon the testimony of Davies, given in his favour by a similar passage.

> She loaths the watry glass wherein she gaz'd,
> And shuns it still, although *for thirst she dye.*

When the construction of a word is explained, it is necessary to pursue it through its train of PHRASEOLOGY, through those forms where it is used in a manner peculiar to our language, or in senses not to be comprised in the general explanations; as from the verb *make*, arise these phrases, to *make love*, to *make an end*, to *make way*; as he *made way* for his followers, the ship *made way* before the wind; to *make a bed*, to *make merry*, to *make a mock*, to *make presents*, to *make a doubt*, to *make out an assertion*, to *make good* a breach, to *make good* a cause, to *make nothing* of an attempt, to *make lamentation*, to *make a merit*, and many others which will occur in reading with that view, and which only their frequency hinders from being generally remarked.

The great labour is yet to come, the labour of interpreting these words and phrases with brevity, fulness and perspicuity; a task of which the extent and intricacy is sufficiently shown by the miscarriage of those who have generally attempted it. This difficulty is encreased by the necessity of explaining the words in the same language, for there is often only one word for one idea; and though it be easy to translate the words *bright*, *sweet*, *salt*, *bitter*, into another language, it is not easy to explain them.

With regard to the INTERPRETATION many other questions have required consideration. It was some time doubted whether it be necessary to explain the things implied by particular words. As under the term *baronet*, whether instead of this explanation, *a title of honour next in degree to that of baron*, it would be better to mention more particularly the creation, privileges and rank of baronets; and whether under the word *barometer*, instead of being satisfied with observing that it is *an instrument to discover the weight of the air*, it would be fit to spend a few lines upon its invention, construction and principles. It is not to be expected that with the explanation of the one the herald should be satisfied, or the philosopher with that of the other; but since it will be required by common readers, that the explications should be sufficient for common use, and since without some attention to such demands the dictionary cannot become generally valuable, I have determined to consult the best writers for explanations real as well as verbal, and perhaps I may at last have reason to say, after one of the augmenters of Furetier, that my book is more learned than its author.

In explaining the general and popular language, it seems necessary to sort the several senses of each word, and to exhibit first its natural and primitive signification, as

To *arrive*, to reach the shore in a voyage. He *arrived* at a safe harbour.

Then to give its consequential meaning, *to arrive*, to reach any place whether by land or sea; as, he *arrived* at his country seat.

Then its metaphorical sense, to obtain any thing desired; as, he *arrived* at a peerage.

Then to mention any observation that arises from the comparison of one meaning with another; as, it may be remarked of the word *arrive*, that in consequence of its original and etymological sense, it cannot be properly applied but to words signifying something desirable; thus, we say a man *arrived* at happiness, but cannot say without a mixture of irony, he *arrived* at misery.

Ground, the earth, generally as opposed to the air or water. He swam till he reached *ground*. The bird fell to the *ground*.

Then follows the accidental or consequential signification, in which *ground* implies any thing that lies under another; as, he laid colours upon a rough *ground*. The silk had blue flowers on a red *ground*.

Then the remoter or metaphorical signification; as, the *ground* of his opinion was a false computation. The *ground* of his work was his father's manuscript.

After having gone through the natural and figurative senses, it will be proper to subjoin the poetical sense of each word, where it differs from that which is in common use; as, *wanton* applied to any thing of which the motion is irregular without terror, as

In *wanton* ringlets curl'd her hair.

To the poetical sense may succeed the familiar; as of *toast*, used to imply the person whose health is drunk.

The wise man's passion, and the vain man's *toast*. POPE.

The familiar may be followed by the burlesque; as of *mellow*, applied to good fellowship:

In all thy humours whether grave, or *mellow*. ADDISON.

Or of *bite* used for *cheat*:

—More a dupe than wit,
Sappho can tell you, how this man was *bit*. POPE.

And lastly, may be produced the peculiar sense, in which a word is found in any great author. As *faculties* in Shakespeare signifies the powers of authority.

—This Duncan
Has borne his *faculties* so meek, has been
So clear in his great office, that &c.

The signification of adjectives, may be often ascertained by uniting them to substantives, as *simple swain*, *simple sheep*; sometimes the sense of a substantive may be elucidated by the epithets annexed to it in good authors, as the *boundless ocean*, the *open lawns*, and where such advantage can be gained by a short quotation, it is not to be omitted.

The difference of signification in words generally accounted synonimous, ought to be carefully observed; as in *pride*, *haughtiness*, *arrogance*; and the strict and critical meaning ought to be distinguished from that which is loose and popular; as in the word *perfection*, which though in its philosophical and exact sense, it can be of little use among human beings, is often so much degraded from its original signification, that the academicians have inserted in their work *the perfection of a language*, and with a little more licentiousness might have prevailed on themselves to have added *the perfection of a dictionary*.

There are many other characters of words which it will be of use to mention. Some have both an active and passive signification, as *fearful*, that which gives or which feels terror, a *fearful prodigy*, a *fearful hare*. Some have a personal, some a real meaning, as in opposition to *old* we use the adjective *young* of animated beings, and *new* of other things. Some are restrained to the sense of praise, and others to that of disapprobation, so commonly, though not always, we *exhort* to good actions, we *instigate* to ill; we *animate*, *incite* and *encourage* indifferently to good or bad. So we usually *ascribe* good, but *impute* evil; yet neither the use of these words, nor perhaps of any other in our licentious language, is so established as not to be often reversed by the correctest writers. I shall therefore, since the rules of stile, like those of law, arise from precedents often repeated, collect the testimonies on both sides, and endeavour to discover and promulgate the decrees of custom, who has so long possessed, whether by right or by usurpation, the sovereignty of words.

It is necessary likewise to explain many words by their opposition to others; for contraries are best seen when they stand together. Thus the verb *stand* has one sense as opposed to *fall*, and another as opposed to *fly*; for want of attending to which distinction, obvious as it is, the learned Dr. Bentley has squandered his criticism to no purpose, on these lines of *Paradise Lost*:

> — — — In heaps
> Chariot and charioteer lay over-turn'd,
> And fiery foaming steeds. What *stood, recoil'd*,
> O'erwearied, through the faint Satanic host,
> Defensive scarce, or with pale fear surpris'd,
> *Fled* ignominious — — —

"Here," says the critick, "as the sentence is now read, we find that what *stood, fled*," and therefore he proposes an alteration, which he might have spared if he had consulted a dictionary, and found that nothing more was affirmed than that those *fled* who did *not fall*.

In explaining such meanings as seem accidental and adventitious, I shall endeavour to give an account of the means by which they were introduced. Thus, to *eke out* any thing, signifies to lengthen it beyond its just dimensions by some low artifice, because the word *eke* was the usual refuge of our old writers when they wanted a syllable. And *buxom*, which means only *obedient*, is now made, in familiar phrases, to stand for *wanton*, because in an antient form of marriage, before the reformation, the bride promised complaisance and obedience in these terms: "I will be bonair and *buxom* in bed and at board."

I know well, my Lord, how trifling many of these remarks will appear separately considered, and how easily they may give occasion to the contemptuous merriment of sportive idleness, and the gloomy censures of arrogant stupidity; but dulness it is easy to despise, and laughter it is easy to repay. I shall not be solicitous what is thought of my work, by such as know not the difficulty or importance of philological studies, nor shall think those that have done nothing qualified to condemn me for doing little. It may not, however, be improper to remind them, that no terrestrial greatness is more than an aggregate of little things, and to inculcate after the Arabian proverb, that drops added to drops constitute the ocean.

There remains yet to be considered the DISTRIBUTION of words into their proper classes, or that part of lexicography which is strictly critical.

The popular part of the language, which includes all words not appropriated to particular sciences, admits of many distinctions and subdivisions; as, into words of general use; words employed chiefly in poetry; words obsolete; words which are admitted only by particular writers, yet not in themselves improper; words used only in burlesque writing; and words impure and barbarous.

Words of general use will be known by having no sign of particularity, and their various senses will be supported by authorities of all ages.

The words appropriated to poetry will be distinguished by some mark prefixed, or will be known by having no authorities but those of poets.

Of antiquated or obsolete words, none will be inserted but such as are to be found in authors who wrote since the accession of Elizabeth, from which we date the golden age of our language; and of these many might be omitted, but that the reader may require, with an appearance of reason, that no difficulty should be left unresolved in books which he finds himself invited to read, as confessed and established models of stile. These will be likewise pointed out by some note of exclusion, but not of disgrace.

The words which are found only in particular books, will be known by the single name of him that has used them; but such will be omitted, unless either their propriety, elegance, or force, or the reputation of their authors affords some extraordinary reason for their reception.

Words used in burlesque and familiar compositions, will be likewise mentioned with their proper authorities, such as *dudgeon* from Butler, and *leasing* from Prior, and will be diligently characterized by marks of distinction.

Barbarous or impure words and expressions, may be branded with some note of infamy, as they are carefully to be eradicated wherever they are found; and they occur too frequently, even in the best writers. As in Pope,

> — — — *in* endless error *hurl'd.*
> '*Tis these* that early taint the female soul.

In Addison,

> Attend to what a *lesser* muse indites.

And in Dryden:

> A dreadful quiet felt, and *worser* far
> Than arms — — —

If this part of the work can be well performed, it will be equivalent to the proposal made by Boileau to the academicians, that they should review all their polite writers, and correct such impurities as might be found in them, that their authority might not contribute, at any distant time, to the depravation of the language.

With regard to questions of purity, or propriety, I was once in doubt whether I should not attribute too much to myself in attempting to decide them, and whether my province was to extend beyond the proposition of the question, and the display of the suffrages on each side; but I have been since determined by your Lordship's opinion, to interpose my own judgment, and shall therefore endeavour to support what appears to me most consonant to grammar and reason. Ausonius thought that modesty forbad him to plead inability for a task to which Caesar had judged him equal.

> Cur me posse negem posse quod ille putat?[4]

And I may hope, my Lord, that since you, whose authority in our language is so generally acknowledged, have commissioned me to declare my own opinion, I shall be considered as exercising a kind of vicarious jurisdiction, and that the power which might have been denied to my own claim, will be readily allowed me as the delegate of your Lordship.

In citing authorities, on which the credit of every part of this work must depend, it will be proper to observe some obvious rules, such as of preferring writers of the first reputation to those of an inferior rank; of noting the quotations with accuracy; and of selecting, when it can be conveniently done, such sentences, as, besides their immediate use, may give pleasure or instruction by conveying some elegance of language, or some precept of prudence, or piety.

It has been asked, on some occasions, who shall judge the judges? And since with regard to this design, a question may arise by what authority the authorities are selected, it is necessary to obviate it, by declaring that many of the writers whose testimonies will be alleged, were selected by Mr. Pope, of whom I may be justified in affirming, that were he still alive, solicitous as he was for the success of this work, he would not be displeased that I have undertaken it.

It will be proper that the quotations be ranged according to the ages of their authors, and it will afford an agreeable amusement, if to the words and phrases which are not of our own growth, the name of the writer who first introduced them can be affixed, and if, to words which are now antiquated, the authority be subjoined of him who last admitted them. Thus for *scathe* and *buxom*, now obsolete, Milton may be cited.

— — — The mountain oak
Stands *scath'd* to heaven — — —
— — — He with broad sails
Winnow'd the *buxom* air — — —

By this method every word will have its history, and the reader will be informed of the gradual changes of the language, and have before his eyes the rise of some words, and the fall of others. But observations so minute and accurate are to be desired rather than expected, and if use be carefully supplied, curiosity must sometimes bear its disappointments.

This, my Lord, is my idea of an English dictionary, a dictionary by which the pronunciation of our language may be fixed, and its attainment facilitated; by which its purity may be preserved, its use ascertained, and its duration lengthened. And though, perhaps, to correct the language of nations by books of grammar, and amend their manners by discourses of morality, may be tasks equally difficult; yet as it is unavoidable to wish, it is natural likewise to hope, that your Lordship's patronage may not be wholly lost; that it may contribute to the preservation of antient, and the improvement of modern writers; that it may promote the reformation of those translators, who for want of understanding the characteristical difference of tongues, have formed a chaotic dialect of heterogeneous phrases; and awaken to the care of purer diction some men of genius, whose attention to argument makes them negligent of stile, or whose rapid imagination, like the Peruvian torrents, when it brings down gold, mingles it with sand.

When I survey the Plan which I have laid before you, I cannot, my Lord, but confess, that I am frighted at its extent, and, like the soldiers of Cæsar, look on Britain as a new world, which it is almost madness to invade. But I hope, that though I should not complete the conquest, I shall at least discover the coast, civilize part of the inhabitants, and make it easy for some other adventurer to proceed farther, to reduce them wholly to subjection, and settle them under laws.

We are taught by the great Roman orator, that every man should propose to himself the highest degree of excellence, but that he may stop with honour at the second or third: though therefore my performance should fall below the excellence of other dictionaries, I may obtain, at least, the praise of having endeavoured well, nor shall I think it any reproach to my diligence, that I have retired without a triumph from a contest with united academies and long successions of learned compilers. I cannot hope in the warmest moments, to preserve so much caution through so long a work, as not often to sink into negligence, or to obtain so much knowledge of all its parts, as not frequently to fail by ignorance. I expect that sometimes the desire of accuracy, will urge me to superfluities, and sometimes the fear of prolixity betray me to omissions; that in the extent of such variety I shall be often bewildred, and in the mazes of such intricacy, be frequently entangled; that in one part refinement will be subtilized beyond exactness, and evidence dilated in another beyond perspicuity. Yet I do not despair of approbation from those who knowing the uncertainty of conjecture, the scantiness of knowledge, the fallibility of memory, and the unsteadiness of attention, can compare the causes of error with the means of avoiding it, and the extent of art with the capacity of man; and whatever be the event of my endeavours, I shall not easily regret an attempt which has procured me the honour of appearing thus publickly,

My Lord, Your Lordship's Most Obedient and Most Humble Servant, SAM. JOHNSON.

Notes

1. For the most part, words ending in *-c* are printed without a final -k in the Plan, though in the *Dictionary* the *-ck* spelling is recommended (see the opening entry in letter K). Similarly, several words which in the *Dictionary* are spelled with *-our* (*errour, terrour, inferiour, oratour*) are here spelled with *-or.*
2. *daisy.*
3. *chameleon.*
4. See note 2 on p. xliv.

The Preface to *A Dictionary of the English Language*

It is the fate of those who toil at the lower employments of life, to be rather driven by the fear of evil, than attracted by the prospect of good; to be exposed to censure, without hope of praise; to be disgraced by miscarriage, or punished for neglect, where success would have been without applause, and diligence without reward.

Among these unhappy mortals is the writer of dictionaries; whom mankind have considered, not as the pupil, but the slave of science, the pionier of literature, doomed only to remove rubbish and clear obstructions from the paths of Learning and Genius, who press forward to conquest and glory, without bestowing a smile on the humble drudge that facilitates their progress. Every other authour may aspire to praise; the lexicographer can only hope to escape reproach, and even this negative recompense has been yet granted to very few.

I have, notwithstanding this discouragement, attempted a dictionary of the *English* language, which, while it was employed in the cultivation of every species of literature, has itself been hitherto neglected, suffered to spread, under the direction of chance, into wild exuberance, resigned to the tyranny of time and fashion, and exposed to the corruptions of ignorance, and caprices of innovation.

When I took the first survey of my undertaking, I found our speech copious without order, and energetick without rules: wherever I turned my view, there was perplexity to be disentangled, and confusion to be regulated; choice was to be made out of boundless variety, without any established principle of selection; adulterations were to be detected, without a settled test of purity; and modes of expression to be rejected or received, without the suffrages of any writers of classical reputation or acknowledged authority.

Having therefore no assistance but from general grammar, I applied myself to the perusal of our writers; and noting whatever might be of use to ascertain or illustrate any word or phrase, accumulated in time the materials of a dictionary, which, by degrees, I reduced to method, establishing to myself, in the progress of the work, such rules as experience and analogy suggested to me; experience, which practice and observation were continually increasing; and analogy, which, though in some words obscure, was evident in others.

In adjusting the ORTHOGRAPHY, which has been to this time unsettled and fortuitous, I found it necessary to distinguish those irregularities that are inherent in our tongue, and perhaps coeval with it, from others which the ignorance or negligence of later writers has produced. Every language has its anomalies, which, though inconvenient, and in themselves once unnecessary, must be tolerated among the imperfections of human things, and which require only to be registred, that they may not be increased, and ascertained, that they may not be confounded: but every language has likewise its improprieties and absurdities, which it is the duty of the lexicographer to correct or proscribe.

As language was at its beginning merely oral, all words of necessary or common use were spoken before they were written; and while they were unfixed by any visible signs, must have been spoken with great diversity, as we now observe those who cannot read to catch sounds imperfectly, and utter them negligently. When this wild and barbarous jargon was first reduced to an alphabet, every penman endeavoured to express, as he could, the sounds which he was accustomed to pronounce or to receive, and vitiated in writing such words as were already vitiated in speech. The powers of the letters, when they were applied to a new language, must have been vague and unsettled, and therefore different hands would exhibit the same sound by different combinations.

From this uncertain pronunciation arise in a great part the various dialects of the same country, which will always be observed to grow fewer, and less different, as books are multiplied; and from this arbitrary representation of sounds by letters, proceeds that diversity of spelling observable in the *Saxon* remains, and I suppose in the first books of every nation, which perplexes or destroys analogy, and produces anomalous formations, which, being once incorporated, can never be afterward dismissed or reformed.

Of this kind are the derivatives *length* from *long*, *strength* from *strong*, *darling* from *dear*, *breadth* from *broad*, from *dry*, *drought*, and from *high*, *height*, which *Milton*, in zeal for analogy, writes *highth*; *Quid te exempta juvat spinis de pluribus una*;[1] to change all would be too much, and to change one is nothing.

This uncertainty is most frequent in the vowels, which are so capriciously pronounced, and so differently modified, by accident or affectation, not only in every province, but in every mouth, that to them, as is well known to etymologists, little regard is to be shewn in the deduction of one language from another.

Such defects are not errours in orthography, but spots of barbarity impressed so deep in the *English* language, that criticism can never wash them away; these, therefore, must be permitted to remain untouched: but many words have likewise been altered by accident, or depraved by ignorance, as the pronunciation of the vulgar has been weakly followed; and some still continue to be variously written, as authours differ in their care or skill: of these it was proper to enquire the true orthography, which I have always considered as depending on their derivation, and have therefore referred them to their original languages: thus I write *enchant, enchantment, enchanter*, after the *French*, and *incantation* after the *Latin*; thus *entire* is chosen rather than *intire*, because it passed to us not from the *Latin integer*, but from the *French entier*.

Of many words it is difficult to say whether they were immediately received from the *Latin* or the *French*, since at the time when we had dominions in *France*, we had *Latin* service in our churches. It is, however, my opinion, that the *French* generally supplied us; for we have few *Latin* words, among the terms of domestick use, which are not *French*; but many *French*, which are very remote from *Latin*.

Even in words of which the derivation is apparent, I have been often obliged to sacrifice uniformity to custom; thus I write, in compliance with a numberless majority, *convey* and *inveigh*, *deceit* and *receipt*, *fancy* and *phantom*; sometimes the derivative varies from the primitive, as *explain* and *explanation*, *repeat* and *repetition*.

Some combinations of letters having the same power are used indifferently without any discoverable reason of choice, as in *choak, choke*; *soap, sope*; *fewel, fuel*, and many others; which I have sometimes inserted twice, that those who search for them under either form, may not search in vain.

In examining the orthography of any doubtful word, the mode of spelling by which it is inserted in the series of the dictionary, is to be considered as that to which I give, perhaps not often rashly, the preference. I have left, in the examples, to every authour his own practice unmolested, that the reader may balance suffrages, and judge between us: but this question is not always to be determined by reputed or by real learning; some men, intent upon greater things, have thought little on sounds and derivations; some, knowing in the ancient tongues, have neglected those in which our words are commonly to be sought. Thus *Hammond* writes *fecibleness* for *feasibleness*, because I suppose he imagined it derived immediately from the *Latin*; and some words, such as *dependant, dependent*; *dependance, dependence*, vary their final syllable, as one or other language is present to the writer.

In this part of the work, where caprice has long wantoned without controul, and vanity sought praise by petty reformation, I have endeavoured to proceed with a scholar's reverence for antiquity, and a grammarian's regard to the genius of our tongue. I have attempted few alterations, and among those few, perhaps the greater part is from the modern to the ancient practice; and I hope I may be allowed to recommend to those, whose thoughts have been, perhaps, employed too anxiously on verbal singularities, not to disturb, upon narrow views, or for minute propriety, the orthography of their fathers. It has been asserted, that for the law to be *known*, is of more importance than to be *right*. Change, says *Hooker*, is not made without inconvenience, even from worse to better. There is in constancy and stability a general and lasting advantage, which will always overbalance the slow improvements of gradual correction. Much less ought our written language to comply with the corruptions of oral utterance, or copy that which every variation of time or place makes different from itself, and imitate those changes, which will again be changed, while imitation is employed in observing them.

This recommendation of steadiness and uniformity does not proceed from an opinion, that particular combinations of letters have much influence on human happiness; or that truth may not be successfully taught by modes of spelling fanciful and erroneous: I am not yet so lost in lexicography, as to forget that *words are the daughters of earth, and that things are the sons of heaven*. Language is only the instrument of science, and words are but the signs of ideas: I wish, however, that the instrument might be less apt to decay, and that signs might be permanent, like the things which they denote.

In settling the orthography, I have not wholly neglected the pronunciation, which I have directed, by printing an accent upon the acute or elevated syllable. It will sometimes be found, that the accent is placed by the authour quoted, on a different syllable from that marked in the alphabetical series; it is then to be understood, that custom has varied, or that the authour has, in my opinion, pronounced wrong. Short directions are sometimes given where the sound of letters is irregular; and if they are sometimes omitted, defect in such minute observations will be more easily excused, than superfluity.

In the investigation both of the orthography and signification of words, their ETYMOLOGY was necessarily to be considered, and they were therefore to be divided into primitives and derivatives. A primitive word, is that which can be traced no further to any *English* root; thus *circumspect*, *circumvent*, *circumstance*, *delude*, *concave*, and *complicate*, though compounds in the *Latin*, are to us primitives. Derivatives, are all those that can be referred to any word in *English* of greater simplicity.

The derivatives I have referred to their primitives, with an accuracy sometimes needless; for who does not see that *remoteness* comes from *remote*, *lovely* from *love*, *concavity* from *concave*, and *demonstrative* from *demonstrate*? but this grammatical exuberance the scheme of my work did not allow me to repress. It is of great importance in examining the general fabrick of a language, to trace one word from another, by noting the usual modes of derivation and inflection; and uniformity must be preserved in systematical works, though sometimes at the expence of particular propriety.

Among other derivatives I have been careful to insert and elucidate the anomalous plurals of nouns and preterites of verbs, which in the *Teutonick* dialects are very frequent, and, though familiar to those who have always used them, interrupt and embarrass the learners of our language.

The two languages from which our primitives have been derived are the *Roman* and *Teutonick*: under the *Roman* I comprehend the *French* and provincial tongues; and under the *Teutonick* range the *Saxon*, *German*, and all their kindred dialects. Most of our polysyllables are *Roman*, and our words of one syllable are very often *Teutonick*.

In assigning the *Roman* original, it has perhaps sometimes happened that I have mentioned only the *Latin*, when the word was borrowed from the *French*; and considering myself as employed only in the illustration of my own language, I have not been very careful to observe whether the *Latin* word be pure or barbarous, or the *French* elegant or obsolete.

For the *Teutonick* etymologies I am commonly indebted to *Junius* and *Skinner*, the only names which I have forborn to quote when I copied their books; not that I might appropriate their labours or usurp their honours, but that I might spare a perpetual repetition by one general acknowledgment. Of these, whom I ought not to mention but with the reverence due to instructors and benefactors, *Junius* appears to have excelled in extent of learning, and *Skinner* in rectitude of understanding. *Junius* was accurately skilled in all the northern languages, *Skinner* probably examined the ancient and remoter dialects only by occasional inspection into dictionaries; but the learning of *Junius* is often of no other use than to show him a track by which he may deviate from his purpose, to which *Skinner* always presses forward by the shortest way. *Skinner* is often ignorant, but never ridiculous: *Junius* is always full of knowledge; but his variety distracts his judgment, and his learning is very frequently disgraced by his absurdities.

The votaries of the northern muses will not perhaps easily restrain their indignation, when they find the name of *Junius* thus degraded by a disadvantageous comparison; but whatever reverence is due to his diligence, or his attainments, it can be no criminal degree of censoriousness to charge that etymologist with want of judgment, who can seriously derive *dream* from *drama*, because *life is a drama, and a drama is a dream*; and who declares with a tone of defiance, that no man can fail to derive *moan* from *μόνος*, *monos*, who considers that grief naturally loves to be *alone.*[2]

Our knowledge of the northern literature is so scanty, that of words undoubtedly *Teutonick* the original is not always to be found in any ancient language; and I have therefore inserted *Dutch* or *German* substitutes, which I consider not as radical but parallel, not as the parents, but sisters of the *English*.

The words which are represented as thus related by descent or cognation, do not always agree in sense; for it is incident to words, as to their authours, to degenerate from their ancestors, and to change their manners when they change their country. It is sufficient, in etymological enquiries, if the senses of kindred words be found such as may easily pass into each other, or such as may both be referred to one general idea.

The etymology, so far as it is yet known, was easily found in the volumes where it is particularly and professedly delivered; and, by proper attention to the rules of derivation, the orthography was soon adjusted. But to COLLECT the WORDS of our language was a task of greater difficulty: the deficiency of dictionaries was immediately apparent; and when they were exhausted, what was yet wanting must be sought by fortuitous and unguided excursions into books, and gleaned as industry should find, or chance should offer it, in the boundless chaos of a living speech. My search, however, has been either skilful or lucky; for I have much augmented the vocabulary.

As my design was a dictionary, common or appellative, I have omitted all words which have relation to proper names; such as *Arian*, *Socinian*, *Calvinist*, *Benedictine*, *Mahometan*; but have retained those of a more general nature, as *Heathen*, *Pagan*.

Of the terms of art I have received such as could be found either in books of science or technical dictionaries; and have often inserted, from philosophical writers, words which are supported perhaps only by a single authority, and which being not admitted into general use, stand yet as candidates or probationers, and must depend for their adoption on the suffrage of futurity.

The words which our authours have introduced by their knowledge of foreign languages, or ignorance of their own, by vanity or wantonness, by compliance with fashion, or lust of innovation, I have registred as they occurred, though commonly only to censure them, and warn others against the folly of naturalizing useless foreigners to the injury of the natives.

I have not rejected any by design, merely because they were unnecessary or exuberant; but have received those which by different writers have been differently formed, as *viscid*, and *viscidity*, *viscous*, and *viscosity*.

Compounded or double words I have seldom noted, except when they obtain a signification different from that which the components have in their simple state. Thus *highwayman*, *woodman*, and *horsecourser*, require an explication; but of *thieflike* or *coachdriver* no notice was needed, because the primitives contain the meaning of the compounds.

Words arbitrarily formed by a constant and settled analogy, like diminutive adjectives in *ish*, as *greenish*, *bluish*, adverbs in *ly*, as *dully*, *openly*, substantives in *ness*, as *vileness*, *faultiness*, were less diligently sought, and many sometimes have been omitted, when I had no authority that invited me to insert them; not that they are not genuine and regular offsprings of *English* roots, but because their relation to the primitive being always the same, their signification cannot be mistaken.

The verbal nouns in *ing*, such as the *keeping* of the *castle*, the *leading* of the *army*, are always neglected, or placed only to illustrate the sense of the verb, except when they signify things as well as actions, and have therefore a plural number, as *dwelling*, *living*; or have an absolute and abstract signification, as *colouring*, *painting*, *learning*.

The participles are likewise omitted, unless, by signifying rather qualities than action, they take the nature of adjectives; as a *thinking* man, a man of prudence; a *pacing* horse, a horse that can pace: these I have ventured to call *participial adjectives*. But neither are these always inserted, because they are commonly to be understood, without any danger of mistake, by consulting the verb.

Obsolete words are admitted, when they are found in authours not obsolete, or when they have any force or beauty that may deserve revival.

As composition is one of the chief characteristicks of a language, I have endeavoured to make some reparation for the universal negligence of my predecessors, by inserting great numbers of compounded words, as may be found under *after*, *fore*, *new*, *night*, *fair*, and many more. These, numerous as they are, might be multiplied, but that use and curiosity are here satisfied, and the frame of our language and modes of our combination amply discovered.

Of some forms of composition, such as that by which *re* is prefixed to note *repetition*, and *un* to signify *contrariety* or *privation*, all the examples cannot be accumulated, because the use of these particles, if not wholly arbitrary, is so little limited, that they are hourly affixed to new words as occasion requires, or is imagined to require them.

There is another kind of composition more frequent in our language than perhaps in any other, from which arises to foreigners the greatest difficulty. We modify the signification of many verbs by a particle subjoined; as to *come off*, to escape by a fetch; to *fall on*, to attack; to *fall off*, to apostatize; *to break off*, to stop abruptly; to *bear out*, to justify; to *fall in*, to comply; to *give over*, to cease; to *set off*, to embellish; to *set in*, to begin a continual tenour; to *set out*, to begin a course or journey; to *take off*, to copy; with innumerable expressions of the same kind, of which some appear wildly irregular, being so far distant from the sense of the simple words, that no sagacity will be able to trace the steps by which they arrived at the present use. These I have noted with great care; and though I cannot flatter myself that the collection is complete, I believe I have so far assisted the students of our language, that this kind of phraseology will be no longer insuperable; and the combinations of verbs and particles, by chance omitted, will be easily explained by comparison with those that may be found.

Many words yet stand supported only by the name of *Bailey*, *Ainsworth*, *Philips*, or the contracted *Dict.* for *Dictionaries* subjoined: of these I am not always certain that they are read in any book but the works of lexicographers. Of such I have omitted many, because I had never read them; and many I have inserted, because they may perhaps exist, though they have escaped my notice: they are, however, to be yet considered as resting only upon the credit of former dictionaries. Others, which I considered as useful, or know to be proper, though I could not at present support them by authorities, I have suffered to stand upon my own attestation, claiming the same privilege with my predecessors of being sometimes credited without proof.

The words, thus selected and disposed, are grammatically considered: they are referred to the different parts of speech; traced, when they are irregularly inflected, through their various terminations; and illustrated by observations, not indeed of great or striking importance, separately considered, but necessary to the elucidation of our language, and hitherto neglected or forgotten by *English* grammarians.

That part of my work on which I expect malignity most frequently to fasten, is the *Explanation*; in which I cannot hope to satisfy those, who are perhaps not inclined to be pleased, since I have not always been able to satisfy myself. To interpret a language by itself is very difficult; many words cannot be explained by synonimes, because the idea signified by them has not more than one appellation; nor by paraphrase, because simple ideas cannot be described. When the nature of things is unknown, or the notion unsettled and indefinite, and various in various minds, the words by which such notions are conveyed, or such things denoted, will be ambiguous and perplexed. And such is the fate of hapless lexicography, that not only darkness, but light, impedes and distresses it; things may be not only too little, but too much known, to be happily illustrated. To explain, requires the use of terms less abstruse than that which is to be explained, and such terms cannot always be found; for as nothing can be proved but by supposing something intuitively known, and evident without proof, so nothing can be defined but by the use of words too plain to admit a definition.

Other words there are, of which the sense is too subtle and evanescent to be fixed in a paraphrase; such are all those which are by the grammarians termed *expletives*, and, in dead languages, are suffered to pass for empty sounds, of no other use than to fill a verse, or to modulate a period, but which are easily perceived in living tongues to have power and emphasis, though it be sometimes such as no other form of expression can convey.

My labour has likewise been much increased by a class of verbs too frequent in the *English* language, of which the signification is so loose and general, the use so vague and indeterminate, and the senses detorted so widely from the first idea, that it is hard to trace them through the maze of variation, to catch them on the brink of utter inanity, to circumscribe them by any limitations, or interpret them by any words of distinct and settled meaning: such are *bear*, *break*, *come*, *cast*, *full*, *get*, *give*, *do*, *put*, *set*, *go*, *run*, *make*, *take*, *turn*, *throw*. If of these the whole power is not accurately delivered, it must be remembered, that while our language is yet living, and variable by the caprice of every one that speaks it, these words are hourly shifting their relations, and can no more be ascertained in a dictionary, than a grove, in the agitation of a storm, can be accurately delineated from its picture in the water.

The particles are among all nations applied with so great latitude, that they are not easily reducible under any regular scheme of explication: this difficulty is not less, nor perhaps greater, in *English*, than in other languages. I have laboured them with diligence, I hope with success; such at least as can be expected in a task, which no man, however learned or sagacious, has yet been able to perform.

Some words there are which I cannot explain, because I do not understand them; these might have been omitted very often with little inconvenience, but I would not so far indulge my vanity as to decline this confession: for when *Tully* owns himself ignorant whether *lessus*, in the twelve tables, means a *funeral song*, or *mourning garment*; and *Aristotle* doubts whether *οὔϱευς*, in the Iliad, signifies a *mule*, or *muleteer*, I may freely, without shame, leave some obscurities to happier industry, or future information.

The rigour of interpretative lexicography requires that *the explanation, and the word explained, should be always reciprocal*; this I have always endeavoured, but could not always attain. Words are seldom exactly synonimous; a new term was not introduced, but because the former was thought inadequate: names, therefore, have often many ideas, but few ideas have many names. It was then necessary to use the proximate word, for the deficiency of single terms can very seldom be supplied by circumlocution; nor is the inconvenience great of such mutilated interpretations, because the sense may easily be collected entire from the examples.

In every word of extensive use, it was requisite to mark the progress of its meaning, and show by what gradations of intermediate sense it has passed from its primitive to its remote and accidental signification; so that every foregoing explanation should tend to that which follows, and the series be regularly concatenated from the first notion to the last.

This is specious, but not always practicable; kindred senses may be so interwoven, that the perplexity cannot be disentangled, nor any reason be assigned why one should be ranged before the other. When the radical idea branches out into parallel ramifications, how can a consecutive series be formed of senses in their nature collateral? The shades of meaning sometimes pass imperceptibly into each other; so that though on one side they apparently differ, yet it is impossible to mark the point of contact. Ideas of the same race, though not exactly alike, are sometimes so little different, that no words can express the dissimilitude, though the mind easily perceives it, when they are exhibited together; and sometimes there is such a confusion of acceptations, that discernment is wearied, and distinction puzzled, and perseverance herself hurries to an end, by crouding together what she cannot separate.

These complaints of difficulty will, by those that have never considered words beyond their popular use, be thought only the jargon of a man willing to magnify his labours, and procure veneration to his studies by involution and obscurity. But every art is obscure to those that have not learned it: this uncertainty of terms, and commixture of ideas, is well known to those who have joined philosophy with grammar; and if I have not expressed them very clearly, it must be remembered that I am speaking of that which words are insufficient to explain.

The original sense of words is often driven out of use by their metaphorical acceptations, yet must be inserted for the sake of a regular origination. Thus I know not whether *ardour* is used for *material heat*, or whether *flagrant*, in *English*, ever signifies the same with *burning*; yet such are the primitive ideas of these words, which are therefore set first, though without examples, that the figurative senses may be commodiously deduced.

Such is the exuberance of signification which many words have obtained, that it was scarcely possible to collect all their senses; sometimes the meaning of derivatives must be sought in the mother term, and sometimes deficient explanations of the primitive may be supplied in the train of derivation. In any case of doubt or difficulty, it will be always proper to examine all the words of the same race; for some words are slightly passed over to avoid repetition, some admitted easier and clearer explanation than others, and all will be better understood, as they are considered in greater variety of structures and relations.

All the interpretations of words are not written with the same skill, or the same happiness: things equally easy in themselves, are not all equally easy to any single mind. Every writer of a long work commits errours, where there appears neither ambiguity to mislead, nor obscurity to confound him; and in a search like this, many felicities of expression will be casually overlooked, many convenient parallels will be forgotten, and many particulars will admit improvement from a mind utterly unequal to the whole performance.

But many seeming faults are to be imputed rather to the nature of the undertaking, than the negligence of the performer. Thus some explanations are unavoidably reciprocal or circular, as *hind, the female of the stag*; *stag, the male of the hind:* sometimes easier words are changed into harder, as *burial* into *sepulture* or *interment*, *drier* into *desiccative*, *dryness* into *siccity* or *aridity*, *fit* into *paroxysm*; for the easiest word, whatever it be, can never be translated into one more easy. But easiness and difficulty are merely relative, and if the present prevalence of our language should invite foreigners to this dictionary, many will be assisted by those words which now seem only to increase or produce obscurity. For this reason I have endeavoured frequently to join a *Teutonick* and *Roman* interpretation, as to CHEER to *gladden*, or *exhilarate*, that every learner of *English* may be assisted by his own tongue.

The solution of all difficulties, and the supply of all defects, must be sought in the examples, subjoined to the various senses of each word, and ranged according to the time of their authours.

When first I collected these authorities, I was desirous that every quotation should be useful to some other end than the illustration of a word; I therefore extracted from philosophers principles of science; from historians remarkable facts; from chymists complete processes; from divines striking exhortations; and from poets beautiful descriptions. Such is design, while it is yet at a distance from execution. When the time called upon me to range this accumulation of elegance and wisdom into an alphabetical series, I soon discovered that the bulk of my volumes would fright away the student, and was forced to depart from my scheme of including all that was pleasing or useful in *English* literature, and reduce my transcripts very often to clusters of words, in which scarcely any meaning is retained; thus to the weariness of copying, I was condemned to add the vexation of expunging. Some passages I have yet spared, which may relieve the labour of verbal searches, and intersperse with verdure and flowers the dusty desarts of barren philology.

The examples, thus mutilated, are no longer to be considered as conveying the sentiments or doctrine of their authours; the word for the sake of which they are inserted, with all its appendant clauses, has been carefully preserved; but it may sometimes happen, by hasty detruncation, that the general tendency of the sentence may be changed: the divine may desert his tenets, or the philosopher his system.

Some of the examples have been taken from writers who were never mentioned as masters of elegance or models of stile; but words must be sought where they are used; and in what pages, eminent for purity, can terms of manufacture or agriculture be found? Many quotations serve no other purpose, than that of proving the bare existence of words, and are therefore selected with less scrupulousness than those which are to teach their structures and relations.

My purpose was to admit no testimony of living authours, that I might not be misled by partiality, and that none of my cotemporaries might have reason to complain; nor have I departed from this resolution, but when some performance of uncommon excellence excited my veneration, when my memory supplied me, from late books, with an example that was wanting, or when my heart, in the tenderness of friendship, solicited admission for a favourite name.

So far have I been from any care to grace my pages with modern decorations, that I have studiously endeavoured to collect examples and authorities from the writers before the restoration, whose works I regard as *the wells of English undefiled*, as the pure sources of genuine diction. Our language, for almost a century, has, by the concurrence of many causes, been gradually departing from its original *Teutonick* character, and deviating towards a *Gallick* structure and phraseology, from which it ought to be our endeavour to recal it, by making our ancient volumes the ground-work of stile, admitting among the additions of later times, only such as may supply real deficiencies, such as are readily adopted by the genius of our tongue, and incorporate easily with our native idioms.

But as every language has a time of rudeness antecedent to perfection, as well as of false refinement and declension, I have been cautious lest my zeal for antiquity might drive me into times too remote, and croud my book with words now no longer understood. I have fixed *Sidney*'s work for the boundary, beyond which I make few excursions. From the authours which rose in the time of *Elizabeth*, a speech might be formed adequate to all the purposes of use and elegance. If the language of theology were extracted from *Hooker* and the translation of the Bible; the terms of natural knowledge from *Bacon*; the phrases of policy, war, and navigation from *Raleigh*; the dialect of poetry and fiction from *Spenser* and *Sidney*; and the diction of common life from *Shakespeare*, few ideas would be lost to mankind, for want of *English* words, in which they might be expressed.

It is not sufficient that a word is found, unless it be so combined as that its meaning is apparently determined by the tract and tenour of the sentence; such passages I have therefore chosen, and when it happened that any authour gave a definition of a term, or such an explanation as is equivalent to a definition, I have placed his authority as a supplement to my own, without regard to the chronological order, that is otherwise observed.

Some words, indeed, stand unsupported by any authority, but they are commonly derivative nouns or adverbs, formed from their primitives by regular and constant analogy, or names of things seldom occurring in books, or words of which I have reason to doubt the existence.

There is more danger of censure from the multiplicity than paucity of examples; authorities will sometimes seem to have been accumulated without necessity or use, and perhaps some will be found, which might, without loss, have been omitted. But a work of this kind is not hastily to be charged with superfluities: those quotations which to careless or unskilful perusers appear only to repeat the same sense, will often exhibit, to a more accurate examiner, diversities of signification, or, at least, afford different shades of the same meaning: one will shew the word applied to persons, another to things; one will express an ill, another a good, and a third a neutral sense; one will prove the expression genuine from an ancient authour; another will shew it elegant from a modern: a doubtful authority is corroborated by another of more credit; an ambiguous sentence is ascertained by a passage clear and determinate; the word, how often soever repeated, appears with new associates and in different combinations, and every quotation contributes something to the stability or enlargement of the language.

When words are used equivocally, I receive them in either sense; when they are metaphorical, I adopt them in their primitive acceptation.

I have sometimes, though rarely, yielded to the temptation of exhibiting a genealogy of sentiments, by shewing how one authour copied the thoughts and diction of another: such quotations are indeed little more than repetitions, which might justly be censured, did they not gratify the mind, by affording a kind of intellectual history.

The various syntactical structures occurring in the examples have been carefully noted; the licence or negligence with which many words have been hitherto used, has made our stile capricious and indeterminate; when the different combinations of the same word are exhibited together, the preference is readily given to propriety, and I have often endeavoured to direct the choice.

Thus have I laboured to settle the orthography, display the analogy, regulate the structures, and ascertain the signification of *English* words, to perform all the parts of a faithful lexicographer: but I have not always executed my own scheme, or satisfied my own expectations. The work, whatever proofs of diligence and attention it may exhibit, is yet capable of many improvements: the orthography which I recommend is still controvertible, the etymology which I adopt is uncertain, and perhaps frequently erroneous; the explanations are sometimes too much contracted, and sometimes too much diffused, the significations are distinguished rather with subtilty than skill, and the attention is harrassed with unnecessary minuteness.

The examples are too often injudiciously truncated, and perhaps sometimes, I hope very rarely, alleged in a mistaken sense; for in making this collection I trusted more to memory, than, in a state of disquiet and embarrassment, memory can contain, and purposed to supply at the review what was left incomplete in the first transcription.

Many terms appropriated to particular occupations, though necessary and significant, are undoubtedly omitted; and of the words most studiously considered and exemplified, many senses have escaped observation.

Yet these failures, however frequent, may admit extenuation and apology. To have attempted much is always laudable, even when the enterprize is above the strength that undertakes it: To rest below his own aim is incident to every one whose fancy is active, and whose views are comprehensive; nor is any man satisfied with himself because he has done much, but because he can conceive little. When first I engaged in this work, I resolved to leave neither words nor things unexamined, and pleased myself with a prospect of the hours which I should revel away in feasts of literature, the obscure recesses of northern learning, which I should enter and ransack, the treasures with which I expected every search into those neglected mines to reward my labour, and the triumph with which I should display my acquisitions to mankind. When I had thus enquired into the original of words, I resolved to show likewise my attention to things; to pierce deep into every science, to enquire the nature of every substance of which I inserted the name, to limit every idea by a definition strictly logical, and exhibit every production of art or nature in an accurate description, that my book might be in place of all other dictionaries whether appellative or technical. But these were the dreams of a poet doomed at last to wake a lexicographer. I soon found that it is too late to look for instruments, when the work calls for execution, and that whatever abilities I had brought to my task, with those I must finally perform it. To deliberate whenever I doubted, to enquire whenever I was ignorant, would have protracted the undertaking without end, and, perhaps, without much improvement; for I did not find by my first experiments, that what I had not of my own was easily to be obtained: I saw that one enquiry only gave occasion to another, that book referred to book, that to search was not always to find, and to find was not always to be informed; and that thus to persue perfection, was, like the first inhabitants of Arcadia, to chace the sun, which, when they had reached the hill where he seemed to rest, was still beheld at the same distance from them.

I then contracted my design, determining to confide in myself, and no longer to solicit auxiliaries, which produced more incumbrance than assistance: by this I obtained at least one advantage, that I set limits to my work, which would in time be finished, though not completed.

Despondency has never so far prevailed as to depress me to negligence; some faults will at last appear to be the effects of anxious diligence and persevering activity. The nice and subtle ramifications of meaning were not easily avoided by a mind intent upon accuracy, and convinced of the necessity of disentangling combinations, and separating similitudes. Many of the distinctions which to common readers appear useless and idle, will be found real and important by men versed in the school philosophy, without which no dictionary ever shall be accurately compiled, or skilfully examined.

Some senses however there are, which, though not the same, are yet so nearly allied, that they are often confounded. Most men think indistinctly, and therefore cannot speak with exactness; and consequently some examples might be indifferently put to either signification: this uncertainty is not to be imputed to me, who do not form, but register the language; who do not teach men how they should think, but relate how they have hitherto expressed their thoughts.

The imperfect sense of some examples I lamented, but could not remedy, and hope they will be compensated by innumerable passages selected with propriety, and preserved with exactness; some shining with sparks of imagination, and some replete with treasures of wisdom.

The orthography and etymology, though imperfect, are not imperfect for want of care, but because care will not always be successful, and recollection or information come too late for use.

That many terms of art and manufacture are omitted, must be frankly acknowledged; but for this defect I may boldly allege that it was unavoidable: I could not visit caverns to learn the miner's language, nor take a voyage to perfect my skill in the dialect of navigation, nor visit the warehouses of merchants, and shops of artificers, to gain the names of wares, tools and operations, of which no mention is found in books; what favourable accident, or easy enquiry brought within my reach, has not been neglected; but it had been a hopeless labour to glean up words, by courting living information, and contesting with the sullenness of one, and the roughness of another.

To furnish the academicians *della Crusca* with words of this kind, a series of comedies called *la Fiera*, or *the Fair*, was professedly written by *Buonaroti*; but I had no such assistant, and therefore was content to want what they must have wanted likewise, had they not luckily been so supplied.

Nor are all words which are not found in the vocabulary, to be lamented as omissions. Of the laborious and mercantile part of the people, the diction is in a great measure casual and mutable; many of their terms are formed for some temporary or local convenience, and though current at certain times and places, are in others utterly unknown. This fugitive cant, which is always in a state of increase or decay, cannot be regarded as any part of the durable materials of a language, and therefore must be suffered to perish with other things unworthy of preservation.

Care will sometimes betray to the appearance of negligence. He that is catching opportunities which seldom occur, will suffer those to pass by unreguarded, which he expects hourly to return; he that is searching for rare and remote things, will neglect those that are obvious and familiar: thus many of the most common and cursory words have been inserted with little illustration, because in gathering the authorities, I forbore to copy those which I thought likely to occur whenever they were wanted. It is remarkable that, in reviewing my collection, I found the word SEA unexemplified.

Thus it happens, that in things difficult there is danger from ignorance, and in things easy from confidence; the mind, afraid of greatness, and disdainful of littleness, hastily withdraws herself from painful searches, and passes with scornful rapidity over tasks not adequate to her powers, sometimes too secure for caution, and again too anxious for vigorous effort; sometimes idle in a plain path, and sometimes distracted in labyrinths, and dissipated by different intentions.

A large work is difficult because it is large, even though all its parts might singly be performed with facility; where there are many things to be done, each must be allowed its share of time and labour, in the proportion only which it bears to the whole; nor can it be expected, that the stones which form the dome of a temple, should be squared and polished like the diamond of a ring.

Of the event of this work, for which, having laboured it with so much application, I cannot but have some degree of parental fondness, it is natural to form conjectures. Those who have been persuaded to think well of my design, require that it should fix our language, and put a stop to those alterations which time and chance have hitherto been suffered to make in it without opposition. With this consequence I will confess that I flattered myself for a while; but now begin to fear that I have indulged expectation which neither reason nor experience can justify. When we see men grow old and die at a certain time one after another, from century to century, we laugh at the elixir that promises to prolong life to a thousand years; and with equal justice may the lexicographer be derided, who being able to produce no example of a nation that has preserved their words and phrases from mutability, shall imagine that his dictionary can embalm his language, and secure it from corruption and decay, that it is in his power to change sublunary nature, or clear the world at once from folly, vanity, and affectation.

With this hope, however, academies have been instituted, to guard the avenues of their languages, to retain fugitives, and repulse intruders; but their vigilance and activity have hitherto been vain; sounds are too volatile and subtile for legal restraints; to enchain syllables, and to lash the wind, are equally the undertakings of pride, unwilling to measure its desires by its strength. The *French* language has visibly changed under the inspection of the academy; the stile of *Amelot*'s translation of father *Paul* is observed by *Le Courayer* to be *un peu passè*; and no *Italian* will maintain, that the diction of any modern writer is not perceptibly different from that of *Boccace*, *Machiavel*, or *Caro*.

Total and sudden transformations of a language seldom happen; conquests and migrations are now very rare: but there are other causes of change, which, though slow in their operation, and invisible in their progress, are perhaps as much superiour to human resistance, as the revolutions of the sky, or intumescence of the tide. Commerce, however necessary, however lucrative, as it depraves the manners, corrupts the language; they that have frequent intercourse with strangers, to whom they endeavour to accommodate themselves, must in time learn a mingled dialect, like the jargon which serves the traffickers on the *Mediterranean* and *Indian* coasts. This will not always be confined to the exchange, the warehouse, or the port, but will be communicated by degrees to other ranks of the people, and be at last incorporated with the current speech.

There are likewise internal causes equally forcible. The language most likely to continue long without alteration, would be that of a nation raised a little, and but a little, above barbarity, secluded from strangers, and totally employed in procuring the conveniencies of life; either without books, or, like some of the *Mahometan* countries, with very few: men thus busied and unlearned, having only such words as common use requires, would perhaps long continue to express the same notions by the same signs. But no such constancy can be expected in a people polished by arts, and classed by subordination, where one part of the community is sustained and accommodated by the labour of the other. Those who have much leisure to think, will always be enlarging the stock of ideas, and every increase of knowledge, whether real or fancied, will produce new words, or combinations of words. When the mind is unchained from necessity, it will range after convenience; when it is left at large in the fields of speculation, it will shift opinions; as any custom is disused, the words that expressed it must perish with it; as any opinion grows popular, it will innovate speech in the same proportion as it alters practice.

As by the cultivation of various sciences, a language is amplified, it will be more furnished with words deflected from their original sense; the geometrician will talk of a courtier's zenith, or the excentrick virtue of a wild hero, and the physician of sanguine expectations and phlegmatick delays. Copiousness of speech will give opportunities to capricious choice, by which some words will be preferred, and others degraded; vicissitudes of fashion will enforce the use of new, or extend the signification of known terms. The tropes of poetry will make hourly encroachments, and the metaphorical will become the current sense: pronunciation will be varied by levity or ignorance, and the pen must at length comply with the tongue; illiterate writers will at one time or other, by publick infatuation, rise into renown, who, not knowing the original import of words, will use them with colloquial licentiousness, confound distinction, and forget propriety. As politeness increases, some expressions will be considered as too gross and vulgar for the delicate, others as too formal and ceremonious for the gay and airy; new phrases are therefore adopted, which must, for the same reasons, be in time dismissed. *Swift*, in his petty treatise on the *English* language, allows that new words must sometimes be introduced, but proposes that none should be suffered to become obsolete. But what makes a word obsolete, more than general agreement to forbear it? and how shall it be continued, when it conveys an offensive idea, or recalled again into the mouths of mankind, when it has once by disuse become unfamiliar, and by unfamiliarity unpleasing.

There is another cause of alteration more prevalent than any other, which yet in the present state of the world cannot be obviated. A mixture of two languages will produce a third distinct from both, and they will always be mixed, where the chief part of education, and the most conspicuous accomplishment, is skill in ancient or in foreign tongues. He that has long cultivated another language, will find its words and combinations croud upon his memory; and haste or negligence, refinement or affectation, will obtrude borrowed terms and exotick expressions.

The great pest of speech is frequency of translation. No book was ever turned from one language into another, without imparting something of its native idiom; this is the most mischievous and comprehensive innovation; single words may enter by thousands, and the fabrick of the tongue continue the same, but new phraseology changes much at once; it alters not the single stones of the building, but the order of the columns. If an academy should be established for the cultivation of our stile, which I, who can never wish to see dependance multiplied, hope the spirit of *English* liberty will hinder or destroy, let them, instead of compiling grammars and dictionaries, endeavour, with all their influence, to stop the licence of translatours, whose idleness and ignorance, if it be suffered to proceed, will reduce us to babble a dialect of *France*.

If the changes that we fear be thus irresistible, what remains but to acquiesce with silence, as in the other insurmountable distresses of humanity? it remains that we retard what we cannot repel, that we palliate what we cannot cure. Life may be lengthened by care, though death cannot be ultimately defeated: tongues, like governments, have a natural tendency to degeneration; we have long preserved our constitution, let us make some struggles for our language.

In hope of giving longevity to that which its own nature forbids to be immortal, I have devoted this book, the labour of years, to the honour of my country, that we may no longer yield the palm of philology to the nations of the continent. The chief glory of every people arises from its authours: whether I shall add any thing by my own writings to the reputation of *English* literature, must be left to time: much of my life has been lost under the pressures of disease; much has been trifled away; and much has always been spent in provision for the day that was passing over me; but I shall not think my employment useless or ignoble, if by my assistance foreign nations, and distant ages, gain access to the propagators of knowledge, and understand the teachers of truth; if my labours afford light to the repositories of science, and add celebrity to *Bacon*, to *Hooker*, to *Milton*, and to *Boyle*.

When I am animated by this wish, I look with pleasure on my book, however defective, and deliver it to the world with the spirit of a man that has endeavoured well. That it will immediately become popular I have not promised to myself: a few wild blunders, and risible absurdities, from which no work of such multiplicity was ever free, may for a time furnish folly with laughter, and harden ignorance in contempt; but useful diligence will at last prevail, and there never can be wanting some who distinguish desert; who will consider that no dictionary of a living tongue ever can be perfect, since while it is hastening to publication, some words are budding, and some falling away; that a whole life cannot be spent upon syntax and etymology, and that even a whole life would not be sufficient; that he, whose design includes whatever language can express, must often speak of what he does not understand; that a writer will sometimes be hurried by eagerness to the end, and sometimes faint with weariness under a task, which *Scaliger* compares to the labours of the anvil and the mine; that what is obvious is not always known, and what is known is not always present; that sudden fits of inadvertency will surprize vigilance, slight avocations will seduce attention, and casual eclipses of the mind will darken learning; and that the writer shall often in vain trace his memory at the moment of need, for that which yesterday he knew with intuitive readiness, and which will come uncalled into his thoughts to-morrow.

In this work, when it shall be found that much is omitted, let it not be forgotten that much likewise is performed; and though no book was ever spared out of tenderness to the authour, and the world is little solicitous to know whence proceeded the faults of that which it condemns; yet it may gratify curiosity to inform it, that the *English Dictionary* was written with little assistance of the learned, and without any patronage of the great; not in the soft obscurities of retirement, or under the shelter of academick bowers, but amidst inconvenience and distraction, in sickness and in sorrow: and it may repress the triumph of malignant criticism to observe, that if our language is not here fully displayed, I have only failed in an attempt which no human powers have hitherto completed. If the lexicons of ancient tongues, now immutably fixed, and comprised in a few volumes, be yet, after the toil of successive ages, inadequate and delusive; if the aggregated knowledge, and co-operating diligence of the *Italian* academicians, did not secure them from the censure of *Beni*; if the embodied criticks of *France*, when fifty years had been spent upon their work, were obliged to change its oeconomy, and give their second edition another form, I may surely be contented without the praise of perfection, which, if I could obtain, in this gloom of solitude, what would it avail me? I have protracted my work till most of those whom I wished to please, have sunk into the grave, and success and miscarriage are empty sounds: I therefore dismiss it with frigid tranquillity, having little to fear or hope from censure or from praise.

Notes

1. 'What good to you is one thorn removed from many' (Horace's *Epistles*, II.2.212).
2. The Preface contains a lengthy footnote, omitted here, illustrating Junius' etymological extravagances.

A

DICTIONARY

OF THE

ENGLISH LANGUAGE:

IN WHICH

The WORDS are deduced from their ORIGINALS,

AND

ILLUSTRATED in their DIFFERENT SIGNIFICATIONS

BY

EXAMPLES from the beſt WRITERS.

TO WHICH ARE PREFIXED,

A HISTORY of the LANGUAGE,

AND

AN ENGLISH GRAMMAR.

BY SAMUEL JOHNSON, A. M.

IN TWO VOLUMES.

VOL. I.

Cum tabulis animum cenſoris ſumet honeſti:
Audebit quæcunque parum ſplendoris habebunt,
Et ſine pondere erunt, et honore indigna ferentur.
Verba movere loco; quamvis invita recedant,
Et verſentur adhuc intra penetralia Veſtæ:
Obſcurata diu populo bonus eruet, atque
Proferet in lucem ſpecioſa vocabula rerum,
Quæ priſcis memorata Catonibus atque Cethegis,
Nunc ſitus informis premit et deſerta vetuſtas. HOR.

LONDON,
Printed by W. STRAHAN,
For J. and P. KNAPTON; T. and T. LONGMAN; C. HITCH and L. HAWES;
A. MILLAR; and R. and J. DODSLEY.
MDCCLV.

Abbreviations and symbols

A number of abbreviations are used in the *Dictionary*, chiefly identifying parts of speech, and sections of texts in sources. All abbreviated names of authors and titles within the sources have been expanded for this anthology.

adj.	adjective	prep.	preposition
adv.	adverb	pret.	preterite
B.	book	priv.	privative
C.	chapter	S., SECT.	section
CAN., CANT.	canto	Sax.	Saxon
Dut.	Dutch	STAN., STANZ.	stanza
Fr.	French	subst.	substantive
gen.	genitive	v.a.	verb active (i.e. transitive)
Germ.	German		
Gr.	Greek	v.n.	verb neuter (i.e. intransitive)
Ital.	Italian		
interj., interject.	interjection		
L.	line	ʹ	in a headword shows that the preceding syllable is accented.
Lat.	Latin		
n.s.	noun substantive		
P.	part		
part., particip.	participle, participial	——	in a play quotation, indicates a change of speaker
pass.	passive		
pl., plur.	plural		

Italics in a headword (e.g. ABAʹCTOR) indicate words 'which are still to be considered as foreign' (see Plan).

Note that the letters *i* and *j* are conflated as a single letter in the Dictionary, as are *u* and *v*. For example, *inward* is followed by *job*, *journalist* by *iris*, *unwriting* by *vocabulary*, and *ustorious* by *vulgar*.

A

The first letter of the European alphabets, has, in the English language, three different sounds, which may be termed the broad, open, and slender.

The broad sound resembling that of the German *a* is found, in many of our monosyllables, as *all, wall, malt, salt*; in which *a* is pronounced as *au* in *cause*, or *aw* in *law*. Many of these words were anciently written with *au*, as *fault, waulk*; which happens to be still retained in *fault*. This was probably the ancient sound of the Saxons, since it is almost uniformly preserved in the rustic pronunciation, and the Northern dialects, as *maun* for *man*, *haund* for *hand*.

A open, not unlike the *a* of the Italians, is found in *father, rather*, and more obscurely in *fancy, fast*, &c.

A slender or close, is the peculiar *a* of the English language, resembling the sound of the French *e* masculine, or diphthong *ai* in *païs*, or perhaps a middle sound between them, or between the *a* and *e*; to this the Arabic *a* is said nearly to approach. Of this sound we have examples in the words, *place, face, waste*, and all those that terminate in *ation*; as, *relation, nation, generation*.

A is short, as, *glass, grass*; or long, as, *glaze, graze*: it is marked long, generally, by an *e* final, *plane*, or by an *i* added, as, *plain*.

A, an article set before nouns of the singular number; *a* man, *a* tree; denoting the number *one*, as, *a* man is coming, that is, *no more than one*; or an indefinite indication, as, *a* man may come this way; that is, *any* man. This article has no plural signification. Before a word beginning with a vowel, it is written *an*, as, *an* ox, *an* egg, of which *a* is the contraction.

A is sometimes a noun; as, a great *A*, a little *a*.

A is placed before a participle, or participial noun; and is considered by Wallis as a contraction of *at*, when it is put before a word denoting some action not yet finished; as, I am *a* walking. It also seems to be anciently contracted from *at*, when placed before local surnames; as, Thomas *a* Becket. In other cases, it seems to signify *to*, like the French *à*.

> A *hunting Chloë went*. PRIOR.

> *They go a begging to a bankrupt's door.* DRYDEN.

> *May pure contents for ever pitch their tents*
> *Upon these downs, these meads, these rocks, these mountains,*
> *And peace still slumber by these purling fountains!*
> *Which we may every year*
> *Find when we come a fishing here.*
> WOTTON.

Now the men fell a *rubbing of armour, which a great while had lain oiled; the magazines of munition are viewed; the officers of remains called to account.* WOTTON.

Another falls a *ringing a Pescennius Niger, and judiciously distinguishes the sound of it to be modern.* ADDISON ON MEDALS.

A has a peculiar signification, denoting the proportion of one thing to another. Thus we say, The landlord hath a hundred *a* year; The ship's crew gained a thousand pounds *a* man.

The river Inn, that had been hitherto shut up among mountains, passes generally through a wide open country, during all its course through Bavaria; which is a voyage of two days, after the rate of twenty leagues a *day.* ADDISON ON ITALY.

A is used in burlesque poetry, to lengthen out a syllable, without adding to the sense.

For cloves and nutmegs to the line-a,
And even for oranges to China.
DRYDEN.

A is sometimes, in familiar writings, put by a barbarous corruption for *he.*

A, in composition, seems to have sometimes the power of the French *a* in these phrases, *a droit*, *a gauche*, &c. and sometimes to be contracted from *at*; as, *aside, aslope, afoot, asleep, athirst, aware.*

If this, which he avouches, does appear,
There is no flying hence, nor tarrying here.
I gin to be a *weary of the sun;*
And wish the state of the world were now undone. SHAKESPEARE'S MACBETH.

And now a breeze from shore began to blow,
The sailors ship their oars, and cease to row;
Then hoist their yards a-trip, *and all their sails*
Let fall, to court the wind, and catch the gales. DRYDEN'S CEYX AND ALCYONE.

A is sometimes redundant; as, *arise, arouse, awake*; the same with rise, rouse, wake.

A, in abbreviations, stands for *artium*, or arts; as, A.B. bachelor of arts, *artium baccalaureus*; A.M. master of arts, *artium magister*; or, *anno*; as, A.D. *anno domini.*

ABA'CTOR. *n.s.* [Lat. *abactor*, a driver away.] Those who drive away or steal cattle in herds, or great numbers at once, in distinction from those that steal only a sheep or two. *Blount.*

ABA'SED. *adj.* [with heralds] is a term used of the wings of eagles, when the top looks downwards towards the point of the shield; or when the wings are shut; the natural way of bearing them being spread with the top pointing to the chief of the angle. *Bailey. Chambers.*

A'BATURE. *n.s.* [a hunting term.] Those sprigs of grass which are thrown down by a stag in his passing by. *Dictionaries.*

ABB. *n.s.* The yarn on a weaver's warp; a term among clothiers. *Chambers.*

ABECEDA'RIAN. *n.s.* [from the names of *a*, *b*, *c*, the three first letters of the alphabet.] He that teaches or learns the alphabet, or first rudiments of literature.

This word is used by *Wood* in his *Athenæ Oxonienses*, where mentioning *Farnaby* the critic, he relates, that, in some part of his life, he was reduced to follow the trade of an *abecedarian* by his misfortunes.

A'BECEDARY. *adj.* [See **ABECEDARIAN.**]

1. Belonging to the alphabet.
2. Inscribed with the alphabet.

> *This is pretended from the sympathy of two needles touched with the loadstone, and placed in the center of two* abecedary *circles, or rings of letters, described round about them, one friend keeping one, and another the other, and agreeing upon an hour wherein they will communicate.*
> BROWN'S VULGAR ERROURS, B. II. C. 2.

ABLIGURI'TION. *n.s.* [*abliguritio*, Lat.] A prodigal spending on meat and drink. *Dictionaries.*

ABNODA'TION. *n.s.* [*abnodatio*, Lat.] The act of cutting away knots from trees; a term of gardening. *Dictionaries.*

ABNO'RMOUS. *adj.* [*abnormis*, Lat. out of rule.] Irregular, mishapen. *Dictionaries.*

ABORI'GINES. *n.s.* Lat. The earliest inhabitants of a country; those of whom no original is to be traced; as, the Welsh in Britain.

ABOVE-BOARD. In open sight; without artifice or trick. A figurative expression, borrowed from gamesters, who, when they put their hands under the table, are changing their cards. It is used only in familiar language.

> *It is the part also of an honest man to deal* above-board, *and without tricks.*
> L'ESTRANGE.

> *Though there have not been wanting such heretofore, as have practised these unworthy arts (for as much as there have been villains in all places, and all ages) yet now-a-days they are owned* above-board.
> SOUTH'S SERMONS.[1]

ABRACADA'BRA. A superstitious charm against agues.

To **ABRI'DGE.** *v.a.* [*abreger*, Fr. *abbrevio*, Lat.]

1. To make shorter in words, keeping still the same substance.

> *All these sayings, being declared by Jason of Cyrene in five books, we will essay to* abridge *in one volume.*
> BIBLE 2 MACCABEES, II. 23.

2. To contract, to diminish, to cut short.

> *The determination of the will, upon enquiry, is following the direction of that guide; and he, that has a power to act or not to act, according as such determination directs, is free. Such determination* abridges *not that power wherein liberty consists.*
> LOCKE.

3. To deprive of; in which sense it is followed by the particle *from*, or *of*, preceding the thing taken away.

> *I have disabled mine estate,*
> *By shewing something a more swelling port,*
> *Than my faint means would grant continuance;*
> *Nor do I now make moan to be* abridg'd
> *From such a noble rate.*
> SHAKESPEARE'S MERCHANT OF VENICE.

> *They were formerly, by the common law, discharged from pontage and murage; but this privilege has been* abridged *them since by several statutes.*
> AYLIFFE'S PARERGON JURIS CANONICI.

ABSENTE'E. *n.s.* He that is absent from his station or employment, or country. A word used commonly with regard to Irishmen living out of their country.

> *Then was the first statute made against* absentees, *commanding all such as had land in Ireland, to return and reside thereupon.*
> SIR JOHN DAVIES ON IRELAND.

> *A great part of estates in Ireland are owned by* absentees, *and such as draw over the*

profits raised out of Ireland, refunding nothing.
CHILD'S DISCOURSE ON TRADE.

ABSI'NTHIATED. *part.* [from *absinthium*, Lat. wormwood.] Imbittered, impregnated with wormwood. *Dictionaries.*

To **ABSTA'IN.** *v.n.* [*abstineo*, Lat.] To forbear, to deny one's self any gratification; with the particle *from.*

If thou judge it hard and difficult,
Conversing, looking, loving, to abstain
From *love's due rites, nuptial embraces sweet;*
And, with desires, to languish without hope.
MILTON'S PARADISE LOST, B. X. L. 993.

To be perpetually longing, and impatiently desirous of any thing, so that a man cannot abstain from *it, is to lose a man's liberty, and to become a servant of meat and drink, or smoke.*
TAYLOR'S RULE OF LIVING HOLY.

Even then the doubtful billows scarce abstain
From *the toss'd vessel on the troubled main.* DRYDEN'S VIRGIL.

AC, AK, or **AKE.** Being initials in the names of places, as *Acton*, signify an oak, from the Saxon *ac*, an oak. *Gibson's Camden.*

A'CCENT. *n.s.* [*accentus*, Lat.]
1. The manner of speaking or pronouncing, with regard either to force or elegance.

I know, Sir, I am no flatterer; he that beguiled you in a plain accent *was a plain knave; which, for my part, I will not be.*
SHAKESPEARE'S KING LEAR.

Your accent *is something finer than you could purchase in so removed a dwelling.*
SHAKESPEARE'S AS YOU LIKE IT.

2. In grammar, the marks made upon syllables to regulate their pronunciation.

Accent, *as in the Greek names and usage, seems to have regarded the tune of the voice; the acute* accent *raising the voice in some certain syllables to a higher,* i.e. *more acute pitch or tone, and the grave depressing it lower, and both having some emphasis,* i.e. *more vigorous pronunciation.*
HOLDER'S ELEMENTS OF SPEECH.

3. Poetically, language or words.

How many ages hence
Shall this our lofty scene be acted o'er,
In states unborn, and accents *yet unknown.*
SHAKESPEARE'S JULIUS CÆSAR.

Winds on your wings to heav'n her accents *bear;*
Such words as heav'n alone is fit to hear.
DRYDEN'S VIRGIL'S PASTORALS, 3.

4. A modification of the voice, expressive of the passions or sentiments.

The tender accent *of a woman's cry*
Will pass unheard, will unregarded die;
When the rough seaman's louder shouts prevail,
When fair occasion shews the springing gale. PRIOR.

To **ACCE'NT.** *v.a.* [from *accentus*, Lat.]
1. To pronounce, to speak words with particular regard to the grammatical marks or rules.

Having got somebody to mark the last syllable but one, where it is long, in words above two syllables (which is enough to regulate her pronunciation, and accenting *the words) let her read daily in the gospels, and avoid understanding them in Latin, if she can.* LOCKE ON EDUCATION, §177.

2. In poetry, to pronounce or utter in general.

O my unhappy lines! you that before
Have serv'd my youth to vent some wanton cries,

And, now congeal'd with grief, can scarce implore
Strength to accent, *Here my Albertus lies!*
WOTTON.

3. To write or note the accents.

ACCE'PTION. [*acception*, Fr. from *acceptio*, Lat.] The received sense of a word; the meaning.

That this hath been esteemed the due and proper acception *of this word, I shall testify by one evidence, which gave me the first hint of this notion.*
HAMMOND ON FUNDAMENTALS.

A'CCIDENCE. *n.s.* [a corruption of *accidents*, from *accidentia*, Lat.] The little book containing the first rudiments of grammar, and explaining the properties of the eight parts of speech.

I do confess I do want eloquence,
And never yet did learn mine accidence.
TAYLOR THE WATER-POET.

ACCO'MPTANT. *n.s.* [*accomptant*, Fr.] A reckoner, computer. See ACCOUNTANT.

As the accompt runs on, generally the accomptant *goes backward.*
SOUTH'S SERMONS.

ACCO'MPTING-DAY. The day on which the reckoning is to be settled.

To whom thou much dost owe, thou much must pay;
Think on the debt against th' accompting-day. SIR J. DENHAM.

To **ACCO'ST.** *v.a.* [*accoster*, Fr.] To speak to first; to address; to salute.

You mistake, knight: accost *her, front her, board her, woo her, assail her.*
SHAKESPEARE'S TWELFTH NIGHT.

At length, collecting all his serpent wiles,
With soothing words renew'd, him thus accosts. PARADISE REGAIN'D.

I first accosted *him: I su'd, I sought,*
And, with a loving force, to Pheneus brought. DRYDEN'S ÆNEID.

ACCOU'NTANT. *n.s.* [See ACCOMPTANT.] A computer; a man skilled or employed in accounts.

The different compute of divers states; the short and irreconcileable years of some; the exceeding errour in the natural frame of others; and the false deductions of ordinary accountants *in most.*
BROWN'S VULGAR ERROURS.

ACCO'UNT-BOOK. *n.s.* A book containing accounts.

I would endeavour to comfort myself upon the loss of friends, as I do upon the loss of money; by turning to my account-book, *and seeing whether I have enough left for my support.* SWIFT, LETTER LXII.

ACCO'UNTING. *n.s.* [from *account.*] The act of reckoning, or making up of accounts.

This method faithfully observed, must keep a man from breaking, or running behind hand in his spiritual estate; which, without frequent accountings, *he will hardly be able to prevent.* SOUTH'S SERMONS.

To **ACCO'UPLE.** *v.a.* [*accoupler*, Fr.] To join, to link together.[2]

He sent a solemn embassage to treat a peace and league with the king; accoupling *it with an article in the nature of a request.* BACON'S HENRY VII.

To **ACCO'URT.** *v.a.* [See To COURT.] To entertain with courtship, or courtesy; a word now not in use.

Who all this while were at their wanton rest,
Accourting *each her friend with lavish feast.* FAIRY QUEEN, B. II. C. II.

ACCUBA'TION. *n.s.* [from *accubo*, to lye down to, Lat.] The antient posture of leaning at meals.

It will appear, that accubation, *or lying down at meals, was a gesture used by very many nations.*
BROWN'S VULGAR ERROURS, B. V.

To **ACCU'MB.** *v.a.* [*accumbo*, Lat.] To lie at the table, according to the ancient manner.

A'CE. *n.s.* [*As* not only signified a piece of money, but any integer, from whence is derived the word *ace*, or unit. Thus *As* signified the whole inheritance. *Arbuthnot on Coins.*]
1. An unit; a single point on cards or dice.

When lots are shuffled together in a lap, urn, or pitcher; or if a man blindfold casts a die, what reason in the world can he have to presume, that he shall draw a white stone rather than a black, or throw an ace *rather than a sise.* SOUTH'S SERMONS.

2. A small quantity.[3]

He will not bate an ace *of absolute certainty; but however doubtful or improbable the thing is, coming from him it must go for an indisputable truth.* GOVERNMENT OF THE TONGUE, §11.

I'll not wag an ace *farther: the whole world shall not bribe me to it.* DRYDEN'S SPANISH FRIAR.

ACE'RB. *adj.* [*acerbus*, Lat.] Acid, with an addition of roughness, as most fruits are before they are ripe. *Quincy.*

ACE'RBITY. *n.s.* [*acerbitas*, Lat.]
1. A rough sower taste.
2. Applied to men, sharpness of temper; severity.

True it is, that the talents for criticism, namely, smartness, quick censure, vivacity of remark, indeed all but acerbity, *seem rather the gifts of youth than of old age.* POPE'S INTRODUCTION TO DUNCIAD.

ACHE. *n.s.* [*ace*, Sax. 'ἄχος, Gr. now generally written *ake*, and in the plural *akes*, of one syllable; the primitive manner being preserved chiefly in poetry, for the sake of the measure.] A continued pain. See **AKE**.

I'll rack thee with old cramps;
Fill all thy bones with aches, *make thee roar,*
That beasts shall tremble at thy din.
SHAKESPEARE'S TEMPEST.

A coming show'r your shooting corns presage,
Old aches *throb, your hollow tooth will urge.* SWIFT'S MISCELLANIES.

ACHOR. *n.s.* [*achor*, Lat. 'αχώρ, Gr. *furfur.*] A species of the herpes; it appears with a crusty scab, which causes an itching on the surface of the head, occasioned by a salt sharp serum oozing through the skin. *Quincy.*

A'CONITE. *n.s.* [*aconitum*, Lat.] Properly the herb wolfs-bane, but commonly used in poetical language for poison in general.

Our land is from the rage of tygers freed,
Nor nourishes the lion's angry seed;
Nor pois'nous aconite *is here produc'd,*
Or grows unknown, or is, when known, refus'd. DRYDEN'S VIRGIL.

Despair, that aconite *does prove,*
And certain death to others, love,
That poison never yet withstood,
Does nourish mine, and turns to blood.
GRANVILLE'S POEMS.

ACO'USTICKS. *n.s.* ['Ακουστικά, of 'ακουώ, Gr. to hear.]
1. The doctrine or theory of sounds.
2. Medicines to help the hearing.

To **ACQUIE'SCE.** *v.n.* [*acquiescer*, Fr. *acquiescere*, Lat.] To rest in, or remain satisfied with, without opposition or discontent.[4]

Neither a bare approbation of, nor a mere wishing, nor unactive complacency in; nor, lastly, a natural inclination to things virtuous and good, can pass before God for a man's willing of such things; and, consequently, if men, upon this account, will needs take up and acquiesce *in an airy ungrounded persuasion, that they will those*

things which really they not will, they fall thereby into a gross and fatal delusion.
SOUTH'S SERMONS.

He hath employed his transcendent wisdom and power, that by these he might make way for his benignity, as the end wherein they ultimately acquiesce.
GREW'S COSMOLOGIA SACRA. B. I.

ACQUIE'SCENCE. *n.s.* [from *acquiesce.*]
1. A silent appearance of content, distinguished on one side from avowed consent, on the other from opposition.

Neither from any of the nobility, nor of the clergy, who were thought most averse from it, there appeared any sign of contradiction to that; but an entire acquiescence *in all the bishops thought fit to do.*
CLARENDON.

2. Satisfaction, rest, content.

Many indeed have given over their pursuits after fame, either from disappointment, or from experience of the little pleasure which attends it, or the better informations or natural coldness of old-age; but seldom from a full satisfaction and acquiescence *in their present enjoyments of it.*
ADDISON'S SPECTATOR, NO 256.

3. Submission.[5]

The greatest part of the world take up their persuasions concerning good and evil, by an implicit faith, and a full acquiescence *in the word of those, who shall represent things to them under these characters.*
SOUTH'S SERMONS.

A'CRE. *n.s.* [*Æcre*, Sax.] A quantity of land containing in length forty perches, and four in breadth, or four thousand eight hundred and forty square yards. *Dictionaries.*

Search ev'ry acre *in the high-grown field,*
And bring him to our eye.
SHAKESPEARE'S KING LEAR.

ACROAMA'TICAL. *adj.* [*'ακροάομαι*, Gr. I bear.] Of or pertaining to deep learning; the opposite of exoterical.

An ACRO'STICK. *n.s.* [from *'ἄκρος* and *στίχος*, Gr.] A poem in which the first letter of every line being taken, makes up the name of the person or thing on which the poem is written.

ACRO'STICK. *adj.*
1. That which relates to an acrostick.
2. That which contains acrosticks.

Leave writing plays, and choose for thy command
Some peaceful province in acrostick *land:*
There thou may'st wings display, and altars raise,
And torture one poor word ten thousand ways. DRYDEN.

To A'CTIVATE. *v.a.* [from *active.*] To make active. This word is perhaps used only by the author alleged.

As snow and ice, especially being holpen, and their cold activated *by nitre or salt, will turn water into ice, and that in a few hours; so it may be, it will turn wood or stiff clay into stone, in longer time.*
BACON'S NATURAL HISTORY, NO 83.

ACTUO'SE. *adj.* [from *act.*] That which hath strong powers of action; a word little used.

ACU'LEATE. *adj.* [*aculeatus*, Lat.] That which has a point or sting; prickly; that which terminates in a sharp point.

A'DAGE. *n.s.* [*adagium*, Lat.] A maxim handed down from antiquity; a proverb.

Shallow unimproved intellects, that are confident pretenders to certainty; as if,

contrary to the adage, *science had no friend but ignorance.*
GLANVILLE'S SCEPSIS SCIENTIFICA, C. 2.

Fine fruits of learning! old ambitious fool,
Dar'st thou apply that adage *of the school;*
As if 'tis nothing worth that lies conceal'd;
And science is not science till reveal'd?
DRYDEN'S PERSIUS, SATIRE I.

ADA'GIO. *n.s.* [Italian.] A term used by musicians, to mark a slow time.

A'DDLE. *adj.* [from *aðel*, a disease, Sax. according to *Skinner* and *Junius*; perhaps from *yðel*, idle, barren, unfruitful.] Originally applied to eggs, and signifying such as produce nothing, but grow rotten under the hen; thence transferred to brains that produce nothing.

There's one with truncheon, like a ladle,
That carries eggs too fresh or addle;
And still at random, as he goes,
Among the rabble rout bestows.
HUDIBRAS, P. II. CANT. II.

After much solitariness, fasting, or long sickness, their brains were addle, *and their bellies as empty of meat as their heads of wit.* BURTON ON MELANCHOLY.

Thus far the poet; but his brains grow addle:
And all the rest is purely from this noddle.
DRYDEN'S DON SEBASTIAN.

To **A'DDLE.** *v.a.* [from *addle, adj.*] To make addle; to corrupt; to make barren.

This is also evidenced in eggs, whereof the sound ones sink, and such as are addled *swim; as do also those that are termed hypenemiæ, or wind-eggs.*
BROWN'S VULGAR ERROURS, B. IV.

A'DDLE-PATED. *adj.* Having addled brains. See **ADDLE**.

Poor slaves in metre, dull and addle-pated,
Who rhyme below even David's psalms translated.
DRYDEN'S ABSALOM AND ACHITOPHEL.

ADIEU'. *adv.* [from *à Dieu*, used elliptically for *à Dieu je vous commende*, used at the departure of friends.] The form of parting, originally importing a commendation to the Divine care, but now used, in a popular sense, sometimes to things inanimate; farewell.

Ne gave him leave to bid that aged fire
Adieu, *but nimbly ran her wonted course.*
FAIRY QUEEN, B. II.

Use a more spacious ceremony to the noble lords; you restrained yourself within the list of too cold an adieu; *be more expressive to them.*
SHAKESPEARE'S ALL'S WELL THAT ENDS WELL.

While now I take my last adieu,
Heave thou no sigh, nor shed a tear;
Lest yet my half-clos'd eye may view
On earth an object worth its care.
PRIOR.

A'DIPOUS. *adj.* [*adiposus*, Lat.] Fat.

A'DJUTANT. *n.s.* A petty officer, whose duty is to assist the major, by distributing the pay, and overseeing the punishment, of the common men.

To **ADMO'NISH.** *v.a.* [*admoneo*, Lat.] To warn of a fault; to reprove gently; to counsel against wrong practices; to put in mind of a fault or a duty; with the particle *of*, or *against*, which is more rare, or the infinitive mood of a verb.

One of his cardinals, who better knew the intrigues of affairs, admonished *him against that unskilful piece of ingenuity.*
DECAY OF PIETY.

He of their wicked ways
Shall them admonish, *and before them set*
The paths of righteousness.
MILTON'S PARADISE LOST, B. XI.

But when he was admonished *by his subject to descend, he came down, gently*

circling in the air, and singing, to the ground.
DRYDEN'S DEDICATION OF VIRGIL'S PASTORALS.

ADOLE'SCENCE. *n.s.* [*adolescentia*, Lat.] The age succeeding childhood, and succeeded by puberty; more largely, that part of life in which the body has not yet reached its full perfection. See **ADOLESCENCY.**

The sons must have a tedious time of childhood and adolescence, *before they can either themselves assist their parents, or encourage them with new hopes of posterity.* BENTLEY'S SERMONS.

ADOLE'SCENCY. *n.s.* The same with *adolescence.*[6]

He was so far from a boy, that he was a man born, and at his full stature, if we believe Josephus, who places him in the last adolescency, *and makes him twenty-five years old.*
BROWN'S VULGAR ERROURS, B. V. C. 8.

ADRE'AD. *adv.* [from *a* and *dread*; as, *aside*, *athirst*, *asleep*.]
In a state of fear; frighted; terrified: now obsolete.

And thinking to make all men adread *to such a one an enemy, who would not spare, nor fear to kill so great a prince.*
SIDNEY, B. II.

ADVA'NTAGE-GROUND. *n.s.* Ground that gives superiority, and opportunities of annoyance or resistance.

This excellent man, who stood not upon the advantage-ground *before, from the time of his promotion to the archbishoprick, or rather from that of his being commissioner of the treasury, exceedingly provoked, or underwent the envy, and reproach, and malice of men of all qualities and conditions; who agreed in nothing else.*
CLARENDON.

A'DVENT. *n.s.* [from *adventus*; that is, *adventus Redemptoris.*] The name of one of the holy seasons, signifying the *coming*; that is, the *coming* of our Saviour; which is made the subject of our devotion during the four weeks before Christmas.[7]

A'DVERSARY. *n.s.* [*adversaire*, Fr. *adversarius*, Lat.] An opponent; antagonist; enemy: generally applied to those that have verbal or judicial quarrels; as, controvertists or litigants: sometimes to an opponent in single combat. It may sometimes imply an open profession of enmity; as we say, a secret enemy is worse than an open *adversary.*

Yet am I noble, as the adversary
I come to cope.
SHAKESPEARE'S KING LEAR.

Those rites and ceremonies of the church, therefore, which were the self-same now that they were, when holy and virtuous men maintained them against profane and deriding adversaries, *her own children have in derision.* HOOKER, B. I. § 1.

Mean while th' adversary *of God and man,*
Satan, with thoughts inflam'd, of highest design,
Puts on swift wings.
MILTON'S PARADISE LOST, B. II. L. 620.

An adversary, *on the contrary, makes a stricter search into us, and discovers every flaw and imperfection in our tempers. A friend exaggerates a man's virtues; an enemy inflames his crimes.*
ADDISON'S SPECTATOR, NO 399.

ADVE'RSATIVE. *adj.* [*adversativus*, Lat.] A term of grammar, applied to a word which makes some opposition or variety; as in this sentence: *This diamond is orient,* but *it is rough. But* is an *adversative* conjunction.

To **ADVERTI'SE.** *v.a.* [*advertir*, Fr.]
It is now spoken with the accent upon

the last syllable; but appears to have been anciently accented on the second. **1.** To inform another; to give intelligence; with an accusative of the person informed.

The bishop did require a respite,
Wherein he might the king his lord advertise,
Whether our daughter were legitimate.
SHAKESPEARE'S HENRY VIII.

As I by friends am well advertised,
Sir Edmund Courtney, and the haughty prelate,
Bishop of Exeter, his elder brother,
With many more confederates are in arms. SHAKESPEARE'S RICHARD III.

2. To inform; to give notice; with *of* before the subject of information.

The death of Selymus nothing suspected, Ferhates, understanding that Solyman expected more assured advertisement, sent unto the other Bassas; unto whom he declared the death of the emperor: of *which they, by another messenger,* advertised *Solyman; firming those letters with all their hands and seals.*
KNOLLES'S HISTORY OF THE TURKS.

They were to advertise *the chief hero* of *the distresses of his subjects, occasioned by his absence, to crave his succour, and solicite him to hasten his return.*
DRYDEN'S PREFACE TO DUFRESNOY.

3. To give notice of any thing, by means of an advertisement in the publick prints; as, *He* advertised *his loss.*

ADU'LT. *n.s.* A person above the age of infancy, or grown to some degree of strength; sometimes full grown: a word used chiefly by medicinal writers.

The depression of the cranium, without a fracture, can but seldom occur; and then it happens to children, whose bones are more pliable and soft than those of adults.
SHARP'S SURGERY.

To ADU'LTER. *v.a.* [*adulterer*, Fr. *adultero*, Lat.] To commit adultery with another: a word not classical.

His chaste wife
He adulters *still: his thoughts lye with a whore.* BEN JONSON.

ADU'LTERANT. *n.s.* [*adulterans*, Lat.] The person or thing which adulterates.

To ADU'LTERATE. *v.a.* [*adulterer*, Fr. *adultero*, Lat.]
1. To commit adultery.

But fortune, oh!
Adulterates *hourly with thine uncle John;*
And with her golden hand hath pluckt on France. SHAKESPEARE'S KING JOHN.

2. To corrupt by some foreign admixture; to contaminate.

Common pot-ashes, bought of them that sell it in shops, who are not so foolishly knavish, as to adulterate *them with salt-petre, which is much dearer than pot-ashes.* BOYLE.

Could a man be composed to such an advantage of constitution, that it should not at all adulterate *the images of his mind; yet this second nature would alter the crasis of his understanding.*
GLANVILLE'S SCEPSIS SCIENTIFICA, C. XVI.

The present war has so adulterated *our tongue with strange words, that it would be impossible for one of our great grandfathers to know what his posterity have been doing.* SPECTATOR.

ADU'LTERER. *n.s.* [*adulter*, Lat.] The person guilty of adultery.

With what impatience must the muse behold,
The wife by her procuring husband sold;
For tho' the law makes null th' adulterer's *deed*
Of lands to her, the cuckold may succeed.
DRYDEN'S JUVENAL.

ADU'LTERESS. *n.s.* [from *adulterer.*] A woman that commits adultery.

> *The Spartan lady replied, when she was asked, What was the punishment for* adulteresses? *There are no such things here.* GOVERNMENT OF THE TONGUE, §3.

> *A robe of tissue, stiff with golden wire;*
> *An upper vest, once Helen's rich attire;*
> *From Argos by the fam'd* adult'ress *brought;*
> *With golden flow'rs and winding foliage wrought.* DRYDEN'S VIRGIL.

ADU'LTERINE. *n.s.* [*adulterine*, Fr. *adulterinus*, Lat.] A child born of an adulteress: a term of canon law.

ADU'LTEROUS. *adj.* [*adulter*, Lat.] Guilty of adultery.

> *Th'* adulterous *Antony, most large*
> *In his abominations, turns you off,*
> *And gives his potent regiment to a trull,*
> *That noses it against us.*
> SHAKESPEARE'S ANTONY AND CLEOPATRA.

> *An* adulterous *person is tied to restitution of the injury, so far as it is reparable; and to make provision for the children, that they may not injure the legitimate.* TAYLOR.

> *Think on whose faith th'* adult'rous *youth rely'd;*
> *Who promis'd, who procur'd the Spartan bride?* DRYDEN'S ÆNEID.

ADU'LTERY. *n.s.* [*adulterium*, Lat.] The act of violating the bed of a married person.

> *All thy domestic griefs at home be left,*
> *The wife's* adult'ry, *with the servant's theft;*
> *And (the most racking thought, which can intrude)*
> *Forget false friends, and their ingratitude.*
> DRYDEN'S JUVENAL.

To **ADU'MBRATE.** *v.a.* [*adumbro*, Lat.] To shadow out; to give a slight likeness; to exhibit a faint resemblance, like that which shadows afford of the bodies which they represent.

> *Heaven is designed for our reward, as well as rescue; and therefore is* adumbrated *by all those positive excellencies, which can endear or recommend.* DECAY OF PIETY.

AFFIDA'VIT. *n.s.* [*affidavit* signifies, in the language of the common law, *he made oath.*] A declaration upon oath.

> *You said, if I return'd next 'size in Lent,*
> *I should be in remitter of your grace;*
> *In th' interim my letters should take place*
> *Of* affidavits. DONNE.

> *Count Rechteren should have made* affidavit, *that his servants had been affronted, and then Monsieur Mesnager would have done him justice.* SPECTATOR, NO 481.

A'FFLUENCE. *n.s.* [*affluence*, Fr. *affluentia*, Lat.]

1. The act of flowing to any place; concourse. It is almost always used figuratively.

> *I shall not relate the* affluence *of young nobles from hence into Spain, after the voice of our prince being there had been noised.* WOTTON.

2. Exuberance of riches; stream of wealth; plenty.

> *Those degrees of fortune, which give fulness and* affluence *to one station, may be want and penury in another.* ROGERS.

> *Let joy or ease, let* affluence *or content,*
> *And the gay conscience of a life well spent,*
> *Calm ev'ry thought, inspirit ev'ry grace.*
> POPE.

To **AFFRO'NT.** *v.a.* [*affronter*, Fr. that is, *ad frontem stare*; *ad frontem & contumeliam allidere*, to insult a man to his face.]

1. To meet face to face; to encounter. This seems the genuine and original sense of the word, which was formerly indifferent to good or ill.

We have closely sent for Hamlet hither,
That he, as 'twere by accident, may here
Affront *Ophelia.*
SHAKESPEARE'S HAMLET.

The seditious, the next day, affronted *the king's forces at the entrance of a highway; whom when they found both ready and resolute to fight, they desired enterparlance, and in the meantime they began to fortify.* SIR JOHN HAYWARD.

2. To meet, in an hostile manner, front to front.

His holy rites and solemn feasts profan'd,
And with their darkness durst affront *his light.* PARADISE LOST.

3. To offer an open insult; to offend avowedly. With respect to this sense, it is observed by *Cervantes*, that, if a man strikes another on the back, and then runs away, the person so struck is injured, but not *affronted*; an *affront* always implying a justification of the act.

But harm precedes not sin only our foe,
Tempting affronts *us with his foul esteem*
Of our integrity.
MILTON'S PARADISE LOST, B. IX.

I would learn the cause, why Torrismond,
Within my palace walls, within my hearing,
Almost within my sight, affronts *a prince,*
Who shortly shall command him.
DRYDEN'S SPANISH FRIAR.

This brings to mind Faustina's fondness for the gladiator, and is interpreted as satire. But how can one imagine, that the Fathers would have dared to affront *the wife of Aurelius.* ADDISON.

A'FTER. *adv.*
1. In succeeding time. It is used of time mentioned as succeeding some other. So we cannot say, I shall be happy *after*, but *hereafter*; but we say, I was first made miserable by the loss, but was *after* happier.

Far be it from me, to justify the cruelties which were at first used towards them, which had their reward soon after.
BACON.

The chief were those who, from the pit of hell
Roaming to seek their prey on earth, durst fix
Their seats long after *next the seat of God.*
PARADISE LOST.

2. Following another.

Let go thy hold, when a great wheel runs down a hill, lest it break thy neck with following it; but the great one that goes upward, let him draw thee after.
SHAKESPEARE'S KING LEAR.

AFTER is compounded with many words, but almost always in its genuine and primitive signification; some, which occurred, will follow, by which others may be explained.

A'FTER ACCEPTATION. [from *after* and *acceptation*.] A sense afterwards, not at first admitted.

'Tis true, some doctors in a scantier space,
I mean, in each apart, contract the place:
Some, who to greater length extend the line,
The church's after acceptation *join.*
DRYDEN'S HIND AND PANTHER.

A'FTER ALL. When all has been taken into the view; when there remains nothing more to be added; at last; in fine; in conclusion.[8]

They have given no good proof in asserting this extravagant principle; for which, after all, *they have no ground or colour, but a passage or two of scripture, miserably perverted, in opposition to many express texts.* ATTERBURY'S SERMONS.

But, after all, *if they have any merit, it is to be attributed to some good old authors, whose works I had leisure to study.*
POPE ON PASTORAL POETRY.

A'FTERCROP. *n.s.* [from *after* and *crop.*] The second crop or harvest of the same year.

> Aftercrops *I think neither good for the land, nor yet the hay good for cattle.* MORTIMER'S HUSBANDRY.

A'FTER-DINNER. *n.s.* [from *after* and *dinner.*] The hour passing just after dinner, which is generally allowed to indulgence and amusement.

> *Thou hast nor youth nor age,*
> *But, as it were, an* afterdinner's *sleep,*
> *Dreaming on both.*
> SHAKESPEARE'S MEASURE FOR MEASURE.

A'FTERMATH. *n.s.* [from *after,* and *math,* from *mow.*] The latter math; the second crop of grass mown in autumn. See **AFTERCROP**.

A'FTERWARD. *adv.* [from *after,* and *wearð,* Sax.] In succeeding time; sometimes written *afterwards,* but less properly.

> *Uses not thought upon before, may* afterward *spring up, and be reasonable causes of retaining that, which former considerations did formerly procure to be instituted.* HOOKER.

> *An anxious distrust of the divine goodness, makes a man more and more unworthy of it; and miserable beforehand, for fear of being so* afterward. L'ESTRANGE.

A'GARICK. *n.s.* [*agaricum,* Lat.] A drug of use in physick, and the dying trade. It is divided into male and female; the male is used only in dying, the female in medicine: the male grows on oaks, the female on larches.

> *There are two excrescences which grow upon trees; both of them in the nature of mushrooms: the one the Romans call* boletus, *which groweth upon the roots of oaks, and was one of the dainties of their table; the other is medicinal, that is called* agarick, *which groweth upon the tops of oaks; though it be affirmed by some, that it groweth also at the roots.* BACON.

AGA'ST. *adj.* [This word, which is usually, by later authours, written *aghast,* is, not improbably, the true word derived from *agaze,* which has been written *aghast,* from a mistaken etymology. See **AGHAST**.] Struck with terrour; amazed; frighted to astonishment.

> *Thus roving on*
> *In confus'd march forlorn, th' advent'rous bands,*
> *With shudd'ring horrour pale, and eyes* agast,
> *View'd first their lamentable lot, and found*
> *No rest.*
> MILTON'S PARADISE LOST, B. II. L. 616.

To **AGA'ZE.** *v.a.* [*from a* and *gaze,* to set *a gazing*; as, *amaze, amuse,* and others.] To strike with amazement; to stupify with sudden terrour. The verb is now out of use.

> *So as they travell'd, so they gan espy*
> *An armed knight toward them gallop fast,*
> *That seemed from some feared foe to fly,*
> *Or other grisly thing that him* agast.
> FAIRY QUEEN.

AGHA'ST. *adj.* [either the participle of *agaze,* (see **AGAZE**.) and then to be written *agazed,* or *agast,* or from *a* and *gast,* a ghost, which the present orthography favours; perhaps they were originally different words.] Struck with horrour, as at the sight of a spectre; stupified with terrour. It is generally applied to the external appearance.

> *Who sighing sore, as if her heart in twaine*
> *Had riven been, and all her heart-strings brast,*
> *With dreary drooping eyne look'd up like one* aghast. SPENSER.

> *The aged earth* aghast,
> *With terrour of that blast,*

Shall from the surface to the centre shake.
MILTON'S CHRIST'S NATIVITY.

Aghast *he wak'd, and, starting from his bed,*
Cold sweat in clammy drops his limbs o'erspread. DRYDEN'S ÆNEID.

I laugh to think how your unshaken Cato
Will look aghast, *while unforeseen destruction*
Pours in upon him thus from every side.
ADDISON'S CATO.

AGITA'TOR. *n.s.* [from *agitate.*] He that agitates any thing; he who manages affairs: in which sense seems to be used the *agitators* of the army.

A'GUE. *n.s.* [*aigu*, Fr. acute.] An intermitting fever, with cold fits succeeded by hot. The cold fit is, in popular language, more particularly called the *ague*, and the hot the fever.

Our castle's strength
Will laugh a siege to scorn. Here let them lie,
Till famine and the ague *eat them up.*
SHAKESPEARE'S MACBETH.

Though
He feels the heats of youth, and colds of age,
Yet neither tempers nor corrects the other;
As if there were an ague *in his nature,*
That still inclines to one extreme.
DENHAM'S SOPHY.

AHA', AHA! *interjection.* A word intimating triumph and contempt.

They opened their mouth wide against me, and said, Aha, aha! *our eye hath seen it.*
BIBLE PSALMS, XXXV. 21.

To **AIL.** *v.a.* [*eglan*, Sax. to be troublesome.]

1. To pain; to trouble; to give pain.

And the angel of God called to Hagar out of heaven, and said unto her, what aileth *thee, Hagar? fear not: for God hath heard the voice of the lad where he is.*
BIBLE GENESIS, XXI. 17.

2. It is used, in a sense less determinate, for *to affect* in any manner; as, *something* ails *me that I cannot sit still; what* ails *the man that he laughs without reason?*

Love smil'd, and thus said, Want join'd to desire is unhappy;
But if he nought do desire, what can Heraclitus ail? SIDNEY.

What ails *me, that I cannot lose thy thought!*
Command the empress hither to be brought,
I, in her death, shall some diversion find,
And rid my thoughts at once of woman-kind.
DRYDEN'S TYRANNICK LOVE.

3. To feel pain; to be incommoded.

4. It is remarkable, that this word is never used but with some indefinite term, or the word *nothing*; as, What ails *him?* What *does he* ail? *He* ails something; *he* ails nothing. Something ails *him;* nothing ails *him.* Thus we never say, a fever *ails* him, or he *ails* a fever, or use definite terms with this verb.

A'IRLING. *n.s.* [from *air*, for gayety.] A young, light, thoughtless, gay person.

Some more there be, slight airlings, *will be won*
With dogs, and horses, and perhaps a whore. BEN JONSON'S CATILINE.

AISLE. *n.s.* [Thus the word is written by *Addison*, but perhaps improperly; since it seems deducible only from either *aile*, a wing, or *allée*, a path; and is therefore to be written *aile.*] The walks in a church, or wings of a quire.

The abbey is by no means so magnificent as one would expect from its endowments. The church is one huge nef, with a double aisle *to it; and, at each end, is a large quire.*
ADDISON.

To **AKE.** *v.n.* [from ᾽ἄχος, Gr. and therefore more grammatically written *ache.* See **ACHE.**]

1. To feel a lasting pain, generally of the internal pains; distinguished from smart, which is commonly used of uneasiness in the external parts; but this is no accurate account.

To sue, and be deny'd, such common grace,
My wounds ake *at you!*
SHAKESPEARE'S TIMON.

Let our finger ake, *and it endues*
Our other healthful members with a sense
Of pain. SHAKESPEARE'S OTHELLO.

Were the pleasure of drinking accompanied, the very moment, with that sick stomach and aking *head, which, in some men, are sure to follow, I think, no body would ever let wine touch his lips.* LOCKE.

His limbs must ake, *with daily toils opprest,*
Ere long-wish'd night brings necessary rest. PRIOR.

2. It is frequently applied, in an improper sense, to the heart; as, *the heart akes*; to imply grief or fear. *Shakespeare* has used it, still more licentiously, of the soul.

Here shame dissuades him, there his fear prevails,
And each, by turns, his aking *heart assails.*
ADDISON'S OVID'S METAMORPHOSES.

My soul akes
To know when two authorities are up,
Neither supreme, how soon confusion
May enter.
SHAKESPEARE'S CORIOLANUS.

ALAMO'DE. *adv.* [*à la mode*, Fr.] According to the fashion: a low word. It is used likewise by the shopkeepers for a kind of thin silken manufacture.

A'LEBERRY. *n.s.* [from *ale* and *berry.*] A beverage made by boiling ale with spice and sugar, and sops of bread: a word only used in conversation.

A'LECONNER. *n.s.* [from *ale* and *con.*] An officer in the city of London, whose business is to inspect the measures of publick houses. Four of them are chosen or rechosen annually by the common-hall of the city; and whatever might be their use formerly, their places are now regarded only as sine-cures for decayed citizens.

A'LEHOUSE. *n.s.* [from *ale* and *house.*] A house where ale is publickly sold; a tipling-house. It is distinguished from a tavern, where they sell wine.

Thou most beauteous inn,
Why should hard-favour'd grief be lodg'd in thee,
When triumph is become an alehouse *guest?* SHAKESPEARE'S RICHARD II.

One would think it should be no easy matter to bring any man of sense in love with an alehouse; *indeed of so much sense, as seeing and smelling amounts to; there being such strong encounters of both, as would quickly send him packing, did not the love of good fellowship reconcile to these nusances.* SOUTH.

Thee shall each alehouse, *thee each gilhouse mourn,*
And answ'ring ginshops sowrer sighs return. POPE'S DUNCIAD.

ALE'MBICK. *n.s.* A vessel used in distilling, consisting of a vessel placed over a fire, in which is contained the substance to be distilled, and a concave closely fitted on, into which the fumes arise by the heat; this cover has a beak or spout, into which the vapours rise, and by which they pass into a serpentine pipe, which is kept cool by making many convolutions in a tub of water; here the vapours are condensed, and what entered the pipe in fumes, comes out in drops.

Though water may be rarefied into invisible vapours, yet it is not changed into air, but only scattered into minute parts; which meeting together in the alembick, *or in the receiver, do presently return into such water as they constituted before.* BOYLE.

A'LGATES. *adv.* [from *all* and *gate*. *Skinner*. *Gate* is the same as *via*; and still used for *way* in the Scottish dialect.] On any terms; every way: now obsolete.

Nor had the boaster ever risen more,
But that Rinaldo's horse ev'n then down fell,
And with the fall his leg oppress'd so sore,
That, for a space, there must he algates *dwell.* FAIRFAX.

A'*LIAS*. *adv.* A Latin word, signifying otherwise; often used in the trials of criminals, whose danger has obliged them to change their names; as, Simpson *alias* Smith, *alias* Baker; that is, *otherwise* Smith, *otherwise* Baker.

ALL FOURS. *n.s.* [from *all* and *four*.] A low game at cards, played by two; so named from the four particulars by which it is reckoned, and which, joined in the hand of either of the parties, are said to make all fours.

A'LLEGORY. *n.s.* [*'αλληγορία*.] A figurative discourse, in which something other is intended, than is contained in the words literally taken; as, *wealth is the daughter of diligence, and the parent of authority*.

Neither must we draw out our allegory *too long, lest either we make ourselves obscure, or fall into affectation, which is childish.* BEN JONSON'S DISCOVERY.

This word nympha meant nothing else but, by allegory, *the vegetative humour or moisture that quickeneth and giveth life to trees and flowers, whereby they grow.* PEACHAM.

ALLE'GRO. *n.s.* A word, denoting one of the six distinctions of time. It expresses a sprightly motion, the quickest of all, except Presto. It originally means *gay*, as in *Milton*.

ALLO'DIUM. *n.s.* [A word of very uncertain derivation, but most probably of German original.] A possession held in absolute independence, without any acknowledgment of a lord paramount. It is opposed to *fee*, or *feudum*, which intimates some kind of dependance. There are no allodial lands in England, all being held either mediately or immediately of the king.

ALLU'SION. *n.s.* [*allusio*, Lat.] That which is spoken with reference to something supposed to be already known, and therefore not expressed; a hint; an implication. It has the particle *to*.

Here are manifest allusions *and footsteps of the dissolution of the earth, as it was in the deluge, and will be in its last ruin.* BURNET'S THEORY.

This last allusion *gall'd the Panther more,*
Because indeed it rubb'd upon the sore. DRYDEN.

Expressions now out of use, allusions *to customs lost to us, and various particularities, must needs continue several passages in the dark.* LOCKE'S ESSAY ON ST. PAUL'S EPISTLES.

ALO'NE. *adv.*

1. This word is seldom used but with the word *let*, if even then it be an adverb, and implies sometimes an ironical prohibition, to help a man who is able to manage the affair himself.[9]

Let us alone *to guard Corioli,*
If they set down before's; 'fore they remove,
Bring up your army.
SHAKESPEARE'S CORIOLANUS.

Let *you* alone, *cunning artificer;*
See how his gorget peers above his gown,
To tell the people in what danger he was.
BEN JONSON'S CATILINE.

2. To let alone; to forbear; to leave unfinished.

His client stole it, but he had better have let *it* alone; *for he lost his cause by his jest.*
ADDISON'S SPECTATOR, NO 408.

To **A'LTER.** *v.a.* [*alterer*, Fr. from *alter*, Lat.]
1. To change; to make otherwise than it is. *To alter*, seems more properly to imply a change made only in some part of a thing; as, to *alter* a writing, may be, to blot or interpolate it; to *change* it, may be, to substitute another in its place.[10]

Do you note
How much her grace is alter'd *on the sudden?*
How long her face is drawn? how pale she looks,
And of an earthly cold?
SHAKESPEARE'S HENRY VIII.

Acts appropriated to the worship of God by his own appointment, must continue so, till himself hath otherwise declared: for who dares alter *what God hath appointed?*
STILLINGFLEET'S DEFENCE OF DISCOURSE ON ROMISH IDOLATRY.

2. To take off from a persuasion or sect.

For the way of writing plays in verse, I find it troublesome and slow; but I am no way altered *from my opinion of it, at least with any reasons which have opposed it.*
DRYDEN.

ALTI'LOQUENCE. *n.s.* [*altus* and *loquor*, Lat.] High speech; pompous language.

A.M. Stands for *artium magister*, or master of arts; the second degree of our universities, which, in some foreign countries, is called doctor of philosophy.

AMA'RITUDE. *n.s.* [*amaritudo*, Lat.] Bitterness.

What amaritude *or acrimony is deprehended in choler, it acquires from a commixture of melancholy, or external malign bodies.*
HARVEY ON CONSUMPTIONS.

AMATO'RCULIST. *n.s.* [*amatorculus*, Lat.] A little insignificant lover; a pretender to affection.

A'MAZON. *n.s.* [α and μάζος.] The Amazons were a race of women famous for valour, who inhabited Caucasus; they are so called from their cutting off their breasts, to use their weapons better. A warlike woman; a virago.

Stay, stay thy hands, thou art an amazon,
And fightest with the sword.
SHAKESPEARE'S HENRY VI.

AMBA'GES. *n.s.* [Lat.] A circuit of words; a circumlocutory form of speech; a multiplicity of words; an indirect manner of expression.

They gave those complex ideas names, that they might the more easily record and discourse of things they were daily conversant in, without long ambages *and circumlocutions; and that the things, they were continually to give and receive information about, might be the easier and quicker understood.* LOCKE.

AMBER DRINK. *n.s.* Drink of the colour of amber, or resembling amber in colour and transparency.

All your clear amber drink *is flat.*
BACON'S NATURAL HISTORY.

A'MBIGU. *n.s.* [French.] An entertainment, consisting not of regular courses, but of a medley of dishes set on together.

When straiten'd in your time, and servants few,
You'd richly then compose an ambigu;
Where first and second course, and your desert,
All in our single table have their part.
KING'S ART OF COOKERY.

A'MBRY. *n.s.* [a word corrupted from *almonry.*]

1. The place where the almoner lives, or where alms are distributed.

2. The place where plate, and utensils for housekeeping, are kept; also a cupboard for keeping cold victuals: a word still used in the northern counties, and in Scotland.

To **AME'ND.** *v.a.* [*amender*, Fr. *emendo*, Lat.]

1. To correct; to change any thing that is wrong to something better.

2. To reform the life, or leave wickedness. In these two cases we usually write *mend*. See MEND.

Amend *your ways and your doings, and I will cause you to dwell in this place.* BIBLE JEREMIAH, VII. 3.

To **AME'ND.** *v.n.* To grow better. To *amend* differs from to *improve*; to *improve* supposes or not denies that the thing is well already, but to *amend* implies something wrong.

As my fortune either amends *or impairs, I may declare it unto you.* SIDNEY.

At his touch
Such sanctity hath heaven given his hand,
They presently amend.
SHAKESPEARE'S MACBETH.

AME'NDE. *n.s.* [French.] This word, in French, signifies a fine, by which recompense is supposed to be made for the fault committed. We use, in a cognate signification, the word *amends.*

A'MICABLE. *adj.* [*amicabilis*, Lat.] Friendly; kind. It is commonly used of more than one; as, they live in an *amicable* manner; but we seldom say, an *amicable* action, or an *amicable* man, though it be so used in this passage.

O grace serene! oh virtue heav'nly fair,
Divine oblivion of low-thoughted care!
Fresh blooming hope, gay daughter of the sky!
And faith, our early immortality!
Enter each mild, each amicable *guest;*
Receive and wrap me in eternal rest.
POPE'S ELOISE TO ABELARD.

A'MITY. *n.s.* [*amitie*, Fr. *amicitia*, Lat.] Friendship, whether publick between nations, opposed to war, or among the people, opposed to discord, or between private persons.

The prophet David did think, that the very meeting of men together, and their accompanying one another to the house of God, should make the bond of their love insoluble, and tie them in a league of inviolable amity. HOOKER, B. V. §38.

The monarchy of Great Britain was in league and amity *with all the world.* SIR JOHN DAVIES ON IRELAND.

You have a noble and a true conceit
Of godlike amity; *which appears most strongly*
In bearing thus the absence of your lord.
SHAKESPEARE'S MERCHANT OF VENICE.

And ye, oh Tyrians, with immortal hate
Pursue this race, this service dedicate
To my deplored ashes; let there be
'Twixt us and them no league nor amity.
SIR JOHN DENHAM.

A'MNESTY. *n.s.* ['αμνηστία.] An act of oblivion; an act by which crimes against the government, to a certain time, are so obliterated, that they can never be brought into charge.

I never read of a law enacted to take away the force of all laws, by which a man may safely commit upon the last of June, what he would infallibly be hanged for, if he committed it on the first of July; by which the greatest criminals may escape, provided they continue long enough in power, to antiquate their crimes, and, by stifling them a while, deceive the legislature into an amnesty. SWIFT.

AMO'UR. *n.s.* [*amour*, Fr. *amor*, Lat.] An affair of gallantry; an intrigue: generally used of vicious love. The *ou* sounds like *oo* in *poor*.

No man is of so general and diffusive a lust, as to prosecute his amours *all the world over; and let it burn never so outrageously, yet the impure flame will either die of itself, or consume the body that harbours it.* SOUTH'S SERMONS.

The restless youth search'd all the world around;
But how can Jove in his amours *be found?*
ADDISON'S OVID'S METAMORPHOSES.

A'MPER. *n.s.* [*ampre*, Sax.] A tumour, with inflammation; bile: a word said, by *Skinner*, to be much in use in Essex; but, perhaps, not found in books.

AMPHITHE'ATRE. *n.s.* [of 'αμφιθέατρον, of 'αμφι and θεᾶομαι.] A building in a circular or oval form, having its area encompassed with rows of seats one above another; where spectators might behold spectacles, as stage-plays, or gladiators. The theatres of the ancients were built in the form of a semicircle, only exceeding a just semicircle by one fourth part of the diameter; and the amphitheatre is two theatres joined together; so that the longest diameter of the amphitheatre, was to the shortest, as one and a half to one.

Within, an amphitheatre *appear'd*
Rais'd in degrees; to sixty paces rear'd,
That when a man was plac'd in one degree,
Height was allow'd for him above to see.
DRYDEN'S FABLES.

Conceive a man placed in the burning iron chair at Lyons, amid the insults and mockeries of a crouded amphitheatre, *and still keeping his seat; or stretched upon a grate of iron, over coals of fire, and breathing out his soul, among the exquisite sufferings of such a tedious execution, rather than renounce his religion, or blaspheme his Saviour.*
ADDISON ON THE CHRISTIAN RELIGION.

A'MPLIFIER. *n.s.* [from *To amplify*.] One that enlarges any thing; one that exaggerates; one that represents any thing with a large display of the best circumstances; it being usually taken in a good sense.

Dorillaus could need no amplifier's *mouth for the highest point of praise.*
SIDNEY, B. II.

To **A'MPUTATE.** *v.a.* [*amputo*, Lat.] To cut off a limb: a word used only in chirurgery.

Amongst the cruizers in private frigates from Dunkirk, it was complained, that their surgeons were too active in amputating *those fractured members.*
WISEMAN'S SURGERY.

To **AMU'SE.** *v.a.* [*amuser*, Fr.]
1. To entertain with tranquillity; to fill with thoughts that engage the mind, without distracting it. To *divert* implies something more lively, and to *please*, something more important. It is therefore frequently taken in a sense bordering on contempt.

They think they see visions, and are arrived to some extraordinary revelations; when, indeed, they do but dream dreams, and

amuse *themselves with the fantastick ideas of a busy imagination.*
DECAY OF PIETY.

I cannot think it natural for a man, who is much in love, to amuse *himself with trifles.* WALSH.

2. To draw on from time to time; to keep in expectation; as, he *amused* his followers with idle promises.

A'NA. *n.s.* Books so called from the last syllables of their titles; as *Scaligerana, Thuaniana*; they are loose thoughts, or casual hints, dropped by eminent men, and collected by their friends.

ANA'CHRONISM. *n.s.* [from 'ανά and χρόνος.] An errour in computing time, by which events are misplaced with regard to each other. It seems properly to signify an errour by which an event is placed too early; but is generally used for any errour in chronology.

This leads me to the defence of the famous anachronism, *in making Æneas and Dido contemporaries: for it is certain, that the hero lived almost two hundred years before the building of Carthage.*
DRYDEN'S VIRGIL, DEDICATION.

A'NAGRAM. *n.s.* ['ανά and γράμμα.] A conceit arising from the letters of a name transposed; as this, of *W,i,l,l,i,a,m, N,o,y,* attorney-general to Charles I. a very laborious man, *I moyl in law.*[11]

Though all her parts be not in th' usual place,
She hath yet the anagrams *of a good face:*
If we might put the letters but one way,
In that lean dearth of words, what could we say? DONNE.

Thy genius calls thee not to purchase fame
In keen iambicks, but mild anagram.
DRYDEN.

ANA'LYSIS. *n.s.* ['ανάλυσις.]
1. A separation of a compound body into the several parts of which it consists.

There is an account of dew falling, in some places, in the form of butter, or grease, which grows extremely fetid; so that the analysis *of the dew of any place, may, perhaps, be the best method of finding such contents of the soil as are within the reach of the sun.* ARBUTHNOT.

2. A consideration of any thing in parts, so as that one particular is first considered, then another.

Analysis *consists in making experiments and observations, and in drawing general conclusions from them by induction, and admitting of no objections against the conclusions, but such as are taken from experiments, or other certain truths.*
NEWTON'S OPTICKS.

3. A solution of any thing, whether corporeal or mental, to its first elements; as, of a sentence to the single words; of a compound word, to the particles and words which form it; of a tune, to single notes; of an argument, to simple propositions.

We cannot know any thing of nature, but by an analysis *of its true initial causes; till we know the first springs of natural motions, we are still but ignorants.*
GLANVILLE'S SCEPSIS SCIENTIFICA.

A'NCIENT. *adj.* [*ancien,* Fr. *antiquus,* Lat.]
1. Old; that happened long since; of old time; not modern. *Ancient* and *old* are distinguished; *old* relates to the duration of the thing itself, as, an *old* coat, a coat much worn; and *ancient,* to time in general, as, an *ancient* dress, a habit used in former times. But this is not always observed; for we mention *old customs*; but though *old* be sometimes opposed to

modern, *ancient* is seldom opposed to *new*.[12]

> Ancient *tenure is that whereby all the manours belonging to the crown, in St. Edward's or William the Conquerour's days, did hold. The number and names of which manours, as all others belonging to common persons, he caused to be written in a book, after a survey made of them, now remaining in the exchequer, and called doomsday book; and such as by that book appeared to have belonged to the crown at that time, are called* ancient *demesnes.*
> COWELL.

2. Old; that has been of long duration.

> *With the* ancient *is wisdom, and in length of days understanding.*
> BIBLE JOB, XII. 12.

> *Thales affirms, that God comprehended all things, and that God was of all things the most* ancient, *because he never had any beginning.*
> RALEIGH'S HISTORY OF THE WORLD.

> *Industry*
> *Gave the tall* ancient *forest too his axe.*
> THOMSON'S SUMMER.

3. Past; former.

> *I see thy fury: if I longer stay,*
> *We shall begin our* ancient *bickerings.*
> SHAKESPEARE'S HENRY VI.

AND. *conjunction.*

1. The particle by which sentences or terms are joined, which it is not easy to explain by any synonimous word.

> *Sure his honesty*
> *Got him small gains, but shameless flattery*
> And *filthy beverage,* and *unseemly thift,*
> And *borrow base,* and *some good lady's gift.* SPENSER'S HUBBERD'S TALE.

> *What shall I do to be for ever known,*
> And *make the age to come my own?*
> COWLEY.

> *The Danes unconquer'd offspring march behind;*
> And *Morini, the last of human kind.*
> DRYDEN.

> *It shall ever be my study to make discoveries of this nature in human life,* and *to settle the proper distinctions between the virtues* and *perfections of mankind,* and *those false colours* and *resemblances of them that shine alike in the eyes of the vulgar.* ADDISON'S TATLER.

2. *And* sometimes signifies *though*, and seems a contraction of *and if*.

> *It is the nature of extreme self-lovers, as they will set an house on fire,* and *it were but to roast their eggs.* BACON.

3. In *and if*, the *and* is redundant, and is omitted by all later writers.

> *I pray thee, Launce,* an' if *thou seest my boy,*
> *Bid him make haste.*
> SHAKESPEARE'S TWO GENTLEMEN OF VERONA.

ANE'NT. *prep.* A word used in the Scotch dialect.
1. Concerning; about; as, *he said nothing* anent *this particular.*
2. Over against; opposite to; as, *he lives* anent *the market-house.*

A'NGLICISM. *n.s.* [from *Anglus*, Lat.] A form of speech peculiar to the English language; an English idiom.

ANIMO'SITY. *n.s.* [*animositas*, Lat.] Vehemence of hatred; passionate malignity. It implies rather the disposition to break out into outrages, than the outrage itself.

> *They were sure to bring passion,* animosity, *and malice enough of their own, what evidence soever they had from others.*
> CLARENDON, B. VIII.

> *If there is not some method found out for allaying these heats and* animosities *among the fair sex, one does not know to what outrages they may proceed.*
> ADDISON'S FREEHOLDER, NO 23.

> *No religious sect ever carried their aversions for each other to greater heights than our*

state parties have done; who, the more to inflame their passions, have mixed religious and civil animosities *together; borrowing one of their appellations from the church.* SWIFT ON THE SENTIMENTS OF A CHURCH OF ENGLAND MAN.

A'NNO DOMINI. [Lat.] In the year of our Lord; as, *anno domini*, or *A.D.* 1751; that is, in the seventeen hundred and fifty first year from the birth of our Saviour.

ANO'MALOUS. *adj.* [*α priv.* and 'ἀμαλος.] Irregular; out of rule; deviating from the general method or analogy of things: It is applied, in grammar, to words deviating from the common rules of inflection; and, in astronomy, to the seemingly irregular motions of the planets.

There will arise anomalous *disturbances not only in civil and artificial, but also in military officers.* BROWN'S VULGAR ERROURS.

He being acquainted with some characters of every speech, you may at pleasure make him understand anomalous *pronunciation.* HOLDER'S ELEMENTS OF SPEECH.

Metals are gold, silver, copper, tin, lead, and iron: to which we may join that anomalous *body, quicksilver or mercury.* LOCKE'S ELEMENTS OF NATURAL PHILOSOPHY.

ANO'THERGUESS. *adj.* [This word, which though rarely used in writing, is somewhat frequent in colloquial language, I conceive to be corrupted from *another guise*; that is, of a different *guise*, or manner, or form.] Of a different kind.

Oh Hocus! where art thou? It used to go in anotherguess *manner in thy time.* ARBUTHNOT'S HISTORY OF JOHN BULL.

A'NSWER-JOBBER. *n.s.* [from *answer* and *jobber.*] He that makes a trade of writing answers.

What disgusts me from having any thing to do with answer-jobbers, *is, that they have no conscience.* SWIFT.

ANTA'LGICK. *adj.* [from 'αντί, against, and 'ἄλγος, pain.] That which softens pain; anodyne.

ANTAPHRODI'TICK. *adj.* [from 'αντί, against, and 'ἀφροδίτη, Venus.] That which is efficacious against the venereal disease.

ANTAPOPLE'CTICK. *adj.* ['αντί, against, and 'αποπληξις, an apoplexy.] Good against an apoplexy.

ANTARTHRI'TICK. *adj.* ['αντί, against, and 'ἀρθιτις, the gout.] Good against the gout.

ANTASTHMA'TICK. *adj.* [from 'αντί and 'ἄσθμα.] Good against the asthma.

ANTECE'DENT. *adj.* [*antecedens*, Lat.]

1. Going before; preceding. *Antecedent* is used, I think, only with regard to time; *precedent*, with regard both to time and place.

To assert, that God looked upon Adam's fall as a sin, and punished it, when, without any antecedent *sin of his, it was impossible for him not to fall, seems a thing that highly reproaches essential equity and goodness.* SOUTH.

2. It has *to* before the thing which is supposed to follow.

No one is so hardy as to say, God is in his debt; that he owed him a nobler being: for existence must be antecedent to *merit.* COLLIER OF ENVY.

Did the blood first exist, antecedent to *the formation of the heart? But that is to set the effect before the cause.* BENTLEY.

ANTHROPOPHAGI'NIAN. *n.s.* A ludicrous word, formed by *Shakespeare* from *anthropophagi*, for the sake of a formidable sound.

Go, knock, and call; he'll speak like an anthropophaginian *unto thee; knock, I say.*
SHAKESPEARE'S MERRY WIVES OF WINDSOR.

A'NTICK. *adj.* [probably from *antiquus*, ancient, as things out of use appear old.] Odd; ridiculously wild; buffoon in gesticulation.

What! dares the slave
Come hither cover'd with an antick *face,*
And fleer and scorn at our solemnity?
SHAKESPEARE'S ROMEO AND JULIET.

Of all our antick *fights, and pageantry,*
Which English idiots run in crouds to see.
DRYDEN.

The prize was to be conferred upon the whistler, that could go through his tune without laughing, though provoked by the antick *postures of a merry Andrew, who was to play tricks.*
ADDISON'S SPECTATOR, NO 179.

ANTI'PODES. *n.s. It has no singular.* [from ἀντί, against, and πόδες, feet.] Those people who, living on the other side of the globe, have their feet directly opposite to ours.

We should hold day with the antipodes,
If you would walk in absence of the sun.
SHAKESPEARE'S MERCHANT OF VENICE.

So shines the sun, tho' hence remov'd, as clear
When his beams warm th' antipodes, *as here.* WALLER.

ANTI'QUITY. *n.s.* [*antiquitas*, Lat.]
1. Old times; time past long ago.

I mention Aristotle, Polybius, and Cicero, the greatest philosopher, the most impartial historian, and the most consummate statesman of all antiquity.
ADDISON'S FREEHOLDER, NO 51.

2. The people of old times; the ancients.

That such pillars were raised by Seth, all antiquity *has avowed.*
RALEIGH'S HISTORY OF THE WORLD.

3. The works or remains of old times.

As for the observation of Machiavel, traducing Gregory the Great, that he did what in him lay, to extinguish all heathen antiquities: *I do not find that those zeals last long; as it appeared in the succession of Sabinian, who did revive the former* antiquities. BACON'S ESSAYS.

4. Old age: a ludicrous sense.

Is not your voice broken? your wind short? your chin double? your wit single? and every part about you blasted with antiquity? *and will you yet call yourself young?* SHAKESPEARE'S HENRY IV.

5. Ancientness; as, this ring is valuable for its *antiquity*.

APE. *n.s.* [*ape*, Icelandish.]
1. A kind of monkey remarkable for imitating what he sees.

I will be more newfangled than an ape, *more giddy in my desires than a monkey.*
SHAKESPEARE'S AS YOU LIKE IT.

Writers report, that the heart of an ape *worn near the heart, comforteth the heart, and increaseth audacity. It is true, that the* ape *is a merry and bold beast.*
BACON'S NATURAL HISTORY.

With glittering gold and sparkling gems they shine,
But apes *and monkeys are the gods within.* GRANVILLE.

2. An imitator; used generally in the bad sense.

Julio Romano, who, had he himself eternity, and could put breath into his work, would beguile nature of her custom: so perfectly he is her ape.
SHAKESPEARE'S WINTER'S TALE.

APE'RITIVE. *adj.* [from *aperio*, Lat. to open.] That which has the quality of opening the excrementious passages of the body.

They may make broth, with the addition of aperitive *herbs.*
HARVEY ON CONSUMPTIONS.

API'TPAT. *adv.* [a word formed from the motion.] With quick palpitation.

O there he comes – Ay, my Hector of Troy, welcome my bully, my back; agad my heart has gone apitpat *for you.*
CONGREVE'S OLD BATCHELOR.

APO'STLE. *n.s.* [*apostolus*, Lat. *'απόστολος.*] A person sent with mandates by another. It is particularly applied to them whom our Saviour deputed to preach the gospel.

But all his mind is bent to holiness;
His champions are the prophets and
apostles. SHAKESPEARE'S HENRY IV.

I am far from pretending infallibility; that would be to erect myself into an apostle: *a presumption in any one that cannot confirm what he says by miracles.*
LOCKE.

We know but a small part of the notion of an apostle, *by knowing barely that he is sent forth.* WATTS'S LOGICK.

APPARA'TUS. *n.s.* [Latin.] Things provided as means to any certain end, as the tools of a trade; the furniture of a house; ammunition for war; equipage; show.

There is an apparatus *of things previous, to be adjusted before I come to the calculation itself.*
WOODWARD'S NATURAL HISTORY.

Ourselves are easily provided for; it is nothing but the circumstantials, the apparatus *or equipage of human life, that costs so much.* POPE'S LETTERS TO GAY.

To **APPE'AR.** *v.n.* [*appareo*, Lat.]
1. To be in sight; to be visible; sometimes with the particle *in.*[13]

As the leprosy appeareth *in the skin of the flesh.* BIBLE LEVITICUS, XIII. 43.

And half her knee, and half her breast
appear,
By art, like negligence, disclos'd and bare.
PRIOR.

2. To become visible as a spirit.

For I have appeared *unto thee for this purpose, to make thee a minister and a witness.* BIBLE ACTS, XXVI. 16.

3. To stand in the presence of another; generally used of standing before some superiour.

When shall I come and appear *before God?* BIBLE PSALMS, XLII. 2.

4. To be the object of observation.

Let thy work appear *unto thy servants, and thy glory unto their children.*
BIBLE PSALMS, XC. 16.

5. To exhibit one's self before a court of justice.

Keep comfort to you, and this morning see
You do appear *before them.*
SHAKESPEARE'S HENRY VIII.

6. To be made clear by evidence.

Egfrid did utterly waste and subdue it, as appears *out of Beda's complaint against him; and Edgar brought it under his obedience, as* appears *by an ancient record.*
SPENSER'S IRELAND.

7. To seem in opposition to reality.

His first and principal care being to appear *unto his people, such as he would have them be, and to be such as he* appeared.
SIDNEY, B. II.

My noble master will appear
Such as he is, full of regard and honour.
SHAKESPEARE'S JULIUS CÆSAR.

8. To be plain beyond dispute.

From experiments, useful indications may be taken, as will appear *by what follows.*
ARBUTHNOT ON ALIMENTS.

APPLI'ABLE. *adj.* [from *apply.*] That which may be applied. For this word the moderns use *applicable*; which see.

Limitations all such principles have, in regard of the varieties of the matter whereunto they are appliable.
HOOKER, B. V.

All that I have said of the heathen idolatry is appliable *to the idolatry of another sort of men in the world.* SOUTH.

A'PPLICABLE. *adj.* [from *apply.*] That which may be applied, as properly relating to something.

What he says of the portrait of any particular person is applicable *to poetry. In the character, there is a better or worse likeness; the better is a panegyrick, and the worse a libel.*
DRYDEN'S DUFRESNOY, PREFACE.

It were happy for us, if this complaint were applicable *only to the heathen world.*
ROGERS.

To **APPO'SE.** *v.a.* [*appono*, Lat.] To put questions to. This word is not now in use, except that, in some schools, to put grammatical questions to a boy is called, to *pose* him; and we now use *pose* for *puzzle.*[14]

Some procure themselves to be surprised at such times as it is like the party that they work upon, will come upon them: and to be found with a letter in their hand, or doing somewhat which they are not accustomed; to the end they may be apposed *of those things which of themselves they are desirous to utter.*
BACON.

APPRO'OF. *n.s.* [from *approve*, as *proof* from *prove.*] Approbation; commendation: a word rightly derived, but old.

O most perilous mouths,
That bear in them one and the self-same tongue
Either of condemnation or approof!
SHAKESPEARE'S MEASURE FOR MEASURE.

To **A'PRICATE.** *v.n.* [*apricor*, Lat.] To bask in the sun. *Dictionaries.*

APRI'CITY. *n.s.* [*apricitas*, Lat.] Warmth of the sun; sunshine. *Dictionaries.*

APRIL. *n.s.* [*Aprilis*, Lat. *Avril*, Fr.] The fourth month of the year, January counted first.

April *is represented by a young man in green, with a garland of myrtle and hawthorn buds; in one hand primroses and violets, in the other the sign Taurus.*
PEACHAM ON DRAWING.

Men are April *when they woo, December when they wed: Maids are May when they are maids, but the sky changes when they are wives.*
SHAKESPEARE'S AS YOU LIKE IT.

A'PRON. *n.s.* [A word of uncertain etymology, but supposed by some to be contracted from *afore one.*] A cloth hung before, to keep the other dress clean.

Give us gold, good Timon: hast thou more? ——
—— *Hold up, you sluts,*
Your aprons *mountant.*
SHAKESPEARE'S TIMON.

The nobility think scorn to go in leather aprons. SHAKESPEARE'S HENRY VI.

How might we see Falstaff, and not ourselves be seen? ——
Put on two leather jerkins and aprons, *and wait upon him at his table as drawers.*
SHAKESPEARE'S HENRY IV.

In both these figures the vest is gathered up before them, like an apron, *which you must suppose filled with fruits, as well as the cornucopiæ.* ADDISON ON MEDALS.

APRON. [in gunnery.] A piece of lead which covers the touchhole of a great gun.

APRON *of a goose.* The fat skin which covers the belly.

A'PRON-MAN. *n.s.* [from *apron* and *man.*] A man that wears an apron; a workman; an artificer.

You have made good work,
You and your apron-men, *that stood so much*
Upon the voice of occupation, and
The breath of garlick eaters.
SHAKESPEARE'S CORIOLANUS.

AQUA MIRABILIS. [Latin.] The wonderful water, is prepared of cloves, galangals, cubebs, mace, cardomums, nutmegs, ginger, and spirit of wine, digested twenty four hours, then distilled. It is a good and agreeable cordial.[15]

A'QUEDUCT. *n.s.* [*aquæductus,* Lat.] A conveyance made for carrying water from one place to another; made on uneven ground, to preserve the level of the water, and convey it by a canal. Some aqueducts are under ground, and others above it, supported by arches.

Among the remains of old Rome, the grandeur of the commonwealth shews itself chiefly in temples, highways, aqueducts, *walls and bridges of the city.*
ADDISON'S REMARKS ON ITALY.

Hither the rills of water are convey'd
In curious aqueducts, *by nature laid*
To carry all the humour.
BLACKMORE, CREATION.

A.R. *anno regni*; that is, the year of the reign: as, *A.R.G.R.* 20. *Anno regni Georgii regis vigesimo,* in the twentieth year of the reign of king George.

ARBITRA'TION. *n.s.* [from *arbitror,* Lat.] The determination of a cause by a judge mutually agreed on by the parties contending.

ARCH. *adj.* [from *'ἀρχος*, chief.]
1. Chief; of the first class.

The tyrannous and bloody act is done;
The most arch *deed of piteous massacre,*
That ever yet this land was guilty of.
SHAKESPEARE'S RICHARD III.

There is sprung up
An heretick, an arch *one, Cranmer.*
SHAKESPEARE'S HENRY VIII.

2. Waggish; mirthful; triflingly mischievous. This signification it seems to have gained, by being frequently applied to the boy most remarkable for his pranks; as the *arch* rogue, &c.[16]

Eugenio set out from the same university, and about the same time with Corusades; he had the reputation of an arch *lad at school.* SWIFT'S FATES OF CLERGY.

ARCH, in composition, signifies chief, or of the first class, [from *'ἀρχος*, or *'ἀρχι.*] as, *archangel, archbishop.* It is pronounced variously with regard to the *ch*, which before a consonant sound as in *cheese*, as *archdeacon*; before a vowel like *k*, as *archangel.*

A'RCHIVES. *n.s. without a singular.* [*archiva,* Lat.] The places where records or ancient writings are kept. It is perhaps sometimes used for the writings themselves.

Though we think our words vanish with the breath that utters them, yet they become records in God's court, and are laid up in his archives, *as witnesses either for or against us.*
GOVERNMENT OF THE TONGUE, §1.

I shall now only look a little into the Mosaick archives, *to observe what they furnish us with upon this subject.*
WOODWARD.

A'REA. *n.s.* [Latin.]
1. The surface contained between any lines or boundaries.

The area *of a triangle is found by knowing the height and the base.* WATTS'S LOGICK.

2. Any open surface, as the floor of a room; the open part of a church; the vacant part or stage of an amphitheatre. An inclosed place, as lists, or a bowling-green, or grass-plot.

Let us conceive a floor or area *of goodly length, with the breadth somewhat more than half the longitude.* WOTTON.

The Alban lake is of an oval figure, and, by reason of the high mountains that encompass it, looks like the area *of some vast amphitheatre.* ADDISON ON ITALY.

In areas *vary'd with Mosaic art,*
Some whirl the disk, and some the jav'lin dart. POPE'S ODYSSEY.

A'RGUER. *n.s.* [from *argue.*] A reasoner; a disputer; a controvertist.

Men are ashamed to be proselytes to a weak arguer, *as thinking they must part with their reputation as well as their sin.* DECAY OF PIETY.

A'RGUTE. *adj.* [*arguto*, Ital. *argutus*, Lat.]
1. Subtile; witty; sharp.
2. Shrill.

A'RIA. *n.s.* [Ital. in musick.] An air, song, or tune.

To **ARI'ETATE.** *v.n.* [*arieto*, Lat.]
1. To butt like a ram.
2. To strike in imitation of the blows which rams give with their heads.

ARIETA'TION. *n.s.* [from *arietate.*]
1. The act of butting like a ram.
2. The act of battering with an engine called a ram.

The strength of the percussion, wherein ordnance do exceed all arietations *and ancient inventions.* BACON'S ESSAYS.

3. The act of striking, or conflicting in general.

Now those heterogeneous atoms, by themselves, hit so exactly into their proper residence, in the midst of such tumultuary motions, and arietations *of other particles.* GLANVILLE'S SCEPSIS SCIENTIFICA.

ARIE'TTA. *n.s.* [Ital. in musick.] A short air, song, or tune.

ARISTO'CRACY. *n.s.* ['άϱιστος, greatest, and ϰϱατέω, to govern.] That form of government which places the supreme power in the nobles, without a king, and exclusively of the people.

The aristocracy *of Venice hath admitted so many abuses through the degeneracy of the nobles, that the period of its duration seems to approach.* SWIFT.

ARM'S END. *n.s.* A phrase taken from boxing, in which the weaker man may overcome the stronger, if he can keep him from closing.

Such a one as can keep him at arm's end, *need never wish for a better companion.* SIDNEY'S ARCADIA.

For my sake be comfortable, hold death awhile at the arm's end. SHAKESPEARE'S AS YOU LIKE IT.

ARMI'SONOUS. *adj.* [*armisonus*, Lat.] Rustling with armour.

A'RMLET. *n.s.* [from *arm.*]
1. A little arm; as, an armlet of the sea.
2. A piece of armour for the arm.
3. A bracelet for the arm.

And, when she takes thy hand, and doth seem kind,
Doth search what rings and armlets *she can find.* DONNE.[17]

A'RQUEBUSE. *n.s.* [Fr. spelt falsely *harquebuss.*] A hand gun. It seems to have anciently meant much the same as our carabine, or fusee.

A harquebuse, *or ordnance, will be farther heard from the mouth of the piece, than backwards or on the sides.*
BACON'S NATURAL HISTORY NO 204.

A'RRANT. *adj.* [a word of uncertain etymology, but probably from *errant*, which being at first applied to its proper signification to vagabonds, as an *errant* or *arrant rogue*, that is, a *rambling rogue*, lost, in time, its original signification, and being by its use understood to imply something bad, was applied at large to any thing that was mentioned with hatred or contempt.] Bad in a high degree.

Country folks, who hallooed and hooted after me, as at the arrantest *coward that ever shewed his shoulders to the enemy.*
SIDNEY, B. II.

A vain fool grows forty times an arranter *sot than before.*
L'ESTRANGE'S FABLES.

And let him every deity adore,
If his new bride prove not an arrant
whore.
DRYDEN'S JUVENAL.

A'RROW. *n.s.* [*arewe*, Sax.] The pointed weapon which is shot from a bow. Darts are thrown by the hand, but in poetry they are confounded.

I swear to thee by Cupid's strongest bow,
By his best arrow *with the golden head.*
SHAKESPEARE'S MIDSUMMER NIGHT'S DREAM.

Here were boys so desperately resolved, as to pull arrows *out of their flesh, and deliver them to be shot again by the archers on their side.* SIR J. HAYWARD.

ARSE. *n.s.* [*earse*, Sax.] The buttocks, or hind part of an animal. *To hang an* ARSE. A vulgar phrase, signifying to be tardy, sluggish, or dilatory.

For Hudibras wore but one spur,
As wisely knowing, could he stir
To active trot one side of 's horse,
The other would not hang an arse.
HUDIBRAS, CANT. 1.

ART. *n.s.* [*arte*, Fr. *ars*, Lat.]

1. The power of doing something not taught by nature and instinct; as, to *walk* is natural, to *dance* is an *art*.

Art *is properly an habitual knowledge of certain rules and maxims, by which a man is governed and directed in his actions.*
SOUTH.

Blest with each grace of nature and of art.
POPE.

Ev'n copious Dryden wanted, or forgot,
The last and greatest art, *the* art *to blot.*
POPE.

2. A science; as, the liberal arts.

Arts *that respect the mind were ever reputed nobler than those that serve the body.* BEN JONSON'S DISCOVERY.

3. A trade.

This observation is afforded us by the art *of making sugar.* BOYLE.

4. Artfulness; skill; dexterity.

The art *of our necessities is strange,*
That can make vile things precious.
SHAKESPEARE'S KING LEAR.

5. Cunning.
6. Speculation.

I have as much of this in art *as you;*
But yet my nature could not bear it so.
SHAKESPEARE'S JULIUS CÆSAR.

ARTI'CULATE. *adj.* [from *articulus*, Lat.]

1. Distinct,[18] as the parts of a limb by joints; not continued in one tone, as *articulate* sounds; that is, sounds varied and changed at proper pauses, in opposition to the voice of animals, which admit no such variety. An *articulate* pronunciation, a manner of speaking

clear and distinct, in which one sound is not confounded with another.

In speaking under water, when the voice is reduced to an extreme exility, yet the articulate *sounds, the words, are not confounded.* BACON'S NATURAL HISTORY NO 195.

The first, at least, of these I thought deny'd
To beasts; whom God, on their creation-day,
Created mute to all articulate *sound.*
MILTON'S PARADISE LOST.

2. Branched out into articles. This is a meaning little in use.

His instructions were extreme curious and articulate; *and, in them, more articles touching inquisition, than negotiation: requiring from his ambassadors an answer in distinct articles to his questions.* BACON'S HENRY VII.

ASCE'NSION. *n.s.* [*ascensio*, Lat.]
1. The act of ascending or rising; frequently applied to the visible elevation of our Saviour to heaven.

Then rising from his grave,
Spoil'd principalities, and pow'rs, triumph'd
In open shew; and, with ascension *bright,*
Captivity led captive through the air.
PARADISE LOST, B. X.

2. The thing rising, or mounting.

Men err in the theory of inebriation, conceiving the brain doth only suffer from vaporous ascensions *from the stomach.* BROWN'S VULGAR ERROURS.

ASCE'NSION, in astronomy, is either *right* or *oblique*. *Right ascension* of the sun, or a star, is that degree of the equinoctial, counted from the beginning of Aries, which rises with the sun or star in a right sphere. *Oblique ascension* is an arch of the equator intercepted between the first point of Aries, and that point of the equator which rises together with a star in an oblique sphere.

ASCE'NSION DAY. The day on which the ascension of our Saviour is commemorated, commonly called Holy Thursday; the Thursday but one before Whitsuntide.

A'SHLAR. *n.s.* [with masons.] Free stones as they come out of the quarry, of different lengths, breadths, and thicknesses.

ASPE'RITY. *n.s.* [*asperitas*, Lat.]
1. Unevenness; roughness of surface.

Sometimes the pores and asperities *of dry bodies are so incommensurate to the particles of the liquor, that they glide over the surface.* BOYLE.

2. Roughness of sound; harshness of pronunciation.
3. Roughness, or ruggedness of temper; moroseness; sourness; crabbedness.

The charity of the one, like kindly exhalations, will descend in showers of blessings; but the rigour and asperity *of the other, in a severe doom upon ourselves.* GOVERNMENT OF THE TONGUE.

Avoid all unseemliness and asperity *of carriage; do nothing that may argue a peevish or froward spirit.* ROGERS.

To **ASPE'RSE.** *v.a.* [*aspergo*, Lat.] To bespatter with censure or calumny.

In the business of Ireland, besides the opportunity to asperse *the king, they were safe enough.* CLARENDON, B. VIII.

Curb that impetuous tongue, nor rashly vain,
And singly mad, asperse *the sov'reign reign.* POPE'S ILIAD.

Unjustly poets we asperse,
Truth shines the brighter clad in verse.
SWIFT.

ASPHA'LTOS. *n.s.* ['ασφαλτός, bitumen.] A solid, brittle, black, bituminous, inflammable substance, resembling pitch, and chiefly found swimming on the surface of the *Lacus*

Asphaltites, or Dead sea, where anciently stood the cities of Sodom and Gomorrah. It is cast up from time to time, in the nature of liquid pitch, from the earth at the bottom of this sea; and, being thrown upon the water, swims like other fat bodies, and condenses gradually[19] by the heat of the sun, and the salt that is in it. It burns with great vehemence. The Arabs use it for pitching their ships; and much of it was employed in the embalming of the ancients.

To **A'SPIRATE.** *v.a.* [*aspiro*, Lat.] To pronounce with aspiration, or full breath; as we aspirate *horse*, *house*, and *hog*.

To **A'SPIRATE.** *v.n.* [*aspiro*, Lat.] To be pronounced with full breath.

Where a vowel ends a word, the next begins either with a consonant, or what is its equivalent; for our w and h aspirate.
DRYDEN'S DEDICATION TO ÆNEID.

ASQU'INT. *adv.* [from *a* and *squint.*] Obliquely; not in the strait line of vision.

A single guide may direct the way better than five hundred, who have contrary views, or look asquint, *or shut their eyes.*
SWIFT'S PROJECT FOR THE ADVANCEMENT OF RELIGION.

ASS. *n.s.* [*asinus*, Lat.]
1. An animal of burden, remarkable for sluggishness, patience, hardiness, coarseness of food, and long life.

You have among you many a purchas'd slave,
Which, like your asses, *and your dogs and mules,*
You use in abject and in slavish part,
Because you bought them.
SHAKESPEARE'S MERCHANT OF VENICE.

2. A stupid, heavy, dull fellow; a dolt.

I do begin to perceive that I am made an ass.
SHAKESPEARE'S MERRY WIVES OF WINDSOR.

That such a crafty mother
Should yield the world to this ass! *– a woman that*
Bears all down with her brain; and her son
Cannot take two from twenty for his heart,
And leave eighteen.
SHAKESPEARE'S CYMBELINE.

ASSE'MBLAGE. *n.s.* [*assemblage*, Fr.] A collection; a number of individuals brought together. It differs from *assembly*, by being applied only, or chiefly, to things; *assembly* being used only, or generally, of persons.

All that we amass together in our thoughts is positive, and the assemblage *of a great number of positive ideas of space or duration.* LOCKE.

O Hartford, fitted or to shine in courts
With unaffected grace, or walk the plains,
With innocence and meditation join'd
In soft assemblage, *listen to my song.*
THOMSON'S SPRING.[20]

A'SSHEAD. *n.s.* [from *ass* and *head.*] One slow of apprehension; a blockhead.

Will you help an asshead, *and a coxcomb, and a knave, a thin-faced knave, a gull.*
SHAKESPEARE'S HAMLET.[21]

ASSIGNA'TION. *n.s.* [*assignation*, French.]
1. An appointment to meet; used generally of love appointments.

The lovers expected the return of this stated hour with as much impatience as if it had been a real assignation. SPECTATOR.

Or when a whore, in her vocation,
Keeps punctual to an assignation.
SWIFT.

2. A making over a thing to another.

ASSI'STANT. *n.s.* [from *assist.*]

1. A person engaged in an affair not as principal, but as auxiliary or ministerial.

Some young towardly noblemen or gentlemen were usually sent as assistants *or attendants, according to the quality of the persons.*
BACON'S ADVICE TO SIR GEORGE VILLIERS.

2. Sometimes it is only a softer word for an attendant.

The pale assistants *on each other star'd,*
With gaping mouths for issuing words prepar'd. DRYDEN.

ASSI'ZE. *n.s.* [*assise*, a sitting, Fr.]

1. An assembly of knights and other substantial men, with the bailiff or justice, in a certain place, and at a certain time.
2. A jury.
3. An ordinance or statute.
4. The court, place, or time, where and when the writs and processes of assize are taken. *Cowel.*

The law was never executed by any justices of assize, *but the people left to their own laws.* SIR J. DAVIES ON IRELAND.

At each assize *and term we try*
A thousand rascals of as deep a dye.
DRYDEN'S JUVENAL.

5. Any court of justice.

The judging God shall close the book of fate,
And there the last assizes *keep,*
For those who wake, and those who sleep.
DRYDEN.

6. *Assize of bread, ale*, &c. Measure, or quantity. Thus it is said, *when wheat is of such a price, the bread shall be of such* assize.
7. Measure; rate: for which we now use *size*. See **SIZE**.

On high hill's top I saw a stately frame,
An hundred cubits high by just assize,
With hundred pillars.
SPENSER'S VISION OF BELLAY.

To **ASSO'T.** *v.a.* [from *sot*; *assoter*, Fr.] To infatuate; to besot: a word out of use.

But whence they sprung, or how they were begot,
Uneath is to assure, uneath to weene
That monstrous errour which doth some assot. FAIRY QUEEN.

ASSUEFA'CTION. *n.s.* [*assuefacio*, Lat.] The state of being accustomed to any thing.

Right and left, as parts inservient unto the motive faculty, are differenced by degrees from use and assuefaction, *or according whereto the one grows stronger.*
BROWN'S VULGAR ERROURS.

A'STERISM. *n.s.* [*asterismus*, Lat.]

1. A constellation.

Poetry had filled the skies with asterisms, *and histories belonging to them; and then astrology devises the feigned virtues and influences of each.*
BENTLEY'S SERMONS.

2. An asterisk, or mark. This is a very improper use.

Dwell particularly on passages with an asterism *; *for the observations which follow such a note, will give you a clear light.* DRYDEN'S DUFRESNOY.

To **ASTO'UND.** *v.a.* [*estonner*, Fr.] To astonish; to confound with fear or wonder. This word is now somewhat obsolete.

These thoughts may startle well, but not astound
The virtuous mind, that ever walks attended
By a strong siding champion, conscience.
PARADISE REGAIN'D.

To **ASTRI'CT.** *v.a.* [*astringo*, Lat.] To contract by applications, in opposition to relax: a word not so much used as *constringe*.

The solid parts were to be relaxed or astricted, *as they let the humours pass either in too small or too great quantities.* ARBUTHNOT ON ALIMENTS.

ASTRI'NGENCY. *n.s.* [from *astringe.*] The power of contracting the parts of the body; opposed to the power of *relaxation*.

Astriction prohibiteth dissolution; as, in medicines, astringents inhibit putrefaction: and, by astringency, *some small quantity of oil of vitriol will keep fresh water long from putrefying.*
BACON'S NATURAL HISTORY, NO 342.

Acid, acrid, austere, and bitter substances, by their astringency, *create horrour, that is, stimulate the fibres.* ARBUTHNOT.

ASTRO'LOGY. *n.s.* [*astrologia*, Lat.] The practice of foretelling things by the knowledge of the stars; an art now generally exploded, as without reason.[22]

I know it hath been the opinion of the learned, who think of the art of astrology, *that the stars do not force the actions or wills of men.* SWIFT.

ASTRO-THEOLOGY. *n.s.* [from *astrum*, a star, and *theologia*, divinity.] Divinity founded on the observation of the celestial bodies.

That the diurnal and annual revolutions are the motions of the terraqueous globe, not of the sun, I shew in the preface of my Astro-Theology.
DERHAM'S PHYSICO-THEOLOGY.

ATHLE'TICK. *adj.* [from *athleta*, Lat. 'αθλητής, a wrestler.]
1. Belonging to wrestling.
2. Strong of body; vigorous; lusty; robust.

Seldom shall one see in rich families that athletick *soundness and vigour of constitution, which is seen in cottages, where nature is cook, and necessity caterer.*
SOUTH.

Science distinguishes a man of honour from one of those athletick *brutes, whom undeservedly we call heroes.* DRYDEN.

ATI'LT. *adv.* [from *a* and *tilt.*]
1. In the manner of a tilter; with the action of a man making a thrust at an antagonist.

In the city Tours,
Thou ran'st atilt, *in honour of my love,*
And stol'st away the ladies hearts from
France. SHAKESPEARE'S HENRY VI.

To run atilt *at men, and wield*
Their naked tools in open field.
HUDIBRAS, P. I. C. I.

2. In the posture of a barrel raised or tilted behind, to make it run out.

Such a man is always atilt; *his favours come hardly from him.* SPECTATOR.

A'TLAS. *n.s.*
1. A collection of maps, so called probably from a picture of Atlas supporting the heavens, prefixed to some collection.
2. A large square folio; so called from these folios, which, containing maps, were made large and square.
3. Sometimes the supporters of a building.
4. A rich kind of silk or stuff made for women's cloaths.

I have the conveniency of buying Dutch atlasses *with gold and silver, or without.*
SPECTATOR, NO 288.

ATRABILA'RIAN. *adj.* [from *atra bilis*, black choler.] Melancholy; replete with black choler.

The atrabilarian *constitution, or a black, viscous, pitchy consistence of the fluids, makes all secretions difficult and sparing.*
ARBUTHNOT ON DIET.

ATTA'CHMENT. *n.s.* [*attachement*, Fr.]

1. Adherence; attention; regard.

The Jews are remarkable for an attachment *to their own country.* ADDISON'S FREEHOLDER, NO 5.

The Romans burnt this last fleet, which is another mark of their small attachment *to the sea.* ARBUTHNOT ON COINS.

2. An apprehension of a man to bring him to answer an action; and sometimes it extends to his moveables.

3. *Foreign attachment*, is the attachment of a foreigner's goods found within a city, to satisfy creditors within a city.

A'TTER. *n.s.* [*ater*, Sax. venom.] Corrupt matter. A word much used in Lincolnshire. *Skinner*.

A'TTITUDE. *n.s.* [*attitude*, Fr. from *atto*, Ital.] The posture or action in which a statue or painted figure is placed.

Bernini would have taken his opinion upon the beauty and attitude *of a figure.* PRIOR'S DEDICATION.

They were famous originals that gave rise to statues, with the same air, posture, and attitudes. ADDISON.

ATTRA'CT. *n.s.* [from *to attract.*] Attraction; the power of drawing.

Feel darts and charms, attracts *and flames,*
And woe and contract in their names.
HUDIBRAS.

ATTRA'CTICAL. *adj.* [from *attract.*] Having the power to draw to it.

Some stones are endued with an electrical or attractical *virtue.*
RAY ON THE CREATION.

ATTRA'CTIVE. *adj.* [from *attract.*]

1. Having the power to draw any thing.

What if the sun
Be centre to the world; and other stars,
By his attractive *virtue, and their own,*
Incited, dance about him various rounds.
PARADISE LOST.

Some the round earth's cohesion to secure,
For that hard task employ magnetick power;
Remark, say they, the globe, with wonder own
Its nature, like the fam'd attractive *stone.*
BLACKMORE.

Bodies act by the attractions of gravity, magnetism, and electricity; and these instances make it not improbable but there may be more attractive *powers than these.* NEWTON'S OPTICS.

2. Inviting; alluring; enticing.

Happy is Hermia, wheresoe'er she lies;
For she hath blessed and attractive *eyes.*
SHAKESPEARE'S MIDSUMMER NIGHT'S DREAM.

I pleas'd, and with attractive *graces won,*
The most averse, thee chiefly.
PARADISE LOST, B. II.

ATTRI'TION. *n.s.* [*attritio*, Lat.]

1. The act of wearing things, by rubbing one against another.

This vapour, ascending incessantly out of the abyss, and pervading the strata of gravel, and the rest, decays the bones and vegetables lodged in those strata; this fluid, by its continual attrition, *fretting the said bodies.*
WOODWARD'S NATURAL HISTORY.

The change of the aliment is effected by attrition *of the inward stomach, and dissolvent liquor assisted with heat.*
ARBUTHNOT ON ALIMENTS.

2.[23] [With divines.] Grief for sin, arising only from the fear of punishment; the lowest degree of repentance.

AVA'ST. *adv.* [from *basta*, Ital. it is enough.] Enough; cease. A word used among seamen.

A'UCTION. *n.s.* [*auctio*, Lat.]

1. A manner of sale in which one

person bids after another, till so much is bid as the seller is content to take.
2. The things sold by auction.

Ask you why Phrine the whole auction *buys;*
Phrine foresees a general excise. POPE.

A'VENUE. *n.s.* [*avenue*, Fr. It is sometimes pronounced with the accent on the second syllable, as *Watts* observes; but it is generally placed on the first.]
1. A way by which any place may be entered.

Good guards were set up at all the avenues *of the city, to keep all people from going out.* CLARENDON, B. VIII.

Truth is a strong-hold, and diligence is laying siege to it: so that it must observe all the avenues *and passes to it.* SOUTH.

2. An alley, or walk of trees before a house.

AULD. *adj.* [*ald*, Sax.] A word now obsolete; but still used in the Scotch dialect.

'Tis pride that pulls the country down;
Then take thine auld *cloak about thee.*
SHAKESPEARE'S OTHELLO.

AVO'IDANCE. *n.s.* [from *avoid.*]
1. The act of avoiding.

It is appointed to give us vigour in the pursuit of what is good, or in the avoidance *of what is hurtful.* WATTS'S LOGICK.

2. The course by which any thing is carried off.

For avoidances, *and drainings of water, where there is too much, we shall speak of.* BACON'S NATURAL HISTORY, NO 600.

AVO'IDER. *n.s.* [from *avoid.*]
1. The person that avoids or shuns any thing.
2. The person that carries any thing away.
3. The vessel in which things are carried away.

AVO'IDLESS. *adj.* [from *avoid.*] Inevitable; that which cannot be avoided.

That avoidless *ruin in which the whole empire would be involved.*
DENNIS'S LETTERS.

A'USPICE. *n.s.* [*auspicium*, Lat.]
1. The omens of any future undertaking drawn from birds.
2. Protection; favour shewn by prosperous men.[24]

Great father Mars, and greater Jove,
By whose high auspice *Rome hath stood*
So long. BEN JONSON'S CATILINE.

3. Influence; good derived to others from the piety of their patron.

But so may he live long, that town to sway,
Which by his auspice *they will nobler make,*
As he will hatch their ashes by his stay.
DRYDEN'S ANNUS MIRABILIS.

To **A'USTRALIZE.** *v.n.* [from *auster*, the south wind, Lat.] To tend towards the south.

Steel and good iron discover a verticity, or polary faculty; whereby they do septentriate at one extreme, and australize *at another.*
BROWN'S VULGAR ERROURS, B. II. C. 2.

AUTO'GRAPHY. *n.s.* [*'αυτογραφόν*, from *'αυτος*, and *γράφω*, to write.] A particular person's own writing; or the original of a treatise, in opposition to a copy.

AUTOMA'TICAL. *adj.* [from *automaton.*] Belonging to an automaton; having the power of moving themselves.

AUTO'PTICAL. *adj.* [from *autopsy.*] Perceived by one's own eyes.

AUXILIARY *Verb.* A verb that helps to conjugate other verbs.

In almost all languages, some of the commonest nouns and verbs have many irregularities; such are the common auxiliary *verbs,* to be *and* to have, to do *and* to be done, *&c.* WATTS.

AWA'RE. *adv.* [from *a* and *ware*; an old word for *cautious*; it is however, perhaps an *adjective*; *gewarian*, Sax.] Vigilant; in a state of alarm; attentive.[25]

Ere I was aware, *I had left myself nothing but the name of a king.* SIDNEY.

Ere sorrow was aware, *they made his thoughts bear away something else besides his own sorrow.* SIDNEY'S ARCADIA.

Temptations of prosperity insinuate themselves; so that we are but little aware *of them, and less able to withstand them.* ATTERBURY'S SERMONS.

A'WFUL. *adj.* [from *awe* and *full.*]
1. That which strikes with awe, or fills with reverence.

So awful, *that with honour thou may'st love*
Thy mate; who sees, when thou art seen least wise.
MILTON'S PARADISE LOST, B. VIII. L. 577.

I approach thee thus, and gaze
Insatiate; I thus single; nor have fear'd
Thy awful *brow, more* awful *thus retir'd,*
Fairest resemblance of thy Maker fair!
MILTON'S PARADISE LOST, B. IX.

2. Worshipful; in authority; invested with dignity. This sense is obsolete.

Know then, that some of us are gentlemen,
Such as the fury of ungovern'd youth
Thrust from the company of awful *men.*
SHAKESPEARE'S TWO GENTLEMEN OF VERONA.

3. Struck with awe; timorous; scrupulous. This sense occurs but rarely.

It is not nature and strict reason, but a weak and awful *reverence for antiquity, and the vogue of fallible men.*
WATTS'S IMPROVEMENT OF THE MIND.

A'WFULLY. *adv.* [from *awful.*] In a reverential manner.

It will concern a man, to treat this great principle awfully *and warily, by still observing what it commands, but especially what it forbids.* SOUTH.

A'WFULNESS. *n.s.* [from *awful.*]
1. The quality of striking with awe; solemnity.

These objects naturally raise seriousness; and night heightens the awfulness *of the place, and pours out her supernumerary horrours upon every thing.*
ADDISON'S SPECTATOR NO 110.

2. The state of being struck with awe.[26]

An help to prayer, producing in us reverence and awfulness *to the divine majesty of God.*
TAYLOR'S RULE OF LIVING HOLY.

To **AWHA'PE.** *v.a.* [This word I have met with only in *Spenser*, nor can I discover whence it is derived; but imagine, that the Teutonick language had anciently *wapen*, to strike, or some such word, from which *weapons*, or offensive arms, took their denomination.] To strike; to confound.

Ah! my dear gossip, answer'd then the ape,
Deeply do your sad words my wits awhape,
Both for because your grief doth great appear,
And eke because myself am touched near.
HUBBERD'S TALE.

AWK. *adj.* [a barbarous contraction of the word *awkward.*] Odd; out of order.

We have heard as arrant jangling in the pulpits, as the steeples; and professors ringing as awk *as the bells to give notice of the conflagration.* L'ESTRANGE.

A'WLESS. *adj.* [from *awe*, and the negative *less.*]
1. Without reverence.[27]

Against whose fury, and th' unmatched force,
The awless *lion could not wage the fight.* SHAKESPEARE'S KING JOHN.

He claims the bull with awless *insolence,*
And having seiz'd his horns, accosts the prince.
DRYDEN.

2. Without the power of causing reverence.

Ah me! I see the ruin of my house;
The tyger now hath seiz'd the gentle hind:
Insulting tyranny begins to jut
Upon the innocent and awless *throne.*
SHAKESPEARE'S RICHARD III.

AY. *adv.* [perhaps from *aio*, Lat.]

1. Yes; an adverb of answering affirmatively.

Return you thither? ——
—— Ay, *madam, with the swiftest wing of speed.*
SHAKESPEARE'S ALL'S WELL THAT ENDS WELL.

What say'st thou? Wilt thou be of our consort?
Say ay; *and be the captain of us all.*
SHAKESPEARE'S TWO GENTLEMEN OF VERONA.

2. It is a word by which the sense is enforced; even; yes, certainly; and more than that.

Remember it, and let it make thee crest-fall'n;
Ay, and allay this thy abortive pride.
SHAKESPEARE'S HENRY VI.

B

The second letter of the English alphabet, is pronounced as in most other European languages, by pressing the whole length of the lips together, and forcing them open with a strong breath. It has a near affinity with the other labial letters, and is confounded by the Germans with *P*, and by the Gascons with *V*; from which an epigrammatist remarks, that *bibere* and *vivere* are in Gascony the same. The Spaniards, in most words, use *B* or *V* indifferently.

BABO'ON. *n.s.* [*babouin*, Fr. It is supposed by *Skinner* to be the augmentation of *babe*, and to import a *great babe.*] A monkey of the largest kind.

> *You had looked through the grate like a geminy of* baboons.
> SHAKESPEARE'S MERRY WIVES OF WINDSOR.

> *He cast every human feature out of his countenance, and became a* baboon.
> ADDISON'S SPECTATOR NO 174.

BA'CHELOR. *n.s.* [This is a word of very uncertain etymology, it not being well known what was its original sense. *Junius* derives it from *βάκιλος*, foolish; *Menage*, from *bas chevalier*, a knight of the lowest rank; *Spelman*, from *baculus*, a staff; *Cujas*, from *buccella*, an allowance of provision. The most probable derivation seems to be from *bacca laurus*, the berry of a laurel or bay; bachelors being young, are of good hopes, like laurels in the berry.[28] In Latin, *baccalaureus*.]

1. A man unmarried.

> *Such separation*
> *Becomes a virtuous* bachelor *and a maid.*
> SHAKESPEARE'S MIDSUMMER NIGHT'S DREAM.

> *The haunting of those dissolute places, or resort to courtesans, are no more punished in married men than in* bachelors.
> BACON'S NEW ATLANTIS.

> *A true painter naturally delights in the liberty which belongs to the* bachelor's *estate.* DRYDEN'S DUFRESNOY.

> *Let sinful* bachelors *their woes deplore,*
> *Full well they merit all they feel, and more.* POPE.

2. A man who takes his first degrees at the university in any profession.

> *Being a boy, new* bachelor *of arts, I chanced to speak against the pope.*
> ASCHAM'S SCHOOLMASTER.

I appear before your honour, in behalf of Martinus Scriblerus, bachelor *of physick.* ARBUTHNOT AND POPE'S MARTIN SCRIBLERUS.

3. A knight of the lowest order. This is a sense now little used.

BA'CKFRIEND. *n.s.* [from *back* and *friend.*] A friend backwards; that is, an enemy in secret.

Set the restless importunities of talebearers and backfriends *against fair words and professions.* L'ESTRANGE.

Far is our church from encroaching upon the civil power; as some who are back-friends *to both, would maliciously insinuate.* SOUTH.

BADGER. *n.s.* [*bedour*, Fr.] An animal that earths in the ground, used to be hunted.

That a brock, or badger, *hath legs of one side shorter than the other, is very generally received not only by theorists and unexperienced believers, but most who behold them daily.*
BROWN'S VULGAR ERROURS, B. III.

BADGER LEGGED. *adj.* [from *badger* and *legged.*] Having legs of an unequal length, as the badger is supposed to have.

His body crooked all over, big-bellied, badger legged, *and his complexion swarthy.* L'ESTRANGE.

BA'LDERDASH. *n.s.* [probably of *bald*, Sax. bold, and *dash*, to mingle.] Any thing jumbled together without judgment; rude mixture; a confused discourse.

To **BA'LDERDASH.** *v.a.* [from the noun.] To mix or adulterate any liquor.

BALL. *n.s.* [*bal*, Fr. from *ballare*, low Lat. from *βαλλίζειν*, to dance.] An entertainment of dancing, at which the preparations are made at the expence of some particular person.

If golden sconces hang not on the walls,
To light the costly suppers and the balls.
DRYDEN.

He would make no extraordinary figure at a ball; *but I can assure the ladies, for their consolation, that he has writ better verses on the sex than any man.* SWIFT.

BA'LLIARDS. *n.s.* [from *ball* and *yard*, or stick to push it with.] A play at which a ball is driven by the end of a stick; now corruptly called *billiards.*[29]

With dice, with cards, with balliards, *far unfit,*
With shuttlecocks misseeming manly wit.
HUBBERD'S TALE.

BALLO'N, BALLO'ON. *n.s.* [*ballon*, Fr.]

1. A large round short-necked vessel used in chymistry.

2. In architecture; a ball or globe placed on the top of a pillar.

3. In fireworks; a ball of pasteboard, stuffed with combustible matter, which, when fired, mounts to a considerable height in the air, and then bursts into bright sparks of fire, resembling stars.

BA'LUSTER. *n.s.* [according to *Du Cange*, from *balaustrium*, low Lat. a bathing place.] A small column or pilaster, from an inch and three quarters to four inches square or diameter. Their dimensions and forms are various; they are frequently adorned with mouldings; they are placed with rails on stairs, and in the fronts of galleries in churches.

This should first have been planched over, and railed about with balusters.
CAREW'S SURVEY OF CORNWAL.

BA'LUSTRADE. *n.s.* [from *baluster.*] An assemblage of one or more rows of little turned pillars, called balusters, fixed upon a terras, or the top of a building, for separating one part from another.

BA'MBOO. *n.s.* An Indian plant of the reed kind. It has several shoots, much larger than our ordinary reeds, which are knotty, and separated from space to space by joints. They are said by some, but by mistake, to contain sugar; the *bamboo* being much larger than the sugar-cane. The leaves grow out of each knot, and are prickly. They are four or five inches long, and an inch in breadth, somewhat pointed, and ribbed through the whole length with green and sharp fibres. Its flowers grow in ears, like those of wheat.[30]

To **BAMBO'OZLE.** *v.a.* [a cant word not used in pure or in grave writings.] To deceive; to impose upon; to confound.

> *After Nick had* bamboozled *about the money, John called for counters.*
> ARBUTHNOT'S JOHN BULL.

BA'NDOG. *n.s.* [from *ban* or *band*, and *dog*. The original of this word is very doubtful. *Caiux, De Canibus Britannicis*, derives it from *band*, that is, *a dog chained up*. *Skinner* inclines to deduce it from *bana*, a *murderer*. May it not come from *ban* a *curse*, as we say a *curst cur*; or rather from *baund*, swelled or large, a *Danish* word; from whence, in some counties, they call a great nut a *ban-nut*.] A kind of large dog.

> *The time of night when Troy was set on fire,*
> *The time when screech-owls cry, and* bandogs *howl.*
> SHAKESPEARE'S HENRY VI. P. II.

> *Or privy, or pert, if any bin,*
> *We have great* bandogs *will tear their skin.* SPENSER'S PASTORALS.

BA'NK-BILL. *n.s.* [from *bank* and *bill*] A note for money laid up in a bank, at the sight of which the money is paid.

> *Let three hundred pounds be paid her out of my ready money, or* bank-bills.
> SWIFT'S LAST WILL.

BA'NKER. *n.s.* [from *bank.*] One that trafficks in money; one that keeps or manages a bank.

> *Whole droves of lenders croud the* banker*'s doors,*
> *To call in money.*
> DRYDEN'S SPANISH FRIAR.

> *By powerful charms of gold and silver led,*
> *The Lombard* bankers *and the change to waste.* DRYDEN.

BA'NNOCK. *n.s.* A kind of oaten or pease meal cake, mixed with water, and baked upon an iron plate over the fire; used in the northern counties, and in Scotland.

BA'NTLING. *n.s.* [if it has any etymology, it is perhaps corrupted from the old word *bairn*, *bairnling*, a little child.] A little child: a low word.

> *If the object of their love*
> *Chance by Lucina's aid to prove,*
> *They seldom let the* bantling *roar,*
> *In basket, at a neighbour's door.* PRIOR.

BA'RBARISM. *n.s.* [*barbarismus*, Lat.]

1. A form of speech contrary to the purity and exactness of any language.

> *The language is as near approaching to it, as our modern* barbarism *will allow; which is all that can be expected from any now extant.*
> DRYDEN'S JUVENAL, DEDICATION.

2. Ignorance of arts; want of learning.

> *I have for* barbarism *spoke more*

Than for that angel knowledge you can say.
SHAKESPEARE'S LOVE'S LABOUR LOST.

The genius of Raphael having succeeded to the times of barbarism *and ignorance, the knowledge of painting is now arrived to perfection.*
DRYDEN'S DUFRESNOY, PREFACE.

3. Brutality; savageness of manners; incivility.

Moderation ought to be had in tempering and managing the Irish, to bring them from their delight of licentious barbarism *unto the love of goodness and civility.*
SPENSER'S STATE OF IRELAND.

Divers great monarchies have risen from barbarism *to civility, and fallen again to ruin.* SIR J. DAVIES ON IRELAND.

4. Cruelty; barbarity; unpitying hardness of heart.[31]

They must per force have melted,
And barbarism *itself have pity'd him.*
SHAKESPEARE'S RICHARD II.

To **BA'RBECUE.** *v.a.* A term used in the West-Indies for dressing a hog whole; which, being split to the backbone, is laid flat upon a large gridiron, raised about two foot above a charcoal fire, with which it is surrounded.

Oldfield, with more than harpy throat endu'd,
Cries, send me, gods, a whole hog barbecu'd. POPE.

BARBER-CHIRURGEON. *n.s.* A man who joins the practice of surgery to the barber's trade; such as were all surgeons formerly, but now it is used only for a low practiser of surgery.

He put himself into barber-chirurgeons *hands, who, by unfit applications, rarified the tumour.* WISEMAN'S SURGERY.

BARBER-MONGER. *n.s.* A word of reproach in Shakespeare, which seems to signify a fop; a man decked out by his barber.

Draw, you rogue; for though it be night, the moon shines; I'll make a sop of the moonshine of you; you whoreson, cullionly, barber-monger, *draw.*
SHAKESPEARE'S KING LEAR.

BARGAINEE'. *n.s.* [from *bargain.*] He or she that accepts a bargain.

BA'RGAINER. *n.s.* [from *bargain.*] The person who profers, or makes a bargain.

BARLEY BROTH. *n.s.* [from *barley* and *broth.*] A low word, sometimes used for strong beer.

Can sodden water,
A drench for surreyn'd jades, their barley broth,
Decoct their cold blood to such valiant heat? SHAKESPEARE'S HENRY V.

BARLEY CORN. *n.s.* [from *barley* and *corn.*] A grain of barley; the beginning of our measure of length; the third part of an inch.

A long, long journey, choak'd with brakes and thorns,
Ill measur'd by ten thousand barley corns. TICKELL.

BA'RREL. *n.s.* [*baril*, Welch.]

1. A round wooden vessel to be stopped close.

It hath been observed by one of the ancients, that an empty barrel *knocked upon with the finger, giveth a diapason to the sound of the like* barrel *full.*
BACON'S NATURAL HISTORY, NO 186.

Trembling to approach
The little barrel, *which he fears to broach.*
DRYDEN'S PERSIUS.

2. A particular measure in liquids. A *barrel* of wine is thirty one gallons and a half; of ale, thirty two gallons; of beer, thirty six gallons, and of beer vinegar, thirty four gallons.

3. In dry measure. A *barrel* of Essex butter contains one hundred and six

pounds; of Suffolk butter, two hundred and fifty six. A *barrel* of herrings should contain thirty two gallons wine measure, holding usually a thousand herrings.

Several colleges, instead of limiting their rents to a certain sum, prevailed with their tenants to pay the price of so many barrels *of corn, as the market went.* SWIFT.

4. Any thing hollow, as the barrel of a gun; that part which holds the shot.

Take the barrel *of a long gun perfectly bored, set it upright with the breech upon the ground, and take a bullet exactly fit for it; then if you suck at the mouth of the barrel ever so gently, the bullet will come up so forcibly, that it will hazard the striking out your teeth.*
DIGBY ON BODIES.

5. A cylinder; frequently that cylinder about which any thing is wound.

Your string and bow must be accommodated to your drill; if too weak, it will not carry about the barrel.
MOXON'S MECHANICAL EXERCISES.

6. *Barrel of the ear*, is a cavity behind the tympanum, covered with a fine membrane. *Dictionaries.*

BASILICK. *n.s.* [*basilique*, Fr. *βασιλική.*] A large hall, having two ranges of pillars, and two isles or wings, with galleries over them. These *basilicks* were first made for the palaces of princes, and afterwards converted into courts of justice, and lastly into churches; whence a *basilick* is generally taken for a magnificent church, as the *basilick* of St. Peter at Rome.

BAT-FOWLING. *n.s.* [from *bat* and *fowl.*] A particular manner of birdcatching in the night time, while they are at roost upon perches, trees, or hedges. They light torches or straw, and then beat the bushes; upon which the birds flying to the flames, are caught either with nets, or otherwise.

You would lift the moon out of her sphere, if she would continue in it five weeks without changing. —— We should so, and then go a bat-fowling.
SHAKESPEARE'S TEMPEST.

Bodies lighted at night by fire, must have a brighter lustre given them than by day; as sacking of cities, bat-fowling, *&c.*
PEACHAM ON DRAWING.

BATTA'LION. *n.s.* [*bataillon*, Fr.]
1. A division of an army; a troop; a body of forces. It is now confined to the infantry, and the number is uncertain, but generally from five to eight hundred men. Some regiments consist of one *battalion*, and others are divided into two, three or more.

When sorrows come, they come not single spies,
But in battalions.
SHAKESPEARE'S HAMLET.

In this battalion *there were two officers, called Thersites and Pandarus.*
TATLER, NO 56.

The pierc'd battalions *disunited fall,*
In heaps on heaps: one fate o'erwhelms them all. POPE.

2. An army. This sense is not now in use.

Six or seven thousand is their utmost power.
—— Why, our battalion *trebles that account.*
SHAKESPEARE'S RICHARD III.

BA'TTEN. *n.s.* A word used only by workmen.

A batten *is a scantling of wooden stuff, two, three or four inches broad, seldom above one thick, and the length unlimited.*
MOXON'S MECHANICAL EXERCISES.

BA'UBEE. *n.s.* A word used in Scotland, and the northern counties, for a halfpenny.

Tho' in the draw'rs of my japan bureau,
To lady Gripeall I the Cæsars show,
'Tis equal to her ladyship or me,
A copper Otho, or a Scotch baubee.
BRAMSTON'S MAN OF TASTE.

BA'WBLING. *adj.* [from *bawble.*] Trifling; contemptible: a word not now in use, except in conversation.

A bawbling *vessel was he captain of,*
For shallow draught and bulk unprized;
With which such scathful grapple did he make,
With the most noble bottom of our fleet.
SHAKESPEARE'S TWELFTH NIGHT.

BA'YONET. *n.s.* [*bayonette*, Fr.] A short sword or dagger fixed at the end of a musket, by which the foot hold off the horse.

One of the black spots is long and slender, and resembles a dagger or bayonet.
WOODWARD ON FOSSILS.

BE'ACON. *n.s.* [*beacon*, Sax. from *becn*, a signal, and *becnan*, whence beckon, to make a signal.]

1. Something raised on an eminence, to be fired on the approach of an enemy, to alarm the country.

His blazing eyes, like two bright shining shields,
Did burn with wrath, and sparkled living fire;
As two broad beacons *set in open fields,*
Send forth their flames.
FAIRY QUEEN, B. I.

Modest doubt is called
The beacon *of the wise.*
SHAKESPEARE'S TROILUS AND CRESSIDA.

The king seemed to account of the designs of Perkin as a may-game; yet had given order for the watching of beacons *upon the coasts, and erecting more where they stood too thin.* BACON'S HENRY VII.

No flaming beacons *cast their blaze afar,*
The dreadful signal of invasive war.
GAY'S RURAL SPORTS.

2. Marks erected, or lights made in the night, to direct navigators in their courses, and warn them from rocks, shallows and sandbanks.

BEAR-GARDEN. *n.s.* [from *bear* and *garden.*]

1. A place in which bears are kept for sport.

Hurrying me from the playhouse, and the scenes there, to the bear-garden, *to the apes, and asses, and tygers.*
STILLINGFLEET.

I could not forbear going to a place of renown for the gallantry of Britons, namely to the bear-garden.
SPECTATOR, NO 436.[32]

2. Any place of tumult or misrule.

BEAR-GARDEN. *adj.* A word used in familiar or low phrase for *rude* or *turbulent*; as, a *bear-garden fellow*; that is, a man rude enough to be a proper frequenter of the bear-garden. *Bear-garden sport*, is used for gross inelegant entertainment.

BEAST. *n.s.* [*beste*, Fr. *bestia*, Lat.]

1. An animal distinguished from birds, insects, fishes, and man.

The man that once did sell the lion's skin,
While the beast *liv'd, was kill'd with hunting him.* SHAKESPEARE.

Beasts *of chase are the buck, the doe, the fox, the martern, and the roe.* Beasts *of the forest are the hart, the hind, the hare, the boar, and the wolf.* Beasts *of warren are the hare and cony.* COWEL.

2. An irrational animal, opposed to man; as man and beast.

I dare do all that may become a man;
Who dares do more, is none. ——
—— What beast *was't then*
That made you break this enterprize to me? MACBETH.

Medea's charms were there, Circean feasts,
With bowls that turn'd enamour'd youths
to beasts. DRYDEN.

3. A brutal savage man, a man acting in any manner unworthy of a reasonable creature.

BE'ASTINGS. See **BEESTINGS.**

BE'ATER. *n.s.* [from *beat.*]

1. An instrument with which any thing is comminuted or mingled.

Beat all your mortar with a beater *three or four times over, before you use it; for thereby you incorporate the sand and lime well together.*
MOXON'S MECHANICAL EXERCISES.

2. A person much given to blows.

The best schoolmaster of our time, was the greatest beater.
ASCHAM'S SCHOOLMASTER.

BEAU. *n.s.* [*beau*, Fr. It is sounded like *bo*, and has often the French plural *beaux.*] A man of dress; a man whose great care is to deck his person.

What, will not beaux *attempt to please the fair?* DRYDEN.

The water nymphs are too unkind
To Vill'roy; are the land nymphs so?
And fly they all, at once combin'd
To shame a general, and a beau?
PRIOR.

You will become the delight of nine ladies in ten, and the envy of ninety-nine beaux *in a hundred.*
SWIFT'S DIRECTIONS TO FOOTMEN.

BE'AVER. *n.s.* [*bievre*, Fr.]

1. An animal, otherwise named the *castor*, amphibious, and remarkable for his art in building his habitation; of which many wonderful accounts are delivered by travellers. His skin is very valuable on account of the fur.

The beaver *being hunted, biteth off his stones, knowing that for them only his life is sought.* HAKEWELL ON PROVIDENCE.

They placed this invention upon the beaver, *for the sagacity and wisdom of that animal; indeed from its artifice in building.*
BROWN'S VULGAR ERROURS, C. 4.

2. A hat of the best kind; so called from being made of the fur of beaver.

You see a smart rhetorician turning his hat, moulding it into different cocks, examining the lining and the button during his harangue: A deaf man would think he was cheapening a beaver, *when he is talking of the fate of a nation.*
ADDISON'S SPECTATOR.

The broker here his spacious beaver *wears,*
Upon his brow sit jealousies and cares.
GAY'S TRIVIA.

3. The part of a helmet that covers the face. [*baviere*, Fr.]

His dreadful hideous head
Close couched on the beaver, *seem'd to throw,*
From flaming mouth, bright sparkles firy red. FAIRY QUEEN.

Big Mars seems bankrupt in their beggar'd host,
And faintly through a rusty beaver *peeps.*
SHAKESPEARE'S HENRY V.

He was slain upon a course at tilt, the splinters of the staff going in at his beaver.
BACON'S ESSAYS, NO 36.

BEAUTY-SPOT. *n.s.* [from *beauty* and *spot.*] A spot placed to direct the eye to something else, or to heighten some beauty; a foil; a patch.

The filthiness of swine makes them the beauty-spot *of the animal creation.*
GREW'S COSMOLOGIA SACRA, B. III. C. 2. §49.

To **BECA'LM.** *v.a.* [from *calm.*]

1. To still the elements.

The moon shone clear on the becalmed *flood.* DRYDEN.

2. To keep a ship from motion.

A man becalmed *at sea, out of sight of land, in a fair day, may look on the sun, or sea, or ship, a whole hour, and perceive no motion.* LOCKE.

3. To quiet the mind.

Soft whisp'ring airs, and the lark's mattin song,
Then woo to musing, and becalm *the mind*
Perplex'd with irksome thoughts.
PHILIPS.

Banish his sorrows, and becalm *his soul*
With easy dreams.
ADDISON'S CATO.

4. To *becalm* and to *calm* differ in this, that *to calm* is to stop motion, and *to becalm* is to with-hold from motion.

To **BEDA'BBLE.** *v.a.* [from *dabble.*] To wet; to besprinkle. It is generally applied to persons, in a sense including inconvenience.

Never so weary, never so in woe,
Bedabbled *with the dew, and torn with briars,*
I can no further crawl, no further go.
SHAKESPEARE'S MIDSUMMER NIGHT'S DREAM.

To **BEDA'GGLE.** *v.a.* [from *daggle.*] To bemire; to soil cloaths, by letting them reach the dirt in walking.

BE'DPRESSER. *n.s.* [from *bed* and *press.*] A heavy lazy fellow.

This sanguine coward, this bedpresser, *this horseback-breaker, this huge hill of flesh.* SHAKESPEARE'S HENRY IV. P. I.

BEDSWE'RVER. *n.s.* [from *bed* and *swerve.*] One that is false to the bed; one that ranges or swerves from one bed to another.

She's a bedswerver, *even as bad as those,*
That vulgars give bold'st titles to.
SHAKESPEARE'S WINTER'S TALE.

BEE. *n.s.* [*beo*, Saxon.]
1. The animal that makes honey, remarkable for its industry and art.

So work the honey bees,
Creatures that, by a ruling nature, teach
The art of order to a peopled kingdom.
SHAKESPEARE'S HENRY V.

From the Moorish camp,
There has been heard a distant humming noise,
Like bees *disturb'd, and arming in their hives.* DRYDEN.

A company of poor insects, whereof some are bees, *delighted with flowers, and their sweetness; others beetles, delighted with other viands.* LOCKE.

2. An industrious and careful person. This signification is only used in familiar language.

BE'EMOL. *n.s.* This word I have found only in the example, and know nothing of the etymology, unless it be a corruption of *bymodule*, from *by* and *modulus*, a note; that is, a note out of the regular order.

There be intervenient in the rise of eight, in tones, two beemols, *or half notes; so as, if you divide the tones equally, the eight is but seven whole and equal notes.*
BACON'S NATURAL HISTORY.

BEER. *n.s.* [*bîr*, Welch.] Liquour made of malt and hops. It is distinguished from ale, either by being older or smaller.

Here's a pot of good double beer, *neighbour; drink.*
SHAKESPEARE'S HENRY VI. P. II.

It were good to try clarifying with almonds in new beer.
BACON'S NATURAL HISTORY, NO 768.

Flow, Welsted! flow, like thine inspirer, beer;
Tho' stale, not ripe; tho' thin, yet never clear;
So sweetly mawkish, and so smoothly dull;
Heady, not strong; and foaming, tho' not full. POPE.

BE'ESTINGS. See **BIESTINGS.**

BEETLEHE'ADED. *adj.* [from *beetle* and *head.*] Loggerheaded; wooden headed; having a head stupid, like the head of a wooden beetle.

A whoreson, beetleheaded, *flap-ear'd knave.*
SHAKESPEARE'S TAMING OF THE SHREW.

To **BEFO'OL.** *v.a.* [from *be* and *fool.*] To infatuate; to fool; to deprive of understanding; to lead into errour.

Men befool *themselves infinitely, when, by venting a few sighs, they will needs persuade themselves that they have repented.* SOUTH.

Jeroboam thought policy the best piety, though in nothing more befooled; *the nature of sin being not only to defile, but to infatuate.* SOUTH.

To **BEGI'N.** *v.n.* I *began*, or *begun*; I have *begun*. [*beginnan*, Sax. from *be*, or *by to*, and *gangan*, *gaan*, or *gan*, to go.]

1. To enter upon something new: applied to persons.

Begin *every day to repent; not that thou shouldst at all defer it; but all that is past ought to seem little to thee, seeing it is so in itself.* Begin *the next day with the same zeal, fear, and humility, as if thou hadst never* begun *before.* TAYLOR.

I'll sing of heroes and of kings;
Begin *my muse.* COWLEY.

2. To commence any action or state; to do the first act, or first part of an act; to make the first step from not doing to doing.

They began *at the ancient men which were before the house.*
BIBLE EZEKIEL, IX. 6.

Of these no more you hear him speak;
He now begins *upon the Greek:*
These rang'd and show'd, shall, in their turns,
Remain obscure as in their urns. PRIOR.

Beginning *from the rural gods, his hand*
Was lib'ral to the pow'rs of high command. DRYDEN'S FABLES.

Rapt into future times, the bard begun,
A virgin shall conceive.
POPE'S MESSIAH.

3. To enter upon existence; as, the world *began*; the practice *began.*[33]

4. To have its original.

And thus the hard and stubborn race of man,
From animated rock and flint began.
BLACKMORE.

From Nimrod first the savage chase began;
A mighty hunter, and his game was man.
POPE.

5. To take rise.

Judgment must begin *at the house of God.*
BIBLE 1 PETER, IV. 17.

The song begun *from Jove.* DRYDEN.

All began,
All ends in love of God, and love of man.
POPE.

6. To come into act.

Now and then a sigh he stole,
And tears began *to flow.* DRYDEN.

To **BEGI'RD.** *v.a.* I *begirt*, or *begirded*; I have *begirt*. [from *be* and *gird.*]

1. To bind with a girdle.

Or should she confident,
As sitting queen ador'd on beauty's throne,
Descend, with all her winning charms begirt,
T' enamour.
MILTON'S PARADISE LOST, B. II. L. 213.[34]

2. To surround; to encircle; to encompass.

Begird *th' almighty throne,*
Beseeching, or besieging.
MILTON'S PARADISE LOST, B. V. L. 868.

At home surrounded by a servile croud,

Prompt to abuse, and in detraction loud:
Abroad begirt *with men, and swords, and spears;*
His very state acknowledging his fears.
PRIOR.

3. To shut in with a siege; to beleaguer; to block up.

It was so closely begirt *before the king's march into the west, that the council humbly desired his majesty, that he would relieve it.* CLARENDON, B. VIII.

To **BEGI'RT.** *v.a.* [This is, I think, only a corruption of *begird*; perhaps by the printer.] To begird. See **BEGIRD.**

And, Lentulus, begirt *you Pompey's house,*
To seize his sons alive; for they are they
Must make our peace with him.
BEN JONSON'S CATILINE.

To **BEGRE'ASE.** *v.a.* [from *be* and *grease.*] To soil or dawb with unctuous or fat matter.

To **BEGRI'ME.** *v.a.* [from *be* and *grime.* See **GRIME** and **GRIM.**] To soil with dirt deep impressed; to soil in such a manner that the natural hue cannot easily be recovered.

Her name, that was as fresh
As Dian's visage, is now begrim'd, *and black*
As my own face.
SHAKESPEARE'S OTHELLO.

BEHI'NDHAND. *adv.* [from *behind* and *hand.*]

1. In a state in which rents or profits, or any advantage, is anticipated; so that less is to be received, or more performed, than the natural or just proportion.

Your trade would suffer, if your being behindhand *has made the natural use so high, that your tradesman cannot live upon his labour.* LOCKE.

2. Not upon equal terms, with regard to forwardness. In this sense, it is followed by *with.*

Consider, whether it is not better to be half a year behindhand *with the fashionable part of the world, than to strain beyond his circumstances.* SPECTATOR, NO 488.

3. Shakespeare uses it as an adjective, but licentiously, for backward; tardy.

And these thy offices,
So rarely kind, are as interpreters
Of my behindhand *slackness.*
SHAKESPEARE'S WINTER'S TALE.

BEHO'LD. *interject.* [from the verb.] See; lo: a word by which attention is excited, or admiration noted.

Behold! *I am with thee, and will keep thee.*
BIBLE GENESIS, XXVIII. 15.

When out of hope, behold *her! not far off,*
Such as I saw her in my dream, adorn'd
With what all earth or heaven could bestow,
To make her amiable.
MILTON'S PARADISE LOST, B. VIII. L. 481.

BEHO'OVEFUL. *adj.* [from *behoof.*] Useful; profitable; advantageous. This word is somewhat antiquated.

It is very behooveful *in this country of Ireland, where there are waste deserts full of grass, that the same should be eaten down.* SPENSER ON IRELAND.

Laws are many times full of imperfections; and that which is supposed behooveful *unto men, proveth oftentimes most pernicious.* HOOKER, B. IV.§14.

Madam, we have culled such necessaries
As are behooveful *for our state tomorrow.*
SHAKESPEARE'S ROMEO AND JULIET.

It may be most behooveful *for princes, in matters of grace, to transact the same publickly: so it is as requisite, in matters of judgment, punishment, and censure, that the same be transacted privately.*
CLARENDON.

BE'LAMIE. *n.s.* [*bel amie*, Fr.] A friend; an intimate. This word is out of use.

Wise Socrates
Pour'd out his life, and last philosophy,
To the fair Critias, his dearest belamie.
FAIRY QUEEN B. II. C. VII.

BE'LAMOUR. *n.s.* [*bel amour*, Fr.] Gallant; consort; paramour: obsolete.

Lo, lo, how brave she decks her bounteous bow'r,
With silken curtains, and gold coverlets,
Therein to shrowd her sumptuous belamour. FAIRY QUEEN B. II.

BELA'TED. *adj.* [from *be* and *late.*] Benighted; out of doors late at night.

Fairy elves,
Whose midnight revels, by a forest side,
Or fountain, some belated *peasant sees,*
Or dreams he sees.
MILTON'S PARADISE LOST, B. I. L. 781.

Or near Fleetditch's oozy brinks,
Belated, *seems on watch to lie.* SWIFT.

BELDA'M. *n.s.* [*belle dame*, which, in old French, signified probably an old woman, as *belle age*, old age.]

1. An old woman; generally a term of contempt, marking the last degree of old age, with all its faults and miseries.

Then sing of secret things that came to pass,
When beldam *nature in her cradle was.*
MILTON.

2. A hag.

Why, how now, Hecat, you look angerly? ——
—— *Have I not reason,* beldams, *as you are?*
Saucy and overbold?
SHAKESPEARE'S MACBETH.

The resty sieve wagg'd ne'er the more;
I wept for woe, the testy beldam *swore.*
DRYDEN.

To **BELO'WT.** *v.a.* [from *be* and *lowt*, a word of contempt.] To treat with opprobrious language; to call names.[35]

Sieur Gaulard, when he heard a gentleman report, that, at a supper, they had not only good cheer, but also savoury epigrams, and fine anagrams, returning home, rated and belowted *his cook, as an ignorant scullion, that never dressed him either epigrams or anagrams.* CAMDEN'S REMAINS.

BELSWA'GGER. *n.s.* A cant word for a whoremaster.

You are a charitable belswagger; *my wife cried out fire, and you called out for engines.* DRYDEN'S SPANISH FRIAR.

BENE'FICENT. *adj.* [from *beneficus*, *beneficentior*, Lat.] Kind; doing good. It differs from *benign*, as the act from the disposition; *beneficence* being kindness, or *benignity*, exerted in action.

Such a creature could not have his origination from any less than the most wise and beneficent *being, the great God.*
HALE'S ORIGIN OF MANKIND.

But Phœbus, thou, to man beneficent,
Delight'st in building cities. PRIOR.

BENEFI'CIARY. *adj.* [from *benefice.*] Holding something in subordination to another; having a dependent and secondary possession, without sovereign power.

The duke of Parma was tempted by no less promise, than to be made a feudatory, or beneficiary *king of England, under the seignory in chief of the pope.*
BACON'S WAR WITH SPAIN.

BENEFI'CIARY. *n.s.* He that is in possession of a benefice.

A benefice is either said to be a benefice with the cure of souls, or otherwise. In the first case, if it be annexed to another benefice, the beneficiary *is obliged to serve the parish church in his own proper person.* AYLIFFE'S PARERGON.

BENGA'L. *n.s.* [from *Bengal* in the East Indies.] A sort of thin slight stuff, made of silk and hair, for womens apparel.

To **BENU'M.** *v.a.* [*benumen*, Saxon.]

1. To make torpid; to take away the sensation and use of any part by cold, or by some obstruction.

So stings a snake that to the fire is brought,
Which harmless lay with cold benumm'd *before.* FAIRFAX, B. II. STANZA 85.

The winds blow moist and keen, which bids us seek
Some better shroud, some better warmth, to cherish
Our limbs benumm'd.
MILTON'S PARADISE LOST, B. X. L. 1069.

My sinews slacken, and an icy stiffness
Benums my blood. DENHAM'S SOPHY.

It seizes upon the vitals, and benums *the senses; and where there is no sense, there can be no pain.* SOUTH.

Will they be the less dangerous, when warmth shall bring them to themselves, because they were once frozen and benummed *with cold?*
L'ESTRANGE, FABLES IX.

2. To stupify.

These accents were her last: the creeping death
Benumm'd *her senses first, then stopp'd her breath.* DRYDEN.

To **BEPI'SS.** *v.a.* [from *piss.*] To wet with urine.

One caused, at a feast, a bagpipe to be played, which made the knight bepiss *himself, to the great diversion of all then present, as well as confusion of himself.*
DERHAM'S PHYSICO-THEOLOGY.

BE'RGMASTER. *n.s.* [from *berg*, Sax. and *master.*] The bailiff, or chief officer, among the Derbyshire miners.

BERLI'N. *n.s.* [from *Berlin*, the city where they were first made.] A coach of a particular form.

Beware of Latin authors all!
Nor think your verses sterling,
Though with a golden pen you scrawl,
And scribble in a berlin. SWIFT.

To **BESHRE'W.** *v.a.* [The original of this word is somewhat obscure; as it evidently implies *to wish ill*, some derive it from *beschryen*, Germ. to enchant. *Topsel*, in his *Book of Animals*, deduces it from the *shrew mouse*, an animal, says he, so poisonous, that its bite is a severe curse. A *shrew* likewise signifies a scolding woman; but its origin is not known.]

1. To wish a curse to.

Nay, quoth the cock; but I beshrew *us both,*
If I believe a saint upon his oath.
DRYDEN'S FABLES.

2. To happen ill to.

Beshrew *thee, cousin, which did'st lead me forth*
Of that sweet way I was in to despair.
SHAKESPEARE'S RICHARD II.

Now much beshrew *my manners, and my pride,*
If Hermia meant to say Lysander lied.
SHAKESPEARE.

To **BESI'EGE.** *v.a.* [from *siege.*] To beleaguer; to lay siege to; to beset with armed forces; to endeavour to win a town or fortress, by surrounding it with an army, and forcing the defendants, either by violence or famine, to give admission.

And he shall besiege *thee in all thy gates, until thy high and fenced walls come down.*
BIBLE DEUTERONOMY, XXVIII. 52.

The queen, with all the northern earls and lords,

Intend here to besiege *you in your castle.*
SHAKESPEARE'S HENRY VI.

BESTRA'UGHT. *particip.* [Of this *participle* I have not found the *verb*; by analogy we may derive it from *bestract*; perhaps it is corrupted from *distraught.*] Distracted; mad; out of one's senses; out of one's wits.

Ask Marian, the fat alewife, if she knew me not. What! I am not bestraught.
SHAKESPEARE'S TAMING OF THE SHREW.

BET. *n.s.* [*weddian*, to wager; *wed*, a wager, Sax. from which the etymologists derive *bet*. I should rather imagine it to come from *betan*, to mend, encrease, or *better*, as a *bet* encreases the original wager.] A wager; something laid to be won upon certain conditions.

The hoary fool, who many days
Has struggl'd with continu'd sorrow,
Renews his hope, and blindly lays
The desp'rate bet *upon tomorrow.*
PRIOR.

His pride was in piquette,
Newmarket fame, and judgment at a bet.
POPE.

BE'TTY. *n.s.* [probably a cant word, without etymology.] An instrument to break open doors.

Record the stratagems, the arduous exploits, and the nocturnal scalades of needy heroes, describing the powerful betty, *or the artful picklock.*
ARBUTHNOT'S HISTORY OF JOHN BULL.

To **BEWI'LDER.** *v.a.* [from *wild.*] To lose in pathless places; to confound for want of a plain road; to perplex; to entangle; to puzzle.

We parted thus; I homeward sped my way,
Bewilder'd *in the wood till dawn of day.*
DRYDEN'S FABLES.

We no solution of our question find;
Your words bewilder, *not direct the mind.*
BLACKMORE.

Our understanding traces 'em in vain,
Lost and bewilder'd *in the fruitless search.*
ADDISON'S CATO.

It is good sometimes to lose and bewilder *ourselves in such studies.*
WATTS'S IMPROVEMENT OF THE MIND.

BIB. *n.s.* A small piece of linen put upon the breasts of children, over their cloaths.

I would fain know, why it should not be as noble a task, to write upon a bib *and hanging-sleeves, as on the* bulla *and* prætexta.
ADDISON ON ANCIENT MEDALS.

To **BIB.** *v.n.* [*bibo*, Lat.] To tipple; to sip; to drink frequently.

He playeth with bibbing *mother Meroë, as though she were so named, because she would drink mere wine without water.*
CAMDEN.

To appease a froward child, they gave him drink as often as he cried; so that he was constantly bibbing, *and drank more in twenty four hours than I did.* LOCKE.

BIBA'CIOUS. *adj.* [*bibax*, Lat.] Much addicted to drinking. *Dictionaries.*[36]

BIBA'CITY. *n.s.* [*bibacitas*, Lat.] The quality of drinking much.

BI'BBER. *n.s.* [from *to bib.*] A tippler; a man that drinks often.

BI'BLE. *n.s.* [from βίβλιον, a book; called, by way of excellence, *The Book.*] The sacred volume in which are contained the revelations of God.

If we pass from the apostolic to the next ages of the church, the primitive christians looked on their bibles *as their most important treasure.*
GOVERNMENT OF THE TONGUE, §3.

We must take heed how we accustom ourselves to a slight and irreverent use of the name of God, and of the phrases and expressions of the holy bible, *which ought not to be applied upon every slight occasion.* TILLOTSON, SERMON I.

In questions of natural religion, we should confirm and improve, or connect our reasonings, by the divine assistance of the bible. WATTS'S LOGICK.

BIBLIO'GRAPHER. *n.s.* [from $\beta\iota\beta\lambda\acute{o}\varsigma$, and $\gamma\varrho\acute{\alpha}\phi\omega$, to write.] A writer of books; a transcriber. *Dictionaries.*

BIBLIOTHE'CAL. *adj.* [from *bibliotheca*, Lat.] Belonging to a library. *Dictionaries.*

BI'BULOUS. *adj.* [*bibulus*, Lat.] That which has the quality of drinking moisture; spungy.

Strow'd bibulous *above, I see the sands,*
The pebbly gravel next, and guttur'd rocks. THOMSON.

BICA'PSULAR. *adj.* [*bicapsularis*, Lat.] A plant whose seed vessel is divided into two parts.

BICE. *n.s.* The name of a colour used in painting. It is either green or blue.

Take green bice, *and order it as you do your blue* bice, *you may diaper upon it with the water of deep green.* PEACHAM.

BIDE'NTAL. *adj.* [*bidens*, Lat.] Having two teeth.

Ill management of forks is not to be helped, when they are only bidental. SWIFT.

BI'ESTINGS. *n.s.* [*bysting*, Saxon.] The first milk given by a cow after calving, which is very thick.

And twice besides, her biestings *never fail*
To store the dairy with a brimming pale.
DRYDEN'S VIRGIL.

BI'GLY. *adv.* [from *big.*] Tumidly; haughtily; with a blustering manner.

Would'st thou not rather choose a small renown,
To be the may'r of some poor paltry town;
Bigly *to look, and barb'rously to speak;*
To pound false weights, and scanty measures break?
DRYDEN'S JUVENAL, SATIRE X.

BI'LINGSGATE. *n.s.* [A cant word, borrowed from *Bilingsgate* in London, a place where there is always a croud of low people, and frequent brawls and foul language.] Ribaldry; foul language.

There stript, fair rhet'rick languish'd on the ground,
And shameful bilingsgate *her robes adorn.*
DUNCIAD, B. IV.

BILI'NGUOUS. *adj.* [*bilinguis*, Lat.] Having, or speaking two tongues.

BI'LLIARDS. *n.s. without a singular.* [*billard*, Fr. of which that language has no etymology; and therefore they probably derived from England both the play and the name; which is corrupted from *balyards*; yards or sticks with which a ball is driven along a table. Thus *Spenser*:

Balyards *much unfit,*
And shuttlecocks misseeming manly wit.
HUBBERD'S TALE.].

A game at which a ball is forced against another on a table.

Let it alone; let's to billiards.
SHAKESPEARE'S ANTONY AND CLEOPATRA.

Even nose and cheek, withal,
Smooth as is the billiard *ball.*
BEN JONSON'S UNDERWOODS.

Some are forced to bound or fly upwards, almost like ivory balls meeting on a billiard *table.* BOYLE.

When the ball obeys the stroke of a billiard *stick, it is not any action of the ball, but bare passion.* LOCKE.

BIN. *n.s.* [*binne*, Sax.] A place where bread, or corn, or wine, is reposited.

The most convenient way of picking hops, is into a long square frame of wood, called a bin. MORTIMER'S HUSBANDRY.

As when from rooting in a bin,
All pouder'd o'er from tail to chin,
A lively maggot sallies out,
You know him by his hazel snout.
SWIFT.

BIO'GRAPHER. *n.s.* [*βίος* and *γράφω*.] A writer of lives; a relator not of the history of nations, but of the actions of particular persons.

Our Grubstreet biographers *watch for the death of a great man, like so many undertakers, on purpose to make a penny of him.*
ADDISON'S FREEHOLDER, NO 35.

BI'RTHDAY. *n.s.* [from *birth* and *day*.]

1. The day on which any one is born.

Orient light,
Exhaling first from darkness, they beheld
Birthday *of heaven and earth.*
MILTON'S PARADISE LOST, B. VII.

2. The day of the year in which any one was born, annually observed.

This is my birthday; *as this very day*
Was Cassius born.
SHAKESPEARE'S JULIUS CÆSAR.

They tell me, 'tis my birthday, *and I'll keep it*
With double pomp of sadness:
'Tis what the day deserves, which gave me breath. DRYDEN.

Your country dames,
Whose cloaths returning birthday *claims.*
PRIOR.

BI'RTHNIGHT. *n.s.* [from *birth* and *night*.]

1. The night in which any one is born.

Th' angelick song in Bethlehem field,
On thy birthnight, *that sung the Saviour born.* PARADISE REGAIN'D.

2. The night annually kept in memory of any one's birth.

A youth more glitt'ring than a birthnight *beau.* POPE.

BIT. *n.s.* [from *bite*.]

1. As much meat as is put into the mouth at once.

How many prodigal bits *have slaves and peasants*
This night englutted?
SHAKESPEARE'S TIMON OF ATHENS.

Follow your function, go and batten on cold bits. SHAKESPEARE.

The mice found it troublesome to be still climbing the oak for every bit *they put in their bellies.* L'ESTRANGE.

By this the boiling kettle had prepar'd,
And to the table sent the smoaking lard,
A sav'ry bit, *that serv'd to relish wine.*
DRYDEN'S FABLES.

John was the darling; he had all the good bits, *was crammed with good pullet, chicken, and capon.*
ARBUTHNOT'S JOHN BULL.

2. A small piece of any thing.

Then clap four slices of pilaster on't,
That, lac'd with bits *of rustick, makes a front.* POPE.

He bought at thousands, what with better wit
You purchase as you want, and bit *by* bit.
POPE'S EPISTLES.

His majesty has power to grant a patent for stamping round bits *of copper, to every subject he hath.* SWIFT.

3. A Spanish West Indian silver coin, valued at sevenpence halfpenny.

4. *A bit the better or worse.* In the smallest degree.

There are few that know all the tricks of these lawyers; for aught I can see, your case is not a bit *clearer than it was seven years ago.*
ARBUTHNOT'S HISTORY OF JOHN BULL.

BLAB. *n.s.* [from the verb.] A teltale; a thoughtless babbler; a treacherous betrayer of secrets.

The secret man heareth many confessions; for who will open himself to a blab, *or babbler?* BACON, ESSAY 6.

To have reveal'd
Secrets of man, the secrets of a friend,
Contempt and scorn of all, to be excluded
All friendship, and avoided as a blab.
MILTON'S AGONISTES.

Whoever shews me a very inquisitive body, I'll shew him a blab, *and one that shall make privacy as publick as a proclamation.* L'ESTRANGE.

I should have certainly gone about shewing my letters, under the charge of secrecy, to every blab *of my acquaintance.*
SWIFT'S LETTERS.

BLACK-GUARD. *adj.* [from *black* and *guard.*] A cant word amongst the vulgar; by which is implied a dirty fellow; of the meanest kind.

Let a black-guard *boy be always about the house, to send on your errands, and go to market for you on rainy days.* SWIFT.

BLACK-LEAD. *n.s.* [from *black* and *lead.*] A mineral found in the lead-mines, much used for pencils; it is not fusible, or not without a very great heat.

You must first get your black-lead *sharpened finely, and put fast into quills, for your rude and first draught.*
PEACHAM.

BLA'CKSMITH. *n.s.* [from *black* and *smith.*] A smith that works in iron; so called from being very smutty.

The blacksmith *may forge what he pleases.* HOWEL.

Shut up thy doors with bars and bolts; it will be impossible for the blacksmith *to make them so fast, but a cat and a whore-master will find a way through them.*
SPECTATOR, NO 205.

BLADE. *n.s.* [*blæð, bleð,* Sax. *bled,* Fr.] The spire of grass before it grows to seed; the green shoots of corn which rise from the seed. This seems to me the primitive signification of the word *blade*; from which, I believe, the *blade* of a sword was first named, because of its similitude in shape; and, from the *blade* of a sword, that of other weapons or tools.

There is hardly found a plant that yieldeth a red juice in the blade *or ear, except it be the tree that beareth sanguis draconis.*
BACON.

Sends in his feeding flocks betimes, t' invade
The rising bulk of the luxuriant blade.
DRYDEN'S GEORGICKS.

If we were able to dive into her secret recesses, we should find that the smallest blade *of grass, or most contemptible weed, has its particular use.*
SWIFT ON THE FACULTIES OF THE MIND.

Hung on every spray, on every blade
Of grass, the myriad dewdrops twinkle round. THOMSON.

To **BLAME.** *v.a.* [*blâmer,* Fr.]
1. To censure; to charge with a fault: it generally implies a slight censure.

Our pow'r
Shall do a court'sy to our wrath, which men
May blame, *but not controul.*
SHAKESPEARE'S KING LEAR.

Porphyrius, you too far did tempt your fate;
'Tis true, your duty to me it became;
But praising that, I must your conduct blame. DRYDEN'S TYRANNICK LOVE.

Each finding, like a friend,
Something to blame, *and something to commend.* POPE.

2. To *blame* has usually the particle *for* before the fault.

The reader must not blame *me for*

making use here, all along of the word sentiment. LOCKE.

3. Sometimes, but rarely, *of.*

Tomoreus he blam'd *of inconsiderate rashness, for that he would busy himself in matters not belonging to his vocation.*
KNOLLES'S HISTORY OF THE TURKS.

BLAME. *n.s.* [from the verb.]
1. Fault; imputation of a fault.[37]

In arms, the praise of success is shared amongst many; yet the blame *of misadventures is charged upon one.*
SIR J. HAYWARD.

They lay the blame *on the poor little ones, sometimes passionately enough, to divert it from themselves.* LOCKE.

2. Crime; that which produces or deserves censure.

Who would not judge us to be discharged of all blame, *which are confest to have no great fault, even by their very word and testimony, in whose eyes no fault of ours hath ever hitherto been accustomed to seem small.* HOOKER, B. V. §27.

I unspeak mine own detraction; here abjure
The taints and blames *I laid upon myself,*
For strangers to my nature.
SHAKESPEARE'S MACBETH.

3. Hurt.

Therewith upon his crest,
With rigour so outrageous he smit,
That a large share it hew'd out of the rest,
And glancing down his shield, from blame *him fairly blest.*
FAIRY QUEEN, B. I. CANT. II. STANZA 18.

4. There is a peculiar structure of this word, in which it is not very evident whether it be a *noun* or a verb; but I conceive it to be the *noun. To blame,* in French, *à tort.*

You were to blame, *I must be plain with you,*
To part so slightly with your wife's first gift.
SHAKESPEARE'S MERCHANT OF VENICE.

I do not ask whether they were mistaken; but, on supposition they were not, whether they were to blame *in the manner.*
STILLINGFLEET.

Now we should hold them much to blame,
If they went back before they came.
PRIOR.

To **BLA'NDISH.** *v.a.* [*blandior,* Lat.] To smooth; to soften. I have met with this word in no other passage.

Must'ring all her wiles,
With blandish'd *parleys, feminine assaults,*
Tongue-batteries, she surceas'd not day nor night,
To storm me over-watch'd, and weary'd out. MILTON'S AGONISTES, L. 402.

BLI'NDMAN'S BUFF. *n.s.* A play in which some one is to have his eyes covered, and hunt out the rest of the company.

Disguis'd in all the mask of night,
We left our champion on his flight:
At blindman's buff *to grope his way,*
In equal fear of night and day.
HUDIBRAS, P. III. C. II.

He imagines I shut my eyes again; but surely he fancies I play at blindman's buff *with him; for he thinks I never have my eyes open.*
STILLINGFLEET'S DEFENCE OF DISCOURSE ON ROMISH IDOLATRY.

BLI'NDWORM. *n.s.* [from *blind* and *worm.*] A small viper, the least of our English serpents, but venemous.[38]

You spotted snakes, with double tongue,
Thorny hedgehogs, be not seen;
Newts and blindworms, *do no wrong;*
Come not near our fairy queen.
SHAKESPEARE'S MIDSUMMER NIGHT'S DREAM.

The greater slow worm, called also the

blindworm, is commonly thought to be blind, because of the littleness of his eyes.
GREW'S MUSÆUM.

BLI'NKARD. *n.s.* [from *blink.*]
1. One that has bad eyes.
2. Something twinkling.

In some parts we see many glorious and eminent stars, in others few of any remarkable greatness, and, in some, none but blinkards, *and obscure ones.*
HAKEWELL ON PROVIDENCE.

BLO'BBER. *n.s.* [from *blob.*] A word used in some counties for a bubble.

There swimmeth also in the sea a round slimy substance, called a blobber, *reputed noisome to the fish.* CAREW.

BLO'CKHEAD. *n.s.* [from *block* and *head.*] A stupid fellow; a dolt; a man without parts.

Your wit will not so soon out as another man's will; it is strongly wedged up in a blockhead.
SHAKESPEARE'S CORIOLANUS.

We idly sit like stupid blockheads,
Our hands committed to our pockets.
HUDIBRAS, P. III. C. II.

A blockhead *rubs his thoughtless skull,*
And thanks his stars he was not born a fool. POPE.

BLOOD-LETTER. *n.s.* [from *blood-let.*] A phlebotomist; one that takes away blood medically.

This mischief happening to aneurisms, proceedeth from the ignorance of the blood-letter, *who, not considering the errour committed in letting blood, binds up the arm carelessly.*
WISEMAN'S SURGERY.

BLOODY-MINDED. *adj.* [from *bloody* and *mind.*] Cruel; inclined to bloodshed.

I think you'll make me mad: truth has been at my tongue's end this half hour, and I have not the power to bring it out, for fear of this bloody-minded *colonel.*
DRYDEN'S SPANISH FRIAR.

BLO'OMY. *adj.* [from *bloom.*] Full of blooms; flowery.

O nightingale! that on yon bloomy *spray*
Warblest at eve, when all the woods are still. MILTON.

Departing spring could only stay to shed
Her bloomy *beauties on the genial bed,*
But left the manly summer in her stead.
DRYDEN.

Hear how the birds, on ev'ry bloomy *spray,*
With joyous musick wake the dawning day. POPE.

BLO'SSOM. *n.s.* [*blosme,* Sax.] The flower that grows on any plant, previous to the seed or fruit. We generally call those flowers *blossoms,* which are not much regarded in themselves, but as a token of some following production.

Cold news for me:
Thus are my blossoms *blasted in the bud,*
And caterpillars eat my leaves away.
SHAKESPEARE'S HENRY IV.

Merrily, merrily shall I live now,
Under the blossom *that hangs on the bough.* SHAKESPEARE'S TEMPEST.

The pulling off many of the blossoms *of a fruit tree, doth make the fruit fairer.*
BACON'S NATURAL HISTORY, NO 449.

To his green years your censure you would suit,
Not blast the blossom, *but expect the fruit.* DRYDEN.

Sweeter than spring,
Thou sole surviving blossom *from the root,*
That nourish'd up my fortune.
THOMSON'S AUTUMN.

To **BLOTE.** *v.a.* To smoke, or dry by the smoke; as *bloted* herrings, or red herrings.

BLO'WER. *n.s.* [from *blow.*] A melter of tin.

Add his care and cost in buying wood, and in fetching the same to the blowing-house, together with the blowers, *two or three months extreme and encreasing labour.* CAREW'S SURVEY.

BLU'NDERBUSS. *n.s.* [from *blunder.*] A gun that is charged with many bullets, so that, without any exact aim, there is a chance of hitting the mark.

There are blunderbusses *in every loop-hole, that go off of their own accord, at the squeaking of a fiddle.* DRYDEN.

BLU'NDERER. *n.s.* [from *blunder.*] A man apt to commit blunders; a blockhead.

Another sort of judges will decide in favour of an authour, or will pronounce him a mere blunderer, *according to the company they have kept.*
WATTS'S IMPROVEMENT OF THE MIND.

To **BOARD.** *v.n.* To live in a house, where a certain rate is paid for eating.

That we might not part,
As we at first did board *with thee,*
Now thou wouldst taste our misery.
HERBERT.

We are several of us, gentlemen and ladies, who board *in the same house; and, after dinner, one of our company stands up, and reads your paper to us all.*
SPECTATOR, NO 961.

BOARD-WAGES. *n.s.* [from *board* and *wages.*] Wages allowed to servants to keep themselves in victuals.

What more than madness reigns,
When one short sitting many hundreds drains,
And not enough is left him, to supply
Board-wages, *or a footman's livery.*
DRYDEN'S JUVENAL'S SATIRES I.

BOAT. *n.s.* [*bat,* Saxon.]
1. A vessel to pass the water in. It is usually distinguished from other vessels, by being smaller and uncovered, and commonly moved by rowing.

I do not think that any one nation, the Syrian excepted, to whom the knowledge of the ark came, did find out at once the device of either ship or boat, *in which they durst venture themselves upon the seas.*
RALEIGH'S ESSAYS.

An effeminate scoundrel multitude!
Whose utmost daring is to cross the Nile,
In painted boats, *to fright the crocodile.*
TATE'S JUVENAL'S SATIRES XV.

2. A ship of a small size; as, a *passage boat, pacquet boat, advice boat, fly boat.*

BOB. *n.s.* [from the verb neuter.]
1. Something that hangs so as to play loosely; generally an ornament at the ear; a pendant; an ear-ring.

The gaudy gossip, when she's set agog,
In jewels drest, and at each ear a bob.
DRYDEN'S JUVENAL'S SATIRES VI.

2. The word repeated at the end of a stanza.

To bed, to bed, will be the bob *of the song.* L'ESTRANGE.

3. A blow.

I am sharply taunted, yea, sometimes with pinches, nips, and bobs.
ASCHAM'S SCHOOLMASTER.[39]

BO'BCHERRY. *n.s.* [from *bob* and *cherry.*] A play among children, in which the cherry is hung so as to bob against the mouth.

Bobcherry *teaches at once two noble virtues, patience and constancy; the first, in adhering to the pursuit of one end; the latter, in bearing a disappointment.*
ARBUTHNOT AND POPE'S MARTIN SCRIBLERUS.

BO'BWIG. *n.s.* [from *bob* and *wig.*] A short wig.

A young fellow riding towards us full gallop, with a bobwig *and a black silken bag tied to it, stopt short at the coach, to ask us how far the judges were behind.* SPECTATOR, NO 129.

BO'ILARY. *n.s.* [from *to boil.*] A place at the salt-works where the salt is boiled.

BOLD. *adj.* [*bald*, Saxon.]

1. Daring; brave; stout; courageous; magnanimous; fearless; intrepid.

The wicked flee when no man pursueth; but the righteous are bold *as a lion.*
BIBLE PROVERBS, XXVIII. 1.

I have seen the councils of a noble country grow bold, *or timorous, according to the fits of his good or ill health that managed them.* TEMPLE.

2. Executed with spirit, and without mean caution.

These, nervous, bold; *those, languid and remiss.* ROSCOMMON.

The cathedral church is a very bold *work, and a masterpiece in Gothick architecture.*
ADDISON ON ITALY.

3. Confident; not scrupulous; not timorous.

We were bold *in our God to speak unto you the gospel of God with much contention.*
BIBLE 1 THESSALONIANS, II. 2.

I can be bold *to say, that this age is adorned with some men of that judgment, that they could open new and undiscovered ways to knowledge.* LOCKE.

4. Impudent; rude.

In thy prosperity he will be as thyself, and will be bold *over thy servants. If thou be brought low, he will be against thee.*
BIBLE ECCLESIASTICUS, VI. 11.

5. Licentious; such as shew great liberty of fiction.[40]

Which no bold *tales of Gods or monsters swell,*
But human passions, such as with us dwell. WALLER.

6. Standing out to the view; striking to the eye.

Catechreses and hyperboles are to be used judiciously, and placed in poetry, as heightenings and shadows are in painting, to make the figures bolder, *and cause it to stand off to sight.*
DRYDEN'S STATE OF INNOCENCE, PREFACE.

7. Open; smooth; even; level: a sailor's term.

Her dominions lie scattered, and have bold *accessible coasts.*
HOWEL'S VOCAL FOREST.

8. *To make bold.* To take freedoms: a phrase not grammatical, though common. *To be bold* is better; as, *I was bold to speak.*

I have made bold *to send to your wife;*
My suit is, that she will to Desdemona
Procure me some access.
SHAKESPEARE'S OTHELLO.

Making *so* bold,
My fears forgetting manners, to unseal
Their grand commission.
SHAKESPEARE'S HAMLET.

And were y' as good as George a Green,
I shall make bold *to turn agen.*
HUDIBRAS, P. II. C. II.

I durst not make *thus* bold *with Ovid, lest some future Milbourn should arise.*
DRYDEN'S FABLES, PREFACE.

Some men have the fortune to be esteemed wits, only for making bold *to scoff at these things, which the greatest part of mankind reverence.* TILLOTSON.

To **BO'LSTER.** *v.a.* [from the noun.]

1. To support the head with a bolster.
2. To afford a bed to.

Mortal eyes do see them bolster,
More than their own.
SHAKESPEARE'S OTHELLO.

3. To hold wounds together with a compress.

The practice of bolstering *the cheeks forward, does little service to the wound, and is very uneasy to the patient.* SHARP.

4. To support; to hold up; to maintain. This is now an expression somewhat coarse and obsolete.

We may be made wiser by the publick persuasions grafted in men's minds, so they be used to further the truth, not to bolster *errour.* HOOKER, B. III. §4.

The lawyer sets his tongue to sale for the bolstering *out of unjust causes.* HAKEWELL ON PROVIDENCE.

It was the way of many to bolster *up their crazy, doating consciences with confidences.* SOUTH.

BO'LTHEAD. *n.s.* A long strait-necked glass vessel, for chymical distillations, called also a *matrass*, or *receiver.*

This spirit abounds in salt, which may be separted, by putting the liquour into a bolt-head, *with a long and narrow neck.* BOYLE'S SCEPTICAL CHYMISTRY.

BO'LUS. *n.s.* [*βόλος.*] A form of medicine, in which the ingredients are made up into a soft mass, larger than pills, to be swallowed at once.

Keep their bodies soluble the while by clysters, lenitive boluses *of cassia and manna, with syrup of violets.* WISEMAN.

By poets we are well assur'd,
That love, alas! can ne'er be cur'd;
A complicated heap of ills,
Despising boluses *and pills.* SWIFT.

BO'NESETTER. *n.s.* [from *boneset.*] A chirurgeon; one who particularly professes the art of restoring broken or luxated bones.

At present my desire is only to have a good bonesetter. DENHAM'S SOPHY.

BO'NNY. *adj.* [from *bon, bonne,* Fr. It is a word now almost confined to the Scottish dialect.]

1. Handsome; beautiful.

Match to match I have encounter'd him,
And made a prey for carrion kites and crows,
Ev'n of the bonny *beast he lov'd so well.*
SHAKESPEARE'S HENRY VI.

Thus wail'd the louts in melancholy strain,
Till bonny *Susan sped across the plain.*
GAY'S PASTORALS.

2. Gay; merry; frolicksome; cheerful; blithe.

Then sigh not so, but let them go,
And be you blithe and bonny.
SHAKESPEARE'S MUCH ADO ABOUT NOTHING.

3. It seems to be generally used in conversation for *plump.*

BOOKLE'ARNED. *adj.* [from *book* and *learned.*] Versed in books, or literature: a term implying some slight contempt.

Whate'er these booklearn'd *blockheads say,*
Solon's the veri'st fool in all the play.
DRYDEN'S PERSIUS.

He will quote passages out of Plato and Pindar, at his own table, to some book-learned *companion, without blushing.* SWIFT.

BO'OTCATCHER. *n.s.* [from *boot* and *catch.*] The person whose business at an inn is to pull off the boots of passengers.

The ostler and the bootcatcher *ought to partake.* SWIFT.

BO'OTY. *n.s.* [*buyt,* Dutch; *butin,* Fr.]

1. Plunder; pillage; spoils gained from the enemy.

One way a band select from forage drives
A herd of beeves, fair oxen, and fair kine,
Their booty.
MILTON'S PARADISE LOST, B. XI. L. 650.

His conscience is the hue and cry that pursues him; and when he reckons that he has gotten a booty, *he has only caught a Tartar.* L'ESTRANGE.

For, should you to extortion be inclin'd,
Your cruel guilt will little booty *find.*
DRYDEN'S JUVENAL'S SATIRES, VIII.

2. Things gotten by robbery.[41]

If I had a mind to be honest, I see, fortune would not suffer me; she drops booties *in my mouth.*
SHAKESPEARE'S WINTER'S TALE.

3. *To play booty.* To play dishonestly, with an intent to lose. The French use, *Je suis botte*, when they mean to say, *I will not go.*

We understand what we ought to do; but when we deliberate, we play booty *against ourselves: our consciences direct us one way, our corruptions hurry us another.*
L'ESTRANGE.

I have set this argument in the best light, that the ladies may not think I write booty. DRYDEN.

BOPE'EP. *n.s.* [from *bo* and *peep.*] To look out, and draw back as if frighted,[42] or with the purpose to fright some other.

Then they for sudden joy did weep,
And I for sorrow sung,
That such a king should play bopeep,
And go the fools among.
SHAKESPEARE'S KING LEAR.

Rivers,
That serve instead of peaceful barriers,
To part th' engagements of their warriours,
Where both from side to side may skip,
And only encounter at bopeep.
HUDIBRAS, P. III. C. III.

There the devil plays at bopeep, *puts out his horns to do mischief, then shrinks them back for safety.*
DRYDEN'S SPANISH FRIAR.

BOTCH. *n.s.* [*bozza*, pronounced *botza*, Ital.]

1. A swelling, or eruptive discoloration of the skin.

Time, which rots all, and makes botches *pox,*
And, plodding on, must make a calf an ox,
Hath made a lawyer.
DONNE.

Botches *and blains must all his flesh imboss,*
And all his people.
MILTON'S PARADISE LOST, B. XII. L. 180.

It proves far more incommodious, which, if it were propelled in boils, botches, *or ulcers, as in the scurvy, would rather conduce to health.*
HARVEY ON CONSUMPTIONS.

2. A part in any work ill finished, so as to appear worse than the rest.

With him,
To leave no rubs or botches *in the work,*
Fleance, his son, must embrace the fate.
SHAKESPEARE'S MACBETH.

3. An adscititious, adventitious part clumsily added.

If both those words are not notorious botches, *I am much deceived; though the French translator thinks otherways.*
DRYDEN'S DEDICATION, ÆNEID.

A comma ne'er could claim
A place in any British name;
Yet, making here a perfect botch,
Thrusts your poor vowel from his notch.
SWIFT.

BO'TTLESCREW. *n.s.* [from *bottle* and *screw.*] A screw to pull out the cork.

A good butler always breaks off the point of his bottlescrew *in two days, by trying which is hardest, the point of the screw, or the neck of the bottle.* SWIFT.

BO'UNCER. *n.s.* [from *bounce.*] A boaster; a bully; an empty threatner.

BOURN. *n.s.* [*borne*, Fr.]
1. A bound; a limit.

Bourn, *bound of land, tilth, vineyard, none.* SHAKESPEARE'S TEMPEST.

That undiscover'd country, from whose bourn
No traveller e'er returns.
SHAKESPEARE'S HAMLET.

False,
As dice are to be wish'd, by one that fixes
No bourn *'twixt his and mine.*
SHAKESPEARE'S WINTER'S TALE.

I know each lane, and every alley green,
And every bosky bourn *from side to side.*
MILTON.

2. [from *burn*, Saxon.] A brook; a torrent: whence many towns, seated near brooks, have names ending in *bourn*. It is not now used in either sense; though the second continues in the Scottish dialect.

Ne swelling Neptune, ne loud thund'ring Jove,
Can change my cheer, or make me ever mourn;
My little boat can safely pass this perilous bourn. FAIRY QUEEN.

BO'UTISALE. *n.s.* [I suppose from *bouty*, or *booty*, and *sale.*] A sale at a cheap rate; as booty or plunder is commonly sold.

To speak nothing of the great boutisale *of colleges and chantries.* SIR J. HAYWARD.

BOWL. *n.s.* [*buelin*, Welch; which signifies, according to *Junius*, any thing made of horn, as drinking cups anciently were. It is pronounced *bole.*]
1. A vessel to hold liquids, rather wide than deep; distinguished from a cup, which is rather deep than wide.

Give me a bowl *of wine;*
I have not that alacrity of spirit,
Nor cheer of mind, that I was wont to have. RICHARD III.

If a piece of iron be fastened on the side of a bowl *of water, a loadstone, in a boat of cork, will presently make into it.*
BROWN'S VULGAR ERROURS, B. II. C. III.

The sacred priests, with ready knives, bereave
The beasts of life, and in full bowls *receive*
The streaming blood.
DRYDEN'S ÆNEID.

While the bright Sein, t' exalt the soul,
With sparkling plenty crowns the bowl,
And wit and social mirth inspires.
FENTON TO LORD GOWER.

2. The hollow part of any thing.

If you are allowed a large silver spoon for the kitchen, let half the bowl *of it be worn out with continual scraping.*
SWIFT'S DIRECTIONS TO THE COOK.

3. A basin, or fountain.

But the main matter is so to convey the water, as it never stay either in the bowl *or in the cistern.* BACON'S ESSAYS.

BRAID. *adj.* [To *brede*, in Chaucer, is to *deceive.*] An old word, which seems to signify *deceitful.*

Since Frenchmen are so braid,
Marry 'em that will. I'll live and die a maid.
SHAKESPEARE'S ALL'S WELL THAT ENDS WELL.

BRA'INSICK. *adj.* [from *brain* and *sick.*] Diseased in the understanding; addleheaded; giddy; thoughtless.

Nor once deject the courage of our minds,
Because Cassandra's mad; her brainsick *raptures*
Cannot distaste the goodness of a quarrel.
TROILUS AND CRESSIDA.

They were brainsick *men, who could neither endure the government of their king, nor yet thankfully receive the authours of their deliverance.*
KNOLLES'S HISTORY OF THE TURKS.

BRA'INSICKLY. *adv.* [from *brainsick.*] Weakly; headily.

Why, worthy thane,
You do unbend your noble strength to think
So brainsickly *of things.*
SHAKESPEARE'S MACBETH.

BRA'INSICKNESS. *n.s.* [from *brainsick.*] Indiscretion; giddiness.

BRA'NGLE. *n.s.* [uncertainly derived.] Squabble; wrangle.

The payment of tythes in this kingdom, is subject to many frauds, brangles, *and other difficulties, not only from papists and dissenters, but even from those who profess themselves protestants.* SWIFT.

To **BRA'NGLE.** *v.n.* [from the noun.] To wrangle; to squabble.

When polite conversing shall be improved, company will be no longer pestered with dull story-tellers, nor brangling *disputers.* SWIFT'S INTRODUCTION TO GENTEEL CONVERSATION.

BRA'NGLEMENT. *n.s.* [from *brangle.*] The same with *brangle.*

BRASS. *n.s.* [*bras*, Sax. *pres*, Welch.]

1. A yellow metal, made by mixing copper with lapis calaminaris. It is used, in popular language, for any kind of metal in which copper has a part.

Brass *is made of copper and calaminaris.* BACON.

Men's evil manners live in brass, *their virtues*
We write in water.
SHAKESPEARE'S HENRY VIII.

Let others mold the running mass
Of metals, and inform the breathing brass. DRYDEN.

2. Impudence.

BRA'VO. *n.s.* [*bravo*, Ital.] A man who murders for hire.

For boldness, like the bravoes *and banditti, is seldom employed, but upon desperate services.*
GOVERNMENT OF THE TONGUE.

No bravoes *here profess the bloody trade,*
Nor is the church the murd'rer's refuge made. GAY'S TRIVIA.

BRAWN. *n.s.* [of uncertain etymology.]

1. The fleshy or musculous part of the body.

The brawn *of the arm must appear full, shadowed on one side, then shew the wrist-bone thereof.* PEACHAM.

But most their looks on the black monarch bend,
His rising muscles and his brawn *commend;*
His double biting ax, and beamy spear,
Each asking a gigantick force to rear.
DRYDEN'S FABLES.

2. The arm, so called from its being musculous.

I'll hide my silver beard in a gold beaver,
And in my vantbrace put this wither'd brawn. SHAKESPEARE.

I had purpose
Once more to hew thy target from thy brawn. SHAKESPEARE.

3. Bulk; muscular strength.

Thy boist'rous hands are then of use, when I,
With this directing head, those hands apply;
Brawn *without brain is thine.*
DRYDEN'S FABLES.

4. The flesh of a boar.

The best age for the boar is from two years to five years old, at which time it is best to geld him, or sell him for brawn.
MORTIMER.

5. A boar.

BREAD-CHIPPER. *n.s.* [from *bread* and *chip.*] One that chips bread; a baker's servant.[43]

No abuse, Hal, on my honour; no abuse.
—— Not to dispraise me, and call me pantler, and bread-chipper, *and I know not what?*
SHAKESPEARE'S HENRY IV. P. II.

BRE'AKNECK. *n.s.* [from *break* and *neck.*] A fall in which the neck is broken; a steep place endangering the neck.

I must
Forsake the court; to do't or no, is certain
To me a breakneck.
SHAKESPEARE'S WINTER'S TALE.

BRE'AKPROMISE. *n.s.* [from *break* and *promise.*] One that makes a practice of breaking his promise.

I will think you the most atheistical break-promise, *and the most hollow lover.*
SHAKESPEARE'S AS YOU LIKE IT.

BRE'ASTCASKET. *n.s.* [from *breast* and *casket.*] With mariners. The largest and longest caskets, which are a sort of strings placed in the middle of the yard.

BRE'ASTKNOT. *n.s.* [from *breast* and *knot.*] A knot or bunch of ribbands worn by women on the breast.

Our ladies have still faces, and our men hearts, why may we not hope for the same atchievements from the influence of this breastknot?
ADDISON'S FREEHOLDER, NO 11.

BREED. *n.s.* [from the verb.]
1. A cast; a kind; a subdivision of species.

I bring you witnesses,
Twice fifteen thousand hearts of England's breed. SHAKESPEARE.

The horses were young and handsome, and of the best breed *in the north.*
SHAKESPEARE'S HENRY VIII.

Walled towns, stored arsenals, and ordnance; all this is but a sheep in a lion's skin, except the breed *and disposition of the people be stout and warlike.*
BACON'S ESSAYS, NO 30.

Infectious streams of crowding sins began,
And through the spurious breed *and guilty nation ran.* ROSCOMMON.

Rode fair Ascanius on a fiery steed,
Queen Dido's gift, and of the Tyrian breed. DRYDEN.

A cousin of his last wife's was proposed; but John would have no more of the breed.
ARBUTHNOT'S HISTORY OF JOHN BULL.

2. Progeny; offspring.

If thou wilt lend this money, lend it not
As to thy friend; for when did friendship take
A breed *of barren metal of his friend?*
SHAKESPEARE'S MERCHANT OF VENICE.

3. A number produced at once; a hatch.

She lays them in the sand, where they lie till they are hatched; sometimes above an hundred at a breed. GREW'S MUSÆUM.

BRE'EDBATE. *n.s.* [from *breed* and *bate.*] One that breeds quarrels; an incendiary.

An honest, willing, kind fellow, as ever servant shall come in house withal; and, I warrant you, no teltale, nor no breedbate.
SHAKESPEARE'S MERRY WIVES OF WINDSOR.

BRIBE. *n.s.* [*Bribe*, in French, originally signifies a piece of bread, and is applied to any piece taken from the rest; it is therefore likely, that a *bribe* originally signified, among us, a share of any thing unjustly got.] A reward given to pervert the judgment, or corrupt the conduct.

You have condemn'd and noted Lucius Pella,
For taking bribes *here of the Sardians.*
SHAKESPEARE'S JULIUS CÆSAR.

Nor less may Jupiter to gold ascribe,
When he turn'd himself into a bribe.
WALLER.

If a man be covetous, profits or bribes *may put him to the test.* L'ESTRANGE.

There's joy when to wild will you laws prescribe,
When you bid fortune carry back her bribe. DRYDEN.

BRI'DEMEN, BRI'DEMAIDS. *n.s.* The attendants on the bride and bridegroom.

BRI'DLEHAND. *n.s.* [from *bridle* and *hand.*] The hand which holds the bridle in riding.

In the turning, one might perceive the bridlehand *something gently stir; but, indeed, so gently, as it did rather distil virtue than use violence.* SIDNEY, B. II.

The heat of summer put his blood into a ferment, which affected his bridlehand *with great pain.* WISEMAN'S SURGERY.

BRI'LLIANT. *adj.* [*brillant,* Fr.] Shining; sparkling; splendid; full of lustre.

So have I seen in larder dark
Of veal a lucid loin,
Replete with many a brilliant *spark,*
As wise philosophers remark,
At once both stink and shine. DORSET.

BRI'LLIANT. *n.s.* A diamond of the finest cut, formed into angles, so as to refract the light, and shine more.

In deference to his virtues, I forbear
To shew you what the rest in orders were;
This brilliant *is so spotless and so bright,*
He needs not foil, but shines by his own proper light. DRYDEN.

BRI'MMER. *n.s.* [from *brim.*] A bowl full to the top.

When healths go round, and kindly brimmers *flow,*
Till the fresh garlands on their foreheads glow. DRYDEN.

BRI'MSTONY. *adj.* [from *brimstone.*] Full of brimstone; containing sulphur; sulphureous.

BRISK. *adj.* [*brusque,* Fr.]

1. Lively; vivacious; gay; sprightly; applied to men.

Pr'ythee, die, and set me free,
Or else be
Kind and brisk, *and gay like me.*
SIR J. DENHAM.

A creeping young fellow, that had committed matrimony with a brisk *gamesome lass, was so altered in a few days, that he was liker a sceleton than a living man.* L'ESTRANGE.

Why shou'd all honour then be ta'en
From lower parts, to load the brain:
When other limbs we plainly see,
Each in his way, as brisk *as he?* PRIOR.

2. Powerful; spirituous.

Our nature here is not unlike our wine;
Some sorts, when old, continue brisk *and fine.* DENHAM.

Under ground, the rude Riphæan race
Mimick brisk *cyder, with the brake's product wild,*
Sloes pounded, hips, and servis' harshest juice. PHILIPS.

It must needs be some exteriour cause, and the brisk *acting of some objects without me, whose efficacy I cannot resist.* LOCKE.

3. Vivid; bright.[44]

Objects appeared much darker, because my instrument was overcharged; had it magnified thirty or twenty five times, it would have made the object appear more brisk *and pleasant.* NEWTON'S OPTICKS.

BRI'STOL STONE. A kind of soft diamond found in a rock near the city of Bristol.

Of this kind of crystal are the better and larger sort of Bristol stones, *and the Kerry stones of Ireland.* WOODWARD.

To **BRO'ADEN.** *v.n.* [from *broad.*] To grow broad. I know not whether this word occurs, but in the following passage.

Low walks the sun, and broadens *by degrees,*
Just o'er the verge of day.
THOMSON'S SUMMER, L. 1605.

BRO'KEN MEAT. Fragments; meat that has been cut.

Get three or four chairwomen to attend you constantly in the kitchen, whom you pay at small charges; only with the broken meat, *a few coals, and all the cinders.* SWIFT.

BRO'WNBILL. *n.s.* [from *brown* and *bill.*] The ancient weapon of the English foot; why it is called *brown*, I have not discovered; but we now say *brown musket* from it.

And brownbills, *levied in the city,*
Made bills to pass the grand committee.
HUDIBRAS.

BRO'WNSTUDY. *n.s.* [from *brown* and *study.*] Gloomy meditations; study in which we direct our thoughts to no certain point.

They live retired, and then they doze away their time in drowsiness and brownstudies; *or, if brisk and active, they lay themselves out wholly in making common places.*
NORRIS.

To **BROWSE.** *v.a.* [*brouser*, Fr.] To eat branches, or shrubs.

And being down, is trod in the durt
Of cattle, and broused, *and sorely hurt.*
SPENSER'S PASTORALS.

Thy palate then did deign
The roughest berry on the rudest hedge:
Yea, like the stag, when snow the pasture sheets,
The barks of trees thou browsedst.
SHAKESPEARE'S ANTONY AND CLEOPATRA.

To **BRUISE.** *v.a.* [*briser*, Fr.] To crush or mangle with the heavy blow of something not edged or pointed; to crush by any weight; to beat into gross powder; to beat together coarsely.

Fellows in arms, and my most loving friends,
Bruis'd *underneath the yoke of tyranny.*
SHAKESPEARE'S RICHARD III.

And fix far deeper in his head their stings,
Than temporal death shall bruise *the victor's heel,*
Or theirs whom he redeems.
PARADISE LOST, B. XII. L. 433.

As in old chaos heav'n with earth confus'd,
And stars with rocks together crush'd and bruis'd. WALLER.

They beat their breasts with many a bruising *blow,*
Till they turn'd livid, and corrupt the snow. DRYDEN'S FABLES.

BRUISE. *n.s.* [from the verb.] A hurt with something blunt and heavy.

One arm'd with metal, th' other with wood,
This fit for bruise, *and that for blood.*
HUDIBRAS.

I since have labour'd
To bind the bruises *of a civil war,*
And stop the issues of their wasting blood.
DRYDEN.

BRUNE'TT. *n.s.* [*brunette*, Fr.] A woman with a brown complexion.

Your fair women therefore thought of this fashion, to insult the olives and the brunettes.
ADDISON'S GUARDIAN, NO 109.

To **BRUSH.** *v.n.*

1. To move with haste: a ludicrous word, applied to men.

Nor wept his fate, nor cast a pitying eye,
Nor took him down, but brush'd *regardless by.* DRYDEN.

The French had gather'd all their force,
And William met them in their way;
Yet off they brush'd, *both foot and horse.*
PRIOR.

2. To fly over; to skim lightly.

Nor love is always of a vicious kind,

But oft to virtuous acts inflames the mind,
Awakes the sleepy vigour of the soul,
And, brushing *o'er, adds motion to the pool.* DRYDEN'S FABLES.

BRU'TENESS. *n.s.* [from *brute.*] Brutality; a word not now used.

Thou dotard vile,
That with thy bruteness *shend'st thy comely age.* FAIRY QUEEN.

To **BRU'TIFY.** *v.a.* [from *brute.*] To make a man a brute.

O thou salacious woman! am I then brutified? *Ay; feel it here; I sprout, I bud, I blossom, I am ripe horn mad.*
CONGREVE'S OLD BATCHELOR.

BUB. *n.s.* [a cant word.] Strong malt liquour.

Or if it be his fate to meet
With folks who have more wealth than wit,
He loves cheap port, and double bub,
And settles in the humdrum club.
PRIOR.

To **BU'BBLE.** *v.n.* [from the noun.]
1. To rise in bubbles.

Alas! a crimson river of warm blood,
Like to a bubbling *fountain stirr'd with wind,*
Doth rise and fall.
SHAKESPEARE'S TITUS ANDRONICUS.

Adder's fork, and blindworm's sting,
Lizard's leg, and owlet's wing:
For a charm of pow'rful trouble,
Like a hellbroth boil and bubble.
SHAKESPEARE'S MACBETH.

Still bubble *on, and pour forth blood and tears.* DRYDEN.

2. To run with a gentle noise.

For thee the bubbling *springs appear'd to mourn,*
And whispering pines made vows for thy return. DRYDEN.

The same spring suffers at some times a very manifest remission of its heat: at others, as manifest an increase of it; yea, sometimes to that excess, as to make it boil and bubble *with extreme heat.*
WOODWARD'S NATURAL HISTORY.

Not bubbling *fountains to the thirsty swain,*
Not show'rs to larks, or sunshine to the bee,
Are half so charming as thy sight to me.
POPE.

To **BU'BBLE.** *v.a.* To cheat: a cant word.

He tells me, with great passion, that she has bubbled *him out of his youth; and that she has drilled him on to five and fifty.*
ADDISON'S SPECTATOR, NO 89.

Charles Mather could not bubble *a young beau better with a toy.*
ARBUTHNOT'S HISTORY OF JOHN BULL.

BU'BBLER. *n.s.* [from *bubble.*] A cheat.

What words can suffice to express, how infinitely I esteem you, above all the great ones in this part of the world; above all the Jews, jobbers, and bubblers.
DIGBY TO POPE.

BUCANI'ERS. *n.s.* A cant word for the privateers, or pirates, of America.

To **BUDGE.** *v.n.* [*bouger*, Fr.] To stir; to move off the place: a low word.

All your prisoners
In the lime grove, which weatherfends your cell,
They cannot budge *till your release.*
SHAKESPEARE'S TEMPEST.

The mouse ne'er shun'd the cat, as they did budge
From rascals worse than they.
SHAKESPEARE'S CORIOLANUS.

I thought th' hadst scorn'd to budge
For fear. HUDIBRAS, CANT. II.

BUDGE. *adj.* [of uncertain etymology.] Surly; stiff; formal.

O foolishness of men! that lend their ears
To those budge *doctors of the stoicks.*
MILTON.

BU'DGET. *n.s.* [*bogette*, Fr.]
1. A bag, such as may be easily carried.

If tinkers may have leave to live,
And bear the sowskin budget;
Then my account I well may give,
And in the stocks avouch it.
SHAKESPEARE'S WINTER'S TALE.

Sir Robert Clifford, in whose bosom, or budget, *most of Perkin's secrets were laid up, was come into England.* BACON.

His budget *with corruptions cramm'd,*
The contributions of the damn'd.
SWIFT.

2. It is used for a store, or stock.

It was nature, in fine, that brought off the cat, when the fox's whole budget *of inventions failed him.* L'ESTRANGE.

BU'FFLEHEADED. *adj.* [from *buffle* and *head.*] A man with a large head, like a buffalo; dull; stupid; foolish.

BULL, in composition, generally notes the large size of any thing, as *bull-head*, *bulrush*, *bull-trout*; and is therefore only an inclusive particle, without much reference to its original signification.

BULL-BAITING. *n.s.* [from *bull* and *bait.*] The sport of baiting bulls with dogs.

What am I the wiser for knowing that Trajan was in the fifth year of his tribuneship, when he entertained the people with a horse-race or bull-baiting?
ADDISON ON ANCIENT MEDALS.

BULL-BEGGAR. *n.s.* [This word probably came from the insolence of those who begged, or raised money by the pope's bull.] Something terrible; something to fright children with.

These fulminations from the Vatican were turned into ridicule; and, as they were called bull-beggars, *they were used as words of scorn and contempt.*
AYLIFFE'S PARERGON.

BULL-DOG. *n.s.* [from *bull* and *dog.*] A dog of a particular form, remarkable for his courage. He is used in baiting the bull; and this species is so peculiar to Britain, that they are said to degenerate when they are carried to other countries.

All the harmless part of him is no more than that of a bull-dog; *they are tame no longer than they are not offended.*
ADDISON'S SPECTATOR, NO 438.

BU'LLY. *n.s.* [*Skinner* derives this word from *burly*, as a corruption in the pronunciation; which is very probably right: or from *bulky*, or *bull-eyed*; which are less probable. May it not come from *bull*, the pope's letter, implying the insolence of those who came invested with authority from the papal court?] A noisy, blustering, quarrelling fellow: it is generally taken for a man that has only the appearance of courage.

Mine host of the garter. —— What says my bully *rook? Speak scholarly and wisely.*
SHAKESPEARE'S MERRY WIVES OF WINDSOR.

All on a sudden the doors flew open, and in comes a crew of roaring bullies, *with their wenches, their dogs, and their bottles.*
L'ESTRANGE'S FABLES.

'Tis so ridic'lous, but so true withal,
A bully *cannot sleep without a brawl.*
DRYDEN'S JUVENAL'S SATIRES, III.

A scolding hero is, at the worst, a more tolerable character than a bully *in petticoats.*
ADDISON'S FREEHOLDER, NO 38.

The little man is a bully *in his nature, but,*

when he grows cholerick, I confine him till his wrath is over.
ADDISON'S SPECTATOR.

BU'MPKIN. *n.s.* [This word is of uncertain etymology; *Henshaw* derives it from *pumpkin*, a kind of worthless gourd, or melon. This seems harsh.[45] *Bump* is used amongst us for a knob, or lump; may not *bumpkin* be much the same with *clodpate, loggerhead, block*, and *blockhead.*] An awkward heavy rustick; a country lout.

The poor bumpkin, *that had never seen nor heard of such delights before, blessed herself at the change of her condition.*
L'ESTRANGE'S FABLES.

A heavy bumpkin, *taught with daily care,*
Can never dance three steps with a becoming air. DRYDEN.

In his white cloak the magistrate appears,
The country bumpkin *the same liv'ry wears.* DRYDEN.

It was a favour to admit them to breeding; they might be ignorant bumpkins *and clowns, if they pleased.* LOCKE.

BU'NTER. *n.s.* A cant word for a woman who picks up rags about the street; and used, by way of contempt, for any low vulgar woman.

BUREAU'. *n.s.* [*bureau*, Fr.] A chest of drawers.[46] It is pronounced as if it were spelt *buro.*

For not the desk with silver nails,
Nor bureau *of expence,*
Nor standish well japan'd, avails
To writing of good sense. SWIFT.

BU'RNING-GLASS. *n.s.* [from *burning* and *glass.*] A glass which collects the rays of the sun into a narrow compass, and so increases their force.

The appetite of her eye did seem to scorch me up like a burning-glass.
SHAKESPEARE'S MERRY WIVES OF WINDSOR.

Love is of the nature of a burning-glass, *which, kept still in one place, fireth; changed often, it doth nothing.*
SUCKLING.

O diadem, thou centre of ambition,
Where all its different lines are reconciled,
As if thou wert the burning-glass *of glory.*
DRYDEN AND LEE.

BU'RSAR. *n.s.* [*bursarius*, Lat.]
1. The treasurer of a college.
2. Students sent as exhibitioners to the universities in Scotland by each presbytery, from whom they have a small yearly allowance for four years.

BU'RSTENESS. *n.s.* [from *burst.*] A rupture, or hernia.

BU'TTER. *n.s.* [*buttere*, Sax. *butyrum*, Lat.]
1. An unctuous substance made by agitating the cream of milk, till the oil separates from the whey.

And he took butter *and milk, and the calf which he had dressed, and set before them.* BIBLE GENESIS, XVIII. 8.

2. *Butter of antimony.* A chymical preparation, made by uniting the acid spirits of sublimate corrosive with regulus of antimony. It is a great caustick. *Harris.*
3. *Butter of tin*, is made with tin and sublimate corrosive. This preparation continually emits fumes. *Harris.*

BU'TTERFLY. *n.s.* [*butterflege*, Saxon.] A beautiful insect, so named because it first appears at the beginning of the season for butter.

Eftsoons that damsel, by her heav'nly might,
She turned into a winged butterfly,
In the wide air to make her wand'ring flight. SPENSER.

Tell old tales, and laugh
At gilded butterflies; *and hear poor rogues*

Talk of court news.
SHAKESPEARE'S KING LEAR.

And so befel, that as he cast his eye
Among the colworts on a butterfly,
He saw false Reynard.
DRYDEN'S FABLES.

That which seems to be a powder upon the wings of a butterfly, *is an innumerable company of extreme small feathers, not to be discerned without a microscope.*
GREW.

BU'XOM. *adj.* [*bucsum*, Sax. from *bugan*, to bend. It originally signified *obedient*, as *John de Trevisa*, a clergyman, tells his patron, that he is *obedient and buxom to all his commands.* In an old form of marriage used before the Reformation, the bride promised to be *obedient and buxom in bed and at board*; from which expression, not well understood, its present meaning seems to be derived.]

1. Obedient; obsequious.

He did tread down, and disgrace all the English, and set up and countenance the Irish; thinking thereby to make them more tractable and buxom *to his government.*
SPENSER'S IRELAND.

He, with broad sails,
Winnow'd the buxom *air.* MILTON.

2. Gay; lively; brisk.

I'm born
Again a fresh child of the buxom *morn,*
Heir of the sun's first beams. CRASHAW.

Zephyr, with Aurora playing,
As he met her once a maying,
Fill'd her with thee, a daughter fair,
So buxom, *blithe, and debonnair.*
MILTON.

Sturdy swains,
In clean array, for rustick dance prepare,
Mixt with the buxom *damsels, hand in hand,*
They frisk and bound. PHILIPS.

3. Wanton; jolly.

Almighty Jove descends, and pours
Into his buxom *bride his fruitful show'rs.*
DRYDEN'S VIRGIL.

She feign'd the rites of Bacchus! cry'd aloud,
And to the buxom *god the virgin vow'd.*
DRYDEN'S ÆNEID.

BY, in composition, implies something out of the direct way; and, consequently, some obscurity, as a *by-road*; something irregular, as a *by-end*; or something collateral, as a *by-concernment*; or private, as a *by-law.* This composition is used at pleasure, and will be understood by the examples following.

BY-COFFEEHOUSE. *n.s.* A coffeehouse in an obscure place.

I afterwards entered a by-coffeehouse, *that stood at the upper end of a narrow lane, where I met with a nonjuror.*
ADDISON'S SPECTATOR, NO 403.

BY-CONCERNMENT. *n.s.* An affair which is not the main business.

Our plays, besides the main design, have under-plots, or by-concernments, *or less considerable persons and intrigues, which are carried on with the motion of the main plot.*
DRYDEN ON DRAMATICK POETRY.

BY-END. *n.s.* Private interest; secret advantage.

All people that worship for fear, profit, or some other by-end, *fall within the intendement of this fable.* L'ESTRANGE.

BY-LAW. *n.s.*

By-laws *are orders made in court-leets, or court-barons, by common assent, for the good of those that make them, farther than the publick law binds.* COWEL.

There was also a law, to restrain the by-laws *and ordinances of corporations.*
BACON'S HENRY VII.

In the beginning of this record is inserted

the law or institution; to which are added two by-laws, *as a comment upon the general law.*
ADDISON'S SPECTATOR, NO 608.

BY-NAME. *n.s.* A nickname; name of reproach, or accidental appellation.

Robert, eldest son to the Conquerour, used short hose, and thereupon was by-named *Court-hose, and shewed first the use of them to the English.*
CAMDEN'S REMAINS.

BY-PAST. *adj.* Past; a term of the Scotch dialect.

Wars, pestilences, and diseases, have not been fewer for these three hundred years by-past, *than ever they have been since we have had records.*
CHEYNE'S PHILOSOPHICAL PRINCIPLES.

BY-ROAD. *n.s.* An obscure unfrequented path.

Through slipp'ry by-roads, *dark and deep,*
They often climb, and often creep.
SWIFT.

BY-SPEECH. *n.s.* An incidental or casual speech, not directly relating to the point.

When they come to allege what word and what law they meant, their common ordinary practice is to quote by-speeches *in some historical narration or other, and to use them as if they were written in most exact form of law.*
HOOKER, B. III. §4.

BY-WORD. *n.s.* A saying; a proverb.

Duke of York, be king;
And bashful Henry be deposed; whose cowardice
Hath made us by-words *to our enemies.*
SHAKESPEARE'S HENRY VI. P III.

I knew a wise man, that had it for a by-word, *when he saw men hasten to a conclusion, Stay a little, that we may make an end the sooner.*
BACON'S ESSAYS, NO 26.

We are become a by-word *among the nations for our ridiculous feuds and animosities.*
ADDISON'S FREEHOLDER, NO 50.

It will be his lot often, to look singular, in loose and licentious times, and to become a by-word *and a reproach, on that account, among the men of wit and pleasure.*
ATTERBURY.

C

The third letter of the alphabet, has two sounds; one like *k*, as, *call*, *clock*, *craft*, *coal*, *companion*, *cuneiform*; the other as *s*, as, *Cæsar*, *cessation*, *cinder*. It sounds like *k* before *a*, *o*, *u*, or a consonant; and like *s*, before *e*, *i*, and *y*.

CA'BARET. *n.s.* [French.] A tavern.

Suppose this servant passing by some cabaret, *or tennis-court, where his comrades were drinking or playing, should stay with them, and drink or play away his money.*
BRAMHALL AGAINST HOBBES.

CA'CKEREL. *n.s.* A fish, said to make those who eat it laxative.

CA'DGER. *n.s.* A huckster; one who brings butter, eggs, and poultry, from the country to market.

CÆSU'RA. *n.s.* [Lat.] A figure in poetry, by which a short syllable after a complete foot is made long.

CAG. *n.s.* A barrel or wooden vessel, containing four or five gallons.

To **CAJO'LE.** *v.a.* [*cageoller*, Fr.] To flatter; to sooth; to coax: a low word.

Thought he, 'tis no mean part of civil
State-prudence, to cajole *the devil.*
HUDIBRAS, CANT. II. P. III.

The one affronts him, while the other cajoles *and pities him; takes up his quarrel, shakes his head at it, clasps his hand upon his breast, and then protests and protests.*
L'ESTRANGE.

CA'LDRON. *n.s.* [*chauldron*, Fr. from *calidus*, Lat.] A pot; boiler; a kettle.

In the midst of all
There placed was a caldron *wide and tall,*
Upon a mighty furnace, burning hot.
FAIRY QUEEN, B. II.

Some strip the skin, some portion out the spoil;
The limbs, yet trembling, in the caldrons *boil;*
Some on the fire the reeking entrails broil.
DRYDEN'S ÆNEID.

In the late eruptions, this great hollow was like a vast caldron, *filled with glowing and melted matter, which, as it boiled over in*

any part, ran down the sides of the mountain.
ADDISON'S REMARKS ON ITALY.

CALM. *adj.* [*calme*, Fr. *kalm*, Dutch.]
1. Quiet; serene; not stormy; not tempestuous; applied to the elements.

Calm *was the day, and, through the trembling air,*
Sweet breathing Zephyrus did softly play
A gentle spirit, that lightly did allay
Hot Titan's beams, which then did glister fair. SPENSER.

2. Undisturb'd; unruffled; applied to the passions.

It is no ways congruous, that God should be frightening men into truth, who were made to be wrought upon by calm *evidence, and gentle methods of persuasion.*
ATTERBURY.

The queen her speech with calm *attention hears,*
Her eyes restrain the silver-streaming tears. POPE'S ODYSSEY.

CA'LMY. *adj.* [from *calm.*] Calm; peaceful.[47]

And now they nigh approached to the sted,
Where as those mermaides dwelt: it was a still
And calmy *bay, on th' one side sheltered*
With the broad shadow of an hoary hill.
FAIRY QUEEN, B. II.

CA'MERADE. *n.s.* [from *camera*, a chamber, Lat.] One that lodges in the same chamber; a bosom companion. By corruption we now use *comrade.*

Camerades *with him, and confederates in his worthy design.*
RYMER'S TRAGEDIES OF LAST AGE.

CAMISA'DO. *n.s.* [*camisa*, a shirt, Ital. *camisium*, low Lat.] An attack made by soldiers in the dark; on which occasion they put their shirts outward, to be seen by each other.

They had appointed the same night, whose darkness would have encreased the fear, to have given a camisado *upon the English.*
HAYWARD.

CAN. *v.n.* [*konnen*, Dutch. It is sometimes, though rarely, used alone; but is in constant use as an expression of the potential mood; as, I *can* do, thou *canst* do, I *could* do, thou *couldest* do. It has no other terminations.]
1. To be able; to have power.

In place there is licence to do good and evil, whereof the latter is a curse; for, in evil, the best condition is not to will; the second not to can. BACON'S ESSAYS, NO 11.

O, there's the wonder!
Mecænas and Agrippa, who can *most*
With Cæsar, are his foes. His wife Octavia,
Driv'n from his house, sollicits her revenge,
And Dolabella, who was once his friend.
DRYDEN'S ALL FOR LOVE.

He can *away with no company, whose discourse goes beyond what claret and dissoluteness inspires.* LOCKE.

2. It expresses the potential mood; as, I *can* do it.

If she can *make me blest? She only* can*:*
Empire, and wealth, and all she brings beside,
Are but the train and trappings of her love. DRYDEN.

3. It is distinguished from *may*, as *power* from *permission*; I *can* do it; it is in my power: I *may* do it; it is allowed me: but, in poetry, they are confounded.[48]
4. *Can* is used of the person with the *verb active*, where *may* is used; of the thing, with the *verb passive*; as, I *can* do it; it *may* be done.

CA'NCELLATED. *particip. adj.* [from *cancel.*] Cross-barred; marked with lines crossing each other.

The tail of the castor is almost bald, though the beast is very hairy; and cancellated, *with some resemblance to the scales of fishes.* GREW'S MUSÆUM.

CA'NCER. *n.s.* [*cancer*, Lat.]

1. A crabfish.

2. The sign of the summer solstice.

When now no more th' alternate twins are fir'd,
And Cancer *reddens with the solar blaze,*
Short is the doubtful empire of the night.
THOMSON.

3. A virulent swelling, or sore, not to be cured.

Any of these three may degenerate into a schirrus, and that schirrus into a cancer. WISEMAN.

As when a cancer *on the body feeds,*
And gradual death from limb to limb proceeds;
So does the chilness to each vital part,
Spread by degrees, and creeps into the heart. ADDISON'S OVID.

To **CA'NCERATE.** *v.n.* [from *cancer.*] To grow cancerous; to become a cancer.

But striking his fist upon the point of a nail in the wall, his hand cancerated, *he fell into a fever, and soon after died on't.* L'ESTRANGE'S FABLES.

CA'NDLE. *n.s.* [*candela*, Lat.]

1. A light made of wax or tallow, surrounding a wick of flax or cotton.

Here burns my candle *out, ay, here it dies,*
Which, while it lasted, gave King Henry light. SHAKESPEARE.

We see that wax candles *last longer than tallow candles, because wax is more firm and hard.* BACON'S NATURAL HISTORY.

Take a child, and, setting a candle *before him, he shall find his pupil to contract very much, to exclude the light, with the brightness whereof it would otherwise be dazzled.* RAY.

2. Light, or luminary.

By these bless'd candles *of the night,*
Had you been there, I think you would have begg'd
The ring of me, to give the worthy doctor.
SHAKESPEARE'S MERCHANT OF VENICE.

CANDLEWA'STER. *n.s.* [from *candle* and *waste.*] That which consumes candles; a spendthrift.

Patch grief with proverbs, make misfortune drunk
With candlewasters.
SHAKESPEARE'S MUCH ADO ABOUT NOTHING.

CA'NNON. *n.s.* [*cannon*, Fr. from *canna*, Lat. a pipe, meaning a large tube.]

1. A great gun for battery.

2. A gun larger than can be managed by the hand. They are of so many sizes, that they decrease in the bore from a ball of forty-eight pounds to a ball of five ounces.

As cannons *overcharg'd with double cracks,*
So they redoubled strokes upon the foe.
SHAKESPEARE'S MACBETH.

He had left all the cannon *he had taken; and now he sent all his great cannon to a garrison.* CLARENDON.

The making, or price, of these gunpowder instruments, is extremely expensive, as may be easily judged by the weight of their materials; a whole cannon *weighing commonly eight thousand pounds; a half* cannon, *five thousand; a culverin, four thousand five hundred; a demi-culverin, three thousand; which, whether it be in iron or brass, must needs be very costly.* WILKINS'S MATHEMATICAL MAGICK.

CANT. *n.s.* [probably from *cantus*, Lat. implying the odd tone of voice used by vagrants; but imagined by some to be corrupted from *quaint.*]

1. A corrupt dialect used by beggars and vagabonds.

2. A particular form of speaking

peculiar to some certain class or body of men.

I write not always in the proper terms of navigation, land service, or in the cant *of any profession.* DRYDEN.

If we would trace out the original of that flagrant and avowed impiety, which has prevailed among us for some years, we should find, that it owes its rise to that cant *and hypocrisy, which had taken possession of the people's minds in the times of the great rebellion.*
ADDISON'S FREEHOLDER, NO 37.

Astrologers, with an old paltry cant, *and a few pot-hooks for planets, to amuse the vulgar, have too long been suffered to abuse the world.*
SWIFT'S PREDICTIONS FOR THE YEAR 1701.

A few general rules, with a certain cant *of words, has sometimes set up an illiterate heavy writer, for a most judicious and formidable critick.*
ADDISON'S SPECTATOR, NO 291.

3. A whining pretension to goodness, in formal and affected terms.

Of promise prodigal, while pow'r you want,
And preaching in the self-denying cant.
DRYDEN'S AURENGZEBE.

4. Barbarous jargon.

The affectation of some late authours, to introduce and multiply cant *words, is the most ruinous corruption in any language.*
SWIFT.

5. Auction.

Numbers of these tenants, or their descendants, are now offering to sell their leases by cant, *even those which were for lives.*
SWIFT.

To **CANT.** *v.n.* [from the noun.] To talk in the jargon of particular professions, or in any kind of formal affected language, or with a peculiar and studied tone of voice.

Men cant *endlessly about materia and forma; hunt chimeras by rules of art, or dress up ignorance in words of bulk or sound, which may stop up the mouth of enquiry.*
GLANVILLE'S SCEPSIS SCIENTIFICA.

That uncouth affected garb of speech, or canting *language rather, if I may so call it, which they have of late taken up, is the signal distinction and characteristical note of that, which, in that their new language, they call the godly party.* SANDERSON.

The busy, subtile serpents of the law,
Did first my mind from true obedience draw;
While I did limits to the king prescribe,
And took for oracles that canting *tribe.*
ROSCOMMON.

Unskill'd in schemes by planets to foreshow,
Like canting *rascals, how the wars will go.*
DRYDEN'S JUVENAL.

CA'NTER. *n.s.* [from *cant.*] A term of reproach for hypocrites, who talk formally of religion, without obeying it.

CANTERBURY GALLOP. [In horsemanship.] The hard gallop of an ambling horse, commonly called a canter; and probably derived from the monks riding to Canterbury on easy ambling horses.

CAPU'CHED. *adj.* [from *capuce,* Fr. a hood.] Covered over as with a hood.

They are differently cucullated and capuched *upon the head and back, and, in the cicada, the eyes are more prominent.*
BROWN'S VULGAR ERROURS, B. IV. C. III.

CAPUCHI'N. *n.s.* A female garment, consisting of a cloak and hood, made in imitation of the dress of capuchin monks; whence its name is derived.

CAR. *n.s.* [*car,* Welch; *karre,* Dut. *cræt,* Sax. *carrus,* Lat.]

1. A small carriage of burden, usually drawn by one horse or two.

When a lady comes in a coach to our shops, it must be followed by a car *loaded with Mr. Wood's money.* SWIFT.

2. In poetical language, a chariot;[49] a chariot of war, or triumph.

Henry is dead, and never shall revive:
Upon a wooden coffin we attend,
And death's dishonourable victory,
We with our stately presence glorify,
Like captives bound to a triumphant car.
SHAKESPEARE'S HENRY VI.

Wilt thou aspire to guide the heav'nly car,
And with thy daring folly burn the world.
SHAKESPEARE.

And the gilded car *of day,*
His glowing axle doth allay
In the steep Atlantick stream. MILTON.

See, where he comes, the darling of the war!
See millions crouding round the gilded car*!* PRIOR.

3. The Charles's wain, or Bear; a constellation.

Ev'ry fixt and ev'ry wand'ring star,
The Pleiads, Hyads, and the Northern Car. DRYDEN.

CA'RABINE, CA'RBINE. *n.s.* [*carabine*, Fr.] A small sort of fire-arm, shorter than a fusil, and carrying a ball of twenty-four in the pound, hung by the light horse at a belt over the left shoulder. It is a kind of medium between the pistol and the musket, having its barrel two foot and a half long.

CA'RDINAL. *n.s.* One of the chief governours of the Romish church, by whom the pope is elected out of their own number, which contains six bishops, fifty priests, and fourteen deacons, who constitute the sacred college, and are chosen by the pope.

A cardinal *is so stiled, because serviceable to the apostolick see, as an axle or hinge on which the whole government of the church turns; or as they have, from the pope's grant, the hinge and government of all the affairs of the Romish church.*
AYLIFFE'S PARERGON.

You hold a fair assembly;
You are a churchman, or, I'll tell you, cardinal,
I should judge now unhappily.
SHAKESPEARE'S HENRY VIII.

CA'RDMATCH. *n.s.* [from *card* and *match.*] A match made by dipping pieces of card in melted sulphur.

Take care, that those may not make the most noise who have the least to sell; which is very observable in the venders of cardmatches.
ADDISON'S SPECTATOR, NO 251.

CA'RECRAZED. *adj.* [from *care* and *craze.*] Broken with care and solicitude.

These both put off, a poor petitioner,
A carecraz'd *mother of a many children.*
SHAKESPEARE'S RICHARD III.

CA'RELESS. *adj.* [from *care.*]

1. Without care; without solicitude; unconcerned; negligent; inattentive; heedless; regardless; thoughtless; neglectful; unheeding; unthinking; unmindful; with *of* or *about.*

Knowing that if the worst befal them, they shall lose nothing but themselves; whereof they seem very careless.
SPENSER'S IRELAND.

Nor lose the good advantage of his grace,
By seeming cold, or careless *of his will.*
SHAKESPEARE'S HENRY IV.

A woman the more curious she is about her face, is commonly the more careless *about her house.* BEN JONSON.

A father, unnaturally careless *of his child, sells or gives him to another man.*
LOCKE.

2. Cheerful; undisturbed.

Thus wisely careless, *innocently gay,*
Cheerful he play'd. POPE.

In my cheerful morn of life,
When nurs'd by careless *solitude I liv'd,*
And sung of nature with unceasing joy,
Pleas'd have I wander'd through your rough domain.
THOMSON'S AUTUMN, L. 5.

3. Unheeded; thoughtless; unconsidered.

The freedom of saying as many careless *things as other people, without being so severely remarked upon.* POPE.

4. Unmoved by; unconcerned at.

Careless *of thunder from the clouds that break,*
My only omens from your looks I take.
GRANVILLE.

CA'ROL. *n.s.* [*carola*, Ital. from *choreola*, Lat.]

1. A song of joy and exultation.

And let the Graces dance unto the rest,
For they can do it best:
The whiles the maidens do their carol *sing,*
To which the woods shall answer, and their echo ring.
SPENSER'S EPITHALAMIUM.

Even in the old testament, if you listen to David's harp, you shall hear as many herse-like airs as carols. BACON.

Oppos'd to her, on t' other side advance
The costly feast, the carol, *and the dance,*
Minstrels and musick, poetry and play,
And balls by night, and tournaments by day. DRYDEN'S FABLES.

2. A song of devotion.

No night is now with hymn or carol *blest.*
SHAKESPEARE.

They gladly thither haste; and, by a choir
Of squadron'd angels, hear his carol *sung.*
PARADISE LOST, B. XII.

3. A song in general.

The carol *they began that hour,*
How that a life was but a flower,
In the spring time.
SHAKESPEARE'S AS YOU LIKE IT.

CA'RPENTER. *n.s.* [*charpentier*, Fr.] An artificer in wood; a builder of houses and ships. He is distinguished from a joiner, as the carpenter performs larger and stronger work.

This work performed with advisement good,
Godfrey his carpenters, *and men of skill,*
In all the camp, sent to an aged wood.
FAIRFAX, B. III.

In building Hiero's great ship, there were three hundred carpenters *employed for a year together.* WILKINS'S DÆDALUS.

In burden'd vessels, first with speedy care,
His plenteous stores do season'd timbers send,
Thither the brawny carpenters *repair,*
And, as the surgeons of maim'd ships, attend. DRYDEN.

CA'RRY-TALE. *n.s.* [from *carry* and *tale.*] A talebearer.

Some carry-tale, *some pleaseman, some slight zany,*
Told our intents before.
SHAKESPEARE'S LOVE'S LABOUR'S LOST.

CARTE BLANCHE. [French.] A blank paper; a paper to be filled up with such conditions as the person to whom it is sent thinks proper.

CASH. *n.s.* [*caisse*, Fr. a chest.] Money; properly ready money; money in the chest, or at hand.

A thief, bent to unhoard the cash
Of some rich burgher.
PARADISE LOST, B. II. L. 188.

He is at an end of all his cash; *he has both his law and his daily bread now upon trust.* ARBUTHNOT'S JOHN BULL.

He sent the thief, that stole the cash, *away,*
And punish'd him that put it in his way.
POPE.

CA'STAWAY. *n.s.* [from *cast* and *away.*] A person lost, or abandoned by providence.[50]

Neither given any leave to search in particular who are the heirs of the kingdom of God, who castaways. HOOKER, B. V.

Lest that by any means, when I have preached to others, I myself should be a castaway.
BIBLE 1 CORINTHIANS, IX. 27.

CA'STAWAY. *adj.* [from the subst.] Useless; of no value.

We only prize, pamper, and exalt this vassal and slave of death, or only remember, at our castaway *leisure, the imprisoned immortal soul.*
RALEIGH'S HISTORY.

CA'STLE. *n.s.* [*castellum*, Lat.]
1. A strong house, fortified against assaults.

The castle *of Macduff I will surprise.*
SHAKESPEARE'S MACBETH.

To forfeit all your goods, lands, tenements, And castles.
SHAKESPEARE'S HENRY VIII.

2. CASTLES *in the air.* [*chateaux d'Espagne*, Fr.] Projects without reality.

These were but like castles in the air, *and in men's fancies vainly imagined.*
RALEIGH'S HISTORY OF THE WORLD.

CASTLE SOAP. *n.s.* [I suppose corrupted from *Castile soap*.] A kind of soap.

I have a letter from a soap-boiler, desiring me to write upon the present duties on Castle soap.
ADDISON'S SPECTATOR, NO 488.

To CA'STRATE. *v.a.* [*castro*, Lat.]
1. To geld.
2. To take away the obscene parts of a writing.

CAT. *n.s.* [*katz*, Teuton. *chat*, Fr.] A domestick animal that catches mice, commonly reckoned by naturalists the lowest order of the leonine species.

'Twas you incens'd the rabble:
Cats, *that can judge as fitly of his worth,*
As I can of those mysteries, which heav'n
Will not have earth to know.
SHAKESPEARE'S CORIOLANUS.

Thrice the brinded cat *hath mew'd.*
SHAKESPEARE'S MACBETH.

A cat, *as she beholds the light, draws the ball of her eye small and long, being covered over with a green skin, and dilates it at pleasure.*
PEACHAM ON DRAWING.

CATA'STROPHE. *n.s.* [*καταστροφή*.]
1. The change or revolution, which produces the conclusion or final event of a dramatick piece.

Pat! —— He comes like the catastrophe *of the old comedy.*
SHAKESPEARE'S KING LEAR.

That philosopher declares for tragedies, whose catastrophes *are unhappy, with relation to the principal characters.*
DENNIS.

2. A final event; a conclusion generally unhappy.

Here was a mighty revolution, the most horrible and portentuous catastrophe *that nature ever yet saw; an elegant and habitable earth quite shattered.*
WOODWARD'S NATURAL HISTORY.

CA'TCAL. *n.s.* [from *cat* and *call*.] A squeaking instrument, used in the playhouse to condemn plays.

A young lady, at the theatre, conceived a passion for a notorious rake that headed a party of catcals. SPECTATOR, NO 602.

Three catcals *be the bribe*
Of him, whose chatt'ring shames the monkey tribe. POPE.

CA'TCHWORD. *n.s.* [from *catch* and *word*. With printers.] The word at the corner of the page under the last line, which is repeated at the top of the next page.

CA'TER. *n.s.* [*quatre*, Fr.] The four of cards and dice.

CA'TER-COUSIN. *n.s.* A corruption of *quatre-cousin*, from the ridiculousness of calling cousin or relation to so remote a degree.

His master and he, saving your worship's reverence, are scarce cater-cousins. SHAKESPEARE'S MERCHANT OF VENICE.

Poetry and reason, how come these to be cater-cousins? RYMER'S TRAGEDIES OF THE LAST AGE.

CATERPI'LLAR. *n.s.* [This word *Skinner* and *Minshew* are inclined to derive from *chatte peluse*, a weasel; it seems easily deducible from *cates*, food, and *piller*, Fr. to rob; the animal that eats up the fruits of the earth.] A worm which, when it gets wings, is sustained by leaves and fruits.

The caterpillar *breedeth of dew and leaves; for we see infinite* caterpillars *breed upon trees and hedges, by which the leaves of the trees or hedges are consumed.* BACON.

Auster is drawn with a pot pouring forth water, with which descend grasshoppers, caterpillars, *and creatures bred by moisture.* PEACHAM ON DRAWING.

CATHE'TER. *n.s.* [καθετήϱ.] A hollow and somewhat crooked instrument, to thrust into the bladder, to assist in bringing away the urine, when the passage is stopped by a stone or gravel.

A large clyster, suddenly injected, hath frequently forced the urine out of the bladder; but if it fail, a catheter *must help you.* WISEMAN'S SURGERY.

CA'TPIPE. *n.s.* [from *cat* and *pipe*.] The same with *catcal*; an instrument that makes a squeaking noise.

Some songsters can no more sing in any chamber but their own, than some clerks can read in any book but their own; put them out of their road once, and they are mere catpipes *and dunces.* L'ESTRANGE.

CA'UDLE. *n.s.* [*chaudeau*, Fr.] A mixture of wine and other ingredients, given to women in childbed, and sick persons.

Ye shall have a hempen caudle *then, and the help of a hatchet.* SHAKESPEARE'S HENRY VI. P. II.

He had good broths; caudle, *and such like; and I believe he did drink some wine.* WISEMAN'S SURGERY.

CAVALI'ER. *n.s.* [*cavalier*, Fr.]

1. A horseman; a knight.
2. A gay sprightly military man.

For who is he, whose chin is but enrich'd
With one appearing hair, that will not follow
These cull'd and choice drawn cavaliers *to*
France? SHAKESPEARE'S HENRY VIII.

3. The appellation of the party of king Charles the first.

Each party grows proud of that appellation, which their adversaries at first intend as a reproach: of this sort were the Guelfs and Gibelines, Hugenots, and Cavaliers. SWIFT.

CAVALI'ER. *adj.* [from the subst.]

1. Gay; sprightly; warlike.
2. Generous; brave.

The people are naturally not valiant, and not much cavalier. *Now it is the nature of cowards to hurt, where they can receive none.* SUCKLING.

3. Disdainful; haughty.

CAVILLA'TION. *n.s.* [from *cavil*.] The disposition to make captious objection; the practice of objecting.

I might add so much concerning the large odds between the case of the eldest churches, in regard of heathens, and ours, in respect of the church of Rome, that very cavillation *itself should be satisfied.* HOOKER, B. IV. §7.

CA'VILLER. *n.s.* [*cavillator*, Lat.] A man fond of making objections; an unfair adversary; a captious disputant.

The candour which Horace shews, is that which distinguishes a critick from a caviller; *he declares, that he is not offended at those little faults, which may be imputed to inadvertency.*
ADDISON'S GUARDIAN, NO 110.

There is, I grant, room still left for a caviller *to misrepresent my meaning.*
ATTERBURY'S PREFACE TO HIS SERMONS.

CA'USEY, CAUSEWAY. *n.s.* [*chaussee*, Fr. This word, by a false notion of its etymology, has been lately written *causeway*.] A way raised and paved; a way raised above the rest of the ground.

To Shuppim the lot came forth westward by the causey.
BIBLE 1 CHRONICLES, XXVI. 16.

Th' other way Satan went down,
The causeway *to hell-gate.*
PARADISE LOST, B. X. L. 415.

But that broad causeway *will direct your way,*
And you may reach the town by noon of day. DRYDEN.

Whose causeway *parts the vale with shady rows;*
Whose seats the weary traveller repose.
POPE.

CA'YMAN. *n.s.* The American name for the alligator or crocodile.[51]

To **CEIL.** *v.a.* [*cælo*, Lat.] To overlay, or cover the inner roof of a building.

And the greater house he ceiled *with fir-tree, which he overlaid with fine gold.*
BIBLE 2 CHRONICLES, III. 5.

How will he, from his house ceiled *with cedar, be content with his Saviour's lot, not to have where to lay his head?*
DECAY OF PIETY.

To **CE'LEBRATE.** *v.a.* [*celebro*, Lat.]

1. To praise; to commend; to give praise to; to make famous.

The songs of Sion were psalms and pieces of poetry, that adored or celebrated *the Supreme Being.*
ADDISON'S SPECTATOR.

I would have him read over the celebrated *works of antiquity, which have stood the test of so many different ages.*
ADDISON.

2. To distinguish by solemn rites; to perform solemnly.

He slew all them that were gone to celebrate *the sabbath.*
BIBLE 2 MACCABEES, V. 26.

On the feast day, the father cometh forth, after divine service, into a large room, where the feast is celebrated. BACON.

3. To mention in a set or solemn manner, whether of joy or sorrow.

This pause of pow'r, 'tis Ireland's hour to mourn;
While England celebrates *your safe return.* DRYDEN.

CE'NOTAPH. *n.s.* [κένος and τάφος.] A monument for one buried elsewhere.

Priam, to whom the story was unknown,
As dead, deplor'd his metamorphos'd son;
A cenotaph *his name and title kept,*
And Hector round the tomb with all his brothers wept. DRYDEN'S FABLES.

The Athenians, when they lost any men at sea, raised a cenotaph, *or empty monument.* NOTES ON ODYSSEY.

CENSE. *n.s.* [*census*, Lat.] Publick rates.[52]

We see what floods of treasure have flowed into Europe by that action; so that the cense, *or rates of Christendom, are raised since ten times, yea twenty times told.*
BACON.

CENT. *n.s.* [*centum*, Lat. a hundred.] A hundred; as, five *per cent*, that is, five in the hundred.

CE'NTIPEDE. *n.s.* [from *centum* and *pes.*] A poisonous insect in the West Indies, commonly called by the English *forty legs.*

CENTRI'FUGAL. *adj.* [from *centrum* and *fugio*, Lat.] Having the quality acquired by bodies in motion, of receding from the centre.

They described an hyperbola, by changing the centripetal into a centrifugal *force.*
CHEYNE'S PHILOSOPHICAL PRINCIPLES.

CENTRI'PETAL. *adj.* [from *centrum* and *peto*, Lat.] Having a tendency to the center; having gravity.

The direction of the force, whereby the planets revolve in their orbits, is towards their centres; and this force may be very properly called attractive, in respect of the central body, and centripetal, *in respect of the revolving body.* CHEYNE.

CENTURIA'TOR. *n.s.* [from *century.*] A name given to historians, who distinguish times by centuries; which is generally the method of ecclesiastical history.

The centuriators *of Magdeburg were the first that discovered this grand imposture.*
AYLIFFE'S PARERGON.

CE'REBEL. *n.s.* [*cerebellum*, Lat.] Part of the brain.

In the head of man, the base of the brain and cerebel, *yea, of the whole scull, is set parallel to the horizon.* DERHAM.

CE'RTAIN. *adj.* [*certus*, Lat.]
1. Sure; indubitable; unquestionable; undoubted; that which cannot be questioned, or denied.

This it is equally certain *of, whether these ideas be more or less general.* LOCKE.

Those things are certain *among men, which cannot be denied, without obstinacy and folly.*
TILLOTSON.

2. Resolved; determined.

However I with thee have fix'd my lot,
Certain *to undergo like doom of death,*
Consort with thee.
MILTON'S PARADISE LOST, B. IX. L. 953.

3. In an indefinite sense, some; as, a *certain* man told me this.

How bad soever this fashion may justly be accounted, certain *of the same countrymen do pass far beyond it.*
CAREW'S SURVEY.

I got them in my country's service, when
Some certain *of your brethren roar'd, and ran*
From noise of our own drums.
SHAKESPEARE'S CORIOLANUS.

Let there be certain *leather bags made of several bignesses, which, for the matter of them, should be tractable.* WILKINS.

4. Undoubting; put past doubt.

This form before Alcyone present,
To make her certain *of the sad event.*
DRYDEN..[53]

CERULI'FICK. *adj.* [from *ceruleous.*] Having the power to produce a blue colour.

The several species of rays, as the rubifick, cerulifick, *and others are separated one from another.*
GREW'S COSMOLOGIA SACRA.

CESS. *n.s.* [probably corrupted from *cense*; See **CENSE**; though imagined by *Junius* to be derived from *saisire*, to seize.]
1. A levy made upon the inhabitants of a place, rated according to their property.

The like cess *is also charged upon the country sometimes for victualling the soldiers, when they lie in garrison.*
SPENSER.

2. The act of laying rates.

3. [from *cesse*, Fr.] It seems to have been used by *Shakespeare* for bounds, or limits.

I pr'ythee, Tom, beat Cutts's saddle, put a few flocks in the point; the poor jade is wrung in the withers out of all cess. SHAKESPEARE'S HENRY IV. P. I.

CH has, in words purely English, or fully naturalized, the sound of *tch*; a peculiar pronunciation, which it is hard to describe in words. In some words derived from the French, it has the sound of *sh*, as *chaise*; and, in some derived from the Greek, the sound of *k*, as *cholerick*.

CHAFE. *n.s.*[from the verb.] A heat; a rage; a fury; a passion; a fume; a pett; a fret; a storm.

When Sir Thomas More was speaker of the parliament, with his wisdom and eloquence, he so crossed a purpose of cardinal Wolsey's, that the cardinal, in a chafe, *sent for him to Whitehall.* CAMDEN'S REMAINS.

At this the knight grew high in chafe,
And staring furiously on Ralph,
He trembled. HUDIBRAS, P. II. C. II.

To **CHA'FFER.** *v.n.* [*kauffen*, Germ. to buy.] To treat about a bargain; to haggle; to bargain.

Nor rode himself to Paul's, the publick fair,
To chaffer *for preferments with his gold,*
Where bishopricks and sinecures are sold.
DRYDEN'S FABLES.

The chaffering *with dissenters, and dodging about this or t'other ceremony, is but like opening a few wickets, and leaving them a-jar.* SWIFT.

In disputes with chairmen, when your master sends you to chaffer *with them, take pity, and tell your master that they will not take a farthing less.* SWIFT.

To **CHA'FFER.** *v.a.* [The active sense is obsolete.]

1. To buy.

He chaffer'd *chairs in which churchmen were set,*
And breach of laws to privy farm did let.
SPENSER.

2. To exchange.

Approaching nigh, he never staid to greet,
Ne chaffer *words, proud courage to provoke.* FAIRY QUEEN.

CHA'FFERY. *n.s.* [from *chaffer.*] Traffick; the practice of buying and selling.

The third is, merchandize and chaffery, *that is, buying and selling.*
SPENSER'S STATE OF IRELAND.

CHA'FINGDISH. *n.s.* [from *chafe* and *dish.*] A vessel to make any thing hot in; a portable grate for coals.

Make proof of the incorporation of silver and tin in equal quantities, whether it will endure the ordinary fire which belongeth to chafingdishes, *posnets, and such other silver vessels.*
BACON'S PHYSICAL REMAINS.

CHAGRI'N. *n.s.* [*chagrine*, Fr.] Ill humour; vexation; fretfulness; peevishness. It is pronounced *shagreen*.

Hear me, and touch Belinda with chagrin*;*
That single act gives half the world the spleen. POPE.

I grieve with the old, for so many additional inconveniencies and chagrins, *more than their small remain of life seemed destined to undergo.* POPE'S LETTERS.

CHA'INSHOT. *n.s.* [from *chain* and *shot.*] Two bullets or half bullets, fastened together by a chain, which, when they fly open, cut away whatever is before them.

In sea fights oftentimes, a buttock, the brawn of the thigh, and the calf of the leg, are torn off by the chainshot, *and splinters.* WISEMAN'S SURGERY.

CHAISE. *n.s.* [*chaise*, Fr.] A carriage of pleasure drawn by one horse.

Instead of the chariot he might have said the chaise *of government; for a* chaise *is driven by the person that sits in it.*
ADDISON'S WHIG EXAMINER.

CHA'LDER, CHALDRON, CHAUDRON. *n.s.* A dry English measure of coals, consisting of thirty six bushels heaped up, according to the sealed bushel kept at Guildhall, London.

The chauldron *should weigh two thousand pounds.* CHAMBERS.

To **CHA'MBER.** *v.n.* [from the noun.]

1. To be wanton; to intrigue.

Let us walk honestly as in the day, not in rioting and drunkenness, not in chambering *and wantonness.*
BIBLE ROMANS, XIII. 13.

2. To reside as in a chamber.

The best blood chamber'd *in his bosom.*
SHAKESPEARE'S RICHARD II.

CH'ANGEFUL. *adj.* [from *change* and *full.*] Full of change; inconstant; uncertain; mutable; subject to variation; fickle.

Unsound plots, and changeful *orders, are daily devised for her good, yet never effectually prosecuted or performed.*
SPENSER ON IRELAND.

Britain, changeful *as a child at play,*
Now calls in princes, and now turns away.
POPE.

To **CHAP.** *v.a.* [*kappen*, Dutch, to cut. This word seems originally the same with *chop*; nor were they probably distinguished at first, otherwise than by accident; but they have now a meaning something different, though referable to the same original sense.] To break into hiatus, or gapings.

It also weakened more and more the arch of the earth, drying it immoderately, and chapping *it in sundry places.*
BURNET'S THEORY OF THE EARTH.

Then would unbalanc'd heat licentious reign,
Crack the dry hill, and chap *the russet plain.* BLACKMORE.

CHARACTERI'STICK. *n.s.* That which constitutes the character; that which distinguishes any thing or person from others.

I shall here endeavour to shew, how this vast invention exerts itself, in a manner superiour to that of any poet, as it is the great and peculiar characteristick *which distinguishes him from all others.*
POPE'S ESSAY ON HOMER.

To **CHA'RACTERIZE.** *v.a.* [from *character.*]

1. To give a character or an account of the personal qualities of any man.

It is some commendation, that we have avoided publickly to characterize *any person, without long experience.* SWIFT.

2. To engrave, or imprint.

They may be called anticipations, prenotions, or sentiments characterized *and engraven in the soul, born with it, and growing up with it.*
HALE'S ORIGIN OF MANKIND.

3. To mark with a particular stamp or token.

There are faces not only individual, but gentilitious and national; European, Asiatick, Chinese, African, and Grecian faces are characterized.
ARBUTHNOT ON AIR.

To **CHARK.** *v.a.* To burn to a black cinder, as wood is burned to make charcoal.

Excess, either with an apoplexy, knocks a man on the head, or, with a fever, like fire in a strong-water shop, burns him down to

the ground; or if it flames not out, charks *him to a coal.*
GREW'S COSMOLOGIA SACRA, B. III. C. V. § 10.

CHA'RLATAN. *n.s.* [*charlatan*, Fr. *ciarlatano*, Ital. from *ciarlare*, to chatter.] A quack; a mountebank; an empirick.

Saltimbanchoes, quacksalvers, and charlatans, *deceive them in lower degrees.*
BROWN'S VULGAR ERROURS. B. I. C. 3.

For charlatans *can do no good,*
Until they're mounted in a crowd.
HUDIBRAS.

CHART. *n.s.* [*charta*, Lat.] A delineation or map of coasts, for the use of sailors. It is distinguished from a *map*, by representing only the coasts.

The Portuguese, when they had doubled the Cape of Good-Hope, found skilful pilates, using astronomical instruments, geographical charts, *and compasses.*
ARBUTHNOT ON COINS.

CHARTER-PARTY. *n.s.* [*chartre partie*, Fr.] A paper relating to a contract, of which each party has a copy.

Charter-parties, *or contracts, made even upon the high sea, touching things that are not in their own nature maritime, belong not to the admiral's jurisdiction.*
HALE'S COMMON LAW OF ENGLAND.

CHASE-GUN. *n.s.* [from *chase* and *gun.*] Guns in the forepart of the ship, fired upon those that are pursued.

Mean time the Belgians tack upon our rear,
And raking chase-guns *through our stern they send.* DRYDEN.

CHASTE. *adj.* [*chaste*, Fr. *castus*, Lat.]
1. Pure from all commerce of sexes; as a chaste virgin.
2. With respect to language; pure; uncorrupt; not mixed with barbarous phrases.
3. Without obscenity.

Among words which signify the same principal ideas, some are clean and decent, others unclean; some chaste, *others obscene.* WATTS'S LOGICK.

4. True to the marriage bed.

Love your children, be discreet, chaste, *keepers at home.* TITUS, II. 5.

CHASTI'SEMENT. *n.s.* [*chastiment*, Fr.] Correction; punishment. These words are all commonly, though not always, used of domestick or parental punishment.

Shall I so much dishonour my fair stars,
On equal terms to give him chastisement?
SHAKESPEARE'S RICHARD II.

He held the chastisement *of one which molested the see of Rome, pleasing to God.*
RALEIGH'S ESSAYS.

For seven years what can a child be guilty of, but lying, or ill-natur'd tricks; the repeated commission of which shall bring him to the chastisement *of the rod.*
LOCKE.

He receives a fit of sickness as the kind chastisement *and discipline of his heavenly father, to wean his affections from the world.* BENTLEY.

To CHA'TTER. *v.n.* [*caqueter*, Fr.]
1. To make a noise as a pie, or other unharmonious bird.

Nightingales seldom sing, the pie still chattereth. SIDNEY.

So doth the cuckow, when the mavis sings,
Begin his witless note apace to chatter.
SPENSER'S SONNETS.

There was a crow sat chattering *upon the back of a sheep; Well, sirrah, says the sheep, you durst not have done this to a dog.*
L'ESTRANGE.

Your birds of knowledge, that in dusky air
Chatter *futurity.*
DRYDEN AND LEE'S OEDIPUS.

2. To make a noise by collision of the teeth.

Stood Theodore surpriz'd in deadly fright,
With chatt'ring *teeth, and bristling hair upright.* DRYDEN.

Dip but your toes into cold water,
Their correspondent teeth will chatter.
PRIOR.

3. To talk idly or carelesly.

Suffer no hour to pass away in a lazy idleness, an impertinent chattering, *or useless trifles.* WATTS'S LOGICK.

CHE'CKMATE. *n.s.* [*echec et mat*, Fr.] The movement on the chess-board, that kills the opposite men, or hinders them from moving.

Love they him called, that gave me the checkmate,
But better might they have behote him hate.
SPENSER.

CHEESE. *n.s.* [*caseus*, Lat. *cyse*, Saxon.] A kind of food made by pressing the curd of coagulated milk, and suffering the mass to dry.

I will rather trust a Fleming with my butter, parson Hugh the Welchman with my cheese, *than my wife with herself.*
SHAKESPEARE'S MERRY WIVES OF WINDSOR.

CHE'ESECAKE. *n.s.* [from *cheese* and *cake.*] A cake made of soft curds, sugar and butter.

Effeminate he sat, and quiet;
Strange product of a cheesecake *diet.*
PRIOR.

Where many a man at variance with his wife,
With soft'ning mead and cheesecake *ends the strife.* KING'S ART OF COOKERY.

CHE'ESY. *adj.* [from *cheese.*] Having the nature or form of cheese.

Acids mixed with them precipitate a tophaceous chalky matter, but not a cheesy *substance.*
ARBUTHNOT ON ALIMENTS.

CHESS. *n.s.* [*echec*, Fr.] A nice and abstruse game, in which two sets of men are moved in opposition to each other.

This game the Persian magi did invent,
The force of Eastern wisdom to express;
From thence to busy Europeans sent,
And styl'd by modern Lombards pensive chess. DENHAM.

So have I seen a king on chess,
(His rooks and knights withdrawn,
His queen and bishops in distress)
Shifting about, grow less and less,
With here and there a pawn. DRYDEN.

CHICA'NE. *n.s.* [*chicane*, Fr. derived by *Menage* from the Spanish word *chico*, little.]

1. The art of protracting a contest by petty objection and artifice.

The general part of the civil law concerns not the chicane *of private cases, but the affairs and intercourse of civilized nations, grounded upon the principles of reason.*
LOCKE ON EDUCATION.

His attornies have hardly one trick left; they are at an end of all their chicane.
ARBUTHNOT'S HISTORY OF JOHN BULL.

2. Artifice in general. This sense is only in familiar language.

Unwilling then in arms to meet,
He strove to lengthen the campaign,
And save his forces by chicane. PRIOR.

The **CHI'CKENPOX.** *n.s.* An exanthematous distemper, so called from its being of no very great danger.

CHI'EFRIE. *n.s.* [from *chief.*] A small rent paid to the lord Paramount.

They shall be well able to live upon those lands, to yield her majesty reasonable chiefrie, *and also give a competent maintenance unto the garrisons.*
SPENSER'S IRELAND.

Would the reserved rent at this day be any more than a small chiefrie. SWIFT.

CHILBLA'IN. *n.s.* [from *chill*, cold, and *blain*; so that *Temple* seems mistaken in his etymology, or has written it wrong to serve a purpose.] Sores made by frost.

I remembered the cure of childblanes *when I was a boy, (which may be called the children's gout) by burning at the fire.* TEMPLE.

CHI'LDERMAS DAY. [from *child* and *mass.*] The day of the week, throughout the year, answering to the day on which the feast of the holy Innocents is solemnized, which weak and superstitious persons think an unlucky day.

So you talk not of hares, or such uncouth things; for that proves as ominous to the fisherman, as the beginning of a voyage on the day when childermas day *fell, doth to the mariner.*
CAREW'S SURVEY OF CORNWALL.

CHIMNEY-CORNER. *n.s.* [from *chimney* and *corner.*] The fireside; the seat on each end of the firegrate; usually noted in proverbial language for being the place of idlers.

Yet some old men
Tell stories of you in their chimney-corner. DENHAM'S SOPHY.

CHI'NCOUGH. *n.s.* [perhaps more properly *kincough*, from *kincken*, to pant, Dut. and *cough.*] A violent and convulsive cough, to which children are subject.

I have observed a chincough, *complicated with an intermitting fever.*
FLOYER ON THE HUMOURS.

CHIRA'GRICAL. *adj.* [*chiragra*, Lat.] Having the gout in the hand; subject to the gout in the hand.

Chiragrical *persons do suffer in the finger as well as in the rest, and sometimes first of all.*
BROWN'S VULGAR ERRORS, B. IV. C. 5.

CHIRO'GRAPHER. *n.s.* [χείϱ, the hand, γϱάφω, to write.] He that exercises or professes the act or business of writing.

Thus passeth it from this office to the chirographer's, *to be engrossed.*
BACON'S OFFICE OF ALIENATION.

CHIRO'GRAPHIST. *n.s.* [See **CHIROGRAPHER.**] This word is used in the following passage, I think improperly, for one that tells fortunes, by examining the hand: the true word is *chirosophist*, or *chiromancer*.

Let the phisiognomists examine his features; let the chirographists *behold his palm; but, above all, let us consult for the calculation of his nativity.*
ARBUTHNOT AND POPE'S MARTIN SCRIBLERUS.

CHIRO'MANCER. *n.s.* [See **CHIROMANCY.**] One that foretells future events by inspecting the hand.

The middle sort, who have not much to spare,
To chiromancers' *cheaper art repair,*
Who clap the pretty palm, to make the lines more fair.
DRYDEN'S JUVENAL, SATIRE VI.

CHI'ROMANCY. *n.s.* [χείϱ, the hand, and μάντις, a prophet.] The art of foretelling the events of life, by inspecting the hand.

There is not much considerable in that doctrine of chiromancy *that spots in the top of the nails, do signify things past; in the middle, things present; and at the bottom, events to come.*
BROWN'S VULGAR ERROURS, B. V. C. 22.

CHIRU'RGEON. *n.s.* [χείϱουϱγος, from χείϱ, the hand, and ἔϱγον, work.]

One that cures ailments, not by internal medicines, but outward applications. It is now generally pronounced, and by many written, *surgeon.*

When a man's wounds cease to smart, only because he has lost his feeling, they are nevertheless mortal, for his not seeing his need of a chirurgeon.
SOUTH'S SERMONS.

CHI'TCHAT. *n.s.* [corrupted by reduplication from *chat.*] Prattle; idle prate; idle talk. A word only used in ludicrous conversation.

I am a member of a female society, who call ourselves the chitchat *club.*
SPECTATOR, NO. 560.

CHI'VALROUS. *adj.* [from *chivalry.*] Relating to chivalry, or errant knighthood; knightly; warlike; adventurous; daring. A word now out of use.

And noble minds of yore allied were
In brave pursuit of chivalrous *emprise.*
FAIRY QUEEN, B. I.

CHO'COLATE-HOUSE. *n.s.* [*chocolate* and *house.*] A house where company is entertained with chocolate.

Ever since that time, Lisander has been twice a day at the chocolate-house.
TATLER, NO. 54.

CHOIR. *n.s.* [*chorus,* Latin.]
1. An assembly or band of singers.

They now assist the choir
Of angels, who their songs admire.
WALLER.

2. The singers in divine worship.

The choir,
With all the choicest musick of the kingdom,
Together sung Te Deum.
SHAKESPEARE'S HENRY VIII.

3. The part of the church where the choristers or singers are placed.

The lords and ladies, having brought the queen
To a prepar'd place in the choir, *fell off*
At distance from her.
SHAKESPEARE'S HENRY VIII.

CHOKE-PEAR. *n.s.* [from *choke* and *pear.*]
1. A rough, harsh, unpalatable pear.
2. Any aspersion or sarcasm, by which another is put to silence. A low term.

Pardon me for going so low as to talk of giving choke-pears. CLARISSA.

CHOP-HOUSE. *n.s.* [*chop* and *house.*] A mean house of entertainment, where provision ready dressed is sold.

I lost my place at the chop-house, *where every man eats in publick a mess of broth, or chop of meat, in silence.* SPECTATOR.

CHO'PIN. *n.s.* [French.]
1. A French liquid measure, containing nearly a pint of Winchester.
2. A term used in Scotland for a quart, of wine measure.

CHO'PPING. *participial adj.* [In this sense, of uncertain etymology.] An epithet frequently applied to infants, by way of ludicrous commendation: imagined by *Skinner* to signify *lusty*, from *cas*, Sax. by others to mean a child that would bring money at a market. Perhaps a greedy, hungry child, likely to live.

Both Jack Freeman and Ned Wild,
Would own the fair and chopping *child.*
FENTON.

CHORO'GRAPHER. *n.s.* [from χωρή, a region, and γράφω, to describe.] He that describes particular regions or countries.

CHORO'GRAPHY. *n.s.* [See CHOROGRAPHER.] The art or

practice of describing particular regions, or laying down the limits and boundaries of particular provinces. It is less in its object than geography, and greater than topography.

CHRISM. *n.s.* [χρίζμα, an ointment.] Unguent; or unction: it is only applied to sacred ceremonies.

One act never to be repeated, is not the thing that Christ's eternal priesthood, denoted especially by his unction or chrism, *refers to.*
HAMMOND'S PRACTICAL CATECHISM.

CHRI'SOM. *n.s.* [See **CHRISM.**] A child that dies within a month after its birth. So called from the chrisom-cloath, a cloath anointed with holy unguent, which the children anciently wore till they were christened.

When the convulsions were but few, the number of chrisoms *and infants was greater.*
GRAUNT'S BILLS OF MORTALITY.

A **CHRISTMAS-BOX.** *n.s.* [from *christmas* and *box.*] A box in which little presents are collected at Christmas.

When time comes round, a Christmas-box *they bear,*
And one day makes them rich for all the year. GAY'S TRIVIA.

CHUCK-FARTHING. *n.s.* [*chuck* and *farthing.*] A play, at which the money falls with a chuck into the hole beneath.

He lost his money at chuck-farthing, *shuffle-cap, and all-fours.*
ARBUTHNOT'S HISTORY OF JOHN BULL.

CHUM. *n.s.* [*chom*, Armorick, to live together.] A chamber fellow; a term used in the universities.

CHURCH-ALE. *n.s.* [from *church* and *ale.*] A wake, or feast, commemoratory of the dedication of the church.

For the church-ale, *two young men of the parish are yearly chosen to be wardens, who make collection among the parishioners of what provision it pleaseth them to bestow.*
CAREW.

CHYLE. *n.s.* [χύλος.] The white juice formed in the stomach by digestion of the aliment, and afterwards changed into blood.

This powerful ferment, mingling with the parts,
The leven'd mass to milky chyle *converts.*
BLACKMORE'S CREATION.

The chyle *itself cannot pass through the smallest vessels.*
ARBUTHNOT ON ALIMENTS.

CHY'MIST. *n.s.* [See **CHYMISTRY.**] A professor of chymistry; a philosopher by fire.

The starving chymist, *in his golden views*
Supremely blest.
POPE'S ESSAY ON MAN, EPISTLE II.

CHY'MISTRY. *n.s.* [derived by some from χῦμος, juice, or χύω, to melt; by others from an oriental word, *kema*, black. According to the etymology, it is written with *y* or *e.*] An art whereby sensible bodies contained in vessels, or capable of being contained therein, are so changed, by means of certain instruments, and principally fire, that their several powers and virtues are thereby discovered, with a view to philosophy, or medicine. *Boerhaave.*

Operations of chymistry *fall short of vital force: no chymist can make milk or blood of grass.*
ARBUTHNOT ON ALIMENTS.

CI'METER. *n.s.* [*cimitarra*, Span. and Portug. from *chimeteir*, Turkish.

Bluteau's Portuguese Dictionaries.] A sort of sword used by the Turks; short; heavy; and recurvated, or bent backward. This word is sometimes erroneously spelt *scimitar*, and *scymeter*; as in the following examples.

By this scimitar,
That slew the sophy and a Persian prince,
That won three fields of sultan Solyman.
SHAKESPEARE'S MERCHANT OF VENICE.

Our armours now may rust, our idle scymiters
Hang by our sides for ornament, not use.
DRYDEN'S DON SEBASTIAN.

CINDER-WENCH, CINDER-WOMAN. *n.s.* [*cinder* and *woman.*] A woman whose trade is to rake in heaps of ashes for cinders.

'Tis under so much nasty rubbish laid,
To find it out's the cinder-woman's *trade.*
ESSAY ON SATIRE.

She had above five hundred suits of fine cloaths, and yet went abroad like a cinder-wench.
ARBUTHNOT'S HISTORY OF JOHN BULL.

In the black form of cinder-wench *she came,*
When love, the hour, the place had banish'd shame. GAY.

CIRCUMFORA'NEOUS. *adj.* [*circumforaneus*, Lat.] Wandering from house to house. As a *circumforaneous* fidler; one that plays at doors.

CIRCUMGYRA'TION. *n.s.* [from *circumgyrate.*] The act of running round.

The sun turns round his own axis in twenty-five days, which arises from his first being put into such a circumgyration.
CHEYNE'S PHILOSOPHICAL PRINCIPLES.

CIRCUMLOCU'TION. *n.s.* [*circumlocutio*, Latin.]

1. A circuit or compass of words; periphrasis.

Virgil, studying brevity, could bring these words into a narrow compass, which a translator cannot render without circumlocutions. DRYDEN.

I much prefer the plain Billingsgate way of calling names, because it would save abundance of time, lost by circumlocution.
SWIFT'S MISCELLANIES.

2. The use of indirect expressions.

These people are not to be dealt withal, but by a train of mystery and circumlocution.
L'ESTRANGE.

CIRCUMROTA'TION. *n.s.* [*circum* and *roto*, Lat.]

1. The act of whirling round with a motion like that of a wheel. Circumvolution.

2. The state of being whirled round.

CIRCUMSPE'CTION. *n.s.* [from *circumspect.*] Watchfulness on every side; cautious; general attention.

Observe the sudden growth of wickedness, from want of care and circumspection *in the first impressions.*
CLARENDON.

So saying, his proud step he scornful turn'd,
But with sly circumspection.
MILTON'S PARADISE LOST, B. IV.

To **CIRCUMVE'ST.** *v.a.* [*circumvestio*, Lat.] To cover round with a garment.

Who on this base the earth did'st firmly found,
And mad'st the deep to circumvest *it round.* WOTTON.

***CI'RCUS*, CIRQUE.** *n.s.* [*circus*, Latin.] An open space or area for sports, with seats round for the spectators.

A pleasant valley, like one of those circuses, *which, in great cities somewhere, doth give a pleasant spectacle of running horses.*
SIDNEY, B. II.

The one was about the cirque *of Flora, the other upon the Tarpeian mountain.*
STILLINGFLEET.

See the cirque *falls! th' unpillar'd temple nods;*
Streets pav'd with heroes, Tyber choak'd with gods. POPE.

CIT. *n.s.* [contracted from *citizen.*] An inhabitant of a city, in an ill sense. A pert low townsman; a pragmatical trader.

We bring you now to show what different things,
The cits *or clowns are from the courts of kings.* JONSON.

Study your race, or the soil of your family will dwindle into cits *or squires, or run up into wits or madmen.* TATLER.

Barnard, thou art a cit, *with all thy worth;*
But Bug and D—l, their honours, and so forth. POPE'S HORACE.

CI'TIZEN. *n.s.* [*civis*, Lat. *citoyen*, French.]

1. A freeman of a city; not a foreigner; not a slave.

All inhabitants within these walls are not properly citizens, *but only such as are called freemen.*
RALEIGH'S HISTORY OF THE WORLD.

2. A townsman; a man of trade; not a gentleman.

When he speaks not like a citizen,
You find him like a soldier.
SHAKESPEARE'S CORIOLANUS.

3. An inhabitant; a dweller in any place.

Far from noisy Rome, secure, he lives;
And one more citizen *to Sibyl gives.*
DRYDEN'S JUVENAL.

CI'TIZEN. *adj.* [This is only in *Shakespeare.*] Having the qualities of a citizen; as cowardice, meanness.

So sick I am not, yet I am not well;
But not so citizen *a wanton, as*
To seem to die ere sick.
SHAKESPEARE'S CYMBELINE.

CIVI'LIAN. *n.s.* [*civilis*, Lat.] One that professes the knowledge of the old Roman law, and of general equity.

The professors of that law, called civilians, *because the civil law is their guide, should not be discountenanced nor discouraged.*
BACON'S ADVICE TO VILLIERS.

A depending kingdom is a term of art, unknown to all ancient civilians, *and writers upon government.* SWIFT.

CI'VILLY. *adv.* [from *civil.*]

1. In a manner relating to government, or to the rights or character of a member of a community; not naturally; not ecclesiastically; not criminally.[54]

Men that are civil lead their lives after one common law; for that a multitude should, without harmony amongst themselves, concur in the doing of one thing; for this is civilly *to live; or should manage community of life, it is not possible.*
HOOKER, B. I. P. 46.

That accusation, which is publick, is either civilly *commenced for the private satisfaction of the party injured; or else criminally, that is, for some publick punishment.*
AYLIFFE.

2. Politely; complaisantly; gently; without rudeness; without brutality.

I will deal civilly *with his poems: nothing ill is to be spoken of the dead.*
DRYDEN'S PREFACE TO HIS FABLES.

I would have had Almeria and Osmyn parted civilly; *as if it was not proper for lovers to do so.*
COLLIER'S VIEW OF THE STAGE.

He thought them folks that lost their way,
And ask'd them civilly *to stay.* PRIOR.

3. Without gay or gaudy colours.

The chambers were handsome and cheerful, and furnished civilly.
BACON'S NEW ATLANTIS.

To **CLA'TTER.** *v.a.*

1. To strike any thing so as to make it sound and rattle.

I only with an oaken staff will meet thee,
And raise such outcries on thy clatter'd *iron,*
That thou oft' shalt wish thyself at Gath.
MILTON'S AGONISTES.

When all the bees are gone to settle,
You clatter *still your brazen kettle.*
SWIFT.

2. To dispute, jar, or clamour. *Martin.* A low word.

A **CLA'TTER.** *n.s.* [from the verb.]

1. A rattling noise made by the frequent and quick collision of sonorous bodies. A *clatter* is a *clash* often repeated with great quickness, and seems to convey the idea of a sound sharper and shriller than *rattle.* [See the verb.]

I have seen a monkey overthrow all the dishes and plates in a kitchen, merely for the pleasure of seeing them tumble, and hearing the clatter *they made in their fall.*
SWIFT TO LORD BOLINGBROKE.

2. It is used for any tumultuous and confused noise.

By this great clatter, *one of greatest note*
Seems bruited.
SHAKESPEARE'S MACBETH.

Grow to be short,
Throw by your clatter,
And handle the matter.
BEN JONSON'S UNDER-WOODS.

O Rourk's jolly boys
Ne'er dreamt of the matter,
'Till rous'd by the noise,
And musical clatter. SWIFT.

The jumbling particles of matter,
In chaos make not such a clatter.
SWIFT.

A **CLE'ANSER.** *n.s.* [*clænsere*, Sax.] That which has the quality of evacuating any foul humours; or digesting a sore; a detergent.

If there happens an imposthume, honey, and even honey of roses, taken inwardly, is a good cleanser.
ARBUTHNOT ON ALIMENTS.

CLEAR. *adj.* [*clair*, Fr. *klaer*, Dut. *clarus*, Latin.]

1. Bright; transpicuous; pellucid; transparent; luminous; without opacity or cloudiness; not nebulous; not opacous; not dark.

The stream is so transparent, pure and clear,
That had the self-enamour'd youth gaz'd here,
He but the bottom, not his face had seen.
DENHAM.

A tun about was ev'ry pillar there;
A polish'd mirrour shone not half so clear.
DRYDEN'S FABLES.[55]

2. Free from clouds; serene; as a clear day.

3. Without mixture; pure; unmingled.

4. Perspicuous; not obscure; not hard to be understood; not ambiguous.

We pretend to give a clear *account how thunder and lightning is produced.*
TEMPLE.

Many men reason exceeding clear *and rightly, who know not how to make a syllogism.* LOCKE.

5. Indisputable; evident; undeniable.

Remain'd to our almighty foe
Clear *victory; to our part loss, and rout*
Through all the empyrean.
MILTON'S PARADISE LOST, B. II.

6. Apparent; manifest; not hid; not dark.

Unto God, who understandeth all their secret cogitations, they are clear *and manifest.* HOOKER, B. III. SECT. 1.

The pleasure of right reasoning is still the greater, by how much the consequences are more clear, *and the chains of them more long.*
BURNET'S THEORY OF THE EARTH.

7. Unspotted; guiltless; irreproachable.

Duncan has been so clear *in his great office.* SHAKESPEARE.

Think that the clearest *gods, who make them honours*
Of mens impossibilities, have preserv'd thee. SHAKESPEARE'S KING LEAR.

Tho' the peripatetick philosophy has been most eminent in this way, yet other sects have not been wholly clear *of it.* LOCKE.

Statesman, yet friend to truth, in soul sincere,
In action faithful, and in honour clear.
POPE.

8. Unprepossessed; not preoccupied; impartial.

Leucippe, of whom one look, in a clear *judgment, would have been more acceptable than all her kindness, so prodigally bestowed.* SIDNEY, B. II.

9. Free from distress, prosecution, or imputed guilt.

The cruel corp'ral whisper'd in my ear,
Five pounds, if rightly tipt, would set me clear. GAY.

10. Free from deductions or incumbrances.

Hope, if the success happens to fail, is clear *gains, as long as it lasts.*
COLLIER AGAINST DESPAIR.

Whatever a foreigner, who purchases land here, gives for it, is so much every farthing clear *gain to the nation; for that money comes* clear *in, without carrying out any thing for it.* LOCKE.

I often wish'd that I had clear,
For life, six hundred pounds a year.
SWIFT.

11. Unincumbered; without let or hindrance; vacant; unobstructed.

If he be so far beyond his health,
Methinks he should the sooner pay his debts,
And make a clear *way to the gods.*
SHAKESPEARE'S TIMON.

A post boy winding his horn at us, my companion gave him two or three curses, and left the way clear *for him.*
ADDISON.

A clear *stage is left for Jupiter to display his omnipotence, and turn the fate of armies alone.* POPE'S ESSAY ON HOMER.

12. Out of debt.

13. Unintangled; at a safe distance from any danger or enemy.

Finding ourselves too slow of sail, we put on a compelled valour, and in the grapple I boarded them: on the instant they got clear *of our ship.* SHAKESPEARE'S HAMLET.

It requires care for a man with a double design to keep clear *of clashing with his own reasonings.* L'ESTRANGE.

14. Canorous; sounding distinctly, plainly; articulately.

I much approved of my friend's insisting upon the qualifications of a good aspect and a clear *voice.*
ADDISON'S SPECTATOR.

15. With *from*; free; guiltless.

I am clear *from the blood of this woman.*
BIBLE SUSAN, 46.

None is so fit to correct their faults, as he who is clear *from any in his own writings.*
DRYDEN'S JUVENAL, DEDICATION.

16. Sometimes with *of*.

The air is clearer *of gross and damp exhalations.* TEMPLE.

17. Used of persons. Distinguishing; judicious; intelligible: this is scarcely used but in conversation.

To **CLE'ARSTARCH.** *v.a.* [from *clear* and *starch.*] To stiffen with starch.

He took his present lodging at the mansion-house of a taylor's widow, who washes, and can clearstarch *his bands.* ADDISON.

CLI'CKER. *n.s.* [from *click.*] A low word for the servant of a salesman, who stands at the door to invite customers.

CLIENTE'LE. *n.s.* [*clientela*, Lat.] The condition or office of a client. A word scarcely used.

> *There's Varus holds good quarters with him;*
> *And, under the pretext of* clientele,
> *Will be admitted.*
> BEN JONSON'S CATILINE.

CLI'MATE. *n.s.* [*κλίμα.*]

1. A space upon the surface of the earth, measured from the equator to the polar circles; in each of which spaces the longest day is half an hour longer than in that nearer to the equator. From the polar circles to the poles climates are measured by the increase of a month.

2. In the common and popular sense, a region, or tract of land, differing from another by the temperature of the air.

> *Betwixt th' extremes, two happier* climates *hold*
> *The temper that partakes of hot and cold.*
> DRYDEN'S OVID.

> *On what new happy* climate *are we thrown?* DRYDEN.

> *This talent of moving the passions cannot be of any great use in the northern* climates. SWIFT.

CLINCH. *n.s.* [from the verb.]

1. A word used in a double meaning; a pun; an ambiguity; a duplicity of meaning, with an identity of expression.[56]

> *Such as they are, I hope they will prove, without a* clinch, *luciferous searching after the nature of light.* BOYLE.

> *Pure* clinches *the suburbian muse affords,*
> *And Panton waging harmless war with words.* DRYDEN.

> *Here one poor word a hundred* clinches *makes.* POPE.

2. That part of the cable which is fastened to the ring of the anchor.

CLI'NICAL, CLINICK. *adj.* [*κλίνω*, to lie down.] Those that keep their beds; those that are sick, past hopes of recovery. A *clinical convert*, one that is converted on his death-bed. This word occurs often in the works of *Taylor*.

CLOCK. *n.s.* [*clocc*, Welsh, from *clôch*, a bell, Welsh and Armorick; *cloche*, French.]

1. The instrument which, by a series of mechanical movements, tells the hour by a stroke upon a bell.

> *If a man be in sickness or pain, the time will seem longer without a* clock *or hour-glass than with it.* BACON.

> *The picture of Jerome usually described at his study, is with a* clock *hanging by.*
> BROWN'S VULGAR ERROURS, B. V. C. 17.

> *I told the* clocks, *and watch'd the wasting light.* DRYDEN.

2. It is an usual expression to say, *What is it of the clock*, for *What hour is it?* Or *ten o'clock*, for *the tenth hour.*

> What is't o'clock? ——
> —— *Upon the stroke of four.*
> SHAKESPEARE'S RICHARD III.

> *Macicaus set forward about* ten o'clock *in the night, towards Andrussa.*
> KNOLLES'S HISTORY OF THE TURKS.

> *About* nine of the clock *at night the king marched out of the North-port.*
> CLARENDON, B. VIII.

3. The clock of a stocking; the flowers or inverted work about the ankle.

> *His stockings with silver* clocks *were ravished from him.*
> SWIFT ON MODERN EDUCATION.

4. CLOCK is also the name of an insect; a sort of beetle. *Dictionaries.*

CLOUGH. *n.s.* [in commerce.] An allowance of two pounds in every hundred weight for the turn of the scale, that the commodity may hold out weight when sold by retail.

CLU'MSY. *adj.* [This word, omitted in the other etymologists, is rightly derived by *Bailey* from *lompsch*, Dutch, stupid. In English, *lump*, *clump*, *lumpish*, *clumpish*, *clumpishly*, *clumsily*, *clumsy*.] Awkward; heavy; artless; unhandy; without dexterity, readiness, or grace. It is used either of persons or actions, or things.

The matter ductile and sequacious, apt to be moulded into such shapes and machines, even by clumsy *fingers.* RAY.

But thou in clumsy *verse, unlick'd, unpointed,*
Hast shamefully defy'd. DRYDEN.

That clumsy *outside of a porter,*
How could it thus conceal a courtier?
SWIFT.

COACH. *n.s.* [*coche*, Fr. *kotczy*, among the Hungarians, by whom this vehicle is said to have been invented. *Minshew*.] A carriage of pleasure, or state, distinguished from a chariot by having seats fronting each other.

Basilius attended for her in a coach, *to carry her abroad to see some sports.*
SIDNEY, B. II.

A better would you fix?
Then give humility a coach *and six.*
POPE'S ESSAY ON MAN.

Suppose that last week my coach *was within an inch of overturning in a smooth even way, and drawn by very gentle horses.* SWIFT.

To **COACH.** *v.a.* [from the noun.] To carry in a coach.

The needy poet sticks to all he meets,
Coach'd, *carted, trod upon; now loose, now fast,*
And carry'd off in some dog's tail at last.
POPE'S DUNCIAD.

COACH-BOX. *n.s.* [*coach* and *box*.] The seat on which the driver of the coach sits.

Her father had two coachmen: when one was in the coach-box, *if the coach swung but the least to one side, she used to shriek.*
ARBUTHNOT'S HISTORY OF JOHN BULL.

CO'ALERY. *n.s.* [from *coal*.] A place where coals are dug.

Two fine stalactitæ were found hanging from a black stone, at a deserted vault in Benwell coalery.
WOODWARD ON FOSSILS.

To **COAX.** *v.a.* To wheedle; to flatter; to humour. A low word.

The nurse had changed her note; for she was then muzzling and coaxing *the child; that's a good dear, says she.* L'ESTRANGE.

I coax! *I wheedle! I'm above it.*
FARQUHAR'S RECRUITING OFFICER.

CO'CKFIGHT. *n.s.* [*cock* and *fight*.] A battle or match of cocks.

In cockfights, *to make one cock more hardy, and the other more cowardly.*
BACON'S NATURAL HISTORY, NO. 990.

At the seasons of football and cockfighting, *these little republicks reassume their national hatred to each other.* ADDISON.

CO'CKHORSE. *adj.* [*cock* and *horse*.] On horseback; triumphant; exulting.

Alma, they strenuously maintain,
Sits cockhorse *on her throne the brain.*
PRIOR.

CO'FFEEHOUSE. *n.s.* [*coffee* and *house*.] A house of entertainment where coffee is sold, and the guests are supplied with news papers.

At ten, from coffeehouse *or play,*
Returning, finishes the day. PRIOR.

It is a point they do not concern themselves

about, farther than perhaps as a subject in a coffeehouse. SWIFT.

CO'FFEEMAN. *n.s.* [*coffee* and *man.*] One that keeps a coffeehouse.

Consider your enemies the Lacedemonians; did ever you hear that they preferred a coffeeman *to Agesilaus?* ADDISON.

To **COG.** *v.a.* [A word of uncertain original, derived by *Skinner* from *coquel-iner*, French.]

1. To flatter; to wheedle; to sooth by adulatory speeches.

I'll mountebank their loves,
Cog *their hearts from them, and come*
home belov'd
Of all the trades in Rome.
SHAKESPEARE'S CORIOLANUS.

2. To obtrude by falsehood.

The outcry is, that I abuse his demonstration by a falsification, by cogging *in the word.* TILLOTSON, PREFACE.

I have cogged *in the word to serve my turn.* STILLINGFLEET.

Fustian tragedies, or insipid comedies, have, by concerted applauses, been cogged *upon the town for masterpieces.* DENNIS.

3. *To* COG *a die.* To secure it, so as to direct its fall; to falsify.

But then my study was to cog *the dice,*
And dext'rously to throw the lucky sice.
DRYDEN'S PERSIUS SATIRES.

For guineas in other men's breeches,
Your gamesters will palm and will cog.
SWIFT.

Ye gallants of Newgate, whose fingers are
nice
In diving in pockets, or cogging *of dice.*
SWIFT.

To **COG.** *v.n.* To lye; to wheedle.

Mrs. Ford, I cannot cog; I cannot prate,
Mrs. Ford: now shall I sin in my wish.
SHAKESPEARE'S MERRY WIVES OF WINDSOR.

COG. *n.s.* The tooth of a wheel, by which it acts upon another wheel.

To **COG.** *v.a.* [from the noun.] To fix cogs in a wheel.

To **CO'HOBATE.** *v.a.* To pour the distilled liquor upon the remaining matter, and distill it again.

The juices of an animal body are, as it were, cohobated, *being excreted and admitted again into the blood with the fresh aliment.*
ARBUTHNOT ON ALIMENTS.

COKE. *n.s.* [Perhaps from *coquo*, *Skinner.*] Fewel made by burning pit-coal under earth, and quenching the cinders; as charcoal is made with wood. It is frequently used in drying malt.

CO'LANDER. *n.s.* [*colo*, to strain, Lat.] A sieve either of hair, twigs or metal, through which a mixture to be separated is poured, and which retains the thicker parts.[57]

Take a thick woven osiar colander,
Through which the pressed wines are
strained clear. MAY.

All the viscera of the body are but as so many colanders *to separate several juices from the blood.*
RAY ON THE CREATION.

The brains from nose and mouth, and
either ear,
Came issuing forth, as through a colander
The curdled milk. DRYDEN.

COLD. *n.s.* [from the adjective.]

1. The cause of the sensation of cold; the privation of heat; the figorifick power.

Fair lined slippers for the cold.
SHAKESPEARE.

Heat and cold *are nature's two hands, whereby she chiefly worketh: and heat we have in readiness, in respect of the fire; but for* cold *we must stay 'till it cometh, or seek it in deep caves, or high mountains; and*

when all is done, we cannot obtain it in any great degree.
BACON'S NATURAL HISTORY, NO. 69.

2. The sensation of cold; coldness; chilness.

When she saw her lord prepar'd to part,
A deadly cold *ran shiv'ring to her heart.*
DRYDEN'S FABLES.

3. A disease caused by cold; the obstruction of perspiration.

What disease hast thou? —— A whorson cold, *sir; a cough.*
SHAKESPEARE'S HENRY IV. P. 2.

Let no ungentle cold *destroy*
All taste we have of heav'nly joy.
ROSCOMMON.

Those rains, so covering the earth, might providentially contribute to the disruption of it, by stopping all the pores, and all evaporation, which would make the vapours within struggle violently, as we get a fever by a cold. BURNET.

To **COLLA'PSE.** *v.n.* [*collabor, collapsus*, Latin.] To fall together; to close so as that one side touches the other.

In consumptions and atrophy the liquids are exhausted, and the sides of the canals collapse; *therefore the attrition is increased, and consequently the heat.*
ARBUTHNOT ON DIET.

COLLA'PSION. *n.s.* [from *collapse.*]
1. The state of vessels closed.
2. The act of closing or collapsing.

CO'LLEAGUE. *n.s.* [*collega*, Lat.] A partner in office or employment. Anciently accented on the last syllable.

Easy it might be seen that I intend
Mercy colleague *with justice, sending thee.* MILTON'S PARADISE LOST.

The regents, upon demise of the crown, would keep the peace without colleagues.
SWIFT.

COLLE'CTIBLE. *adj.* [from *collect.*] That which may be gathered from the premises by just consequence.

Whether thereby be meant Euphrates, is not collectible *from the following words.*
BROWN'S VULGAR ERROURS, B. VI. C. 8.

COLLE'CTIVELY. *adv.* [from *collective.*] In a general mass; in a body; not singly; not numbered by individuals; in the aggregate; accumulatively; taken together; in a state of combination or union.

Although we cannot be free from all sin collectively, *in such sort that no part thereof shall be found inherent in us, yet distributively all great actual offences, as they offer themselves one by one, both may and ought to be by all means avoided.*
HOOKER, B. V. SECT. 48.

Singly and apart many of them are subject to exception, yet collectively *they make up a good moral evidence.* HALE.

The other part of the water was condensed at the surface of the earth, and sent forth collectively *into standing springs and rivers.*
WOODWARD'S NATURAL HISTORY.

CO'LON. *n.s.* [κώλον.]
1. A point [:] used to mark a pause greater than that of a comma, and less than that of a period. Its use is not very exactly fixed, nor is it very necessary, being confounded by most with the semicolon. It was used before punctuation was refined, to mark almost any sense less than a period. To apply it properly, we should place it, perhaps, only where the sense is continued without dependence of grammar or construction; as, *I love him, I despise him: I have long ceased to trust, but shall never forbear to succour him.*
2. The greatest and widest of all the intestines, about eight or nine hands breadth long. It begins where the ilium

ends, in the cavity of the os ilium on the right side; from thence ascending by the kidney, on the same side, it passes under the concave side of the liver, to which it is sometimes tied, as likewise to the gall-bladder, which tinges it yellow in that place: then it runs under the bottom of the stomach to the spleen in the left side, to which it is also knit: from thence it turns down to the left kidney; and thence passing, in form of an S, it terminates at the upper part of the os sacrum, in the rectum. *Quincy.*

> *Now, by your cruelty hard bound,*
> *I strain my guts, my* colon *wound.*
> SWIFT.

> *The contents of the* colon *are of a sower, fetid, acid smell in rabbits.*
> FLOYER ON THE HUMOURS.

CO'LONEL. *n.s.* [Of uncertain etymology. *Skinner* imagines it originally *colonialis*, the leader of a colony. *Minshew* deduces it from *colonna*, a pillar; as *patriæ columen*; *exercitus columen*. Each is plausible.] The chief commander of a regiment; a field officer of the highest rank, next to the general officers. It is now generally sounded with only two distinct syllables, *col'nel.*

> *The chiefest help must be the care of the* colonel, *that hath the government of all his garrison.* SPENSER ON IRELAND.

> *Captain or* colonel, *or knight in arms,*
> *Whose chance on these defenceless doors may seize,*
> *If deed of honour did thee ever please,*
> *Guard them, and him within protect from harms.* MILTON.

CO'LUMN. *n.s.* [*columna*, Latin.]

1. A round pillar.

> *Some of the old Greek* columns, *and altars were brought from the ruins of Apollo's temple at Delos.* PEACHAM.

> *Round broken* columns *clasping ivy twin'd.* POPE.

2. Any body of certain dimensions pressing vertically upon its base.

> *The whole weight of any* column *of the atmosphere, and likewise the specifick gravity of its bases, are certainly known by many experiments.*
> BENTLEY'S SERMONS.

3. [In the military art.] The long file or row of troops, or of baggage, of an army in its march. An army marches in one, two, three, or more columns, according as the ground will allow.

4. [With printers.] A column is half a page, when divided into two equal parts by a line passing through the middle, from the top to the bottom; and, by several parallel lines, pages are often divided into three or more columns.

COMB. *n.s.* [*camb*, Saxon; *kam*, Dutch.]

1. An instrument to separate and adjust the hair.

> *By fair Ligea's golden* comb,
> *Wherewith she sits on diamond rocks,*
> *Sleeking her soft alluring locks.*
> MILTON.

> *I made an instrument in fashion of a* comb, *whose teeth, being in number sixteen, were about an inch and a half broad, and the intervals of the teeth about two inches wide.* NEWTON.

2. The top or crest of a cock, so called from its pectinated indentures.

> *Cocks have great* combs *and spurs, hens little or none.* BACON.

> *High was his* comb, *and coral-red withal,*
> *With dents embattl'd, like a castle-wall.*
> DRYDEN.

3. The cantons in which the bees lodge their honey. Perhaps from the same word which makes the termination of towns, and signifies hollow or deep.

This in affairs of state,
Employ'd at home, abides within the gate,
To fortify the combs, *to build the wall,*
To prop the ruins, lest the fabrick fall.
DRYDEN'S VIRGIL'S GEORGICKS.

COMBINA'TION. *n.s.* [from *combine.*]

1. Union for some certain purpose; association; league. A combination is of private persons, a confederacy of states or sovereigns.

This cunning cardinal
The articles o' th' combination *drew,*
As himself pleas'd.
SHAKESPEARE'S HENRY VIII.

2. It is now generally used in an ill sense; but was formerly indifferent.

They aim to subdue all to their own will and power, under the disguises of holy combinations. KING CHARLES.

3. Union of bodies, or qualities; commixture; conjunction.

These natures, from the moment of their first combination, *have been and are for ever inseparable.* HOOKER, B. V. S. 52.

Resolution of compound bodies by fire, does not so much enrich mankind as it divides the bodies; as upon the score of its making new compounds by new combinations. BOYLE.

Ingratitude is always in combination *with pride and hard-heartedness.* SOUTH'S SERMONS.

4. Copulation of ideas in the mind.

They never suffer any ideas to be joined in their understandings, in any other or stronger combination *than what their own nature and correspondence give them.* LOCKE.

5. COMBINATION is used in mathematicks, to denote the variation or alteration of any number of quantities, letters, sounds, or the like, in all the different manners possible. Thus the number of possible changes or *combinations* of the twenty-four letters of the alphabet, taken first two by two, then three by three, &c. amount to 1,391,724, 288,887,252,999,425,128,493,402,200. CHAMBERS.

COME'DIAN. *n.s.* [from *comedy.*]

1. A player or actor of comick parts.

2. A player in general; a stage-player; an actress or actor.

Melissarion, pretty honey-bee, when of a comedian *she became a wealthy man's wife, would be saluted madam Pithias, or Prudence.* CAMDEN'S REMAINS.

Comedians *on the stage shew all their skill,*
And after do as love and fortune will.[58]

3. A writer of comedies.

Scaliger willeth us to admire Plautus as a comedian, *but Terence as a pure and elegant speaker.* PEACHAM OF POETRY.

CO'MEDY. *n.s.* [*comedia*, Lat.] A dramatick representation of the lighter faults of mankind.[59]

Your honour's players
Are come to play a pleasant comedy.
SHAKESPEARE'S TAMING OF THE SHREW.

A long, exact, and serious comedy,
In every scene some moral let it teach,
And, if it can, at once both please and preach. POPE.

CO'MELY. *adj.* [from *become*; or from *cweman*, Sax. to please.]

1. Graceful; decent; having dignity or grandeur of mien or look. Comeliness seems to be that species of beauty which excites reverence rather than pleasure.

If the principal part of beauty is in decent motion, no marvel though persons in years seem many times more amiable; for no youth can be comely *but by pardon, and considering the youth as to make up the comeliness.* BACON, ESSAY 44.

He that is comely *when old and decrepit, surely was very beautiful when he was young.* SOUTH.

Thou art a comely, *young, and valiant knight.* DRYDEN.

2. Used of things, decent; according to propriety.

Oh, what a world is this, when what is comely
Envenoms him that bears it!
SHAKESPEARE'S AS YOU LIKE IT.

This is a happier and more comely *time,*
Than when these fellows ran about the streets,
Crying confusion.
SHAKESPEARE'S CORIOLANUS.

CO'MICK. *adj.* [*comicus*, Lat. *comique*, French.]

1. Relating to comedy.

When I venture at the comick *stile,*
Thy scornful lady seems to mock my toil.
WALLER.

A comick *subject loves an humble verse,*
Thyestes scorns a low and comick *stile;*
Yet comedy sometimes may raise her voice. ROSCOMMON.

Thy tragick muse gives smiles, thy comick *sleep.* DRYDEN.

2. Raising mirth.

Stately triumphs, mirthful comick *shows,*
Such as befit the pleasure.
SHAKESPEARE'S HENRY VI. P. III.

COMING-IN. *n.s.* Revenue; income.

Here's a small trifle of wives, eleven widows and nine maids is a simple coming-in *for one man.* SHAKESPEARE.

What are thy rents? what are thy comings-in?
O ceremony, shew me but thy worth:
What is thy toll, O adoration?
SHAKESPEARE'S HENRY V.

CO'MMA. *n.s.* [*κόμμα*.]

1. The point which notes the distinction of clauses, and order of construction in the sentence, marked thus [,].

Comma's *and points they set exactly right.* POPE.

2. The ninth part of a tone, or the interval whereby a semitone or a perfect tone exceeds the imperfect tone. It is a term used only in theorical musick, to shew the exact proportions between concords. *Harris.*

COMMA'NDRESS. *n.s.* [from *commander.*] A woman vested with supreme authority.

To prescribe the order of doing in all things is a peculiar prerogative, which wisdom hath, as queen or sovereign commandress, *over all other virtues.*
HOOKER, B. V. SECT. 8.

Be you commandress *therefore, princess, queen*
Of all our forces, be thy word a law.
FAIRFAX, B. II.

COMMENSURABI'LITY. *n.s.* [from *commensurable.*] Capacity of being compared with another, as to the measure; or of being measured by another. Thus an inch and a yard are commensurable, a yard containing a certain number of inches. The diameter and circumference of a circle are incommensurable, not being reduceable to any common measure. Proportion.

Some place the essence thereof in the proportion of parts, conceiving it to consist in a comely commensurability *of the whole unto the parts, and the parts between themselves.* BROWN.

To CO'MMIGRATE. *v.n.* [*con* and *migro*, Latin.] To remove in a body, or by consent, from one country to another.

CO'MMON. *n.s.* [*communis*, Latin.]

1. Belonging equally to more than one.

Though life and sense be common *to man and brutes, and their operations in many things alike; yet by this form he lives the life of a man, and not of a brute, and hath the sense of a man, and not of a brute.* HALE'S ORIGIN OF MANKIND.

He who hath received damage, has, besides the right of punishment common *to him with other men, a particular right to seek reparation.* LOCKE.

2. Having no possessor or owner.

Where no kindred are to be found, we see the possession of a private man revert to the community, and so become again perfectly common, *no body having a right to inherit them; nor can any one have a property in them, otherwise than in other things common by nature.* LOCKE.

3. Vulgar; mean; not distinguished by any excellence; often seen; easy to be had; of little value; not rare; not scarce.

Or as the man whom princes do advance,
Upon their gracious mercy-seat to sit,
Doth common *things, of course and circumstance,*
To the reports of common men commit.
DAVIES.

4. Publick; general; serving the use of all.

He was advised by a parliament-man not to be strict in reading all the common *prayer, but make some variation.* WALTON.

I need not mention the old common *shore of Rome, which ran from all parts of the town, with the current and violence of an ordinary river.* ADDISON ON ITALY.

5. Of no rank; mean; without birth or descent.

Look, as I blow this feather from my face,
And as the air blows it to me again,
Such is the lightness of you common *men.*
SHAKESPEARE'S HENRY VI.

Flying bullets now,
To execute his rage, appear too slow;
They miss, or sweep but common *souls away,*
For such a loss Opdam his life must pay.
WALLER.

6. Frequent; usual; ordinary.

There is an evil which I have seen common *among men.* BIBLE ECCLESIASTES, VI. 1.

The Papists were the most common *place, and the butt against whom all the arrows were directed.* CLARENDON.

Neither is it strange that there should be mysteries in divinity, as well as in the commonest *operations in nature.* SWIFT.

7. Prostitute.

'Tis a strange thing, the impudence of some women! was the word of a dame, who herself was common. L'ESTRANGE.

Hipparchus was going to marry a common *woman, but consulted Philander upon the occasion.* SPECTATOR, NO. 475.

8. [In grammar.] Such verbs as signify both action and passion are called *common*; as *aspernor*, *I despise*, or *am despised*; and also such nouns as are both masculine and feminine, as *parens*.

COMMON LAW contains those customs and usages which have, by long prescription, obtained in this nation the force of laws. It is distinguished from the statute law, which owes its authority to acts of parliament.

CO'MMONAGE. *n.s.* [from *common.*] The right of feeding on a common; the joint right of using any thing in common with others.

COMMUNICA'TION. *n.s.* [from *communicate.*]

1. The act of imparting benefits or knowledge.

Both together serve completely for the reception and communication *of learned knowledge.* HOLDER'S ELEMENTS OF SPEECH.

2. Common boundary or inlet; passage or means, by which from one place there is a way without interruption to another.

The map shews the natural communication *providence has formed between the rivers and lakes of a country at so great a distance from the sea.*
ADDISON ON ITALY.

The Euxine sea is conveniently situated for trade, by the communication *it has both with Asia and Europe.* ARBUTHNOT.

3. Interchange of knowledge; good intelligence between several persons.

Secrets may be carried so far, as to stop the communication *necessary among all who have the management of affairs.* SWIFT.

4. Conference; conversation.

Abner had communication *with the elders of Israel, saying, ye fought for David in times past to be king over you: now then do it.* BIBLE 2 SAMUEL, III. 17.

The chief end of language, in communication, *being to be understood, words serve not for that end, when any word does not excite in the hearers the same idea which it stands for in the mind of the speaker.*
LOCKE.

To **COMMU'TE.** *v.a.* [*commuto*, Latin.]

1. To exchange; to put one thing in the place of another; to give or receive one thing for another.

This will commute *our tasks, exchange these pleasant and gainful ones, which God assigns, for those uneasy and fruitless ones we impose on ourselves.*
DECAY OF PIETY.

2. To buy off, or ransom one obligation by another.

Some commute *swearing for whoring; as if forbearance of the one were a dispensation for the other.* L'ESTRANGE.

To **COMMU'TE.** *v.n.* To attone; to bargain for exemption.

Those institutions which God designed for means to further men in holiness, they look upon as a privilege to serve instead of it, and to commute *for it.*
SOUTH'S SERMONS.

To **COMPA'RE.** *v.a.* [*comparo*, Latin.]

1. To make one thing the measure of another; to estimate the relative goodness or badness, or other qualities, of any one thing, by observing how it differs from something else.

I will hear Brutus speak. ——
I will hear Cassius, and compare *their reasons.* SHAKESPEARE.

They measuring themselves by themselves, and comparing *themselves among themselves, are not wise.*
BIBLE 2 CORINTHIANS, X. 12.

No man can think it grievous, who considers the pleasure and sweetness of love, and the glorious victory of overcoming evil with good; and then compares *these with the restless torment, and perpetual tumults, of a malicious and revengeful spirit.*
TILLOTSON, SERMON VI.

He that has got the ideas of numbers, and hath taken the pains to compare *one, two, and three to six, cannot chuse but know they are equal.* LOCKE.

Thus much of the wrong judgment men make of present and future pleasure and pain, when they are compared *together, and so the absent considered as future.*
LOCKE.

2. It may be observed, that when the comparison intends only similitude or illustration by likeness, we use *to* before the thing brought for illustration; as, he *compared* anger *to* a fire.

Solon compared *the people unto the sea, and orators and counsellors to the winds; for that the sea would be calm and quiet, if the winds did not trouble it.*
BACON'S APOPHTHEGMS.

3. When two persons or things are compared, to discover their relative proportion of any quality, *with* is used before the thing used as a measure.

Black Macbeth
Will seem as pure as snow, being compar'd
With my confineless harms.
SHAKESPEARE'S MACBETH.

To compare
Small things with greatest.
MILTON'S PARADISE REGAIN'D, B. IV.

He carv'd in iv'ry such a maid so fair,
As nature could not with his art compare.
DRYDEN.

If he compares *this translation with the original, he will find that the three first stanzas are rendered almost word for word.*
ADDISON'S SPECTATOR, NO. 229.

4. *To compare* is, in *Spenser*, used after the Latin *comparo*, for to get; to procure; to obtain.

But, both from back and belly, still did spare
To fill his bags, and riches to compare.
FAIRY QUEEN, B. I.

COMPA'TIBLE. *adj.* [corrupted, by an unskilful compliance with pronunciation, from *competible*, from *competo*, Latin, to suit, to agree. *Competible* is found in good writers, and ought always to be used.]
1. Suitable to; fit for; consistent with; not incongruous to.

The object of the will is such a good as is compatible *to an intellectual nature.*
HALE'S ORIGIN OF MANKIND.

2. Consistent; agreeable.

Our poets have joined together such qualities as are by nature the most compatible; *valour with anger, meekness with piety, and prudence with dissimulation.*
BROOME.

COMPE'NDIOUS. *adj.* [from *compendium.*] Short; summary; abridged; direct; comprehensive; holding much in a narrow space; near; by which time is saved, and circuition cut off.

They had learned more compendious *and expeditious ways, whereby they shortened their labours, and so gained time.*
WOODWARD'S NATURAL HISTORY.

COMPE'NDIUM. *n.s.* [Latin.] Abridgment; summary; breviate; abbreviature; that which holds much in a narrow room; the near way.

After we are grown well acquainted with a short system or compendium *of a science, which is written in the plainest and most simple manner, it is then proper to read a larger regular treatise on that subject.*
WATTS'S IMPROVEMENT OF THE MIND.

COMPE'TIBLE. *adj.* [from *competo*, Latin. For this word a corrupt orthography has introduced *compatible.*] Suitable to; consistent with.

It is not competible *with the grace of God so much as to incline any man to do evil.*
HAMMOND ON FUNDAMENTALS.

Those are properties not at all competible *to body or matter, though of never so pure a mixture.* GLANVILLE.

CO'MPLIMENT. *n.s.* [*compliment*, Fr.] An act, or expression of civility, usually understood to include some hypocrisy, and to mean less than it declares.[60]

He observed few compliments *in matter of arms, but such as proud anger did indite to him.* SIDNEY, B. II.

My servant, sir? 'Twas never merry world
Since lowly feigning was call'd compliment:
Y' are servant to the duke Orsino, youth.
SHAKESPEARE.

One whom the musick of his own vain tongue
Doth ravish, like inchanting harmony:

A man of compliments, *whom right and wrong*
Have chose as umpire of their meeting.
SHAKESPEARE.

What honour that,
But tedious waste of time, to sit and hear
So many hollow compliments *and lies,*
Outlandish flatteries?
MILTON'S PARADISE REGAIN'D, B. IV.

Virtue and religion, heaven and eternal happiness, are not trifles to be given up in a compliment, *or sacrificed to a jest.* ROGERS, SERMON X.

COMPOTA'TION. *n.s.* [*compotatio*, Lat.] The act of drinking or tippling together.

Secrecy to words spoke under the rose, only mean, in compotation, *from the ancient custom in symposiack meetings, to wear chaplets of roses.* BROWN'S VULGAR ERROURS.

If thou wilt prolong
Dire compotation, *forthwith reason quits*
Her empire to confusion and misrule,
And vain debates; then twenty tongues at once
Conspire in senseless jargon; naught is heard
But din and various clamour, and mad rant. PHILLIPS.

COMPRESSIBI'LITY. *n.s.* [from *compressible.*] The quality of being compressible; the quality of admitting to be brought by force into a narrower compass; as air may be compressed, but water can by no violence be reduced to less space than it naturally occupies.

To **COMPTRO'LL.** *v.a.* [This word is written by some authors, who did not attend to the etymology, for *controll*; and some of its derivatives are written in the same manner.] To controll; to over-rule; to oppose.

COMPU'TER. *n.s.* [from *compute.*] Reckoner; accountant; calculator.

The kalendars of these computers, *and the accounts of these days, are different.* BROWN'S VULGAR ERROURS, B. VI. C. 4.

I have known some such ill computers, *as to imagine the many millions in stocks so much real wealth.* SWIFT.

CO'MPUTIST. *n.s.* [*computiste*, Fr.] Calculator; one skilled in the art of numbers or computation.

The treasurer was a wise man, and a strict computist. WOTTON.

We conceive we have a year in three hundred and sixty-five days exact: computists *tell us, that we escape six hours.* BROWN.

CON. A Latin inseparable preposition, which, at the beginning of words, signifies union or association; as *concourse*, a running together; to *convene*, to come together.

CONCE'RNING. *prep.* [from *concern*: this word, originally a participle, has before a noun the force of a preposition.] Relating to; with relation to.

There is not any thing more subject to errour than the true judgment concerning *the power and forces of an estate.* BACON.

The ancients had no higher recourse than to nature, as may appear by a discourse concerning *this point in Strabo.* BROWN.

None can demonstrate that there is such an island as Jamaica, yet, upon testimony, I am free from all doubt concerning *it.* TILLOTSON, PREFACE.

To **CONCOA'GULATE.** *v.a.* [from *con* and *coagulate.*] To curdle or congeal one thing with another.

The saline parts of those, upon their

solution by the rain, may work upon those other substances, formerly concoagulated *with them.* BOYLE'S EXPERIMENTS.

They do but coagulate themselves, without concoagulating *with them any water.* BOYLE'S HISTORY OF FIRMNESS.

CONCO'CTION. *n.s.* [from *concoct.*] Digestion in the stomach; maturation by heat; the acceleration of any thing towards purity and perfection.

This hard rolling is between concoction *and a simple maturation.* BACON'S NATURAL HISTORY, NO. 324.

The constantest notion of concoction *is, that it should signify the degrees of alteration of one body into another, from crudity to perfect* concoction, *which is the ultimity of that action or process.* BACON'S NATURAL HISTORY, NO. 324.

He, though he knew not which soul spake,
Because both meant, both spake the same,
Might thence a new concoction *take,*
And part far purer than he came.
DONNE.

CONCO'RDANCE. *n.s.* [*concordantia*, Latin.]

1. Agreement.
2. A book which shews in how many texts of scripture any word occurs.

I shall take it for an opportunity to tell you, how you are to rule the city out of a concordance. SOUTH'S SERMONS, DEDICATION.

Some of you turn over a concordance, *and there, having the principal word, introduce as much of the verse as will serve your turn.* SWIFT.

An old concordance *bound long since.* SWIFT.

3. A concord in grammar; one of the three chief relations in speech. It is not now in use in this sense.

After the three concordances *learned, let the master read unto him the epistles of Cicero.* ASCHAM'S SCHOOLMASTER.

CONCREMA'TION. *n.s.* [from *concremo*, Lat. to burn together.] The act of burning many things together. *Dictionaries.*

CO'NCREMENT. *n.s.* [from *concresco*, Latin.] The mass formed by concretion; a collection of matter growing together.

There is the cohesion of the matter into a more loose consistency, like clay, and thereby it is prepared to the concrement *of a pebble or flint.* HALE'S ORIGIN OF MANKIND.

CONCRE'SCENCE. *n.s.* [from *concresco*, Lat.] The act or quality of growing by the union of separate particles.

Seeing it is neither a substance perfect, nor inchoate, how any other substance should thence take concrescence *hath not been taught.* RALEIGH'S HISTORY OF THE WORLD.

CONCU'SSION. *n.s.* [*concussio*, Lat.] The act of shaking; agitation; tremefaction.

It is believed that great ringing of bells in populous cities, hath dissipated pestilent air; which may be from the concussion *of the air.* BACON'S NATURAL HISTORY, NO. 127.

There want not instances of such an universal concussion *of the whole globe, as must needs imply an agitation of the whole abyss.* WOODWARD'S NATURAL HISTORY, P. III.[61]

The strong concussion *on the heaving tide,*
Roll'd back the vessel to the island's side.
POPE'S ODYSSEY.

CONDI'GN. *adj.* [*condignus*, Latin.] Worthy of a person; suitable; deserved;

merited: it is always used of something deserved by crimes.

Unless it were a bloody murtherer,
I never gave them condign *punishment.*
SHAKESPEARE'S HENRY VI.

Consider who is your friend, he that would have brought him to condign *punishment, or he that has saved him.* ARBUTHNOT.

CO'NDIMENT. *n.s.* [*condimentum*, Latin.] Seasoning; sauce; that which excites the appetite by a pungent taste.

As for radish and the like, they are for condiments, *and not for nourishment.* BACON'S NATURAL HISTORY.

Many things are swallowed by animals rather for condiment, *gust, or medicament, than any substantial nutriment.* BROWN.

To **CO'NDITE.** *v.a.* [*condio*, Lat.] To pickle; to preserve by salts or aromaticks.

Much after the same manner as the sugar doth, in the conditing *of pears, quinces, and the like.* GREW'S MUSÆUM.

The most innocent of them are but like condited *or pickled mushrooms, which, carefully corrected, may be harmless, but can never do good.* TAYLOR'S RULE OF LIVING HOLY.

To **CONDO'LE.** *v.n.* [*condoleo*, Latin.] To lament with those that are in misfortune; to express concern for the miseries of others. It has *with* before the person for whose misfortune we profess grief.

Your friends would have cause to rejoice, rather than condole *with you.* TEMPLE.

I congratulate with the republick of beasts upon this honour done to their king; and must condole *with us poor mortals, who, by distance, are rendered incapable of paying our respects.* ADDISON'S GUARDIAN, NO. 118.

To **CONDO'LE.** *v.a.* To bewail with another.

I come not, Sampson, to condole *thy chance,*
As these perhaps, yet wish it had not been,
Though for no friendly intent.
MILTON'S AGONISTES, L. 1076.

Why should our poet petition Isis for her safe delivery, and afterwards condole *her miscarriage.* DRYDEN.

CONDO'LENCE. *n.s.* [*condolance*, French.] The expression of grief for the sorrows of another; the civilities and messages of friends upon any loss or misfortune.

The reader will excuse this digression, due by way of condolence *to my worthy brethren.* ARBUTHNOT'S PREFACE TO JOHN BULL.

To **CONFA'BULATE.** *v.n.* [*confabulo*, Lat.] To talk easily or carelessly together; to chat; to prattle.

CONFARREA'TION. *n.s.* [*confarreatio*, Lat. from *far*, corn.] The solemnization of marriage by eating bread together.

By the ancient laws of Romulus, the wife was by confarreation *joined to the husband.* AYLIFFE'S PARERGON.

To **CONFE'R.** *v.n.* [*confero*, Lat. *conferer*, French.] To discourse with another upon a stated subject; to ventilate any question by oral discussion; to converse solemnly; to talk gravely together; to compare sentiments.

You will hear us confer *of this, and by an auricular assurance have your satisfaction.* SHAKESPEARE'S KING LEAR.

Reading makes a full man, conference a ready man, and writing an exact man; and therefore, if a man write little, he had need have a great memory; if he confer *little, he had need have a present wit; and if he read little, he had need have much cunning, to seem to know that he doth not.* BACON.

When they had commanded them to go aside out of the council, they conferred *among themselves.* BIBLE ACTS, IV. 15.

He was thought to confer *with the lord Colepeper upon the subject; but had some particular thoughts, upon which he then* conferred *with nobody.*
CLARENDON, B. VIII.

The Christian princess in her tent
  confers
With fifty of your learn'd philosophers;
Whom with such eloquence she does
  persuade,
That they are captives to her reasons
  made. DRYDEN'S TYRANNICK LOVE.

CO'NFESSOR. *n.s.* [*confesseur*, French.]

1. One who makes profession of his faith in the face of danger. He who dies for religion is a martyr; he who suffers for it is a confessor.

The doctrine in the thirty-nine articles is so orthodoxly settled, as cannot be questioned without danger to our religion, which hath been sealed with the blood of so many martyrs and confessors.
BACON'S ADVICE TO VILLIERS.

Was not this an excellent confessor *at least, if not a martyr in this cause?*
STILLINGFLEET.

The patience and fortitude of a martyr or confessor *lie concealed in the flourishing times of Christianity.*
ADDISON'S SPECTATOR.

It was the assurance of a resurrection that gave patience to the confessor, *and courage to the martyr.* ROGERS, SERMON VIII.

2. He that hears confessions, and prescribes rules and measures of penitence.

See that Claudio
Be executed by nine to-morrow morning:
Bring him his confessor, *let him be*
  prepar'd;
For that's the utmost of his pilgrimage.
SHAKESPEARE.

If you find any sin that lies heavy upon you, disburthen yourself of it into the bosom of your confessor, *who stands between God and you to pray for you.*
TAYLOR.

One must be trusted; and he thought her
  fit,
As passing prudent, and a parlous wit:
To this sagacious confessor *he went,*
And told her.
DRYDEN'S WIFE OF BATH.

3. He who confesses his crimes. *Dictionaries.*

CONFORMA'TION. *n.s.* [French; *conformatio*, Latin.]

1. The form of things as relating to each other; the particular texture, and consistence of the parts of a body, and their disposition to make a whole; as, *light of different colours is reflected from bodies according to their different* conformation.

Varieties are found in the different natural shapes of the mouth, and several conformations *of the organs.*
HOLDER'S ELEMENTS OF SPEECH.

Where there happens to be such a structure and conformation *of the earth, as that the fire may pass freely unto these spiracles, it then readily gets out.*
WOODWARD'S NATURAL HISTORY.

2. The act of producing suitableness, or conformity to any thing.[62]

Virtue and vice, sin and holiness, and the conformation *of our hearts and lives to the duties of true religion and morality, are things of more consequence than the furniture of understanding.* WATTS.

CONFO'UNDED. *participial adj.* [from *confound.*] Hateful; detestable; enormous; odious: a low cant word.

A most confounded *reason for his brutish conception.* GREW.

Sir, I have heard another story,
He was a most confounded *Tory;*
And grew, or he is much bely'd,
Extremely dull before he dy'd. SWIFT.

To **CONGLA'CIATE.** *v.n.* [*conglaciatus*, Latin.] To turn to ice.

No other doth properly conglaciate *but water; for the determination of quicksilver is properly fixation, and that of milk coagulation.*
BROWN'S VULGAR ERROURS, B. II. C. 1.

To **CO'NGLOBATE.** *v.a.* [*conglobatus*, Latin.] To gather into a hard firm ball.

The testicle, as is said, is one large conglobated *gland, consisting of soft fibres, all in one convolution.*
GREW'S COSMOLOGIA SACRA.

To **CONGLO'MERATE.** *v.a.* [*conglomero*, Lat.] To gather into a ball, like a ball of thread; to inweave into a round mass.

The liver is one great conglomerated *gland, composed of innumerable small glands, each of which consisteth of soft fibres, in a distinct or separate convolution.*
GREW'S COSMOLOGIA SACRA.

To **CONGRA'TULATE.** *v.a.* [*gratulor*, Latin.]

1. To compliment upon any happy event; to express joy for the good of another.

I congratulate *our English tongue, that it has been enriched with words from all our neighbours.* WATTS'S LOGICK.

2. It has sometimes the accusative case of the cause of joy, and *to* before the person.

An ecclesiastical union within yourselves, I am rather ready to congratulate *to you.*
SPRATT'S SERMONS.

The subjects of England may congratulate *to themselves, that the nature of our government and the clemency of our king secure us.*
DRYDEN'S PREFACE TO AURENGZEBE.

CONGRA'TULATE. *v.n.* To rejoice in participation.

I cannot but, with much pleasure, congratulate *with my dear country, which hath outdone all Europe in advancing conversation.*
SWIFT'S INTRODUCTION TO GENTEEL CONVERSATION.

To **CONJO'BBLE.** *v.a.* [from *con*, together, and *jobbernol*, the head.] To concert; to settle; to discuss. A low cant word.

What would a body think of a minister that should conjobble *matters of state with tumblers, and confer politicks with tinkers?* L'ESTRANGE.

CO'NJURER. *n.s.* [from *conjure.*]

1. An enchanter; one that uses charms.

Good doctor Pinch, you are a conjurer;
Establish him in his true sense again.
SHAKESPEARE'S COMEDY OF ERROURS.

Figures in the book
Of some dread conjurer, *that would enforce nature.* DONNE.

Thus has he done you British consorts right,
Whose husbands, should they pry like mine to-night,
Would never find you in your conduct slipping,
Though they turn'd conjurers *to take you tripping.* ADDISON.

2. An impostor who pretends to secret arts; a cunning man.

From the account the loser brings,
The conj'rer *knows who stole the things.*
PRIOR.

3. By way of irony; a man of shrewd conjecture; a man of sagacity.

Though ants are very knowing, I don't take them to be conjurers; *and therefore*

they could not guess that I had put some corn in that room.
ADDISON, GUARDIAN, NO. 156.

CONNOISSE'UR. *n.s.* [French.] A judge; a critick: it is often used of a pretended critick.

Your lesson learnt, you'll be secure
To get the name of connoisseur.
SWIFT.

CO'NSCRIPT. *adj.* [from *conscribo*, Latin.] A term used in speaking of the Roman senators, who were called *Patres conscripti*, from their names being written in the register of the senate.

To **CONSE'NT.** *v.n.* [*consentio*, Latin.]
1. To be of the same mind; to agree.[63]
2. To co-operate to the same end.
3. To yield; to give consent; to allow; to admit. With *to*.

Ye comets, scourge the bad revolting stars
That have consented *unto Henry's death.*
SHAKESPEARE'S HENRY VI.

In this we consent *unto you, if ye will be as we be.* BIBLE GENESIS.

Their num'rous thunder would awake
Dull earth, which does with heav'n consent
To all they wrote. WALLER.

CONSENTA'NEOUS. *adj.* [*consentaneus*, Latin.] Agreeable to; consistent with.

In the picture of Abraham sacrificing his son, Isaac is described a little boy; which is not consentaneous *unto the circumstance of the text.*
BROWN'S VULGAR ERROURS, B. V. C. 8.

It will cost no pains to bring you to the knowing, nor to the practice, it being very agreeable and consentaneous *to every one's nature.*
HAMMOND'S PRACTICAL CATECHISM.

CONSENTA'NEOUSLY. *adv.* [from *consentaneous.*] Agreeably; consistently; suitably.

Paracelsus did not always write so consentaneously *to himself, that his opinions were confidently to be collected from every place of his writings, where he seems to express it.* BOYLE.

CONSENTA'NEOUSNESS. *n.s.* [from *consentaneous.*] Agreement; consistence. *Dictionaries.*

CONSE'NTIENT. *adj.* [*consentiens*, Latin.] Agreeing; united in opinion; not differing in sentiment.

The authority due to the consentient *judgment and practice of the universal church.*
OXFORD REASONS AGAINST THE COVENANT.

CONSE'RVANCY. *n.s.* [from *conservans*, Latin.] Courts held by the Lord Mayor of London for the preservation of the fishery on the river Thames, are called *Courts of Conservancy.*

CONSERVA'TION. *n.s.* [*conservatio*, Latin.]
1. The act of preserving; care to keep from perishing; continuance; protection.

Though there do indeed happen some alterations in the globe, yet they are such as tend rather to the benefit and conservation *of the earth, and its productions, than to the disorder and destruction of both.*
WOODWARD'S NATURAL HISTORY.

2. Preservation from corruption.

It is an enquiry of excellent use, to enquire of the means of preventing or staying of putrefaction; for therein consisteth the means of conservation *of bodies.*
BACON'S NATURAL HISTORY.

CONSE'RVATIVE. *adj.* [from *conservo*, Latin.] Having the power of opposing diminution or injury.

The spherical figure, as to all heavenly bodies, so it agreeeth to light, as the most perfect and conservative *of all others.*
PEACHAM.

CONSE'RVATORY. *n.s.* [from *conservo*, Latin.] A place where any thing is kept in a manner proper to its peculiar nature; as, fish in a pond, corn in a granary.

A conservatory *of snow and ice, such as they use for delicacy to cool wine in summer.*
BACON'S NATURAL HISTORY, NO. 70.

You may set your tender trees and plants, with the windows and doors of the green-houses and conservatories *open, for eight or ten days before April.*
EVELYN'S KALENDAR.

The water dispensed to the earth and atmosphere by the great abyss, that subterranean conservatory *is by that means restored back.*
WOODWARD'S NATURAL HISTORY.

CONSI'DERATE. *adj.* [*consideratus*, Latin.]

1. Serious; given to consideration; prudent; not rash; not negligent.

I will converse with iron-witted fools,
And unrespective boys: none are for me,
That look into me with consid'rate *eyes.*
SHAKESPEARE'S RICHARD III.

Æneas is patient, considerate, *and careful of his people.*
DRYDEN'S FABLES, PREFACE.

I grant it to be in many cases certain, that it is such as a considerate *man may prudently rely and proceed upon, and hath no just cause to doubt of.*
TILLOTSON, PREFACE.

The expediency in the present juncture, may appear to every considerate *man.*
ADDISON'S FREEHOLDER, NO. 16.

2. Having respect to; regardful.[64]

Though they will do nothing for virtue, yet they may be presumed more considerate *of praise.*
DECAY OF PIETY.

3. Moderate; not rigorous. This sense is much used in conversation.

CO'NSOLATE. *v.a.* [*consolor*, Latin] To comfort; to console; to ease in misery.[65]

I will be gone,
That pitiful rumour may report my flight,
To consolate *thine ear.*
SHAKESPEARE'S ALL'S WELL THAT ENDS WELL.

What may somewhat consolate *all men that honour virtue, we do not discover the latter scene of his misery in authors of antiquity.*
BROWN'S VULGAR ERROURS, B. VII. C. 17.

To **CONSO'LE.** *v.a.* [*consolor*, Lat.] To comfort; to cheer; to free from the sense of misery.

Others the syren sisters compass round,
And empty heads console *with empty sound.* POPE'S DUNCIAD.

CO'NSONANT. *n.s.* [*consonans*, Latin.] A letter which cannot be sounded, or but imperfectly, by itself.

In all vowels the passage of the mouth is open and free, without any appulse of an organ of speech to another: but in all consonants *there is an appulse of the organs, sometimes (if you abstract the* consonants *from the vowels) wholly precluding all sound; and, in all of them, more or less checking and abetting it.*
HOLDER'S ELEMENTS OF SPEECH.

He considered these as they had a greater mixture of vowels or consonants, *and accordingly employed them as the verse required a greater smoothness.*
POPE'S ESSAY ON HOMER.

CONSTERNA'TION. *n.s.* [from *consterno*, Latin.] Astonishment; amazement; alienation of mind by a surprise; surprise; wonder.

They find the same holy consternation *upon themselves that Jacob did at Bethel, which he called the gate of heaven.* SOUTH.

The natives, dubious whom
They must obey, in consternation *wait,*
'Till rigid conquest will pronounce their liege. PHILIPS.

To **CO'NSTIPATE.** *v.a.* [from *constipo*, Latin.]

1. To croud together into a narrow room; to thicken; to condense.

Of cold, the property is to condense and constipate. BACON.

It may, by amassing, cooling, and constipating *of waters, turn them into rain.* RAY ON THE CREATION.

There might arise some vertiginous motions or whirlpools in the matter of the chaos, whereby the atoms might be thrust and crouded to the middle of those whirlpools, and there constipate *one another into great solid globes.* BENTLEY.

2. To stuff up, or stop by filling up the passages.

It is not probable that any aliment should have the quality of intirely constipating *or shutting up the capillary vessels.* ARBUTHNOT ON ALIMENTS.

3. To bind the belly; or make costive.

CONSU'MABLE. *adj.* [from *consume.*] Susceptible of destruction; possible to be wasted, spent, or destroyed.

It does truly agree in this common quality ascribed unto both, of being incombustible, and not consumable *by fire; but yet there is this inconvenience, that it doth contract so much fuliginous matter from the earthy parts of the oil, though it was tried with some of the purest oil which is ordinary to be bought, that in a very few days it did choak and extinguish the flame.* WILKINS'S MATHEMEMATICAL MAGICK.

Our growing rich or poor depends only on, which is greater or less, our importation or exportation of consumable *commodities.* LOCKE.

To **CONSU'ME.** *v.a.* [*consumo*, Latin.] To waste; to spend; to destroy.

Where two raging fires meet together,
They do consume *the thing that feeds their fury.* SHAKESPEARE.

Thou shalt carry much seed out into the field, and shalt gather but little in; for the locusts shall consume *it.* BIBLE DEUTERONOMY, XXVIII.

Thus in soft anguish she consumes *the day,*
Nor quits her deep retirement. THOMSON'S SPRING.

To **CONSU'ME.** *v.n.* To waste away; to be exhausted.

These violent delights have violent ends,
And in their triumph die; like fire and powder,
Which, as they meet, consume. SHAKESPEARE'S ROMEO AND JULIET.

To **CONTA'BULATE.** *v.a.* [*contabulo*, Latin.] To floor with boards.

CONTABULA'TION. *n.s.* [*contabulatio*, Latin.] A joining of boards together; a boarding a floor.

CONTE'NT. *n.s.* [from the verb.]

1. Moderate happiness; such satisfaction as, though it does not fill up desire, appeases complaint.

Nought's had, all's spent,
Where our desire is got without content. SHAKESPEARE'S MACBETH.

One thought content *the good to be enjoy'd;*
This every little accident destroy'd. DRYDEN.

A wise content *his even soul secur'd;*

By want not shaken, nor by wealth allur'd. SMITH ON PHILIPS.

2. Acquiescence; satisfaction in a thing unexamined.

Others for language all their care express,
And value books, as women men, for dress:
Their praise is still – the style is excellent;
The sense they humbly take upon content.
POPE'S EPISTLES.

3. [From *contentus*, contained.] That which is contained, or included in any thing.

Though my heart's content *firm love doth bear,*
Nothing of that shall from mine eyes appear. SHAKESPEARE.

Scarcely any thing can be certainly determined of the particular contents *of any single mass of ore by mere inspection.*
WOODWARD'S NATURAL HISTORY, P. IV.

These experiments are made on the blood of healthy animals: in a lax and weak habit such a serum might afford other contents.
ARBUTHNOT ON ALIMENTS.

4. The power of containing; extent; capacity.

This island had then fifteen hundred strong ships, of great content. BACON.

It were good to know the geometrical content, *figure, and situation of all the lands of a kingdom, according to natural bounds.*
GRAUNT'S BILLS OF MORTALITY.

5. That which is comprised in a writing. In this sense the plural only is in use.

I have a letter from her
Of such contents, *as you will wonder at.*
SHAKESPEARE.

I shall prove these writings not counterfeits, but authentick, and the contents true, and worthy of a divine original.
GREW'S COSMOLOGIA SACRA, B. IV. C. 1. S. 1.

The contents *of both books come before those of the first book, in the thread of the story.*
ADDISON'S SPECTATOR, NO. 267.

CO'NTEXT. *n.s.* [*contextus*, Latin.] The general series of a discourse; the parts of the discourse that precede and follow the sentence quoted.

That chapter is really a representation of one, which hath only the knowledge, not practice of his duty; as is manifest from the context.
HAMMOND ON FUNDAMENTALS.

CONTE'XT. *adj.* [from *contex.*] Knit together; firm.

Hollow and thin, for lightness; but withal context *and firm, for strength.*
DERHAM'S PHYSICO-THEOLOGY.

CONTE'XTURE. *n.s.* [from *contex.*] The disposition of parts one amongst others; the composition of any thing out of separate parts; the system; the constitution; the manner in which any thing is woven or formed.

He was not of any delicate contexture; *his limbs rather sturdy than dainty.*
WOTTON.

Every species, afterwards expressed, was produced from that idea, forming that wonderful contexture *of created beings.*
DRYDEN'S DUFRESNOY, PREFACE.

Hence 'gan relax,
The ground's contexture; *hence Tartarian dregs,*
Sulphur, and nitrous spume, enkindling fierce,
Bellow'd within their darksome caves.
PHILIPS.

This apt, this wise contexture *of the sea,*
Makes it the ships, driv'n by the winds, obey;
Whence hardy merchants sail from shore to shore. BLACKMORE.

To **CONTRADI'CT.** *v.a.* [*contradico*, Latin.]

1. To oppose verbally; to assert the contrary to what has been asserted.

It is not lawful to contradict *a point of history which is known to all the world, as to make Hannibal and Scipio contemporaries with Alexander.*
DRYDEN'S DEDICATION, ÆNEID.

2. To be contrary to; to repugn; to oppose.

No truth can contradict *any truth.*
HOOKER, B. II. SECT. 7.

I contradict *your banes:*
If you will marry, make your loves to me.
SHAKESPEARE'S KING LEAR.

CO'NTRAST. *n.s.* [*contraste*, Fr.] Opposition and dissimilitude of figures, by which one contributes to the visibility or effect of another.

To **CO'NTRAST.** *v.a.* [from the noun.]
1. To place in opposition, so that one figure shews another to advantage.
2. To shew another figure to advantage by its colour or situation.

The figures of the groups must not be all on a side, that is, with their face and bodies all turned the same way; but must contrast *each other by their several positions.*
DRYDEN'S DUFRESNOY.

CONTRAVALLA'TION. *n.s.* [from *contra* and *vallo*, Latin.] The fortification thrown up, by the besiegers, round a city, to hinder the sallies of the garrison.

When the late czar of Muscovy first acquainted himself with mathematical learning, he practised all the rules of circumvallation and contravallation *at the siege of a town in Livonia.* WATTS'S LOGICK.

CONTRISTA'TION. *n.s.* [from *contristate.*] The act of making sad; the state of being made sad; sorrow; heaviness of heart; sadness; sorrowfulness; gloominess; grief; moan; mournfulness; trouble; discontent; melancholy.[66]

Incense and nidorous smells, such as were of sacrifices, were thought to intoxicate the brain, and to dispose men to devotion; which they may do by a kind of sadness and contristation *of the spirits, and partly also by heating and exalting them.*
BACON'S NATURAL HISTORY, NO. 932.

CONTRI'TE. *adj.* [*contritus*, Latin.]
1. Bruised; much worn.
2. Worn with sorrow; harrassed with the sense of guilt; penitent. In the books of divines *contrite* is sorrowful for sin, from the love of God and desire of pleasing him; and *attrite* is sorrowful for sin, from the fear of punishment.

I Richard's body have interred now;
And on it have bestow'd more contrite *tears,*
Than from it issu'd forced drops of blood.
SHAKESPEARE'S HENRY V.

With tears
Wat'ring the ground, and with our sighs the air
Frequenting, sent from hearts contrite, *in sign*
Of sorrow unfeign'd, and humiliation meek. MILTON'S PARADISE LOST.

The contrite *sinner is restored to pardon, and, through faith in Christ, our repentance is intitled to salvation.*
ROGERS'S SERMONS.

CO'NTROVERSY. *n.s.* [*controversia*, Latin.]
1. Dispute; debate; agitation of contrary opinions: a dispute is commonly oral, and a controversy in writing.

How cometh it to pass that we are so rent with mutual contentions, and that the church is so much troubled? If men had been willing to learn, all these controversies *might have died the very day they were first brought forth.* HOOKER, B. I.

Without controversy *great is the mystery of godliness.* BIBLE 1 TIMOTHY.

Wild controversy *then, which long had slept,*
Into the press from ruin'd cloisters leapt.
DENHAM.

This left no room for controversy *about the title, nor for encroachment on the right of others.* LOCKE.

2. A suit in law.

If there be a controversy *between men, and they come unto judgment, that the judges may judge them, then they shall justify the righteous and condemn the wicked.* BIBLE DEUTERONOMY, XXV. 1.

3. A quarrel.

The Lord hath a controversy *with the nations.* BIBLE JEREMIAH, XXV. 31.

4. Opposition; enmity: this is an unusual sense.

The torrent roar'd, and we did buffet it
With lusty sinews; throwing it aside,
And stemming it with hearts of
controversy.
SHAKESPEARE'S JULIUS CÆSAR.

CO'NVENT. *n.s.* [*conventus*, Latin.]

1. An assembly of religious persons; a body of monks or nuns.

He came to Leicester;
Lodg'd in the abbey, where the reverend abbot,
With all his convent, *honourably receiv'd him.* SHAKESPEARE'S HENRY VIII.

2. A religious house; an abbey; a monastery; a nunnery.

One seldom finds in Italy a spot of ground more agreeable than ordinary, that is not covered with a convent. ADDISON.

CONVE'RSABLE. *adj.* [from *converse*. It is sometimes written *conversible*, but improperly; *conversant*, *conversation*, *conversable*.] Qualified for conversation; fit for company; well adapted to the reciprocal communication of thoughts; communicative.

That fire and levity which makes the young ones scarce conversible, *when tempered by years, makes a gay old age.* GUARDIAN, NO. 101.

To **CONVE'RSE.** *v.n.* [*converser*, Fr. *conversor*, Latin.]

1. To cohabit with; to hold intercourse with; to be a companion to: followed by *with*.

Men then come to be furnished with fewer or more simple ideas from without, according as the objects they converse *with afford greater or less variety.* LOCKE.

By approving the sentiments of a person with whom he conversed, *in such particulars as were just, he won him over from those points in which he was mistaken.* ADDISON'S FREEHOLDER.

For him who lonely loves
To seek the distant hills, and there
converse
With nature.
THOMSON'S SUMMER, L. 130.

2. To be acquainted with; to be familiar to.[67]

I will converse *with iron-witted fools,*
And unrespective boys: none are for me,
That look into me with considerate eyes.
SHAKESPEARE'S RICHARD III.

3. To convey the thoughts reciprocally in talk.

Go therefore half this day, as friend with friend,
Converse *with Adam.*
MILTON'S PARADISE LOST, B. V. L. 230.

Much less can bird with beast, or fish with fowl,
So well converse.
MILTON'S PARADISE LOST, B. VIII. L. 396.

4. To discourse familiarly upon any subject: with *on* before the thing.

We had conversed *so often* on *that subject, and he had communicated his thoughts of it so fully to me, that I had not the least remaining difficulty.*
DRYDEN'S DUFRESNOY.

5. To have commerce with a different sex.

Being asked by some of her sex, in how long a time a woman might be allowed to pray to the gods, after having conversed *with a man? If it were a husband, says she, the next day; if a stranger, never.* GUARDIAN, NO. 165.

CONU'NDRUM. *n.s.* A low jest; a quibble; a mean conceit: a cant word.

Mean time he smoaks, and laughs at merry tale,
Or pun ambiguous, or conundrum *quaint.* PHILIPS.

CO'NVOLUTED. *part.* [of the verb I have found no example.] Twisted; rolled upon itself.

This differs from Muscovy-glass only in this, that the plates of that are flat and plain, whereas these are convoluted *and inflected.* WOODWARD ON FOSSILS.

CO'NY. *n.s.* [*kanin*, Germ. *connil* or *connin*, Fr. *cuniculus*, Latin.] A rabbit; an animal that burroughs in the ground.

With a short-legg'd hen,
Lemons and wine for sauce; to these a cony
Is not to be despair'd of, for our money.
BEN JONSON'S EPIGRAMS.

The husbandman suffers by hares and conys, *which eat the corn, trees.* MORTIMER'S HUSBANDRY.

COOK-MAID. *n.s.* [*cook* and *maid*.] A maid that dresses provisions.

A friend of mine was lately complaining to me, that his wife had turned off one of the best cook-maids *in England.* ADDISON'S FREEHOLDER, NO. 32.

COO'RDINATE. *adj.* [*con* and *ordinatus*, Latin.] Holding the same rank; not being subordinate. Thus shell-fish may be divided into two *coordinate* kinds, crustateous and testaceous; each of which is again divided into many species, *subordinate* to the kind, but *coordinate* to each other.

The word Analysis signifies the general and particular heads of a discourse, with their mutual connexions, both coordinate *and subordinate, drawn out into one or more tables.* WATTS.

COP. *n.s.* [*kop*, Dut. *cop*, Sax.] The head; the top of any thing; any thing rising to a head. As a *cop*, vulgarly *cock* of hay; a *cob-castle*, properly *cop-castle*, a small castle or house on a hill. A *cob* of cherrystones for *cop*, a pile of stones one laid upon another; a tuft on the head of birds.

COPA'YVA. *n.s.* [It is sometimes written *capivi*, *copivi*, *capayva*, *copayva*, *cupayva*, *cupayba*.] A gum which distils from a tree in Brasil. It is much used in disorders of the urinary passages.

CO'PPED. *adj.* [from *cop*.] Rising to a top or head.

It was broad in its basis, and rose copped *like a sugarloaf.* WISEMAN'S SURGERY.

CO'PULA. *n.s.* [Latin.] The word which unites the subject and predicate of a proposition; as, *books* are *dear*.

The copula *is the form of a proposition; it represents the act of the mind, affirming or denying.* WATTS'S LOGICK.

To **COQUE'T.** *v.a.* [from the noun.] To entertain with compliments and amorous tattle; to treat with an appearance of amorous tenderness.

You are coquetting *a maid of honour, my lord looking on to see how the gamesters play, and I railing at you both.* SWIFT.

To **COQU'ET.** *v.n.* To act the lover.[68]

Phyllis, who but a month ago
Was marry'd to the Tunbridge beau,
I saw coquetting *t'other night,*
In publick, with that odious knight.
SWIFT.

COQU'ETTE. *n.s.* [*coquette*, Fr. from *coquart*, a prattler.] A gay, airy girl; a girl who endeavours to attract notice.

> *The light* coquettes *in sylphs aloft repair,*
> *And sport and flutter in the fields of air.*
> POPE'S RAPE OF THE LOCK.

> *A* coquette *and a tinder-box are sparkled.* ARBUTHNOT AND POPE.

CO'RDIAL. *n.s.* [from *cor*, the heart, Latin.]
1. A medicine that increases the force of the heart, or quickens the circulation.
2. Any medicine that increases strength.

> *A* cordial, *properly speaking, is not always what increaseth the force of the heart; for, by increasing that, the animal may be weakened, as in inflammatory diseases. Whatever increaseth the natural or animal strength, the force of moving the fluids and muscles, is a* cordial: *these are such substances as bring the serum of the blood into the properest condition for circulation and nutrition; as broths made of animal substances, milk, ripe fruits, and whatever is endued with a wholsome but not pungent taste.* ARBUTHNOT ON ALIMENTS.

3. Any thing that comforts, gladdens, and exhilerates.

> *Then with some* cordials *seek for to appease*
> *The inward languor of my wounded heart,*
> *And then my body shall have shortly ease;*
> *But such sweet* cordials *pass physicians art.* SPENSER.

> *Comfort, like* cordials *after death, comes late.* DRYDEN.

> *Your warrior offspring that upheld the crown,*
> *The scarlet honour of your peaceful gown,*
> *Are the most pleasing objects I can find,*
> *Charms to my sight, and* cordials *to my mind.* DRYDEN.

CO'RMORANT. *n.s.* [*cormoran*, Fr. from *corvus marinus*, Latin.]
1. A bird that preys upon fish. It is nearly of the bigness of a capon, with a wry bill and broad feet, black on his body, but greenish about his wings. He is eminently greedy and rapacious.

> *Let fame, that all hunt after in their lives,*
> *Live register'd upon our brazen tombs;*
> *When, spight of* cormorant *devouring time,*
> *Th' endeavour of this present breath may buy*
> *That honour which shall 'bate his scythe's keen edge.* SHAKESPEARE.

> *Those called birds of prey, as the eagle, hawk, puttock, and* cormorant.
> PEACHAM ON DRAWING.

> *Thence up he flew, and on the tree of life*
> *Sat like a* cormorant.
> MILTON'S PARADISE LOST, B. IV. L. 194.

> *Not far from thence is seen a lake, the haunt*
> *Of coots, and of the fishing* cormorant.
> DRYDEN'S FABLES.

2. A glutton.

CORN-FLAG. *n.s.* [*corn* and *flag*.] It hath a fleshy double tuberose root: the leaves are like those of the fleur-de-lys: the flower consists of one leaf, shaped like a lily, open at the top, in two lips; the upper imbricated, the under divided into five segments: the ovary becomes an oblong fruit, divided into three cells, filled with roundish seeds wrapt up in a cover. *Miller* enumerates eleven species of this plant, some with red flowers, and some with white. It is a proper ornament for borders.[69]

CO'RONER. *n.s.* [from *corona*.] An officer whose duty is to enquire, on the part of the king, how any violent death was occasioned; for which purpose a jury of twelve persons is impannelled.

Go thou and seek the coroner, *and let him sit o' my uncle; for he's in the third degree of drink; he's drowned.*
SHAKESPEARE.

CO'RONET. *n.s.* [*coronetta*, Ital. the diminutive of *corona*, a crown.] An inferiour crown worn by the nobility. The coronet of a duke is adorned with strawberry leaves; that of a marquis has leaves with pearls interposed; that of an earl raises the pearls above the leaves; that of a viscount is surrounded with only pearls; that of a baron has only four pearls.

The rest was drawn into a coronet *of gold, richly set with pearl.* SIDNEY.

In his livery
Walk'd crowns and coronets, *realms and islands were*
As plates dropt from his pocket.
SHAKESPEARE'S ANTONY AND CLEOPATRA.

All the rest are countesses.
—— *Their* coronets *say so.*
SHAKESPEARE'S HENRY VIII.

Under a coronet *his flowing hair,*
In curls, on either cheek play'd.
MILTON'S PARADISE LOST.

Nor could our nobles hope their bold attempt,
Who ruin'd crowns, would coronets *exempt.* DRYDEN.

Peers and dukes, and all their sweeping train,
And garters, stars, and coronets *appear.*
POPE'S RAPE OF THE LOCK.

CO'RPORAL. *n.s.* [corrupted from *caporal*, French.] The lowest officer of the infantry, whose office is to place and remove the sentinels.

The cruel corp'ral *whisper'd in my ear,*
Five pounds, if rightly tipt, would set me clear. GAY.

CO'RPORAL *of a Ship*. An officer that hath the charge of setting the watches and sentries, and relieving them; who sees that all the soldiers and sailors keep their arms near and clean, and teaches them how to use them. He has a mate under him. *Harris.*

CO'RPORAL. *adj.* [*corporel*, Fr. *corpus*, Latin.]

1. Relating to the body; belonging to the body.

To relief of lazars and weak age,
Of indigent faint souls, past corporal *toil,*
A hundred alms-houses, right well supplied. SHAKESPEARE'S HENRY V.

Render to me some corporal *sign about her,*
More evident than this.
SHAKESPEARE'S CYMBELINE.

That God hath been otherwise seen, with corporal *eyes, exceedeth the small proportion of my understanding.*
RALEIGH.

They enjoy greater sensual pleasures, and feel fewer corporal *pains, and are utter strangers to all those anxious and tormenting thoughts, which perpetually haunt and disquiet mankind.*
ATTERBURY.

2. Material; not spiritual. In the present language, when *body* is used philosophically in opposition to spirit, the word *corporeal* is used, as a *corporeal* being; but otherwise *corporal. Corporeal* is having a body; *corporal* relating to the body. This distinction seems not ancient.

Whither are they vanish'd?
Into the air: and what seem'd corporal
Melted, as breath, into the wind.
SHAKESPEARE'S MACBETH.

And from these corporal *nutriments, perhaps,*
Your bodies may at last turn all to spirit.
MILTON'S PARADISE LOST.

CORPO'REAL. *adj.* [*corporeus*, Latin.]

1. Having a body; not immaterial. See CORPORAL.

The swiftness of those circles attribute,
Though numberless, to his omnipotence,
That to corporeal *substances could add*
Speed almost spiritual.
MILTON'S PARADISE LOST, B. VIII.

Having surveyed the image of God in the soul, we are not to omit those characters that God imprinted upon the body, as much as a spiritual substance could be pictured upon a corporeal. SOUTH'S SERMONS.

God being supposed to be a pure spirit, cannot be the object of any corporeal *sense.* TILLOTSON.

The course is finish'd which thy fates decreed,
And thou from thy corporeal *prison freed.*
DRYDEN'S FABLES.

Fix thy corporeal *and internal eye*
On the young gnat, or new-engender'd fly.
PRIOR.

2. It is used by Swift inaccurately for *corporal.*

I am not in a condition to make a true step even on Aimsbury Downs; and I declare, that a corporeal *false step is worse than a political one.* SWIFT.

CORPUSCULA'RIAN. *adj.* [from *corpusculum*, Lat.] Relating to bodies; comprising bodies. It is the distinguishing epithet of that philosophy which attempts the rational solution of all physical appearances by the action of one body upon another.

As to natural philosophy I do not expect to see any principles proposed, more comprehensive and intelligible than the corpuscularian *or mechanical.* BOYLE.

This may be said, that the modern corpuscularians *talk, in most things, more intelligibly than the peripateticks.* BENTLEY.

The mechanical or corpuscular *philosophy, though peradventure the eldest, as well as the best in the world, had lain dead for many ages in contempt and oblivion.* BENTLEY'S SERMONS.

CORRE'CTIONER. *n.s.* [from *correction.*] One that has been in the house of correction; a jayl-bird. This seems to be the meaning in *Shakespeare.*

I will have you foundly swinged for this, you blue-bottle rogue! you filthy famished correctioner. SHAKESPEARE'S HENRY IV.

CO'RRODY. *n.s.* [from *corrodo*, Latin.] A defalcation from an allowance or salary for some other than the original purpose.

In those days even noble persons, and other meaner men, ordered corrodies *and pensions to their chaplains and servants out of churches.* AYLIFFE'S PARERGON.

To CO'RRUGATE. *v.a.* [*corrugo*, Latin.] To wrinkle or purse up; as the skin is drawn into wrinkles by cold, or any other cause. *Quincy.*

The cramp cometh of contraction of sinews: it cometh either by cold or dryness; for cold and dryness do both of them contract and corrugate. BACON'S NATURAL HISTORY, NO. 964.

COSMO'GRAPHY. *n.s.* [*κόσμος* and *γράφω.*] The science of the general system or affections of the world, distinct from geography, which delivers the situation and boundaries of particular countries.

Here it might see the world without travel; it being a lesser scheme of the creation, nature contracted, a little cosmography, *or map of the universe.* SOUTH'S SERMONS.

CO'TTAGE. *n.s.* [from *cot.*] A hut; a mean habitation; a cot; a little house.

The sea-coast shall be dwellings and

cottages *for shepherds, and folds for flocks.* BIBLE ZEPHANIAH, II. 6.

They were right glad to take some corner of a poor cottage, *and there to serve God upon their knees.* HOOKER, B. IV. S. 2.

The self-same sun that shines upon his court,
Hides not his visage from our cottage, *but*
Looks on both alike.
SHAKESPEARE'S WINTER'S TALE.

Let the women of noble birth and great fortunes nurse their children, look to the affairs of the house, visit poor cottages, *and relieve their necessities.*
TAYLOR'S HOLY LIVING.

It is difficult for a peasant, bred up in the obscurities of a cottage, *to fancy in his mind the unseen splendors of a court.*
SOUTH'S SERMONS.

Beneath our humble cottage *let us haste,*
And here, unenvied, rural dainties taste.
POPE'S ODYSSEY.

CO'TTAGER. *n.s.* [from *cottage*]

1. One who lives in a hut or cottage.

Let us from our farms,
Call forth our cottagers *to arms.*
SWIFT.

The most ignorant Irish cottager *will not sell his cow for a groat.*
SWIFT'S ADDRESS TO PARLIAMENT.

2. A cottager, in law, is one that lives on the common, without paying rent, and without any land of his own.

The husbandmen and plowmen be but as their work-folks and labourers, or else mere cottagers, *which are but housed beggars.*
BACON'S HENRY VII.

The yeomenry, or middle people, of a condition between gentlemen and cottagers. BACON'S HENRY VII.

CO'UCHEE. *n.s.* [French.] Bedtime; the time of visiting late at night.

None of her sylvan subjects made their court;
Levees and couchees *pass'd without resort.* DRYDEN.

COVER-SHAME. *n.s.* [*cover* and *shame.*] Some appearance used to conceal infamy.

Does he put on holy garments for a cover-shame *of lewdness?*
DRYDEN'S SPANISH FRYAR.

COUGH. *n.s.* [*kuch*, Dutch.] A convulsion of the lungs, vellicated by some sharp serosity. It is pronounced *coff.*

In consumptions of the lungs, when nature cannot expel the cough, *men fall into fluxes of the belly, and then they die.*
BACON'S NATURAL HISTORY, NO. 63.

For his dear sake long restless nights you bore,
While rattling coughs *his heaving vessels tore.* SMITH.

To **COUGH.** *v.n.* [*kuchen*, Dutch.] To have the lungs convulsed; to make a noise in endeavouring to evacuate the peccant matter from the lungs.

Thou didst drink
The stale of horses, and the gilded puddle
Which beasts would cough *at.*
SHAKESPEARE'S ANTHONY AND CLEOPATRA.

Thou hast quarrelled with a man for coughing *in the street, because he hath wakened thy dog that hath lain asleep in the sun.*
SHAKESPEARE'S ROMEO AND JULIET.

The first problem enquireth why a man doth cough, *but not an ox or cow; whereas the contrary is often observed.* BROWN.

If any humour be discharged upon the lungs, they have a faculty of clearing themselves, and casting it up by coughing.
RAY ON THE CREATION.

There are who to my person pay their court,
I cough *like Horace, and though lean, am short.* POPE'S EPISTLES.

To **COUGH.** *v.a.* To eject by a cough; to expectorate.

If the matter be to be discharged by expectoration, it must first pass into the substance of the lungs, then into the aspera arteria, or weasand, and from thence be coughed *up, and spit out by the mouth.* WISEMAN'S SURGERY.

CO'UGHER. *n.s.* [from *cough.*] One that coughs. *Dictionaries.*

COUNTERBU'FF. *n.s.* [*counter* and *buff.*] A blow in a contrary direction; a stroke that produces a recoil.

He at the second gave him such a counterbuff, *that, because Phalantus was not to be driven from the saddle, the saddle with broken girths was driven from the horse.* SIDNEY.

Go, captain Stub, lead on, and show
What house you come of, by the blow
You give sir Quintin, and the cuff
You 'scape o' th' sandbags counterbuff.
BEN JONSON.

CO'UNTERCASTER. *n.s.* [from *counter*, for a false piece of money, and *caster.*] A word of contempt for an arithmetician; a book-keeper; a caster of accounts; a reckoner.

I, of whom his eyes had seen the proof
At Rhodes, at Cyprus, must be let and calm'd
By debtor and creditor, this countercaster.
SHAKESPEARE'S OTHELLO.

COUNTERMA'RCH. *n.s.* [from the verb.]

1. Retrocession; march backward; march in a different direction from the former.

How are such an infinite number of things placed with such order in the memory, notwithstanding the tumults, marches, and countermarches *of the animal spirits?* COLLIER ON THOUGHT.

2. Change of measures; alteration of conduct.

They make him do and undo, go forward and backwards by such countermarches *and retractions, as we do not willingly impute to wisdom.* BURNET'S THEORY OF THE EARTH.

COUNTERNO'ISE. *n.s.* [*counter* and *noise.*] A sound by which any other noise is overpowered.

They endeavoured, either by a constant succession of sensual delights, to charm and lull asleep, or else, by a counternoise *of revellings and riotous excesses, to drown the softer whispers of their conscience.* CALAMY'S SERMONS.

CO'UNTERPANE. *n.s.* [*contre-point*, French.] A coverlet for a bed, or any thing else woven in squares. It is sometimes written, according to etymology, *counterpoint.*

In ivory coffers I have stufft my crowns;
In cypress chests my arras counterpanes.
SHAKESPEARE.

CO'UNTERPOINT. *n.s.* A coverlet woven in squares, commonly spoken *counterpain.* See **COUNTERPANE.**

To **COUNTERRO'L.** *v.a.* [*counter* and *roll.* This is now generally written as it is spoken, *control.*] To preserve the power of detecting frauds by a counter account.

COUPLE-BEGGAR. *n.s.* [*couple* and *beggar.*] One that makes it his business to marry beggars to each other.

No couple-beggar *in the land,*
E'er join'd such numbers hand in hand.
SWIFT.

CO'URIER. *n.s.* [*courier*, French.] A messenger sent in haste; an express; a runner.

I met a courier, *one mine ancient friend.* SHAKESPEARE'S TIMON.

This thing the wary bassa well perceiving, for more assurance, by speedy couriers *advertised Solyman of the taking of Tauris, and of the enemy's purpose, requesting him with all speed to repair with his army to Tauris.* KNOLLES'S HISTORY.

To **COURT.** *v.a.* [from the noun.]
1. To woo; to solicit a woman to marriage.

Follow a shadow, it flies you;
Seem to fly it, it will pursue:
So court a mistress, she denies you;
Let her alone, she will court *you.*
BEN JONSON'S FOREST.

Fir'd with her love, and with ambition led,
The neighb'ring princes court *her nuptial bed.* DRYDEN'S ÆNEID.

Alas! Sempronius, wouldst thou talk of love
To Marcia, whilst her father's life's in danger?
Thou might'st as well court *the pale trembling vestal,*
While she beholds the holy flame expiring.
ADDISON'S CATO.

Ev'n now, when silent scorn is all they gain,
A thousand court *you, though they* court *in vain.* POPE.

2. To solicit; to seek.

Their own ease and satisfaction would quickly teach children to court *commendation, and avoid doing what they found condemned.*
LOCKE ON EDUCATION, SECT. 59.

3. To flatter; to endeavour to please.

COURT-DRESSER. *n.s.* [*court* and *dresser.*] One that dresses the court, or persons of rank; a flatterer.

There are many ways of fallacy; such arts of giving colours, appearances and resemblances, by this court-dresser, *fancy.*
LOCKE.

CO'USIN. *n.s.* [*cousin*, Fr. *consanguineus*, Lat.]
1. Any one collaterally related more remotely than a brother or sister.

Macbeth unseam'd him from the nape to th' chops,
And fix'd his head upon our battlements.
—— Oh, valiant cousin! *worthy gentleman.*
SHAKESPEARE'S MACBETH.

Tybalt, my cousin! *O, my brother's child!*
Unhappy sight! alas, the blood is spill'd
Of my dear kinsman.
SHAKESPEARE'S ROMEO AND JULIET.

Thou art, great lord, my father's sister's son,
And cousin *german to great Priam's seed.*
SHAKESPEARE'S TROILUS AND CRESSIDA.

2. A title given by the king to a nobleman, particularly to those of the council.

COXCO'MICAL. *adj.* [from *coxcomb.*] Foppish; conceited: a low word unworthy of use.

Because, as he was a very natural writer, and they were without prejudice, without prepossession, without affectation, and without the influence of coxcomical, *senseless cabal, they were at liberty to receive the impressions which things naturally made on their minds.* DENNIS.

CRACK. *n.s.* [*kraeck*, Dutch.]
1. A sudden disruption, by which the parts are separated but a little way from each other.
2. The chink, fissure, or vacuity made by disruption; a narrow breach.

Contusions, when great, do usually produce a fissure or crack *of the skull, either in the same part where the blow was inflicted, or in the contrary part.* WISEMAN.

At length it would crack in many places; and those cracks, *as they dilated, would appear of a pretty good, but yet obscure and dark sky-colour.*
NEWTON'S OPTICKS.

3. The sound of any body bursting or falling.

If I say sooth, I must report, they were
As cannons overcharg'd with double cracks. SHAKESPEARE'S MACBETH.

Now day appears, and with the day the king,
Whose early care had robb'd him of his rest:
Far off the cracks *of falling houses ring,*
And shrieks of subjects pierce his tender breast. DRYDEN.

4. Any sudden and quick sound.

A fourth? – start eye!
What will the line stretch out to th' crack *of doom?* SHAKESPEARE.

Vulcan was employed in hammering out thunderbolts, that every now and then flew up from the anvil with dreadful cracks *and flashes.*
ADDISON'S GUARDIAN, NO. 103.

5. Any breach, injury, or diminution; a flaw.[70]

And let us, Paladour, though now our voices
Have got the mannish crack, *sing him to th' ground.* SHAKESPEARE.

I cannot
Believe this crack *to be in my dread mistress,*
So sovereignly being honourable.
SHAKESPEARE'S WINTER'S TALE.

6. Craziness of intellect.

7. A man crazed.

I have invented projects for raising millions, without burthening the subject; but cannot get the parliament to listen to me, who look upon me as a crack *and a projector.*
ADDISON'S SPECTATOR.

8. A whore; in low language.

9. A boast.

Leasings, backbitings, and vain-glorious cracks,
All those against that fort did bend their batteries. SPENSER.

10. A boaster. This is only in low phrase.

CRA'MBO. *n.s.* [a cant word, probably without etymology.] A play at which one gives a word, to which another finds a rhyme; a rhyme.

So Mævius, when he drain'd his skull
To celebrate some suburb trull,
His similes in order set,
And ev'ry crambo *he could get.* SWIFT.

CRASS. *adj.* [*crassus*, Latin.] Gross; coarse; not thin; not comminuted; not subtle; not consisting of small parts.

Metals are intermixed with the common terrestrial matter, so as not to be discoverable by human industry; or, if discoverable, so diffused and scattered amongst the crasser *and more unprofitable matter, that it would never be possible to separate and extract it.*
WOODWARD'S NATURAL HISTORY.

CRA'VER. *n.s.* [from *crave.*] A weak-hearted spiritless fellow. It is used in *Clarissa.*

To **CRAUNCH.** *v.a.* [*schrantsen*, Dutch; whence the vulgar say more properly to *scraunch.*] To crush in the mouth. The word is used by *Swift.*

CRA'YON. *n.s.* [*crayon*, French.]
1. A kind of pencil; a roll of paste to draw lines with.

Let no day pass over you without drawing a line; that is to say, without working, without giving some strokes of the pencil or the crayon. DRYDEN'S DUFRESNOY.

2. A drawing or design done with a pencil or crayon.

CREDE'NDA. *n.s.* [Latin.] Things to be believed; articles of faith; distinguished in theology from *agenda*, or practical duties.

These were the great articles and credenda *of Christianity, that so much startled the world.* SOUTH'S SERMONS.

CREDE'NTIAL. *n.s.* [from *credens*, Latin.] That which gives a title to credit; the warrant upon which belief or authority is claimed.

A few persons of an odious and despised

country could not have filled the world with believers, had they not shown undoubted credentials *from the Divine Person who sent them on such a message.*
ADDISON ON THE CHRISTIAN RELIGION.

CRE'EPER. *n.s.* [from *creep.*]
1. A plant that supports itself by means of some stronger body.

Plants that put forth their sap hastily, have bodies not proportionable to their length; therefore they are winders or creepers; *as ivy, briony, and woodbine.*
BACON'S NATURAL HISTORY.

2. An iron used to slide along the grate in kitchens.
3. A kind of patten or clog worn by women.

CREE'PHOLE. *n.s.* [*creep* and *hole.*]
1. A hole into which any animal may creep to escape danger.
2. A subterfuge; an excuse.

CREE'PINGLY. *adv.* [from *creeping.*] Slowly; after the manner of a reptile.

The joy, which wrought into Pygmalion's mind, was even such as, by each degree of Zelmane's words, creepingly *entered into Philoclea's.* SIDNEY, B. II.

CREE'PLE[71] *n.s.* [from *creep.*] A lame person, a cripple.

She to whom this world must itself refer
As suburbs or the microcosm of her,
She, she is dead, she's dead when thou know'st this,
Thou know'st how lame a creeple *this world is.* DONNE.

CREMA'TION. *n.s.* [*crematio,* Latin.] A burning.

CRE'MOR. *n.s.* [Latin.] A milky substance; a soft liquor resembling cream.

The food is swallowed into the stomach, where, mingled with dissolvent juices, it is reduced into a chyle or cremor. RAY.

CRE'NATED. *adj.* [from *crena,* Latin] Notched; indented.

The cells are prettily crenated, *or notched quite round the edges; but not straited down to any depth.*
WOODWARD ON FOSSILS.

CRI'CKET. *n.s.* [*krekel,* from *kreken,* to make a noise, Dutch.]
1. An insect that squeaks or chirps about ovens and fireplaces.

Didst thou not hear a noise? ——
—— *I heard the owl scream, and the* crickets *cry.*
SHAKESPEARE'S MACBETH.

Far from all resort of mirth,
Save the cricket *on the hearth.*
MILTON.

The solemn death-watch click'd the hour she dy'd,
And shrilling crickets *in the chimney cry'd.* GAY'S PASTORALS.

2. [from *cryce,* Saxon, a stick.] A sport, at which the contenders drive a ball with sticks in opposition to each other.

The judge, to dance, his brother serjeant call;
The senator at cricket *urge the ball.*
POPE'S DUNCIAD, B. IV.

3. [from *kriechen,* Germ. to creep.] A low seat or stool.

CRI'NCUM. *n.s.* [a cant word.] A cramp; a contraction; whimsy.

For jealousy is but a kind
Of clap and crincum *of the mind.*
HUDIBRAS, P. III. CANT. 1.

CRINI'GEROUS. *adj.* [*criniger,* Latin.] Hairy; overgrown with hair. *Dictionaries.*

CRI'SIS. *n.s.* [*κρίσις.*]
1. The point in which the disease kills, or changes to the better.

Wise leeches will not vain receipts obtrude;
Deaf to complaints, they wait upon the ill,
'Till some safe crisis *authorize their skill.*
DRYDEN.

2. The point of time at which any affair comes to the height.

This hour's the very crisis *of your fate;*
Your good or ill, your infamy or fame,
And all the colour of your life depends
On this important now.
DRYDEN'S SPANISH FRYAR.

The undertaking, which I am now laying down, was entered upon in the very crisis *of the late rebellion, when it was the duty of every Briton to contribute his utmost assistance to the government, in a manner suitable to his station and abilities.* ADDISON'S FREEHOLDER, NO. 55.

CRI'TICK. *n.s.* [κριτικος.]
1. A man skilled in the art of judging of literature; a man able to distinguish the faults and beauties of writing.

This settles truer ideas in men's minds of several things, whereof we read the names in ancient authors, than all the large and laborious arguments of criticks. LOCKE.

Criticks *I saw, that other names deface,*
And fix their own with labour in their place. POPE.

Where an author has many beauties consistent with virtue, piety, and truth, let not little criticks *exalt themselves, and shower down their ill-nature.* WATTS.[72]

2. A censurer; a man apt to find fault.

My chief design, next to seeing you, is to be a severe critick *on you and your neighbour.* SWIFT.

CRI'TICK. *adj.* Critical; relating to criticism; relating to the art of judging of literary performances.

Thence arts o'er all the northern world advance,
But critick *learning flourish'd most in France.* POPE.

CRI'TICK. *n.s.*
1. A critical examination; critical remarks; animadversions.

I should be glad if I could persuade him to continue his good offices, and write such another critick *on any thing of mine.* DRYDEN.

I should as soon expect to see a critique *on the poesy of a ring, as on the inscription of a medal.* ADDISON ON MEDALS.

2. Science of criticism.

If ideas and words were distinctly weighed, and duly considered, they would afford us another sort of logick and critick *than what we have been hitherto acquainted with.* LOCKE.

What is every year of a wise man's life, but a censure and critique *on the past?* POPE.

Not that my quill to criticks *was confin'd,*
My verse gave ampler lessons to mankind. POPE.

To **CRI'TICK.** *v.n.* [from *critick.*] To play the critick; to criticise.

They do but trace over the paths that have been beaten by the antients; or comment, critick, *and flourish upon them.* TEMPLE.

To **CROSS-EXAMINE.** *v.a.* [*cross* and *examine.*] To try the faith of evidence by captious questions of the contrary party.

If we may but cross-examine *and interrogate their actions against their words, these will soon confess the invalidity of their solemnest confessions.* DECAY OF PIETY.

The judges shall, as they think fit, interrogate or cross-examine *the witnesses.* SPECTATOR, NO. 608.

To **CRO'SSBITE.** *v.a.* [from the noun.] To contravene by deception.

No rhetorick must be spent against cross-biting *a country evidence, and frighting him out of his senses.* COLLIER.

That many knotty points there are,
Which all discuss, but few can clear;
As nature slily had thought fit,
For some by-ends, to cross-bite *wit.*
PRIOR.

CROWD. *n.s.* [*cruð*, Saxon.]
1. A multitude confusedly pressed together.
2. A promiscuous medly, without order or distinction.

He could then compare the confusion of a multitude to that tumult he had observed in the Icarian sea, dashing and breaking among its crowd *of islands.*
ESSAY ON HOMER.

3. The vulgar; the populace.

He went not with the crowd *to see a shrine,*
But fed us by the way, with food divine.
DRYDEN'S FABLES.

4. [from *crwth*, Welsh.] A fiddle.

His fiddle is your proper purchase,
Won in the service of the churches;
And by your doom must be allow'd
To be, or be no more, a crowd.
HUDIBRAS, P. I. CANT. 2.

CRU'CIAL. *adj.* [*crux, crucis*, Latin.] Transverse; intersecting one another.

Whoever has seen the practice of the crucial *incision, must be sensible of the false reasoning used in its favour.* SHARP.

To **CRU'CIATE.** *v.a.* [*crucio*, Latin.] To torture; to torment; to excruciate.

CRU'CIBLE. *n.s.* [*crucibulum*, low Latin.] A chymist's melting pot, made of earth; so called, because they were formerly marked with a cross.

Take a quantity of good silver, and put it in a crucible *or melting cruse, and set them on fire, well covered round about with coals.* PEACHAM ON DRAWING.

CRU'ET. *n.s.* [*kruicke*, Dutch.] A vial for vinegar or oyl, with a stopple.

Within thy reach I set the vinegar!
And fill'd the cruet *with the acid tide,*
While pepper-water worms thy bait
supply'd. SWIFT.

CRUISE. *n.s.* [*kruicke*, Dutch.] A small cup.

I have not a cake, but an handful of meal in a barrel, and a little oil in a cruise.
BIBLE 1 KINGS, XVII. 12.

The train prepare a cruise *of curious*
mold,
A cruise *of fragrance, form'd of burnish'd*
gold. POPE'S ODYSSEY.

A **CRUISE.** *n.s.* [*croise*, Fr. from the original *cruisers*, who bore the cross, and plundered only infidels.] A voyage in search of plunder.

To **CRUISE.** *v.n.* [from the noun.] To rove over the sea in search of opportunities to plunder; to wander on the sea without any certain course.

CRUSTA'CEOUS. *adj.* [from *crusta*, Lat.] Shelly, with joints; not testaceous; not with one continued uninterrupted shell. Lobster is *crustaceous*, oyster testaceous.

It is true that there are some shells, such as those of lobsters, crabs, and others of crustaceous *kinds, that are very rarely found at land.*
WOODWARD'S NATURAL HISTORY.

CU'CKOO. *n.s.* [*cwccw*, Welsh; *cocu*, Fr. *kockock*, Dutch.]
1. A bird which appears in the Spring; and is said to suck the eggs of other birds, and lay her own to be hatched in their place; from which practice, it was usual to alarm a husband at the approach of an adulterer by calling *cuckoo*, which, by mistake, was in time applied to the husband. This bird is remarkable for the uniformity of his note, from which his name in most tongues seems to have been formed.

Finding Mopsa, like a cuckoo *by a nightingale, alone with Pamela, I came in.* SIDNEY.

The merry cuckoo, *messenger of Spring,*
His trumpet shrill hath thrice already
sounded. SPENSER.

The plainsong cuckoo *gray,*
Whose note full many a man doth mark,
And dares not answer, nay.
SHAKESPEARE.

Take heed, have open eye; for thieves do
foot by night:
Take heed ere Summer comes, or cuckoo
birds affright. SHAKESPEARE.

I deduce,
From the first note the hollow cuckoo *sings,*
The symphony of Spring; and touch a
theme
Unknown to fame, the passion of the
grove. THOMSON'S SPRING.

2. It is a name of contempt.

Why, what a rascal art thou then, to praise him so for running? ——
—— A horseback, ye cuckoo; *—— but a-foot, he will not budge a foot.*
SHAKESPEARE'S HENRY IV. P. I.

CUE. *n.s.* [*queue*, a tail, French.]
1. The tail or end of any thing; as, the long curl of a wig.
2. The last words of a speech which the player who is to answer catches, and regards as intimation to begin.

Pyramus, you begin: when you have spoken your speech, enter into that brake; and so every one according to his cue.
SHAKESPEARE'S MIDSUMMER NIGHT'S DREAM.

3. A hint; an intimation; a short direction.

What's Hecuba to him, or he to Hecuba,
That he should weep for her? What would
he do,
Had he the motive and the cue *for passion*
That I have? He would drown the stage
with tears. SHAKESPEARE.

Let him know how many servants there are, of both sexes, who expect vails; and give them their cue *to attend in two lines, as he leaves the house.* SWIFT.

4. The part which any man is to play in his turn.

Hold your hands,
Both you of my inclining, and the rest:
Were it my cue *to fight, I should have*
known it
Without a prompter.
SHAKESPEARE'S OTHELLO.

Neither is Otto here a much more talking gentleman: nothing appears in his cue *to move pity, or any way make the audience of his party.*
RYMER'S TRAGEDIES OF THE LAST AGE.

5. Humour; temper of mind: a low word.

CU'LPRIT. *n.s.* [about this word there is great dispute. It is used by the judge at criminal trials, who, when the prisoner declares himself not guilty, and puts himself upon his trial, answers; *Culprit, God send thee a good deliverance.* It is likely that it is a corruption of *Qu'il paroît, May it so appear*, the wish of the judge being that the prisoner may be found innocent.] A man arraigned before his judge.

The knight appear'd, and silence they
proclaim;
Then first the culprit *answer'd to his name;*
And, after forms of law, was last requir'd
To name the thing that woman most
desir'd. DRYDEN.

An author is in the condition of a culprit; *the publick are his judges: by allowing too much, and condescending too far, he may injure his own cause; and by pleading and asserting too boldly, he may displease the court.*
PRIOR'S PREFACE TO SOLOMON.

CU'LTURE. *n.s.* [*cultura*, Latin.]
1. The act of cultivation; the act of tilling the ground; tillage.

Give us seed unto our heart, and culture *to our understanding, that there may come fruit of it.* BIBLE 2 ESDRAS, VIII. 6.

These three last were slower than the ordinary wheat of itself, and this culture *did rather retard than advance.* BACON.

The plough was not invented 'till after the deluge; the earth requiring little or no care or culture, *but yielding its increase freely, and without labour and toil.* WOODWARD.

Where grows? – Where grows it not? If vain our toil,
We ought to blame the culture, *not the soil.*
Fix'd to no spot is happiness sincere.
POPE'S ESSAY ON MAN.

They rose as vigorous as the sun;
Then to the culture *of the willing glebe.*
THOMSON'S SPRING.

2. Art of improvement and melioration.

One might wear any passion out of a family by culture, *as skilful gardeners blot a colour out of a tulip that hurts its beauty.* TATLER, NO. 75.

CU'NNINGMAN. *n.s.* [*cunning* and *man.*] A man who pretends to tell fortunes, or teach how to recover stolen goods.

He sent him for a strong detachment
Of beadle, constable, and watchmen,
T' attack the cunningman, *for plunder*
Committed falsly on his lumber.
HUDIBRAS, P. III. CANT 1.

To **CUP.** *v.a.* [from the noun.]
1. To supply with cups: this sense is obsolete.

Plumpy Bacchus, with pink eyne,
In thy vats our cares be drown'd:
With thy grapes our hairs be crown'd!
Cup *us, 'till the world go round.*
SHAKESPEARE'S ANTONY AND CLEOPATRA.

2. To fix a glass-bell or cucurbite upon the skin, to draw the blood in scarification.

The clotted blood lies heavy on his heart,
Corrupts, and there remains in spite of art:
Nor breathing veins, nor cupping *will prevail;*
All outward remedies and inward fail.
DRYDEN'S FABLES.

You have quartered all the foul language upon me, that could be raked out of the air of Billingsgate, without knowing who I am; or whether I deserve to be cupped *and scarified at this rate.* SPECTATOR, NO. 595.

Blistering, cupping, *and bleeding are seldom of use but to the idle and intemperate.*
ADDISON'S SPECTATOR, NO. 195.

Him the damn'd doctors and his friends immur'd;
They bled, they cupp'd, *they purg'd; in short they cur'd.* POPE.

CU'PPER. *n.s.* [from *cup.*] One who applies cupping-glasses; a scarifier.

CUPPING-GLASS. *n.s.* [from *cup* and *glass.*] A glass used by scarifiers to draw out the blood by rarefying the air.

A bubo, in this case, ought to be drawn outward by cupping-glasses, *and brought to suppuration.* WISEMAN'S SURGERY.

CU'RRANT. *n.s.*
1. The tree hath no prickles; the leaves are large: the flower consists of five leaves, placed in form of a rose: the ovary, which arises from the center of the flower-cup, becomes a globular fruit, produced in bunches.
2. A small dried grape, properly written *corinth.*

They butter'd currants *on fat veal bestow'd,*
And rumps of beef with virgin honey stew'd;
Insipid taste, old friend, to them who Paris know,
Where rocombole, shallot, and the rank garlick grow. KING.

CU'RRENCY. *n.s.* [from *current.*]

1. Circulation; power of passing from hand to hand.

The currency *of those half-pence would, in the universal opinion of our people, be utterly destructive to this kingdom.* SWIFT.

2. General reception.

3. Fluency; readiness of utterance; easiness of pronunciation.

4. Continuance; constant flow; uninterrupted course.

The currency *of time to establish a custom, ought to be with a continuando from the beginning to the end of the term prescribed.* AYLIFFE'S PARERGON.

5. General esteem; the rate at which any thing is vulgarly valued.

He that thinketh Spain to be some great over-match for this estate, assisted as it is, and, may be, is no good mintman, but takes greatness of kingdoms according to their bulk and currency, *and not after intrinsick value.* BACON'S WAR WITH SPAIN.

6. The papers stamped in the English colonies by authority, and passing for money.

CU'RRISH. *adj.* [from *cur.*] Having the qualities of a degenerate dog; brutal; sour; quarrelsome; malignant; churlish; uncivil; untractable; impracticable.

Sweet speaking oft a currish *heart reclaims.* SIDNEY, B. II.

No care of justice, nor no rule of reason,
No temperance, nor no regard of season,
Did thenceforth ever enter in his mind,
But cruelty, the sign of currish *kind.*
HUBBERD'S TALE.

In fashions wayward, and in love unkind;
For Cupid deigns not wound a currish *mind.* FAIRFAX, B. IV.

I would she were in heaven, so she could
Entreat some pow'r to change this currish *Jew.* SHAKESPEARE.

She says your dog was a cur; and tells you, currish *thanks is good enough for such a present.* SHAKEPEARE'S TWO GENTLEMEN OF VERONA.

CU'RTAIN. *n.s.* [*cortina*, Latin.]

1. A cloath contracted or expanded at pleasure, to admit or exclude the light; to conceal or discover any thing; to shade a bed; to darken a room.

Their curtains *ought to be kept open, so as to renew the air.* ARBUTHNOT ON DIET.

So through white curtains *shot a tim'rous ray,*
And op'd those eyes that must eclipse the day. POPE.

Thy hand, great dulness! let's the curtain *fall,*
And universal darkness buries all.
POPE'S DUNCIAD, B. III.

2. *To draw the* CURTAIN. To close it so as to shut out the light, or conceal the object.

I must draw a curtain *before the work for a while, and keep your patience a little in suspence, 'till materials are prepared.* BURNET'S THEORY OF THE EARTH.

Once more I write to you, and this once will be the last: the curtain *will soon be* drawn *between my friend and me, and nothing left but to wish you a long good night.* POPE.

3. To open it so as to discern the object.

Had I forgot thee? Oh, come in, Æmilia:
Soft, by and by; let me the curtains *draw.*
Where art thou? What's the matter with thee now? SHAKESPEARE.

So soon as the all-cheering sun
Should in the farthest East begin to draw
The shady curtain *from Aurora's bed.*
SHAKESPEARE'S ROMEO AND JULIET.

Peace, the lovers are asleep:
They, sweet turtles! folded lie
In the last knot that love could tie:
Let them sleep, let them sleep on,
'Till this stormy night be gone;
And th' eternal morrow dawn,
Then the curtain *will be drawn,*
And they waken with that light,
Whose day shall never sleep in night.
CRASHAW.

4. [In fortification.] That part of the wall or rampart that lies between two bastions. *Military Dictionaries.*

The governour, not discouraged, suddenly of timber and boards raised up a curtain *twelve foot high, at the back of his soldiers.*
KNOLLES'S HISTORY OF THE TURKS.

CURTAIN-LECTURE. *n.s.* [from *curtain* and *lecture.*] A reproof given by a wife to her husband in bed.

What endless brawls by wives are bred!
The curtain-lecture *makes a mournful bed.* DRYDEN'S JUVENAL.

She ought to exert the authority of the curtain-lecture, *and, if she finds him of a rebellious disposition, to tame him.*
ADDISON.

CU'STARD. *n.s.* [*cwstard*, Welsh.] A kind of sweetmeat made by boiling eggs with milk and sugar, 'till the whole thickens into a mass. It is a food much used in city feasts.

He cram'd them 'till their guts did ake,
With cawdle, custard, *and plumb cake.*
HUDIBRAS, CANT. II.

Now may'rs and shrieves all hush'd and satiate lay;
Yet eat, in dreams, the custard *of the day.*
POPE'S DUNCIAD.

CU'TTER. *n.s.* [from *cut.*]

1. An agent or instrument that cuts any thing.

2. A nimble boat that cuts the water.

3. [73] The teeth that cut the meat.

The molares, or grinders are behind, nearest the center of motion, because there is a greater strength or force required to chew the meat than to bite a piece; and the cutters *before, that they may be ready to cut off a morsel from any solid food, to be transmitted to the grinders.*
RAY ON THE CREATION.

4. An officer in the Exchequer that provides wood for the tallies, and cuts the sum paid upon them; and then casts the same into the court to be written upon. *Cowel.*

CYCLOPÆDI'A. *n.s.* [*κύκλος* and *παδεία.*] A circle of knowledge; a course of the sciences.

D

Is a consonant nearly approaching in sound to *T*, but formed by a stronger appulse of the tongue to the upper part of the mouth. The sound of *D* in *English* is uniform, and it is never mute.

To **DAB.** *v.a.* [*dauber*, Fr.] To strike gently with something soft or moist.

> *A sore should never be wiped by drawing a piece of tow or rag over it, but only by* dabbing *it with fine lint.* SHARP.

A **DAB.** *n.s.* [from the verb.]

1. A small lump of any thing.
2. A blow with something moist or soft.
3. Something moist or slimy thrown upon one.
4. [In low language.] An artist; a man expert at something. This is not used in writing.
5. A kind of small flat fish.

> *Of flat fish there are rays, flowks,* dabs, *plaice.* CAREW.

DA'DAL.[74] *adj.* [*dædalus*, Latin.]

1. Various; variegated.
2. Skilful: this is not the true meaning, nor should be imitated.

> *Nor hath*
> *The* dædal *hand of nature only pour'd*
> *Her gifts of outward grace.* PHILIPS.

DA'GGERSDRAWING. *n.s.* [*dagger* and *draw.*] The act of drawing daggers; approach to open violence.

> *They always are at* daggersdrawing,
> *And one another clapperclawing.*
> HUDIBRAS, P. II. CANT. 2.

> *I have heard of a quarrel in a tavern, where all were at* daggersdrawing, *'till one desired to know the subject of the quarrel.*
> SWIFT.

DA'MNABLE. *adj.* [from *damn.*]

1. Deserving damnation; justly doomed to never-ending punishment.

> *It gives him occasion of labouring with greater earnestness elsewhere, to entangle unwary minds with the snares of his* damnable *opinion.*
> HOOKER, B. 5. SECT. 42.

> *He's a creature unprepar'd, unmeet for death;*

And, to transport him in the mind he is,
Were damnable.
SHAKESPEARE'S MEASURE FOR MEASURE.

As he does not reckon every schism of a damnable *nature, so he is far from closing with the new opinion of those who make it no crime.* SWIFT.

2. It is sometimes indecently used in a low and ludicrous sense; odious; pernicious.

Oh thou damnable *fellow! did not I pluck thee by the nose for thy speeches?* SHAKESPEARE'S MEASURE FOR MEASURE.

To **DA'MNIFY.** *v.a.* [from *damnifico*, Latin.]

1. To endamage; to injure; to cause loss to any.

He, who has suffered the damage, has a right to demand in his own name, and he alone can remit satisfaction: the damnified *person has the power of appropriating the goods or service of the offender, by right of self-preservation.* LOCKE.

2. To hurt; to impair.

When now he saw himself so freshly rear,
As if late fight had nought him damnify'd,
He was dismay'd, and 'gan his fate to
fear. FAIRY QUEEN.

DA'MPY. *adj.* [from *damp.*] Dejected; gloomy; sorrowful.

The lords did dispel dampy *thoughts, which the remembrance of his uncle might raise, by applying him with exercises and disports.* HAYWARD.

DA'NDIPRAT. *n.s.* [*dandin*, French.] A little fellow; an urchin: a word used sometimes in fondness, sometimes in contempt.

DA'NGLER. *n.s.* [from *dangle.*] A man that hangs about women only to waste time.

A dangler *is of neither sex.*
RALPH'S MISCELLANY.

To **DAP.** *v.n.* [corrupted from *dip.*] To let fall gently into the water: a word, I believe, only used by anglers.

I have taught him how to catch a chub, by dapping *with a grasshopper.*
WALTON'S ANGLER.

DA'PPER. *adj.* [*dapper*, Dutch] Little and active; lively without bulk. It is usually spoken in contempt.

And on the tawny sands and shelves,
Trip the pert fairies and the dapper *elves.*
MILTON.

A pert dapper *spark of a magpye, fancied the birds would never be governed 'till himself should sit at the helm.*
L'ESTRANGE.

DA'RING. *adj.* [from *dare.*] Bold; adventurous; fearless; courageous; intrepid; brave; stout.

The last Georgick has indeed many metaphors, but not so daring *as this; for human thoughts and passions may be more naturally ascribed to a bee than to an inanimate plant.*
ADDISON'S ESSAYS ON THE GEORGICKS.

The song too daring, *and the theme too*
great. PRIOR.

Grieve not, O daring *prince! that noble*
heart. POPE.

DA'RINGLY. *adv.* [from *daring.*] Boldly; courageously; fearlessly; impudently; outrageously.

Some of the great principles of religion are every day openly and daringly *attacked from the press.* ATTERBURY.

Your brother, fir'd with success,
Too daringly *upon the foe did press.*
HALIFAX.

DATE. *n.s.* [*datte*, Fr. from *datum*, Latin.]

1. The time at which a letter is written, marked at the end or the beginning.

2. The time at which any event happened.

3. The time stipulated when any thing shall be done.

His days and times are past,
And my reliance on his fracted dates
Has smit my credit.
SHAKESPEARE'S TIMON.

My father's promise ties me not to time;
And bonds, without a date, *they say are void.* DRYDEN.

4. End; conclusion.

What time would spare, from steel receives its date;
And monuments, like men, submit to fate.
POPE.

5. Duration; continuance.

Could the declining of this fate, O friend,
Our date *to immortality extend?*
DENHAM.

Then raise,
From the conflagrant mass, purg'd, and refin'd,
New heav'ns, new earth, ages of endless date,
Founded in righteousness.
MILTON'S PARADISE LOST.

6. [from *dactylus.*] The fruit of the date-tree.

Hold, take these keys, and fetch more spices, nurse.
—— They call for dates *and quinces in the pastry.* SHAKESPEARE.

To **DAWN.** *v.n.* [supposed by the etymologists to have been originally to *dayen*, or advance towards day.]

1. To grow luminous; to begin to grow light.

I have been troubled in my sleep this night;
But dawning *day new comfort hath inspir'd.*
SHAKESPEARE'S TITUS ANDRONICUS.

As it began to dawn, *towards the first day of the week, came Mary Magdalene to see the sepulchre.*
BIBLE MATTHEW, XXVIII. 1.

All night I slept, oblivious of my pain;
Aurora dawn'd, *and Phœbus shin'd in vain.* POPE'S ODYSSEY.

2. To glimmer obscurely.

A Romanist, from the very first dawning *of any notions in his understanding, hath this principle constantly inculcated, viz. that he must believe as the church.* LOCKE.

3. To begin, yet faintly; to give some promises of lustre or eminence.

While we behold such dauntless worth appear
In dawning *youth, and souls so void of fear.* DRYDEN'S ÆNEID.

Thy hand strikes out some free design,
When life awakes and dawns *at every line.* POPE.

DAWN. *n.s.* [from the verb.]

1. The time between the first appearance of light and the sun's rise, reckoned from the time that the sun comes within eighteen degrees of the horizon.

Then on to-morrow's dawn *your care employ,*
To search the land, and where the cities lie,
And what the men; but give this day to joy. DRYDEN'S ÆNEID.

2. Beginning; first rise.

These tender circumstances diffuse a dawn *of serenity over the soul.* POPE.

But such their guiltless passion was,
As in the dawn *of time inform'd the heart*
Of innocence, and undissembling truth.
THOMSON'S SUMMER.

To **DAZE.** *v.a.* [*dwæs*, Saxon.] To overpower with light; to strike with too strong lustre; to hinder the act of seeing by too much light suddenly introduced.

They smote the glistering armies as they stand,
With quiv'ring beams, which daz'd *the wond'ring eye.*
FAIRFAX, B. I. STANZA 73.

Poor human kind, all daz'd *in open day,*

Err after bliss, and blindly miss their way.
DRYDEN.

DEAD-DOING. *participial adj.* [*dead* and *do.*] Destructive; killing; mischievous; having the power to make dead.

Hold, O dear lord, your dead-doing *hand;*
Then loud he cry'd, I am your humble thrall. FAIRY QUEEN.

They never care how many others
They kill, without regard of mothers,
Or wives or children, so they can
Make up some fierce, dead-doing *man.*
HUDIBRAS, P. I. CAN. 11.

DEAD-RECKONING. *n.s.* [a sea-term.] That estimation or conjecture which the seamen make of the place where a ship is, by keeping an account of her way by the log, by knowing the course they have steered by the compass, and by rectifying all with allowance for drift or lee-way; so that this reckoning is without any observation of the sun, moon, and stars, and is to be rectified as often as any good observation can be had.

DEALBA'TION. *n.s.* [*dealbatio*, Lat.] The act of bleaching or whitening; rendering things white, which were not so before: a word which is now almost grown into disuse.

All seed is white in viviparous animals, and such as have preparing vessels, wherein it receives a manifold dealbation.
BROWN'S VULGAR ERROURS, B. VI. C. 10.

DEAMBULA'TION. *n.s.* [*deambulatio*, Latin.] The act of walking abroad.

DE'ARBOUGHT. *adj.* [*dear* and *bought.*] Purchased at an high price.

O fleeting joys
Of Paradise, dearbought *with lasting woe.*
MILTON'S PARADISE LOST.

Such dearbought *blessings happen ev'ry day,*
Because we know not for what things to pray. DRYDEN'S FABLES.

Forget not what my ransom cost,
Nor let my dearbought *soul be lost.*
ROSCOMMON.

DE'ATHWATCH. *n.s.* [*death* and *watch.*] An insect that makes a tinkling noise like that of a watch, and is superstitiously imagined to prognosticate death.

The solemn deathwatch *click'd the hour she dy'd.* GAY.

We learn to presage approaching death in a family by ravens and little worms, which we therefore call a deathwatch.
WATTS.

DEBA'SEMENT. *n.s.* [from *debase.*] The act of debasing or degrading.

It is a wretched debasement *of that sprightly faculty, the tongue, thus to be made the interpreter to a goat or boar.*
GOVERNMENT OF THE TONGUE, SECT. 12.

DEBA'SER. *n.s.* [from *debase.*] He that debases; he that adulterates; he that degrades another; he that sinks the value of things, or destroys the dignity of persons.

To **DECA'NT.** *v.a.* [*decanto*, Lat. *decanter*, Fr.] To pour off gently by inclination.

Take aqua fortis, and dissolve in it ordinary coined silver, and pour the coloured solution into twelve times as much fair water, and then decant *or filtrate the mixture, that it may be very clear.*
BOYLE.

They attend him daily as their chief,
Decant *his wine, and carve his beef.*
SWIFT.

DECANTA'TION. *n.s.* [*decantation*, Fr.] The act of decanting or pouring off clear.

DECA'NTER. *n.s.* [from *decant.*] A glass vessel made for pouring off liquor clear from the lees.

DECE'MBER. *n.s.* [*december*, Latin.] The last month of the year; but named *december*, or the *tenth* month, when the year began in March.

Men are April when they woo, and December *when they wed.*
SHAKESPEARE'S AS YOU LIKE IT.

What should we speak of,
When we are old as you? When we shall hear
The rain and wind beat dark December.
SHAKESPEARE'S CYMBELINE.

DECENNO'VAL, DECENNO'VARY. *adj.* [*decem* and *novem*, Latin.] Relating to the number nineteen.

Meton, of old, in the time of the Peloponesian war, constituted a decennoval *circle, or of nineteen years; the same which we now call the golden number.*
HOLDER ON TIME.

Seven months are retrenched in this whole decennovary *progress of the epacts, to reduce the accounts of her motion and place to those of the sun.*
HOLDER ON TIME.

DECEPTIBI'LITY. *n.s.* [from *deceit.*] Liableness to be deceived.

Some errours are so fleshed in us, that they maintain their interest upon the deceptibility *of our decayed natures.*
GLANVILLE.

DECE'PTIBLE. *adj.* [from *deceit.*] Liable to be deceived; open to imposture; subject to fraud.

The first and father cause of common errour, is the common infirmity of human nature; of whose deceptible *condition, perhaps, there should not need any other eviction than the frequent errours we shall ourselves commit.* BROWN.

DECE'PTION. *n.s.* [*deceptio*, Latin.]

1. The act or means of deceiving; cheat; fraud; fallacy.

Being thus divided from truth in themselves, they are yet farther removed by advenient deception.
BROWN'S VULGAR ERROURS.

All deception *is a misapplying of those signs, which, by compact or institution, were made the means of mens signifying or conveying their thoughts.*
SOUTH'S SERMONS.

2. The state of being deceived.

Reason, not impossibly, may meet
Some specious object by the foe suborn'd,
And fall into deception *unaware.*
MILTON'S PARADISE LOST.

DECE'PTIOUS. *adj.* [from *deceit.*] Deceitful; apt to deceive.

Yet there is a credence in my heart,
That doth invert th' attest of eyes and ears;
As if those organs had deceptious *functions,*
Created only to calumniate.
SHAKESPEARE'S TROILUS AND CRESSIDA.

DECE'PTIVE. *adj.* [from *deceit.*] Having the power of deceiving. *Dictionaries.*

DECE'PTORY. *adj.* [from *deceit.*] Containing means of deceit. *Dictionaries.*

DE'CKER. *n.s.* [from *deck.*] A dresser; one that apparels or adorns; a coverer.

To **DECLA'IM.** *v.n.* [*declamo*, Latin.] To harangue; to speak to the passions; to rhetoricate; to speak set orations.

What are his mischiefs, consul? You declaim
Against his manners, and corrupt your own. BEN JONSON'S CATILINE.

The splendid declaimings *of novices and men of heat.* SOUTH.

It is usual for masters to make their boys declaim *on both sides of an argument.* SWIFT.

Dress up all the virtues in the beauties of oratory, and declaim *aloud on the praise of goodness.* WATTS'S IMPROVEMENT.

DECLINA'TION. *n.s.* [*declinatio*, Latin.]

1. Descent; change from a better to a worse state; decay.[75]

The queen, hearing of the declination *of a monarchy, took it so ill, as she would never after hear of his suit.* BACON, ESSAY 23.

Hope waits upon the flow'ry prime;
And Summer, though it be less gay,
Yet is not look'd on as a time
Of declination *or decay.* WALLER.

2. The act of bending down; as, a declination of the head.

3. Variation from rectitude; oblique motion; obliquity.

Supposing there were a declination *of atoms, yet will it not effect what they intend; for then they do all decline, and so there will be no more concourse than if they did perpendicularly descend.* RAY ON THE CREATION.

This declination *of atoms in their descent, was itself either necessary or voluntary.* BENTLEY.

4. Variation from a fixed point.

There is no declination *of latitude, nor variation of the elevation of the pole, notwithstanding what some have asserted.* WOODWARD'S NATURAL HISTORY.

5. [In navigation.] The variation of the needle from the true meridian of any place to the East or West.

6. [In astronomy.] The *declination* of a star we call its shortest distance from the equator.

BROWN'S VULGAR ERROURS, B. I. C. 13.

7. [In grammar.] The declension or inflection of a noun through its various terminations.

8. DECLINATION *of a Plane* [in dialing], is an arch of the horizon, comprehended either between the plane and the prime vertical circle, if accounted from the East or West; or else between the meridian and the plane, if accounted from the North or South. *Harris.*

DECO'RUM. *n.s.* [Latin.] Decency; behaviour contrary to licentiousness, contrary to levity; seemliness.

If your master
Would have a queen his beggar, you must tell him,
That majesty, to keep decorum, *must*
No less beg than a kingdom.
SHAKESPEARE'S ANTONY AND CLEOPATRA.

I am far from suspecting simplicity, which is bold to trespass in points of decorum. WOTTON.

Beyond the fix'd and settled rules
Of vice and virtue in the schools,
The better sort should set before 'em
A grace, a manner, a decorum. PRIOR.

Gentlemen of the army should be, at least, obliged to external decorum*: a profligate life and character should not be a means of advancement.* SWIFT.

He kept with princes due decorum;
Yet never stood in awe before 'em.
SWIFT.

DECO'YDUCK. *n.s.* A duck that lures others.

There is likewise a sort of ducks, called decoyducks, *that will bring whole flights of fowl to their retirements, where are conveniences made for catching them.* MORTIMER'S HUSBANDRY.

DECU'MBITURE. *n.s.* [from *decumbo*, Latin.]

1. The time at which a man takes to his bed in a disease.

2. [In astrology.] A scheme of the heavens erected for that time, by which the prognosticks of recovery or death are discovered.

If but a mile she travel out of town,
The planetary hour must first be known,
And lucky moment: if her eye but akes,
Or itches, its decumbiture *she takes.*
DRYDEN'S JUVENAL'S SATIRES, VI.

DECU'RION. *n.s.* [*decurio*, Lat.] A commander over ten; an officer subordinate to the centurion.

He instituted decurions *through both these colonies, that is, one over every ten families.* TEMPLE.

DEE'MSTER. *n.s.* [from *deem.*] A judge; a word yet in use in Jersey and the Isle of Man.

To **DEFA'LCATE.** *v.a.* [from *falx, falcis*, a sickle; *defalquer*, French.] To cut off; to lop; to take away part of a pension or salary. It is generally used of money.

DEFALCA'TION. *n.s.* [from *defalcaie.*] Diminution; abatement; excision of any part of a customary allowance.

The tea table is set forth with its customary bill of fare, and without any defalcation. ADDISON'S SPECTATOR, NO. 487.

To **DEFA'LK.** *v.a.* [See **DEFALCATE.**] To cut off; to lop away.

What he defalks *from some insipid sin, is but to make some other more gustful.* DECAY OF PIETY.

To **DE'FECATE.** *v.a.* [*defæco*, Latin.]

1. To purge liquors from lees or foulness; to purify; to cleanse.

I practised a way to defecate *the dark and muddy oil of amber.* BOYLE'S HISTORY OF FIRMNESS.

The blood is not sufficiently defecated *or clarified, but remains muddy.* HARVEY ON CONSUMPTIONS.

Provide a brazen tube
Inflext; self-taught and voluntary flies
The defecated *liquor, through the vent*
Ascending; then, by downward tract convey'd,
Spouts into subject vessels, lovely clear.
PHILIPS.

2. To purify from any extraneous or noxious mixture; to clear; to brighten.

We defecate *the notion from materiality, and abstract quantity, place, and all kind of corporeity from it.* GLANVILLE'S SCEPSIS SCIENTIFICA.

We are puzzled with contradictions, which are no absurdities to defecate *faculties.* GLANVILLE'S SCEPSIS SCIENTIFICA, C. 13.

DEFE'CTIVE or *deficient Nouns* [in grammar.] Indeclinable nouns, or such as want a number, or some particular case.

DEFE'CTIVE *Verb* [in grammar.] A verb which wants some of its tenses.

DEFENSA'TIVE. *n.s.* [from *defence.*]

1. Guard; defence.

A very unsafe defensative *it is against the fury of the lion, and surely no better than virginity, or blood royal, which Pliny doth place in cock-broth.* BROWN'S VULGAR ERROURS, B. III.

If the bishop has no other defensatives *but excommunication, no other power but that of the keys, he may surrender up his pastoral staff.* SOUTH'S SERMONS.

2. [In surgery.] A bandage, plaister, or

the like, used to secure a wound from outward violence.

DEFI'CIENT. *adj.* [*deficiens*, from *deficio*, Latin.] Failing; wanting; defective; imperfect.

O woman! best are all things as the will
Of God ordain'd them: his creating hand
Nothing imperfect or deficient *left.*
MILTON'S PARADISE LOST.

Figures are either simple or mixed: the simple be either circular or angular; and of circular, either complete, as circles, or deficient, *as ovals.*
WOTTON'S ARCHITECTURE.

Neither Virgil nor Homer were deficient *in any of the former beauties.*
DRYDEN'S FABLES, PREFACE.

Several views, postures, stands, turns, limitations and exceptions, and several other thoughts of the mind, for which we have either none, or very deficient *names, are diligently to be studied.* LOCKE.

DEFI'CIENT *Verbs.* See **DEFECTIVE** *Verbs.*

DEFI'CIENT *Nouns.* See **DEFECTIVE** *Nouns.*

To **DEFRA'UD.** *v.a.* [*defraudo*, Latin.] To rob or deprive by a wile or trick; to cheat; to cozen; to deceive; to beguile. With *of* before the thing taken by fraud.

That no man go beyond and defraud *his brother in any matter, because that the Lord is the avenger of all such, as we also have forewarned you and testified.*
BIBLE THESSALONIANS, IV. 6.

My son, defraud *not the poor of his living, and make not the needy eyes to wait long.*
BIBLE ECCLESIASTICUS, IV. 1.

They seem, after a sort, even to mourn, as being injured and defrauded of *their right, when places, not sanctified as they are, prevent them unnecessarily in that pre-eminence and honour.*
HOOKER, B. V. S. 16.

Then they, who brothers better claim disown,
Expel their parents, and usurp the throne;
Defraud *their clients, and, to lucre sold,*
Sit brooding on unprofitable gold.
DRYDEN'S ÆNEID, 6.

But now he seiz'd Briseis' heav'nly charms,
And of *my valour's prize* defrauds *my arms.* POPE'S ILIAD.

There is a portion of our lives which every wise man may justly reserve for his own particular use, without defrauding *his native country.*
DRYDEN'S DEDICATION TO KING ARTHUR.

To **DEGRA'DE.** *v.a.* [*degrader*, French.]

1. To put one from his degree; to deprive him of his office, dignity, or title.

He should
Be quite degraded, *like a hedgeborn swain,*
That doth presume to boast of gentle blood. SHAKESPEARE'S HENRY VI.

2. To lessen; to diminish the value of.

Nor shalt thou, by descending to assume
Man's nature, lessen or degrade *thine own.*
MILTON'S PARADISE LOST.

All higher knowledge in her presence falls
Degraded.
MILTON'S PARADISE LOST, B. VIII. L. 551.

DEGRE'E. *n.s.* [*degré*, French, from *gradus*, Latin.]

1. Quality; rank; station; place of dignity.

Surely men of low degree *are vanity, and men of high* degree *are a lie: to be laid in the balance, they are altogether lighter than vanity.* BIBLE PSALMS, LXII. 9.

It was my fortune, common to that age,
To love a lady fair, of great degree,
The which was born of noble parentage,
And set in highest seat of dignity.
FAIRY QUEEN, B. II. CANT. 4.

I embrace willingly the ancient received course and conveniency of that discipline, which teacheth inferior degrees *and orders in the church of God.*
HOOKER'S DEDICATION.

Well then, Coleville is your name; a knight is your degree, *and your place the dale.*
SHAKESPEARE'S HENRY IV. P. II.

Degree *being vizarded,*
Th' unworthiest shews as fairly in the mask. SHAKESPEARE.

This noble youth to madness lov'd a dame
Of high degree, *Honoria was her name.*
DRYDEN.

Farmers in degree,
He a good husband, a good housewife she.
DRYDEN.

But is no rank, no station, no degree,
From this contagious taint of sorrow free?
PRIOR.

2. The state and condition in which a thing is.[76]

The book of wisdom noteth degrees *of idolatry, making that of worshipping petty and vile idols more gross than simply the worshipping of the creature.*
BACON'S HOLY WAR.

3. A step or preparation to any thing.

Her first degree *was by setting forth her beauties, truly in nature not to be misliked, but as much advanced to the eye as abased to the judgment by art.* SIDNEY, B. II.

Which sight the knowledge of myself might bring,
Which to true wisdom is the first degree.
DAVIES.

4. Order of lineage; descent of family.

King Latinus, in the third degree,
Had Saturn author of his family.
DRYDEN'S ÆNEID. B. VII. L. 72.

5. The orders or classes of the angels.

The several degrees *of angels may probably have larger views, and be endowed with capacities able to set before them, as in one picture, all their past knowledge at once.*
LOCKE.

6. Measure; proportion.

If you come to separate them, and that all the parts are equally heard as loud as one another, they will stun you to that degree, *that you would fancy your ears were torn in pieces.* DRYDEN'S DUFRESNOY.

Poesy
Admits of no degrees; *but must be still*
Sublimely good, or despicably ill.
ROSCOMMON.

7. [In geometry.] The three hundred and sixtieth part of the circumference of a circle. The space of one degree in the heavens is accounted to answer to sixty miles.

In minds and manners, twins oppos'd we see;
In the same sign, almost the same degree.
DRYDEN'S PERSIUS SATIRES.

To you who live in chill degree,
As map informs, of fifty-three.
DRYDEN'S EPISTLES.

8. [In arithmetick.] A *degree* consists of three figures, viz. of three places comprehending units, tens and hundreds; so three hundred and sixty-five is a degree.
COCKER'S ARITHMETICK.

9. The division of the lines upon several sorts of mathematical instruments.

10. [In musick.] The intervals of sounds, which are usually marked by little lines. *Dictionaries.*

11. [In physick and chymistry.] The vehemence or slackness of the hot or cold quality of a plant, mineral, or other mixt body.

The second, third, and fourth degrees *of heat are more easily introduced than the first: every one is both a preparative and a step to the next.* SOUTH'S SERMONS.

DE'LICES. *n.s. pl.* [*deliciæ*, Latin.] Pleasures. This word is merely French.

And now he has pour'd out his idle mind

In dainty delices *and lavish joys,*
Having his warlike weapons cast behind,
And flowers in pleasures and vain pleasing toys. FAIRY QUEEN.

DELI'NQUENCY. *n.s.* [*delinquentia*, Latin.] A fault; a failure in duty; a misdeed.

They never punish the greatest and most intolerable delinquency *of the tumults, and their exciters.* KING CHARLES.

Can
Thy years determine like the age of man,
That thou should'st my delinquencies *exquire,*
And with variety of tortures tire?
SANDYS'S PARAPHRASE OF JOB.

A delinquent ought to be cited in the place or jurisdiction where the delinquency *was committed by him.*
AYLIFFE'S PARERGON.

DE'MI. *inseparable particle.* [*demi*, Fr. *dimidium*, Latin.] Half; one of two equal parts. This word is only used in composition; as *demigod*, that is, half human, half divine.

DEMI-DEVIL. *n.s.* [*demi* and *devil.*] Partaking of infernal nature; half a devil.

Will you, I pray, demand that demi-devil,
Why he hath thus ensnar'd my soul and body? SHAKESPEARE'S OTHELLO.

DEMI-MAN. *n.s.* [*demi* and *man.*] Half a man. A term of reproach.

We must adventure this battle, lest we perish by the complaints of this barking demi-man.
KNOLLES'S HISTORY OF THE TURKS.

DEMI'SE. *n.s.* [from *demetre*, *demis*, *demise*, French.] Death; decease. It is seldom used but in formal and ceremonious language.

About a month before the demise *of queen Anne, the author retired.* SWIFT.

DEMO'CRACY. *n.s.* [*δημοκρατία.*] One of the three forms of government; that in which the sovereign power is neither lodged in one man, nor in the nobles, but in the collective body of the people.

While many of the servants, by industry and virtue, arrive at riches and esteem, then the nature of the government inclines to a democracy. TEMPLE.

The majority having the whole power of the community, may employ all that power in making laws, and executing those laws; and there the form of the government is a perfect democracy. LOCKE.

DEMONO'LOGY. *n.s.* [*δαίμων* and *λόγοζ.*] Discourse of the nature of devils. Thus king James entitled his book concerning witches.

DEMONSTRA'TION. *n.s.* [*demonstratio*, Latin.]

1. The highest degree of deducible or argumental evidence; the strongest degree of proof; such proof as not only evinces the position proved to be true, but shews the contrary position to be absurd and impossible.

What appeareth to be true by strong and invincible demonstration, *such as wherein it is not by any way possible to be deceived, thereunto the mind doth necessarily assent.* HOOKER.

Where the agreement or disagreement of any thing is plainly and clearly perceived, it is called demonstration. LOCKE.

2. Indubitable evidence of the senses or reason.

Which way soever we turn ourselves, we are encountered with clear evidences and sensible demonstrations *of a Deity.*
TILLOTSON.

DENSE. *adj.* [*densus*, Latin.] Close; compact; approaching to solidity; having small interstices between the constituent particles.

The cause of cold is the density of the body;

for all dense *bodies are colder than most other bodies, as metals, stone, glass; and they are longer in heating than softer bodies.* BACON.

In the air the higher you go, the less it is compressed, and consequently the less dense *it is; and so the upper part is exceedingly thinner than the lower part which we breathe.* LOCKE.

To **DE'NSHIRE.** *v.a.* A barbarous term of husbandry.

Burning of land, or burn-bating, is commonly called denshiring, *that is, Devenshiring or Denbighshiring, because most used or first invented there.*
MORTIMER'S HUSBANDRY.

DEO'BSTRUENT. *n.s.* [*deobstruens*, Latin.] A medicine that has the power to resolve viscidities, or to open by any means the animal passages.

All sopes are attenuating and deobstruent, *resolving viscid substances.*
ARBUTHNOT ON ALIMENTS.

To **DEO'PPILATE.** *v.a.* [*de* and *oppilo*, Latin.] To deobstruct; to clear a passage; to free from obstructions.

DEOPPILA'TION. *n.s.* [from *deoppilate.*] The act of clearing obstructions; the removal of whatever obstructs the vital passages.

Though the grosser parts be excluded again, yet are the dissoluble parts extracted, whereby it becomes effectual in deoppilations.
BROWN'S VULGAR ERROURS, B. II. C. 21.

DEO'PPILATIVE. *adj.* [from *deoppilate.*] Deobstruent.

A physician prescribed him a deoppilative *and purgative apozem.*
HARVEY ON CONSUMPTION.

DEOSCULA'TION. *n.s.* [*deosculatio*, Latin.] The act of kissing.

We have an enumeration of the several acts of worship required to be performed to images, viz. processions, genuflections, thurifications and deosculations.
STILLINGFLEET.

DEPA'RTMENT. *n.s.* [*departement*, French.] Separate allotment; province or business assigned to a particular person.[77]

The Roman fleets, during their command at sea, had their several stations and departments*: the most considerable was the Alexandrian fleet, and the second was the African.* ARBUTHNOT.

DEPE'NDANT. *adj.* [from *depend.*] In the power of another.

On God, as the most high, all inferior causes in the world are dependant.
HOOKER, B. V. S. 23.

DEPE'NDANT. *n.s.* [from *depend.*] One who lives in subjection, or at the discretion of another; a retainer.

A great abatement of kindness appears as well in the general dependants, *as in the duke himself also, and your daughter.*
SHAKESPEARE'S KING LEAR.

For a six-clerk a person recommended a dependant *upon him, who paid six thousand pounds ready money.*
CLARENDON.

His dependants *shall quickly become his proselytes.*
SOUTH.

DEPE'NDENCE, DEPE'NDENCY. *n.s.* [from *depend*, Latin. This word, with many others of the same termination, are indifferently written with *ance* or *ence*, *ancy* or *ency*, as the authors intended to derive them from the Latin or French.]

1. A thing or person at the disposal or discretion of another.

We invade the rights of our neighbours, not upon account of covetousness, but of dominion, that we may create dependencies. COLLIER ON PRIDE.

2. State of being subordinate, or subject in some degree to the discretion of another; the contrary to sovereignty.

Let me report to him
Your sweet dependency, *and you shall find*
A conqu'ror that will pray in aid for kindness,
Where he for grace is kneel'd to.
SHAKESPEARE'S ANTONY AND CLEOPATRA.

At their setting out they must have their commission, or letters patents from the king, that so they may acknowledge their dependency *upon the crown of England.* BACON TO VILLIERS.

3. That which is not principal; that which is subordinate.

We speak of the sublunary worlds, this earth, and its dependencies, *which rose out of a chaos about six thousand years ago.* BURNET'S THEORY OF THE EARTH.

4. Concatination; connexion; rise of consequents from premises.

Her madness hath the oddest frame of sense;
Such a dependency *of thing on thing,*
As e'er I heard in madness.
SHAKESPEARE'S MEASURE FOR MEASURE.

5. Relation of any thing to another, as of an effect to its cause.

I took pleasure to trace out the cause of effects, and the dependence *of one thing upon another in the visible creation.* BURNET'S THEORY OF THE EARTH.

6. Trust; reliance; confidence.

The expectation of the performance of our desire, is that we call dependence *upon him for help and assistance.* STILLINGFLEET.

DEPE'NDENT. *adj.* [*dependens*, Latin. This, as many other words of like termination, are written with *ent* or *ant*, as they are supposed to flow from the Latin or French.][78] Hanging down.

In the time of Charles the Great, and long since, the whole furrs in the tails were dependent; *but now that fashion is left, and the spots only worn, without the tails.* PEACHAM.

DEPE'NDENT. *n.s.* [from *dependens*, Latin.] One subordinate; one at the discretion or disposal of another.

We are indigent, defenceless beings; the creatures of his power, and the dependents *of his providence.* ROGERS.

DEPORTA'TION. *n.s.* [*deportatio*, Latin.]

1. Transportation; exile into a remote part of the dominion, with prohibition to change the place of residence.

2. Exile in general.

An abjuration, which is a deportation *for ever into a foreign land, was anciently with us a civil death.* AYLIFFE'S PARERGON.

To **DEPU'RE.** *v.a.* [*depurer*, French.]

1. To cleanse; to free from impurities.

2. To purge; to free from some noxious quality.

It produced plants of such imperfection and harmful quality, as the waters of the general flood could not so wash out or depure, *but that the same defection hath had continuance in the very generation and nature of mankind.* RALEIGH.

To **DEQUA'NTITATE.** *v.a.* [from *de* and *quantitas*, Latin.] To diminish the quantity of.

This we affirm of pure gold; for that which is current, and passeth in stamp amongst us, by reason of its allay, which is a proportion of silver or copper mixed therewith, is actually dequantitated *by fire, and possibly by frequent extinction.* BROWN'S VULGAR ERROURS, B. II. C. 2.

DE'SCANT. *n.s.* [*discanto*, Italian.]
1. A song or tune composed in parts.

Nay, now you are too flat,
And mar the concord with too harsh a
descant. SHAKESPEARE.

The wakeful nightingale
All night long her amorous descant *sung.*
MILTON'S PARADISE LOST.

2. A discourse; a disputation; a disquisition branched out into several divisions or heads. It is commonly used as a word of censure, or contempt.

Look you get a prayer-book in your hand,
And stand between two churchmen, good
my lord;
For on that ground I'll build a holy
descant.
SHAKESPEARE'S RICHARD III.

Such kindness would supplant our unkind reportings, and severe descants *upon our brethren.*
GOVERNMENT OF THE TONGUE.

DESE'RVER. *n.s.* [from *deserve.*] A man who merits rewards. It is used, I think, only in a good sense.

Their love is never link'd to the deserver,
'Till his deserts are pass'd.
SHAKESPEARE'S ANTONY AND CLEOPATRA.

Heavy, with some high minds, is an overweight of obligation; or otherwise great deservers *do perchance grow intolerable presumers.* WOTTON.

Emulation will never be wanting amongst poets, when particular rewards and prizes are proposed to the best deservers.
DRYDEN'S DUFRESNOY, PREFACE.

DESI'GNEDLY. *adv.* [from *design.*] Purposely; intentionally; by design or purpose; not ignorantly; not inadvertently; not fortuitously.

The next thing is sometimes designedly *to put them in pain; but care must be taken that this be done when the child is in good humour.* LOCKE.

Uses made things; that is to say, some things were made designedly, *and on purpose, for such an use as they serve to.*
RAY ON THE CREATION.

DESK. *n.s.* [*disch*, a table, Dutch.] An inclining table for the use of writers or readers, made commonly with a box or repository under it.

Tell her in the desk,
That's cover'd o'er with Turkish tapestry,
There is a purse of ducats.
SHAKESPEARE'S COMEDY OF ERROURS.

He is drawn leaning on a desk, *with his bible before him.* WALTON'S ANGLER.

I have also been obliged to leave unfinished in my desk *the heads of two essays.*
POPE.

Not the desk *with silver nails,*
Nor bureau of expence,
Nor standish well japann'd, avails
To writing of good sense. SWIFT.

DESPI'SABLE. *adj.* [from *despise.*] Contemptible; despicable; regarded with contempt. A word scarcely used but in low conversation.

I am extremely obliged to you for taking notice of a poor old distressed courtier, commonly the most despisable *thing in the world.* ARBUTHNOT TO POPE.

DE'SPOT. *n.s.* [*δήσποτίς.*] An absolute prince; one that governs with unlimited authority. This word is not in use, except as applied to some Dacian prince; as, the *despot* of Servia.

To **DESPU'MATE.** *v.n.* [*despumo*, Latin.] To throw off parts in foam; to froth; to work.

DESPUMA'TION. *n.s.* [from *despumate.*] The act of throwing off excrementitious parts in scum or foam.

DESTINA'TION. *n.s.* [from *destinate.*] The purpose for which any thing is appointed; the ultimate design.

The passages through which spirits are conveyed to the members, being almost infinite, and each of them drawn through so many meanders, wherein other spirits are a journeying, it is wonderful that they should perform their regular destinations *without losing their way.*
GLANVILLE'S SCEPSIS SCIENTIFICA.

There is a great variety of apprehensions and fancies of men, in the destination *and application of things to several ends and uses.* HALE'S ORIGIN OF MANKIND.

DE'SULTORY, DESULTORIOUS. *adj.* [*desultorius*, Lat.] Roving from thing to thing; unsettled; immethodical; unconstant.[79]

'Tis not for a desultory *thought to attone for a lewd course of life, nor for any thing but the superinducing of a virtuous habit upon a vitious one, to qualify an effectual conversion.* L'ESTRANGE.

Let but the least trifle cross his way, and his desultorious *fancy presently takes the scent, leaves the unfinished and half-mangled notion, and skips away in pursuit of the new game.* NORRIS.

Take my desultory *thoughts in their native order, as they rise in my mind, without being reduced to rules, and marshalled according to art.*
FELTON ON THE CLASSICKS.

To **DET'ER.** *v.a.* [*deterreo*, Latin.] To discourage from any thing;[80] to fright from any thing.

I never yet the tragick strain assay'd,
Deterr'd *by thy inimitable maid.*
WALLER.

Many and potent enemies tempt and deter *us from our duty, yet our case is not hard, so long as we have a greater strength on our side.* TILLOTSON, SERMON 6.

Beauty or unbecomingness are of more force to draw or deter *imitation, than any discourses which can be made to them.*
LOCKE.

The ladies may not be deterred *from corresponding with me by this method.*
ADDISON'S GUARDIAN, NO. 114.

My own face deters *me from my glass;*
And Kneller only shews what Celia was.
PRIOR.

DETE'RMENT. *n.s.* [from *deter.*] Cause of discouragement; that by which one is deterred.[81]

This will not be thought a discouragement unto spirits, which endeavour to advantage nature by art; nor will the ill success of some be made a sufficient determent *unto others.*
BROWN'S VULGAR ERROURS, B. VI. C. 8.

These are not all the determents *that opposed my obeying you.* BOYLE.

To **DETE'RGE.** *v.a.* [*detergo*, Latin.] To cleanse a sore; to purge any part from feculence or obstructions.

Consider the part and habit of body, and add or diminish your simples as you design to deterge *or incarn.* WISEMAN.

Sea salt preserves bodies, through which it passeth, from corruption, and it detergeth *the vessels, and keeps the fluids from putrefaction.*
ARBUTHNOT ON ALIMENTS.

DETE'RGENT. *adj.* [from *deterge.*] That which cleanses.

The food ought to be nourishing and detergent. ARBUTHNOT.

DETERRA'TION. *n.s.* [*de* and *terra*, Latin; *deterrer*, French.] Discovery of any thing by removal of the earth that hides it; the act of unburying.

This concerns the raising of new mountains, deterrations *or the devolution of earth down upon the valleys, from the hills and higher grounds.*
WOODWARD'S NATURAL HISTORY.

DEUCE. *n.s.* [*deux*, French.]
1. Two: A word used in games.

You are a gentleman and a gamester; then, I am sure, you know how much the gross sum of deuce *ace amounts to.*
SHAKESPEARE.

2. The devil. See **DEUSE.**

To **DEVE'LOP.** *v.a.* [*developer*, French.] To disengage from something that enfolds and conceals; to disentangle; to clear from its covering.

Take him to develop, *if you can,*
And hew the block off, and get out the man. DUNCIAD.

DE'VIOUS. *adj.* [*devius*, Latin.]
1. Out of the common track.

Creusa kept behind: by choice we stray
Through ev'ry dark and ev'ry devious *way.* DRYDEN'S ÆNEID.

In this minute devious *subject I have been necessitated to explain myself in more words, than to some few may seem needful.*
HOLDER'S ELEMENTS OF SPEECH.

2. Wandering; roving; rambling.

Every muse,
And every blooming pleasure, wait without
To bless the wildly devious *morning walk.*
THOMSON'S SUMMER.

3. Erring; going astray from rectitude.

One devious *step, at first setting out, frequently leads a person into a wilderness of doubt and error.* CLARISSA.[82]

DEUSE. *n.s.* [more properly than *deuce, Junius*, from *Dusius*, the name of a certain species of evil spirits.] The devil: a ludicrous word.

'Twas the prettiest prologue, as he wrote it;
Well, the deuce *take me if I ha'nt forgot it.* CONGREVE.

DEW-BURNING. *adj.* [from *dew* and *burning*.] The meaning of this compound is doubtful. Perhaps it alludes to the sparkling of dew.

He, now to prove his late renewed might,
High-brandishing his bright dew-burning *blade,*
Upon his crested scalp so sore did smite,
That to the scull a yawning wound it made. FAIRY QUEEN.

DIABE'TES. *n.s.* [διαβάιτης.] A morbid copiousness of urine; a fatal colliquation by the urinary passages.

An increase of that secretion may accompany the general colliquations; as in fluxes, hectick sweats and coughs, diabetes, *and other consumptions.*
DERHAM'S PHYSICO-THEOLOGY.

DI'AL. *n.s.* [*diale, Skinner.*] A plate marked with lines, where a hand or shadow shews the hour.

O, gentlemen, the time of life is short:
To spend that shortness basely were too long,
Though life did ride upon a dial's *point,*
Still ending at th' arrival of an hour.
SHAKESPEARE'S HENRY IV.

If the motion be very slow, we perceive it not: we have no sense of the accretive motion of plants or animals; and the sly shadow steals away upon the dial, *and the quickest eye can discover no more but that it is gone.*
GLANVILLE'S SCEPSIS SCIENTIFICA, C. 11.

DIAL-PLATE. *n.s.* [*dial* and *plate.*] That on which hours or lines are marked.

He tells us that the two friends, being each of them possessed of one of these needles, made a kind of dial-plate, *inscribing it with the four and twenty letters, in the same manner as the hours of the day are marked upon the ordinary* dial-plate.
ADDISON'S SPECTATOR, NO. 241.

DIALE'CT. *n.s.* [διάλεκτος.]
1. The subdivision of a language; as the Attic, Doric, Ionic, Æolic dialects.
2. Stile; manner of expression.

When themselves do practise that whereof

they write, they change their dialect; *and those words they shun, as if there were in them some secret sting.*
HOOKER, B. V. S. 22.

3. Language; speech.

In her youth
There is a prone and speechless dialect,
Such as moves men.
SHAKESPEARE'S MEASURE FOR MEASURE.

If the conferring of a kindness did not bind the person, upon whom it was conferred, to the returns of gratitude, why, in the universal dialect *of the world, are kindnesses still called obligations?*
SOUTH'S SERMONS.

DIA'LLING. *n.s.* [from *dial.*] The sciaterick science; the knowledge of shadow; the act of constructing dials on which the shadow may shew the hour.

DIA'LIST. *n.s.* [from *dial.*] A constructer of dials.

Scientifick dialists, *by the geometrick considerations of lines, have found out rules to mark out the irregular motion of the shadow in all latitudes, and on all planes.*
MOXON.

DI'APER. *n.s.* [*diapre*, French, of uncertain etymology.]

1. Linen cloth woven in flowers, and other figures.[83]

Not any damsel, which her vaunteth most
In skilful knitting of soft silken twine;
Nor any weaver, which his work doth boast
In diaper, *in damask, or in lyne,*
Might in their diverse cunning ever dare
With this so curious net-work to compare.
SPENSER.

2. A napkin; a towel.

Let one attend him with a silver bason
Full of rose-water, and bestrew'd with flowers;
Another bear the ewer, a third a diaper.
SHAKESPEARE.

To **DI'APER.** *v.a.* [from the noun.]

1. To variegate; to diversify; to flower.

For fear the stones her tender foot should wrong,
The ground he strew'd with flowers all along,
And diaper'd *like the discoloured mead.*
SPENSER.

Flora useth to cloath our grand-dame earth with a new livery, diapered *with various flowers, and chequered with delightful objects.* HOWEL'S VOCAL FORREST.

2. To draw flowers upon cloaths.

If you diaper *upon folds, let your work be broken, and taken, as it were, by the half; for reason tells you, that your fold must cover somewhat unseen.*
PEACHAM ON DRAWING.

DI'BSTONE.[84] *n.s.* A little stone which children throw at another stone.

I have seen little girls exercise whole hours together, and take abundance of pains to be expert at dibstones, *as they call it.*
LOCKE.

DI'CKENS. A kind of adverbial exclamation, importing, as it seems, much the same with the *devil*; but I know not whence derived.

Where had you this pretty weathercock?
—— I cannot tell what the dickens *his name is my husband had him of.*
SHAKESPEARE'S MERRY WIVES OF WINDSOR.

What a dickens *does he mean by a trivial sum?*
But han't you found it, sir?
CONGREVE'S OLD BATCHELOR.

DI'CTION. *n.s.* [*diction*, French; *dictio*, Latin.] Stile; language; expression.

There appears in every part of his diction, *or expression, a kind of noble and bold purity.* DRYDEN.

DI'CTIONARY. *n.s.* [*dictionarium*, Latin.] A book containing the words of any language in alphabetical order, with explanations of their meaning; a lexicon; a vocabulary; a word-book.

Some have delivered the polity of spirits, and left an account that they stand in awe of charms, spells, and conjurations; that they are afraid of letters and characters, notes and dashes, which, set together, do signify nothing; and not only in the dictionary *of man, but in the subtler vocabulary of satan.* BROWN'S VULGAR ERROURS, B. I. C. 10.

Is it such a horrible fault to translate simulacra images? I see what a good thing it is to have a good catholick dictionary. STILLINGFLEET.

An army, or a parliament, is a collection of men; a dictionary, *or nomenclature, is a collection of words.* WATTS.

DIET-DRINK. *n.s.* [*diet* and *drink.*] Medicated liquors; drink brewed with medicinal ingredients.

The observation will do that better than the lady's diet-drinks, *or apothecary's medicines.* LOCKE.

DI'FFICIL. *adj.* [*difficilis,* Latin.]
1. Difficult; hard; not easy; not obvious. Little used.

That that should give motion to an unwieldy bulk, which itself hath neither bulk nor motion, is of as difficil *apprehension as any mystery in nature.* GLANVILLE'S SCEPSIS SCIENTIFICA, C. 4.

Latin was not more difficil,
Than to a blackbird 'tis to whistle. HUDIBRAS.

2. Scrupulous; hard to be persuaded.

The cardinal finding the pope difficil *in granting the dispensation, doth use it as a principal argument, concerning the king's merit towards that see, that he had touched none of those deniers which had been levied by popes in England.* BACON.

DI'FFICILNESS. *n.s.* [from *difficil.*] Difficulty to be persuaded; incompliance; impracticability.[85]

There be that in their nature do not affect the good of others: the lighter sort of malignity turneth but to a crossness, or forwardness, or aptness to oppose, or difficilness, *or the like; but the deeper sort, to envy and mere mischief.* BACON'S ESSAYS.

DI'FFICULT. *adj.* [*difficilis,* Latin.]
1. Hard; not easy; not facil.

It is difficult *in the eyes of this people.* BIBLE ZACHARY.

2. Troublesome; vexatious.
3. Hard to please; peevish; morose.

DI'FFICULTLY. *adv.* [from *difficult.*] Hardly; with difficulty.

A man who has always indulged himself in the full enjoyment of his station, will difficultly *be persuaded to think any methods unjust that offer to continue it.* ROGERS'S SERMONS.

DI'FFICULTY. *n.s.* [from *difficult; difficultè,*[86] French.]
1. Hardness; contrariety to easiness or facility.

The religion which, by this covenant, we engage ourselves to observe, is a work of labour and difficulty; *a service that requires our greatest care and attention to the discharge of it.* ROGERS, SERMON 13.

2. That which is hard to accomplish; that which is not easy.

They mistake difficulties *for impossibilities: a pernicious mistake certainly; and the more pernicious, for that men are seldom convinced of it, 'till their convictions do them no good.* SOUTH'S SERMONS.

3. Distress; opposition.

Thus, by degrees, he rose to Jove's imperial seat:
Thus difficulties *prove a soul legitimately great.* DRYDEN.

4. Perplexity in affairs; uneasiness of circumstances.

They lie at present under some difficulties, *by reason of the emperor's displeasure, who has forbidden the importation of their manufactures.* ADDISON ON ITALY.

5. Objection; cavil.

Men should consider, that raising difficulties *concerning the mysteries in religion, cannot make them more wise, learned, or virtuous.* SWIFT.

DI'FFORM. *adj.* [from *forma*, Latin.] Contrary to uniform; having parts of different structure; dissimilar; unlike; irregular; as a difform flower, one of which the leaves are unlike each other.

The unequal refractions of difform *rays proceed not from any contingent irregularities; such as are veins, an uneven polish, or fortuitous position of the pores of glass.* NEWTON.

DIGLADIA'TION. *n.s.* [*digladiatio*, Latin.] A combat with swords; any quarrel or contest.

Aristotle seems purposely to intend the cherishing of controversial digladiations, *by his own affection of an intricate obscurity.* GLANVILLE'S SCEPSIS SCIENTIFICA, C. 19.

DI'GNITARY. *n.s.* [from *dignas*, Latin.] A clergyman advanced to some dignity; to some rank above that of a parochial priest.

If there be any dignitaries, *whose preferments are perhaps not liable to the accusation of superfluity, they may be persons of superior merit.* SWIFT.

DI'LATORY. *adj.* [*dilatoire*, French; *dilatorius*, Lat.] Tardy; slow; given to procrastination; addicted to delay; sluggish; loitering.

An inferior council, after former tedious suits in a higher court, would be but dilatory, *and so to little purpose.* HAYWARD.

What wound did ever heal but by degrees?
Thou know'st we work by wit, and not by witchcraft;
And wit depends on dilatory *time.*
SHAKESPEARE'S OTHELLO.

These cardinals trifle with me: I abhor
This dilatory *sloth, and tricks of Rome.*
SHAKESPEARE'S HENRY VIII.

Dilatory *fortune plays the jilt*
With the brave, noble, honest, gallant man,
To throw herself away on fools and knaves. OTWAY'S ORPHEUS.

A dilatory *temper commits innumerable cruelties without design.*
ADDISON'S SPECTATOR, NO. 469.

DILE'MMA. *n.s.* [*διλημμα.*]

1. An argument equally conclusive by contrary suppositions. A young rhetorician applied to an old sophist to be taught the art of pleading, and bargained for a certain reward to be paid, when he should gain a cause. The master sued for his reward, and the scholar endeavoured to elude his claim by a dilemma: If I gain my cause, I shall withhold your pay, because the judge's award will be against you; if I lose it, I may withhold it, because I shall not yet have gained a cause. On the contrary, says the master, if you gain your cause, you must pay me, because you are to pay me when you gain a cause; if you lose it, you must pay me, because the judges will award it.

A dilemma, *that bishop Morton the chancellor used, to raise benevolence, some called his fork, and some his crutch.*
BACON'S HENRY VII.

Hope, whose weak being ruin'd is
Alike if it succeed, and if it miss;
Whom good or ill does equally confound,
And both the horns of fate's dilemma *wound.* COWLEY.

2. A difficult or doubtful choice; a vexatious alternative.

A strong dilemma *in a desp'rate case!*
To act with infamy, or quit the place.
SWIFT.

A dire dilemma*; either way I'm sped;*
If foes, they write, if friends, they read me dead. POPE.

DIMI'NUTIVE. *n.s.* [from the adjective.]

1. A word formed to express littleness; as *lapillus*, in Latin, a *little stone*; *maisonette*, in French, a *little house*; *manniken*, in English, a *little man.*

He afterwards proving a dainty and effeminate youth, was commonly called, by the diminutive *of his name, Peterkin or Perkin.* BACON'S HENRY VII.

Sim, while but Sim, in good repute did live;
Was then a knave, but in diminutive.
COTTON.

2. A small thing: a sense not now in use.

Follow his chariot; monster-like, be shewn
For poor'st diminutives, *for doits!*
SHAKESPEARE'S ANTONY AND CLEOPATRA.

To **DINE.** *v.n.* [*diner*, French.] To eat the chief meal about the middle of the day.

Perhaps some merchant hath invited him,
And from the mart he's somewhere gone to dinner:
Good sister, let us dine, *and never fret.*
SHAKESPEARE.

Myself, he, and my sister,
To-day did dine *together.*
SHAKESPEARE'S COMEDY OF ERROURS.

He would dine *with him the next day.*
CLARENDON.

Thus, of your heroes and brave boys,
With whom old Homer makes such noise,
The greatest actions I can find,
Are, that they did their work and din'd.
PRIOR.

DINING-ROOM. *n.s.* [*dine* and *room.*] The principal apartment of the house; the room where entertainments are made.

He went out from the dining-room *before he had fallen into errour by the intemperance of his meat, or the deluge of drink.*
TAYLOR'S RULE OF LIVING HOLY.

DI'NNER. *n.s.* [*diner*, French.] The chief meal; the meal eaten about the middle of the day.

Let me not stay a jot for dinner:
Go, get it ready.
SHAKESPEARE'S KING LEAR.

Before dinner *and supper, as often as it is convenient, or can be had, let the publick prayers of the church, or some parts of them, be said publickly in the family.*
TAYLOR.

The jolly crew, unmindful of the past,
The quarry share, their plenteous dinner *haste.* DRYDEN'S ÆNEID.

DIRE'CTORY. *n.s.* [from *director.*] The book which the factious preachers published in the rebellion for the direction of their sect in acts of worship.

As to the ordinance concerning the directory, *we cannot consent to the taking away of the book of common prayer.*
OXFORD REASONS AGAINST THE COVENANT.

DIRT-PIE. *n.s.* [*dirt* and *pie.*] Forms moulded by children of clay, in imitation of pastry.

Thou set'st thy heart upon that which has newly left off making of dirt-pies, *and is but preparing itself for a green-sickness.*
SUCKLING.

DISAFFE'CTED. *part. adj.* [from *disaffect.*] Not disposed to zeal or affection. Usually applied to those who are enemies to the government.

By denying civil worship to the emperor's statues, which the custom then was to give,

they were proceeded against as disaffected *to the emperor.*
STILLINGFLEET'S DEFENCE OF DISCOURSE ON ROMISH IDOLATRY.

To **DISANNU'L.** *v.a.* [*dis* and *annul.* This word is formed contrary to analogy by those who not knowing the meaning of the word *annul*, intended to form a negative sense by the needless use of the negative particle. It ought therefore to be rejected as ungrammatical and barbarous.] To annul; to deprive of authority; to vacate; to make null; to make void; to nullify.

The Jews ordinances for us to resume, were to check our Lord himself, which hath disannulled *them.* HOOKER, B. IV. §11.

That gave him power of disannulling *of laws, and disposing of mens fortunes and estates, and the like points of absolute power, being in themselves harsh and odious.* BACON, HENRY VII.

To be in both worlds full,
Is more than God was, who was hungry here:
Wouldst thou his laws of fasting disannul?
HERBERT.

Wilt thou my judgments disannul? *Defame*
My equal rule, to clear thyself of blame?
SANDYS.

DI'SARD. *n.s.* [*disi*, *disig*, Saxon, a fool, *Skinner*; *diseur*, French, *Junius.*] A prattler; a boasting talker. This word is inserted both by *Skinner* and *Junius*; but I do not remember it.

To **DISBA'RK.** *v.a.* [*debarquer*, French.] To land from a ship; to put on shore.

Together sail'd they, fraught with all the things
To service done by land that might belong,
And, when occasion serv'd, disbarked *them.* FAIRFAX, B. I.

The ship we moor on these obscure abodes;
Disbark *the sheep, an offering to the gods.*
POPE'S ODYSSEY.

DISCI'PLE. *n.s.* [*discipulus*, Latin.] A scholar; one that professes to receive instructions from another.

He rebuked disciples, *who would call for fire from heaven upon whole cities, for the neglect of a few.* KING CHARLES.

The commemorating the death of Christ, is the professing ourselves the disciples *of the crucified Saviour; and that engageth us to take up his cross and follow him.*
HAMMOND.

A young disciple *should behave himself so well, as to gain the affection and the ear of his instructor.* WATTS.

To **DISCOMME'ND.** *v.a.* [*dis* and *commend.*] To blame; to censure; to mention with disapprobation.

Absolutely we cannot discommend, *we cannot absolutely approve, either willingness to live, or forwardness to die.*
HOOKER.

Now you will all be wits; and he, I pray,
And you, that discommend *it, mend the play.* DENHAM.

Neither do I discommend *the lofty stile in tragedy, which is naturally pompous and magnificent.*
DRYDEN'S SPANISH FRYAR, DEDICATION.

To **DISCOMMO'DE.** *v.a.* [*dis* and *commode*, French.] To put to inconvenience; to molest; to incommode.

To **DISCONCE'RT.** *v.a.* [*dis* and *concert.*]

1. To unsettle the mind; to discompose.

You need not provoke their spirits by outrages: a careless gesture, a word, or a look, is enough to disconcert *them.*
COLLIER.

2. To break a scheme; to defeat a machination.

DISCO'VERER. *n.s.* [from *discover.*]

1. One that finds any thing not known before; a finder out.

If more be found out, they will not recompence the discoverer's *pains, but will be fitter to be cast out.*
HOLDER'S ELEMENTS OF SPEECH.

Places receive appellations according to the language of the discoverer, *from observations made upon the people.*
NOTES ON ODYSSEY.

The Cape of Good Hope was doubled in those early times; and that the Portuguese were not the first discoverers *of that navigation.* ARBUTHNOT ON COINS.

An old maiden gentlewoman is the greatest discoverer *of judgments; she can tell you what sin it was that set such a man's house on fire.*
ADDISON'S SPECTATOR, NO. 483.

2. A scout; one who is put to descry the posture or number of an enemy; speculator.

Here stand, my lords, and send discoverers *forth,*
To know the numbers of our enemies.
SHAKESPEARE'S HENRY VI.

DISCOU'RSER. *n.s.* [from *discourse.*]

1. A speaker; an haranguer.

The tract of every thing,
Would by a good discourser *lose some life,*
Which action's self was tongue to.
SHAKESPEARE.

2. A writer on any subject; a dissertator.

Philologers and critical discoursers, *who look beyond the obvious exteriors of things, will not be angry at our narrower explorations.*
BROWN'S PREFACE TO VULGAR ERROURS.

But it seems to me, that such discoursers *do reason upon short views, and a very moderate compass of thought.* SWIFT.

DISCU'MBENCY. *n.s.* [*discumbens,* Latin.] The act of leaning at meat, after the ancient manner.

The Greeks and Romans used the custom of discumbency *at meals, which was upon their left side; for so their right hand was free and ready for all service.*
BROWN'S VULGAR ERROURS.

To **DISEMBA'RK.** *v.a.* [*dis* and *embark.*] To carry to land.

I must unto the road, to disembark
Some necessaries.
SHAKESPEARE'S TWO GENTLEMEN OF VERONA.

To **DISEMBA'RK.** *v.n.* To land; to go on land.

There disembarking *on the green sea-side,*
We land our cattle, and the spoil divide.
POPE'S ODYSSEY.

To **DISEMBI'TTER.** *v.a.* [*dis* and *embitter.*] To sweeten; to free from bitterness; to clear from acrimony.[87]

Encourage such innocent amusements as may disembitter *the minds of men, and make them mutually rejoice in the same agreeable satisfactions.*
ADDISON'S FREEHOLDER, NO. 34.

To **DISFO'REST.** *v.a.* [*dis* and *forest.*] To reduce land from the privileges of a forest to the state of common land.

To **DISGLO'RIFY.** *v.a.* [*dis* and *glorify.*] To deprive of glory; to treat with indignity.

So Dagon shall be magnify'd, and God,
Besides whom is no god, compar'd with idols,
Disglorify'd, *blasphem'd, and had in scorn.* MILTON'S AGONISTES.

DISGU'ST. *n.s.* [*degout,* French.]

1. Aversion of the palate from any thing.

2. Ill-humour; malevolence; offence conceived.

The manner of doing is of more consequence than the thing done, and upon that depends the satisfaction or disgust *wherewith it is received.* LOCKE.

Thence dark disgust *and hatred, winding wiles,*
Coward deceit, and ruffian violence.
THOMSON'S SPRING.

To **DISGU'ST.** *v.a.* [*degouter*, French; *degusto*, Latin.]

1. To raise aversion in the stomach; to distaste.

2. To strike with dislike; to offend. It is variously constructed with *at* or *with.*

If a man were disgusted *at marriage, he would never recommend it to his friend.* ATTERBURY.

Those unenlarged souls are disgusted *with the wonders which the microscope has discovered.*
WATTS'S IMPROVEMENT OF THE MIND.

3. To produce aversion: with *from.*

What disgusts *me from having to do with answer-jobbers is, that they have no conscience.* SWIFT.

DISGU'STFUL. *adj.* [*disgust* and *full.*] Nauseous; that which causes aversion.

I have finished the most disgustful *task that ever I undertook.* SWIFT.

To **DISHE'RIT.** *v.a.* [*dis* and *inherit.*] To cut off from hereditary succession; to debar from an inheritance.

He tries to restore to their rightful heritage such good old English words as have been long time out of use, almost disherited.
SPENSER'S PASTORALS.

How they were rank'd shall rest untold by me,
With nameless nymphs that liv'd in ev'ry tree;
Nor how the Dryads and the woodland train,
Disherited, *ran howling o'er the plain.*
DRYDEN'S FABLES.

To **DISHE'VEL.** *v.a.* [*decheveler*, French.] To spread the hair disorderly; to throw the hair of a woman negligently about her head. It is not often used but in the passive participle.

A gentle lady all alone,
With garments rent and hair dishevelled,
Wringing her hands, and making piteous moan. SPENSER'S FAIRY QUEEN.

After followed great numbers of women weeping, with dishevelled *hair, scratching their faces and tearing themselves after the manner of the country.* KNOLLES.

A troop of Trojans mix'd with these appear,
And mourning matrons with dishevell'd *hair.* DRYDEN'S ÆNEID.

The flames involv'd in smoak
Of incence, from the sacred altar broke,
Caught her dishevell'd *hair and rich attire.* DRYDEN'S ÆNEID.

You this morn beheld his ardent eyes,
Saw his arm lock'd in her dishevell'd *hair.*
SMITH'S PHÆDRA AND HIPPOLITUS.

DISHU'MOUR. *n.s.* [*dis* and *humour.*] Peevishness; ill humour; uneasy state of mind.

Speaking impatiently to servants, or any thing that betrays inattention or dishumour, *are also criminal.*
SPECTATOR, NO. 424.

DISINTERE'SSED. *n.s.* [*dis* and *interesse*, French. It is written *disinterested* by those who derive it immediately from *interest*, and I think more properly.] Without regard to private advantage; not biassed by particular views; impartial.

Not that tradition's parts are useless here,
When general, old, disinteress'd, *and clear.* DRYDEN.

DISINTERE'SSMENT. *n.s.* [*dis* and *interessement*, French.] Disregard to private advantage; disinterest; disinterestedness. This word like *charges* in the same sentence, is merely gallick.

He has managed some of the charges of the kingdom with known ability, and laid them down with entire disinteressment. PRIOR'S POSTSCRIPT.

DISI'NTEREST. *n.s.* [*dis* and *interest.*]

1. What is contrary to one's wish or prosperity; that which any one is concerned to prevent.

They judge it the great disinterest *to Rome.* GLANVILLE.

2. Indifference to profit; superiority to regards of private advantage.

DISI'NTERESTED. *adj.* [from *disinterest.*]

1. Superior to regard of private advantage; not influenced by private profit.

My lord, as disinterested *as you appear to the world, I am convinced, that no man is more in the power of prevailing favourite passion than yourself.* SWIFT.

2. Without any concern in an affair; without fear or hope.

DISKI'NDNESS. *n.s.* [*dis* and *kindness.*]

1. Want of kindness; want of affection; want of benevolence.

2. Ill turn; injury; act of malignity; detriment.

This discourse is so far from doing any diskindness *to the cause, that it does it a real service.* WOODWARD'S NATURAL HISTORY.

DISLI'KE. *n.s.* [from the verb.]

1. Disinclination; absence of affection; the contrary to fondness.

He then them took, and tempering goodly well
Their contrary dislikes *with loved means,*
Did place them all in order, and compel
To keep themselves within their sundry reigns,
Together link'd with adamantine chains.
SPENSER.

Your dislikes *to whom I would be pleasing,*
Do cloud my joys with danger and with sorrow. SHAKESPEARE.

God's grace, that principle of his new birth, gives him continual dislike *to sin.* HAMMOND'S PRACTICAL CATECHISM.

Sorrow would have been as silent as thoughts, as severe as philosophy. It would have rested in inward senses, tacit dislikes. SOUTH'S SERMONS.

Our likings or dislikes *are founded rather upon humour and fancy than upon reason.* L'ESTRANGE.

The jealous man is not angry if you dislike another; but if you find those faults which are in his own character, you discover not only your dislike *of another, but of himself.* ADDISON.

2. Discord; dissention; disagreement. This sense is not now in use.

This said Aletes, and a murmur rose
That shew'd dislike *among the christian peers.* FAIRFAX.

To **DISLI'KE.** *v.a.* [*dis* and *like.*] To disapprove; to regard without affection; to regard with ill-will or disgust.

What most he should dislike, *seems pleasant to him;*
What like, offensive.
SHAKESPEARE'S KING LEAR.

Ye dislike, *and so undo*
The players, and disgrace the poet too.
DENHAM'S PROLOGUE TO SOPHY.

Whosoever dislikes *the digressions, or grows weary of them, may throw them away.* TEMPLE.

DISLI'KEFUL. *adj.* [*dislike* and *full.*] Disaffected; malign.

I think it best, by an union of manners, and conformity of minds, to bring them to be one people, and to put away the dislikeful *conceit of the one and the other.* SPENSER'S IRELAND.

To **DISLI'KEN.** *v.a.* [*dis* and *like.*] To make unlike.

Muffle your face,
Dismantle you; and, as you can, disliken
The truth of your own seeming.
SHAKESPEARE'S WINTER'S TALE.

DISLI'KENESS. *n.s.* [*dis* and *likeness.*] Dissimilitude; not resemblance; unlikeness.

That which is not designed to represent any thing but itself, can never be capable of a wrong representation, nor mislead us from the true apprehension of any thing by its dislikeness *to it; and such, excepting those of substances, are all our own complex ideas.* LOCKE.

DISLI'KER. *n.s.* [from *dislike.*] A disapprover; one that is not pleased.

There is a point, which whoever can touch, will never fail of pleasing a majority, so great that the dislikers *will be forced to fall in with the herd.* SWIFT.

To **DISMO'RTGAGE.** *v.a.* [*dis* and *mortgage.*] To redeem from mortgage.

He dismortgaged *the crown demesnes, made an increase of munition, arms and treasure, and left behind a mass of gold.* HOWEL'S VOCAL FORREST.

DISO'RIENTATED. *adj.* [*dis* and *orient.*] Turned from the East; turned from the right direction; thrown out of the proper place. *Harris.*

To **DISPLO'DE.** *v.a.* [*displodo,* Latin.] To disperse with a loud noise; to vent with violence.

In view
Stood rank'd of seraphim another row,
In posture to displode *their second fire*
Of thunder.
MILTON'S PARADISE LOST, B. VI. L. 605.

DISPLO'SION. *n.s.* [from *displosus,* Lat.] The act of disploding; a sudden burst or dispersion with noise and violence.

To **DISPRE'AD.** *v.a.* [*dis* and *spread.*] To spread different ways. In this word, and a few others, *dis* has the same force as in Latin composition, and means, different ways; in different directions.[88]

As morning sun her beams dispreaden *clear,*
And in her face fair truth and mercy doth appear. FAIRY QUEEN.

Over him, art striving to compare
With nature, did an arbour green dispread,
Framed of wanton ivy, flowing fair,
Through which the fragrant eglantine did spread
His pricking arms, entrail'd with roses red.
FAIRY QUEEN.

Above, below, around, with art dispread,
The sure inclosure folds the genial bed.
POPE'S ODYSSEY.

DISPU'NISHABLE. *adj.* [*dis* and *punishable.*] Without penal restraint.

No leases of any part of the said lands shall ever be made, other than leases for years not exceeding thirty-one, in possession, and not in reversion or remainder, and not dispunishable *of waste.*
SWIFT'S LAST WILL.

To **DISPU'RSE.** *v.a.* [*dis* and *purse.*] To pay; to disburse. It is not certain that the following passage should not be written *disburse.*

Many a pound of my own proper store,
Because I would not tax the needy commons,
Have I dispursed *to the garrisons,*
And never ask'd for restitution.
SHAKESPEARE'S HENRY VI.

DISRE'LISH. *n.s.* [*dis* and *relish.*]

1. Bad taste; nauseousness.

Oft they assay'd,
Hunger and thirst constraining; drugg'd as oft
With hatefullest disrelish, *writh'd their jaws,*
With soot and cinders fill'd.
MILTON'S PARADISE LOST, B. X.

2. Dislike of the palate; squeamishness.

Bread or tobacco may be neglected, where they are shewn not to be useful to health, because of an indifferency or disrelish *to them.* LOCKE.

DISSA'TISFACTION. *n.s.* [*dis* and *satisfaction.*] The state of being dissatisfied; discontent; want of something to compleat the wish.

He that changes his condition, out of impatience and dissatisfaction, *when he has tried a new one, wishes for his old again.* L'ESTRANGE.

The ambitious man has little happiness, but is subject to much uneasiness and dissatisfaction.
ADDISON'S SPECTATOR.

In vain we try to remedy the defects of our acquisition, by varying the object: the same dissatisfaction *pursues us through the circle of created goods.* ROGERS, SERMON 5.

DISSA'TISFACTORINESS. *n.s.* [from *dissatisfactory.*] Inability to give content.

DISSATISFA'CTORY. *adj.* [from *dissatisfy.*] That which is unable to give content.

To **DISSE'VER.** *v.a.* [*dis* and *sever.* In this word the particle *dis* makes no change in the signification, and therefore the word, though supported by great authorities, ought to be ejected from our language.] To part in two; to break; to divide; to sunder; to separate; to disunite.

Shortly had the storm so dissevered *the company, which the day before had tarried together, that most of them never met again, but were swallowed up.*
SIDNEY, B. II.

The dissevering *of fleets hath been the overthrow of many actions.*
RALEIGH'S ESSAYS.

All downright rains dissever *the violence of outrageous winds, and level the mountainous billows.* RALEIGH.

Dissever *your united strengths,*
And part your mingled colours once again.
SHAKESPEARE'S KING JOHN.

The meeting points the sacred hair dissever
From the fair head, for ever and for ever.
POPE.

To **DI'SSIPATE.** *v.a.* [*dissipatus,* Latin.]

1. To scatter every way; to disperse.

The heat at length grows so great, that it again dissipates *and bears off those very corpuscles which before it brought.*
WOODWARD'S NATURAL HISTORY.

The circling mountains eddy in,
From the bare wild, the dissipated *storm.*
THOMSON'S AUTUMN.

2. To scatter the attention.

This slavery to his passions produced a life irregular and dissipated.
SAVAGE'S LIFE.

3. To spend a fortune.

The wherry that contains
Of dissipated *wealth the poor remains.*
LONDON.

DI'SSOLUTENESS. *n.s.* [from *dissolute.*] Looseness; laxity of manners; debauchery.

If we look into the common management, we shall have reason to wonder, in the great dissoluteness *of manners which the world complains of, that there are any footsteps at all left of virtue.* LOCKE.

To **DISSU'NDER.** *v.a.* [*dis* and *sunder*. This is a barbarous word. See **DISSEVER.**] To sunder; to separate.

But when her draught the sea and earth
dissunder'd,
The troubl'd bottoms turn'd up, and she
thunder'd. CHAPMAN.

DI'STANCE. *n.s.* [*distance*, French; *distantia*, Latin.]

1. *Distance* is space considered barely in length between any two beings, without considering any thing else between them. LOCKE.

It is very cheap, notwithstanding the great distance *between the vineyards and the towns that sell the wine.* ADDISON ON ITALY.

As he lived but a few miles distance *from her father's house, he had frequent opportunities of seeing her.* ADDISON.

2. Remoteness in place.

Cæsar is still disposed to give us terms,
And waits at distance *'till he hears from*
Cato. ADDISON'S CATO.

These dwell at such convenient distance,
That each may give his friend assistance.
PRIOR.

3. The space kept between two antagonists in fencing.

We come to see thee fight; to see thy pass, thy stock, thy reverse, thy distance. SHAKESPEARE'S MERRY WIVES OF WINDSOR.

4. Contrariety; opposition.

Banquo was your enemy,
So is he mine; and in such bloody distance,
That every minute of his being thrusts
Against my near'st of life.
SHAKESPEARE'S MACBETH.

5. A space marked on the course where horses run.

This was the horse that ran the whole field out of distance, *and won the race.* L'ESTRANGE.

6. Space of time.

You must do it by distance *of time.* BIBLE 2 ESDRAS, V. 47.

I help my preface by a prescript, to tell that there is ten years distance *between one and the other.* PRIOR.

7. Remoteness in time either past or future.

We have as much assurance of these things, as things future and at a distance *are capable of.* TILLOTSON'S SERMONS.

To judge right of blessings prayed for, and yet at a distance, *we must be able to know things future.* SMALRIDGE'S SERMONS.

8. Ideal disjunction; mental separation.

The qualities that affect our senses are, in the things themselves, so united and blended, that there is no separation, no distance *between them.* LOCKE.

9. Respect; distant behaviour.

I hope your modesty
Will know, what distance *to the crown is*
due. DRYDEN.

'Tis by respect and distance *that authority is upheld.* ATTERBURY.

If a man makes me keep my distance, *the comfort is, he keeps his at the same time.* SWIFT.

10. Retraction of kindness; reserve; alienation.

On the part of heav'n,
Now alienated! distance *and distaste,*
Anger, and just rebuke, and judgment
giv'n. MILTON'S PARADISE LOST.

DISTE'NTION. *n.s.* [*distentio*, Latin.]

1. The act of stretching in breadth.

Wind and distention *of the bowels are signs of a bad digestion in the intestines; for in dead animals, when there is no digestion at all, the* distention *is in the greatest extremity.* ARBUTHNOT.

2. Breadth; space occupied by the thing distended.

3. The act of separating one part from another; divarication.

Our leggs do labour more in elevation than in distention.
WOTTON'S ARCHITECTURE.

DISVALUA'TION. *n.s.* [*dis* and *valuation.*] Disgrace; diminution of reputation.

What can be more to the disvaluation *of the power of the Spaniard, than that eleven thousand English should, within two months, have marched into the heart of his countries?*
BACON'S WAR WITH SPAIN.

To **DISVA'LUE.** *v.a.* [*dis* and *value.*] To undervalue; to set a low price upon.

Her reputation was disvalu'd
In levity.
SHAKESPEARE'S MEASURE FOR MEASURE.

The very same pride which prompts a man to vaunt and overvalue what he is, does as forcibly incline him to contemn and disvalue *what he has.*
GOVERNMENT OF THE TONGUE.

DISU'SAGE. *n.s.* [*dis* and *usage.*] The gradual cessation of use or custom.

They cut off presently such things as might be extinguished without danger, leaving the rest to be abolished by disusage *through tract of time.* HOOKER, B. IV. S. 14.

DISU'SE. *n.s.* [*dis* and *use.*]
1. Cessation of use; dessuetude; want of practice.

The disuse *of the tongue is the only effectual remedy against these.*
ADDISON'S GUARDIAN, NO. 12.

2. Cessation of custom.

That obligation upon the lands did not prescribe, or come into disuse, *but by fifty consecutive years.* ARBUTHNOT.

DISWI'TTED. *adj.* [*dis* and *wit.*] Deprived of the wits; mad; distracted. A word not in use.

She ran away alone;
Which when they heard, there was not one
But hasted after to be gone,
As she had been diswitted.
DRAYTON'S NYMPHID.

DI'VER. *n.s.* [from *dive.*]
1. One that sinks voluntarily under water.

If perseverance gain the diver's *prize,*
Not everlasting Blackmore this denies.
POPE'S DUNCIAD.

2. One that goes under water in search of treasure.

It is evident, from the relation of divers *and fishers for pearls, that there are many kinds of shell-fish which lie perpetually concealed in the deep, skreened from our sight.* WOODWARD.

3. He that enters deep into knowledge or study.

He would have him, as I conceive it, to be no superficial and floating artificer; but a diver *into causes, and into the mysteries of proportion.*
WOTTON'S ARCHITECTURE.

To **DI'ZEN.** *v.a.* [This word seems corrupted from *dight.*] To dress; to deck; to rig out. A low word.

Your ladyship lifts up the sash to be seen;
For sure I had dizen'd *you out like a queen.* SWIFT.

DI'ZZARD. *n.s.* [from *dizzy.*] A blockhead; a fool. *Dictionaries.*

DO'CTOR. *n.s.* [*doctor*, Latin.]
1. One that has taken the highest degree in the faculties of divinity, law, or physick. In some universities they have doctors of musick. In its original import it means a man so well versed in his faculty, as to be qualified to teach it.

No woman had it, but a civil doctor,
Who did refuse three thousand ducats of me,

And begg'd the ring.
SHAKESPEARE'S MERCHANT OF VENICE.

Then stood there up one in the council, a pharisee, named Gamaliel, a doctor *of laws.* BIBLE ACTS, V. 34.

2. A man skilled in any profession.

Then subtle doctors *scriptures made their pride,*
Casuists, like cocks, struck out each other's eyes. DENHAM.

Each proselyte would vote his doctor *best,*
With absolute exclusion to the rest.
DRYDEN'S HIND AND PANTHER.

3. A physician; one who undertakes the cure of diseases.

By med'cine life may be prolong'd, yet death
Will seize the doctor *too.*
SHAKESPEARE'S CYMBELINE.

How does your patient, doctor*?*
—— Not so sick, my lord,
As she is troubl'd with thick coming fancies. SHAKESPEARE'S MACBETH.

Children will not take those medicines from the doctor's *hand, which they will from a nurse or mother.*
GOVERMENT OF TONGUE.

To 'pothecaries let the learn'd prescribe,
That men may die without a double bribe:
Let them, but under their superiors, kill,
When doctors *first have sign'd the bloody bill.* DRYDEN.

He that can cure by recreation, and make pleasure the vehicle of health, is a doctor *at it in good earnest.* COLLIER.

In truth, nine parts in ten of those who recovered, owed their lives to the strength of nature and a good constitution, while such a one happened to be the doctor.
SWIFT.

4. Any able or learned man.

The simplest person, that can but apprehend and speak sense, is as much judge of it as the greatest doctor *in the school.*
DIGBY OF BODIES.

DO'DKIN. *n.s.* [*duytken*, Dutch.] A doitkin or little doit; a contemptuous name for a low coin.

I would not buy them for a dodkin.
LILY'S GRAMMAR CONSTRUED.

DOG. *n.s.* [*dogghe*, Dutch.]

1. A domestick animal remarkably various in his species; comprising the mastiff, the spaniel, the buldog, the greyhound, the hound, the terrier, the cur, with many others. The larger sort are used as a guard; the less for sports.

Such smiling rogues as these sooth every passion:
Renege, affirm, and turn their halcyon beaks
With ev'ry gale and vary of their masters,
As knowing nought, like dogs, *but following.*
SHAKESPEARE'S KING LEAR.

Why should we not think a watch and pistol as distinct species one from another, as a horse and a dog. LOCKE.

The clamour roars of men and boys, and dogs,
Ere the soft fearful people, to the flood
Commit their woolly sides.
THOMSON'S SPRING, L. 375.

2. A constellation called Sirius, or Canicula, rising and setting with the sun during the canicular days, or dog days.

Among the southern constellations two there are who bear the name of the dog*; the one in sixteen degrees latitude, containing on the left thigh a star of the first magnitude, usually called Procyon, or Anticanus.*
BROWN'S VULGAR ERROURS, B. IV.

It parts the twins and crab, the dog *divides,*
And Argo's keel that broke the frothy tides. CREECH.

3. A reproachful name for a man.

I never heard a passion so confus'd,
So strange, outrageous, and so variable,

As the dog *Jew did utter in the streets.* SHAKESPEARE'S MERCHANT OF VENICE.

Beware of dogs, *beware of evil workers.* BIBLE PHILIPPIANS, III. 2.

4. *To give or send to the* DOGS; to throw away. *To go to the* DOGS; to be ruined, destroyed, or devoured.

Had whole Colepeper's wealth been hops and hogs,
Could he himself have sent it to the dogs*?*
POPE'S EPISTLES.

5. It is used as the term for the male of several species; as, the *dog* fox, the *dog* otter.

If ever I thank any man, I'll thank you; but that they call compliments is like the encounter of two dog *apes.* SHAKESPEARE.

6. *Dog* is a particle added to any thing to mark meanness, or degeneracy, or worthlessness; as *dog* rose.

DOG-TRICK. *n.s.* [*dog* and *trick.*] An ill turn; surly or brutal treatment.

Learn better manners, or I shall serve you a dog-trick*: come, down upon all four immediately; I'll make you know your rider.* DRYDEN'S DON SEBASTIAN.

DO'GBOLT. *n.s.* [*dog* and *bolt.*] Of this word I know not the meaning, unless it be, that when meal or flower is sifted or bolted to a certain degree, the coarser part is called *dogbolt*, or flower for *dogs.*

His only solace was, that now
His dogbolt *fortune was so low,*
That either it must quickly end,
Or turn about again, and mend.
HUDIBRAS, P. I. CANT. 3.

DOGCHEAP. *adj.* [*dog* and *cheap.*] Cheap as dogs meat; cheap as the offal bought for dogs.

Good store of harlots, say you, and dogcheap*?* DRYDEN.

DOGKE'NNEL. *n.s.* [*dog* and *kennel.*] A little hut or house for dogs.

A certain nobleman, beginning with a dogkennel, *never lived to finish the palace he had contrived.* DRYDEN.

I am desired to recommend a dogkennel *to any that shall want a pack.* TATLER, NO. 62.

DOLL. *n.s.*
1. A contraction of Dorothy.[89]
2. A little girl's puppet or baby.

DO'LLAR. *n.s.* [*daler*, Dutch.] A Dutch and German coin of different value, from about two shillings and sixpence to four and sixpence.

He disburs'd, at St. Colmeskill isle,
Ten thousand dollars *for our gen'ral use.*
SHAKESPEARE'S MACBETH.

DOMI'NICAL. *adj.* [*dominicalis*, Latin.] That which notes the Lord's day, or Sunday.

The cycle of the moon serves to shew the epacts, and that of the sun the dominical *letter, throughout all their variations.* HOLDER ON TIME.

DOOMSDAY-BOOK. *n.s.* [*doomsday* and *book.*] A book made by order of William the Conqueror, in which the estates of the kingdom were registered.

The Danes also brought in a reckoning of money by ores, per oras, which is mentioned in doomsday-book. CAMDEN.

DO'RNICK. *n.s.* [of Deornick in Flanders, where first made.] A species of linen cloath used in Scotland for the table.

To **DORR.** *v.a.* [*tor*, stupid, Teutonick.] To deafen or stupify with noise. This word I find only in *Skinner.*

DORR. *n.s.* [so named probably from the noise which he makes.] A kind of flying insect, remarkable for flying with a loud noise.

The dorr, *or hedge-chafer's chief marks are these: his head is small, like that of the common beetle: this and his eyes black: his shoulder-piece, and the middle of his belly, also black; but just under the wing-shells spotted with white. His wing-shells, legs, and the end of his tail, which is long and flat-pointed, of a light chesnut: his breast, especially, covered with a downy hair.* GREW'S MUSÆUM.

DORSI'FEROUS, DORSI-PAROUS. *n.s.* [*dorsum* and *fero*, or *pario*, Latin.] Having the property of bearing or bringing forth on the back. It is used of plants that have the seeds on the back of their leaves, as fern; and may be properly used of the American frog, which brings forth young from her back.

DOSE. *n.s.* [*δόσις*.][90]

1. So much of any medicine as is taken at one time. *Quincy.*

The too vig'rous dose *too fiercely wrought,*
And added fury to the strength it brought.
DRYDEN'S VIRGIL.

In a vehement pain of the head he prescribed the juice of the thapsia in warm water, without mentioning the dose. ARBUTHNOT.

2. As much of any thing as falls to a man's lot.

No sooner does he peep into
The world, but he has done his doe;
Married his punctual dose *of wives,*
Is cuckolded, and breaks, or thrives.
HUDIBRAS, P. II.

3. It is often used of the utmost quantity of strong liquor that a man can swallow. He has his *dose*, that is, he can carry off no more.

DO'SSIL. *n.s.* [corrupted from *dorsel*, something laid upon the part.] A pledget; a nodule or lump of lint, to be laid on a sore.

Her complaints put me upon dressing with such medicaments as basilicon, with præcipitate, upon a dossil. WISEMAN.

DO'TARD. *n.s.* [from *dote.*] A man whose age has impaired his intellects; a man in his second childhood; called in some provinces a *twichild.*

Dotard, *said he, let be thy deep advise,*
Seems that through many years thy wits thee fail,
And that weak old hath left thee nothing wise,
Else never should thy judgement be so frail. FAIRY QUEEN.

The sickly dotard *wants a wife,*
To draw off his last dregs of life. PRIOR.

DOUBLE is much used in composition, generally for *doubly*, two ways; as *double edged*, having an edge on each side; or for twice the number or quantity, as *double died*, twice died.

To **DOUBLE-DIE.** *v.a.* [*double* and *die.*] To die twice over.

Yes, I'll to the royal bed,
Where first the mysteries of our love were acted,
And double-die *it with imperial crimson.*
DRYDEN AND LEE'S OEDIPUS.

DOUBLE-MINDED. *adj.* [from *double* and *mind.*] Deceitful; insidious.[91]

A double-minded *man is unstable in all his ways.* BIBLE JAMES, I. 8.

DOUBLE-TONGUED. *adj.* [*double* and *tongue.*] Deceitful; giving contrary accounts of the same thing.

The deacons must be grave, not double-tongued, *not given to much wine, not greedy of filthy lucre.*
BIBLE 1 TIMOTHY, III. 8.

For much she fear'd the Tyrians, double-tongu'd,
And knew the town to Juno's care belong'd. DRYDEN'S VIRGIL.

DO'VETAIL. *n.s.* [*dove* and *tail.*] A form of joining two bodies together, where that which is inserted has the form of a wedge reversed, and therefore cannot fall out.

DO'WNFAL. *n.s.* [*down* and *fall.*]

1. Ruin; calamity; fall from rank or state.

Why do'st thou say king Richard is depos'd?
Dar'st thou, thou little better thing than earth,
Divine his downfal?
SHAKESPEARE'S RICHARD II.

We have seen some, by the ways by which they had designed to rise uncontrollably, to have directly procured their utter downfal. SOUTH'S SERMONS.

2. A sudden fall, or body of things falling.

Each downfal *of a flood the mountains pour*
From their rich bowels, rolls a silver stream. DRYDEN'S INDIAN EMPEROR.

3. Destruction of fabricks.

Not more aghast the matrons of renown,
When tyrant Nero burn'd th' imperial town,
Shriek'd for the downfal *in a doleful cry,*
For which their guiltless lords were doom'd to die. DRYDEN.

DO'WNHIL. *n.s.* [*down* and *hill.*] Declivity; descent.

Heavy the third, and stiff, he sinks apace;
And though 'tis downhil *all, but creeps along the race.* DRYDEN.

DO'WNLOOKED. *adj.* [*down* and *look.*] Having a dejected countenance; gloomy; sullen; melancholy.

Jealousy suffus'd, with jaundice in her eyes,
Discolouring all she view'd, in tawney dress'd;
Downlook'd, *and with a cuckow on her fist.* DRYDEN'S FABLES.

DO'WNSITTING. *n.s.* [*down* and *sit.*] Rest; repose; the act of sitting down, or going to rest.

Thou knowest my downsitting *and mine uprising; thou understandest my thoughts afar off.* BIBLE PSALMS, CXXXIX. 2.

DRAD. *adj.* [for *dread*, or the preterit of *To dread.*] Terrible; formidable; dreaded.

Th' utmost sand-breach they shortly fetch,
Whilst the drad *danger does behind remain.* FAIRY QUEEN.

DRA'MA. *n.s.* [δϱάμα.] A poem accommodated to action; a poem in which the action is not related, but represented; and in which therefore such rules are to be observed as make the representation probable.

Many rules of imitating nature Aristotle drew from Homer, which he fitted to the drama; *furnishing himself also with observations from the theatre, when it flourished under Eschylus, Euripides, and Sophocles.* DRYDEN'S ÆNEID, DEDICATION.

DRAMA'TICAL, DRAMATICK. *adj.* [from *drama.*] Represented by action; not narrative.

I hope to make it appear, that in the great dramatick *poem of nature, is a necessity of introducing a God.* BENTLEY.

DRA'STICK. *adj.* [δϱάστικος.] Powerful; vigorous; efficacious.

It is used of a medicine that works with speed; as jalap, scammony, and the stronger purges. *Quincy.*

DRAUGHTHOUSE. *n.s.* [*draught* and *house.*] A house in which filth is deposited.

And they brake down the image of Baal,

and brake down the house of Baal, and made it a draughthouse.
BIBLE 2 KINGS, X. 27.

DRAWBACK. *n.s.* [*draw* and *back.*] Money paid back for ready payment, or any other reason.

In poundage and drawbacks *I lose half my rent;*
Whatever they give me, I must be content.
SWIFT.

DRA'WBRIDGE. *n.s.* [*draw* and *bridge.*] A bridge made to be lifted up, to hinder or admit communication at pleasure.

Half the buildings were raised on the continent, and the other half on an island, continued together by a drawbridge.
CAREW'S SURVEY OF CORNWAL.

DRA'WINGROOM. *n.s.* [*draw* and *room.*]

1. The room in which company assembles at court.

What you heard of the words spoken of you in the drawing-room *was not true: the sayings of princes are generally as ill related as the sayings of wits.* POPE.

2. The company assembled there.

DRA'YPLOUGH. *n.s.* [*dray* and *plough.*] A plough of a particular kind.

The drayplough *is the best plough in Winter for miry clays.*
MORTIMER'S HUSBANDRY.

DRA'ZEL. *n.s.* [perhaps corrupted from *drossel*, the scum or dross of human nature; or from *droslesse*, French, a whore.]

A low, mean, worthless wretch.
As the devil uses witches,
To be their cully for a space,
That, when the time's expir'd, the drazels
For ever may become his vassals.
HUDIBRAS, P. III. CANT. 1.

DRE'GGY. *adj.* [from *dregs.*] Containing dregs; consisting of dregs; muddy; feculent.

These num'rous veins, such is the curious frame,
Receive the pure insinuating stream;
But no corrupt or dreggy *parts admit,*
To form the blood, or feed the limbs unfit.
BLACKMORE'S CREATION.

Ripe grapes, being moderately pressed, their juice may, without much dreggy *matter, be squeezed out.* BOYLE.

DREGS. *n.s.* [*dresten*, Saxon; *dreggian*, Islandick.]

1. The sediment of liquors; the lees; the grounds; the feculence.

Fain would we make him author of the wine,
If for the dregs *we could some other blame.* DAVIES.

They often tread destruction's horrid path,
And drink the dregs *of the revenger's wrath.* SANDYS.

We from the dregs *of life think to receive,*
What the first sprightly running could not give. DRYDEN.

Such run on poets in a raging vein,
Ev'n to the dregs *and squeezings of the brain.* POPE.

2. Any thing by which purity is corrupted.

The king by this journey purged a little the dregs *and leaven of the northern people, that were before in no good affections towards him.* BACON.

3. Dross; sweepings; refuse.

Heav'n's favourite thou, for better fate's design'd,
Than we the dregs *and rubbish of mankind.* DRYDEN'S JUVENAL.

What diffidence we must be under, whether God will regard our sacrifice, when we have nothing to offer him but the dregs *and refuse of life, the days of loathing and satiety, and the years in which we have no pleasure.* ROGERS'S SERMONS.

To **DRI'BBLE.** *v.n.* [This word seems to have come from *drop* by successive alterations, such as are usual in living languages. *Drop, drip, dripple, dribble,* from thence *drivel* and *driveler. Drip* may indeed be the original word, from the Danish *drypp.*]

1. To fall in drops.

Semilunar processes on the surface, owe their form to the dribbling *of water that passed over it.* WOODWARD ON FOSSILS.

A dribbling, *difficulty, and a momentary suppression of urine, may be caused by the stone's shutting up the orifice of the bladder.* ARBUTHNOT ON ALIMENTS.

2. To fall weakly and slowly.

Believe not that the dribbling *dart of love*
Can pierce a compleat bosom.
SHAKESPEARE'S MEASURE FOR MEASURE.

3. To slaver as a child or ideot.

To **DRI'BBLE.** *v.a.* To throw down in drops.

Let the cook follow with a ladle full of soup, and dribble *it all the way up stairs.* SWIFT'S RULES TO SERVANTS.

DRI'BLET. *n.s.* [from *dribble.*] A small sum; odd money in a sum.

Twelve long years of exile born,
Twice twelve we number'd since his blest return:
So strictly wert thou just to pay,
Even to the dribblet *of a day.* DRYDEN.

DRILL. *n.s.* [from the verb.]

1. An instrument with which holes are bored. It is pressed hard against the thing bored, and turned round with a bow and string.

The way of tempering steel to make gravers, drills, *and mechanical instruments, we have taught artificers.* BOYLE.

Drills *are used for the making such holes as punches will not conveniently serve for; as a piece of work that hath already its shape, and must have an hole or more made in it.* MOXON'S MECHANICAL EXERCISES.

2. An ape; a baboon.

Shall the difference of hair be a mark of a different internal specifick constitution between a changeling and a drill, *when they agree in shape and want of reason?* LOCKE.

3. A small dribbling brook. This I have found no where else, and suspect it should be *rill.*

Springs through the pleasant meadows pour their drills,
Which snake-like glide between the bordering hills. SANDYS.

DRI'NKMONEY. *n.s.* [*drink* and *money.*] Money given to buy liquor.

Peg's servants were always asking for drinkmoney. ARBUTHNOT.

DRI'PPINGPAN. *n.s.* [*drip* and *pan.*] The pan in which the fat of roast meat is caught.

When the cook turns her back, throw smoaking coals into the drippingpan. SWIFT.

DROLL. *n.s.* [*droler,* French.]

1. One whose business is to raise mirth by petty tricks; a jester; a buffoon; a jackpudding.

As he was running home in all haste, a droll *takes him up by the way.* L'ESTRANGE.

Why, how now, Andrew! cries his brother droll;
To-day's conceit, methinks, is something dull. PRIOR.

Democritus, dear droll, *revisit earth,*
And with our follies glut thy heighten'd mirth. PRIOR.

2. A farce; something exhibited to raise mirth.

Some as justly fame extols,

For lofty lines in Smithfield drolls.
SWIFT.

DROP SERENE. *n.s.* [*gutta serena,* Latin] A disease of the eye, proceeding from an inspissation of the humour.

So thick a drop serene *hath quench'd their orbs,*
Or dim suffusion veil'd!
MILTON'S PARADISE LOST, B. III.

DRO'TCHEL. *n.s.* [corrupted perhaps from *dretchel. To dretch*, in *Chaucer*, is to *idle*, to *delay*. *Droch*, in *Frisick*, is *delay*.] An idle wench; a sluggard. In Scottish it is still used.

To **DRUDGE.** *v.n.* [*dreccan*, to vex, Saxon; *draghen*, to carry, Dutch.] To labour in mean offices; to toil without honour or dignity; to work hard; to slave.

And to crack'd fiddle, and hoarse tabour,
In merriment, did drudge *and labour.*
HUDIBRAS, P. I.

The poor sleep little: we must learn to watch
Our labours late, and early every morning,
Mid'st Winter frosts; then clad and fed with sparing,
Rise to our toils, and drudge *away the day.* OTWAY.

Advantages obtained by industry directed by philosophy, can never be expected from drudging *ignorance.*
GLANVILLE'S SCEPSIS SCIENTIFICA.

Soon he came to court,
Proffering for hire his service at the gate,
To drudge, *draw water, and to run or wait.* DRYDEN'S FABLES.

I made no such bargain with you, to live always drudging.
DRYDEN'S DEDICATION TO ÆNEID.

What is an age, in dull renown drudg'd *o'er!*
One little single hour of love is more.
GRANVILLE.

DRUDGE. *n.s.* [from the verb.] One employed in mean labour; a slave; one doomed to servile occupation.

To conclude, this drudge *of the devil, this diviner, laid claim to me.*
SHAKESPEARE'S COMEDY OF ERROURS.

He sits above, and laughs the while
At thee, ordain'd his drudge, *to execute*
Whate'er his wrath shall bid.
MILTON'S PARADISE LOST, B. II.

Art thou our slave,
Our captive, at the publick mill our drudge,
And dar'st thou, at our sending and command,
Dispute thy coming.
MILTON'S AGONISTES, L. 392.

He is content to be their drudge,
And on their errands gladly trudge.
HUDIBRAS, P. III. CANT. 1.

The hard master makes men serve him for nought, who rewards his drudges *and slaves with nothing but shame and sorrow, and misery.* TILLOTSON, SERMON 4.

DRU'DGER. *n.s.* [from *drudge.*]
1. A mean labourer.
2. The drudging-box; the box out of which flower is thrown on roast meat. *Dictionaries.*

DRU'DGERY. *n.s.* [from *drudge.*] Mean labour; ignoble toil; dishonourable work; servile occupation.

My old dame will be undone for one to do her husbandry, and her drudgery.
SHAKESPEARE'S HENRY IV. P. II.

Were there not instruments for drudgery *as well as offices of* drudgery? *Were there not people to receive orders as well as others to give and authorize them?* L'ESTRANGE.

You do not know the heavy grievances,
The toils, the labours, weary drudgeries,
Which they impose.
SOUTHERN'S OROONOKO.

To thee that drudgery *of pow'r I give;*

Cares be thy lot: reign thou, and let me live. DRYDEN'S AURENGZEBE.

Paradise was a place of bliss, as well as immortality, without drudgery, *and without sorrow.* LOCKE.

Even drudgery *himself,*
As at the car he sweats, or dusty hews
The palace-stone, looks gay.
THOMSON'S SUMMER, L. 1445.

It is now handled by every dirty wench, and condemned to do her drudgery.
SWIFT'S MEDITATIONS ON A BROOMSTICK.

DRU'NKARD. *n.s.* [from *drunk.*] One given to excessive use of strong liquors; one addicted to habitual ebriety.

Some blood drawn on me would beget opinion
Of my more fierce endeavour. I've seen drunkards
Do more than this in sport.
SHAKESPEARE'S KING LEAR.

My bowels cannot hide her woes,
But, like a drunkard, *I must vomit them.*
SHAKESPEARE'S TITUS ANDRONICUS.

God will not take the drunkard's *excuse, that he has so long accustomed himself to intemperate drinking, that now he cannot leave it off.* SOUTH'S SERMONS.

DUBITA'TION. *n.s.* [*dubitatio*, Latin.] The act of doubting; doubt.

Many of the ancients denied the antipodes; but the experience of our enlarged navigation can now assert them beyond all dubitation.
BROWN'S VULGAR ERROURS, B. I. C. 7.

Dubitation *may be called a negative perception; that is, when I perceive that what I see, is not what I would see.*
GREW.

DU'CAT. *n.s.* [from *duke.*] A coin struck by dukes: in silver valued at about four shillings and six pence; in gold at nine shillings and six pence.

I cannot instantly raise up the gross
Of full three thousand ducats.
SHAKESPEARE'S MERCHANT OF VENICE.

There was one that died in debt: it was reported, where his creditors were, that he was dead: one said, he hath carried five hundred ducats *of mine into the other world.* BACON.

To **DUCKO'Y.** *v.a.* [mistaken for *decoy*: the decoy being commonly practised upon *ducks*, produced the errour.] To entice to a snare.

This fish hath a slender membranous string, which he projects and draws in at pleasure, as a serpent doth his tongue: with this he duckoys *little fishes, and then preys upon them.* GREW'S MUSÆUM.

To **DU'LCIFY.** *v.a.* [*dulcifier*, French.] To sweeten; to set free from acidity, saltness, or acrimony of any kind.

A decoction of wild gourd, or colocynthis, though somewhat qualified, will not from every hand be dulcified *into aliment, by an addition of flower or meal.*
BROWN'S VULGAR ERROURS.

I dressed him with a pledgit, dipt in a dulcified *tincture of vitriol.*
WISEMAN'S SURGERY.

Spirit of wine dulcifies *spirit of salt; nitre, or vitriol have other bad effects.*
ARBUTHNOT ON ALIMENTS.

DULL. *adj.* [*dwl*, Welsh; *dole*, Saxon; *dol*, mad, Dutch.]

1. Stupid; doltish; blockish; unapprehensive; indocile; slow of understanding.

Such is their evil hap to play upon dull *spirited men.* HOOKER.

He that hath learned no wit by nature, nor art, may complain of gross breeding, or comes of a very dull *kindred.*
SHAKESPEARE.

Sometimes this perception, in some kind of bodies, is far more subtile than the sense; so

that the sense is but a dull *thing in comparison of it.*
BACON'S NATURAL HISTORY.

Every man, even the dullest, *is thinking more than the most eloquent can teach him how to utter.* DRYDEN.

2. Blunt; obtuse.

Meeting with time, Slack thing, said I,
Thy scythe is dull; *whet it, for shame.*
HERBERT.

3. Unready; aukward.

Gynecia a great while stood still, with a kind of dull *amazement looking stedfastly upon her.* SIDNEY.

O help thou my weak wit, and sharpen my dull *tongue.*
FAIRY QUEEN, B. I. STANZ. 2.

Memory is so necessary to all conditions of life, that we are not to fear it should grow dull *for want of exercise, if exercise would make it stronger.* LOCKE.

4. Hebetated; not quick.

This people's heart is waxed gross, and their ears are dull *of hearing.*
BIBLE MATTHEW, XIII. 15.

5. Sad; melancholy.
6. Sluggishly; heavy; slow of motion.

Thenceforth the waters waxed dull *and slow,*
And all that drunk thereof did faint and feeble grow.
FAIRY QUEEN.

7. Gross; cloggy; vile.

She excels each mortal thing
Upon the dull *earth dwelling.*
SHAKESPEARE'S TWO GENTLEMEN OF VERONA.

8. Not exhilerating; not delightful; as, *to make dictionaries is* dull *work.*
9. Not bright; as, *the mirror is* dull, *the fire is* dull.

I'll not be made a soft and dull *ey'd fool,*
To shake the head, relent, and sigh, and yield
To Christian intercessors.
SHAKESPEARE'S MERCHANT OF VENICE.

10. Drowsy; sleepy.

DUN. *adj.* [*dun*, Saxon.]
1. A colour partaking of brown and black.

By mixing such powders we are not to expect a strong and full white, such as is that of paper; but some dusky obscure one, such as might arise from a mixture of light and darkness, or from white and black, that is, a grey, or dun, *or russet brown.*
NEWTON'S OPTICKS.

2. Dark; gloomy.

Come, thick night!
And pall thee in the dunnest *smoke of hell,*
That my keen knife see not the wound it makes;
Nor heav'n peep through the blanket of the dark,
To cry hold! hold!
SHAKESPEARE'S MACBETH.

He then survey'd
Hell, and the gulph between, and Satan there
Coasting the wall of heav'n on this side,
In the dun *air sublime.*
MILTON'S PARADISE LOST, B. III. L. 69.

To **DUN.** *v.a.* [*dunan*, Saxon, to clamour.] To claim a debt with vehemence and importunity.

Borrow of thy back, and borrow of thy belly: they'll never ask thee again. I shall be dunning *thee every day.* BACON.

I remember what she won:
And hath she sent so soon to dun? SWIFT.

When thou dun'st *their parents, seldom they,*
Without a suit before the tribune, pay.
DRYDEN'S JUVENAL.

DUN. *n.s.* [from the verb.] A clamorous, importunate, troublesome creditor.

Thus, while my joyless minutes tedious flow,

With looks demure, and silent pace, a dun,
Horrible monster! hated by gods and men,
To my aerial citadel ascends. PHILLIPS.

It grieves my heart to be pulled by the sleeve by some rascally dun, *Sir, remember my bill.*
ARBUTHNOT'S HISTORY OF JOHN BULL.

DU'NNER. *n.s.* [from *dun.*] One employed in soliciting petty debts.

They are ever talking of new silks, and serve the owners in getting them customers, as their common dunners *do in making them pay.* SPECTATOR, NO. 454.

To **DWAULE.** *v.a.* [*dwelian*, Sax. to wander; *dwaelen*, Dut.] To be delirious: a provincial word mentioned by *Junius.*

DY'SPHONY. *n.s.* [*δυσφωνία.*] A difficulty in speaking, occasioned by an ill disposition of the organs. *Dictionaries.*

E

Has two sounds; long, as *scĕne*, and short, as *men*. *E* is the most frequent vowel in the English language; for it not only is used like the rest in the beginning or end of words, but has the peculiar quality of lengthening the foregoing vowel, as *căn, cāne*; *măn, māne*; *găp, gāpe*; *glăd, glāde*; *brĕd, brēde*; *chĭn, chīne*; *whĭp, wīpe*; *thĭn, thīne*; *nŏd, nōde*; *tŭn, tūne*; *plŭm, plūme*. Yet it sometimes occurs final, where yet the foregoing vowel is not lengthened; as *gŏne, knowlĕdge, ĕdge, gĭve*. Anciently almost every word ended with *e*; as for *can, canne*; for *year, yeare*; for *great, greate*; for *need, neede*; for *flock, flocke*. It is probable that this *e* final had at first a soft sound, like the female *e* of the French; and that afterwards it was in poetry either mute or vocal, as the verse required, 'till at last it became universally silent.

Ea has the sound of *e* long: the *e* is commonly lengthened rather by the immediate addition of *a* than by the apposition of *e* to the end of the word; as *mĕn, mēan*; *sĕll, sēal*; *mĕt, mēat*; *nĕt, nēat*.

EA'GLESPEED. *n.s.* [*eagle* and *speed.*] Swiftness like that of an eagle.

> *Abrupt, with* eaglespeed *she cut the sky,*
> *Instant invisible to mortal eye.*
> POPE'S ODYSSEY, B. I.

EA'GRE. *n.s.* [*æger*, in Runick, is the *ocean*; *eggia*, in Islandick, is to *agitate*, to *incite.*] A tide swelling above another tide, observable in the river Severn.

> *For as an* eagre *rides in triumph o'er the tide,*
> *The tyrant passions, hope and fear,*
> *Did in extremes appear,*
> *And flash'd upon the soul with equal force.* DRYDEN.

EAME. *n.s.* [*eam*, Saxon; *eom*, Dutch] Uncle: a word still used in the wilder parts of Staffordshire.

> *Daughter, says she, fly, fly; behold, thy dame*
> *Foreshows the treason of thy wretched* eame*!* FAIRFAX.

EA'RWITNESS. *n.s.* [*ear* and *witness.*] One who attests, or can attest any thing as heard by himself.

> *All present were made* earwitnesses, *even of each particular branch of a common indictment.* HOOKER, B. V. S. 36.

> *The histories of mankind, written by eye or* earwitnesses, *are built upon this principle.* WATTS'S LOGICK.

EA'RLY. *adj.* [*ær*, Saxon, before] Soon with respect to something else: as, in the morning, with respect to the sun; in time, with respect to creation; in the season, in comparison with other products.

> *I am a tainted wether of the flock,*
> *Meetest for death: the weakest kind of fruit*
> *Drops* earliest *to the ground, and so let me.* SHAKESPEARE.

> *It is a curiosity to have several fruits upon one tree; and the more when some of them come* early, *and some come late, so that*

you may have upon the same tree ripe fruits all Summer.
BACON'S NATURAL HISTORY, NO. 501.

God made all the world, that he might be worshipped in some parts of the world; and therefore, in the first and most early *times of the church, what care did he manifest to have such places erected to his honour?*
SOUTH'S SERMONS.

And yet my numbers please the rural throng,
Rough satyrs dance, and Pan approves the song;
The nymphs, forsaking ev'ry cave and spring,
Their early *fruit and milk-white turtles bring.* POPE.

Sickness is early *old age: it teaches us a diffidence in our earthly state, and inspires us with the thoughts of a future.* POPE.

Oh soul of honour!
Oh early *heroe!*
SMITH'S PHÆDRA AND HIPPOLITUS.

EA'RLY. *adv.* [from the adjective.] Soon; betimes.

Early *before the morn with crimson ray*
The windows of bright heav'n opened had.
FAIRY QUEEN.

None in more languages can show
Those arts, which you so early *know.*
WALLER.

The princess makes her issue like herself, by instilling early *into their minds religion, virtue and honour.*
ADDISON'S FREEHOLDER.

EA'RTHLING. *n.s.* [from *earth.*] An inhabitant of the earth; a mortal; a poor frail creature.

To earthlings, *the footstool of God, that stage which he raised for a small time, seemeth magnificent.* DRUMMOND.

EAST. *n.s.* [*eost*, Saxon; *heos*, Erse.]
1. The quarter where the sun rises.[92]

They counting forwards towards the East, *did allow 180 degrees to the Portugals eastward.* ABBOT.

2. The regions in the eastern parts of the world.

I would not be the villain that thou thinkest,
For the whole space that's in the tyrant's grasp,
And the rich East *to boot.*
SHAKESPEARE'S MACBETH.

EA'TINGHOUSE. *n.s.* [*eat* and *house.*] A house where provisions are sold ready dressed.

An hungry traveller stept into an eatinghouse *for his dinner.*
L'ESTRANGE.

To **EA'VESDROP.** *v.a.* [*eaves* and *drop.*] To catch what comes from the eaves; in common phrase, to listen under windows.

EBRI'ETY. *n.s.* [*ebrietas*, Latin.] Drunkenness; intoxication by strong liquors.

Bitter almonds, as an antidote against ebriety, *hath commonly failed.*
BROWN'S VULGAR ERROURS, B. II. C. 6.

ECCOPRO'TICKS. *n.s.* [*'έκ* and *κόπρος.*] Such medicines as gently purge the belly, so as to bring away no more than the natural excrements lodged in the intestines.

The body ought to be maintained in its daily excretions by such means as are eccoprotick.
HARVEY ON THE PLAGUE.

ECLE'CTICK. *adj.* [*'εκλέκτικος.*] Selecting; chusing at will.

Cicero gives an account of the opinions of philosophers; but was of the eclectick *sect, and chose out of each such positions as came nearest truth.*
WATTS'S IMPROVEMENT OF THE MIND.

ECO'NOMY. *n.s.* [*'οικονομία.* This word is often written, from its derivation, *œconomy*; but *œ* being no diphthong in English, it is placed here with the authorities for different orthography.]

1. The management of a family; the government of a houshold.

> *By St. Paul's* economy *the heir differs nothing from a servant, while he is in his minority; so a servant should differ nothing from a child in the substantial part.*
> TAYLOR'S RULE OF LIVING HOLY.

2.[93] Frugality; discretion of expence; laudable parsimony.

> *Particular sums are not laid out to the greatest advantage in his* economy*; but are sometimes suffered to run waste, while he is only careful of the main.*
> DRYDEN'S STATE OF INNOCENCE, PREFACE.

> *I have no other notion of* economy, *than that it is the parent of liberty and ease.*
> SWIFT TO LORD BOLINGBROKE.

3. Disposition of things; regulation.

> *All the divine and infinitely wise ways of* economy *that God could use towards a rational creature, oblige mankind to that course of living which is most agreeable to our nature.* HAMMOND.

4. The disposition or arrangement of any work.

> *In the Greek poets, as also in Plautus, we shall see the* economy *and disposition of poems better observed than in Terence.*
> BEN JONSON'S DISCOVERIES.

> *If this* economy *must be observed in the minutest parts of an epick poem, what soul, though sent into the world with great advantages of nature, cultivated with the liberal arts and sciences, can be sufficient to inform the body of so great a work?*
> DRYDEN'S DEDICATION TO THE ÆNEID.

5. System of motions; distribution of every thing active or passive to its proper place.

> *These the strainers aid,*
> *That, by a constant separation made,*
> *They may a due* economy *maintain,*
> *Exclude the noxious parts, the good retain.*
> BLACKMORE'S CREATION.

E'CURIE. *n.s.* [French; *equus*, Latin.] A place covered for the lodging or housing of horses.

EDA'CIOUS. *adj.* [*edax*, Latin.] Eating; voracious; devouring; predatory; ravenous; rapacious; greedy.

E'DGETOOL. *n.s.* [*edge* and *tool.*] A tool made sharp to cut.

> *There must be no playing with things sacred, nor jesting with* edgetools.
> L'ESTRANGE.

> *Nurses from their children keep* edgetools.
> DORSET.

> *I shall exercise upon steel, and its several sorts; and what sort is fittest for* edgetools, *which for springs.*
> MOXON'S MECHANICAL EXERCISES.

EFFE'CT. *n.s.* [*effectus*, Latin.]

1. That which is produced by an operating cause.

> *You may see by her example, in herself wise, and of others beloved, that neither folly is the cause of vehement love, nor reproach the* effect. SIDNEY, B. II.

> Effect *is the substance produced, or simple idea introduced into any subject, by the exerting of power.* LOCKE.

> *We see the pernicious* effects *of luxury in the antient Romans, who immediately found themselves poor as soon as this vice got footing among them.*
> ADDISON ON ITALY.

2. Consequence; event.

> *No man, in* effect, *doth accompany with others, but he learneth, ere he is aware, some gesture, or voice, or fashion.*
> BACON'S NATURAL HISTORY, NO. 236.

> *To say of a celebrated piece that there are faults in it, is, in* effect, *to say that the author of it is a man.*
> ADDISON'S GUARDIAN.

3. Purpose; intention; general intent.

They spake to her to that effect.
BIBLE 2 CHRONICLES, XXXIV. 22.

4. Consequence intended; success; advantage.

Christ is become of no effect *unto you.*
BIBLE GALATIANS, V. 4.

He should depart only with a title, the effect *whereof he should not be possessed of, before he had very well deserved it.*
CLARENDON, B. VIII.

The custom or institution has hitherto proved without effect, *and has neither extinguished the practice of such crimes, nor lessened the numbers of such criminals.*
TEMPLE.

5. Completion; perfection.

Semblant art shall carve the fair effect,
And full atchievement of thy great designs.
PRIOR.

6. Reality; not mere appearance.

In shew, a marvellous indifferently composed senate ecclesiastical was to govern, but in effect *one only man should, as the spirit and soul of the residue, do all in all.* HOOKER.

State and wealth, the business and the crowd,
Seems at this distance but a darker cloud;
And is to him, who rightly things esteems,
No other in effect *than what it seems.*
DENHAM.

7. [In the plural.] Goods; moveables.

What form of prayer
Can serve my turn? Forgive me my foul murther!
That cannot be, since I am still possest
Of those effects *for which I did the murther,*
My crown, mine own ambition, and my queen. SHAKESPEARE.

The emperor knew that they could not convey away many of their effects.
ADDISON'S SPECTATOR, NO. 499.

To **EFFO'RM.** *n.s.* [*efformo*, Latin.] To make in any certain manner; to shape; to fashion.

Merciful and gracious, thou gavest us being, raising us from nothing, and efforming *us after thy own image.* TAYLOR.

EFFO'SSION. *n.s.* [*effosumo*, Latin.] The act of digging up from the ground; deterration.

He set apart annual sums for the recovery of manuscripts, the effossion *of coins, and the procuring of mummies.*
ARBUTHNOT.

E'FFRONTERY. *n.s.* [*effronterie*, Fr.] Impudence; shamelessness; contempt of reproach.

They could hardly contain themselves within one unworthy act, who had effrontery *enough to commit or countenance it.* KING CHARLES.

Others with ignorance and insufficiency have self-admiration and effrontery *to set up themselves.*
WATTS'S IMPROVEMENT OF THE MIND.

A bold man's effrontery, *in company with women, must be owing to his low opinion of them, and his high one of himself.*
CLARISSA.

EFFU'MABILITY. *n.s.* [*fumus*, Latin.] The quality of flying away, or vapouring in fumes.[94]

They seem to define mercury by volatility, or, if I may coin such a word, effumability.
BOYLE'S SCEPTICAL CHYMISTRY.

E. G. [*exempli gratia.*] For the sake of an instance or example.

E'GOTISM. *n.s.* [from *ego*, Latin.] The fault committed in writing by the frequent repetition of the word *ego*, or *I*; too frequent mention of a man's self, in writing or conversation.

The most violent egotism *which I have met with, in the course of my reading, is that of cardinal Wolsey's;* ego & rex meus, *I and my king.* SPECTATOR, NO. 562.

To **E'GOTIZE.** *v.n.* [from *ego.*] To talk much of one's self.

EJE'CTMENT. *n.s.* [from *eject.*] A legal writ by which any inhabitant of a house, or tenant of an estate, is commanded to depart.

EIGH. *interj.* An expression of sudden delight.

EIGHT. *adj.* [*eahta*, Saxon; *ahta*, Gothick; *acht*, Scottish.] Twice four. A word of number.

This island contains eight *score and* eight *miles in circuit.* SANDYS'S JOURNEY.

EIGHTH. *adj.* [from *eight.*] Next in order to the seventh; the ordinal of eight.

Another yet? – A seventh! I'll see no more;
And yet the eighth *appears!*
SHAKESPEARE'S MACBETH.

In the eighth *month should be the reign of Saturn.* BACON.

I stay reluctant seven continu'd years,
And water her ambrosial couch with tears;
The eighth, *she voluntary moves to part,*
Or urg'd by Jove, or her own changeful heart. POPE'S ODYSSEY.

ELA'STICAL, ELASTICK. *adj.* [from 'ελάω.] Having the power of returning to the form from which it is distorted or withheld; springy; having the power of a spring.

By what elastick *engines did she rear*
The starry roof, and roll the orbs in air.
BLACKMORE'S CREATION.

If the body is compact, and bends or yields inward to pression, without any sliding of its parts, it is hard and elastick, *returning to its figure with a force rising from the mutual attraction of its parts.*
NEWTON'S OPTICKS.

The most common diversities of human constitutions arise from the solids, as to their different degrees of strength and tension; in some being too lax and weak, in others too elastick *and strong.*
ARBUTHNOT ON ALIMENTS.

A fermentation must be excited in some assignable place, which may expand itself by its elastical *power, and break through, where it meets with the weakest resistance.*
BENTLEY.

ELBOWCHA'IR. *n.s.* [*elbow* and *chair.*] A chair with arms to support the elbows.

Swans and elbowchairs, *in the opera of Dioclesian, have danced upon the English stage with good success.* GAY.

E'LBOWROOM. *n.s.* [*elbow* and *room.*] Room to stretch out the elbows on each side; perfect freedom from confinement.

Now my soul hath elbowroom;
It would not out at windows nor at doors.
SHAKESPEARE.

The natives are not so many, but that there may be elbowroom *enough for them, and for the adventives also.* BACON.

A politican must put himself into a state of liberty, so to provide elbowroom *for his conscience to have its full play in.*
SOUTH'S SERMONS.

ELE'CTRE. *n.s.* [*electrum*, Latin.]
1. Amber; which, having the quality when warmed by friction of attracting bodies, gave to one species of attraction the name of *electricity*, and to the bodies that so attract the epithet *electrick*.
2. A mixed metal.

Change silver plate or vessel into the compound stuff, being a kind of silver electre, *and turn the rest into coin.*
BACON.

ELECTRI'CITY. *n.s.* [from *electrick.* See **ELECTRE.**] A property in some bodies, whereby, when rubbed so as to grow warm, they draw little bits of paper, or such like substances, to them. *Quincy.*

Such was the account given a few years ago of electricity; but the industry of the present age, first excited by the experiments of *Gray*, has discovered in electricity a multitude of philosophical wonders. Bodies electrified by a sphere of glass, turned nimbly round, not only emit flame, but may be fitted with such a quantity of the electrical vapour, as, if discharged at once upon a human body, would endanger life. The force of this vapour has hitherto appeared instantaneous, persons at both ends of a long chain seeming to be struck at once. The philosophers are now endeavouring to intercept the strokes of lightning.

ELOQUE'NCE. *n.s.* [*eloquentia*, Latin.]

1. The power of speaking with fluency and elegance; oratory.

Action is eloquence, *and the eyes of th' ignorant*
More learned than the ears.
SHAKESPEARE'S CORIOLANUS.

2. Elegant language uttered with fluency.

Say she be mute, and will not speak a word;
Then I'll commend her volubility,
And say she uttereth piercing eloquence.
SHAKESPEARE.

Fit words attended on his weighty sense,
And mild persuasion flow'd in eloquence.
POPE'S ODYSSEY, B. VII.

ELY'SIUM. *n.s.* [Latin.] The place assigned by the heathens to happy souls; any place exquisitely pleasant.

To have thee with thy lips to stop my mouth,
So should'st thou either turn my flying soul,
Or I should breathe it so into thy body,
And then it liv'd in sweet Elysium.
SHAKESPEARE'S HENRY VI.

E'MBASSAGE, E'MBASSY. *n.s.* [It may be observed, that though our authors write almost indiscriminately *embassador* or *ambassador*, *embassage* or *ambassage*; yet there is scarcely an example of *ambassy*, all concurring to write *embassy*.]

1. A publick message; a message concerning business between princes or states.

Fresh embassy *and suits,*
Nor from the state nor private friends, hereafter,
Will I lend ear to.
SHAKESPEARE'S CORIOLANUS.

When he was at Newcastle he sent a solemn embassage *unto James III. king of Scotland, to treat and conclude a peace with him.* BACON'S HENRY VII.

The peace polluted thus, a chosen band
He first commissions to the Latian land,
In threat'ning embassy.
DRYDEN'S ÆNEID.

2. Any solemn message.

He sends the angels on embassies *with his decrees.* TAYLOR.

3. An errand in an ironical sense.

A bird was made fly with such art to carry a written embassage *among the ladies, that one might say, if a live bird, how taught? If dead, how made?* SIDNEY, B. II.

Nimble mischance, that art so light of foot,
Doth not thy embassage *belong to me?*
And am I last that know it.
SHAKESPEARE'S RICHARD II.

E'MBOLISM. *n.s.* ['εμβολισμός.]

1. Intercalation; insertion of days or years to produce regularity and equation of time.

The civil constitutions of the year were after different manners in several nations; some using the sun's year, but in divers fashions; and some following the moon, finding out embolisms or equations, even to the addition of whole months, to make all as even as they could. HOLDER ON TIME.

2. The time inserted; intercalatory time.

To **EMBRO'THEL.** *v.a.* [*brothel, brodel.*] To inclose in a brothel.

Men, which chuse
Law practice for mere gain, boldly repute,
Worse than embrothel'd *strumpets prostitute.* DONNE.

E'MISSARY. *n.s.* [*emissarius,* Latin.]

1. One sent out on private messages; a spy; a secret agent.

Clifford, now become the state informer, was an emissary *and spy of the king's, and he fled over into Flanders with his consent and privity.* BACON'S HENRY VII.

You shall neither eat nor sleep,
No, nor forth your window peep,
With your emissary *eye,*
To fetch in the forms go by.
BEN JONSON'S UNDERWOODS.

The Jesuits send over emissaries, *with instructions to personate themselves members of the several sects amongst us.* SWIFT.

2. One that emits or sends out. A technical sense.

Wherever there are emissaries, *there are absorbent vessels in the skin; and, by the absorbent vessels, mercury will pass into the blood.* ARBUTHNOT ON ALIMENTS.

To **EMPE'OPLE.** *v.a.* [from *people.*] To form into a people or community.

He wonder'd much, and 'gan enquire
What stately building durst so high extend
Her lofty towers unto the starry sphere,
And what unknown nation there
empeopled *were.* FAIRY QUEEN.

E'MPHASIS. *n.s.* [᾿έμφασις.] A remarkable stress laid upon a word or sentence; particular force impressed by stile or pronunciation.

Oh, that brave Cæsar!
—— Be choak'd with such another emphasis.
SHAKESPEARE'S ANTONY AND CLEOPATRA.

Emphasis *not so much regards the time as a certain grandeur, whereby some letter, syllable, word, or sentence is rendered more remarkable than the rest, by a more vigorous pronunciation, and a longer stay upon it.*
HOLDER'S ELEMENTS OF SPEECH.

These questions have force and emphasis, *if they be understood of the antediluvian earth.*
BURNET'S THEORY OF THE EARTH.

EMPI'RICAL, EMPIRICK. *adj.* [from the noun.]

1. Versed in experiments.

By fire
Of sooty coal, the empirick *alchymist*
Can turn, or holds it possible to turn,
Metals of drossiest ore to perfect gold.
MILTON'S PARADISE LOST.

2. Known only by experience; practised only by rote, without rational grounds.

The most sovereign prescription in Galen is but empirick *to this preservative.*
SHAKESPEARE'S CORIOLANUS.

In extremes, bold counsels are the best;
Like empirick *remedies, they last are try'd,*
And by th' event condemn'd or justify'd.
DRYDEN'S AURENGZEBE.

EMPI'RICALLY. *adv.* [from *empirical.*]

1. Experimentally; according to experience.

We shall empirically *and sensibly deduct the causes of blackness from originals, by which we generally observe things denigrated.*
BROWN'S VULGAR ERROURS, B. VI. C. 12.

2. Without rational grounds; charlatanically; in the manner of quacks.

EMPI'RICISM. *n.s.* [from *empirick.*] Dependence on experience without knowledge or art; quackery.

EMPLA'STER. *n.s.* ['ἐμπλαστρον. This word is now always pronounced, and generally written *plaster.*] An application to a sore of an oleaginous or viscous substance, spread upon cloth. See **PLASTER.**

All emplasters, *applied to the breasts, ought to have a hole for the nipples.*
WISEMAN'S SURGERY.

To **EMPU'ZZLE.** *v.a.* [from *puzzle.*] To perplex; to put to a stand.

It hath empuzzled *the enquiries of others to apprehend, and enforced them unto strange conceptions to make out.*
BROWN.

E'MULOUS. *adj.* [*æmulus*, Latin.]

1. Rivalling; engaged in competition.

What the Gaul or Moor could not effect,
Nor emulous *Carthage, with their length of spite,*
Shall be the work of one.
BEN JONSON'S CATILINE.

She is in perpetual diffidence, or actual enmity with her, but always emulous *and suspectful of her.*
HOWEL'S VOCAL FORREST.

2. Desirous of superiority; desirous to rise above another; desirous of any excellence possessed by another. With *of* before the object of emulation.

By strength
They measure all, of other excellence
Not emulous, *nor care who them excels.*
MILTON'S PARADISE LOST.

By fair rewards our noble youth we raise
To emulous *merit, and to thirst of praise.*
PRIOR.

Good Howard, emulous *of the Grecian art.* PRIOR.

3. Factious; contentious.

Whose glorious deeds, but in these fields of late,
Made emulous *missions 'mongst the gods themselves,*
And drave great Mars to faction.
SHAKESPEARE'S TROILUS AND CRESSIDA.

To **ENA'MBUSH.** *v.a.* [from *ambush.*] To hide in ambush; to hide with hostile intention.

They went within a vale, close to a flood, whose stream
Us'd to give all their cattle drink, they there enambush'd *them.*
CHAPMAN'S ILIADS, B. I.

ENCO'MPASSMENT. *n.s.* [from *encompass.*] Circumlocution; remote tendency of talk.

Finding
By this encompassment *and drift of question,*
That they do know my son, come you more near. SHAKESPEARE.

ENCO'RE. *adv.* [French.] Again; once more. A word used at publick shows when a singer, or fiddler, or buffoon is desired by the audience to do the same thing again.

To the same notes thy sons shall hum or snore,
And all thy yawning daughters cry encore. DUNCIAD, B. IV.

ENCYCLOPE'DIA, ENCYCLOPE'DY. *n.s.* ['εγκυκλοπάιδια.] The circle of sciences; the round of learning.

Every science borrows from all the rest, and we cannot attain any single one without the encyclopædy.
GLANVILLE'S SCEPSIS SCIENTIFICA, C. 25.

This art may justly claim a place in the encyclopædia, *especially such as serves for*

a model of education for an able politician.
ARBUTHNOT'S HISTORY OF JOHN BULL.

ENDE'ARMENT. *n.s.* [from *endear.*]

1. The cause of love; means by which any thing is endeared.

Her first endearments, *twining round the soul.* THOMSON.

2. The state of being endeared; the state of being loved.

Is not the separate property of a thing the great cause of its endearment *amongst all mankind?* SOUTH'S SERMONS.

When a man shall have done all that he can to make one his friend, and emptied his purse to create endearment *between them, he may, in the end, be forced to write vanity and frustration.* SOUTH'S SERMONS.

E'NDLESS. *adj.* [from *end.*]

1. Without end; without conclusion or termination.

Nothing was more endless *than the common method of comparing eminent writers by an opposition of particular passages in them.*
POPE'S PREFACE TO THE ILIAD.

2. Infinite in longitudinal extent.

As it is pleasant to the eye to have an endless *prospect, so it is some pleasure to a finite understanding to view unlimited excellencies.* TILLOTSON.

3. Infinite in duration; perpetual.

None of the heathens, how curious soever in searching out all kinds of outward ceremonies, could ever once endeavour to resemble herein the church's care for the endless *good of her children.*
HOOKER, B. V. S. 18.

But after labours long, and sad delay,
Brings them to joyous rest, and endless
bliss. FAIRY QUEEN.

All our glory extinct, and happy state,
Here swallow'd up in endless *misery!*
MILTON'S PARADISE LOST.

4. Incessant; continual.

All the priests and friars in my realm,
Shall in procession sing her endless *praise.*
SHAKESPEARE'S HENRY VI.

Each pleasing Blount shall endless *smiles bestow,*
And soft Belinda's blush for ever glow.
POPE.

E'NEMY. *n.s.* [*ennemi*, French; *inimicus*, Latin.]

1. A publick foe.

All these statutes speak of English rebels and Irish enemies, *as if the Irish had never been in condition of subjects, but always out of the protection of the law.*
DAVIES ON IRELAND.

The enemy *thinks of raising threescore thousand men for the next Summer.*
ADDISON ON THE STATE OF THE WAR.

2. A private opponent; an antagonist.

3. Any one who regards another with malevolence; not a friend.

Kent, in disguise,
Follow'd his enemy *king, and did him service*
Improper for a slave.
SHAKESPEARE'S KING LEAR.

4. One that dislikes.

He that designedly uses ambiguities, ought to be looked on as an enemy *to truth and knowledge.* LOCKE.

Bold is the critick, who dares prove
These heroes were no friends to love;
And bolder he who dares aver,
That they were enemies *to war.* PRIOR.

5. [In theology.] The fiend; the devil.

Defend us from the danger of the enemy.
COMMON PRAYER.

E'NERGY. *n.s.* [’ενέϱγεια]

1. Power not exerted in action.

They are not effective of any thing, nor leave no work behind them, but are energies *merely; for their working upon mirrours, and places of echo, doth not alter any thing in those bodies.* BACON.

2. Force; vigour; efficacy; influence.

Whether with particles of heav'nly fire
The God of nature did his soul inspire;
Or earth, but new divided from the sky,
And pliant still, retain'd th' ethereal energy. DRYDEN.

God thinketh with operation infinitely perfect, with an omnipotent as well as an eternal energy.
GREW'S COSMOLOGIA SACRA.

Beg the blessed Jesus to give an energy *to your imperfect prayers, by his most powerful intercession.*
SMALRIDGE'S SERMONS.

What but God!
Inspiring God! who, boundless spirit all,
And unremitting energy, *pervades,*
Adjusts, sustains, and agitates the whole.
THOMSON'S SPRING.

3. Faculty; operation.

Matter, though divided into the subtilest parts, moved swiftly, is senseless and stupid, and makes no approach to vital energy.
RAY ON THE CREATION.

How can concussion of atoms beget self-consciousness, and other powers and energies *that we feel in our minds?*
BENTLEY.

4. Strength of expression; force of signification; spirit; life.

Who did ever, in French authors, see
The comprehensive English energy.
ROSCOMMON.

Swift and ready, and familiar communication is made by speech; and, when animated by elocution, it acquires a greater life and energy, *ravishing and captivating the hearers.* HOLDER.

Many words deserve to be thrown out of our language, and not a few antiquated to be restored, on account of their energy *and sound.* SWIFT.

E'NGINE. *n.s.* [*engin*, French; *ingegno*, Italian.]

1. Any mechanical complication, in which various movements and parts concur to one effect.

2. A military machine.

This is our engine, *towers that overthrows;*
Our spear that hurts, our sword that wounds our foes. FAIRFAX.

3. Any instrument.

The sword, the arrow, the gun, with many terrible engines *of death, will be well employed.* RALEIGH'S ESSAYS.

He takes the scissars, and extends
The little engine *on his fingers ends.*
POPE'S RAPE OF THE LOCK.

4. Any instrument to throw water upon burning houses.

Some cut the pipes, and some the engines *play;*
And some, more bold, mount ladders to the fire. DRYDEN.

5. Any means used to bring to pass, or to effect. Usually in an ill sense.

Prayer must be divine and heavenly, which the devil with all his engines *so violently opposeth.*
DUPPA'S RULES FOR DEVOTION.

6. An agent for another. In contempt.

They had th' especial engines *been, to rear*
His fortunes up into the state they were.
DANIEL.

ENGINE'ER. *n.s.* [*engingnier*, French.] One who manages engines; one who directs the artillery of an army.

For 'tis the sport to have the engineer
Hoist with his own petard.
SHAKESPEARE'S HAMLET.

Him thus enrag'd,
Descrying from afar, some engineer,
Dext'rous to guide th' unerring charge, design'd
By one nice shot to terminate the war.
PHILLIPS.

An author, who points his satire at a great man, is like the engineer *who signalized himself by this ungenerous practice.*
ADDISON'S FREEHOLDER, NO. 19.

E'NGINERY. *n.s.* [from *engine.*]

1. The act of managing artillery.

They may descend in mathematicks to fortification, architecture, enginery, *or navigation.* MILTON ON EDUCATION.

2. Engines of war; artillery.

We saw the foe
Approaching, gross and huge, in hollow cube
Training his dev'lish enginery.
MILTON.

E'NGLISH. *adj.* [*engles*, Saxon.] Belonging to England; thence English is the language of England.

He hath neither Latin, French, nor Italian; and you may come into the court, and swear that I have a poor pennyworth in the English.
SHAKESPEARE'S MERCHANT OF VENICE.

Of English *talc, the coarser sort is called plaister, or parget; the finer, spoad.*
WOODWARD.

To **E'NGLISH.** *v.a.* [from the noun.] To translate into English.

We find not a word in the text can properly be rendered anise, which is what the Latins call anethum, and properly Englished *dill.*
BROWN'S VULGAR ERROURS, B. VII. C. 7.

To **ENJO'IN.** *v.a.* [*enjoindre*, French.] To direct; to order; to prescribe. It is more authoritative than *direct*, and less imperious than *command.*

To satisfy the good old man,
I would bend under any heavy weight
That he'll enjoin *me to.*
SHAKESPEARE'S MUCH ADO ABOUT NOTHING.

Monks and philosophers, and such as do continually enjoin *themselves.*
BACON'S NATURAL HISTORY, NO. 292.

It endeavours to secure every man's interest, by enjoining *that truth and fidelity be inviolably preserved.*
TILLOTSON'S SERMONS.

ENODA'TION. *n.s.* [*enodatio*, Latin.]

1. The act of untying a knot.
2. Solution of a difficulty. *Dictionaries.*

ENO'RMOUS. *adj.* [*enormis*, Latin.]

1. Irregular; out of rule; not regulated by any stated measures; excursive beyond the limits of a regular figure.

Nature here
Wanton'd, as in her prime; and plaid at will
Her virgin fancies, pouring forth more sweets,
Wild above rule, or art, enormous *bliss!*
MILTON'S PARADISE LOST.

The enormous *part of the light in the circumference of every lucid point, ought to be less discernible in shorter telescopes than in longer, because the shorter transmit less light to the eye.* NEWTON'S OPTICKS.

2. Disordered; confused.

I shall find time
From this enormous *state, and seek to give*
Losses their remedies.
SHAKESPEARE'S KING LEAR.

3. Wicked beyond the common measure.

4. Exceeding in bulk the common measures: always used with some degree of dislike, or horror, or wonder.

A giant-shepherd here his flock maintains,
Far from the rest, and solitary reigns,
A form enormous*! far unlike the race*
Of human birth, in stature, or in face.
POPE'S ODYSSEY.

ENO'UGH. *adj.* [*genoh*, Saxon; *ganah*, Gothick; *genoeg*, Dut. It is not easy to determine whether this word be an adjective or adverb; perhaps, when it is joined with a substantive, it is an adjective, of which *enow* is the plural.

In other situations it seems an adverb; except that after the verb *to have*, or *to be*, either expressed or understood, it may be accounted a substantive. It is pronounced as if it were written *enuf.*] In a sufficient measure; so as may satisfy; so as may suffice.

> *Why wou'dst thou go, with one consent they cry,*
> *When thou hadst gold* enough, *and Emily.* DRYDEN.

> *When there was not room* enough *for their herds, they by consent separated, and enlarged their pasture.* LOCKE.

ENO'W. The plural of *enough*. In a sufficient number.

> *The earth hath since born* enow *bleeding witnesses, that it was no want of true courage.* SIDNEY, B. II.

> *The walls of the church there are* enow *contented to build, and to underset it with goodly pillars: the marbles are polished, the roofs shine with gold, the altar hath precious stones to adorn it, and of Christ's ministers no choice at all.*
> HOOKER, B. V. S. 15.

> *As if*
> *Man had not selfish foes* enow *besides,*
> *That, day and night, for his destruction wait.* MILTON'S PARADISE LOST.

> *My conquering brother will have slaves* enow,
> *To pay his cruel vows for victory.*
> DRYDEN'S DON SEBASTIAN.

> *There are at Rome* enow *modern works of architecture to employ any reasonable man.*
> ADDISON ON ANCIENT MEDALS.

ENSU'RANCE. *n.s.* [from *ensure.*]
1. Exemption from hazard, obtained by the payment of a certain sum.
2. The sum paid for security.

ENSU'RANCER. *n.s.* [from *ensurance.*] He who undertakes to exempt from hazard.

> *The vain* ensurancers *of life,*
> *And they who most perform'd, and promis'd less,*
> *Ev'n Short and Hobbes, forsook th' unequal strife.* DRYDEN.

ENTERPA'RLANCE. *n.s.* [*entre* and *parler*, French.] Parley; mutual talk; conference.

> *During the* enterparlance *the Scots discharged against the English without harm, but not without breach of the laws of the field.* HAYWARD.

E'NTERPRISER. *n.s.* [from *enterprise.*] A man of enterprise; one who undertakes great things; one who engages himself in important and dangerous designs.

> *They commonly proved great* enterprisers *with happy success.*
> HAYWARD ON EDWARD VI.

ENTHU'SIASM. *n.s.* ['ενθουσιασμός.]
1. A vain belief of private revelation; a vain confidence of divine favour or communication.

> Enthusiasm *is founded neither on reason nor divine revelation, but rises from the conceits of a warmed or overweening brain.* LOCKE.

2. Heat of imagination; violence of passion; confidence of opinion.
3. Elevation of fancy; exaltation of ideas.

> *Imaging is, in itself, the very height and life of poetry, which, by a kind of* enthusiasm, *or extraordinary emotion of soul, makes it seem to us that we behold those things which the poet paints.*
> DRYDEN'S JUVENAL, PREFACE.

E'NTIERTY. *n.s.* [*entiertè*, French.] The whole; not barely a part.

> *Sometime the attorney thrusteth into the writ the uttermost quantity; or else setteth down an* entierty, *where but a moiety was to be passed.*
> BACON'S OFFICE OF ALIENATION.

ENTI'RENESS. *n.s.* [from *entire.*]

1. Totality; compleatness; fulness.

In an arch where each single stone, which, if severed from the rest, would be perhaps defenceless, is sufficiently secured by the solidity and entireness *of the whole fabrick, of which it is a part.* BOYLE.

2. Honesty; integrity.

ENTREME'TS. *n.s.* [French.] Small plates set between the main dishes.

Chards of beet are plants of white beet transplanted, producing great tops, which, in the midst, have a large white main shoot, which is the true chard used in pottages and entremets.
MORTIMER'S ART OF HUSBANDRY.

To **ENVE'NOM.** *v.a.* [from *venom*]

1. To tinge with poison; to poison; to impregnate with venom. It is never used of the person to whom poison is given, but of the draught, meat, or instrument by which it is conveyed.

The treacherous instrument is in thy hand,
Unbated and envenom'd.
SHAKESPEARE.

Alcides, from Oechalia, crown'd
With conquest, felt th' envenom'd *robe, and tore,*
Through pain, up by the roots Thessalian pines. MILTON.

Nor with envenom'd *tongue to blast the same*
Of harmless men. PHILLIPS.

2. To make odious.

Oh, what a world is this, when what is comely
Envenoms *him that bears it!*
SHAKESPEARE'S AS YOU LIKE IT.

3. To enrage.

With her full force she threw the pois'nous dart,
And fix'd it deep within Amata's heart;
That thus envenom'd *she might kindle rage,*
And sacrifice to strife her house and husband's age. DRYDEN.

EPHE'MERA. *n.s.* ['εφήμερος.]

1. A fever that terminates in one day.
2. An insect that lives only one day.

E'PIC. *adj.* [*epicus*, Latin; 'επος.] Narrative; comprising narrations, not acted, but rehearsed. It is usually supposed to be heroick, or to contain one great action atchieved by a hero.

Holmes, whose name shall live in epic *song,*
While music numbers, or while verse has feet. DRYDEN.

The epic *poem is more for the manners, and the tragedy for the passions.*
DRYDEN.

From morality they formed that kind of poem and fable which we call epic.
POPE'S VIEW OF EPIC POEMS.

EPIDE'MICAL, EPIDEMICK. *n.s.* ['επί and δήμος.]

1. That which falls at once upon great numbers of people, as a plague.

It was conceived not to be an epidemick *disease, but to proceed from a malignity in the constitution of the air, gathered by the predispositions of seasons.*
BACON'S HENRY VII.

As the proportion of acute and epidemical *diseases shews the aptness of the air to sudden and vehement impressions, so the chronical diseases shew the ordinary temper of the place.*
GRAUNT'S BILLS OF MORTALITY.

2. Generally prevailing; affecting great numbers.

The more epidemical *and prevailing this evil is, the more honourable are those who shine as exceptions.*
SOUTH'S SERMONS.

He ought to have been busied in losing his money, or in other amusements equally laudable and epidemick *among persons of honour.* SWIFT.

3. General; universal.

They're citizens o' th' world, they're all in all;
Scotland's a nation epidemical.
CLEAVELAND.

EQUINE'CESSARY. *adj.* [*æquus* and *necessarius*, Latin.] Needful in the same degree.

For both to give blows and to carry,
In fights, are equinecessary.
HUDIBRAS, P. I. CANT. 3.

EQUINO'CTIAL. *n.s.* [*æquus*, and *nox*, Latin.] The line that encompasses the world at an equal distance from either pole, to which circle when the sun comes, he makes equal days and nights all over the globe.

EQUIPE'NDENCY. *n.s.* [*æquus* and *pendeo*, Latin.] The act of hanging in equipoise; not determined either way.

Doubtless the will of man, in the state of innocence, had an entire freedom, a perfect equipendency *and indifference to either part of the contradiction, to stand or not to stand.* SOUTH.

EQUI'PMENT. *n.s.* [from *equip.*]
1. The act of equipping or accoutering.
2. Accoutrement; equipage.

To **ERA'SE.** *v.a.* [*raser*, French.] To destroy; to exscind; to expunge; to rub out.

The heads of birds, for the most part, are given erased; *that is, plucked off.*
PEACHAM ON BLAZONING.

ERA'SEMENT. *n.s.* [from *erase.*]
1. Destruction; devastation.
2. Expunction; abolition.

ERO'SION. *n.s.* [*erosio*, Latin.]
1. The act of eating away.
2. The state of being eaten away; canker; corrosion.

As sea-salt is a sharp solid body, when taken in too great quantities, in a constant diet of salt meat, it breaks the vessels, produceth erosions *of the solid parts, and all the symptoms of the sea-scurvy.*
ARBUTHNOT ON ALIMENTS.

E'RRAND. *n.s.* [*ærenð*, Saxon; *arend*, Danish.] A message; something to be told or done by a messenger; a mandate; a commission. It is generally used now only in familiar language.

Servants being commanded to go, shall stand still, 'till they have their errand *warranted unto them.*
HOOKER, B. II. S. 8.

But hast thou done thy errand *to Baptista?*
—— I told him that your father was in Venice.
SHAKESPEARE.

A quean! have I not forbid her my house?
She comes of errands, *does she?*
SHAKESPEARE'S MERRY WIVES OF WINDSOR.

When he came, behold the captains of the host were sitting, and he said, I have an errand *to thee, O captain.*
BIBLE 2 KINGS IX. 5.

From them I go
This uncouth errand *sole.*
MILTON'S PARADISE LOST, B. II.

His eyes,
That run through all the heav'ns, or down to th' earth,
Bear his swift errands, *over moist and dry,*
O'er sea and land.
MILTON'S PARADISE LOST, B. III. L. 652.

Well thou do'st to hide from common sight
Thy close intrigues, too bad to bear the light;
Nor doubt I, but the silver-footed dame,
Tripping from sea, on such an errand *came.* DRYDEN'S HOMER.

ERRA'NT. *adj.* [*errans*, Latin; *errant*, French.]
1. Wandering; roving; rambling. Particularly applied to an order of

knights much celebrated in romances, who roved about the world in search of adventures.

There are just seven planets, or errant *stars, in the lower orbs of heaven; but it is now demonstrable unto sense, that there are many more.*
BROWN'S VULGAR ERROURS, B. IV. C. 12.

Chief of domestick knights and errant,
Either for chartel or for warrant.
HUDIBRAS.

2. Vile; abandoned; completely bad. See **ARRANT.**

Any way, so thou wilt do it, good impertinence:
Thy company, if I slept not very well
A-nights, would make me an errant *fool with questions.* JONSON'S CATILINE.

ERRA'TA. *n.s.* [Latin.] The faults of the printer inserted in the beginning or end of the book.

If he meet with faults, besides those that the errata *take notice of, he will consider the weakness of the author's eyes.* BOYLE.

ESCO'T. *n.s.* [French.] A tax paid in boroughs and corporations towards the support of the community, which is called scot and lot.

To **ESSA'Y.** *v.a.* [*essayer*, French.]

1. To attempt; to try; to endeavour.

While I this unexampled task essay,
Pass awful gulphs, and beat my painful way,
Celestial dove, divine assistance bring.
BLACKMORE'S CREATION.

No conquest she, but o'er herself desir'd;
No arts essay'd, *but not to be admir'd.*
POPE, EPISTLE 5.

2. To make experiment of.

3. To try the value and purity of metals.

The standard in our mint being now settled, the rules and methods of essaying *suited to it should remain unvariable.*
LOCKE.

ESTA'BLISHMENT. *n.s.* [from *establish*; *etablissement*, French.]

1. Settlement; fixed state.

All happy peace, and goodly government,
Is settled there in sure establishment.
FAIRY QUEEN, B. II. C. 11.

2. Confirmation of something already done; ratification.

He had not the act penned by way of recognition of right; as, on the other side, he avoided to have it by new law; but chose rather a kind of middle way, by way of establishment. BACON'S HENRY VII.

3. Settled regulation; form; model of a government or family.

Now come unto that general reformation, and bring in that establishment *by which all men should be contained in duty.*
SPENSER'S STATE OF IRELAND.

4. Foundation; fundamental principle; settled law.

The sacred order to which you belong, and even the establishment *on which it subsists, have often been struck at; but in vain.*
ATTERBURY'S SERMONS.

5. Allowance; income; salary.

His excellency, who had the sole disposal of the emperor's revenue, might easily provide against that evil, by gradually lessening your establishment.
GULLIVER'S TRAVELS.[95]

E'STRICH. *n.s.* [commonly written *ostrich.*] The largest of birds.

To be furious,
Is to be frighted out of fear; and, in that mood,
The dove will peck the estridge.
SHAKESPEARE'S ANTHONY AND CLEOPATRA.

The peacock, not at thy command, assumes
His glorious train; nor estrich *her rare plumes.* SANDYS.

ETCH. *n.s.* A country word, of which I know not the meaning.

When they sow their etch *crops, they sprinkle a pound or two of clover on an acre.* MORTIMER'S HUSBANDRY.

Where you find dunging of land makes it rank, lay dung upon the etch, *and sow it with barley.* MORTIMER'S HUSBANDRY.

E'THER. *n.s.* [*æther*, Latin; 'άιθηϱ.]
1. An element more fine and subtle than air; air refined or sublimed.

If any one should suppose that ether, *like our air, may contain particles which endeavour to recede from one another; for I do not know what this* ether *is; and that its particles are exceedingly smaller than those of air, or even than those of light, the exceeding smallness of its particles may contribute to the greatness of the force, by which those particles may recede from one another.* NEWTON'S OPTICKS.

The parts of other bodies are held together by the eternal pressure of the ether, *and can have no other conceivable cause of their cohesion and union.* LOCKE.

2. The matter of the highest regions above.

There fields of light and liquid ether *flow,*
Purg'd from the pond'rous dregs of earth below. DRYDEN.

E'THNICK. *adj.* ['έθνικος.] Heathen; Pagan; not Jewish; not Christian.

Such contumely as the ethnick *world durst not offer him, is the peculiar insolence of degenerated Christians.* GOVERNMENT OF TONGUE.

I shall begin with the agreement of profane, whether Jewish or ethnick, *with the Sacred Writings.* GREW'S COSMOLOGIA SACRA.

ETHOLO'GICAL. *adj.* ['ήθος and λόγος.] Treating of morality.

ETYMOLO'GICAL. *adj.* [from *etymology.*] Relating to etymology; relating to the derivation of words.

Excuse this conceit, this etymological *observation.* LOCKE.

ETYMO'LOGIST. *n.s.* [from *etymology.*] One who searches out the original of words; one who shows the derivation of words from their original.

ETYMO'LOGY. *n.s.* [*etymologia*, Lat. 'έτυμος and λόγος.]
1. The descent or derivation of a word from its original; the deduction of formations from the radical word; the analysis of compound words into primitives.

Consumption is generally taken for any universal diminution and colliquation of the body, which acception its etymology *implies.* HARVEY ON CONSUMPTIONS.

When words are restrained, by common usage, to a particular sense, to run up to etymology, *and construe them by Dictionaries, is wretchedly ridiculous.* COLLIER'S VIEW OF THE STAGE.

Pelvis is used by comick writers for a looking-glass, by which means the etymology *of the word is visible, and pelvidera will signify a lady who looks in her glass.* ADDISON'S SPECTATOR.

If the meaning of a word could be learned by its derivation or etymology, *yet the original derivation of words is oftentimes very dark.* WATTS'S LOGICK.

2. The part of grammar which delivers the inflections of nouns and verbs.

EVERDU'RING. *adj.* [*ever* and *during.*] Eternal; enduring without end.

Our souls, piercing through the impurity of flesh, behold the highest heavens, and thence bring knowledge to contemplate the everduring *glory and termless joy.* RALEIGH.

Heav'n open'd wide
Her everduring *gates, harmonious sound!*
On golden hinges moving.
MILTON'S PARADISE LOST, B. VII.

EVERMO'RE. *adv.* [*ever* and *more.*] Always; eternally. *More* seems an expletive accidentally added, unless it signified originally *from this time*: as, *evermore, always henceforward*; but this sense has not been strictly preserved.

It govern'd was, and guided evermore,
Through wisdom of a matron grave and hoare. FAIRY QUEEN.

Sparks by nature evermore *aspire,*
Which makes them now to such a highness flee. DAVIES.

Religion prefers those pleasures which flow from the presence of God for evermore, *infinitely before the transitory pleasures of this world.* TILLOTSON, SERMON I.

E'VESDROPPER.[96] *n.s.* [*eves* and *dropper.*] Some mean fellow that skulks about a house in the night.

What makes you listening there? Get farther off; I preach not to thee, thou wicked evesdropper.
DRYDEN'S SPANISH FRYAR.

Do but think how decent a habit you have on, and how becoming your function it is to be disguised like a slave, and an evesdropper, *under the women's windows.*
DRYDEN'S DON SEBASTIAN.

EUGH. *n.s.* [This word is so written by most writers; but since the original *iw*, Saxon, or Welsh *ywen*, more favours the easier orthography of *yew*, I have referred it thither.] A tree.

At the first stretch of both his hands he drew,
And almost join'd the horns of the tough eugh. DRYDEN'S ÆNEID.

EVILSPE'AKING. *n.s.* [*evil* and *speaking.*] Slander; defamation; calumny; censoriousness.

Wherefore laying aside all malice and all guile, and hypocrisies and envies, and all evilspeakings. BIBLE 1 PETER, II. 1.

EVILWI'SHING. *adj.* [*evil* and *wish.*] Wishing evil to; having no good will.

They having heard of this sudden going out with so small a company, in a country full of evilwishing *minds towards him, followed him.* SIDNEY, B. II.

EX. A Latin preposition often prefixed to compounded words; sometimes meaning *out*, as *exhaust*, to draw *out*; sometimes only enforcing the meaning, and sometimes producing little alteration.

EXA'CTLY. *adv.* [from *exact.*] Accurately; nicely; thoroughly.

Both of 'em knew mankind exactly *well; for both of 'em began that study in themselves.*
DRYDEN'S DON SEBASTIAN.

The religion they profess is such, that the more exactly *it is sifted by pure unbiassed reason, the more reasonable still it will be found.* ATTERBURY'S SERMONS.

EXAMINA'TION. *n.s.* [*examinatio*, Latin.] The act of examining by questions, or experiment; accurate disquisition.

I have brought him forth, that, after examination *had, I might have somewhat to write.* BIBLE ACTS, XXV. 26.

Different men leaving out or putting in several simple ideas, according to their various examination, *skill, or observation of the subject, have different essences.*
LOCKE.

EXCANTA'TION. *n.s.* [*excanto*, Latin.] Disenchantment by a countercharm.

EXCARNIFICA'TION. *n.s.* [*excarnifico*, Latin.] The act of taking away the flesh.

EXCELLE'NCE, EXCELLENCY. *n.s.* [*excellence*, French; *excellentia*, Latin.]

1. The state of abounding in any good quality.

2. Dignity; high rank in existence.

Is it not wonderful, that base desires should so extinguish in men the sense of their own excellency, *as to make them willing that their souls should be like to the souls of beasts, mortal and corruptible with their bodies?* HOOKER, B. V. S. 2.

I know not why a fiend may not deceive a creature of more excellency *than himself, but yet a creature.*
DRYDEN'S JUVENAL, DEDICATION.

3. The state of excelling in any thing.

I have, amongst men of parts and business, seldom heard any one commended for having an excellency *in musick.* LOCKE.

4. That in which one excels.

The criticisms have been made rather to discover beauties and excellencies *than their faults and imperfections.*
ADDISON'S SPECTATOR.

5. Purity; goodness.

She loves him with that excellence,
That angels love good men with.
SHAKESPEARE'S HENRY VIII.

6. A title of honour. It is now usually applied to generals of an army, ambassadors, and governors.

They humbly sue unto your excellence,
To have a goodly peace concluded of.
SHAKESPEARE'S HENRY VI.

EXCI'SE. *n.s.* [*accijs*, Dutch; *excisum*, Latin.] A hateful tax levied upon commodities, and adjudged not by the common judges of property, but wretches hired by those to whom excise is paid.

The people should pay a ratable tax for their sheep, and an excise *for every thing which they should eat.* HAYWARD.

Ambitious now to take excise
Of a more fragrant paradise.
CLEAVELAND.

Excise,
With hundred rows of teeth, the shark exceeds,
And on all trades like Cassawar she feeds.
MARVEL.

Can hire large houses, and oppress the poor,
By farm'd excise.
DRYDEN'S JUVENAL, SATIRE 3.

EXCLAMA'TION. *n.s.* [*exclamatio*, Latin]

1. Vehement outcry; clamour; outrageous vociferation.

The ears of the people are continually beaten with exclamations *against abuses in the church.* HOOKER, DEDICATION.

Either be patient, and intreat me fair,
Or with the clamorous report of war
Thus will I drown your exclamations.
SHAKESPEARE'S RICHARD III.

2. An emphatical utterance; a pathetical sentence.

O Musidorus! Musidorus! but what serve exclamations, *where there are no ears to receive the sound?* SIDNEY, B. II.

3. A note by which a pathetical sentence is marked thus !

To **EXCO'GITATE.** *v.a.* [*excogito*, Latin.] To invent; to strike out by thinking.

If the wit of man had been to contrive this organ for himself, what could he have possibly excogitated *more accurate?*
MORE'S ANTIDOTE AGAINST ATHEISM.

The tradition of the origination of mankind seems to be universal; but the particular methods of that origination, excogitated *by the heathen, were particular.*
HALE'S ORIGIN OF MANKIND.

We shall find them to be little else than excogitated *and invented models, not much arising from the true image of the things themselves.*
HALE'S ORIGIN OF MANKIND.

EXCU'SE. *n.s.* [from the verb. The last syllable of the verb is sounded as if written *excuze*, that of the noun with the natural sound.]

1. Plea offered in extenuation; apology.

I was set upon by some of your servants, whom because I have in my just defence evil entreated, I came to make my excuse *to you.* SIDNEY.

Be gone, I will not hear thy vain excuse;
But, as thou lov'st thy life, make speed from hence. SHAKESPEARE.

As good success admits no examination, so the contrary allows of no excuse, *how reasonable or just soever.* RALEIGH.

We find out some excuse *or other for deferring good resolutions, 'till our intended retreat is cut off by death.* ADDISON.

2. The act of excusing or apologising.

Heav'n put it in thy mind to take it hence,
That thou might'st win the more thy father's love,
Pleading so wisely in excuse *of it.*
SHAKESPEARE'S HENRY IV.

3. Cause for which one is excused.

Let no vain hope your easy mind seduce;
For rich ill poets are without excuse.
ROSCOMMON.

Nothing but love this patience could produce;
And I allow your rage that kind excuse.
DRYDEN'S AURENGZEBE.

EXCU'SELESS. *adj.* [from *excuse.*] That for which no excuse or apology can be given.

The voluntary enslaving myself is excuseless. DECAY OF PIETY.

EXE'MPTION. *n.s.* [from *exempt.*] Immunity; privilege; freedom from imposts or burdensome employments.

The like exemption *hath the writ to enquire of a man's death, which also must be granted freely.*
BACON'S OFFICE OF ALIENATION.

The Roman laws gave particular exemptions *to such as built ships, or traded in corn.* ARBUTHNOT ON COINS.

EXE'QUIES. *n.s.* without a singular. [*exequiæ*, Lat.] Funeral rites; the ceremony of burial; the procession of burial. For this word *obsequies* is often used, but not so properly.

Let's not forget
The noble duke of Bedford late deceas'd,
But see his exequies *fulfill'd in Roan.*
SHAKESPEARE'S HENRY VI.

The tragical end of the two brothers, whose exequies *the next successor had leisure to perform.*
DRYDEN'S DEDICATION TO ÆNEID.

To **EXFO'LIATE.** *v.n.* [*ex* and *folium*, Latin.] To shell off; separate, as a corrupt bone from the sound part. A term of chirurgery.

Our work went on successfully, the bone exfoliating *from the edges.*
WISEMAN'S SURGERY.

EXHIBI'TION. *n.s.* [from *exhibit.*]

1. The act of exhibiting; display; setting forth.

What are all mechanick works, but the sensible exhibition *of mathematick demonstrations?*
GREW'S COSMOLOGIA SACRA, B. II.

2. Allowance; salary; pension.[97]

I crave fit disposition for my wife,
Due preference of place and exhibition,
As levels with her breeding.
SHAKESPEARE'S OTHELLO.

What maintenance he from his friends receives,
Like exhibition *thou shalt have from me.*
SHAKESPEARE.

All was assigned to the army and garrisons there, and she received only a pension or exhibition *out of his coffers.* BACON.

He is now neglected, and driven to live in exile upon a small exhibition. SWIFT.

E'XIGENT. *n.s.* [*exigens*, Latin.]
1. Pressing business; occasion that requires immediate help.

In such an exigent *I see not how they could have staid to deliberate about any other regiment than that which already was devised to their hands.*
HOOKER, PREFACE.

The council met, your guards to find you sent,
And know your pleasure in this exigent.
WALLER.

2. [A law term.] A writ sued when the defendant is not to be found, being part of the process leading to an outlawry. *Shakespeare* uses it for any extremity. *Hanmer.*
3. End.

These eyes, like lamps whose wasting oil is spent,
Wax dim, as drawing to their exigent.
SHAKESPEARE'S HENRY VI.

E'XIT. *n.s.* [*exit*, Latin.]
1. The term set in the margin of plays to mark the time at which the player goes off the stage.
2. Recess; departure; act of quitting the stage; act of quitting the theatre of life.

All the world's a stage,
And all the men and women meerly players:
They have their exits *and their entrances,*
And one man in his time plays many parts. SHAKESPEARE.

A regard for fame becomes a man more towards the exit *than at his entrance into life.* SWIFT.

Many of your old comrades live a short life, and make a figure at their exit. SWIFT.

3. Passage out of any place.

In such a pervious substance as the brain, they might find an easy either entrance or exit, *almost every where.* GLANVILLE.

4. Way by which there is a passage out.

The fire makes its way, forcing the water forth through its ordinary exits, *wells, and the outlets of rivers.* WOODWARD.

EXO'RBITANT. *adj.* [*ex* and *orbito*, Latin.]
1. Going out of the prescribed track; deviating from the course appointed or rule established.[98]

What signifies the fiction of the tortoise riding upon the wings of the wind, but to prescribe bounds and measures to our exorbitant *passions?* L'ESTRANGE.

These phenomena are not peculiar to the earthquakes which have happened in our times, but have been observed in all ages, and particularly those exorbitant *commotions of the waters of the globe.*
WOODWARD'S NATURAL HISTORY.

2. Anomalous; not comprehended in a settled rule or method.

The Jews, who had laws so particularly determining in all affairs what to do, were notwithstanding continually inured with causes exorbitant, *and such as their laws had not provided for.*
HOOKER, B. III. S. 11.

3. Enormous; beyond due proportion; excessive.

Their subjects would live in great plenty, were not the impositions so very exorbitant; *for the courts are too splendid for the territories.* ADDISON'S REMARKS ON ITALY.

So endless and exorbitant *are the desires of men, that they will grasp at all, and can form no scheme of perfect happiness with less.*
SWIFT ON THE DISSENTIONS IN ATHENS AND ROME.

EXPE'NSE. *n.s.* [*expensum*, Latin.]
Cost; charges; money expended.

Hence comes that wild and vast expense,
That hath enforc'd Rome's virtue thence,
Which simple poverty first made.
BEN JONSON'S CATILINE.

A feast prepar'd with riotous expense,

Much cost, more care, and most magnificence. DRYDEN.

I can see no reason by which we were obliged to make those prodigious expenses. SWIFT.

EXPE'NSEFUL. *adj.* [*expense* and *full.*] Costly; chargeable; expensive.

No part of structure is either more expenceful *than windows or more ruinous, as being exposed to all violence of weather.* WOTTON'S ARCHITECTURE.

EXPE'NSELESS. *adj.* [from *expense.*] Without cost.

A physician may save any army by this frugal and expenseless *means only.* MILTON ON EDUCATION.

What health promotes, and gives unenvy'd peace,
Is all expenseless, *and procur'd with ease.*
BLACKMORE'S CREATION.

EXPE'NSIVE. *adj.* [from *expense.*]
1. Given to expense; extravagant; luxurious.

Frugal and industrious men are friendly to the established government, as the idle and expensive *are dangerous.* TEMPLE.

2. Costly; requiring expense: as, *expensive* dress; an *expensive* journey.
3. Liberal; generous; distributive.

This requires an active, expensive, *indefatigable goodness, such as our apostle calls a work and labour of love.* SPRATT.

E'XPLETIVE. *n.s.* [*expletivum*, Latin.] Something used only to take up room; something of which the use is only to prevent a vacancy.

These are not only useful expletives *to matter, but great ornaments of style.* SWIFT.

Oft the ear the open vowels tire,
While expletives *their feeble aid do join.*
POPE'S ESSAY ON CRITICISM.

Another nicety is in relation to expletives, *whether words or syllables, which are made use of purely to supply a vacancy:* do, *before verbs plural, is absolutely such; and future refiners may explode* did *and* does. POPE.

To **EXPLO'DE.** *v.a.* [*explodo*, Latin.]
1. To drive out disgracefully with some noise of contempt; to treat with open contempt; to treat not only with neglect, but open disdain or scorn.

Him old and young
Exploded, *and had seiz'd with violent hands,*
Had not a cloud descending snatch'd him thence
Unseen amid' the throng.
MILTON'S PARADISE LOST, B. XI.

Thus was th' applause they meant,
Turn'd to exploding *hiss, triumph to shame,*
Cast on themselves from their own mouths. MILTON'S PARADISE LOST.

Old age explodes *all but morality.* ROSCOMMON.

There is pretended, that a magnetical globe or terrella, being placed upon its poles, would have a constant rotation; but this is commonly exploded, *as being against all experience.* WILKINS'S DÆDALUS.

Shall that man pass for a proficient in Christ's school, who would have been exploded *in the school of Zeno or Epictetus.* SOUTH'S SERMONS.

Provided that no word, which a society shall give a sanction to, be afterwards antiquated and exploded, *they may receive whatever new ones they shall find occasion for.*
SWIFT'S LETTER TO THE LORD HIGH TREASURER.

2. To drive out with noise and violence.

But late the kindled powder did explode
The massy ball, and the brass tube unload. BLACKMORE.

EXPLO'DER. *n.s.* [from *explode.*] An hisser; one who drives out any person or thing with open contempt.

To **EXPO'STULATE.** *v.n.* [*expostulo*, Latin.] To canvass with another; to altercate; to debate without open rupture.

More bitterly could I expostulate,
Save that for reverence of some alive
I give a sparing limit to my tongue.
SHAKESPEARE'S RICHARD III.

The emperor's ambassador did expostulate *with the king, that he had broken his league with the emperor.* HAYWARD.

It is madness for friendless and unarmed innocence to expostulate *with invincible power.* L'ESTRANGE.

Durst I expostulate *with providence, I then might ask.* COTTON.

The bishop will expostulate, *and the tenant will have regard to the reasonableness of the demand, rather than engage in a suit.* SWIFT.

To **EXPROBRA'TE.** *v.a.* [*exprobro*, Latin.] To charge upon with reproach; to impute openly with blame; to upbraid.

To exprobrate *their stupidity, he induces the providence of storks: now, if the bird had been unknown, the illustration had been obscure, and the exprobration not so proper.* BROWN.

To **EXPRO'PRIATE.** *v.a.* [*ex* and *proprius*, Latin.] To make no longer our own; to hold no longer as a property. Not in use.

When you have resigned, or rather consigned, your expropriated *will to God, and thereby entrusted him to will for you, all his dispensations towards you are, in effect, the acts of your own will.*
BOYLE'S SERAPHICK LOVE.

EXPU'RGATORY. *adj.* [*expurgatorius*, Latin.] Employed in purging away what is noxious: as, the *expurgatory* index of the Romanists directs the abolition or expunction of passages admitted by any authors contrary to popery.

There wants expurgatory *animadversions, whereby we might strike out great numbers of hidden qualities; and having once a conceded list, we might with more safety attempt their reasons.*
BROWN'S VULGAR ERROURS, B. II. C. 7.

EXQU'ISITELY. *adv.* [from *exquisite.*] Perfectly; completely: in either a good or ill sense.

We see more exquisitely *with one eye shut than with both open; for that the spirits visual unite themselves, and become stronger.*
BACON'S NATURAL HISTORY, NO. 86.

A collection of rare manuscripts, exquisitely *written in Arabick, and sought in the most remote parts by Epenius, the most excellent linguist.* WOTTON.

The soldier then, in Grecian arts unskill'd,
Returning rich with plunder from the field,
If cups of silver or of gold he brought,
With jewels set, and exquisitely *wrought,*
To glorious trappings strait the plate he turn'd,
And with the glitt'ring spoil his horse adorn'd. DRYDEN.

The poetry of opera's is generally as exquisitely *ill as the musick is good.*
ADDISON'S REMARKS ON ITALY.

EXTE'NDLESSNESS. *n.s.* [from *extend.*] Unlimited extension. In this sense it is once found; but, I think, with little propriety.

Certain moleculæ seminales must keep the world from an infinitude, and extendlessness *of excursions every moment into new figures and animals.*
HALE'S ORIGIN OF MANKIND.

EXTI'NGUISHER. *n.s.* [from *extinguish.*] A hollow cone put upon a candle to quench it.

If it should ever offer to flame out again, I would use the conicum as an extinguisher *to smother it.*
MORE'S DIVINE DIALOGUES.

Of it a broad extinguisher *he makes,*
And hoods the flames that to their quarry strove. DRYDEN.

'Tis better to cover the vital flame with an extinguisher *of honour, than let it consume 'till it burns blue, and lies agonizing within the socket.*
COLLIER ON THE VALUE OF LIFE.

EXTO'RTION. *n.s.* [from *extort.*]
1. The act or practice of gaining by violence and rapacity.

That goodness
Of gleaning all the land's wealth into one,
Into your own hands, cardinal, by extortion.
SHAKESPEARE'S HENRY VIII.

Oppression and extortion *did maintain the greatness, and oppression and* extortion *did extinguish the greatness of that house.*
DAVIES ON IRELAND.

2. Force by which any thing is unjustly taken away.

Because the lords had power to impose this charge, the freeholders were glad to give a great part of their lands to hold the rest free from that extortion.
DAVIES ON IRELAND.

A succeeding king's just recovery of rights from unjust usurpations and extortions, *shall never be prejudiced by any act of mine.*
KING CHARLES.

EXTRADI'CTIONARY. *adj.* [*extra* and *dictio*, Latin.] Not consisting in words but realities.

Of these extradictionary *and real fallacies, Aristotle and logicians make six; but we observe men are commonly deceived by four thereof.*
BROWN'S VULGAR ERROURS, B. I. C. 4.

EXTRAO'RDINARY. *adj.* [*extraordinarius*, Lat. This word and its derivatives are generally pronounced *extrordinary*, whereby the *a* is liquified into the *o*.]
1. Different from common order and method; not ordinary.

Evils must be judged inevitable, if there be no apparent ordinary way to avoid them; because where council and advice bear rule of God's extraordinary *power, without* extraordinary *warrant, we cannot presume.* HOOKER, B. V. S. 9.

At that time Spain had no other wars, save those which were grown into an ordinary: now they have coupled therewith the extraordinary *of the Valtoline and the Palatinate.*
BACON'S WAR WITH SPAIN.

Let us see what extraordinary *armies have been transmitted thither, and what ordinary forces have been maintained there.*
DAVIES'S STATE OF IRELAND.

2. Different from the common course of law.

If they proceeded in a martial or any other extraordinary *way, without any form of law, his majesty should declare his justice and affection to an old faithful servant.*
CLARENDON.

3. Eminent; remarkable; more than common.

The house was built of fair and strong stone, not affecting so much any extraordinary *kind of fineness, as an honourable representing of a firm stateliness.*
SIDNEY.

The Indians worshipped rivers, fountains, rocks, or great stones, &c. and all things which seemed to have something extraordinary *in them.*
STILLINGFLEET'S DEFENCE OF DISCOURSE ON ROMISH IDOLATRY.

EXTRAVE'RSION. *n.s.* [*extra* and *versio*, Latin.] The act of throwing out; the state of being thrown out.

Nor does there intervene heat to afford them any colour to pretend that there is made an extraversion *of the sulphur, or of any of the two other supposed principles.* BOYLE.

EXTRE'ME. *adj.* [*extremus*, Latin. This word is sometimes corrupted by the superlative termination, of which it is by no means capable, as it has in itself the superlative signification.]

1. Greatest; of the highest degree.

He that will take away extreme *heat by setting the body in extremity of cold, shall undoubtedly remove the disease; but together with it the diseased too.* HOOKER, B. IV. S. 8.

The Lord shall smite thee with a fever, an inflammation, and an extreme *burning.* BIBLE DEUTERONOMY, XXVIII. 22.

They thought it the extremest *of evils to put themselves at the mercy of those hungry and disorderly people.* BACON.

2. Utmost.

The hairy fool
Stood on th' extremest *verge of the swift brook,*
Augmenting it with tears.
SHAKESPEARE'S AS YOU LIKE IT.

Miseno's cape and Bauli last he view'd,
That on the sea's extremest *borders stood.*
ADDISON ON ITALY.

3. Last; that beyond which there is nothing.

Farewel, ungrateful and unkind! I go,
Condemn'd by thee, to those sad shades below:
I go th' extremest *remedy to prove,*
To drink oblivion, and to drench my love.
DRYDEN.

4. Pressing in the utmost degree.

Cases of necessity being sometime but urgent, sometime extreme, *the consideration of publick utility is urged equivalent to the easier kind of necessity.* HOOKER, B. V. S. 9.[99]

To **E'XTRICATE.** *v.a.* [*extrico*, Latin.] To disembarrass; to set free any one in a state of perplexity; to disentangle.

We run into great difficulties about free created agents, which reason cannot well extricate *itself out of.* LOCKE.

These are great reliefs to nature, as they give her an opportunity of extricating *herself from her oppressions, and recovering the several tones and springs of her distended vessels.* ADDISON'S SPECTATOR, NO. 195.

EXU'BERANCE. *n.s.* [*exuberatio*, Latin.] Overgrowth; superfluous shoots; useless abundance; luxuriance.

Men esteem the overflowing of gall the exuberance *of zeal, and all the promises of the faithful combatant they confidently appropriate.* DECAY OF PIETY.

Though he expatiates on the same thoughts in different words, yet in his similes that exuberance *is avoided.* GARTH.

EYESE'RVANT. *n.s.* [*eye* and *servant.*] A servant that works only while watched.

EYESE'RVICE. *n.s.* [*eye* and *service.*] Service performed only under inspection.

Servants, obey in all things your master; not with eyeservice, *as men pleasers, but in singleness of heart.* BIBLE COLOSSIANS, III.

EY'ESHOT. *n.s.* [*eye* and *shot.*] Sight; glance; view.

I must carry off my prize as others do; and not think of sharing the booty before I am

free from danger, and out of eyeshot *from the other windows.*
DRYDEN'S DON SEBASTIAN.

I have preserved many a young man from her eyeshot *by this means.*
SPECTATOR, NO. 284.

EY'EWINK. *n.s.* [*eye* and *wink.*] A wink, as a hint or token.

They would have won any woman's heart; and, I warrant you, they could never get an eyewink *of her.* SHAKESPEARE.

F

A consonant generally reckoned by authors, and admitted by *Scaliger*, among the semi-vowels, and according to that opinion distinguished in the enumeration of the alphabet by a name beginning with a vowel, yet has so far the nature of a mute, that it is easily pronounced before a liquid in the same syllable. It has in English an invariable sound, formed by compression of the whole lips and a forcible breath. Its kindred letter is V, which, in the Islandick alphabet, is only distinguished from it by a point in the body of the letter.

To **FA'BRICATE.** *v.a.* [*fabricor*, Latin.]
1. To build; to construct.
2. To forge; to devise falsely. This sense is retained among the Scottish lawyers; for when they suspect a paper to be forged, they say it is *fabricate*.

FABULO'SITY. *n.s.* [*fabulositas*, Latin.] Lyingness; fulness of stories; fabulous invention.

> *In their* fabulosity *they would report, that they had observations for twenty thousand years.*
> ABBOT'S DESCRIPTION OF THE WORLD.

FA'BULOUS. *adj.* [*fabulosus*, Latin.] Feigned; full of fables, or invented tales.

> *A person terrified with the imagination of spectres, is more reasonable than one who thinks the appearance of spirits* fabulous *and groundless.*
> ADDISON'S SPECTATOR, NO. 110.

FACEPAI'NTER. *n.s.* [*face* and *painter.*] A drawer of portraits; a painter who draws from the life.

FACE'TIOUS. *adj.* [*facetieux*, French; *facetiæ*, Lat.] Gay; cheerful; lively; merry; witty. It is used both of persons and sentiments.

> *Socrates, informed of some derogating speeches used of him behind his back, made this* facetious *reply, Let him beat me too when I am absent.*
> GOVERNMENT OF THE TONGUE, S. 6.

FA'CTIOUS. *adj.* [*factieux*, French.]
1. Given to faction; loud and violent in a party; publickly dissensious; addicted to form parties and raise publick disturbances.

> *He is a traitor; let him to the Tower,*
> *And crop away that* factious *pate of his.*
> SHAKESPEARE'S HENRY VI.

> *Be* factious *for redress of all these griefs.*
> SHAKESPEARE'S JULIUS CÆSAR.

2. Proceeding from publick dissensions; tending to publick discord.

Grey-headed men and grave, with warriors mix'd,
Assemble; and harangues are heard; but soon
In factious *opposition.*
MILTON'S PARADISE LOST, B. XI. L. 664.

Factious *tumults overbore the freedom and honour of the two houses.*
KING CHARLES.

Why these factious *quarrels, controversies, and battles amongst themselves, when they were all united in the same design?*
DRYDEN'S JUVENAL, DEDICATION.

FA'CTORY. *n.s.* [from *factor.*]
1. A house or district inhabited by traders in a distant country.
2. The traders embodied in one place.

FAIN. *adj.* [*feagn*, Saxon.]
1. Glad; merry; chearful; fond. It is still retained in Scotland in this sense.

And in her hand she held a mirrour bright,
Wherein her face she often viewed fain.
FAIRY QUEEN.

My lips will be fain *when I sing unto thee, and so will my soul whom thou hast delivered.* BIBLE PSALM LXXI.

2. Forced; obliged; compelled. [This signification seems to have arisen from the mistake of the original signification in some ambiguous expressions; as, *I was* fain *to do this*, would equally suit with the rest of the sentence, whether it was understood to mean *I was compelled*, or *I was glad to do it for fear of worse*. Thus the primary meaning seems to have been early lost.]

Every weight to shroud it did constrain,
And this fair couple eke to shroud themselves were fain.
FAIRY QUEEN, B. I. CANT. 1. STAN. 6.

Whosoever will hear, he shall find God; whosoever will study to know, shall be also fain *to believe.*
HOOKER, B. V.

I was fain *to forswear it; they would else have married me to the rotten medlar.*
SHAKESPEARE'S MEASURE FOR MEASURE.

When Hildebrand had accursed Henry IV. there were none so hardy as to defend their lord; wherefore he was fain *to humble himself before Hildebrand.*
RALEIGH'S ESSAYS.

The learned Castalio was fain *to make trenchers at Basle, to keep himself from starving.* LOCKE.

FA'INTING. *n.s.* [from *faint.*]
Deliquium; temporary loss of animal motion.

These faintings *her physicians suspect to proceed from contusions.*
WISEMAN'S SURGERY.

FA'INTLING. *adj.* [from *faint.*]
Timorous; feebleminded. A burlesque or low word.

There's no having patience, thou art such a faintling *silly creature.*
ARBUTHNOT'S HISTORY OF JOHN BULL.

FA'INTNESS. *n.s.* [from *faint.*]
1. Languour; feebleness; want of strength.

If the prince of the lights of heaven, which now as a giant doth run his unwearied courses, should through a languishing faintness *begin to stand.*
HOOKER, B. I. S. 3.

This proceeded not from any violence of pain, but from a general languishing and faintness *of spirits, which made him think nothing worth the trouble of one careful thought.* TEMPLE.

2. Inactivity; want of vigour.

This evil proceeds rather of the unsoundness of the counsels laid for the reformation, or of faintness *in following and effecting the*

same, than of any such fatal course appointed of God.
SPENSER'S STATE OF IRELAND.

3. Timorousness; dejection.

The paleness of this flow'r
Bewray'd the faintness *of my master's heart.* SHAKESPEARE'S HENRY VI.

FA'INTY. *adj.* [from *faint.*] Weak; feeble; languid; debilitated; enfeebled.

When Winter frosts constrain the field with cold,
The fainty *root can take no steady hold.*
DRYDEN'S VIRGIL'S GEORGICKS.

The ladies gasp'd, and scarcely could respire;
The breath they drew, no longer air, but fire:
The fainty *knights were scorch'd, and knew not where*
To run for shelter; for no shade was near.
DRYDEN.

FAIR. *n.s.* [*foire*, French; *feriæ*, or *forum*, Latin.] An annual or stated meeting of buyers and sellers; a time of traffick more frequented than a market. The privilege of holding fairs in England is granted by the king.

With silver, iron, tin and lead they traded in thy fairs.
BIBLE EZEKIEL, XXVII. 12.

His corn, his cattle, were his only care,
And his supreme delight a country fair.
DRYDEN.

The ancient Nundinæ, or fairs *of Rome, were kept every ninth day: afterwards the same privileges were granted to the country markets, which were at first under the power of the consuls.*
ARBUTHNOT ON COINS.

FA'LDSTOOL. *n.s.* [*fald* or *fold* and *stool.*] A kind of stool placed at the south-side of the altar, at which the kings of England kneel at their coronation.

FALLA'CIOUS. *adj.* [*fallax*, Latin; *fallacieux*, French.]

1. Producing mistake; sophistical. It is never used of men, but of writings, propositions, or things.

They believed and assented to things neither evident nor certain, nor yet so much as probable, but actually false and fallacious; *such as were the absurd doctrines and stories of their rabbies.*
SOUTH'S SERMONS.

2. Deceitful; mocking expectation.

Soon as the force of that fallacious *fruit,*
That with exhilarating vapour bland
About their spirits had play'd, and inmost pow'rs
Made err, was now exhal'd.
MILTON'S PARADISE LOST, B. IX.

False philosophy inspires
Fallacious *hope.* MILTON.

FA'LLINGSICKNESS. *n.s.* [*fall* and *sickness.*] The epilepsy; a disease in which the patient is without any warning deprived at once of his senses, and falls down.

Did Cæsar swoon? —— He fell down in the market-place, and foam'd at mouth, and was speechless. —— He hath the fallingsickness.
SHAKESPEARE'S JULIUS CÆSAR.

The dogfisher is good against the fallingsickness. WALTON.

FA'LSIFIER. *n.s.* [from *falsify.*]

1. One that counterfeits; one that makes any thing to seem what it is not.

It happens in theories built on too obvious or too few experiments, what happens to falsifiers *of coin; for counterfeit money will endure some one proof, others another, but none of them all proofs.* BOYLE.

2. A liar; one that contrives falshoods.

Boasters are naturally falsifiers, *and the people, of all others, that put their shams the worst together.*
L'ESTRANGE'S FABLES.

To **FA'LTER.** *v.n.* [*faltar*, to be wanting, Spanish; *vaulttur*, a stammerer, Islandick, which is probably a word from the same radical.]

1. To hesitate in the utterance of words.

With faltering *tongue, and trembling ev'ry vein,*
Tell on, quoth she. FAIRY QUEEN, B. I.

The pale assistants on each other star'd,
With gaping mouths for issuing words prepar'd;
The still-born sounds upon the palate hung,
And dy'd imperfect on the falt'ring *tongue.* DRYDEN.

He changes, gods! and falters *at the question:*
His fears, his words, his looks declare him guilty. SMITH.

2. To fail in any act of the body.

This earth shall have a feeling; and these stones
Prove armed soldiers, ere her native king
Shall falter *under foul rebellious arms.*
SHAKESPEARE'S RICHARD II.

3. To fail in any act of the understanding.

How far ideots are concerned in the want or weakness of any or all faculties, an exact observation of their several ways of faltering *would discover.* LOCKE.

To **FA'LTER.** *v.a.* To sift; to cleanse. This word seems to be merely rustick or provincial.

Barley for malt must be bold, dry, sweet, and clean faltered *from foulness, seeds and oats.* MORTIMER'S HUSBANDRY.

FANA'TICISM. *n.s.* [from *fanatick.*] Enthusiasm; religious frenzy.

A church whose doctrines are derived from the clear fountains of the Scriptures, whose polity and discipline are formed upon the most uncorrupted models of antiquity, which has stood unshaken by the most furious assaults of popery on the one hand, and fanaticism *on the other; has triumphed over all the arguments of its enemies, and has nothing now to contend with but their slanders and calumnies.*
ROGERS'S SERMONS.

FANA'TICK. *adj.* [*fanaticus*, Latin; *fanatique*, Fr.] Enthusiastick; struck with a superstitious frenzy.

After these appear'd
A crew, who, under names of old renown,
Osiris, Isis, Orus, and their train,
With monst'rous shapes and sorceries abus'd
Fanatick *Egypt, and her priests, to seek*
Their wand'ring gods disguis'd in brutish forms. MILTON'S PARADISE LOST.

FANA'TICK. *n.s.* [from the adjective.] An enthusiast; a man mad with wild notions of religion.

The double armature of St. Peter is a more destructive engine than the tumultary weapon snatcht up by a fanatick.
DECAY OF PIETY.

FANCYMO'NGER. *n.s.* [from *fancy.*] One who deals in tricks of imagination.

There is a man haunts the forest, that abuses our young plants with carving Rosalind on their barks; hangs odes upon hawthorns, and elegies on brambles; all, forsooth, deifying the name of Rosalind. If I could meet that fancymonger, *I would give him some good counsel; for he seems to have the quotidian of love upon him.*
SHAKESPEARE'S AS YOU LIKE IT.

FA'NCYSICK. *adj.* [*fancy* and *sick.*] One whose imagination is unsound; one whose distemper is in his own mind.

'Tis not necessity, but opinion, that makes men miserable; and when we come once to be fancysick, *there's no cure for it.*
L'ESTRANGE.

FA'NGLED. *adj.* [from *fangle.*] This word seems to signify gaudy; ridiculously shewy; vainly decorated. This is still retained in Scotland: as, he's new *fangled*, or whimsical, and very fond of novelty.[100]

Quick wits be in desire new fangled, *and in purpose unconstant.* ASCHAM.

A book! oh, rare one!
Be not, as in this fangled *world, a garment*
Nobler than that it covers.
SHAKESPEARE'S CYMBELINE.

FAR-FE'TCH. *n.s.* [*far* and *fetch.*] A deep stratagem. A ludicrous word.

But Jesuits have deeper reaches,
In all their politick farfetches;
And from their Coptick priest, Kircherus,
Found out this mystick way to jeer us.
HUDIBRAS, P. III.

FAR-FE'TCHED. *adj.* [*far* and *fetch.*]

1. Brought from places remote.

Of these things others quickly will dispose,
Whose pains have earn'd the farfetch'd *spoil.* MILTON'S PARADISE LOST.

By his command we boldly cross'd the line,
And bravely fought where southern stars arise:
We trac'd the farfetch'd *gold unto the mine,*
And that which brib'd our fathers made our prize. DRYDEN.

2. Studiously sought; elaborately strained; not easily or naturally introduced.

York, with all his farfetch'd *policy.*
SHAKESPEARE'S HENRY VI.

For farfetch'd *rhymes make puzzled angels strain,*
And in low prose dull Lucifer complain.
SMITH.

Under this head we may rank those words, which signify different ideas, by a sort of an unaccountable farfetched *analogy, or distant resemblance, that fancy has introduced between one thing and another; as when we say, the meat is green when it is half roasted.* WATTS'S LOGICK.

FARCE. *n.s.* [from the verb; or from *farcer*, French, to mock.] A dramatick representation written without regularity, and stuffed with wild and ludicrous conceits.

There is yet a lower sort of poetry and painting, which is out of nature; for a farce *is that in poetry which grotesque is in a picture: the persons and actions of a* farce *are all unnatural, and the manners false; that is, inconsistent with the characters of mankind: grotesque painting is the just resemblance of this.*
DRYDEN'S DUFRESNOY.

What should be great, you turn to farce.
PRIOR.

They object against it as a farce, *because the irregularity of the plot should answer to the extravagance of the characters, which they say this piece wants, and therefore is no* farce. GAY.

FA'RTHER. *adv.* [This word is now generally considered as the comparative degree of *far*; but by no analogy can *far* make *farther* or *farthest*: it is therefore probable, that the ancient orthography was nearer the true, and that we ought to write *further* and *furthest*, from *forth*, *forther*, *forthest*, forðor, furðer, Saxon; the *o* and *u*, by resemblance of sound, being first confounded in speech, and afterwards in books.] At a greater distance; to a greater distance; more remotely; beyond; moreover.

To make a perfect judgment of good pictures, when compared with one another, besides rules, there is farther *required a long conversation with the best pieces.*
DRYDEN'S DUFRESNOY.

They contented themselves with the opinions, fashions and things of their country, without looking any farther.
LOCKE.

FA'RTHINGALE. *n.s.* [This word has much exercised the etymology of

Skinner, who at last seems to determine that it is derived from *vertu garde*: if he had considered what *vert* signifies in Dutch, he might have found out the true sense.] A hoop; circles of whalebone used to spread the petticoat to a wide circumference.

With silken coats, and caps, and golden rings,
With ruffs, and cuffs, and farthingales, *and things.* SHAKESPEARE.

Tell me,
What compass will you wear your farthingale? SHAKESPEARE.

Arthur wore in hall
Round table, like a farthingal.
HUDIBRAS, P. I. CANT. 1.

Some will have it that it portends the downfal of the French king; and observe, that the farthingale *appeared in England a little before the ruin of the Spanish monarchy.* ADDISON.

She seems a medley of all ages,
With a huge farthingale *to swell her fustian stuff,*
A new commode, a topknot, and a ruff.
SWIFT.

FA'SHIONIST. *n.s.* [from *fashion.*] A follower of the mode; a fop; a coxcomb. *Dictionaries.*

FASTI'DIOUS. *adj.* [*fastidiosus*, Latin; *fastidieux*, *fastidieuse*, French.] Disdainful; squeamish; delicate to a vice; insolently nice.

Reasons plainly delivered, and always after one manner, especially with fine and fastidious *minds, enter but heavily and dully.*
BACON'S COLLECTION OF GOOD AND EVIL.

Let their fastidious *vain*
Commission of the brain,
Run on and rage, sweat, censure, and condemn,
They were not made for thee, less thou for them. BEN JONSON.

A squeamish fastidious *niceness, in meats and drinks, must be cured by starving.*
L'ESTRANGE.

All hopes, raised upon the promises or supposed kindnesses of the fastidious *and fallacious great ones of the world, shall fail.* SOUTH'S SERMONS.

FA'TAL. *adj.* [*fatalis*, Latin; *fatal*, French]

1. Deadly; mortal; destructive; causing destruction.

O fatal *maid! thy marriage is endow'd*
With Phrygian, Latian, and Rutilian blood. DRYDEN'S ÆNEID.

A palsy in the brain is most dangerous; when it seizeth the heart, or organs of breathing, fatal.
ARBUTHNOT ON DIET.

2. Proceeding by destiny; inevitable; necessary.

Others delude their trouble by a graver way of reasoning, that these things are fatal *and necessary, it being in vain to be troubled at that which we cannot help.*
TILLOTSON'S SERMONS.

3. Appointed by destiny.

It was fatal *to the king to fight for his money; and though he avoided to fight with enemies abroad, yet he was still enforced to fight for it with rebels at home.*
BACON'S HENRY VII.

Fatal *course*
Had circled his full orb.
MILTON'S PARADISE LOST, B. V.

It was
Still fatal *to stout Hudibras,*
In all his feats of arms, when least
He dreamt of it, to prosper best.
HUDIBRAS, P. I. CANT. 3.

Behold the destin'd place of your abodes;
For thus Anchises prophecy'd of old,
And this our fatal *place of rest foretold.*
DRYDEN'S ÆNEID, B. VII.

O race divine!
For beauty still is fatal *to the line.*
DRYDEN.

FA'UCET. *n.s.* [*fausset*, French; *fauces*, Latin.] The pipe inserted into a vessel to give vent to the liquor, and stopped up by a peg or spigot. It is sometimes improperly written *fosset*.

You were out a good wholesome forenoon in hearing a cause between an orange-wife and a fosset-*seller, and adjourned a controversy of three-pence to a second audience.* SHAKESPEARE.

If you are sent down to draw drink, and find it will not run, blow strongly into the faucet, *and it will immediately pour into your mouth.*
SWIFT'S DIRECTIONS TO THE BUTLER.

FAULT. *n.s.* [*faut*, *faute*, Fr. *faltar*, to be deficient, Spanish. The *l* is sometimes sounded, and sometimes mute. In conversation it is generally suppressed.]

1. Offence; slight crime; somewhat liable to censure or objection.

The prophet chuseth rather to charge them with the fault *of making a law unto themselves, than the crime of transgressing a law which God had made.*
HOOKER, B. III. S. 6.

He finds no fault *with their opinion about the true God, but only that it was not clear and distinct enough.* STILLINGFLEET.

He that but conceives a crime in thought,
Contracts the danger of an actual fault*:*
Then what must he expect that still proceeds
To commit sin, and work up thoughts to deeds. DRYDEN.

If you like not my poem, the fault *may possibly be in my writing; but more probably 'tis in your morals, which cannot bear the truth of it.* DRYDEN.

They wholly mistake the nature of criticism, who think its business is principally to find fault. DRYDEN.

To be desirous of a good name, and careful to do every thing, that we innocently may, to obtain it, is so far from being a fault, *even in private persons, that it is their great and indispensible duty.*
ATTERBURY'S SERMONS.

Before his sacred name flies ev'ry fault,
And each exalted stanza teems with thought. POPE.

Which of our thrum-cap'd ancestors found fault,
For want of sugar-tongs or spoons for salt?
KING.

Being void of all friendship and enmity, they never complain, nor find fault *with the times.* SWIFT.

2. Defect; want; absence.

I could tell to thee, as to one it pleases me, for fault *of a better, to call my friend, I could be sad, and sad indeed too.*
SHAKESPEARE'S HENRY IV. P. II.

There is no straw given unto thy servants, and they say unto us, make brick; and behold, thy servants are beaten; but the fault *is in thine own people.*
BIBLE EXODUS, V. 16.

3. Puzzle; difficulty: as, the enquirer is at a *fault*.

To **FEAGUE.** *v.a.* [*Gower* uses *To feige*, free to censure; *fegen*, German, to sweep; *fyken*, Dutch, to strike.] To whip; to chastise; to beat. In Scottish *feake*, to slutter; to be idly or officiously busy.[101]

FE'ASTRITE. *n.s.* [*feast* and *rite*.] Custom observed in entertainments.

His hospitable gate,
Unbarr'd to all, invites a numerous train
Of daily guests; whose board with plenty crown'd,
Revives the feastrites *old.* PHILLIPS.

FE'ATHERDRIVER. *n.s.* [*feather* and *drive*.] One who cleanses feathers by whisking them about.

A featherdriver *had the residue of his lungs filled with the fine dust or down of feathers.*
DERHAM'S PHYSICO-THEOLOGY.

FE'ATHERSELLER. *n.s.* [*feather* and *seller.*] One who sells feathers for beds.

FE'CULENT. *adj.* [*fæculentus*, Lat. *feculent*, French.] Foul; dreggy; excrementitious.

But both his hands, most filthy feculent,
Above the water were on high extent,
And fain'd to wash themselves incessantly,
Yet nothing cleaner were for such intent.
FAIRY QUEEN.

We may affirm them to be to the body as the light of a candle to the gross and feculent *snuff, which as it is not pent up in it, so neither doth it partake of its stench and impurity.* GLANVILLE'S APOLOGY.

FEET. *n.s.* The plural of *foot.*

His brother's image to his mind appears,
Inflames his heart with rage, and wings his feet *with fears.* POPE'S STATIUS.

FELLOW-CO'MMMONER. *n.s.*

1. One who has the same right of common.

He cannot appropriate, he cannot inclose, without the consent of all his fellowcommoners, *all mankind.* LOCKE.

2. A commoner at Cambridge of the higher order, who dines with the fellows.

FELLOW-HE'LPER. *n.s.* Coadjutor; one who concurs in the same business.

We ought to receive such, that we might be fellowhelpers *to the truth.*
BIBLE 3 JOHN, VIII.

FE'MALE. *n.s.* [*femelle*, French; *femella*, Latin.] A she; one of the sex which brings young.[102]

God created man in his own image, male and female *created he them.*
BIBLE GENESIS, I. 27.

Man, more divine,
Lord of the wide world, and wide wat'ry seas,
Indu'd with intellectual sense and soul,
Are masters to their females, *and their lords.* SHAKESPEARE.

FE'NDER. *n.s.* [from *fend*]

1. An iron plate laid before the fire to hinder coals that fall from rolling forward to the floor.

2. Any thing laid or hung at the side of a ship to keep off violence.

FENERA'TION. *n.s.* [*fœneratio*, Latin.] Usury; the gain of interest; the practice of increasing money by lending.

The hare figured not only pusilanimity and timidity from its temper, but feneration *and usury from its fecundity and superfetation.*
BROWN'S VULGAR ERROURS, B. III. C. 17.

FERIA'TION. *n.s.* [*feriatio*, Lat.] The act of keeping holiday; cessation from work.

As though there were any feriation *in nature, this season is commonly termed the physicians vacation.*
BROWN'S VULGAR ERROURS.

To **FERME'NT.** *v.a.* [*fermento*, Latin; *fermenter*, French.] To exalt or rarify by intestine motion of parts.

Ye vig'rous swains! while youth ferments *your blood,*
And purer spirits swell the sprightly flood,
Now range the hills, the thickest woods beset,
Wind the shrill horn, or spread the waving net. POPE.

To **FERME'NT.** *v.n.* To have the parts put into intestine motion.

FE'RULA. *n.s.* [*ferule*, Fr. from *ferula*, giant fennel, Lat.] An instrument of correction with which young scholars are beaten on the hand: so named because anciently the stalks of fennel were used for this purpose.

These differ as much as the rod and ferula. SHAW'S GRAMMAR.

To **FE'RULE.** *v.a.* To chastise with the ferula.

FESCUE. *n.s.* [*veese*, Dutch; *festu*, French.] A small wire by which those who teach to read point out the letters.

Teach him an alphabet upon his fingers, making the points of his fingers of his left hand both on the inside to signify some letter, when any of them is pointed at by the forefinger of the right hand, or by any kind of fescue. HOLDER.

Teach them how manly passions ought to move;
For such as cannot think, can never love;
And since they needs will judge the poet's art,
Point 'em with fescues *to each shining part.* DRYDEN.

FE'STIVE. *adj.* [*festivus*, Latin.] Joyous; gay; befitting a feast.

The glad circle round them yield their souls
To festive *mirth and wit that knows no gall.* THOMSON.

FESTI'VITY. *n.s.* [*festivitas*, Latin, from *festive*.]

1. Festival; time of rejoicing.

The daughter of Jephtha came to be worshipped as a deity, and had an annual festivity *observed unto her honour.* BROWN.

There happening a great and solemn festivity, *such as the sheep-shearing used to be, David condescends to beg of a rich man some small repast.* SOUTH.

2. Gaiety; joyfulness; temper or behaviour befitting a feast.

To those persons there is no better instrument to cause the remembrance, and to endear the affection to the article, than the recommending it by festivity *and joy of a holyday.* TAYLOR.

To **FE'TTLE.** *v.n.* [A cant word from *feel*.] To do trifling business; to ply the hands without labour.

When your master is most busy in company, come in and pretend to fettle *about the room; and if he chides, say you thought he rung the bell.* SWIFT'S DIRECTIONS TO THE FOOTMAN.

FE'VER. *n.s.* [*fievre*, French; *febris*, Latin.] A disease in which the body is violently heated, and the pulse quickened, or in which heat and cold prevail by turns. It is sometimes continual, sometimes intermittent.

Think'st thou the firy fever *will go out*
With titles blown from adulation?
Will it give place to flexure and low bending? SHAKESPEARE'S HENRY V.

Duncan is in his grave;
After life's fitful fever *he sleeps well.*
SHAKESPEARE'S MACBETH.

Should not a ling'ring fever *be remov'd,*
Because it long has rag'd within my blood? DRYDEN.

He had never dreamed in his life, 'till he had the fever *he was then newly recovered of.* LOCKE.

FE'UTERER. *n.s.* A dogkeeper: perhaps the cleaner of the kennel.

FE'WEL. *n.s.* [*feu*, French.] Combustible matter; materials for keeping fire: as firewood, coal.

If a spark of error have thus far prevailed, falling even where the wood was green, and farthest off from any inclination unto furious attempts, must not the peril thereof be greater in men, whose minds are as dry fewel, *apt beforehand unto tumults, seditions and broils?* HOOKER, DEDICATION.

Others may give the fewel *or the fire;*
But they the breath, that makes the flame, inspire. DENHAM.

A known quantity of fewel, *all kindled at*

once, will cause water to boil, which being lighted gradually will never be able to do it. BENTLEY'S SERMONS.

FI'DDLEFADDLE. *adj.* Trifling; giving trouble, or making a bustle about nothing.

She was a troublesome fiddlefaddle *old woman, and so ceremonious that there was no bearing of her.*
ARBUTHNOT'S JOHN BULL.

To **FIDGE,** To **FI'DGET.** *v.n.* [A cant word.] To move nimbly and irregularly. It implies in Scotland agitation.

Tim, thou'rt the Punch to stir up trouble in;
You wriggle, fidge, *and make a rout,*
Put all your brother puppets out;
Run on in a perpetual round,
To teaze, perplex, disturb, confound.
SWIFT.

FI'ELDMARSHAL. *n.s.* [*field* and *marshal.*] Commander of an army in the field.

FI'ELDOFFICER. *n.s.* [*field* and *officer.*] An officer whose command in the field extends to a whole regiment: as the colonel, lieutenant-colonel, and major.

FI'ERCENESS. *n.s.* [from *fierce.*]
1. Ferocity; savageness.

The same defect of heat which gives a fierceness *to our natures, may contribute to that roughness of our language.*
SWIFT'S LETTER TO THE LORD HIGH TREASURER.

2. Eagerness for blood; fury.

Suddenly there came out of a wood a monstrous lion, with a she-bear not far from him, of little less fierceness.
SIDNEY.

3. Quickness to attack; keenness in anger and resentment.

The Greeks are strong, and skilful to their strength,
Fierce to their skill, and to their fierceness *valiant.* SHAKESPEARE.

4. Violence; outrageous passion.

His pride and brutal fierceness *I abhor;*
But scorn your mean suspicions of me more. DRYDEN'S AURENGZEBE.

FI'GURABLE. *adj.* [from *figuro*, Latin.] Capable of being brought to certain form, and retained in it. Thus lead is *figurable*, but not water.

The differences of impressible and not impressible, figurable *and not* figurable, *scissible and not scissible, are plebeian notions.* BACON'S NATURAL HISTORY.

FI'GURATIVE. *adj.* [*figuratif-ve*, Fr. from *figura*, Latin.]
1. Representing something else; typical; representative.

This, they will say, was figurative, *and served by God's appointment but for a time, to shadow out the true everlasting glory of a more divine sanctity; where into Christ being long since entered, it seemeth that all these curious exornations should rather cease.* HOOKER, B. V. S. 15.

2. Changed by rhetorical figures from the primitive meaning; not literal.

How often have we been railed at for understanding words in a figurative *sense, which cannot be literally understood without overthrowing the plainest evidence of sense and reason.*
STILLINGFLEET'S DEFENCE OF DISCOURSE ON ROMISH IDOLATRY.

This is a figurative *expression, where the words are used in a different sense from what they signify in their first ordinary intention.* ROGERS, SERMON 14.

3. Full of figures; full of rhetorical exornations; full of changes from the original sense.

Sublime subjects ought to be adorned with

the sublimest and with the most figurative *expressions.*
DRYDEN'S JUVENAL, PREFACE.

FIGURE-FLINGER. *n.s.* [*figure* and *fling.*] A pretender to astrology and prediction.

Quacks, figure-flingers, *pettifoggers, and republican plotters cannot well live without it.* COLLIER OF CONFIDENCE.

To **FILE.** *v.a.* [from *filum*, a thread.] **1.** To string upon a thread or wire. Whence to *file a bill* is to offer it in its order to the notice of the judge.

From the day his first bill was filed *he began to collect reports.*
ARBUTHNOT AND POPE'S MARTIN SCRIBLERUS.

2. [from *feolan*, Saxon.] To cut with a file.

They which would file *away most from the largeness of that offer, do in more sparing terms acknowledge little less.*
HOOKER, B. V. S. 27.

His humour is lofty, his discourse peremptory, his tongue filed, *and his eye ambitious.*
SHAKESPEARE'S LOVE'S LABOUR'S LOST.

Let men be careful how they attempt to cure a blemish by filing *or cutting off the head of such an overgrown tooth.* RAY.

3. [from *filan.*] To foul; to sully; to pollute. This sense is retained in Scotland.[103]

For Banquo's issue have I fil'd *my mind,*
For them the gracious Duncan have I
murder'd. SHAKESPEARE'S MACBETH.

His weeds, divinely fashioned,
All fil'd *and mangl'd.*
CHAPMAN'S ILIADS, B. XVIII.

To **FILE.** *v.n.* [from the noun.] To march in a file, not abreast, but one behind another.

All ran down without order or ceremony, 'till we drew up in good order, and filed *off.* TATLER, NO. 86.

Did all the grosser atoms at the cell
Of chance file *off to form the pond'rous*
ball,
And undetermin'd into order fall?
BLACKMORE'S CREATION.

To **FI'LLIP.** *v.a.* [A word, says *Skinner*, formed from the sound. This resemblance I am not able to discover, and therefore am inclined to imagine it corrupted from *fill up*, by some combination of ideas which cannot be recovered.] To strike with the nail of the finger by a sudden spring or motion.

If I do, filip *me with a three-man beetle.*
SHAKESPEARE'S HENRY IV.

Then let the pebbles on the hungry beach
Fillip *the stars: then let the mutinous winds*
Strike the proud cedars 'gainst the fiery
sun. SHAKESPEARE'S CORIOLANUS.

We see, that if you fillip *a lutestring, it sheweth double or treble.*
BACON'S NATURAL HISTORY, NO. 183.

FI'LLIP. *n.s.* [from the verb.] A jerk of the finger let go from the thumb.

FINDFA'ULT. *n.s.* [*find* and *fault.*] A censurer; a caviller.

We are the makers of manners, Kate; and the liberty that follows our places, stops the mouth of all findfaults. SHAKESPEARE.

To **FINEDRA'W.** *v.a.* [*fine* and *draw.*] To sow up a rent with so much nicety that it is not perceived.

FINEFI'NGERED. *adj.* [*fine* and *finger.*] Nice; artful; exquisite.

The most finefinger'd *workman on the*
ground,
Arachne, by his means was vanquished.
SPENSER.

FINE'SSE. *n.s.* [French.] Artifice; stratagem: an unnecessary word which is creeping into the language.

A circumstance not much to be stood upon, in case it were not upon some finess. HAYWARD.

F'INGLEFANGLE. *n.s.* [from *fangle.*] A trifle: a burlesque word.

We agree in nothing but to wrangle,
About the slightest finglefangle.
HUDIBRAS, P. III. CAN. 3.

FI'REBALL. *n.s.* [*fire* and *ball.*] Grenado; ball filled with combustibles, and bursting where it is thrown.

Judge of those insolent boasts of conscience, which, like so many fireballs, *or mouth grenadoes, are thrown at our church.* SOUTH'S SERMONS.

The same great man hath sworn to make us swallow his coin in fireballs. SWIFT.

FI'REBRUSH. *n.s.* [*fire* and *brush.*] The brush which hangs by the fire to sweep the hearth.

When you are ordered to stir up the fire, clean away the ashes from betwixt the bars with the firebrush. SWIFT.

FI'RECROSS. *n.s.* [*fire* and *cross.*] A token in Scotland for the nation to take arms: the ends thereof burnt black, and in some parts smeared with blood. It is carried like lightning[104] from one place to another. Upon refusal to send it forward, or to rise, the last person who has it shoots the other dead.

He sent his heralds through all parts of the realm, and commanded the firecross *to be carried; namely, two firebrands set in fashion of a cross, and pitched upon the point of a spear.* HAYWOOD.

FI'REMAN. *n.s.* [*fire* and *man.*]
1. One who is employed to extinguish burning houses.

The fireman *sweats beneath his crooked arms;*
A leathern casque his vent'rous head defends,
Boldly he climbs where thickest smoke ascends. GAY.

2. A man of violent passions.

I had last night the fate to drink a bottle with two of these firemen. TATLER, NO. 61.

FI'RESHOVEL. *n.s.* [*fire* and *shovel.*] The instrument with which the hot coals are thrown up in kitchens.

Nim and Bardolph are sworn brothers in filching; and in Calais they stole a fireshovel. SHAKESPEARE'S HENRY V.

Culinary utensils and irons often feel the force of fire; as tongs, fireshovels, *prongs, and irons.* BROWN'S VULGAR ERROURS.

The neighbours are coming out with forks and fireshovels, *and spits, and other domestick weapons.* DRYDEN'S SPANISH FRYAR.

To **FISH.** *v.n.*
1. To be employed in catching fishes.
2. To endeavour at any thing by artifice.

While others fish, *with craft, for great opinion,*
I, with great truth, catch meer simplicity.
SHAKESPEARE.

To **FISH.** *v.a.* To search water in quest of fish, or any thing else.

Some have fished *the very jakes for papers left there by men of wit.* SWIFT.

Oft, as he fish'd *her nether realms for wit,*
The goddess favour'd him, and favours yet. POPE'S DUNCIAD.

FI'SHERTOWN. *n.s.* [*fisher* and *town.*] A town inhabited by fishermen.

Others of them, in that time, burned that fishertown *Mousehole.* CAREW'S SURVEY OF CORNWAL.

Lime in Dorsetshire, a little fishertown. CLARENDON, B. VII.

FI'SHKETTLE. *n.s.* [*fish* and *kettle.*] A caldron made long for the fish to be boiled without bending.

It is probably that the way of embalming amongst the Egyptians was by boiling the body, in a long caldron like a fishkettle, *in some kind of liquid balsam.*
GREW'S MUSÆUM.

FIT. *n.s.* [from *fight*, *Skinner*, every fit of a disease being a struggle of nature; from *viit*, in Flemish, frequent, *Junius.*]
1. A paroxysm or exacerbation of any intermittent distemper.

Small stones and gravel collect and become very large in the kidneys, in which case a fit *of the stone in that part is the cure.*
SHARP'S SURGERY.

2. Any short return after intermission; interval.

Sometimes 'tis grateful to the rich to try
A short vicissitude, and fit *of poverty.*
DRYDEN'S HORACE.

Men that are habitually wicked may now and then, by fits *and starts, feel certain motions of repentance.* L'ESTRANGE.

By fits *my swelling grief appears,*
In rising sighs and falling tears.
ADDISON ON ITALY.

Thus o'er the dying lamp th' unsteady flame
Hangs quivering on a point, leaps off by fits,
And falls again as loth to quit its hold.
ADDISON'S CATO.

Religion is not the business of some fits *only and intervals of our life, to be taken up at certain days and hours, and laid aside for the rest of our time; but a system of precepts to be regarded in all our conduct.*
ROGERS'S SERMONS.

All fits *of pleasure we balanced by an equal degree of pain or languor: 'tis like spending this year part of the next year's revenue.*
SWIFT.

3. Any violent affection of mind or body.

The life did flit away out of her nest,
And all his senses were with deadly fit
opprest. FAIRY QUEEN.

An ambitious man subjects himself to others, and puts it in the power of every malicious tongue to throw him into a fit *of melancholy.* ADDISON'S SPECTATOR.

4. Disorder; distemperature.

For your husband,
He's noble, wise, judicious, and best knows
The fits *o' th' season.*
SHAKESPEARE'S MACBETH.

5. It is used, without an epithet of discrimination, for the hysterical disorders of women, and the convulsions of children; and by the vulgar for the epilepsy.

Mrs. Bull was so much enraged, that she fell downright into a fit.
ARBUTHNOT'S HISTORY OF JOHN BULL.[105]

FITZ. *n.s.* [Norman, from *fils*, a son, Fr.] A son. Only used in law and genealogy: as *Fitzherbert*, the son of Herbert; *Fitzthomas*, the son of Thomas; *Fitzroy*, the son of the king. It is commonly used of illegitimate children.

FIVE. *adj.* [*fif*, Saxon.] Four and one; half of ten.

And five *of them were wise, and* five *were foolish.* BIBLE MATTHEW.

No person, no incident, but must be of use to carry on the main design: all things else are like six fingers to the hand, when nature, which is superfluous in nothing, can do her work with five.
DRYDEN'S DUFRESNOY.

Five *herds,* five *bleating flocks, his pastures fill'd;*
His lands a hundred yoke of oxen till'd.
DRYDEN'S ÆNEID.

Our British youth lose their figure by that time they are five *and twenty.*
ADDISON'S GUARDIAN, NO. 111.

FI'ZGIG. *n.s.* A kind of dart or harpoon with which seamen strike fish.

Can'st thou with fizgigs *pierce him to the quick,*
Or in his skull thy barbed trident stick.
SANDYS'S JOB.[106]

FLAM. *n.s.* [A cant word of no certain etymology.] A falsehood; a lye; an illusory pretext.

A flam *more senseless than the rog'ry*
Of old aruspicy and aug'ry.
HUDIBRAS, P. II. CANT. 3.

'Till these men can prove the things, ordered by our church, to be either intrinsically unlawful or indecent, all pretences or pleas of conscience to the contrary are nothing but cant and cheat, flam *and delusion.* SOUTH'S SERMONS.

What are most of the histories of the world but lyes? Lyes immortalized and consigned over as a perpetual abuse and flam *upon posterity.* SOUTH'S SERMONS.

To **FLAM.** *v.a.* [from the noun.] To deceive with a lye. Merely cant.

For so our ignorance was flamm'd,
To damn ourselves t' avoid being damn'd.
HUDIBRAS, P. III.

God is not to be flammed *off with lyes, who knows exactly what thou can'st do, and what not.* SOUTH'S SERMONS.

To **FLAP.** *v.a.* [from the noun.]
1. To beat with a flap, as flies are beaten.

A hare, hard put to it by an eagle, took sanctuary in a ditch with a beetle: the eagle flapt *off the former, and devoured the other.* L'ESTRANGE.

Yet let me flap *this bug with gilded wings,*
This painted child of dirt, that stinks and stings. POPE.

2. To move with a flap or noise made by the stroke of any thing broad.

With fruitless toil
Flap *filmy pinions oft, to extricate*
Their feet in liquid shackles bound.
PHILLIPS.

Three times, all in the dead of night,
A bell was heard to ring;
And shrieking at her window thrice
The raven flapp'd *his wing.* TICKELL.

To **FLAP.** *v.n.*
1. To ply the wings with noise.

'Tis common for a duck to run flapping *and fluttering away, as if maimed, to carry people from her young.* L'ESTRANGE.

The dira flapping *on the shield of Turnus, and fluttering about his head, disheartened him in the duel.*
DRYDEN'S ÆNEID, DEDICATION.

2. To fall with flaps, or broad parts depending.

When suffocating mists obscure the morn,
Let thy worst wig, long us'd to storms, be worn;
This knows the powder'd footman, and with care
Beneath his flapping *hat secures his hair.*
GAY'S TRIVIA.

FLA'PDRAGON. *n.s.* [from a dragon supposed to breathe fire.]
1. A play in which they catch raisins out of burning brandy, and, extinguishing them by closing the mouth, eat them.
2. The thing eaten at flapdragon.

He plays at quoits well, and eats conger and fennel, and drinks candles ends for flapdragons, *and rides the wild mare with the boys.*
SHAKESPEARE'S HENRY IV. P. II.

FLASK. *n.s.* [*flasque*, French.]
1. A bottle; a vessel.

Then for the Bourdeaux you may freely ask;
But the Champaigne is to each man his flask. KING.

2. A powder-horn.

Powder in a skilless soldier's flask
Is set on fire. SHAKESPEARE.

FLA'SKET. *n.s.* [from *flask.*] A vessel in which viands are served.

Another plac'd
The silver stands, with golden flaskets *grac'd.* POPE'S ODYSSEY.

To **FLA'TTER.** *v.a.* [*flater*, French.]
1. To sooth with praises; to please with blandishments; to gratify with servile obsequiousness; to gain by false compliments.

When I tell him he hates flatterers,
He says he does; being then most flattered.
SHAKESPEARE'S JULIUS CÆSAR.

His nature is too noble for the world;
tHe would not flatter *Neptune for his trident,*
Or Jove for's power to thunder: his heart's his mouth;
What his breast forges, that his tongue must vent. SHAKESPEARE.

He that flattereth *his neighbour, spreadeth a net for his feet.*
BIBLE PROVERBS, XXIX. 5.

He flattereth *himself in his own eyes, until his iniquity be found hateful.*
BIBLE PSALMS, XXXVI. 2.

After this way of flattering *their willing benefactors out of part, they contrived another of forcing their unwilling neighbours out of all their possessions.*
DECAY OF PIETY.

Averse alike to flatter *or offend.* POPE.

They flatter'd *ev'ry day, and some days eat.* POPE.

I scorn to flatter *you or any man.*
DR. NEWTON'S DEDICATION TO MILTON.

2. To praise falsely.

Flatter'd *crimes of a licentious age,*
Provoke our censure. YOUNG.

3. To please; to sooth. This sense is purely Gallick.

A consort of voices supporting themselves by their different parts make a harmony, pleasingly fills the ears and flatters *them.*
DRYDEN'S DUFRESNOY.

4. To raise false hopes.

He always vacant, always amiable,
Hopes thee, of flatt'ring *gales*
Unmindful. MILTON.

FLEA. *n.s.* [*flea*, Saxon; *vloye*, Dutch; *fleach*, Scottish.] A small red insect remarkable for its agility in leaping, which sucks the blood of larger animals.

While wormwood hath seed, get a handful or twain,
To save against March to make flea *to refrain:*
Where chamber is sweeped, and wormwood is strown,
No flea *for his life dare abide to be known.* TUSSER'S HUSBANDRY.

Fleas *breed principally of straw or mats, where there hath been a little moisture.*
BACON'S NATURAL HISTORY.

A valiant flea, *that dares eat his breakfast on the lip of a lion.*
SHAKESPEARE'S HENRY V.

FLEET. *n.s.* [*flota*, Saxon.] A company of ships; a navy.

Our pray'rs are heard; our master's fleet *shall go*
As far as winds can bear, or waters flow.
PRIOR.

FLEET. *n.s.* [*fleot*, Saxon, an estuary, or arm of the sea.] A creek; an inlet of water. A provincial word, from which the Fleet-prison and Fleet-street are named.

They have a very good way in Essex of draining of lands that have land-floods or fleets *running through them, which make a kind of a small creek.*
MORTIMER'S HUSBANDRY.

FLESH. *n.s.* [*flæc*, *flæsc*, Saxon; *vleesch*, Dutch; *fêol*, Erse.]
1. The body distinguished from the soul.

As if this flesh, *which walls about our life,*
Were brass impregnable.
SHAKESPEARE'S RICHARD II.

A disease that's in my flesh,
Which I must needs call mine.
SHAKESPEARE'S KING LEAR.

And thou, my soul, which turn'st with curious eye
To view the beams of thine own form divine,
Know, that thou can'st know nothing perfectly,
While thou art clouded with this flesh *of mine.* DAVIES.

2. The muscles distinguished from the skin, bones, tendons.

A spirit hath not flesh *and bones.*
BIBLE NEW TESTAMENT.

3. Animal food distinguished from vegetable.

Flesh *should be forborne as long as he is in coats, or at least 'till he is two or three years old.* LOCKE.

Flesh, *without being qualified with acids, is too alkalescent a diet.*
ARBUTHNOT ON ALIMENTS.

Acidity in the infant may be cured by a flesh *diet in the nurse.*
ARBUTHNOT ON ALIMENTS.

4. The body of beasts or birds used in food, distinct from fishes.

There is another indictment upon thee, for suffering flesh *to be eaten in thy house, contrary to the law.*
SHAKESPEARE'S HENRY IV.

We mortify ourselves with the diet of fish; and think we fare coarsely, if we abstain from the flesh *of other animals.*
BROWN'S VULGAR ERROURS.

5. Animal nature.

The end of all flesh *is come before me.*
BIBLE GENESIS, VI. 13.

6. Carnality; corporal appetites.

Name not religion; for thou lov'st the flesh. SHAKESPEARE.

Fasting serves to mortify the flesh, *and subdue the lusts thereof.*
SMALRIDGE'S SERMONS.

7. A carnal state; worldly disposition.[107]

They that are in the flesh *cannot please God.* BIBLE ROMANS, VIII. 8.

The flesh *lusteth against the spirit, and the spirit against the* flesh.
BIBLE GALATIANS, V. 16.

8. Near relation.

Let not our hand be upon him; for he is our flesh. BIBLE GENESIS.

When thou seest the naked, cover him; and hide not thyself from thine own flesh.
BIBLE ISAIAH, LVIII. 7.

9. The outward or literal sense. The Orientals termed the immediate or literal signification of any precept or type *the flesh*, and the remote or typical meaning *the spirit.* This is frequent in St. *Paul.*

Ye judge after the flesh.
BIBLE JOHN, VIII. 15.

FLE'SHMONGER. *n.s.* [from *flesh.*] One who deals in flesh; a pimp.

Was the duke a fleshmonger, *a fool, and a coward, as you then reported him?*
SHAKESPEARE'S MEASURE FOR MEASURE.

FLE'SHPOT. *n.s.* [*flesh* and *pot.*] A vessel in which flesh is cooked; thence plenty of flesh.

If he takes away the fleshpots, *he can also alter the appetite.*
TAYLOR'S RULE FOR LIVING HOLY.

FLE'SHQUAKE. *n.s.* [*flesh* and *quake.*] A tremor of the body: a word formed by *Jonson* in imitation of earthquake.

They may, blood-shaken then,
Feel such a fleshquake *to possess their powers,*
As they shall cry like ours:
In sound of peace or wars,

No harp e'er hit the stars.
BEN JONSON'S NEW-INN.

FLI'ER. *n.s.* [from *fly.*]
1. One that runs away; a fugitive; a runaway.

Cam'st thou from where they made the stand?
—— I did;
Though you, it seems, came from the fliers. SHAKESPEARE'S CYMBELINE.

The gates are ope, now prove good seconds;
'Tis for the followers fortune widens them,
Not for the fliers.
SHAKESPEARE'S CORIOLANUS.

Now the fliers *from and forsakers of their places, carry the parliamentary power along with them.* KING CHARLES.

2. That part of a machine which, by being put into a more rapid motion than the other parts, equalizes and regulates the motion of the rest; as in a jack.

The flier, *tho't had leaden feet,*
Turn'd so quick, you scarce could see't.
SWIFT.

FLI'MSY. *adj.* [Of this word I know not any original, and suspect it to have crept into our language from the cant of manufacturers.]
1. Weak; feeble; without strength of texture.
2. Mean; spiritless; without force.

Proud of a vast extent of flimsy *lines.*
POPE, EPISTLE II.

FLIPP. *n.s.* [A cant word.] A liquor much used in ships, made by mixing beer with spirits and sugar.

The tarpawlin and swabber is lolling at Madagascar, with some drunken sunburnt whore, over a can of flip. DENNIS.

To **FLIRT.** *v.a.* [*Skinner* thinks it formed from the sound.]
1. To throw any thing with a quick elastick motion.

Dick the scavenger
Flirts *from his cart the mud in Walpole's face.* SWIFT.

2. To move with quickness.

Permit some happier man
To kiss your hand, or flirt *your fan.*
DORSET.

To **FLIRT.** *v.n.*
1. To jeer; to gibe at one.
2. To run about perpetually; to be unsteady and fluttering.

FLIRT. *n.s.* [from the verb.]
1. A quick elastick motion.

In unfurling the fan are several little flirts *and vibrations, as also gradual and deliberate openings.*
ADDISON'S SPECTATOR.

Before you pass th' imaginary sights
While the spread fan o'ershades your closing eyes,
Then give one flirt, *and all the vision flies.*
POPE.

2. A sudden trick.

Have licence to play,
At the hedge a flirt,
For a sheet or a shirt.
BEN JONSON'S GYPSIES.

3. A pert young hussey.

Scurvy knave, I am none of his flirt *gills; I am none of his skains mates.*
SHAKESPEARE'S ROMEO AND JULIET.

Several young flirts *about town had a design to cast us out of the fashionable world.*
ADDISON'S GUARDIAN, NO. 109.

FLIRTA'TION. *n.s.* [from *flirt.*] A quick sprightly motion. A cant word among women.

A muslin flounce, made very full, would give a very agreeable flirtation *air.*
POPE.

To **FLIT.** *v.n.* [from *To fleet*; or from *flitter*, Danish, to remove.]
1. To fly away.

Likest it seemeth, in my simple wit,
Unto the fair sunshine in Summer's day,
That when a dreadful storm away is flit,
Through the broad world doth spread his goodly ray. SPENSER.

His grudging ghost did strive
With the frail flesh; at last it flitted *is,*
Whither the souls do die of men that live amiss. FAIRY QUEEN.

2. To remove; to migrate. In Scotland it is still used for removing from one place to another at quarter-day, or the usual term.

So hardly he the flitted *life does win,*
Unto her native prison to return.
FAIRY QUEEN, CANT. 7.

It became a received opinion, that the souls of men, departing this life, did flit *out one body into some other.* HOOKER.

3. To flutter; to rove on the wing.

He made a glancing shot, and miss'd the dove;
Yet miss'd so narrow, that he cut the cord
Which fasten'd, by the foot, the flitting *bird.* DRYDEN'S ÆNEID.

Fear the just gods, and think of Scylla's fate!
Chang'd to a bird, and sent to flit *in air.*
POPE.

4. To be flux or unstable.

Himself up high he lifted from the ground,
And with strong flight did forcibly divide
The yielding air, which nigh too feeble found
Her flitting *parts, and element unsound.*
FAIRY QUEEN, B. I.

He stopt at once the passage of his wind,
And the free soul to flitting *air resign'd.*
DRYDEN'S ÆNEID.

FLO'REN. *n.s.* [so named, says *Camden*, because made by Florentines.] A gold coin of Edward III. in value six shillings.

FLO'RIN. *n.s.* [French.] A coin first made by the Florentines. That of Germany is in value 2 s. 4 *d.* that of Spain 4 s. 4 *d.* halfpenny; that of Palermo and Sicily 2 *s.* 6 *d.* that of Holland 2 *s.*

In the Imperial chamber the proctors have half a florin *taxed and allowed them for every substantial recess.* AYLIFFE.

FLO'TSON. *n.s.* [from *flote.*] Goods that swim without an owner on the sea.

FLUE. *n.s.* [A word of which I know not the etymology, unless it be derived from *flew* or *fly.*]
1. A small pipe or chimney to convey air, heat, or smoke.
2. Soft down or fur, such as may fly in the wind.

FLU'ENT. *adj.* [*fluens*, Latin.]
1. Liquid.

It is not malleable; but yet is not fluent, *but stupified.* BACON.

2. Flowing; in motion; in flux.

Motion being a fluent *thing, and one part of its duration being absolutely independent upon another, it doth not follow that because any thing moves this moment, it must necessarily continue to do so the next.* RAY ON THE CREATION.

3. Ready; copious; voluble.

Those have some natural dispositions, which have better grace in youth than in age, such as is a fluent *and luxurious speech.* BACON.

I shall lay before you all that's within me,
And with most fluent *utterance.*
DENHAM'S SOPHY.

FLU'MMERY. *n.s.* A kind of food made by coagulation of wheatflower or oatmeal.

Milk and flummery *are very fit for children.* LOCKE.

To **FLU'STER.** *v.a.* [from *To flush.*] To make hot and rosy with drinking; to make half drunk.

Three lads of Cyprus, noble swelling spirits,
Have I to-night fluster'd *with flowing cups,*
And they watch too.
SHAKESPEARE'S OTHELLO.

To **FLUX.** *v.a.*

1. To melt.
2. To salivate; to evacuate by spitting.

He might fashionably and genteelly have been duelled or fluxed *into another world.* SOUTH.

FOAL. *n.s.* [*fola*, Saxon.] The offspring of a mare, or other beast of burthen. The custom now is to use *colt* for a young horse, and *foal* for a young mare; but there was not originally any such distinction.

Also flew his steed,
And with his winged heels did tread the wind,
As he had been a foal *of Pegasus's kind.*
FAIRY QUEEN, B. I.

Twenty she-asses and ten foals.
BIBLE GENESIS, XXXII. 15.

FOH. *interject.* [from *fah*, Saxon, an enemy.] An interjection of abhorrence: as if one should at sight of any thing hated cry out *a foe!*

Not to affect many proposed matches
Of her own clime, complection and degree,
Whereto we see in all things nature tends,
Foh! *one may smell in such a will most rank,*
Foul disproportions, thoughts unnatural.
SHAKESPEARE'S OTHELLO.

FOO'DFUL. *adj.* [*food* and *full.*] Fruitful; full of food; plenteous.

There Tityus was to see, who took his birth
From heav'n, his nursing from the foodful *earth.* DRYDEN.

FOO'DY. *adj.* [from *food.*] Eatable; fit for food.

To vessels, wine she drew;
And into well sew'd sacks pour'd foody *meal.* CHAPMAN.

FOOLHA'PPY. *adj.* [*fool* and *happy.*] Lucky without contrivance or judgment.

As when a ship, that flies fair under sail,
An hidden rock escaped unawares,
That lay in wait her wreck for to bewail;
The mariner, yet half amazed, stares
At perils past, and yet in doubt ne dares
To joy at his foolhappy *oversight.*
FAIRY QUEEN, B. I. CANT. 6.

FOOLHA'RDY. *adj.* [*fool* and *hardy.*] Daring without judgment; madly adventurous; foolishly bold.

One mother, when as her foolhardy *child*
Did come too near, and with his talons play,
Half dead through fear, her little babe revil'd. FAIRY QUEEN.

Some would be so foolhardy *as to presume to be more of the cabinet-council of God Almighty than the angels.* HOWEL.

If any yet be so foolhardy,
T' expose themselves to vain jeopardy;
If they come wounded off, and lame,
No honour's got by such a maim.
HUDIBRAS, P. I. CANT. 1.

FOO'LTRAP. *n.s.* [*fool* and *trap.*] A snare to catch fools in: as a flytrap.

Betts, at the first, were fooltraps, *where the wise*
Like spiders lay in ambush for the flies.
DRYDEN.

FOOT. *n.s.* plural *feet.* [*fot*, Saxon; *voet*, Dutch; *fut*, Scottish.]

1. The part upon which we stand.

The queen that bore thee,
Oft'ner upon her knees than on her feet,
Died ev'ry day she liv'd.
SHAKESPEARE'S MACBETH.

His affection to the church was so notorious, that he never deserted it 'till both it and he were over-run and trod under foot. CLARENDON.

2. That by which any thing is supported in the nature of a foot.[108]

3. The lower part; the base.

Yond' towers, whose wanton tops do buss the clouds,
Must kiss their own feet.
SHAKESPEARE'S TROILUS AND CRESSIDA.

Fretting, by little and little, washes away and eats out both the tops and sides and feet *of mountains.*
HAKEWILL ON PROVIDENCE.

4. The end; the lower part.

What dismal cries are those?
—— Nothing; a trifling sum of misery,
New added to the foot *of thy account:*
Thy wife is seiz'd by force, and born away.
DRYDEN'S CLEOMEN.

5. The act of walking.

Antiochus departed, weening in his pride to make the land navigable, and the sea passable by foot.
BIBLE 2 MACCABEES, V. 21.

6. *On* FOOT. Walking; without carriage.

Israel journeyed about six hundred thousand on foot. BIBLE EXODUS, XII.

7. A posture of action.

The centurions and their charges distinctly billeted, already in the entertainment, and to be on foot *at an hour's warning.*
SHAKESPEARE'S CORIOLANUS.

8. Infantry; footmen in arms. In this sense it has no plural.

Lusias gathered threescore thousand choice men of foot, *and five thousand horsemen.*
BIBLE 1 MACCABEES, IV. 28.

Himself with all his foot *entered the town, his horse being quartered about it.*
CLARENDON, B. VIII.

Thrice horse and foot *about the fires are led,*
And thrice with loud laments they wail the dead. DRYDEN.

9. State; character; condition.

See on what foot *we stand; a scanty shore,*
The sea behind, our enemies before.
DRYDEN'S ÆNEID.

In specifying the word Ireland, it would seem to insinuate that we are not upon the same foot *with our fellow subjects in England.*
SWIFT'S DRAPIER'S LETTERS.

What colour of excuse can be for the contempt with which we treat this part of our species, that we should not put them upon the common foot *of humanity, that we should only set an insignificant fine upon the man who murders them?*
ADDISON.

10. Scheme; plan; settlement.

There is no wellwisher to his country without a little hope, that in time the kingdom may be on a better foot.
SWIFT.

I ask, whether upon the foot *of our constitution, as it stood in the reign of the late king James, a king of England may be deposed?* SWIFT.

11. A state of incipient existence.

If such a tradition were at any time set on foot, *it is not easy to imagine how it should at first gain entertainment; but much more difficult how it should come to be universally propagated.*
TILLOTSON'S SERMONS.

12. It seems to have been once proverbially used for the level, the square, par.

Were it not for this easy borrowing upon interest, men's necessities would draw upon them a most sudden undoing, in that they would be forced to sell their means, be it lands or goods, far under foot.
BACON'S ESSAYS.

13. A certain number of syllables constituting a distinct part of a verse.

Feet, *in our English versifying, without quantity and joints, be sure signs that the verse is either born deformed, unnatural, or lame.* ASCHAM'S SCHOOLMASTER.

Did'st thou hear these verses?
—— O yes, I heard them all, and more too; for some o' them had in them more feet *than the verses would bear.*
SHAKESPEARE.

14. Motion; action.

While other jests are something rank on foot,
Her father hath commanded her to slip
Away with Slender to marry.
SHAKESPEARE'S MERRY WIVES OF WINDSOR.

In the government of the world the number and variety of the ends on foot, *with the secret nature of most things to which they relate, must make a distinct remark of their congruity, in some cases very difficult, and in some unattainable.* GREW.

15. A measure containing twelve inches. When it signifies measure it has often, but vitiously, *foot* in the plural.

An orange, lemon, and apple, wrapt in a linnen cloth, being buried for a fortnight's space four foot *deep within the earth, came forth no ways mouldy or rotten.* BACON.

16. Step.

This man's son would, every foot *and anon, be taking some of his companions into the orchard.* L'ESTRANGE.

FOO'TPAD. *n.s.* [*foot* and *pad.*] A highwayman that robs on foot, not on horseback.

FOO'TPATH. *n.s.* [*foot* and *path.*] A narrow way which will not admit horses or carriages.

Know'st thou the way to Dover?
—— *Both stile and gate, horseway and* footpath.
SHAKESPEARE'S KING LEAR.

FOP. *n.s.* [A word probably made by chance, and therefore without etymology.] A simpleton; a coxcomb; a man of small understanding and much ostentation; a pretender; a man fond of show, dress, and flutter; an impertinent.

A whole tribe of fops,
Got 'tween asleep and wake.
SHAKESPEARE'S KING LEAR.

When such a positive abandon'd fop,
Among his numerous absurdities,
Stumbles upon some tolerable line,
I fret to see them in such company.
ROSCOMMON.

The leopard's beauty, without the fox's wit, is no better than a fop *in a gay coat.* L'ESTRANGE.

In a dull stream, which moving slow,
You hardly see the current flow;
When a small breeze obstructs the course,
It whirls about for want of force,
And in its narrow circle gathers
Nothing but chaff, and straws, and feathers:
The current of a female mind
Stops thus, and turns with ev'ry wind;
Thus whirling round, together draws
Fools, fops, *and rakes, for chaff and straws.* SWIFT.

FO'PDOODLE. *n.s.* [*fop* and *doodle.*] A fool; an insignificant wretch.

Where sturdy butchers broke your noddle,
And handled you like a fopdoodle.
HUDIBRAS, P. II.

FO'PPLING. *n.s.* [from *fop.*] A petty fop; an under-rate coxcomb.

Thy works in Chloe's toilet gain a part,
And, with his tailor, share the foppling's *heart.* TICKELL.

FO'RCER. *n.s.* [from *force.*]

1. That which forces, drives, or constrains.

2. The embolus of a pump working by pulsion, in contradistinction to a sucker, which acts by attraction.

The usual means for the ascent of water is either by suckers or forcers.
WILKINS'S DÆDALUS.

FORD. *n.s.* [*ford*, Saxon, from *faran*, to pass.]

1. A shallow part of a river when it may be passed without swimming.

Her men the paths rode through made by her sword;

They pass the stream, when she had found the ford. FAIRFAX.

2. It sometimes signifies the stream, the current, without any consideration of passage or shallowness.

Medusa with Gorgonian terror guards
The ford, *and of itself the water flies*
All taste of living wight.
MILTON'S PARADISE LOST, B. II.

Rise, wretched widow! rise; nor undeplor'd
Permit my ghost to pass the Stygian ford*:*
But rise, prepar'd in black to mourn thy perish'd lord. DRYDEN.

FORE. *adv.*

1. Anteriorly; in the part which appears first to those that meet it.

Each of them will bear six demiculverins and four saikers, needing no other addition than a slight spar deck fore *and aft, which is a slight deck throughout.*
RALEIGH'S ESSAYS.

2. *Fore* is a word much used in composition to mark priority of time, of which some examples shall be given.[109]

FO'RECAST. *n.s.* [from the verb.] Contrivance beforehand; scheme; plan; antecedent policy.

Alas! that Warwick had no more forecast,
But while he thought to steal the single ten,
The king was slily finger'd from the deck!
SHAKESPEARE'S HENRY VI.

He makes this difference to arise from the forecast *and predetermination of the gods.*
ADDISON ON ANCIENT MEDALS.

The last, scarce ripen'd into perfect man,
Saw helpless him from whom their life began:
Mem'ry and forecast *just returns engage;*
That pointed back to youth, this on to age.
POPE.

FORECA'STER. *n.s.* [from *forecast.*] One who contrives beforehand.

FOREIMA'GINE. *v.a.* [*fore* and *imagine.*] To conceive or fancy before proof.

We are within compass of a foreimagined *possibility in that behalf.*
CAMDEN'S REMAINS.

To **FOREJU'DGE.** *v.a.* [*fore* and *judge.*] To judge beforehand; to be prepossessed.

FORE'NSICK. *adj.* [*forensis*, Latin.] Belonging to courts of judicature.

Person is a forensick *term, appropriating actions and their merit; and so belongs only to intelligent agents, capable of a law, and happiness and misery. This personality extends itself beyond present existence to what is past, only by consciousness.*
LOCKE.

The forum was a publick place in Rome, where lawyers and orators made their speeches before the proper judges in matters of property, or in criminal cases: thence all sorts of disputations in courts of justice, where several persons make their distinct speeches, may come under the name of forensick *disputes.*
WATTS'S IMPROVEMENT OF THE MIND.

To **FORESA'Y.** *v.a.* [*fore* and *say.*] To predict; to prophesy; to foretell.

Let ordinance
Come as the gods foresay *it.*
SHAKESPEARE'S CYMBELINE.

To **FORESE'E.** *v.a.* [*fore* and *see.*] To see beforehand; to see what has not yet happened; to have prescience; to foreknow.

With Cupid she foresees *and goes god Vulcan's pace.* SIDNEY.

The first of them could things to come foresee*;*
The next, could of things present best advise;
The third, things past could keep in memory. FAIRY QUEEN.

If there be any thing foreseen *that is not usual, be armed for it by any hearty though a short prayer, and an earnest resolution beforehand, and then watch when it comes.* TAYLOR.

At his foreseen *approach, already quake*
The Caspian kingdoms and Meotian lake:
Their seers behold the tempest from afar,
And threat'ning oracles denounce the war.
DRYDEN'S ÆNEID.

FO'RESKIRT. *n.s.* [*fore* and *skirt.*] The pendulous or loose part of the coat before.

A thousand pounds a year for pure respect!
No other obligation?
That promises more thousands: honour's train
Is longer than his foreskirt.
SHAKESPEARE'S HENRY VIII.

FORETO'OTH. *n.s.* [*fore* and *tooth.*] The tooth in the anterior part of the mouth; the incisor.

The foreteeth *should be formed broad, and with a thin sharp edge like chizzles.*
RAY ON THE CREATION.

FOREVOU'CHED. *part.* [*fore* and *vouch.*] Affirmed before; formerly told.

Sure her offence
Must be of such unnatural degree,
That monsters it; or your forevouch'd *affection*
Fall'n into taint.
SHAKESPEARE'S KING LEAR.

FORK. *n.s.* [*furca*, Latin; *fforch*, Welsh; *fourche*, French.]

1. An instrument divided at the end into two or more points or prongs, used on many occasions.

At Midsummer down with the brembles and brakes,
And after abroad with thy forks *and thy rakes.* TUSSER'S HUSBANDRY.

The vicar first, and after him the crew,
With forks *and staves the felon to pursue,*
Ran Coll our dog.
DRYDEN'S NUN'S PRIEST.

I dine with forks *that have but two prongs.* SWIFT.

2. It is sometimes used for the point of an arrow.

The bow is bent and drawn: make from the shaft.
—— Let it fall rather, though the fork *invade*
The region of my heart.
SHAKESPEARE'S KING LEAR.

3. A point of a fork.

Several are amazed at the wisdom of the ancients that represented a thunderbolt with three forks, *since nothing could have better explained its triple quality of piercing, burning, and melting.*
ADDISON ON ANCIENT MEDALS.

FO'RKY. *adj.* [from *fork.*] Forked; furcated; opening into two parts.

The smiling infant in his hand shall take
The crested basilisk and speckled snake;
Pleas'd the green lustre of the scales survey,
And with their forky *tongue and pointless sting shall play.* POPE'S MESSIAH.

FO'RMALIST. *n.s.* [*formaliste*, French, from *form.*] One who practises external ceremony; one who prefers appearance to reality; one who seems what he is not.

It is a ridiculous thing, and fit for a satyr to persons of judgment, to see what shifts formalists *have, and what prospectives to make superficies to seem a body that hath depth and bulk.* BACON, ESSAY 27.

A grave, stanch, skilfully managed face, set upon a grasping aspiring mind, having got many a sly formalist *the reputation of a primitive and severe piety.*
SOUTH'S SERMONS.

To **FO'RMALIZE.** *v.a.* [*formaliser*, French, from *formal.*]

1. To model; to modify. A word not now in use.

The same spirit which anointed the blessed soul of our Saviour Christ, doth so formalize, *unite, and actuate his whole*

race, as if both he and they were so many limbs compacted into one body.
HOOKER, B. V. S. 56.

2. To affect formality; to be fond of ceremony.

FORNICA'TOR. *n.s.* [*fornicateur*, French, from *fornix*, Latin.] One that has commerce with unmarried women.

A fornicator *or adulterer steals the soul as well as dishonours the body of his neighbour.*
TAYLOR'S RULE OF LIVING HOLY.

FORNICA'TRESS. *n.s.* [from *fornicator.*] A woman who without marriage cohabits with a man.

See you the fornicatress *be remov'd;*
Let her have needful but not slavish means. SHAKESPEARE.

FORT. *n.s.* [*fort*, French.] A fortified house; a castle.

They erected a fort, *which they called the* fort de l'or; *and from thence they bolted like beasts of the forest.* BACON.

Now to their fort *they are about to send*
For the loud engines which their isle defend. WALLER.

He that views a fort *to take it,*
Plants his artillery 'gainst the weakest part. DENHAM'S SOPHY.

My fury does, like jealous forts, *pursue*
With death, ev'n strangers who but come to view. DRYDEN.

FO'RTLET. *n.s.* [from *fort.*] A little fort.

FO'RTUNEBOOK. *n.s.* [*fortune* and *book.*] A book consulted to know fortune or future events.

Thou know'st a face, in whose each look
Beauty lays ope love's fortunebook;
On whose fair revolutions wait
The obsequious motions of love's fate.
CRASHAW.

FORTUNEHU'NTER. *n.s.* [*fortune* and *hunt.*] A man whose employment is to enquire after women with great portions to enrich himself by marrying them.

We must, however, distinguish between fortunehunters *and fortunestealers.*
SPECTATOR, NO. 312.

FO'SSEWAY. *n.s.* [*fosse* and *way.*] One of the great Roman inroads through England, so called from the ditches on each side.

FO'ULFACED. *adj.* [*foul* and *faced.*] Having an ugly or hateful visage.

If black scandal, or foulfac'd *reproach,*
Attend the sequel of your imposition,
Your mere enforcement shall acquittance me
From all the impure blots and stains thereof. SHAKESPEARE'S RICHARD III.

FOULMOU'THED. *adj.* [*foul* and *mouth.*] Scurrilous; habituated to the use of opprobrious terms and epithets.

My lord, he speaks most vilely of you, like a foulmouth'd *man as he is, and said he would cudgel you.*
SHAKESPEARE'S HENRY IV.

It was allowed by every body, that so foulmouthed *a witness never appeared in any cause.* ADDISON.

My reputation is too well established in the world to receive any hurt from such a foulmouthed *scoundrel as he.*
ARBUTHNOT.

Now singing shrill, and scolding oft between,
Scolds answer foulmouth'd *scolds; bad neighbourhood I ween.* SWIFT.

FO'ULNESS. *n.s.* [from *foul.*]
1. The quality of being foul; filthiness; nastiness.

The ancients were wont to make garments that were not destroyed but purified by fire;

and whereas the spots or foulness *of other cloaths are washed out, in these they were usually burnt away.*
WILKINS'S MATHEMATICAL MAGICK.

2. Pollution; impurity.

It is no vicious blot, murder, or foulness,
No unchaste action, or dishonour'd step,
That hath depriv'd me of your grace and favour. SHAKESPEARE.

There is not so chaste a nation as this, nor so free from all pollution or foulness: *it is the virgin of the world.* BACON.

3. Hatefulness; atrociousness.

He by an affection sprung up from excessive beauty, should not delight in horrible foulness. SIDNEY.

Consul, you are too mild:
The foulness *of some facts takes thence all mercy:*
Report it to the senate.
BEN JONSON'S CATILINE.

It is the wickedness of a whole life, discharging all its filth and foulness *into this one quality, as into a great sink or common shore.* SOUTH'S SERMONS.

4. Ugliness; deformity.

He's fallen in love with your foulness, *and she'll fall in love with my anger.*
SHAKESPEARE'S AS YOU LIKE IT.

The fury laid aside
Her looks and limbs, and with new methods tried
The foulness *of th' infernal form to hide.*
DRYDEN'S ÆNEID.

5. Dishonesty; want of candour.

Piety is opposed to hypocrisy and insincerity, and all falseness or foulness *of intentions; especially to that personated devotion, under which any kind of impiety is wont to be disguised.*
HAMMOND'S FUNDAMENTALS.

FOXHU'NTER. *n.s.* [*fox* and *hunter.*] A man whose chief ambition is to shew his bravery in hunting foxes. A term of reproach used of country gentlemen.

The foxhunters *went their way, and then out steals the fox.*
L'ESTRANGE, FABLE 104.

John Wildfire, foxhunter, *broke his neck over a six-bar gate.*
SPECTATOR, NO. 561.

FRA'GMENTARY. *adj.* [from *fragment.*] Composed of fragments. A word not elegant, nor in use.

She, she is gone; she's gone: when thou know'st this,
What fragmentary *rubbish this world is,*
Thou know'st, and that it is not worth a thought;
He knows it too too much that thinks it nought. DONNE.

FRAISE. *n.s.* [French, the caul of an animal.] A pancake with bacon in it.

FRA'NION. *n.s.* [Of this word I know not the derivation.] A paramour; a boon companion.

First, by her side did sit the bold Sansloy,
Fit mate for such a mincing minion,
Who in her looseness took exceeding joy,
Might not be found a franker franion.
FAIRY QUEEN, B. II.

FRA'NKLIN. *n.s.* [from *frank.*] A steward; a bailiff of land. It signifies originally a little gentleman, and is not improperly Englished a gentleman servant.[110]

A spacious court they see,
Both plain and pleasant to be walked in,
Where them does meet a franklin *fair and free.* FAIRY QUEEN.

FREAK. *n.s.* [*frech*, German, saucy, petulant; *fræc*, Saxon, fugitive.]

1. A sudden and causeless change of place.
2. A sudden fancy; a humour; a whim; a capricious prank.

O! but I fear the fickle freaks, *quoth she,*
Of fortune, and the odds of arms in field.
FAIRY QUEEN.

When that freak *has taken possession of a fantastical head, the distemper is incurable.* L'ESTRANGE, FABLE 100.

She is so restless and peevish that she quarrels with all about her, and sometimes in a freak *will instantly change her habitation.* SPECTATOR, NO. 427.

To vex me more, he took a freak
To slit my tongue, and make me speak.
SWIFT.

To **FREAK.** *v.a.* [A word, I suppose, Scotch, brought into England by *Thomson.*] To variegate; to checquer.

There furry nations harbour:
Sables of glossy black, and dark embrown'd,
Or beauteous, freak'd *with many a*
mingled hue. THOMSON.

FRE'AKISH. *adj.* [from *freak.*] Capricious; humoursome.

It may be a question, whether the wife or the woman was the more freakish *of the two; for she was still the same uneasy fop.* L'ESTRANGE, FABLE 173.

FREESCHO'OL. *n.s.* [*free* and *school.*] A school in which learning is given without pay.

To give a civil education to the youth of this land in the time to come, provision was made by another law, that there should be one freeschool *at least erected in every diocess.* DAVIES.

Two clergymen stood candidates for a small freeschool *in —shire, where a gentleman of interest in the country, who happened to have a better understanding than his neighbours, procured the place for him who was the better scholar.* SWIFT.

FREETHI'NKER. *n.s.* [*free* and *think.*] A libertine; a contemner of religion.

Atheist is an old-fashion'd word: I'm a freethinker, *child.* ADDISON'S DRUMMER.

Of what use is freedom of thought, if it will not produce freedom of action, which is the sole end, how remote soever in appearance, of all objections against Christianity? And therefore the freethinkers *consider it as an edifice, wherein all the parts have such a mutual dependance on each other, that if you pull out one single nail, the whole fabrick must fall to the ground.* SWIFT'S ARGUMENT AGAINST ABOLISHING CHRISTIANITY.

To **FRE'NCHIFY.** *v.a.* [from *French.*] To infect with the manner of France; to make a coxcomb.

They misliked nothing more in king Edward the Confessor than that he was Frenchified; *and accounted the desire of foreign language then to be a foretoken of bringing in foreign powers, which indeed happened.* CAMDEN'S REMAINS.

Has he familiarly dislik'd
Your yellow starch, or said your doublet
Was not exactly Frenchified.
SHAKESPEARE'S AS YOU LIKE IT.

FRE'SCO. *n.s.* [Italian.]

1. Coolness; shade; duskiness, like that of the evening or morning.

Hellish sprites
Love more the fresco *of the nights.*
PRIOR.

2. A picture not drawn in glaring light, but in dusk.

Here thy well-study'd marbles fix our eye;
A fading fresco *here demands a sigh.*
POPE.

FRESHWA'TER. [A compound word of *fresh* and *water*, used as an adjective.] Raw; unskilled; unacquainted. A low term borrowed from the sailors, who stigmatise those who come first to sea as *freshwater* men or novices.

The nobility, as freshwater *soldiers which had never seen but some light skirmishes, in their vain bravery made light account of the Turks.*
KNOLLES'S HISTORY OF THE TURKS.

To **FRI'BBLE.** *v.n.* To trifle.

Though cheats, yet more intelligible
Than those that with the stars do fribble.
HUDIBRAS, P. II.

FRI'BBLER. *n.s.* [from the verb.] A trifler.

A fribbler *is one who professes rapture for the woman, and dreads her consent.*
SPECTATOR, NO. 288.

FRICASSE'E. *n.s.* [French.] A dish made by cutting chickens or other small things in pieces, and dressing them with strong sauce.

Oh, how would Homer praise their dancing dogs,
Their stinking cheese, and fricacy *of frogs!*
He'd raise no fables, sing no flagrant lye,
Of boys with custard choak'd at Newberry. KING.

FRIEND. *n.s.* [*vriend*, Dutch; *freond*, Saxon. This word, with its derivatives, is pronounced *frend*, *frendly*: the *i* totally neglected.]

1. One joined to another in mutual benevolence and intimacy: opposed to foe or enemy.

Friends *of my soul, you twain*
Rule in this realm, and the gor'd state sustain. SHAKESPEARE.

Some man is a friend *for his own occasion, and will not abide in the day of thy trouble.*
BIBLE ECCLESIASTICUS, VI. 8.

God's benison go with you, and with those
That would make good of bad, and friends *of foes.* SHAKESPEARE.

Wonder not to see this soul extend
The bounds, and seek some other self, a friend. DRYDEN.

2. One without hostile intentions.

Who comes so fast in silence of the night?
—— A friend.
—— What friend? *your name?*
SHAKESPEARE'S THE MERCHANT OF VENICE.

3. One reconciled to another: this is put by the custom of the language somewhat irregularly in the plural number.

He's friends *with Cæsar,*
In state of health thou say'st, and thou say'st free. SHAKESPEARE.

My son came then into my mind; and yet my mind
Was then scarce friends *with him.*
SHAKESPEARE'S KING LEAR.

4. An attendant, or companion.

The king ordains their entrance, and ascends
His regal seat, surrounded by his friends.
DRYDEN'S ÆNEID.

5. Favourer; one propitious.

Aurora riding upon Pegasus, sheweth her swiftness, and how she is a friend *to poetry and all ingenious inventions.*
PEACHAM.

6. A familiar compellation.

Friend, *how camest thou in hither?*
BIBLE MATTHEW, XXII. 12.

What supports me, do'st thou ask?
The conscience, friend, *t'have lost mine eyes o'erply'd*
In liberty's defence. MILTON.

FRI'GAT. *n.s.* [*frigate*, French; *fregata*, Italian.]

1. A small ship. Ships under fifty guns are generally termed *frigats*.

The treasure they fought for was, in their view, embezzled in certain frigats.
RALEIGH'S APOLOGY.

On high-rais'd decks the haughty Belgians ride,
Beneath whose shade our humble frigats *go.* DRYDEN.

2. Any small vessel on the water.

Behold the water work and play
About her little frigat, *therein making way.* FAIRY QUEEN.

FRI'GHTFULLY. *adv.* [from *frightful.*]
1. Dreadfully; horribly.

This will make a prodigious mass of water, and looks frightfully *to the imagination; 'tis huge and great.* BURNET.

2. Disagreeably; not beautifully. A woman's word.

Then to her glass; and Betty, pray,
Don't I look frightfully *to-day?* SWIFT.

FRIGORI'FICK. *adj.* [*frigorificus, frigus* and *facio*, Lat.] Causing cold. A word used in science.

Frigorifick *atoms or particles mean those nitrous salts which float in the air in cold weather, and occasion freezing.* QUINCY.

FRI'PPERER. *n.s.* [from *frippier*, French.] One who deals in old things vamped up.

FRISK. *n.s.* [from the verb.] A frolick; a fit of wanton gaiety.

FRI'SKER. *n.s.* [from *frisk.*] A wanton; one not constant or settled.

Now I will wear this, and now I will wear that;
Now I will wear I cannot tell what:
All new fashions be pleasant to me:
Now I am a frisker, *all men on me look;*
What should I do but set cock on the hoop? CAMDEN.

FRITH. *n.s.* [*fretum*, Latin.]
1. A strait of the sea where the water being confined is rough.

What desp'rate madman then would venture o'er
The frith, *or haul his cables from the shore?* DRYDEN'S VIRGIL.

Batavian fleets
Defraud us of the glittering finny swarms
That heave our friths, *and crowd upon our shores.* THOMSON.

2. A kind of net. I know not whether this sense be now retained.

The Wear is a frith, *reaching through the Ose, from the land to low water mark, and having in it a bunt or cod with an eye-hook; where the fish entering, upon their coming back with the ebb, are stopt from issuing out again.* CAREW.

FROG. *n.s.* [*frogga*, Saxon.]
1. A small animal with four feet, living both by land and water, and placed by naturalists among mixed animals, as partaking of beast and fish.[111] There is likewise a small green frog that perches on trees, said to be venomous.

Poor Tom, that eats the swimming frog, *the toad, the todpole.*
SHAKESPEARE'S KING LEAR.

Auster is drawn with a pot or urn, pouring forth water, with which shall descend frogs. PEACHAM ON DRAWING.

2. The hollow part of the horse's hoof.

FROISE. *n.s.* [from the French *froisser*, as the pancake is crisped or crimpled in frying.] A kind of food made by frying bacon inclosed in a pancake.

FRO'NTBOX. *n.s.* [*front* and *box.*] The box in the playhouse from which there is a direct view to the stage.

How vain are all these glories, all our pains,
Unless good sense preserve what beauty gains!
That men may say, when we the frontbox *grace,*
Behold the first in virtue, as in face.
POPE'S RAPE OF THE LOCK.

FRO'NTIER. *n.s.* [*frontiere*, French.] The marches; the limit; the utmost verge of any territory; the border: properly that which terminates not at the sea, but fronts another country.

Draw all the inhabitants of those borders away, or plant garrisons upon all those frontiers *about him.*
SPENSER ON IRELAND.

I upon my frontiers *here*
Keep residence,
That little which is left so to defend.
MILTON'S PARADISE LOST.

FRO'NTLET. *n.s.* [from *frons*, Latin; *fronteau*, French.] A bandage worn upon the forehead.

How now, daughter, what makes that frontlet *on? You are too much of late i' th' frown.* SHAKESPEARE'S KING LEAR.

They shall be as frontlets *between thine eyes.* BIBLE DEUTERONOMY, VI. 8.

To the forehead frontlets *were applied, to restrain and intercept the influx.*
WISEMAN'S SURGERY.

FRONTROO'M. *n.s.* [*front* and *room.*] An apartment in the forepart of the house.

If your shop stands in an eminent street, the frontrooms *are commonly more airy than the backrooms; and it will be inconvenient to make the* frontroom *shallow.*
MOXON'S MECHANICAL EXERCISES.

To **FROUNCE.** *v.a.* [from the noun.] To frizzle or curl the hair about the face. This word was at first probably used in contempt.

Some frounce *their curled hair in courtly guise,*
Some prank their ruffs, and others timely dight
Their gay attire.
FAIRY QUEEN, B. I. CANT. 4.

Some warlike sign must be used; either a slovenly buskin, or an overstaring frounced *head.* ASCHAM'S SCHOOLMASTER.

Thus, night, oft see me in thy pale career,
'Till civil suited morn appear;
Not trick'd and frounc'd *as she was wont,*
With the Attick boy to hunt. MILTON.

F. R. S. *Fellow* of the *Royal Society.*

Who this profess,
Shine in the dignity of F. R. S. POPE.

FRUITGRO'VES. *n.s.* [*fruit* and *groves.*] Shades, or close plantations of fruit trees.

The faithful slave,
Whom to my nuptial train Icarius gave,
To tend the fruitgroves?
POPE'S ODYSSEY, B. IV.

FRUIT-TIME. *n.s.* [*fruit* and *time.*] The Autumn; the time for gathering fruit.

FRUME'NTY. *n.s.* [*frumentum*, corn, Latin.] Food made of wheat boiled in milk.

FRUSTRA'NEOUS. *adj.* [*frustra*, Latin.] Vain; useless; unprofitable; without advantage.

Their attempts being so frustraneous, *and the demonstrations to the contrary so perspicuous, it is a marvel that any man, virtuously and piously disposed, should be so partially and zealously affected in a cause that has neither truth nor any honest usefulness in it.*
MORE'S DIVINE DIALOGUES.

He timely withdraws his frustraneous *baffled kindnesses, and sees the folly of endeavouring to stroke a tyger into a lamb, or to court an Ethiopian out of his colour.*
SOUTH'S SERMONS.

FU'LCIMENT. *n.s.* [*fulcimen*, *fulcimentum*, Latin.] That on which a body rests, which acts or is acted upon at each end, as a balance or a lever.

The power that equiponderates with any weight, must have the same proportion unto it as there is betwixt their several distances from the center or fulciment.
WILKINS.

FU'LHAM. *n.s.* A cant word for false dice. *Hanmer.*

Let vultures gripe thy guts, for gourd and
Fulham's *hold,*
And high and low beguile the rich and
poor. SHAKESPEARE.

FULL is much used in composition to intimate any thing arrived at its highest state, or utmost degree.

FULL-EY'ED. [*full* and *eye.*] Having large prominent eyes.

FULL-FE'D. [*full* and *fed.*] Sated; fat; saginated.

All as a partridge plump, full-fed *and*
fair,
She form'd this image of well-bodied air.
POPE'S DUNCIAD.

FU'LLINGMILL. *n.s.* [*full* and *mill.*] A mill where the water raises hammers which beat the cloath 'till it be cleansed.

By large hammers, like those used for paper and fullingmills, *they beat their hemp.* MORTIMER.

FU'LSOME. *adj.* [from *fulle*, Saxon, foul.]

1. Nauseous; offensive.

The skilful shepherd peel'd me
certain wands;
And in the doing of the deed of kind,
He stuck them up before the
fulsome *ewes.* SHAKESPEARE.

He that brings fulsome *objects to my*
view,
With nauseous images my fancy fills,
And all goes down like oxymel of squills.
ROSCOMMON.

Now half the youth of Europe are in
arms,
How fulsome *must it be to stay*
behind,
And die of rank diseases here at home?
OTWAY'S ORPHAN.

2. Of a rank odious smell.

White satyrion is of a dainty smell, and bean-flowers: again, if the plant puts forth white flowers only, and those not thin or dry, they are commonly of rank and fulsome *smell.* BACON'S NATURAL HISTORY, NO. 507.

3.[112] Tending to obscenity.

A certain epigram, which is ascribed to the emperor, is more fulsome *than any passage I have met with in our poet.* DRYDEN.

FUME'TTE. *n.s.* [French.] A word introduced by cooks, and the pupils of cooks, for the stink of meat.

A haunch of ven'son made her sweat,
Unless it had the right fumette. SWIFT.

FU'MID. *adj.* [*fumidus*, Latin.] Smoky; vaporous.

A crass and fumid *exhalation is caused from the combat of the sulphur and iron with the acid and nitrous spirits of aquafortis.* BROWN'S VULGAR ERROURS, B. II. C. 5.

FUN. *n.s.* [A low cant word.] Sport; high merriment; frolicksome delight.

Don't mind me, though, for all my fun *and*
jokes,
You bards may find us bloods good-natur'd
folks. MOORE.

FUNK. *n.s.* A stink. A low word.

FU'RNITURE. *n.s.* [*fourniture*, Fr. from *furnish.*]

1. Moveables; goods put in a house for use or ornament.

No man can transport his large retinue, his sumptuous fare, and his rich furniture *into another world.* SOUTH'S SERMONS.

There are many noble palaces in Venice: their furniture *is not commonly very rich, if we except the pictures from the hands of the best masters.* ADDISON.

2. Appendages.

By a general conflagration mankind shall be destroyed, with the form and all the furniture *of the earth.* TILLOTSON.

3. Equipage; embellishments; decorations.

Young Clarion, with vauntful lustyhed,
After his guise did cast abroad to fare,
And thereto 'gan his furnitures *prepare.*
SPENSER.

The duke is coming: see, the barge be ready,
And fit it with such furniture *as suits*
The greatness of his person.
SHAKESPEARE'S HENRY VIII.

The ground must be of a mixt brown, and large enough, or the horse's furniture *must be of very sensible colours.* DRYDEN.

FU'SIL. *n.s.* [*fusil*, French.]
1. A firelock; a small neat musquet.
2. [In heraldry, from *fusus*, Latin.] Something like a spindle.

Fusils *must be made long, and small in the middle, in the ancient coat of Mountague, argent three* fusils *in sesse gules.*
PEACHAM ON BLAZONING.

FUSS. *n.s.* [A low cant word.] A tumult; a bustle.

End as it befits your station;
Come to use and application;
Nor with senates keep a fuss*:*
I submit, and answer thus. SWIFT.

FU'TILE. *adj.* [*futile*, French; *futilis*, Latin.]
1. Talkative; loquacious.

One futile *person, that maketh it his glory to tell, will do more hurt than many that know it their duty to conceal.* BACON.

2. Trifling; worthless; of no weight.

FUTI'LITY. *n.s.* [*futilité*, French, from *futile*.]
1. Talkativeness; loquacity.

This fable does not strike so much at the futility *of women, as at the incontinent levity of a prying humour.*
L'ESTRANGE.

2. Triflingness; want of weight; want of solidity.

Trifling futility *appears in their signs of the zodiack, and their mutual relations and aspects.* BENTLEY.

To **FUZZ.** *v.n.* [without etymology.] To fly out in small particles.

FY. *interj.* [*fy*, French and Flemish; *φεῦ*, Greek; *vah*, Lat.] A word of blame and disapprobation.

And fy *on fortune, mine avowed foe,*
Whose wrathful wreaks themselves do now allay. FAIRY QUEEN.

Fy, *my lord,* fy*! a soldier, and afraid? What need we fear who knows it, when none can call our power to account?*
SHAKESPEARE'S MACBETH.

A bawd, sir, fy *upon him!*
SHAKESPEARE'S MEASURE FOR MEASURE.

But fy, *my wand'ring muse, how thou do'st stray!*
Expectance calls thee now another way.
MILTON.

Nay, fy, *what mean you in this open place?*
Unhand me, or, I swear, I'll scratch your face:
Let go, for shame; you make me mad for spite:
My mouth's my own; and if you kiss, I'll bite. DRYDEN.

Fy, *madam, he cried, we must be past all these gaities.* TATLER, NO. 54.

G

Has two sounds, one from the Greek *Γ*, and the Latin, which is called that of the hard G, because it is formed by a pressure somewhat hard of the forepart of the tongue against the upper gum. This sound G retains before *a*, *o*, *u*, *l*, *r*; as, *gate*, *go*, *gull*. The other sound, called that of the soft G, resembles that of *J*, and is commonly, though not always, found before *e*, *i*; as, *gem*, *gibbet*. Before *n*, at the end of a word, *g* is commonly melted away; as in the French, from which these words are commonly derived: thus, for *benign*, *malign*, *condign*, we pronounce *benine*, *maline*, *condine*. It is often silent in the middle of words before *h*; as, *might*. The Saxon *g* seems to have had generally the sound of *y* consonant; whence *gate* is by rusticks still pronounced *yate*.

GA'FFER. *n.s.* [*gefere*, companion, Saxon.] A word of respect now obsolete, or applied only in contempt to a mean person.

For gaffer *Treadwell told us by the bye,*
Excessive sorrow is exceeding dry.
GAY'S PASTORALS.

GALA'XY. *n.s.* [γαλαξία; *galaxie*, Fr.] The milky way; a stream of light in the sky.

A broad and ample road, whose dust is gold,
And pavement stars, as stars to thee appear,
Seen in the galaxy.
MILTON'S PARADISE LOST, B. VII.

A brown, for which heaven would disband
The galaxy, *and stars be tann'd.*
CLEAVELAND.

Men doubt, because they stand so thick i' th' sky,
If those be stars that paint the galaxy.
COWLEY.

We dare not undertake to shew what advantage is brought to us by those innumerable stars in the galaxy.
BENTLEY'S SERMONS.

GALE. *n.s.* [*gahling*, hasty, sudden, German.] A wind not tempestuous, yet stronger than a breeze.

What happy gale
Blows you to Padua here, from old Verona? SHAKESPEARE.

Winds
Of gentlest gale *Arabian odours fann'd*
From their soft wings, and Flora's earliest smells. MILTON.

Fresh gales *and gentle air.* MILTON.

Umbria's green retreats,
Where western gales *eternally reside.*
ADDISON.

GALLE'ON. *n.s.* [*galion*, French.] A large ship with four or sometimes five decks, now in use only among the Spaniards.

I assured them that I would stay for them at Trinidado, and that no force should drive me thence, except I were sunk or set on fire by the Spanish galleons.
RALEIGH'S APOLOGY.

The number of vessels were one hundred and thirty, whereof galleasses and galleons *seventy-two, goodly ships, like floating towers or castles.*
BACON'S WAR WITH SPAIN.

GA'LLERY. *n.s.* [*galerie*, French, derived by *Du Cange* from *galeria*, low Latin, a fine room.]
1. A kind of walk along the floor of a house, into which the doors of the apartments open; in general, any building of which the length much exceeds the breadth.

In most part there had been framed by art such pleasant arbors, that, one answering another, they became a gallery *aloft from tree to tree, almost round about, which below gave a perfect shadow.*
SIDNEY, B. I.

High lifted up were many lofty towers,
And goodly galleries *fair overlaid.*
FAIRY QUEEN, B. I.

Your gallery
Have we pass'd through, not without much content. SHAKESPEARE.

The row of return on the banquet side, let it be all stately galleries, *in which* galleries *let there be three cupola's.* BACON.

A private gallery *'twixt th' apartments led,*
Not to the foe yet known. DENHAM.

Nor is the shape of our cathedral proper for our preaching auditories, but rather the figure of an amphitheatre, with galleries *gradually overlooking each other; for into this condition the parish-churches of London are driving apace, as appears by the many* galleries *every day built in them.* GRAUNT.

There are covered galleries *that lead from the palace to five different churches.*
ADDISON ON ITALY.

2. The seats in the playhouse above the pit, in which the meaner people sit.

While all its throats the gallery *extends,*
And all the thunder of the pit ascends.
POPE'S EPISTLE OF HORACE.

GA'LLICISM. *n.s.* [*gallicisme*, French, from *gallicus*, Latin.] A mode of speech peculiar to the French language: such as, he *figured* in controvery; he *held* this conduct; he *held* the same language that another had *held* before: with many other expressions to be found in the pages of *Bolinbroke.*

In English I would have Gallicisms *avoided, that we may keep to our own language, and not follow the French mode in our speech.*
FELTON ON THE CLASSICKS.

GA'LLIPOT. *n.s.* [*gleye*, Dutch, shining earth. *Skinner*. The true derivation is from *gala*, Spanish, finery. *Gala*, or gallypot, is a fine painted pot.] A pot painted and glazed, commonly used for medicines.

Plato said his master Socrates was like the apothecary's gallipots, *that had on the outsides apes, owls, and satyrs; but within, precious drugs.*
BACON, APOPHTHEGM 227.

Here phials in nice discipline are set;
There gallipots *are rang'd in alphabet*
GARTH'S DISPENSATORY.

Alexandrinus thought it unsafe to trust the real secret of his phial and gallipot *to any man.* SPECTATOR, NO. 426.

Thou that do'st Æsculapius deride,
And o'er his gallipots *in triumph ride.*
FENTON.

GA'MBLER. *n.s.* [A cant word, I suppose, for game or gamester.] A knave whose practice it is to invite the unwary to game and cheat them.

GAOL. *n.s.* [*geol*, Welsh; *geole*, French.] A prison; a place of confinement. It is always pronounced and too often written *jail*, and sometimes *goal*.

Then am I the prisoner, and his bed my gaol. SHAKESPEARE'S KING LEAR.

Have I been ever free, and must my house
Be my retentive enemy, my gaol?
SHAKESPEARE'S TIMON.

If we mean to thrive and do good, break open the gaols, *and let out the prisoners.* SHAKESPEARE'S HENRY VI. P. II.

GA'OLDELIVERY. *n.s.* [*gaol* and *deliver*.] The judicial process, which by condemnation or acquittal of persons confined evacuates the prison.

Then doth th' aspiring soul the body leave,
Which we call death; but were it known to all,
What life our souls do by this death receive,
Men would it birth or gaoldelivery *call.*
DAVIES.

These make a general gaoldelivery *of souls, not for punishment.* SOUTH.

To **GAR.** *v.a.* [*giera*, Islandick.] To cause; to make.[113] It is still in use in Scotland.

Tell me, good Hobbinol, what gars *thee greet?*
What! hath some wolf thy tender lambs ytorn?
Or is thy bagpipe broke, that sounds so sweet?
Or art thou of thy loved loss forlorne.
SPENSER'S PASTORALS.

To **GARGARI'ZE.** *v.a.* [*γαργαρίζω*; *gargariser*, French.] To wash the mouth with medicated liquors.

Vinegar, put to the nostrils, or gargarized, *doth ease the hiccough; for that it is astringent, and inhibiteth the motion of the spirit.* BACON'S NATURAL HISTORY.

This being relaxed, may make a shaking of the larynx; as when we gargarize. HOLDER'S ELEMENTS OF SPEECH.

GA'RRAN. *n.s.* [Erse. It imports the same as gelding. The word is still retained in Scotland.] A small horse; a hobby. A Highland horse which when brought into the North of England takes the name of *galloway*.

When he comes forth he will make their cows and garrans *to walk, if he doth no other harm to their persons.* SPENSER.

Every man would be forced to provide Winter-fodder for his team, whereas common garrans *shift upon grass the year round; and this would force men to the enclosing of grounds, so that the race of* garrans *would decrease.* TEMPLE.

GAS. *n.s.* [A word invented by the chymists.] It is used by Van Helmont, and seems designed to signify, in general, a spirit not capable of being coagulated: but he uses it loosely in many senses, and very unintelligibly and inconsistently. *Harris.*

To **GASP.** *v.n.* [from *gape*, *Skinner*; from *gispe*, Danish, to sob, *Junius*.]
1. To open the mouth wide to catch breath.

The sick for air before the portal gasp.
DRYDEN'S VIRGIL'S GEORGICKS.

They rais'd a feeble cry with trembling notes;
But the weak voice deceiv'd their gasping *throats.* DRYDEN.

The gasping *head flies off; a purple flood*
Flows from the trunk.
DRYDEN'S ÆNEID.

The ladies gasp'd, *and scarcely could respire;*
The breath they drew no longer air, but fire. DRYDEN.

A scantling of wit lay gasping *for life, and groaning beneath a heap of rubbish.*
DRYDEN'S SPANISH FRYAR.

Pale and faint,
He gasps *for breath; and, as his life flows from him,*

Demands to see his friends.
ADDISON'S CATO.

2. To emit breath by opening the mouth convulsively.

I lay me down to gasp *my latest breath;*
The wolves will get a breakfast by my death. DRYDEN.

He staggers round, his eyeballs roll in death,
And with short sobs he gasps *away his breath.* DRYDEN'S ÆNEID.

3. To long for. This sense is, I think, not proper, as nature never expresses desire by gasping.

The Castilian and his wife had the comfort to be under the same master, who, seeing how dearly they loved one another, and gasped *after their liberty, demanded a most exorbitant price for their ransom.* SPECTATOR, NO. 198.

GAUDE. *n.s.* [The etymology of this word is uncertain: *Skinner* imagines it may come from *gaude*, French, a yellow flower, yellow being the most gaudy colour. *Junius*, according to his custom, talks of 'άγανος; and Mr. *Lye* finds *gaude*, in *Douglass*, to signify deceit or fraud, from *gwawdio*, Welsh, to cheat. It seems to me most easily deducible from *gaudium*, Latin, joy; the cause of joy; a token of joy: thence aptly applied to any thing that gives or expresses pleasure. In Scotland this word is still retained, both as a showy bawble, and the person fooled. It is also retained in Scotland to denote a yellow flower.] An ornament; a fine thing; any thing worn as a sign of joy.

He stole th' impression of her fantasy,
With bracelets of thy hair, rings, gaudes, *conceits,*
Knacks, trifles, nosegays, sweetmeats.
SHAKESPEARE.

The sun is in the heav'n, and the proud day,
Attended with the pleasures of the world,
Is all too wanton, and too full of gaudes,
To give me audience.
SHAKESPEARE'S KING LEAR.

My love to Hermia
Is melted as the snow; seems to me now
As the remembrance of an idle gaude,
Which in my childhood I did doat upon.
SHAKESPEARE.

Some bound for Guiney, golden sand to find,
Bore all the gaudes *the simple natives wear;*
Some for the pride of Turkish courts design'd,
For folded turbants finest holland bear.
DRYDEN'S ANNUS MIRABILIS.

GAWK. *n.s.* [*geac*, Saxon.]

1. A cuckow.

2. A foolish fellow. In both senses it is retained in Scotland.

GA'ZETTE. *n.s.* [*gazetta* is a Venetian halfpenny, the price of a news paper, of which the first was published at Venice.] A paper of news; a paper of publick intelligence. It is accented indifferently on the first or last syllable.

And sometimes when the loss is small,
And danger great, they challenge all;
Print new additions to their seats,
And emendations in gazettes.
HUDIBRAS, P. III. CANT. 3.

An English gentleman, without geography, cannot well understand a gazette.
LOCKE.

One cannot hear a name mentioned in it that does not bring to mind a piece of a gazette. ADDISON'S GUARDIAN.

All, all but truth, falls dead-born from the press;
Like the last gazette, *or the last address.*
POPE.

GAZETTE'ER. *n.s.* [from *gazette*.]

1. A writer of news.

2. It was lately a term of the utmost infamy, being usually applied to wretches who were hired to vindicate the court.[114]

Satire is no more: I feel it die:
No gazetteer *more innocent than I.*
POPE.

GA'ZINGSTOCK. *n.s.* [*gaze* and *stock.*] A person gazed at with scorn or abhorrence.

These things are offences to us, by making us gazingstocks *to others, and objects of their scorn and derision.* RAY.

GEE. A term used by waggoners to their horses when they would have them go faster.

GE'MMARY. *adj.* [from *gem.*] Pertaining to gems or jewels.

The principle and gemmary *affection is its translucency: as for irradiancy, which is found in many gems, it is not discoverable in this.*
BROWN'S VULGAR ERROURS, B. I. C. 2.

GE'NERAL. *adj.* [*general*, French; *generalis*, Latin.]

1. Comprehending many species or individuals; not special; not particular.

To conclude from particulars to generals *is a false way of arguing.*
NOTES TO POPE'S ODYSSEY.

2. Lax in signification; not restrained to any special or particular import.

Where the author speaks more strictly and particularly on any theme, it will explain the more loose and general *expressions.*
WATTS'S IMPROVEMENT OF THE MIND.

3. Not restrained by narrow or distinctive limitations.

A general *idea is an idea in the mind, considered there as separated from time and place, and so capable to represent any particular being that is conformable to it.*
LOCKE.

4. Relating to a whole class or body of men, or a whole kind of any being.

They, because some have been admitted without trial, make that fault general *which is particular.* WHITGIFTE.

5. Publick; comprising the whole.

Nor would we deign him burial of his men,
'Till he disburs'd, at Saint Colmeskill isle,
Ten thousand dollars to our gen'ral *use.*
SHAKESPEARE'S MACBETH.

Nor sail'd they to express how much they prais'd,
That for the general *safety he despis'd*
His own.
MILTON'S PARADISE LOST, B. II.

6. Not directed to any single object.

If the same thing be peculiarly evil, that general *aversion will be turned into a particular hatred against it.* SPRATT.

7. Extensive, though not universal.

8. Common; usual.

I've been bold,
For that I knew it the most general *way.*
SHAKESPEARE'S TIMON.

9. *General* is appended to several offices: as, *Attorney General, Solicitor General, Vicar General.*

GE'NIO. *n.s.* [*genio*, Italian; *genius*, Latin.] A man of a particular turn of mind.

Some genio's *are not capable of pure affection; and a man is born with talents for it as much as for poetry, or any other science.* TATLER, NO. 53.

GE'NTRY. *n.s.* [*gentlery*, *gentry*, from *gentle.*]

1. Birth; condition.[115]

You are certainly a gentleman,
Clerk-like experienc'd, which no less adorns
Our gentry *than our parents' noble name,*
In whose success we are gentle.
SHAKESPEARE'S WINTER'S TALE.

2. Class of people above the vulgar; those between the vulgar and the nobility.

They slaughtered many of the gentry, *for whom no sex or age could be accepted for excuse.* SIDNEY.

Let states, that aim at greatness, take heed how their nobility and gentry *multiply too fast.* BACON.

How chearfully the hawkers cry
A satire, and the gentry *buy.* SWIFT.

3. A term of civility real or ironical.

The many-colour'd gentry *there above,*
By turns are rul'd by tumult and by love. PRIOR.

4. Civility; complaisance. Obsolete.

Shew us so much gentry *and good-will,*
As to extend your time with us a-while. SHAKESPEARE'S HAMLET.

GE'NUS. *n.s.* [Latin.] In science, a class of being, comprehending under it many species: as quadruped is a genus comprehending under it almost all terrestrial beasts.

A general idea is called by the schools genus, *and it is one common nature agreeing to several other common natures: so animal is a* genus, *because it agrees to horse, lion, whale, and butterfly.* WATTS'S LOGICK.

If minerals are not convertible into another species, though of the same genus, *much less can they be surmised reducible into a species of another* genus. HARVEY ON CONSUMPTIONS.

GEORGE. *n.s.* [*Georgius*, Latin.]

1. A figure of St. George on horseback worn by the knights of the garter.

Look on my George, *I am a gentleman;*
Rate me at what thou wilt. SHAKESPEARE'S HENRY VI. P. II.

2. A brown loaf. Of this sense I know not the original.

Cubb'd in a cabbin, on a mattress laid,
On a brown george, *with lousy swobbers, fed.* DRYDEN'S PERSIUS.

GI'BBERISH. *n.s.* [Derived by *Skinner* from *gaber*, French, to cheat; by others conjectured to be formed by corruption from *jabber*. But as it was anciently written *gebrish*, it is probably derived from the chymical cant, and originally implied the jargon of *Geber* and his tribe.] Cant; the private language of rogues and gipsies; words without meaning.

Some, if they happen to hear an old word, albeit very natural and significant, cry out straitway, that we speak no English, but gibberish. SPENSER.

Some of both sexes writing down a number of letters, just as it came into their heads; upon reading this gibberish, *that which the men had wrote sounded like High Dutch, and the other by the women like Italian.* SWIFT.

GI'DDY. *adj.* [*gidig*, Saxon. I know not whether this word may not come from *gad*, to wander, to be in motion, *gad, gid, giddy*.]

1. Vertiginous; having in the head a whirl, or sensation of circular motion, such as happens by disease or drunkenness.

Them rev'ling thus the Tentyrites invade,
By giddy *heads and stagg'ring legs betray'd.* TATE'S JUVENAL.

2. Rotatory; whirling; running round with celerity.

As Ixion fix'd, the wretch shall feel
The giddy *motion of the whirling mill.* POPE.

3. Inconstant; mutable; unsteady; changeful.

Our fancies are more giddy *and unfirm,*
More longing, wavering, sooner lost and won,
Than womens are. SHAKESPEARE'S TWELFTH NIGHT.

It may be gnats and flies have their imagination more mutable and giddy, *as small birds likewise have.* BACON'S NATURAL HISTORY.

Thanks to giddy *chance, which never bears*
That mortal bliss should last for length of years,

She cast us headlong from our high estate,
And here in hope of thy return we wait.
DRYDEN'S FABLES.

The giddy *vulgar, as their fancies guide,*
With noise say nothing, and in parts divide. DRYDEN'S ÆNEID.

You are as giddy *and volatile as ever, the reverse of Pope, who hath always loved a domestick life.* SWIFT TO GAY.

4. That which causes giddiness.

The frequent errors of the pathless wood,
The giddy *precipice, and the dang'rous flood.* PRIOR.

The sylphs through mystick mazes guide their way,
Through all the giddy *circle they pursue.*
POPE.

5. Heedless; thoughtless; uncautious; wild.

Too many giddy *foolish hours are gone,*
And in fantastick measures danc'd away.
ROWE'S JANE SHORE.

How inexcusable are those giddy *creatures, who, in the same hour, leap from a parent's window to a husband's bed.* CLARISSA.

6. Tottering; unfixed.

As we pac'd along
Upon the giddy *footing of the hatches,*
Methought that Glo'ster stumbled.
SHAKESPEARE'S RICHARD III.

7. Intoxicated; elated to thoughtlessness; overcome by any overpowering inticement.

Art thou not giddy *with the fashion too, that thou hast shifted out of thy tale into telling me of the fashion?*
SHAKESPEARE.

Like one of two contending in a prize,
That thinks he hath done well in people's eyes;
Hearing applause and universal shout,
Giddy *in spirit, gazing still in doubt,*
Whether those peals of praise be his or no.
SHAKESPEARE.

GI'DDYBRAINED. *adj.* [*giddy* and *brain.*] Careless; thoughtless.

Turn him out again, you unnecessary, useless, giddybrain'd *ass!*
OTWAY'S VENICE PRESERVED.

GI'DDYHEADED. *adj.* [*giddy* and *head.*] Without thought or caution; without steadiness or constancy.

And sooner may a gulling weather spy,
By drawing forth heav'n's scheme descry
What fashion'd hats or ruffs, or suits, next year,
Our giddyheaded *antick youth will wear.*
DONNE.

That men are so misaffected, melancholy, giddyheaded, *hear the testimony of Solomon.* BURTON ON MELANCHOLY.

To **GI'GGLE.** *v.n.* [*gichgelen*, Dutch.] To laugh idly; to titter; to grin with merry levity. It is retained in Scotland.

GI'NGERBREAD. *n.s.* [*ginger* and *bread.*] A kind of farinaceous sweetmeat made of dough, like that of bread or biscuit, sweetened with treacle, and flavoured with ginger and some other aromatick seeds. It is sometimes gilt.

An' I had but one penny in the world, thou should'st have it to buy gingerbread.
SHAKESPEARE'S LOVE'S LABOUR LOST.

Her currans there and gooseberries were spread,
With the enticing gold of gingerbread.
KING'S COOKERY.

'Tis a loss you are not here, to partake of three weeks frost, and eat gingerbread *in a booth by a fire upon the Thames.*
SWIFT.

To **GIRN.** *v.n.* Seems to be a corruption of *grin*. It is still used in Scotland, and is applied to a crabbed, captious, or peevish person.

GI'ZZARD. *n.s.* [*gesier*, French; *gigeria*, Latin. It is sometimes called *gizzern.*]

1. The strong musculous stomach of a fowl.

Fowls have two ventricles, and pick up stones to convey them into their second ventricle, the gizzerne. MORE.

In birds there is no mastication in the mouth; but in such as are not carnivorous, it is immediately swallowed into the crop, a kind of antestomach, where it is moistened by some proper juice from the glandules distilling in there, and thence transferred into the gizzard, *or musculous stomach.* RAY.

Flutt'ring there they nestle near the throne,
And lodge in habitations not their own;
By their high crops and corny gizzards *known.* DRYDEN.

2. It is proverbially used for apprehension or conception of mind: as, he *frets his gizzard*, he harrasses his imagination.

But that which does them greatest harm,
Their spiritual gizzards *are too warm;*
Which puts the overheated sots
In fevers still.
HUDIBRAS, P. III. CANT. 11.

Satisfaction and restitution lie so cursedly hard upon the gizzards *of our publicans, that the blood in their veins is not half so dear to them as the treasure they have in their coffers.* L'ESTRANGE.

GLAIRE. *n.s.* [*glær*, Saxon, amber; *glar*, Danish, glass; *glaire*, French; *glarea*, Latin.]

1. The white of an egg.

Take the glaire *of eggs, and strain it as short as water.*
PEACHAM ON DRAWING.

2. A kind of halbert. *Dictionaries.*

To **GLAIRE.** *v.a.* [*glairer*, French; from the noun.] To smear with the white of an egg. This word is still used by the bookbinders.

GLASS. *n.s.* [*glæs*, Saxon; *glas*, Dutch, as *Pezon* imagines from *glâs*, British, green. In Erse it is called *klânn*, and this primarily signifies clean or clear, being so denominated from its transparency.]

1. An artificial substance made by fusing fixed salts and flint or sand together, with a vehement fire.

The word glass *cometh from the Belgick and High Dutch:* glass, *from the verb glansen, which signifies amongst them to shine; or perhaps from glacies in the Latin, which is ice, whose colour it resembles.*
PEACHAM ON DRAWING.

Glass *is thought so compact and firm a body that it is indestructible by art or nature, and is also of so close a texture that the subtlest chymical spirits cannot pervade it.* BOYLE.

Show'rs of granadoes rain, by sudden burst
Disploding murd'rous bowels, fragments of steel
And stones, and glass *and nitrous grain adust.* PHILLIPS.

2. A glass vessel of any kind.

I'll see no more;
And yet the eighth appears, who bears a glass
Which shews me many more.
SHAKESPEARE'S MACBETH.

3. A looking-glass; a mirrour.

He was the mark and glass, *copy and book,*
That fashion'd others.
SHAKESPEARE'S HENRY IV. P. II.

He spreads his subtile nets from sight,
With twinkling glasses, *to betray*
The larks that in the meshes light.
DRYDEN'S HORACE.

4. *An Hour* GLASS. A glass used in measuring time by the flux of sand.

Were my wife's liver
Infected as her life, she would not live
The running of one glass.
SHAKESPEARE'S WINTER'S TALE.

5.[116] A cup of glass used to drink in.

To this last costly treaty,
That swallow'd so much treasure, and like a glass

Did break i' th' rinsing.
SHAKESPEARE'S HENRY VIII.

When thy heart
Dilates with fervent joys, and eager soul
Prompts to pursue the sparkling glass, *besure*
'Tis time to shun it. PHILLIPS.

6. The quantity of wine usually contained in a glass; a draught.

While a man thinks one glass *more will not make him drunk, that one* glass *hath disabled him from well discerning his present condition.*
TAYLOR'S RULE OF LIVING HOLY.

The first glass *may pass for health, the second for good-humour, the third for our friends; but the fourth is for our enemies.*
TEMPLE.

7. A perspective glass.

Like those who have surveyed the moon by glasses, *I can only tell of a new and shining world above us; but not relate the riches and glories of the place.* DRYDEN.

To **GLAVER.** *v.n.* [*glave*, Welsh, flattery; *gliwan*, Saxon, to flatter. It is still retained in Scotland.] To flatter; to wheedle. A low word.

Kingdoms have their distempers, intermissions, and paroxysms, as well as natural bodies; and a glavering *council is as dangerous on the one hand as a wheedling priest, or a flattering physician is on the other.* L'ESTRANGE'S FABLES.

GLE'BY. *adj.* [from *glebe.*] Turfy; perhaps in the following passage fat or fruitful, if it has indeed any meaning.

Pernicious flatt'ry! thy malignant seeds
In an ill hour, and by a fatal hand
Sadly diffus'd o'er virtue's gleby *land,*
With rising pride amidst the corn appear,
And choke the hopes and harvest of the year. PRIOR.

GLEED. *n.s.* [from *glowan*, Saxon, to glow.] A hot glowing coal. A provincial and obsolete word.

To **GLEEK.** *v.a.* [*gligman*, in Saxon, is a mimick or a droll.]

1. To sneer; to gibe; to droll upon.

I can gleek *upon occasion.*
SHAKESPEARE'S MIDSUMMER NIGHT'S DREAM.

I have seen you gleeking *or galling at this gentleman twice or thrice.*
SHAKESPEARE'S HENRY V.

2. In Scotland it is still retained, and signifies to fool or spend time idly, with something of mimickry or drollery.

GLI'TTERAND. Shining; sparkling. A participle used by *Chaucer* and the old English poets. This participial termination is still retained in Scotland.

To **GLOSS.** *v.n.* [*gloser*, Fr. from the noun.]

1. To comment.

Thou detain'st Briseis in thy bands,
By priestly glossing *on the gods commands.* DRYDEN'S FABLES.

2. To make sly remarks.

Her equals first observ'd her growing zeal,
And laughing gloss'd, *that Abra serv'd so well.* PRIOR.

To **GLOSS.** *v.a.*

1. To explain by comment.

No woman shall succeed in Salique land;
Which Salique land the French unjustly gloss
To be the realm of France.
SHAKESPEARE'S HENRY V.

In parchment then, large as the fields, he draws
Assurances, big as gloss'd *civil laws.*
DONNE.

2. To palliate by specious exposition or representation.

Is this the paradise, in description whereof so much glossing *and deceiving eloquence hath been spent?* HOOKER'S SERMONS.

Do I not reason wholly on your conduct?
You have the art to gloss *the foulest cause.*
PHILLIPS'S BRITON.

3. To embellish with superficial lustre.

But thou, who lately of the common strain
Wert one of us, if still thou do'st retain
The same ill habits, the same follies too,
Gloss'd *over only with a saint-like show,*
Then I resume the freedom which I gave,
Still thou art bound to vice, and still a slave. DRYDEN'S PERSIUS.

GLO'SSARY. *n.s.* [*glossarium*, Latin; *glossaire*, French.] A dictionary of obscure or antiquated words.

According to Varro, the most learned of the Romans, when delubrum was applied to a place, it signified such a one, in quo dei simulachrum dedicatum est; and also in the old glossaries. STILLINGFLEET.

I could add another word to the glossary. BAKER.

To **GLOUT.** *v.n.* [A low word of which I find no etymology.] To pout; to look sullen. It is still used in Scotland.

She lurks in midst of all her den, and streaks
From out a ghastly whirlpool all her necks,
Where, glowting *round her rock, to fish she falls.* CHAPMAN.

Glouting *with sullen spight, the fury shook*
Her clotted locks, and blasted with each look. GARTH.

GLUM. *adj.* [A low cant word formed by corrupting *gloom.*] Sullen; stubbornly grave.

Some, when they hear a story, look glum, *and cry, Well, what then?* GUARDIAN.

GNA'RLED. *adj.* [*gnar*, *nar*, or *nurr*, is in Staffordshire a hard knot of wood which boys drive with sticks.] Knotty.

Merciful heav'n!
Thou rather with thy sharp and sulph'rous bolt
Split'st the unwedgeable and gnarled *oak,*
Than the soft myrtle.
SHAKESPEARE'S MEASURE FOR MEASURE.

To **GNAW.** *v.a.* [*gnagan*, Saxon; *knaghen*, Dutch.]

1. To eat by degrees; to devour by slow corrosion.

To you such scabb'd harsh fruit is giv'n, as raw
Young soldiers at their exercisings gnaw.
DRYDEN'S JUVENAL.

2. To bite in agony or rage.

Alas, why gnaw *you so your nether lip?*
Some bloody passion shakes your very frame. SHAKESPEARE'S OTHELLO.

They gnawed *their tongues for pain.*
BIBLE REVELATION, XVI. 10.

He comely fell, and dying gnaw'd *the ground.* DRYDEN.

3. To wear away by biting.

Gnawing *with my teeth my bonds asunder,*
I gain'd my freedom.
SHAKESPEARE'S COMEDY OF ERROURS.

Like rotten fruit I fall, worn like a cloth
Gnawn *into rags by the devouring moth.*
SANDYS.

A lion, hampered in a net, called to a mouse to help him out of the snare: the mouse gnawed *the threads to pieces, and set the lion at liberty.* L'ESTRANGE.

4. To fret; to waste; to corrode.
5. To pick with the teeth.

His bones clean pick'd; his very bones they gnaw. DRYDEN.

GO-BY. *n.s.* Delusion; artifice; circumvention; over-reach.

Except an apprentice is instructed how to adulterate and varnish, and give you the go-by *upon occasion, his master may be charged with neglect.*
COLLIER ON PRIDE.

GO-CART. *n.s.* [*go* and *cart.*] A machine in which children are inclosed to teach them to walk, and which they push forward without danger of falling.

Young children, who are try'd in
Go-carts, *to keep their steps from sliding,*
When members knit, and legs grow stronger,
Make use of such machine no longer.
PRIOR.

GOAL. *n.s.* [*gaule*, French, a long pole set up to mark the bounds of the race.]

1. The landmark set up to bound a race; the point marked out to which racers run.

As at the Olympian games, or Pythian fields,
Part curb their fiery steeds, or shun the goal
With rapid wheels.
MILTON'S PARADISE LOST, B. II.

And the slope sun his upward beam
Shoots against the dusky pole,
Pacing toward the other goal. MILTON.

2. The starting post.

Hast thou beheld, when from the goal *they start,*
The youthful charioteers with heaving heart
Rush to the race?
DRYDEN'S VIRGIL'S GEORGICKS.

3. The final purpose; the end to which a design tends.

Our poet has always the goal *in his eye, which directs him in his race: some beautiful design, which he first establishes, and then contrives the means, which will naturally conduct him to his end.*
DRYDEN'S OVID, PREFACE.

Each individual seeks a sev'ral goal;
But heav'n's great view is one, and that the whole. POPE.

So man, who here seems principal alone,
Perhaps acts second to some sphere unknown;
Touches some wheel, or verges to some goal;
'Tis but a part we see, and not a whole.
POPE'S ESSAY ON MAN.

4. It is sometimes improperly written for *gaol*, or *jail.*

GOB. *n.s.* [*gobe*, French.] A small quantity. A low word.

Do'st think I have so little wit as to part with such a gob *of money?*
L'ESTRANGE.

To **GO'BBLE.** *v.a.* [*gober*, to swallow, old French.] To swallow hastily with tumult and noise.

The sheep were so keen upon the acorns, that they gobbled *up now and then a piece of the coat along with them.*
L'ESTRANGE.

Of last year's corn in barn great store;
Fat turkeys gobbling *at the door.*
PRIOR.

The time too precious now to waste,
And supper gobbled *up in haste,*
Again afresh to cards they run. SWIFT.

GO'DLING. *n.s.* [from *god.*] A little divinity; a diminutive god.

Thy puny godlings *of inferior race,*
Whose humble statues are content with brass. DRYDEN'S JUVENAL.

GO'LDFINCH. *n.s.* [*goldfinc*, Saxon.] A singing bird, so named from his golden colour. This is called in Staffordshire a *proud taylor*.

Of singing birds they have linnets, goldfinches, *ruddocks, Canary-birds, blackbirds, thrushes, and divers others.*
CAREW.

A goldfinch *there I saw, with gaudy pride*
Of painted plumes, that hopp'd from side to side. DRYDEN.

GO'LDFINDER. *n.s.* [*gold* and *find.*] One who finds gold. A term ludicrously applied to those that empty jakes.

His empty paunch that he might fill,
He suck'd his vittels through a quill;

Untouch'd it pass'd between his grinders,
Or't had been happy for goldfinders.
SWIFT.

GOO'D-CONDITIONED. *adj.* Without ill qualities or symptoms. Used both of things and persons, but not elegantly.

No surgeon, at this time, dilates an abscess of any kind by injections, when the pus is good-conditioned. SHARP'S SURGERY.

GOOD-NOW. *interjection.*
1. In good time; *a la bonne heure.* A gentle exclamation of intreaty. It is now a low word.

Good-now *sit down, and tell me, he that knows,*
Why this same watch?
SHAKESPEARE'S HAMLET.

2. A soft exclamation of wonder.

Good-now, good-now, *how your devotions jump with mine!*
DRYDEN'S SPANISH FRYAR.

GOOSE. *n.s.* plural *geese.* [*gos*, Saxon; *goes*, Dutch, *gawe*, Erse, sing. *gewey*, plural.]
1. A large waterfowl proverbially noted, I know not why, for foolishness.

Thou cream-faced lown,
Where got'st thou that goose *look?*
SHAKESPEARE'S MACBETH.

Since I pluckt geese, *play'd truant, and whipt top, I knew not what 'twas to be beaten 'till lately.* SHAKESPEARE.

Smile you my speeches, as I were a fool?
Goose, *if I had you upon Sarum plain,*
I'd drive ye cackling home to Camelot.
SHAKESPEARE'S KING LEAR.

Birds most easy to be drawn are waterfowl; as the goose *and swan.*
PEACHAM ON DRAWING.

Nor watchful dogs, nor the more wakeful geese,
Disturb with nightly noise the sacred peace. DRYDEN'S FABLES.

2. A taylor's smoothing iron.

Come in, taylor: here you may roast your goose. SHAKESPEARE.

To **GO'SPEL.** *v.n.* [from the noun.] To fill with sentiments of religion. This word in *Shakespeare*, in whom alone I have found it, is used, though so venerable in itself, with some degree of irony: I suppose from the gospellers, who had long been held in contempt.

Are you so gospell'd
To pray for this good man, and for his issue,
Whose heavy hand hath bow'd you to the grave? SHAKESPEARE.

GO'SPELLER. *n.s.* [from *gospel.*] A name of the followers of *Wicklif*, who first attempted a reformation from popery, given them by the Papists in reproach, from their professing to follow and preach only the gospel.

These gospellers *have had their golden days,*
Have troden down our holy Roman faith.
ROWE'S JANE SHORE.

To **GO'VERN.** *v.a.* [*gouverner*, French; *guberno*, Latin.]
1. To rule as a chief magistrate.

This inconvenience is more hard to be redressed in the governor than the governed; *as a malady in a vital part is more incurable than in an external.*
SPENSER ON IRELAND.

Slaves to our passions we become, and then
It grows impossible to govern *men.*
WALLER.

2. To regulate; to influence; to direct.

The welfare of that is the chief point, which he is to carry always in his eye, and by which he is to govern *all his counsels, designs, and actions.*
ATTERBURY'S SERMONS.

3. To manage; to restrain.

Go after her, she's desperate; govern *her.*
SHAKESPEARE'S KING LEAR.

4. [In grammar.] To have force with regard to syntax: as, *amo governs* the accusative case.
5. To pilot; to regulate the motions of a ship.

GO'VERNANTE.[117] *n.s.* [*gouvernante*, French.] A lady who has the care of young girls of quality. The more usual and proper word is *governess.*

GO'VERNESS. *n.s.* [*gouverneresse*, old French, from *govern.*]
1. A female invested with authority.

The moon, the governess *of floods,*
Pale in her anger, washes all the air,
That rheumatick diseases do abound.
SHAKESPEARE.

2. A tutoress; a woman that has the care of young ladies.

He presented himself unto her, falling down upon both his knees, and holding up his hands, as the old governess *of Danae is painted, when she suddenly saw the golden shower.* SIDNEY.

His three younger children were taken from the governess *in whose hands he put them.* CLARENDON, B. VIII.

3. A tutoress; an instructress; a directress.

Great affliction that severe governess *of the life of man brings upon those souls she seizes on.* MORE AGAINST ATHEISM.

GOUT. *n.s.* [*goutte*, French.]
1. The arthritis; a periodical disease attended with great pain.

The gout *is a disease which may affect any membranous part, but commonly those which are at the greatest distance from the heart or the brain, where the motion of the fluids is the slowest, the resistance, friction, and stricture of the solid parts the greatest, and the sensation of pain, by the dilaceration of the nervous fibres, extreme.*
ARBUTHNOT ON DIET.

One that's sick o' th' gout, *had rather*
Groan so in perplexity than be cur'd
By th' sure physician death.
SHAKESPEARE'S CYMBELINE.

This very rev'rend lecher, quite worn out
With rheumatisms, and crippled with his gout,
Forgets what he in youthful times has done,
And swinges his own vices in his son.
DRYDEN'S JUVENAL.

2. A drop. [*goutte*, French; *gutta*, Latin.] *Gut* for *drop* is still used in Scotland by physicians.

I see thee still,
And on the blade o' th' dudgeon gouts *of blood,*
Which was not so before.
SHAKESPEARE'S MACBETH.

GO'WNMAN. *n.s.* [*gown* and *man.*] A man devoted to the acts of peace; one whose proper habit is a gown.

Let him with pedants
Pore out his life amongst the lazy gownmen. ROWE.

Thus will that whole bench, in an age or two, be composed of mean, fawning gownmen, *dependants upon the court for a morsel of bread.* SWIFT.

To **GRA'BBLE.** *v.n.* [probably corrupted from *grapple.*] To grope; to feel eagerly with the hands.

My blood chills about my heart at the thought of these rogues, with their bloody hands grabbling *in my guts, and pulling out my very entrails.*
ARBUTHNOT'S HISTORY OF JOHN BULL.

GRA'MMAR. *n.s.* [*grammaire*, French; *grammatica*, Latin; *γραμματική.*]
1. The science of speaking correctly; the art which teaches the relations of words to each other.

We make a countryman dumb, whom we will not allow to speak but by the rules of grammar. DRYDEN'S DUFRESNOY.

Men, speaking language according to the

grammar *rules of that language, do yet speak improperly of things.* LOCKE.

2. Propriety or justness of speech; speech according to grammar.

Varium & mutabile semper femina, is the sharpest satire that ever was made on woman; for the adjectives are neuter, and animal must be understood to make them grammar. DRYDEN.

3. The book that treats of the various relations of words to one another.

GRA'MMAR *School. n.s.* A school in which the learned languages are grammatically taught.

Thou hast most traitorously corrupted the youth of the realm in erecting a grammar school. SHAKESPEARE'S HENRY VI.

The ordinary way of learning Latin in a grammar school *I cannot encourage.* LOCKE.

GRAMMA'RIAN. *n.s.* [*grammairien*, French, from *grammar.*] One who teaches grammar; a philologer.

Many disputes the ambiguous nature of letters hath created among the grammarians.
HOLDER'S ELEMENTS OF SPEECH.

They who have called him the torture of grammarians, *might also have called him the plague of translators.* DRYDEN.

GRAMMA'TICAL. *adj.* [*grammatical*, Fr. *grammaticus*, Latin.]

1. Belonging to grammar.

The beauty of virtue still being set before their eyes, and that taught them with far more diligent care than grammatical *rules.* SIDNEY, B. II.

I shall take the number of consonants, not from the grammatical *alphabets of any language, but from the diversity of sounds framed by single articulations with appulse.* HOLDER.

2. Taught by grammar.

They seldom know more than the grammatical *construction, unless born with a poetical genius.*
DRYDEN'S DUFRESNOY.

GRAMMA'TICALLY. *adv.* [from *grammatical.*] According to the rules or science of grammar.

When a sentence is distinguished into the nouns, the verbs, pronouns, adverbs, and other particles of speech which compose it, then it is said to be analysed grammatically. WATTS.

As grammar teacheth us to speak properly, so it is the part of rhetorick to instruct how to do it elegantly, by adding beauty to that language that before was naked and grammatically *true.*
BAKER'S REFLECTIONS ON LEARNING.

GRAMMATICA'STER. *n.s.* [Latin.] A mean verbal pedant; a low grammarian.

I have not vexed their language with the doubts, the remarks, and eternal triflings of the French grammaticasters.
RYMER'S TRAGEDIES OF THE LAST AGE.

GRA'SHOPPER. *n.s.* [*grass* and *hop.*] A small insect that hops in the Summer grass. The *cicada* of the Latins, or *cicala* of the Italians, is often by the poets translated *grashopper*, but improperly.

Her waggon spokes made of long spinners legs,
The cover of the wings of grashoppers.
SHAKESPEARE'S ROMEO AND JULIET.

Grashoppers *eat up the green of whole countries.* BACON.

Where silver lakes, with verdant shadows crown'd,
Disperse a grateful chilness all around;
The grashopper *avoids the untainted air,*
Nor in the midst of Summer ventures there. ADDISON.

The women were of such an enormous stature, that we appeared as grashoppers *before them.* ADDISON'S SPECTATOR.

GRASS. *n.s.* [*græs*, Saxon.] The common herbage of the field on which cattle feed; an herb with long narrow leaves.

Ye are grown fat as the heifer at grass, *and bellow as bulls.*
BIBLE JEREMIAH, L. 11.

The trade of beef for foreign exportation was prejudiced, and almost sunk; for the flesh being young, and only grass *fed, was thin, light and moist, and not of a substance to endure the salt, or be preserved by it, for long voyages, or a slow consumption.* TEMPLE.

You'll be no more your former you;
But for a blooming nymph will pass,
Just fifteen, coming Summer's grass.
SWIFT.

GRATE. *n.s.* [*crates*, Latin.]
1. A partition made with bars placed near to one another, or crossing each other: such as are in cloysters or prisons.

I have grated upon my good friends for three reprieves for you, and your couch-fellow, Nim; or else you had look'd through the grates, *like a geminy of baboons.*
SHAKESPEARE.

Out at a little grate *his eyes he cast*
Upon those bord'ring hills, and open plain. DANIEL'S CIVIL WAR.

A fan has on it a nunnery of lively black-eyed vestals, who are endeavouring to creep out at the grates. ADDISON.

2. The range of bars within which fires are made.

My dear is of opinion that an old fashioned grate *consumes coals, but gives no heat.*
SPECTATOR, NO. 30.

GRATIFICA'TION. *n.s.* [*gratificatio*, Latin.]
1. The act of pleasing.

They are incapable of any design above the present gratification *of their palates.*
SOUTH'S SERMONS.

2. Pleasure; delight.

How hardly is his will brought to change all its desires and aversions, and to renounce those gratifications *in which he has been long used to place his happiness?*
ROGERS'S SERMONS.

3. Reward; recompence. A low word.

GRA'VER. *n.s.* [*graveur*, French, from *grave*.]
1. One whose business is to inscribe or carve upon hard substances; one who copies pictures upon wood or metal to be impressed on paper.

If he makes a design to be graved, he is to remember that the gravers *dispose not their colours as the painters do; and that, by consequence, he must take occasion to find the reason of his design in the natural shadows of the figures, which he has disposed to cause the effect.*
DRYDEN'S DUFRESNOY.

2. The stile or tool used in graving.

With all the care wherewith I tried upon it the known ways of softening gravers, *I could not soften this.* BOYLE.

The toilsome hours in diff'rent labour slide,
Some work the file, and some the graver *guide.* GAY.

GRA'VY. *n.s.* The serous juice that runs from flesh not much dried by the fire.

They usually boil and roast their meat until it falls almost off from the bones; but we love it half raw, with the blood trickling down from it, delicately terming it the gravy, *which in truth looks more like an ichorous or raw bloody matter.*
HARVEY ON CONSUMPTIONS.

There may be a stronger broth made of vegetables than of any gravy *soup.*
ARBUTHNOT ON ALIMENTS.

GREAVES. *n.s.* [from *gréves*, French.] Armour for the legs; a sort of boots. It wants the singular number.

He had greaves *of brass upon his legs.*
BIBLE 1 SAMUEL, XVII. 6.

A shield make for him, and a helm, fair greaves, *and curets such*
As may renown thy workmanship, and honour him as much.
CHAPMAN'S ILIADS, B. XVIII.

GRE'CISM. *n.s.* [*gnæcismus*, Latin.] An idiom of the Greek language.

GRE'EDY. *adj.* [*gædig*, Sax. *graadig*, Dan. *gretig*, Dutch.]

1. Ravenous; voracious; hungry.

As a lion that is greedy *of his prey.*
BIBLE PSALMS, XVII. 12.

Be not unsatiable in any dainty thing, nor too greedy *upon meats.*
BIBLE ECCLESIASTICUS, XXXVII. 29.

He made the greedy *ravens to be Elias's caterers, and bring him food.*
KING CHARLES.

2. Eager; vehemently desirous. It is now commonly taken in an ill sense.

Greedy *to know, as is the mind of man,*
Their cause of death, swift to the fire she ran. FAIRFAX.

The ways of every one that is greedy *of gain.* BIBLE PROVERBS.

Stern look'd the fiend, as frustrate of his will,
Not half suffic'd, and greedy *yet to kill.*
DRYDEN.

While the reaper fills his greedy *hands,*
And binds the golden sheaves in brittle bands. DRYDEN'S VIRGIL.

GRE'ENWOOD. *n.s.* [*green* and *wood.*] A wood considered as it appears in the Spring or Summer. It is sometimes used as one word.

Among wild herbs under the greenwood *shade.* FAIRFAX.

It happen'd on a Summer's holiday,
That to the greenwood *shade he took his way;*
For Cymon shunn'd the church.
DRYDEN'S CYMON AND IPHIGENIA.

GRE'NADIER. *n.s.* [*grenadier*, Fr. from *grenade.*] A tall foot soldier, of whom there is one company in every regiment: such men being employed to throw grenades.

Peace allays the shepherd's fear
Of wearing cap of grenadier.
GAY'S PASTORALS.

GRE'YHOUND. *n.s.* [*grighund*, Saxon.] A tall fleet dog that chases in sight.

First may a trusty greyhound *transform himself into a tyger.* SIDNEY, B. I.

So on the downs we see, near Wilton fair,
A hast'ned hare from greedy greyhounds *go.* SIDNEY.

Th' impatient greyhound, *slipt from far,*
Bounds o'er the glebe to catch the fearful hare. DRYDEN.

GRIM. *adj.* [*grimma*, Saxon.]

1. Having a countenance of terrour; horrible; hideous; frightful.

The innocent prey in haste he does forsake,
Which quit from death, yet quakes in every limb,
With change of fear to see the lion look so grim. FAIRY QUEEN.

Thou hast a grim *appearance, and thy face*
Bears a command in't.
SHAKESPEARE'S CORIOLANUS.

Their dear causes
Would to the bleeding and the grim *alarm*
Excite the mortified man.
SHAKESPEARE'S MACBETH.

What if the breath that kindled those grim *fires,*
Awak'd, should blow them into sevenfold rage? MILTON.

Expert to turn the sway
Of battle, open when and where to close
The ridges of grim *war.*
MILTON'S PARADISE LOST, B. VI.

He that dares to die,
May laugh at the grim *face of law and scorn,*

The cruel wrinkle of a tyrant brow.
DENHAM'S SOPHY.

Their swarthy hosts would darken all our plains,
Doubling the native horrour of the war,
And making death more grim.
ADDISON'S CATO.

2. Ugly; ill-looking.

Grim *visag'd war hath smooth'd his wrinkl'd front.* SHAKESPEARE.

Venus was like her mother; for her father is but grim.
SHAKESPEARE.

GRIME. *n.s.* [from *grim.*] Dirt deeply insinuated; sullying blackness not easily cleansed.

Swart, like my shoe, but her face nothing so clean kept; for why? she sweats: a man may go over shoes in the grime *of it.*
SHAKESPEARE'S COMEDY OF ERROURS.

Collow is the word by which they denote black grime *of burnt coals or wood.*
WOODWARD ON FOSSILS.

To **GRIME.** *v.a.* [from the noun.] To dirt; to sully deeply.

My face I'll grime *with filth,*
Blanket my loins, elf all my hair in knots.
SHAKESPEARE.

GRIPE. *n.s.* [from the verb.]
1. Grasp; hold; seizure of the hand or paw.

Therefore still on high
He over him did hold his cruel claws,
Threatning with greedy gripe *to do him dy.* FAIRY QUEEN.

They put a barren sceptre in my gripe,
Thence to be wrench'd with an unlineal hand. SHAKESPEARE'S MACBETH.

Should I
Slaver with lips, as common as the stairs
That mount the Capitol; join gripes *with hands*
Made hardy with hourly falshood as with labour. SHAKESPEARE.

He gave me his hand,
And, with a feeble gripe, *says, dear, my lord,*
Command my service.
SHAKESPEARE'S HENRY V.

I fell; and with my weight the helm constrain'd,
Was drawn along, which yet my gripe *retain'd.* DRYDEN'S ÆNEID.

2. Squeeze; pressure.

Fir'd with this thought, at once he strain'd the breast;
'Tis true, the harden'd breast resists the gripe,
And the cold lips return a kiss unripe.
DRYDEN'S FABLES.

3. Oppression; crushing power.

I take my cause
Out of the gripes *of cruel men, and give it*
To a most noble judge, the king my master.
SHAKESPEARE'S HENRY VIII.

4. Affliction; pinching distress.

Adam, at the news
Heart-struck with chilling gripe *of sorrow stood,*
That all his senses bound!
MILTON'S PARADISE LOST, B. XI.

Can'st thou bear cold and hunger? Can these limbs,
Fram'd for the tender offices of love,
Endure the bitter gripes *of smarting poverty?* OTWAY.

5. [In the plural.] Belly-ach; colick.

In the jaundice the choler is wanting; and the icterical have a great sourness and gripes, *with windiness.* FLOYER.

GRI'PER. *n.s.* [from *gripe.*] Oppressor; usurer; extortioner.

Others pretend zeal, and yet are professed usurers, gripers, *monsters of men, and harpies.* BURTON ON MELANCHOLY.

GRO'CER. *n.s.* [This should be written *grosser*, from *gross*, a large quantity; a *grocer* originally being one who dealt by wholesale; or from *grossus*, a fig, which their present state seems to favour.]

A grocer *is a man who buys and sells tea, sugar and plumbs and spices for gain.* WATTS'S LOGICK.

But still the offspring of your brain shall prove
The grocer's *care, and brave the rage of Jove.* GARTH.

GRO'CERY. *n.s.* [from *grocer.*] Grocers ware, such as tea; sugar; raisins; spice.

His troops, being now in a country where they were not expected, met with many cart-loads of wine, grocery, *and tobacco.* CLARENDON, B. VIII.

GRO'TTO. *n.s.* [*grotte*, French; *grotta*, Italian.] A cavern or cave made for coolness. It is not used properly of a dark horrid cavern.

Their careless chiefs to the cool grotto's *run,*
The bow'rs of kings, to shade them from the sun. DRYDEN.

This was found at the entry of the grotto *in the Peak.* WOODWARD ON FOSSILS.

GRO'UND-BAIT. *n.s.* [from *ground* and *bait.*] A bait made of barley or malt boiled; which, being thrown into the place where you design to angle, sinks to the bottom, and draws the fish to it.

Take the depth of the place where you mean after to cast your groundbait, *and to fish.* WALTON'S ANGLER.

GROUND-RENT. *n.s.* Rent paid for the privilege of building on another man's ground.

A foot in front, and thirty-three five sevenths deep, would bring in a ground-rent *of five pounds.* ARBUTHNOT ON COINS.

GROUND-ROOM. *n.s.* A room on the level with the ground.

I beseeched him hereafter to meditate in a ground-room; *for that otherwise it would be impossible for an artist of any other kind to live near him.* TATLER, NO. 88.

To **GROWL.** *v.n.* [*grollen*, Flemish.]

1. To snarl or murmur like an angry cur.

They roam amid' the fury of their heart,
And growl *their horrid loves.*
THOMSON'S SPRING.

Dogs in this country are of the size of common mastiffs, and by nature never bark, but growl *when they are provoked.* ELLIS'S VOYAGE.

2. To murmur; to grumble.

Othello, neighbours – how he would roar about a foolish handkerchief! and then he would growl *so manfully.* GAY.

To **GRU'BBLE.** *v.n.* [*grubelen*, German, from *grub.*] To feel in the dark.

Thou hast a colour;
Now let me rowl and grubble *thee:*
Blind men say white feels smooth, and black feels rough:
Thou hast a rugged skin; I do not like thee. DRYDEN.

GRUEL. *n.s.* [*gruau*, *gruelle*, French.] Food made by boiling oatmeal in water; any kind of mixture made by boiling ingredients in water.

Finger of birth-strangl'd babe,
Ditch-deliver'd by a drab;
Make the gruel *thick and slab.*
SHAKESPEARE'S MACBETH.

Was ever Tartar fierce or cruel
Upon the strength of water gruel*?*
PRIOR.

Gruel *made of grain, broths, malt-drink not much hopped, posset-drinks, and in general whatever relaxeth.*
ARBUTHNOT.

GUBERNA'TION. *n.s.* [*gubernatio*, Lat.] Government; superintendency; superiour direction.

Perhaps there is little or nothing in the government of the kingdoms of nature and grace, but what is transacted by the man Jesus, inhabited by the divine power and wisdom, and employed as a medium or conscious instrument of this extensive gubernation.
WATTS'S IMPROVEMENT OF THE MIND.

GU'DGEON. *n.s.* [*goujon*, French.]
1. A small fish found in brooks and rivers, easily caught, and therefore made a proverbial name for a man easily cheated.

'Tis true, no turbets dignify my boards;
But gudgeons, *flounders, what my Thames affords.* POPE.

This he did to draw you in, like so many gudgeons, *to swallow his false arguments.* SWIFT.

2. Something to be caught to a man's own disadvantage; a bait; an allurement: gudgeons being commonly used as baits for pike.

But fish not with this melancholy bait,
For this fool's gudgeon, *this opinion.*
SHAKESPEARE'S MERCHANT OF VENICE.

To **GUGGLE.** *v.n.* [*gorgoliare*, Italian.] To sound as water running with intermissions out of a narrow mouthed vessel.

GUI'NEA. *n.s.* [from *Guinea*, a country in *Africa* abounding with gold.] A gold coin valued at one and twenty shillings.

By the word gold I must be understood to design a particular piece of matter; that is, the last guinea *that was coined.* LOCKE.

GUINE'ADROPPER. *n.s.* [*guinea* and *drop*.] One who cheats by dropping guineas.

Who now the guineadropper's *bait regards,*
Trick'd by the sharper's dice, or juggler's cards. GAY.

GU'LLYHOLE. *n.s.* [from *gully* and *hole*.] The hole where the gutters empty themselves in the subterraneous sewer.

GULO'SITY. *n.s.* [*gulosus*, Latin.] Greediness; gluttony; voracity.

They are very temperate, seldom offending in ebriety, or excess of drink; nor erring in gulosity, *or superfluity of meats.*
BROWN'S VULGAR ERROURS, B. IV. C. 10.

GUMMO'SITY. *n.s.* [from *gummous*.] The nature of gum; gumminess.

Sugar and honey make windy liquors, and the elastick fermenting particles are detained by their innate gummosity.
FLOYER.

GUN. *n.s.* [Of this word there is no satisfactory etymology. Mr. *Lye* observes that *gun* in Iceland signifies *battle*; but when guns came into use we had no commerce with Iceland.] The general name for firearms; the instrument from which shot is discharged by fire.

These dread curses, like the sun 'gainst glass,
Or like an overcharged gun, *recoil*
And turn upon thyself.
SHAKESPEARE'S HENRY VI. P. II.

The emperor, smiling, said that never emperor was yet slain with a gun.
KNOLLES'S HISTORY OF THE TURKS.

The bullet flying, makes the gun *recoil.*
CLEAVELAND.

In vain the dart or glitt'ring sword we shun,
Condemn'd to perish by the slaught'ring gun. GRANVILLE.

GU'NPOWDER. *n.s.* [*gun* and *powder*.] The powder put into guns to be fired. It consists of about twenty parts of nitre, three parts of sulphur, and three of charcoal. The proportions are not exactly kept.

> Gunpowder *consisteth of three ingredients, saltpetre, small-coal and brimstone.* BROWN'S VULGAR ERROURS, B. II.

> *Burning by* gunpowder *frequently happens at sea.* WISEMAN.

GU'STO. *n.s.* [Italian.]

1. The relish of any thing; the power by which any thing excites sensations in the palate.

> *Pleasant* gustos *gratify the appetite of the luxurious.* DERHAM.

2. Intellectual taste; liking.

> *In reading what I have written, let them bring no particular* gusto *along with them.* DRYDEN.

To **GU'TTLE.** *v.n.* [from *gut*.] To feed luxuriously; to gormandise. A low word.

> *His jolly brother, opposite in sense,*
> *Laughs at his thrift; and, lavish of expence,*
> *Quaffs, crams, and* guttles *in his own defence.* DRYDEN.

To **GU'TTLE.** *v.a.* [from *gut*.] To swallow.[118]

> *The fool spit in his porridge, to try if they'd hiss: they did not hiss, and so he* guttled *them up, and scalded his chops.* L'ESTRANGE.

GYMNA'STICALLY. *adv.* [from *gymnastick*.] Athletically; fitly for strong exercise.

> *Such as with agility and vigour have not the use of either, who are not* gymnastically *composed, nor actively use those parts.* BROWN'S VULGAR ERROURS, B. IV. C. 5.

GYMNA'STICK. *adj.* [*γυμναστικός*; *gymnastique*, French.] Pertaining to athletick exercises; consisting of leaping, wrestling, running, throwing the dart, or quoit.

> *The Cretans wisely forbid their servants* gymnasticks *as well as arms; and yet your modern footmen exercise themselves daily, whilst their enervated lords are softly lolling in their chariots.* ARBUTHNOT AND POPE'S MARTIN SCRIBLERUS.

GY'MNICK. *adj.* [*γυμνικός*; *gymnique*, French.] Such as practise the athletick or gymnastick exercises.

> *Have they not sword-players, and ev'ry sort*
> *Of* gymnick *artists, wrestlers, riders, runners.* MILTON.

H

Is in English, as in other languages, a note of aspiration, sounded only by a strong emission of the breath, without any conformation of the organs of speech, and is therefore by many grammarians accounted no letter. The *h* in English is scarcely ever mute at the beginning of a word, or where it immediately precedes a vowel; as *house*, *behaviour*: where it is followed by a consonant it has no sound, according to the present pronunciation: but anciently, as now in Scotland, it made the syllable guttural; as *right*, *bought*.

HA. *interject.* [*ha*, Latin.]
1. An expression of wonder, surprise, sudden question, or sudden exertion.

> *You shall look fairer ere I give or hazard:*
> *What says the golden chest?* ha! *let me see.*
> SHAKESPEARE.

> Ha! *what art thou! thou horrid headless trunk!*
> *It is my Hastings!*
> ROWE'S JANE SHORE.

2. An expression of laughter.[119]

> *He saith among the trumpets* ha, ha, *and he smelleth the battle afar off.*
> BIBLE JOB, XXXIX. 25.

> Ha, ha, *'tis what so long I wish'd and vow'd;*
> *Our plots and delusions*
> *Have wrought such confusions,*
> *That the monarch's a slave to the crowd.*
> DRYDEN'S ALBION.

HA'BNAB. *adv.* [*hap ne hap*, or *nap*; as *would ne would*, *will ne will*; that is, *let it happen or not.*] At random; at the mercy of chance; without any rule or certainty of effect.

> *He circles draws and squares,*
> *With cyphers, astral characters;*
> *Then looks 'em o'er to understand 'em,*
> *Although set down* habnab *at random.*
> HUDIBRAS, P. II.

HA'GGESS. *n.s.* [from *hog* or *hack.*] A mass of meat, generally pork chopped, and inclosed in a membrane. In Scotland it is commonly made in a sheep's maw of the entrails of the same animal, cut small, with suet and spices.

To **HA'GGLE.** *v.a.* [corrupted from *hackle* or *hack.*] To cut; to chop; to mangle.[120]

> *Suffolk first died, and York all* haggled *o'er*
> *Comes to him where in gore he lay insteep'd.* SHAKESPEARE HENRY V.

To **HA'GGLE.** *v.n.* To be tedious in a bargain; to be long in coming to the price.

HAIRLA'CE. *n.s.* [*hair* and *lace.*] The fillet with which women tie up their hair.

Worms are commonly resembled to a woman's hairlace *or fillet, thence called tenia.* HARVEY ON CONSUMPTIONS.

If Molly happens to be careless,
And but neglects to warm her hairlace,
She gets a cold as sure as death. SWIFT.

HALF-PENY. *n.s.* plural *half-pence.* [*half* and *peny.*] A copper coin, of which two make a peny.

There shall be in England seven half-peny *loaves sold for a peny.*
SHAKESPEARE'S HENRY VI. P. II.[121]

Bardolph stole a lute-case, bore it twelve leagues, and sold it for three half-pence.
SHAKESPEARE'S HENRY V.

I thank you; and sure, dear friend, my thanks are too dear of a half-peny.
SHAKESPEARE.

He cheats for half-pence, *and he doffs his coat*
To save a farthing in a ferryboat.
DRYDEN'S PERSIUS.

Never admit this pernicious coin, no not so much as one single half-peny. SWIFT.

You will wonder how Wood could get his majesty's broad seal for so great a sum of bad money, and that the nobility here could not obtain the same favour, and make our own half-pence *as we used to do.* SWIFT.

HALF-SCHOLAR. *n.s.* Imperfectly learned.

We have many half-scholars *now-a-days, and there is much confusion and inconsistency in the notions and opinions of some persons.*
WATTS'S IMPROVEMENT OF THE MIND.

HALF-SIGHTED. *adj.* [*half* and *sight.*] Seeing imperfectly; having weak discernment.

The officers of the king's houshold had need be provident, both for his honour and thrift: they must look both ways, else they are but half-sighted.
BACON'S ADVICE TO VILLIERS.

HALLUCINA'TION. *n.s.* [*hallucinatio*, Latin.] Errour; blunder; mistake; folly.

A wasting of flesh, without cause, is frequently termed a bewitched disease; but questionless a meer hallucination *of the vulgar.* HARVEY ON CONSUMPTIONS.

This must have been the hallucination *of the transcriber, who probably mistook the dash of the I for a T.*
ADDISON'S SPECTATOR.

HA'LSER. *n.s.* [from *hals*, neck, and *seel*, a rope. It is now in marine pronunciation corrupted to *hawser.*] A rope less than a cable.

A beechen mast then in the hollow base
They hoisted, and with well-wreath'd halsers *hoise*
Their white sails.
CHAPMAN'S ODYSSEY, B. II.

No halsers *need to bind these vessels here,*
Nor bearded anchors; for no storms they fear. DRYDEN'S VIRGIL.

HA'MMOCK. *n.s.* [*hamaca*, Saxon.] A swinging bed.

Prince Maurice of Nassau, who had been accustomed to hammocks, *used them all his life.* TEMPLE.

HA'MPER. *n.s.* [Supposed by *Minshew* to be contracted from *hand panier*; but *hanaperium* appears to have been a word long in use, whence *hanaper*, *hamper.*] A large basket for carriage.

What powder'd wigs! what flames and darts!

What hampers *full of bleeding hearts.* SWIFT.

HA'NAPER. *n.s.* [*hanaperium*, low Latin.] A treasury; an exchequer. The clerk of the hanaper *receives* the fees due to the king for the seal of charters and patents.

The fines for all original writs were wont to be immediately paid into the hanaper *of the Chancery.* BACON.

HA'ND-BARROW. *n.s.* A frame on which any thing is carried by the hands of two men, without wheeling on the ground.

A hand-barrow, *wheelbarrow, shovel and spade.* TUSSER.

Set the board whereon the hive standeth on a hand-barrow, *and carry them to the place you intend.* MORTIMER'S HUSBANDRY.

HAND-BASKET. *n.s.* A portable basket.

You must have woollen yarn to tie grafts with, and a small hand-basket *to carry them in.* MORTIMER'S HUSBANDRY.

HA'NDICRAFT. *n.s.* [*hand* and *craft.*] Manual occupation; work performed by the hand.

The nurseries for children of ordinary gentlemen and handicrafts *are managed after the same manner.* GULLIVER'S TRAVELS.

The cov'nants thou shalt teach by candle-light,
When puffing smiths, and ev'ry painful trade
Of handicrafts, *in peaceful beds are laid.*
DRYDEN'S JUVENAL.

Particular members of convents have excellent mechanical genius's, and divert themselves with painting, sculpture, architecture, gardening, and several kinds of handicrafts. ADDISON.

HA'NDKERCHIEF. *n.s.* [*hand* and *kerchief.*] A piece of silk or linen used to wipe the face, or cover the neck.

She found her sitting in a chair, in one hand holding a letter, in the other her handkerchief, *which had lately drunk up the tears of her eyes.* SIDNEY, B. II.

He was torn to pieces with a bear: this avouches the shepherd's son, who has not only his innocence, but a handkerchief *and rings of his, that Paulina knows.* SHAKESPEARE'S WINTER'S TALE.

They did not make use of handkerchiefs, *but of the lacinia or border of the garment, to wipe their face.* ARBUTHNOT.

HANDS *off.* A vulgar phrase for keep off; forbear.

They cut a stag into parts; but as they were entering upon the dividend, hands off, *says the lion.* L'ESTRANGE'S FABLES.

HA'NDSEL. *n.s.* [*hansel*, a first gift, Dutch.] The first act of using any thing; the first act of sale.[122]

The apostles term it the pledge of our inheritance, and the hansel *or earnest of that which is to come.* HOOKER.

Thou art joy's handsel; *heav'n lies flat in thee,*
Subject to ev'ry mounter's bended knee.
HERBERT.

HA'NDWRITING. *n.s.* [*hand* and *writing.*] A cast or form of writing peculiar to each hand.

That you beat me at the mart, I have your hand to show;
If the skin were parchment, and the blows you gave me ink,
Your own handwriting *would tell you what I think.* SHAKESPEARE.

To no other cause than the wise providence of God can be referred the diversity of handwritings. COCKBURN.

HA'NDYDANDY. *n.s.* A play in which children change hands and places.

See how yond justice rails upon yond simple thief! Hark in thine ear: change places, and, handydandy, *which is the justice, which is the thief.* SHAKESPEARE'S KING LEAR.

Neither cross and pile, nor ducks and drakes, are quite so ancient as handydandy. ARBUTHNOT AND POPE'S MARTIN SCRIBLERUS.

HAN'T, for *has not*, or *have not.*

That roguish leer of your's makes a pretty woman's heart ake: you han't *that simper about the mouth for nothing.* ADDISON.

HAP-HAZARD. *n.s.* Chance; accident.[123]

The former of these is the most sure and infallible way; but so hard that all shun it, and had rather walk as men do in the dark by hap-hazard, *than tread so long and intricate mazes for knowledge sake.* HOOKER, B. I. S. 7.

We live at haphazard, *and without any insight into causes and effects.* L'ESTRANGE.

We take our principles at hap-hazard *upon trust, and without ever having examined them; and then believe a whole system, upon a presumption that they are true.* LOCKE.

HARA'NGUE. *n.s.* [*harangue*, French. The original of the French word is much questioned: *Menage* thinks it a corruption of *hearing*, English; *Junius* imagines it to be *discours au rang*, to a circle, which the Italian *arringo* seems to favour. Perhaps it may be from *orare*, or *orationare*, *orationer*, *oraner*, *aranger*, *haranguer.*] A speech; a popular oration.

Gray-headed men, and grave, with warriors mix'd,
Assemble, and harangues *are heard; but soon*
In factious opposition.
MILTON'S PARADISE LOST, B. XI.

Nothing can better improve political schoolboys than the art of making plausible or implausible harangues, *against the very opinion for which they resolve to determine.* SWIFT.

A multitude of preachers neglect method in their harangues. WATTS'S IMPROVEMENT OF THE MIND.

To **HARA'NGUE.** *v.n.* [*haranguer*, French.] To make a speech; to pronounce an oration.

HARA'NGUER. *n.s.* [from *harangue.*] An orator; a publick speaker: generally with some mixture of contempt.

HARDHA'NDED. *adj.* [*hard* and *hand.*] Coarse; mechanick; one that has hands hard with labour.

—— Hardhanded *men that work in Athens here,*
Which never labour'd in their minds 'till now. SHAKESPEARE.

HA'RDHEAD. *n.s.* [*hard* and *head.*] Clash of heads; manner of fighting in which the combatants dash their heads together.

I have been at hardhead *with your butting citizens; I have routed your herd, I have disperst them.* DRYDEN'S SPANISH FRYAR.

HARDLA'BOURED. *adj.* [*hard* and *labour.*] Elaborate; studied; diligently wrought.

How chearfully the hawkers cry
A satire, and the gentry buy!
While my hardlabour'd *poem pines;*
Unfold upon the printer's lines. SWIFT.

HA'RDWARE. *n.s.* [*hard* and *ware.*] Manufactures of metal.

HA'RDWAREMAN. *n.s.* [*hardware* and *man*.] A maker or seller of metalline manufactures.

One William Wood, an hardwareman, *obtains by fraud a patent in England to coin 108,000 l. in copper to pass in Ireland, leaving us liberty to take or refuse.* SWIFT.

HARE. *n.s.* [*hara*, Saxon; *karh*, Erse.]
1. A small quadruped, with long ears and short tail, that moves by leaps, remarkable for timidity, vigilance, and fecundity; the common game of hunters.

Dismay'd not this
Our captains Macbeth and Banquo?
—— Yes,
As sparrows, eagles; or the hare, *the lion.*
SHAKESPEARE'S MACBETH.

We view in the open champaign a brace of swift greyhounds coursing a good stout and well breathed hare. MORE.

Your dressings must be with Galen's powder and hare's *fur.*
WISEMAN'S SURGERY.

Poor is the triumph o'er the timid hare.
THOMSON'S AUTUMN.

2. A constellation.

The hare *appears, whose active rays supply*
A nimble force, and hardly wings deny.
CREECH.

HA'RLEQUIN. *n.s.* [This name is said to have been given by *Francis* of France to a busy buffoon, in ridicule of his enemy *Charles le quint*. *Menage* derives it more probably from a famous comedian that frequented M. *Harlay*'s house, whom his friends called *Harlequino*, little Harley. *Trevoux*.] A buffoon who plays tricks to divert the populace; a Jack-pudding; a zani.

The joy of a king for a victory must not be like that of a harlequin *upon a letter from his mistress.* DRYDEN.

The man in graver tragick known,
Though his best part long since was done,
Still on the stage desires to tarry;
And he who play'd the harlequin,
After the jest still loads the scene,
Unwilling to retire, though weary.
PRIOR.

HA'RNESS. *n.s.* [*harnois*, French, supposed from *iern* or *hiern*, Runnick; *hiairn*, Welsh and Erse, iron.]
1. Armour; defensive furniture of war.[124]

A goodly knight, all dress'd in harness *meet,*
That from his head no place appeared to his feet. FAIRY QUEEN.

Doff thy harness, *youth:*
I am to-day i' th' vein of chivalry.
SHAKESPEARE'S TROILUS AND CRESSIDA.

Of no right, nor colour like to right,
He doth fill fields with harness.
SHAKESPEARE'S HENRY IV. P. I.

Were I a great man, I should fear to drink:
Great men should drink with harness *on their throats.* SHAKESPEARE.

2. The traces of draught horses, particularly of carriages of pleasure or state: of other carriages we say *geer*.

Or wilt thou ride? Thy horses shall be trapp'd,
Their harness *studded all with gold and pearl.* SHAKESPEARE.

Their steeds around,
Free from their harness, *graze the flow'ry ground.* DRYDEN.

HA'RPING. *Iron. n.s.* [from *harpago*, Latin.] A bearded dart with a line fastened to the handle, with which whales are struck and caught.

The boat which on the first assault did go,
Struck with a harping iron *the younger foe;*
Who, when he felt his side so rudely gor'd,
Loud as the sea that nourish'd him he roar'd. WALLER.

HARPONE'ER. *n.s.* [*harponeur*, French, from *harpoon.*] He that throws the harpoon in whalefishing.

HARPO'ON. *n.s.* [*harpon*, French.] A harping iron.

HASK. *n.s.* This seems to signify a case or habitation made of rushes or flags.

Phœbus, weary of his yearly task,
Established hath his steeds in lowly lay,
And taken up his inn in fishes hask.
SPENSER'S PASTORALS.

HA'SSOCK. *n.s.* [*haseck*, German. *Skinner.*]

1. A thick mat on which men kneel at church.

He found his parishioners very irregular; and in order to make them kneel, and join in the responses, he gave every one of them a hassock *and common prayer book.* ADDISON.

2. In Scotland it is applied to any thing made of rushes or privet, on which a person may sit: it is therefore probable that *hassock* and *hask* are the same.

HA'STY-PUDDING. *n.s.* A pudding made of milk and flower, boiled quick together; as also of oatmeal and water boiled together.

Sure hasty-pudding *is thy chiefest dish,*
With bullock's liver, or some stinking fish.
DORSET.

HA'TCASE. *n.s.* [*hat* and *case.*] A slight box for a hat.

I might mention a hatcase, *which I would not exchange for all the beavers in Great Britain.* ADDISON'S SPECTATOR.

HATCH. *n.s.* [from the verb.]

1. A brood excluded from the egg.
2. The act of exclusion from the egg.
3. Disclosure; discovery.

Something's in his soul,
O'er which his melancholy sits on brood;
And, I do doubt, the hatch *and the disclose*
Will be some danger.
SHAKESPEARE'S HAMLET.

4. [*Hæca*, Saxon; *hecke*, Dutch, a bolt.] The half door; the opening over the door.[125]

Something about, a little from the right,
In at the window, or else o'er the hatch.
SHAKESPEARE'S KING JOHN.

5. [In the plural.] The doors or openings by which they descend from one deck or floor of a ship to another.

To the king's ship, invisible as thou art,
There shalt thou find the mariners asleep
Under the hatches.
SHAKESPEARE'S TEMPEST.

There she's hid;
The mariners all under hatches *stow'd.*
SHAKESPEARE'S TEMPEST.

So seas, impell'd by winds with added pow'r,
Assault the sides, and o'er the hatches *tow'r.* DRYDEN.

A ship was fasten'd to the shore;
The plank was ready laid for safe ascent,
For shelter there the trembling shadow bent,
And skip'd and sculk'd, and under hatches *went.* DRYDEN.

6. *To be under* HATCHES. To be in a state of ignominy, poverty, or depression.

He assures us how this fatherhood began in Adam, continued its course 'till the flood, got out of the ark with Noah, made and supported all the kings of the earth, 'till the captivity in Egypt, and then the poor fatherhood was under hatches. LOCKE.

7. *Hatches.* Floodgates. *Ainsworth.*

HA'TCHET-FACE. *n.s.* An ugly face; such, I suppose, as might be hewn out of a block by a hatchet.

An ape his own dear image will embrace;
An ugly beau adores a hatchet-face.
DRYDEN.

To **HA'TTER.** *v.a.* [Perhaps corrupted from *batter.*] To harass; to weary; to wear out with fatigue.

He's hatter'd *out with pennance.*
DRYDEN.

HA'TTER. *n.s.* [from *hat.*] A maker of hats.

A hatter *sells a dozen of hats for five shillings a piece.* SWIFT.

HA'VEN. *n.s.* [*haven*, Dutch; *havre*, French.]

1. A port; a harbour; a safe station for ships.

Only love was threatened and promised to him, and so to his cousin, as both the tempest and haven *of their best years.*
SIDNEY, B. II.

Order for sea is given:
They have put forth the haven.
SHAKESPEARE'S ANTONY AND CLEOPATRA.

After an hour and a half sailing, we entered into a good haven, *being the port of a fair city.* BACON'S NEW ATLANTIS.

The queen beheld, as soon as day appear'd,
The navy under sail, the haven *clear'd.*
DENHAM.

We may be shipwreckt by her breath:
Love, favour'd once with that sweet gale,
Doubles his haste, and fills his sail,
'Till he arrive, where she must prove
The haven, *or the rock of love.*
WALLER.

2. A shelter; an asylum.

All places, that the eye of heaven visits,
Are to a wise man ports and happy havens. SHAKESPEARE'S RICHARD II.

HA'VENER. *n.s.* [from *haven.*] An overseer of a port.

These earls and dukes appointed their special officers, as receiver, havener, *and customer.*
CAREW'S SURVEY OF CORNWAL.

HA'VER is a common word in the northern counties for oats: as, *haver* bread for oaten bread.[126]

When you would anneal, take a blue stone, such as they make haver *or oat cakes upon, and lay it upon the cross bars of iron.*
PEACHAM.

HAW. *n.s.* [*hag*, Saxon.]

1. The berry and seed of the hawthorn.

Now sow and go harrow, where ridge ye did draw
The seed of the bremble with kernel and haw. TUSSER.

Years of store of haws *and hips commonly portend cold Winters.*
BACON'S NATURAL HISTORY.

His quarrel to the hedge was, that his thorns and his brambles did not bring forth raisins, rather than haws *and blackberries.*
L'ESTRANGE.

2. An excrescence in the eye.

3. [*haga*, Saxon; *haw*, a garden, Danish.] A small piece of ground adjoining to an house. In Scotland they call it *haugh.*

Upon the haw *at Plymouth is cut out in the ground the portraiture of two men, with clubs in their hands, whom they term Gog and Magog.*
CAREW'S SURVEY OF CORNWAL.

HAZE. *n.s.* [The etymology unknown.] Fog; mist.

HA'ZY. *adj.* [from *haze.*] Dark; foggy; misty.

Our clearest day here is misty and hazy; *we see not far, and what we do see is in a bad light.*
BURNET'S THEORY OF THE EARTH.

Oft engender'd by the hazy *North,*
Myriads on myriads, insect armies waft.
THOMSON.

HE. *pronoun.* gen. *him*; plur. *they*; gen. *them*. [*hy*, Dutch; *he*, Saxon. It seems to have borrowed the plural from *ðis*, plural *ðas*, dative *ðisum*.]

1. The man that was named before.

All the conspirators, save only he,
Did that they did in envy of great Cæsar.
SHAKESPEARE.

If much you note him,
You shall offend him, *and increase his passion;*
Feed and regard him *not.*
SHAKESPEARE'S MACBETH.

I am weary of this moon; would he *would change.* SHAKESPEARE.

Adam spoke;
So cheer'd he *his fair spouse, and she was cheer'd.* MILTON.

When Adam wak'd, he *on his side*
Leaning half rais'd hung over her.
MILTON.

Thus talking, hand in hand along they *pass'd*
On to their blissful bow'rs. MILTON.

Extol
Him *first,* him *last,* him *midst.*
MILTON.

2. The man; the person. It sometimes stands without reference to any foregoing word.

He *is never poor*
That little hath, but he *that much desires.*
DANIEL.

3. Man or male being.

Such mortal drugs I have; but Mantua's law
Is death to any he *that utters them.*
SHAKESPEARE'S ROMEO AND JULIET.

Ay, crook-back, here I stand to answer thee, or any he *the proudest of thy sort.*
SHAKESPEARE'S HENRY VI. P. III.

Tros and his race the sculptor shall employ,
And he *the god who built the walls of Troy.* DRYDEN'S VIRGIL.

4. Male: as, a *he* bear, a *he* goat. It is used where the male and female have not different denominations.

The he's *in birds have the fairest feathers.*
BACON'S NATURAL HISTORY.

5. In the two last senses *he* is rather a noun than pronoun.

HE'ADACH. *n.s.* [*head* and *ach.*] Pain in the head.

From the cruel headach,
Riches do not preserve. SIDNEY, B. I.

Nothing more exposes to headachs, *colds, catarrhs, and coughs, than keeping the head warm.* LOCKE.

In the headach *he orders the opening of the vein of the forehead.* ARBUTHNOT.

At some dear idle time,
Not plagu'd with headachs, *or the want of rhyme.* POPE.

HE'ADLONG. *adv.* [*head* and *long.*]

1. With the head foremost. It is often doubtful whether this word be adjective or adverb.

I'll look no more,
Lest my brain turn, and the deficient sight
Topple down headlong.
SHAKESPEARE'S KING LEAR.

Who, while he steering view'd the stars, and bore
His course from Africk to the Latian shore,
Fell headlong *down.*
DRYDEN'S ÆNEID. B. VI.

Headlong *from thence the glowing fury springs*
And o'er the Theban palace spreads her wings. POPE.

2. Rashly; without thought; precipitately.

To give Ahab such warning, as might infallibly have prevented his destruction, was esteemed by him evil; and to push him on headlong *into it, because he was fond of it, was accounted good.*
SOUTH'S SERMONS.

Some ask for envy'd pow'r, which publick hate

Pursues and hurries headlong *to their fate;*
Down go the titles.
DRYDEN'S JUVENAL'S SATIRES, X.

3. Hastily; without delay or respite.

Unhappy offspring of my teeming womb!
Dragg'd headlong *from thy cradle to thy tomb.* DRYDEN.

4. It is very negligently used by *Shakespeare.*

Hence will I drag thee headlong *by the heels*
Unto a dunghill, which shall be thy grave.
SHAKESPEARE'S HENRY VI.

HE'ADWORKMAN. *n.s.* [*head, work* and *man.*] The foreman, or chief servant over the rest.

Can Wood be otherwise regarded than as the mechanick, the headworkman, *to prepare his furnace, metal, and stamps?*
SWIFT'S ADDRESS TO PARLIAMENT.

HEARSE. *n.s.* [of unknown etymology.]
1. A carriage in which the dead are conveyed to the grave.
2. A temporary monument set over a grave.

To add to your laments,
Wherewith you now bedew king Henry's hearse,
I must inform you of a dismal fight.
SHAKESPEARE'S HENRY VI.

HEART-BREAKER. *n.s.* A cant name for a woman's curls, supposed to break the heart of all her lovers.

Like Sampson's heartbreakers, *it grew*
In time to make a nation rue.
HUDIBRAS, P. I.

HEART-FELT. *adj.* Felt in the conscience.

What nothing earthly gives, or can destroy,
The soul's calm sun-shine, and the heart-felt *joy,*
Is virtue's prize.
POPE'S ESSAY ON MAN.

HEART-STRUCK. *adj.*
1. Driven to the heart; infixed for ever in the mind.

Who is with him?
—— *None but the fool who labours to out-jest*
His heart-struck *injuries.*
SHAKESPEARE'S KING LEAR.

2. Shocked with fear or dismay.

He added not; for Adam, at the news
Heart-struck, *with chilling gripe of sorrow stood,*
That all his senses bound!
MILTON'S PARADISE LOST, B. XI.

HE'ATER. *n.s.* [from *heat.*] An iron made hot, and put into a box-iron, to smooth and plait linnen.

HE'ATHEN. *n.s.* [*heyden*, German.] The gentiles; the pagans; the nations unacquainted with the covenant of grace.

Deliver us from the heathen, *that we may give thanks to thy holy name.*
BIBLE 1 CHRONICLES, XVI. 35.

If the opinions of others, whom we think well of, be a ground of assent, men have reason to be heathens *in Japan, mahometans in Turkey, papists in Spain, and protestants in England.* LOCKE.

In a paper of morality, I consider how I may recommend the particular virtues I treat of, by the precepts or examples of the ancient heathens.
ADDISON'S SPECTATOR.

HE'BDOMAD. *n.s.* [*hebdomas*, Latin.] A week; a space of seven days.

Computing by the medical month, the first hebdomad *or septenary consists of six days, seventeen hours and a half.* BROWN.

To **HEBE'TATE.** *v.a.* [*hebeto*, Latin; *hebeter*, French.] To dull; to blunt; to stupify.

The eye, especially if hebetated, *might cause the same perception.* HARVEY ON CONSUMPTIONS.

Beef may confer a robustness on the limbs of my son, but will hebetate *and clog his intellectuals.* ARBUTHNOT AND POPE'S MARTIN SCRIBLERUS.

HE'BRAISM. *n.s.* [*hebraisme*, French; *hebraismus*, Latin.] A Hebrew idiom.

Milton has infused a great many Latinisms, as well as Græcisms, and sometimes Hebraisms, *into his poem.* SPECTATOR.

HE'BRAIST. *n.s.* [*hebræus*, Latin.] A man skilled in Hebrew.

HE'BRICIAN. *n.s.* [from *Hebrew*.] One skilful in Hebrew.

The words are more properly taken for the air or ether than the heavens, as the best Hebrecians *understand them.* RALEIGH.

The nature of the Hebrew verse, as the meanest Hebrician *knoweth, consists of uneven feet.* PEACHAM.

HECTICAL, HE'CTICK. *adj.* [*hectique*, French, from ʻέξις.]

1. Habitual; constitutional.

This word is joined only to that kind of fever which is slow and continual, and ending in a consumption, is the contrary to those fevers which arise from a plethora, or too great fulness from obstruction, because it is attended with too lax a state of the excretory passages, and generally those of the skin; whereby so much runs off as leaves not resistance enough in the contractile vessels to keep them sufficiently distended, so that they vibrate oftener, agitate the fluids the more, and keep them thin and hot. *Quincy.*

A hectick *fever hath got hold*
Of the whole substance, not to be
controul'd. DONNE.

2. Troubled with a morbid heat.

No hectick *student scars the gentle maid.* TAYLOR.

HEDGE, prefixed to any word, notes something mean, vile, of the lowest class: perhaps from a *hedge*, or *hedge-born man*, a man without any known place of birth.

There are five in the first shew: the pedant, the braggart, the hedge-*priest, the fool, and the boy.* SHAKESPEARE.

The clergy do much better than a little hedge, *contemptible, illiterate vicar can be presumed to do.* SWIFT.

A person, who, by his stile and literature, seems to have been the corrector of a hedge-*press in Little Britain, proceeded gradually to an author.* SWIFT.

HEDGE-NOTE. *n.s.* [*hedge* and *note*.] A word of contempt for low writing.

When they began to be somewhat better bred, they left these hedge-notes *for another sort of poem, which was also full of pleasant raillery.* DRYDEN'S JUVENAL, DEDICATION.

HE'EL-PIECE. *n.s.* [*heel* and *piece*.] A piece fixed on the hinder part of the shoe, to supply what is worn away.

To HE'EL-PIECE. *v.a.* [*heel* and *piece*.] To put a piece of leather on a shoe-heel.

Some blamed Mrs. Bull for new heel-piecing *her shoes.* ARBUTHNOT.

HEIGH-HO. *interj.*

1. An expression of slight languour and uneasiness.

Heigh-ho*! an't be not four by the day, I'll be hang'd.* SHAKESPEARE.

2. It is used by *Dryden*, contrarily to custom, as a voice of exultation.

We'll toss off our ale 'till we cannot stand,
And heigh-ho *for the honour of old*
England. DRYDEN.

HE'IRLOOM. *n.s.* [*heir* and *geloma*, goods, Sax.] Any furniture or moveable decreed to descend by inheritance, and therefore inseparable from the freehold.

Achilles' sceptre was of wood,
Transmitted to the hero's line;
Thence through a long descent of kings
Came an heirloom, *as Homer sings.*
SWIFT.

HELTER-SKELTER. *adv.* [As *Skinner* fancies, from *heolster sceado*, the darkness of hell; hell, says he, being a place of confusion.] In a hurry; without order; tumultuously.

Sir John, I am thy Pistol, and thy friend;
And helter-skelter *have I rode to England,*
And tidings do I bring.
SHAKESPEARE'S HENRY V.

He had no sooner turned his back but they were at it helter-skelter, *throwing books at one another's heads.* L'ESTRANGE.

HEM. *n.s.* [*hem*, Saxon.]
1. The edge of a garment doubled and sewed to keep the threads from spreading.

Rowlers must be made of even cloth, white and gentle, without hem, *seam, or thread hanging by.* WISEMAN.

2. [*Hemmen*, Dutch.] The noise uttered by a sudden and violent expiration of the breath.

I would try if I could cry hem, *and have him.* SHAKESPEARE.

He loves to clear his pipes in good air, and is not a little pleased with any one who takes notice of the strength which he still exerts in his morning hems.
ADDISON'S SPECTATOR.

3. *interject.* Hem! [Latin.]

HE'NCHMAN. *n.s.* [*hync*, a servant, and *man*, *Skinner*; *hengst*, a horse, and *man*, *Spelman*.] A page; an attendant. Obsolete.

Why should Titania cross her Oberon?
I do but beg a little changeling boy,
To be my henchman.
SHAKESPEARE'S MIDSUMMER'S NIGHT'S DREAM.

Three henchmen *were for ev'ry knight assign'd,*
All in rich livery clad, and of a kind.
DRYDEN.

HERD. *n.s.* [*heord*, Saxon.]
1. A number of beasts together. It is peculiarly applied to black cattle. *Flocks* and *herds* are *sheep* and *oxen* or *kine*.

Note a wild and wanton herd,
Or race of youthful and unhandled colts,
Fetching mad bounds.
SHAKESPEARE'S MERCHANT OF VENICE.

There find a herd *of heifers, wand'ring o'er*
The neighbouring hill, and drive them to the shore. ADDISON.

2. A company of men, in contempt or detestation.

Survey the world, and where one Cato shines,
Count a degenerate herd *of Catilines.*
DRYDEN'S JUVENAL.

I do not remember where ever God delivered his oracles by the multitude, or nature truths by the herd. LOCKE.

3. It anciently signified a keeper of cattle, and in Scotland it is still used. [*hyrd*, Saxon.] A sense still retained in composition: as *goatherd*.

HEREA'FTER. *adv.* [*here* and *after*.]
1. In time to come; in futurity.

How worthy he is, I will leave to appear hereafter, *rather than story him in his own hearing.*
SHAKESPEARE'S CYMBELINE.

The grand-child, with twelve sons increas'd, departs
From Canaan, to a land hereafter *call'd Egypt.*
MILTON'S PARADISE LOST, B. XII.

Hereafter *he from war shall come,*
And bring his Trojans peace. DRYDEN.

2. In a future state.

HEREA'T. *adv.* [*here* and *at.*] At this.

One man coming to the tribune, to receive his donative, with a garland in his hand, the tribune, offended hereat, *demanded what this singularity could mean.* HOOKER, B. II.

HEREBY'. *adv.* [*here* and *by.*] By this.

In what estate the fathers rested, which were dead before, it is not hereby *either one way or other determined.* HOOKER.

Hereby *the Moors are not excluded by beauty, there being in this description no consideration of colours.* BROWN.

The acquisition of truth is of infinite concernment: hereby *we become acquainted with the nature of things.* WATTS.

HEREO'UT. *adv.* [*here* and *out.*]
1. Out of this place.

A bird all white, well feather'd on each wing,
Here-out *up to the throne of God did fly.*
SPENSER.

2. All the words compounded of *here* and a preposition, except *hereafter*, are obsolete, or obsolescent; never used in poetry, and seldom in prose, by elegant writers, though perhaps not unworthy to be retained.

HE'RESIARCH. *n.s.* [*heresiarque*, French; 'άιϱεσις and 'αϱχή.] A leader in heresy; the head of a herd of hereticks.

The pope declared him not only an heretick, but an heresiarch. STILLINGFLEET.

HE'RIOT. *n.s.* [*heregild*, Saxon.] A fine paid to the lord at the death of a landholder, commonly the best thing in the landholder's possession.

This he detains from the ivy; for he should be the true possessory lord thereof, but the olive dispenseth with his conscience to pass it over with a compliment and an heriot *every year.* HOWEL'S VOCAL FOREST.

Though thou consume but to renew,
Yet love, as lord, doth claim a heriot *due.*
CLEAVELAND.

I took him up, as your heriot, *with intention to have made the best of him, and then have brought the whole produce of him in a purse to you.* DRYDEN'S DON SEBASTIAN.

HE'RO. *n.s.* [*heros*, Latin; 'ηϱώς.]
1. A man eminent for bravery.

In which were held, by sad decease,
Heroes *and* heroesses.
CHAPMAN'S ODYSSEY.

I sing of heroes *and of kings,*
In mighty numbers mighty things.
COWLEY.

Heroes *in animated marble frown.*
POPE.

In this view he ceases to be an hero, *and his return is no longer a virtue.*
POPE'S ODYSSEY, NOTES.

These are thy honours, not that here thy bust
Is mix'd with heroes, *or with kings thy dust.* POPE.

Heroes, *kings,*
Joy thy wish'd approach to see.
WELSTED.

2. A man of the highest class in any respect.

HE'ROESS. *n.s.* [from *hero*; *herois*, Latin.] A heroine; a female hero.[127]

In which were held, by sad decease,

Heroes and heroesses.
CHAPMAN'S ODYSSEY.

HE'ROINE. *n.s.* [from *hero*; *heroine*, French.] A female hero. Anciently, according to English analogy, *heroess*.

But inborn worth, that fortune can controul,
New-strung, and stiffer bent her softer soul;
The heroine *assum'd the woman's place,*
Confirm'd her mind, and fortify'd her face. DRYDEN.

Then shall the British stage
More noble characters expose to view,
And draw her finish'd heroines *from you.*
ADDISON.

HE'RONRY, HERONSHAW. *n.s.* [from *heron*; commonly pronounced *hernry*.] A place where herons breed.

They carry their load to a large heronry *above three miles.*
DERHAM'S PHYSICO-THEOLOGY.

HERSE. *n.s.* [*hersia*, low Latin; supposed to come from *herian*, to praise.][128]

1. A temporary monument raised over a grave.

2. The carriage in which corpses are drawn to the grave.

When mourning nymphs attend their Daphnis' herse,
Who does not weep that reads the moving verse? ROSCOMMON.

Crowds of dead in decent pomp are born;
Their friends attend the herse, *the next relations mourn.*
DRYDEN'S VIRGIL'S GEORGICKS, B. IV.

On all the line a sudden vengeance waits,
And frequent herses *shall besiege your gates.* POPE.

HEY. *interj.* [from *high*.] An expression of joy, or mutual exhortation; the contrary to the Latin *hei*.

Shadwell from the town retires,
To bless the wood with peaceful lyrick;
Then hey *for praise and panegyrick.*
PRIOR.

HE'YDAY. *interj.* [for *high day*] An expression of frolick and exultation, and sometimes of wonder.

Thou'lt say anon he is some kin to thee,
Thou spend'st such heyday *wit in praising him.* SHAKESPEARE.

'Twas a strange riddle of a lady,
Not love, if any lov'd her, heyday!
HUDIBRAS, P. I.

HICCIUS DOCCIUS. *n.s.* [corrupted, I fancy, from *hic est doctus*, this or here is the learned man. Used by jugglers of themselves.] A cant word for a juggler; one that plays fast and loose.

An old dull sot, who told the clock
For many years at Bridewell dock,
At Westminster and Hicks's hall,
And hiccius doccius *play'd in all;*
Where, in all governments and times,
H' had been both friend and foe to crimes.
HUDIBRAS, P. III.

HICCO'UGH. *n.s.* [*hicken*, Danish.] A convulsion of the stomach producing sobs.

So by an abbey's skeleton of late
I heard an eccho supererogate
Through imperfection, and the voice restore,
As if she had the hiccough *o'er and o'er.*
CLEAVELAND.

Sneezing cureth the hiccough, *and is profitable unto women in hard labour.*
BROWN'S VULGAR ERROURS.

If the stomach be hurt, singultus or hiccough *follows, with vomiting and nausea.* WISEMAN'S SURGERY.

To **HI'CCOUGH.** *v.n.* [from the noun.] To sob with convulsion of the stomach.

To **HI'CKUP.** *v.n.* [corrupted from *hiccough.*] To sob with a convulsed stomach.

Quoth he, to bid me not to love,
Is to forbid my pulse to move,
My beard to grow, my ears to prick up,
Or, when I'm in a fit, to hickup.
HUDIBRAS, P. II.

HIDE and **SEEK.** *n.s.* A play in which some hide themselves, and another seeks them.

The boys and girls would venture to come and play at hide and seek *in my hair.* GULLIVER'S TRAVELS.

To **HI'GGLE.** *v.n.* [of uncertain etymology; probably corrupted from *haggle.*]

1. To chaffer; to be penurious in a bargain.

In good offices and due retributions we may not be pinching and niggardly: it argues an ignoble mind, where we have wronged, to higgle *and dodge in the amends.* HALE.

Base thou art!
To higgle *thus for a few blows,*
To gain thy knight an op'lent spouse.
HUDIBRAS, P. II.

Why all this higgling *with thy friend about such a paultry sum? Does this become the generosity of the noble and rich John Bull?* ARBUTHNOT'S HISTORY OF JOHN BULL.

2. To go selling provisions from door to door. This seems the original meaning.

HIGGLEDY-PIGGELDY. *adv.* A cant word, corrupted from *higgle*, which denotes any confused mass, as higglers carry a huddle of provisions together.

HI'GGLER. *n.s.* [from *higgle.*] One who sells provisions by retail.

HIGH-FLI'ER. *n.s.* One that carries his opinions to extravagance.

She openly professeth herself to be a high-flier; *and it is not improbably she may also be a papist at heart.* SWIFT.

HIGH-RE'D. Deeply red.

Oil of turpentine, though clear as water, being digested upon the purely white sugar of lead, has in a short time afforded a high-red *tincture.*
BOYLE ON COLOURS.

HIGH-VI'CED. Enormously wicked.

Be as a planetary plague, when Jove
Will o'er some high-vic'd *city hang his poison*
In the sick air.
SHAKESPEARE'S TIMON OF ATHENS.

HINGE. *n.s.* [or *hingle*, from *hangle* or *hang.*]

1. Joints upon which a gate or door turns.

At the gate
Of heav'n arriv'd, the gate self-open'd wide,
On golden hinges *turning.*
MILTON'S PARADISE LOST, B. V.

Then from the hinge *their strokes the gates divorce,*
And where the way they cannot find, they force. DENHAM.

Heav'n's imperious queen shot down from high;
At her approach the brazen hinges *fly,*
The gates are forc'd. DRYDEN'S ÆNEID.

2. The cardinal points of the world, East, West, North, and South.

If when the moon is in the hinge *at East,*
The birth breaks forward from its native rest;
Full eighty years, if you two years abate,
This station gives.
CREECH'S MANILIUS.

And these being hinges *of the world, create*
New powers in stars.
CREECH'S MANILIUS.

3. A governing rule or principle.

The other hinge *of punishment might turn upon a law, whereby all men, who did not*

marry by the age of five and twenty, should pay the third part of their revenue.
TEMPLE.

4. *To be off the* HINGES. To be in a state of irregularity and disorder.

The man's spirit is out of order and off the hinges; *and 'till that be put into its right frame, he will be perpetually disquieted.*
TILLOTSON, SERMON 4.

To **HIP.** *v.a.* [from *hip.*]
1. To sprain or shoot the hip.

His horse was hipp'd, *with an old motly saddle, and the stirrups of no kindred.*
SHAKESPEARE'S TAMING OF THE SHREW.

2. HIP-HOP. A cant word formed by the reduplication of *hop.*

Your different tastes divide our poets cares;
One foot the sock, t'other the buskin wears:
Thus while he strives to please, he's forc'd to do't,
Like Volscius hip-hop *in a single boot.*
CONGREVE.

To **HISS.** *v.n.* [*hissen,* Dutch.] To utter a noise like that of a serpent and some other animals. It is remarkable, that this word cannot be pronounced without making the noise which it signifies.

In the height of this bath to be thrown into the Thames, and cool'd glowing hot, in that surge, like a horseshoe; think of that; hissing *hot.*
SHAKESPEARE'S MERRY WIVES OF WINDSOR.

The merchants shall hiss *at thee.*
BIBLE EZEKIEL, XXVII. 36.

See the furies arise:
See the snakes that they rear,
How they hiss *in their hair.*
DRYDEN'S ALEXANDER'S FEAST.

Against the steed he threw
His forceful spear, which, hissing *as it flew,*
Pierc'd through the yielding planks.
DRYDEN.

To **HISS.** *v.a.* [*hiscean,* Saxon.]
1. To condemn by hissing; to explode.

Every one will hiss *him out to his disgrace.*
BIBLE ECCLESIASTICUS, XXII. 1.

Men shall pursue with merited disgrace;
Hiss, *clap their hands, and from his country chase.* SANDYS.

She would so shamefully fail in the last act, that, instead of a plaudite, she would deserve to be hissed *off the stage.* MORE.

I have seen many successions of men, who have shot themselves into the world, some bolting out upon the stage with vast applause, and others hissed *off, and quitting it with disgrace.* DRYDEN.

Will you venture your all upon a cause, which would be hissed *out of all the courts as ridiculous?* COLLIER ON DUELLING.

2. To procure hisses or disgrace.

Thy mother plays, and I
Play too; but so disgrac'd a part, whose issue
Will hiss *me to my grave.*
SHAKESPEARE'S WINTER'S TALE.

What's the newest grief?
—— *That of an hour's age doth* hiss *the speaker,*
Each minute teems a new one.
SHAKESPEARE'S MACBETH.

HISS. *n.s.* [from the verb.]
1. The voice of a serpent, and of some other animals.
2. Censure; expression of contempt used in theatres.

He heard
On all sides, from innumerable tongues,
A dismal universal hiss, *the sound*
Of publick scorn!
MILTON'S PARADISE LOST, B. X.

Fierce champion fortitude, that knows no fears
Of hisses, *blows, or want, or loss of ears.*
POPE'S DUNCIAD.

HIST. *interj.* [Of this word I know not the original: probably it may be a corruption of *hush, hush it, husht, hist.*[129]] An exclamation commanding silence.

Hist! *Romeo,* hist! *O for a falc'ner's voice,*
To lure this tassel gentle back again.
SHAKESPEARE'S ROMEO AND JULIET.

Mute silence hist *along!*
'Less Philomel will deign a song,
In her sweetest saddest plight,
Smoothing the rugged brow of night.
MILTON.

Hist, hist, *says another that stood by, away, doctor; for here's a whole pack of dismals coming.* SWIFT.

HI'STORY. *n.s.* [*'ιστοϱία*; *historia*, Latin; *histoire*, French.]

1. A narration of events and facts delivered with dignity.

Justly Cæsar scorns the poet's lays;
It is to history *he trusts for praise.*
POPE.

2. Narration; relation.

The history *part lay within a little room.*
WISEMAN'S SURGERY.

What histories *of toil could I declare?*
But still long-weary'd nature wants repair.
POPE'S ODYSSEY.

3. The knowledge of facts and events.

History, *so far as it relates to the affairs of the Bible, is necessary to divines.*
WATTS'S IMPROVEMENT OF THE MIND.

HISTRIO'NICAL, HISTRIONICK. *adj.* [from *histrio*, Latin; *histrion*, Fr.] Befitting the stage; suitable to a player; becoming a buffoon; theatrical.

To **HITCH.** *v.n.* [*hiegan*, Saxon, or *hocher*, French. *Skinner.*] To catch; to move by jerks. I know not where it is used but in the following passage.[130]

Whoe'er offends, at some unlucky time
Slides in a verse, or hitches *in a rhyme;*
Sacred to ridicule his whole life long,
And the sad burthen of some merry song.
POPE'S HORACE.

HO'BNOB. This is probably corrupted from *habnab* by a coarse pronunciation. See **HABNAB.**

His incensement at this moment is so implacable, that satisfaction can be none, but pangs of death and sepulchre: hobnob *is his word; give't, or take't.*
SHAKESPEARE'S TWELFTH NIGHT.

HOGWA'SH. *n.s.* [*hog* and *wash.*] The draff which is given to swine.

Your butler purloins your liquor, and the brewer sells you hogwash.
ARBUTHNOT'S HISTORY OF JOHN BULL.

HOLDERFO'RTH. *n.s.* [*hold* and *forth.*] An haranguer; one who speaks in publick.

Whence some tub holdersforth *have made*
In powd'ring tubs the richest trade.
HUDIBRAS, P. III.

He was confirmed in this opinion upon seeing the holderforth.
ADDISON'S FREEHOLDER.

HO'LLY. *n.s.* [*holeyn*, Saxon.] A plant.

The leaves are set about the edges with long, sharp, stiff prickles: the berries are small, round, and generally of a red colour, containing four triangular striated seeds in each. Of this tree there are several species; some variegated in the leaves, some with yellow berries, and some with white. *Miller.*

Fairest blossoms drop with every blast;
But the brown beauty will like hollies *last.*
GAY.

Some to the holly *hedge*
Nestling repair, and to the thicket some;
Some to the rude protection of the thorn.
THOMSON'S SPRING.

HO'MELY. *adv.* Plainly; coarsely; rudely.

Thus like the god his father, homely *drest,*
He strides into the hall a horrid guest.
DRYDEN'S ÆNEID.

HO'MER. *n.s.* A measure of about three pints.

An homer *of barley-seed shall be valued at fifty shekels of silver.*
BIBLE LEVITICUS, XXVII. 16.

HO'MICIDE. *n.s.* [*homicide*, French; *homicidium*, Latin.]

1. Murder; manquelling.

The apostles command to abstain from blood: construe this according to the law of nature, and it will seem, that homicide *only is forbidden; but construe it in reference to the law of the Jews, about which the question was, and it shall easily appear to have a clean other sense, and a truer, when we expound it of eating, and not of shedding blood.* HOOKER, B. IV.

2. Destruction. In the following lines it is not proper.

What wonder is't that black detraction thrives!
The homicide *of names is less than lives.*
DRYDEN.

3. [*Homicide*, Fr. *homicida*, Lat.] A murderer; a manslayer.

Your beauty, that did haunt me in my sleep,
To undertake the death of all the world,
So might I live one hour in your sweet bosom.
—— *If I thought that, I tell thee,* homicide,
These nails should rend that beauty from my cheeks. SHAKESPEARE.

Hector comes, the homicide, *to wield*
His conqu'ring arms, with corps to strew the field. DRYDEN.

HOMO'NYMOUS. *adj.* [*homonyme*, Fr. *'ομώνυμος*.] Denominating different things; equivocal; ambiguous.

As words signifying the same thing are called synonymous, so equivocal words, or those which signify several things, are called homonymous, *or ambiguous; and when persons use such ambiguous words, with a design to deceive, it is called equivocation.*
WATTS'S LOGICK.

HOMO'NYMY. *n.s.* [*homonymie*, French; *'ομονυμία*.] Equivocation; ambiguity.

To **HONE.** *v.n.* [*hongian*, Saxon.] To pine; to long for any thing.

HON'EY-COMBED. *adj.* [*honey* and *comb*.] Spoken of a piece of ordnance flawed with little cavities by being ill cast.

A mariner having discharged his gun, which was honey-combed, *and loading it suddenly again, the powder took fire.*
WISEMAN.

HO'NEY-MOON. *n.s.* [*honey* and *moon*.] The first month after marriage, when there is nothing but tenderness and pleasure.

A man should keep his finery for the latter season of marriage, and not begin to dress 'till the honey-moon *is over.* ADDISON.

To **HOOP.** *v.n.* [from *wopgan* or *wopyan*, Gothick; or *houpper*, French, derived from the Gothick. This word is generally written *whoop*, which is more proper, if we deduce it from the Gothick; and *hoop*, if we derive it from the French.] To shout; to make an outcry by way of call or pursuit.

HO'OPING-COUGH. *n.s.* [or *whooping-cough*, from *hoop*, to shout.] A convulsive cough, so called from its noise; the chine cough.

HO'PEFUL. *adj.* [*hope* and *full*.]

1. Full of qualities which produce hope; promising; likely to obtain success; likely to come to maturity; likely to gratify desire, or answer expectation.

He will advance thee:
I know his noble nature, not to let

Thy hopeful *service perish.*
SHAKESPEARE'S HENRY VIII.

You serve a great and gracious master, and there is a most hopeful *young prince whom you must not desert.* BACON.

What to the old can greater pleasure be,
Than hopeful *and ingenious youth to see?*
DENHAM.

They take up a book in their declining years, and grow very hopeful *scholars by that time they are threescore.* ADDISON.

2. Full of hope; full of expectation of success. This sense is now almost confined to Scotland, though it is analogical, and found in good writers.

Men of their own natural inclination hopeful *and strongly conceited, whatsoever they took in hand.* HOOKER, B. V.

I was hopeful *the success of your first attempts would encourage you to make trial also of more nice and difficult experiments.* BOYLE.

Whatever ills the friendless orphan bears,
Bereav'd of parents in his infant years,
Still must the wrong'd Telemachus sustain,
If hopeful *of your aid, he hopes in vain.*
POPE'S ODYSSEY.

HORI'ZON. *n.s.* [*'ορίζων.*] The line that terminates the view. The horizon is distinguished into sensible and real: the sensible horizon is the circular line which limits the view; the real is that which would bound it, if it could take in the hemisphere. It is falsely pronounced by Shakespeare *hórizon.*

When the morning sun shall raise his car
Above the border of this horizon,
We'll forward towards Warwick and his mates. SHAKESPEARE.

She began to cast with herself from what coast this blazing star should first appear, and at what time it must be upon the horizon *of Ireland.*
BACON'S HENRY VII.

Far in th' horizon *to the North appear'd,*
From skirt to skirt, a fiery region.
MILTON'S PARADISE LOST.

In his East the glorious lamp was seen,
Regent of day; and all th' horizon *round*
Invested with bright rays.
MILTON'S PARADISE LOST, B. VII.

The morning lark, the messenger of day,
Saluted in her song the morning gray;
And soon the sun arose with beams so bright,
That all th' horizon *laugh'd to see the joyous sight.* DRYDEN.

When the sea is worked up in a tempest, so that the horizon *on every side is nothing but foaming billows and floating mountains, it is impossible to describe the agreeable horrour that rises from such a prospect.* ADDISON'S SPECTATOR.

HO'ROLOGE, HOROLOGY. *n.s.* [*horologium*, Latin.] Any instrument that tells the hour: as a clock; a watch; an hourglass.

'Tis evermore the prologue to his sleep;
He'll watch the horologue *a double set,*
If drink rock not his cradle.
SHAKESPEARE'S OTHELLO.

Before the days of Jerome there were horologies, *that measured the hours not only by drops of water in glasses, called clepsydra, but also by sand in glasses, called clepsammia.* BROWN.

HO'RRID. *adj.* [*horridus*, Latin.]

1. Hideous; dreadful; shocking.

Oh!
Give colour to my pale cheek with thy blood,
That we the horrider *may seem to those*
Which chance to find us.
SHAKESPEARE'S CYMBELINE.

Not in the legions
Of horrid *hell can come a devil more damn'd,*
In evils to top Macbeth.
SHAKESPEARE'S MACBETH.

2. Shocking; offensive; unpleasing: in womens cant.

Already I your tears survey,
Already hear the horrid *things they say.*
POPE.

3. Rough; rugged.

Horrid *with fern, and intricate with thorn,*
Few paths of human feet or tracks of beasts were worn. DRYDEN.

HORRI'SONOUS. *adj.* [*horrisonus*, Latin.] Sounding dreadfully. *Dictionaries.*

HO'RSELITTER. *n.s.* [*horse* and *litter.*] A carriage hung upon poles between two horses, in which the person carried lyes along.

He that before thought he might command the waves of the sea, was now cast on the ground, and carried in an horselitter. BIBLE 2 MACCABEES, IX. 8.

HO'SPITAL. *n.s.* [*hospital*, French; *hospitalis*, Latin.]

1. A place built for the reception of the sick, or support of the poor.

They who were so careful to bestow them in a college when they were young, would be so good as to provide for them in some hospital *when they are old.* WOTTON.

I am about to build an hospital, *which I will endow handsomely for twelve old husbandmen.* ADDISON'S SPECTATOR.

2. A place for shelter or entertainment.[131]

They spy'd a goodly castle, plac'd
Foreby a river in a pleasant dale,
Which chusing for that evening's hospital,
They thither march'd.
FAIRY QUEEN, B. II.

HOSPITA'LITY. *n.s.* [*hospitalité*, French.] The practice of entertaining strangers.

The Lacedemonians forbidding all access of strangers into their coasts, are, in that respect, deservedly blamed, as being enemies to that hospitality *which, for common humanity sake, all the nations on earth should embrace.* HOOKER, B. I.

My master is of a churlish disposition,
And little recks to find the way to heav'n
By doing deeds of hospitality.
SHAKESPEARE'S AS YOU LIKE IT.

How has this spirit of faction broke all the laws of charity, neighbourhood, alliance, and hospitality? SWIFT.

HO'STLER. *n.s.* [*hosteller*, from *hostel.*] One who has the care of horses at an inn.

The cause why they are now to be permitted is want of convenient inns for lodging travellers on horseback, and hostlers *to tend their horses by the way.* SPENSER ON IRELAND.

HO'STRY. *n.s.* [corrupted from *hostelry.*] A place where the horses of guests are kept.

Swift rivers are with sudden ice constrain'd,
And studded wheels are on its back sustain'd;
An hostry *now for waggons, which before*
Tall ships of burden on its bosom bore.
DRYDEN'S GEORGICKS.

HO'TBED. *n.s.* A bed of earth made hot by the fermentation of dung.

The bed we call a hotbed *is this: there was taken horsedung, old and well rotted; this was laid upon a bank half a foot high, and supported round about with planks, and upon the top was cast sifted earth two fingers deep.*
BACON'S NATURAL HISTORY.

Preserve the hotbed *as much as possible from rain.* EVELYN.

HOTCO'CKLES. *n.s.* [*hautes coquilles*, French.] A play in which one covers his eyes, and guesses who strikes him.

The chytindra is certainly not our hotcockles; *for that was by pinching, not by striking.*
ARBUTHNOT AND POPE'S MARTIN SCRIBLERUS.

As at hotcockles *once I laid me down,*
And felt the weighty hand of many a clown,
Buxoma gave a gentle tap, and I
Quick rose, and read soft mischief in her eye. GAY'S PASTORALS.

HO'THOUSE. *n.s.* [*hot* and *house.*]

1. A bagnio; a place to sweat and cup in.

Now she professes a hothouse, *which, I think, is a very ill house too.* SHAKESPEARE'S MEASURE FOR MEASURE.

2. A brothel.

Where lately harbour'd many a famous whore,
A purging bill, now fix'd upon the door,
Tells you it is a hothouse; *so it may,*
And still be a whorehouse: th' are synonyma. BEN JONSON.

HOU'SEHOLDSTUFF. *n.s.* [*household* and *stuff.*] Furniture of an house; utensils convenient for a family.

In this war that he maketh, he still flieth from his foe, and lurketh in the thick woods, waiting for advantages: his cloke is his bed, yea and his housholdstuff. SPENSER ON IRELAND.

A great part of the building was consumed, with much costly housholdstuff. BACON'S HENRY VII.

The poor woman had her jest for her housholdstuff, *and paid her physician with a conceit for his money.* L'ESTRANGE.

HOU'SEKEEPER. *n.s.* [*house* and *keep.*]

1. Householder; master of a family.

To be said an honest man and a good housekeeper, *goes as fairly as to say a graceful man and a great scholar.* SHAKESPEARE.

If I may credit housekeepers *and substantial tradesmen, all sorts of provisions and commodities are risen excessively.* LOCKE.

2. One who lives in plenty.[132]

The people are apter to applaud housekeepers *than house-raisers.* WOTTON.

3. One who lives much at home.

How do you both? You are manifest housekeepers. *What are you sewing here?* SHAKESPEARE'S CORIOLANUS.

4. A woman servant that has care of a family, and superintends the other maid servants.

Merry folks, who want by chance
A pair to make a country-dance,
Call the old housekeeper, *and get her*
To fill a place for want of better. SWIFT.

5. A housedog.

Distinguish the housekeeper, *the hunter.* SHAKESPEARE'S MACBETH.

HO'USEWIFE. *n.s.* [*house* and *wife.* This is now frequently written *huswife*, or *hussy.*]

1. The mistress of a family.

You will think it unfit for a good housewife *to stir in or to busy herself about her housewifry.* SPENSER ON IRELAND.

I have room enough, but the kind and hearty housewife *is dead.* POPE TO SWIFT.

2. A female œconomist.

Fitting is a mantle for a bad man, and surely for a bad housewife *it is no less convenient; for some of them, that be wandering women, it is half a wardrobe.* SPENSER ON IRELAND.

Let us sit and mock the good housewife, *fortune, from her wheel, that her gifts may henceforth be disposed equally.* SHAKESPEARE.

Farmers in degree,
He a good husband, a good housewife *she.* DRYDEN.

Early housewives *leave the bed,*
When living embers on the hearth are spread. DRYDEN.

The fairest among the daughters of Britain shew themselves good stateswomen as well as good housewives. ADDISON'S FREEHOLD

3. One skilled in female business.

He was bred up under the tuition of a tender mother, 'till she made him as good an housewife *as herself: he could preserve apricocks, and make jellies.*
ADDISON'S SPECTATOR.

HOWD'YE. [Contracted from *how do ye.*] In what state is your health. A message of civility.

Years make men more talkative, but less writative; so that I now write no letters but of plain business, or plain howd'ye's, *to those few I am forced to correspond with.*
POPE.

HU'GGERMUGGER. *n.s.* [corrupted perhaps from *hug er morcker*, or hug in the dark. *Morcker* in Danish is darkness, whence our *murky*. It is written by *Sir Thomas More*, *hoker moker*. *Hoker*, in *Chaucer*, is *peevish*, *crossgrained*, of which *moker* may be only a ludicrous reduplication. *Hooke* is likewise in German *a corner*, and *moky* is in English *dark*. I know not how to determine.] Secrecy; bye-place.

Now hold in huggermugger *in their hand,*
And all the rest do rob of goods and land.
HUBBERD'S TALE.

But if I can but find them out,
Where e'er th' in huggermugger *lurk,*
I'll make them rue their handy-work.
HUDIBRAS, P. I.

There's a distinction betwixt what's done openly and barefaced, and a thing that's done in huggermugger, *under a seal of secrecy and concealment.*
L'ESTRANGE'S FABLES.

To **HUM.** *v.a.* [*hommelen*, Dutch.]

1. To make the noise of bees.

The humming *of bees is an unequal buzzing.* BACON.

An airy nation flew,
Thick as the humming *bees that hunt the golden dew*
In Summer's heat.
DRYDEN'S ÆNEID, B. VI.

So weary bees in little cells repose;
But if night-robbers lift the well-stor'd hive,
An humming *through their waxen city grows.* DRYDEN.

2. To make an inarticulate and buzzing sound.

I think he'll hear me: yet to bite his lip,
And hum *at good Cominius, much unhearts me.* SHAKESPEARE.

Upon my honour, sir, I heard a humming,
And that a strange one too, which did awake me. SHAKESPEARE.

The cloudy messenger turns me his back,
And hums; *as who should say, you'll rue.*
SHAKESPEARE'S MACBETH.

3. To pause in speaking, and supply the interval with an audible emission of breath.

Having pump'd up all his wit,
And humm'd *upon it, thus he writ.*
HUDIBRAS, P. III.

I still acquiest,
And never humm'd *and haw'd sedition,*
Nor snuffled treason.
HUDIBRAS, P. III. CANT. 2.

The man lay humming *and hawing a good while; but, in the end, he gave up himself to the physicians.* L'ESTRANGE.

Still humming *on, their drowsy course they keep,*
And lash'd so long, like tops, are lash'd asleep. POPE.

4.[133] To sing low.

The musical accents of the Indians, to us, are but inarticulate hummings; *as are ours to their otherwise tuned organs.*
GLANVILLE'S APOLOGY.

Hum *half a tune.* POPE.

5. To applaud. Approbation was commonly expressed in publick assemblies by a hum, about a century ago.

HUM. *interject.* A sound implying doubt and deliberation.

Let not your ears despise the heaviest sound
That ever yet they heard.
—— Hum! *I guess at it.*
SHAKESPEARE'S MACBETH.

See sir Robert —— hum!
And never laugh for all my life to come.
POPE.

HU'MANIST. *n.s.* [*humaniste*, French.] A philologer; a grammarian.

HUMA'NITY. *n.s.* [*humanité*, French; *humanitas*, Latin.]

1. The nature of man.

Look to thyself; reach not beyond humanity. SIDNEY.

A rarer spirit never did steer humanity. SHAKESPEARE.

The middle of humanity *thou never knewest, but the extremity of both ends.* SHAKESPEARE'S TIMON OF ATHENS.

To preserve the Hebrew intire and uncorrupt, there hath been used the highest caution humanity *could invent.* BROWN.

2. Humankind; the collective body of mankind.

If he can untie those knots, he is able to teach all humanity, *and will do well to oblige mankind by his informations.* GLANVILLE.

3. Benevolence; tenderness.

All men ought to maintain peace, and the common offices of humanity *and friendship in diversity of opinions.* LOCKE.

How few, like thee, enquire the wretched out,
And court the offices of soft humanity?
Like thee reserve their raiment for the naked,
Reach out their bread to feed the crying orphan,
Or mix their pitying tears with those that weep? ROWE.

4. Philology; grammatical studies.[134]

HUMECTA'TION. *n.s.* [*humectation*, Fr. from *humectate.*] The act of wetting; moistening.

Plates of brass, applied to a blow, will keep it down from swelling: the cause is repercussion, without humectation, *or entrance of any body.* BACON'S NATURAL HISTORY.

That which is concreted by exsiccation, or expression of humidity, will be resolved by humectation, *as earth and clay.* BROWN'S VULGAR ERROURS.

HUMICUBA'TION. *n.s.* [*humi* and *cubo*, Latin.] The act of lying on the ground.

Fasting and sackcloth, and ashes and tears, and humicubations, *used to be companions of repentance.* BRAMHALL.

HUNKS. *n.s.* [*hunskur*, sordid, Islandick.] A covetous sordid wretch; a miser; a curmudgeon.

The old hunks *was well served, to be tricked out of a whole hog for the securing of his puddings.* L'ESTRANGE.

She has a husband, a jealous, covetous, old hunks. DRYDEN.

Irus has given all the intimations of being a close hunks, *worth money.* ADDISON'S SPECTATOR.

HU'RLY, HURLYBURLY. *n.s.* [I have been told that this word owes its original to two neighbouring families named *Hurly* and *Burly*, or *Hurleigh* and *Burleigh*, which filled their part of the kingdom with contests and violence. If this account be rejected,[135] the word must be derived from *hurl*, *hurly*, and *burly*, a ludicrous reduplication. *Hurlade*, French; *hurlubrelu*, inconsiderately.] Tumult; commotion; bustle.

Winds take the ruffian billows by the top,
That with the hurley *death itself awakes.*
SHAKESPEARE'S HENRY IV.

Poor discontents,
Which gape and rub the elbow at the news
Of hurlyburly *innovation.*
SHAKESPEARE'S HENRY IV, P. I.

Methinks, I see this hurly *all on foot.*
SHAKESPEARE'S KING JOHN.

All places were filled with tumult and hurly-burly, *every man measured the danger by his own fear; and such a pitiful cry was in every place, as in cities presently to be besieged.* KNOLLES.

HUSH. *interj.* [Without etymology.] Silence! be still! no noise!

The king hath done you wrong; but hush*! 'tis so.* SHAKESPEARE.

There's something else to do; hush *and be mute,*
Or else our spell is marr'd.
SHAKESPEARE'S TEMPEST.

HU'SHMONEY. *n.s.* [*hush* and *money.*] A bribe to hinder information; pay to secure silence.

A dext'rous steward, when his tricks are found,
Hushmoney *sends to all the neighbours round;*
His master, unsuspicious of his pranks,
Pays all the cost, and gives the villain thanks. SWIFT.

HU'SSY. *n.s.* [corrupted from *housewife*: taken in an ill sense.] A sorry or bad woman; a worthless wench. It is often used ludicrously in slight disapprobation.

Get you in, hussy, *go: now will I personate this hopeful young jade.*
SOUTHERN'S INNOCENT ADULTERY.

HU'SWIFE. *n.s.* [corrupted from *housewife.*]

1. A bad manager; a sorry woman. It is common to use *housewife* in a good, and *huswife* or *hussy* in a bad sense.

Bianca,
A huswife, *that, by selling her desires,*
Buys herself bread and cloth.
SHAKESPEARE'S OTHELLO.

2. An œconomist; a thrifty woman.

Why should you want?
The bounteous huswife, *nature, on each bush*
Lays her fulness before you.
SHAKESPEARE.

HUZZA'. *interj.* A shout; a cry of acclamation.

The huzzas *of the rabble are the same to a bear that they are to a prince.*
L'ESTRANGE.

It was an unfair thing in you to keep a parcel of roaring bullies about me day and night, with huzzas *and hunting horns never let me cool.*
ARBUTHNOT'S HISTORY OF JOHN BULL.

All fame is foreign, but of true desert;
Plays round the head, but comes not to the heart:
One self-approving hour whole years outweighs
Of stupid starers and of loud huzzas.
POPE'S ESSAY ON MAN.

To **HUZZA'.** *v.n.* [from the interjection.] To utter acclamation.

A caldron of fat beef, and stoop of ale,
On the huzzaing *mob shall still prevail.*
KING'S COOKERY.

To **HUZZA'.** *v.a.* To receive with acclamation.

He was huzzaed *into the court by several thousands of weavers and clothiers.*
ADDISON.

HY'PER. *n.s.* [A word barbarously curtailed by *Prior* from *hypercritick.*] A hypercritick; one more critical than necessity requires. *Prior* did not know the meaning of the word.

Criticks I read on other men,
And hypers *upon them again.* PRIOR.

HYPERCRI'TICK. *n.s.* [*hyper-critique*, Fr. ʽυπερ and κρίτικος.] A critick exact or captious beyond use or reason.

Those hypercriticks *in English poetry differ from the opinion of the Greek and Latin judges of antiquity, from the Italians and French, and from the general taste of all ages.* DRYDEN.

HYPERCRI'TICAL. *adj.* [from *hypercritick.*] Critical beyond necessity or use.

We are far from imposing those nice and hypercritical *punctilio's, which some astrologers oblige our gardeners to.* EVELYN.

Such hypercritical *readers will consider my business was to make a body of refined sayings, only taking care to produce them in the most natural manner.* SWIFT.

HYSTE'RICAL, HYSTERICK. *adj.* [*hysterique*, French; *'υστερικός.*] **1.** Troubled with fits; disordered in the regions of the womb.

In hysterick *women the rarity of symptoms doth oft strike such an astonishment into spectators, that they report them possessed with the devil.* HARVEY ON CONSUMPTIONS.

Many hysterical *women are sensible of wind passing from the womb.* FLOYER ON THE HUMOURS.

2. Proceeding from disorders in the womb.

Parent of vapours, and of female wit,
Who gave th' hysterick *or poetick fit.* POPE'S RAPE OF THE LOCK.

This terrible scene made too violent an impression upon a woman in her condition, and threw her into a strong hysterick *fit.* ARBUTHNOT AND POPE'S MARTIN SCRIBLERUS.

HYSTE'RICKS. *n.s.* [*'υστερικός.*] Fits of women, supposed to proceed from disorders in the womb.

I

Is in English considered both as a vowel and consonant; though, since the vowel and consonant differ in their form as well as sound, they may be more properly accounted two letters.

I vowel has a long sound, as *fine*, *thine*, which is usually marked by an *e* final; and a short sound, as *fin*, *thin*. Prefixed to *e* it makes a diphthong of the same sound with the soft *i*, or double *e*, *ee*: thus *field*, *yield*, are spoken as *feeld*, *yeeld*; except *friend*, which is spoken *frend*. Subjoined to *a* or *e* it makes them long, as *fail*, *neigh*; and to *o* makes a mingled sound, which approaches more nearly to the true notion of a diphthong, or sound composed of the sounds of two vowels, than any other combination of vowels in the English language, as *oil*, *coin*. The sound of *i* before another *i*, and at the end of a word, is always expressed by *y*.

J consonant has invariably the same sound with that of *g* in *giant*; as *jade*, *jet*, *jilt*, *jolt*, *just*.

To **JA'BBER.** *v.n.* [*gabberen*, Dutch.] To talk idly; to prate without thinking; to chatter.

> *We scorn, for want of talk, to* jabber
> *Of parties.* SWIFT.

JACK Pudding**.** *n.s.* [*jack* and *pudding.*] A zani; a merry Andrew.

> *Every* jack pudding *will be ridiculing palpable weaknesses which they ought to cover.* L'ESTRANGE.
>
> *A buffoon is called by every nation by the name of the dish they like best: in French jean pottage, and in English* jack pudding. GUARDIAN.
>
> Jack pudding, *in his party-colour'd jacket,*
> *Tosses the glove, and jokes at ev'ry packet.*
> GAY.

JAGG. *n.s.* [from the verb.] A protuberance or denticulation.

> *The figure of the leaves is divided into so many* jaggs *or escallops, and curiously indented round the edges.* RAY.
>
> *Take off all the staring straws, twigs, and* jaggs *in the hive, and make them as smooth as possible.*
> MORTIMER'S HUSBANDRY.

JA'GGY. *adj.* [from *jagg.*] Uneven; denticulated.

> *His tow'ring crest was glorious to behold;*
> *His shoulders and his sides were scal'd with gold;*
> *Three tongues he brandish'd when he charg'd his foes;*
> *His teeth stood* jaggy *in three dreadful rows.* ADDISON.
>
> *Amid' those angles, infinitely strain'd,*
> *They joyful leave their* jaggy *salts behind.*
> THOMSON'S AUTUMN.

JAIL. *n.s.* [*geol*, French.] A gaol; a prison; a place where criminals are confined. See **GAOL.** It is written either way; but commonly by latter writers *jail*.

Away with the dotard, to the jail *with him.* SHAKESPEARE.

A dependant upon him paid six pound ready money, which, poor man, he lived to repent in a jail. CLARENDON.

He sigh'd and turn'd his eyes, because he knew
'Twas but a larger jail *he had in view.*
DRYDEN.

One jail *did all their criminals restrain,*
Which now the walls of Rome can scarce contain. DRYDEN.

JAKES. *n.s.* [Of uncertain etymology.] A house of office.

I will tread this unbolted villain into mortar, and daub the walls of jakes *with him.* SHAKESPEARE'S KING LEAR.

Their sordid avarice rakes
In excrements, and hires the very jakes.
DRYDEN'S JUVENAL.

Some have fished the very jakes *for papers left there by men of wit.* SWIFT.

IA'MBICK. *n.s.* [*iambique*, French; *iambicus*, Latin.] Verses composed of iambick feet, or a short and long syllable alternately: used originally in satire, therefore taken for satire.

In thy felonious heart though venom lies,
It does but touch thy Irish pen, and dies:
Thy genius calls thee not to purchase fame
In keen iambicks, *but mild anagram.*
DRYDEN.

JA'NNOCK. *n.s.* [probably a corruption of *bannock.*] Oatbread. A northern word.

JA'NTY. *adj.* [corrupted from *gentil*, French.] Showy; fluttering.

This sort of woman is a janty *slattern: she hangs on her cloaths, plays her head, and varies her posture.* SPECTATOR.

To **JA'VEL,** or Jable. *v.a.* To bemire; to soil over with dirt through unnecessary traversing and travelling. This word is still retained in Scotland and the northern counties.

JAUNT. *n.s.* [from the verb.] Ramble; flight; excursion. It is commonly used ludicrously, but solemnly by *Milton.*

Our Saviour meek, and with untroubled mind,
After his airy jaunt, *though hurry'd sore,*
Hungry and cold, betook him to his rest.
MILTON'S PARADISE REGAIN'D.

He sends me out on many a jaunt,
Old houses in the night to haunt.
HUDIBRAS, P. III.

They parted, and away posts the cavalier in quest of his new mistress: his first jaunt *is to court.* L'ESTRANGE.

If you are for a merry jaunt, *I'll try for once who can foot it farthest.*
DRYDEN'S SPANISH FRYAR.

Thus much of the scheme of my design in this part have I run over, and led my reader a long and tedious jaunt, *in tracing out these metallick and mineral bodies.*
WOODWARD.

I'CEHOUSE. *n.s.* [*ice* and *house.*] A house in which ice is reposited against the warm months.

I'D. Contracted for *I would.*

I'DIOM. *n.s.* [*idiome*, French; *'ιδίωμα.*] A mode of speaking peculiar to a language or dialect; the particular cast of a tongue; a phrase; phraseology.

He did romanize our tongue, leaving the words translated as much Latin as he found them; wherein he followed their language, but did not comply with the idiom *of ours.* DRYDEN.

Some that with care true eloquence shall teach,
And to just idioms *fix our doubtful speech.* PRIOR.

I'DIOTISM. *n.s.* [*idiotisme*, French; *'ιδιωτισμός.*]

1. Peculiarity of expression; mode of expression peculiar to a language.

Scholars sometimes in common speech, or writing, in their native language, give terminations and idiotisms *suitable to their native language unto words newly invented.* HALE.

2. Folly; natural imbecillity of mind.

JE'OPARDY. *n.s.* [This word is supposed to be derived from *j'ai perdu*, or *jeu perdu. Skinner* and *Junius.*] Hazard; danger; peril. A word not now in use.

And would ye not poor fellowship expel,
Myself would offer you t' accompany,
In this adventure's chanceful jeopardy.
HUBBERD'S TALE.

Thy rage shall burn thee up, and thou shalt turn
To ashes ere our blood shall quench that fire:
Look to thyself, thou art in jeopardy.
SHAKESPEARE'S KING JOHN.

This colour will be reprehended or encountered, by imputing to all excellencies in compositions a kind of poverty, or at least a casualty or jeopardy. BACON.

I'GNIS FA'TUUS. *n.s.* [Latin.] Will with the wisp; Jack with the lanthorn.

Vapours arising from putrified waters are usually called ignes fatui.
NEWTON'S OPTICKS.

IGNI'VOMOUS. *adj.* [*ignivomus*, Latin.] Vomiting fire.

Vulcanos and ignivomous *mountains are some of the most terrible shocks of the globe.*
DERHAM'S PHYSICO-THEOLOGY.

To **IGNO'RE.** *v.a.* [*ignorer*, French; *ignoro*, Latin.] Not to know; to be ignorant of. This word *Boyle* endeavoured to introduce; but it has not been received.

I ignored *not the stricter interpretation, given by modern criticks to divers texts, by me alleged.* BOYLE.

Philosophy would solidly be established, if men would more carefully distinguish those things that they know from those that they ignore. BOYLE.

To **JIG.** *v.n.* [from the noun.] To dance carelesly; to dance. Expressed in contempt.

As for the jigging *part and figures of dances, I count that little.* LOCKE.

J'IGGUMBOB. *n.s.* [A cant word.] A trinket; a knick-knack; a slight contrivance in machinery.

He rifled all his pokes and fobs
Of gimcracks, whims, and jiggumbobs.
HUDIBRAS, P. III.

ILK. *adv.* [*ealc*, Saxon.] Eke; also. It is still retained in Scotland, and denotes each: as, *ilk ane of you*, every one of you. It also signifies the same; as, *Macintosh of that ilk*, denotes a gentleman whose surname and the title of his estate are the same.

Shepherds, should it not yshend
Your roundels fresh, to hear a doleful verse
Of Rosalind, who knows not Rosalind,
That Colin made? ilk *can I you rehearse.*
SPENSER.

To **ILLA'QUEATE.** *v.a.* [*illaqueo*, Latin.] To entangle; to entrap; to ensnare.

I am illaquated, *but not truly captivated into an assent to your conclusion.*
MORE'S DIVINE DIALOGUES.

ILLI'TERATE. *adj.* [*illiteratus*, Latin.] Unlettered; untaught; unlearned; unenlightened by science.

The duke was illiterate, *yet had learned at court to supply his own defects, by the drawing unto him of the best instruments of experience.* WOTTON.

Th' illiterate *writer, empirick like, applies*

To minds diseas'd unsafe chance remedies:
The learn'd in schools, where knowledge first began,
Studies with care th' anatomy of man;
Sees virtue, vice, and passions in their cause,
And fame from science, not from fortune draws. DRYDEN.

In the first ages of Christianity not only the learned and the wise, but the ignorant and illiterate *embraced torments and death.* TILLOTSON'S SERMONS.

ILLNA'TURE. *n.s.* [*ill* and *nature.*] Habitual malevolence; want of humanity.

Illnature *inclines a man to those actions that thwart and sour and disturb conversation, and consists of a proneness to do ill turns, attended with a secret joy upon the sight of any mischief that befals another, and of an utter insensibility of any kindness done him.* SOUTH'S SERMONS.

IMA'GINER. *n.s.* [from *imagine.*] One who forms ideas.

The juggler took upon him to know that such an one should point in such a place of a garter that was held up; and still he did it, by first telling the imaginer, *and after bidding the actor think.* BACON'S NATURAL HISTORY.

IMBE'CILE. *adj.* [*imbecilis*, Latin; *imbecille*, French.] Weak; feeble; wanting strength of either mind or body.

To **IMBE'CILE.** *v.a.* [from the adjective. This word is corruptly written *embezzle.*] To weaken a stock or fortune by clandestine expences or unjust appropriations.

Princes must in a special manner be guardians of pupils and widows, not suffering their persons to be oppressed, or their states imbeciled. TAYLOR'S RULE OF LIVING HOLY.

To **IMBI'BE.** *v.a.* [*imbibo*, Latin; *imbiber*, French.]

1. To drink in; to draw in.

A pot of ashes will receive more hot water than cold, forasmuch as the warm water imbibeth *more of the salt.* BROWN.

The torrent merciless imbibes
Commissions, perquisites, and bribes. SWIFT.

Illumin'd wide,
The dewy-skirted clouds imbibe *the sun.* THOMSON'S AUTUMN.

2. To admit into the mind.

Those, that have imbibed *this error, have extended the influence of this belief to the whole gospel, which they will not allow to contain any thing but promises.* HAMMOND.

It is not easy for the mind to put off those confused notions and prejudices it has imbibed *from custom.* LOCKE.

Conversation with foreigners enlarges our minds, and sets them free from many prejudices we are ready to imbibe *concerning them.* WATTS'S IMPROVEMENT OF THE MIND.

3. To drench; to soak. This sense, though unusual, perhaps unexampled, is necessary in the English, unless the word *imbue* be adopted, which our writers seem not willing to receive.

Metals, corroded with a little acid, turn into rust, which is an earth tasteless and indissolvable in water; and this earth, imbibed *with more acid, becomes a metallick salt.* NEWTON.

IMBRI'CATED. *adj.* [from *imbrex*, Latin.] Indented with concavities; bent and hollowed like a roof or gutter-tile.

To **IMBRO'WN.** *v.a.* [from *brown.*] To make brown; to darken; to obscure; to cloud.

Where the morning sun first warmly smote
The open field, and where the unpierc'd shade

Imbrown'd *the noontide bow'rs.*
MILTON'S PARADISE LOST.

The walking crew,
At thy request, support the miry shoe;
The foot grows black that was with dirt imbrown'd,
And in thy pocket gingling half-pence sound. GAY.

Another age shall see the golden ear
Imbrown *the slope, and nod on the parterre.* POPE.

Imbrown'd *with native bronze, lo! Henly stands.* POPE.

To **IMBU'E.** *v.a.* [*imbuo*, Latin. This word, which seems wanted in our language, has been proposed by several writers, but not yet adopted by the rest. *Imbu*, French, the participal adj. is only used.] To tincture deep; to imbibe with any liquor or die.

I would render this treatise intelligible to every rational man, however little versed in scholastick learning; among whom I expect it will have a fairer passage, than among those that are deeply imbued *with other principles.* DIGBY.

Cloaths which have once been throughly embued *with black, cannot well afterwards be dyed into lighter colour.* BOYLE.

Where the mineral matter is great, so as to take the eye, the body appears imbued *and tinctured with the colour.* WOODWARD.

IMITA'TION. *n.s.* [*imitatio*, Latin; *imitation*, French.]

1. The act of copying; attempt to resemble.

Since a true knowledge of nature gives us pleasure, a lively imitation *of it, either in poetry or painting, must produce a much greater; for both these arts are not only true* imitations *of nature, but of the best nature.* DRYDEN.

2. That which is offered as a copy.

3. A method of translating looser than paraphrase, in which modern examples and illustrations are used for ancient, or domestick for foreign.

In the way of imitation, *the translator not only varies from the words and sense, but forsakes them as he sees occasion; and, taking only some general hints from the original, runs division on the groundwork.* DRYDEN.

IMME'DIACY. *n.s.* [*immediateté*, French, from *immediate.*] Personal greatness; power of acting without dependance. This is a harsh word, and sense peculiar I believe to *Shakespeare.*

He led our pow'rs,
Bore the commission of my place and person;
The which immediacy *may well stand up,*
And call itself your brother.
SHAKESPEARE'S KING LEAR.

IMMO'MENT. *adj.* [*in* and *moment.*] Trifling; of no importance or value. A barbarous word.

I some lady-trifles have reserv'd,
Immoment *toys, things of such dignity*
As we greet modern friends withal.
SHAKESPEARE'S ANTONY AND CLEOPATRA.

IMMU'SICAL. *adj.* [*in* and *musical.*] Unmusical; inharmonious.

All sounds are either musical, which are ever equal, or immusical, *which are ever unequal, as the voice in speaking, and whisperings.*
BACON'S NATURAL HISTORY.

When we consider the immusical *note of all swans we ever beheld or heard of, we cannot consent.* BROWN.

IMPA'RTIBLE. *adj.* [*impartible*, Fr. from *impart.*] Communicable; to be conferred or bestowed. This word is elegant, though used by few writers.

The same body may be conceived to be more or less impartible *than it is active or heavy.* DIGBY.

IMPE'RTINENT. *adj.* [*impertinent*, Fr. *in* and *pertinens*, Latin.]

1. Of no relation to the matter in hand; of no weight.

The law of angels we cannot judge altogether impertinent *unto the affairs of the church of God.* HOOKER.

The contemplation of things that are impertinent *to us, and do not concern us, are but a more specious idleness.* TILLOTSON.

2. Importunate; intrusive; meddling.

'Tis not a sign two lovers are together, when they can be so impertinent *as to enquire what the world does.* POPE.

3. Foolish; trifling.[136]

IMPE'RTINENT. *n.s.* A trifler; a meddler; an intruder.

Governours would have enough to do to trouble their heads with the politicks of every meddling officious impertinent. L'ESTRANGE'S FABLES.

I'MPETRATION. *n.s.* [*impetration*, Fr. *impetratio*, from *impetro*, Latin.] The act of obtaining by prayer or intreaty.[137]

The blessed sacrament is the mystery of the death of Christ, and the application of his blood, which was shed for the remission of sins, and is the great means of impetration, *and the meritorious cause of it.* TAYLOR.

It is the greatest solemnity of prayer, the most powerful liturgy, and means of impetration *in this world.* TAYLOR.

IMPLE'X. *adj.* [*implexus*, Latin.] Intricate; entangled; complicated.[138]

Every poem is either simple or implex*: it is called simple when there is no change of fortune in it;* implex, *when the fortune of the chief actor changes from bad to good, or from good to bad.* SPECTATOR.

IMPO'ROUS. *adj.* [*in* and *porous.*] Free from pores; free from vacuities or interstices; close of texture; completely solid.

It has its earthly and salinous parts so exactly resolved, that its body is left imporous, *and not discreted by atomical terminations.* BROWN'S VULGAR ERROURS.

If atoms should descend plumb down with equal velocity, being all perfectly solid and imporous, *they would never the one overtake the other.* RAY ON THE CREATION.

To **IMPO'RT.** *v.a.* [*importo*, Latin.]

1. To carry into any country from abroad: opposed to *export*.

For Elis I would sail with utmost speed,
T' import *twelve mares, which there*
luxurious feed. POPE.

2. To imply; to infer.

Himself not only comprehended all our necessities, but in such sort also framed every petition as might most naturally serve for many; and doth, though not always require, yet always import *a multitude of speakers together.* HOOKER.

The name of discipline importeth *not as they would fain have it construed; but the self-same thing it signifieth, which the name of doctrine doth.* HOOKER.

This question we now asked, imported, *as that we thought this land a land of magicians.* BACON.

3. To produce in consequence.

Something he left imperfect in the state,
Which since his coming forth is thought of, which
Imports *the kingdom so much fear and danger,*
That his return was most requir'd.
SHAKESPEARE'S KING LEAR.

4. [*Importer*, *importe*, French. Impersonally.] To be of moment: as, it imports, it is of weight or consequence.

Her length of sickness, with what else more serious
Importeth *thee to know, this bears.*
SHAKESPEARE'S ANTONY AND CLEOPATRA.

Let the heat be such as may keep the metal perpetually molten; for that above all importeth *to the work.* BACON.

Number in armies importeth *not much, where the people is of weak courage.* BACON'S ESSAYS.

This to attain, whether heav'n move, or earth,
Imports *not, if thou reckon right.*
MILTON'S PARADISE LOST.

It may import *us in this calm to hearken more than we have done to the storms that are now raising abroad.* TEMPLE.

If I endure it, what imports *it you?*
DRYDEN'S SPANISH FRYAR.

IMPO'RTLESS. *adj.* [from *import.*] Of no moment or consequence. This is a word not in use, but not inelegant.

We less expect
That matter needless, of importless *burthen,*
Divide thy lips.
SHAKESPEARE'S TROILUS AND CRESSIDA.

I'MPOST. *n.s.* [*impost, impôt,* French; *impositum,* Latin.] A tax; a toll; a custom paid.

Taxes and imposts *upon merchants do seldom good to the king's revenue; for that that he wins in the hundred, he loseth in the shire.* BACON'S ESSAYS.

IMPREJU'DICATE. *adj.* [*in, præ,* and *judico,* Latin.] Unprejudiced; not prepossessed; impartial.

The solid reason of one man with imprejudicate *apprehensions, begets as firm a belief as the authority or aggregated testimony of many hundreds.* BROWN.

IMPREPARA'TION. *n.s.* [*in* and *preparation.*] Unpreparedness; want of preparation.

Impreparation *and unreadiness when they find in us, they turn it to the soothing up of themselves.* HOOKER.

IMPROBABI'LITY. *n.s.* [from *improbable.*] Unlikelihood; difficulty to be believed.

The difficulty being so great, and the improbability *of attempting this successfully, it was but reason that a solid foundation should be laid.* HAMMOND.

As to the improbabilities *of a spirit appearing, I boldly answer him, that a heroick poet is not tied to the bare representation of what is true, or exceeding probable.* DRYDEN.

IMPRO'PER. *adj.* [*impropre,* Fr. *improprius,* Latin.]

1. Not well adapted; unqualified.

As every science requires a peculiar genius, so likewise there is a genius peculiarly improper *for every one.* BURNET.

2. Unfit; not conducive to the right end.

The methods used in an original disease would be very improper *in a gouty case.* ARBUTHNOT ON DIET.

3. Not just; not accurate.

He disappear'd, was rarify'd;
For 'tis improper *speech to say he dy'd:*
He was exhal'd. DRYDEN.

IMPRO'VABLE. *adj.* [from *improve.*] Capable of being advanced from a good to a better state; capable of melioration.

Adventures in knowledge are laudable, and the essays of weaker heads afford improvable *hints unto better.* BROWN.

We have stock enough, and that too of so improvable *a nature, that is, capable of infinite advancement.* DECAY OF PIETY.

Man is accommodated with moral principles, improvable *by the exercise of his faculties.*
HALE'S ORIGIN OF MANKIND.

Animals are not improvable *beyond their proper genius: a dog will never learn to mew, nor a cat to bark.*
GREW'S COSMOLOGIA SACRA.

I have a fine spread of improvable *lands, and am already planting woods and draining marshes.*
ADDISON'S SPECTATOR.

I'MPUDENT. *adj.* [*impudent*, Fr. *impudens*, Latin.] Shameless; wanting modesty.

It is not a confident brow, nor the throng of words that come with such more than impudent *sawciness from you, can thrust me from a level consideration.*
SHAKESPEARE'S HENRY IV.

When we behold an angel, not to fear,
Is to be impudent.
DRYDEN'S SPANISH FRYAR.

INA'CCURATE. *adj.* [*in* and *accurate.*] Not exact; not accurate. It is used sometimes of persons, but more frequently of performances.

INA'NITY. *n.s.* [from *inanis*, Latin.] Emptiness; void space.

This opinion excludes all such inanity, *and admits no vacuities but so little ones as no body whatever can come to, but will be bigger than they, and must touch the corporal parts which those vacuities divide.* DIGBY ON BODIES.

INA'PPETENCY. *n.s.* [*in* and *appetentia*, Latin.] Want of stomach or appetite.

INARTI'CULATE. *adj.* [*inarticulé*, Fr. *in* and *articulate.*] Not uttered with distinctness like that of the syllables of human speech.

Observe what inarticulate *sounds resemble any of the particular letters.*
WILKINS'S MATHEMATICAL MAGICK.

By the harmony of words we elevate the mind to a sense of devotion; as our solemn musick, which is inarticulate *poesy, does in churches.* DRYDEN.

To INAU'GURATE. *v.a.* [*inauguro*, Latin.] To consecrate; to invest with a new office by solemn rites; to begin with good omens; to begin.

Those beginnings of years were propitious to him, as if kings did chuse remarkable days to inaugurate *their favours, that they may appear acts as well of the time as of the will.* WOTTON.

To INCA'RCERATE. *v.a.* [*incarcero*, Latin.] To imprison; to confine. It is used in the Scots law to denote imprisoning or confining in a gaol; otherwise it is seldom found.

The pestilent contagion may be propagated by those dense bodies, that easily incarcerate *the infected air; as woollen cloaths.*
HARVEY ON CONSUMPTIONS.

INCA'RNATE. *participial adj.* [*incarnat*, Fr. from the verb.]

1. Cloathed with flesh; embodied in flesh.

Undoubtedly even the nature of God itself, in the person of the son, is incarnate, *and hath taken to itself flesh.* HOOKER.

They say he cried out of women.
—— *Yes, that he did, and said they were devils* incarnate. SHAKESPEARE.

A most wise sufficient means of redemption and salvation, by the satisfactory death and obedience of the incarnate *son of God, Jesus Christ, God blessed for ever.*
SANDERSON.

Here shalt thou sit incarnate, *here shalt reign*
Both God and man.
MILTON'S PARADISE LOST, B. III.

2. It may be doubted whether *Swift* understood this word.

But he's possest,
Incarnate *with a thousand imps.*
SWIFT.

3. In Scotland *incarnate* is applied to any thing tinged of a deep red colour, from its resemblance to a flesh colour.

INCH. *n.s.* [*inceaxon*; *uncia*, Latin.]
1. A measure of length supposed equal to three grains of barley laid end to end; the twelfth part of a foot.

A foot is the sixth part of the stature of man, a span one eighth of it, and a thumb's breadth or inch *one seventy-second.* HOLDER ON TIME.

2. A proverbial name for a small quantity.

The plebeians have got your fellow tribune;
They'll give him death by inches.
SHAKESPEARE'S CORIOLANUS.

As in lasting, so in length is man,
Contracted to an inch, *who was a span.*
DONNE.

Is it so desirable a condition to consume by inches, *and lose one's blood by drops?*
COLLIER.

He should never miss, in all his race,
Of time one minute, or one inch *of space.*
BLACKMORE.

The commons were growing by degrees into power and property, gaining ground upon the patricians inch *by* inch. SWIFT.

3. A nice point of time.

Beldame, I think, we watch'd you at an inch. SHAKESPEARE.

INCLI'NATORY. *adj.* [from *incline.*] Having a quality of inclining to one or other.

If that inclinatory *virtue be destroyed by a touch from the contrary pole, that end which before was elevated will then decline.* BROWN'S VULGAR ERROURS.

INCLI'NATORILY. *adv.* [from *inclinatory.*] Obliquely; with inclination to one side or the other; with some deviation from North and South.

Whether they be refrigerated inclinatorily, *or somewhat equinoxially, that is, toward the eastern or western points, they discover some verticity.*
BROWN'S VULGAR ERROURS.

INCO'G. *adv.* [corrupted by mutilation from *incognito*, Latin.] Unknown; in private.

But if you're rough, and use him like a dog,
Depend upon it, he'll remain incog.
ADDISON.

INCO'GNITO. *adv.* [*incognitus*, Latin.] In a state of concealment.

'Twas long ago
Since gods came down incognito.
PRIOR.

INCO'MPARABLY. *adv.* [from *incomparable.*]
1. Beyond comparison; without competition.

A founder it had, whom I think incomparably *the wisest man that ever the French church did enjoy, since the hour it enjoyed him.* HOOKER.

Self-preservation will oblige a man voluntarily to undergo any less evil, to secure himself but from the probability of an evil incomparably *greater.*
SOUTH'S SERMONS.

2. Excellently; to the highest degree. A low phrase.

There are the heads of Antoninus Pius, the Faustina's, and Marcus Aurelius, all incomparably *well cut.* ADDISON ON ITALY.

INCOMPOSSIBI'LITY. *n.s.* [from *incompossible.*] Quality of being not possible but by the negation or destruction of something; inconsistency with something.

The manifold incompossibilities *and lubricities of matter cannot have the same fitnesses in any modification.* MORE.

Though the repugnancy of infinitude be equally incompetible to continued or successive motion, and depends upon the incompossibility *of the very nature of things successive or extensive with infinitude, yet that* incompossibility *is more conspicuous in discrete quantity, that*

ariseth from individuals already actually distinguished.
HALE'S ORIGIN OF MANKIND.

INCOMPREHENSIBI'LITY. *n.s.* [*incomprehensibilité*, Fr. from *incomprehensible.*] Unconceivableness; superiority to human understanding.

INCONSPI'CUOUS. *adj.* [*in* and *conspicuous.*] Indiscernible; not perceptible by the sight.

When an excellent experimenter had taken pains in accurately filling up a tube of mercury, we found that yet there remained store of inconspicuous *bubbles.* BOYLE.

INCONSU'MPTIBLE. *adj.* [*in* and *consumptus*, Lat.] Not to be spent; not to be brought to an end; not to be destroyed by fire. This seems a more elegant word than *inconsumable.*

Before I give any answer to this objection of pretended inconsumptible *lights, I would gladly see the effect undoubtedly proved.*
DIGBY ON BODIES.

INCO'NTINENT. *adj.* [*incontinens*, Lat. *in* and *continent.*]

1. Unchaste; indulging unlawful pleasure.

In these degrees have they made a pair of stairs to marriage, which they will climb incontinent, or else be incontinent *before marriage.*
SHAKESPEARE'S AS YOU LIKE IT.

Men shall be lovers of their own selves, false accusers, incontinent, *fierce.*
BIBLE 2 TIMOTHY, III. 3.

2. Shunning delay; immediate. This is a meaning now obsolete.

They ran towards the far rebounded noise,
To weet what wight so loudly did lament;
Unto the place they came incontinent.
FAIRY QUEEN.

Come, mourn with me for what I do lament,
And put on sullen black incontinent.
SHAKESPEARE'S RICHARD II.

He says he will return incontinent.
SHAKESPEARE'S OTHELLO.

INCONVE'RSABLE. *adj.* [*in* and *conversable.*] Incommunicative; ill qualified by temper for conversation; unsocial.

He is a person very inconversable.
MORE.

INCO'RRIGIBLE. *adj.* [*incorrigible*, Fr. *in* and *corrigible.*] Bad beyond correction; depraved beyond amendment by any means; erroneous beyond hope of instruction.[139]

The loss is many times irrecoverable, and the inconvenience incorrigible.
MORE'S DIVINE DIALOGUES.

What are their thoughts of things, but variety of incorrigible *error?*
L'ESTRANGE.

Provok'd by those incorrigible *fools,*
I left declaiming in pedantick schools.
DRYDEN'S JUVENAL.

Whilst we are incorrigible, *God may in vengeance continue to chastise us with the judgment of war.*
SMALRIDGE'S SERMONS.

The most violent party-men are such as have discovered least sense of religion or morality; and when such are laid aside, as shall be found incorrigible, *it will be no difficulty to reconcile the rest.* SWIFT.

I'NCUBUS. *n.s.* [Latin; *incube*, Fr.] The night-mare.

The incubus *is an inflation of the membranes of the stomach, which hinders the motion of the diaphragma, lungs, pulse, and motion, with a sense of a weight oppressing the breast.*
FLOYER ON THE HUMOURS.

To **INCU'RVATE.** *v.a.* [*incurvo*, Latin.] To bend; to crook.

Sir Isaac Newton has shewn, by several

experiments of rays passing by the edges of bodies, that they are incurvated *by the action of these bodies.*
CHEYNE'S PHILOSOPHICAL PRINCIPLES.

INDAGA'TION. *n.s.* [from *indagate.*] Search; enquiry; examination.

Paracelsus directs us, in the indagation *of colours, to have an eye principally upon salts.* BOYLE.

Part hath been discovered by himself, and some by human indagation.
BROWN'S VULGAR ERROURS.

INDE'CENCY. *n.s.* [*indecence,* French.] Any thing unbecoming; any thing contrary to good manners; something wrong, but scarce criminal.

He will in vain endeavour to reform indecency *in his pupil, which he allows in himself.* LOCKE.

INDEFI'NITUDE. *n.s.* [from *indefinite.*] Quantity not limited by our understanding, though yet finite.

They arise to a strange and prodigious multitude, if not indefinitude, *by their various positions, combinations, and conjunctions.*
HALE'S ORIGIN OF MANKIND.

INDEPE'NDENT. *adj.* [*independant,* Fr. *in* and *dependent.*]

1. Not depending; not supported by any other; not relying on another; not controlled. It is used with *on, of,* or *from* before the object; of which *on* seems most proper, since we say to *depend on,* and consequently *dependent on.*

Creation must needs infer providence, and God's making the world irrefragably proves that he governs it too; or that a being of dependent nature remains nevertheless independent *upon him in that respect.*
SOUTH'S SERMONS.

Since all princes of independent *governments are in a state of nature, the world never was without men in that state.*
LOCKE.

The town of St. Gaul is a protestant republick, independent *of the abbot, and under the protection of the cantons.* ADDISON.

2. Not relating to any thing else, as to a superiour cause or power.

The consideration of our understanding, which is an incorporeal substance independent *from matter; and the contemplation of our own bodies, which have all the stamps and characters of excellent contrivance; these alone do very easily guide us to the wise Author of all things.*
BENTLEY'S SERMONS.

INDEPE'NDENT. *n.s.* One who in religious affairs holds that every congregation is a complete church, subject to no superiour authority.

We shall, in our sermons, take occasion to justify such passages in our liturgy as have been unjustly quarrelled at by presbyterians, independents, *or other puritan sectaries.* SANDERS.

A very famous independent *minister was head of a college in those times.*
ADDISON'S SPECTATOR.

INDIGITA'TION. *n.s.* [from *indigitate.*] The act of pointing out or showing.

Which things I conceive no obscure indigitation *of providence.*
MORE AGAINST ATHEISM.

INDISTU'RBANCE. *n.s.* [*in* and *disturb.*] Calmness; freedom from disturbance.

What is called by the stoicks apathy, and by the scepticks indisturbance, *seems all but to mean great tranquillity of mind.*
TEMPLE.

To **INDO'CTRINATE.** *v.a.* [*endoctriner,* old French.] To instruct; to tincture with any science, or opinion.

Under a master that discoursed excellently, and took much delight in indoctrinating *his young unexperienced favourite, Buckingham had obtained a quick conception of speaking very gracefully and pertinently.* CLARENDON.

They that never peept beyond the common belief, in which their easy understandings were at first indoctrinated, *are strongly assured of the truth and co-operative excellency of their receptions.* GLANVILLE'S SCEPSIS SCIENTIFICA.

INDOCTRINA'TION. *n.s.* [from *indoctrinate.*] Instruction; information.

Although postulates are very accommodable unto junior indoctrinations, *yet are these authorities but temporary, and not to be embraced beyond the minority of our intellectuals.* BROWN.

INDRA'UGHT. *n.s.* [*in* and *draught.*]

1. An opening in the land into which the sea flows.

Ebbs and floods there could be none, when there was no indraughts, *bays, or gulphs to receive a flood.* RALEIGH.

2. Inlet; passage inwards.

Navigable rivers are so many indraughts *to attain wealth.* BACON'S ADVICE TO VILLIERS.

INDU'BIOUS. *adj.* [*in* and *dubious.*] Not doubtful; not suspecting; certain.

Hence appears the vulgar vanity of reposing an indubious *confidence in those antipestilential spirits.* HARVEY.

INDU'LGENCE, INDULGENCY. *n.s.* [*indulgence*, Fr. from *indulge.*]

1. Fondness; fond kindness.

Restraint she will not brook;
And left to herself, if evil thence ensue,
She first his weak indulgence *will accuse.*
MILTON'S PARADISE LOST.

The glories of our isle,
Which yet like golden ore, unripe in beds,
Expect the warm indulgency *of heaven.*
DRYDEN'S KING ARTHUR.

2. Forbearance; tenderness; opposite to rigour.

They err, that through indulgence *to others, or fondness to any sin in themselves, substitute for repentance any thing less.* HAMMOND ON FUNDAMENTALS.

In known images of life, I guess
The labour greater, as th' indulgence *less.*
POPE.

3. Favour granted.

If all these gracious indulgences *are without any effect on us, we must perish in our own folly.* ROGERS.

4. Grant of the church of Rome, not defined by themselves.

Thou, that giv'st whores indulgences *to sin,*
I'll canvas thee.
SHAKESPEARE'S HENRY VI.

Indulgences, *dispenses, pardons, bulls,*
The sport of winds. MILTON.

In purgatory, indulgences, *and supererogation, the assertors seem to be unanimous in nothing but in reference to profit.* DECAY OF PIETY.

Leo X. is deservedly infamous for his base prostitution of indulgences. ATTERBURY.

INDU'STRIOUS. *adj.* [*industrieux*, Fr. *industrius*, Lat.]

1. Diligent; laborious; assiduous. Opposed to *slothful.*

He himself, being excellently learned, and industrious *to seek out the truth of all things concerning the original of his own people, hath set down the testimony of the ancients truly.* SPENSER ON IRELAND.

Let our just censures
Attend the true event, and put we on
Industrious *soldiership.*
SHAKESPEARE'S MACBETH.

His thoughts were low:
To vice industrious; *but to nobler deeds*
Timorous and slothful.
MILTON'S PARADISE LOST.

2.[140] Designed; done for the purpose.

The industrious *perforation of the tendons of the second joints of fingers and toes, draw the tendons of the third joints through.* MORE'S DIVINE DIALOGUES.

Observe carefully all the events which happen either by an occasional concurrence of various causes, or by the industrious *application of knowing men.*
WATTS'S IMPROVEMENT OF THE MIND.

I'NDUSTRY. *n.s.* [*industrie*, Fr. *industria*, Lat.] Diligence; assiduity.[141]

The sweat of industry *would dry and die,*
But for the end it works to.
SHAKESPEARE'S CYMBELINE.

See the laborious bee
For little drops of honey flee,
And there with humble sweets content her
industry. COWLEY.

Providence would only initiate mankind into the useful knowledge of her treasures, leaving the rest to employ our industry, *that we might not live like idle loiterers.*
MORE'S ANTIDOTE AGAINST ATHEISM.

I'NFANCY. *n.s.* [*infantia*, Latin.]
1. The first part of life. Usually extended by naturalists to seven years.

Dare we affirm it was ever his meaning, that unto their salvation, who even from their tender infancy *never knew any other faith or religion than only Christian, no kind of teaching can be available, saving that which was so needful for the first universal conversion of Gentiles, hating Christianity?* HOOKER.

Pirithous came t' attend
This worthy Theseus, his familiar friend:
Their love in early infancy *began,*
And rose as childhood ripen'd into man.
DRYDEN.

The insensible impressions on our tender infancies *have very important and lasting consequences.* LOCKE.

2. Civil infancy, extended by the English law to one and twenty years.
3. First age of any thing; beginning; original; commencement.

In Spain our springs, like old mens children, be
Decay'd and wither'd from their infancy.
DRYDEN'S INDIAN EMPEROR.

The difference between the riches of Roman citizens in the infancy *and in the grandeur of Rome, will appear by comparing the first valuation of estates with the estates afterwards possessed.*
ARBUTHNOT ON COINS.

INFATUA'TION. *n.s.* [from *infatuate.*] The act of striking with folly; deprivation of reason.

Where men give themselves over to the defence of wicked interests and false propositions, it is just with God to smite the greatest abilities with the greatest infatuations. SOUTH'S SERMONS.

INFA'USTING. *n.s.* [from *infaustus*, Lat.] The act of making unlucky. An odd and inelegant word.

As the king did in some part remove the envy from himself, so he did not observe that he did withal bring a kind of malediction and infausting *upon the marriage, as an ill prognostick.*
BACON'S HENRY VII.

INFESTI'VITY. *n.s.* [*in* and *festivity.*] Mournfulness; want of cheerfulness.

INFI'RMARY. *n.s.* [*infirmerie*, French.] Lodgings for the sick.

These buildings to be for privy lodgings on both sides, and the end for privy galleries, whereof one should be for an infirmary, *if any special person should be sick.*
BACON.

INFI'RMITY. *n.s.* [*infirmité*, French.]

1. Weakness of sex, age, or temper.

Infirmity,
Which waits upon worn times, hath something seiz'd
His wish'd ability.
SHAKESPEARE'S WINTER'S TALE.

Discover thine infirmity,
That warranteth by law to be thy privilege:
I am with child, ye bloody homicides.
SHAKESPEARE'S HENRY VI.

If he had done or said any thing amiss, he desired their worships to think it was his infirmities.
SHAKESPEARE'S JULIUS CÆSAR.

Are the infirmities *of the body, pains, and diseases his complaints? His faith reminds him of the day when this corruptible shall put on incorruption, and this mortal immortality.* ROGERS.

2. Failing; weakness; fault.

A friend should bear a friend's infirmities;
But Brutus makes mine greater than they are. SHAKESPEARE.

Many infirmities *made it appear more requisite, that a wiser man should have the application of his interest.* CLARENDON.

How difficult is it to preserve a great name, when he that has acquired it, is so obnoxious to such little weaknesses and infirmities, *as are no small diminution to it, when discovered.*
ADDISON'S SPECTATOR.

3. Disease; malady.

General laws are like general rules of physick, according whereunto, as now, no wise man will desire himself to be cured, if there be joined with his disease some special accident, in regard that thereby others in the same infirmity, *but without the like accident, may.* HOOKER.

INFLE'CTION. *n.s.* [*inflectio*, Latin.]

1. The act of bending or turning.

Neither the divine determinations, persuasions, or inflexions *of the understanding or will of rational creatures, doth deceive the understanding, pervert the will, or necessitate either to any moral evil.* HALE.

2. Modulation of the voice.

His virtue, his gesture, his countenance, his zeal, the motion of his body, and the inflection *of his voice, who first uttereth them as his own, is that which giveth the very essence of instruments available to eternal life.* HOOKER.

3. Variation of a noun or verb.

The same word in the original tongue, by divers inflections *and variations, makes divers dialects.* BREREWOOD.

INFO'RMER. *n.s.* [from *inform*.]

1. One who gives intelligence.

This writer is either byassed by an inclination to believe the worst, or a want of judgment to chuse his informers.
SWIFT.

2. One who discovers offenders to the magistrate.

There were spies and informers *set at work to watch the company.* L'ESTRANGE.

Let no court sycophant pervert my sense,
Nor sly informer *watch these words to draw*
Within the reach of treason. POPE.

Informers *are a detestable race of people, although sometimes necessary.* SWIFT.

INFO'RMOUS. *adj.* [*informe*, Fr. *informis*, Latin.] Shapeless; of no regular figure.

That a bear brings forth her young informous *and unshapen, which she fashioneth after by licking them over, is an opinion not only common with us at present, but hath been delivered by ancient writers.* BROWN'S VULGAR ERROURS.

INGANNA'TION. *n.s.* [*ingannare*, Italian.] Cheat; fraud; deception; juggle; delusion; imposture; trick; slight. A word neither used nor necessary.

Whoever shall resign their reasons, either from the root of deceit in themselves, or inability to resist such trivial ingannations *from others, are within the line of vulgarity.* BROWN.

INGENU'ITY. *n.s.* [*ingenuité*, Fr. from *ingenuous.*]

1. Openness; fairness; candour; freedom from dissimulation.

Such of high quality, or other of particular note, as shall fall under my pen, I shall not let pass without their due character, being part of my professed ingenuity. WOTTON.

My constancy I to the planets give;
My truth, to them who at the court do live;
Mine ingenuity *and openness*
To jesuits; to buffoons my pensiveness.
DONNE.

I know not whether it be more shame or wonder, that men can so put off ingenuity, *and the native greatness of their kind, as to descend to so base, so ignoble a vice.* GOVERNMENT OF THE TONGUE.

If a child, when questioned for any thing, directly confess, you must commend his ingenuity, *and pardon the fault, be it what it will.* LOCKE.

2. [From *ingenious.*] Wit; invention; genius; subtilty; acuteness.

These are but the frigidities of wit, and become not the genius of manly ingenuities. BROWN'S VULGAR ERROURS.

The ancient atomical hypothesis might have slept for ever, had not the ingenuity *of the present age recalled it from its urn and silence.* GLANVILLE'S SCEPSIS SCIENTIFICA.

Such sots have neither parts nor wit, ingenuity *of discourse, nor fineness of conversation, to entertain or delight any one.* SOUTH.

A pregnant instance how far virtue surpasses ingenuity, *and how much an honest simplicity is preferable to fine parts and subtile speculations.* WOODWARD.

INGE'STION. *n.s.* [from *ingest.*] The act of throwing into the stomach.

It has got room enough to grow into its full dimension, which is performed by the daily ingestion *of milk and other food, that's in a short time after digested into blood.* HARVEY.

INHE'RITOR. *n.s.* [from *inherit.*] An heir; one who receives any thing by succession.

You, like a letcher, out of whorish loins,
Are pleas'd to breed out your inheritors.
SHAKESPEARE.

The sole inheritor
Of all perfections that a man may owe.
SHAKESPEARE.

The very conveyances of his lands will hardly lie in this box; and must the inheritor *himself have no more?* SHAKESPEARE.

Marriage without consent of parents they do not make void, but they mulct it in the inheritors; *for the children of such marriages are not admitted to inherit above a third part of their parents inheritance.* BACON'S NEW ATLANTIS.

INHE'RITRESS. *n.s.* [from *inheritor.*] An heiress; a woman that inherits.

Having given artificially some hopes to marry Anne, inheritress *to the duchy of Bretagne.* BACON'S HENRY VII.

INHE'RITRIX. *n.s.* [from *inheritor.*] An heiress. This is now more commonly used, though *inheritress* be a word more analogically English.

Charles the great
Establish'd then this law, to wit, No feme
Should be inheritrix *in Salike land.*
SHAKESPEARE'S HENRY V.

I'NJURY. *n.s.* [*injuria*, Lat. *injure*, Fr.]

1. Hurt without justice.

The town of Bouline, and other places, were

acquired by just title of victory; and therefore in keeping of them no injury *was offered.* HAYWARD.

Riot ascends above their loftiest tow'rs,
And injury *and outrage.* MILTON.

2. Mischief; detriment.

Many times we do injury *to a cause by dwelling upon trifling arguments.* WATTS'S LOGICK.

3. Annoyance.

Great injuries *such vermin as mice and rats do in the fields.* MORTIMER.

4. Contumelious language; reproachful appellation.[142]

Casting off the respects fit to be continued between great kings, he fell to bitter invectives against the French king; and, by how much he was the less able to do, talking so much the more, spake all the injuries *he could devise of Charles.* BACON.

I'NKLING. *n.s.* [This word is derived by *Skinner* from *inklincken*, to sound within. This sense is still retained in Scotland: as, *I heard not an* inkling.] Hint; whisper; intimation.

Our business is not unknown to the senate: they have had inkling *what we intend to do, which now we'll shew them in deeds.* SHAKESPEARE'S CORIOLANUS.

We in Europe, notwithstanding all the remote discoveries and navigations of this last age, never heard of any of the least inkling *or glimpse of this island.* BACON'S NEW ATLANTIS.

They had some inkling *of secret messages betwen the marquis of Newcastle and young Hotham.* CLARENDON, B. VIII.

Aboard a Corinthian vessel he got an inkling *among the ship's crew of a conspiracy.* L'ESTRANGE'S FABLES.

To **INLA'W.** *v.a.* [*in* and *law.*] To clear of outlawry or attainder.

It should be a great incongruity to have them to make laws, who themselves were not inlawed. BACON'S HENRY VII.

INNHO'LDER. *n.s.* [*inn* and *hold.*] A man who keeps an inn; an innkeeper.

I'NNINGS. *n.s.* Lands recovered from the sea. *Ainsworth.*

INNKE'EPER. *n.s.* [*inn* and *keeper.*] One who keeps lodgings and provisions for the entertainment of travellers.

Clergymen must not keep a tavern, nor a judge be an innkeeper. TAYLOR'S RULE OF HOLY LIVING.

A factious innkeeper, *in the reign of Henry VII. was hanged, drawn, and quartered.* ADDISON'S FREEHOLDER.

We were not so inquisitive about the inn as the innkeeper; *and provided our landlord's principles were sound, did not take any notice of the staleness of his provisions.* ADDISON.

INNUE'NDO. *n.s.* [*innuendo*, from *innuo*, Latin.] An oblique hint.

As if the commandments, that require obedience and forbid murder, were to be indicted for a libellous innuendo *upon all the great men that come to be concerned.* L'ESTRANGE.

Mercury, though employed on a quite contrary errand, owns it a marriage by an innuendo. DRYDEN.

Pursue your trade of scandal-picking,
Your hints that Stella is no chicken;
Your innuendo's, *when you tell us,*
That Stella loves to talk with fellows.
SWIFT.

INQUINA'TION. *n.s.* [*inquinatio*, Lat. from *inquinate.*] Corruption; pollution.

Their causes and axioms are so full of imagination, and so infected with the old received theories, as they are mere inquinations *of experience, and concoct it not.* BACON.

The middle action, which produceth such imperfect bodies, is fitly called by some of the ancients inquination, *or inconcoction, which is a kind of putrefaction.*
BACON'S NATURAL HISTORY.

INSCRU'TABLE. *adj.* [*inscrutabilis*, Lat. *inscrutable*, Fr.] Unsearchable; not to be traced out by inquiry or study.

A jest unseen, inscrutable, *invisible,*
As a weather-cock on a steeple.
SHAKESPEARE'S TWO GENTLEMEN OF VERONA.

This king had a large heart, inscrutable *for good, and was wholly bent to make his kingdom and people happy.* BACON.

O how inscrutable! *his equity*
Twins with his power. SANDYS.

Hereunto they have recourse as unto the oracle of life, the great determinator of virginity, conception, fertility, and the inscrutable *infirmities of the whole body.*
BROWN'S VULGAR ERROURS.

We should contemplate reverently the works of nature and grace, the inscrutable *ways of providence, and all the wonderful methods of God's dealing with men.*
ATTERBURY.

INSECTO'LOGER. *n.s.* [*insect* and *λόγος*.] One who studies or describes insects.[143]

The insect itself is, according to modern insectologers, *of the ichneumon-fly kind.*
DERHAM'S PHYSICO-THEOLOGY.

INSI'DIOUS. *adj.* [*insidieux*, French; *insidiosus*, Latin.] Sly; circumventive; diligent to entrap; treacherous.

Since men mark all our steps, and watch our haltings, let a sense of their insidious *vigilance excite us so to behave ourselves, that they may find a conviction of the mighty power of Christianity towards regulating the passions.*
ATTERBURY'S SERMONS.

They wing their course
And dart on distant coasts, if some sharp rock,
Or shoal insidious, *breaks not their career.* THOMSON.

To INSI'ST. *v.n.* [*insister*, French; *insisto*, Latin.]

1. To stand or rest upon.

The combs being double, the cells on each side the partition are so ordered, that the angles on one side insist *upon the centers of the bottom of the cells on the other side.*
RAY.

2. Not to recede from terms or assertions; to persist in.

Upon such large terms, and so absolute,
As our conditions shall insist *upon,*
Our peace shall stand as firm as rocky mountains. SHAKESPEARE.

3. To dwell upon in discourse.

Were there no other act of hostility but that which we have hitherto insisted on, *the intercepting of her supplies were irreparably injurious to her.* DECAY OF PIETY.

INSI'STENT. *adj.* [*insistens*, Latin.] Resting upon any thing.

The breadth of the substruction must be at least double to the insistent *wall.*
WOTTON.

INSI'TIENCY. *n.s.* [*in* and *sitio*, Latin.] Exemption from thirst.

What is more admirable than the fitness of every creature, for the use we make of him? The docility of an elephant, and the insitiency *of a camel for travelling in desarts.*
GREW.

I'NSOLENCE, INSOLENCY. *n.s.* [*insolence*, Fr. *insolentia*, Latin.] Pride exerted in contemptuous and overbearing treatment of others; petulant contempt.

They could not restrain the insolency *of O'Neal, who, finding none now to with-*

stand him, made himself lord of those few people that remained.
SPENSER ON IRELAND.

Such a nature,
Tickled with good success, disdains the shadow
Which he treads on at noon; but I do wonder
His insolence *can brook to be commanded*
Under Cominius. SHAKESPEARE.

Flown with insolence *and wine.*
MILTON.

Publick judgments are the banks and shores upon which God breaks the insolency *of sinners, and stays their proud waves.*
TILLOTSON.

The steady tyrant man,
Who with the thoughtless insolence *of power,*
For sport alone, pursues the cruel chace.
THOMSON.

The fear of any violence, either against her own person or against her son, might deter Penelope from using any endeavours to remove men of such insolence *and power.*
BROOME.

To **I'NSOLENCE.** *v.a.* [from the noun.] To insult; to treat with contempt. A very bad word.

The bishops, who were first faulty, insolenced *and assaulted.* KING CHARLES.

I'NSOLENT. *adj.* [*insolent*, Fr. *insolens*, Latin.] Contemptuous of others; haughty; overbearing.

We have not pillaged those rich provinces which we rescued: victory itself hath not made us insolent *masters.* ATTERBURY.

INSPE'CTOR. *n.s.* [Latin.]

1. A prying examiner.

With their new light our bold inspectors *press,*
Like Cham, to shew their father's nakedness. DENHAM.

2. A superintendent.

They may travel under a wise inspector *or tutor to different parts, that they may bring home useful knowledge.* WATTS.

To **INSPI'SSATE.** *v.a.* [*in* and *spissus*, Lat.] To thicken; to make thick.

Sugar doth inspissate *the spirits of the wine, and maketh them not so easy to resolve into vapour.*
BACON'S NATURAL HISTORY.

This oil farther inspissated *by evaporation, turns by degrees into balm.*
ARBUTHNOT ON ALIMENTS.

I'NSTITUTIST. *n.s.* [from *institute.*] Writer of institutes, or elemental instructions.

Green gall the institutists *would persuade us to be an effect of an over-hot stomach.*
HARVEY ON CONSUMPTIONS.

INSTRU'CTER. *n.s.* [from *instruct.*] A teacher; an instituter; one who delivers precepts or imparts knowledge.[144]

You have ten thousand instructors *in Christ.* BIBLE 1 CORINTHIANS, IV. 15.

After the flood arts to Chaldea fell,
The father of the faithful there did dwell,
Who both their parent and instructor *was.* DENHAM.

O thou, who future things can'st represent
As present, heav'nly instructor*!*
MILTON'S PARADISE LOST, B. XI.

Poets, the first instructors *of mankind,*
Brought all things to their native proper use. ROSCOMMON.

They see how they are beset on every side, not only with temptations, but instructors *to vice.* LOCKE ON EDUCATION.

We have precepts of duty given us by our instructors. ROGERS.

Several instructors *were disposed among this little helpless people.*
ADDISON'S GUARDIAN, NO. 105.

INSUFFLA'TION. *n.s.* [*in* and *sufflo*, Latin.] The act of breathing upon.

Imposition of hands is a custom of parents in blessing their children, but taken up by the apostles instead of that divine insufflation *which Christ used.* HAMMOND'S FUNDAMENTALS.

I'NSULATED. *adj.* [*insula*, Lat.] Not contiguous on any side.

INTE'LLIGENCE, INTELLIGENCY. *n.s.* [*intelligence*, French; *intelligentia*, Latin.]

1. Commerce of information; notice; mutual communication; account of things distant or secret.

It was perceived there had not been in the catholicks, either at Armenia or at Seleucia, so much foresight as to provide that true intelligence *might pass between them of what was done.* HOOKER, B. V.

A mankind witch! hence with her, out of door!
A most intelligency *bawd!*
SHAKESPEARE.

He furnished his employed men liberally with money, to draw on and reward intelligences; *giving them also in charge to advertise continually what they found.* BACON'S HENRY VII.

The advertisements of neighbour princes are always to be regarded, for that they receive intelligence *from better authors than persons of inferior note.* HAYWARD.

Let all the passages
Be well secur'd, that no intelligence
May pass between the prince and them.
DENHAM'S SOPHY.

Those tales had been sung to lull children asleep, before ever Berosus set up his intelligence *office at Coos.* BENTLEY.

2. Commerce of acquaintance; terms on which men live one with another.

Factious followers are worse to be liked, which follow not upon affection to him with whom they range themselves; whereupon commonly ensueth that ill intelligence *that we see between great personages.* BACON.

He lived rather in a fair intelligence *than any friendship with the favourites.* CLARENDON.

3. Spirit; unbodied mind.

How fully hast thou satisfied me, pure Intelligence *of heav'n, angel!* MILTON'S PARADISE LOST.

There are divers ranks of created beings intermediate between the glorious God and man, as the glorious angels and created intelligences. HALE.

They hoped to get the favour of the houses, and by the favour of the houses they hoped for that of the intelligencies, *and by their favour for that of the supreme God.* STILLINGFLEET.

The regularity of motion, visible in the great variety and curiosity of bodies, is a demonstration that the whole mass of matter is under the conduct of a mighty intelligence. COLLIER.

Satan, appearing like a cherub to Uriel, the intelligence *of the sun circumvented him even in his own province.* DRYDEN.

4. Understanding; skill.

Heaps of huge words, up hoarded hideously,
They think to be chief praise of poetry;
And thereby wanting due intelligence,
Have marr'd the face of goodly poesie.
SPENSER.

INTELLIGE'NCER. *n.s.* [from *intelligence.*] One who sends or conveys news; one who gives notice of private or distant transactions; one who carries messages between parties.

His eyes, being his diligent intelligencers, *could carry unto him no other news but discomfortable.* SIDNEY.

Who hath not heard it spoken
How deep you were within the books of heav'n?
To us, th' imagin'd voice of heav'n itself;
The very opener and intelligencer
Between the grace and sanctities of heav'n,

And our dull workings.
SHAKESPEARE'S HENRY IV.

If they had instructions to that purpose, they might be the best intelligencers *to the king of the true state of his whole kingdom.* BACON.

They are the best sort of intelligencers; *for they have a way into the inmost closets of princes.* HOWEL.

They have news-gatherers and intelligencers, *who make them acquainted with the conversation of the whole kingdom.*
SPECTATOR.

INTE'NDANT. *n.s.* [French.] An officer of the highest class, who oversees any particular allotment of the publick business.

Nearchus, who commanded Alexander's fleet, and Onesicrates, his intendant *general of marine, have both left relations of the Indies.* ARBUTHNOT.

INTERCI'PIENT. *n.s.* [*intercipiens*, Latin.] An intercepting power; something that causes a stoppage.

They commend repellents, but not with much astringency, unless as intercipients *upon the parts above, lest the matter should thereby be impacted in the part.*
WISEMAN.

INTERCI'SION. *n.s.* [*inter* and *cædo*, Lat.] Interruption.

By cessation of oracles we may understand their intercision, *not abcission, or consummate desolation.*
BROWN'S VULGAR ERROURS.

To **INTERCLU'DE.** *v.n.* [*intercludo*, Latin.] To shut from a place or course by something intervening; to intercept.

The voice is sometimes intercluded *by a hoarseness, or viscuous phlegm cleaving to the aspera arteria.* HOLDER.

INTERCLU'SION. *n.s.* [*interclusus*, Latin.] Obstruction; interception.

INTERCOLUMNIA'TION. *n.s.* [*inter* and *columna*, Latin.] The space between the pillars.

The distance or intercolumniation *may be near four of his own diameter, because the materials commonly laid over this pillar were rather of wood than stone.*
WOTTON.

To **INTERCO'MMON.** *v.n.* [*inter* and *common.*] To feed at the same table.

Wine is to be forborn in consumptions, for that the spirits of the wine do prey upon the roscid juice of the body, and intercommon *with the spirits of the body, and so rob them of their nourishment.*
BACON'S NATURAL HISTORY.

INTERJA'CENCY. *n.s.* [from *interjacens*, Latin.]

1. The act or state of lying between.

England and Scotland is divided only by the interjacency *of the Tweed, and some desert ground.* HALE.

2. The thing lying between.

Its fluctuations are but motions, which winds, storms, shoars, and every interjacency *irregulates.*
BROWN'S VULGAR ERROURS.

INTERKNO'WLEDGE. *n.s.* [*inter* and *knowledge.*] Mutual knowledge.

All nations have interknowledge *one of another, either by voyage into foreign parts, or by strangers that come to them.*
BACON'S NEW ATLANTIS.

To **INTERLE'AVE.** *v.a.* [*inter* and *leave.*] To chequer a book by the insertion of blank leaves.

To **INTERLI'NE.** *v.a.* [*inter* and *line.*]

1. To write in alternate lines.

When, by interlining *Latin and English one with another, he has got a moderate knowledge of the Latin tongue, he may then be advanced farther.* LOCKE.

2. To correct by something written between the lines.

He cancell'd an old will, and forg'd a new;
Made wealthy at the small expence of signing,
With a wet seal, and a fresh interlining.
DRYDEN'S JUVENAL.

Three things render a writing suspected: the person producing a false instrument, the person that frames it, and the interlining *and rasing out of words contained in such instruments.* AYLIFFE'S PARERGON.

The muse invok'd, sit down to write,
Blot out, correct, and interline. SWIFT.

To **INTERLO'PE.** *v.n.* [*inter* and *loopen*, Dutch, to run.] To run between parties and intercept the advantage that one should gain from the other; to traffick without a proper licence; to forestall; to anticipate irregularly.

The patron is desired to leave off this interloping *trade, or admit the knights of the industry to their share.* TATLER.

INTERLO'PER. *n.s.* [from *interlope.*] One who runs into business to which he has no right.

The swallow was a fly-catcher, and was no more an interloper *upon the spider's right, than the spider was upon the swallow's.* L'ESTRANGE.

I'NTERLUDE. *n.s.* [*inter* and *ludus*, Latin.] Something plaid at the intervals of festivity; a farce.

When there is a queen, and ladies of honour attending her, there must sometimes be masques, and revels, and interludes.
BACON'S ADVICE TO VILLIERS.

The enemies of Socrates hired Aristophanes to personate him on the stage, and, by the insinuations of those interludes, *conveyed a hatred of him into the people.*
GOVERNMENT OF THE TONGUE.

Dreams are but interludes, *which fancy makes;*
When monarch reason sleeps, this mimick wakes. DRYDEN.

INTERME'DDLER. *n.s.* [from *intermeddle.*] One that interposes officiously; one that thrusts himself into business to which he has no right.

There's hardly a greater pest to government and families, than officious tale-bearers, and busy intermeddlers. L'ESTRANGE.

Our two great allies abroad, and our stock-jobbers at home, direct her majesty not to change her secretary or treasurer, who, for the reasons that these officious intermeddlers *demanded their continuance, ought never to have been admitted into the least trust.* SWIFT.

Shall saucy intermeddlers *say,*
Thus far, and thus, are you allow'd to punish? A. PHILLIPS.

INTERMIGRA'TION. *n.s.* [*intermigration*, Fr. *inter* and *migro*, Lat.] Act of removing from one place to another, so as that of two parties removing each takes the place of the other.

Men have a strange variety in colour, stature, and humour; and all arising from the climate, though the continent be but one, as to point of access, mutual intercourse, and possibility of intermigrations.
HALE'S ORIGIN OF MANKIND.

I'NTERSTICE. *n.s.* [*interstitium*, Lat. *interstice*, Fr.]

1. Space between one thing and another.

The sun shining through a large prism upon a comb placed immediately behind the prism, his light, which passed through the interstices *of the teeth fell upon a white paper: the breadths of the teeth were equal to their* interstices, *and seven teeth together with their* interstices *took up an inch in breadth.* NEWTON'S OPTICKS.

The force of the fluid will separate the smallest particles which compose the fibres, so as to leave vacant interstices *in those places where they cohered before.* ARBUTHNOT.

2. Time between one act and another.

I will point out the interstices *of time which ought to be between one citation and another.* AYLIFFE'S PARERGON.

INTERVI'EW. *n.s.* [*entrevue*, French.] Mutual sight; sight of each other. It is commonly used for a formal and appointed meeting or conference.

The day will come, when the passions of former enmity being allayed, we shall with ten times redoubled tokens of reconciled love shew ourselves each towards other the same, which Joseph and the brethren of Joseph were at the time of their interview *in Egypt.* HOOKER.

His fears were, that the interview *betwixt*
England and France might, through their amity,
Breed him some prejudice.
SHAKESPEARE'S HENRY VIII.

Such happy interview, *and fair event*
Of love, and youth not lost, songs, garlands, flow'rs,
And charming symphonies, attach'd the heart
Of Adam.
MILTON'S PARADISE LOST, B. XI.

To **INTERWI'SH.** *v.a.* [*inter* and *wish.*] To wish mutually to each other.

The venom of all stepdames, gamester's gall,
What tyrants and their subjects interwish,
All ill fall on that man. DONNE.

To **I'NTONATE.** *v.a.* [*intono*, Lat.] To thunder. *Dictionaries.*

INTONA'TION. *n.s.* [*intonation*, Fr. from *intonate.*] The act of thundering. *Dictionaries.*

To **INTO'NE.** *v.n.* [from *intono*, or rather from *tone*; *intonner*, French.] To make a slow protracted noise.

So swells each wind-pipe; ass intones *to ass*
Harmonick twang.
POPE'S DUNCIAD, B. II.

INTRENCHANT. *adj.* [This word, which is, I believe, found only in *Shakespeare*, is thus explained by one of his editors: The *intrenchant* air means the air which suddenly encroaches and closes upon the space left by any body which had passed through it. *Hanmer.* I believe *Shakespeare* intended rather to express the idea of indivisibility or invulnerableness, and derived *intrenchant*, from *in* privative, and *trencher*, to cut; *intrenchant* is indeed properly *not cutting*, rather than *not to be cut*; but this is not the only instance in which *Shakespeare* confounds words of active and passive signification.] Not to be divided; not to be wounded; indivisible.

As easy may'st thou the intrenchant *air*
With thy keen sword impress, as make me bleed. SHAKESPEARE.

INTRI'GUER. *n.s.* [*intrigueur*, Fr. from *intrigue.*] One who busies himself in private transactions; one who forms plots; one who persues women.

I desire that intriguers *will not make a pimp of my lion, and convey their thoughts to one another.* ADDISON.

INTROSPE'CTION. *n.s.* [from *introspect.*] A view of the inside.

The actings of the mind or imagination itself, by way of reflection or introspection *of themselves, are discernible by man.*
HALE'S ORIGIN OF MANKIND.

I was forced to make an introspection *into my own mind, and into that idea of beauty which I have formed in my own imagination.* DRYDEN.

INTROVE'NIENT. *adj.* [*intro* and *venio*, Latin.] Entering; coming in.

Scarce any condition which is not exhausted and obscured, from the commixture of introvenient *nations, either by commerce or conquest.*
BROWN'S VULGAR ERROURS.

INTURGE'SCENCE. *n.s.* [*in* and *turgesco*, Latin.] Swelling; the act or state of swelling.

Not by attenuation of the upper part of the sea, but inturgescencies *caused first at the bottom, and carrying the upper part of it before them.*
BROWN'S VULGAR ERROURS.

INVALI'DITY. *n.s.* [*in* and *validity*; *invalidité*, French.]
1. Weakness; want of cogency.
2. Want of bodily strength. This is no English meaning.

He ordered, that none who could work should be idle; and that none who could not work, by age, sickness, or invalidity, *should want.* TEMPLE.

INVE'NTION. *n.s* [*invention*, French; *inventio*, Latin.]
1. Fiction.[145]

O for a muse of fire, that would ascend
The brightest heaven of invention*!*
SHAKESPEARE'S HENRY V, PROLOGUE.

By improving what was writ before,
Invention *labours less, but judgment more.* ROSCOMMON.

Invention *is a kind of muse, which, being possessed of the other advantages common to her sisters, and being warmed by the fire of Apollo, is raised higher than the rest.*
DRYDEN.

The chief excellence of Virgil is judgment, of Homer is invention. POPE.

2. Discovery.

Nature hath provided several glandules to separate this juice from the blood, and no less than four pair of channels to convey it into the mouth, which are of a late invention, *and called ductus salivales.*
RAY ON THE CREATION.

3. Excogitation; act of producing something new.

Mine is th' invention *of the charming lyre;*
Sweet notes and heav'nly numbers I inspire. DRYDEN.

4. Forgery.

We hear our bloody cousins, not confessing
Their cruel parricide, filling their hearers
With strange invention.
SHAKESPEARE'S MACBETH.

If thou can'st accuse,
Do it without invention *suddenly.*
SHAKESPEARE'S HENRY VI.

5. The thing invented.

The garden, a place not fairer in natural ornaments than artificial inventions.
SIDNEY.

Th' invention *all admir'd; and each how he*
To be th' inventor miss'd, so easy it seem'd
Once found, which yet unfound most would have thought
Impossible. MILTON'S PARADISE LOST.

INVE'NTOR. *n.s.* [*inventor*, Latin.]
1. A finder out of something new.

We have the statue of your Columbus, that discovered the West Indies, also the inventor *of ships: your Monk, that was the* inventor *of ordnance, and of gunpowder.*
BACON.

Studious they appear
Of arts that polish life; inventors *rare,*
Unmindful of their maker.
MILTON'S PARADISE LOST.

Th' invention all admir'd, and each how he
To be the inventor *miss'd.* MILTON.

Why are these positions charged upon me as their sole author and inventor, *and the reader led into a belief that they were never before maintained by any person of virtue?* ATTERBURY.

2. A contriver; a framer. In an ill sense.

In this upshot, purposes mistook,
Fall'n on th' inventors *heads.*
SHAKESPEARE'S HAMLET.

INVE'NTRESS. *n.s.* [*inventrice*, Fr. from *inventor.*] A female that invents.

The arts, with all their retinue of lesser trades, history and tradition tell us when they had their beginning; and how many of their inventors and inventresses *were deified.* BURNET.

Cecilia came,
Inventress *of the vocal frame:*
The sweet enthusiast, from her sacred store,
Enlarg'd the former narrow bounds.
DRYDEN.

I'NVOICE. *n.s.* [This word is perhaps corrupted from the French word *envoyez*, send.] A catalogue of the freight of a ship, or of the articles and price of goods sent by a factor.

I'NWARD. *n.s.*

1. Any thing within, generally the bowels. Seldom has this sense a singular.

Then sacrificing, laid
The inwards, *and their fat, with incense strew'd*
On the cleft wood, and all due rites perform'd. MILTON.

They esteem them most profitable, because of the great quantity of fat upon their inwards. MORTIMER'S HUSBANDRY.

2. Intimate; near acquaintance.

Sir, I was an inward *of his; a sly fellow was the duke; and I know the cause of his withdrawing.* SHAKESPEARE.

JOB. *n.s.* [A low word now much in use, of which I cannot tell the etymology.]

1. Petty, piddling work; a piece of chance work.

He was now with his old friends in the state of a poor disbanded officer after peace, like an old favourite of a cunning minister after the job *is over.* ARBUTHNOT.

No cheek is known to blush, no heart to throb,
Save when they lose a question, or a job.
POPE.

Such patents as these never were granted with a view of being a job, *for the interest of a particular person to the damage of the publick.* SWIFT.

2. A low mean lucrative busy affair.

3. A sudden stab with a sharp instrument.

To **JOB.** *v.a.*

1. To strike suddenly with a sharp instrument.

As an ass with a galled back was feeding in a meadow, a raven pitched upon him, and there sat jobbing *of the sore.* L'ESTRANGE.

2. To drive in a sharp instrument.

Let peacocke and turkey leave jobbing *their bex.* TUSSER.

The work would, where a small irregularity of stuff should happen, draw or job *the edge into the stuff.* MOXON.

To **JOB.** *v.n.* To play the stockjobber; to buy and sell as a broker.

The judge shall job, *the bishop bite the town,*
And mighty dukes pack cards for half a crown. POPE.

JOBBERNO'WL. *n.s.* [most probably from *jobbe*, Flemish, dull, and *nowl*, *hnol*, Saxon, a head.] Loggerhead; blockhead.

And like the world, men's jobbernowls
Turn round upon their ears, the poles.
HUDIBRAS, P. III.

JO'GGER. *n.s.* [from *jog.*] One who moves heavily and dully.

They, with their fellow joggers *of the plough.* DRYDEN.

JOKE. *n.s.* [*jocus*, Latin.] A jest; something not serious.

Link towns to towns with avenues of oak,
Inclose whole downs in walls, 'tis all a joke!
Inexorable death shall level all. POPE.

Why should publick mockery in print, or a merry joke *upon a stage, be a better test of truth than severe railing sarcasms and publick persecutions?*
WATTS'S IMPROVEMENT OF THE MIND.

To **JOLL.** *v.a.* [from *joll*, the head.] To beat the head against any thing; to clash with violence.

Howsoe'er their hearts are sever'd in religion, their heads are both one: they may joll *horns together like any deer i' th' herd.* SHAKESPEARE.

The tortoises envied the easiness of the frogs, 'till they saw them jolled *to pieces and devoured for want of a buckler.*
L'ESTRANGE.

JO'URNAL. *n.s.* [*journal*, French; *giornale*, Italian.]

1. A diary; an account kept of daily transactions.

Edward kept a most judicious journal *of all the principal passages of the affairs of his estate.* HAYWARD ON EDWARD VI.

Time has destroyed two noble journals *of the navigation of Hanno and of Hamilcar.*
ARBUTHNOT ON COINS.

2. Any paper published daily.

JO'URNALIST. *n.s.* [from *journal.*] A writer of journals.

I'RIS. *n.s.* [Latin.]

1. The rainbow.

Beside the solary iris, *which God shewed unto Noah, there is another lunary, whose efficient is the moon.* BROWN.

2. Any appearance of light resembling the rainbow.

When both bows appeared more distinct, I measured the breadth of the interior iris *2 gr. 10'; and the breadth of the red, yellow, and green in the exterior* iris, *was to the breadth of the same colours in the interior 3 to 2.* NEWTON'S OPTICKS.

3. The circle round the pupil of the eye.

4. The flower-de-luce.

Iris *all hues, roses and jessamine.*
MILTON.

To **IRK.** *v.a.* [*yrk*, work, Islandick.] This word is used only impersonally, *it* irks *me*; *mihi pœnæ est*, it gives me pain; or, I am weary of it. Thus the authors of the Accidence say, *tædet*, it *irketh.*

Come, shall we go and kill us venison?
And yet it irks *me, the poor dappled fools*
Should, in their own confines, with forked heads,
Have their round haunches gor'd.
SHAKESPEARE.

It irks *his heart he cannot be reveng'd.*
SHAKESPEARE'S HENRY VI.

I'RON. *adj.*

1. Made of iron.

In iron *walls they deem'd me not secure.*
SHAKESPEARE'S HENRY VI.

Get me an iron *crow, and bring it straight*
Unto my cell.
SHAKESPEARE'S ROMEO AND JULIET.

Some are of an iron *red, shining, and polite; others not polite, but as if powdered with* iron *dust.* WOODWARD.

Poll-cats and weesels do a great deal of injury to warrens: the way of taking them is in hutches, and iron *traps.* MORTIMER.

2. Resembling iron in colour.

A piece of stone of a dark iron *grey colour, but in some parts of a ferruginous colour.*
WOODWARD ON FOSSILS.

Some of them are of an iron *red, and very bright.* WOODWARD.

3. Harsh; severe; rigid; miserable; calamitous: as, the iron age, for an age of hardship and wickedness. These

ideas may be found more or less in all the following examples.

Three vigorous virgins, waiting still behind,
Assist the throne of th' iron *scepter'd king.*
CRASHAW.

O sad virgin, that thy power
Might bid the soul of Orpheus sing
Such notes as warbled to the string,
Drew iron *tears from Pluto's cheek,*
And made hell grant what love did seek.
MILTON.

In all my iron *years of wars and dangers,*
From blooming youth down to decaying age,
My fame ne'er knew a stain of dishonour.
ROWE.

Jove crush the nations with an iron *rod,*
And ev'ry monarch be the scourge of God.
POPE'S ODYSSEY.

4. Indissoluble; unbroken.

Rash Elpenor, in an evil hour,
Dry'd an immeasurable bowl, and thought
T' exhale his surfeit by irriguous sleep,
Imprudent: him death's iron *sleep opprest.*
PHILLIPS.

5. Hard; impenetrable.

I will converse with iron *witted fools,*
And unrespective boys: none are for me,
That look into me with consid'rate eyes.
SHAKESPEARE'S RICHARD III.

I'RONY. *adj.* [from *iron.*] Made of iron; partaking of iron.

The force they are under is real, and that of their fate but imaginary: it is not strange if the irony *chains have more solidity than the contemplative.*
HAMMOND'S FUNDAMENTALS.

Some springs of Hungary, highly impregnated with vitriolick salts, dissolve the body of one metal, suppose iron, put into the spring; and deposite, in lieu of the irony *particles carried off, coppery particles.*
WOODWARD ON FOSSILS.

I'RONY. *n.s.* [*ironie*, Fr. *'ειρωνεία.*] A mode of speech in which the meaning is contrary to the words: as, *Bolingbroke was a holy man.*

So grave a body, upon so solemn an occasion, should not deal in irony, *or explain their meaning by contraries.*
SWIFT.

IRRE'LATIVE. *adj.* [*in* and *relativus*, Latin.] Having no reference to any thing; single; unconnected.

Separated by the voice of God, things in their species came out in uncommunicated varieties, and irrelative *seminalities.*
BROWN'S VULGAR ERROURS.

IRREPLE'VIABLE. *adj.* [*in* and *replevy.*] Not to be redeemed. A law term.

IRRESI'STLESS. *adj.* [A barbarous ungrammatical conjunction of two negatives.] Irresistible; resistless.

Those radiant eyes, whose irresistless *flame*
Strikes envy dumb, and keeps sedition tame,
They can to gazing multitudes give law,
Convert the factious, and the rebel awe.
GRANVILLE.

IRRI'SION. *n.s.* [*irrisio*, Lat. *irrision*, French.] The act of laughing at another.

This person, by his indiscreet and unnatural irrision, *and exposing of his father, incurs his indignation and curse.*
WOODWARD'S NATURAL HISTORY.

IS. [*is*, Saxon.]

1. The third person singular of *to be*: I am, thou art, he *is.*

He that is *of God, heareth God's words.*
BIBLE JOHN, VIII. 47.

Be not afraid of them, for they cannot do evil; neither is *it in them to do good.*
BIBLE JEREMIAH, X. 5.

My thought, whose murther yet is *but fantastical,*
Shakes so my single state of man, that function

Is smother'd in surmise; and nothing is,
But what is *not.*
SHAKESPEARE'S MACBETH.

2. It is sometimes expressed by *'s.*

There's some among you have beheld me fighting. SHAKESPEARE.

I'SICLE. *n.s.* [More properly *icicle*, from *ice*; but *ice* should rather be written *ise*; *iss*, Saxon.] A pendent shoot of ice.

Do you know this lady?
—— The moon of Rome; chaste as the isicle
That's curdled by the frost from purest snow
Hanging on Dian's temple.
SHAKESPEARE.

The frosts and snows her tender body spare;
Those are not limbs for isicles *to tear.*
DRYDEN.

ITCH. *n.s.* [*gicha*, Saxon.]
1. A cutaneous disease extremely contagious, which overspreads the body with small pustules filled with a thin serum, and raised as microscopes have discovered by a small animal. It is cured by sulphur.

Lust and liberty
Creep in the minds and marrows of our youths,
That 'gainst the stream of virtue they may strive,
And drown themselves in riot, itches, *blains.* SHAKESPEARE'S TIMON.

The Lord will smite thee with the scab and with the itch, *whereof thou can'st not be healed.*
BIBLE DEUTERONOMY, XXVIII. 27.

As if divinity had catch'd
The itch, *on purpose, to be scratch'd.*
HUDIBRAS.

2. The sensation of uneasiness in the skin, which is eased by rubbing.
3. A constant teazing desire.

A certain itch *of meddling with other people's matters, puts us upon shifting.*
L'ESTRANGE.

He had still pedigree in his head, and an itch *of being thought a divine king.*
DRYDEN.

From servants company a child is to be kept, not by prohibitions, for that will but give him an itch *after it, but by other ways.* LOCKE.

At half mankind when gen'rous Manly raves,
All know 'tis virtue; for he thinks them knaves:
When universal homage Umbra pays,
All see 'tis vice, and itch *of vulgar praise.*
POPE.

JUG. *n.s.* [*jugge*, Danish.] A large drinking vessel with a gibbous or swelling belly.

You'd rail upon the hostess of the house,
Because she bought stone jugs *and no seal'd quarts.* SHAKESPEARE.

He fetch'd 'em drink,
Fill'd a large jug *up to the brink.*
SWIFT'S MISCELLANIES.

To **JU'GGLE.** *v.n.* [*jougler* or *jongler*, Fr. *jocari*, Lat.]
1. To play tricks by slight of hand; to show false appearances of extraordinary performances.

The ancient miracle of Memnon's statue seems to be a juggling *of the Ethiopian priests.* DIGBY ON BODIES.

2. To practise artifice or imposture.

Be these juggling *fiends no more believ'd,*
That palter with us in a double sense.
SHAKESPEARE'S MACBETH.

Is't possible the spells of France should juggle
Men into such strange mockeries?
SHAKESPEARE'S HENRY VIII.

They ne'er forswore themselves, nor lied,
Disdain'd to stay for friends consents;

Nor juggl'd *about settlements.*
HUDIBRAS, P. III.

To **JUKE.** *v.n.* [*jucher*, French.]
1. To perch upon any thing: as, birds.
2. *Juking*, in Scotland, denotes still any complaisance by bending of the head.

Two asses travelled; the one laden with oats, the other with money: the money-merchant was so proud of his trust, that he went juking *and tossing of his head.*
L'ESTRANGE.

JU'NCATE. *n.s.* [*juncade*, French; *gioncata*, Italian.]
1. Cheesecake; a kind of sweetmeat of curds and sugar.
2. Any delicacy.

A goodly table of pure ivory,
All spread with juncates, *fit to entertain*
The greatest prince.
SPENSER, SONNET 77.

With stories told of many a feat,
How fairy Mab the juncates *eat.*
MILTON.

3. A furtive or private entertainment. It is now improperly written *junket* in this sense, which alone remains much in use. See **JUNKET.**

JU'NKET. *n.s.* [properly *juncate.* See **JUNCATE.**]
1. A sweetmeat.

You know, there wants no junkets *at the feast.* SHAKESPEARE.

2. A stolen entertainment.

JU'RIST. *n.s.* [*juriste*, Fr. *jura*, Lat.] A civil lawyer; a man who professes the science of the law; a civilian.

This is not to be measured by the principles of jurists. BACON.

K

A letter borrowed by the English from the Greek alphabet. It has before all the vowels one invariable sound: as, *keen*, *ken*, *kill*; but is not much in use, except after[146] *c* at the end of words: as, *knock*, *clock*, *crack*, *back*, *brick*, *stick*, *pluck*, *check*, which were written anciently with *e* final: as, *clocke*, *checke*, *tricke*. It is also in use between a vowel and the silent *e* final: as, *cloke*, *broke*, *brake*, *pike*, *duke*, *eke*. It likewise ends a word after a diphthong: as, *look*, *break*, *shock*, *beek*. The English never use *c* at the end of a word. *K* is silent in the present pronunciation before *n*: as, *knife*, *knee*, *knell*.

KAM. *adj.* Crooked. *Kam*, in Erse, is squint-eyed, and applied to any thing awry: clean *kam* signifies crooked, athwart, awry, cross from the purpose. *A-schembo*, Italian, hence our English *a-kimbo*. Clean *kam* is, by vulgar pronunciation, brought to *kim kam*.

The blood he hath lost, he dropt it for his country:
And what is left, to lose it by his country,
Were to us all that do't and suffer it,
A brand to th' end o' th' world.
—— *This is clean* kam.
—— *Meerly awry.* SHAKESPEARE.

KAYLE. *n.s.* [*quille*, French.]

1. Ninepin; kettlepins, of which *skittles* seems a corruption.

And now at keels *they try a harmless chance,*
And now their cur they teach to fetch and dance. SIDNEY.

The residue of the time they wear out at coits, kayles, *or the like idle exercises.*
CAREW'S SURVEY OF CORNWALL.

2. A kind of play still retained in Scotland, in which nine holes ranged in three's are made in the ground, and an iron bullet rolled in among them.

KE'CKSY. *n.s.* [commonly *kex*, *cigue*, French; *cicuta*, Latin. *Skinner*.] *Skinner* seems to think *kecksy* or *kex* the same as hemlock. It is used in Staffordshire both for hemlock, and any other hollow jointed plant.

Nothing teems
But hateful docks, rough thistles, kecksies, *burs,*
Losing both beauty and utility.
SHAKESPEARE'S HENRY V.

To **KE'ELHALE.** *v.a.* [*keel* and *hale*.] To punish in the seamen's way, by dragging the criminal under water on one side of the ship and up again on the other.

KELL. *n.s.* A sort of pottage. *Ainsworth.* It is so called in Scotland, being a soupe made with shreded greens.

To **KEMB.** *v.a.* [*cœmban*, Saxon; *kammen*, German: now written, perhaps less properly, *to comb.*] To separate or disentangle by a denticulated instrument.

Yet are the men more loose than they,
More kemb'd *and bath'd, and rubb'd and trim'd,*
More sleek. BEN JONSON.

Thy head and hair are sleek;
And then thou kemb'st *the tuzzes on thy cheek.* DRYDEN.

KE'NNEL. *n.s.* [*chenil*, French.]
1. A cot for dogs.

A dog sure, if he could speak, had wit enough to describe his kennel. SIDNEY.

From forth the kennel *of thy womb hath crept*
A hell-hound, that doth hunt us all to death. SHAKESPEARE.

The seditious remain within their station, which, by reason of the nastiness of the beastly multitude, might be more fitly termed a kennel *than a camp.* HAYWARD.

2. A number of dogs kept in a kennel.

A little herd of England's tim'rous deer,
Maz'd with a yelping kennel *of French curs.* SHAKESPEARE.

3. The hole of a fox, or other beast.
4. [*Kennel*, Dutch; *chenal*, Fr. *canalis*, Latin.] The watercourse of a street.

Bad humours gather to a bile; or, as divers kennels *flow to one sink, so in short time their numbers increased.* HAYWARD.

He always came in so dirty, as if he had been dragged through the kennel *at a boarding-school.* ARBUTHNOT.

KE'TTLE. *n.s.* [*cetl*, Saxon; *ketel*, Dutch.] A vessel in which liquor is boiled. In the kitchen the name of *pot* is given to the boiler that grows narrower towards the top, and of *kettle* to that which grows wider. In authors they are confounded.

The fire thus form'd, she sets the kettle *on;*
Like burnish'd gold the little seether shone.
DRYDEN.

KI'CKSHAW. *n.s.* [This word is supposed, I think with truth, to be only a corruption of *quelque chose*, something; yet *Milton* seems to have understood it otherwise; for he writes it *kickshoe*, and seems to think it used in contempt of dancing.]
1. Something uncommon; fantastical; something ridiculous.

Shall we need the monsieurs of Paris to take our hopeful youth into their slight and prodigal custodies, and send them over back again transformed into mimicks, apes, and kickshoes? MILTON.

2. A dish so changed by the cookery that it can scarcely be known.

Some pigeons, a couple of short-legged hens, a joint of mutton, and any pretty little tiny kickshaws.
SHAKESPEARE'S HENRY IV.

In wit, as well as war, they give us vigour;
Cressy was lost by kickshaws *and soup-meagre.* FENTON.

KI'MBO. *adj.* [*a schembo*, Italian.] Crooked; bent; arched.

The kimbo *handles seem with bears-foot carv'd,*
And never yet to table have been serv'd.
DRYDEN'S VIRGIL.

He observed them edging towards one another to whisper; so that John was forced to sit with his arms a kimbo, *to keep them asunder.*
ARBUTHNOT'S HISTORY OF JOHN BULL.

KI'NDLY. *adj.* [from *kind*; probably from *kind* the substantive.]

. Homogeneal; congeneal; kindred; of he same nature.

This competency I beseech God I may be able to digest into kindly *juice, that I may grow thereby.*
HAMMOND.

These soft fires
Not only enlighten, but with kindly *heat,*
Of various influence, foment and warm,
Temper or nourish.
MILTON'S PARADISE LOST, B. IV.

2. The foregoing sense seems to have been originally implied by this word; but following writers, inattentive to its etymology, confounded it with *kind*.
3. Bland; mild; softening.

Through all the living regions do'st thou move,
And scatter'st, where thou goest, the kindly *seeds of love.* DRYDEN.

Ye heav'ns, from high the dewy nectar pour,
And in soft silence shed the kindly *show'r!*
POPE.

KI'SSINGCRUST. *n.s.* [*kissing* and *crust.*] Crust formed where one loaf in the oven touches another.

These bak'd him kissingcrusts, *and those*
Brought him small beer.
KING'S COOKERY.

KIT. *n.s.* [*kitte*, Dutch.]
. A large bottle. *Skinner*.
2. A small diminutive fiddle.

'Tis kept in a case fitted to it, almost like a dancing-master's kit.
GREW'S MUSÆUM.

3. A small wooden vessel, in which Newcastle salmon is sent up to town.

KI'TCHENSTUFF. *n.s.* [*kitchen* and *stuff.*] The fat of meat scummed off the pot, or gathered out of the dripping-pan.

As a thrifty wench scrapes kitchenstuff,
And barreling the droppings and the snuff
Of wasting candles, which in thirty year,
Reliquely kept, perchance buys wedding cheer. DONNE.

Instead of kitchenstuff *some cry*
A gospel preaching ministry. HUDIBRAS.

KI'TCHENWENCH. *n.s.* [*kitchen* and *wench.*] Scullion; maid employed to clean the instruments of cookery.

Laura to his lady was but a kitchenwench. SHAKESPEARE.

Roasting and boiling leave to the kitchenwench. SWIFT.

To KLICK. *v.n.* [from *clack.*]
1. To make a small sharp noise.
2. In Scotland it denotes to pilfer or steal away suddenly with a snatch.

KNACK. *n.s.* [*cnec*, Welsh, sly knavery; *cnaringe*, skill, Sax.]
1. A little machine; a petty contrivance; a toy.

When I was young, I was wont
To load my she with knacks*: I would have ransack'd*
The pedlar's silken treasury, and have pour'd it
To her acceptance.
SHAKESPEARE'S WINTER'S TALE.

For thee, fond boy,
If I may ever know thou do'st but sigh
That thou no more shalt see this knack, *as never*
I mean thou shalt, we'll bar thee from success. SHAKESPEARE.

This cap was moulded on a porringer,
A velvet dish; fie, fie, 'tis lewd and filthy:
Why 'tis a cockle, or a walnut shell,
A knack, *a toy, a trick, a baby's cap.*
SHAKESPEARE.

But is't not presumption to write verse to you,
Who make the better poems of the two?
For all these pretty knacks *that you compose,*
Alas, what are they but poems in prose!
DENHAM.

He expounded both his pockets,
And found a watch, with rings and lockets;
A copper-plate, with almanacks
Engrav'd upon't, with other knacks.
HUDIBRAS.

2. A readiness; an habitual facility; a lucky dexterity.

I'll teach you the knacks
Of eating of flax,
And out of their noses
Draw ribbands and posies.
BEN JONSON'S GYPSIES.

The knack *of fast and loose passes with foolish people for a turn of wit; but they are not aware all this while of the desperate consequences of an ill habit.*
L'ESTRANGE.

There is a certain knack *in the art of conversation that gives a good grace to many things, by the manner and address of handling them.* L'ESTRANGE.

Knaves, who in full assemblies have the knack
Of turning truth to lies, and white to black. DRYDEN.

My author has a great knack *at remarks: in the end he makes another, about our refining in controversy, and coming nearer and nearer to the church of Rome.*
ATTERBURY.

The dean was famous in his time,
And had a kind of knack *at rhime.*
SWIFT.

3. A nice trick.

For how should equal colours do the knack*?*
Cameleons who can paint in white and black? POPE.

KNA'CKER. *n.s.* [from *knack.*]
1. A maker of small work.

One part for plow-wright, cartwright, knacker, *and smith.*
MORTIMER'S HUSBANDRY.

2. A ropemaker. [*Restio*, Latin.] *Ainsworth.*

To **KNIGHT.** *v.a.* [from the noun.] To create one a knight, which is done by the king, who gives the person kneeling a blow with a sword, and bids him rise up *sir.*

Favours came thick upon him: the next St George's day he was knighted.
WOTTON.

The lord protector knighted *the king; and immediately the king stood up, took the sword from the lord protector, and dubbed the lord mayor of London knight.*
HAYWARD.

The hero William, and the martyr Charles,
One knighted *Blackmore, and one pension'd Quarles.* POPE.

KNIGHT of the Post. A hireling evidence.

There are knights of the post, *and holy cheats enough, to swear the truth of the broadest contradictions, where pious frauds shall give them an extraordinary call.*
SOUTH'S SERMONS.

KNIGHT of the Shire. One of the representatives of a county in parliament: he formerly was a military knight, but now any man having an estate in land of six hundred pounds a year is qualified.

KNO'WLEDGE. *n.s.* [from *know.*]
1. Certain perception; indubitable apprehension.

Knowledge, *which is the highest degree of the speculative faculties, consists in the perception of the truth of affirmative or negative propositions.* LOCKE.

2. Learning; illumination of the mind.

Ignorance is the curse of God,
Knowledge *the wing wherewith we fly to heav'n.* SHAKESPEARE.

3. Skill in any thing.

Do but say to me what I should do,

That in your knowledge *may by me be done,*
And I am prest unto it.
SHAKESPEARE'S MERCHANT OF VENICE.

4. Acquaintance with any fact or person.

The dog straight fawned upon his master for old knowledge. SIDNEY.

That is not forgot,
Which ne'er I did remember; to my knowledge
I never in my life did look on him.
SHAKESPEARE'S RICHARD II.

5. Cognisance; notice.

Why have I found grace in thine eyes, that thou shouldst take knowledge *of me, seeing I am a stranger?* BIBLE RUTH, II. 10.

A state's anger should not take
Knowledge *either of fools or women.*
BEN JONSON'S CATILINE.

6. Information; power of knowing.

I pulled off my headpiece, and humbly entreated her pardon, or knowledge *why she was cruel.* SIDNEY.

To **KNU'CKLE.** *v.n.* [from the noun.] To submit: I suppose from an odd custom of striking the under side of the table with the knuckles, in confession of an argumental defeat.

To **KYD.** *v.n.* [corrupted probably from *cuð*, Saxon.] To know.

But ah, unjust and worthless Colin Clout,
That kydst *the hidden kinds of many a weed;*
Yet kydst *not one to cure thy sore heart root,*
Whose rankling wound as yet doth rifely bleed. SPENSER.

L

A liquid consonant, which preserves always the same sound in English. In the Saxon it was aspirated; as *hlaf, loaf; hlœfdig, lady.* At the end of a monosyllable it is always doubled; as, *shall; still; full,* except after a diphthong; as, *fail; feel; veal; cool.* In a word of more syllables it is written single; as, *channel; canal; tendril.* It is sometimes put before *e,* and sounded feebly after it; as *bible; title.*

LA. *interject.* [corrupted by an effeminate pronunciation from *lo.*] See; look; behold.

> La *you! if you speak ill of the devil,*
> *How he takes it at heart.*
> SHAKESPEARE'S TWELFTH NIGHT.

LA'BORATORY. *n.s.* [*laboratoire,* French.] A chemist's workroom.

> *It would contribute to the history of colours, if chemists would in their* laboratory *take a heedful notice, and give us a faithful account, of the colours observed in the steam of bodies, either sublimed or distilled.* BOYLE ON COLOURS.

> *The flames of love will perform those miracles they of the furnace boast of, would they employ themselves in this* laboratory. DECAY OF PIETY.

LACE. *n.s.* [*lacet,* French; *laqueus,* Latin.]

1. A string; a cord.

> *There the fond fly entangled, struggled long,*
> *Himself to free thereout; but all in vain:*
> *For striving more, the more in* laces *strong*
> *Himself he tied, and wrapt his winges twain*
> *In limy snares, the subtil loops among.*
> SPENSER.

2. A snare; a gin.

> *The king had snared been in love's strong* lace. FAIRFAX.

3. A platted string, with which women fasten their clothes.

> *O! cut my* lace, *lest my heart cracking, it*
> *Break too.*
> SHAKESPEARE'S WINTER'S TALE.

> *Doll ne'er was call'd to cut her* lace,
> *Or throw cold water in her face.* SWIFT.

4. Ornaments of fine thread curiously woven.

> *Our English dames are much given to the wearing of costly* laces; *and, if they be brought from Italy, they are in great esteem.*
> BACON'S ADVICE TO VILLIERS.

5. Textures of thread, with gold or silver.

He wears a stuff, whose thread is coarse and round,
But trimm'd with curious lace.
HERBERT.

6. Sugar. A cant word.

If haply he the sect pursues,
That read and comment upon news;
He takes up their mysterious face,
He drinks his coffee without lace. PRIOR.

LA'CKLINEN. *adj.* [*lack* and *linen.*] Wanting shirts.

I scorn you, scurvy companion; what? your poor, base, rascally, cheating, lacklinen *mate; away, you mouldy rogue, away; I'm made for your master.*
SHAKESPEARE'S HENRY IV.

LACO'NICK. *adj.* [*laconicus*, Lat. *laconique*, Fr.] Short; brief; from *Lacones*, the Spartans, who used few words.

I grow laconick *even beyond laconicism; for sometimes I return only yes, or no, to questionary or petitionary epistles of half a yard long.* POPE TO SWIFT.

LAD. *n.s.* [*leode*, Saxon, which commonly signifies people, but sometimes, says Mr. *Lye*, a boy.]

1. A boy; a stripling, in familiar language.

We were
Two lads, *that thought there was no more behind,*
But such a day to-morrow as to-day,
And to be boy eternal.
SHAKESPEARE'S WINTER'S TALE.

The poor lad *who wants knowledge, must set his invention on the rack, to say something where he knows nothing.*
LOCKE.

Too far from the ancient forms of teaching several good grammarians have departed, to the great detriment of such lads *as have been removed to other schools.* WATTS.

2. A boy, in pastoral language.

For grief whereof the lad *would after joy,*
But pin'd away in anguish, and self-will'd annoy. FAIRY QUEEN.

The shepherd lad,
Whose offspring on the throne of Judah sat
So many ages.
MILTON'S PARADISE REGAIN'D, B. II. L. 439.

LAG. *n.s.*

1. The lowest class; the rump; the fag end.

The rest of your foes, O gods, the senators of Athens, together with the common lag *of people, what is amiss in them, make suitable for destruction.*
SHAKESPEARE'S TIMON OF ATHENS.

2. He that comes last, or hangs behind.

The last, the lag *of all the race.*
DRYDEN'S VIRGIL'S ÆNEIS.

What makes my ram the lag *of all the flock.* POPE.

LAM'BATIVE. *n.s.* A medicine taken by licking with the tongue.

I stitch'd up the wound, and applied astringents, with compress and retentive bandage, then put him into bed, and let him blood in the arm, advising a lambative, *to be taken as necessity should require.*
WISEMAN'S SURGERY.

LAMBS-WOOL. *n.s.* [*lamb* and *wool.*] Ale mixed with the pulp of roasted apples.

A cup of lambs-wool *they drank to him there.*
SONG OF THE KING AND THE MILLER.

LA'MMAS. *n.s.* [This word is said by *Bailey*, I know not on what authority, to be derived from a custom, by which the tenants of the archbishop of York were obliged, at the time of mass, on the first of August, to bring a lamb to the altar. In Scotland they are said to wean lambs on this day. It may else be corrupted from *lattermath.*] The first of August.

In 1578 was that famous lammas *day, which buried the reputation of Don John of Austria.* BACON.

LAMP. *n.s.* [*lampe*, French; *lampas*, Latin.]

1. A light made with oil and a wick.

O thievish night,
Why should'st thou, but for some felonious end,
In thy dark lanthorn thus close up the stars
That nature hung in heaven, and fill'd their lamps
With everlasting oil, to give due light
To the misled and lonely traveller?
MILTON.

In lamp *furnaces I used spirit of wine instead of oil, and with the same flame has melted foliated gold.* BOYLE.

2. Any kind of light, in poetical language, real or metaphorical.

Thy gentle eyes send forth a quick'ning spirit,
And feed the dying lamp *of life within me.*
ROWE.

Cynthia, fair regent of the night,
O may thy silver lamp *from heaven's high bow'r,*
Direct my footsteps in the midnight hour.
GAY.

LAMPO'ON. *n.s.* [*Bailey* derives it from *lampons*, a drunken song. It imports, *let us drink*, from the old French *lamper*, and was repeated at the end of each couplet at carousals. *Trevoux.*] A personal satire; abuse; censure written not to reform but to vex.

They say my talent is satire; if so, it is a fruitful age: they have sown the dragon's teeth themselves, and it is but just they should reap each other in lampoons. DRYDEN.

Make satire a lampoon. POPE.

LANCEPE'SADE. *n.s.* [*lance spezzate*, French.] The officer under the corporal: not now in use among us.

To th' Indies of her arm he flies,
Fraught both with east and western prize,
Which, when he had in vain essay'd,
Arm'd like a dapper lancepesade
With Spanish pike, he broach'd a pore.
CLEAVELAND.

To **LANCH.** *v.a.* [*lancer*, French. This word is too often written *launch*: it is only a vocal corruption of *lance.*] To dart; to cast as a lance; to throw; to let fly.

See whose arm can lanch *the surer bolt,*
And who's the better Jove.
DRYDEN AND LEE'S OEDIPUS.

Me, only me, the hand of fortune bore,
Unblest to tread that interdicted shore:
When Jove tremendous in the sable deeps,
Launch'd *his red light'ning at our scatter'd ships.* POPE.

LA'NDING-PLACE. *n.s.* [from *land.*] The top of stairs.

Let the stairs to the upper rooms be upon a fair, open newel, and a fair landing-place *at the top.* BACON.

The landing-place *is the uppermost step of a pair of stairs, viz. the floor of the room you ascend upon.* MOXON.

There is a stair-case that strangers are generally carried to see, where the easiness of the ascent, the disposition of the lights, and the convenient landing, *are admirably well contrived.*
ADDISON'S REMARKS ON ITALY.

What the Romans called vestibulum was no part of the house, but the court and landing-place *between it and the street.*
ARBUTHNOT ON COINS.

LA'NDLOPER. *n.s.* [*land* and *loopen*, Dutch.] A landman; a term of reproach used by seamen of those who pass their lives on shore.

LAND-TAX. *n.s.* [*land* and *tax.*] Tax laid upon land and houses.

If mortgages were registered, land-taxes *might reach the lender to pay his proportion.* LOCKE.

LAND-WAITER. *n.s.* [*land* and *waiter.*] An officer of the customs, who is to watch what goods are landed.

Give a guinea to a knavish land-waiter, *and he shall connive at the merchant for cheating the queen of an hundred.* SWIFT'S EXAMINER, NO. 27.

LA'NGUAGE. *n.s.* [*language,* French; *lingua,* Latin.]

1. Human speech.

We may define language, *if we consider it more materially, to be letters, forming and producing words and sentences; but if we consider it according to the design thereof, then* language *is apt signs for communication of thoughts.* HOLDER.

2. The tongue of one nation as distinct from others.

O! good my lord, no Latin;
I am not such a truant since my coming,
As not to know the language *I have liv'd in.* SHAKESPEARE.

He not from Rome alone, but Greece,
Like Jason, brought the golden fleece;
To him that language, *though to none*
Of th' others, as his own was known. DENHAM.

3. Stile; manner of expression.

Though his language *should not be refin'd,*
It must not be obscure and impudent. ROSCOMMON.

Others for language *all their care express,*
And value books, as women, men, for dress:
Their praise is still – the stile is excellent;
The sense, they humbly take upon content. POPE.

LA'NGUAGED. *adj.* [from the noun.] Having various languages.

He wand'ring long a wider circle made,
And many languag'd *nations has survey'd.* POPE.

LA'NGUAGE-MASTER. *n.s.* [*language* and *master.*] One whose profession is to teach languages.

The third is a sort of language-master, *who is to instruct them in the stile proper for a minister.* SPECTATOR, NO. 305.

LA'RDER. *n.s.* [*lardier,* old French; from *lard.*] The room where meat is kept or salted.

This similitude is not borrowed of the larder *house, but out of the school house.* ASCHAM'S SCHOOLMASTER.

Flesh is ill kept in a room that is not cool; whereas in a cool and wet larder *it will keep longer.* BACON.

So have I seen in larder *dark,*
Of veal a lucid loin. DORSET.

Old age,
Morose, perverse in humour, diffident
The more he still abounds, the less content:
His larder *and his kitchen too observes,*
And now, lest he should want hereafter, starves. KING.

LASS. *n.s.* [from *lad* is formed *laddess,* by contraction *lass. Hickes.*] A girl; a maid; a young woman: used now only of mean girls.

Now was the time for vig'rous lads to show
What love or honour could invite them to;
A goodly theatre, where rocks are round
With reverend age, and lovely lasses *crown'd.* WALLER.

A girl was worth forty of our widows; and an honest, downright, plain-dealing lass *it was.* L'ESTRANGE.

They sometimes an hasty kiss
Steal from unwary lasses; *they with scorn,*
And neck reclin'd, resent. PHILIPS.

LA'TIN. *adj.* [*Latinus.*] Written or spoken in the language of the old Romans.

Augustus himself could not make a new Latin *word.* LOCKE.

LA'TIN. *n.s.* An exercise practised by school-boys, who turn English into Latin.

In learning farther his syntaxis, he shall not use the common order in schools for making of Latins. ASCHAM.

LATI'NITY. *n.s.* [*Latinité*, French; *latinitas*, Latin.] Purity of Latin stile; the Latin tongue.

If Shakespeare was able to read Plautus with ease, nothing in Latinity *could be hard to him.* DENNIS'S LETTERS.

To **LA'TINIZE.** [*Latiniser*, French; from Latin.] To use words or phrases borrowed from the Latin.

I am liable to be charged that I latinize *too much.* DRYDEN.

He uses coarse and vulgar words, or terms and phrases that are latinized, *scholastick, and hard to be understood.* WATTS.

LA'TTER. *adj.* [This is the comparative of *late*, though universally written with *tt*, contrary to analogy, and to our own practice in the superlative *latest.* When the thing of which the comparison is made is mentioned, we use *later*; as, *this fruit is* later *than the rest*; but *latter* when no comparison is expressed; as, *those are* latter *fruits.* –

Volet usus
Quem penes arbitrium est, & vis, & norma loquendi.][147]

1. Happening after something else.
2. Modern; lately done or past.

Hath not navigation discovered, in these latter *ages, whole nations at the bay of Soldania.* LOCKE.

3. Mentioned last of two.

The difference between reason and revelation, and in what sense the latter *is superior.* WATTS.

LA'VATORY. *n.s.* [from *lavo*, Latin.] A wash; something in which parts diseased are washed.

Lavatories, *to wash the temples, hands, wrists, and jugulars, do potently profligate, and keep off the venom.* HARVEY.

To **LAUNCH.** *v.a.*

1. To push to sea.

All art is used to sink episcopacy, and launch *presbytery, in England.* KING CHARLES.

With stays and cordage last he rigg'd the ship,
And roll'd on leavers, launch'd *her in the deep.* POPE.

2. To dart from the hand. This perhaps, for distinction sake, might better be written *lanch.*

The King of Heav'n, obscure on high,
Bar'd his red arm, and launching *from the sky*
His writhen bolt, not shaking empty smoke,
Down to the deep abyss the flaming fellow strook. DRYDEN.

LAUREA'TION. *n.s.* [from *laureate.*] It denotes, in the Scottish universities, the act or state of having degrees conferred, as they have in some of them a flowery crown, in imitation of laurel among the antients.

LAWN. *n.s.* [*land*, Danish; *lawn*, Welsh; *lande*, French.]

1. An open space between woods,

Betwixt them lawns, *or level downs, and flocks,*
Grazing the tender herb, were interpos'd. MILTON'S PARADISE LOST.

His mountains were in a few years shaded with young trees, that gradually shot up into groves, woods, and forests, intermixed with walks, and lawns, *and gardens.* ADDISON'S SPECTATOR, NO. 58.

Stern beasts in trains that by his truncheon fell,

Now grisly forms shoot o'er the lawns *of hell.* POPE.

Interspers'd in lawns *and opening glades,*
Thin trees arise that shun each other's shades. POPE.

2. [*Linon*, French.] Fine linen, remarkable for being used in the sleeves of bishops.

Should'st thou bleed,
To stop the wounds my finest lawn *I'd tear,*
Wash them with tears, and wipe them with my hair. PRIOR.

From high life high characters are drawn,
A saint in crape is twice a saint in lawn.
POPE.

What awe did the slow solemn knell inspire:
The duties by the lawn *rob'd prelate pay'd,*
And the last words, that dust to dust convey'd! TICKELL.

LEADER. *n.s.* [from *lead.*]

1. One that leads, or conducts.

2. Captain; commander.

In my tent
I'll draw the form and model of our battle,
Limit each leader *to his several charge,*
And part in just proportion our small strength. SHAKESPEARE.

I have given him for a leader *and commander to the people.*
BIBLE ISAIAH, LV. 4.

Those who escaped by flight excused their dishonour, not without a sharp jest against some of their leaders, *affirming, that, as they had followed them into the field, so it was good reason they should follow them out.* HAYWARD.

When our Lycians see
Our brave examples, they admiring say,
Behold our gallant leaders. DENHAM.

The brave leader *of the Lycian crew.*
DRYDEN.

3. One who goes first.

Nay keep your way, little gallant; you were wont to be a follower now you are a leader. SHAKESPEARE.

4. One at the head of any party or faction: as the detestable Wharton was the *leader* of the whigs.

The understandings of a senate are enslaved by three or four leaders, *set to get or to keep employments.* SWIFT.

LEADING-STRINGS. *n.s.* [*lead* and *string.*] Strings by which children, when they learn to walk, are held from falling.

Sound may serve such, ere they to sense are grown,
Like leading-strings, *'till they can walk alone.* DRYDEN.

Was he ever able to walk without leading-strings, *or swim without bladders, without being discovered by his hobbling and his sinking?* SWIFT.

LE'CTURE. *n.s.* [*lecture*, French.]

1. A discourse pronounced upon any subject.

Mark him, while Dametas reads his rustick lecture *unto him, how to feed his beasts before noon, and where to shade them in the extreme heat.* SIDNEY, B. II.

Wrangling pedant,
When in musick we have spent an hour,
Your lecture *shall have leisure for as much.* SHAKESPEARE.

When letters from Cesar were given to Rusticus, he refused to open them till the philosopher had done his lectures.
TAYLOR'S HOLY LIVING.

Virtue is the solid good, which tutors should not only read lectures *and talk of, but the labour and art of education should furnish the mind with, and fasten there.*
LOCKE.

Numidia will be blest by Cato's lectures.
ADDISON'S CATO.

2. The act or practice of reading; perusal.

In the lecture *of holy scripture, their apprehensions are commonly confined unto the literal sense of the text.* BROWNE.

3. A magisterial reprimand.

LE'CTURER. *n.s.* [from *lecture.*] An instructor; a teacher by way of lecture;[148] a preacher in a church hired by the parish to assist the rector or vicar.

> *If any minister refused to admit into his church a* lecturer *recommended by them, and there was not one orthodox or learned man recommended, he was presently required to attend upon the committee.*
> CLARENDON.

LEECH. *n.s.* [*læc*, Saxon.]

1. A physician; a professor of the art of healing: whence we still use *cowleech.*

> *A* leech, *the which had great insight*
> *In that disease of grieved conscience,*
> *And well could cure the same; his name was patience.*
> SPENSER'S FAIRY QUEEN, B. I.

> *Her words prevail'd, and then the learned* leach
> *His cunning hand 'gan to his wounds to lay,*
> *And all things else the which his art did teach.* FAIRY QUEEN.

> *Physick is their bane.*
> *The learned* leaches *in despair depart,*
> *And shake their heads, desponding of their art.* DRYDEN.

> *Wise* leeches *will not vain receipts obtrude;*
> *Deaf to complaints they wait upon the ill,*
> *Till some safe crisis.* DRYDEN.

> *The hoary wrinkled* leech *has watch'd and toil'd,*
> *Tried every health restoring herb and gum,*
> *And wearied out his painful skill in vain.*
> ROWE'S JANE SHORE.

> *A skilful* leach,
> *They say, had wrought this blessed deed;*
> *This* leach *Arbuthnot was yclept.*
> GAY'S PASTORALS.

2. A kind of small water serpent, which fastens on animals, and sucks the blood: it is used to draw blood where the lancet is less safe, whence perhaps the name.

> *I drew blood by* leeches *behind his ear.*
> WISEMAN'S SURGERY.

> *Sticking like* leeches, *till they burst with blood,*
> *Without remorse insatiably.*
> ROSCOMMON.

LE'GEND. *n.s.* [*legenda*, Latin.]

1. A chronicle or register of the lives of saints.

> Legends *being grown in a manner to be nothing else but heaps of frivolous and scandalous vanities, they have been even with disdain thrown out, the very nests which bred them abhorring them.*
> HOOKER, B. V.

> *There are in Rome two sets of antiquities, the christian and the heathen; the former, though of a fresher date, are so embroiled with fable and* legend, *that one receives but little satisfaction.*
> ADDISON'S REMARKS ON ITALY.

2. Any memorial or relation.

> *And in this* legend *all that glorious deed*
> *Read, whilst you arm you; arm you whilst you read.* FAIRFAX, B. I.

3. An incredible unauthentick narrative.

> *Who can show the* legends, *that record*
> *More idle tales, or fables so absurd.*
> BLACKMORE.

> *It is the way and means of attaining to heaven, that makes profane scorners so willingly let go the expectation of it. It is not the articles of the creed, but the duty to God and their neighbour, that is such an inconsistent incredible* legend.
> BENTLEY'S SERMONS.

4. Any inscription; particularly on medals or coins.

Compare the beauty and comprehensiveness of legends *on ancient coins.*
ADDISON ON MEDALS.

To **LE'NIFY.** *v.a.* [*lenifier*, old French; *lenio*, Latin.] To assuage; to mitigate.

It is used for squinancies and inflammations in the throat, whereby it seemeth to have a mollifying and lenifying *virtue.*
BACON'S NATURAL HISTORY, NO. 554.

All soft'ning simples, known of sov'reign use,
He presses out, and pours their noble juice;
These first infus'd, to lenify *the pain,*
He tugs with pincers, but he tugs in vain.
DRYDEN.

LESS. A negative or privative termination. [*leas*, Saxon; *loos*, Dutch.] Joined to a substantive, it implies the absence or privation of the thing expressed by that substantive: as, a *witless* man, a man without wit; *childless*, without children; *fatherless*, deprived of a father; *pennyless*, wanting money.

LESS. *adj.* [*leas*, Saxon.] The comparative of little: opposed to greater.[149]

Mary, the mother of James the less.
BIBLE MARK, XV. 40.

Yet could he not his closing eyes withdraw,
Though less *and* less *of Emily he saw.*
DRYDEN.

He that thinks he has a positive idea of infinite space will find, that he can no more have a positive idea of the greatest than he has of the least space; for in this latter we are capable only of a comparative idea of smallness, which will always be less than *any one whereof we have the positive idea.*
LOCKE.

All the ideas that are considered as having parts, and are capable of increase by the addition of any equal or less *parts, affords us, by their repetition, the idea of infinity.*
LOCKE.

'Tis less *to conquer, than to make wars cease,*
And, without fighting, awe the world to peace. HALIFAX.

LE'SSER. *adj.* A barbarous corruption of *less*, formed by the vulgar from the habit of terminating comparatives in *er*; afterwards adopted by poets, and then by writers of prose.[150]

What great despite doth fortune to thee bear,
Thus lowly to abase thy beauty bright,
That it should not deface all other lesser *light.*
FAIRY QUEEN.

It is the lesser *blot, modesty finds,*
Women to change their shapes than men their minds.
SHAKESPEARE'S TWO GENTLEMEN OF VERONA.

The mountains, and higher parts of the earth, grow lesser *and* lesser *from age to age: sometimes the roots of them are weakened by subterraneous fires, and sometimes tumbled by earthquakes into those caverns that are under them.*
BURNET'S THEORY OF THE EARTH.

Cain, after the murder of his brother, cries out, Every man that findeth me shall slay me. By the same reason may a man, in the state of nature, punish the lesser *breaches of that law.* LOCKE.

Any heat whatsoever promotes the ascent of mineral matter, but more especially of that which is subtile, and is consequently moveable more easily, and with a lesser *power.*
WOODWARD'S NATURAL HISTORY.

The larger here, and there the lesser *lambs,*
The new-fall'n young herd bleating for their dams. POPE.

LEUCOPHLE'GMACY. *n.s.* [from *leucophlegmatick.*] Paleness, with viscid juices and cold sweatings.

Spirits produce debility, flatulency, fevers, leucophlegmacy, *and dropsies.*
ARBUTHNOT ON ALIMENTS.

LE'VEE. *n.s.* [French.]
1. The time of rising.
2. The concourse of those who croud round a man of power in a morning.

The servile rout their careful Cæsar praise;
Him they extol, they worship him alone,
They croud his levees, *and support his throne.* DRYDEN.

Woud'st thou be first minister of state?
To have thy levees *crouded with resort,*
Of a depending, gaping, servile court.
DRYDEN'S JUVENAL.

None of her Sylvan subjects made their court,
Levees *and couchees pass'd without resort.*
DRYDEN.

LEVEROOK. *n.s.* [*lafere*, Saxon.] This word is retained in Scotland, and denotes the lark.

The smaller birds have their particular seasons; as, the leverook.
WALTON'S ANGLER.

If the lufft faa 'twill smoore aw the leverooks. SCOTCH PROVERB.

LEXICO'GRAPHER. *n.s.* [*λεξικόν* and *γράφω*; *lexicographe*, French.] A writer of dictionaries; a harmless drudge, that busies himself in tracing the original, and detailing the signification of words.

Commentators and lexicographers *acquainted with the Syriac language, have given these hints in their writings on scripture.*
WATTS'S IMPROVEMENT OF THE MIND.

LEXICO'GRAPHY. *n.s.* [*λεξικόν* and *γράφω*.] The art or practice of writing dictionaries.

LE'XICON. *n.s.* [*λεξικόν*.] A dictionary; a book teaching the signification of words.

Though a linguist should pride himself to have all the tongues that Babel cleft the world into, yet if he had not studied the solid things in them as well as the words and lexicons, *yet he were nothing so much to be esteemed a learned man as any yeoman competently wise in his mother dialect only.* MILTON.

LIAR. *n.s.* [from *lie*. This word would analogically be *lier*; but this orthography has prevailed, and the convenience of distinction from *lier*, he who lies down, is sufficient to confirm it.] One who tells falshood; one who wants veracity.

She's like a liar, *gone to burning hell!*
'Twas I that kill'd her.
SHAKESPEARE'S OTHELLO.

He approves the common liar, *fame,*
Who speaks him thus at Rome.
SHAKESPEARE'S ANTONY AND CLEOPATRA.

I do not reject his observation as untrue, much less condemn the person himself as a liar, *whensoever it seems to be contradicted.* BOYLE.

Thy better soul abhors a liar's *part,*
Wise is thy voice, and noble is thy heart.
POPE'S ODYSSEY.

LI'BERTINE. *n.s.* [*libertin*, French.]
1. One unconfined; one at liberty.

When he speaks,
The air, a charter'd libertine, *is still;*
And the mute wonder lurketh in men's ears,
To steal his sweet and honied sentences.
SHAKESPEARE'S HENRY V.

2. One who lives without restraint or law.

Man, the lawless libertine, *may rove*
Free and unquestion'd.
ROWE'S JANE SHORE.

Want of power is the only bound that a libertine *puts to his views upon any of the sex.* CLARISSA.

3. One who pays no regard to the precepts of religion.

They say this town is full of couzenage,

As nimble jugglers, that deceive the eye;
Disguised cheaters, prating mountebanks,
And many such like libertines *of sin.*
SHAKESPEARE.

That word may be applied to some few libertines *in the audience.*
COLLIER'S VIEW OF THE STAGE.

4. [In law; *libertinus*, Lat.] A freedman; or rather, the son of a freedman.

Some persons are forbidden to be accusers on the score of their sex, as women; others on the score of their age, as pupils and infants; others on the score of their conditions, as libertines *against their patrons.* AYLIFFE'S PARERGON.

LIBRA'RIAN. *n.s.* [*librarius*, Latin.]
1. One who has the care of a library.
2. One who transcribes or copies books.

Charybdis thrice swallows, and thrice refunds, the waves: this must be understood of regular tides. There are indeed but two tides in a day, but this is the error of the librarians.
BROOME'S NOTES ON THE ODYSSEY.

LICH. *n.s.* [*lice*, Saxon.] A dead carcase; whence *lichwake*, the time or act of watching by the dead; *lichgate*, the gate through which the dead are carried to the grave; *Lichfield*, the field of the dead, a city in Staffordshire, so named from martyred christians. *Salve magna parens.*[151] *Lichwake* is still retained in Scotland in the same sense.

LI'ER. *n.s.* [from *to lie.*] One that rests or lies down; or remains concealed.

There were liers *in ambush against him behind the city.*
BIBLE JOSHUA, VIII. 14.

LI'FESTRING. *n.s.* [*life* and *string.*] Nerve; strings imagined to convey life.

These lines are the veins, the arteries,
The undecaying lifestrings *of those hearts*
That still shall pant, and still shall exercise
The motion spirit and nature both impart.
DANIEL.

LIFT. *n.s.* [from the verb.]
1. The act of lifting; the manner of lifting.[152]

In the lift *of the feet, when a man goeth up the hill, the weight of the body beareth most upon the knees.* BACON.

In races, it is not the large stride, or high lift, *that makes the speed.*
BACON'S ESSAYS.

The goat gives the fox a lift, *and out he springs.* L'ESTRANGE.

2. [In Scottish.] The sky: for in a starry night they say, *How clear the* lift *is!*
3. Effect; struggle. *Dead lift* is an effort to raise what with the whole force cannot be moved; and figuratively any state of impotence and inability.

Myself and Trulla made a shift
To help him out at a dead lift.
HUDIBRAS, P. I.

Mr. Doctor had puzzled his brains
In making a ballad, but was at a stand.
For you freely must own, you were at a dead lift. SWIFT.

4. *Lift*, in Scotland, denotes a load or surcharge of any thing; as also, if one be disguised much with liquor, they say, *He has got a great* lift.
5. *Lifts* of a sail are ropes to raise or lower them at pleasure.

LIGHTHO'USE. *n.s.* [*light* and *house.*] An high building, at the top of which lights are hung to guide ships at sea.

He charged himself with the risque of such vessels as carried corn in winter; and built a pharos or lighthouse. ARBUTHNOT.

Build two poles to the meridian, with immense lighthouses *on the top of them.*
ARBUTHNOT AND POPE.

LIGHTMI'NDED. *adj.* [*light* and *mind.*] Unsettled; unsteady.

He that is hasty to give credit is lightminded.
BIBLE ECCLESIASTICUS, XIX. 4.

LI'GHTNESS. *n.s.* [from *light.*]
1. Levity; want of weight; absence of weight.

Some are for masts of ships, as fir and pine, because of their length, straightness, and lightness.
BACON'S NATURAL HISTORY.

Suppose many degrees of littleness and lightness *in particles, so as many might float in the air a good while before they fell.*
BURNET'S THEORY OF THE EARTH.

2. Inconstancy; unsteadiness.

For, unto knight there is no greater shame,
Than lightness *and inconstancy in love.*
FAIRY QUEEN.

Of two things they must chuse one; namely, whether they would, to their endless disgrace, with ridiculous lightness, *dismiss him, whose restitution they had in so importunate manner desired, or else condescend unto that demand.* HOOKER.

As I blow this feather from my face,
Obeying with my wind when I do blow,
And yielding to another when it blows,
Commanded always by the greatest gust;
Such is the lightness *of you common men.*
SHAKESPEARE.

3. Unchastity; want of conduct in women.

Is it the disdain of my estate, or the opinion of my lightness, *that have emboldened such base fancies towards me?*
SIDNEY, B. II.

Can it be,
That modesty may more betray our sense,
Than woman's lightness.
SHAKESPEARE'S MEASURE FOR MEASURE.

4. Agility; nimbleness.

LIGHTS. *n.s.* [supposed to be called so from their lightness in proportion to their bulk.] The lungs; the organs of breathing.

The complaint was chiefly from the lights, *a part as of no quick sense, so no seat for any sharp disease.* HAYWARD.

LI'KING. *n.s.* [from *like.*]
1. Good state of body; plumpness.

I'll repent, and that suddenly, while I am in some liking; *I shall be out of heart shortly, and then I shall have no strength to repent.* SHAKESPEARE'S HENRY IV.

Their young ones are in good liking; *they grow up with corn.*
BIBLE JOB, XXXIX. 4.

Cappadocian slaves were famous for their lustiness; and, being in good liking, *were set on a stall when exposed to sale, to shew the good habit of their body.*
DRYDEN'S NOTES TO PERSIUS.

2. State of trial.

The royal soul, that, like the lab'ring moon,
By charms of art was hurried down;
Forc'd with regret to leave her native sphere,
Came but awhile on liking *here.*
DRYDEN.

3. Inclination.

Why do you longer feed on loathed light,
Or liking *find to gaze on earthly mold.*
FAIRY QUEEN.

LI'MITARY. *adj.* [from *limit.*] Placed at the boundaries as a guard or superintendant.

Then, when I am thy captive, talk of chains,
Proud limitary *cherub!*
MILTON'S PARADISE LOST.

LI'MOUS. *adj.* [*limosus*, Latin.] Muddy; slimy.

That country became a gained ground by the muddy and limous *matter brought*

down by the Nilus, which settled by degrees unto a firm land.
BROWN'S VULGAR ERROURS.

They esteemed this natural melancholick acidity to be the limous *or slimy fœculent part of the blood.* FLOYER.

LI'NCTUS. *n.s.* [from *lingo*, Latin.] Medicine licked up by the tongue.

To **LI'NGER.** *v.n.* [from *leng*, Saxon, *long*.]

1. To remain long in languor and pain.

Like wretches, that have linger'd *long,*
We'll snatch the strongest cordial of our love. DRYDEN.

Better to rush at once to shades below,
Than linger *life away, and nourish woe.*
POPE'S ODYSSEY.

2. To hesitate; to be in suspense.

Perhaps thou ling'rest, *in deep thoughts detain'd*
Of th' enterprize so hazardous and high.
PARADISE REGAIN'D.

3. To remain long. In an ill sense.

Let order die,
And let this world no longer be a stage
To feed contention in a ling'ring *act.*
SHAKESPEARE'S HENRY IV.

Ye breth'ren of the lyre, and tuneful voice,
Lament his lot; but at your own rejoice.
Now live secure, and linger *out your days;*
The gods are pleas'd alone with Purcel's lays. DRYDEN.

Your very fear of death shall make ye try
To catch the shade of immortality;
Wishing on earth to linger, *and to save*
Part of its prey from the devouring grave.
PRIOR.

4. To remain long without any action or determination.

We have lingered *about a match between Anne Page and my cousin Slender, and this day we shall have our answer.*
SHAKESPEARE'S MERRY WIVES OF WINDSOR.

5. To wait long in expectation or uncertainty.

I must sollicit
All his concerns as mine:
And if my eyes have pow'r, he should not sue
In vain, nor linger *with a long delay.*
DRYDEN'S CLEOMENES.

6. To be long in producing effect.

She doth think, she has strange ling'ring *poisons.* SHAKESPEARE.

LI'NGO. *n.s.* [Portuguese.] Language; tongue; speech. A low cant word.

I have thoughts to learn somewhat of your lingo, *before I cross the seas.*
CONGREVE'S WAY OF THE WORLD.

LINGUA'CIOUS. *adj.* [*linguax*, Latin.] Full of tongue; loquacious; talkative.

LINGUADE'NTAL. *adj.* [*lingua* and *dens*, Latin.] Uttered by the joint action of the tongue and teeth.

The linguadentals *f, v, as also the* linguadentals *th, dh, he will soon learn.*
HOLDER'S ELEMENTS OF SPEECH.

LI'NGUIST. *n.s.* [from *lingua*.] A man skilful in languages.

Though a linguist *should pride himself to have all the tongues that Babel cleft the world into, yet, if he had not studied the solid things in them, as well as the words and lexicons, he were nothing so much to be esteemed a learned man, as any yeoman or tradesman competently wise in his mother dialect only.*
MILTON ON EDUCATION.

Our linguist *received extraordinary rudiments towards a good education.*
ADDISON'S SPECTATOR.

LI'NKBOY. *n.s.* [*link* and *boy*.] A boy that carries a torch to accommodate passengers with light.

What a ridiculous thing it was, that the

continued shadow of the earth should be broken by sudden miraculous disclusions of light, to prevent the officiousness of the linkboy. MORE'S DIVINE DIALOGUES.

Though thou art tempted by the linkman's *call,*
Yet trust him not along the lonely wall.
GAY.

In the black form of cinder wench she came.
O may no linkboy *interrupt their love.*
GAY'S TRIVIA.

LIP. *n.s.* [*lippe*, Saxon.]
1. The outer part of the mouth, the muscles that shoot beyond the teeth, which are of so much use in speaking, that they are used for all the organs of speech.

Those happiest smiles
That play'd on her ripe lip, *seem'd not to know*
What guests were in her eyes.
SHAKESPEARE'S KING LEAR.

No falshood shall defile my lips *with lies,*
Or with a vail of truth disguise.
SANDYS ON JOB.

Her lips *blush deeper sweets.*
THOMSON'S SPRING.

2. The edge of any thing.

In many places is a ridge of mountains some distance from the sea, and a plain from their roots to the shore; which plain was formerly covered by the sea, which bounded against those hills as its first ramparts, or as the ledges or lips *of its vessel.*
BURNET'S THEORY OF THE EARTH.

In wounds, the lips *sink and are flaccid; a gleet followeth, and the flesh within withers.* WISEMAN'S SURGERY.

3. To make a lip; to hang the lip in sullenness and contempt.

A letter for me! It gives me an estate of seven years health; in which time I will make a lip *at the physician.*
SHAKESPEARE'S CORIOLANUS.

LIPLA'BOUR. *n.s.* [*lip* and *labour.*] Action of the lips without concurrence of the mind; words without sentiments.

Fasting, when prayer is not directed to its own purposes, is but liplabour.
TAYLOR'S RULE OF HOLY LIVING.

LI'PWISDOM. *n.s.* [*lip* and *wisdom.*] Wisdom in talk without practice.

I find that all is but lipwisdom, *which wants experience; I now, woe is me, do try what love can do.* SIDNEY, B. I.

LI'QUOR. *n.s.* [*liquor*, Latin; *liqueur*, French.]
1. Any thing liquid: it is commonly used of fluids inebriating, or impregnated with something, or made by decoction.

Nor envy'd them the grape
Whose heads that turbulent liquor *fills with fumes.* MILTON.

Sin taken into the soul, is like a liquor *poured into a vessel; so much of it as it fills, it also seasons.*
SOUTH'S SERMONS.

2. Strong drink; in familiar language.

To **LISP.** *v.n.* [*þlisp*, Saxon.] To speak with too frequent appulses of the tongue to the teeth or palate, like children.

Come, I cannot cog, and say, thou art this and that, like a many of these lisping *hawthorn buds, that come like women in mens apparel, and smell like Bucklersbury in simpling time.*
SHAKESPEARE'S MERRY WIVES OF WINDSOR.

Scarce had she learnt to lisp *a name*
Of martyr, yet she thinks it shame
Life should so long play with that breath,
Which spent can buy so brave a death.
CRASHAW.

They ramble not to learn the mode,
How to be drest, or how to lisp *abroad.*
CLEAVELAND.

Appulse partial, giving some passage to breath, is made to the upper teeth, and

causes a lisping *sound, the breath being strained through the teeth.*
HOLDER'S ELEMENTS OF SPEECH.

As yet a child, nor yet a fool to fame,
I lisp'd *in numbers, for the numbers came.* POPE.

LI'TTER. *n.s.* [*litiere*, French.]
1. A kind of vehiculary bed; a carriage capable of containing a bed hung between two horses.

To my litter *strait;*
Weakness possesseth me.
SHAKESPEARE'S KING JOHN.

He was carried in a rich chariot litterwise, *with two horses at each end.*
BACON'S NEW ATLANTIS.

The drowsy frighted steeds,
That draw the litter *of close curtain'd sleep.* MILTON.

Here modest matrons in soft litters *driv'n,*
In solemn pomp appear.
DRYDEN'S ÆNEID.

Litters *thick besiege the donor's gate,*
And begging lords and teeming ladies wait
The promis'd dole.
DRYDEN'S JUVENAL.

2. The straw laid under animals, or on plants.

To crouch in litter *of your stable planks.*
SHAKESPEARE.

Take off the litter *from your kernel beds.*
EVELYN.

Their litter *is not toss'd by sows unclean.*
DRYDEN'S VIRGIL.

3. A brood of young.

I do here walk before thee like a sow that hath overwhelmed all her litter *but one.*
SHAKESPEARE'S HENRY IV.

Reflect upon that numerous litter *of strange, senseless opinions, that crawl about the world.* SOUTH'S SERMONS.

A wolf came to a sow, and very kindly offered to take care of her litter.
L'ESTRANGE'S FABLES.

Full many a year his hateful head had been
For tribute paid, nor since in Cambria seen:
The last of all the litter *'scap'd by chance,*
And from Geneva first infested France.
DRYDEN.

4. Any number of things thrown sluttishly about.

Strephon, who found the room was void,
Stole in, and took a strict survey
Of all the litter *as it lay.* SWIFT.

5. A birth of animals.

Fruitful as the sow that carry'd
The thirty pigs at one large litter *farrow'd.*
DRYDEN'S JUVENAL.

LI'VRE. *n.s.* [French.] The sum by which the French reckon their money, equal nearly to our shilling.

LI'ZARD. *n.s.* [*lisarde*, French; *lacertus*, Latin.] An animal resembling a serpent, with legs added to it.

There are several sorts of lizards; *some in Arabia of a cubit long. In America they eat* lizards; *it is very probable likewise that they were eaten sometimes in Arabia and Judæa, since Moses ranks them among the unclean creatures.* CALMET.

Thou'rt like a foul mis-shapen stigmatick,
Mark'd by the destinies to be avoided,
As venomous toads, or lizards *dreadful stings.* SHAKESPEARE.

Adder's fork, and blind worm's sting,
Lizard's *leg, and owlet's wing.*
SHAKESPEARE'S MACBETH.

LO. *interject.* [*la*, Saxon.] Look; see; behold. It is a word used to recall the attention generally to some object of sight; sometimes to something heard, but not properly; often to something to be understood.

Lo! *within a ken our army lies.*
SHAKESPEARE.

Now must the world point at poor Catharine,

And say, lo! *there is mad Petruchio's wife.* SHAKESPEARE.

Lo! *I have a weapon,*
A better never did itself sustain
Upon a soldier's thigh.
SHAKESPEARE'S OTHELLO.

Thou did'st utter,
I am yours for ever.
—— *Why* lo *you now, I've spoke to the purpose twice.* SHAKESPEARE.

For lo! *he sung the world's stupenduous birth.* ROSCOMMON.

Lo! *heav'n and earth combine*
To blast our bold design.
DRYDEN'S ALBION.

LOAF. *n.s.* [from *hlal* or *laf*, Saxon.]
1. A mass of bread as it is formed by the baker: a loaf is thicker than a cake.

Easy it is
Of a cut loaf *to steal a shive, we know.*
SHAKESPEARE.

The bread and bread corn in the town sufficed not for six days: hereupon the soldiers entered into proportion; and, to give example, the lord Clinton limited himself to a loaf *a day.* HAYWARD.

With equal force you may break a loaf *of bread into more and less parts than a lump of lead of the same bigness.* DIGBY.

2. Any mass into which a body is wrought.

Your wine becomes so limpid, that you may bottle it with a piece of loaf *sugar in each bottle.* MORTIMER.

LOB. *n.s.*
1. Any one heavy, clumsy, or sluggish.

Farewel, thou lob *of spirits, I'll be gone,*
Our queen and all her elves come here anon. SHAKESPEARE.

2. Lob's pound; a prison. Probably a prison for idlers, or sturdy beggars.

Crowdero, whom in irons bound,
Thou basely threw'st into lob's *pound.*
HUDIBRAS.

3. A big worm.

For the trout the dew worm, which some also call the lob *worm, and the brandling are the chief.* WALTON'S ANGLER.

LO'CKET. *n.s.* [*loquet*, French.] A small lock; any catch or spring to fasten a necklace, or other ornament.

Where knights are kept in narrow lists,
With wooden lockets *'bout their wrists.*
HUDIBRAS, P. II.

LOCOMO'TIVE. *adj.* [*locus* and *moveo*, Lat.] Changing place; having the power of removing or changing place.

I shall consider the motion, or locomotive *faculty of animals.*
DERHAM'S PHYSICO-THEOLOGY.

In the night too oft he kicks,
Or shows his locomotive *tricks.* PRIOR.

An animal cannot well be defined from any particular, organical part, nor from its locomotive *faculty, for some adhere to rocks.*
ARBUTHNOT ON ALIMENTS.

LOFT. *n.s.* [*lloft*, Welsh; or from *lift.*]
1. A floor.

There is a traverse placed in a loft *above.*
BACON.

2. The highest floor.

To lull him in his slumber soft,
A trickling stream from high rock tumbling down,
And ever drizzling rain upon the loft,
Mixt with a murmuring wind.
FAIRY QUEEN, B. I.

3. Rooms on high.

Passing through the spheres of watchful fire,
And hills of snow, and lofts *of piled thunder.* MILTON.

A weasel once made shift to slink
In at a corn loft, *through a chink.*
POPE.

LO'GOMACHY. *n.s.* [λογομαχία.] A contention in words; a contention about words.

Forced terms of art did much puzzle sacred theology with distinctions, cavils, quiddities; and so transformed her to a meer kind of sophistry and logomachy. HOWEL.

To **LOLL.** *v.n.* [Of this word the etymology is not known. Perhaps it might be contemptuously derived from *lollard*, a name of great reproach before the reformation; of whom one tenet was, that all trades not necessary to life are unlawful.]

1. To lean idly; to rest lazily against any thing.

So hangs, and lolls, *and weeps upon me; so shakes and pulls me.*
SHAKESPEARE'S OTHELLO.

He is not lolling *on a lewd love bed,*
But on his knees at meditation.
SHAKESPEARE'S RICHARD III.

Close by a softly murm'ring stream,
Where lovers us'd to loll *and dream.*
HUDIBRAS, P. I.

To loll *on couches, rich with cytron steds,*
And lay your guilty limbs in Tyrian beds.
DRYDEN.

Void of care he lolls *supine in state,*
And leaves his business to be done by fate.
DRYDEN'S PERSIUS.

But wanton now, and lolling *at our ease,*
We suffer all the invet'rate ills of peace.
DRYDEN.

A lazy, lolling *sort*
Of ever listless loit'rers.
DUNCIAD, B. IV.

2. To hang out. Used of the tongue hanging out in weariness or play.

The triple porter of the Stygian seat,
With lolling *tongue lay fawning at thy feet.* DRYDEN.

With harmless play amidst the bowls he pass'd,
And with his lolling *tongue assay'd the taste.* DRYDEN.

LONGI'MANOUS. *adj.* [*longue-main*, French; *longimanus*, Lat.] Long-handed; having long hands.

The villainy of this Christian exceeded the persecution of heathens, whose malice was never so longimanous *as to reach the soul of their enemies, or to extend unto the exile of their elysiums.*
BROWN'S VULGAR ERROURS, B. VII.

LONGI'METRY. *n.s.* [*longus* and μετρέω; *longimetrie*, French.] The art or practice of measuring distances.

Our two eyes are like two different stations in longimetry, *by the assistance of which the distance between two objects is measured.*
CHEYNE'S PHILOSOPHICAL PRINCIPLES.

LO'OBY. *n.s.* [Of this word the derivation is unsettled. *Skinner* mentions *lapp*, German, *foolish*; and *Junius*, *llabe*, a clown, Welsh, which seems to be the true original.] A lubber; a clumsy clown.

The vices trace
From the father's scoundrel race.
Who could give the looby *such airs?*
Were they masons, were they butchers?
SWIFT.

LOOK. *interj.* [properly the imperative mood of the verb: it is sometimes *look ye.*] See! lo! behold! observe.

Look, *where he comes, and my good man too; he's as far from jealousy as I am from giving him cause.* SHAKESPEARE.

Look *you, he must seem thus to the world: fear not your advancement.*
SHAKESPEARE.

Look, *when the world hath fewest barbarous people, but such as will not marry, except they know means to live, as it is almost everywhere at this day, except Tartary, there is no danger of inundations of people.* BACON'S ESSAYS.

Look *you! we that pretend to be subject to a constitution, must not carve out our own quality; for at this rate a cobler may make himself a lord.* COLLIER ON PRIDE.

LOON. *n.s.* [This word, which is now used only in Scotland, is the English word *lown.*] A sorry fellow; a scoundrel; a rascal.

Thou cream-fac'd loon*!*
Where got'st thou that goose look?
SHAKESPEARE'S MACBETH.

The false loon, *who could not work his will*
By open force, employ'd his flatt'ring skill:
I hope, my lord, said he, I not offend;
Are you afraid of me that are your friend?
DRYDEN.

This young lord had an old cunning rogue, or, as the Scots call it, a false loon *of a grandfather, that one might call a Jack of all trades.*
ARBUTHNOT'S HISTORY OF JOHN BULL.

LOORD. *n.s.* [*loerd*, Dutch; from *lourdant*, French; *lurdan*, Erse; a heavy, stupid, or witless fellow. *D. Trevoux* derives *lourdant* from *lorde* or *lourde*, a village in Gascoigny, the inhabitants of which were formerly noted robbers, say they. But dexterity in robbing implies some degree of subtility, from which the Gascoigns are so far removed, that, at this day, they are aukward and heavy to a proverb. The Erse imports some degree of knavery, but then it is used in a ludicrous sense, as in English, you pretty rogue; though in general it denotes reproachful heaviness, or stupid laziness. *Spenser*'s Scholiast says, *loord* was wont, among the old Britons, to signify a lord; and therefore the Danes, that usurped their tyranny here in Britain, were called, for more dread than dignity, *lurdans*, i.e. lord Danes, whose insolence and pride was so outrageous in this realm, that if it fortuned a Briton to be going over a bridge, and saw the Dane set foot upon the same, he must return back till the Dane was clean over, else he must abide no less than present death: but being afterward expelled, the name of *lurdane* became so odious unto the people whom they had long oppressed, that, even at this day, they use for more reproach to call the quartan ague the fever *lurdane*. So far the Scholiast, but erroneously. From *Spenser*'s own words, it signifies something of stupid dulness rather than magisterial arrogance. *Macbean.*] A drone.

Siker, thou's but a lazy loord,
And rekes much of thy swinke,
That with fond terms and witless words
To bleer mine eyes do'st think.
SPENSER'S PASTORALS.

LOT. *n.s.* [*hlaut*, Gothick; *hlot*, Saxon; *lot*, Dutch.]

1. Fortune; state assigned.

Kala at length concluded my ling'ring lot*;*
Disdain me not, although I be not fair,
Who is an heir of many hundred sheep,
Doth beauty keep which never sun can burn,
Nor storms do turn. SIDNEY, B. I.

Our own lot *is best; and by aiming at what we have not, we lose what we have already.* L'ESTRANGE'S FABLES.

Prepar'd I stand; he was but born to try
The lot *of man, to suffer and to die.*
POPE'S ODYSSEY.

2. A die, or any thing used in determining chances.

Aaron shall cast lots *upon the two goats; one* lot *for the Lord, and the other* lot *for the scape-goat.*
BIBLE LEVITICUS, XVI. 8.

Their tasks in equal portions she divides,
And where unequal, there by lots *decides.*
DRYDEN'S VIRGIL.

Ulysses bids his friends to cast lots, *to shew,*

that he would not voluntarily expose them to so imminent danger.
NOTES ON THE ODYSSEY.

3. It seems in *Shakespeare* to signify a lucky or wished chance.

If you have heard your general talk of Rome,
And of his friends there, it is lots *to blanks*
My name hath touch'd your ears; it is
Menenius. SHAKESPEARE.

4. A portion; a parcel of goods as being drawn by lot: as, what *lot* of silks had you at the sale?
5. Proportion of taxes: as, to pay scot and *lot.*

LO'VELILY. *adv.* [from *lovely.*] Amiably; in such a manner as to excite love.

Thou look'st
Lovelily *dreadful.*
OTWAY'S VENICE PRESERV'D.

LO'VER. *n.s.* [from *love.*]
1. One who is in love.

Love is blind, and lovers *cannot see*
The pretty follies that themselves commit.
SHAKESPEARE.

Let it be never said, that he whose breast
Is fill'd with love, should break a lover's
rest. DRYDEN.

2. A friend; one who regards with kindness.

Your brother and his lover *have embrac'd.*
SHAKESPEARE.

I tell thee, fellow,
Thy general is my lover*: I have been*
The book of his good act, whence men have
read
His fame unparallel'd haply amplified.
SHAKESPEARE.

3. One who likes any thing.

To be good and gracious, and a lover *of knowledge, are amiable things.*
BURNET'S THEORY OF THE EARTH.

LO'VETALE. *n.s.* [*love* and *tale.*] Narrative of love.

The lovetale
Infected Sion's daughters with like heat;
Whose wanton passions in the sacred porch
Ezekiel saw.
MILTON'S PARADISE LOST, B. I.

Cato's a proper person to entrust
A lovetale *with.* ADDISON'S CATO.

LO'VETHOUGHT. *n.s.* [*love* and *thought.*] Amorous fancy.

Away to sweet beds of flowers,
Lovethoughts *lie rich when canopied with*
bowers. SHAKESPEARE.

LO'VETOY. *n.s.* [*love* and *toy.*] Small presents given by lovers.

Has this amorous gentleman presented himself with any lovetoys, *such as gold snuff-boxes.*
ARBUTHNOT AND POPE'S MARTIN SCRIBLERUS.

LO'VETRICK. *n.s.* [*love* and *trick.*] Art of expressing love.

Other disports than dancing jollities;
Other lovetricks *than glancing with the*
eyes. DONNE.

LOUIS D'OR. *n.s.* [French.] A golden coin of France, valued at about seventeen shillings.[153]

If he is desired to change a louis d'or, *he must consider of it.*
SPECTATOR, NO. 305.

LO'WBELL. *n.s.* [*laeye*, Dutch; *leg*, Saxon; or *log*, Islandick, a flame, and *bell.*]

A kind of fowling in the night, in which the birds are wakened by a bell, and lured by a flame into a net. *Lowe* denotes a flame in Scotland; and *to lowe*, to flame.

LOWN. *n.s.* [*liun*, Irish; *loen*, Dutch, a stupid drone.] A scoundrel; a rascal.

King Stephen was a worthy peer,
His breeches cost him but a crown,
He thought them sixpence all too dear,

And therefore call'd the taylor lown. SHAKESPEARE.

LOWTHO'UGHTED. *adj.* [*low* and *thought.*] Having the thoughts with-held from sublime or heavenly meditations; mean of sentiment; narrow mindedness.

Above the smoak and stir of this dim spot,
Which men call earth, and with lowthoughted *care,*
Strive to keep up a frail and feverish being. MILTON.

O grace serene! Oh virtue heav'nly fair!
Divine oblation of lowthoughted *care!*
Fresh blooming hope, gay daughter of the sky,
And faith our early immortality! POPE.

LOWSPIRITED. *adj.* [*low* and *spirit.*] Dejected; depressed; not lively; not vivacious; not spritely.

Severity carried to the highest pitch breaks the mind; and then, in the place of a disorderly young fellow, you have a lowspirited *moped creature.* LOCKE.

LP. a contraction for *lordship.*

LU'BRICK. *adj.* [*lubricus,* Latin.]

1. Slippery; smooth on the surface.

A throng
Of short thick sobs, whose thund'ring volleys float
And roul themselves over her lubrick *throat,*
In panting murmurs. CRASHAW.

2. Uncertain; unsteady.

I will deduce him from his cradle through the deep and lubrick *waves of state, till he is swallowed in the gulph of fatality.* WOTTON.

3. Wanton; lewd. [*lubrique,* French.]

Why were we hurry'd down
This lubrick *and adult'rate age;*
Nay, added fat pollutions of our own,
T' encrease the steaming ordures of the stage. DRYDEN.

LU'BRICOUS. *adj.* [*lubricus,* Latin.]

1. Slippery; smooth.

The parts of water being voluble and lubricous *as well as fine, it easily insinuates itself into the tubes of vegetables, and by that means introduces into them the matter it bears along with it.* WOODWARD'S NATURAL HISTORY.

2. Uncertain.

The judgment being the leading power, if it be stored with lubricous *opinions instead of clearly conceived truths, and peremptorily resolved in them, the practice will be as irregular as the conceptions.* GLANVILLE'S SCEPSIS SCIENTIFICA.

LUCUBRA'TION. *n.s.* [*lucubratio,* Latin.] Study by candlelight; nocturnal study; any thing composed by night.

Thy lucubrations *have been perused by several of our friends.* TATLER, NO. 78.

L'UDICROUS. *adj.* [*ludicer,* Lat.] Burlesque; merry; sportive; exciting laughter.

Plutarch quotes this as an instance of Homer's judgment; in closing a ludicrous *scene with decency and instruction.* NOTES ON THE ODYSSEY.

LU'DICROUSLY. *adv.* [from *ludicrous.*] Sportively; in burlesque; in a manner that may excite laughter.

LUFF. *n.s.* [in Scotland.] The palm of the hand; as, clap me arles in my *luff.*

LU'GGAGE. *n.s.* [from *lug.*] Any thing cumbrous and unwieldy that is to be carried away; any thing of more weight than value.

Come bring your luggage *nobly on your back.* SHAKESPEARE.

What do you mean
To doat thus on such luggage?
SHAKESPEARE'S TEMPEST.

Think not thou to find me slack, or need

Thy politick maxims, or that cumbersome
Luggage *of war there shewn me.*
MILTON'S PARADISE REGAIN'D.

How durst thou with that sullen luggage
O' th' self, old ir'n; and other baggage,
T' oppose thy lumber against us?
HUDIBRAS, P. I.

The mind of man is too light to bear much certainty among the ruffling winds of passion and opinion; and if the luggage *be prized equally with the jewels, none will be cast out till all be shipwrecked.*
GLANVILLE.

A lively faith will bear aloft the mind,
And leave the luggage *of good works behind.* DRYDEN.

I am gathering up my luggage, *and preparing for my journey.*
SWIFT TO POPE.

LU'NACY. *n.s.* [from *luna*, the moon.] A kind of madness influenced by the moon; madness in general.

Love is merely madness, and deserves as well a dark house and a whip as madmen do; and the reason why they are not so punished and cured is, that the lunacy *is so ordinary, that the whippers are in love too.* SHAKESPEARE'S AS YOU LIKE IT.

Your kindred shun your house,
As beaten hence by your strange lunacy.
SHAKESPEARE.

There is difference of lunacy: *I had rather be mad with him, that, when he had nothing, thought all the ships that came into the haven his, than with you, who, when you have so much coming in, think you have nothing.* SUCKLING.

L'UNATICK. *adj.* [*lunaticus*, Latin.] Mad; having the imagination influenced by the moon.

Bedlam beggars, from low farms,
Sometimes with lunatick *bans, sometimes with prayers,*
Enforce their charity.
SHAKESPEARE.

LU'NATICK. *n.s.* A madman.

The lunatick, *the lover, and the poet,*
Are of imagination all compact:
One sees more devils than vast hell can hold;
The madman.
SHAKESPEARE'S MIDSUMMER NIGHT'S DREAM.

I dare ensure any man well in his wits, for one in the thousand that he shall not die a lunatick *in Bedlam within these seven years; because not above one in about one thousand five hundred have done so.*
GRAUNT'S BILLS.

See the blind beggar dance, the cripple sing,
The sot a hero, lunatick *a king.* POPE.

The residue of the yearly profits shall be laid out in purchasing a piece of land, and in building thereon an hospital for the reception of idiots and lunaticks. SWIFT.

LUNCH, LUNCHEON. *n.s.* [*Minshew* derives it from *louja*, Spanish; *Skinner* from *kleinken*, a small piece, Teutonick. It probably comes from *clutch* or *clunch.*] As much food as one's hand can hold.

When hungry thou stood'st staring, like an oaf,
I slic'd the luncheon *from the barley loaf;*
With crumbled bread I thicken'd well the mess. GAY.

To **LURCH.** *v.n.* [*loeren*, Dutch; or rather from the noun.]

1. To shift; to play tricks.

I myself, sometimes leaving the fear of heav'n on my left-hand, and hiding mine honour in my necessity, am fain to shuffle, to hedge, and to lurch. SHAKESPEARE.

2. To lie in wait: we now rather use *lurk.*

While the one was upon wing, the other stood lurching *upon the ground, and flew away with the fish.* L'ESTRANGE.

To **LURCH.** *v.a.* [*lurcor*, Latin.]

1. To devour; to swallow greedily.

Too far off from great cities may hinder business; or too near lurcheth *all provisions, and maketh every thing dear.* BACON'S ESSAYS.

2. To defeat; to disappoint. A word now used only in burlesque. [from the game *lurch.*]

He waxed like a sea;
And, in the brunt of seventeen battles since,
He lurcht *all swords o' th' garland.*
SHAKESPEARE'S CORIOLANUS.

God never designed the use of them to be continual; by putting such an emptiness in them, as should so quickly fail and lurch *the expectation.* SOUTH'S SERMONS.

This is a sure rule, that will never deceive or lurch *the sincere communicant.* SOUTH'S SERMONS.

3. To steal privily; to filch; to pilfer.

LU'STRING. *n.s.* [from *lustre.*] A shining silk; commonly pronounced *lutestring.*

LY'RICK. *n.s.* A poet who writes songs to the harp.

The greatest conqueror in this nation, after the manner of the old Grecian lyricks, *did not only compose the words of his divine odes, but set them to musick himself.* ADDISON.

M

Has, in English, one unvaried sound, by compression of the lips; as, *mine*, *tame*, *camp*: it is never mute.

MACARO'ON. *n.s.* [*macarone*, Italian.]

1. A coarse, rude, low fellow; whence *macaronick* poetry, in which the language is purposely corrupted.

> *Like a big wife, at sight of lothed meat,*
> *Ready to travail; so I sigh and sweat,*
> *To hear this* macaroon *talk on in vain.*
> DONNE.

2. [*Macaron*, French, from *μάκαϱ*.] A kind of sweet biscuit, made of flower, almonds, eggs, and sugar.

MACHI'NE. *n.s.* [*machina*, Latin; *machine*, French. This word is pronounced *masheen*.]

1. Any complicated piece of workmanship.[154]

> *We are led to conceive this great* machine *of the world to have been once in a state of greater simplicity, as to conceive a watch to have been once in its first materials.* BURNET.

> *In a watch's fine* machine,
> *The added movements which declare*
> *How full the moon, how old the year,*
> *Derive their secundary pow'r*
> *From that which simply points the hour.*
> PRIOR.

2. An engine.

> *In the hollow side,*
> *Selected numbers of their soldiers hide;*
> *With inward arms the dire* machine *they load,*
> *And iron bowels stuff the dark abode.*
> DRYDEN.

3. Supernatural agency in poems.

> *The marvellous fable includes whatever is supernatural, and especially the* machines *of the gods.* POPE.

MACHI'NERY. *n.s.* [from *machine*.]

1. Enginery; complicated workmanship; self-moved engines.

2. The *machinery* signifies that part

which the deities, angels, or demons, act in a poem. POPE'S RAPE OF THE LOCK

MAGAZI'NE. *n.s.* [*magazine*, French, from the Arabick *machsan*, a treasure.]

1. A storehouse, commonly an arsenal or armoury, or repository of provisions.

If it should appear fit to bestow shipping in those harbours, it shall be very needful that there be a magazine *of all necessary provisions and munitions.* RALEIGH'S ESSAYS.

Plain heroick magnitude of mind;
Their armories and magazines *contemns.*
MILTON'S AGONISTES.

Some o'er the publick magazines *preside,*
And some are sent new forage to provide.
DRYDEN'S VIRGIL.

Useful arms in magazines *we place,*
All rang'd in order, and disposed with grace. POPE.

His head was so well stored a magazine*, that nothing could be proposed which he was not master of.* LOCKE.

2. Of late this word has signified a miscellaneous pamphlet, from a periodical miscellany named the *Gentleman's Magazine*, by *Edward Cave.*[155]

MA'GICK. *n.s.* [*magia*, Latin.]

1. The art of putting in action the power of spirits: it was supposed that both good and bad spirits were subject to magick; yet magick was in general held unlawful; sorcery; enchantment.

She once being looft,
The noble ruin of her magick, *Antony,*
Claps on his sea-wing.
SHAKESPEARE'S ANTONY AND CLEOPATRA.

What charm, what magick, *can over-rule the force of all these motives.* ROGERS.

2. The secret operations of natural powers.

The writers of natural magick *do attribute much to the virtues that come from the parts of living creatures, as if they did infuse some immaterial virtue into the part severed.* BACON'S NATURAL HISTORY.

MA'GNET. *n.s.* [*magnes*, Latin.] The lodestone; the stone that attracts iron.

Two magnets, *heav'n and earth, allure to bliss,*
The larger loadstone that, the nearer this.
DRYDEN.

It may be reasonable to ask, whether obeying the magnet *be essential to iron?*
LOCKE.

MA'IDMARIAN. *n.s.* [*puer ludius*, Latin.] A kind of dance, so called from a buffoon dressed like a man, who plays tricks to the populace.

A set of morrice-dancers danced a maidmarian *with a tabor and pipe.* TEMPLE.

MA'INMAST. *n.s.* [*main* and *mast.*] The chief or middle mast.

One dire shot,
Close by the board the prince's mainmast *bore.* DRYDEN.

A Dutchman, upon breaking his leg by a fall from a mainmast, *told the standers by, it was a mercy it was not his neck.*
SPECTATOR, NO. 574.

MA'INPRISE. *n.s.* [*main* and *pris*, French.] Delivery into the custody of a friend, upon security given for appearance; bail.

Sir William Bremingham was executed for treason, though the earl of Desmond was left to mainprize. DAVIES.

Give its poor entertainer quarter;
And, by discharge or mainprise, *grant*
Deliv'ry from this base restraint.
HUDIBRAS, P. II.

MA'INSAIL. *n.s.* [*main* and *sail.*] The sail of the mainmast.

They committed themselves unto the sea, and hoisted up the mainsail *to the wind, and made toward shore.*
BIBLE ACTS, XXVII.

MA'INSHEET. *n.s.* [*main* and *sheet.*] The sheet or sail of the mainmast.

Strike, strike the top-sail; let the mainsheet *fly,*
And furl your sails. DRYDEN.

MA'INYARD. *n.s.* [*main* and *yard.*] The yard of the mainmast.

With sharp hooks they took hold of the tackling which held the mainyard *to the mast, then rowing they cut the tackling, and brought the* mainyard *by the board.* ARBUTHNOT.

MA'INTOP. *n.s.* [*main* and *top.*] The top of the mainmast.

From their maintop *joyful news they hear*
Of ships, which by their mould bring new supplies. DRYDEN.

Dictys could the maintop-*mast bestride,*
And down the ropes with active vigour slide. ADDISON.

MA'KEBATE. *n.s.* [*make* and *debate.*] Breeder of quarrels.

Love in her passions, like a right makebate, *whispered to both sides arguments of quarrel.* SIDNEY.

Outrageous party-writers are like a couple of makebates, *who inflame small quarrels by a thousand stories.* SWIFT.

MALECONTE'NT, MALECONTENTED. *adj.* [*male* and *content.*] Discontented; dissatisfied.

Brother Clarence, how like you our choice,
That you stand pensive, as half malecontent. SHAKESPEARE.

Poor Clarence! Is it for a wife
That thou art malecontent? *I will provide thee.* SHAKESPEARE.

The king, for the better securing his state against mutinous and malecontented *subjects, who might have their refuge in Scotland, sent a solemn ambassage unto James III. to conclude a peace.*
BACON'S HENRY VII.

They cannot signalize themselves as malecontents, *without breaking through all the softer virtues.*
ADDISON'S FREEHOLDER.

The usual way in despotick governments is to confine the malecontent *to some castle.*
ADDISON'S FREEHOLDER.

MALEFA'CTOR. *n.s.* [*male* and *facio,* Latin.] An offender against law; a criminal; a guilty person.

A jaylor to bring forth
Some monstrous malefactor.
SHAKESPEARE'S ANTONY AND CLEOPATRA.

Fear his word,
As much as malefactors *do your sword.*
ROSCOMMON.

It is a sad thing when men shall repair to the ministry, not for preferment but refuge; like malefactors *flying to the altar, only to save their lives.* SOUTH'S SERMONS.

If their barking dog disturb her ease,
Th' unmanner'd malefactor *is arraign'd.*
DRYDEN'S JUVENAL.

The malefactor *goat was laid*
On Bacchus' altar, and his forfeit paid.
DRYDEN.

MALVERSA'TION. *n.s.* [French.] Bad shifts; mean artifices; wicked and fraudulent tricks.

MAM, MAMMA. *n.s.* [*mamma,* Latin: this word is said to be found for the compellation of *mother* in all languages; and is therefore supposed to be the first syllables that a child pronounces.] The fond word for mother.

Poor Cupid sobbing scarce could speak;
Indeed, mamma, *I did not know ye:*
Alas! how easy my mistake?

I took you for your likeness Cloe.
PRIOR.

Little masters and misses are great impediments to servants; the remedy is to bribe them, that they may not tell tales to papa and mamma.
SWIFT'S RULES TO SERVANTS.

MA'NAGEMENT. *n.s.* [*menagement*, French.]

1. Conduct; administration.

Mark with what management *their tribes divide;*
Some stick to you, and some to t'other side. DRYDEN.

An ill argument introduced with deference, will procure more credit than the profoundest science with a rough, insolent, and noisy management.
LOCKE ON EDUCATION.

The wrong management *of the earl of Godolphin was the only cause of the union.* SWIFT'S MISCELLANIES.

2. Practice; transaction; dealing.

He had great managements *with ecclesiasticks in the view of being advanced to the pontificate.* ADDISON ON ITALY.

MA'NAGER. *n.s.* [from *manage.*]

1. One who has the conduct or direction of any thing.

A skilful manager *of the rabble, so long as they have but ears to hear, needs never enquire whether they have any understanding.* SOUTH'S SERMONS.

The manager *opens his sluice every night, and distributes the water into the town.*
ADDISON.

An artful manager, *that crept between*
His friend and shame, and was a kind of screen. POPE.

2. A man of frugality; a good husband.

A prince of great aspiring thoughts: in the main, a manager *of his treasure, and yet bountiful, from his own motion, wherever he discerns merit.*
TEMPLE'S MISCELLANY.

The most severe censor cannot but be pleased with the prodigality of Ovid's wit; though he could have wished, that the master of it had been a better manager.
DRYDEN.

MA'NAGERY. *n.s.* [*menagerie*, French.]

1. Conduct; direction; administration.

They who most exactly describe that battle, give so ill an account of any conduct or discretion in the managery *of that affair, that posterity would receive little benefit in the most particular relation of it.*
CLARENDON, B. VIII.

2. Husbandry; frugality.

The court of Rome has, in other instances, so well attested its good managery, *that it is not credible crowns are conferred gratis.*
DECAY OF PIETY.

3. Manner of using.

No expert general will bring a company of raw, untrained men into the field, but will, by little bloodless skirmishes, instruct them in the manner of the fight, and teach them the ready managery *of their weapons.*
DECAY OF PIETY.

To MA'NCIPATE. *v.a.* [*mancipo*, Latin.] To enslave; to bind; to tie.

Although the regular part of nature is seldom varied, yet the meteors, which are in themselves more unstable, and less mancipated *to stated motions, are oftentimes employed to various ends.*
HALE'S ORIGIN OF MANKIND.

MANCIPA'TION. *n.s.* [from *mancipate.*] Slavery; involuntary obligation.

MA'NGO. *n.s.* [*mangostan*, Fr.] A fruit of the isle of Java, brought to Europe pickled.

The fruit with the husk, when very young, makes a good preserve, and is used to pickle like mangoes. MORTIMER.

What lord of old wou'd bid his cook prepare

Mangoes, potargo, champignons, cavare. KING.

MA'NNER. *n.s.* [*maniere*, French.]

1. Form; method.

In my divine Emilia make me blest.
Find thou the manner, *and the means prepare,*
Possession, more than conquest, is my care. DRYDEN.

2. Custom; habit; fashion.

As the manner *of some is.* BIBLE NEW TESTAMENT.

3. Certain degree.

It is in a manner *done already;*
For many carriages he hath dispatch'd
To the sea-side.
SHAKESPEARE'S KING JOHN.

The bread is in a manner *common.* BIBLE 1 SAMUEL XXI. 5.

If the envy be general in a manner *upon all the ministers of an estate, it is truly upon the state itself.* BACON'S ESSAYS.

This universe we have possest, and rul'd
In a manner *at our will, th' affairs of earth.* PARADISE REGAIN'D.

Antony Augustinus does in a manner *confess the charge.* BAKER'S REFLECTIONS ON LEARNING.

4. Sort; kind.

All manner *of men assembled here in arms against God's peace and the king's: we charge you to repair to your dwelling-places.* SHAKESPEARE'S HENRY VI. P. I.

A love that makes breath poor, and speech unable,
Beyond all manner *of so much I love you.* SHAKESPEARE.

What manner *of men were they whom ye slew?* BIBLE JUDGES.

The city may flourish in trade, and all manner *of outward advantages.* ATTERBURY.

5. Mien; cast of the look.

Air and manner *are often more expressive than words.* CLARISSA.

Some men have a native dignity in their manner, *which will procure them more regard by a look, than others can obtain by the most imperious commands.* CLARISSA.

6. Peculiar way.[156]

If I melt into melancholy while I write, I shall be taken in the manner; *and I sit by one too tender to these impressions.* DONNE'S LETTERS.

It can hardly be imagined how great a difference was in the humour, disposition, and manner, *of the army under Essex, and the other under Waller.* CLARENDON, B. VIII.

Some few touches of your lordship, which I have endeavoured to express after your manner, *have made whole poems of mine to pass with approbation.* DRYDEN'S JUVENAL.

As man is known by his company, so a man's company may be known by his manner *of expressing himself.* SWIFT.

7. Way; sort.

The temptations of prosperity insinuate themselves after a gentle, but very powerful, manner. ATTERBURY.

8. Character of the mind.

His princes are as much distinguished by their manners *as by their dominions; and even those among them, whose characters seem wholly made up of courage, differ from one another as to the particular kinds.* ADDISON.

9. Manners in the plural. General way of life; morals; habits.

The kinds of musick have most operation upon manners: *as, to make them warlike; to make them soft and effeminate.* BACON'S NATURAL HISTORY, NO. 114.

Every fool carries more or less in his face the signature of his manners, *though more legible in some than others.* L'ESTRANGE'S FABLES.

We bring our manners *to the blest abodes,*
And think what pleases us must please the gods. DRYDEN.

10. [In the plural.] Ceremonious behaviour; studied civility.

The time will not allow the compliment,
Which very manners *urge.*
SHAKESPEARE'S KING LEAR.

These bloody accidents must excuse my manners,
That so neglected you.
SHAKESPEARE'S OTHELLO.

Our griefs and not our manners *reason now.* SHAKESPEARE.

Ungracious wretch,
Fit for the mountains and the barbarous caves,
Where manners *ne'er were preach'd.*
SHAKESPEARE.

Dear Kate, you and I cannot be confined within the weak list of a country's fashion: we are the makers of manners, *Kate.*
SHAKESPEARE'S HENRY V.

Good manners *bound her to invite*
The stranger dame to be her guest that night. DRYDEN.

None but the careless and the confident would rush rudely into the presence of a great man: and shall we, in our applications to the great God, take that to be religion, which the common reason of mankind will not allow to be manners*?*
SOUTH'S SERMONS.

Your passion bends
Its force against your nearest friends;
Which manners, *decency, and pride,*
Have taught you from the world to hide.
SWIFT.

MA'NUAL. *n.s.* A small book, such as may be carried in the hand.

This manual *of laws, stiled the confessor's laws, contains but few heads.*
HALE'S COMMON LAW OF ENGLAND.

In those prayers which are recommended to the use of the devout persons of your church, in the manuals *and offices allowed them in our own language, they would be careful to have nothing they thought scandalous.* STILLINGFLEET.

MANUFA'CTURE. *n.s.* [*manus* and *facio*, Latin; *manufacture*, French.]

1. The practice of making any piece of workmanship.

2. Any thing made by art.

Heav'n's pow'r is infinite: earth, air, and sea,
The manufacture *mass the making pow'r obey.* DRYDEN.

The peasants are clothed in a coarse kind of canvas, the manufacture *of the country.*
ADDISON ON ITALY.

MANUFA'CTURER. *n.s.* [*manufacturier*, French; *manufacturus*, Lat.] A workman; an artificer.

In the practices of artificers and the manufacturers *of various kinds, the end being proposed, we find out ways of composing things for the several uses of human life.*
WATTS.

To MANU'RE. *v.a.* [*manouvrer*, French.]

1. To cultivate by manual labour.

They mock our scant manuring, *and require*
More hands than ours to lop their wanton growth. MILTON.

2. To dung; to fatten with composts.

Fragments of shells, reduced by the agitation of the sea to powder, are used for the manuring *of land.* WOODWARD.

Revenge her slaughter'd citizens,
Or share their fate: the corps of half her senate
Manure *the fields of Thessaly, while we*
Sit here, deliberating in cold debates.
ADDISON'S CATO.

MANYLA'NGUAGED. *adj.* [*many* and *language.*] Having many languages.

Seek Atrides on the Spartan shore;

He, wand'ring long, a wider circle made,
And manylanguag'd *nations has survey'd.*
POPE'S ODYSSEY.

MANYTI'MES, an adverbial phrase. Often; frequently.

They are Roman catholick in the device and legend, which are both of them many-times *taken out of the scriptures.*
ADDISON ON ANCIENT MEDALS.

MA'RGIN. *n.s.* [*margo*, Latin; *marge*, French.]

1. The border; the brink; the edge; the verge.

He drew his flaming sword, and struck
At him so fiercely, that the upper marge
Of his sevenfold shield away it took.
FAIRY QUEEN, B. II.

Never since
Met we on hill, in dale, forest, or mead,
Or on the beached margent *of the sea.*
SHAKESPEARE.

An airy crowd came rushing where he stood,
Which fill'd the margin *of the fatal flood.*
DRYDEN'S ÆNEID.

2. The edge of a page left blank, or fill'd with a short note.

As much love in rhime,
As would be cramm'd up in a sheet of paper
Writ on both sides the leaf, margent *and all.* SHAKESPEARE.

Reconcile those two places, which both you and the margins *of our bibles acknowledge to be parallel.* HAMMOND.

He knows in law, nor text, nor margent.
SWIFT.

3. The edge of a wound or sore.

All the advantage to be gathered from it is only from the evenness of its margin, *the purpose will be as fully answered by keeping that under only.*
SHARP'S SURGERY.

MA'RKET. *n.s.* [anciently written *mercat*, of *mercatus*, Lat.]

1. A publick time of buying and selling.

It were good that the privilege of a market *were given, the rather to enable them to their defence; for there is nothing doth sooner cause civility than many* market *towns, by reason the people repairing often thither will learn civil manners.*
SPENSER ON IRELAND.

Mistress, know yourself, down on your knees,
And thank heav'n, fasting, for a good man's love:
For I must tell you friendly in your ear,
Sell when you can, you are not for all markets. SHAKESPEARE.

They counted our life a pastime, and our time here a market *for gain.*
BIBLE WISDOM, XV. 12.

If one bushel of wheat and two bushels of barley will, in the market, *be taken one for another, they are of equal worth.* LOCKE.

2. Purchase and sale.

With another year's continuance of the war, there will hardly be money left in this kingdom to turn the common markets, *or pay rents.* TEMPLE.

The precious weight
Of pepper and Sabæan incense take,
And with post-haste thy running market *make,*
Be sure to turn the penny.
DRYDEN'S PERSIUS.

3. Rate; price. [*marché*, French.]

'Twas then old soldiers, cover'd o'er with scars,
Thought all past services rewarded well,
If, to their share, at least two acres fell,
Their country's frugal bounty; so of old
Was blood and life at a low market *sold.*
DRYDEN'S JUVENAL.

MA'RKET-BELL. *n.s.* [*market* and *bell.*] The bell to give notice that trade may begin in the market.

Enter, go in, the marketbell *is rung.*
SHAKESPEARE'S HENRY VI.

MA'RROW, in the Scottish dialect, to this day, denotes a fellow, companion, or associate; as also equal match he *met with his* marrow.

Though buying and selling doth wonderful wel,
Yet chopping and changing I cannot commend
With theef of his marrow *for fear of il end.* TUSSER.

MA'RSHALSEA. *n.s.* [from *marshal.*] The prison in Southwark belonging to the marshal of the king's houshold.

MA'RVEL. *n.s.* [*merveille*, French.] A wonder; any thing astonishing. Little in use.

A marvel *it were, if a man could espy, in the whole scripture, nothing which might breed a probable opinion, that divine authority was the same way inclinable.* HOOKER.

I am scarce in breath, my lord.
—— No marvel, *you have so bestir'd your valour; you cowardly rascal!* SHAKESPEARE'S KING LEAR.

No marvel
My lord protector's hawks do towre so well. SHAKESPEARE.

MASH. *n.s.* [*masche*, Dutch.]

1. The space between the threads of a net, commonly written *mesh.*

To defend one's self against the stings of bees, have a net knit with so small mashes, *that a bee cannot get through.* MORTIMER'S HUSBANDRY.

2. Any thing mingled or beaten together into an undistinguished or confused body. [from *mischen*, Dutch, to mix, or *mascher*, French.]

3. A mixture for a horse.

Put half a peck of ground malt into a pale, then put to it as much scalding water as will wet it well; stir it about for half an hour till the water is very sweet, and give it the horse lukewarm: this mash *is to be given to a horse after he has taken a purge, to make it work the better; or in the time of great sickness, or after hard labour.* FARRIER'S DICTIONARY.

When mares foal, they feed them with mashes, *and other moist food.* MORTIMER'S HUSBANDRY.

MASK. *n.s.* [*masque*, French.]

1. A cover to disguise the face; a visor.

Now love pulled off his mask, *and shewed his face unto her, and told her plainly that she was his prisoner.* SIDNEY.

Since she did neglect her looking-glass,
And throw her sun-expelling mask *away;*
The air hath starv'd the roses in her cheeks,
And pitch'd the lily tincture of her face. SHAKESPEARE.

Could we suppose that a mask *represented never so naturally the general humour of a character, it can never suit with the variety of passions that are incident to every single person in the whole course of a play.* ADDISON ON ITALY.

2. Any pretence or subterfuge.

Too plain thy nakedness of soul espy'd,
Why dost thou strive the conscious shame to hide,
By masks *of eloquence, and veils of pride?* PRIOR.

3. A festive entertainment, in which the company is masked.

Will you prepare for this masque *to-night.* SHAKESPEARE.

4. A revel; a piece of mummery; a wild bustle.

They in the end agreed,
That at a masque *and common revelling,*
Which was ordain'd, they should perform the deed. DANIEL.

This thought might lead me through this world's vain mask,
Content, though blind, had I no other guide. MILTON.

5. A dramatick performance, written in

a tragick stile without attention to rules or probability.

Thus I have broken the ice to invention, for the lively representation of floods and rivers necessary for our painters and poets in their picturs, poems, comedies, and masks. PEACHAM.

MASTER-TEETH. *n.s.* [*master* and *teeth.*] The principal teeth.

Some living creatures have their master-teeth *indented one within another like saws; as lions and dogs.* BACON.

MA'STICATORY. *n.s.* [*masticatoire*, French.] A medicine to be chewed only, not swallowed.

Remember masticatories *for the mouth.* BACON.

Salivation and masticatories *evacuate considerably; salivation many pints of phlegm in a day, and very much by chewing tobacco.* FLOYER ON HUMOURS.

MA'STIFF. *n.s. mastives*, plural. [*mastin*, French; *mastino*, Italian.] A dog of the largest size; a bandog; dogs kept to watch the house.

As savage bull, whom two fierce mastives *bait,*
When rancour doth with rage him once engore,
Forgets with wary ward them to await,
But with his dreadful horns them drives afore. FAIRY QUEEN.

When rank Thersites opes his mastiff *jaws,*
We shall hear musick, wit, and oracle. SHAKESPEARE.

When we knock at a farmer's door, the first answer shall be his vigilant mastiff. MORE'S ANTIDOTE AGAINST ATHEISM.

Soon as Ulysses near th' enclosure drew,
With open mouths the furious mastives *flew.* POPE'S ODYSSEY.

Let the mastiffs *amuse themselves about a sheep's skin stuffed with hay, provided it will keep them from worrying the flock.* SWIFT.

MATCH. *n.s.* [*meche*, French; *miccia*, Italian; probably from *mico*, to shine, Latin: surely not, as *Skinner* conjectures, from the Saxon *maca*, a companion, because a match is companion to a gun.]

1. Any thing that catches fire; generally a card, rope, or small chip of wood dipped in melted sulphur.

Try them in several bottles matches, *and see which of them last longest without stench.* BACON.

He made use of her trees as of matches *to set Druina a fire.* HOWEL'S VOCAL FOREST.

Being willing to try something that would not cherish much fire at once, and would keep fire much longer than a coal, we took a piece of match, *such as soldiers use.* BOYLE.

2. [From *μάχη*, a fight, or from *maca*, Saxon, one equal to another.] A contest; a game; any thing in which there is contest or opposition.

Shall we play the wantons with our woes,
And make some pretty match *with shedding tears?* SHAKESPEARE.

The goat was mine, by singing fairly won.
A solemn match *was made; he lost the prize.* DRYDEN.

3. [From *maca*, Saxon.] One equal to another; one able to contest with another.

Government mitigates the inequality of power among particular persons, and makes an innocent man, though of the lowest rank, a match *for the mightiest of his fellow-subjects.* ADDISON'S FREEHOLDER.

The old man has met with his match. SPECTATOR.

The natural shame that attends vice, makes

them zealous to encourage themselves by numbers, and form a party against religion: it is with pride they survey their increasing strength, and begin to think themselves a match *for virtue.* ROGERS.

4. One that suits or tallies with another.

5. A marriage.

The match
Were rich and honourable; besides, the gentleman
Is full of virtue, bounty, worth, and qualities,
Beseeming such a wife as your fair daughter. SHAKESPEARE.

Love doth seldom suffer itself to be confined by other matches *than those of its own making.* BOYLE.

With him she strove to join Lavinia's hand,
But dire portents the purpos'd match *withstand.* DRYDEN.

6. One to be married.

She inherited a fair fortune of her own, and was very rich in a personal estate, and was looked upon as the richest match *of the West.* CLARENDON, B. VIII.

MATHEMATI'CIAN. *n.s.* [*mathematicus*, Lat. *mathematicien*, French.] A man versed in the mathematicks.

One of the most eminent mathematicians *of the age assured me, that the greatest pleasure he took in reading Virgil was in examining Æneas's voyage by the map.* ADDISON'S SPECTATOR.

MA'TRIX. *n.s.* [Lat. *matrice*, Fr.] Womb; a place where any thing is generated or formed.

If they be not lodged in a convenient matrix, *they are not excited by the efficacy of the sun.* BROWN'S VULGAR ERROURS.

MA'UDLIN. *adj.* [*Maudlin* is the corrupt appellation of *Magdelen*, who being drawn by painters with swoln eyes, and disordered look, a drunken countenance, seems to have been so named from a ludicrous resemblance to the picture of *Magdelen.*] Drunk; fuddled.

And the kind maudling *crowd melts in her praise.* SOUTHERN'S SPARTAN DAME.

And largely, what she wants in words, supplies
With maudlin *eloquence of trickling eyes.* ROSCOMMON.

To MA'UNDER. *v.n.* [*maudire*, French.] To grumble; to murmur.

He made me many visits, maundring *as if I had done him a discourtesy in leaving such an opening.* WISEMAN'S SURGERY.

MAY, auxiliary verb, preterite *might*. [*magan*, Saxon; *moghen*, Dutch.]

1. To be at liberty; to be permitted; to be allowed; as, you *may* do for me [*per me licet*] all you can.

He that is sent out to travel with the thoughts of a man, designing to improve himself, may *get into the conversation of persons of condition.* LOCKE ON EDUCATION.

2. To be possible; with the words *may be*.

Be the workmen what they may *be, let us speak of the work.* BACON'S ESSAYS.

3. To be by chance.

It may *be, I shall otherwise bethink me.* SHAKESPEARE.

How old may *Phillis be, you ask,*
Whose beauty thus all hearts engages?
To answer is no easy task,
For she has really two ages. PRIOR.

4. To have power.

This also tendeth to no more but what the king may *do: for what he* may *do is of two kinds; what he* may *do as just, and what he* may *do as possible.* BACON.

Make the most of life you may.
BOURNE.

5. A word expressing desire.

May *you live happily and long for the service of your country.*
DRYDEN'S DEDICATION TO THE ÆNEIS.

ME. *pronoun.*

1. The oblique case of *I.*

Me, *only* me, *the hand of fortune bore,*
Unblest to tread an interdicted shore.
POPE'S ODYSSEY.

For me *the fates severely kind, ordain*
A cool suspense. POPE.

2. *Me* is sometimes a kind of ludicrous expletive.

He thrusts me *himself into the company of three or four gentlemanlike dogs, under the duke's table.* SHAKESPEARE.

He presently, as greatness knows itself,
Steps me *a little higher than his vow*
Made to my father, while his blood was poor. SHAKESPEARE.

I, having been acquainted with the smell before, knew it was Crab, and goes me *to the fellow that whips the dogs.*
SHAKESPEARE'S TWO GENTLEMEN OF VERONA.

I followed me *close, came in foot and hand, and, with a thought, seven of the eleven I paid.* SHAKESPEARE'S HENRY IV.

3. It is sometimes used ungrammatically for *I*; as, *methinks.*

Me *rather had, my heart might feel your love,*
Than my unpleas'd eye see your courtesy.
SHAKESPEARE.

MECHA'NICAL, MECHANICK. *adj.* [*mechanicus*, Lat. *mechanique*, French; from μηχανή.]

1. Mean; servile; of mean occupation.[157]

Know you not, being mechanical, *you ought not walk upon a labouring day, without the sign of your profession?*
SHAKESPEARE.

Hang him, mechanical *salt-butter rogue; I will stare him out of his wits; I will hew him with my cudgel.* SHAKESPEARE.

Mechanick *slaves,*
With greasy aprons, rules, and hammers, shall
Uplift us to the view.
SHAKESPEARE'S ANTONY AND CLEOPATRA.

To make a god, a hero, or a king,
Descend to a mechanick *dialect.*
ROSCOMMON.

2. Constructed by the laws of mechanicks.

Many a fair precept in poetry is, like a seeming demonstration in mathematicks, very specious in the diagram, but failing in the mechanick *operation.* DRYDEN.

The main business of natural philosophy, is to argue from phenomena without feigning hypotheses, and to deduce causes from effects till we come to the very first cause, which certainly is not mechanical; *and not only to unfold the mechanism of the world, but chiefly to resolve these, and such like questions.* NEWTON'S OPTICKS.

3. Skilled in mechanicks.

MECHA'NICK. *n.s.* A manufacturer; a low workman.

Do not bid me
Dismiss my soldiers, or capitulate
Again with Rome's mechanicks.
SHAKESPEARE'S CORIOLANUS.

A third proves a very heavy philosopher, who possibly would have made a good mechanick, *and have done well enough at the useful philosophy of the spade or the anvil.* SOUTH.

MECHANI'CIAN. *n.s.* [*mechanicien*, French.] A man professing or studying the construction of machines.

Some were figured like male, others like female screws, as mechanicians *speak.*
BOYLE.

MECHA'NISM. *n.s.* [*mechanisme*, French.]

1. Action according to mechanick laws.

After the chyle has passed through the lungs, nature continues her usual mechanism, *to convert it into animal substances.*
ARBUTHNOT ON ALIMENTS.

He acknowledges nothing besides matter and motion; so that all must be performed either by mechanism *or accident, either of which is wholly unaccountable.*
BENTLEY.

2. Construction of parts depending on each other in any complicated fabrick.

MEDICI'NAL. *adj.* [*medicinalis*, Latin: this word is now commonly pronounced *medícinal*, with the accent on the second syllable; but more properly, and more agreeably to the best authorities, *medicínal*.]
1. Having the power of healing; having physical virtue.

Come with words as medicinal *as true,*
Honest as either; to purge him of that humour
That presses him from sleep.
SHAKESPEARE'S WINTER'S TALE.

Thoughts my tormentors arm'd with deadly stings,
Mangle my apprehensive tenderest parts;
Exasperate, exulcerate and raise
Dire inflammation, which no cooling herb
Nor medicinal *liquor can assuage.*
MILTON'S AGONISTES.

The second causes took the swift command,
The medicinal *head, the ready hand;*
All but eternal doom was conquer'd by their art. DRYDEN.

2. Belonging to physick.

Learn'd he was in med'cinal *lore,*
For by his side a pouch he wore,
Replete with strange hermetick powder,
That wounds nine miles point-blank with solder. BUTLER.

Such are called medicinal-*days by some writers, wherein no crisis or change is expected, so as to forbid the use of medicines: but it is most properly used for those days wherein purging, or any other evacuation, is more conveniently complied with.*
QUINCY.

Medicinal-*hours are those wherein it is supposed that medicines may be taken, commonly reckoned in the morning fasting, about an hour before dinner, about four hours after dinner, and going to bed; but times are to be governed by the symptoms and aggravation of the distemper.*
QUINCY.

ME'DICINE. *n.s.* [*medicine*, Fr. *medicina*, Latin. It is generally pronounced as if only of two syllables, *med'cine.*]Physick; any remedy administered by a physician.

O, my dear father! restauration, hang
Thy medicine *on my lips; and let this kiss*
Repair those violent harms.
SHAKESPEARE'S KING LEAR.

Let's make us medicines *of our great revenge,*
To cure this deadly grief.
SHAKESPEARE'S MACBETH.

A merry heart doth good like a medicine*; but a broken spirit drieth the bones.*
BIBLE PROVERBS, XVII. 22.

I wish to die, yet dare not death endure;
Detest the med'cine, *yet desire the cure.*
DRYDEN.

MEDITERRA'NE, MEDITERRANEAN, MEDITERRANEOUS. *adj.* [*medius* and *terra*; *mediterranée*, Fr.]
1. Encircled with land.

In all that part that lieth on the north side of the mediterrane *sea, it is thought not to be the vulgar tongue.* BREREWOOD.

2. Inland; remote from the sea.

It is found in mountains and mediterraneous *parts; and so it is a fat and unctuous sublimation of the earth.*
BROWN.

We have taken a less height of the mountains than is requisite, if we respect the mediterraneous *mountains, or those that are at a great distance from the sea.* BURNET.

ME'DLY. *n.s.* [from *meddle* for *mingle.*] A mixture; a miscellany; a mingled mass. It is commonly used with some degree of contempt.

Some imagined that the powder in the armory had taken fire; others, that troops of horsemen approached: in which medly *of conceits they bare down one upon another, and jostled many into the tower ditch.* HAYWARD.

Love is a medley *of endearments, jars,*
Suspicions, quarrels, reconcilements, wars;
Then peace again. WALSH.

They count their toilsome marches, long fatigues,
Unusual fastings, and will bear no more
This medley *of philosophy and war.*
ADDISON'S CATO.

Mahomet began to knock down his fellow citizens, and to fill all Arabia with an unnatural medley *of religion and bloodshed.* FREEHOLDER, NO. 50.

There are that a compounded fluid drain
From different mixtures: the blended streams,
Each mutually correcting each, create
A pleasurable medley. PHILIPS.

MEETING-HOUSE. *n.s.* [*meeting* and *house.*] Place where Dissenters assemble to worship.

His heart misgave him that the churches were so many meeting-houses; *but I soon made him easy.* ADDISON.

ME'GRIM. *n.s.* [from *Hemicrany, migrain, megrim, 'ημικρανία.*] Disorder of the head.

In every megrim *or vertigo there is an obtenebration joined with a semblance of turning round.*
BACON'S NATURAL HISTORY.

There screen'd in shades from day's detested glare,
Spleen sighs for ever on her pensive bed,
Pain at her side, and megrim *at her head.*
POPE.

To **MELI'ORATE.** *v.a.* [*meliorer,* Fr. from *melior.*] To better; to improve.

Grafting meliorates *the fruit; for that the nourishment is better prepared in the stock than in the crude earth.* BACON.

But when we graft, or buds inoculate,
Nature by art we nobly meliorate.
DENHAM.

A man ought by no means to think, that he should be able so much as to alter or meliorate *the humour of an ungrateful person by any acts of kindness.*
SOUTH'S SERMONS.

Castration serves to meliorate *the flesh of those beasts that suffer it.* GRAUNT.

Much labour is requir'd in trees.
Well must the ground be digg'd, and better dress'd,
New soil to make, and meliorate *the rest.*
DRYDEN'S VIRGIL.

MELIORA'TION. *n.s.* [*melioration,* Fr. from *meliorate.*] Improvement; act of bettering.

For the melioration *of musick there is yet much left, in this point of exquisite consorts, to try.* BACON.

MEMORA'NDUM. *n.s.* [Latin.] A note to help the memory.

I resolved to new pave every street within the liberties, and entered a memorandum *in my pocket-book accordingly.*
GUARDIAN, NO. 166.

Nature's fair table-book, our tender souls,
We scrawl all o'er with old and empty rules,
Stale memorandums *of the schools.*
SWIFT'S MISCELLANIES.

MEN-PLE'ASER. *n.s.* [*men* and *pleaser.*] One too careful to please others.

Servants be obedient to them that are your masters: not with eye-service, as men-pleasers; *but as the servants of Christ, doing the will of God from the heart.* BIBLE EPHESIANS, VI. 6.

MENA'GE. *n.s.* [French.] A collection of animals.

I saw here the largest menage *that I met with any-where.* ADDISON ON ITALY.

To **MEND.** *v.a.* [*emendo*, Latin.]

1. To repair from breach or decay.

They gave the money to the workmen to repair and mend *the house.* BIBLE 2 CHRONICLES, XXXIV. 10.

2. To correct; to alter for the better.

The best service they could do to the state, was to mend *the lives and manners of the persons who composed it.* TEMPLE'S MISCELLANY.

You need not despair, by the assistance of his growing reason, to master his timorousness, and mend *the weakness of his constitution.* LOCKE ON EDUCATION.

Though in some lands the grass is but short, yet it mends *garden herbs and fruit.* MORTIMER'S HUSBANDRY.

Their opinion of Wood, and his project, is not mended. SWIFT.

3. To help; to advance.

Whatever is new is unlooked for; and ever it mends *some, and impairs others: and he that is holpen takes it for a fortune, and he that is hurt for a wrong.* BACON.

If, to avoid succession in eternal existence, they recur to the punctum stans of the schools, they will thereby very little mend *the matter, or help us to a more positive idea of infinite duration.* LOCKE.

4. To improve; to increase.

Death comes not at call; justice divine
Mends *not her slowest pace, for pray'r, or cries.* MILTON.

When upon the sands the traveller,
Sees the high sea come rolling from afar,
The land grow short, he mends *his weary pace,*
While death behind him covers all the place. DRYDEN.

He saw the monster mend *his pace; he springs,*
As terror had increas'd his feet with wings. DRYDEN.

To **MEND.** *v.n.* To grow better; to advance in any good; to be changed for the better.

Name a new play and he's the poet's friend;
Nay, show'd his faults – but when wou'd poets mend?
POPE'S ESSAY ON CRITICISM.

MENO'LOGY. *n.s.* [*μηνολόγιον*; *menologe*, French.] A register of months.

In the Roman martyrology we find, at one time, many thousand martyrs destroyed by Dioclesian: the menology *saith they were twenty thousand.* STILLINGFLEET.

To **ME'NTION.** *v.a.* [*mentionner*, Fr. from the noun.] To write or express in words or writing.

I will mention *the loving-kindnesses of the Lord, and the praises of the Lord.* BIBLE ISAIAH, LXIII. 7.

These mentioned *by their names were princes in their families.* BIBLE 1 CHRONICLES, IV. 38.

The rest of the acts of Jehoshaphat are written in the book of Jehu, who is mentioned *in the book of Kings.* BIBLE 2 CHRONICLES.

All his transgressions shall not be mentioned. BIBLE EZEKIEL, XVIII.

MEPHI'TICAL. *adj.* [*mephitis*, Lat.] Ill favoured; stinking.

Mephitical *exhalations are poisonous or noxious steams issuing out of the earth, from what cause soever.* QUINCY.

ME'RCURY. *n.s.* [*mercurius*, Latin.]
1. The chemist's name for quicksilver is mercury. *Hill.*

The gall of animals and mercury *kill worms; and the water in which* mercury *is boiled has this effect.* ARBUTHNOT.

2. Sprightly qualities.

Thus the mercury *of man is fix'd,*
Strong grows the virtue with his nature mix'd;
The dross cements what else were too refin'd,
And in one int'rest body acts with mind.
POPE.

3. A news-paper. *Ainsworth.*
4. It is now applied, in cant phrase, to the carriers of news and pamphlets.

MERETRI'CIOUS. *adj.* [*meretricius*, *meretrix*, Latin.] Whorish; such as is practised by prostitutes; alluring by false show.

Our degenerate understandings having suffered a sad divorce from their dearest object, defile themselves with every meretricious *semblance, that the variety of opinion presents them with.*
GLANVILLE'S SCEPSIS SCIENTIFICA.

Not by affected, meretricious *arts,*
But strict harmonious symmetry of parts.
ROSCOMMON.

To **ME'RRIMAKE.** *v.a.* To feast; to be jovial.

With thee 'twas Marian's dear delight
To moil all day, and merrimake *at night.*
GAY'S PASTORALS.

MERRY-A'NDREW. *n.s.* A buffoon; a zany; a jack-pudding.

He would be a statesman because he is a buffoon; as if there went no more to the making of a counsellor than the faculties of a merry-andrew *or tumbler.*
L'ESTRANGE.

The first who made the experiment was a merry-andrew. SPECTATOR, NO. 599.

ME'RRYTHOUGHT. *n.s.* [*merry* and *thought.*] A forked bone on the body of fowls; so called because boys and girls pull in play at the two sides, the longest part broken off betokening priority of marriage.

Let him not be breaking merrythoughts *under the table with my cousin.*
EACHARD'S CONTEMPT OF THE CLERGY.

MESH. *n.s.* [*maesche*, Dutch; *mache*, old French: it were therefore better written, as it is commonly pronounced, *mash.*] The interstice of a net; the space between the threads of a net.

The drovers hang square nets athwart the tide, thorough which the shoal of pilchard passing, leave many behind entangled in the meashes.
CAREW'S SURVEY OF CORNWALL.

Such a hare is madness the youth, to skip o'er the meshes *of good counsel the cripple.*
SHAKESPEARE'S MERCHANT OF VENICE.

He spreads his subtle nets from sight,
With twinkling glasses to betray
The larks that in the meshes *light.*
DRYDEN.

With all their mouths the nerves the spirits drink,
Which through the cells of the fine strainers sink:
These all the channel'd fibres ev'ry way,
For motion and sensation, still convey:
The greatest portion of th' arterial blood,
By the close structure of the parts withstood,
Whose narrow meshes *stop the grosser flood.* BLACKMORE.

ME'SSAGE. *n.s.* [*message*, Fr.] An errand; any thing committed to another to be told to a third.

She doth display
The gate with pearls and rubies richly dight,

Through which her words so wise do make their way,
To bear the message *of her spright.*
SPENSER, SONNET 81.

May one, that is a herald and a prince,
Do a fair message *to his kingly ears!*
SHAKESPEARE.

She is fair, and, fairer than that word,
Of wond'rous virtues; sometimes from her eyes
I did receive fair speechless messages.
SHAKESPEARE.

Gently hast thou told
Thy message, *which might else in telling wound,*
And in performing end us.
MILTON'S PARADISE LOST, B. XI.

Let the minister be low, his interest inconsiderable, the word will suffer for his sake; the message *will still find reception according to the dignity of the messenger.* SOUTH.

The welcome message *made, was soon receiv'd;*
'Twas to be wish'd and hop'd, but scarce believ'd. DRYDEN.

ME'TAPHOR. *n.s.* [*metaphore*, Fr. *μετάφορα*.] The application of a word to an use to which, in its original import, it cannot be put: as, he *bridles* his anger; he *deadens* the sound; the spring *awakes* the flowers. A metaphor is a simile comprized in a word; the spring putting in action the powers of vegetation, which were torpid in the winter, as the powers of a sleeping animal are excited by awaking him.

The work of tragedy is on the passions, and in a dialogue; both of them abhor strong metaphors, *in which the epopœa delights.* DRYDEN'S DEDICATION TO VIRGIL'S ÆNEIS.

METEORO'LOGIST. *n.s.* [from *meteorology*.] A man skilled in meteors, or studious of them.

The meteorologists *observe, that amongst the four elements which are the ingredients of all sublunary creatures, there is a notable correspondency.*
HOWEL'S VOCAL FOREST.

METEORO'LOGY. *n.s.* [*μετέωρα* and *λέγω*.] The doctrine of meteors.

In animals we deny not a natural meteorology, *or innate presentation of wind and weather.* BROWN'S VULGAR ERROURS.

ME'THODIST. *n.s.* [from *method*.]

1. A physician who practises by theory.

Our wariest physicians, not only chemists but methodists, *give it inwardly in several constitutions and distempers.* BOYLE.

2. One of a new kind of puritans lately arisen, so called from their profession to live by rules and in constant method.

METRO'POLIS. *n.s.* [*metropolis*, Latin; *metropole*, French; *μήτηρ* and *πόλις*.] The mother city; the chief city of any country or district.

His eye discovers unaware
The goodly prospect of some foreign land,
First seen: or some renown'd metropolis,
With glistering spires and pinnacles adorn'd. MILTON.

Reduc'd in careful watch
Round their metropolis.
MILTON'S PARADISE LOST, B. X.

We stopped at Pavia, that was once the metropolis *of a kingdom, but at present a poor town.* ADDISON ON ITALY.

ME'ZZOTINTO. *n.s.* [Italian.] A kind of graving, so named as nearly resembling paint, the word importing half-painted: it is done by beating the whole into asperity with a hammer, and then rubbing it down with a stone to the resemblance intended.

MI'ASM. *n.s.* [from *μιαίνω*, *inquino* to infect.] Such particles or atoms as are supposed to arise from distempered, putrefying, or poisonous bodies, and to affect people at a distance.

> *The plague is a malignant fever, caused through pestilential* miasms *insinuating into the humoral and consistent parts of the body.* HARVEY ON CONSUMPTIONS.

MICROCO'SM. *n.s.* [*μίκϱος* and *κόσμος*.] The little world. Man is so called as being imagined, by some fanciful philosophers, to have in him something analogous to the four elements.

> *You see this in the map of my*
> microcosm.
> SHAKESPEARE'S CORIOLANUS.

> *She to whom this world must itself*
> *refer,*
> *As suburbs, or the* microcosm *of her;*
> *She, she is dead; she's dead, when thou*
> *know'st this,*
> *Thou know'st how lame a creeple this*
> *world is.* DONNE.

> *As in this our* microcosm, *the heart*
> *Heat, spirit, motions gives to every part:*
> *So Rome's victorious influence did*
> *disperse*
> *All her own virtues through the universe.*
> DENHAM.

> *Philosophers say, that man is a* microcosm, *or little world, resembling in miniature every part of the great; and the body natural may be compared to the body politick.* SWIFT.

MI'GHTY. *adv.* In a great degree. Not to be used but in very low language.

> *Lord of his new hypothesis he reigns:*
> *He reigns; How long? Till some usurper*
> *rise,*
> *And he too mighty thoughtful,* mighty *wise:*
> *Studies new lines.* PRIOR.

MI'LKSCORE. *n.s.* [*milk* and *score.*] Account of milk owed for, scored on a board.

> *He ordered the lord high treasurer to pay off the debts of the crown, particularly a* milkscore *of three years standing.*
> ADDISON'S FREEHOLDER, NO. 36.

> *He is better acquainted with the* milkscore *than his steward's accounts.*
> ADDISON'S SPECTATOR, NO. 482.

MI'LL-TEETH. *n.s.* [*mill* and *teeth.*] The grinders; dentes molares, double teeth.

> *The best instruments for cracking bones and nuts are grinders or* mill-teeth.
> ARBUTHNOT ON ALIMENTS.

MIME. *n.s.* [*mime*, Fr. *μίμος*; *mimus*, Latin.] A buffoon who practises gesticulations, either representative of some action, or merely contrived to raise mirth.

> *Think'st thou,* mime, *this is great?*
> BEN JONSON.

MI'MICK. *n.s.* [*mimicus*, Latin.]

1. A ludicrous imitator; a buffoon who copies another's act or manner so as to excite laughter.

> *Like poor Andrew I advance,*
> *False* mimick *of my master's dance:*
> *Around the cord a while I sprawl,*
> *And thence, though slow, in earnest fall.*
> PRIOR.

2. A mean or servile imitator.

> *Of France the* mimick, *and of Spain the*
> *prey.* ANONYMOUS.

MI'NER. *n.s.* [*mineur*, Fr. from *mine.*]

1. One that digs for metals.

> *By me kings palaces are push'd to ground,*
> *And* miners *crush'd beneath their mines*
> *are found.* DRYDEN.

2. One who makes military mines.

> *As the bombardeer levels his mischief at cities, the* miner *busies himself in ruining private houses.* TATLER.

MI'NIM. *n.s.* [from *minimus*, Lat.]
1. A small being; a dwarf.

Not all
Minims *of nature; some of serpent-kind,*
Wond'rous in length, and corpulence, involv'd
Their snaky folds, and added wings.
MILTON'S PARADISE LOST.

2. This word is applied, in the northern countries, to a small sort of fish, which they pronounce *mennim*.

To **MI'NISH.** *v.a.* [from *diminish*; *minus*, Latin.] To lessen; to lop; to impair.

Ye shall not minish *ought from your bricks of your daily task.*
BIBLE EXODUS, V. 19.

They are minished *and brought low through oppression.*
BIBLE PSALMS, CVII. 39.

Another law was to bring in the silver of the realm to the mint, in making all clipt, minished, *or impaired coins of silver, not to be current in payments.*
BACON'S HENRY VII.

MI'NISTERY. *n.s.* [*ministerium*, Lat.] Office; service. This word is now contracted to *ministry*, but used by *Milton* as four syllables.

They that will have their chamber filled with a good scent, make some odoriferous water be blown about it by their servants mouths that are dextrous in that ministery. DIGBY.

This temple to frequent
With ministeries *due, and solemn rites.*
MILTON, B. XII.

MI'NNOCK. *n.s.* Of this word I know not the precise meaning.[158] It is not unlikely that *minnock* and *minx* are originally the same word.

An ass's nole I fixed on his head;
Anon his Thisbe must be answered,
And forth my minnock *comes.*
SHAKESPEARE.

To **MI'NORATE.** *v.a.* [from *minor*, Lat.] To lessen; to diminish. A word not yet admitted into the language.

This it doth not only by the advantageous assistance of a tube, but by shewing in what degrees distance minorates *the object.*
GLANVILLE'S SCEPSIS SCIENTIFICA.

MI'NSTER. *n.s.* [*minstere*, Saxon.] A monastery; an ecclesiastical fraternity; a cathedral church. The word is yet retained at York and Lichfield.

MI'NUM. *n.s.*
1. [With printers.] A small sort of printing letter.
2. [With musicians.] A note of slow time, two of which make a semibrief, as two crotchets make a minum; two quavers a crotchet, and two semiquavers a quaver. *Bailey.*

Oh, he's the courageous captain of compliments; he fights as you sing pricksongs, keeps time, distance, and proportion; rests his minum, *one, two, and the third in your bosom.*
SHAKESPEARE'S ROMEO AND JULIET.

MI'NUTE. *n.s.* [*minutum*, Latin.]
1. The sixtieth part of an hour.

This man so complete,
Who was enroll'd 'mongst wonders, and when we,
Almost with list'ning ravish'd, could not find
His hour of speech a minute.
SHAKESPEARE'S HENRY VIII.

2. Any small space of time.

They walk'd about me ev'ry minute *while;*
And if I did but stir out of my bed,
Ready they were to shoot me to the heart.
SHAKESPEARE.

The speed of gods
Time counts not, though with swiftest minutes *wing'd.*
MILTON'S PARADISE LOST, B. X.

Gods! that the world should turn

On minutes *and on moments.*
DENHAM'S SOPHY.

Experience does every minute *prove the sad truth of this assertion.*
SOUTH'S SERMONS.

Tell her, that I some certainty may bring;
I go this minute *to attend the king.*
DRYDEN'S AURENGZEBE.

3. The first draught of any agreement in writing; this is common in the Scottish law: as, have you made a *minute* of that contract?

MI'NUTE-BOOK. *n.s.* [*minute* and *book.*] Book of short hints.

MI'NUTE-GLASS. *n.s.* [*minute* and *glass.*] Glass of which the sand measures a minute.

MI'NUTE-WATCH. *n.s.* [*minute* and *watch.*] A watch in which minutes are more distinctly marked than in common watches which reckon by the hour.

Casting our eyes upon a minute-watch, *we found that from the beginning of the pumping, about two minutes after the coals had been put in glowing, to the total disappearing of the fire, there had passed but three minutes.* BOYLE.

MIRADO'R. *n.s.* [Spanish, from *mirar*, to look.] A balcony; a gallery whence ladies see shews.

Mean time your valiant son, who had before
Gain'd fame, rode round, to ev'ry mirador*;*
Beneath each lady's stand a stop he made,
And bowing, took th' applauses which they paid. DRYDEN.

MI'RKSOME. *n.s.* [*morck*, dark, Danish. In the derivatives of this set, no regular orthography is observed: it is common to write *murky*, to which the rest ought to conform.] Dark; obscure.

Through mirksome *air her ready way she makes.* FAIRY QUEEN.

MIS, an inseparable particle used in composition to mark an ill sense, or depravation of the meaning: as, *chance*, luck; *mischance*, ill luck; *computation*, reckoning; *miscomputation*, false reckoning; *to like*, to be pleased; *to mislike*, to be offended; from *mes* in Teutonick and French, used in the same sense. Of this it is difficult to give all the examples; but those that follow will sufficiently explain it.

MISACCEPTA'TION. *n.s.* [*mis* and *acceptation.*] The act of taking in a wrong sense.

To MISASSI'GN. *v.a.* [*mis* and *assign*] To assign erroneously.

We have not misassigned *the cause of this phenomenon.* BOYLE.

To MISCA'L. *v.a.* [*mis* and *call.*] To name improperly.

My heart will sigh when I miscal *it so.*
SHAKESPEARE'S RICHARD II.

The third act, which connects propositions and deduceth conclusions from them, the schools call discourse; and we shall not miscal *it if we name it reason.*
GLANVILLE'S SCEPSIS SCIENTIFICA.

What you miscal *their folly is their care.*
DRYDEN.

MISCITA'TION. *n.s.* [*mis* and *citation.*] Unfair or false quotation.

Being charged with miscitation *and unfair dealing, it was requisite to say something; for honesty is a tender point.*
COLLIER'S VIEW OF THE STAGE.

To MISCI'TE. *v.a.* [*mis* and *cite.*] To quote wrong.

To **MISDEME'AN.** *v.a.* [*mis* and *demean.*] To behave ill.

From frailty
And want of wisdom, you, that best should teach us,
Have misdemean'd *yourself.*
SHAKESPEARE'S HENRY VIII.

MISDEME'ANOR. *n.s.* [*mis* and *demean.*] Offence; ill behaviour; something less than an atrocious crime.

The house of commons have only power to censure the members of their own house, in point of election or misdemeanors, *in or towards that house.* BACON.

It is no real disgrace to the church merely to lose her privileges, but to forfeit them by her fault or misdemeanor. SOUTH.

These could never have touched the head, or stopped the source of these unhappy misdemeanors, *for which the punishment was sent.*
WOODWARD'S NATURAL HISTORY, P. II.

MISINFORMA'TION. *n.s.* [from *misinform.*] False intelligence; false accounts.

Let not such be discouraged as deserve well, by misinformation *of others, perhaps out of envy or treachery.* BACON.

The vengeance of God, and the indignation of men, will join forces against an insulting baseness, when backed with greatness, and set on by misinformation.
SOUTH'S SERMONS.

To **MI'SLE.** *v.n.* [from *mist.*] To rain in imperceptible drops, like a thick mist: properly *mistle.*

Enough, thou mourned hast,
Now ginnes to mizzle, *hie we homeward fast.* SPENSER.

The very small drops of a misling *rain descending through a freezing air, do each of them shoot into one of those figured icicles.*
GREW'S COSMOLOGIA SACRA, B. I.

This cold precipitates the vapours either in dews, or, if the vapours more copiously ascend, they are condensed into misling, *or into showers of small rain, falling in numerous, thick, small drops.*
DERHAM'S PHYSICO-THEOLOGY.

In misling *days when I my thresher heard,*
With nappy beer I to the barn repair'd.
GAY'S PASTORALS.

To **MISPE'L.** *v.a.* [*mis* and *spell.*] To spell wrong.

She became a protest enemy to the arts and sciences, and scarce ever wrote a letter to him without wilfully mispelling *his name.*
SPECTATOR, NO. 635.

To **MISPO'INT.** *v.a.* [*mis* and *point.*] To confuse sentences by wrong punctuation.

To **MISRECI'TE.** *v.a.* [*mis* and *recite.*] To recite not according to the truth.

He misrecites *the argument, and denies the consequence, which is clear.*
BISHOP BRAMHALL AGAINST HOBBES.

To **MISREPRESE'NT.** *v.a.* [*mis* and *represent.*] To represent not as it is; to falsify to disadvantage: *mis* often signifies not only error, but malice or mischief.

Two qualities necessary to a reader before his judgment should be allowed are, common honesty and common sense; and that no man could have misrepresented *that paragraph, unless he were utterly destitute of one or both.* SWIFT.

While it is so difficult to learn the springs of some facts, and so easy to forget the circumstances of others, it is no wonder they should be so grosly misrepresented *to the publick by curious and inquisitive heads, who proceed altogether upon conjectures.*
SWIFT.

MISS. *n.s.* [contracted from *mistress. Bailey.*]

1. The term of honour to a young girl.

Where there are little masters and misses *in a house, they are great impediments to the diversions of the servants.* SWIFT.

2. A strumpet; a concubine; a whore; a prostitute.

All women would be of one piece,
The virtuous matron and the miss.
HUDIBRAS, P. III.

This gentle cock, for solace of his life,
Six misses *had besides his lawful wife.*
DRYDEN.

MI'SSIVE. n.s. [French.]
1. A letter sent: it is retained in Scotland in that sense.

Great aids came in to him; partly upon missives, *and partly voluntaries from many parts.* BACON'S HENRY VII.

2. A messenger.[159]

Rioting in Alexandria, you
Did pocket up my letters; and with taunts
Did gibe my missive *out of audience.*
SHAKESPEARE.

While wrapt in the wonder of it came missives *from the king, who all hail'd me thane of Cawdor.*
SHAKESPEARE'S MACBETH.

To **MISTA'TE.** *v.a.* [*mis* and *state.*] To state wrong.

They mistate *the question, when they talk of pressing ceremonies.*
BISHOP SANDERSON.

To **MISTE'ACH.** *v.a.* [*mis* and *teach.*] To teach wrong.

Such guides shall be set over the several congregations as will be sure to misteach *them.* BISHOP SANDERSON.

The extravagances of the lewdest life are the more consummate disorders of a mistaught *or neglected youth.*
L'ESTRANGE'S FABLES.

MI'STRESS. *n.s.* [*maistresse, maîtresse,* French.]
1. A woman who governs: correlative to subject or to servant.

Here stood he in the dark, his sharp sword out,
Mumbling of wicked charms, conj'ring the moon
To stand's auspicious mistress.
SHAKESPEARE'S KING LEAR.

Let us prepare
Some welcome for the mistress *of the house.* SHAKESPEARE.

Like the lily,
That once was mistress *of the field and flourish'd,*
I'll hang my head and perish.
SHAKESPEARE'S HENRY VIII.

He'll make your Paris louvre shake for it,
Were it the mistress *court of mighty Europe.* SHAKESPEARE.

I will not charm my tongue; I'm bound to speak;
My mistress *here lies murther'd in her bed.* SHAKESPEARE'S OTHELLO.

The late queen's gentlewoman! a knight's daughter!
To be her mistress' mistress! *the queen's queen.* SHAKESPEARE.

Rome now is mistress *of the whole world,*
sea and land, to either pole.
BEN JONSON'S CATILINE.

Wonder not, sov'reign mistress! *if perhaps*
Thou can'st, who art sole wonder; much less arm
Thy looks, the heav'n of mildness, with disdain. MILTON.

Those who assert the lunar orb presides
O'er humid bodies, and the ocean guides;
Whose waves obsequious ebb, or swelling run
With the declining or encreasing moon;
With reason seem her empire to maintain
As mistress *of the rivers and the main.*
BLACKMORE.

What a miserable spectacle, for a nation that had been mistress *at sea so long!*
ARBUTHNOT ON COINS.

2. A woman who possesses faculties uninjured.[160]

There had she enjoyed herself while she was

mistress *of herself, and had no other thoughts but such as might arise out of quiet senses.* SIDNEY, B. II.

Ages to come, that shall your bounty hear,
Will think you mistress *of the Indies were;*
Though streighter bounds your fortune did confine,
In your large heart was found a wealthy mine. WALLER.

3. A woman skilled in any thing.

A letter desires all young wives to make themselves mistresses *of Wingate's Arithmetick.*
ADDISON'S SPECTATOR, NO. 92.

4. A woman teacher.

Erect publick schools, provided with the best and ablest masters and mistresses. SWIFT.

5. A woman beloved and courted.

They would not suffer the prince to confer with, or very rarely to see, his mistress, *whom they pretended he should forthwith marry.* CLARENDON.

Nice honour still engages to requite
False mistresses *and proud with slight for slight.* GRANVILLE.

6. A term of contemptuous address.

Look you, pale mistress,
Do you perceive the ghastness of her eye?
SHAKESPEARE.

7. A whore; a concubine.

MI'TTENS. *n.s.* [*mitaines*, French.][161]
1. Coarse gloves for the Winter.

December must be expressed with a horrid aspect, as also January clad in Irish rug, holding in furred mittens *the sign of Capricorn.* PEACHAM ON DRAWING.

2. Gloves that cover the arm without covering the fingers.
3. To handle one without *mittens*. To use one roughly. A low phrase. *Ainsworth.*

MI'ZMAZE. *n.s.* [A cant word, formed from *maze* by reduplication.] A maze; a labyrinth.

Those who are accustomed to reason have got the true key of books, and the clue to lead them through the mizmaze *of variety of opinions and authors to truth.*
LOCKE.

MOB. *n.s.* [contracted from *mobile*, Latin.] The croud; a tumultuous rout.

Parts of different species jumbled together, according to the mad imagination of the dawber; a very monster in a Bartholomew-fair, for the mob *to gape at.* DRYDEN.

Dreams are but interludes, which fancy makes,
When monarch reason sleeps, this mimick wakes;
Compounds a medley of disjointed things,
A court of coblers, and a mob *of kings.*
DRYDEN.

A cluster of mob *were making themselves merry with their betters.*
ADDISON'S FREEHOLDER, NO. 44.

MO'BBY. *n.s.* An American drink made of potatoes.

MO'BILE. *n.s.* [*mobile*, French.] The populace; the rout; the mob.

Long experience has found it true of the unthinking mobile, *that the closer they shut their eyes the wider they open their hands.* SOUTH'S SERMONS.

The mobile *are uneasy without a ruler, they are restless with one.*
L'ESTRANGE'S FABLES.

MODERA'TION. *n.s.* [*moderatio*, Latin.]
1. Forbearance of extremity; the contrary temper to party violence; state of keeping a due mean betwixt extremes.

Was it the purpose of these churches, which abolished all popish ceremonies, to come back again to the middle point of evenness and moderation? HOOKER, B. IV.

A zeal in things pertaining to God, according to knowledge, and yet duly tempered with candor and prudence, is the true notion of that much talked of, much misunderstood virtue, moderation. ATTERBURY'S SERMONS.

In moderation *placing all my glory,*
While tories call me whig, and whigs a tory. POPE.

2. Calmness of mind; equanimity. [*moderation*, Fr.]

Equally inur'd
By moderation *either state to bear,*
Prosperous, or adverse.
MILTON'S PARADISE LOST, B. XI.

3. Frugality in expence. *Ainsworth.*

MO'DERNS. *n.s.* Those who have lived lately, opposed to the ancients.

There are moderns *who, with a slight variation, adopt the opinion of Plato.* BOYLE ON COLOURS.

Some by old words to fame have made pretence;
Ancients in phrase, mere moderns *in their sense!* POPE.

MO'DERNISM. *n.s.* [from *modern.*] Deviation from the ancient and classical manner. A word invented by *Swift.*

Scribblers send us over their trash in prose and verse, with abominable curtailings and quaint modernisms. SWIFT.

To **MO'DERNISE.** *v.a.* [from *modern.*] To adapt ancient compositions to modern persons or things; to change ancient to modern language.

MO'HOCK. *n.s.* The name of a cruel nation of America given to ruffians who infested, or rather were imagined to infest, the streets of London.

From milk-sop he starts up mohock. PRIOR.

Who has not trembled at the mohock's *name?* GAY.

Thou hast fallen upon me with the rage of a mad dog, or a mohock. DENNIS.

MO'IDORE. *n.s.* [*moede*, Fr.] A Portugal coin, rated at one pound seven shillings.

MOIL. *v.a.* [*mouiller*, French.]

1. To dawb with dirt.

All they which were left were moiled *with dirt and mire by reason of the deepness of the rotten way.* KNOLLES.

2. To weary.

No more tug one another thus, nor moil *yourselves, receive*
Prize equal. CHAPMAN'S ILIAD.

To **MOIL.** *v.n.* [*mouiller*, French.]

1. To labour in the mire.

Moil *not too much under-ground, for the hope of mines is very uncertain.* BACON'S ESSAYS.

2. To toil; to drudge.

They toil and moil *for the interest of their masters, that in requital break their hearts; and the freer they are of their flesh, the more scandalous is the bondage.* L'ESTRANGE.

Oh the endless misery of the life I lead! cries the moiling *husband; to spend all my days in ploughing.* L'ESTRANGE.

Now he must moil, *and drudge, for one he loaths.* DRYDEN.

With thee 'twas Marian's dear delight
To moil *all day, and merry-make at night.* GAY'S PASTORALS.

MOME'NTALLY. *adv.* [from *momentum*, Latin.] For a moment.

Air but momentally *remaining in our bodies, hath no proportionable space for its conversion, only of length enough to refrigerate the heart.*
BROWN'S VULGAR ERROURS, B. III.

MOMENTA'NEOUS, MOMENTANY. *adj.* [*momentanée*, Fr. *momentaneus*, Lat.] Lasting but a moment.

Small difficulties, when exceeding great

good is sure to ensue; and, on the other side, momentany *benefits, when the hurt which they draw after them is unspeakable, are not at all to be respected.*
HOOKER, B. I.

Flame above is durable and consistent; but with us it is a stranger and momentany.
BACON'S NATURAL HISTORY, NO. 31.

MO'MENTARY. *adj.* [from *moment.*] Lasting for a moment; done in a moment.

Momentary *as a sound,*
Swift as a shadow, short as any dream.
SHAKESPEARE.

Scarce could the shady king
The horrid sum of his intentions tell,
But she, swift as the momentary *wing*
Of light'ning, or the words he spoke, left hell. CRASHAW.

Swift as thought the flitting shade
Through air his momentary *journey made.* DRYDEN.

Onions, garlick, pepper, salt and vinegar, taken in great quantities, excite a momentary *heat and fever.* ARBUTHNOT.

MO'NASTERY. *n.s.* [*monastere,* Fr. *monasterium,* Lat.] House of religious retirement; convent. It is usually pronounced, and often written, *monastry.*

Then courts of kings were held in high renown;
There, virgins honourable vows receiv'd,
But chaste as maids in monasteries *liv'd.*
DRYDEN.

In a monastery *your devotions cannot carry you so far toward the next world, as to make this lose the sight of you.* POPE.

MO'NEYSCRIVENER. *n.s.* [*money* and *scrivener.*] One who raises money for others.

Suppose a young unexperienced man in the hands of moneyscriveners; *such fellows are like your wire-drawing mills, if they get hold of a man's finger, they will pull in his whole body at last.*
ARBUTHNOT'S HISTORY OF JOHN BULL.

MO'NITOR. *n.s.* [Latin.] One who warns of faults, or informs of duty; one who gives useful hints. It is used of an upper scholar in a school commissioned by the master to look to the boys in his absence.

You need not be a monitor *to the king; his learning is eminent: be but his scholar, and you are safe.* BACON.

It was the privilege of Adam innocent to have these notions also firm and untainted, to carry his monitor *in his bosom, his law in his heart, and to have such a conscience as might be its own casuist.*
SOUTH'S SERMONS.

We can but divine who it is that speaks; whether Persius himself, or his friend and monitor, *or a third person.* DRYDEN.

The pains that come from the necessities of nature, are monitors *to us to beware of greater mischiefs.* LOCKE.

MO'NKERY. *n.s.* [from *monk.*] The monastick life.

Neither do I meddle with their evangelical perfection of vows, nor the dangerous servitude of their rash and impotent votaries, nor the inconveniences of their monkery.
HALL.

MO'NSIEUR. *n.s.* [French.] A term of reproach for a Frenchman.

A Frenchman his companion;
An eminent monsieur, *that, it seems, much loves*
A Gallian girl.
SHAKESPEARE'S CYMBELINE.

MONTE'TH. *n.s.* [from the name of the inventor.] A vessel in which glasses are washed.

New things produce new words, and thus Monteth
Has by one vessel sav'd his name from death. KING.

MO'PPET, MOPSEY. *n.s.* [perhaps from *mop.*] A puppet made of rags, as a mop is made; a fondling name for a girl.

Our sovereign lady: made for a queen?
With a globe in one hand, and a sceptre in t'other?
A very pretty moppet!
DRYDEN'S SPANISH FRYAR.

MO'RBID. *n.s.* [*morbidus*, Latin.] Diseased; in a state contrary to health.

Though every human constitution is morbid, *yet are there diseases consistent with the common functions of life.* ARBUTHNOT.

MO'RBIDNESS. *n.s.* [from *morbid.*] State of being diseased.

MO'RBIFICAL, MORBIFICK. *n.s.* [*morbus* and *facio*, Lat. *morbifique*, Fr.] Causing diseases.

The air appearing so malicious in this morbifick *conspiracy, exacts a more particular regard; wherefore initiate consumptives must change their air.* HARVEY ON CONSUMPTIONS.

This disease is cured by the critical resolution, concoction, and evacuation of the morbifick *matter.* ARBUTHNOT.

MORBO'SE. *n.s.* [*morbosus*, Latin.] Proceeding from disease; not healthy.

Malphighi, under galls, comprehends all preternatural and morbose *tumours and excrescencies of plants.* RAY ON CREATION.

MORBO'SITY. *n.s.* [from *morbosus*, Lat.] Diseased state. A word not in use.

The inference is fair, from the organ to the action, that they have eyes, therefore some sight was designed, if we except the casual impediments or morbosities *in individuals.* BROWN.

MO'RELAND. *n.s.* [*morland*, Saxon; *mor*, a mountain, and *land.*] A mountainous or hilly country: a tract of Staffordshire is called the Morlands.[162]

MO'RNING-GOWN. *n.s.* A loose gown worn before one is formally dressed.

Seeing a great many in rich morning-gowns, *he was amazed to find that persons of quality were up so early.* ADDISON.

MO'RTGAGE. *n.s.* [*mort* and *gage*, French.]

1. A dead pledge; a thing put into the hands of a creditor.

Th' estate runs out, and mortgages *are made,*
Their fortune ruin'd, and their fame betray'd. DRYDEN.

The Romans do not seem to have known the secret of paper credit, and securities upon mortgages. ARBUTHNOT.

The broker,
Bent on some mortgage, *to avoid reproach,*
He seeks bye-streets, and saves th' expensive coach. GAY.

2. The state of being pledged.

The land is given in mortgage *only, with full intention to be redeemed within one year.*
BACON'S OFFICE OF ALIENATION.

To **MO'RTGAGE.** *v.a.* [from the noun.] To pledge; to put to pledge; to make over to a creditor as a security.

Let men contrive how they disentangle their mortgaged *souls.* DECAY OF PIETY.

They make the widows mortgag'd *ox their prey.* SANDYS.

Their not abating of their expensive way of living, has forced them to mortgage *their best manors.* ARBUTHNOT.

MORTIFICA'TION. *n.s.* [*mortification*, Fr. from *mortify.*]

1. The state of corrupting, or losing the vital qualities; gangrene.

It appeareth in the gangrene, or mortifi-

cation *of flesh, either by opiates, or intense colds.*
BACON'S NATURAL HISTORY NO. 333.

My griefs ferment and rage,
Nor less than wounds immedicable,
Rankle and fester, and gangrene,
To black mortification.
MILTON'S AGONISTES, L. 617.

2. Destruction of active qualities.

Inquire what gives impediment to union or restitution, which is called mortification; *as when quicksilver is mortified with turpentine.*
BACON'S PHYSICAL REMAINS.

3. The act of subduing the body by hardships and macerations.

A diet of some fish is more rich and alkalescent than that of flesh, and therefore very improper for such as practise mortification.
ARBUTHNOT ON ALIMENTS.

4. Humiliation; subjection of the passions.

The mortification *of our lusts has something in it that is troublesome, yet nothing that is unreasonable.* TILLOTSON.

5. Vexation; trouble.

It is one of the most vexatious mortifications *of a studious man, to have his thoughts disordered by a tedious visit.*
L'ESTRANGE.

We had the mortification *to lose the fight of Munich, Augsburg, and Ratisbon.*
ADDISON ON ITALY.

MO'TTO. *n.s.* [*motto*, Italian.] A sentence added to a device, or prefixed to any thing written.

It may be said to be the motto *of human nature, rather to suffer than to die.*
L'ESTRANGE'S FABLES.

We ought to be meek-spirited, till we are assured of the honesty of our ancestors; for covetousness and circumvention make no good motto *for a coat.* COLLIER.

It was the motto *of a bishop eminent for his piety and good works in king Charles the second's reign, Inservi Deo & lætare, Serve God and be chearful.*
ADDISON'S FREEHOLDER.

MOUNT. *n.s.* [*mont*, French; *mons*, Latin.]

1. A mountain; a hill.

Jacob offered sacrifice upon the mount.
BIBLE GENESIS, XXXI. 54.

Behold yon mountain's hoary height,
Made higher with new mounts *of snow.*
DRYDEN.

2. An artificial hill raised in a garden, or other place.

He might see what mounts *they had in short time cast, and what a number there was of brave and warlike soldiers.*
KNOLLES'S HISTORY OF THE TURKS.

3. A publick treasure; a bank. Now obsolete.

These examples confirmed me in a resolution to spend my time wholly in writing; and to put forth that poor talent God hath given me, not to particular exchanges, but to banks or mounts *of perpetuity, which will not break.* BACON.

MOUNTAINE'ER. *n.s.* [from *mountain.*]

1. An inhabitant of the mountains.

A few mountaineers *may escape, enough to continue human race; and yet illiterate rusticks, as* mountaineers *always are.*
BENTLEY'S SERMONS.

Amiternian troops, of mighty fame,
And mountaineers, *that from Severus*
came. DRYDEN'S ÆNEID.

2. A savage; a free booter; a rustick.

Yield, rustick mountaineer.
SHAKESPEARE'S CYMBELINE.

No savage, fierce banditti, or mountaineer,
Will dare to soil her virgin purity.
MILTON.

MOUSE. plural *mice. n.s.* [*mus*, Saxon; *mus*, Latin.] The smallest of all beasts; a little animal haunting houses and corn fields, destroyed by cats.

The eagle England being in prey,
To her unguarded nest the weazel Scot
Comes sneaking, and so sucks her princely eggs;
Playing the mouse *in absence of the cat.*
SHAKESPEARE.

These shall be unclean; the weasle, the mouse, *and the tortoise.*
BIBLE LEVITICUS, XI. 29.

Where mice *and rats devour'd poetick bread,*
And with heroick verse luxuriously were fed. DRYDEN.

This structure of hair I have observed in the hair of cats, rats, and mice.
DERHAM'S PHYSICO-THEOLOGY.

MO'UTH-FRIEND. *n.s.* [*mouth* and *friend.*] One who professes friendship without intending it.

May you a better feast never behold,
You knot of mouth-friends*: smoke and lukewarm water*
Is your perfection. SHAKESPEARE.

MOW. *n.s.* [probably corrupted from *mouth*; *mouë*, French.] Wry mouth; distorted face. This word is now out of use, but retained in Scotland.

The very abjects came together against me unawares, making mows *at me.*
PSALM XXXV. 15, COMMON PRAYER.

Apes and monkeys,
'Twixt two such she's, would chatter this way, and
Contemn with mows *the other.*
SHAKESPEARE'S CYMBELINE.

Those that would make mowes *at him while my father lived, give twenty ducats apiece for his picture in little.*
SHAKESPEARE.

MO'YLE. *n.s.* A mule; an animal generated between the horse and the ass.

Ordinary husbandmen should quit breeding of horses, and betake themselves to moyles*; a beast which will fare hardly, live very long, draw indifferently well, carry great burthens, and hath also a pace swift and easy enough.* CAREW.

'Twould tempt a moyle *to fury.* MAY.

MU'CHWHAT. *adv.* [*much* and *what.*] Nearly.

The motion being conveyed from the brain of man to the fancy of another, it is there received; and the same kind of strings being moved, and muchwhat *after the same manner as in the first imaginant.*
GLANVILLE'S SCEPSIS SCIENTIFICA, C. 24.

The bigness of her body and bill, as likewise the form of them, is muchwhat *as swallows.*
MORE'S ANTIDOTE AGAINST ATHEISM.

If we will disbelieve every thing, because we cannot certainly know all things, we shall do muchwhat *as wisely as he who would not use his legs because he had no wings to fly.* LOCKE.

Unless he can prove cœlibatum a man or a woman, this Latin will be muchwhat *the same with a solecism.* ATTERBURY.

MU'CKENDER. *n.s.* [*mouchoir*, French; *mocadero*, Spanish; *muccinium*, low Latin.] A handkerchief.

For thy dull fancy a muckender *is fit,*
To wipe the slabberings of thy snotty wit.
DORSET.

To **MU'CKER.** *v.n.* [from *muck.*] To scramble for money; to hoard up; to get or save meanly: a word used by *Chaucer*, and still retained in conversation.

MUD. *n.s.* [*modder*, Dutch.] The slime and uliginous matter at the bottom of still water.

The purest spring is not so free from mud*,*
As I am clear from treason.
SHAKESPEARE'S HENRY VI, P. III.

Water in mud *doth putrefy, as not able to preserve itself.*
BACON'S NATURAL HISTORY, NO. 696.

The channel was dried up, and the fish left dead and sticking in the mud.
L'ESTRANGE.

The force of the fluid will separate the smallest particles, so as to leave vacant interstices, which will be again filled up by particles carried on by the succeeding fluid, as a bank by the mud *of the current, which must be reduced to that figure which gives least resistance to the current.* ARBUTHNOT.

A fountain in a darksome wood,
Nor stain'd with falling leaves nor rising
mud. ADDISON.

To **MU'DDLE.** *v.a.* [from *mud.*]
1. To make turbid; to foul; to make muddy.

The neighbourhood told him, he did ill to muddle *the water and spoil the drink.*
L'ESTRANGE'S FABLES.

Yet let the goddess smile or frown,
Bread we shall eat, or white or brown;
And in a cottage, or a court,
Drink fine champagne, or muddl'd *port.*
PRIOR.

2. To make half drunk; to cloud or stupify.

I was for five years often drunk, always muddled*; they carried me from tavern to tavern.*
ARBUTHNOT'S HISTORY OF JOHN BULL.

Epicurus seems to have had his brains so muddled *and confounded, that he scarce ever kept in the right way, though the main maxim of his philosophy was to trust to his senses, and follow his nose.*
BENTLEY'S SERMONS.

MUFF. *n.s.* [*muff*, Swedish.] A soft cover for the hands in Winter.

Feel but the difference soft and rough,
This a gantlet, that a muff.
CLEAVELAND.

What! no more favours, not a ribbon more,
Not fan, not muff. SUCKLING.

The lady of the spotted muff *began.*
DRYDEN.

A child that stands in the dark upon his mother's muff*, says he stands upon something, he knows not what.* LOCKE.

MUG. *n.s.* [*Skinner* derives it from *mwgl*, Welsh, warm.] A cup to drink in.

Ah Bowzybee, why didst thou stay so long?
The mugs *were large, the drink was*
wond'rous strong. GAY.

MU'GGY, MUGGISH. *adj.* [A cant word.] Moist; damp; mouldy.

Cover with stones, or muggy *straw, to keep it moist.* MORTIMER'S HUSBANDRY.

MU'GHOUSE. *n.s.* [*mug* and *house.*] An alehouse; a low house of entertainment.

Our sex has dar'd the mughouse *chiefs to*
meet,
And purchas'd fame in many a well fought
street. TICKELL.

MULIE'BRITY. *n.s.* [*muliebris*, Lat.] Womanhood; the contrary to virility; the manners and character of woman.

MULTA'NGULAR. [*multus* and *angulus*, Lat.] Many cornered; having many corners; polygonal.

MULTO'CULAR. *adj.* [*multus* and *oculus*, Latin.] Having more eyes than two.

Flies are multocular*, having as many eyes as there are perforations in their corneæ.*
DERHAM'S PHYSICO-THEOLOGY.

MU'MMER. *n.s.* [*mumme*, Danish.] A masker; one who performs frolicks in a personated dress.

If you chance to be pinch'd with the colick, you make faces like mummers.
SHAKESPEARE'S CORIOLANUS.

Jugglers and dancers, anticks, mummers.
MILTON.

I began to smoke that they were a parcel of mummers. ADDISON.

Peel'd, patch'd and pyebald, linsey-woolsey brothers;
Grave mummers!
POPE'S DUNCIAD, B. III.

To **MUMP.** *v.a.* [*mompelin*, Dutch.]
1. To nibble; to bite quick; to chew with a continued motion.

Let him not pry nor listen,
Nor frisk about the house
Like a tame mumping *squirrel with a bell on.* OTWAY.

2. To talk low and quick.
3. [In cant language.] To go a begging. *Ainsworth.*

MUNI'CIPAL. *adj.* [*municipal*, Fr. *municipalis*, *municipium*, Lat.] Belonging to a corporation.

A counsellor, bred up in the knowledge of the municipal *and statute laws, may honestly inform a just prince how far his prerogative extends.* DRYDEN.

MU'RDER. *n.s.* [*morðor*, *morðer*, Sax. *murdrum*, law Lat. The etymology requires that it should be written, as it anciently often was, *murther*; but of late the word itself has commonly, and its derivatives universally, been written with *d*.] The act of killing a man unlawfully; the act of killing criminally.

Kill men i' th' dark! where be these bloody thieves?
Ho murder! murder!
SHAKESPEARE'S OTHELLO.

Now witchcraft celebrates
Pale Hecate's offerings; and wither'd murder,
With Tarquin's ravishing strides, towards his design
Moves like a ghost.
SHAKESPEARE'S MACBETH.

Blood hath been shed ere now, i' th' olden time,
Ere human statute purg'd the general weal;
Ay, and since too, murders *have been perform'd*
Too terrible for th' ear.
SHAKESPEARE'S MACBETH.

Slaughter grows murder *when it goes too far,*
And makes a massacre what was a war.
DRYDEN.

The killing of their children had, in the account of God, the guilt of murder, *as the offering them to idols had the guilt of idolatry.* LOCKE.

MU'RMUR. *n.s.* [*murmur*, Lat. *murmure*, Fr.]
1. A low shrill noise.

Flame as it moveth within itself, or is blown by a bellows, giveth a murmur *or interiour sound.*
BACON'S NATURAL HISTORY.

When the wing'd colonies first tempt the sky,
Or setting, seize the sweets the blossoms yield,
Then a low murmur *runs along the field.*
POPE.

2. A complaint half suppressed; a complaint not openly uttered.

Some discontents there are; some idle murmurs;
How idle murmurs!
The doors are all shut up; the wealthier sort,
With arms across, and hats upon their eyes,
Walk to and fro before their silent shops.
DRYDEN.

MU'SKROSE. *n.s.* [*musk* and *rose*.] A rose so called, I suppose, from its fragrance.

In May and June come roses of all kinds, except the musk, *which comes later.*
BACON'S ESSAYS.

Thyrsis, whose artful strains have oft delay'd
The huddling brook to hear his madrigal,
And sweeten'd every muskrose *of the dale.* MILTON.

The muskrose *will, if a lusty plant, bear flowers in Autumn without cutting.*
BOYLE.

MUSSITA'TION. *n.s.* [*mussito*, Lat.] Murmur; grumble.

MUSTA'CHES. *n.s.* [*mustaches*, French.] Whiskers; hair on the upper lip.

This was the manner of the Spaniards, to cut off their beards, save only their mustaches, *which they wear long.* SPENSER.

MUTE. *adj.* [*muet*, French; *mutus*, Latin.]

1. Silent; not vocal; not having the use of voice.

Why did he reason in my soul implant,
And speech, th' effect of reason? To the mute
My speech is lost; my reason to the brute.
DRYDEN.

Mute *solemn sorrow, free from female noise,*
Such as the majesty of grief destroys.
DRYDEN.

2. Having nothing to say.

Say she be mute, *and will not speak a word,*
Then I'll commend her volubility.
SHAKESPEARE.

All sat mute,
Pondering the danger with deep thoughts.
MILTON.

All the heav'nly choir stood mute,
And silence was in heav'n.
MILTON'S PARADISE LOST, B. III.

The whole perplex'd ignoble crowd,
Mute *to my questions, in my praises loud,*
Echo'd the word. PRIOR.

MUTE. *n.s.*

1. One that has no power of speech.

Either our history shall with full mouth
Speak freely of our acts; or else our grave,
Like Turkish mute, *shall have a tongueless mouth.* SHAKESPEARE.

Your mute *I'll be;*
When my tongue blabs, then let mine eyes not see. SHAKESPEARE.

He that never hears a word spoken, no wonder if he remain speechless; as one must do, who from an infant should be bred up amongst mutes, *and have no teaching.* HOLDER.

Let the figures, to which art cannot give a voice, imitate the mutes *in their actions.* DRYDEN'S DUFRESNOY.

2. A letter which without a vowel can make no sound.

Grammarians note the easy pronunciation of a mute *before a liquid, which doth not therefore necessarily make the preceding vowel long.*
HOLDER'S ELEMENTS OF SPEECH.

To **MUTE.** *v.n.* [*mutir*, French.] To dung as birds.

Mine eyes being open, the sparrows muted *warm dung into mine eyes.*
BIBLE TOBIT, II. 10.

I could not fright the crows,
Or the least bird from muting *on my head.* BEN JONSON.

The bird not able to digest the fruit, from her inconverted muting *ariseth this plant.* BROWN'S VULGAR ERROURS.

MY'OLOGY. *n.s.* [*myologie*, French.] The description and doctrine of the muscles.

To instance in all the particulars, were to write a whole system of myology.
CHEYNE'S PHILOSOPHICAL PRINCIPLES.

MY'RIAD. *n.s.* [*μύριας*.]

1. The number of ten thousand.
2. Proverbially any great number.

Assemble thou,
Of all those myriads, *which we lead, the chief.* MILTON.

Are there legions of devils who are continually designing and working our ruin? there are also myriads *of good angels who are more cheerful and officious to do us good.*
TILLOTSON.

Safe sits the goddess in her dark retreat;
Around her, myriads *of ideas wait,*
And endless shapes. PRIOR.

N

A semivowel, has in English an invariable sound; as, *no*, *name*, *net*; it is sometimes after *m* almost lost; as, *condemn*, *contemn*.

To **NAB.** *v.a.* [*nappa*, Swedish.] To catch unexpectedly; to seize without warning. A word seldom used but in low language.

NAG. *n.s.* [*nagge*, Dutch.]

1. A small horse. A horse in familiar language.

A hungry lion would fain have been dealing with good horse-flesh; but the nag *would be too fleet.* L'ESTRANGE.

Thy nags, *the leanest things alive,*
So very hard thou lov'st to drive.
PRIOR.

2. A paramour; in contempt.

Your ribauld nag *of Egypt*
Hoists sails, and flies.
SHAKESPEARE'S ANTONY AND CLEOPATRA.

NA'PTAKING. *n.s.* [*nap* and *take.*] Surprize; seizure on a sudden; unexpected onset, like that made on men asleep.

Naptakings, *assaults, spoilings, and firings, have in our forefather's days, between us and France, been very common.* CAREW.

NA'PPINESS. *n.s.* [*nappy.*] The quality of having a nap.

NA'PKIN. *n.s.* [from *nap*; which etymology is oddly favoured by *Virgil*, *Tonsisque ferunt mantilia villis;*[163] *naperia*, Italian.]

1. Cloaths used at table to wipe the hands.

By art were weaved napkins, *shirts, and coats, inconsumptible by fire.*
BROWN'S VULGAR ERROURS.

The same matter was woven into a napkin *at Louvain, which was cleansed by being burnt in the fire.* WILKINS.

Napkins, *Heliogabalus had of cloth of gold, but they were most commonly of linnen, or soft wool.* ARBUTHNOT.

2. A handkerchief. Obsolete. This sense is retained in Scotland.

I am glad I have found this napkin;
This was her first remembrance from the moor. SHAKESPEARE.

NA'TIONAL. *adj.* [*national*, Fr. from *nation.*]

1. Publick; general; not private; not particular.

They in their earthly Canaan plac'd,
Long time shall dwell and prosper: but when sins
National *interrupt their public peace.*
MILTON'S PARADISE LOST.

Such a national *devotion inspires men with sentiments of religious gratitude, and swells their hearts with joy and exultation.* ADDISON'S FREEHOLDER, NO. 49.

The astonishing victories our armies have been crowned with, were in some measure the blessings returned upon that national *charity which has been so conspicuous.* ADDISON.

God, in the execution of his judgments, never visits a people with public and general calamities, but where their sins are public and national *too.* ROGERS'S SERMONS.

2. Bigotted to one's own country.

NA'TURALIST. *n.s.* [from *natural.*] A student in physicks, or natural philosophy.

Admirable artifice! wherewith Galen, tho' a mere naturalist, *was so taken, that he could not but adjudge the honour of a hymn to the wise creator.* MORE.

It is not credible, that the naturalist *could be deceived in his account of a place that lay in the neighbourhood of Rome.* ADDISON ON ITALY.

NA'TURE. *n.s.* [*natura*, Latin; *nature*, French.]

1. An imaginary being supposed to preside over the material and animal world.

Thou, nature, *art my goddess; to thy law*
My services are bound.
SHAKESPEARE'S KING LEAR.

When it was said to Anaxagoras, the Athenians have condemned you to die; he said again, and nature *them.* BACON.

Let the postilion nature *mount, and let*
The coachman art be set. COWLEY.

Heav'n bestows
At home all riches that wise nature *needs.*
COWLEY.

Simple nature *to his hope has giv'n,*
Beyond the cloud-topt hill an humbler heav'n. POPE.

2. The native state or properties of any thing, by which it is discriminated from others.

Between the animal and rational province, some animals have a dark resemblance of the influxes of reason: so between the corporeal and intellectual world, there is man participating much of both natures. HALE'S ORIGIN OF MANKIND.

3. The constitution of an animated body.

Nature, *as it grows again tow'rd earth,*
Is fashion'd for the journey, dull and heavy. SHAKESPEARE.

We're not ourselves,
When nature, *being opprest, commands the mind*
To suffer with the body.
SHAKESPEARE'S KING LEAR.

4. Disposition of mind; temper.

Nothing could have subdu'd nature
To such a lowness but his unkind daughters. SHAKESPEARE.

A credulous father, and a brother noble,
Whose nature *is so far from doing harms,*
That he suspects none; on whose foolish honesty
My practices ride easy.
SHAKESPEARE'S KING LEAR.

5. The regular course of things.

My end
Was wrought by nature, *not by vile offence.* SHAKESPEARE.

6. The compass of natural existence.

If their dam may be judge, the young apes are the most beautiful things in nature. GLANVILLE.

7. [164] Natural affection, or reverence; native sensations.

Have we not seen
The murd'ring son ascend his parent's bed,
Thro' violated nature *force his way,*
And stain the sacred womb where once he lay? POPE.

8. The state or operation of the material world.

He binding nature *fast in fate,*
Left conscience free and will. POPE.

9. Sort; species.

A dispute of this nature *caused mischief in abundance betwixt a king and an archbishop.* DRYDEN.

10. Sentiments or images adapted to nature, or conformable to truth and reality.

Only nature *can please those tastes which are unprejudiced and refined.* ADDISON.

Nature *and Homer were he found the same.* POPE.

11. Physics; the science which teaches the qualities of things.

Nature *and* nature's *laws lay hid in night,*
God said, let Newton be, and all was light. POPE.

NA'VELGALL. *n.s. Navelgall* is a bruise on the top of the chine of the back, behind the saddle, right against the navel, occasioned either by the saddle being split behind, or the stuffing being wanting, or by the crupper buckle sitting down in that place, or some hard weight or knobs lying directly behind the saddle.

NA'UGHTINESS. *n.s.* [from *naughty.*] Wickedness; badness. Slight wickedness or parvescuity, as of children.

No remembrance of naughtiness *delights but mine own; and methinks the accusing his traps might in some manner excuse my fault, which certainly I loth to do.* SIDNEY, B. II.

NEAF. *n.s.* [*nefi*, Islandick.] A fist. It is retained in Scotland; and in the plural *neaves.*

Give me thy neaf, *Monsieur Mustardseed.* SHAKESPEARE.

NEB. *n.s.* [*nebbe*, Saxon.]

1. Nose; beak; mouth. Retained in the north.

How she holds up the neb! *the bill to him,*
And arms her with the boldness of a wife. SHAKESPEARE.

Take a glass with a belly and a long neb. BACON.

2. [In Scotland.] The bill of a bird. See NIB.

NE'BULA. *n.s.* [Lat.] It is applied to appearances, like a cloud in the human body; as also to films upon the eyes.

NE'CKBEEF. *n.s.* [*neck* and *beef.*] The coarse flesh of the neck of cattle, sold to the poor at a very cheap rate.

They'll sell (as cheap as neckbeef*) for counters at cards.* SWIFT.

NE'CKCLOATH. *n.s.* [*neck* and *cloath.*] That which men wear on their neck.

Will she with huswife's hand provide thy meat,
And ev'ry sunday morn thy neckcloath *plait?* GAY.

NE'CKERCHIEF, NECKATEE. *n.s.* A gorget; handkerchief for a woman's neck.

To **NEESE.** *v.n.* [*nyse*, Danish; *niesen*, Dutch.] To sneese; to discharge flatulencies by the nose. Retained in Scotland.

He went up and stretched himself upon him; and the child neesed *seven times, and opened his eyes.* BIBLE 2 KINGS, IV. 35.

By his neesings *a light doth shine, and his eyes are like the eye-lids of the morning.* BIBLE JOB, XLI. 18.

NE'POTISM. *n.s.* [*nepotisme*, French; *nepos*, Latin.] Fondness for nephews.

To this humour of nepotism *Rome owes its present splendor; for it would have been impossible to have furnished out so many glorious palaces with such a profusion of pictures and statues, had not the riches of the people fallen into different families.* ADDISON ON ITALY.

NET. *n.s.* [*nati*, Gothick; *net*, Saxon.] A texture woven with large interstices or meshes, used commonly as a snare for animals.

Poor bird! thoud'st never fear the net, *nor lime,*
The pitfall nor the gin.
SHAKESPEARE'S MACBETH.

He made nets *of chequer-work for the chapiters, upon the top of the pillars.* BIBLE 1 KINGS, VII. 17.

Impatience intangles us like the fluttering of a bird in a net, *but cannot at all ease our trouble.* TAYLOR'S HOLY LIVING.

The vegetative tribes,
Wrapt in a filmy net, *and clad with leaves.* THOMSON.[165]

NE'TWORK. *n.s.* [*net* and *work*.] Any thing reticulated or decussated, at equal distances, with interstices between the intersections.

Nor any skill'd in workmanship emboss'd;
Nor any skill'd in loops of fing'ring fine;
Might in their diverse cunning ever dare,
With this so curious network *to compare.* SPENSER.

A large cavity in the sinciput was filled with ribbons, lace, and embroidery, wrought together in a curious piece of network. ADDISON'S SPECTATOR.

NEW-YEAR'S-GIFT. *n.s.* [*new*, *year*, and *gift*.] Present made on the first day of the year.

If I be served such a trick, I'll have my brains taken out and buttered, and give them to a dog for a new-year's-gift. SHAKESPEARE'S MERRY WIVES OF WINDSOR.

When he sat on the throne distributing new-year's-gifts, *he had his altar of incense by him, that before they received gifts they might cast a little incense into the fire; which all good christians refused to do.* STILLINGFLEET.

NIB. *n.s.* [*ned*, Saxon, the face; *nebbe*, Dutch, the bill.]

1. The bill or beck of a bird. See **NEB**.
2. The point of any thing, generally of a pen.

A tree called the bejuco, which twines about other trees, with its end hanging downwards, travellers cut the nib *off it, and presently a spout of water runs out from it as clear as crystal.* DERHAM.

NICE. *adj.* [*nese*, Saxon, soft.]

1. Accurate in judgment to minute exactness; superfluously exact. It is often used to express a culpable delicacy.

Such a man was Argalus, as hardly the nicest *eye can find a spot in.* SIDNEY.

He that stands upon a slipp'ry place,
Makes nice *of no vile hold to stay him up.*
SHAKESPEARE'S KING JOHN.

Nor be so nice *in taste myself to know,*
If what I swallow be a thrush or no.
DRYDEN'S PERSIUS.

Thus critics, of less judgment than caprice,

Curious, not knowing, not exact, but nice,
Form short ideas, and offend in arts,
As most in manners, by a love to parts.
POPE ON CRITICISM.

Our author, happy in a judge so nice,
Produc'd his play, and begg'd the knight's advice. POPE.

2. Delicate; scrupulously and minutely cautious.

The letter was not nice, *but full of charge*
Of dear import.
SHAKESPEARE'S ROMEO AND JULIET.

Dear love! continue nice *and chaste;*
For if you yield, you do me wrong;
Let duller wits to love's end haste,
I have enough to woo thee long. DONNE.

Of honour men at first like women nice,
Raise maiden scruples at unpractis'd vice.
EARL HALLIFAX.

Having been compiled by Gratian, in an ignorant age, we ought not to be too nice *in examining it.* BAKER.

3. Fastidious; squeamish.

God hath here
Varied his bounty so with new delights,
As may compare with heaven; and to taste,
Think not I shall be nice.
MILTON'S PARADISE LOST.

4. Easily injured; delicate.

With how much ease is a young muse betray'd?
How nice *the reputation of the maid?*
ROSCOMMON.

5. Formed with minute exactness.

Indulge me but in love, my other passions
Shall rise and fall by virtue's nicest *rules.*
ADDISON'S CATO.

6. Requiring scrupulous exactness.

Supposing an injury done, it is a nice *point to proportion the reparation to the degree of the indignity.* L'ESTRANGE.

My progress in making this nice *and troublesome experiment, I have set down more at large.* NEWTON'S OPTICKS.

7. Refined.

A nice *and subtile happiness I see*
Thou to thyself proposest, in the choice
Of thy associates, Adam; and wilt taste
No pleasure, tho' in pleasure solitary.
MILTON'S PARADISE LOST.

8. Having lucky hits. This signification is not in use.

When my hours
Were nice *and lucky, men did ransom lives*
Of me for jests.
SHAKESPEARE'S ANTONY AND CLEOPATRA.

NICHE. *n.s.* [French.] A hollow in which a statue may be placed.

Niches, *containing figures of white stone or marble, should not be coloured in their concavity too black.* WOTTON.

They not from temples, nor from gods refrain,
But the poor lares from the niches *seize,*
If they be little images that please.
DRYDEN.

On the south a long majestic race
Of Ægypt's priests, the gilded niches *grace.*
POPE.

The heirs to titles and large estates are well enough qualified to read pamphlets against religion and high-flying; whereby they fill their niches, *and carry themselves through the world with that dignity which best becomes a senator and a squire.*
SWIFT'S MISCELLANIES.

NICKNA'ME. *n.s.* [*nom de nique,* French.] A name given in scoff or contempt; a term of derision; an opprobious or contemptuous appellation.

The time was when men were had in price for learning; now letters only make men vile. He is upbraidingly called a poet, as if it were a contemptible nickname.
BEN JONSON.

My mortal enemy hath not only falsely surmised me to be a feigned person, giving me nicknames, *but also hath offered large*

sums of money to corrupt the princes with whom I have been retained.
BACON'S HENRY VII.

So long as her tongue was at liberty, there was not a word to be got from her, but the same nickname *in derision.*
L'ESTRANGE.

NIDGET. *n.s.* [corrupted from *nithing* or *niding.* The opprobrious term with which the man was anciently branded who refused to come to the royal standard in times of exigency.] A coward; a dastard.

There was one true English word of greater force than them all, now out of all use; it signifieth no more than abject, baseminded, false-hearted, coward, or nidget.
CAMDEN.

NIDO'ROUS. *adj.* [*nidoreux*, from *nidor.*] Resembling the smell or taste of roasted fat.

Incense and nidorous *smells, such as of sacrifices, were thought to intoxicate the brain, and to dispose men to devotion; which they may do by a kind of contristation of the spirits, and partly also by heating and exalting them.* BACON.

The signs of the functions of the stomach being depraved, are eructations either with the taste of the aliment, acid, nidorose, *or fœtid, resembling the taste of rotten eggs.*
ARBUTHNOT ON ALIMENTS.

NI'DOROSITY. *n.s.* [from *nidorous.*] Eructation with the taste of undigested roast-meat.

The cure of this nidorosity *is, by vomiting and purging.*
FLOYER ON THE HUMOURS.

NIGHTBRA'WLER. *n.s.* [*night* and *brawler.*] One who raises disturbances in the night.

You unlace your reputation,
And spend your rich opinion for the name
Of a night-brawler.
SHAKESPEARE'S OTHELLO.

NI'GHTDOG. *n.s.* [*night* and *dog.*] A dog that hunts in the night. Used by deer-stealers.

When night-dogs *run, all sorts of deer are chased.* SHAKESPEARE.

NI'GHTFARING. *n.s.* [*night* and *fare.*] Travelling in the night.

Will-a-Wisp misleads night-faring *clowns,*
O'er hills, and sinking bogs, and pathless downs. GAY.

NI'GHTFOUNDERED. *n.s.* [from *night* and *founder.*] Lost or distressed in the night.

Either some one like us night-foundered *here,*
Or else some neighbour woodman, or at worst,
Some roving robber calling to his fellows.
MILTON.

NI'GHTMAN. *n.s.* [*night* and *man.*] One who carries away ordure in the night.

NI'GHTWARD. *adj.* [*night* and *ward.*] Approaching towards night.

Their night-ward *studies, wherewith they close the day's work.*
MILTON ON EDUCATION.

NI'MIETY. *n.s.* [*nimietas*, school Latin.] The state of being too much.

NI'NEPENCE. *n.s.* [*nine* and *pence.*] A silver coin valued at ninepence.

Three silver pennies, and a nine-pence *bent.* GAY'S PASTORALS.

NI'NNYHAMMER. *n.s.* [from *ninny.*] A simpleton.

Another vents her passion in scurrilous terms; an old ninny-hammer, *a dotard, a nincompoop, is the best language she can afford me.*
ADDISON'S GUARDIAN, NO. 109.

Have you no more manners than to rail at Hocus, that has saved that clod-pated,

numskull'd, ninny-hammer *of yours from ruin, and all his family.*
ARBUTHNOT'S JOHN BULL.

NI'ZY. *n.s.* A dunce; a simpleton. A low word.

NOCK. *n.s.* [*nocchia*, Italian.]
1. A slit; a nick; a notch.
2. The fundament. *Les fesses.*

When the date of nock *was out,*
Off dropt the sympathetick snout.
HUDIBRAS.

NOCTA'MBULO. *n.s.* [*nox* and *ambulo*, Latin.] One who walks in his sleep.

Respiration being carried on in sleep, is no argument against its being voluntary. What shall we say of noctambulo*'s? There are voluntary motions carried on without thought, to avoid pain.*
ARBUTHNOT ON AIR.

NO'CTUARY. *n.s.* [from *noctis*, Latin.] An account of what passes by night.

I have got a parcel of visions and other miscellanies in my noctuary, *which I shall send you to enrich your paper.*
ADDISON'S SPECTATOR, NO. 586.

NODA'TION. *n.s.* [from *nodo.*] The state of being knotted, or act of making knots.

NOMENCLA'TOR. *n.s.* [Lat. *nomenclateur*, Fr.] One who calls things or persons by their proper names.

There were a set of men in old Rome called nomenclators*; that is, men who could call every man by his name.*
ADDISON'S GUARDIAN, NO. 107.

Are envy, pride, avarice, and ambition, such ill nomenclators *that they cannot furnish appellations for their owners?*
SWIFT.

NO'MINATIVE. [in grammar, *nominatif*, Fr.] The case that primarily designates the name of any thing, and is called *right*, in opposition to the other cases called *oblique*.

NONCONFO'RMIST. *n.s.* [*non* and *conformist.*] One who refuses to join in the established worship.

On his death-bed he declared himself a non-conformist, *and had a fanatic preacher to be his spiritual guide.*
SWIFT.

NONJU'RING. *adj.* [*non* and *juro*, Latin.] Belonging to those who will not swear allegiance to the Hanoverian family.

This objection was offered me by a very pious, learned, and worthy gentleman of the nonjuring *party.* SWIFT.

NONNA'TURALS. *n.s.* [*non naturalia.*] Physicians reckon these to be six, viz. air, meat and drink, sleep and watching, motion and rest, retention and excretion, and the passions of the mind.

The six nonnaturals *are such as neither naturally constitutive, nor merely destructive, do preserve or destroy according unto circumstance.*
BROWN'S VULGAR ERROURS.

NO'NPLUS. *n.s.* [*non* and *plus*, Latin.] Puzzle; inability to say or do more. A low word.

Let it seem never so strange and impossible, the nonplus *of my reason will yield a fairer opportunity to my faith.* SOUTH.

One or two rules, on which their conclusions depend, in most men have governed all their thoughts: take these from them and they are at a loss, and their understanding is perfectly at a nonplus.
LOCKE.

Such an artist did not begin the matter at a venture, and when put to a nonplus, *pause and hesitate which way he should proceed; but he had first in his comprehensive intel-*

lect a compleat idea of the whole organical body. BENTLEY.

NO'NSENSE. *n.s.* [*non* and *sense.*]

1. Unmeaning or ungrammatical language.

'Till understood, all tales,
Like nonsense, *are not true nor false.*
HUDIBRAS, P. III.

Many copies dispersed gathering new faults, I saw more nonsense *than I could have crammed into it.* DRYDEN.

This nonsense *got into all the following editions by a mistake of the stage editors.* POPE'S NOTES ON SHAKESPEARE.

2. Trifles; things of no importance.[166]

What's the world to him,
'Tis nonsense *all.* THOMSON.

NOO'NING. *n.s.* [from *noon.*] Repose at noon.

NO'STRUM. *n.s.* [Latin.] A medicine not yet made publick, but remaining in some single hand.

Very extraordinary, and one of his nostrums, *let it be writ upon his monument, Hic jacet auctor hujus argumenti; for no body ever used it before.* STILLINGFLEET.

What drop or nostrum *can this plague remove?* POPE.

NO'TARY. *n.s.* [*notaire*, Fr. from *notarius*, Latin.] An officer whose business it is to take notes of any thing which may concern the publick.

There is a declaration made to have that very book, and no other set abroad, wherein their present authorised notaries *do write those things fully and only, which being written and there read, are by their own open testimony acknowledged to be their own.* HOOKER.

Go with me to a notary, *seal me there*
Your bond.
SHAKESPEARE'S MERCHANT OF VENICE.

One of those with him, being a notary, *made an entry of this act.*
BACON'S NEW ATLANTIS.

So I but your recorder am in this,
Or mouth and speaker of the universe,
A ministerial notary; *for 'tis*
Not I, but you and fame that make this verse. DONNE.

They have in each province, intendants and notaries. TEMPLE.

NOTORI'ETY. *n.s.* [*notorieté*, Fr. from *notorious.*] Publick knowledge; publick exposure.

We see what a multitude of pagan testimonies may be produced for all those remarkable passages: and indeed of several, that more than answer your expectation, as they were not subjects in their own nature so exposed to publick notoriety.
ADDISON ON THE CHRISTIAN RELIGION.

NOTO'RIOUS. *adj.* [*notorius*, Lat. *notoire*, Fr.] Publickly known; evident to the world; apparent; not hidden. It is commonly used of things known to their disadvantage; whence by those who do not know the true signification of the word, an atrocious crime is called a *notorious* crime, whether publick or secret.

What need you make such ado in cloaking a matter too notorious. WHITGIFTE.

The goodness of your intercepted packets
You writ to the pope against the king; your goodness,
Since you provoke me, shall be most notorious.
SHAKESPEARE.

I shall have law in Ephesus,
To your notorious *shame.*
SHAKESPEARE'S COMEDY OF ERROURS.

In the time of king Edward III. the impediments of the conquest of Ireland are notorious. DAVIES.

What notorious *vice is there that doth not blemish a man's reputation?*
TILLOTSON.

The inhabitants of Naples have been always very notorious *for leading a life of laziness and pleasure, which arises partly out of the plenty of their country, and partly out of the temper of their climate.*
ADDISON ON ITALY.

The bishops have procured some small advancement of rents; although it be notorious *that they do not receive the third penny of the real value.*
SWIFT'S MISCELLANIES.

NOTWITHSTA'NDING. *conj.* [This word, though in conformity to other writers called here a conjunction, is properly a participal adjective, as it is compounded of *not* and *withstanding*, and answers exactly to the Latin *non obstante*; it is most properly and analogically used in the ablative case absolute with a noun; as, *he is rich notwithstanding his loss*; it is not so proper to say, *he is rich notwithstanding he has lost much*; yet this mode of writing is too frequent, *Addison* has used it: but when a sentence follows, it is more grammatical to insert *that*; as, *he is rich notwithstanding* that *he has lost much*. When *notwithstanding* is used absolutely, the expression is elliptical, *this* or *that* being understood, as in the following passages of *Hooker*.]

1. Without hindrance or obstruction from.

Those on whom Christ bestowed miraculous cures, were so transported that their gratitude made them, notwithstanding *his prohibition, proclaim the wonders he had done for them.* DECAY OF PIETY.

2. Although. This use is not proper.

A person languishing under an ill habit of body, may lose several ounces of blood, notwithstanding *it will weaken him for a time, in order to put a new ferment into the remaining mass, and draw into it fresh supplies.* ADDISON.

3. Nevertheless; however.

They which honour the law as an image of the wisdom of God himself, are notwithstanding *to know that the same had an end in Christ.* HOOKER, B. IV.

The knowledge is small, which we have on earth concerning things that are done in heaven: notwithstanding *this much we know even of saints in heaven, that they pray.* HOOKER, B. V. S. 23.

He hath a tear for pity, and a hand
Open as day, for melting charity:
Yet notwithstanding, *being incens'd, he's flint;*
As humourous as winter.
SHAKESPEARE'S HENRY IV.

NO'VEL. *n.s.* [*nouvelle*, French.]

1. A small tale, generally of love.

Nothing of a foreign nature; like the trifling novels *which Ariosto inserted in his poems.* DRYDEN.

Her mangl'd fame in barb'rous pastime lost,
The coxcomb's novel *and the drunkard's toast.* PRIOR.

2. A law annexed to the code.

By the civil law, no one was to be ordained a presbyter till he was thirty-five years of age: though by a later novel *it was sufficient, if he was above thirty.*
AYLIFFE'S PARERGON.

NO'VELIST. *n.s.* [from *novel*.]

1. Innovator; assertor of novelty.

Telesius, who hath renewed the philosophy of Parmenides, is the best of novelists.
BACON'S NATURAL HISTORY, NO. 69.

Aristotle rose,
Who nature's secrets to the world did teach,
Yet that great soul our novelists *impeach.*
DENHAM.

The fooleries of some affected novelist *have discredited new discoveries.*
GLANVILLE'S SCEPSIS SCIENTIFICA.

2. A writer of novels.

NOVE'RCAL. *adj.* [*novercalis*, from *noverca*, Latin.] Having the manner of a stepmother; beseeming a stepmother.

When the whole tribe of birds by incubation, produce their young, it is a wonderful deviation, that some few families should do it in a more novercal *way.* DERHAM.

NOUN. *n.s.* [*nom*, French; *nomen*, Latin.] The name of any thing in grammar.

A noun *is the name of a thing, whether substance, mode or relation, which in speech is used to signify the same when there is occasion to affirm or deny any thing about it, or to express any relation it has in discourse to any other thing.* CLARKE'S LATIN GRAMMAR.

Thou hast men about thee, that usually talk of a noun *and a verb, and such abominable words as no christian ear can endure to hear.* SHAKESPEARE'S HENRY VI.

The boy, who scarce has paid his entrance down,
To his proud pedant, or declin'd a noun.
DRYDEN.

NOWADAYS. *adv.* [This word, though common and used by the best writers, is perhaps barbarous.] In the present age.

Not so great as it was wont of yore,
It's nowadays, *ne half so straight and sore.* HUBBERD.

Reason and love keep little company together nowadays.
SHAKESPEARE'S MIDSUMMER'S NIGHT DREAM.

It was a vestal and a virgin fire, and differed as much from that which passes by this name nowadays, *as the vital heat from the burning of a fever.*
SOUTH'S SERMONS.

Such are those principles, which by reason of the bold cavils of perverse and unreasonable men, we are nowadays *put to defend.*
TILLOTSON, SERMON 1.

What men of spirit nowadays,
Come to give sober judgment of new plays.
GARRICK'S EPISTLES.

NO'WISE. *n.s.* [*no* and *wise*: this is commonly spoken and written by ignorant barbarians, *noways.*] Not in any manner or degree.

A power of natural gravitation, without contact or impulse, can in nowise *be attributed to mere matter.* BENTLEY.

NUGA'CITY. *n.s.* [*nugacis*, Latin.] Futility; trifling talk or behaviour.

NULL. *n.s.* Something of no power, or no meaning. Marks in ciphered writing which stand for nothing, and are inserted only to puzzle, are called *nulls.*

If part of the people be somewhat in the election, you cannot make them nulls *or ciphers in the privation or translation.*
BACON'S WAR WITH SPAIN.

NULLIBI'ETY. *n.s.* [from *nullibi*, Latin.] The state of being nowhere.

NU'NCHION. *n.s.* A piece of victuals eaten between meals.

Laying by their swords and trunchions,
They took their breakfasts or their nunchions. HUDIBRAS.

NUT. *n.s.* [*hnut*, Saxon; *noot*, Dutch; *noix*, Fr.]

1. The fruit of certain trees; it consists of a kernel covered by a hard shell. If the shell and kernel are in the center of a pulpy fruit, they then make not a nut but a stone.

One chanc'd to find a nut
In the end of which a hole was cut,
Which lay upon a hazel-root,
There scatter'd by a squirrel;
Which out the kernel gotten had;
When quoth this Fay, dear queen be glad,
Let Oberon be ne'er so mad,
I'll set you safe from peril.
DRAYTON'S NYMPHID.

Nuts *are hard of digestion, yet possess some good medicinal qualities.*
ARBUTHNOT ON ALIMENTS.

2. A small body with teeth, which correspond with the teeth of wheels.

The force of this faculty may be more conveniently used by the multiplication of several wheels, together with nuts *belonging unto each, that are used for the roasting of meat.*
WILKIN'S MATHEMATICAL MAGICK.

Clocks and jacks, though the screws and teeth of the wheels and nuts *be never so smooth, yet if they be not oiled, will hardly move.* RAY ON THE CREATION.

O

Has in English a long sound; as, *drone*, *groan*, *stone*, *alone*, *cloke*, *broke*, *coal*, *droll*; or short, *got*, *knot*, *shot*, *prong*, *long*. It is usually denoted long by a servile *a* subjoined; as *moan*, or by *e* at the end of the syllable; as, *bone*: when these vowels are not appended, it is generally short, except before *ll*; as, *droll*, *scroll*, and even then sometimes short; as, *loll*.

1. O is used as an interjection of wishing or exclamation.

> O *that we, who have resisted all the designs of his love, would now try to defeat that of his anger!* DECAY OF PIETY.

> O! *were he present, that his eyes and hands*
> *Might see, and urge, the death which he commands.* DRYDEN.

2. O is used with no great elegance by *Shakespeare* for a circle or oval.

> *Can this cockpit hold*
> *The vasty field of France? or may we cram*
> *Within this wooden* O, *the very casks*
> *That did affright the air at Agincourt?*
> SHAKESPEARE.

OAF. *n.s.* [This word is variously written; *auff*, *ofe*, and *oph*; it seems a corruption of *ouph*, a demon or fairy, in German *alf*, from which *elf*: and means properly the same with *changeling*; a foolish child left by malevolent *ouphs* or *fairies*, in the place of one more witty, which they steal away.]
1. A changeling; a foolish child left by the fairies.

> *These, when a child haps to be got,*
> *Which after proves an idiot,*
> *When folk perceives it thriveth not,*
> *The fault therein to smother:*
> *Some silly doating brainless calf,*
> *That understands things by the half,*
> *Says that the fairy left this* oaf,
> *And took away the other.*
> DRAYTON'S NYMPHID.

2. A dolt; a blockhead; an idiot.

OATH. *n.s.* [*aith*, Gothick; *að*, Saxon. The distance between the noun *oath*, and the verb *swear*, is very observable, as it may shew that our oldest dialect is formed from different languages.] An affirmation, negation, or promise, corroborated by the attestation of the Divine Being.

> *Read over Julia's heart, thy first best love,*

For whose dear sake thou then did'st rend thy faith
Into a thousand oaths; *and all those* oaths
Descended into perjury to love me.
SHAKESPEARE.

He that strikes the first stroke, I'll run him up to the hilts as I am a soldier.
—— *An* oath *of mickle might; and fury shall abate.* SHAKESPEARE.

We have consultations, which inventions shall be published, which not: and take an oath *of secrecy for the concealing of those which we think fit to keep secret.* BACON.

Those called to any office of trust, are bound by an oath *to the faithful discharge of it: but an* oath *is an appeal to God, and therefore can have no influence, except upon those who believe that he is.* SWIFT.

OATS. *n.s.* [*aten*, Saxon.] A grain, which in England is generally given to horses, but in Scotland supports the people.

It is of the grass leaved tribe; the flowers have no petals, and are disposed in a loose panicle: the grain is eatable. The meal makes tolerable good bread. *Miller.*

The oats *have eaten the horses.* SHAKESPEARE.

It is bare mechanism, no otherwise produced than the turning of a wild oatbeard, *by the insinuation of the particles of moisture.* LOCKE.

For your lean cattle, fodder them with barley straw first, and the oat *straw last.* MORTIMER'S HUSBANDRY.

His horse's allowance of oats *and beans, was greater than the journey required.* SWIFT.

OBEQUITA'TION. *n.s.* [from *obequito*, Latin.] The act of riding about.

OBERRA'TION. *n.s.* [from *oberro*, Latin.] The act of wandering about.

OBLI'GEE. *n.s.* [from *oblige.*] The person bound by a legal or written contract.

OBLI'GER. *n.s.* He who binds by contract.

OBMUTE'SCENCE. *n.s.* [from *obmutesco*, Latin.] Loss of speech.

A vehement fear often produceth obmutescence. BROWN.

OBNO'XIOUS. *n.s.* [*obnoxius*, Latin.]

1. Subject.

I propound a character of justice in a middle form, between the speculative discourses of philosophers, and the writings of lawyers, which are tied and obnoxious *to their particular laws.* BACON'S HOLY WAR.

2. Liable to punishment.

All are obnoxious, *and this faulty land,*
Like fainting Hester, does before you stand,
Watching your sceptre. WALLER.

We know ourselves obnoxious *to God's severe justice, and that he is a God of mercy and hateth sin; and therefore that we might not have the least suspicion of his unwillingness to forgive, he hath sent his only begotten son into the world, by his dismal sufferings and cursed death, to expiate our offences.* CALAMY'S SERMONS.

Thy name, O Varus, if the kinder pow'rs
Preserve our plains, and shield the Mantuan tow'rs,
Obnoxious *by Cremona's neighb'ring crime,*
The wings of swans, and stronger pinion'd rhyme
Shall raise aloft. DRYDEN.

3. [167] Liable; exposed.

Long hostility had made their friendship weak in itself, and more obnoxious *to jealousies and distrusts.* HAYWARD.

But what will not ambition and revenge
Descend to? who aspires, must down as low
As high he soar'd; obnoxious *first or last,*
To basest things.
MILTON'S PARADISE LOST.

Beasts lie down,
To dews obnoxious *on the grassy floor.*
DRYDEN.

OBSE'SSION. *n.s.* [*obsessio*, Latin.]
1. The act of besieging.
2. The first attack of Satan, antecedent to possession.

OBSTETRICA'TION. *n.s.* [from *obstetricor*, Lat.] The office of a midwife.

OBSTIPA'TION. *n.s.* [from *obstipo*, Lat.] The act of stopping up any passage.

OBSTUPEFA'CTION. *n.s.* [*obstupefacio*, Latin.] The act of inducing stupidity, or interruption of the mental powers.

OBTENEBRA'TION. *n.s.* [*ob* and *tenebræ*, Latin.] Darkness; the state of being darkened; the act of darkening; cloudiness.

In every megrim or vertigo, there is an obtenebration *joined with a semblance of turning round.*
BACON'S NATURAL HISTORY.

OBTURA'TION. *n.s.* [from *obturatus*, Lat.] The act of stopping up any thing with something smeared over it.

OBVE'NTION. *n.s.* [*obvenio*, Latin.] Something happening not constantly and regularly, but uncertainly; incidental advantage.

When the country grows more rich and better inhabited, the tythes and other obventions, *will also be more augmented and better valued.*
SPENSER ON IRELAND.

OCCU'LT. *adj.* [*occulte*, Fr. *occultus*, Lat.] Secret; hidden; unknown; undiscoverable.

If his occult *guilt*
Do not itself unkennel in one speech,
It is a damned ghost that we have seen.
SHAKESPEARE'S HAMLET.

An artist will play a lesson on an instrument without minding a stroke; and our tongues will run divisions in a tune not missing a note, even when our thoughts are totally engaged elsewhere: which effects are to be attributed to some secret act of the soul, which to us is utterly occult, *and without the ken of our intellects.*
GLANVILLE'S SCEPSIS SCIENTIFICA, C. IV.

These instincts we call occult *qualities; which is all one with saying that we do not understand how they work.*
L'ESTRANGE.

These are manifest qualities, and their causes only are occult. *And the Aristotelians gave the name of* occult *qualities not to manifest qualities, but to such qualities only as they supposed to lie hid in bodies, and to be the unknown causes of manifest effects.* NEWTON'S OPTICKS.

O'CULIST. *n.s.* [from *oculus*, Latin.] One who professes to cure distempers of the eyes.

If there be a speck in the eye, we take them off; but he were a strange oculist *who would pull out the eye.* BACON.

I am no oculist, *and if I should go to help one eye and put out the other, we should have but an untoward business of it.*
L'ESTRANGE.

ODONTA'LGICK. *adj.* ['οδών and 'άλγος.] Pertaining to the tooth-ach.

O'DORATE. *adj.* [*odoratus*, Latin.] Scented; having a strong scent, whether fœtid or fragrant.

Smelling is with a communication of the breath, or vapour of the object odorate. BACON'S NATURAL HISTORY.

O'DOROUS. *adj.* [*odorus*, Lat.] Fragrant; perfumed; sweet of scent.

Such fragrant flowers do give most odorous *smell,*
But her sweet odour did them all excel. SPENSER.

Their private roofs on od'rous *timber borne,*
Such as might palaces for kings adorn. WALLER.

We smell, because parts of the odorous *body touch the nerves of our nostrils.* CHEYNE'S PHILOSOPHICAL PRINCIPLES.

OE. This combination of vowels does not properly belong to our language, nor is ever found but in words derived from the Greek, and not yet wholly conformed to our manner of writing: *oe* has in such words the sound of *E.*

OFF. *adv.* [*af*, Dutch.]
1. Of this adverb the chief use is to conjoin it with verbs: as, to *come off*; to *fly off*; to *take off*; which are found under the verbs.
2. It is generally opposed to *on*: as, to lay *on*; to take *off*. In this case it signifies, disunion; separation; breach of continuity.

Since the wisdom of their choice is rather to have my cap than my heart, I will practice the insinuating nod, and be off *to them most counterfitly.* SHAKESPEARE'S CORIOLANUS.

Where are you, Sir John? come, off *with your boots.* SHAKESPEARE.

See
The lurking gold upon the fatal tree;
Then rend it off. DRYDEN, ÆNEID. VI.

A piece of silver coined for a shilling, that has half the silver clipped off, *is no more a shilling than a piece of wood, which was once a sealed yard, is still a yard, when one half of it is broke* off. LOCKE.

3. It signifies distance.

West of this forest, scarcely off *a mile,*
In goodly form comes on the enemy. SHAKESPEARE.

About thirty paces off *were placed harquebusiers.* KNOLLES.

4. In painting or statuary it signifies projection or relief.

'Tis a good piece;
This comes off *well and excellent.* SHAKESPEARE.

5. It signifies evanescence; absence or departure.

Competitions intermit, and go off *and on as it happens, upon this or that occasion.* L'ESTRANGE.

6. It signifies any kind of disappointment; defeat; interruption; adverse division: as, the affair is *off*; the match is *off*.
7. In favour.[168]

The questions no way touch upon puritanism, either off *or on.* SANDERSON.

8. From; not toward.

Philoclea, whose delight of hearing and seeing was before a stay from interrupting her, gave herself to be seen unto her with such a lightening of beauty upon Zelmane, that neither she could look on, nor would look off. SIDNEY, B. II.

9. Off hand; not studied.

Several starts of fancy off *hand look well enough.* L'ESTRANGE.

OFFE'NDER. *n.s.* [from *offend.*]
1. A criminal; one who has committed a crime; a transgressor; a guilty person.

All that watch for iniquity are cut off, that make a man an offender *for a word.* BIBLE ISAIAH XXIX. 21.

So like a fly the poor offender *dies;*
But like the wasp, the rich escapes and flies. DENHAM.

How shall I lose the sin, yet keep the sense,
And love th' offender, *yet detest th' offence?* POPE.

The conscience of the offender *shall be sharper than an avenger's sword.* CLARISSA.

2. One who has done an injury.

All vengeance comes too short,
Which can pursue th' offender.
SHAKESPEARE'S KING LEAR.

OFFE'NDRESS. *n.s.* [from *offender.*] A woman that offends.

Virginity murthers itself, and should be buried in highways out of all sanctified limit, as a desperate offendress *against nature.* SHAKESPEARE'S ALL'S WELL THAT ENDS WELL.

O'FFING. *n.s.* [from *off.*] The act of steering to a distance from the land.

To **O'GLE.** *v.a.* [*oogh*, an eye, Dutch.] To view with side glances, as in fondness; or with a design not to be heeded.

From their high scaffold with a trumpet cheek,
And ogling *all their audience, then they speak.* DRYDEN.

If the female tongue will be in motion, why should it not be set to go right? Could they talk of the different aspects and conjunctions of the planets, they need not be at the pains to comment upon oglings *and clandestine marriages.* ADDISON'S GUARDIAN, NO. 155.

Whom is he ogling *yonder? himself in his looking-glass.* MARTINUS SCRIBLERIUS.

O'GLIO. *n.s.* [from *olla*, Spanish.] A dish made by mingling different kinds of meat; a medley; a hotchpotch.

These general motives of the common good, I will not so much as once offer up to your lordship, though they have still the upper end; yet, like great oglio's, *they rather make a shew than provoke appetite.* SUCKLING.

Where is there such an oglio *or medley of various opinions in the world again, as those men entertain in their service, without any scruple as to the diversity of their sects and opinions?* KING CHARLES.

He that keeps an open house, should consider that there are oglio's *of guests, as well as of dishes, and that the liberty of a common table is as good as a tacit invitation to all sorts of intruders.* L'ESTRANGE.

OH. *interject.* An exclamation denoting pain, sorrow, or surprise.

He,
Like a full acorn'd boar, a churning on,
Cry'd, oh! *and mounted.*
SHAKESPEARE'S CYMBELINE.

Oh *me! all the horse have got over the river, what shall we do?* WALTON'S ANGLER.

My eyes confess it,
My every action speaks my heart aloud;
But oh, *the madness of my high attempt*
Speaks louder yet!
DRYDEN'S SPANISH FRIAR.

OI'LMAN. *n.s.* [*oil* and *man.*] One who trades in oils and pickles.

OI'LSHOP. *n.s.* [*oil* and *shop.*] A shop where oils and pickles are sold.

O'LDEN. *adj.* [from *old*; perhaps the Saxon plural.] Ancient. This word is not now in use.

Blood hath been shed ere now, i'th' olden *time,*
Ere human statute purg'd the gen'ral weal. SHAKESPEARE.

O'LIO. *n.s.* [*olla*, Span.] A mixture; a medly. See **OGLIO**.

Ben Johnson, in his Sejanus and Catiline, has given us this olio *of a play, this unnatural mixture of comedy and tragedy.* DRYDEN ON DRAMATIC POETRY.

I am in a very chaos to think I should so forget myself.

But I have such an olio *of affairs, I know not what to do.*
CONGREVE'S WAY OF THE WORLD.

O'LITORY. *n.s.* [*olitor*, Latin.] Belonging to the kitchen garden.

Gather your olitory *seeds.*
EVELYN'S KALENDAR.

O'MELET. *n.s.* [*omelette*, Fr.] A kind of pancake made with eggs.

OMNIFA'RIOUS. *adj.* [*omnifariam*, Lat.] Of all varieties or kinds.

These particles could never of themselves, by omnifarious *kinds of motion, whether fortuitous or mechanical, have fallen into this visible system.*
BENTLEY'S SERMONS.

But if thou omnifarious *drinks wou'dst brew;*
Besides the orchard, ev'ry hedge and bush
Affords assistance. PHILIPS.

O'NSET. *n.s.* [*on* and *set.*]

1. Attack; storm; assault; first brunt.

As well the soldier dieth, which standeth still, as he that gives the bravest onset.
SIDNEY, B. II.

All breathless, weary, faint,
Him spying, with fresh onset *he assail'd,*
And kindling new his courage, seeming queint,
Struck him so hugely, that through great constraint
He made him stoop.
FAIRY QUEEN, B. II.

The shout
Of battle now began, and rushing sound
Of onset.
MILTON'S PARADISE LOST, B. VI.

Sometimes it gains a point; and presently it finds itself baffled and beaten off; yet still it renews the onset, *attacks the difficulty afresh; plants this reasoning and that argument, like so many intellectual batteries, till at length it forces a way into the obstinate enclosed truth.* SOUTH.

Without men and provisions it is impossible to secure conquests that are made in the first onsets *of an invasion.*
ADDISON.

Observe
The first impetuous onsets *of his grief;*
Use every artifice to keep him stedfast.
PHILIPS.

2. Something added by way of ornamental appendage. This sense, says *Nicholson*, is still retained in Northumberland, where *onset* means a *tuft*.

I will with deeds requite thy gentleness;
And for an onset, *Titus, to advance*
Thy name and honourable family,
Lavinia will I make my empress.
SHAKESPEARE'S TITUS ANDRONICUS.

ONTO'LOGY. *n.s.* [*'όντα* and *λόγος*.] The science of the affections of being in general; metaphysicks.

The modes, accidents and relations that belong to various beings, are copiously treated of in metaphysicks, or more properly ontology. WATTS'S LOGICK.

OPENEY'ED. *adj.* [*open* and *eye.*] Vigilant; watchful.

While you here do snoring lie,
Openeyed *conspiracy*
His time doth take.
SHAKESPEARE'S TEMPEST.

OPERA'TOR. *n.s.* [*operateur*, Fr. from *operate.*] One that performs any act of the hand; one who produces any effect.

An imaginary operator *opening the first with a great deal of nicety, upon a cursory view appeared like the head of another.*
ADDISON'S SPECTATOR, NO. 275.

To administer this dose, there cannot be fewer than fifty thousand operators, *allowing one* operator *to every thirty.*
SWIFT.

O'PIATE. *n.s.* A medicine that causes sleep.

They chose atheism as an opiate, *to still*

those frightning apprehensions of hell, by inducing a dulness and lethargy of mind, rather than to make use of that native and salutary medicine, a hearty repentance. BENTLEY'S SERMONS.

OPINA'TOR. *n.s.* [*opinor*, Lat.] One who holds an opinion.

Consider against what kind of opinators *the reason above given is levelled.* HALE'S ORIGIN OF MANKIND.

OPINIA'TRETY, OPINIATRY. *n.s.* [*opiniatreté*, French.] Obstinacy; inflexibility; determination of mind; stubbornness. This word, though it has been tried in different forms, is not yet received, nor is it wanted.

Lest popular opiniatry *should arise, we will deliver the chief opinions.* BROWN'S VULGAR ERROURS, B. VII.

The one sets the thoughts upon wit and false colours, and not upon truth; the other teaches fallacy, wrangling and opiniatry. LOCKE'S EDUCATION.

So much as we ourselves consider and comprehend of truth and reason, so much we possess of real and true knowledge. The floating of other men's opinions in our brains, make us not one jot the more knowing, though they happen to be true: what in them was science, is in us but opiniatrety. LOCKE.

I can pass by opiniatry *and the busy meddling of those who thrust themselves into every thing.* WOODWARD'S LETTERS.

I was extremely concerned at his opiniatrety *in leaving me; but he shall not get rid so.* POPE.

OPI'NIONATIVE. *adj.* [from *opinion.*] Fond of preconceived notions; stubborn.

Striking at the root of pedantry and opinionative *assurance, would be no hindrance to the world's improvement.* GLANVILLE.

One would rather chuse a reader without art, than one ill instructed with learning, but opinionative *and without judgment.* BURNET'S THEORY OF THE EARTH.

OPI'NIONIST. *n.s.* [*opinioniste*, Fr. from *opinion.*] One fond of his own notions.

Every conceited opinionist *sets up an infallible chair in his own brain.* GLANVILLE TO ALBIUS.

O'PTICK. *adj.* [*'οπτικὴ*; *optique*, Fr.]

1. Visual; producing vision; subservient to vision.

May not the harmony and discord of colours arise from the proportions of the vibrations propagated through the fibres of the optic *nerves into the brain, as the harmony and discord of sounds arise from the proportions of the vibrations of the air?* NEWTON'S OPTICKS.

2. Relating to the science of vision.

Where our master handleth the contractions of pillars, we have an optic *rule, that the higher they are the less should be always their diminution aloft, because the eye itself doth naturally contract all objects, according to the distance.* WOTTON'S ARCHITECTURE.

O'PTICK. *n.s.* An instrument of sight; an organ of sight.

Can any thing escape the perspicacity of those eyes which were before light, and in whose opticks *there is no opacity.* BROWN.

Our corporeal eyes we find
Dazzle the opticks *of our mind.*
DENHAM.

You may neglect, or quench, or hate the flame,
Whose smoke too long obscur'd your rising name,
And quickly cold indiff'rence will ensue,
When you love's joys thro' honour's optick *view.* PRIOR.

Why has not man a microscopick eye?
For this plain reason, man is not a fly.

Say what the use, were finer opticks *giv'n,*
T'inspect a mite, not comprehend the heav'n. POPE.

OPTI'MITY. *n.s.* [from *optimus.*] The state of being best.

O'RANGEWIFE. *n.s.* [*orange* and *wife.*] A woman who sells oranges.

You wear out a good wholesome forenoon in hearing a cause between an orangewife *and a fosset seller.* SHAKESPEARE.

O'RATOUR. *n.s.* [*orateur,* Fr. *orator,* Lat.]

1. A publick speaker; a man of eloquence.

Poor queen and son! your labour is but lost;
For Warwick is a subtle orator.
SHAKESPEARE'S HENRY VI.

As when of old some orator *renown'd,*
In Athens or free Rome, where eloquence
Flourish'd, since mute! to some great cause address'd,
Stood in himself collected; while each part,
Motion, each act, won audience.
MILTON'S PARADISE LOST.

The constant design of both these orators *in all their speeches, was to drive some one particular point.* SWIFT.

I have listened to an orator *of this species, without being able to understand one single sentence.* SWIFT.

Both orators *so much renown'd,*
In their own depths of eloquence were drown'd. DRYDEN.

2. A petitioner. This sense is used in addresses to chancery.

ORBITY. *n.s.* [*orbus,* Latin.] Loss, or want of parents or children.

O'RCHESTRE. *n.s.* [French. ’ὀρχήστρα.] The place where the musicians are set at a publick show.

O'RDEAL. *n.s.* [*ordal,* Sax. *ordalium,* low Lat. *ordalie,* Fr.] A trial by fire or water, by which the person accused appealed to heaven, by walking blindfold over hot bars of iron; or being thrown, I suppose, into the water; whence the vulgar trial of witches.

Their ordeal *laws they used in doubtful cases, when clear proofs wanted.*
HAKEWILL ON PROVIDENCE.

In the time of king John, the purgation per ignem et aquam, or the trial by ordeal *continued; but it ended with this king.*
HALE.

O'RDINARY. *n.s.*

1. Established judge of ecclesiastical causes.

The evil will
Of all their parishioners they had constrain'd,
Who to the ordinary *of them complain'd.*
HUBBERD.

If fault be in these things any where justly found, law hath refered the whole disposition and redress thereof to the ordinary *of the place.* HOOKER, B. V. S. 12.

2. Settled establishment.

Spain had no other wars save those which were grown into an ordinary; *now they have coupled therewith the extraordinary of the Valtoline and Palatinate.* BACON.

3. Actual and constant office.

Villiers had an intimation of the king's pleasure to be his cup-bearer at large; and the summer following he was admitted in ordinary.
WOTTON.

4. Regular price of a meal.

Our courteous Antony,
Being barber'd ten times o'er, goes to the feast;
And for his ordinary *pays his heart*
For what his eyes eat only.
SHAKESPEARE'S ANTONY AND CLEOPATRA.

5. A place of eating established at a certain price.

They reckon all their errors for accomplish-

ments; and all the odd words they have picked up in a coffee-house, or a gaming ordinary, *are produced as flowers of style.* SWIFT.

ORGANIZA'TION. *n.s.* [from *organize.*] Construction in which the parts are so disposed as to be subservient to each other.

Every man's senses differ as much from others in their figure, colour, site, and infinite other peculiarities in the organization, *as any one man's can from itself, through divers accidental variations.* GLANVILLE'S SCEPSIS SCIENTIFICA, C. XXVI.

That being then one plant, which has such an organization of parts in one coherent body, partaking of one common life, it continues to be the same plant, though that life be communicated to new particles of matter, in a like continued organization. LOCKE.

ORGA'SM. *n.s.* [*orgasme*, Fr. *'ὀργασμος.*] Sudden vehemence.

By means of the curious lodgment and inosculation of the auditory nerves, the orgasms *of the spirits should be allayed, and perturbations of the mind quieted.* DERHAM'S PHYSICO-THEOLOGY.

ORNI'SCOPIST. *n.s.* [*'ὄρνις* and *'ἔσκοπα.*] One who examines the flight of birds in order to foretel futurity.

ORNI'THOLOGY. *n.s.* [*'ὄρνις* and *λόγος.*] A discourse on birds.

O'RRERY. *n.s.* An instrument which by many complicated movements represents the revolutions of the heavenly bodies. It was first made by Mr. Rowley, a mathematician born at Litchfield, and so named from his patron the earl of Orrery: by one or other of this family almost every art has been encouraged or improved.

ORTS. *n.s.* seldom with a singular. [This word is derived by *Skinner* from *ort*, German, the *fourth part of any thing*; by Mr. *Lye* more reasonably from *orda*, Irish, a fragment. In Anglo Saxon, *ord* signifies the beginning; whence in some provinces *odds* and *ends*; for *ords* and *ends* signify remnants, scattered pieces, refuse; from *ord* thus used probably came *ort.*] Refuse; things left or thrown away.

He must be taught, and train'd, and bid go forth;
A barren-spirited fellow, one that feeds
On abject orts *and imitations.*
SHAKESPEARE'S JULIUS CÆSAR.

The fractions of her faith, orts *of her love,*
The fragments, scraps, the bits, and greasy reliques
Of her o'er eaten faith, are bound to Diomede. SHAKESPEARE.

Much good do't you then;
Brave plush and velvet men,
Can feed on orts *and safe in your stage-cloths,*
Dare quit, upon your oaths,
The stagers, and the stage-wrights too.
BEN JONSON.

ORTHO'GRAPHY. *n.s.* [*'ὀρθος* and *γράφω*; *orthographie*, Fr.]

1. The part of grammar which teaches how words should be spelled.

This would render languages much more easy to be learned, as to reading and pronouncing, and especially as to the writing them, which now as they stand we find to be troublesome, and it is no small part of grammar which treats of orthography *and right pronunciation.* HOLDER.

2. The art or practice of spelling.

In London they clip their words after one manner about the court, another in the city, and a third in the suburbs; all which reduced to writing, would entirely confound orthography. SWIFT.

3. The elevation of a building delineated.

You have the orthography *or upright of this ground-plat, and the explanation thereof with a scale of feet and inches.* MOXON'S MECHANICAL EXERCISES.

O'RTOLAN. *n.s.* [French.] A small bird accounted very delicious.

Nor ortolans *nor godwits.* COWLEY.

OSCI'TANCY. *n.s.* [*oscitantia*, Lat.]

1. The act of yawning.
2. Unusual sleepiness; carelessness.

If persons of so circumspect a piety, have been thus overtaken, what security can there be for our wreckless oscitancy? GOVERNMENT OF THE TONGUE.

It might proceed from the oscitancy *of transcribers, who, to dispatch their work the sooner, used to write all numbers in cyphers.* ADDISON'S SPECTATOR, NO. 470.

OTACOU'STICK. *n.s.* [ὦτα and 'ακούω; *otacoustique*, Fr.] An instrument to facilitate hearing.

In a hare, which is very quick of hearing, it is supplied with a bony tube; which, as a natural otacoustick, *is so directed backward, as to receive the smallest and most distant sound that comes behind her.* GREW'S COSMOLOGIA SACRA, B. I.

O'THERGATES. *adv.* [*other* and *gate*, for way.] In another manner.

If sir Toby had not been in drink, he would have tickled you othergates *than he did.* SHAKESPEARE'S TWELFTH NIGHT.

O'THERGUISE. *adj.* [*other* and *guise*. This is often mistaken, and sometimes written *otherguess.*] Of another kind.

O'THERWHERE. *adv.* [*other* and *where.*] In other places.

As Jews they had access to the temple and synagogues, but as Christians they were of necessity forced otherwhere *to assemble themselves.* HOOKER, B. V. S. 11.

His godlike acts, and his temptations fierce,
And former sufferings, otherwhere *are*
found. MILTON.

O'THERWHILE. *adv.* [*other* and *while.*] At other times.

O'THERWISE. *adv.* [*other* and *wise.*]

1. In an indifferent manner.

They only plead, that whatsoever God revealeth, as necessary for all Christian men to do and believe, the same we ought to embrace, whether we have received it by writing or otherwise, *which no man denieth.* HOOKER, B. I.

The whole church hath not tied the parts unto one and the same thing, they being therein left each to their own choice, may either do as others do, or else otherwise, *without any breach of duty at all.* HOOKER, B. IV. S. 13.

In these good things, what all others should practise, we should scarce know to practise otherwise. SPRAT.

Thy father was a worthy prince,
And merited, alas! a better fate;
But heaven thought otherwise.
ADDISON'S CATO.

2. By other causes.

Sir John Norris failed in the attempts of Lisborn, and returned with the loss, by sickness and otherwise, *of eight thousand men.* RALEIGH.

3. In other respects.

It is said truly, that the best men otherwise, *are not always the best in regard of society.* HOOKER, B. I.

Men seldom consider God any otherwise *than in relation to themselves, and therefore want some extraordinary benefits to excite their attention and engage their love.* ROGER.

To **O'VER-ACT.** *v.a.* [*over* and *act.*] To act more than enough.

You over-act, *when you should underdo:*
A little call yourself again, and think.
BEN JONSON.

Princes courts may over-act *their reverence, and make themselves laughed at for their foolishness and extravagant relative worship.* STILLINGFLEET.

Good men often blemish the reputation of their piety, by over-acting *some things in religion; by an indiscreet zeal about things wherein religion is not concerned.* TILLOTSON.

To **O'VER-BALANCE.** *v.a.* To weigh down; to preponderate.

Not doubting but by the weight of reason I should counterpoise the over-balancings *of any factions.* KING CHARLES.

The hundred thousand pounds per annum, wherein we over-balance *them in trade, must be paid us in money.* LOCKE.

When these important considerations are set before a rational being, acknowledging the truth of every article, should a bare single possibility be of weight enough to over-balance *them.* ROGERS, SERMON XII.

To **O'VER-BUY.** *v.a.* [*over* and *buy.*] To buy too dear.

He, when want requires, is only wise,
Who slights not foreign aids, nor over-buys;
But on our native strength, in time of need, relies. DRYDEN.

To **O'VER-DRIVE.** *v.a.* [*over* and *drive.*] To drive too hard, or beyond strength.

The flocks and herds with young, if men should over-drive *one day, all will die.* BIBLE GENESIS, XXXIII. 13.

To **OVER-EMPTY.** *v.a.* [*over* and *empty.*] To make too empty.

The women would be loth to come behind the fashion in new-fangledness of the manner, if not in costliness of the matter, which might over-empty *their husbands purses.* CAREW.

O'VER-FORWARDNESS. *n.s.* [*over* and *forwardness.*] Too great quickness; too great readiness.

By an over-forwardness *in courts to give countenance to frivolous exceptions, though they make nothing to the true merit of the cause, it often happens that causes are not determined according to their merits.* HALE.

O'VER-GREAT. *adj.* [*over* and *great.*] Too great.

Though putting the mind unprepared upon an unusual stress ought to be avoided; yet this must not run it, by an over-great *shyness of difficulties, into a lazy sauntring about obvious things.* LOCKE.

O'VER-HEAD. *adv.* [*over* and *head.*] Aloft; in the zenith; above; in the cieling.[169]

Over-head *the moon*
Sits arbitress, and nearer to the earth
Wheels her pale course.
MILTON'S PARADISE LOST, B. I.

The four stars over-head, *represent the four children.* ADDISON.

To **OVERLA'BOUR.** *v.a.* [*over* and *labour.*] To take too much pains on any thing; to harrass with toil.

She without noise will over-see
His children and his family;
And order all things till he come,
Sweaty and over-labour'd *home.*
DRYDEN.

OVERLA'SHINGLY. *n.s.* [*over* and *lash.*] With exaggeration. A mean word, now obsolete.

Although I be far from their opinion who write too overlashingly, *that the Arabian tongue is in use in two third parts of the inhabited world, yet I find that it extendeth where the religion of Mahomet is professed.* BREREWOOD.

OVERMU'CH. *adj.* [*over* and *much.*] Too much; more than enough.

It was the custom of those former ages, in their over-much *gratitude, to advance the first authors of any useful discovery among the number of their gods.* WILKINS.

An over-much *use of salt, besides that it occasions thirst and* over-much *drinking, has other ill effects.* LOCKE.

OVERMU'CH. *adv.* In too great a degree.

The fault which we find in them is, that they over-much *abridge the church of her power in these things. Whereupon they re-charge us, as if in these things we gave the church a liberty which hath no limits or bounds.* HOOKER.

Perhaps
I also erred, in over-much *admiring*
What seem'd in thee so perfect, that I thought
No evil durst attempt thee.
MILTON'S PARADISE LOST, B. IX.

Deject not then so over-much *thyself,*
Who hast of sorrow thy full load besides.
MILTON.

OVERMU'CH. *n.s.* More than enough.

By attributing over-much *to things*
Less excellent, as thou thyself perceiv'st.
MILTON.

With respect to the blessings the world enjoys, even good men may ascribe over-much *to themselves.* GREW.

OVERMU'CHNESS. *n.s.* [from *over-much.*] Exuberance; superabundance.

There are words that do as much raise a stile, as others can depress it; superlation and over-muchness *amplifies. It may be above faith, but not above a mean.* BEN JONSON.

OVERNI'GHT. *n.s.* [*over* and *night.* This seems to be used by *Shakespeare* as a noun, but by *Addison* more properly, as I have before placed it, as a noun with a preposition.] Night before bed-time.

If I had given you this at over-night,
She might have been o'erta'en.
SHAKESPEARE.

Will confesses, that for half his life his head ached every morning with reading men over-night. ADDISON.

To **OVERNA'ME.** *v.a.* [*over* and *name.*] To name in a series.

Over-name *them; and as thou namest them I will describe them.*
SHAKESPEARE'S MERCHANT OF VENICE.

To **OVERSE'E.** *v.a.* [*over* and *see.*]
1. To superintend; to overlook.

He had charge my discipline to frame,
And tutors nouriture to oversee.
FAIRY QUEEN.

She without noise will oversee
His children and his family. DRYDEN.

2. To overlook; to pass by unheeded; to omit.

I who resolve to oversee
No lucky opportunity,
Will go to council to advise
Which way t' encounter, or surprise.
HUDIBRAS, P. III.

OVERSE'EN. *part.* [from *oversee.*] Mistaken; deceived.

A common received error is never utterly overthrown, till such times as we go from signs unto causes, and shew some manifest root or fountain thereof common unto all, whereby it may clearly appear how it hath come to pass that so many have been overseen. HOOKER, B. I. S. 8.

They rather observed what he had done, and suffered for the king and for his country, without farther enquiring what he had omitted to do, or been overseen *in doing.* CLARENDON.

OVERSE'ER. *n.s.* [from *oversee.*]
1. One who overlooks; a superintendent.

There are in the world certain voluntary overseers *of all books, whose censure, in this respect, would fall sharp on us.* HOOKER, B. V. S. 31.

Jehiel and Azariah were overseers *under Cononiah.* BIBLE 2 CHRONICLES, XXXI. 13.

To entertain a guest, with what a care
Wou'd he his houshold ornaments prepare;
Harrass his servants, and as o'erseer *stand,*
To keep them working with a threat'ning wand.
Clean all my plate, he cries. DRYDEN.

2. An officer who has the care of the parochial provision for the poor.

The church-wardens and overseers *of the poor might find it possible to discharge their duties, whereas now in the greater out-parishes many of the poorer parishioners, through neglect, do perish for want of some heedful eye to overlook them.* GRAUNT'S BILLS OF MORTALITY.

OVERSO'ON. *adv.* [*over* and *soon.*] Too soon.

The lad may prove well enough, if he over-soon *think not too well of himself, and will bear away that he heareth of his elders.* SIDNEY, B. II.

OVERTHWA'RT. *adj.* [*over* and *thwart.*]
1. Opposite; being over against.

We whisper, for fear our overthwart *neighbours*
Should hear us, and betray us to the government. DRYDEN.

2. Crossing any thing perpendicularly.
3. Perverse; adverse; contradictious.

Two or three acts disposed them to cross and oppose any proposition; and that overthwart *humour was discovered to rule in the breasts of many.* CLARENDON.

O'VERTURE. *n.s.* [*ouverture*, French.]
1. Opening; disclosure; discovery.

I wish
You had only in your silent judgment try'd it,
Without more overture.
SHAKESPEARE'S WINTER'S TALE.

2. Proposal; something offered to consideration.

Mac Murugh moved Henry to invade Ireland, and made an overture *unto him for obtaining of the sovereign lordship thereof.* DAVIES ON IRELAND.

All these fair overtures, *made by men well esteemed for honest dealing, could not take place.* HAYWARD.

We with open breast
Stand ready to receive them, if they like
Our overture, *and turn not back perverse.*
MILTON.

The earl of Pembroke, who abhorred the war, promoted all overtures *towards accommodation with great importunity.* CLARENDON.

If a convenient supply offers itself to be seised by force or gained by fraud, human nature persuades us to hearken to the inviting overture. ROGERS, SERMON 2.

Suppose five hundred men proposing, debating, and voting, according to their own little or much reason, abundance of indigested and abortive, many pernicious and foolish overtures *would arise.* SWIFT.

OVERYEA'RED. *adj.* [*over* and *year.*] Too old.

Among them dwelt
A maid, whose fruit was ripe, not overyeared. FAIRFAX.

OUGHT. *verb imperfect.* [This word the etymologists make the preterite of *owe*, but it has often a present signification.]

1. [Preterite of *owe.*] Owed; was bound to pay; have been indebted.

Apprehending the occasion, I will add a continuance to that happy motion, and besides give you some tribute of the love and duty I long have ought *you.* SPELMAN.

This blood which men by treason sought,
That followed, sir, which to myself I ought. DRYDEN.

2. To be obliged by duty.

Judges ought *to remember, that their office is to interpret law, and not to make or give law.* BACON.

Morals criticks ought *to show.* POPE.

She acts just as she ought,
But never, never reach'd one generous thought. POPE.

3. To be fit; to be necessary.

If grammar ought *to be taught, it must be to one that can speak the language already.* LOCKE.

OUT, in composition, generally signifies something beyond or more than another.

Out-*fawn as much, and* out-*comply,*
And seem as scrupulously just,
To bait the hooks for greater trust.
HUDIBRAS, P. II. CANT. 3.

To **OUTBA'LANCE.** *v.a.* [*out* and *balance.*] To over-weigh; to preponderate.

Let dull Ajax bear away my right,
When all his days outbalance *this one night.* DRYDEN.

OU'TERLY. *adv.* [from *outer.*] Towards the outside.

In the lower jaw, two tusks like those of a boar, standing outerly, *an inch behind the cutters.* GREW'S MUSÆUM.

To **OUTFA'WN.** *v.a.* [*out* and *fawn.*] To excel in fawning.

In affairs of less import,
That neither do us good nor hurt,
And they receive as little by,
Outfawn *as much and out-comply.*
HUDIBRAS.

To **OUTKNA'VE.** *v.a.* [*out* and *knave.*] To surpass in knavery.

The world calls it out-witting a man, when he's only outknaved. L'ESTRANGE.

OUTLA'NDISH. *adj.* [*out* and *land.*] Not native; foreign.

Yourself transplant
A while from hence: perchance outlandish *ground*
Bears no more wit than ours; but yet more scant
Are those diversions there which here abound. DONNE.

Tedious waste of time to sit and hear
So many hollow compliments and lies,
Outlandish *flatteries.*
MILTON'S PARADISE REGAIN'D, B. IV.

Upon the approach of the king's troops under General Wills, who was used to the outlandish *way of making war, we put in practice passive obedience.* ADDISON.

OU'TMOST. *adj.* [*out* and *most.*] Remotest from the middle.

Chaos retir'd,
As from her outmost *works a broken foe.*
MILTON.

If any man suppose that it is not reflected by the air, but by the outmost *superficial parts of the glass, there is still the same difficulty.* NEWTON'S OPTICKS.

The generality of men are readier to fetch a reason from the immense distance of the starry heavens, and the outmost *walls of the world.* BENTLEY'S SERMONS.

OUTPA'RISH. *n.s.* [*out* and *parish.*] Parish not lying within the walls.

In the greater outparishes *many of the poorer parishioners, through neglect, do perish for want of some heedful eye to overlook them.* GRAUNT'S MORTALITY.

OUTRA'GIOUS. *adj.* [*outrageux*, French. It should, I think, be written *outrageous*; but the custom seems otherwise.]

1. Violent; furious; raging; exorbitant; tumultuous; turbulent.

Under him they committed divers the most outragious *villanies, that a base multitude can imagine.* SIDNEY.

As she went her tongue did walk,
In foul reproach and terms of vile despight,
Provoking him by her outragious *talk,*
To heap more vengeance on that wretched wight. FAIRY QUEEN.

They view'd the vast immeasurable abyss,
Outragious *as a sea, dark, wasteful, wild.* MILTON.

When he knew his rival freed and gone,
He swells with wrath; he makes outragious *moan:*
He frets, he fumes, he stares, he stamps the ground;
The hollow tow'r with clamours rings around. DRYDEN.

2. Excessive; passing reason or decency.

My characters of Antony and Cleopatra, though they are favourable to them, have nothing of outragious *panegyrick.* DRYDEN'S DUFRESNOY.

3. Enormous; atrocious.

Think not, although in writing I prefer'd
The manner of thy vile outragious *crimes,*
That therefore I have forg'd.
SHAKESPEARE'S HENRY VI.

To **OUTSI'T.** *v.a.* [*out* and *sit.*] To sit beyond the time of any thing.

He that prolongs his meals and sacrifices his time, as well as his other conveniences, to his luxury, how quickly does he outsit *his pleasure?* SOUTH.

To **OUTSTA'ND.** *v.a.* [*out* and *stand.*]

1. To support; to resist.

Each could demolish the other's work with ease enough, but not a man of them tolerably defend his own; which was sure never to outstand *the first attack that was made.* WOODWARD.

2. To stand beyond the proper time.

I have outstood *my time, which is material*
To th' tender of our present.
SHAKESPEARE'S CYMBELINE.

To **OUTSTA'ND.** *v.n.* To protuberate from the main body.

OUTSTREE'T. *n.s.* [*out* and *street.*] Street in the extremities of a town.

To **OUTVI'E.** *v.a.* [*out* and *vie.*] To exceed; to surpass.

For folded flocks, on fruitful plains,
Fair Britain all the world outvies.
DRYDEN.

The farmers used to make gratias to the English merchants, endeavouring sometimes to out-vie *one another in such indulgencies.* ADDISON.

One of these petty sovereigns will be still endeavouring to equal the pomp of greater princes, as well as to out-vie *those of his own rank.* ADDISON.

OUTWA'LL. *n.s.* [*out* and *wall.*]

1. Outward part of a building.
2. Superficial appearance.

For confirmation that I am much more
Than my out-wall, *open this purse and take*
What it contains.
SHAKESPEARE'S KING LEAR.

OYE'S. *n.s.* [*oyez*, hear ye, French.] Is the introduction to any proclamation or advertisement given by the publick criers both in England and Scotland. It is thrice repeated.

Fairies, black, grey, green, and white,
Attend your office and your quality.
Crier hobgoblin make the fairy O yes.
SHAKESPEARE.

O yes! *if any happy eye*
This roving wanton shall descry;
Let the finder surely know
Mine is the wag. CRASHAW.

P

Is a labial consonant, formed by a slight compression of the anterior part of the lips; as, *pull*, *pelt*. It is confounded by the Germans and Welsh with *b*: it has an uniform sound: it is sometimes mute before *t*; as, *accompt*, *receipt*; but the mute *p* is in modern orthography commonly omitted.

PACK. *n.s.* [*pack*, Dutch.]

1. A large bundle of any thing tied up for carriage.

Themistocles said to the king of Persia, that speech was like cloth of Arras, opened and put abroad, whereby the imagery appears in figures; whereas in thoughts they lie but as in packs. BACON, ESSAYS 28.

Had sly Ulysses at the sack
Of Troy, brought thee his pedlar's pack.
CLEAVELAND.

Our knight did bear no less a pack
Of his own buttocks on his back.
HUDIBRAS, P. I.

2. A burden; a load.

I rather chose
To cross my friend in his intended drift,
Than, by concealing it, heap on your head
A pack *of sorrows.*
SHAKESPEARE'S MERCHANT OF VENICE.

But when they took notice how stupid a beast it was, they loaded it with packs *and burdens, and set boys upon the back of it.*
L'ESTRANGE.

3. A due number of cards.

Women to cards may be compar'd, we play
A round or two, when us'd we throw away,
Take a fresh pack. GRANVILLE.

It is wonderful to see persons of sense passing away a dozen hours together in shuffling and dividing a pack *of cards.*
ADDISON.

4. A number of hounds hunting together.

Two ghosts join their packs *to hunt her o'er the plain.* DRYDEN.

The fury fires the pack; *they snuff, they vent,*
And feed their hungry nostrils with the scent. DRYDEN.

The savage soul of game is up at once,
The pack *full-opening various.*
THOMSON'S SUMMER.

5. A number of people confederated in any bad design or practice.

You panderly rascals! there's a knot, a gang, a pack, *a conspiracy, against me.* SHAKESPEARE'S MERRY WIVES OF WINDSOR.

Never such a pack *of knaves and villains, as they who now governed in the parliament.* CLARENDON.

Bickerstaff is more a man of honour, than to be an accomplice with a pack *of rascals that walk the streets on nights.* SWIFT.

6. Any great number, as to quantity and pressure: as a pack or world of troubles. *Ainsworth.*

PA'CKCLOATH. *n.s.* [*pack* and *cloath.*] A cloath in which goods are tied up.

PACT. *n.s.* [*pact*, Fr. *pactum*, Latin.] A contract; a bargain; a covenant.

The queen, contrary to her pact *and agreement concerning the marriage of her daughter, delivered her daughters out of sanctuary unto king Richard.* BACON.

PA'CTION. *n.s.* [*paction*, Fr. *pactio*, Latin.] A bargain; a covenant.

The French king sent for Matthew earl of Levenox, encouraging him to remove the earl of Arraine from the regency of Scotland, and reverse such pactions *as he had made.* HAYWARD.

There never could be any room for contracts or pactions, *between the supreme being and his intelligent creatures.* CHEYNE.

PA'DDER. *n.s.* [from *pad.*] A robber; a foot highwayman.

Spurr'd as jockies use, to break,
Or padders *to secure a neck.*
HUDIBRAS, P. III. CANT. 1.

Worse than all the clatt'ring tiles, and worse
Than thousand padders, *is the poet's curse;*
Rogues that in dog days cannot rhime forbear;
But without mercy read, to make you hear. DRYDEN.

If he advanced himself by a voluntary engaging in unjust quarrels, he has no better pretence to honour than what a resolute and successful padder *may challenge.* COLLIER.

PA'DDOCK. *n.s.* [corrupted from *parrack.*] A small inclosure for deer.

PALA'CIOUS. *adj.* [from *palace.*] Royal; noble; magnificent.

London encreases daily, turning of great palacious *houses into small tenements.* GRAUNT'S BILLS OF MORTALITY.

PALIFICA'TION. *n.s.* [*palus*, Latin.] The act or practice of making ground firm with piles.

I have said nothing of palification *or piling of the groundplot commanded by Vitruvius, when we build upon a moist soil.* WOTTON.

PA'LLET. *n.s.* [*paillet*, in *Chaucer*, which was probably the French word from *paille*, straw, and secondarily, a bed.]

1. A small bed; a mean bed.

Why rather, sleep, liest thou in smoaky cribs,
Upon uneasy pallets *stretching thee,*
And husht with buzzing night flies to thy slumber;
Than in the perfum'd chambers of the great,
Under the canopies of costly state,
And lull'd with sounds of sweetest melody?
SHAKESPEARE.

His secretary was laid in a pallet *near him for ventilation of his thoughts.* WOTTON'S BUCKINGHAM.

If your stray attendance be yet lodg'd,
Or shroud within these limits, I shall know
Ere morrow wake, or the low-roosted lark
From her thatch't pallet *rouse.* MILTON.

2. [*palette*, French.] A small measure, formerly used by chirurgeons.

A surgeon drew from a patient in four days, twenty-seven pallets, *every* pallet *containing three ounces.* HAKEWILL.

PALLMA'LL. *n.s.* [*pila* and *malleus*, Lat. *pale maille*, French] A play in which the ball is struck with a mallet through an iron ring.

PALME'TTO. *n.s.* A species of the palm-tree: It grows in the West-Indies to be a very large tree; with the leaves the inhabitants thatch their houses. These leaves, before they are expanded, are cut and brought into England to make womens plaited hats; and the berries of these trees were formerly much used for buttons.

Broad o'er my head the verdant cedars wave,
And high palmettos *lift their graceful shade.* THOMSON.

PA'LMISTRY. *n.s.* [*palma*, Latin.] 1. The cheat of foretelling fortune by the lines of the palm.

We shall not query what truth there is in palmistry, *or divination, from those lines of our hands of high denomination.* BROWN'S VULGAR ERROURS, B. V.

Here while his canting drone-pipe scan'd,
The mystick figures of her hand,
He tipples palmistry, *and dines*
On all her fortune-telling lines.
CLEAVELAND.

With the fond maids in palmistry *he deals;*
They tell the secret first which he reveals.
PRIOR.

2. *Addison* uses it for the action of the hand.

Going to relieve a common beggar, he found his pocket was picked; that being a kind of palmistry *at which this vermin are very dextrous.* ADDISON'S SPECTATOR.

PALPITA'TION. *n.s.* [*palpitation*, Fr. from *palpitate.*] Beating or panting; that alteration in the pulse of the heart, upon frights or any other causes, which makes it felt: for a natural uniform pulse goes on without distinction.

The heart strikes five hundred sort of pulses in an hour; and hunted into such continual palpitations, *through anxiety and distraction, that fain would it break.* HARVEY.

I knew the good company too well to feel any palpitations *at their approach.* TATLER, NO. 86.

Anxiety and palpitations *of the heart, are a sign of weak fibres.* ARBUTHNOT ON ALIMENTS.

Her bosom heaves
With palpitations *wild.*
THOMSON'S SPRING.

PAM. *n.s.* [probably from *palm*, victory; as *trump* from *triumph.*] The knave of clubs.

Ev'n mighty pam *that kings and queens o'erthrew,*
And mow'd down armies in the fights of lu. POPE.

PAMPHLETEE'R. *n.s.* [from *pamphlet.*] A scribbler of small books.

The squibs are those who in the common phrase are called libellers, lampooners, and pamphleteers. TATLER.

With great injustice I have been pelted by pamphleteers. SWIFT.

PA'NCAKE. *n.s.* [*pan* and *cake.*] Thin pudding baked in the frying-pan.

A certain knight swore by his honour they were good pancakes, *and swore by his honour the mustard was naught.* SHAKESPEARE.

The flour makes a very good pancake, *mixed with a little wheat flour.* MORTIMER'S HUSBANDRY.

PANA'DO. *n.s.* [from *panis*, bread.] Food made by boiling bread in water.

Their diet ought to be very sparing; gruels, panados, *and chicken broth.* WISEMAN'S SURGERY.

PANCRA'TICAL. *adj.* [*παν* and *κρατός.*] Excelling in all the gymnastick exercises.

He was the most pancratical *man of Greece, and, as Galen reporteth, able to persist erect upon an oily plank, and not to be removed by the force of three men.* BROWN.

PA'NDECT. *n.s.* [*pandecta*, Latin.]
1. A treatise that comprehends the whole of any science.

It were to be wished, that the commons would form a pandect *of their power and privileges, to be confirmed by the entire legislative authority.* SWIFT.

2. The digest of the civil law.

PANDICULA'TION. *n.s.* [*pandiculans*, Lat.] The restlessness, stretching, and uneasiness that usually accompany the cold fits of an intermitting fever.

Windy spirits, for want of a due volatilization, produce in the nerves a pandiculation, *or oscitation, or stupor, or cramp in the muscles.*
FLOYER ON THE HUMOURS.

PA'NTOMIME. *n.s.* [πᾶς and *μίμος*; *pantomime*, Fr.]
1. One who has the power of universal mimickry; one who expresses his meaning by mute action; a buffoon.

Not that I think those pantomimes,
Who vary action with the times,
Are less ingenious in their art,
Than those who duly act one part.
HUDIBRAS.

2. A scene; a tale exhibited only in gesture and dumb-shew.

He put off the representation of pantomimes *till late hours, on market-days.*
ARBUTHNOT.

Exulting folly hail'd the joyful day,
And pantomime *and song confirm'd her sway.* ANONYMOUS.

PAPA'VEROUS. *adj.* [*papavereus*, from *papaver*, Lat. a poppy.] Resembling poppies.

Mandrakes afford a papaverous *and unpleasant odour, whether in the leaf or apple.* BROWN'S VULGAR ERROURS.

PAR. *n.s.* [Latin.] State of equality; equivalence; equal value. This word is not elegantly used, except as a term of traffick.

To estimate the par, *it is necessary to know how much silver is in the coins of the two countries, by which you charge the bill of exchange.* LOCKE.

My friend is the second after the treasurer; the rest of the great officers are much upon a par. GULLIVER'S TRAVELS.

PA'RAGRAPH. *n.s.* [*paragraphe*, Fr. *παραγραφή*.] A distinct part of a discourse.

Of his last paragraph, *I have transcribed the most important parts.* SWIFT.

PARAGRA'PHICALLY. *adv.* [from *paragraph*.] By paragraphs; with distinct breaks or divisions.

PA'RAMOUR. *n.s.* [*par* and *amour*, Fr.]
1. A lover or woer.

Upon the floor
A lovely bevy of fair ladies sat,
Courted of many a jolly paramour,
The which them did in modestwise amate,
And each one sought his lady to aggrate.
FAIRY QUEEN.

No season then for her
To wanton with the sun her lusty paramour. MILTON.

2. A mistress. It is obsolete in both senses, though not inelegant or unmusical.

Shall I believe
That unsubstantial death is amorous,
And that the lean abhorred monster keeps

Thee here in dark to be his paramour. SHAKESPEARE.

PARAPHERNA'LIA. *n.s.* [Lat. *paraphernaux*, Fr.] Goods in the wife's disposal.

PA'RAPHRAST. *n.s.* [*paraphraste*, Fr. παραφραστής.] A lax interpreter; one who explains in many words.

The fittest for publick audience are such, as following a middle course between the rigor of literal translators and the liberty of paraphrasts, *do, with great shortness and plainess, deliver the meaning.* HOOKER.

The chaldean paraphrast *renders Gerah by Meath.* ARBUTHNOT.

To **PARBREAK.** *v.n.* [*brecker*, Dutch.] To vomit.

PARENTA'TION. *n.s.* [from *parento*, Latin.] Something done or said in honour of the dead.

PARE'NTHESIS. *n.s.* [*parenthese*, Fr. παρά, 'εν and τίθημι.] A sentence so included in another sentence, as that it may be taken out, without injuring the sense of that which incloses it: being commonly marked thus, ( ).

In vain is my person excepted by a parenthesis *of words, when so many hands are armed against me with swords.* KING CHARLES.

In his Indian relations, are contained strange and incredible accounts; he is seldom mentioned, without a derogatory parenthesis, *in any author.* BROWN'S VULGAR ERROURS.

Thou shalt be seen,
Tho' with some short parenthesis *between,*
High on the throne of wit. DRYDEN.

Don't suffer every occasional thought to carry you away into a long parenthesis, *and thus stretch out your discourse, and divert you from the point in hand.* WATTS'S LOGICK.

PA'RGET. *n.s.* Plaster laid upon roofs of rooms.

Gold was the parget, *and the cieling bright*
Did shine all scaly with great plates of gold;
The floor with jasp and emerald was
dight. SPENSER.

Of English talc, the coarser sort is called plaster or parget; *the finer, spaad.* WOODWARD.

PA'RGETER. *n.s.* [from *pargeo.*] A plasterer.

PA'RITOR. *n.s.* [for *apparitor.*] A beadle; a summoner of the courts of civil law.

You shall be summon'd by an host of paritours; *you shall be sentenced in the spiritual court.* DRYDEN.

PA'RKER. *n.s.* [from *park.*] A park-keeper. *Ainsworth.*

PA'RLOUR. *n.s.* [*parloir*, French; *parlatorio*, Italian.]

1. A room in monasteries, where the religious meet and converse.

2. A room in houses on the first floor, elegantly furnished for reception or entertainment.

Can we judge it a thing seemly for a man to go about the building of an house to the God of heaven, with no other appearance than if his end were to rear up a kitchen or a parlour *for his own use?* HOOKER.

Back again fair Alma led them right,
And soon into a goodly parlour *brought.*
FAIRY QUEEN.

It would be infinitely more shameful, in the dress of the kitchen, to receive the entertainments of the parlour. SOUTH.

Roof and sides were like a parlour *made,*
A soft recess, and a cool summer shade.
DRYDEN.

PA'RLOUS. *adj.* [This might seem to come from *parler*, Fr. to speak; but *Junius* derives it, I think, rightly, from *perilous*, in which sense it answers to the Latin *improbus.*] Keen; sprightly; waggish.

Midas durst communicate
To none but to his wife his ears of state;
One must be trusted, and he thought her fit,
As passing prudent, and a parlous *wit.*
DRYDEN.

To **PARSE.** *v.a.* [from *pars*, Latin.] To resolve a sentence into the elements or parts of speech. It is a word only used in grammar schools.

Let him construe the letter into English, and parse *it over perfectly.*
ASCHAM'S SCHOOLMASTER.

Let scholars reduce the words to their original, to the first case of nouns, or first tense of verbs, and give an account of their formations and changes, their syntax and dependencies, which is called parsing.
WATTS'S IMPROVEMENT OF THE MIND.

PARTI'CULARLY. *v.a.* [from *particular.*]

1. Distinctly; singly; not universally.

Providence, that universally casts its eye over all the creation, is yet pleased more particularly *to fasten it upon some.*
SOUTH'S SERMONS.

2. In an extraordinary degree.

This exact propriety of Virgil, I particularly *regarded as a great part of his character.*
DRYDEN.

With the flower and the leaf I was so particularly *pleased, both for the invention and the moral, that I commend it to the reader.* DRYDEN.

PARTY-JU'RY. *n.s.* [in law.] A jury in some trials half foreigners and half natives.

PA'RTY-MAN. *n.s.* [*party* and *man.*] A factious person; an abettor of a party.

PA'SQUIL, PA'SQUIN, PA'SQUINADE. *n.s.* [from *pasquino*, a statue at Rome, to which they affix any lampoon or paper of satirical observation.] A lampoon.

He never valued any pasquils *that were dropped up and down, to think them worthy of his revenge.* HOWEL.

The pasquils, *lampoons, and libels, we meet with now-a-days, are a sort of playing with the four and twenty letters, without sense, truth, or wit.* TATLER, NO. 92.

PA'SSENGER. *n.s.* [*passager*, French.]

1. A traveller; one who is upon the road; a wayfarer.

All the way, the wanton damsel found
New mirth, her passenger *to entertain.*
FAIRY QUEEN.

What hollowing, and what stir is this?
These are my mates that make their wills their law,
Have some unhappy passenger *in chase.*
SHAKESPEARE.

The nodding horror of whose shady brows
Threats the forlorn and wand'ring passenger. MILTON.

Apelles, when he had finished any work, exposed it to the sight of all passengers, *and concealed himself to hear the censure of his faults.* DRYDEN'S DUFRESNOY.

2. One who hires in any vehicle the liberty of travelling.

The diligent pilot in a dangerous tempest doth attend the unskilful words of a passenger. SIDNEY.

PA'SSINGBELL. *n.s.* [*passing* and *bell.*] The bell which rings at the hour of departure, to obtain prayers for the passing soul: it is often used for the bell, which rings immediately after death.

Those loving papers,
Thicken on you now, as pray'rs ascend
To heaven in troops at a good man's passingbell. DONNE.

A talk of tumult, and a breath

Would serve him as his passingbell *to death.* DANIEL.

Before the passingbell *begun,*
The news through half the town has run.
SWIFT.

PASTE. *n.s.* [*paste*, French.]
1. Any thing mixed up so as to be viscous and tenacious: such as flour and water for bread or pies; or various kinds of earth mingled for the potter.

Except you could bray Christendom in a mortar, and mould it into a new paste, *there is no possibility of an holy war.* BACON'S HOLY WAR.

With particles of heav'nly fire
The God of nature did his soul inspire;
Which wise Prometheus temper'd into paste,
And, mixt with living streams, the godlike image cast. DRYDEN.

When the gods moulded up the paste *of man,*
Some of their dough was left upon their hands. DRYDEN.

He has the whitest hand that ever you saw, and raises paste *better than any woman.* ADDISON'S SPECTATOR, NO. 482.

2. Flour and water boiled together so as to make a cement.
3. Artificial mixture, in imitation of precious stones.

PA'STEBOARD. *n.s.* [*paste* and *board.*] Masses made anciently by pasting one paper on another: now made sometimes by macerating paper and casting it in moulds, sometimes by pounding old cordage, and casting it in forms.

Tintoret made chambers of board and pasteboard, *proportioned to his models, with doors and windows, through which he distributed, on his figures, artificial lights.* DRYDEN.

I would not make myself merry even with a piece of pasteboard, *that is invested with a publick character.* ADDISON.

PA'STRY. *n.s.* [*pastisserie*, Fr. from *paste.*]
1. The act of making pies.

Let never fresh machines your pastry *try,*
Unless grandees or magistrates are by,
Then you may put a dwarf into a pye.
KING.

2. Pies or baked paste.

Remember
The seed cake, the pastries *and the furmenty pot.* TUSSER.

They call for dates and quinces in the pastry. SHAKESPEARE.

Beasts of chase, or fowls of game,
In pastry *built, or from the spit, or boil'd,*
Gris amber steam'd.
MILTON'S PARADISE REGAIN'D.

3. The place where pastry is made.

PAT. *adj.* [from *pas*, Dutch, *Skinner.*] Fit; convenient; exactly suitable either as to time or place. This is a low word, and should not be used but in burlesque writings.

Pat pat; *and here's a marvellous convenient place for our rehearsal.*
SHAKESPEARE'S MIDSUMMER NIGHT'S DREAM.

Now I might do it pat, *now he is praying.*
SHAKESPEARE.

They never saw two things so pat,
In all respects, as this and that.
HUDIBRAS, P. II.

Zuinglius dreamed of a text, which he found very pat *to his doctrine of the Eucharist.* ATTERBURY.

He was surely put to't at the end of a verse,
Because he could find no word to come pat *in.* SWIFT.

PATCH. *n.s.* [*pezzo*, Italian.]
1. A piece sewed on to cover a hole.

Patches *set upon a little breach,*
Discredit more in hiding of the flaw,

Than did the flaw before it was so patch'd. SHAKESPEARE.

If the shoe be ript, or patches *put;*
He's wounded! see the plaister on his foot. DRYDEN.

They suffer their minds to appear in a piebald livery of coarse patches *and borrowed shreds, such as the common opinion of those they converse with clothe them in.* LOCKE.

2. A piece inserted in mosaick or variegated work.

3. A small spot of black silk put on the face.

How! providence! and yet a Scottish crew!
Then madam nature wears black patches *too.* CLEAVELAND.

If to every common funeral,
By your eyes martyr'd, such grace were allow'd,
Your face wou'd wear not patches, *but a cloud.* SUCKLING.

They were patched differently, and cast hostile glances upon one another, and their patches *were placed in different situations as party-signals to distinguish friends from foes.* ADDISON.

This the morning omens seem'd to tell;
Thrice from my trembling hand the patch-*box fell.* POPE.

4. A small particle; a parcel of land.

We go to gain a little patch *of ground,*
That hath in it no profit but the name. SHAKESPEARE.

5. A paltry fellow. Obsolete.

What a py'd ninny's this? thou scurvy patch! SHAKESPEARE.

PATH. *n.s.* [*pað*, Saxon.] Way; road; track. In conversation it is used of a narrow way to be passed on foot; but in solemn language means any passage.

For darkness, where is the place thereof? that thou shouldst know the paths *to the house thereof.* BIBLE JOB, XXXVIII. 20.

On the glad earth the golden age renew,
And thy great father's path *to heav'n pursue.* DRYDEN.

The dewy paths *of meadows we will tread,*
For crowns and chaplets. DRYDEN'S THEOCRITUS.

There is but one road by which to climb up, and they have a very severe law against any that enters the town by another path, *lest any new one should be worn on the mountain.* ADDISON'S REMARKS ON ITALY.

PATHE'TICAL, PATHETICK. [*παθητικός*; *pathetique*, Fr.] Affecting the passions; passionate; moving.

His page that handful of wit;
'Tis a most pathetical *neat.* SHAKESPEARE.

How pathetick *is that expostulation of Job, when, for the trial of his patience, he was made to look upon himself in this deplorable condition.* SPECTATOR, NO. 571.

Tully considered the dispositions of a sincere and less mercurial nation, by dwelling on the pathetick *part.* SWIFT.

While thus pathetick *to the prince he spoke,*
From the brave youth the streaming passion broke. POPE.

PA'TRON. *n.s.* [*patron*, Fr. *patronus*, Latin.]

1. One who countenances, supports or protects. Commonly a wretch who supports with insolence, and is paid with flattery.

I'll plead for you, as for my patron. SHAKESPEARE.

Ne'er let me pass in silence Dorset's name;
Ne'er cease to mention the continu'd debt,
Which the great patron *only would forget.* PRIOR.

2. A guardian saint.

Thou amongst those saints, whom thou do'st see,
Shall be a saint, and thine own nation's friend
And patron. FAIRY QUEEN, B. I.

St. Michael is mentioned as the patron *of the Jews, and is now taken by the Christians, as the protector general of our religion.* DRYDEN.

3. Advocate; defender; vindicator.

We are no patrons *of those things; the best defence whereof is speedy redress and amendment.* HOOKER, B. II. S. 1.

Whether the minds of men have naturally imprinted on them the ideas of extension and number, I leave to those who are the patrons *of innate principles.* LOCKE.

4. One who has donation of ecclesiastical preferment.

PA'TTEN. *n.s.* [*patin*, Fr.] A shoe of wood with an iron ring, worn under the common shoe by women to keep them from the dirt.

Their shoes and pattens *are snouted and piked more than a finger long, crooking upwards, which they call crackowes, which were fastened to the knees with chains of gold and silver.* CAMDEN'S REMAINS.

Good housewives
Underneath th' umbrella's oily shed,
Safe through the wet on clinking pattens *tread.* GAY.

PAVI'LION. *n.s.* [*pavillon*, French.] A tent; a temporary or moveable house.

Flowers being under the trees, the trees were to them a pavillion, *and the flowers to the trees a mosaical floor.* SIDNEY.

She did lie
In her pavilion, *cloth of gold, of tissue.*
SHAKESPEARE.

He, only he, heaven's blew pavilion *spreads,*
And on the ocean's dancing billows treads.
SANDYS.

It was usual for the enemy, when there was a king in the field, to demand by a trumpet in what part of the camp he resided, that they might avoid firing upon the royal pavilion.
ADDISON'S FREEHOLDER, NO. 23.

The glowing fury springs,
Once more invades the guilty dome, and shrouds
Its bright pavilions *in a veil of clouds.*
POPE.

PA'YDAY. *n.s.* [*pay* and *day*.] Day on which debts are to be discharged or wages paid.

Labourers pay away all their wages, and live upon trust till next payday.
LOCKE.

PEA'RLEYED. *adj.* [*pearl* and *eye*.] Having a speck in the eye.

PEAT. *n.s.* [from *petit*, Fr.] A little fondling; a darling; a dear play thing. It is now commonly called *pet*.

A pretty peat! *it is best put finger in the eye,*
An she knew why.
SHAKESPEARE'S TAMING OF THE SHREW.

A citizen and his wife
Both riding on one horse, upon the way
I overtook; the wench a pretty peat.
DONNE.

PECCADI'LLO. [Spanish; *peccadille*, French.] A petty fault; a slight crime; a venial offence.

He means those little vices, which we call follies and the defects of the human understanding, or at most the peccadillos *of life, rather than the tragical vices to which men are hurried by their unruly passions.*
DRYDEN.

'Tis low ebb with his accusers, when such peccadilos *as these are put in to swell the charge.* ATTERBURY.

PE'CCANT. *adj.* [*peccant*, Fr. *peccans*, Latin.]
1. Guilty; criminal.

From them I will not hide
My judgments, how with mankind I proceed;

As how with peccant *angels late they saw.* MILTON.

That such a peccant *creature should disapprove and repent of every violation of the rules of just and honest, this right reason could not but infer.* SOUTH'S SERMONS.

2. Ill disposed; corrupt; bad; offensive to the body; injurious to health. It is chiefly used in medical writers.

With laxatives preserve your body sound,
And purge the peccant *humours that abound.* DRYDEN.

Such as have the bile peccant *or deficient are relieved by bitters, which are a sort of subsidiary gall.* ARBUTHNOT.

3. Wrong; bad; deficient; unformal.

Nor is the party cited bound to appear, if the citation be peccant *in form or matter.* AYLIFFE'S PARERGON.

PECU'LATION. *n.s.* [*peculatus*, Latin; *peculat*, Fr.] Robbery of the publick; theft of publick money.

PED. *n.s.*
1. A small packsaddle. A *ped* is much shorter than a pannel, and is raised before and behind, and serves for small burdens.

A pannel and wanty, packsaddle and ped. TUSSER.

2. A basket; a hamper.

A hask is a wicker ped, *wherein they use to carry fish.* SPENSER.

PEDERE'RO. *n.s.* [*pedrero*, Spanish, from *piedra*, a stone with which they charged it.] A small cannon managed by a swivel. It is frequently written *paterero*.

PEDE'STRIOUS. *adj.* [*pedestris*, Latin.] Not winged; going on foot.

Men conceive they never lie down, and enjoy not the position of rest, ordained unto all pedestrious *animals.* BROWN.

PEE'PHOLE, PEEPINGHOLE. *n.s.* [*peep* and *hole*.] Hole through which one may look without being discovered.

By the peepholes *in his crest,*
Is it not virtually confest,
That there his eyes took distant aim. PRIOR.

The fox spied him through a peepinghole *he had found out to see what news.* L'ESTRANGE.

PE'LTING. *adj.* This word in *Shakespeare* signifies, I know not why, mean; paltry; pitiful.

Could great men thunder, Jove could ne'er be quiet;
For every pelting *petty officer*
Would use his heav'n for thunder. SHAKESPEARE.

Fogs falling in the land,
Have every pelting *river made so proud,*
That they have overborn their continents. SHAKESPEARE.

They from sheepcotes and poor pelting *villages*
Enforce their charity. SHAKESPEARE.

A tenement or pelting *farm.* SHAKESPEARE.

PENCE. *n.s.* The plural of *penny*; formed from *pennies*, by a contraction usual in the rapidity of colloquial speech.

The same servant found one of his fellow servants, which owed him an hundred pence, *and took him by the throat.* BIBLE MATTHEW.

PENGUIN. *n.s.* [*anser magellanicus*, Latin.]
1. A bird. This bird was found with this name, as is supposed, by the first discoverers of America; and *penguin* signifying in Welsh a white head, and the head of this fowl being white, it has been imagined, that America was peopled from Wales; whence *Hudibras*:

British Indians nam'd from penguins. *Grew* gives another account of the name, deriving it from *pinguis*, Lat. *fat*; but is, I believe, mistaken.

The penguin *is so called from his extraordinary fatness: for though he be no higher than a large goose, yet he weighs sometimes sixteen pounds: his wings are extreme short and little, altogether unuseful for flight, but by the help whereof he swims very swiftly.* GREW'S MUSÆUM.

2. A fruit.

The penguin *is very common in the West Indies, where the juice of its fruit is often put into punch, being of a sharp acid flavour: there is also a wine made of the juice of this fruit, but it will not keep good long.* MILLER.

PENITE'NTIARY. *n.s.* [*penitencier*, Fr. *pœnitentiarius*, low Latin.]

1. One who prescribes the rules and measures of pennance.

Upon the loss of Urbin, the duke's undoubted right, no penitentiary, *though he had enjoined him never so straight pennance to expiate his first offence, would have counselled him to have given over pursuit of his right, which he prosperously re-obtained.* BACON.

The great penitentiary *with his counsellors prescribes the measure of pennance.* AYLIFFE'S PARERGON.

2. A penitent; one who does pennance.

A prison restrained John Northampton's liberty, who, for abusing the same in his unruly mayoralty of London, was condemned hither as a perpetual penitentiary. CAREW.

To maintain a painful fight against the law of sin, is the work of the penitentiary. HAMMOND.

3. The place where pennance is enjoined. *Ainsworth.*

PENKNIFE. *n.s.* [*pen* and *knife.*] A knife used to cut pens.

Some schoolmen, fitter to guide penknives *than swords, precisely stand upon it.* BACON.

PE'NNER. *n.s.* [from *pen.*]

1. A writer.

2. A pencase. *Ainsworth.* So it is called in Scotland.

PE'NNY. *n.s.* plural *pence.* [*penig*, Saxon.]

1. A small coin, of which twelve make a shilling: a penny is the radical denomination from which English coin is numbered, the copper halfpence and farthings being only *nummerum famuli*, a subordinate species of coin.

She sighs and shakes her empty shoes in vain,
No silver penny *to reward her pain.* DRYDEN.

One frugal on his birth-day fears to dine,
Does at a penny's *cost in herbs repine.* DRYDEN.

2. Proverbially. A small sum.

You shall hear
The legions, now in Gallia, sooner landed
In our not fearing Britain, than have tidings
Of any penny *tribute paid.*
SHAKESPEARE'S CYMBELINE.

We will not lend thee a penny. SHAKESPEARE.

Because there is a latitude of gain in buying and selling, take not the utmost penny *that is lawful, for although it be lawful, yet it is not safe.* TAYLOR'S LIVING HOLY.

3. Money in general.

Pepper and Sabean incense take;
And with post-haste thy running markets make;
Be sure to turn the penny. DRYDEN.

It may be a contrivance of some printer, who hath a mind to make a penny. SWIFT'S MISCELLANIES.

PE'NSION. *n.s.* [*pension*, Fr.] An allowance made to any one without an equivalent. In England it is generally understood to mean pay given to a state hireling for treason to his country.

A charity bestowed on the education of her young subjects has more merit than a thousand pensions *to those of a higher fortune.*
ADDISON'S GUARDIAN, NO. 105.

He has liv'd with the great without flattery, and been a friend to men in power without pensions. POPE.

To **PE'NSION.** *v.a.* [from the noun.] To support by an arbitrary allowance.

One might expect to see medals of France in the highest perfection, when there is a society pensioned *and set apart for the designing of them.*
ADDISON ON ANCIENT MEDALS.

The hero William and the martyr Charles,
One knighted Blackmore, and one
pension'd *Quarles.* POPE.

PE'NSIONARY. *adj.* [*pensionnaire*, French.] Maintained by pensions.

Scorn his houshold policies,
His silly plots and pensionary *spies.*
DONNE.

They were devoted by pensionary *obligations to the olive.*
HOWEL'S VOCAL FOREST.

PE'NSIONER. *n.s.* [from *pension.*]
1. One who is supported by an allowance paid at the will of another; a dependant.

Prices of things necessary for sustentation, grew excessive to the hurt of pensioners, *soldiers, and all hired servants.*
CAMDEN.

Hovering dreams,
The fickle pensioners *of Morpheus' train.*
MILTON.

The rector is maintained by the perquisites of the curate's office, and therefore is a kind of pensioner *to him.* COLLIER.

2. A slave of state hired by a stipend to obey his master.

In Britain's senate he a seat obtains,
And one more pensioner *St. Stephen*
gains. POPE.

PE'NSIVE. *adj.* [*pensif*, French; *pensivo*, Italian.]
1. Sorrowfully thoughtful; sorrowful; mournfully serious; melancholy.

Think it still a good work, which they in their pensive *care for the well bestowing of time account waste.* HOOKER.

Are you at leisure, holy father, ——
—— *My leisure serves me,* pensive
daughter, now. SHAKESPEARE.

Anxious cares the pensive *nymph opprest,*
And secret passions labour'd in her breast.
POPE.

2. It is generally and properly used of persons; but *Prior* has applied it to things.

We at the sad approach of death shall know
The truth, which from these pensive
numbers flow,
That we pursue false joy, and suffer real
woe. PRIOR.

PE'NTHOUSE. *n.s.* [*pent*, from *pente*, Fr. and *house.*] A shed hanging out aslope from the main wall.

This is the penthouse *under which Lorenzo desir'd us to make a stand.*
SHAKESPEARE'S MERCHANT OF VENICE.

Sleep shall neither night nor day
Hang upon his penthouse *lid.*
SHAKESPEARE.

The Turks lurking under their penthouse, *laboured with mattocks to dig up the foundation of the wall.* KNOLLES.

A blow was received by riding under a penthouse. WISEMAN.

Those defensive engines, made by the

Romans into the form of penthouses *to cover the assailants from the weapons of the besieged, would he presently batter in pieces with stones and blocks.* WILKINS.

My penthouse *eye-brows and my shaggy beard*
Offend your sight; but these are manly signs. DRYDEN.

The chill rain
Drops from some penthouse *on her wretched head.* ROWE.

PEREGRINA'TION. *n.s.* [from *peregrinus*, Lat.] Travel; abode in foreign countries.

It was agreed between them, what account he should give of his peregrination *abroad.* BACON'S HENRY VII.

That we do not contend to have the earth pass for a paradise, we reckon it only as the land of our peregrination, *and aspire after a better country.* BENTLEY'S SERMONS.

PERE'NNIAL. *adj.* [*perennis*, Latin.]

1. Lasting through the year.

If the quantity were precisely the same in these perennial *fountains, the difficulty would be greater.* CHEYNE.

2. Perpetual; unceasing.

The matter wherewith these perennial *clouds are raised, is the sea that surrounds them.* HARVEY.

PERE'NNITY. *n.s.* [from *perennitas*, Lat.] Equality of lasting through all seasons; perpetuity.

That springs have their origin from the sea, and not from rains and vapours, I conclude from the perennity *of divers springs.* DERHAM'S PHYSICO-THEOLOGY.

PERFU'MER. *n.s.* [from *perfume.*] One whose trade is to sell things made to gratify the scent.

A moss the perfumers *have out of apple trees, that hath an excellent scent.* BACON'S NATURAL HISTORY.

First issued from perfumers *shops*
A croud of fashionable fops. SWIFT.

PE'RILOUS. *adj.* [*perileux*, Fr. from *peril.*]

1. Dangerous; hazardous; full of danger.

Alterations in the service of God, for that they impair the credit of religion, are therefore perilous *in common-weals, which have no continuance longer than religion hath all reverence done unto it.* HOOKER, B. V. S. 2.

Her guard is chastity,
She that has that is clad in compleat steel,
And like a quiver'd nymph with arrows keen
May trace huge forests and unharbour'd heaths,
Infamous hills and sandy perilous *wilds.* MILTON.

Dictate propitious to my duteous ear,
What arts can captivate the changeful seer:
For perilous *th' assay, unheard the toil*
T' elude the prescience of a God by guile. POPE.

Into the perilous *flood*
Bear fearless. THOMSON.

2. It is used by way of emphasis, or ludicrous exaggeration of any thing bad.

Thus was th' accomplish'd squire endu'd
With gifts and knowledge per'lous *shrewd.* HUDIBRAS.

3. Smart; witty. In this sense it is, I think, only applied to children, and probably obtained its signification from the notion, that children eminent for wit, do not live; a witty boy was therefore a *perilous* boy, or a boy in danger. It is vulgarly *parlous.*

'Tis a per'lous *boy,*
Bold, quick, ingenious, forward, capable;
He's all the mother's from the top to toe. SHAKESPEARE.

PE'RIWIG. *n.s.* [*perruque*, Fr.] Adscititious hair; hair not natural, worn by way of ornament or concealment of baldness.

Her hair is auburn, mine is perfect yellow,
If that be all the difference in his love,
I'll get me such a colour'd periwig.
SHAKESPEARE.

It offends me to hear a robusteous periwig-*pated fellow tear a passion to tatters, to split the ears of the groundlings.* SHAKESPEARE.

The sun's
Dishevel'd beams and scatter'd fires
Serve but for ladies periwigs *and tires*
In lovers sonnets. DONNE.

Madam time, be ever bald,
I'll not thy periwig *be call'd.*
CLEAVELAND.

For vailing of their visages his highness and the marquis bought each a periwig, *somewhat to overshadow their foreheads.* WOTTON.

They used false hair or periwigs.
ARBUTHNOT ON COINS.

From her own head Megara takes
A periwig *of twisted snakes,*
Which in the nicest fashion curl'd,
Like toupets. SWIFT'S MISCELLANIES.

To **PE'RIWIG.** *v.a.* [from the noun.] To dress in false hair.

Now when the winter's keener breath began
To crystallize the Baltick ocean,
To glaze the lakes, to bridle up the floods,
And periwig *with snow the bald-pate woods.* SYLVESTER.

Near the door an entrance gapes,
Crouded round with antick shapes,
Discord periwig'd *with snakes,*
See the dreadful strides she takes.
SWIFT'S MISCELLANIES.

PERMI'T. *n.s.* A written permission from an officer for transporting of goods from place to place, showing the duty on them to have been paid.

PERPOTA'TION. *n.s.* [*per* and *poto*, Latin.] The act of drinking largely.

PERSONA'TION. *n.s.* [from *personate.*] Counterfeiting of another person.

This being one of the strangest examples of a personation *that ever was, it deserveth to be discovered and related at the full.*
BACON'S HENRY VII.

PE'RSPECTIVE. *n.s.* [*perspectif*, Fr. *perspicio*, Lat.]

1. A glass through which things are viewed.

If it tend to danger, they turn about the perspective, *and shew it so little, that he can scarce discern it.* DENHAM.

It may import us in this calm, to hearken to the storms raising abroad; and by the best perspectives, *to discover from what coast they break.* TEMPLE.

You hold the glass, but turn the perspective,
And farther off the lessen'd object drive.
DRYDEN.

Faith for reason's glimmering light shall give
Her immortal perspective. PRIOR.

2. The science by which things are ranged in picture, according to their appearance in their real situation.

Medals have represented their buildings according to the rules of perspective.
ADDISON ON ANCIENT MEDALS.

3. View; visto.

Lofty trees, with sacred shades,
And perspectives *of pleasant glades,*
Where nymphs of brightest form appear.
DRYDEN.

PE'RSPECTIVE. *adj.* Relating to the science of vision; optick; optical.

We have perspective *houses, where we make demonstrations of all lights and radiations; and out of things uncoloured and transparent, we can represent unto you all several colours.* BACON.

PERT. *adj.* [*pert*, Welsh; *pert*, Dutch; *appert*, French.]

1. Lively; brisk; smart.

Awake the pert *and nimble spirit of mirth;*
Turn melancholy forth to funerals.
SHAKESPEARE.

On the tawny sands and shelves,
Trip the pert *fairies and the dapper elves.*
MILTON.

2. Saucy; petulant; with bold and garrulous loquacity.

All servants might challenge the same liberty, and grow pert *upon their masters; and when this sauciness became universal, what less mischief could be expected than an old Scythian rebellion?*
COLLIER ON PRIDE.

A lady bids me in a very pert *manner mind my own affairs, and not pretend to meddle with their linnen.* ADDISON.

Vanessa
Scarce list'ned to their idle chat,
Further than sometimes by a frown,
When they grew pert, *to pull them down.*
SWIFT.

To **PERVE'RT.** *v.a.* [*perverto*, Lat. *pervertir*, Fr.]

1. To distort from the true end or purpose.

Instead of good they may work ill, and pervert *justice to extreme injustice.*
SPENSER'S STATE OF IRELAND.

If thou seest the oppression of the poor, and violent perverting *of justice in a province, marvel not.*
BIBLE ECCLESIASTICUS, V. 8.

If then his providence
Out of our evil seek to bring forth good,
Our labour must be to pervert *that end,*
And out of good still to find means of evil.
MILTON.

He has perverted *my meaning by his glosses; and interpreted my words into blasphemy, of which they were not guilty.*
DRYDEN.

Porphyry has wrote a volume to explain this cave of the nymphs with more piety than judgment; and another person has perverted *it into obscenity; and both allegorically.* BROOME.

2. To corrupt; to turn from the right; opposed to *convert*, which is to turn from the wrong to the right.

The heinous and despiteful act
Of Satan, done in Paradise, and how
He in the serpent had perverted *Eve,*
Her husband she, to taste the fatal fruit,
Was known in heav'n.
MILTON'S PARADISE LOST.

PERVE'RTER. *n.s.* [from *pervert.*]

1. One that changes any thing from good to bad; a corrupter.

Where a child finds his own parents his perverters, *he cannot be so properly born, as damned into the world.* SOUTH.

2. One who distorts any thing from the right purpose.

He that reads a prohibition in a divine law, had need be well satisfied about the sense he gives it, lest he incur the wrath of God, and be found a perverter *of his law.*
STILLINGFLEET.

PERU'KE. *n.s.* [*peruque*, Fr.] A cap of false hair; a periwig

I put him on a linen cap, and his peruke *over that.* WISEMAN.

To **PERU'KE.** *v.a.* [from the noun.] To dress in adscititious hair.

PERU'KEMAKER. *n.s.* [*peruke* and *maker.*] A maker of perukes; a wigmaker.

PE'SSARY. *n.s.* [*pessarie*, Fr.] Is an oblong form of medicine, made to thrust up into the uterus upon some extraordinary occasions.

Of cantharides he prescribes five in a

pessary, *cutting off their heads and feet, mixt with myrrh.* ARBUTHNOT.

PEST. *n.s.* [*peste*, Fr. *pestis*, Lat.]
1. Plague; pestilence.

Let fierce Achilles
The god propitiate, and the pest *assuage.* POPE.

2. Any thing mischievous or destructive.

The pest *a virgin's face and bosom bears,*
High on her crown a rising snake appears,
Guards her black front, and hisses in her hairs. POPE.

At her words the hellish pest
Forbore. MILTON'S PARADISE LOST.

Of all virtues justice is the best;
Valour without it is a common pest. WALLER.

PE'STERER. *n.s.* [from *pester.*] One that pesters or disturbs.

PE'STHOUSE. *n.s.* [from *pest* and *house.*] An hospital for persons infected with the plague.

PET. *n.s.* [This word is of doubtful etymology; from *despit*, Fr. or *impetus*, Lat. perhaps it may be derived some way from *petit*, as it implies only a little fume or fret.]
1. A slight passion; a slight fit of anger.

If all the world
Should in a pet *of temperance feed on pulse,*
Drink the clear stream, and nothing wear but freeze,
Th' all-giver would be unthankt, would be unprais'd. MILTON.

If we cannot obtain every vain thing we ask, our next business is to take pet *at the refusal.* L'ESTRANGE.

Life, given for noble purposes, must not be thrown up in a pet, *nor whined away in love.* COLLIER.

They cause the proud their visits to delay,
And send the godly in a pet *to pray.* POPE.

2. A lamb taken into the house, and brought up by hand. A cade lamb. [Probably from *petit*, little.][170] *Hanmer.*

PETRO'L, PETROLEUM. *n.s.* [*petrole*, Fr.] Petrol or petroleum is a liquid bitumen, black, floating on the water of springs. *Woodward.*

PETTIFO'GGER. *n.s.* [corrupted from *pettivoguer*; *petit* and *voguer*, Fr.] A petty small-rate lawyer.

The worst conditioned and least cliented petivoguers *get, under the sweet bait of revenge, more plentiful prosecution of actions.* CAREW'S SURVEY OF CORNWALL.

Your pettifoggers *damn their souls*
To share with knaves in cheating fools. HUDIBRAS.

Consider, my dear, how indecent it is to abandon your shop and follow pettifoggers; *there is hardly a plea between two country esquires about a barren acre, but you draw yourself in as bail, surety or solicitor.* ARBUTHNOT'S HISTORY OF JOHN BULL.

Physicians are apt to despise empiricks, lawyers, pettifoggers, *merchants and pedlars.* SWIFT.

PE'WTER. *n.s.* [*peauter*, Dutch.]
1. A compound of metals; an artificial metal.

Coarse pewter *is made of fine tin and lead.* BACON.

The pewter, *into which no water could enter, became more white, and liker to silver, and less flexible.* BACON.

Pewter *dishes, with water in them, will not melt easily, but without it they will; nay, butter or oil, in themselves inflammable, yet, by their moisture, will do the like.* BACON.

2. The plates and dishes in a house.

The eye of the mistress was wont to make her pewter *shine.* ADDISON.

PHILO'LOGER. *n.s.* [φιλόλογος.] One whose chief study is language; a grammarian; a critick.

> Philologers *and critical discoursers, who look beyond the shell and obvious exteriors of things, will not be angry with our narrower explorations.* BROWN.

> *You expect, that I should discourse of this matter like a naturalist, not a* philologer. BOYLE.

> *The best* philologers *say, that the original word does not only signify domestick, as opposed to foreign, but also private, as opposed to common.* SPRAT'S SERMONS.

PHILO'LOGICAL. *adj.* [from *philology.*] Critical; grammatical.

> *Studies, called* philological, *are history, language, grammar, rhetorick, poesy and criticism.* WATTS.

> *He who pretends to the learned professions, if he doth not arise to be a critick himself in* philological *matters, should frequently converse with dictionaries, paraphrasts, commentators or other criticks, which may relieve any difficulties.* WATTS.

PHILO'LOGIST. *n.s.* [φιλόλογος.] A critick; a grammarian.

PHILO'LOGY. *n.s.* [φιλολογία; *philologie*, Fr.] Criticism; grammatical learning.

> *Temper all discourses of* philology *with interspersions of morality.* WALKER.

PHI'LOMOT. *adj.* [corrupted from *feuille morte*, a dead leaf.] Coloured like a dead leaf.

> *One of them was blue, another yellow, and another* philomot, *the fourth was of a pink colour, and the fifth of a pale green.* ADDISON'S SPECTATOR, NO. 265.

PHILO'SOPHER. *n.s.* [*philosophus*, Lat. *philosophe*, Fr.] A man deep in knowledge, either moral or natural.

> *Many sound in belief have been also great* philosophers. HOOKER'S ECCLESIASTICAL POLITY.

> *That stone*
> Philosophers *in vain so long have sought.* MILTON.

> *Adam, in the state of innocence, came into the world a* philosopher, *which sufficiently appeared by his writing the natures of things upon their names; he could view essences in themselves, and read forms without the comment of their respective properties.* SOUTH'S SERMONS.

> *They all our fam'd* philosophers *defie,*
> *And would our faith by force of reason try.* DRYDEN.

> *If the* philosophers *by fire had been so wary in their observations and sincere in their reports, as those, who call themselves* philosophers, *ought to have been, our acquaintance with the bodies here about us had been yet much greater.* LOCKE.

PHI'LOSOPHY. *n.s.* [*philosophie*, Fr. *philosophia*, Latin.]

1. Knowledge natural or moral.

> *I had never read, heard nor seen any thing, I had never any taste of* philosophy *nor inward feeling in myself, which for a while I did not call to my succour.* SIDNEY.

> Hang up philosophy;
> *Unless* philosophy *can make a Juliet,*
> *Displant a town, reverse a prince's doom,*
> *It helps not.* SHAKESPEARE.

> *The progress you have made in* philosophy, *hath enabled you to benefit yourself with what I have written.* DIGBY.

2. Hypothesis or system upon which natural effects are explained.

> *We shall in vain interpret their words by the notions of our* philosophy, *and the doctrines in our schools.* LOCKE.

3. Reasoning; argumentation.

> *Of good and evil much they argu'd then*
> *Vain wisdom all and false* philosophy. MILTON.

His decisions are the judgment of his passions and not of his reason, the philosophy *of the sinner and not of the man.* ROGERS'S SERMONS.

4. The course of sciences read in the schools.

PHIZ. *n.s.* [This word is formed by a ridiculous contraction from *physiognomy*, and should therefore, if it be written at all, be written *phyz.*] The face, in a sense of contempt.

His air was too proud, and his features amiss,
As if being a traitor had alter'd his phiz.
STEPNEY.

PHLEME. *n.s.* [from *phlæbotomus*, Lat.] A fleam, so it is commonly written; an instrument which is placed on the vein and driven into it with a blow; particularly in bleeding of horses.

PHO'NICKS. *n.s.* [from *φωνή.*] The doctrine of sounds.

PHRASE. *n.s.* [*φϱάσις.*]
1. An idiom; a mode of speech peculiar to a language.
2. An expression; a mode of speech.

Now mince the sin,
And mollify damnation with a phrase*:*
Say you consented not to Sancho's death,
But barely not forbad it. DRYDEN.

To seat the Lord, and depart from evil, are phrases *which the scripture useth to express the sum of religion.* TILLOTSON.

3. Stile; expression.

Thou speak'st
In better phrase *and matter than thou didst.* SHAKESPEARE.

To **PHRASE.** *v.a.* [from the noun.] To stile; to call; to term.

These suns,
For so they phrase *them, by their heralds challenged*
The noble spirits to arms.
SHAKESPEARE'S HENRY VIII.

PHRASEO'LOGY. *n.s.* [*φϱάσις* and *λέγω.*]
1. Stile; diction.

The scholars of Ireland seem not to have the least conception of a stile, but run on in a flat phraseology, *often mingled with barbarous terms.*
SWIFT'S MISCELLANIES.

2. A phrase book. *Ainsworth.*

PHYSIO'LOGY. *n.s.* [*φύσις* and *λέγω*; *physiologie*, Fr.] The doctrine of the constitution of the works of nature.

Disputing physiology *is of no accommodation to your designs.*
GLANVILLE'S SCEPSIS SCIENTIFICA.

Philosophers adapted their description of the deity to the vulgar, otherwise the conceptions of mankind could not be accounted for from their physiology.
BENTLEY'S SERMONS.

PICKAPACK. *adv.* [from *pack*, by a reduplication very common in our language.] In manner of a pack.

In a hurry she whips up her darling under her arms, and carries the other a pickapack *upon her shoulders.* L'ESTRANGE.

PI'CKBACK. *adj.* [corrupted perhaps from *pickpack.*] On the back.

As our modern wits behold,
Mounted a pickback *on the old,*
Much farther off. HUDIBRAS.

PI'CKLEHERRING. *n.s.* [*pickle* and *herring.*] A jack-pudding; a merry-andrew; a zany; a buffoon.

Another branch of pretenders to this art, without horse or pickleherring, *lie snug in a garret.* SPECTATOR, NO. 572.

The pickleherring *found the way to shake him, for upon his whistling a country jig, this unlucky wag danced to it with such a variety of grimaces, that the countryman could not forbear smiling, and lost the prize.* ADDISON'S SPECTATOR.

PICKTOO'TH. *n.s.* [*pick* and *tooth.*] An instrument by which the teeth are cleaned.

If a gentleman leaves a picktooth *case on the table after dinner, look upon it as part of your vails.* SWIFT.

PICKTHA'NK. *n.s.* [*pick* and *thank.*] An officious fellow, who does what he is not desired; a whispering parasite.

With pleasing tales his lord's vain ears he fed,
A flatterer, a pickthank, *and a lyer.*
FAIRFAX.

Many tales devis'd,
Oft the ear of greatness needs must hear,
By smiling pickthanks *and base newsmongers.* SHAKESPEARE.

The business of a pickthank *is the basest of offices.* L'ESTRANGE.

If he be great and powerful, spies and pickthanks *generally provoke him to persecute and tyrannize over the innocent and the just.* SOUTH'S SERMONS.

PICTO'RIAL. *adj.* [from *pictor*, Lat.] Produced by a painter. A word not adopted by other writers, but elegant and useful.

Sea horses are but grotesco delineations, which fill up empty spaces in maps, as many pictorial *inventions, not any physical shapes.* BROWN'S VULGAR ERROURS.

To **PIDDLE.** *v.n.* [This word is obscure in its etymology; *Skinner* derives it from *picciolo*, Italian; or *petit*, Fr. little; Mr. *Lye* thinks the diminutive of the Welsh *breyta*, to eat; perhaps it comes from *peddle*, for *Skinner* gives for its primitive signification, to deal in little things.]

1. To pick at table; to feed squeamishly, and without appetite.

From stomach sharp, and hearty feeding,
To piddle *like a lady breeding.*
SWIFT'S MISCELLANIES.

2. To trifle; to attend to small parts rather than to the main. *Ainsworth.*

PI'EPOWDER *court. n.s.* [from *pied*, foot, and *pouldre*, dusty.] A court held in fairs for redress of all disorders committed therein.

PI'GGIN. *n.s.* In the northern provinces, a small vessel.

PI'GMY. *n.s.* [*pigmée*, Fr. *pigmæus*, Lat.] A small nation, fabled to be devoured by the cranes; thence any thing mean or inconsiderable.[171]

When cranes invade, his little sword and shield
The pigmy *takes.* DRYDEN'S JUVENAL.

The criticks of a more exalted taste, may discover such beauties in the antient poetry, as may escape the comprehension of us pigmies *of a more limited genius.* GARTH.

But that it wanted room,
It might have been a pigmy's *tomb.*
SWIFT.

PI'LLION. *n.s.* [from *pillow.*]
1. A soft saddle set behind a horseman for a woman to sit on.

The housse and pillion *both were gone;*
Phyllis, it seems, was fled with John.
SWIFT.

2. A pad; a pannel; a low saddle.

I thought that the manner had been Irish, as also the furniture of his horse, his shank pillion *without stirrups.* SPENSER.

3. The pad of the saddle that touches the horse.

PI'LSER. *n.s.* The moth or fly that runs into a candle flame. *Ainsworth.*

PI'NMONEY. *n.s.* [*pin* and *money.*] Money allowed to a wife for her private expences without account.

The woman must find out something else to mortgage, when her pinmoney *is gone.* ADDISON'S GUARDIAN.

PIO'NEER. *n.s.* [*pionier*, from *pion*, obsolete Fr. *pion*, according to *Scaliger*, comes from *peo* for *pedito*, a foot soldier, who was formerly employed in digging for the army. A *pioneer* is in Dutch, *spagenier*, from *spage*, a spade; whence *Junius* imagines that the French borrowed *pagenier*, which was afterwards called *pioneer.*] One whose business is to level the road, throw up works, or sink mines in military operations.

Well said, old mole, can'st work i' th' ground so fast?
A worthy pioneer?
SHAKESPEARE'S HAMLET.

Three try new experiments, such as themselves think good; these we call pioneers *or miners.* BACON.

His pioneers
Even the paths, and make the highways plain. FAIRFAX.

Of labouring pioneers
A multitude with spades and axes arm'd,
To lay hills plain, fell woods or vallies fill.
MILTON.

The Romans, after the death of Tiberius, sent thither an army of pioneers *to demolish the buildings, and deface the beauties of the island.*
ADDISON'S REMARKS ON ITALY.

PI'PING. *adj.* [from *pipe.* This word is only used in low language.]
1. Weak; feeble; sickly: from the weak voice of the sick.

I, in this weak piping *time of peace,*
Have no delight to pass away the time,
Unless to spy my shadow in the sun.
SHAKESPEARE.

2. Hot; boiling: from the sound of any thing that boils.

PI'PKIN. *n.s.* [diminutive of *pipe*, a large vessel.] A small earthern boiler.

A pipkin *there like Homer's tripod walks.*
POPE.

Some officer might give consent
To a large cover'd pipkin *in his tent.*
KING.

PI'RATE. *n.s.* [πειϱατής; *pirata*, Lat. *pirate*, Fr.]
1. A sea-robber.

Wrangling pirates *that fall out*
In sharing that which you have pill'd from me. SHAKESPEARE.

Pirates *all nations are to prosecute, not so much in the right of their own fears, as upon the band of human society.* BACON.

Relate, if business or the thirst of gain
Engage your journey o'er the pathless main,
Where savage pirates *seek through seas unknown*
The lives of others, vent'rous of their own.
POPE.

2. Any robber; particularly a bookseller who seizes the copies of other men.

PISH. *interj.* A contemptuous exclamation. This is sometimes spoken and written *pshaw.* I know not their etymology, and imagine them formed by chance.

There was never yet philosopher
That could endure the toothach patiently;
However they have writ,
And made a pish *at chance or sufferance.*
SHAKESPEARE.

She frowned and cried pish, *when I said a thing that I stole.*
SPECTATOR, NO. 268.

PI'SSBURNT. *adj.* Stained with urine.

PISTE. *n.s.* [French.] The track or tread a horseman makes upon the ground he goes over.

PI'STON. *n.s.* [*piston*, Fr.] The movable part in several machines; as in pumps and syringes, whereby the suction or attraction is caused; an embolus.

PITAPAT. *n.s.* [probably from *pas a pas*, or *patte patte*, Fr.]

1. A flutter; a palpitation.

A lion meets him, and the fox's heart went pitapat. L'ESTRANGE.

2. A light quick step.

Now I hear the pitapat *of a pretty foot through the dark alley: no, 'tis the son of a mare that's broken loose, and munching upon the melons.*
DRYDEN'S DON SEBASTIAN.

PI'TCHFORK. *n.s.* [*pitch* and *fork.*] A fork with which corn is thrown upon the waggon.

An old lord in Leicestershire amused himself with mending pitchforks *and spades for his tenants gratis.* SWIFT.

PI'TFALL. *n.s.* [*pit* and *fall.*] A pit dug and covered, into which a passenger falls unexpectedly.

Poor bird! thoud'st never fear the net nor lime,
The pitfall *nor the gin.*
SHAKESPEARE'S MACBETH.

Thieves dig concealed pitfalls *in his way.*
SANDYS.

These hidden pitfalls *were set thick at the entrance of the bridge, so that throngs of people fell into them.* ADDISON.

PI'TTANCE. *n.s.* [*pitance*, Fr. *pietantia*, Italian.]

1. An allowance of meat in a monastry.
2. A small portion.

Then at my lodging,
The worst is this, that at so slender warning
You're like to have a thin and slender pittance. SHAKESPEARE.

The ass saved a miserable pittance *for himself.* L'ESTRANGE.

I have a small pittance *left, with which I might retire.* ARBUTHNOT.

Many of them lose the greatest part of the small pittance *of learning they received at the university.* SWIFT'S MISCELLANIES.

PLACA'RD, PLACART. *n.s.* [*plakaert*, Dutch; *placard*, Fr.] An edict; a declaration; a manifesto.

To **PLA'CATE.** *v.a.* [*placeo*, Lat.] To appease; to reconcile. This word is used in Scotland.

That the effect of an atonement and reconciliation was to give all mankind a right to approach and rely on the protection and beneficence of a placated *deity, is not deducible from nature.* FORBES.

PLAGUILY. *adv.* [from *plaguy.*] Vexatiously; horribly. A low word.

This whispering bodes me no good; but he has me so plaguily *under the lash, I dare not interrupt him.* DRYDEN.

You look'd scornful, and snift at the dean;
But he durst not so much as once open his lips,
And the doctor was plaguily *down in the hips.* SWIFT.

PLA'GUY. *adj.* [from *plague.*] Vexatious; troublesome. A low word.

Of heats,
Add one more to the plaguy *bill.*
DONNE.

What perils do environ
The man that meddles with cold iron,
What plaguy *mischiefs and mishaps*
Do dog him still with after-claps.
HUDIBRAS.

PLA'INWORK. *n.s.* [*plain* and *work.*] Needlework as distinguished from embroidery; the common practice of sewing or making linen garments.

She went to plainwork, *and to purling brooks.* POPE.

PLANTA'TION. *n.s.* [*plantatio*, from *planto*, Latin.]

1. The act or practice of planting.
2. The place planted.

As swine are to gardens and orderly plantations, *so are tumults to parliaments.* KING CHARLES.

Some peasants
Of the same soil their nursery prepare,
With that of their plantation; *lest the tree*
Translated should not with the soil agree. DRYDEN.

Whose rising forests, not for pride or show,
But future buildings, future navies grow:
Let his plantations *stretch from down to down,*
First shade a country, and then raise a town. POPE.

Virgil, with great modesty in his looks, was seated by Calliope in the midst of a plantation *of laurel.* ADDISON.

3. A colony.

Planting of countries is like planting of woods; the principal thing, that hath been the destruction of most plantations, *hath been the base and hasty drawing of profit in the first years; speedy profit is not to be neglected, as far as may stand with the good of the* plantation. BACON'S ESSAYS.

4. Introduction; establishment.

Episcopacy must be cast out of this church, after possession here, from the first plantation *of christianity in this island.* KING CHARLES.

PLA'NTER. *n.s.* [*planteur*, Fr. from *plant*.]

1. One who sows, sets or cultivates; cultivator.

There stood Sabinus, planter *of the vines,*
And studiously surveys his gen'rous wines. DRYDEN.

What do thy vines avail,
Or olives, when the cruel battle mows
The planters, *with their harvest immature?* PHILIPS.

That product only which our passions bear,
Eludes the planter's *miserable care.* PRIOR.

2. One who cultivates ground in the West Indian colonies.

A planter *in the West Indies might muster up, and lead all his family out against the Indians, without the absolute dominion of a monarch, descending to him from Adam.* LOCKE.

He to Jamaica seems transported,
Alone, and by no planter *courted.* SWIFT'S MISCELLANIES.

3. One who disseminates or introduces.

Had these writings differed from the sermons of the first planters *of christianity in history or doctrine, they would have been rejected by those churches which they had formed.* ADDISON.

PLA'STER. *n.s.* [*plastre*. Fr. from πλαζω.]

1. Substance made of water and some absorbent matter, such as chalk or lime well pulverised, with which walls are overlaid or figures cast.

In the same hour came forth fingers of a man's hand, and wrote upon the plaster *of the wall.* BIBLE DANIEL, V. 5.

In the worst inn's worst room, with mat half-hung,
The floors of plaster, *and the walls of dung.* POPE.

Maps are hung up so high, to cover the naked plaster *or wainscot.* WATTS'S IMPROVEMENT OF THE MIND.

2. [*Emplastrum*, Lat. in English, formerly *emplaster*.] A glutinous or adhesive salve.

Seeing the sore is whole, why retain we the plaster? HOOKER.

You rub the sore,
When you should bring the plaster.
SHAKESPEARE.

It not only moves the needle in powder, but likewise, if incorporated with plasters, *as we have made trial.* BROWN.

Plasters, *that had any effect, must be by dispersing or repelling the humours.* TEMPLE'S MISCELLANIES.

PLA'STICK. *adj.* [*πλαστικός.*] Having the power to give form.

Benign creator! let thy plastick *hand*
Dispose its own effect. PRIOR.

There is not any thing strange in the production of the said formed metals, nor other plastick *virtue concerned in shaping them into those figures, than merely the configuration of the particles.* WOODWARD'S NATURAL HISTORY.

PLA'YBOOK. *n.s.* [*play* and *book.*] Book of dramatick compositions.

Your's was a match of common good liking, without any mixture of that ridiculous passion, which has no being but in playbooks *and romances.* SWIFT.

PLA'YDAY. *n.s.* [*play* and *day.*] Day exempt from tasks or work.

I thought the life of every lady
Should be one continual playday;
Balls and masquerades and shows.
SWIFT'S MISCELLANIES.

PLA'YDEBT. *n.s.* [*play* and *debt.*] Debt contracted by gaming.

There are multitudes of leases upon single lives, and playdebts *upon joint lives.* ARBUTHNOT.

She has several playdebts *on her hand, which must be discharged very suddenly.* SPECTATOR, NO. 295.

PLA'YGAME. *n.s.* [*play* and *game.*] Play of children.

That liberty alone gives the true relish to their ordinary playgames. LOCKE.

PLA'YPLEASURE. *n.s.* [*play* and *pleasure.*] Idle amusement.

He taketh a kind of playpleasure *in looking upon the fortunes of others.* BACON'S ESSAYS.

PLA'YSOME. *adj.* [*play* and *some.*] Wanton; full of levity.

PLEA'SEMAN. *n.s.* [*please* and *man.*] A pickthank; an officious fellow.

Some carry tale, some pleaseman, *some slight zany,*
That knows the trick to make my lady laugh,
Told our intents.
SHAKESPEARE'S LOVE'S LABOUR'S LOST.

PLE'NIST. *n.s.* [from *plenus*, Lat.] One that holds all space to be full of matter.

Those spaces, which the vacuists would have empty, because devoid of air, the plenists *do not prove replenished with subtle matter by any sensible effects.* BOYLE.

PLE'THORA. *n.s.* [from *πλήθωρα.*] The state in which the vessels are fuller of humours than is agreeable to a natural state or health; arises either from a diminution of some natural evacuations, or from debauch and feeding higher or more in quantity than the ordinary powers of the viscera can digest: evacuations and exercise are its remedies.

The diseases of the fluids are a plethora, *or too great abundance of laudable juices.* ARBUTHNOT ON ALIMENTS.

PLI'CATURE, PLICATION. *n.s.* [*plicatura*, from *plico*, Lat.] Fold; double. *Plication* is used somewhere in *Clarissa.*

PLOU'GHBOY. *n.s.* [*plough* and *boy*.] A boy that follows the plough; a coarse ignorant boy.

> A ploughboy, *that has never seen any thing but thatched houses and his parish church, imagines that thatch belongs to the very nature of a house.* WATTS'S LOGICK.

PLUMP. *n.s.* [from the adjective.] A knot; a tuft; a cluster; a number joined in one mass.[172]

> *England, Scotland, Ireland lie all in a* plump *together, not accessible but by sea.* BACON.

> *Warwick having espied certain* plumps *of Scottish horsemen ranging the field, returned towards the arriere to prevent danger.* HAYWARD.

> *We rested under a* plump *of trees.* SANDYS.

> *Spread upon a lake, with upward eye*
> *A* plump *of fowl behold their foe on high;*
> *They close their trembling troop, and all attend*
> *On whom the sowsing eagle will descend.*
> DRYDEN.

PLU'MPER. *n.s.* [from *plump*.] Something worn in the mouth to swell out the cheeks.

> *She dext'rously her* plumpers *draws,*
> *That serve to fill her hollow jaws.*
> SWIFT'S MISCELLANIES.

PLU'RALIST. *n.s.* [*pluraliste*, Fr. from *plural*.] One that holds more ecclesiastical benefices than one with cure of souls.

> *If the* pluralists *would do their best to suppress curates, their number might be so retrenched, that they would not be in the least formidable.* COLLIER ON PRIDE.

PO'CKETBOOK. *n.s.* [*pocket* and *book*.] A paper book carried in the pocket for hasty notes.

> *Licinius let out the offals of his meat to interest, and kept a register of such debtors in his* pocketbook. ARBUTHNOT.

> *Note down the matters of doubt in some* pocketbook, *and take the first opportunity to get them resolved.* WATTS.

PO'CKETGLASS. *n.s.* [*pocket* and *glass*.] Portable looking-glass.

> *Powders and* pocketglass, *and beans.* PRIOR.

> *And vanity with* pocketglass,
> *And impudence with front of brass.*
> SWIFT'S MISCELLANIES.

PO'CKHOLE. *n.s.* [*pock* and *hole*.] Pit or scar made by the smallpox.

> *Are these but warts and* pockholes *in the face*
> *O' th' earth?* DONNE.

POCU'LENT. *adj.* [*poculum*, Lat.] Fit for drink.

> *Some of these herbs, which are not esculent, are notwithstanding* poculent; *as hops and broom.* BACON.

POI'GNANT. *adj.* [*poignant*, Fr.]

1. Sharp; stimulating the palate.

> *No* poignant *sauce she knew, nor costly treat,*
> *Her hunger gave a relish to her meat.*
> DRYDEN.

> *The studious man, whose will was never determined to* poignant *sauces and delicious wine, is, by hunger and thirst, determined to eating and drinking.* LOCKE.

2. Severe; piercing; painful.

> *If God makes use of some* poignant *disgrace to let out the poisonous vapour, is not the mercy greater than the severity of the cure?* SOUTH'S SERMONS.

> *Full three long hours his tender body did sustain*
> *Most exquisite and* poignant *pain.*
> NORRIS'S MISCELLANY.

3. Irritating; satirical; keen.

PO'LICE. *n.s.* [French.] The regulation and government of a city or country, so far as regards the inhabitants.

PO'LICED. *adj.* [from *police.*] Regulated; formed into a regular course of administration.

Where there is a kingdom altogether unable or indign to govern, it is a just cause of war for another nation, that is civil or policed, *to subdue them.* BACON'S HOLY WAR.

POLI'TE. *adj.* [*politus*, Latin.]

1. Glossy; smooth.

Some of them are diaphanous, shining and polite; *others not* polite, *but as if powder'd over with fine iron dust.* WOODWARD.

If any sort of rays, falling on the polite *surface of any pellucid medium, be reflected back, the fits of easy reflexion, which they have at the point of reflexion, shall still continue to return.*
NEWTON'S OPTICKS.

The edges of the sand holes, being worn away, there are left all over the glass a numberless company of very little convex polite *risings like waves.*
NEWTON'S OPTICKS.

2. Elegant of manners.

A nymph of quality admires our knight,
He marries, bows at court, and grows
polite. POPE.

POLI'TENESS. *n.s.* [*politesse*, Fr. from *polite.*] Elegance of manners; gentility; good breeding.

I have seen the dullest men aiming at wit, and others, with as little pretensions, affecting politeness *in manners and discourse.* SWIFT.

PO'LTRON. *n.s.* [*pollice truncato*, from the thumb cut off; it being once a practice of cowards to cut off their thumbs, that they might not be compelled to serve in war. *Saumaise. Menage* derives it from the Italian *poltro*, a bed; as cowards feign themselves sick a bed: others derive it from *poletro* or *poltro*, a young unbroken horse.] A coward; a nidgit; a scoundrel.

Patience is for poltrons. SHAKESPEARE.

They that are bruis'd with wood or fists,
And think one beating may for once
Suffice, are cowards and poltrons.
HUDIBRAS, P. II.

For who but a poltron *possess'd with fear,*
Such haughty insolence can tamely bear.
DRYDEN.

PO'LY. [*πολύ.*] A prefix often found in the composition of words derived from the Greek, and intimating multitude: as, *polygon*, a figure of many angles; *polypus*, an animal with many feet.

PONK. *n.s.* [Of this word I know not the original.] A nocturnal spirit; a hag.

Ne let the ponk, *nor other evil sprights,*
Ne let mischievous witches. SPENSER.

PO'NTAGE. *n.s.* [*pons, pontis*, bridge.] Duty paid for the reparation of bridges.

In right of the church, they were formerly by the common law discharged from pontage *and murage.* AYLIFFE.

POO'RNESS. *n.s.* [from *poor.*]

1. Poverty; indigence; want.

If a prince should complain of the poorness *of his exchequer, would he be angry with his merchants, if they brought him a cargo of good bullion.*
BURNET'S THEORY OF THE EARTH.

2. Meanness; lowness; want of dignity.

The Italian opera seldom sinks into a poorness *of language, but, amidst all the meanness of the thoughts, has something beautiful and sonorous in the expression.*
ADDISON.

There is a kind of sluggish resignation, as well as poorness *and degeneracy of spirit, in a state of slavery.* ADDISON.

3. Sterility; barrenness.

The poorness *of the herbs shews the* poorness *of the earth, especially if in colour more dark.* BACON.

Enquire the differences of metals which contain other metals, and how that agrees with the poorness *or riches of the metals in themselves.* BACON.

POP. *n.s.* [*poppysma*, Lat.] A small smart quick sound. It is formed from the sound.

I have several ladies, who could not give a pop *loud enough to be heard at the farther end of the room, who can now discharge a fan, that it shall make a report like a pocket-pistol.*
ADDISON'S SPECTATOR, NO. 102.

PORCH. *n.s.* [*porche*, Fr. *porticus*, Lat.]
1. A roof supported by pillars before a door; an entrance.

Ehud went forth through the porch, *and shut the doors of the parlour.*
BIBLE JUDGES, III. 23.

Not infants in the porch *of life were free,*
The sick, the old, that could but hope a day
Longer by nature's bounty, not let stay.
BEN JONSON.

2. A portico; a covered walk.

All this done,
Repair to Pompey's porch, *where you shall find us.* SHAKESPEARE.

PO'RKLING. *n.s.* [from *pork.*] A young pig.

A hovel
Will serve thee in winter, moreover than that,
To shut up thy porklings, *thou meanest to fat.* TUSSER.

PO'RRIDGE. *n.s.* [more properly *porrage*; *porrata*, low Latin, from *porrum*, a leek.] Food made by boiling meat in water; broth.

I had as lief you should tell me of a mess of porridge. SHAKESPEARE.

PO'RTER. *n.s.* [*portier*, Fr. from *porta*, Lat. a gate.]
1. One that has the charge of the gate.

Porter, *remember what I give in charge,*
And, when you've so done, bring the keys to me. SHAKESPEARE.

Arm all my houshold presently, and charge
The porter *he let no man in till day.*
BEN JONSON.

Nic. Frog demanded to be his porter, *and his fishmonger, to keep the keys of his gates, and furnish the kitchen.* ARBUTHNOT.

2. One who waits at the door to receive messages.

A fav'rite porter *with his master vie,*
Be brib'd as often, and as often lie. POPE.

3. [*Porteur*, Fr. from *porto*, Lat. to carry.] One who carries burthens for hire.

It is with kings sometimes as with porters, *whose packs may jostle one against the other, yet remain good friends still.*
HOWEL.

By porter, *who can tell, whether I mean a man who bears burthens, or a servant who waits at a gate?* WATTS.

PO'RTRESS. *n.s.* [from *porter.*] A female guardian of a gate. *Janitrix.*

The portress *of hell-gate reply'd.*
MILTON'S PARADISE LOST.

The shoes put on, our faithful portress
Admits us in to storm the fortress;
While like a cat with walnuts shod,
Stumbling at ev'ry step she trod.
SWIFT'S MISCELLANIES.

PO'SER. *n.s.* [from *pose.*] One that asketh questions to try capacities; an examiner.

He that questioneth much, shall learn much; but let his questions not be troublesome, for that is fit for a poser. BACON.

PO'SITURE. *n.s.* [*positura*, Lat.] The manner in which any thing is placed.

Supposing the positure *of the party's hand who did throw the dice, and supposing all other things, which did concur to the production of that cast, to be the very same they were, there is no doubt but in this case the cast is necessary.* BRAMHALL.

PO'SSE. *n.s.* [Latin.] An armed power; from *posse comitatus*, the power of the shires. A low word.

The posse *comitatus, the power of the whole county, is legally committed unto him.* BACON.

As if the passion that rules, were the sheriff of the place, and came with all the posse, *the understanding is seized.* LOCKE.

POSSE'SSOUR. *n.s.* [*possessor*, Lat. *possesseur*, Fr.] Owner; master; proprietor.

Thou profoundest hell
Receive thy new possessor. MILTON.

A considerable difference lies between the honour of men for natural and acquired excellencies and divine graces, that those having more of human nature in them, the honour doth more directly redound to the possessor *of them.* STILLINGFLEET.

'Twas the interest of those, who thirsted after the possessions of the clergy, to represent the possessors *in as vile colours as they could.* ATTERBURY'S SERMONS.

PO'STAGE. *n.s.* [from *post.*] Money paid for conveyance of a letter.

Fifty pounds for the postage *of a letter! to send by the church, is the dearest road in Christendom.* DRYDEN.

POSTBOY. *n.s.* [*post* and *boy.*] Courier; boy that rides post.

This genius came thither in the shape of a postboy, *and cried out, that Mons was relieved.* TATLER.

POSTE'RIORITY. *n.s.* [*posteriorité*, Fr. from *posterior.*] The state of being after; opposite to *priority.*

Although the condition of sex and posteriority *of creation might extenuate the error of a woman, yet it was unexcusable in the man.* BROWN'S VULGAR ERROURS.

There must be a posteriority *in time of every compounded body, to these more simple bodies out of which it is constituted.* HALE'S ORIGIN OF MANKIND.

POSTHA'CKNEY. *n.s.* [*post* and *hackney.*] Hired posthorses.

Espying the French ambassador with the king's coach attending him, made them balk the beaten road and teach posthackneys *to leap hedges.* WOTTON.

PO'STHOUSE. *n.s.* [*post* and *house.*] Post office; house where letters are taken and dispatched.

An officer at the posthouse *in London places every letter he takes in, in the box belonging to the proper road.* WATTS.

PO'STIL. *n.s.* [*postille*, Fr. *postilla*, Lat.] Gloss; marginal notes.

To **PO'STIL.** *v.a.* [from the noun.] To gloss; to illustrate with marginal notes.

I have seen a book of account of Empson's, that had the king's hand almost to every leaf by way of signing, and was in some places postilled *in the margin with the king's hand.* BACON'S HENRY VII.

POSTI'LLER. *n.s.* [from *postil.*] One who glosses or illustrates with marginal notes.

It hath been observed by many holy writers, commonly delivered by postillers *and commentators.* BROWN.

Hence you phantastick postillers *in song,*
My text defeats your art, ties nature's tongue. CLEAVELAND.

POSTI'LION. *n.s.* [*postillon*, French.]

1. One who guides the first pair of a set of six horses in a coach.

A young batchelor of arts came to town recommended to a chaplain's place; but none being vacant, modestly accepted of that of a postilion. TATLER, NO. 52.

2. One who guides a post chaise.

POSTLIMI'NIOUS. *adj.* [*postliminium*, Lat.] Done or contrived subsequently.

The reason why men are so short and weak in governing, is, because most things fall out to them accidentally, and come not into any compliance with their pre-conceiv'd ends, but are forced to comply subsequently, and to strike in with things as they fall out, by postliminious *after-applications of them to their purposes.* SOUTH'S SERMONS.

PO'STOFFICE. *n.s.* [*post* and *office*.] Office where letters are delivered to the post; a posthouse.

If you don't send to me now and then, the postoffice *will think me of no consequence; for I have no correspondent but you.* GAY TO SWIFT.

If you are sent to the postoffice *with a letter, put it in carefully.* SWIFT.

PO'STURE. *n.s.* [*posture*, Fr. *positura*, Latin.]

1. Place; situation.

Although these studies are not so pleasing as contemplations physical or mathematical, yet they recompense with the excellency of their use in relation to man, and his noblest posture *and station in this world, a state of regulated society.* HALE.

According to the posture *of our affairs in the last campaign, this prince could have turned the balance on either side.* ADDISON.

2. Voluntary collocation of the parts of the body with respect to each other.

He starts,
Then lays his finger on his temple; strait
Springs out into fast gait; then stops again,
Strikes his breast hard, and then anon he casts
His eyes against the moon, in most strange postures. SHAKESPEARE.

Where there are affections of reverence, there will be postures *of reverence.* SOUTH'S SERMONS.

The posture *of a poetick figure is the description of his heroes in the performance of such or such an action.* DRYDEN.

In the meanest marble statue, one sees the faces, postures, *airs and dress of those that lived so many ages before us.* ADDISON.

3. State; disposition.

The lord Hopton left Arundel-castle, before he had put it into the good posture *he intended.* CLARENDON, B. VIII.

I am at the same point and posture *I was, when they forced me to leave Whitehall.* KING CHARLES.

In this abject posture *have ye sworn*
T' adore the conqueror. MILTON.

The several postures *of his devout soul in all conditions of life, are displayed with great simplicity.* ATTERBURY.

To **PO'STURE.** *v.a.* [from the noun.] To put in any particular place or disposition.

The gillfins are so postured, *as to move from back to belly and e contra.* GREW.

POSTUREMA'STER. *n.s.* [*posture* and *master*.] One who teaches or practises artificial contortions of the body.

When the students have accomplished themselves in this part, they are to be delivered into the hands of a kind of posturemaster. SPECTATOR, NO. 305.

POTA'RGO. *n.s.* A West Indian pickle.

What lord of old would bid his cook prepare

Mangos, potargo, *champignons, cavarre.* KING.

PO'TCOMPANION. *n.s.* A fellow drinker; a good fellow at carousals.

PO'TGUN. *n.s.* [by mistake or corruption used for *popgun.*] A gun which makes a small smart noise.

An author, thus who pants for fame,
Begins the world with fear and shame,
When first in print, you see him dread
Each potgun *levell'd at his head.*
SWIFT'S MISCELLANIES.

PO'THERB. *n.s.* [*pot* and *herb.*] An herb fit for the pot.

Sir Tristram telling us tobacco was a potherb, *bid the drawer bring in t'other halfpint.* TATLER, NO. 57.

Egypt baser than the beasts they worship;
Below their potherb *gods that grow in gardens.* DRYDEN.

Of alimentary leaves, the olera or potherbs *afford an excellent nourishment; amongst those are the cole or cabbage kind.* ARBUTHNOT.

Leaves eaten raw are termed sallad; if boiled, they become potherbs*: and some of those plants, which are* potherbs *in one family, are sallad in another.* WATTS.

PO'TLID. *n.s.* [*pot* and *lid.*] The cover of a pot.

The columella is a fine, thin, light, bony tube; the bottom of which spreads about, and gives it the resemblance of a wooden potlid *in country houses.* DERHAM.

PO'TTAGE. *n.s.* [*potage,* Fr. from *pot.*] Any thing boiled or decocted for food. See **PORRIDGE**.

Jacob sod pottage, *and Esau came from the field faint.* BIBLE GENESIS.

POTVA'LIANT. *adj.* [*pot* and *valiant.*] Heated with courage by strong drink.

POU'NDAGE. *n.s.* [from *pound.*]

1. A certain sum deducted from a pound; a sum paid by the trader to the servant that pays the money, or to the person who procures him customers.

In poundage *and drawbacks I lose half my rent.* SWIFT.

2. Payment rated by the weight of the commodity.

Tonnage and poundage, *and other duties upon merchandizes, were collected by order of the board.* CLARENDON.

POU'NDER. *n.s.* [from *pound.*]

1. The name of a heavy large pear.

Alcinous' orchard various apples bears,
Unlike are bergamots and pounder *pears.*
DRYDEN.

2. Any person or thing denominated from a certain number of pounds: as, *a ten pounder*; a gun that carries a bullet of ten *pounds* weight; or in ludicrous language a man with ten *pounds* a year; in like manner, a note or bill is called a twenty *pounder* or ten *pounder*, from the sum it bears.

None of these forty or fifty pounders *may be suffered to marry, under the penalty of deprivation.* SWIFT.

3. A pestle. *Ainsworth.*

PO'WDER. *n.s.* [*poudre,* Fr.]

1. Dust; any body comminuted.

The calf which they had made, he burnt in the fire, and ground it to powder.
BIBLE EXODUS, XXXII. 20.

2. Gunpowder.

The seditious being furnished with artillery, powder *and shot, battered Bishopsgate.* HAYWARD.

As to the taking of a town, there were few conquerors could signalize themselves that way, before the invention of powder *and fortifications.* ADDISON.

3. Sweet dust for the hair.

When th' hair is sweet through pride or lust,
The powder *doth forget the dust.*
HERBERT.

Our humbler province is to tend the fair,
To save the powder *from too rude a gale.*
POPE.

PO'WDERBOX. *n.s.* [*powder* and *box.*] A box in which powder for the hair is kept.

There stands the toillette,
The patch, the powderbox, *pulville, perfumes.* GAY.

PO'WDERHORN. *n.s.* [*powder* and *horn.*] A horn case in which powder is kept for guns.

You may stick your candle in a bottle or a powderhorn. SWIFT.

PO'WDERMILL. *n.s.* [*powder* and *mill.*] The mill in which the ingredients for gunpowder are ground and mingled.

Upon the blowing up of a powdermill, *the windows of adjacent houses are bent and blown outwards, by the elastick force of the air within exerting itself.* ARBUTHNOT.

POWDERING-TUB. *n.s.* [*powder* and *tub.*]

1. The vessel in which meat is salted.

When we view those large bodies of oxen, what can we better conceit them to be, than so many living and walking powdering-tubs, *and that they have animam salis.* MORE.

2. The place in which an infected lecher is physicked to preserve him from putrefaction.

To the spital go,
And from the powd'ring-tub *of infamy*
Fetch forth the lazar kite Doll Tearsheet.
SHAKESPEARE.

POX. *n.s.* [properly *pocks*, which originally signified a small bag or pustule; of the same original, perhaps, with *powke* or *pouch*. We still use *pock*, for a single pustule; *poccas*, Sax. *pocken*, Dutch.]

1. Pustules; efflorescencies; exanthematous eruptions.

2. The venereal disease. This is the sense when it has no epithet.

Though brought to their ends by some other apparent disease, yet the pox *hath been judged the foundation.* WISEMAN.

Wilt thou still sparkle in the box,
Still ogle in the ring?
Can'st thou forget thy age and pox.
DORSET.

PRA'VITY. *n.s.* [*pravitas*, Lat.] Corruption; badness; malignity.

Doubt not but that sin
Will reign among them, as of thee begot;
And therefore was law given them, to evince
Their natural pravity.
MILTON'S PARADISE LOST, B. XII.

More people go to the gibbet for want of timely correction, than upon any incurable pravity *of nature.* L'ESTRANGE.

I will shew how the pravity *of the will could influence the understanding to a disbelief of Christianity.* SOUTH.

PREA'CHMENT. *n.s.* [from *preach.*] A sermon mentioned in contempt; a discourse affectedly solemn.

Was't you, that revell'd in our parliament,
And made a preachment *of your high descent.* SHAKESPEARE.

All this is but a preachment *upon the text at last.* L'ESTRANGE.

PRECA'RIOUS. *adj.* [*precarius*, Lat. *precaire*, Fr.] Dependent; uncertain, because depending on the will of another; held by courtesy; changeable or alienable at the pleasure of another. No word is more unskilfully used than this with its derivatives. It is used for *uncertain* in all its senses; but it only means *uncertain*, as dependent on others: thus there are authors who mention the *precariousness* of an *account*, of the *weather*, of a *die*.

What subjects will precarious *kings regard,*
A beggar speaks too softly to be heard. DRYDEN.

Those who live under an arbitrary tyrannick power, have no other law but the will of their prince, and consequently no privileges but what are precarious. ADDISON.

This little happiness is so very precarious, *that it wholly depends on the will of others.* ADDISON'S SPECTATOR.

He who rejoices in the strength and beauty of youth, should consider by how precarious *a tenure he holds these advantages, that a thousand accidents may before the next dawn lay all these glories in the dust.* ROGERS'S SERMONS.

PRECA'RIOUSNESS. *n.s.* [from *precarious.*] Uncertainty; dependence on others. The following passage from a book, otherwise elegantly written, affords an example of the impropriety mentioned at the word *precarious.*

Most consumptive people die of the discharge they spit up, which, with the precariousness *of the symptoms of an oppressed diaphragm from a mere lodgement of extravasated matter, render the operation but little adviseable.* SHARP'S SURGERY.

PRECI'NCT. *n.s.* [*præcinctus*, Latin.] Outward limit; boundary.

The main body of the sea being one, yet within divers precincts, *hath divers names; so the catholick church is in like sort divided into a number of distinct societies.* HOOKER.

Through all restraint broke loose, he wings his way
Not far off heav'n, in the precincts *of light,*
Directly towards the new-created world. MILTON.

PRECO'CIOUS. *adj.* [*præcocis*, Lat. *precose*, Fr.] Ripe before the time.

Many precocious *trees, and such as have their spring in the winter, may be found in most parts.* BROWN.

PRECONCEI'T. *n.s.* [*præ* and *conceit.*] An opinion previously formed.

A thing in reason impossible, which notwithstanding through their misfashioned preconceit, *appeared unto them no less certain than if nature had written it in the very foreheads of all the creatures.* HOOKER.

To **PRECONCEI'VE.** *v.a.* [*præ* and *conceive.*] To form an opinion beforehand; to imagine beforehand.

In a dead plain the way seemeth the longer, because the eye hath preconceived *it shorter than the truth; and the frustrations of that maketh it seem so.* BACON.

Fondness of preconceived *opinions is not like to render your reports suspect, nor for want of sagacity or care, defective.* GLANVILL'S SCEPSIS SCIENTIFICA.

The reason why men are so weak in governing is, because most things fall out accidentally, and come not into any compliance with their preconceived *ends, but they are forced to comply subsequently.* SOUTH'S SERMONS.

PRECONCE'PTION. *n.s.* [*præ* and *conception.*] Opinion previously formed.

Custom with most men prevails more than truth, according to the notions and preconceptions, *which it hath formed in our minds, we shape the discourse of reason itself.* HAKEWILL.

PREDIGE'STION. *n.s.* [*præ* and *digestion.*] Digestion too soon performed.

Predigestion, *or hasty digestion, fills the*

body full of crudities and seeds of diseases. BACON'S ESSAYS.

PRE'FACE. *n.s.* [*preface*, Fr. *præfatio*, Lat.] Something spoken introductory to the main design; introduction; something proemial.

This superficial tale
Is but a preface *to her worthy praise.*
SHAKESPEARE.

Sir Thomas More betrayed his depth of judgment in state affairs in his Utopia, than which, in the opinion of Budæus in a preface *before it, our age hath not seen a thing more deep.*
PEACHAM OF POETRY.

Heav'n's high behest no preface *needs;*
Sufficient that thy pray'rs are heard, and death
Defeated of his seizure.
MILTON'S PARADISE LOST, B. XI.

To **PRE'FACE.** *v.n.* [*prefari*, Lat.] To say something introductory.

Before I enter upon the particular parts of her character, it is necessary to preface, *that she is the only child of a decrepid father.* SPECTATOR, NO. 449.

To **PRE'FACE.** *v.a.*

1. To introduce by something proemial.

Thou art rash,
And must be prefac'd *into government.*
SOUTHERN.

2. To face; to cover. A ludicrous sense.

I love to wear cloaths that are flush,
Not prefacing *old rags with plush.*
CLEAVELAND.

PRE'FACER. *n.s.* [from *preface.*] The writer of a preface.

If there be not a tolerable line in all these six, the prefacer *gave me no occasion to write better.* DRYDEN.

PREFI'X. *n.s.* [*præfixum*, Lat.] Some particle put before a word, to vary its signification.

In the Hebrew language the noun has its prefixa *and affixa, the former to signify some few relations, and the latter to denote the pronouns possessive and relative.*
CLARKE.

It is a prefix *of augmentation to many words in that language.*
BROWN'S VULGAR ERROURS.

PREGUSTA'TION. *n.s.* [*præ* and *gusto*, Lat.] The act of tasting before another.

PRE'JUDICE. *n.s.* [*prejudice*, Fr. *prejudicium*, Lat.]

1. Prepossession; judgment formed beforehand without examination. It is used for prepossession in favour of any thing or against it. It is sometimes used with *to* before that which the *prejudice* is against, but not properly.

The king himself frequently considered more the person who spoke, as he was in his prejudice, *than the counsel itself that was given.* CLARENDON, B. VIII.

My comfort is, that their manifest prejudice *to my cause will render their judgment of less authority.* DRYDEN.

There is an unaccountable prejudice *to projectors of all kinds, for which reason, when I talk of practising to fly, silly people think me an owl for my pains.*
ADDISON.

2. Mischief; detriment; hurt; injury. This sense is only accidental or consequential; *a bad thing* being called *a prejudice*, only because *prejudice* is commonly *a bad thing*, and is not derived from the original or etymology of the word: it were therefore better to use it less; perhaps *prejudice* ought never to be applied to any mischief, which does not imply some partiality or prepossession. In some of the following examples its impropriety will be discovered.

I have not spake one the least word,

That might be prejudice *of her present state,*
Or touch of her good person.
SHAKESPEARE'S HENRY VIII.

England and France might, through their amity,
Breed him some prejudice; *for from this league*
Peep'd harms that menac'd him.
SHAKESPEARE'S HENRY VIII.

Factions carried too high and too violently, is a sign of weakness in princes, and much to the prejudice *of their authority and business.* BACON.

How plain this abuse is, and what prejudice *it does to the understanding of the sacred scriptures.* LOCKE.

A prince of this character will instruct us by his example, to fix the unsteadiness of our politicks; or by his conduct hinder it from doing us any prejudice. ADDISON.

To **PREJUDI'CE.** *v.a.* [from the noun.]

1. To prepossess with unexamined opinions; to fill with prejudices.

Half-pillars wanted their expected height,
And roofs imperfect prejudic'd *the sight.*
PRIOR.

Suffer not any beloved study to prejudice *your mind, so far as to despise all other learning.* WATTS.

No snares to captivate the mind he spreads,
Nor bribes your eyes to prejudice *your heads.* ANONYMOUS.

2. To obstruct or injure by prejudices previously raised.

Companies of learned men, be they never so great and reverend, are to yield unto reason; the weight whereof is no whit prejudiced *by the simplicity of his person, which doth alledge it.* HOOKER, B. II. S. 7.

Neither must his example, done without the book, prejudice *that which is well appointed in the book.* WHITGIFTE.

I am not to prejudice *the cause of my fellow-poets, though I abandon my own defence.* DRYDEN.

3. To injure; to hurt; to diminish; to impair; to be detrimental to. This sense, as in the noun, is often improperly extended to meanings that have no relation to the original sense; who can read with patience of an ingredient that *prejudices* a medicine?

The strength of that law is such, that no particular nation can lawfully prejudice *the same by any their several laws and ordinances, more than a man by his private resolutions, the law of the whole commonwealth wherein he liveth.* HOOKER.

The Danube rescu'd, and the empire sav'd,
Say, is the majesty of verse retriev'd?
And would it prejudice *thy softer vein,*
To sing the princes, Louis and Eugene?
PRIOR.

To this is added a vinous bitter, warmer in the composition of its ingredients than the watry infusion; and, as gentian and lemon-peel make a bitter of so grateful a flavour, the only care required in this composition was to chuse such an addition as might not prejudice *it.* LONDON DISPENSATORY.

PRELU'DE. *n.s.* [*prelude*, Fr. *prælu-dium*, Lat.]

1. Some short flight of musick played before a full concert.

2. Something introductory; something that only shews what is to follow.

To his infant arms oppose
His father's rebels and his brother's foes;
Those were the preludes *of his fate,*
That form'd his manhood, to subdue
The hydra of the many-headed hissing crew. DRYDEN.

The last Georgick was a good prelude *to the Æneis, and very well shewed what the poet could do in the description of what was really great.* ADDISON.

One concession to a man is but a prelude *to another.* CLARISSA.

PRELU'DIOUS. *adj.* [from *prelude.*] Previous; introductory.

That's but a preludious *bliss,*
Two souls pickeering in a kiss.
CLEAVELAND.

PRE'MISES. *n.s.* [*præmissa*, Lat. *premisses*, Fr]

1. Propositions antecedently supposed or proved.

They infer upon the premises, *that as great difference as commodiously may be, there should be in all outward ceremonies between the people of God, and them which are not his people.*
HOOKER, B. IV. S. 7.

This is so regular an inference, that whilst the premises *stand firm, it is impossible to shake the conclusion.* DECAY OF PIETY.

She study'd well the point, and found
Her foes conclusions were not sound,
From premises *erroneous brought,*
And therefore the deduction's nought.
SWIFT'S MISCELLANIES.

2. In low language, houses or lands: as, *I was upon the* premisses.

PRE'MIUM. *n.s.* [*præmium*, Lat.] Something given to invite a loan or a bargain.

No body cares to make loans upon a new project; whereas men never fail to bring in their money upon a land-tax, when the premium *or interest allowed them is suited to the hazard they run.*
ADDISON'S FREEHOLDER, NO. 23.

People were tempted to lend, by great premiums *and large interest; and it concerned them to preserve that government, which they had trusted with their money.* SWIFT'S MISCELLANIES.

To **PREMO'NISH.** *v.a.* [*præmoneo*, Lat.] To warn or admonish beforehand.

PREMO'NISHMENT. *n.s.* [from *premonish.*] Previous information.

After these premonishments, *I will come to the compartition itself.*
WOTTON'S ARCHITECTURE.

PREMONI'TION. *n.s.* [from *premonish.*] Previous notice; previous intelligence.

What friendly premonitions *have been spent*
On your forbearance, and their vain event. CHAPMAN.

How great the force of such an erroneous persuasion is, we may collect from our Saviour's premonition *to his disciples, when he tells them, that those who killed them should think they did God service.*
DECAY OF PIETY.

PREPARA'TION. *n.s.* [*preparatio*, Lat. *preparation*, Fr. from *prepare.*]

1. The act of preparing or previously fitting any thing to any purpose.

Nothing hath proved more fatal to that due preparation *for another life, than our unhappy mistake of the nature and end of this.*
WAKE'S PREPARATION FOR DEATH.

2. Previous measures.

I will shew what preparations *there were in nature for this great dissolution, and after what manner it came to pass.*
BURNET'S THEORY OF THE EARTH.

3. Ceremonious introduction.

I make bold to press, with so little preparation, *upon you. —— You're welcome.*
SHAKESPEARE'S MERRY WIVES OF WINDSOR.

4. The act of making or fitting by a regular process.

In the preparations *of cookery, the most volatile parts of vegetables are destroyed.*
ARBUTHNOT ON ALIMENTS.

5. Any thing made by process of operation.

I wish the chymists had been more sparing, who magnify their preparations, *inveigle the curiosity of many, and delude the security of most.*
BROWN'S VULGAR ERROURS.

6. Accomplishment; qualification. Out of use.

Sir John, you are a gentleman of excellent breeding, authentick in your place and person, generally allowed for your many warlike, courtlike and learned preparations. SHAKESPEARE.

PREPOSI'TION. *n.s.* [*præposition*, Fr. *præpositio*, Lat.] In grammar, a particle governing a case.

A preposition *signifies some relation, which the thing signified by the word following it, has to something going before in the discourse; as, Cesar came to Rome.*
CLARKE'S LATIN GRAMMAR.

PREPO'SITOR. *n.s.* [*præpositor*, Lat.] A scholar appointed by the master to overlook the rest.

PRESBYTE'RIAN. *adj.* [*πρεσβύτερος*.] Consisting of elders; a term for a modern form of ecclesiastical government.

Chiefly was urged the abolition of episcopal, and the establishing of presbyterian *government.* KING CHARLES.

PRE'SIDENT. *n.s.* [*præsidens*, Lat. *president*, Fr.]

1. One placed with authority over others; one at the head of others.

As the president *of my kingdom, will I*
Appear there for a man.
SHAKESPEARE'S ANTONY AND CLEOPATRA.

The tutor sits in the chair as president *or moderator, to see that the rules of disputation be observed.* WATTS.

2. Governour; prefect.

How might those captive Israelites, under the oversight and government of Assyrian presidents, *be able to leave the places they were to inhabit.*
BREREWOOD ON LANGUAGES.

3. A tutelary power.

This last complaint th' indulgent ears did pierce
Of just Apollo, president *of verse.* WALLER.

PRE'SIDENTSHIP. *n.s.* [from *president*.] The office and place of president.

When things came to trial of practice, their pastors learning would be at all times of force to overpersuade simple men, who, knowing the time of their own presidentship *to be but short, would always stand in fear of their ministers perpetual authority.* HOOKER'S PREFACE.

PRE'SSGANG. *n.s.* [*press* and *gang*.] A crew that strolls about the streets to force men into naval service.

PRE'STO. *n.s.* [*presto*, Italian.] Quick; at once. A word used by those that show legerdemain.

Presto*! begone! 'tis here again;*
There's ev'ry piece as big as ten. SWIFT.

PRETERLA'PSED. *adj.* [*præterlapsus*, Lat.] Past and gone.

We look with a superstitious reverence upon the accounts of preterlapsed *ages.*
GLANVILL'S SCEPSIS SCIENTIFICA.

Never was there so much of either, in any preterlapsed *age, as in this.* WALKER.

PRE'TERPERFECT. *adj.* [*præteritum perfectum*, Lat.] A grammatical term applied to the tense which denotes time absolutely past.

The same natural aversion to loquacity has of late made a considerable alteration in our language, by closing in one syllable the termination of our preterperfect *tense, as drown'd, walk'd, for drowned, walked.*
ADDISON'S SPECTATOR.

PRE'TERPLUPERFECT. *adj.* [*præteritum plusquam perfectum*, Lat.]

The grammatical epithet for the tense denoting time relatively past, or past before some other past time.

PRETTY. *adj.* [*præt*, finery, Sax. *pretto*, Italian; *prat*, *prattigh*, Dutch.]

1. Neat; elegant; pleasing without surprise or elevation.

Of these the idle Greeks have many pretty *tales.* RALEIGH.

They found themselves involved in a train of mistakes, by taking up some pretty *hypothesis in philosophy.* WATTS.

2. Beautiful without grandeur or dignity.

The pretty *gentleman is the most complaisant creature in the world, and is always of my mind.* SPECTATOR.

3. It is used in a kind of diminutive contempt in poetry, and in conversation: as, *a* pretty *fellow indeed!*

A pretty *task; and so I told the fool,*
Who needs must undertake to please by rule. DRYDEN.

He'll make a pretty *figure in a triumph,*
And serve to trip before the victor's chariot. ADDISON.

4. Not very small. This is a very vulgar use.

A knight of Wales, with shipping and some pretty *company, did go to discover those parts.* ABBOT.

Cut off the stalks of cucumbers, immediately after their bearing, close by the earth, and then cast a pretty *quantity of earth upon the plant, and they will bear next year before the ordinary time.* BACON'S NATURAL HISTORY.

I would have a mount of some pretty *height, leaving the wall of the enclosure breast high.* BACON'S ESSAYS.

Of this mixture we put a parcel into a crucible, and suffered it for a pretty *while to continue red hot.* BOYLE.

A weazle a pretty *way off stood leering at him.* L'ESTRANGE.

PRE'TTY. *adv.* In some degree. This word is used before adverbs or adjectives to intend their signification: it is less than *very*.

The world begun to be pretty *well stocked with people, and human industry drained those unhabitable places.* BURNET.

I shall not enquire how far this lofty method may advance the reputation of learning; but I am pretty *sure 'tis no great addition to theirs who use it.* COLLIER.

A little voyage round the lake took up five days, though the wind was pretty *fair for us all the while.* ADDISON.

I have a fondness for a project, and a pretty *tolerable genius that way myself.* ADDISON'S GUARDIAN, NO. 107.

These colours were faint and dilute, unless the light was trajected obliquely; for by that means they became pretty *vivid.* NEWTON'S OPTICKS.

This writer every where insinuates, and, in one place, pretty *plainly professes himself a sincere christian.* ATTERBURY.

The copper halfpence are coined by the publick, and every piece worth pretty *near the value of the copper.* SWIFT.

The first attempts of this kind were pretty *modest.* BAKER.

PRI'CKLOUSE. *n.s.* [*prick* and *louse.*] A word of contempt for a taylor. A low word.

A taylor and his wife quarreling; the woman in contempt called her husband pricklouse. L'ESTRANGE.

PRI'ESTCRAFT. *n.s.* [*priest* and *craft.*] Religious frauds; management of wicked priests to gain power.

Puzzle has half a dozen common-place topicks; though the debate be about Doway, his discourse runs upon bigotry and priestcraft. SPECTATOR.

From priestcraft *happily set free,*
Lo! ev'ry finish'd son returns to thee. POPE.

PRIE'STRIDDEN. *adj.* [*priest* and *ridden.*] Managed or governed by priests.

Such a cant of high-church and persecution, and being priestridden. SWIFT.

PRIG. *n.s.* [A cant word derived perhaps from *prick*, as he *pricks* up, he is *pert*; or from *prickeared*, an epithet of reproach bestowed upon the presbyterian teachers.] A pert, conceited, saucy, pragmatical, little fellow.

The little man concluded, with calling monsieur Mesnager an insignificant prig. SPECTATOR, NO. 482.

There have I seen some active prig,
To shew his parts, bestride a twig.
SWIFT'S MISCELLANIES.

PRIME'VAL, PRIMEVOUS. *adj.* [*primævus*, Lat.] Original; such as was at first.

Immortal dove,
Thou with almighty energy did'st move
On the wild waves, incumbent did'st display
Thy genial wings, and hatch primeval *day.* BLACKMORE.

All the parts of this great fabrick change;
Quit their old stations and primeval *frame,*
And lose their shape, their essence, and their name. PRIOR.

PRI'SONBASE. *n.s.* A kind of rural play, commonly called *prisonbars.*

The spachies of the court play every friday at ciocho di canni, which is no other than prisonbase *upon horseback, hiting one another with darts, as the others do with their hands.* SANDYS'S TRAVELS.

PRIVA'DO. *n.s.* [Spanish.] A secret friend.

The lady Brampton, an English lady, embarked for Portugal at that time, with some privado *of her own.* BACON.

PRI'VITY. *n.s.* [*privauté*, Fr. from *privy.*]

1. Private communication.

I will unto you in privity *discover the drift of my purpose; I mean thereby to settle an eternal peace in that country, and also to make it very profitable to her majesty.* SPENSER.

2. Consciousness; joint knowledge; private concurrence.

The authority of higher powers have force even in these things which are done without their privity, *and are of mean reckoning.* HOOKER, B. I. S. 7.

Upon this French going out, took he upon him,
Without the privity *o' th' king, t' appoint*
Who should attend him?
SHAKESPEARE'S HENRY VIII.

All the doors were laid open for his departure, not without the privity *of the prince of Orange, concluding that the kingdom might better be settled in his absence.* SWIFT.

3. [In the plural.] Secret parts.

Few of them have any thing to cover their privities. ABBOT.

PRI'VY. *n.s.* Place of retirement; necessary house.

Your fancy
Would still the same ideas give ye,
As when you spy'd her on the privy.
SWIFT.

PRO. [Latin.] For; in defence of; *pro* and *con*, for *pro* and *contra*, for and against. Despicable cant.

Doctrinal points in controversy had been agitated in the pulpits, with more warmth than had used to be; and thence the animosity increased in books pro *and con.* CLARENDON.

Matthew met Richard, when
Of many knotty points they spoke,
And pro *and* con *by turns they took.*
PRIOR.

PROBATUM EST. A Latin expression added to the end of a receipt, signifying it is tried or proved.

Vain the concern that you express,
That uncall'd Alard will possess
Your house and coach both day and night,
And that Macbeth was haunted less
By Banquo's restless sprite:
Lend him but fifty louis d' or,
And you shall never see him more;
Take my advice probatum est?
Why do the gods indulge our store,
But to secure our rest. PRIOR.

PROBE-SCISSORS. *n.s.* [*probe* and *scissor.*] Scissors used to open wounds, of which the blade thrust into the orifice has a button at the end.

The sinus was snipt up with probe-scissors. WISEMAN.

PROBO'SCIS. *n.s.* [*proboscis*, Lat.] A snout; the trunk of an elephant; but it is used also for the same part in every creature, that bears any resemblance thereunto.

The elephant wreath'd to make them sport
His lithe proboscis. MILTON.

PRO'CINCT. *n.s.* [*procinctus*, Lat.] Complete preparation; preparation brought to the point of action.

When all the plain
Cover'd with thick imbattl'd squadrons bright,
Chariots, and flaming arms, and fiery steeds,
Reflecting blaze on blaze, first met his view,
War he perceiv'd, war in procinct.
MILTON.

PRODI'GIOUS. *adj.* [*prodigiosus*, Lat. *prodigieux*, Fr.] Amazing; astonishing; such as may seem a prodigy; portentous; enormous; monstrous; amazingly great.

If e'er he have a child, abortive it be,
Prodigious *and untimely brought to light.* SHAKESPEARE.

An emission of immateriate virtues we are a little doubtful to propound, it being so prodigious; *but that it is constantly avouched by many.* BACON'S NATURAL HISTORY.

It is prodigious *to have thunder in a clear sky.* BROWN.

Then entring at the gate,
Conceal'd in clouds, prodigious *to relate,*
He mix'd, unmark'd, among the busy throng. DRYDEN.

The Rhone enters the lake, and brings along with it a prodigious *quantity of water.* ADDISON'S REMARKS ON ITALY.

It is a scandal to christianity, that in towns, where there is a prodigious *increase in the number of houses and inhabitants, so little care should be taken for churches.* SWIFT.

PROFE'SSOR. *n.s.* [*professeur*, Fr. from *profess.*]

1. One who declares himself of any opinion or party.

When the holiness of the professors *of religion is decayed you may doubt the springing up of a new sect.* BACON'S ESSAYS.

2. One who publickly practises or teaches an art.

Professors *in most sciences, are generally the worst qualified to explain their meanings to those who are not of their tribes.* SWIFT.

3. One who is visibly religious.

Ordinary illiterate people, who were professors, *that shewed a concern for religion, seemed much conversant in St. Paul's Epistles.* LOCKE.

PROFE'SSORSHIP. *n.s.* [from *professor.*] The station or office of a publick teacher.

Dr. Prideaux succeeded him in the

professorship, *being then elected bishop of Worcester, Sanderson succeeded him in the regius* professorship. WALTON.

PROFI'CUOUS. *adj.* [*proficuus*, Lat.] Advantageous; useful.

It is very proficuous, *to take a good large dose.* HARVEY.

To future times
Proficuous, *such a race of men produce,*
As in the cause of virtue firm, may fix
Her throne inviolate. PHILIPS.

PRO'FLUENCE. *n.s.* [from *profluent.*] Progress; course.

In the profluence *or proceedings of their fortunes, there was much difference between them.* WOTTON.

To **PROG.** *v.n.*
1. To rob; to steal.
2. To shift meanly for provisions. A low word.

She went out progging *for provisions as before.* L'ESTRANGE.

PROG. *n.s.* [from the verb.] Victuals; provision of any kind. A low word.

O nephew! your grief is but folly,
In town you may find better prog.
SWIFT'S MISCELLANIES.

Spouse tuckt up doth in pattens trudge it,
With handkerchiefs of prog, *like trull with budget;*
And eat by turns plumcake and judge it.
CONGREVE.

PROGENERA'TION. *n.s.* [*progenero*, Lat.] The act of begetting; propagation.

PROGNOSTICATION. *n.s.* [from *prognosticate.*]
1. The act of foreknowing or foreshowing.

If an oily palm be not a fruitful prognostication, *I cannot scratch mine ear.*
SHAKESPEARE'S ANTONY AND CLEOPATRA.

Raw as he is, and in the hottest day prognostication *proclaims, shall he be set against a brick-wall, the sun looking with a southward eye upon him, where he is to behold him, with flies blown to death.*
SHAKESPEARE'S WINTER'S TALE.

This theory of the earth begins to be a kind of prophecy or prognostication *of things to come, as it hath been hitherto an history of things past.*
BURNET'S THEORY OF THE EARTH.

2. Foretoken.

He bid him farewell, arming himself in a black armour, as a badge or prognostication *of his mind.* SIDNEY.

To **PRO'GRESS.** *v.n.* [*progredior*, Lat.] To move forward; to pass. Not used.

Let me wipe off this honourable dew,
That silverly doth progress *on thy cheeks.*
SHAKESPEARE.

PROJE'CTOR. *n.s.* [from *project.*]
1. One who forms schemes or designs.

The following comes from a projector, *a correspondent as diverting as a traveller; his subject having the same grace of novelty to recommend it.* ADDISON.

Among all the projectors *in this attempt, none have met with so general a success, as they who apply themselves to soften the rigour of the precept.*
ROGERS'S SERMONS.

2. One who forms wild impracticable schemes.

Chymists, and other projectors, *propose to themselves things utterly impracticable.*
L'ESTRANGE.

Astrologers that future fates foreshew,
Projectors, *quacks, and lawyers not a few.*
POPE.

To **PROIN.** *v.a.* [a corruption of *prune.*] To lop; to cut; to trim; to prune.

I sit and proin *my wings*
After flight, and put new stings

To my shafts. BEN JONSON.

The country husbandman will not give the proining *knife to a young plant, as not able to admit the scar.* BEN JONSON.

To **PROLA'TE.** *v.a.* [*prolatum*, Lat.] To pronounce; to utter.

The pressures of war have somewhat cowed their spirits, as may be gathered from the accent of their words, which they prolate *in a whining querulous tone, as if still complaining and crest-fallen.* HOWEL.

PROLA'TION. *n.s.* [*prolatus*, Lat.]

1. Pronunciation; utterance.

Parrots, having been used to be fed at the prolation *of certain words, may afterwards pronounce the same.* RAY.

2. Delay; act of deferring. *Ainsworth.*

PROLIFICA'TION. *n.s.* [*proles* and *facio*, Lat.] Generation of children.

Their fruits, proceeding from simpler roots, are not so distinguishable as the offspring of sensible creatures, and prolifications *descending from double origins.* BROWN.

PROMI'SCUOUS. *adj.* [*promiscuus*, Lat.] Mingled; confused; undistinguished.

Glory he requires, and glory he receives,
Promiscuous *from all nations.*
MILTON'S PARADISE LOST.

Promiscuous *love by marriage was*
restrain'd. ROSCOMMON.

In rush'd at once a rude promiscuous
crowd;
The guards, and then each other overbear,
And in a moment throng the theatre.
DRYDEN.

No man, that considers the promiscuous *dispensations of God's providence in this world, can think it unreasonable to conclude, that after this life good men shall be rewarded, and sinners punished.* TILLOTSON'S SERMONS.

The earth was formed out of that promiscuous *mass of sand, earth, shells, subsiding from the water.* WOODWARD.

Clubs, diamonds, hearts, in wild disorder
seen,
With throngs promiscuous *strow the level*
green. POPE.

A wild, where weeds and flow'rs
promiscuous *shoot.* POPE.

PRO'MPTER. *n.s.* [from *prompt.*]

1. One who helps a publick speaker, by suggesting the word to him when he falters.

Were it my cue to fight, I should have
known it
Without a prompter.
SHAKESPEARE'S OTHELLO.

In florid impotence he speaks,
And as the prompter *breathes, the puppet*
squeaks. POPE.

2. An admonisher; a reminder.

We understand our duty without a teacher, and acquit ourselves as we ought to do without a prompter. L'ESTRANGE.

To **PROMU'LGATE.** *v.a.* [*promulgo*, Lat.] To publish; to make known by open declaration.

Those albeit I know he nothing so much hateth as to promulgate, *yet I hope that this will occasion him to put forth divers other goodly works.* SPENSER.

Those, to whom he entrusted the promulgating *of the gospel, had far different instructions.* DECAY OF PIETY.

It is certain laws, by virtue of any sanction they receive from the promulgated *will of the legislature, reach not a stranger, if by the law of nature every man hath not a power to punish offences against it.* LOCKE.

To **PROMU'LGE.** *v.a.* [from *promulgo*, Lat.] To promulgate; to publish; to teach openly.

The chief design of them is, to establish the

truth of a new revelation in those countries, where it is first promulged *and propagated.* ATTERBURY.

PRONG. *n.s.* [*pronghen*, Dutch, to squeeze. *Minshew.*] A fork.

The cooks make no more ado, but slicing it into little gobbets, prick it on a prong *of iron, and hang it in a furnace.* SANDYS'S JOURNEY.

Whacum his sea-coal prong *threw by,*
And basely turn'd his back to fly.
HUDIBRAS.

Be mindful,
With iron teeth of rakes and prongs *to move*
The crusted earth.
DRYDEN'S VIRGIL'S GEORGICKS.

PROPE'NDENCY. *n.s.* [from *propend.*]
1. Inclination or tendency of desire to any thing.
2. [From *propendo*, Lat. to weigh.] Preconsideration; attentive deliberation; perpendency.

An act above the animal actings, which are transient, and admit not of that attention, and propendency *of actions.* HALE.

To **PROPO'RTION.** *v.a.* [*proportionner*, Fr. from the noun.]
1. To adjust by comparative relation.

Measure is that which perfecteth all things, because every thing is for some end; neither can that thing be available to any end, which is not proportionable thereunto: and to proportion *as well excesses as defects, are opposite.* HOOKER.

Till body up to spirit work, in bounds
Proportion'd *to each kind.* MILTON.

In the loss of an object, we do not proportion *our grief to the real value it bears, but to the value our fancies set upon it.* ADDISON'S SPECTATOR, NO. 256.

2. To form symmetrically.

Nature had proportioned *her without any fault, quickly to be discovered by the senses; yet altogether seemed not to make up that harmony that Cupid delights in.* SIDNEY.

PROPO'RTIONABLE. *adj.* [from *proportion.*] Adjusted by comparative relation; such as is fit.

His commandments are not grievous, because he offers us an assistance proportionable *to the difficulty.* TILLOTSON.

It was enlivened with an hundred and twenty trumpets, assisted with a proportionable *number of other instruments.* ADDISON.

PROSE. *n.s.* [*prose*, Fr. *prosa*, Lat.] Language not restrained to harmonick sounds or set number of syllables; discourse not metrical.

Things unattempted yet in prose *or rhime.* MILTON.

The reformation of prose *was owing to Boccace, who is the standard of purity in the Italian tongue, though many of his phrases are become obsolete.* DRYDEN.

A poet lets you into the knowledge of a device better than a prose *writer, as his descriptions are often more diffuse.* ADDISON.

Prose *men alone for private ends,*
I thought, forsook their ancient friends.
PRIOR.

I will be still your friend in prose*:*
Esteem and friendship to express,
Will not require poetick dress. SWIFT.

My head and heart thus flowing through my quill,
Verse man and prose *man, term me which you will.* POPE.

PRO'SELYTE. *n.s.* [προσήλυτος; *proselite*, Fr.] A convert; one brought over to a new opinion.

He that saw hell in's melancholy dream,

Scar'd from his sins, repented in a fright,
Had he view'd Scotland, had turn'd proselyte. CLEAVELAND.

Men become professors and combatants for those opinions they were never convinced of, nor proselytes *to.* LOCKE.

Where'er you tread,
Millions of proselytes *behind are led,*
Through crowds of new-made converts still you go. GRANVILLE.

What numbers of proselytes *may we not expect.* ADDISON.

To **PRO'SELYTE.** *v.a.* To convert. A bad word.

Men of this temper cut themselves off from the opportunities of proselyting *others, by averting them from their company.* GOVERNMENT OF THE TONGUE.

PROSO'DIAN. *n.s.* [from *prosody.*] One skilled in metre or prosody.

Some have been so bad prosodians, *as from thence to derive malum, because that fruit was the first occasion of evil.* BROWN.

PRO'SODY. *n.s.* [*prosodie*, Fr. *προσῳδία.*] The part of grammar which teaches the sound and quantity of syllables, and the measures of verse.

PRO'STITUTE. *n.s.* [from the verb.]

1. A hireling; a mercenary; one who is set to sale.

At open fulsome bawdry they rejoice,
Base prostitute! *thus dost thou gain thy bread.* DRYDEN.

No hireling she, no prostitute *to praise.* POPE.

2. [*Prostibula*, Lat.] A publick strumpet.

From every point they come,
Then dread no dearth of prostitutes *at Rome.* DRYDEN.

PROTU'BERANCE. *n.s.* [*protubero*, Lat.] Something swelling above the rest; prominence; tumour.

If the world were eternal, by the continual fall and wearing of waters, all the protuberances *of the earth would infinite ages since have been levelled, and the superficies of the earth rendered plain.* HALE'S ORIGIN OF MANKIND.

Mountains seem but so many wens and unnatural protuberances *upon the face of the earth.* MORE.

PROTU'BERANT. *adj.* [from *protuberate.*] Swelling; prominent.

One man's eyes are more protuberant *and swelling out, another's more sunk and depressed.* GLANVILLE'S SCEPSIS SCIENTIFICA.

Though the eye seems round, in reality the iris is protuberant *above the white, else the eye could not have admitted a whole hemisphere at one view.* RAY.

PRO'VERB. *n.s.* [*proverbe*, Fr. *proverbium*, Lat.]

1. A short sentence frequently repeated by the people; a saw; an adage.

The sum of his whole book of proverbs *is an exhortation to the study of this practick wisdom.* DECAY OF PIETY.

It is in praise and commendation of men, as it is in gettings and gains; for the proverb *is true, that light gains make heavy purses; for light gains come thick, whereas great come but now and then.* BACON'S ESSAYS.

The Italian proverb *says of the Genoese, that they have a sea without fish, land without trees, and men without faith.* ADDISON.

2. A word,[173] name or observation commonly received or uttered.

Thou hast delivered us for a spoil, and a proverb *of reproach.*
BIBLE TOBIT, III. 4.

To **PRO'VERB.** *v.a.* [from the noun.] Not a good word.
1. To mention in a proverb.

Am I not sung and proverb'd *for a fool*
In ev'ry street; do they not say, how well
Are come upon him his deserts?
MILTON'S AGONISTES.

2. To provide with a proverb.

Let wantons, light of heart,
Tickle the senseless rushes with their heels:
For I am proverb'd *with a grandsire phrase;*
I'll be a candle-holder and look on.
SHAKESPEARE.

PROVI'NCIAL. *adj.* [*provincial*, Fr. from *province.*]
1. Relating to a province.[174]

The duke dare not more stretch
This finger of mine, than he dare rack his own;
His subject am I not, nor here provincial.
SHAKESPEARE.

2. Appendant to the provincial country.

Some have delivered the polity of spirits, and left an account even to their provincial *dominions.* BROWN.

3. Not of the mother country; rude; unpolished.

They build and treat with such magnificence,
That, like th' ambitious monarchs of the age,
They give the law to our provincial *stage.*
DRYDEN.

A country 'squire having only the provincial *accent upon his tongue, which is neither a fault, nor in his power to remedy, must marry a cast wench.* SWIFT.

4. Belonging only to an archbishop's jurisdiction; not æcumenical.

A law made in a provincial *synod, is properly termed a* provincial *constitution.*
AYLIFFE'S PARERGON.

To **PROVI'NE.** *v.n.* [*provigner*, Fr.] To lay a stock or branch of a vine in the ground to take root for more encrease.

PRO'VOST. *n.s.* [*prafast*, Sax. *provost*, Fr. *provosto*, Ital. *præpositus*, Lat.]
1. The chief of any body: as, the provost of a college.
2. The executioner of an army.

Kingston, provost *marshal of the king's army, was deemed not only cruel but inhuman in his executions.* HAYWARD.

PRO'XIMATE. *adj.* [*proximus*, Lat.] Next in the series of ratiocination; near and immediate: opposed to *remote* and *mediate.*

Writing a theory of the deluge, we were to shew the proximate *natural causes of it.*
BURNET'S THEORY OF THE EARTH.

Substance is the remote genus of bird, because it agrees not only to all kinds of animals, but also to things inanimate; but animal is the proximate *or nearest genus of bird, because it agrees to fewest other things.* WATTS'S LOGICK.

PRUCE. *n.s.* [*Pruce* is the old name for Prussia.] Prussian leather.

Some leathern bucklers use
Of folded hides, and others shields of pruce. DRYDEN.

PRUDE. *n.s.* [*prude*, Fr.] A woman over nice and scrupulous, and with false affectation.

The graver prude *sinks downward to a gnome,*
In search of mischief, still on earth to roam. POPE.

Not one careless thought intrudes,
Less modest than the speech of prudes.
SWIFT.

PRU'DERY. *n.s.* [from *prude.*] Overmuch nicety in conduct.

PRU'DISH. *adj.* [from *prude.*] Affectedly grave.

I know you all expect, from seeing me,
Some formal lecture, spoke with prudish *face.* GARRICK.

PSHAW. *interj.* An expression of contempt.

A peevish fellow has some reason for being out of humour, or has a natural incapacity for delight, and therefore disturbs all with pishes and pshaws. SPECTATOR, NO. 438.

PTI'SAN. *n.s.* [*ptisanne*, Fr. *πτισάνη.*] A medical drink made of barley decocted with raisins and liquorice.

Thrice happy were those golden days of old,
When dear as Burgundy the ptisans *sold;*
When patients chose to die with better will,
Than breathe and pay the apothecary's bill. GARTH.

In fevers the aliments prescribed by Hippocrates, were ptisans *and cream of barley.* ARBUTHNOT.

PUBE'RTY. *n.s.* [*puberté*, Fr. *pubertas*, Lat.] The time of life in which the two sexes begin first to be acquainted.

The cause of changing the voice at the years of puberty *seemeth to be, for that when much of the moisture of the body, which did before irrigate the parts, is drawn down to the spermatical vessels, it leaveth the body more hot than it was, whence cometh the dilatation of the pipes.* BACON.

All the carnivorous animals would have multiplied exceedingly, before these children that escaped could come to the age of puberty. BENTLEY'S SERMONS.

PUBLICAN. *n.s.* [from *publicus*, Lat.]
1. A toll gatherer.

As Jesus sat at meat, many publicans *and sinners came and sat down with him.* BIBLE MATTHEW, IX. 10.

2. A man that keeps a house of general entertainment. In low language.

PU'BLISHER. *n.s.* [from *publish.*]
1. One who makes publick or generally known.

Love of you
Hath made me publisher *of this pretence.* SHAKESPEARE.

The holy lives, the exemplary sufferings of the publishers *of this religion, and the surpassing excellence of that doctrine which they published.* ATTERBURY.

2. One who puts out a book into the world.

A collection of poems appeared, in which the publisher *has given me some things that did not belong to me.* PRIOR.

To **PU'DDER.** *v.n.* [from the noun.] To make a tumult; to make a bustle.

Mathematicians, abstracting their thoughts from names, and setting before their minds the ideas themselves, have avoided a great part of that perplexity, puddering *and confusion, which has so much hindered knowledge.* LOCKE.

To **PU'DDER.** *v.a.* To perplex; to disturb; to confound.

He that will improve every matter of fact into a maxim, will abound in contrary observations, that can be of no other use but to perplex and pudder *him.* LOCKE.

PUDDING. *n.s.* [*potten*, Welsh, an intestine; *boudin*, French; *puding*, Swedish.]
1. A kind of food very variously compounded, but generally made of meal, milk, and eggs.

Sallads, and eggs, and lighter fare
Tune the Italian spark's guitar;
And if I take Dan Congreve right,

Pudding and beef make Britons fight. PRIOR.

2. The gut of an animal.

He'll yield the crow a pudding *one of these days; the king has kill'd his heart.* SHAKESPEARE'S HENRY V.

As sure as his guts are made of puddings. SHAKESPEARE.

3. A bowel stuffed with certain mixtures of meal and other ingredients.

Mind neither good nor bad, nor right nor wrong,
But eat your pudding, *slave, and hold your tongue.* PRIOR.[175]

PU'DDINGPIE. *n.s.* [*pudding* and *pie.*] A pudding with meat baked in it.

Some cry the covenant, instead
Of puddingpies *and gingerbread.*
HUDIBRAS.

PU'DDINGTIME. *n.s.* [*pudding* and *time.*]
1. The time of dinner; the time at which pudding, anciently the first dish, is set upon the table.
2. Nick of time; critical minute.

Mars that still protects the stout,
In puddingtime *came to his aid.*
HUDIBRAS.

PUG. *n.s.* [*piga*, Saxon, a girl. *Skinner.*] A kind name of a monkey, or any thing tenderly loved.

Upon setting him down, and calling him pug, *I found him to be her favourite monkey.* ADDISON'S SPECTATOR.

PUGH. *interj.* [corrupted from *puff*, or borrowed from the sound.] A word of contempt.

PU'GIL. *n.s.* [*pugille*, Fr.] What is taken up between the thumb and two first fingers. *Dictionaries.*

Take violets, and infuse a good pugil *of them in a quart of vinegar.* BACON'S NATURAL HISTORY.

PUKE. *n.s.* [of uncertain derivation.] Vomit; medicine causing vomit.

PU'KER. *n.s.* [from *puke.*] Medicine causing a vomit.

The puker *rue,*
The sweetner sassafras are added too.
GARTH.

PU'LPIT. *n.s.* [*pulpitum*, Lat. *pulpitre*, *pupitre*, Fr.]
1. A place raised on high, where a speaker stands.

Produce his body to the market-place,
And in the pulpit, *as becomes a friend,*
Speak in the order of his funeral.
SHAKESPEARE'S JULIUS CÆSAR.

2. The higher desk in the church where the sermon is pronounced; distinct from the lower desk where prayers are read.

We see on our theatres, the examples of vice rewarded, yet it ought not to be an argument against the art, any more than the impieties of the pulpit *in the late rebellion.* DRYDEN.

Sir Roger has given a handsome pulpit *cloth, and railed in the communion table.* ADDISON'S SPECTATOR, NO. 112.

Bishops were not wont to preach out of the pulpit. AYLIFFE.

Pulpits *their sacred satyr learn'd to spare,*
And vice admir'd to find a flatt'rer there.
POPE.

To **PU'LVIL.** *v.a.* [from the noun.] To sprinkle with perfumes in powder.

Have you pulvilled *the coachman and postilion, that they may not stink of the stable.*
CONGREVE'S WAY OF THE WORLD.

PUN. *n.s.* [I know not whence this word is to be deduced: to *pun*, is to grind or beat with a *pestle*; can *pun* mean an empty sound, like that of a mortar beaten, as *clench*, the old word for *pun*, seems only a corruption of *clink?*] An equivocation; a quibble; an expression where a word has at once different meanings.

It is not the word, but the figure that appears on the medal: cuniculus may stand for a rabbit or a mine, but the picture of a rabbit is not the picture of a mine: a pun *can be no more engraven, than it can be translated.* ADDISON.

But fill their purse, our poet's work is done,
Alike to them by pathos, or by pun.
POPE.

PUNCTI'LIO. *n.s.* A small nicety of behaviour; a nice point of exactness.

Common people are much astonished, when they hear of those solemn contests which are made among the great, upon the punctilios *of a publick ceremony.*
ADDISON.

Punctilio *is out of doors, the moment a daughter clandestinely quits her father's house.*
CLARISSA.

PUNCTUA'TION. *n.s.* [*punctum*, Lat.] The act or method of pointing.

It ought to do it willingly, without being forced to it by any change in the words or punctuation. ADDISON.

PUNK. *n.s.* A whore; a common prostitute; a strumpet.

She may be a punk; *for many of them are neither maid, widow, nor wife.*
SHAKESPEARE'S MEASURE FOR MEASURE.

And made them fight, like mad or drunk,
For dame religion as for punk.
HUDIBRAS.

Near these a nursery erects its head,
Where unfledg'd actors learn to laugh and cry,
Where infant punks *their tender voices try.* DRYDEN.

PU'NSTER. *n.s.* [from *pun.*] A quibbler; a low wit who endeavours at reputation by double meaning.

His mother was cousin to Mr. Swan, gamester and punster *of London.*
ARBUTHNOT AND POPE.

To **PUNT.** *v.n.* To play at basset and ombre.

One is for setting up an assembly for basset, where none shall be admitted to punt, *that have not taken the oaths.* ADDISON.

When a duke to Jansen punts *at White's,*
Or city heir in mortgage melts away,
Satan himself feels far less joy than they.
POPE.

PU'PPETSHOW. *n.s.* [*puppet* and *show.*] A mock drama performed by wooden images moved by wire.

Tim, you have a taste I know,
And often see a puppetshow. SWIFT.

To induce him to be fond of learning, he would frequently carry him to the puppetshow. ARBUTHNOT AND POPE.

A president of the council will make no more impression upon my mind, than the sight of a puppetshow. POPE.

PURBLI'ND. *adj.* [corrupted from *poreblind*, which is still used in Scotland; *pore* and *blind.*] Nearsighted; shortsighted.

Speak to my gossip Venus one fair word,
One nickname to her purblind *son and heir.* SHAKESPEARE.

The truth appears so naked on my side,
That any purblind *eye may find it out.*
SHAKESPEARE.

'Tis known to several
Of head piece extraordinary; lower messes
Perchance, are to this business purblind.
SHAKESPEARE.

Like to purblind *moles, no greater light than that little which they shun.*
DRUMMOND.

Darkness, that here surrounded our purblind *understandings, will vanish at the dawning of eternal day.* BOYLE.

Dropt in blear thick-sighted eyes,
They'd make them see in darkest night,
Like owls, though purblind *in the light.*
HUDIBRAS.

Purblind man
Sees but a part o' th' chain, the nearest links;
His eyes not carrying to that equal beam,
That poises all above.
DRYDEN AND LEE'S OEDIPUS.

PU'RIST. *n.s.* [*puriste*, Fr.] One superstitiously nice in the use of words.

PURL. *n.s.* [this is justly supposed by *Minshew* to be contracted from *purfle.*]
1. An embroidered and puckered border.

Himself came in next after a triumphant chariot made of carnation velvet, enriched with purl *and pearl.* SIDNEY.

The jagging of pinks is like the inequality of oak leaves, but they seldom have any small purls. BACON.

2. [I know not whence derived.] A kind of medicated malt liquor, in which wormwood and aromaticks are infused.

To **PURL.** *v.n.* [of this word it is doubtful what is the primitive signification; if it is refered originally to the appearance of a quick stream, which is always dimpled on the surface, it may come from *purl*, a *pucker* or *fringe*; but if, as the use of authors seem to show, it relates to the sound, it must be derived from *porla*, Swedish, to murmur, according to Mr. *Lye.*] To murmur; to flow with a gentle noise.

Tones are not so apt to procure sleep, as some other sounds; as the wind, the purling *of water, and humming of bees.*
BACON'S NATURAL HISTORY.

Instruments that have returns, as trumpets; or flexions, as cornets; or are drawn up, and put from, as sacbuts, have a purling *sound; but the recorder or flute, that have none of these inequalities, give a clear sound.* BACON.

All fish from sea or shore,
Freshet, or purling *brook, or shell or fin.*
MILTON.

My flow'ry theme,
A painted mistress, or a purling *stream.*
POPE.

Around th' adjoining brook, that purls *along*
The vocal grove, now fretting o'er a rock.
THOMSON.

To **PURL.** *v.a.* To decorate with fringe or embroidery.

When was old Sherewood's head more quaintly curl'd,
Or nature's cradle more enchas'd and purl'd. BEN JONSON.

To **PURR.** *v.a.* To murmur as a cat or leopard in pleasure.

PU'RSY. *adj.* [*poussif*, Fr.] Short-breathed and fat.

In the fatness of these pursy *times,*
Virtue itself of vice must pardon beg,
Yea courb and woo for leave to do it good.
SHAKESPEARE.

Now breathless wrong
Shall sit and pant in your great chairs of ease,
And pursy *insolence shall break his wind*
With fear and horrid flight.
SHAKESPEARE'S TIMON OF ATHENS.

By these, the Medes
Perfume their breaths, and cure old pursy *men.* TEMPLE.

An hostess dowager,
Grown fat and pursy *by retail*
Of pots of beer and bottl'd ale.
HUDIBRAS, P. III.

PU'SHPIN. *n.s.* [*push* and *pin.*] A child's play, in which pins are pushed alternately.

Men, that have wandering thoughts at the

voice of wisdom out of the mouth of a philosopher, deserve as well to be whipt, as boys for playing at pushpin, *when they should be learning.* L'ESTRANGE.

PUSS. *n.s.* [I know not whence derived; *pusio*, Lat. is a dwarf.]

1. The fondling name of a cat.

A young fellow, in love with a cat, made it his humble suit to Venus to turn puss *into a woman.* L'ESTRANGE.

Let puss *practice what nature teaches.* WATTS.

I will permit my son to play at apodidrascinda, which can be no other than our puss *in a corner.* ARBUTHNOT AND POPE.

2. The sportsman's term for a hare.

Poor honest puss,
It grieves my heart to see thee thus;
But hounds eat sheep as well as hares.
GAY.

PU'TAGE. *n.s.* [*putain*, Fr.] In law, prostitution on the woman's part.

PU'TANISM. *n.s.* [*putanisme*, Fr.] The manner of living, or trade of a prostitute. *Dictionaries.*

PY'GMY. *n.s.* [*pygmée*, Fr. *πυγμάιος*.] A dwarf; one of a nation fabled to be only three spans high, and after long wars to have been destroyed by cranes.[176]

If they deny the present spontaneous production of larger plants, and confine the earth to as pygmy *births in the vegetable kingdom, as they do in the other; yet surely in such a supposed universal decay of nature, even mankind itself that is now nourished, though not produced, by the earth, must have degenerated in stature and strength in every generation.* BENTLEY.

Q

Is a consonant borrowed from the Latin or French, for which, though *q* is commonly placed in the Saxon alphabet, the Saxons generally used *cþ*, *cw*; as *cþellan* or *cwellan*, to quell: *qu* is, in English, pronounced as by the Italians and Spaniards *cw*; as *quail*, *quench*, except *quoit*, which is spoken, according to the manner of the French, *coit*: the name of this letter is *cue*, from *queue*, French, tail; its form being that of an O with a tail.

To **QUACK.** *v.n.* [*quacken*, Dutch, to cry as a goose.]

1. To cry like a duck. This word is often written *quaake*, to represent the sound better.

> *Wild-ducks* quack *where grasshoppers did sing.* KING.

2. To chatter boastingly; to brag loudly; to talk ostentatiously.

> *Believe mechanick virtuosi*
> *Can raise them mountains in Potosi,*
> *Seek out for plants with signatures,*
> *To* quack *of universal cures.*
> HUDIBRAS, P. III.

QUACK. *n.s.* [from the verb.]

1. A boastful pretender to arts which he does not understand.

> *The change, schools and pulpits are full of* quacks, *jugglers and plagiaries.* L'ESTRANGE.

> *Some* quacks *in the art of teaching, pretend to make young gentlemen masters of the languages, before they can be masters of common sense.* FELTON ON THE CLASSICKS.

2. A vain boastful pretender to physick; one who proclaims his own medical abilities in publick places.

> *At the first appearance that a French* quack *made in Paris: a little boy walked before him, publishing with a shrill voice, "My father cures all sorts of distempers;" to which the doctor added in a grave manner, "The child says true."* ADDISON.

3. An artful tricking practitioner in physick.

> *Despairing* quacks *with curses fled the place,*
> *And vile attorneys, now an useless race.*
> POPE.

QUA'CKSALVER. *n.s.* [*quack* and *salve.*] One who brags of medicines or salves; a medicaster; a charlatan.

> *Saltimbancoes,* quacksalvers *and charlatans deceive the vulgar in lower degrees;*

were Æsop alive, the piazza and the pont neuf could not speak their fallacies. BROWN.

Many poor country vicars, for want of other means, are driven to their shifts; to turn mountebanks, quacksalvers *and empiricks.* BURTON ON MELANCHOLY.

To **QUAFF.** *v.a.* [of this word the derivation is uncertain: *Junius*, with his usual idleness of conjecture, derives it from the Greek, *κυαφίζειν* in the Eolick dialect used for *κυαφίθειν*. I from *go off*, as *go off, guoff, quoff, quaff.* It comes from *coeffer*, Fr. to be drunk.][177]

To drink; to swallow in large draughts.

He calls for wine; a health, quoth he, as if
H'ad been abroad carousing to his mates
After a storm, quafft *off the muscadel,*
And threw the sops all in the sexton's face.
SHAKESPEARE.

I found the prince,
With such a deep demeanour in great sorrow,
That tyranny, which never quafft *but blood,*
Would, by beholding him, have wash'd his knife
With gentle eye drops.
SHAKESPEARE'S HENRY IV. P. II.

On flow'rs repos'd, and with rich flow'rets crown'd,
They eat, they drink, and in communion sweet
Quaff *immortality and joy.*
MILTON'S PARADISE LOST, B. V.

To **QUA'FFER.** *v.n.* [a low word, I suppose, formed by chance.] To feel out. This seems to be the meaning.

Ducks, having larger nerves that come into their bills than geese, quaffer *and grope out their meat the most.* DERHAM.

QUA'RANTAIN, QUARANTINE. *n.s.* [*quarantain*, Fr.] The space of forty days, being the time which a ship, suspected of infection, is obliged to forbear intercourse or commerce.

Pass your quarantine *among some of the churches round this town, where you may learn to speak before you venture to expose your parts in a city congregation.* SWIFT.

To **QUECK.** *v.n.* To shrink; to show pain; perhaps to complain.

The lads of Sparta were accustomed to be whipped at altars, without so much as quecking. BACON.

QUEER. *adj.* [of this word the original is not known: a correspondent supposes a *queer* man to be one who has a *quære* to his name in a list.] Odd; strange; original; particular.

He never went to bed till two in the morning, because he would not be a queer *fellow; and was every now and then knocked down by a constable, to signalize his vivacity.* SPECTATOR.

QUERIMO'NIOUS. *adj.* [*querimonia*, Latin.] Querulous; complaining.

QUE'RIST. *n.s.* [from *quæro*, Lat.] An enquirer; an asker of questions.

I shall propose some considerations to my gentle querist. SPECTATOR.

The juggling sea god, when by chance trepan'd
By some instructed querist *sleeping on the strand,*
Impatient of all answers, strait became
A stealing brook.
SWIFT'S MISCELLANIES.

QUE'RPO. *n.s.* [corrupted from *cuerpo*, Spanish.] A dress close to the body; a waistcoat.

I would fain see him walk in querpo, *like a cased rabbit, without his holy furr upon his back.* DRYDEN.

QUE'STMAN, QUESTMONGER. *n.s.* [*quest, man*, and

monger.] Starter of lawsuits or prosecutions.

Their principal working was upon penal laws, wherein they spared none, great nor small, but raked over all new and old statutes, having ever a rabble of promoters, questmongers, *and leading jurors at their command.* BACON.

QUI'BBLER. *n.s.* [from *quibble.*] A punster.

To **QUI'CKSET.** *v.a.* [*quick* and *set.*] To plant with living plants.

In making or mending, as needeth thy ditch,
Get set to quickset *it, learn cunningly which.* TUSSER.

A man may ditch and quickset *three poles a day, where the ditch is three foot wide and two foot deep.* MORTIMER.

QUI'CKSET. *n.s.* [*quick* and *set.*] Living plant set to grow.

Plant quicksets *and transplant fruit trees towards the decrease.* EVELYN'S KALENDAR.

Nine in ten of the quickset *hedges are ruined for want of skill.* SWIFT'S MISCELLANIES.

QUI'DDANY. *n.s.* [*cydonium, cydoniatum*, Lat. *quidden*, German, a quince.] Marmalade; confection of quinces made with sugar.

To **QUINCH.** *v.n.* [this word seems to be the same with *queech, winch* and *queck.*] To stir; to flounce as in resentment or pain.

Bestow all my soldiers in such sort as I have, that no part of all that realm shall be able to dare to quinch. SPENSER.

QUI'NTAIN. *n.s.* [*quintain*, Fr.] A post with a turning top. See QUINTIN.

My better parts
Are all thrown down; and that, which here stands up,
Is but a quintain, *a mere lifeless block.*
SHAKESPEARE.

QUI'NTIN. *n.s.* [I know not whence derived; *Minshew* deduces it from *quintus*, Lat. and calls it a game celebrated every fifth year; *palus quintanus*, Lat. *Ainsworth. quintaine*, Fr.] An upright post, on the top of which a cross post turned upon a pin, at one end of the cross post was a broad board, and at the other a heavy sand bag; the play was to ride against the broad end with a lance, and pass by before the sand bag coming round, should strike the tilter on the back.

At quintin *he,*
In honour of his bridaltee,
Hath challeng'd either wide countee;
Come cut and long tail, for there be
Six batchelors as bold as he,
Adjuting to his company,
And each one hath his livery.
BEN JONSON.

QUIRE.[178] *n.s.* [*choeur*, Fr. *choro*, Italian.]

1. A body of singers; a chorus.

The trees did bud and early blossoms bore,
And all the quire *of birds did sweetly sing,*
And told that garden's pleasures in their caroling. FAIRY QUEEN.

Myself have lim'd a bush for her,
And plac'd a quire *of such enticing birds,*
That she will light to listen to their lays.
SHAKESPEARE.

At thy nativity a glorious quire
Of angels in the fields of Bethlehem sung
To shepherds watching at their folds by night,
And told them the Messiah now was born.
MILTON.

I may worship thee
For ay, with temples vow'd and virgin quires. MILTON.

As in beauty she surpass'd the quire,
So nobler than the rest was her attire.
DRYDEN.

2. The part of the church where the service is sung.

I am all on fire,
Not all the buckets in a country quire
Shall quench my rage. CLEAVELAND.

Some run for buckets to the hallow'd quire,
Some cut the pipes, and some the engines play. DRYDEN.

The fox obscene to gaping tombs retires,
And wolves with howling fill the sacred quires. POPE.

3. [*Cahier*, Fr.] A bundle of paper consisting of twenty-four sheets.

QUI'RISTER. *n.s.* [from *quire.*] Chorister; one who sings in concert, generally in divine service.

The coy quiristers, *that lodge within,*
Are prodigal of harmony.
THOMSON'S SPRING.

QUITS. *interj.* [from *quit.*] An exclamation used when any thing is repayed and the parties become even.

To **QUOB.** *v.n.* [a low word.] To move as the embrio does in the womb; to move as the heart does when throbbing.

R

Is called the canine letter, because it is uttered with some resemblance to the growl or snarl of a cur: it has one constant sound in English, such as it has in other languages; as *red*, *rose*, *more*, *muriatick*: in words derived from the Greek, it is followed by an *h*, *rhapsody*: *r* is never mute, unless the second *r* may be accounted mute, where two *rr* are used; as *myrrh*.

RA'CKET. *n.s.* [of uncertain derivation; M. *Casaubon* derives it, after his custom, from *ῥαχία*, the dash of fluctuation against the shore.]

1. An irregular clattering noise.

That the tennis court keeper knows better than I, it is a low ebb of linen with thee, when thou keepest not racket *there.*
SHAKESPEARE'S HENRY IV. P. II.

2. A confused talk, in burlesque language.

Ambition hath removed her lodging, and lives the next door to faction, where they keep such a racket, *that the whole parish is disturbed and every night in an uproar.*
SWIFT.

3. [*Raquette*, Fr.] The instrument with which players strike the ball. Whence perhaps all the other senses.

When we have matcht our rackets *to these balls,*
We will in France play a set,
Shall strike his father's crown into the hazard. SHAKESPEARE.

The body, into which impression is made, either can yield backward or it cannot: if it can yield backward, then the impression made is a motion; as we see a stroke with a racket *upon a ball, makes it fly from it.*
DIGBY ON THE SOUL.

He talks much of the motives to do and forbear, how they determine a reasonable man, as if he were no more than a tennis-ball, to be tossed to and fro by the rackets *of the second causes.*
BRAMHALL AGAINST HOBBS.

To **RA'DICATE.** *v.a.* [*radicatus*, from *radix*, Lat.] To root; to plant deeply and firmly.

Meditation will radicate *these seeds, fix the transient gleam of light and warmth, confirm resolutions of good, and give them a durable consistence in the soul.*
HAMMOND.

Nor have we let fall our pen upon discour-

agement of unbelief, from radicated *beliefs, and points of high prescription.*
BROWN'S VULGAR ERROURS.

If the object stays not on the sense, it makes not impression enough to be remembered; but if it be repeated there, it leaves plenty enough of those images behind it, to strengthen the knowledge of the object: in which radicated *knowledge, if the memory consist, there would be no need of reserving those atoms in the brain.*
GLANVILLE'S DEFENCE.

To **RAFF.** *v.a.* To sweep; to huddle; to take hastily without distinction.

Their causes and effects I thus raff *up together.* CAREW.

RA'FFLE. *n.s.* [*rafle*, Fr. from the verb.] A species of game or lottery, in which many stake a small part of the value of some single thing, in consideration of a chance to gain it.

The toy, brought to Rome in the third triumph of Pompey, being a pair of tables for gaming, made of two precious stones, three foot broad, and four foot long, would have made a fine raffle.
ARBUTHNOT ON COINS.

RAGAMU'FFIN. *n.s.* [from *rag* and I know not what else.] A paltry mean fellow.[179]

I have led my ragamuffins *where they were pepper'd; there's not three of my hundred and fifty left alive; and they are for the town's end to beg during life.*
SHAKESPEARE'S HENRY IV.

Shall we brook that paltry ass
And feeble scoundrel, Hudibras,
With that more paltry ragamuffin,
Ralpho, vapouring and huffing.
HUDIBRAS.

Attended with a crew of ragamuffins, *she broke into his house, turned all things topsy-turvy, and then set it on fire.*
SWIFT.

RA'GEFUL. *adj.* [*rage* and *full.*] Furious; violent.

This courtesy was worse than a bastinado to Zelmane; so that again with rageful *eyes she bad him defend himself; for no less than his life would answer it.* SIDNEY, B. II.

A popular orator may represent vices in so formidable appearances, and set out each virtue in so amiable a form, that the covetous person shall scatter most liberally his beloved idol, wealth, and the rageful *person shall find a calm.* HAMMOND.

RA'GMAN. *n.s.* [*rag* and *man.*] One who deals in rags.

RAI'NDEER. *n.s.* [*hranas*, Saxon; *rangifer*, Latin.] A deer with large horns, which, in the northern regions, draws sledges through the snow.

RAKE. *n.s.* [*rastrum*, Lat. *race*, Sax. *racche*, Dutch.]

1. An instrument with teeth, by which the ground is divided, or light bodies are gathered up.

At Midsummer down with the brembles and brakes,
And after abroad with thy forkes and thy rakes. TUSSER.

O that thy bounteous deity wou'd please
To guide my rake *upon the chinking sound*
Of some vast treasure hidden under ground. DRYDEN.

He examines his face in the stream, combs his ruful locks with a rake. GARTH.

2. [*Racaille*, Fr. the low rabble; or *rekel*, Dutch, a worthless cur dog.] A loose, disorderly, vicious, wild, gay, thoughtless fellow; a man addicted to pleasure.

The next came with her son, who was the greatest rake *in the place, but so much the mother's darling, that she left her husband for the sake of this graceless youth.*
ADDISON.

Rakes *hate sober grave gentlewomen.*
ARBUTHNOT.

Men, some to bus'ness, some to pleasure take;
But ev'ry woman is at heart a rake.
POPE.

The sire saw smiling his own virtues wake;
The mother begg'd the blessing of a rake.
POPE.

RA'KEHEL. *n.s.* [of this word the etymology is doubtful: as it is now written, it is apparently derived from *rake* and *hell*, and may aptly represent a wretch whose life is passed in places of lewdness and wickedness: *Skinner* derives it from *racaille*, French, the rabble; *Junius*, from *rekel*, Dutch, a mongrel dog.] A wild, worthless, dissolute, debauched, sorry fellow.

Out of the frie of these rakehell *horse-boys, growing up in knavery and villainy, are their kern supplied.* SPENSER.

The king, when he heard of Perkins's siege of Exeter, said in sport, that the king of rakehells *was landed in the West, and that he hoped now to see him.* BACON.

A rakehell *of the town, whose character is set off with excessive prodigality, prophaneness, intemperance and lust, is rewarded with a lady of great fortune to repair his own, which his vices had almost ruined.* SWIFT.

RA'KEHELLY. *adv.* [from *rakehell.*] Wild; dissolute.

I scorn the rakehelly *rout of our ragged rhimers, which without learning boast, without judgment jangle, and without reason rage and foam.*
SPENSER'S PASTORALS.

No breaking of windows or glasses for spight,
And spoiling the goods for a rakehelly *prank.* BEN JONSON.

RA'KISH. *adj.* [from *rake.*] Loose; lewd; dissolute.

There seldom can be peculiarity in the love of a rakish *heart.* CLARISSA.

RA'MOUS. *adj.* [from *ramus*, Latin] Branchy; consisting of branches.

Which vast contraction and expansion seems unintelligible, by feigning the particles of air to be springy and ramous, *or rolled up like hoops, or by any other means than a repulsive power.*
NEWTON'S OPTICKS.

A ramous *efforescence, of a fine white spar, found hanging from a crust of like spar, at the top of an old wrought cavern.*
WOODWARD ON FOSSILS.

To **RANT.** *v.n.* [*randen*, Dutch, to rave.] To rave in violent or high sounding language without proportionable dignity of thought.

Look where my ranting *host of the garter comes; there is either liquor in his pate, or money in his purse, when he looks so merrily.*
SHAKESPEARE'S MERRY WIVES OF WINDSOR.

Nay, an thou'lt mouth, I'll rant *as well as thou.* SHAKESPEARE.

They have attacked me; some with piteous moans, others grinning and only shewing their teeth, others ranting *and hectoring, others scolding and reviling.*
STILLINGFLEET.

RA'PPORT. *n.s.* [*rappat*, Fr.] Relation; reference; proportion. A word introduced by the innovator, *Temple*, but not copied by others.

'Tis obvious what rapport *there is between the conceptions and languages in every country, and how great a difference this must make in the excellence of books.*
TEMPLE.

RA'REESHOW. *n.s.* [this word is formed in imitation of the foreign way of pronouncing *rare show.*] A show carried in a box.

The fashions of the town affect us just like a rareeshow, *we have the curiosity to peep at them, and nothing more.* POPE.

Of rareeshows *he sung, and Punch's feats.*
GAY.

RASP. *n.s.* [*raspo*, Italian.] A delicious berry that grows on a species of the bramble; a raspberry.

Sorrel set amongst rasps, *and the* rasps *will be the smaller.*
BACON'S NATURAL HISTORY.

Now will the corinths, now the rasps *supply*
Delicious draughts, when prest to wines.
PHILIPS.

To **RASP.** *v.a.* [*raspen*, Dutch; *rasper*, Fr. *raspare*, Italian.] To rub to powder with a very rough file.

Some authors have advised the rasping *of these bones; but in this case it is needless.*
WISEMAN'S SURGERY.

Having prepared hard woods and ivory for the lathe with rasping, *they pitch it between the pikes.* MOXON.

RASP. *n.s.* [from the verb.] A large rough file, commonly used to wear away wood.

Case-hardening is used by file-cutters, when they make coarse files, and generally most rasps *have formerly been made of iron and case-hardened.*
MOXON'S MECHANICAL EXERCISES.

RA'SPATORY. *n.s.* [*raspatoir*, Fr. from *rasp*.] A chirurgeon's rasp.

I put into his mouth a raspatory, *and pulled away the corrupt flesh, and with cauteries burnt it to a crust.*
WISEMAN'S SURGERY.

RA'THER. *adv.* [this is a comparative from *rath*; *rað*, Saxon, soon. Now out of use. One may still say, by the same form of speaking, *I will* sooner *do this than that*; that is, *I like better to do this*.]

1. More willingly; with better liking.

Almighty God desireth not the death of a sinner, but rather *that he should turn from his wickedness and live.*
COMMON PRAYER.

2. Preferably to the other; with better reason.

'Tis rather *to be thought, that an heir had no such right by divine institution, than that God should give such a right, but yet leave it undeterminate who such heir is.*
LOCKE.

3. In a greater degree than otherwise.

He sought through the world, but sought in vain,
And no where finding, rather *fear'd her slain.* DRYDEN.

4. More properly.

This is an art,
Which does mend nature, change it rather, *but*
The art itself is nature.
SHAKESPEARE'S WINTER'S TALE.

5. Especially.

You are come to me in a happy time,
The rather *for I have some sport in hand.*
SHAKESPEARE.

6. *To have* RATHER. [this is, I think, a barbarous expression of late intrusion into our language, for which it is better to say *will rather*.] To desire in preference.

'Tis with reluctancy he is provoked by our impenitence to apply the discipline of severity and correction; he had rather *mankind should adore him as their patron and benefactor.* ROGERS'S SERMONS.

RAU'CITY. *n.s.* [*raucus*, Lat.] Hoarseness; loud rough noise.

Inequality not stayed upon, but passing, is rather an encrease of sweetness; as in the purling of a wreathed string, and in the raucity *of a trumpet.*
BACON'S NATURAL HISTORY.

RA'WHEAD. *n.s.* [*raw* and *head*.] The name of a spectre, mentioned to fright children.

Hence draw thy theme, and to the stage permit
Rawhead *and bloody bones, and hands and feet,*

Ragousts for Tereus or Thyestes drest. DRYDEN.

Servants awe children, and keep them in subjection, by telling them of rawhead *and* bloodybones. LOCKE.

To **READ.** *v.a.* pret. *read*, part. pass. *read.* [*ræd*, Saxon.]

1. To peruse any thing written.

I have seen her take forth paper, write upon't, read *it, and afterwards seal it.* SHAKESPEARE'S MACBETH.

The passage you must have read, *though since slipt out of your memory.* POPE.

If we have not leisure to read *over the book itself regularly, then by the titles of chapters we may be directed to peruse several sections.* WATTS'S IMPROVEMENT OF THE MIND.

2. To discover by characters or marks.

An armed corse did lye,
In whose dead face he read *great magnanimity.* SPENSER.

3. To learn by observation.

Those about her
From her shall read *the perfect ways of honour.* SHAKESPEARE.

4. To know fully.

O most delicate fiend!
Who is't can read *a woman?*
SHAKESPEARE'S CYMBELINE.

To **READ.** *v.n.*

1. To perform the act of perusing writing.

It shall be with him, and he shall read *therein, that he may learn to fear the Lord.* BIBLE DEUTERONOMY, XVII. 19.

2. To be studious in books.

'Tis sure that Fleury reads. TAYLOR.

3. To know by reading.

I have read *of an eastern king, who put a judge to death for an iniquitous sentence.* SWIFT.

To **REAR.** *v.a.* [*aræran*, Saxon.]

1. To raise up.

All the people shouted with a loud voice, for the rearing *up of the house of the Lord.* BIBLE 1 ESDRAS, V. 62.

Who now shall rear *you to the sun, or rank*
Your tribes. MILTON.

2. To lift up from a fall.

Down again she fell unto the ground,
But he her quickly rear'd *up again.*
FAIRY QUEEN, B. I.

In adoration at his feet I fell
Submiss: he rear'd *me.* MILTON.

3. To move upwards.

Up to a hill anon his steps he rear'd,
From whose high top to ken the prospect round. MILTON.

4. To bring up to maturity.

No creature goeth to generate, whilst the female is busy in sitting or rearing *her young.* BACON'S NATURAL HISTORY.

They were a very hardy breed, and reared *their young ones without any care.* MORTIMER'S HUSBANDRY.

They flourish'd long in tender bliss, and rear'd
A numerous offspring, lovely like themselves. THOMSON.

5. To educate; to instruct.

He wants a father to protect his youth,
And rear *him up to virtue.* SOUTHERN.

They have in every town publick nurseries, where all parents, except cottagers and labourers, are obliged to send their infants to be reared *and educated.* SWIFT.

6. To exalt; to elevate.

Charity decent, modest, easy, kind,
Softens the high, and rears *the abject mind.* PRIOR.

7. To rouse; to stir up.

Into the naked woods he goes,
And seeks the tusky boar to rear,
With well-mouth'd hounds and pointed spear. DRYDEN.[180]

REA'RWARD. *n.s.* [from *rear.*]

1. The last troop.

He from the beginning began to be in the rearward, *and before they left fighting, was too far off.* SIDNEY.

The standard of Dan was the rearward *of the camp.*
BIBLE NUMBERS.

2. The end; the tail; a train behind.

Why follow'd not, when she said Tybalt's dead,
Thy father or thy mother?
But with a rearward *following Tybalt's death,*
Romeo is banished.
SHAKESPEARE'S ROMEO AND JULIET.

3. The latter part. In contempt.

He was ever in the rearward *of the fashion.* SHAKESPEARE.

To **REBE'LLOW.** *v.n.* [*re* and *bellow.*] To bellow in return; to echo back a loud noise.

He loudly bray'd with beastly yelling sound,
That all the fields rebellowed *again.*
FAIRY QUEEN.

The resisting air the thunder broke,
The cave rebellow'd, *and the temple shook.* DRYDEN.

From whence were heard, rebellowing *to the main,*
The roars of lions. DRYDEN'S ÆNEIS.

REBOA'TION. *n.s.* [*reboo*, Lat.] The return of a loud bellowing sound.

REBU'KE. *n.s.* [from the verb.]
1. Reprehension; chiding expression; objurgation.

Why bear you these rebukes, *and answer not?* SHAKESPEARE.

If he will not yield,
Rebuke *and dread correction wait on us,*
And they shall do their office.
SHAKESPEARE'S HENRY IV.

The channels of waters were seen; at thy rebuke, *O Lord, at the blast of the breath of thy nostrils.*
BIBLE PSALMS, XVIII. 15.

Thy rebuke *hath broken my heart; I am full of heaviness.*
BIBLE PSALM LXIX. 21.

The rebukes *and chiding to children, should be in grave and dispassionate words.* LOCKE.

Shall Cibber's son, without rebuke,
Swear like a lord? POPE.

Should vice expect to 'scape rebuke,
Because its owner is a duke?
SWIFT'S MISCELLANIES.

2. In low language, it signifies any kind of check.

He gave him so terrible a rebuke *upon the forehead with his heel, that he laid him at his length.* L'ESTRANGE.

RE'BUS. *n.s.* [*rebus*, Latin.] A word represented by a picture.

Some citizens, wanting arms, have coined themselves certain devices alluding to their names, which we call rebus*: Master Jugge the printer, in many of his books, took, to express his name, a nightingale sitting in a bush with a scrole in her mouth, wherein was written jugge, jugge, jugge.*
PEACHAM.

RE'CEPTIVE. *adj.* [*receptus*, Lat.] Having the quality of admitting what is communicated.

The soul being, as it is active, perfected by love of that infinite good, shall, as it is receptive, *be also perfected with those supernatural passions of joy, peace and delight.*
HOOKER.

The pretended first matter is capable of all forms, and the imaginary space is receptive *of all bodies.* GLANVILLE.

RE'CIPE. *n.s.* [*recipe*, Lat. the term used by physicians, when they direct ingredients.] A medical prescription.

I should enjoin you travel; for absence doth in a kind remove the cause, and answers the physicians first recipe, *vomiting and purging; but this would be too harsh.*
SUCKLING.

Th' apothecary train is wholly blind,
From files a random recipe *they take,*
And many deaths of one prescription make. DRYDEN.

RECI'PIENT. *n.s.* [*recipiens*, Latin.]

1. The receiver; that to which any thing is communicated.

Though the images, or whatever else is the cause of sense, may be alike as from the object, yet may the representations be varied according to the nature of the recipient. GLANVILLE.

2. [*Recipient*, Fr.] The vessel into which spirits are driven by the still.

The form of sound words, dissolved by chymical preparation, ceases to be nutritive; and after all the labours of the alembeck, leaves in the recipient *a fretting corrosive.* DECAY OF PIETY.

RECITA'TION. *n.s.* [from *recite.*] Repetition; rehearsal.

If menaces of scripture fall upon men's persons, if they are but the recitations *and descriptions of God's decreed wrath, and those decrees and that wrath have no respect to the actual sins of men; why should terrors restrain me from sin, when present advantage invites me to it?* HAMMOND.

He used philosophical arguments and recitations. TEMPLE.

RECI'TATIVE, RECITATIVO. *n.s.* [from *recite.*] A kind of tuneful pronunciation, more musical than common speech, and less than song; chaunt.

He introduced the examples of moral virtue, writ in verse, and performed in recitative *musick.* DRYDEN.

By singing peers upheld on either hand,
Then thus in quaint recitativo *spoke.*
DUNCIAD, B. IV.

To **RECI'TE.** *v.a.* [*recito*, Lat. *reciter*, Fr.] To rehearse; to repeat; to enumerate; to tell over.

While Telephus's youthful charms,
His rosy neck, and winding arms,
With endless rapture you recite,
And in the tender name delight.
ADDISON.

The thoughts of gods let Granville's verse recite,
And bring the scenes of op'ning fate to light. POPE.

If we will recite *nine hours in ten,*
You lose your patience.
POPE'S EPISTLES OF HORACE.

To **RECOGNI'SE.** *v.a.* [*recognosco*, Lat.]

1. To acknowledge; to recover and avow knowledge of any person or thing.

The British cannon formidably roars,
While starting from his oozy bed,
Th' asserted ocean rears his reverend head,
To view and recognise *his ancient lord.*
DRYDEN.

Then first he recognis'd *th' æthereal guest,*
Wonder and joy alternate fire his breast.
POPE.

2. To review; to reexamine.

However their causes speed in your tribunals, Christ will recognise *them at a greater.* SOUTH.

RECO'RD. *n.s.* [*record*, Fr. from the verb. The accent of the noun is indifferently on either syllable; of the verb always on the last.] Register; authentick memorial.

Is it upon record? *or else reported*
Successively, from age to age?
SHAKESPEARE'S RICHARD III.

It cannot be
The Volscians dare break with us.
—— *We have* record *that very well it can;*
And three examples of the like have been.
SHAKESPEARE.

The king made a record *of these things, and Mardocheus wrote thereof.*
BIBLE ESTHER, XII. 4.

An ark, and in the ark his testimony,
The records *of his covenant.* MILTON.

Of such a goddess no time leaves record,
Who burn'd the temple where she was
ador'd. DRYDEN.

If he affirms such a monarchy continued to the flood, I would know what records *he has it from.* LOCKE.

Though the attested copy of a record *be good proof, yet the copy of a copy never so well attested will not be admitted as a proof in judicature.* LOCKE.

Thy elder look, great Janus! cast
Into the long records *of ages past;*
Review the years in fairest action drest.
PRIOR.

RE'CREMENT. *n.s.* [*recrementum*, Lat.] Dross; spume; superfluous or useless parts.

The vital fire in the heart requires an ambient body of a yielding nature, to receive the superfluous serosities and other recrements *of the blood.* BOYLE.

RECRIMINA'TION. *n.s.* [*recrimination*, Fr. from *recriminate.*] Return of one accusation with another.

Publick defamation will seem disobliging enough to provoke a return, which again begets a rejoinder, and so the quarrel is carried on with mutual recriminations.
GOVERNMENT OF THE TONGUE.

RECRIMINA'TOR. *n.s.* [from *recriminate.*] He that returns one charge with another.

To **RECRUI'T.** *v.a.* [*recruter*, Fr.]
1. To repair any thing wasted by new supplies.

He was longer in recruiting *his flesh than was usual; but by a milk diet he recovered it.* WISEMAN'S SURGERY.

Increase thy care to save the sinking kind;
With greens and flow'rs recruit *their empty hives,*
And seek fresh forage to sustain their lives.
DRYDEN.

Her cheeks glow the brighter, recruiting *their colour;*
As flowers by sprinkling revive with fresh odour. GRANVILLE.

This sun is set; but see in bright array
What hosts of heavenly lights recruit *the day!*
Love in a shining galaxy appears
Triumphant still. GRANVILLE.

Seeing the variety of motion, which we find in the world is always decreasing, there is a necessity of conserving and recruiting *it by active principles; such as are the cause of gravity, by which planets and comets keep their motions in their orbs, and bodies acquire great motion in falling.*
NEWTON.

2. To supply an army with new men.

He trusted the earl of Holland with the command of that army, with which he was to be recruited *and assisted.*
CLARENDON.

RECUBA'TION. *n.s.* [*recubo*, Latin.] The act of lying or leaning.

Whereas our translation renders it sitting, it cannot have that illation, for the French and Italian translations express neither position of session or recubation.
BROWN.

RECU'MBENT. *adj.* [*recumbens*, Lat.] Lying; leaning.

The Roman recumbent, *or more properly accumbent, posture in eating was introduced after the first Punick war.*
ARBUTHNOT.

RECURVA'TION, RECURVITY. *n.s.* [*recurvo*, Lat.] Flexure backwards.

Ascending first into a caspulary reception of the breast bone by a serpentine recurvation, *it ascendeth again into the neck.* BROWN'S VULGAR ERROURS.

RECU'RVOUS. *adj.* [*recurvus*, Lat.] Bent backward.

I have not observed tails in all; but in

others I have observed long recurvous *tails, longer than their bodies.* DERHAM.

RE'DCOAT. *n.s.* A name of contempt for a soldier.

The fearful passenger, who travels late,
Shakes at the moon-shine shadow of a rush,
And sees a redcoat *rise from ev'ry bush.*
DRYDEN.

RE'DSHANK. *n.s.* [*red* and *shank.*]
1. This seems to be a contemptuous appellation for some of the people of Scotland.

He sent over his brother Edward with a power of Scots and redshanks *unto Ireland, where they got footing.*
SPENSER.

2. A bird. *Ainsworth.*

REDU'NDANT. *adj.* [*redundans,* Latin.]
1. Superabundant; exuberant; superfluous.

His head,
With burnish'd neck of verdant gold, erect
Amidst his circling spires, that on the grass
Floated redundant.
MILTON'S PARADISE LOST, B. IX.

Notwithstanding the redundant *oil in fishes, they do not encrease fat so much as flesh.* ARBUTHNOT ON ALIMENTS.

2. Using more words or images than are useful.

Where the author is redundant, *mark those paragraphs to be retrenched; when he trifles, abandon those passages.* WATTS.

To **REE.** *v.a.* [I know not the etymology.] To riddle; to sift.

After malt is well rubbed and winnowed, you must then ree *it over in a sieve.*
MORTIMER'S HUSBANDRY.

REFE'CTION. *n.s.* [*refection,* Fr. from *refectio,* Lat.] Refreshment after hunger or fatigue.

After a draught of wine, a man may seem lighter in himself from sudden refection, *though he be heavier in the balance, from a ponderous addition.* BROWN.

Fasting is the diet of angels, the food and refection *of souls, and the richest aliment of grace.* SOUTH.

For sweet refection *due,*
The genial viands let my train renew.
POPE.

REFE'CTORY. *n.s.* [*refectoire,* Fr. from *refect.*] Room of refreshment; eating room.

He cells and refectories *did prepare,*
And large provisions laid of winter fare.
DRYDEN.

To **REFI'NE.** *v.a.* [*raffiner,* Fr.]
1. To purify; to clear from dross and recrement.

I will refine *them as silver is refined, and will try them as gold is tried.*
BIBLE ZECHERIAH, XIII. 9.

Weigh ev'ry word, and ev'ry thought refine. ANONYMOUS.

The red Dutch currant yields a rich juice, to be diluted with a quantity of water boiled with refined *sugar.* MORTIMER.

2. To make elegant; to polish; to make accurate.

Queen Elizabeth's time was a golden age for a world of refined *wits, who honoured poesy with their pens.* PEACHAM.

Love refines *the thoughts, and hath his seat*
In reason. MILTON.

The same traditional sloth, which renders the bodies of children, born from wealthy parents, weak, may perhaps refine *their spirits.* SWIFT.

To **REFI'NE.** *v.n.*
1. To improve in point of accuracy or delicacy.

Chaucer refined *on Boccace, and mended stories.* DRYDEN.

Let a lord but own the happy lines;
How the wit brightens, how the sense refines! POPE.

2. To grow pure.

The pure limpid stream, when foul with stains,
Works itself clear, and as it runs refines.
ADDISON.

3. To affect nicety.

He makes another paragraph about our refining *in controversy, and coming nearer still to the church of Rome.* ATTERBURY.

REFI'NEMENT. *n.s.* [from *refine.*]
1. The act of purifying, by clearing any thing from dross and recrementitious matter.

The more bodies are of kin to spirit in subtilty and refinement, *the more diffusive are they.* NORRIS.[181]

2. Improvement in elegance or purity.

From the civil war to this time, I doubt whether the corruptions in our language have not equalled its refinements.
SWIFT.

3. Artificial practice.

The rules religion prescribes are more successful in publick and private affairs, than the refinements *of irregular cunning.*
ROGERS.

4. Affectation of elegant improvement.

The flirts about town had a design to leave us in the lurch, by some of their late refinements. ADDISON'S GUARDIAN.

REFOCILLA'TION. *n.s.* [*refocillo,* Lat.] Restoration of strength by refreshment.

REFORMA'TION. *n.s.* [*reformation,* Fr. from *reform.*]
1. Change from worse to better.

Never came reformation *in a flood*
With such a heady current, scow'ring faults;
Nor ever Hydra-headed wilfulness
So soon did lose his seat, as in this king.
SHAKESPEARE'S HENRY V.

Satire lashes vice into reformation.
DRYDEN.

The pagan converts mention this great reformation *of those who had been the greatest sinners, with that sudden and surprising change, which the christian religion made in the lives of the most profligate.* ADDISON.

2.[182] The change of religion from the corruptions of popery to its primitive state.

The burden of the reformation *lay on Luther's shoulders.* ATTERBURY.

REFO'RMER. *n.s.* [from *reform.*]
1. One who makes a change for the better; an amender.

Publick reformers *had need first practise that on their own hearts, which they purpose to try on others.*
KING CHARLES.

The complaint is more general, than the endeavours to redress it: Abroad every man would be a reformer, *how very few at home.* SPRAT'S SERMONS.

It was honour enough, to behold the English churches reformed; that is, delivered from the reformers. SOUTH.

2. Those who changed religion from popish corruptions and innovations.

Our first reformers *were famous confessors and martyrs all over the world.* BACON.

To **REFRI'GERATE.** *v.a.* [*refrigero, re* and *frigus,* Lat.] To cool.

The great breezes, which the motion of the air in great circles, such as the girdle of the world, produceth, do refrigerate; *and therefore in those parts noon is nothing so hot, when the breezes are great, as about ten of the clock in the forenoon.*
BACON'S NATURAL HISTORY.

Whether they be refrigerated *inclinatorily or somewhat equinoxically, though in a lesser degree, they discover some verticity.*
BROWN'S VULGAR ERROURS.

REFRIGERA'TION. *n.s.* [*refrigeratio,* Lat. *refrigeration,* Fr.] The act of cooling; the state of being cooled.

Divers do stut; the cause may be the refrigeration *of the tongue, whereby it is less apt to move.* BACON.

If the mere refrigeration *of the air would fit it for breathing, this might be somewhat helped with bellows.* WILKINS.

REFRI'GERATORY. *n.s.*

1. That part of a distilling vessel that is placed about the head of a still, and filled with water to cool the condensing vapours; but this is now generally done by a worm or spiral pipe, turning through a tub of cold water. *Quincy.*

2. Any thing internally cooling.

A delicate wine, and a durable refrigeratory. MORTIMER.

To **REGE'NERATE.** *v.a.* [*regenero*, Lat.]

1. To reproduce; to produce anew.

Albeit the son of this earl of Desmond, who lost his head, were restored to the earldom; yet could not the king's grace regenerate *obedience in that degenerate house, but it grew rather more wild.*
DAVIES ON IRELAND.

Through all the soil a genial ferment spreads,
Regenerates *the plants, and new adorns the meads.* BLACKMORE.

An alkali, poured to that which is mixed with an acid, raiseth an effervescence, at the cessation of which, the salts, of which the acid is composed, will be regenerated.
ARBUTHNOT.

2. [*Regenerer*, Fr.] To make to be born anew; to renew by change of carnal nature to a christian life.

No sooner was a convert initiated, but by an easy figure he became a new man, and both acted and looked upon himself as one regenerated *and born a second time into another state of existence.*
ADDISON ON THE CHRISTIAN RELIGION.

RE'GLET. *n.s.* [*reglette*, from *regle*, Fr.] Ledge of wood exactly planed, by which printers separate their lines in pages widely printed.

To **REIMBO'DY.** *v.n.* [*re* and *imbody*, which is more frequently, but not more properly, written *embody.*] To embody again.

Quicksilver, broken into little globes, the parts brought to touch immediately reimbody. BOYLE.

To **REIMBU'RSE.** *v.a.* [*re*, *in* and *bourse*, Fr. a purse.] To repay; to repair loss or expence by an equivalent.

Hath he saved any kingdom at his own expence, to give him a title of reimbursing *himself by the destruction of ours?*
SWIFT'S MISCELLANIES.

RELA'TION. *n.s.* [*relation*, Fr. from *relate.*]

1. Manner of belonging to any person or thing.

Under this stone lies virtue, youth,
Unblemish'd probity and truth;
Just unto all relations *known,*
A worthy patriot, pious son. WALLER.

So far as service imports duty and subjection, all created beings bear the necessary relation *of servants to God.* SOUTH.

Our necessary relations *to a family, oblige all to use their reasoning powers upon a thousand occasions.* WATTS.

2. Respect; reference; regard.

I have been importuned to make some observations on this art, in relation *to its agreement with poetry.* DRYDEN.

Relation *consists in the consideration and comparing one idea with another.*
LOCKE.

3. Connexion between one thing and another.

Augurs, that understand relations, *have*
By magpies, choughs and rooks brought forth

The secret'st man of blood.
SHAKESPEARE'S MACBETH.

Kindred; alliance of kin.

Relations *dear, and all the charities*
Of fathers, son and brother first were known. MILTON.

Be kindred and relation *laid aside,*
And honour's cause by laws of honour try'd. DRYDEN.

Are we not to pity and supply the poor, though they have no relation *to us? no* relation? *that cannot be: the gospel stiles them all our brethren; nay, they have a nearer* relation *to us, our fellow-members; and both these from their* relation *to our Saviour himself, who calls them his brethren.* SPRAT.

Person related by birth or marriage; nsman; kinswoman.

A she-cousin, of a good family and small fortune, passed months among all her relations. SWIFT.

Dependants, friends, relations,
Savag'd by woe, forget the tender tie.
THOMSON.

Narrative; tale; account; narration; cital of facts.

In an historical relation, *we use terms that are most proper.*
BURNET'S THEORY OF THE EARTH.

The author of a just fable, must please more than the writer of an historical relation. DENNIS'S LETTERS.

ELA'Y. *n.s.* [*relais*, Fr.] Horses on e road to relieve others.

E'LEVANT. *adj.* [French.] elieving. *Dictionaries.*

ELI'GIONIST. *n.s.* [from *ligion.*] A bigot to any religious ersuasion.

The lawfulness of taking oaths may be revealed to the quakers, who then will stand upon as good a foot for preferment as any other subject; under such a motly administration, what pullings and hawlings, what a zeal and biass there will be in each religionist *to advance his own tribe, and depress the others.* SWIFT.

RELI'NQUISHMENT. *n.s.* [from *relinquish.*] The act of forsaking.

Government or ceremonies, or whatsoever it be, which is popish, away with it: this is the thing they require in us, the utter relinquishment *of all things popish.* HOOKER.

That natural tenderness of conscience, which must first create in the soul a sense of sin, and from thence produce a sorrow for it, and at length cause a relinquishment *of it, is took away by a customary repeated course of sinning.* SOUTH.

To **RELU'ME.** *v.a.* To light anew; to rekindle.

Relume *her ancient light, nor kindle new.* POPE.

To **RELU'MINE.** *v.a.* To light anew.

Once put out thy light;
I know not where is that Promethean heat,
That can thy light relumine.
SHAKESPEARE'S OTHELLO.

To **REMA'ND.** *v.a.* [*re* and *mando*, Lat.] To send back; to call back.

The better sort quitted their freeholds and fled into England, and never returned, though many laws were made to remand *them back.* DAVIES ON IRELAND.

Philoxenus, for despising some dull poetry of Dionysius, was condemned to dig in the quarries; from whence being remanded, *at his return Dionysius produced some other of his verses, which as soon as Philoxenus had read, he made no reply, but, calling to the waiters, said, carry me again to the quarries.*
GOVERNMENT OF THE TONGUE.

REMA'RKABLE. *adj.* [*remarkable*, Fr.] Observable; worthy of note.

So did Orpheus plainly teach, that the world had beginning in time, from the will of the most high God, whose remarkable *words are thus converted.* RALEIGH.

'Tis remarkable, *that they*
Talk most, who have the least to say.
PRIOR.

What we obtain by conversation soon vanishes, unless we note down what remarkables *we have found.* WATTS.

REME'DIATE. *adj.* [from *remedy.*] Medicinal; affording a remedy. Not in use.

All you, unpublish'd virtues of the earth,
Spring with my tears; be aidant and
remediate
In the good man's distress.
SHAKESPEARE'S KING LEAR.

REME'MBERER. *n.s.* [from *remember.*] One who remembers.

A brave master to servants, and a rememberer *of the least good office; for his flock he transplanted most of them into plentiful soils.* WOTTON.

REMINI'SCENCE. *n.s.* [*reminiscens,* Latin.] Recollection; recovery of ideas.

I cast about for all circumstances that may revive my memory or reminiscence.
HALE'S ORIGIN OF MANKIND.

For the other part of memory, called reminiscence, *which is the retrieving of a thing at present forgot, or but confusedly remembered, by setting the mind to ransack every little cell of the brain; while it is thus busied, how accidentally does the thing sought for offer itself to the mind?*
SOUTH.

REMINISCE'NTIAL. *adj.* [from *reminiscence.*] Relating to reminiscence.

Would truth dispense, we could be content with Plato, that knowledge were but remembrance, that intellectual acquisition were but reminiscential *evocation.* BROWN.

REMI'TTANCE. *n.s.* [from *remit.*
1. The act of paying money at a distan[t]
place.
2. Sum sent to a distant place.

A compact among private persons furnish[e]
out the several remittances.
ADDISON'S REMARKS ON ITALY.

REMO'TION. *n.s.* [from *remotus,* Lat.] The act of removing; the state of being removed to distance.

All this safety were remotion, *and thy defence absence.* SHAKESPEARE.

This act persuades me,
'Tis the remotion *of the duke and her.*
SHAKESPEARE.

The consequent strictly taken, may be a sallacious illation, in reference to antecedency or consequence; as to conclude fro[m] the position of the antecedent unto the position of the consequent, or from the remotion *of the consequent to the* remotion *of the antecedent.*
BROWN'S VULGAR ERROURS.

To **REMU'RMUR.** *v.a.* [*re* and *murmur.*] To utter back in murmurs; to repeat in low hoarse sounds.

Her fate is whisper'd by the gentle breeze,
And told in sighs to all the trembling trees
The trembling trees, in ev'ry plain and
wood,
Her fate remurmur *to the silver flood.*
POPE.

RENCOU'NTER. *n.s.* [*rencontre,* Fr.]
1. Clash; collision.

You may as well expect two bowls should grow sensible by rubbing, as that the rencounter *of any bodies should awaken them into perception.* COLLIER.

2. Personal opposition.

Virgil's friends thought fit to alter a line i[n] Venus's speech, that has a relation to the rencounter. ADDISON.

So when the trumpet sounding gives the sign,
The justling chiefs in rude rencounter *join:*
So meet, and so renew the dextrous fight;
Their clattering arms with the fierce shock resound. GRANVILLE.

. Loose or casual engagement.

The confederates should turn to their advantage their apparent odds in men and horse; and by that means out-number the enemy in all rencounters *and engagements.* ADDISON.

. Sudden combat without premeditation.

ENI'TENCY. *n.s.* [from *renitent.*] hat resistance in solid bodies, when ey press upon, or are impelled one gainst another, or the resistance that a ody makes on account of weight. *uincy.*

ENI'TENT. *adj.* [*renitens*, Lat.] cting against any impulse by elastick ower.

By an inflation of the muscles, they become soft, and yet renitent, *like so many pillows, dissipating the force of the pressure, and so taking away the sense of pain.* RAY.

E'NNET. *n.s.* See **RUNNET**.

A putredinous ferment coagulates all humours, as milk with rennet *is turned.* FLOYER ON THE HUMOURS.

EPA'NDOUS. *adj.* [*repandus*, at.] Bent upwards.

Though they be drawn repandous *or convexedly crooked in one piece, yet the dolphin that carrieth Arion is concavously inverted, and hath its spine depressed in another.* BROWN.

E'PARATION. *n.s.* [*reparation*, r. *reparatio*, from *reparo*, Lat.]

. The act of repairing.

Antonius Philosophus took care of the reparation *of the highways.* ARBUTHNOT ON COINS.

2. Supply of what is wasted.

When the organs of sense want their due repose and necessary reparations, *the soul exerts herself in her several faculties.* ADDISON.

In this moveable body, the fluid and solid parts must be consumed; and both demand a constant reparation. ARBUTHNOT.

3. Recompense for any injury; amends.

The king should be able, when he had cleared himself, to make him reparation. BACON.

I am sensible of the scandal I have given by my loose writings, and make what reparation *I am able.* DRYDEN.

REPARTEE'. *n.s.* [*repartie*, Fr.] Smart reply.

The fools overflowed with smart repartees, *and were only distinguished from the intended wits, by being called coxcombs.* DRYDEN'S DUFRESNOY.

Sullen was Jupiter just now:
And Cupid was as bad as he;
Hear but the youngster's repartee. PRIOR.

To **REPARTEE'.** *v.n.* To make smart replies.

High flights she had, and wit at will,
And so her tongue lay seldom still;
For in all visits who but she,
To argue, or to repartee? PRIOR.

REPEA'TER. *n.s.* [from *repeat.*]
1. One that repeats; one that recites.
2. A watch that strikes the hours at will by compression of a spring.

REPE'RTORY. *n.s.* [*repertoire*, Fr. *repertorium*, Lat.] A treasury; a magazine; a book in which any thing is to be found.

REPO'RTER. *n.s.* [from *report.*] Relater; one that gives an account.

There she appear'd; or my reporter *devis'd well for her.*
SHAKESPEARE'S ANTONY AND CLEOPATRA.

Rumours were raised of great discord among the nobility; for this cause the lords assembled, gave order to apprehend the reporters *of these surmises.* HAYWARD.

If I had known a thing they concealed, I should never be the reporter *of it.*
POPE.

To **REPO'SITE.** *v.a.* [*repositus*, Lat.] To lay up; to lodge as in a place of safety.

Others reposite *their young in holes, and secure themselves also therein, because such security is wanting, their lives being sought.*
DENHAM'S PHYSICO-THEOLOGY.

REPO'SITORY. *n.s.* [*repositoire*, Fr. *repositorium*, Lat.] A place where any thing is safely laid up.

The mind of man, not being capable of having many ideas under view at once, it was necessary to have a repository *to lay up those ideas.* LOCKE.

He can take a body to pieces, and dispose of them, to us not without the appearance of irretrievable confusion, but with respect to his own knowledge into the most regular and methodical repositories.
ROGERS'S SERMONS.

REPRESE'NTATIVE. *n.s.*
1. One exhibiting the likeness of another.

A statue of rumour whispering an idiot in the ear, who was the representative *of credulity.* ADDISON'S FREEHOLDER.

2. One exercising the vicarious power given by another.

I wish the welfare of my country; and my morals and politicks teach me to leave all that to be adjusted by our representatives *above, and to divine providence.*
BLOUNT TO POPE.

3. That by which any thing is shown.

Difficulty must cumber this doctrine, which supposes that the perfections of God are the representatives *to us, of whatever we perceive in the creatures.* LOCKE.

REPRESE'NTER. *n.s.* [from *represent.*]
1. One who shows or exhibits.

Where the real works of nature, or veritable acts of story, are to be described, art, being but the imitator or secondary representer, *must not vary from the verity.* BROWN.

2. One who bears a vicarious character; one who acts for another by deputation.

My muse officious ventures
On the nation's representers. SWIFT.

REPRI'SAL. *n.s.* [*represalia*, low Lat. *represaille*, Fr.] Something seized by way of retaliation for robbery or injury.

The English had great advantage in value of reprisals, *as being more strong and active at sea.* HAYWARD.

Sense must sure thy safest plunder be,
Since no reprisals *can be made on thee.*
POPE.

REPRI'SE. *n.s.* [*reprise*, Fr.] The act of taking something in retaliation of injury.

Your care about your banks infers a fear
Of threat'ning floods and inundations near;
If so, a just reprise *would only be*
Of what the land usurp'd upon the sea.
DRYDEN.

REPTI'LE. *n.s.* An animal that creeps upon many feet.

Terrestial animals may be divided into quadrupeds or reptiles, *which have many feet, and serpents which have no feet.*
LOCKE'S ELEMENTS OF NATURAL PHILOSOPHY.

Holy retreat! Sithence no female hither,

Conscious of social love and nature's
rites,
Must dare approach, from the inferior
reptile,
To woman, form divine. PRIOR.

REPU'BLICAN. *n.s.* [from *repub-ck.*] One who thinks a common-wealth without monarchy the best overnment.

These people are more happy in imagination than the rest of their neighbours, because they think themselves so; though such a chimerical happiness is not peculiar to republicans. ADDISON.

'o **REPU'LLULATE.** *v.n.* [*re* and *ullulo*, Lat. *repulluler*, Fr.] To bud gain.

Though tares repullulate, *there is wheat still left in the field.*
HOWEL'S VOCAL FOREST.

RE'REWARD.[183] *n.s.* The rear or ist troop.

'o **RESCRI'BE.** *v.a.* [*rescribo*, Lat. *escrire*, Fr.]

. To write back.

Whenever a prince on his being consulted rescribes *or writes back Toleramus, he dispenses with that act otherwise unlawful.* AYLIFFE'S PARERGON.

. To write over again.

Calling for more paper to rescribe *them, he shewed him the difference betwixt the ink-box and the sand-box.* HOWEL.

RE'SCRIPT. *n.s.* [*rescrit*, Fr. *escriptum*, Lat.] Edict of an emperour.

One finding a great mass of money digged under ground, and being somewhat doubtful, signified it to the emperor, who made a rescript *thus; Use it.*
BACON'S APOPHTHEGMS.

The popes, in such cases, where canons were silent, did, after the manner of the Roman emperors, write back their determinations, which were stiled rescripts *or decretal epistles, having the force of laws.*
AYLIFFE'S PARERGON.

RESE'NTFUL. *adj.* [*resent* and *full.*] Malignant; easily provoked to anger, and long retaining it.

RESE'RVATORY. *n.s.* [*reservoir*, Fr.] Place in which any thing is reserved or kept.

How I got such notice of that subterranean reservatory *as to make a computation of the water now concealed therein, peruse the propositions concerning earthquakes.*
WOODWARD.

RESERVOI'R. *n.s.* [*reservoir*, Fr.] Place where any thing is kept in store.

There is not a spring or fountain, but are well provided with huge cisterns and reservoirs *of rain and snow-water.* ADDISON.

Who sees pale Mammon pine amidst his
store,
Sees but a backward steward for the poor;
This year a reservoir, *to keep and spare;*
The next, a fountain spouting through his
heir. POPE.

To **RESI'DE.** *v.n.* [*resideo*, Lat. *resider*, Fr.]

1. To have abode; to live; to dwell; to be present.

How can God with such reside?
MILTON.

In no fix'd place the happy souls reside;
In groves we live, and lie on mossy beds.
DRYDEN'S ÆNEIS.

2. [*Resido*, Lat.] To sink; to subside; to fall to the bottom.

Oil of vitriol and petroleum, a drachm of each, turn into a mouldy substance; there residing *in the bottom a fair cloud and a thick oil on the top.* BOYLE.

RE'SIDENT. *adj.* [*residens*, Lat. *resident*, Fr.] Dwelling or having abode in any place.

I am not concerned in this objection; not

thinking it necessary, that Christ should be personally present or resident *on earth in the millenium.*
BURNET'S THEORY OF THE EARTH.

He is not said to be resident *in a place, who comes thither with a purpose of retiring immediately; so also he is said to be absent, who is absent with his family.*
AYLIFFE'S PARERGON.

RE'SIDENT. *n.s.* [from the adj.] An agent, minister, or officer residing in any distant place with the dignity of an ambassador.

The pope fears the English will suffer nothing like a resident *or consul in his kingdoms.* ADDISON.

RESIPI'SCENCE. *n.s.* [*resipiscence*, Fr. *resipiscentia*, low Lat.] Wisdom after the fact; repentance.

RESI'STANCE, RESISTENCE. *n.s.* [*resistance*, Fr. This word, like many others, is differently written, as it is supposed to have come from the Latin or the French.]

1. The act of resisting; opposition.

Demetrius, seeing that the land was quiet, and that no resistance *was made against him, sent away all his forces.*
BIBLE 1 MACCABEES.

2. The quality of not yielding to force or external impression.

The resistance *of bone to cold is greater than of flesh; for that the flesh shrinketh, but the bone resisteth, whereby the cold becometh more eager.* BACON.

Musick so softens and disarms the mind,
That not an arrow does resistance *find.*
WALLER.

The idea of solidity we receive by our touch, and it arises from the resistance *which we find in body to the entrance of any other body into the place it possesses.* LOCKE.

But that part of the resistance, *which arises from the vis inertiæ, is proportional to the density of the matter, and cannot be diminished by dividing the matter into smaller parts, nor by any other means, than by decreasing the density of the medium.*
NEWTON'S OPTICKS.

RESO'RT. *n.s.* [from the verb.]

1. Frequency; assembly; meeting.

Unknown, unquestion'd in that thick
resort. DRYDEN.

2. Concourse; confluence.

The like places of resort *are frequented by men out of place.*
SWIFT'S MISCELLANIES.

3. Act of visiting.

Join with me to forbid him her resort.
SHAKESPEARE.

4. [*Ressort*, Fr.] Movement; active power; spring.[184]

Some know the resorts *and falls of business, that cannot sink into the main of it.* BACON'S ESSAYS.

In fortune's empire blindly thus we go,
We wander after pathless destiny,
Whose dark resorts *since prudence cannot know,*
In vain it would provide for what shall be.
DRYDEN.

RESPIRA'TION. *n.s.* [*respiration*, Fr. *respiratio*, from *respiro*, Lat.]

1. The act of breathing.

Apollonius of Tyana affirmed, that the ebbing and flowing of the sea was the respiration *of the world, drawing in water as breath, and putting it forth again.*
BACON.

Syrups or other expectoratives do not advantage in coughs, by slipping down between the epiglottis; for, as I instanced before, they must necessarily occasion a greater cough and difficulty of respiration.
HARVEY ON CONSUMPTIONS.

The author of nature foreknew the necessity of rains and dews to the present structure of plants, and the uses of respiration *to animals; and therefore created those correspondent properties in the atmosphere.* BENTLEY'S SERMONS.

. Relief from toil.

Till the day
Appear of respiration *to the just,*
And vengeance to the wicked.
MILTON'S PARADISE LOST, B. XII.

.ESTA'GNANT. *adj.* [*restagnans*, at.] Remaining without flow or ıotion.

Upon the tops of high mountains, the air, which bears against the restagnant *quicksilver, is less pressed by the less ponderous incumbent air.* BOYLE.

:ESTAURA'TION. *n.s.* [*restauro*, at.] The act of recovering to the ɔrmer state.

Adam is in us an original cause of our nature, and of that corruption of nature which causeth death; Christ as the cause original of restauration *to life.* HOOKER, B. V. S. 56.

O my dear father! restauration *hang*
Thy medicine on my lips; and let this kiss
Repair those violent harms, that my two sisters
Have in thy reverence made.
SHAKESPEARE'S KING LEAR.

Spermatical parts will not admit a regeneration, much less will they receive an integral restauration. BROWN.

ꞦESTI'FF. *adj.* [*restif*, Fr. *restivo*, tal.]

. Unwilling to stir; resolute against oing forward; obstinate; stubborn. It ; originally used of an horse, that, hough not wearied, will not be driven ɔrward.

All, who before him did ascend the throne,
Labour'd to draw three restive *nations on.*
ROSCOMMON.

This restiff *stubborness is never to be excused under any pretence whatsoever.* L'ESTRANGE.

Some, with studious care,
Their restiff *steeds in sandy plains prepare.* DRYDEN.

The archangel, when discord was restive, *and would not be drawn from her beloved monastery with fair words, drags her out with many stripes.*
DRYDEN'S DEDICATION TO JUVENAL.

So James the drowsy genius wakes
Of Britain, long entranc'd in charms,
Restiff, *and slumb'ring on its arms.*
DRYDEN.

The pamper'd colt will discipline disdain,
Impatient of the lash, and restiff *to the rein.* DRYDEN.

2. Being at rest; being less in motion. Not used.

Palsies oftenest happen upon the left side; the most vigorous part protecting itself, and protruding the matter upon the weaker and restive *side.*
BROWN'S VULGAR ERROURS.

RESTORA'TION. *n.s.* [from *restore*; *restauration*, Fr.]

1. The act of replacing in a former state. This is properly *restauration.*

Hail, royal Albion, hail to thee,
Thy longing people's expectation!
Sent from the gods to set us free
From bondage and from usurpation:
Behold the different climes agree,
Rejoicing in thy restoration.
DRYDEN'S ALBION.

The Athenians, now deprived of the only person that was able to recover their losses, repent of their rashness, and endeavour in vain for his restoration. SWIFT.

2. Recovery.

The change is great in this restoration *of the man, from a state of spiritual darkness, to a capacity of perceiving divine truth.* ROGERS.

RESTO'RATIVE. *n.s.* [from *restore.*] A medicine that has the power of recruiting life.

I will kiss thy lips;
Haply some poison yet doth hang on them,
To make me die with a restorative.
SHAKESPEARE'S ROMEO AND JULIET.

God saw it necessary by such mortifications to quench the boundless rage of an insatiable intemperance, to make the weakness of the flesh, the physick and the restorative *of the spirit.* SOUTH'S SERMONS.

Asses milk is an excellent restorative *in consumptions.* MORTIMER.

He prescribes an English gallon of asses milk, especially as a restorative.
ARBUTHNOT.

RE'STY. *adj.* [*restiff*, Fr.] Obstinate in standing still. See **RESTIFF**.

Come, our stomachs
Will make what's homely savoury, weariness
Can snore upon the flint, when resty *sloth*
Finds the down pillow hard.
SHAKESPEARE'S CYMBELINE.

Men of discretion, whom people in power may with little ceremony load as heavy as they please, find them neither resty *nor vicious.* SWIFT.

RESUPINA'TION. *n.s.* [*resupino*, Lat.] The act of lying on the back.

RETAI'LER. *n.s.* [from *retail.*] One who sells by small quantities.

From these particulars we may guess at the rest, as retailers *do of the whole piece, by taking a view of its ends.* HAKEWILL.

RETE'CTION. *n.s.* [*retectus*, Lat.] The act of discovering to the view.

This is rather a restoration of a body to its own colour, or a retection *of its native colour, than a change.* BOYLE.

RE'TICLE. *n.s.* [*reticulum*, Lat.] A small net. *Dictionaries.*

RETI'CULAR. *adj.* [from *reticulum*, Lat.] Having the form of a small net.

RETI'CULATED. *adj.* [*reticulatus*, Lat.] Made of network; formed with interstitial vacuities.

The intervals of the cavities, rising a little, make a pretty kind of reticulated *work.*
WOODWARD ON FOSSILS.

RE'TIFORM. *adj.* [*retiformis*, Lat.] Having the form of a net.

The uveous coat and inside of the choroides are blackened, that the rays may not be reflected backwards to confound the sight; and if any be by the retiform *coat reflected, they are soon choaked in the black inside of the uvea.* RAY.

RETROCE'SSION. *n.s.* [*retrocessum*, Lat.] The act of going back.

RETROCOPU'LATION. *n.s.* [*retro* and *copulation.*] Post-coition.

From the nature of this position, there ensueth a necessity of retrocopulation.
BROWN'S VULGAR ERROURS.

RETROGRADA'TION. *n.s.* [*retrogradation*, Fr. from *retrograde.*] The act of going backward.

As for the revolutions, stations, and retrogadations *of the planets, observed constantly in most certain periods of time, sufficiently demonstrates, that their motions are governed by counsel.*
RAY ON THE CREATION.

RETROMI'NGENT. *adj.* [*retro* and *mingens*, Lat.] Staling backward.

By reason of the backward position of the feminine parts of quadrupeds, they can hardly admit the substitution of masculine generations, except it be in retromingents.
BROWN.

RETROSPE'CTIVE. *adj.* [from *retrospect.*] Looking backwards.

In vain the grave, with retrospective *eye,*
Would from the apparent what conclude the why. POPE.

RETU'RNABLE. *adj.* Allowed to be reported back. A law term.

It may be decided in that court, where the verdict is returnable. HALE.

He shall have an attachment against the sheriff, directed to the coroner, and returnable *into the king's bench.* AYLIFFE.

RETU'RNER. *n.s.* [from *return.*] One who pays or remits money.

The chapmen, that give highest for this, can make most profit by it, and those are the returners *of our money.* LOCKE.

REVENUE. *n.s.* [*revenu*, Fr. Its accent is uncertain.] Income; annual profits received from lands or other funds.

They privily send over unto them the revenues, *wherewith they are there maintained.*
SPENSER'S STATE OF IRELAND.

She bears a duke's revenues *on her back,*
And in her heart scorns our poverty.
SHAKESPEARE'S HENRY VI.

Only I retain
The name and all th' addition to a king;
The sway, revenue, *beloved sons, be yours.*
SHAKESPEARE.

Many offices are of so small revenue, *as not to furnish a man with what is sufficient for the support of his life.* TEMPLE.

If the woman could have been contented with golden eggs, she might have kept that revenue *on still.* L'ESTRANGE.

His vassals easy, and the owner blest,
They pay a trifle, and enjoy the rest:
Not so a nation's revenues *are paid;*
The servant's faults are on the master laid. SWIFT.

To **REVE'RB.** *v.a.* [*reverbero*, Lat.] To strike against; to reverberate. Not in use.

Reserve thy state, with better judgment check
This hideous rashness:
The youngest daughter does not love thee least;
Nor are those empty hearted, whose loud sound
Reverbs *no hollowness.*
SHAKESPEARE'S KING LEAR.

RE'VERENCER. *n.s.* [from *reverence.*] One who regards with reverence.

The Athenians quite sunk in their affairs, had little commerce with the rest of Greece, and were become great reverencers *of crowned heads.* SWIFT.

To **REVE'RT.** *v.n.* [*revertir*, old Fr.] To return; to fall back.

My arrows,
Too slightly timbred for so loud a wind,
Would have reverted *to my bow again.*
SHAKESPEARE'S HAMLET.

If his tenant and patentee shall dispose of his gift without his kingly assent, the lands shall revert *to the king.* BACON.

REVE'RT. *n.s.* [from the verb.] Return; recurrence. A musical term.

Hath not musick her figures the same with rhetorick? what is a revert *but her antistrophe?* PEACHAM OF MUSICK.

To **REVE'ST.** *v.a.* [*revestir*, *revêtir*, Fr. *revestio*, Lat.]

1. To clothe again.

Her, nathless,
Th' enchanter finding fit for his intents,
Did thus revest, *and deckt with due habiliments.* SPENSER.

When thou of life renewest the seeds,
The withered fields revest *their chearful weeds.* WOTTON.

2. To reinvest; to vest again in a possession or office.

REVE'STIARY. *n.s.* [*revestiaire*, Fr. from *revestio*, Lat.] Place where dresses are reposited.

The effectual power of words the Pythagoreans extolled; the impious Jews ascribed all miracles to a name, which was ingraved in the revestiary *of the temple.* CAMDEN'S REMAINS.

REVI'CTION. *n.s.* [*revictum*, Lat.] Return to life.

If the Rabines prophecy succeed, we shall conclude the days of the phenix, not in its own, but in the last and general flames, without all hope of reviction. BROWN.

To **REVI'CTUAL.** *v.a.* [*re* and *victual.*] To stock with victuals again.

It hath been objected, that I put into Ireland, and spent much time there, taking care to revictual *myself and none of the rest.* RALEIGH'S APOLOGY.

REVIE'W. *n.s.* [*reveue*, Fr. from the verb.] Survey; re-examination.

We make a general review *of the whole work, and a general* review *of nature; that, by comparing them, their full correspondency may appear.*
BURNET'S THEORY OF THE EARTH.

The works of nature will bear a thousand views and reviews; *the more narrowly we look into them, the more occasion we shall have to admire.*
ATTERBURY'S SERMONS.

REVI'SAL. *n.s.* [from *revise.*] Review; reexamination.

The revisal *of these letters has been a kind of examination of conscience to me; so fairly and faithfully have I set down in them the undisguised state of the mind.* POPE.

REVI'SE. *n.s.* [from the verb.]

1. Review; reexamination.

The author is to be excused, who never, in regard to his eyes and other impediments, gives himself the trouble of corrections and revises. BOYLE.

2. Among printers, a second proof of a sheet corrected.

REVI'SION. *n.s.* [*revision*, Fr. from *revise.*] Review.

To **REVIVI'FICATE.** *v.a.* [*revivifier*, Fr. *re* and *vivifico*, Lat.] To recall to life.

REVO'LTER. *n.s.* [from *revolt.*] One who changes sides; a deserter; a renegade.

Fair honour that thou dost thy God, in trusting
He will accept thee to defend his cause,
A murderer, a revolter, *and a robber.*
MILTON'S AGONISTES.

He was not a revolter *from the truth, which he had once embraced.*
ATTERBURY'S SERMONS.

Those, who are negligent or revolters, *shall perish.* SWIFT.

REVU'LSION. *n.s.* [*revulsion*, Fr. *revulsus*, Lat.] The act of revolving or drawing humours from a remote part of the body.

Derivation differs from revulsion *only in the measure of the distance, and the force of the medicines used: if we draw it to some very remote or contrary part, we call it* revulsion; *if only to some neighbouring place, and by gentle means, we call it derivation.* WISEMAN OF TUMOURS.

There is a way of revulsion *to let blood in an adverse part.*
BACON'S NATURAL HISTORY.

I had heard of some strange cures of frenzies, by casual applications of fire to the lower parts, which seems reasonable enough, by the violent revulsion *it may make of humours from the head.*
TEMPLE'S MISCELLANIES.

RHABA'RBARATE. *adj.* [from *rhabarbara*, Lat.] Impregnated or tinctured with rhubarb.

The salt humours must be evacuated by the sennate, rhabarbarate, *and sweet manna purgers, with acids added, or the purging waters.* FLOYER ON THE HUMOURS.

RHA'BDOMANCY. *n.s.* [ῥάβδος and *μαντεία*.] Divination by a wand.

Of peculiar rhabdomancy *is that which is used in mineral discoveries, with a forked hazel, commonly called Moses's rod, which, freely held forth, will stir and play if any mine be under it.*
BROWN'S VULGAR ERROURS.

RHA'PSODIST. *n.s.* [from *rhapsody.*] One who writes without regular dependence of one part upon another.

Ask our rhapsodist, *if you have nothing but the excellence and loveliness of virtue to preach, and no future rewards or punishments, how many vicious wretches will you ever reclaim.*
WATTS'S IMPROVEMENT OF THE MIND.

RHA'PSODY. *n.s.* [ῥαψῳδία; ῥάπτω, to sew, and ᾠδή, a song.] Any number of parts joined together, without necessary dependence or natural connection.

Such a deed, as sweet religion makes
A rhapsody *of words.*
SHAKESPEARE'S HAMLET.

This confusion and rhapsody *of difficulties was not to be supposed in each single sinner.* HAMMOND.

He, that makes no reflexions on what he reads, only loads his mind with a rhapsody *of tales fit for the entertainment of others.* LOCKE.

The words slide over the ears, and vanish like a rhapsody *of evening tales.*
WATTS'S IMPROVEMENT OF THE MIND.

RHE'TORICK. *n.s.* [ῥητορική; *rhetorique*, Fr.]

1. The act of speaking not merely with propriety, but with art and elegance.

We could not allow him an orator, who had the best thoughts, and who knew all the rules of rhetorique, *if he had not acquired the art of using them.*
DRYDEN'S DUFRESNOY.

Of the passions, and how they are moved, Aristotle, in his second book of rhetorick, *hath admirably discoursed in a little compass.*
LOCKE'S THOUGHTS ON READING.

Grammar teacheth us to speak properly, rhetorick *instructs to speak elegantly.*
BAKER'S REFLECTIONS ON LEARNING.

2. The power of persuasion; oratory.

The heart's still rhetorick, *disclos'd with eyes.* SHAKESPEARE.

His sober lips then did he softly part,
Whence of pure rhetorick *whole streams outflow.* FAIRFAX.

Enjoy your dear wit and gay rhetorick,
That hath so well been taught her dazling fence. MILTON.

To **RHETO'RICATE.** *v.n.* [*rhetoricor*, low Lat. from *rhetorick.*] To play the orator; to attack the passions.

'Twill be much more seasonable to reform, than apologize or rhetoricate; *not to suffer themselves to perish in the midst of such solicitations to be saved.*
DECAY OF PIETY.

RHEU'MATISM. *n.s.* [ῥευματισμός; *rheumatisme*, Fr. *rheumatismus*, Lat.] A painful distemper supposed to proceed from acrid humours.

Rheumatism *is a distemper affecting chiefly the membrana communis musculorum, which it makes rigid and unfit for motion; and it seems to be occasioned almost by the same causes, as the mucilaginous glands in the joints are rendered stiff and gritty in the gout.* QUINCY.

The throtling quinsey 'tis my star appoints,
And rheumatisms *I send to rack the joints.* DRYDEN.

RHINO'CEROS. *n.s.* [ῥίν and κέρας; *rhinocerot*, Fr.] A vast beast in the East Indies armed with a horn in his front.

Approach thou like the rugged Russian bear,
The arm'd rhinoceros, *or Hyrcanian tyger;*

Take any shape but that, and my firm nerves
Shall never tremble.
SHAKESPEARE'S MACBETH.

If you draw your beast in an emblem, shew a landscape of the country natural to the beast; as to the rhinoceros *an East Indian landscape, the crocodile, an Egyptian.* PEACHAM.

RI'BALD. *n.s.* [*ribauld*, Fr. *ribaldo*, Italian.] A loose, rough, mean, brutal wretch.

That lewd ribbald, *with vile lust advanced,*
Laid first his filthy hands on virgin clean,
To spoil her dainty corse so fair and sheen.
FAIRY QUEEN.

Your ribauld *nag of Egypt,*
The breeze upon her, like a cow in June,
Hoists sails, and flies.
SHAKESPEARE'S ANTONY AND CLEOPATRA.

The busy day,
Wak'd by the lark, has rous'd the ribald *crows,*
And dreaming night will hide our joys no longer. SHAKESPEARE.

Ne'er one sprig of laurel grac'd these ribbalds,
From flashing Bentley down to pidling Tibbalds. POPE.

To **RI'BROAST.** *v.n.* [*rib* and *roast.*] To beat soundly. A burlesque word.

That done, he rises, humbly bows,
And gives thanks for the princely blows;
Departs not meanly proud, and boasting
Of his magnificent ribroasting. BUTLER.

I have been pinched in flesh, and well ribroasted *under my former masters; but I'm in now for skin and all.* L'ESTRANGE.

RI'DDANCE. *n.s.* [from *rid.*]

1. Deliverance.

Deliverance from sudden death, riddance *from all adversity, and the extent of saving mercy towards all men.* HOOKER.

2. Disencumbrance; loss of something one is glad to lose.

I have too griev'd a heart
To take a tedious leave: thus losers part.
—— A gentle riddance.
SHAKESPEARE'S MERCHANT OF VENICE.

By this, the cock had a good riddance *of his rival.* L'ESTRANGE.

3. Act of clearing away any encumbrances.

Those blossoms, and those dropping gums,
That lie bestrown, unsightly and unsmooth,
Ask riddance, *if we mean to tread with ease.* MILTON.

RI'DINGCOAT. *n.s.* [*riding* and *coat.*] A coat made to keep out weather.

When you carry your master's ridingcoat *in a journey, wrap your own in it.* SWIFT'S DIRECTIONS TO THE GROOM.

RI'DINGHOOD. *n.s.* [*riding* and *hood.*] A hood used by women, when they travel, to bear off the rain.

The palliolum was like our ridinghood, *and served both for a tunick and a coat.* ARBUTHNOT ON COINS.

Good housewives all the winter's rage despise,
Defended by the ridinghood's *disguise.*
GAY.

RIGHT. *interject.* An expression of approbation.

Right, *cries his lordship, for a rogue in need*
To have a taste, is insolence indeed:
In me 'tis noble, suits my birth and state.
POPE.

RING. *n.s.* [*hring*, Saxon.]

1. A circle; an orbicular line.

In this habit
Met I my father with his bleeding rings,

Their precious gems new lost.
SHAKESPEARE.

Bubbles of water, before they began to exhibit their colours to the naked eye, have appeared through a prism girded about with many parallel and horizontal rings. NEWTON.

2. A circle of gold or some other matter worn as an ornament.

A quarrel.
—— About a hoop of gold, a paltry ring.
SHAKESPEARE.

I have seen old Roman rings *so very thick about, and with such large stones in them, that 'tis no wonder a fop should reckon them a little cumbersome in the summer.* ADDISON.

3. A circle of metal to be held by.

The rings *of iron, that on the doors were hung,*
Sent out a jarring sound, and harshly rung. DRYDEN.

Some eagle got the ring *of my box in his beak, with an intent to let it fall, and devour it.* GULLIVER.

4. A circular course.

Chaste Diana,
Goddess presiding o'er the rapid race,
Place me, O place me in the dusty ring,
Where youthful charioteers contend for glory. SMITH.

5. A circle made by persons standing round.

Make a ring *about the corps of Cæsar,*
And let me shew you him, that made the will. SHAKESPEARE.

The Italians, perceiving themselves almost environed, cast themselves into a ring, *and retired back into the city.* HAYWARD.

Round my arbour a new ring *they made,*
And footed it about the secret shade.
DRYDEN.

6. A number of bells harmonically tuned.

A squirrel spends his little rage,
In jumping round a rowling cage;
The cage as either side turn'd up,
Striking a ring *of bells a-top.* PRIOR.

7. The sound of bells or any other sonorous body.

Stop the holes of a hawk's bell, it will make no ring, *but a flat noise or rattle.* BACON.

Hawks bells, that have holes, give a greater ring, *than if the pellet did strike upon brass in the open air.* BACON.

Sullen Moloch fled,
Hath left in shadows dread
His burning idol all of blackest hue;
In vain with cymbals ring,
They call the grisly king. MILTON.

8. A sound of any kind.

The king, full of confidence, as he had been victorious in battle, and had prevailed with his parliament, and had the ring *of acclamations fresh in his ears, thought the rest of his reign should be but play.*
BACON'S HENRY VII.

RIVA'LITY, RIVALRY. *n.s.* [*rivalitas*, Lat. from *rival.*] Competition; emulation.

It is the privilege of posterity to set matters right between those antagonists, who, by their rivalry *for greatness, divided a whole age.* ADDISON.

RI'VER. *n.s.* [*riviere*, Fr. *rivus*, Lat.] A land current of water bigger than a brook.

It is a most beautiful country, being stored throughout with many goodly rivers, *replenished with all sorts of fish.* SPENSER.

The first of these rivers *has been celebrated by the Latin poets for the gentleness of its course, as the other for its rapidity.*
ADDISON'S REMARKS ON ITALY.

To **ROB.** *v.a.* [*rober*, old Fr. *robbare*, Italian.]

1. To deprive of any thing by unlawful force, or by secret theft; to plunder. To be *robbed*, according to the present use of the word, is to be injured by theft secret or violent; to *rob*, is to take away

by unlawful violence; and to *steal*, is to take away privately.

Is't not enough to break into my garden,
And, like a thief, to come to rob *my grounds,*
But thou wilt brave me with these sawcy terms? SHAKESPEARE.

Our sins being ripe, there was no preventing of God's justice from reaping that glory in our calamities, which we robbed *him of in our prosperity.* KING CHARLES.

I have not here designed to rob *him of any part of that commendation, which he has so justly acquired from the whole author, whose fragments only fall to my portion.* DRYDEN.

The water nymphs lament their empty urns,
Bœotia, robb'd *of silver Dirce, mourns.* ADDISON.

2. To set free; to deprive of something bad. Ironical.

Our house is hell, and thou, a merry devil,
Did'st rob *it of some taste of tediousness.* SHAKESPEARE.

3. To take away unlawfully.

Better be disdained of all, than fashion a carriage to rob *love from any.* SHAKESPEARE.

Procure, that the nourishment may not be robbed *and drawn away.* BACON'S NATURAL HISTORY.

Nor will I take from any man his due;
But thus assuming all, he robs *from you.* DRYDEN.

Oh double sacrilege on things divine,
To rob *the relick, and deface the shrine!* DRYDEN.

ROBE'RSMAN, ROBERTSMAN. *n.s.* In the old statutes, a sort of bold and stout robbers or night thieves, said to be so called from Robinhood, a famous robber.

RO'CKET. *n.s.* [*rochetto*, Italian.] An artificial firework, being a cylindrical case of paper filled with nitre, charcoal, and sulphur, and which mounts in the air to a considerable height, and there bursts.

Every rocket *ended in a constellation, strowing the air with a shower of silver spangles.* ADDISON.

When bonefires blaze, your vagrant works shall rise
In rockets, *till they reach the wond'ring skies.* GARTH.

RO'GUY. *adj.* [from *rogue.*] Knavish; wanton. A bad word.

A shepherd's boy had gotten a roguy *trick of crying a wolf, and fooling the country with false alarms.* L'ESTRANGE.

ROI'STER, or roisterer. *n.s.* [from the verb.] A turbulent, brutal, lawless, blustering fellow.

RO'LLER. *n.s.* [*rouleau*, Fr. from *roll.*]

1. Any thing turning on its own axis, as a heavy stone to level walks.

When a man tumbles a roller *down a hill, the man is the violent enforcer of the first motion; but when it is once tumbling, the property of the thing itself continues it.* HAMMOND.

The long slender worms, that breed between the skin and flesh in the isle of Ormuz and in India, are generally twisted out upon sticks or rollers. RAY ON THE CREATION.

They make the string of the pole horizontal towards the lathe, conveying and guiding the string from the pole to the work, by throwing it over a roller. MOXON'S MECHANICAL EXERCISES.

Lady Charlotte, like a stroller,
Sits mounted on the garden roller. SWIFT'S MISCELLANIES.

2. Bandage; fillet.

Fasten not your roller *by tying a knot, lest you hurt your patient.* WISEMAN'S SURGERY.

Bandage being chiefly to maintain the due situation of a dressing, surgeons always turn a roller *with that view.* SHARP.

ROLLYPOOLY. *n.s.* A sort of game, in which, when a ball rolls into a certain place, it wins. A corruption of *roll ball into the pool.*

Let us begin some diversion; what d'ye think of roulypouly *or a country dance?* ARBUTHNOT'S HISTORY OF JOHN BULL.

ROMA'NCE. *n.s.* [*roman*, Fr. *romanza*, Italian.]

1. A military fable of the middle ages; a tale of wild adventures in war and love.

What resounds
In fable or romance *of Uther's son.*
MILTON.

A brave romance *who would exactly frame,*
First brings his knight from some immortal dame. WALLER.

Some romances *entertain the genius; and strengthen it by the noble ideas which they give of things; but they corrupt the truth of history.* DRYDEN'S DUFRESNOY.

2. A lie; a fiction. In common speech.

ROMA'NCER. *n.s.* [from *romance.*] A lier; a forger of tales.

The allusion of the daw extends to all impostors, vain pretenders, and romancers. L'ESTRANGE.

Shall we, cries one, permit
This leud romancer, *and his bantering wit.* TATE'S JUVENAL.

ROMA'NTICK. *adj.* [from *romance.*]

1. Resembling the tales of romances; wild.

Philosophers have maintained opinions, more absurd than any of the most fabulous poets or romantick *writers.* KEIL.

Zeal for the good of one's country a party of men have represented, as chimerical and romantick. ADDISON.

2. Improbable; false.

3. Fanciful; full of wild scenery.

The dun umbrage, o'er the falling stream,
Romantick *hangs.* THOMSON'S SPRING.

ROMP. *n.s.*

1. A rude, awkward, boisterous, untaught girl.

She was in the due mean between one of your affected courtesying pieces of formality, and your romps *that have no regard to the common rules of civility.* ARBUTHNOT.

2. Rough rude play.

Romp *loving miss*
Is haul'd about in gallantry robust.
THOMSON.

ROOMAGE. *n.s.* [from *room.*] Space; place.

Man, of all sensible creatures, has the fullest brain to his proportion, for the lodging of the intellective faculties: it must be a silent character of hope, when there is good store of roomage *and receipt, where those powers are stowed.* WOTTON.

ROO'MINESS. *n.s.* [from *roomy.*] Space; quantity of extent.

RO'PEDANCER. *n.s.* [*rope* and *dancer.*] An artist who dances on a rope.

Salvian, amongst other publick shews, mentions the Petaminarii; probably derived from the Greek πετάσθαι, which signifies to fly, and may refer to such kind of ropedancers.
WILKINS'S MATHEMATICAL MAGICK.

Statius, posted on the highest of the two summits, the people regarded with the same terror, as they look upon a daring ropedancer, *whom they expect to fall every moment.* ADDISON'S GUARDIAN.

Nic bounced up with a spring equal to that of one of your nimblest tumblers or rope-dancers, *and fell foul upon John Bull, to snatch the cudgel he had in his hand.* ARBUTHNOT.

RO'STRATED. *adj.* [*rostratus*, Lat.] Adorned with beaks of ships.

He brought to Italy an hundred and ten rostrated *gallies of the fleet of Mithridates.* ARBUTHNOT.

RO'TGUT. *n.s.* [*rot* and *gut.*] Bad beer.

They overwhelm their panch daily with a kind of flat rotgut, *we with a bitter dreggish small liquor.* HARVEY.

ROTU'NDIFOLIOUS. *adj.* [*rotundus* and *folium*, Lat.] Having round leaves.

RO'VER. *n.s.* [from *rove.*]

1. A wanderer; a ranger.
2. A fickle inconstant man.
3. A robber; a pirate.

This is the case of rovers *by land, as some cantons in Arabia.* BACON'S HOLY WAR.

4. *At* ROVERS. Without any particular aim.

Nature shoots not at rovers: *even inanimates, though they know not their perfection, yet are they not carried on by a blind unguided impetus; but that, which directs them, knows it.*
GLANVILL'S SCEPSIS SCIENTIFICA.

Providence never shoots at rovers: *there is an arrow that flies by night as well as by day, and God is the person that shoots it.*
SOUTH'S SERMONS.

Men of great reading show their talents on the meanest subjects; this is a kind of shooting at rovers. ADDISON.

To **ROU'GHWORK.** *v.a.* [*rough* and *work.*] To work coarsely over without the least nicety.

Thus you must continue, till you have roughwrought *all your work from end to end.*
MOXON'S MECHANICAL EXERCISES.

ROU'NDABOUT. *adj.* [This word is used as an adjective, though it is only an adverb united to a substantive by a colloquial license of language, which ought not to have been admitted into books.]

1. Ample; extensive.

Those sincerely follow reason, but for want of having large, sound, roundabout *sense, have not a full view of all that relates to the question.*
LOCKE ON UNDERSTANDING.

2. Indirect; loose.

Paraphrase is a roundabout *way of translating, invented to help the barrenness, which translators, overlooking in themselves, have apprehended in our tongue.*
FELTON.

ROU'NDHOUSE. *n.s.* [*round* and *house.*] The constable's prison, in which disorderly persons, found in the street, are confined.

They march'd to some fam'd roundhouse.
POPE.

RU'BRICK. *n.s.* [*rubrique*, Fr. *rubrica*, Lat.] Directions printed in books of law and in prayer books; so termed, because they were originally distinguished by being in red ink.

No date prefix'd,
Directs me in the starry rubrick *set.*
MILTON'S PARADISE REGAIN'D.

They had their particular prayers according to the several days and months; and their tables or rubricks *to instruct them.*
STILLINGFLEET.

RUDIME'NTAL. *adj.* [from *rudiment.*] Initial; relating to first principles.

Your first rudimental *essays in spectator-*

ship were made in my shop, where you often practised for hours. SPECTATOR.

RU'FFIAN. *n.s.* [*ruffiano*, Italian; *ruffien*, Fr. a bawd; *roffver*, Danish, to pillage; perhaps it may be best derived from *rough.*] A brutal, boisterous, mischievous fellow; a cut-throat; a robber; a murderer.

Ruffian, *let go that rude uncivil touch,*
Thou friend of an ill fashion!
SHAKESPEARE'S TWO GENTLEMEN OF VERONA.

Have you a ruffian *that will swear? drink? dance?*
Revel the night? rob? murder?
SHAKESPEARE'S HENRY IV.

Sir Ralph Vane's bold answers termed rude and ruffian *like, falling into ears apt to take offence, furthered his condemnation.* HAYWARD.

The boasted ancestors of these great men,
Whose virtues you admire, were all such ruffians,
This dread of nations, this almighty Rome,
That comprehends in her wide empire's bounds
All under heaven, was founded on a rape.
ADDISON'S CATO.

RUGO'SE. *adj.* [*rugosus*, Lat.] Full of wrinkles.

It is a relaxation of the sphincter to such a degree, that the internal rugose *coat of the intestine turneth out, and beareth down.* WISEMAN'S SURGERY.

RU'MMER. *n.s.* [*roemer*, Dutch.] A glass; a drinking cup.

Imperial Rhine bestow'd the generous rummer. PHILIPS.

RU'MOURER. *n.s.* [from *rumour.*] Reporter; spreader of news.

A slave
Reports, the Volscians, with two several powers,
Are entered into the Roman territories.
—— *Go see this* rumourer *whipt: it cannot be.* SHAKESPEARE.

RU'NAGATE. *n.s.* [corrupted from *renegat*, Fr.] A fugitive; rebel; apostate.

The wretch compel'd, a runagate *became,*
And learn'd what ill a miser state doth breed. SIDNEY.

God bringeth the prisoners out of captivity; but letteth the runagates *continue in scarceness.* BIBLE PSALMS, LXVIII. 6.

I dedicate myself to your sweet pleasure,
More noble than that runagate *to your bed.* SHAKESPEARE.

As Cain, after he had slain Abel, had no certain abiding; so the Jews, after they had crucified the son of God, became runagates.
RALEIGH'S HISTORY OF THE WORLD.

RU'NNET. *n.s.* [*gerunnen*, Saxon, coagulated.] A liquor made by steeping the stomach of a calf in hot water, and used to coagulate milk for curds and cheese. It is sometimes written *rennet.*

The milk of the fig hath the quality of runnet *to gather cheese.*
BACON'S NATURAL HISTORY.

It coagulates the blood, as runnet *turns milk.* MORE.

The milk in the stomach of calves, coagulated by the runnet, *is rendered fluid by the gall in the duodenum.* ARBUTHNOT.

RUSE. *n.s.* [French.] Cunning; artifice; little stratagem; trick; wile; fraud; deceit. A French word neither elegant nor necessary.

I might here add much concerning the wiles and ruses, *which these timid creatures use to save themselves.* RAY.

RUSH-CANDLE. *n.s.* [*rush* and *candle.*] A small blinking taper, made by stripping a rush, except one small stripe of the bark which holds the pith together, and dipping it in tallow.

Be it moon or sun, or what you please;

And if you please to call it a rush-candle,
Henceforth it shall be so for me.
SHAKESPEARE.

If your influence be quite dam'd up
With black usurping mists, some gentle taper,
Though a rush-candle *from the wicker hole*
Of some clay habitation, visit us.
MILTON.

RU'STICK. *adj.* [*rusticus*, Lat.]

1. Rural; country.

By Lelius willing missing was the odds of the Iberian side, and continued so in the next by the excellent running of a knight, though fostered so by the muses, as many times the very rustick *people left both their delights and profits to harken to his songs.* SIDNEY, B. II.

2. Rude; untaught; inelegant.

An ignorant clown cannot learn fine language or a courtly behaviour, when his rustick *airs have grown up with him till the age of forty.* WATTS'S LOGICK.

3. Brutal; savage.

My soul foreboded I should find the bow'r
Of some fell monster, fierce with barb'rous pow'r;
Some rustick *wretch, who liv'd in heav'n's despight,*
Contemning laws, and trampling on the right. POPE.

4. Artless; honest; simple.

5. Plain; unadorned.

An altar stood, rustick, *of grassy sord.*
MILTON.

With unguents smooth the polish'd marble shone,
Where ancient Neleus sat, a rustick *throne.* POPE.

RU'STICK. *n.s.* A clown; a swain; an inhabitant of the country.

As nothing is so rude and insolent as a wealthy rustick, *all this his kindness is overlooked, and his person most unworthily railed at.* SOUTH.

S

Has in English the same hissing sound as in other languages, and unhappily prevails in so many of our words that it produces in the ear of a foreigner a continued sibilation.

In the beginning of words it has invariably its natural and genuine sound: in the middle it is sometimes uttered with a stronger appulse of the tongue to the palate, like *z*; as *rose*, *roseate*, *rosy*, *osier*, *nosel*, *resident*, *busy*, *business*. It sometimes keeps its natural sound; as *loose*, *designation*; for which I know not whether any rules can be given.

In the end of monosyllables it is sometimes *s*, as in *this*; and sometimes *z*, as in *as*, *has*; and generally where *es* stands in verbs for *eth*, as *gives*. It seems to be established as a rule, that no noun singular should end with *s* single: therefore in words written with diphthongs, and naturally long, an *e* is nevertheless added at the end, as *goose*, *house*; and where the syllable is short the *s* is doubled, and was once *sse*, as *ass*, anciently *asse*; *wilderness*, anciently *wildernesse*; *distress*, anciently *distresse*.

SA'CKPOSSET. *n.s.* [*sack* and *posset.*] A posset made of milk, sack, and some other ingredients.

Snuff the candles at supper on the table, because the burning snuff may fall into a dish of soup or sackposset. SWIFT.

SA'CRILEGE. *n.s.* [*sacrilege*, Fr. *sacrilegium*, Lat.] The crime of appropriating to himself what is devoted to religion; the crime of robbing heaven; the crime of violating or profaning things sacred.

By what eclipse shall that sun be defac'd,
What mine hath erst thrown down so fair a tower!
What sacrilege *hath such a saint disgrac'd?* SIDNEY.

Then 'gan a cursed hand the quiet womb
Of his great grandmother with steel to wound,
And the hid treasures in her sacred tomb
With sacrilege *to dig.* FAIRY QUEEN.

We need not go many ages back to see the vengeance of God upon some families, raised upon the ruins of churches, and enriched with the spoils of sacrilege. SOUTH'S SERMONS.

SAGA'CITY. *n.s.* [*sagacité*, French; *sagacitas*, Latin.]

1. Quickness of scent.
2. Acuteness of discovery.

It requires too great a sagacity *for vulgar minds to draw the line nicely between virtue and vice.* SOUTH.

Sagacity *finds out the intermediate ideas, to discover what connection there is in each link of the chain, whereby the extremes are held together.* LOCKE.

Many were eminent in former ages for their discovery of it; but though the knowledge they have left be worth our study, yet they left a great deal for the industry and sagacity *of after-ages.* LOCKE.

SA'ILER, SAILOR. *n.s.* [*sailor* is more usual, *sailer* more analogical;

from *sail.*] A seaman; one who practises or understands navigation.

They had many times men of other countries that were no sailors. BACON.

Batter'd by his lee they lay;
The passing winds through their torn canvas play,
And flagging sails on heartless sailors *fall.* DRYDEN.

Young Pompey built a fleet of large ships, and had good sailors, *commanded by experienced captains.* ARBUTHNOT.

Full in the openings of the spacious main
It rides, and, lo, descends the sailer *train.* POPE'S ODYSSEY.

SA'INTLIKE. *adj.* [*saint* and *like.*]

1. Suiting a saint; becoming a saint.

If still thou do'st retain
The same ill habits, the same follies too,
Gloss'd over only with a saintlike *show,*
Still thou art bound to vice.
DRYDEN'S PERSIUS.

2. Resembling a saint.

The king, in whose time it passed, whom catholicks count a saintlike *and immaculate prince, was taken away in the flower of his age.* BACON.

SA'INTLY. *adj.* [from *saint.*] Like a saint; becoming a saint.

I mention still
Him whom thy wrongs, with saintly *patience borne,*
Made famous in a land and times obscure. MILTON'S PARADISE LOST.

SA'INTSHIP. *n.s.* [from *saint.*] The character or qualities of a saint.

He that thinks his saintship *licenses him to censures, is to be looked on not only as a rebel, but an usurper.* DECAY OF PIETY.

This savours something ranker than the tenents of the fifth monarchy, and of sovereignty founded upon saintship. SOUTH.

The devil was piqu'd such saintship *to behold,*
And long'd to tempt him. POPE.

SALAMA'NDER. *n.s.* [*salamandre,* Fr. *salamandra,* Lat.] An animal supposed to live in the fire, and imagined to be very poisonous. *Ambrose Parey* has a picture of the salamander, with a receipt for her bite; but there is no such creature, the name being now given to a poor harmless insect.

The salamander *liveth in the fire, and hath force also to extinguish it.*
BACON'S NATURAL HISTORY.

According to this hypothesis the whole lunar world is a torrid zone, and may be supposed uninhabitable, except they are salamanders *which dwell therein.*
GLANVILLE'S SCEPSIS SCIENTIFICA.

Whereas it is commonly said that a salamander *extinguisheth fire, we have found by experience, that on hot coals it dieth immediately.*
BROWN'S VULGAR ERROURS.

The artist was so encompassed with fire and smoke, that one would have thought nothing but a salamander *could have been safe in such a situation.*
ADDISON'S GUARDIAN.

SA'LESMAN. *n.s.* [*sale* and *man.*] One who sells cloaths ready made.

Poets make characters, as salesmen *cloaths;*
We take no measure of your fops and beaus. SWIFT.

SA'LEWORK. *n.s.* [*sale* and *work.*] Work for sale; work carelesly done.

I see no more in you than in the ordinary
Of nature's salework.
SHAKESPEARE'S AS YOU LIKE IT.

SA'LIENT. *adj.* [*saliens,* Latin.]

1. Leaping; bounding; moving by leaps.

The legs of both sides moving together, as frogs, and salient *animals, is properly called leaping.* BROWN'S VULGAR ERROURS.

2. Beating; panting.

A salient *point so first is call'd the heart,*
By turns dilated, and by turns comprest,

Expels and entertains the purple guest. BLACKMORE.

3. Springing or shooting with a quick motion.

Who best can send on high
The salient *spout, far streaming to the sky.* POPE.

SALI'VOUS. *adj.* [from *saliva.*] Consisting of spittle; having the nature of spittle.

There happeneth an elongation of the uvula, through the abundance of salivous *humour flowing upon it.* WISEMAN.

SA'LMAGUNDI. *n.s.* [It is said to be corrupted from *selon mon gout*, or *sale à mon goût.*] A mixture of chopped meat and pickled herrings with oil, vinegar, pepper, and onions.

SALSOA'CID. *adj.* [*salsus* and *acidus*, Latin.] Having a taste compounded of saltness and sourness.

The salsoacids *help its passing off; as sal prunel.* FLOYER.

SALSU'GINOUS. *adj.* [*salsugo*, Latin.] Saltish; somewhat salt.

The distinction of salts, whereby they are discriminated into acid, volatile, or salsuginous, *if I may so call the fugitive salts of animal substances, and fixed or alcalizate, may appear of much use in natural philosophy.* BOYLE.

SALTA'TION. *n.s.* [*saltatio*, Latin.]

1. The act of dancing or jumping.

The locusts being ordained for saltation, *their hinder legs do far exceed the others.* BROWN'S VULGAR ERROURS.

2. Beat; palpitation.

If the great artery be hurt, you will discover it by its saltation *and florid colour.* WISEMAN'S SURGERY.

SALTI'NBANCO. *n.s.* [*saltare in banco*, to climb on a bench, as a mountebank mounts a bank.] A quack or mountebank.

Saltinbancoes, *quacksalvers, and charlatans deceive them: were Æsop alive, the Piazza and Pont-neuf could not speak their fallacies.* BROWN'S VULGAR ERROURS.

He play'd the saltinbanco's *part,*
Transform'd t' a Frenchman by my art. HUDIBRAS.

SALVABI'LITY. *n.s.* [from *salvable.*] Possibility of being received to everlasting life.

Why do we Christians so fiercely argue against the salvability *of each other, as if it were our wish that all should be damned, but those of our particular sect.* DECAY OF PIETY.

SA'LVATORY. *n.s.* [*salvatoire*, French.] A place where any thing is preserved.

I consider the admirable powers of sensation, phantasy, and memory, in what salvatories *or repositories the species of things past are conserved.* HALE'S ORIGIN OF MANKIND.

SA'LVO. *n.s.* [from *salvo jure*, Latin, a form used in granting any thing: as *salvo jure putei.*] An exception; a reservation; an excuse.

They admit many salvoes, *cautions, and reservations, so as they cross not the chief design.* KING CHARLES.

It will be hard if he cannot bring himself off at last with some salvo *or distinction, and be his own confessor.* L'ESTRANGE.

If others of a more serious turn join with us deliberately in their religious professions of loyalty, with any private salvoes *or evasions, they would do well to consider those maxims in which all casuists are agreed.* ADDISON.

SA'LUTARY. *adj.* [*salutaire*, Fr. *salutaris*, Latin.] Wholsome; healthful; safe; advantageous; contributing to health or safety.

The gardens, yards, and avenues are dry and clean; and so more salutary *as more elegant.* RAY.

It was want of faith in our Saviour's countrymen, which hindered him from shedding among them the salutary *emanations of his divine virtue; and he did not many mighty works there, because of their unbelief.* BENTLEY.

SALUTI'FEROUS. *adj.* [*salutifer*, Latin.] Healthy; bringing health.

The king commanded him to go to the south of France, believing that nothing would contribute more to the restoring of his former vigour than the gentle salutiferous *air of Montpelier.* DENNIS'S LETTERS.

SA'MLET. *n.s.* [*salmonet*, or *salmonlet*.] A little salmon.

Sir Francis Bacon observes the age of a salmon exceeds not ten years, so his growth is very sudden: after he is got into the sea he becomes from a samlet, *not so big as a gudgeon, to be a salmon, in as short a time as a gosling becomes a goose.* WALTON'S ANGLER.

SA'NDBLIND. *adj.* [*sand* and *blind*.] Having a defect in the eyes, by which small particles appear to fly before them.

My true begotten father, being more than sandblind, *high gravelblind, knows me not.* SHAKESPEARE'S MERCHANT OF VENICE.

SA'NDISH. *adj.* [from *sand*.] Approaching to the nature of sand; loose; not close; not compact.

Plant the tenuifolia's and ranunculus's in fresh sandish *earth, taken from under the turf.* EVELYN'S KALENDAR.

SANE. *adj.* [*sanus*, Latin.] Sound; healthy. *Baynard* wrote a poem on preserving the body in a sane and sound state.

SA'PID. *adj.* [*sapidus*, Latin.] Tasteful; palatable; making a powerful stimulation upon the palate.

Thus camels, to make the water sapid, *do raise the mud with their feet.* BROWN'S VULGAR ERROURS.

The most oily parts are not separated by a slight decoction, 'till they are disentangled from the salts; for if what remains of the subject, after the infusion and decoction be continued to be boiled down with the addition of fresh water, a fat, sapid, *odorous, viscous, inflammable, frothy water will constantly be found floating a-top of the boiling liquor.* ARBUTHNOT.

SAPONA'CEOUS, SAPONARY. *adj.* [from *sapo*, Latin, soap.] Sopy; resembling soap; having the qualities of soap.

By digesting a solution of salt of tartar with oil of almonds, I could reduce them to a soft saponary *substance.* BOYLE.

Any mixture of an oily substance with salt, may be called a soap: bodies of this nature are called saponaceous. ARBUTHNOT.

SA'VANNA. *n.s.* [Spanish, according to *Bailey*.] An open meadow without wood; pasture ground in America.

He that rides post through a country may tell how, in general, the parts lie; here a morass, and there a river; woodland in one part, and savanna's *in another.* LOCKE.

Plains immense,
And vast savanna's, *where the wand'ring eye,*
Unfix'd, is in a verdant ocean lost.
THOMSON'S SUMMER.

SAUCE. *n.s.* [*sauce*, *saulse*, French; *salsa*, Italian.]

1. Something eaten with food to improve its taste.

The bitter sauce *of the sport was, that we had our honours for ever lost, partly by our own faults, but principally by his faulty using of our faults.* SIDNEY.

To feed were best at home;
From thence the sauce *to meat is ceremony;*
Meeting were bare without it.
SHAKESPEARE'S MACBETH.

Epicurean cooks
Sharpen with cloyless sauce *his appetite.*
SHAKESPEARE.

Such was the sauce *of Moab's noble feast,*
'Till night far spent invites them to their rest. COWLEY.

He that spends his time in sports, is like him whose meat is nothing but sauces; *they are healthless, chargeable, and useless.* TAYLOR.

High sauces *and rich spices are fetched from the Indies.* BAKER.

2. *To serve one the same* SAUCE. A vulgar phrase to retaliate one injury with another.

SA'UCEBOX. *n.s.* [from *sauce*, or rather from *saucy*.] An impertinent or petulant fellow.

The foolish old poet says, that the souls of some women are made of sea-water: this has encouraged my saucebox *to be witty upon me.* ADDISON'S SPECTATOR.

SAU'CER. *n.s.* [*sauciere*, Fr. from *sauce*.]

1. A small pan or platter in which sauce is set on the table.

Infuse a pugil of new violets seven times, and it shall make the vinegar so fresh of the flower, as, if brought in a saucer, *you shall smell it before it come at you.* BACON.

Some have mistaken blocks and posts
For spectres, apparitions, ghosts,
With saucer *eyes and horns.* HUDIBRAS.

2. A piece or platter of china, into which a tea-cup is set.

SA'VEALL. *n.s.* [*save* and *all*.] A small pan inserted into a candlestick to save the ends of candles.

SA'USAGE. *n.s.* [*saucisse*, French; *salsum*, Latin.] A roll or ball made commonly of pork or veal, and sometimes of beef, minced very small, with salt and spice; sometimes it is stuffed into the guts of fowls, and sometimes only rolled in flower.

To **SAY.** *v.a.* preter. *said.* [*secgan*, Saxon; *seggen*, Dutch.]

1. To speak; to utter in words; to tell.

Say *it out, Diggon, for whatever it hight;*
For nought but well mought him betight,
He is so meek. SPENSER.

In this slumbry agitation what have you heard her say? SHAKESPEARE.

Speak unto Solomon; for he will not say *thee nay.* BIBLE 1 KINGS.

2. To allege.[185]

After all can be said *against a thing, this will still be true, that many things possibly are, which we know not of.* TILLOTSON.

In vain shall we attempt to justify ourselves, as the rich young man in the gospel did, by appealing to the great duties of the law; unless we can say *somewhat more, even that we have been liberal in our distributions to the poor.* ATTERBURY.

3. To tell in any manner.

With flying speed, and seeming great
pretence,
Came messenger with letters which his
message said. FAIRY QUEEN.

To **SAY.** *v.n.*

1. To speak; to pronounce; to utter.[186]

He said *moreover, I have somewhat to* say *unto thee; and she* said, say *on.*
BIBLE 1 KINGS, II. 14.

Say *nothing to any man, but go thy way.*
BIBLE MARK, I. 44.

To the others he said, *go ye after him.*
BIBLE EZEKIEL, IX. 5.

The council-table and star-chamber hold, as Thucydides said *of the Athenians, for honourable that which pleased, and for just that which profited.* CLARENDON.

The lion here has taken his right measures, that is to say, he has made a true judgment. L'ESTRANGE.

He has left his succession as undetermined as if he had said *nothing about it.* LOCKE.

This ought to weigh with those whose reading is designed for much talk and little knowledge, and I have nothing to say *to it.* LOCKE.

Of some propositions it may be difficult to say *whether they affirm or deny; as when we* say, *Plato was no fool.* WATTS.

2. In poetry, *say* is often used before a question; tell.

Say first what cause
Mov'd our grand parents to fall off?
MILTON.

Say, *Stella, feel you no content,*
Reflecting on a life well-spent. SWIFT.

SAY. *n.s.* [from the verb.]

1. A speech; what one has to say.

He no sooner said out his say, *but up rises a cunning snap.* L'ESTRANGE.

2. [For *assay*.] Sample.

Since thy outside looks so fair and warlike,
And that thy tongue some 'say *of breeding breathes,*
By rule of knighthood I disdain.
SHAKESPEARE.

So good a say *invites the eye,*
A little downward to espy
The lively clusters of her breasts.
SIDNEY.

3. Trial by a sample.

This gentleman having brought that earth to the publick 'say *masters, and upon their being unable to bring it to fusion, or make it fly away, he had procured a little of it, and with a peculiar flux separated a third part of pure gold.* BOYLE.

4. [*Soie*, French.] Silk. Obsolete.

5. A kind of woollen stuff.

SCALA'DE, SCALADO. *n.s.* [French; *scalada*, Spanish, from *scala*, Latin, a ladder.] A storm given to a place by raising ladders against the walls.

What can be more strange than that we should within two months have won one town of importance by scalado, *battered and assaulted another, and overthrown great forces in the field?* BACON.

Thou raisedst thy voice to record the stratagems, the arduous exploits, and the nocturnal scalade *of needy heroes, the terror of your peaceful citizens.*
ARBUTHNOT'S HISTORY OF JOHN BULL.

SCA'LARY. *adj.* [from *scala*, Latin.] Proceeding by steps like those of a ladder.

He made at nearer distances certain elevated places and scalary *ascents, that they might better ascend or mount their horses.* BROWN'S VULGAR ERROURS.

SCA'LDHEAD. *n.s.* [*skalladur*, bald, Islandick. *Hickes*.] A loathsome disease; a kind of local leprosy in which the head is covered with a continuous scab.

The serum is corrupted by the infection of the touch of a salt humour, to which the scab, pox, and scaldhead *are referable.*
FLOYER.

To **SCA'MBLE.** *v.n.* [This word, which is scarcely in use, has much exercised the etymological sagacity of *Meric Casaubon*; but, as is usual, to no purpose.]

1. To be turbulent and rapacious; to scramble; to get by struggling with others.

Have fresh chaff in the bin,
And somewhat to scamble *for hog and for hen.* TUSSER.

Scambling, *out-facing, fashion-mong'ring boys,*
That lie, and cog, and flout, deprave and slander. SHAKESPEARE.

That self bill is urg'd, and had against us past,

But that the scambling *and unquiet time*
Did push it out of further question.
SHAKESPEARE'S HENRY V.

He was no sooner entered into the town but a scambling *soldier clapt hold of his bridle, which he thought was in a begging or a drunken fashion.* WOTTON.

2. To shift aukwardly.

Some scambling *shifts may be made without them.* MORE.

SCA'MBLER. *n.s.* [Scottish.] A bold intruder upon one's generosity or table.

SCA'NTLET. *n.s.* [corrupted, as it seems, from *scantling.*] A small pattern; a small quantity; a little piece.

While the world was but thin, the ages of mankind were longer; and as the world grew fuller, so their lives were successively reduced to a shorter scantlet, *'till they came to that time of life which they now have.* HALE.

SCA'NTLING. *n.s.* [*eschantillon*, French; *ciantellino*, Italian.]

1. A quantity cut for a particular purpose.

'Tis hard to find out a woman that's of a just scantling *for her age, humour, and fortune, to make a wife of.* L'ESTRANGE.

2. A certain proportion.

The success,
Although particular, shall give a scantling
Of good or bad unto the general.
SHAKESPEARE'S TROILUS AND CRESSIDA.

3. A small quantity.

Reduce desires to narrow scantlings *and small proportions.*
TAYLOR'S RULE OF LIVING HOLY.

A scantling *of wit lay gasping for life, and groaning beneath a heap of rubbish.* DRYDEN.

In this narrow scantling *of capacity, we enjoy but one pleasure at once.* LOCKE.

SCA'RECROW. *n.s.* [*scare* and *crow.*] An image or clapper set up to fright birds: thence any vain terrour.

Thereat the scarecrow *waxed wond'rous proud,*
Through fortune of his first adventure fair,
And with big thundering voice revil'd him loud. FAIRY QUEEN.

No eye hath seen such scarecrows*: I'll not march through Coventry with them, that's flat.* SHAKESPEARE'S HENRY IV.

We must not make a scarecrow *of the l aw,*
Setting it up to fear the birds of prey,
And let it keep one shape, 'till custom make it
Their pearch, and not their terrour.
SHAKESPEARE.

Many of those great guns, wanting powder and shot, stood but as cyphers and scarecrows. RALEIGH.

A scarecrow *set to frighten fools away.* DRYDEN.

SCA'REFIRE. *n.s.* [*scare* and *fire.*] A fright by fire; a fire breaking out so as to raise terrour.

The drum and trumpet, by their several sounds, serve for many kind of advertisements; and bells serve to proclaim a scarefire, *and in some places water-breaches.* HOLDER.

SCA'RFSKIN. *n.s.* [*scarf* and *skin.*] The cuticle; the epidermis; the outer scaly integuments of the body.

The scarfskin, *being uppermost, is composed of several lays of small scales, which lie thicker according as it is thicker in one part of the body than another: between these the excretory ducts of the miliary glands of the true skin open.* CHEYNE.

To **SCA'RIFY.** *v.a.* [*scarifico*, Lat. *scarifier*, Fr.] To let blood by incisions of the skin, commonly after the application of cupping-glasses.

Washing the salts out of the eschar, and scarifying *it, I dressed it.*
WISEMAN'S SURGERY.

You quarter foul language upon me, without knowing whether I deserve to be cupped and scarified *at this rate.*
SPECTATOR.

SCATE. *n.s.* [*skidor*, Swedish; *skid*, Islandick.] A kind of wooden shoe, with a steel plate underneath, on which they slide over the ice.

SCATH. *n.s.* [*sceað*, Saxon.] Waste; damage; mischief; depopulation. *Scath* in Scotland denotes spoil or damage: as, he bears the *scath* and the scorn. A proverb.

She suborned hath
This crafty messenger, with letters vain,
To work new woe and unprovided scath.
FAIRY QUEEN.

The ear that budded fair is burnt and blasted,
And all my hoped gain is turn'd to scath.
SPENSER.

He bore a spiteful mind against king Edward, doing him all the scath *that he could, and annoying his territories.*
SPENSER.

My proud one doth work the greater scath,
Through sweet allurement of her lovely hue. SPENSER.

They placed them in Rhodes, where daily doing great scath *to the Turk, the great warrior Soliman, with a mighty army, so overlaid them, that he won the island from them.* KNOLLES.

Still preserv'd from danger, harm, and scath,
By many a sea and many an unknown shore. FAIRFAX.

SCA'VENGER. *n.s.* [from *scafan*, to shave, perhaps to sweep, Saxon.] A petty magistrate, whose province is to keep the streets clean.[187]

Since it is made a labour of the mind, as to inform mens judgments, and move their affections, to resolve difficult places of Scripture, to decide and clear off controversies, I cannot see how to be a butcher, scavenger, *or any other such trade, does at all qualify men for this work.* SOUTH'S SERMONS.

Fasting's nature's scavenger. BAYNARD.

Dick the scavenger, *with equal grace,*
Flirts from his cart the mud in Walpole's face. SWIFT.

SCE'LERAT. *n.s.* [French; *sceleratus*, Latin.] A villain; a wicked wretch. A word introduced unnecessarily from the French by a Scottish author.

Scelerats *can by no arts stifle the cries of a wounded conscience.* CHEYNE.

SCE'NARY. *n.s.* [from *scene.*]

1. The appearances of place or things.

He must gain a relish of the works of nature, and be conversant in the various scenary *of a country life.* ADDISON.

2. The representation of the place in which an action is performed.

The progress of the sound, and the scenary *of the bordering regions, are imitated from Æn. vii. on the sounding the horn of Alecto.* POPE.

3. The disposition and consecution of the scenes of a play.

To make a more perfect model of a picture, is, in the language of poets, to draw up the scenary *of a play.* DRYDEN.

SCE'NOGRAPHY. *n.s.* [*σκηνή* and *γράφω*; *scenographie*, Fr.] The art of perspective.

SCHE'MATIST. *n.s.* [from *scheme.*] A projector; one given to forming schemes.

SCHE'MER. *n.s.* [from *scheme.*] A projector; a contriver.

SCE'PTICK. *n.s.* See **SKEPTICK.**

SCI'ENCE. *n.s.* [*science*, French; *scientia*, Latin.]

1. Knowledge.

If we conceive God's sight or science, *before the creation of the world, to be extended to all and every part of the world, seeing every thing as it is, his prescience or foresight of any action of mine, or rather his* science or *sight, from all eternity, lays no necessity on any thing to come to pass, any more than my seeing the sun move hath to do in the moving of it.* HAMMOND.

2. Certainty grounded on demonstration.

So you arrive at truth, though not at science. BERKLEY.

3. Art attained by precepts, or built on principles.

Science *perfects genius, and moderates that fury of the fancy which cannot contain itself within the bounds of reason.* DRYDEN.

4. Any art or species of knowledge.

No science *doth make known the first principles, whereon it buildeth; but they are always taken as plain and manifest in themselves, or as proved and granted already, some former knowledge having made them evident.* HOOKER.

Whatsoever we may learn by them, we only attain according to the manner of natural sciences, *which mere discourse of wit and reason findeth out.* HOOKER.

I present you with a man
Cunning in musick and the mathematicks,
To instruct her fully in those sciences.
SHAKESPEARE.

The indisputable mathematicks, the only science *heaven hath yet vouchsafed humanity, have but few votaries among the slaves of the Stagirite.*
GLANVILLE'S SCEPSIS SCIENTIFICA.

5. One of the seven liberal arts, grammar, rhetorick, logick, arithmetick, musick, geometry, astronomy.

Good sense, which only is the gift of heav'n,
And though no science, *fairly worth the sev'n.* POPE.

SCIO'LIST. *n.s.* [*sciolus*, Latin.] One who knows many things superficially.

'Twas this vain idolizing of authors which gave birth to that silly vanity of impertinent citations: these ridiculous fooleries signify nothing to the more generous discerners, but the pedantry of the affected sciolists.
GLANVILLE'S SCEPSIS SCIENTIFICA.

These passages, in that book, were enough to humble the presumption of our modern sciolists, *if their pride were not as great as their ignorance.* TEMPLE.

SCIO'MACHY. *n.s.* [*schiamachie*, Fr. *σκία* and *μαχή*.] Battle with a shadow. This should be written *skiamachy.*[188]

To avoid this sciomachy, *or imaginary combat of words, let me know, sir, what you mean by the name of tyrant?* COWLEY.

SCI'SSIBLE. *adj.* [from *scissus*, Latin.] Capable of being divided smoothly by a sharp edge.

The differences of impressible and not impressible, scissible *and not* scissible, *and many other passions of matter, are plebeian notions.* BACON.

SCI'SSILE. *adj.* [*scissile*, Fr. *scissilis*, Latin.] Capable of being cut or divided smoothly by a sharp edge.

Animal fat is a sort of amphibious substance, scissile *like a solid, and resolveable by heat.* ARBUTHNOT.

SCI'SSION. *n.s.* [*scission*, French; *scissio*, Latin.] The act of cutting.

Nerves may be wounded by scission *or puncture: the former way they are usually cut through, and wholly cease from action.*
WISEMAN'S SURGERY.

SCI'SSOR. *n.s.* [This word is variously written, as it is supposed to be derived by different writers; of whom some write *cisors*, from *cædo*, or *incido*; others *scissors*, from *scindo*; and some *cisars*, *cizars*, or *scissars*, *ciseaux*, Fr.] A small pair of sheers, or blades moveable on a pivot, and intercepting the thing to be cut.

His beard they have sing'd off with brands of fire;
And ever, as it blaz'd, they threw on him
Great pails of puddled mire to quench the hair:
My master preaches patience to him, and the while
His man with scissars *nicks him for a fool.* SHAKESPEARE.

Wanting the scissars, *with these hands I'll tear,*
If that obstruct my flight, this load of hair. PRIOR.

When the lawyers and tradesmen brought extravagant bills, sir Roger wore a pair of scissars *in his pocket, with which he would snip a quarter of a yard off nicely.* ARBUTHNOT.

SCI'SSURE. *n.s.* [*scissum*, Latin.] A crack; a rent; a fissure.

The breach seems like the scissures *and ruptures of an earthquake, and threatens to swallow all that attempt to close it, and reserves its cure only for omnipotence.* DECAY OF PIETY.

SCONCE. *n.s.* [*schantz*, German.]
1. A fort; a bulwark.

Such fellows are perfect in the great commanders names, and they will learn you by rote where services were done; at such and such a sconce, *at such a breach.* SHAKESPEARE'S HENRY V.

2. The head: perhaps as being the acropolis, or citadel of the body. A low word.

Why does he suffer this rude knave now to knock him about the sconce *with a dirty shovel, and will not tell him of his action of battery?* SHAKESPEARE'S HAMLET.

3. A pensile candlestick, generally with a looking-glass to reflect the light.

Golden sconces *hang upon the walls,*
To light the costly suppers and the balls. DRYDEN'S LUCRETIA.

Triumphant Umbriel, on a sconce's *height,*
Clapp'd his glad wings, and sat to view the fight. POPE.

Put candles into sconces. SWIFT'S DIRECTIONS TO THE BUTLER.

To **SCONCE.** *v.a.* [A word used in the universities, and derived plausibly by *Skinner*, whose etymologies are generally rational, from *sconce*, as it signifies the head; to *sconce* being to fix a fine on any one's head.] To mulct; to fine. A low word which ought not to be retained.

SCOTCH *Hoppers.* *n.s.* A play in which boys hop over lines or scotches in the ground.

Children being indifferent to any thing they can do, dancing and scotch hoppers *would be the same thing to them.* LOCKE.

To **SCRA'MBLE.** *v.n.* [The same with *scrabble*; *scrasselen*, Dutch.]
1. To catch at any thing eagerly and tumultuously with the hands; to catch with haste preventive of another; to contend tumultuously which shall catch any thing.

England now is left
To tug and scramble, *and to part by th' teeth*
The unow'd interest of proud swelling state. SHAKESPEARE.

Of other care they little reck'ning make,
Than how to scramble *at the shearer's feast,*
And shove away the worthy bidden guest. MILTON.

It is not to be supposed, that, when such a tree was shaking, there would be no scrambling *for the fruit.* STILLINGFLEET.

They must have scrambled *with the wild beasts for crabs and nuts.* RAY ON THE CREATION.

. To climb by the help of the hands:
s, he *scrambled* up that rock.

SCRA'MBLE. *n.s.* [from the verb.]
. Eager contest for something, in which one endeavours to get it before another.

As they were in the middle of their gambols, some body threw a handful of apples among them, that set them presently together by the ears upon the scramble. L'ESTRANGE.

Because the desire of money is constantly almost every where the same, its vent varies very little, but as its greater scarcity enhances its price and increases the scramble. LOCKE.

. Act of climbing by the help of the ands.

o **SCRANCH.** *v.a.* [*schrantzer*, utch.] To grind somewhat crackling etween the teeth. The Scots retain it.

CRAPE. *n.s.* [*skrap*, Swedish.] ifficulty; perplexity; distress. This is a w word.

CREEN. *n.s.* [*escran*, French.]
Any thing that affords shelter or oncealment.

Now near enough: your leavy screens *throw down,*
And show like those you are.
SHAKESPEARE'S MACBETH.

Some ambitious men seem as screens *to princes in matters of danger and envy.* BACON.

Our people, who transport themselves, are settled in those interjacent tracts, as a screen *against the insults of the savages.* SWIFT.

My juniors by a year,
Who wisely thought my age a screen,
When death approach'd, to stand between,
The screen *remov'd, their hearts are trembling.* SWIFT.

2. Any thing used to exclude cold or light.

When there is a screen *between the candle and the eye, yet the light passeth to the paper whereon one writeth.* BACON.

One speaks the glory of the British queen,
And one describes a charming Indian screen. POPE.

Ladies make their old cloaths into patch-work for screens *and stools.* SWIFT.

3. A riddle to sift sand.

To **SCREEN.** *v.a.* [from the noun.]
1. To shelter; to conceal; to hide.

Back'd with a ridge of hills,
That screen'd *the fruits of th' earth and seats of men,*
From cold Septentrion blasts.
MILTON'S PARADISE REGAIN'D.

A good magistrate's retinue of state screens *him from the dangers, which he is to incur for the sake of it.* ATTERBURY.

This gentle deed shall fairly be set foremost,
To screen *the wild escapes of lawless passion.* ROWE.

2. [*Cerno crevi*, Latin.] To sift; to riddle.

Let the cases be filled with natural earth, taken the first half spit, from just under the turf of the best pasture ground, mixed with one part of very mellow soil screened. EVELYN.

SCRUB. *n.s.* [from the verb.]
1. A mean fellow, either as he is supposed to scrub himself for the itch, or as he is employed in the mean offices of scouring away dirt.
2. Any thing mean or despicable.

With a dozen large vessels my vault shall be stor'd;
No little scrub *joint shall come on my board.* SWIFT.

3. A worn out broom. *Ainsworth.*

SCRU'PLER. *n.s.* [from *scruple.*] A doubter; one who has scruples.

The scruples which many publick ministers would make of the worthiness of parents to have their children baptised, forced such questioned parents, who did not believe the necessity of having their children baptised by such scruplers, *to carry their children unto other ministers.*
GRAUNT'S BILLS OF MORTALITY.

SCRUTA'TOR. *n.s.* [*scrutateur*, Fr. from *scrutor*, Lat.] Enquirer; searcher; examiner.

In process of time, from being a simple scrutator, *an arch-deacon became to have jurisdiction more amply.* AYLIFFE.

To **SCRUZE.** *v.a.* [Perhaps from *screw*. This word, though now disused by writers, is still preserved, at least in its corruption, to *scrouge*, in the London jargon.] To squeeze; to compress.

Though up he caught him 'twixt his
puissant hands,
And having scruzed *out of his carrion corse*
The loathful life, now loos'd from sinful
bands,
Upon his shoulders carried him.
FAIRY QUEEN.

To **SCULK.**[189] *v.n.* [*sculcke*, Danish.] To lurk in hiding places; to lie close.

It has struck on a sudden into such a reputation, that it scorns any longer to sculk, *but owns itself publickly.*
GOVERNMENT OF THE TONGUE.

Fearing to be seen, within a bed
Of coleworts he conceal'd his wily head;
There sculk'd *'till afternoon, and watch'd*
his time. DRYDEN.

My prophets and my sophists finish'd here
Their civil efforts of the verbal war:
Not so my rabbins and logicians yield;
Retiring still they combat; from the field
Of open arms unwilling they depart,
And sculk *behind the subterfuge of art.*
PRIOR.

No news of Phyl! the bridegroom came,
And thought his bride had sculk'd *for*
shame;
Because her father us'd to say
The girl had such a bashful way.
SWIFT.

The immediate publishers thereof lay sculking *under the wings of an act of parliament.*
LETTER TO PUBLISHER OF THE DUNCIAD.

SCU'RRILOUS. *adj.* [*scurrilis*, Latin.] Grosly opprobrious; using such language as only the license of a buffoon can warrant; loudly jocular; vile; low.

Yet is not their goodness so intolerable, as, on the contrary side, the scurrilous *and more than satyrical immodesty of Martinism.* HOOKER.

Let him approach singing.
—— Forewarn him that he use no scurrilous *words in's tunes.*
SHAKESPEARE'S WINTER'S TALE.

How often is a person, whose intentions are to do good by the works he publishes, treated in as scurrilous *a manner as if he were an enemy to mankind?*
ADDISON'S FREEHOLDER.

Their characters have been often treated with the utmost barbarity and injustice by scurrilous *and enraged orators.* SWIFT.

SEABRE'ACH. *n.s.* [*sea* and *breach.*] Irruption of the sea by breaking the banks.

To an impetuous woman, tempests and seabreaches *are nothing.* L'ESTRANGE.

SE'ACOAST. *n.s.* [*sea* and *coast.*] Shore; edge of the sea.

The venturous mariner that way,
Learning his ship from those white rocks to
save,
Which all along the southern seacoast *lay;*
For safety's sake that same his seamark
made,
And nam'd it Albion. FAIRY QUEEN.

Upon the seacoast *are many parcels of land, that would pay well for the taking in.* MORTIMER'S HUSBANDRY.

EAMA'RK. *n.s.* [*sea* and *mark.*] oint or conspicuous place distinuished at sea, and serving the ariners as directions of their course.

Those white rocks,
Which all along the southern seacoast lay,
Threat'ning unheedy wreck and rash decay,
For safety's sake his seamark *made,*
And nam'd it Albion. FAIRY QUEEN.

Though you do see me weapon'd,
Here is my journey's end, here is my butt,
The very seamark *of my utmost sail.*
SHAKESPEARE'S OTHELLO.

They were executed at divers places upon the seacoast, for seamarks *or lighthouses, to teach Perkins's people to avoid the coast.* BACON'S HENRY VII.

They are remembered with a brand of infamy fixt upon them, and set as seamarks *for those who observe them to avoid.* DRYDEN.

The fault of others sway,
He set as seamarks *for himself to shun.*
DRYDEN.

E'APIECE. *n.s.* [*sea* and *piece.*] A icture representing any thing at sea.

Great painters often employ their pencils upon seapieces. ADDISON'S SPECTATOR.

E'ARISQUE. *n.s.* [*sea* and *risque.*] Iazard at sea.

He was so great an encourager of commerce, that he charged himself with all the searisque *of such vessels as carried corn to Rome in the Winter.* ARBUTHNOT.

E'ASHORE. *n.s.* [*sea* and *shore.*] he coast of the sea.

That seashore *where no more world is found,*
But foaming billows breaking on the ground. DRYDEN.

Fournier gives an account of an earthquake in Peru, that reached three hundred leagues along the seashore. BURNET.

To say a man has a clear idea of any quantity, without knowing how great it is, is as reasonable as to say he has the positive idea of the number of the sands on the seashore. LOCKE.

SE'COND *Sight. n.s.* The power of seeing things future, or things distant: supposed inherent in some of the Scottish islanders.

As he was going out to steal a sheep, he was seised with a fit of second sight*: the face of the country presented him with a wide prospect of new scenes, which he had never seen before.* ADDISON'S FREEHOLDER.

SE'CRETARY. *n.s.* [*secretaire*, Fr. *secretarius*, low Latin.] One entrusted with the management of business; one who writes for another.

Call Gardiner to me, my new secretary. SHAKESPEARE.

That which is most of all profitable is acquaintance with the secretaries, *and employed men of ambassadors.* BACON.

Cottington was secretary *to the prince.* CLARENDON.

SE'CRETIST. *n.s.* [from *secret.*] A dealer in secrets.

Some things I have not yet thought fit so plainly to reveal, not out of any envious design of having them buried with me, but that I may barter with those secretists, *that will not part with one secret but in exchange for another.* BOYLE.

SE'CTARY. *n.s.* [*sectaire*, French; from *sect.*]

1. One who divides from publick establishment, and joins with those distinguished by some particular whims.

My lord, you are a sectary,
That's the plain truth. SHAKESPEARE.

Romish catholick tenets are inconsistent, on the one hand, with the truth of religion professed and protested by the church of England, whence we are called protestants; and the anabaptists, and separatists, and sectaries, *on the other hand, whose tenets are full of schism, and inconsistent with monarchy.* BACON.

The number of sectaries *does not concern the clergy in point of interest or conscience.* SWIFT.

2. A follower; a pupil.

The sectaries *of my celestial skill,*
That wont to be the world's chief ornament,
And learned imps that wont to shoot up still,
They under keep. SPENSER.

SECTA'TOR. *n.s.* [*sectateur*, Fr. *sectator*, Latin.] A follower; an imitator; a disciple.

Hereof the wiser sort and the best learned philosophers were not ignorant, as Cicero witnesseth, gathering the opinion of Aristotle and his sectators. RALEIGH.

To **SEDU'CE.** *v.a.* [*seduco*, Latin; *seduire*, French.] To draw aside from the right; to tempt; to corrupt; to deprave; to mislead; to deceive.

'Tis meet
That noble minds keep ever with their likes;
For who so firm that cannot be seduc'd?
SHAKESPEARE'S JULIUS CÆSAR.

Me the gold of France did not seduce,
Although I did admit it as a motive,
The sooner to effect what I intended.
SHAKESPEARE'S HENRY V.

A beauty-waining and distressed widow,
Seduc'd *the pitch and height of all his thoughts*
To base declension.
SHAKESPEARE'S RICHARD III.

In the latter times some shall depart from the faith, giving heed to seducing *spirits.*
BIBLE 1 TIMOTHY, IV. 1.

I shall never gratify the spightfulness of a few with any sinister thoughts of all their allegiance, whom pious frauds have seduced. KING CHARLES.

Subtle he needs must be who could seduce
Angels. MILTON.

Nor let false friends seduce *thy mind to fame,*
By arrogating Johnson's hostile name;
Let father Flecknoe fire thy mind with praise,
And uncle Ogleby thy envy raise.
DRYDEN.

SEDU'CER. *n.s.* [from *seduce.*] One who draws aside from the right; a tempter; a corrupter.

Grant it me, O king; otherwise a seducer *flourishes, and a poor maid is undone.*
SHAKESPEARE.

There is a teaching by restraining seducers *and so removing the hindrances of knowledge.* SOUTH.

The soft seducer, *with enticing looks,*
The bellowing rivals to the fight provokes.
DRYDEN.

He whose firm faith no reason could remove,
Will melt before that soft seducer, *love.*
DRYDEN.

SE'EDTIME. *n.s.* [*seed* and *time.*] The season of sowing.

While the earth remaineth, seedtime *and harvest shall not cease.*
BIBLE GENESIS, VIII. 22.

If he would have two tributes in one year, he must give them two seedtimes, *and two harvests.* BACON.

The first rain fell upon the seedtime *about October, and was to make the seed to root; the latter was to fill the ear.* BROWN.

Their very seedtime *was their harvest, and by sowing tares they immediately reaped gold.* DECAY OF PIETY.

Day and night,
Seedtime *and harvest, heat and hoary frost,*
Shall hold their course, 'till fire purge all things. MILTON.

He that too curiously observes the face of

the heavens, by missing his seedtime, *will lose the hopes of his harvest.* ATTERBURY.

EE'KSORROW. *n.s.* [*seek* and *orrow.*] One who contrives to give imself vexation.

Afield they go, where many lookers be,
And thou seeksorrow, *Klaius, them among:*
Indeed thou saidst it was thy friend to see,
Strephon, whose absence seem'd unto thee long. SIDNEY.

EMICO'LON. *n.s.* [*semi* and *ώλον.*] Half a colon; a point made ıus [;] to note a greater pause than ıat of a comma.

EMIVO'WEL. *n.s.* [*semi* and *owel.*] A consonant which makes an nperfect sound, or does not demand a otal occlusion of the mouth.

When Homer would represent any agreeable object, he makes use of the smoothest vowels and most flowing semivowels. BROOME'S NOTES TO THE ODYSSEY.

E'NSUALIST. *n.s.* [from *sensual.*] carnal person; one devoted to cor-oral pleasures.

Let atheists and sensualists *satisfy themselves as they are able; the former of which will find, that, as long as reason keeps her ground, religion neither can nor will lose her's.* SOUTH.

E'NSUOUS. *adj.* [from *sense.*] ender; pathetick; full of passion.[190]

To this poetry would be made precedent, as being less subtile and fine; but more simple, sensuous, *and passionate.* MILTON.

E'NTENCE. *n.s.* [*sentence*, French; *ententia*, Latin.]

. Determination or decision, as of a ıdge civil or criminal.

The rule of voluntary agents on earth is the sentence *that reason giveth, concerning the goodness of those things which they are to do.* HOOKER.

If we have neither voice from heaven, that so pronounceth of them, neither sentence *of men grounded upon such manifest and clear proof, that they, in whose hands it is to alter them, may likewise infallibly, even in heart and conscience, judge them so; upon necessity to urge alteration, is to trouble and disturb without necessity.* HOOKER.

How will I give sentence *against them.* BIBLE JEREMIAH, IV. 12.

If matter of fact breaks out with too great an evidence to be denied, why, still there are other lenitives, that friendship will apply, before it will be brought to the decretory rigours of a condemning sentence. SOUTH'S SERMONS.

Let him set out some of Luther's works, that by them we may pass sentence *upon his doctrines.* ATTERBURY.

2. It is usually spoken of condemnation pronounced by the judge; doom.

By the consent of all laws, in capital causes, the evidence must be full and clear; and if so, where one man's life is in question, what say we to a war, which is ever the sentence *of death upon many?* BACON'S HOLY WAR.

What rests but that the mortal sentence *pass?* MILTON.

3. A maxim; an axiom, generally moral.

A sentence *may be defined a moral instruction couched in a few words.* BROOME'S NOTES ON THE ODYSSEY.

4. A short paragraph; a period in writing.

An excellent spirit, knowledge, understanding, and shewing of hard sentences *were found in Daniel.* BIBLE DANIEL, V. 12.

SENTENTIO'SITY. *n.s.* [from *sententious.*] Comprehension in a sentence.

Vulgar precepts in morality carry with them nothing above the line, or beyond the

extemporary sententiosity *of common conceits with us.*
BROWN'S VULGAR ERROURS.

SE'PARATIST. *n.s.* [*separatiste*, Fr. from *separate*.] One who divides from the church; a schismatick; a seceder.

The anabaptists, separatists, *and sectaries tenets are full of schism, and inconsistent with monarchy.* BACON.

Our modern separatists *pronounce all those heretical, or carnal, from whom they have withdrawn.* DECAY OF PIETY.

Says the separatist, *if those, who have the rule over you, should command you any thing about church affairs, you ought not, in conscience, to obey them.*
SOUTH'S SERMONS.

SERA'GLIO. *n.s.* [Italian, perhaps of Oriental original. The *g* is lost in the pronunciation.] A house of women kept for debauchery.

There is a great deal more solid content to be found in a constant course of well living, than in the voluptuousness of a seraglio.
NORRIS.

SERENA'DE. *n.s.* [*serenade*, Fr. *serenata*, Italian, whence, in Milton, *serenate*, from *serenus*, Latin, the lovers commonly attending their mistresses in fair nights.] Musick or songs with which ladies are entertained by their lovers in the night.

Mixt dance, or wanton mask, or midnight ball,
Or serenate, *which the starv'd lover sings*
To his proud fair; best quitted with disdain. MILTON.

Foolish swallow, what do'st thou
So often at my window do,
With thy tuneless serenade? COWLEY.

Shall I the neighbours nightly rest invade,
At her deaf doors, with some vile serenade? DRYDEN.

Will fancies he never should have been the man he is, had not he broke windows, and disturbed honest people with his midnight serenades, *when he was a young fellow.*
ADDISON.

SE'RGEANT. *n.s.* [*sergent*, French; *sergente*, Italian, from *servicus*, Latin.]

1. An officer whose business it is to execute the commands of magistrates.

Had I but time, as this fell sergeant, *death*
Is strict in his arrest, oh, I could tell.
SHAKESPEARE'S HAMLET.

When it was day the magistrates sent the sergeants, *saying, let these men go.*
BIBLE ACTS, XVI. 35.

2. A petty officer in the army.

This is the sergeant,
Who, like a good and hardy soldier, fought. SHAKESPEARE'S MACBETH.

3. A lawyer of the highest rank under a judge.

None should be made sergeants, *but such as probably might be held fit to be judges afterwards.* BACON.

4. It is a title given to some of the king's servants: as, *sergeant chirurgeons*.

SERMOCINA'TION. *n.s.* [*sermocinatio*, Latin.] The act or practice of making speeches.

SE'RPENT. *n.s.* [*serpens*, Latin.] An animal that moves by undulation without legs. They are often venomous. They are divided into two kinds; the *viper*, which brings young, and the *snake*, that lays eggs.

She was arrayed all in lily white,
And in her right hand bore a cup of gold,
With wine and water filled up to the height;
In which a serpent *did himself enfold,*
That horror made to all that did behold.
FAIRY QUEEN.

She struck me with her tongue,
Most serpent *like, upon the very heart.*
SHAKESPEARE'S KING LEAR.

They, or under ground, or circuit wide,

With serpent *error wand'ring, found their way.* MILTON.

Haply piercing through the dark disguise,
The chief I challeng'd: he whose practis'd wit
Knew all the serpent *mazes of deceit,*
Eludes my search. POPE'S ODYSSEY.

SE'RVANT. *n.s.* [*servant*, French; *servus*, Latin.]

1. One who attends another, and acts at his command. The correlative of master.

We are one in fortune; both
Fell by our servants, *by those men we lov'd most.* SHAKESPEARE.

I had rather be a country servant *maid,*
Than a great queen with this condition.
SHAKESPEARE'S RICHARD III.

He disdain'd not
Thenceforth the form of servant *to assume.* MILTON.

For master or for servant *here to call*
Was all alike, where only two were all.
DRYDEN.

2. One in a state of subjection. Unusual.

Being unprepar'd,
Our will became the servant *to defect,*
Which else should free have wrong'd.
SHAKESPEARE'S MACBETH.

3. A word of civility used to superiours or equals.

This subjection, due from all men to all men, is something more than the compliment of course, when our betters tell us they are our humble servants, *but understand us to be their slaves.* SWIFT.

SETA'CEOUS. *adj.* [*seta*, Latin.] Bristly; set with strong hairs; consisting of strong hairs.

The parent insect, with its stiff setaceous *tail, terebrates the rib of the leaf when tender, and makes way for its egg into the very pith.* DERHAM.

SETTE'E. *n.s.* A large long seat with a back to it.

SETTLE. *n.s.* [*setol*, Sax.] A seat; a bench; something to sit on.

From the bottom to the lower settle *shall be two cubits.* BIBLE EZEKIEL, XLIII. 14.

The man, their hearty welcome first exprest,
A common settle *drew for either guest,*
Inviting each his weary limbs to rest.
DRYDEN.

SE'VENNIGHT. *n.s.* [*seven* and *night.*]

1. A week; the time from one day of the week to the next day of the same denomination preceding or following; a week, numbered according to the practice of the old northern nations, as in *fortnight.*

Rome was either more grateful to the beholders, or more noble in itself, than justs with the sword and lance, maintained for a sevennight *together.* SIDNEY.

Iago's footing here anticipates our thoughts
A se'nnight's *speed.*
SHAKESPEARE'S OTHELLO.

Shining woods, laid in a dry room, within a sevennight *lost their shining.*
BACON'S NATURAL HISTORY.

2. We use still the word *sevennight* or *se'nnight* in computing time: as, it happened on Monday was *sevennight*, that is, *on the Monday before last Monday*; it will be done on Monday *sevennight*, that is, *on the Monday after next Monday.*

This comes from one of those untucker'd ladies whom you were so sharp upon on Monday was se'ennight. ADDISON.

SE'VOCATION. *n.s.* [*sevoco*, Latin.] The act of calling aside.

SEWER. *v.n.* [*escuyer trenchant*, French; or *asseour*, old French; from *asseoir*, to set down; for those officers set the dishes on the table. *Newton's Milton.*]

1. An officer who serves up a feast.

> *Marshall'd feast,*
> *Serv'd up in hall with* sewers *and seneshals:*
> *The skill of artifice or office mean.*
> MILTON.

> *The cook and* sewer, *each his talent tries,*
> *In various figures scenes of dishes rise.*
> COWEL.

2. [From *issue, issuer.*] A passage for water to run through, now corrupted to *shore.*

> *The fenmen hold that the* sewers *must be kept so, as the water may not stay too long in the spring till the weeds and sedge be grown up.* BACON.

> *Men suffer their private in judgment to be drawn into the common* sewer, *or stream of the present vogue.* KING CHARLES.

> *As one who long in populous city pent,*
> *Where houses thick, and* sewers *annoy the air,*
> *Forth issuing on a summer's morn, to breathe*
> *Among the pleasant villages and farms*
> *Adjoin'd, from each thing met conceives delight.* MILTON.

3. He that uses a needle.

SEX. *n.s.* [*sexe*, French; *sexus*, Latin.]

1. The property by which any animal is male or female.

> *These two great* sexes *animate the world.*
> MILTON.

> *Under his forming hands a creature grew,*
> *Manlike, but different* sex. MILTON.

2. Womankind; by way of emphasis.

> *Unhappy* sex! *whose beauty is your snare;*
> *Expos'd to trials; made too frail to bear.*
> DRYDEN.

> *Shame is hard to be overcome; but if the* sex *once get the better of it, it gives them afterwards no more trouble.* GARTH.

To **SHAB.** *v.n.* To play mean tricks; a low barbarous cant word.

SHA'BBY. *adj.* [A word that has crept into conversation and low writing; but ought not to be admitted into the language.] Mean; paltry.

> *The dean was so* shabby, *and look'd like a ninny,*
> *That the captain suppos'd he was curate to Jenny.* SWIFT.

SHADE. *n.s.* [*scadu*, Saxon; *schade*, Dutch.]

1. The cloud or opacity made by interception of the light.

> *Spring no obstacle found here nor* shade,
> *But all sunshine.* MILTON.

2. Darkness; obscurity.

> *The weaker light unwillingly declin'd,*
> *And to prevailing* shades *the murmuring world resign'd.* ROSCOMMON.

3. Coolness made by interception of the sun.

> *Antigonus, when told that the enemy had such volleys of arrows that hid the sun, said, that falls out well; for this is hot weather, and so we shall fight in the* shade. BACON.

> *That high mount of God whence light and* shade
> *Shine both.* MILTON.

4. An obscure place, properly in a grove or close wood by which the light is excluded.

> *Let us seek out some desolate* shade, *and there*
> *Weep our sad bosoms empty.*
> SHAKESPEARE.

> *Regions of sorrow, doleful* shades.
> MILTON.

> *Then to the desart takes his flight;*
> *Where still from* shade *to* shade *the son of God,*
> *After forty days fasting, had remain'd.*
> MILTON.

The pious prince then seeks the shade,
Which hides from sight his venerable maid. DRYDEN.

5. Screen causing an exclusion of light or heat; umbrage.

Let the arched knife
Well sharpen'd now assail the spreading shades
Of vegetables, and their thirsty limbs dissever. PHILIPS.

In Brazil are trees which kill those that sit under their shade *in a few hours.* ARBUTHNOT.

6. Protection; shelter.

7. The parts of a picture not brightly coloured.

'Tis ev'ry painter's art to hide from sight,
And cast in shades *what seen would not delight.* DRYDEN.

8. A colour; gradation of light.

White, red, yellow, blue, with their several degrees, or shades *and mixtures, as green come in only by the eyes.* LOCKE.

9. The figure formed upon any surface corresponding to the body by which the light is intercepted.[191]

Envy will merit as its shade *pursue.* POPE.

10. The soul separated from the body; so called as supposed by the ancients to be perceptible to the sight, not to the touch. A spirit; a ghost; manes.

To Trachin swift as thought the flitting shade
Thro' air his momentary journey made. DRYDEN.

Ne'er to these chambers where the mighty rest,
Since their foundation, came a nobler guest;
Nor e'er was to the bow'rs of bliss convey'd
A fairer spirit or more welcome shade. TICKELL.

SHAGRE'EN. *n.s.* [*chagrin*, French.] The skin of a kind of fish, or skin made rough in imitation of it.

To **SHA'GREEN.** *v.a.* [*chagriner*, French] To irritate; to provoke. Both should be written *chagrin*.

SHALL. *v. defective.* [*sceal*, Sax. is originally I *owe*, or I *ought*. In *Chaucer*, *the faithe I* shall *to God*, means *the faith I* owe *to God*: thence it became a sign of the future tense. The French use *devoir*, *dois*, *doit*, in the same manner, with a kind of future signification; and the Swedes have *skall*, and the Islanders *skal*, in the same sense. It has no tenses but *shall* future, and *should* imperfect.

The explanation of *shall*, which foreigners and provincials confound with *will*, is not easy; and the difficulty is increased by the poets, who sometimes give to *shall* an emphatical sense of *will*: but I shall endeavour, *crassa Minervâ*,[192] to show the meaning of *shall* in the future tense.]

1. *I* SHALL *love.* It will so happen that I must love; I am resolved to love.

2. SHALL *I love?* Will it be permitted me to love? Will you permit me to love? Will it happen that I must love?

3. *Thou* SHALT *love.* I command thee to love; it is permitted thee to love: [in poetry or solemn diction] it will happen that thou must love.

4. SHALT *thou love?* Will it happen that thou must love? Will it be permitted to thee to love?

5. *He* SHALL *love.* It will happen that he must love; it is commanded him that he love.

It is a mind, that shall *remain a poison where it is.*
—— Shall *remain!*
Hear you this triton of the minnows? Mark you
His absolute shall?
SHAKESPEARE'S CORIOLANUS.

See Romulus the great:
This prince a priestess of your blood shall *bear,*
And like his sire in arms he shall *appear.*
DRYDEN'S ÆNEIS.

That he shall *receive no benefit from Christ, is the affirmation whereon all his despair is founded; and the one way of removing this dismal apprehension, is to convince him that Christ's death, and the benefits thereof, either do, or, if he perform the condition required of him,* shall *certainly belong to him.* HAMMOND'S FUNDAMENTALS.

6. SHALL *he love?* Is it permitted him to love? In solemn language, Will it happen that he must love?
7. The plural persons follow the signification of the singulars.

SHA'LLOWBRAINED. *adj.* [*shallow* and *brain.*] Foolish; futile; trifling; empty.

It cannot but be matter of just indignation to all good men to see a company of lewd shallowbrained *huffs making atheism, and contempt of religion, the sole badge of wit.* SOUTH.

SHA'MBLING. *adj.* [See **SCAMBLING.**[193]] Moving aukwardly and irregularly. A low bad word.

By that shambling *in his walk, it should be my rich banker, Gomez, whom I knew at Barcelona.* DRYDEN'S SPANISH FRYAR.

So when nurse Nokes to act young Ammon tries,
With shambling *legs, long chin, and foolish eyes,*
With dangling hands he strokes th' imperial robe,
And with a cuckold's air commands the globe. SMITH.

SHA'PESMITH. *n.s.* [*shape* and *smith.*] One who undertakes to improve the form of the body. A burlesque word.

No shapesmith *yet set up and drove a trade,*
To mend the work that providence had made. GARTH.

SHA'REBONE. *n.s.* [*share* and *bone.*] The os pubis; the bone that divides the trunk from the limbs.

The cartilage bracing together the two ossa pubis, or sharebones, *Bartholine faith, is twice thicker and laxer in women than men.* DERHAM.

SHARK. *n.s.* [*canis charcharias,* Latin.]

1. A voracious sea-fish.

His jaws horrifick arm'd with threefold fate,
The direful shark.
THOMSON'S SUMMER.

2. A greedy artful fellow; one who fills his pockets by sly tricks.[194]

David's messengers are sent back to him, like so many sharks *and runnagates, only for endeavouring to compliment an ill-nature out of itself, and seeking that by petition which they might have commanded by their sword.* SOUTH'S SERMONS.

3. Trick; fraud; petty rapine.

Wretches who live upon the shark, *and other mens sins, the common poisoners of youth, equally desperate in their fortunes and their manners, and getting their very bread by the damnation of souls.* SOUTH'S SERMONS.

To **SHARK.** *v.a.* To pick up hastily or slily.

Young Fortinbras,
Of unimproved mettle, hot and full,
Hath in the skirts of Norway, here and there,
Shark'd *up a list of landless resolutes.*
SHAKESPEARE'S HAMLET.

To **SHARK.** *v.n.*

1. To play the petty thief.

The fly leads a lazy, voluptuous, scandalous, sharking *life, hateful wherever she comes.* L'ESTRANGE.

2. To cheat; to trick. *Ainsworth.*

There are cheats by natural inclination as well as by corruption: nature taught this boy to shark, *not discipline.* L'ESTRANGE.

The old generous English spirit, which heretofore made this nation so great in the eyes of all the world, seems utterly extinct; and we are degenerated into a mean, sharking, *fallacious, undermining converse, there being a snare and a trapan almost in every word we hear, and every action we see.* SOUTH.

SHA'RPER. *n.s.* [from *sharp.*] A tricking fellow; a petty thief; a rascal.

Sharpers, *as pikes, prey upon their own kind.* L'ESTRANGE.

He should retrench what he lost to sharpers, *and spent upon puppet-plays, to apply it to that use.* ARBUTHNOT.

I only wear it in a land of Hectors,
Thieves, supercargo's, sharpers, *and directors.* POPE.

SHA'VER. *n.s.* [from *shave.*]
1. A man that practises the art of shaving.
2. A man closely attentive to his own interest.

My lord
Was now dispos'd to crack a jest,
And bid friend Lewis go in quest;
This Lewis is a cunning shaver. SWIFT.

3. A robber; a plunderer.

They fell all into the hands of the cruel mountain people, living for the most part by theft, and waiting for wrecks, as hawks for their prey: by these shavers *the Turks were stript of all they had.* KNOLLES.

SHAW. *n.s.* [*scua*, Saxon; *schawe*, Dutch; *skugga*, Islandick.] A thicket; a small wood. A tuft of trees near Lichfield is called Gentle *shaw.*

SHA'WFOWL. *n.s.* [*shaw* and *fowl.*] An artificial fowl made by fowlers on purpose to shoot at.

SHEE'PBITER. *n.s.* [from *sheepbite.*] A petty thief.

His gate like a sheepbiter *fleering aside.* TUSSER.

Wouldst thou not be glad to have the niggardly rascally sheepbiter *come to some notable shame.* SHAKESPEARE.

There are political sheepbiters *as well as pastoral: betrayers of publick trusts, as well as of private.* L'ESTRANGE.

SHEEPWA'LK. *n.s.* [*sheep* and *walk.*] Pasture for sheep.

He beheld a field,
Part arable and tilth; whereon were sheaves
New reap'd; the other part sheepwalks *and folds.* MILTON.

SHE'RIFF. *n.s.* [*scyregepefa*, Saxon, from *scyre*, a shire, and *reve*, a steward. It is sometimes pronounced *shrieve*, which some poets have injudiciously adopted.] An officer to whom is intrusted in each county the execution of the laws.

A great pow'r of English and of Scots
Are by the sheriff *of Yorkshire overthrown.* SHAKESPEARE.

Concerning ministers of justice, the high sheriffs *of the counties have been very ancient in this kingdom.* BACON.

Now may'rs and shrieves *all hush'd and satiate lay.* POPE.

SHI'FTER. *n.s.* [from *shift.*] One who plays tricks; a man of artifice.

'Twas such a shifter, *that, if truth were known,*
Death was half glad when he had got him down. MILTON.

SHI'LLING. *n.s.* [*scylling*, Sax. and Erse; *schelling*, Dut.] A coin of various value in different times. It is now twelve pence.

Five of these pence made their shilling, *which they called* scilling, *probably from* scilingus, *which the Romans used for the*

fourth part of an ounce; and forty-eight of these scillings *made their pound, and four hundred of these pounds were a legacy for a king's daughter, as appeareth by the last will of king Alfred.*
CAMDEN'S REMAINS.

The very same shilling *may at one time pay twenty men in twenty days, and at another rest in the same hands one hundred days.* LOCKE.

SHILL-I-SHALL-I. A corrupt reduplication of *shall I?* The question of a man hesitating. To stand *shill-I-shall-I*, is to continue hesitating and procrastinating.

I am somewhat dainty in making a resolution, because when I make it, I keep it: I don't stand shill-I-shall-I *then; if I say't, I'll do't.*
CONGREVE'S WAY OF THE WORLD.

SHI'NESS. *n.s.* [from *shy*.] Unwillingness to be tractable or familiar.

An incurable shiness *is the vice of Irish horses, and is hardly ever seen in Flanders, because the Winter forces the breeders there to house and handle their colts.* TEMPLE.

They were famous for their justice in commerce, but extreme shiness *to strangers: they exposed their goods with the price marked upon them, and then retired.*
ARBUTHNOT.

SHIRE. *n.s.* [*scir*, from *sciran*, to divide, Sax. *skyre*, Erse.] A division of the kingdom; a county; so much of the kingdom as is under one sheriff.

His blazing eyes, like two bright shining shields,
Did burn with wrath, and sparkled living fire;
As two broad beacons, set in open fields,
Send forth their flames far off to every shire. FAIRY QUEEN.

The noble youths from distant shires *resort.* PRIOR.

SHI'TTLECOCK. *n.s.* [Commonly and perhaps as properly *shuttlecock*. Of *shittle* or *shuttle* the etymology is doubtful: *Skinner* derives it from *schutteln*, German, to shake; or *sceatan*, Saxon, to throw. He thinks it is called a cock from its feathers. Perhaps it is properly *shuttlecork*, a cork driven to and fro, as the instrument in weaving, and softened by frequent and rapid utterance from *cork* and *cock*.] A cork stuck with feathers, and driven by players from one to another with battledoors.

You need not discharge a cannon to break the chain of his thoughts: the pat of a shittlecock, *or the creaking of a jack, will do his business.* COLLIER.

SHOE'BOY. *n.s.* [*shoe* and *boy*.] A boy that cleans shoes.

If I employ a shoeboy, *is it in view to his advantage, or my own convenience?*
SWIFT.

How each the publick good pursues,
Make all true patriots up to shoeboys,
Huzza their brethren. SWIFT.

SHOE'ING-HORN. *n.s.* [*shoe* and *horn*.]
1. A horn used to facilitate the admission of the foot into a narrow shoe.
2. Any thing by which a transaction is facilitated; any thing used as a medium. In contempt.

Most of our fine young ladies retain in their service supernumerary and insignificant fellows which they use like whifflers, and commonly call shoeing-horns.
SPECTATOR.

I have been an arrant shoeing-horn *for above these twenty years. I served my mistress in that capacity above five of the number before she was shod. Though she had many who made their applications to her, I always thought myself the best shoe in her shop.* SPECTATOR.

SHOE'TYE. *n.s.* [*shoe* and *tye.*] The ribband with which women tie their shoes.

Madam, I do as is my duty,
Honour the shadow of your shoetye.
HUDIBRAS.

SHOG. *n.s.* [from *shock.*] Violent concussion.

Another's diving bow he did adore,
Which, with a shog, *casts all the hair before.* DRYDEN.

He will rather have the primitive man to be produced, in a kind of digesting balneum, where all the heavier lees may subside, and a due æquilibrium be maintained, not disturbed by any such rude and violent shogs *that would ruffle and break all the little stamina of the embryon.* BENTLEY.

To **SHOG.** *v.a.* To shake; to agitate by sudden interrupted impulses.

After it is washed, they put the remnant into a wooden dish, the which they softly shog *to and fro in the water, until the earthy substance be flitted away.* CAREW.

SHOP. *n.s.* [*sceop*, Saxon, a magazine; *eschoppe*, French; *shopa*, low Latin. *Ainsworth.*]

1. A place where any thing is sold.

Our windows are broke down,
And we for fear compell'd to shut our shops. SHAKESPEARE.

Your most grave belly thus answer'd;
True is it, my incorporate friends,
That I receive the general food at first,
Which you do live upon; and fit it is,
Because I am the store-house and the shop
Of the whole body. SHAKESPEARE.

In his needy shop *a tortoise hung,*
An alligator stuft, and other skins
Of ill-shap'd fishes; and about his shelves
A beggarly account of empty boxes.
SHAKESPEARE.

Scarce any sold in shops *could be relied on as faithfully prepared.* BOYLE.

His shop *is his element, and he cannot with any enjoyment of himself live out of it.* SOUTH'S SERMONS.

2. A room in which manufactures are carried on.

We have divers mechanical arts and stuffs made by them; and shops *for such as are not brought into vulgar use.* BACON.

SHOPBOA'RD. *n.s.* [*shop* and *board.*] Bench on which any work is done.

That beastly rabble, that came down
From all the garrets in the town,
And stalls, and shopboards, *in vast swarms,*
With new-chalk'd bills, and rusty arms.
HUDIBRAS.

It dwells not in shops or work-houses; nor till the late age was it ever known, that any one served seven years to a smith or a taylor, that he should commence doctor or divine from the shopboard *or the anvil; or from whistling to a team, come to preach to a congregation.* SOUTH'S SERMONS.

SHO'PMAN. *n.s.* [*shop* and *man.*] A petty trader.

Garth, gen'rous as his muse, prescribes and gives,
The shopman *sells, and by destruction lives.* DRYDEN.

SHO'RTHAND. *n.s.* [*short* and *hand.*] A method of writing in compendious characters.

Your follies and debauches change
With such a whirl, the poets of your age
Are tir'd, and cannot score them on the stage,
Unless each vice in shorthand *they indite,*
Ev'n as notcht 'prentices whole sermons write. DRYDEN.

Boys have but little use of shorthand, *and should by no means practise it, 'till they can write perfectly well.* LOCKE.

In shorthand *skill'd, where little marks comprise*

Whole words, a sentence in a letter lies. CREECH.

As the language of the face is universal, so 'tis very comprehensive: no laconism can reach it: 'tis the shorthand *of the mind, and crowds a great deal in a little room.* COLLIER.

SHO'RY. *adj.* [from *shore.*] Lying near the coast.

There is commonly a declivity from the shore to the middle part of the channel, and those shory *parts are generally but some fathoms deep.* BURNET'S THEORY OF THE EARTH.

SHOULD. *v.n.* [*scude*, Dutch; *sceoldan*, Saxon.]
1. This is a kind of auxiliary verb used in the conjunctive mood, of which the signification is not easily fixed.
2. *I* SHOULD *go.* It is my business or duty to go.
3. *If I* SHOULD *go.* If it happens that I go.
4. *Thou* SHOULD'ST *go.* Thou oughtest to go.
5. *If thou* SHOULD'ST *go.* If it happens that thou goest.
6. The same significations are found in all the other persons singular and plural.

Let not a desperate action more engage you
Than safety should.
BEN JONSON'S CATILINE.

Some praises come of good wishes and respects, when by telling men what they are, they represent to them what they should *be.* BACON.

To do thee honour I will shed their blood,
Which the just laws, if I were faultless,
should. WALLER.

So subjects love just kings, or so they
should. DRYDEN.

I conclude, that things are not as they should *be.* SWIFT.

7. SHOULD *be.* A proverbial phrase of slight contempt or irony.

The girls look upon their father as a clown, and the boys think their mother no better than she should *be.* ADDISON.

8. There is another signification now little in use, in which *should* has scarcely any distinct or explicable meaning. *It should be* differs in this sense very little from *it is.*

There is a fabulous narration, that in the northern countries there should *be an herb that groweth in the likeness of a lamb, and feedeth upon the grass.* BACON'S NATURAL HISTORY.

SHO'ULDERSLIP. *n.s.* [*shoulder* and *slip.*] Dislocation of the shoulder.

The horse will take so much care of himself as to come off with only a strain or a shoulderslip. SWIFT.

SHRILL. [A word supposed to be made *per onomatopœiam*, in imitation of the thing expressed, which indeed it images very happily.] Sounding with a piercing, tremulous, or vibratory sound.

Thy hounds shall make the welkin answer them,
And fetch shrill *echoes from the hollow earth.* SHAKESPEARE.

I have heard
The cock that is the trumpet to the morn,
Doth with his lofty and shrill *sounding throat*
Awake the god of day.
SHAKESPEARE'S HAMLET.

Have I fall'n,
From the dread summit of this chalky bourn!
Look up a height, the shrill *gorg'd lark so far*
Cannot be seen or heard.
SHAKESPEARE'S KING LEAR.

Upsprings the lark,
Shrill *voic'd and loud, the messenger of morn.* THOMSON.

To **SHRUGG.**[195] *v.n.* [*schrichen*, Dutch; to tremble.] To express horror or dissatisfaction by motion of the shoulders or whole body.

Like a fearful deer that looks most about when he comes to the best feed, with a shrugging *kind of tremor through all her principal parts, she gave these words.* SIDNEY.

The touch of the cold water made a pretty kind of shrugging *come over her body like the twinkling of the fairest among the fixed stars.* SIDNEY.

Be quick, thou wert best
To answer other business; shrug'st *thou malice?* SHAKESPEARE.

He grins, smacks, shrugs, *and such an itch endures,*
As prentices or school boys which do know
Of some gay sport abroad, yet dare not go.
DONNE.

They grin, they shrug,
They bow, they snarl, they scratch, they hug. SWIFT.

To **SHRUG.** *v.a.* To contract or draw up.

He shrugs *his shoulders when you talk of securities.* ADDISON.

Zealots will shrug *up their shoulders.*
BLOUNT.

He shrug'd *his sturdy back,*
As if he felt his shoulders ake.
HUDIBRAS.

SHU'FFLECAP. *n.s.* [*shuffle* and *cap.*] A play at which money is shaken in a hat.

He lost his money at chuck farthing, shufflecap, *and all-fours.*
ARBUTHNOT'S HISTORY OF JOHN BULL.

SHU'TTLECOCK. *n.s.* [See SHITTLECOCK.] A cork stuck with feathers, and beaten backward and forward.

With dice, with cards, with balliards far unfit,
With shuttlecocks *misseeming manly wit.*
HUBBERD'S TALE.

SI'CAMORE. *n.s.* [*sicamorus*, Latin.] A tree.

Of trees you have the palm, olive, and sicamore. PEACHAM.

SI'CCITY. *n.s.* [*siccite*, Fr. *siccitas*, from *siccus*, Latin.] Driness; aridity; want of moisture.

That which is coagulated by a firy siccity *will suffer coliquation from an aqueous humidity, as salt and sugar.*
BROWN'S VULGAR ERROURS.

The reason some attempt to make out from the siccity *and driness of its flesh.*
BROWN'S VULGAR ERROURS.

In application of medicaments consider what degree of heat and siccity *is proper.*
WISEMAN'S SURGERY.

SICE. *n.s.* [*six*, French.] The number six at dice.

My study was to cog the dice,
And dext'rously to throw the lucky sice;
To shun ames-ace, that swept my stakes away. DRYDEN.

SI'DEBOARD. *n.s.* [*side* and *board.*] The side table on which conveniences are placed for those that eat at the other table.

At a stately sideboard *by the wine*
That fragrant smell diffus'd.
MILTON'S PARADISE REGAIN'D.

No sideboards *then with gilded plate were dress'd,*
No sweating slaves with massive dishes press'd. DRYDEN.

The snow white damask ensigns are display'd,
And glitt'ring salvers on the sideboard *laid.* KING.

The shining sideboard, *and the burnish'd plate,*
Let other ministers, great Anne, require.
PRIOR.

Scipio Africanus brought from Carthage to Rome, in silver vessels, to the value of 11966 l. 15 s. 9 d. a quantity exceeded afterwards by the sideboards *of many private tables.* ARBUTHNOT.

SI'DEBOX. *n.s.* [*side* and *box.*] Seat for the ladies on the side of the theatre.

Why round our coaches crowd the white-glov'd beaus?
Why bows the sidebox *from its inmost rows?* POPE.

SIDERA'TION. *n.s.* [*sideration*, French; *sideratio*, Latin.] A sudden mortification, or, as the common people call it, a blast; or a sudden deprivation of sense, as in an apoplexy.

The contagious vapour of the very eggs produce a mortification or sideration *in the parts of plants on which they are laid.* RAY ON THE CREATION.

SIGN. *n.s.* [*signe*, French; *signum*, Latin.]

1. A token of any thing; that by which any thing is shown.

Signs *must resemble the things they signify.* HOOKER.

Signs *for communication may be contrived from any variety of objects of one kind appertaining to either sense.* HOLDER.

To express the passions which are seated in the heart by outward signs, *is one great precept of the painters, and very difficult to perform.* DRYDEN'S DUFRESNOY.

When any one uses any term, he may have in his mind a determined idea which he makes it the sign *of, and to which he should keep it steadily annexed.* LOCKE.

2. A wonder; a miracle.[196]

If they will not hearken to the voice of the first sign, *they will not believe the latter* sign. BIBLE EXODUS, IV. 8.

Cover thy face that thou see not; for I have set thee for a sign *unto Israel.*
BIBLE EZEKIEL, XII. 6.

Compell'd by signs *and judgments dire.*
MILTON.

3. A picture hung at a door, to give notice what is sold within.

I found my miss, struck hands, and pray'd him tell,
To hold acquaintance still, where he did dwell;
He barely nam'd the street, promis'd the wine;
But his kind wife gave me the very sign.
DONNE.

Underneath an alehouse' paltry sign.
SHAKESPEARE'S HENRY VI.

True sorrow's like to wine,
That which is good does never need a sign. SUCKLING.

Wit and fancy are not employed in any one article so much as that of contriving signs *to hang over houses.* SWIFT.

4. A monument; a memorial.

The fire devoured two hundred and fifty men, and they became a sign.
BIBLE NUMBERS, XXVI. 10.

5. A constellation in the zodiack.

There stay until the twelve celestial signs
Have brought about their annual reckoning. SHAKESPEARE.

Now did the sign *reign, and the constellation was come, under which Perkin should appear.* BACON'S HENRY VII.

After ev'ry foe subdu'd, the sun
Thrice through the signs *his annual race shall run.* DRYDEN.

6. Note of resemblance.

7. Ensign.

The ensign of Messiah blaz'd,
Aloft by angels borne, his sign *in heaven.*
MILTON.

8. Typical representation; symbol.

The holy symbols or signs *are not barely significative; but what they represent is as certainly delivered to us as the symbols themselves.* BREREWOOD.

9. A subscription of one's name: as, a *sign* manual.

SI'GNAL. *n.s.* [*signal*, French; *sennale*, Spanish.] Notice given by a sign; a sign that gives notice.

The weary sun hath made a golden set,
And, by the bright track of his firy car,
Gives signal *of a goodly day to-morrow.*
SHAKESPEARE'S RICHARD III.

Scarce the dawning day began to spring,
As at a signal *giv'n, the streets with clamours ring.* DRYDEN.

To **SI'GNALIZE.** *v.a.* [*signaler*, French.] To make eminent; to make remarkable.

Many, who have endeavoured to signalize *themselves by works of this nature, plainly discover that they are not acquainted with the most common systems of arts and sciences.* ADDISON'S SPECTATOR.

Some one eminent spirit, having signalized *his valour and fortune in defence of his country, or by the practice of popular arts at home, becomes to have great influence on the people.* SWIFT.

SI'GNATURE. *n.s.* [*signature*, Fr. *signatura*, from *signo*, Lat.]

1. A sign or mark impressed upon anything; a stamp; a mark.

The brain being well furnished with various traces, signatures, *and images, will have a rich treasure always ready to be offered to the soul.* WATTS.

That natural and indelible signature *of God, which human souls, in their first origin, are supposed to be stampt with, we have no need of in disputes against atheism.* BENTLEY.

Vulgar parents cannot stamp their race
With signatures *of such majestick grace.*
POPE'S ODYSSEY.

2. A mark upon any matter, particularly upon plants, by which their nature or medicinal use is pointed out.

All bodies work by the communication of their nature, or by the impression and signatures *of their motions: the diffusion of species visible, seemeth to participate more of the former, and the species audible of the latter.* BACON'S NATURAL HISTORY.

Some plants bear a very evident signature *of their nature and use.*
MORE AGAINST ATHEISM.

Seek out for plants, and signatures,
To quack of universal cures. HUDIBRAS.

Herbs are described by marks and signatures, *so far as to distinguish them from one another.* BAKER ON LEARNING.

3. Proof; evidence.[197]

The most despicable pieces of decayed nature are curiously wrought with eminent signatures *of divine wisdom.*
GLANVILLE.

Some rely on certain marks and signatures *of their election, and others on their belonging to some particular church or sect.* ROGERS'S SERMONS.

4. [Among printers.] Some letter or figure to distinguish different sheets.

SI'LENCE. *interj.* An authoritative restraint of speech.

Sir, have pity; I'll be his surety. ——
—— Silence: *one word more*
Shall make me chide thee, if not hate thee.
SHAKESPEARE.

SI'LLILY. *adv.* [from *silly*.] In a silly manner; simply; foolishly.

I wonder, what thou and I
Did, till we lov'd? were we not wean'd till then,
But suck'd on childish pleasures sillily?
Or slumber'd we in the seven sleepers den?
DONNE.

We are caught as sillily *as the bird in the net.* L'ESTRANGE.

Do, do, look sillily, *good colonel; 'tis a*

decent melancholy after an absolute defeat. DRYDEN'S SPANISH FRIAR.

SI'LLY. *adj.* [*selig*, German. *Skinner.*]
1. Harmless; innocent; inoffensive; plain; artless.
2. Weak; helpless.

After long storms,
In dread of death and dangerous dismay,
With which my silly *bark was tossed sore,*
I do at length descry the happy shore.
SPENSER.

3. Foolish; witless.

Perhaps their loves, or else their sheep,
Was that did their silly *thoughts so busy keep.* MILTON.

The meanest subjects censure the actions of the greatest prince; the silliest *servants, of the wisest master.* TEMPLE.

I have no discontent at living here; besides what arises from a silly *spirit of liberty, which I resolve to throw off.* SWIFT.

Such parts of writings as are stupid or silly, *false or mistaken, should become subjects of occasional criticism.* WATTS.

SI'LLYHOW. *n.s.* [Perhaps from *selig*, happy, and *heoft*, the head.] The membrane that covers the head of the fœtus.

Great conceits are raised, of the membranous covering called the sillyhow, *sometimes found about the heads of children upon their birth.*
BROWN'S VULGAR ERROURS.

SI'MILE. *n.s.* [*simile*, Latin.] A comparison by which any thing is illustrated or aggrandized.

Their rhimes,
Full of protest, of oath, and big compare,
Want similes.
SHAKESPEARE'S TROILUS AND CRESSIDA.

Lucentio slip'd me, like his greyhound,
Which runs himself, and catches for his master:
A good swift simile, *but something currish.* SHAKESPEARE.

In argument,
Similes *are like songs in love,*
They much describe; they nothing prove.
PRIOR.

Poets, to give a loose to a warm fancy, not only expatiate in their similes, *but introduce them too frequently.* GARTH.

SIMPLE. *n.s.* [*simple*, French.] A single ingredient in a medicine; a drug. It is popularly used for an herb.

Of simples *in these groves that grow,*
We'll learn the perfect skill;
The nature of each herb to know,
Which cures, and which can kill.
DRAYTON'S QUEST OF CYNTHIA.

Our foster nurse of nature is repose,
The which he lacks; that to provoke in him,
Are many simples *operative, whose power*
Will close the eye of anguish.
SHAKESPEARE'S KING LEAR.

He would ope his leathern scrip,
And shew me simples *of a thousand names,*
Telling their strange and vigorous faculties. MILTON.

What virtue is in this remedy lies in the naked simple *itself, as it comes over from the Indies.* TEMPLE.

Around its entries nodding poppies grow,
And all cool simples *that sweet rest bestow;*
Night from the plants their sleepy virtue drains,
And passing, sheds it on the silent plains.
DRYDEN.

Med'cine is mine: what herbs and simples *grow*
In fields and forests, all their pow'rs I know,
And am the great physician call'd.
DRYDEN.

To **SIMPLE.** *v.n.* To gather simples.

As once the foaming boar he chas'd,
Lascivious Circe well the youth survey'd,
As simpling *on the flow'ry hills he stray'd.*
GARTH.

SI'MPLER. *n.s.* [from *simple.*] A simplist. An herbarist.

SI'MPLIST. *n.s.* [from *simple.*] One skilled in simples.

A plant so unlike a rose, it hath been mistaken by some good simplists *for amomum.*
BROWN'S VULGAR ERROURS.

SIMULA'TION. *n.s.* [*simulation,* French; *simulatio* from *simulo,* Latin.] That part of hypocrisy which pretends that to be which is not.

Simulation *is a vice rising of a natural falseness, or fearfulness; or of a mind that hath some main faults; which because a man must needs disguise, it maketh him practise* simulation. BACON.

For the unquestionable virtues of her person and mind, he well expressed his love in an act and time of no simulation *towards his end, bequeathing her all his mansion-houses, and a power to dispose of his whole personal estate.* WOTTON.

For distinction sake, a deceiving by word is commonly called a lie; and deceiving by actions, gestures, or behaviour, is called simulation *or hypocrisy.*
SOUTH'S SERMONS.

SI'NISTROUSLY. *adv.* [from *sinistrous.*]

1. With a tendency to the left.

Many in their infancy are sinistrously *disposed, and divers continue all their life left-handed, and have but weak and imperfect use of the right.*
BROWN'S VULGAR ERROURS.

2. Perversely; absurdly.

SINK. *n.s.* [*sinc,* Saxon.]

1. A drain; a jakes

Should by the cormorant belly be restrain'd,
Who is the sink *o' th' body.*
SHAKESPEARE'S CORIOLANUS.

Bad humours gather to a bile, or as divers kennels flow to one sink, *so in short time their numbers increased.* HAYWARD.

Gather more filth than any sink *in town.*
GRANVILLE.

Returning home at night, you'll find the sink
Strike your offended sense with double stink. SWIFT.

2. Any place where corruption is gathered.

What sink *of monsters, wretches of lost minds,*
Mad after change, and desperate in their states,
Wearied and gall'd with their necessities,
Durst have thought it?
BEN JONSON'S CATILINE.

Our soul, whose country's heav'n and God her father,
Into this world, corruption's sink, *is sent;*
Yet so much in her travail she doth gather,
That she returns home wiser than she went. DONNE.

SI'NUS. *n.s.* [Latin.]

1. A bay of the sea; an opening of the land.

Plato supposeth his Atlantis to have sunk all into the sea: whether that be true or no, I do not think it impossible that some arms of the sea, or sinus's, *might have had such an original.*
BURNET'S THEORY OF THE EARTH.

2. Any fold or opening.

SI'ROP, SIRUP. *n.s.* [Arabick] The juice of vegetables boiled with sugar.

Shall I, whose ears her mournful words did seize,
Her words in sirup *laid of sweetest breath,*
Relent. SIDNEY.

Not poppy, nor mandragora,
Nor all the drowsy sirups *of the world*
Shall ever med'cine thee to that sweet sleep,
Which thou owed'st yesterday.
SHAKESPEARE'S OTHELLO.

And first, behold this cordial jalap here,

That flames and dances in his crystal bounds,
With spirits of balm, and fragrant syrops *mixt.* MILTON.

Those expressed juices contain the true essential salt of the plant; for if they be boiled into the consistence of a syrup, *and set in a cool place, the essential salt of the plant will shoot upon the sides of the vessels.* ARBUTHNOT.

SITHE. *n.s.* [*siðe*, Saxon. This word is very variously written by authors: I have chosen the orthography which is at once most simple and most agreeable to etymology.] The instrument of mowing; a crooked blade joined at right angles to a long pole.

Let fame, that all hunt after in their lives,
Live registred upon our brazen tombs;
And then grace us in the disgrace of death:
When, spight of cormorant-devouring time,
Th' endeavour of this present breath may buy
That honour which shall 'bate his scythe's *keen edge;*
And make us heirs of all eternity.
SHAKESPEARE.

Time is commonly drawn upon tombs, in gardens, and other places, an old man, bald, winged with a sithe, *and an hourglass.* PEACHAM ON DRAWING.

There rude impetuous rage does storm and fret;
And there, as master of this murd'ring brood,
Swinging a huge scithe, *stands impartial death,*
With endless business almost out of breath. CRASHAW.

The milk-maid singeth blithe,
And the mower whets his scithe.
MILTON.

The brazen trumpets kindle rage no more;
But useless lances into sythes *shall bend,*
And the broad faulchion in a plough-share end. POPE.

Grav'd o'er their seats the form of time was found,
His scythe *revers'd, and both his pinions bound.* POPE.

But, Stella, say, what evil tongue
Reports you are no longer young?
That time sits with his sythe *to mow*
Where erst sat Cupid with his bow.
SWIFT.

Echo no more returns the chearful sound
Of sharpening scythe.
THOMSON'S SUMMER.

SIX and seven. *n.s.* To be at six and seven, is to be in a state of disorder and confusion.[198]

All is uneven,
And every thing is left at six and seven.
SHAKESPEARE.

In 1588, there sat in the see of Rome a fierce thundring friar, that would set all at six and seven, *or at six and five, if you allude to his name.* BACON.

What blinder bargain e'er was driv'n,
Or wager laid at six and seven.
HUDIBRAS.

John once, turned his mother out of doors, to his great sorrow; for his affairs went on at sixes and sevens. ARBUTHNOT.

The goddess would no longer wait;
But raising from her chair of state,
Left all below at six and seven,
Harness'd her doves and flew to heav'n.
SWIFT.

SIZE. *n.s.* [perhaps rather *cise*, from *incisa*, Latin; or from *assise*, French.]
1. Bulk; quantity of superficies; comparative magnitude.

I ever verified my friends,
With all the size *that verity*
Would without lapsing suffer.
SHAKESPEARE'S CORIOLANUS.

If any decayed ship be new made, it is more fit to make her a size *less than bigger.*
RALEIGH.

The distance judg'd for shot of ev'ry size,

The linstocks touch, the pond'rous ball expires. DRYDEN.

Objects near our view are thought greater than those of a larger size, *that are more remote.* LOCKE.

The martial goddess,
Like thee, Telemachus, in voice and size,
With speed divine, from street to street she flies;
She bids the mariners prepare to stand.
POPE'S ODYSSEY.

2. [*Assise*, old French.] A settled quantity. In the following passage it seems to signify the allowance of the table: whence they say a *sizer* at Cambridge.

'Tis not in thee
To cut off my train, to scant my sizes,
And, in conclusion, to oppose the bolt
Against my coming in.
SHAKESPEARE'S KING LEAR.

3. Figurative bulk; condition.

This agrees too in the contempt of men of a less size *and quality.* L'ESTRANGE.

They do not consider the difference between elaborate discourses, delivered to princes or parliaments, and a plain sermon, intended for the middling or lower size *of people.* SWIFT.

4. [*Sisa*, Italian.] Any viscous or glutinous substance.

SI'ZERS. *n.s.* See **SCISSARS.**[199]

A buttrice and pincers, a hammer and naile,
An apron and sizers *for head and for taile.* TUSSER.

SK'EPTICK. *n.s.* [σκέπτομαι, Gr. *sceptique*, French.] One who doubts, or pretends to doubt of every thing.

Bring the cause unto the bar; whose authority none must disclaim, and least of all those scepticks *in religion.*
DECAY OF PIETY.

Survey
Nature's extended face, then scepticks *say,*
In this wide field of wonders can you find
No art. BLACKMORE.

With too much knowledge for the scepticks *side,*
With too much weakness for the stoicks pride,
Man hangs between.
POPE'S ESSAY ON MAN.

The dogmatist is sure of every thing, and the sceptick *believes nothing.*
WATTS'S LOGICK.

SKILT. *n.s.* [A word used by *Cleaveland*, of which I know not either the etymology or meaning.]

Smeitymnus! ha! what art?
Syriack? Or Arabick? Or Welsh? What skilt?
Ape all the bricklayers that Babel built.
CLEAVELAND.

SKI'MBLESKAMBLE. *adj.* [A cant word formed by reduplication from *scamble.*] Wandering; wild.

A couching lion and a ramping cat,
And such a deal of skimbleskamble *stuff,*
As puts me from my faith.
SHAKESPEARE.

SK'IMMILK. *n.s.* [*skim* and *milk.*] Milk from which the cream has been taken.

Then cheese was brought: says Slouch, this e'en shall roll;
This is skimmilk, *and therefore it shall go.*
KING.

SKONCE. *n.s.* [See **SCONCE.**]

Reinard ransacketh every corner of his wily skonce, *and bestirreth the utmost of his nimble stumps to quit his coat from their jaws.* CAREW.

SKREEN. *n.s.* [*escran*, *escrein*, French, which *Minshew* derives from *secerniculum*, Latin. *Nimis violenter ut solet*,[190] says *Skinner*, which may be true as to one of the senses; but if the first sense of *skreen* be a kind of coarse sieve or riddle, it may perhaps come, if not from *cribrum*, from some of the descendants of *cerno*.]

1. A riddle or coarse sieve.

A skuttle or skreen *to rid soil fro' the corn.* TUSSER.

2. Any thing by which the sun or weather is kept off.

3. Shelter; concealment.

Fenc'd from day, by night's eternal skreen;
Unknown to heav'n, and to myself unseen. DRYDEN.

To **SKREEN.** *v.a.* [from the noun.]

1. To riddle; to sift. A term yet used among masons when they sift sand for mortar.

2. To shade from sun or light, or weather.

3. To keep off light or weather.

The curtains closely drawn, the light to skreen:
Thus cover'd with an artificial night,
Sleep did his office. DRYDEN.

The waters mounted up into the air: their interposition betwixt the earth and the sun skreen *and fence off the heat, otherwise insupportable.*
WOODWARD'S NATURAL HISTORY.

4. To shelter; to protect.

Ajax interpos'd
His sevenfold shield, and skreen'd *Laertes' son,*
When the insulting Trojans urg'd him sore. PHILIPS.

He that travels with them is to skreen *them, and get them out when they have run themselves into the briars.* LOCKE.

His majesty encouraged his subjects to make mouths at their betters, and afterwards skreened *them from punishment.* SPECTATOR.

The scales, of which the scarf-skin is composed, are designed to fence the orifices of the secretory ducts of the miliary glands, and to skreen *the nerves from external injuries.* CHEYNE.

To **SKULK.** *v.n.* To hide; to lurk in fear or malice.

Discover'd, and defeated of your prey,
You skulk'd *behind the fence, and sneak'd away.* DRYDEN.

SKY'ROCKET. *n.s.* [*sky* and *rocket*.] A kind of firework, which flies high and burns as it flies.

I considered a comet, or in the language of the vulgar a blazing star, as a skyrocket *discharged by an hand that is almighty.* ADDISON.

To **SLAM.** *v.a.* [*lema*, Islandick; *schlagen*, Dutch.] To slaughter; to crush. A word not used but in low conversation.

SLA'PDASH. *interj.* [from *slap* and *dash*.] All at once: as any thing broad falls with a slap into the water, and dashes it about. A low word.

And yet, slapdash, *is all again*
In ev'ry sinew, nerve, and vein. PRIOR.

SLATE. *n.s.* [from *slit*: *slate* is in some counties a crack; or from *esclate*, a tile, French.] A grey fossile stone, easily broken into thin plates, which are used to cover houses, or to write upon.

A square cannot be so truly drawn upon a slate *as it is conceived in the mind.*
GREW'S COSMOLOGIA SACRA.

A small piece of a flat slate *the ants laid over the hole of their nest, when they foresaw it would rain.*
ADDISON'S SPECTATOR.

SLEAVE. *n.s.* [Of this word I know not well the meaning: *sleave* silk is explained by *Gouldman floccus sericus*, a lock of silk; and the women still say *sleave the silk*, for *untwist* it. *Ainsworth* calls a weaver's shuttle or reed a *slay*. *To sley* is to part a twist into single fibres.]

I on a fountain light,
Whose brim with pinks was platted,
The banks with daffadillies dight
With grass like sleave *was matted.*
DRAYTON'S CYNTHIA.

SLEAZY. *adj.* [often written *sleezy.*] Weak; wanting substance. This seems to be of the same race with *sleave*, or from to *sley*.

SLEE'VELESS. *adj.* [from *sleeve.*]
1. Wanting sleeves; having no sleeves.

His cloaths were strange, though coarse, and black, tho' bare;
Sleeveless *his jerkin was, and it had been*
Velvet, but 'twas now, so much ground was seen,
Become tufftaffaty. DONNE.

They put on long sleeveless *coats of home-spun cotton.* SANDYS.

Behold yon isle by palmers, pilgrims trod,
Grave mummers! sleeveless *some, and shirt-less others.* POPE.

2. Wanting reasonableness; wanting propriety; wanting solidity. [This sense, of which the word has been long possessed, I know not well how it obtained; *Skinner* thinks it properly *live-less* or *lifeless*: to this I cannot heartily agree, though I know not what better to suggest. Can it come from *sleeve*, a knot, or *skein*, and so signify unconnected, *hanging ill together*? or from *sleeve*, a cover; and therefore means *plainly absurd*; foolish without palliation?]

This sleeveless *tale of transubstantiation was brought into the world by that other fable of the multipresence.* HALL.

My landlady quarrelled with him for sending every one of her children on a sleeveless *errand, as she calls it.* SPECTATOR.

To **SLI'DDER.** *v.n.* [*slidderen*, Dutch.] To slide with interruption.

Go thou from me to fate,
Now die: with that he dragg'd the trembling sire,
Slidd'ring *through clotted blood.*
DRYDEN.

SLI'PPY. *adv.* [from *slip.*] Slippery; easily sliding. A barbarous provincial word.

The white of an egg is ropy, slippy, *and nutritious.* FLOYER.

SLI'PSHOD. *adj.* [*slip* and *shod.*] Having the shoes not pulled up at the heels, but barely slipped on.

The slipshod *'prentice from his master's door*
Had par'd the dirt, and sprinkled round the floor. SWIFT.

SLI'PSLOP. *n.s.* Bad liquor. A low word formed by reduplication of *slop*.

SLI'VER. *n.s.* [from the verb.] A branch torn off. *Sliver*, in Scotland, still denotes a slice cut off: as, he took a large *sliver* of the beef.

There on the pendant boughs, her coronet weed
Clamb'ring to hang, an envious sliver *broke,*
When down her weedy coronet and herself
Fell in the weeping brook.
SHAKESPEARE'S HAMLET.

To **SLOCK.** *v.n.* [*slock*, to quench, Swedish and Scottish.] To slake; to quench.

SLOP. *n.s.* [from the verb.] Mean and vile liquor of any kind. Generally some nauseous or useless medicinal liquor.[200]

The sick husband here wanted for neither slops *nor doctors.* L'ESTRANGE.

But thou, whatever slops *she will have bought,*
Be thankful. DRYDEN'S JUVENAL.

SLOUCH. *n.s.* [*sloff*, Danish, stupid.]
1. A downcast look; a depression of the

head. In Scotland, an ungainly gait, as also the person whose gait it is.

Our doctor has every quality that can make a man useful; but, alas! he hath a sort of slouch *in his walk.* SWIFT.

2. A man who looks heavy and clownish.

Begin thy carrols then, thou vaunting slouch;
Be thine the oaken staff, or mine the pouch. GAY.

SLO'VENLINESS. *n.s.* [from *slovenly.*] Indecent negligence of dress; neglect of cleanliness.

Slovenliness *is the worst sign of a hard student, and civility the best exercise of the remiss; yet not to be exact in the phrase of compliment, or gestures of courtesy.* WOTTON.

SLO'VENRY. *n.s.* [from *sloven.*] Dirtiness; want of neatness.

Our gayness and our gilt are all besmirch'd
With rainy marching in the painful field:
There's not a piece of feather in our host,
And time hath worn us into slovenry.
SHAKESPEARE'S HENRY V.

SLU'BBERDEGULLION. *n.s.* [I suppose a cant word without derivation.] A paltry, dirty, sorry wretch.

Quoth she, although thou hast deserv'd,
Base slubberdegullion, *to be serv'd*
As thou did'st vow to deal with me,
If thou had'st got the victory.
HUDIBRAS.

SLUG. *n.s.* [*slug*, Danish, and *slock*, Dutch, signify a glutton, and thence one that has the sloth of a glutton.]
1. An idler; a drone; a slow, heavy, sleepy, lazy wretch.

Fie, what a slug *is Hastings, that he comes not!* SHAKESPEARE.

2. An hindrance; an obstruction.

Usury dulls and damps all improvements, wherein money would be stirring, if it were not for this slug. BACON.

3. A kind of slow creeping snail.
4. [*Slecg*, an hammerhead, Saxon.] A cylindrical or oval piece of metal shot from a gun.

When fractures are made with bullets or slugs, *there the scalp and cranium are driven in together.*
WISEMAN'S SURGERY.

As, forc'd from wind-guns, lead itself can fly,
And pond'rous slugs *cut swiftly through the sky.* POPE.

To **SLUG.** *v.n.* [from the noun.] To lie idle; to play the drone; to move slowly.

All he did was to deceive good knights,
And draw them from pursuit of praise and fame,
To slug *in sloth and sensual delights,*
And end their days with irrenowned shame. FAIRY QUEEN.

He lay not all night slugging *in a cabbin under his mantle, but used commonly to keep others waking to defend their lives.*
SPENSER.

One went slugging *on with a thousand cares.* L'ESTRANGE.

SLU'GGARD. *n.s.* [from *slug.*] An idler; a drone; an inactive lazy fellow.

Cry mercy, lords, and watchful gentlemen,
That you have ta'en a tardy sluggard *here.* SHAKESPEARE'S RICHARD III.

Up, up, says avarice; thou snor'st again,
Stretchest thy limbs, and yawn'st, but all in vain:
The tyrant lucre no denial takes;
At his command th' unwilling sluggard *wakes.* DRYDEN.

Sprightly May commands our youth to keep
The vigils of her night, and breaks their sluggard *sleep.* DRYDEN.

To **SLU'GGARDIZE.** *v.a.* [from *sluggard.*] To make idle; to make dronish.

Rather see the wonders of the world abroad,
Than, living dully sluggardiz'd *at home,*
Wear out thy youth with shapeless idleness. SHAKESPEARE.

SLU'TTERY. *n.s.* [from *slut.*] The qualities or practice of a slut.

Slutt'ry, *to such neat excellence oppos'd,*
Should make desire vomit emptiness.
SHAKESPEARE'S CYMBELINE.

Where fires thou find'st unrak'd, and hearths unswept,
There pinch the maids as blue as bilberry;
Our radiant queen hates sluts and slutt'ry. SHAKESPEARE.

These make our girls their sluttery *rue,*
By pinching them both black and blue;
And put a penny in their shoe,
The house for cleanly sweeping.
DRAYTON.

A man gave money for a black, upon an opinion that his swarthy colour was rather sluttery *than nature, and the fault of his master that kept him no cleaner.*
L'ESTRANGE.

SMA'LLCOAL. *n.s.* [*small* and *coal.*] Little wood coals used to light fires.

A smallcoal *man, by waking one of these distressed gentlemen, saved him from ten years imprisonment.* SPECTATOR.

When smallcoal *murmurs in the hoarser throat,*
From smutty dangers guard thy threaten'd coat. GAY.

SMA'LLCRAFT. *n.s.* [*small* and *craft.*] A little vessel below the denomination of ship.

Shall he before me sign, whom t' other day
A smallcraft *vessel hither did convey;*
Where stain'd with prunes, and rotten figs, he lay. DRYDEN.

SMA'LLY. *adv.* [from *small.*] In a little quantity; with minuteness; in a little or low degree.

A child that is still, and somewhat hard of wit, is never chosen by the father to be made a scholar, or else when he cometh to the school, is smally *regarded.* ASCHAM.

SMA'LNESS. *n.s.* [from *small.*]

1. Littleness; not greatness.

The parts in glass are evenly spread, but are not so close as in gold; as we see by the easy admission of light, and by the smalness *of the weight.*
BACON'S NATURAL HISTORY.

2. Littleness; want of bulk; minuteness; exility.

Whatsoever is invisible, in respect of the fineness of the body, or the smalness *of the parts, or subtilty of the motion, is little enquired.*
BACON'S NATURAL HISTORY.

The smalness *of the rays of light may contribute very much to the power of the agent by which they are refracted.*
NEWTON.

3. Want of strength; weakness.

SMART. *n.s.* A fellow affecting briskness and vivacity. A cant word.

SMA'TTERER. *n.s.* [from *smatter.*] One who has a slight or superficial knowledge.

These few who preserve any rudiments of learning, are, except one or two smatterers, *the clergy's friends.* SWIFT.

SME'LLFEAST. *n.s.* [*smell* and *feast.*] A parasite; one who haunts good tables.

The ant lives upon her own, honestly gotten; whereas the fly is an intruder, and a common smellfeast *that spunges upon other people's trenchers.* L'ESTRANGE.

SMOCKFA'CED. *adj.* [*smock* and *face.*] Palefaced; maidenly.

Old chiefs reflecting on their former deeds,
Disdain to rust with batter'd invalids;
But active in the foremost ranks appear,
And leave young smockfac'd *beaux to guard the rear.* FENTON.

To **SMO'OTHEN.** *v.a.* [A bad word among mechanicks for *smooth.*] To make even and smooth.

With edged grooving tools they cut down and smoothen *the extuberances left.* MOXON'S MECHANICAL EXERCISES.

SMO'ULDERING, SMOULDRY. [This word seems a participle; but I know not whether the verb *smoulder* be in use: *smoran*, Saxon, to smother; *smoel*, Dutch, hot.] Burning and smoking without vent.

None can breathe, nor see, nor hear at will,
Through smouldry *cloud of duskish stinking smoke,*
That th' only breath him daunts who hath escap'd the stroke. FAIRY QUEEN.

In some close pent room it crept along,
And, smould'ring *as it went, in silence fed;*
'Till th' infant monster, with devouring strong,
Walk'd boldly upright with exalted head. DRYDEN.

SMU'GGLER. *n.s.* [from *smuggle.*] A wretch, who, in defiance of justice and the laws, imports or exports goods either contraband or without payment of the customs.

SNACK. *n.s.* [from *snatch.*] A share; a part taken by compact.

If the master gets the better on't, they come in for their snack. L'ESTRANGE.

For four times talking, if one piece thou take,
That must be cantled, and the judge go snack. DRYDEN.

All my demurs but double his attacks;
At last he whispers, "Do, and we go snacks." POPE.

SNAKE. *n.s.* [*snaca*, Saxon; *snake*, Dutch.] A serpent of the oviparous kind, distinguished from a viper. The snake's bite is harmless. *Snake* in poetry is a general name for a viper.

Glo'ster's shew beguiles him;
As the snake, *roll'd in a flow'ry bank,*
With shining checker'd slough, doth sting a child,
That for the beauty thinks it excellent.
SHAKESPEARE'S HENRY VI.

We have scotch'd the snake, *not kill'd it:*
She'll close, and be herself; whilst our poor malice
Remains in danger of her former teeth.
SHAKESPEARE'S MACBETH.

The parts must have their outlines in waves, resembling the gliding of a snake *upon the ground: they must be smooth and even.* DRYDEN'S DUFRESNOY.

Nor chalk, nor crumbling stones, the food of snakes
That work in hollow earth their winding tracks. DRYDEN.

SNAP. *n.s.* [from the verb.]

1. The act of breaking with a quick motion.
2. A greedy fellow.

He had no sooner said out his say, but up rises a cunning snap, *then at the board.* L'ESTRANGE.

3. A quick eager bite.

With their bills, thwarted crosswise at the end, they would cut an apple in two at one snap. CAREW.

4. A catch; a theft.

SNA'PDRAGON, or *Calf's snout.* *n.s.* [*antirrhinum*, Latin.]

1. A plant.
2. A kind of play, in which brandy is set on fire, and raisins thrown into it, which those who are unused to the sport are afraid to take out; but which may be safely snatched by a quick motion, and put blazing into the

mouth, which being closed, the fire is at once extinguished.

SNAST. *n.s.* The snuff of a candle.

It first burned fair, 'till some part of the candle was consumed, and the sawdust gathering about the snast; *but then it made the* snast *big and long, and burn duskishly, and the candle wasted in half the time of the wax pure.*
BACON'S NATURAL HISTORY.

SNE'AKER. *n.s.* A large vessel of drink.

I have just left the right worshipful and his myrmidons about a sneaker *of five gallons.* SPECTATOR.

SNIP. *n.s.* [from the verb.]

1. A single cut with scissars.

What! this a sleeve?
Here's snip *and nip, and cut, and slish and slash,*
Like to a censor in a barber's shop.
SHAKESPEARE.

The ulcer would not cure farther than it was laid open; therefore with one snip *more I laid it open to the very end.* WISEMAN.

2. A small shred.

Those we keep within compass by small snips *of emplast, hoping to defend the parts about; but, in spite of all, they will spread farther.* WISEMAN'S SURGERY.

3. A share; a snack. A low word.

He found his friend upon the mending hand, which he was glad to hear, because of the snip *that he himself expected upon the dividend.* L'ESTRANGE.

SNU'FFERS. *n.s.* [from *snuff.*] The instrument with which the candle is clipped.

When you have snuffed the candle, leave the snuffers *open.*
SWIFT'S DIRECTIONS TO THE BUTLER.

SOAP. *n.s.* [*sape*, Saxon; *sapo*, Latin.] A substance used in washing, made of a lixivium of vegetable alkaline ashes and any unctuous substance.

Soap *is a mixture of a fixed alkaline salt and oil; its virtues are cleansing, penetrating, attenuating, and resolving; and any mixture of any oily substance with salt may be called a* soap.
ARBUTHNOT ON ALIMENTS.

He is like a refiner's fire, and like fullers soap. MALACHI.

A bubble blown with water, first made tenacious by dissolving a little soap *in it, after a while will appear tinged with a great variety of colours.*
NEWTON'S OPTICKS.

Soap-*earth is found in great quantity on the land near the banks of the river Hermus, seven miles from Smyrna.*
WOODWARD.

Soap-*ashes are much commended, after the* soap-*boilers have done with them, for cold or sour lands.* MORTIMER.

As rain-water diminishes their salt, so the moistening of them with chamber-lee or soap-*suds adds thereto.* MORTIMER.

SOAPBOI'LER. *n.s.* [*soap* and *boil.*] One whose trade is to make soap.

A soapboiler *condoles with me on the duties on castle-soap.*
ADDISON'S SPECTATOR.

SOCK. *n.s.* [*soccus*, Latin; *socc*, Saxon; *socke*, Dutch.]

1. Something put between the foot and shoe.

Ere I lead this life long, I'll sow nether socks, *and mend them, and foot them too.*
SHAKESPEARE'S HENRY IV.

A physician, that would be mystical, prescribeth for the rheum to walk continually upon a camomile alley; meaning he should put camomile within his socks.
BACON.

2. The shoe of the ancient comick actors, taken in poems for comedy, and opposed to buskin or tragedy.

Then to the well trod stage anon,
If Johnson's learned sock *be on,*
Or sweetest Shakespeare, fancy's child,
Warble his native wood-notes wild.
MILTON.

Great Fletcher never treads in buskins here,
Nor greater Johnson dares in socks *appear;*
But gentle Simkin just reception finds
Amidst the monument of vanish'd minds.
DRYDEN.

On two figures of actors in the villa Mathei at Rome, we see the fashion of the old sock *and larva.* ADDISON.

SO'FA. *n.s.* [I believe an eastern word.] A splendid seat covered with carpets.

The king leaped off from the sofa *on which he sat, and cried out, 'tis my Abdullah!* GUARDIAN.

SOHO. *interj.* A form of calling from a distant place.

SOI'LINESS. *n.s.* [from *soil.*] Stain; foulness.

Make proof of the incorporation of silver and tin, whether it yield no soiliness *more than silver.* BACON.

SOI'LURE. *n.s.* [from *soil.*] Stain; pollution.

He merits well to have her,
Not making any scruple of her soilure.
SHAKESPEARE.

To **SO'JOURN.** *v.n.* [*sejourner*, French; *seggiornare*, Italian.] To dwell any where for a time; to live as not at home; to inhabit as not in a settled habitation. Almost out of use.

If, till the expiration of your month,
You will return and sojourn *with my sister,*
Dismissing half your train, come then to me. SHAKESPEARE.

Th' advantage of his absence took the king,
And in the mean time sojourn'd *at my father's.* SHAKESPEARE.

How comes it he is to sojourn *with you? how creeps acquaintance?*
SHAKESPEARE'S CYMBELINE.

Here dwells he; though he sojourn *every where*
In progress, yet his standing house is here.
DONNE.

The sojourning *of Israel, who dwelt in Egypt, was four hundred and thirty years.*
BIBLE EXODUS, XII. 40.

The soldiers first assembled at Newcastle, and there sojourned *three days.*
HAYWARD.

To sojourn *in that land*
He comes invited.
MILTON'S PARADISE LOST.

He who sojourns *in a foreign country, refers what he sees abroad to the state of things at home.* ATTERBURY.

SO'JOURN. *n.s.* [*sejour*, French, from the verb.] A temporary residence; a casual and no settled habitation. This word was anciently accented on the last syllable: *Milton* accents it indifferently.

The princes, France and Burgundy,
Long in our court have made their am'rous sojourn. SHAKESPEARE.

Thee I revisit now,
Escap'd the Stygian pool, though long detain'd
In that obscure sojourn.
MILTON'S PARADISE LOST.

Scarce view'd the Galilean towns,
And once a year Jerusalem, few days
Short sojourn.
MILTON'S PARADISE REGAIN'D.

SO'LECISM. *n.s.* [*σολοικισμός.*] Unfitness of one word to another; impropriety in language. A barbarism may be in one word, a solecism must be of more.

There is scarce a solecism *in writing which the best author is not guilty of, if we be at liberty to read him in the words of some manuscript.* ADDISON.

SOLI'CITOR. *n.s.* [from *solicit.*]

1. One who petitions for another.

Be merry, Cassio;
For thy solicitor *shall rather die,*
Than give thy cause away.
SHAKESPEARE'S OTHELLO.

Honest minds will consider poverty as a recommendation in the person who applies himself to them, and make the justice of his cause the most powerful solicitor *in his behalf.* ADDISON.

2. One who does in Chancery the business which is done by attorneys in other courts.

For the king's attorney and solicitor *general, their continual use for the king's service requires men every way fit.* BACON.

SOLIDU'NGULOUS. *adj.* [*solidus* and *ungula*, Latin] Wholehoofed.

It is set down by Aristotle and Pliny, that an horse and all solidungulous *or whole-hoofed animals have no gall, which we find repugnant unto reason.* BROWN'S VULGAR ERROURS.

SOLIFI'DIAN. *n.s.* [*solus* and *fides*, Latin.] One who supposes only faith, not works, necessary to justification.

It may be justly feared, that the title of fundamentals, being ordinarily confined to the doctrines of faith, hath occasioned that great scandal in the church of God, at which so many myriads of solifidians *have stumbled, and fallen irreversibly, by conceiving heaven a reward of true opinions.* HAMMOND.

SOLI'LOQUY. *n.s.* [*soliloque*, Fr. *solus* and *loquor*, Lat.] A discourse made by one in solitude to himself.

The whole poem is a soliloquy: *Solomon is the person that speaks: he is at once the hero and the author; but he tells us very often what others say to him.* PRIOR.

He finds no respite from his anxious grief,
Then seeks from his soliloquy *relief.*
GARTH'S DISPENSATORY.

If I should own myself in love, you know lovers are always allowed the comfort of soliloquy. SPECTATOR.

SO'LIPEDE. *n.s.* [*solus* and *pedes*, Lat.] An animal whose feet are not cloven.

Solipedes, *or firm footed animals, as horses, asses, and mules, are in mighty number.* BROWN'S VULGAR ERROURS.

SOLITA'IRE. *n.s.* [*solitaire*, French.]

1. A recluse; a hermit.

Often have I been going to take possession of tranquillity, when your conversation has spoiled me for a solitaire. POPE.

2. An ornament for the neck.

SO'LVIBLE. *adj.* [from *solve.*] Possible to be cleared by reason or inquiry.

Intellective memory I call an act of the intellective faculty, because it is wrought by it, though I do not inquire how or where, because it is not solvible. HALE'S ORIGIN OF MANKIND.

SO'LUTIVE. *adj.* [from *solvo*, Latin.] Laxative; causing relaxation.

Though it would not be so abstersive, opening, and solutive *as mead, yet it will be more lenitive in sharp diseases.* BACON.

SO'MERSAULT, SOMERSET. *n.s.* [*Somerset* is the corruption. *Sommer*, a beam, and *sault*, French, a leap.] A leap by which a jumper throws himself from a beam, and turns over his head.

SOMNI'FEROUS. *adj.* [*somnifere*, Fr. *somnifer*, Latin.] Causing sleep; procuring sleep; soperiferous; dormitive.

I wish for some somniferous *potion, that might force me to sleep away the inter-*

mitted time, as it does with men in sorrow. WALTON'S ANGLER.

SOMNI'FICK. *adj.* [*somnus* and *facio*, Latin.] Causing sleep.

SON. *n.s.* [*sunus*, Gothick; *suna*, Saxon; *sohn*, German; *son*, Swedish; *sone*, Dutch; *syn*, Sclavonian.]

1. A male born of one or begotten by one; correlative to father or mother.

She had a son *for her cradle, ere she had a husband for her bed.*
SHAKESPEARE'S KING LEAR.

Cast out this bondwoman and her son.
BIBLE GENESIS, XXI. 10.

He compares the affection of the Divine Being to the indulgence of a wise father, who would have his sons *exercised with labour and pain, that they may gather strength.* ADDISON.

2. Descendant however distant: as, the sons of Adam.

I am the son *of the wise, the* son *of ancient kings.* BIBLE ISAIAH, XIX.

3. Compellation of an old to a young man, or of a confessor to his penitent.

Be plain, good son, *and homely in thy drift;*
Riddling confession finds but riddling shrift. SHAKESPEARE.

4. Native of a country.

Britain then
Sees arts her savage sons *controul.* POPE.

5. The second person of the Trinity.

If thou be the son *of God, come down.*
BIBLE MATTHEW, XXVII. 40.

6. Product of any thing.

Our imperfections prompt our corruption, and loudly tell us we are sons *of earth.*
BROWN'S VULGAR ERROURS.

Earth's tall sons, *the cedar, oak, and pine,*
Their parents undecaying strength declare.
BLACKMORE.

7. In scripture, sons of pride, and sons of light, denoting some quality. 'Tis a Hebraism.

This new fav'rite
Of heav'n, this man of clay, son *of despite.* MILTON.

SONA'TA. *n.s.* [Italian.] A tune.

He whistled a Scotch tune, and an Italian sonata. ADDISON.

Could Pedro, think you, make no trial
Of a sonata *on his viol,*
Unless he had the total gut,
Whence every string at first was cut.
PRIOR.

SO'NGISH. *adj.* [from *song.*] Containing songs; consisting of songs. A low word.

The songish *part must abound in the softness and variety of numbers, its intention being to please the hearing.* DRYDEN.

SOONLY. *adv.* [from *soon.*] Quickly; speedily. This word I remember in no other place; but if *soon* be, as it seems once to have been, an adjective, *soonly* is proper.

A mason meets with a stone that wants no cutting, and, soonly *approving of it, places it in his work.* MORE.

SO'OTERKIN. *n.s.* A kind of false birth fabled to be produced by the Dutch women from sitting over their stoves.

When Jove was, from his teeming head,
Of wit's fair goddess brought to-bed,
There follow'd at his lying-in,
For after-birth, a sooterkin. SWIFT.

SOPE. *n.s.* [See **SOAP.**]

SOPHISTICA'TION. *n.s.* [*sophistication*, Fr. from *sophisticate.*] Adulteration; not genuineness.

Sophistication *is the act of counterfeiting*

or adulterating any thing with what is not so good, for the sake of unlawful gain. QUINCY.

The drugs and simples sold in shops, generally are adulterated by the fraudulent avarice of the sellers, especially if the preciousness may make their sophistication *very beneficial.* BOYLE.

Besides easy submission to sophistications *of sense, we have inability to prevent the miscarriages of our junior reasons.* GLANVILLE.

SOPORI'FEROUS. *adj.* [*sopor* and *fero.*] Productive of sleep; causing sleep; narcotick; opiate; dormitive; somniferous; anodyne; sleepy.

The particular ingredients of those magical ointments are opiate and soporiferous; *for anointing of the forehead, neck, feet, and back-bone, procures dead sleeps.* BACON.

While the whole operation was performing, I lay in a profound sleep, by the force of that soporiferous *medicine infused into my liquor.* GULLIVER'S TRAVELS.

SOPORI'FICK. *adj.* [*sopor* and *facio.*] Causing sleep; opiate; narcotick.

The colour and taste of opium are, as well as its soporifick *or anodyne virtues, mere powers depending on its primary qualities.* LOCKE.

SORE. *n.s.* [*sar*, Saxon; *saur*, Danish.] A place tender and painful; a place excoriated; an ulcer. It is not used of a wound, but of a breach of continuity, either long continued or from internal cause: to be a *sore*, there must be an excoriation; a tumour or bruise is not called a *sore* before some disruption happen.

Let us hence provide
A salve for any sore *that may betide.*
SHAKESPEARE'S HENRY VI.

It is a bad exchange to wound a man's own conscience, to salve state sores. KING CHARLES.

Receipts abound; but searching all thy store,
The best is still at hand to launce the sore,
And cut the head; for till the core be found
The secret vice is fed and gathers ground.
DRYDEN.

By these all festring sores *her councils heal,*
Which time or has disclos'd, or shall reveal. DRYDEN.

Lice and flies, which have a most wonderful instinct to find out convenient places for the hatching and nourishment of their young, lay their eggs upon sores. BENTLEY.

SO'RROW. *n.s.* [*sorg*, Danish.] Grief; pain for something past; sadness; mourning. Sorrow is not commonly understood as the effect of present evil, but of lost good.

Sorrow *is uneasiness in the mind, upon the thought of a good lost, which might have been enjoyed longer; or the tense of a present evil.* LOCKE.

Sorrow *on thee, and all the pack of you;*
That triumph thus upon my misery!
SHAKESPEARE.

A world of woe and sorrow. MILTON.

Some other hour I will to tears allow;
But having you, can show no sorrow *now.*
DRYDEN.

SO'RRY. *adj.* [*sarig*, Saxon.]

1. Grieved for something past. It is generally used of slight or casual miscarriages or vexations, but sometimes of greater things. It does not imply any long continuance of grief.

O, forget
What we are sorry *for ourselves in thee.*
TIMON OF ATHENS.

The king was sorry: *nevertheless for the oath's sake he commanded the Baptist's head to be given her.*
BIBLE MATTHEW, XIV. 9.

I'm sorry *for thee, friend; 'tis the duke's pleasure.* SHAKESPEARE.

We are sorry *for the satire interspersed in some of these pieces, upon a few people, from whom the highest provocations have been received.* SWIFT.

2. [From *saur*, filth, Islandick.] Vile; worthless; vexatious.

A salt and sorry *rheum offends me:*
Lend me thy handkerchief.
SHAKESPEARE'S OTHELLO.

How now, why do you keep alone?
Of sorriest *fancies your companions making,*
Using those thoughts, which should, indeed, have died
With them they think on.
SHAKESPEARE'S MACBETH.

If the union of the parts consist only in rest, it would seem that a bag of dust would be of as firm a consistence as that of marble; and Bajazet's cage had been but a sorry *prison.* GLANVILLE.

Coarse complexions,
And cheeks of sorry *grain will serve to ply*
The sampler, and to teize the housewife's wool. MILTON.

How vain were all the ensigns of his power, that could not support him against one slighting look of a sorry *slave!*
L'ESTRANGE.

If this innocent had any relation to his Thebais, the poet might have found some sorry *excuse for detaining the reader.*
DRYDEN.

If such a slight and sorry *business as that could produce one organical body, one might reasonably expect, that now and then a dead lump of dough might be leavened into an animal.* BENTLEY'S SERMONS.

SO'RTILEGE. *n.s.* [*sortilege*, Fr. *sortilegium*, Latin.] The act or practice of drawing lots.

To **SOSS.** *v.n.* [A cant word.] To sit lazily on a chair; to fall at once into a chair.

The winter sky began to frown,
Poor Stella must pack off to town;
From wholesome exercise and air,
To sossing *in an easy chair.* SWIFT.

SOU'LSHOT. *n.s.* [*soul* and *shot.*] Something paid for a soul's requiem among the Romanists.

In the Saxon times there was a funeral duty to be paid, called pecunia sepulchralis & symbolum animæ, and a Saxon soulshot.
AYLIFFE'S PARERGON.

SOUP. *n.s.* [*soupe*, French.] Strong decoction of flesh for the table.

Spongy morells in strong ragousts are found,
And in the soup *the slimy snail is drown'd.* GAY'S TRIVIA.

Let the cook daub the back of the footman's new livery, or, when he is going up with a dish of soup, *let her follow him softly with a ladle-full.* SWIFT.

SO'UVENANCE. *n.s.* [French.] Remembrance; memory. A French word which with many more is now happily disused.

If thou wilt renounce thy miscreance,
Life will I grant thee for thy valiance,
And all thy wrongs will wipe out of my souvenance. SPENSER.

Gave wond'rous great countenance to the knight,
That of his way he had no souvenance,
Nor care of vow'd revenge. SPENSER.

SPA'DDLE. *n.s.* [Diminutive of *spade.*] A little spade.

Others destroy moles with a spaddle, *waiting in the mornings and evenings for them.* MORTIMER'S HUSBANDRY.

SPARGEFA'CTION. *n.s.* [*spargo*, Lat.] The act of sprinkling.

SPARK. *n.s.* [*spearca*, Saxon; *sparke*, Dutch.]

1. A small particle of fire, or kindled matter

If any marvel how a thing, in itself so weak, could import any great danger, they must consider not so much how small the spark *is that flieth up, as how apt things about it are to take fire.* HOOKER.

I am about to weep; but thinking that
We are a queen, my drops of tears I'll turn
To sparks *of fire.* SHAKESPEARE.

I was not forgetful of the sparks *which some mens distempers formerly studied to kindle in parliaments.* KING CHARLES.

In this deep quiet, from what source unknown,
Those seeds of fire that fatal birth disclose:
And first, few scatt'ring sparks *about were blown,*
Big with the flames that to our ruin rose. DRYDEN.

Oh, may some spark *of your celestial fire*
The last, the meanest of your sons inspire. POPE.

2. Any thing shining.

We have, here and there, a little clear light, some sparks *of bright knowledge.* LOCKE.

3. Any thing vivid or active.

If any spark *of life be yet remaining,*
Down, down to hell, and say, I sent thee thither. SHAKESPEARE.

4. A lively, showy, splendid, gay man. It is commonly used in contempt.

How many huffing sparks *have we seen, that in the same day have been both the idols and the scorn of the same slaves?* L'ESTRANGE.

A spark *like thee, of the mankilling trade*
Fell sick. DRYDEN.

As for the disputes of sharpers, we don't read of any provisions made for the honours of such sparks. COLLIER.

The finest sparks, *and cleanest beaux*
Drip from the shoulders to the toes. PRIOR.

I who have been the poet's spark *to day,*
Will now become the champion of his play. GRANVILLE.

Unlucky as Fungoso in the play,
These sparks *with aukward vanity display*
What the fine gentlemen wore yesterday. POPE.

SPA'RKISH. *adj.* [from *spark.*]

1. Airy; gay. A low word.[201]

Is any thing more sparkish *and better humour'd than Venus's accosting her son in the desarts of Libya?* WALSH.

2. Showy; well dressed; fine.

A daw, to be sparkish, *trick'd himself up with all the gay feathers he could muster.* L'ESTRANGE.

SPATTERDASHES. *n.s.* [*spatter* and *dash.*] Coverings for the legs by which the wet is kept off.

SPEA'KING *Trumpet. n.s.* A stentorophonick instrument; a trumpet by which the voice may be propagated to a great distance.

That with one blast through the whole house does bound,
And first taught speaking trumpet *how to sound.* DRYDEN.

SPECTA'TION. *n.s.* [*spectatio*, Latin.] Regard; respect.

This simple spectation *of the lungs is differenced from that which concomitates a pleurisy.* HARVEY.

SPE'CTRUM. *n.s.* [Latin.] An image; a visible form.

This prism had some veins running along within the glass, from the one end to the other, which scattered some of the sun's light irregularly, but had no sensible effect in encreasing the length of the coloured spectrum. NEWTON'S OPTICKS.

SPECULA'TOR. *n.s.* [from *speculate.*]

1. One who forms theories.

He is dexterous in puzzling others, if they be not through-paced speculators *in those great theories.* MORE.

2. [*Speculateur*, French.] An observer; a contemplator.

Although lapidaries and questuary enquirers affirm it, yet the writers of minerals, and natural speculators, *conceive the stones which bear this name to be a mineral concretion.* BROWN.

3. A spy; a watcher.

All the boats had one speculator, *to give notice when the fish approached.* BROOME'S NOTES ON THE ODYSSEY.

SPEECH. *n.s.* [from *speak.*]

1. The power of articulate utterance; the power of expressing thoughts by vocal words.

There is none comparable to the variety of instructive expressions by speech, *wherewith a man alone is endowed, for the communication of his thoughts.* HOLDER ON SPEECH.

Though our ideas are first acquired by various sensations and reflections, yet we convey them to each other by the means of certain sounds, or written marks, which we call words; and a great part of our knowledge is both obtained and communicated by these means, which are called speech. WATTS.

2. Language; words considered as expressing thoughts.

In speech *be eight parts.* ACCIDENCE.

The acts of God to human ears
Cannot without process of speech *be told.* MILTON.

3. Particular language as distinct from others.

There is neither speech *nor language, but their voices are heard among them.* BIBLE PSALMS, COMMON PRAYER.

4. Any thing spoken.

A plague upon your epileptick visage!
Smile you my speeches *as I were a fool.* SHAKESPEARE'S KING LEAR.

5. Talk; mention.

The duke did of me demand
What was the speech *among the Londoners,*
Concerning the French journey. SHAKESPEARE.

Speech *of a man's self ought to be seldom.* BACON'S ESSAYS.

6. Oration; harangue.

The constant design of these orators, in all their speeches, *was to drive some one particular point.* SWIFT.

7. Liberty to speak.[202]

I, with leave of speech *implor'd, reply'd.* MILTON.

To **SPET.** *v.a.* To bring or pour abundantly. [*Spet* in Scotland is a superabundance of water: as, that tide or fresh was a high *spet.*]

Mysterious dame,
That ne'er art call'd, but when the dragon womb
Of Stygian darkness spets *her thickest gloom,*
And makes one blot of all the air,
Stop thy cloudy ebon chair. MILTON.

SPICK *and* **SPAN.** [This word I should not have expected to have found authorised by a polite writer. *Span-new* is used by *Chaucer*, and is supposed to come from *spannan*, to stretch, Sax. *expandere*, Lat. whence *span. Span-new* is therefore originally used of cloath new extended or dressed at the clothiers, and *spick and span* is newly extended on the *spikes* or tenters: it is however a low word.] Quite new; now first used.

While the honour, thou hast got,
Is spick and span *new, piping hot,*
Strike her up bravely. BUTLER.

They would have these reduced to nothing, and then others created spick and span *new out of nothing.* BURNET.

I keep no antiquated stuff;
But spick and span *I have enough.* SWIFT.

SPI'NSTER. *n.s.* [from *spin.*]
1. A woman that spins.

The spinsters *and the knitters in the sun,*
And the free maids that weave their thread with bones,
Do use to chant it.
SHAKESPEARE'S TWELFTH NIGHT.

2. [In law.] The general term for a girl or maiden woman.

One Michael Cassio,
That never set a squadron in the field,
Nor the division of a battle knows
More than a spinster.
SHAKESPEARE'S OTHELLO.

I desire that a yearly annuity of twenty pounds shall be paid to Rebecca Dingley of the city of Dublin, spinster, *during her life.* SWIFT.

SPI'NSTRY. *n.s.* [from *spinster.*] The work of spinning.

SPI'RE. *n.s.* [*spira*, Latin; *spira*, Italian; *spira*, Swedish.]
1. A curve line; any thing wreathed or contorted; a curl; a twist; a wreath.

His head
Crested aloft, and carbuncle his eyes;
With burnish'd neck of verdant gold, erect
Amidst his circling spires, *that on the grass*
Floated redundant. MILTON.

A dragon's fiery form belied the god,
Sublime on radiant spires *he rode.*
DRYDEN.

Air seems to consist of spires *contorted into small spheres, through the interstices of which the particles of light may freely pass; it is light, the solid substance of the* spires *being very small in proportion to the spaces they take up.* CHEYNE.

2. Any thing growing up taper; a round pyramid, so called perhaps because a line drawn round and round in less and less circles, would be a spire; a steeple.

With glist'ring spires *and pinnacles adorn'd.* MILTON.

He cannot make one spire *of grass more or less than he hath made.*
HALE'S ORIGIN OF MANKIND.

These pointed spires *that wound the ambient sky,*
Inglorious change! shall in destruction lie.
PRIOR.

3. The top or uppermost point.

'Twere no less than a traducement to silence, that
Which to the spire *and top of praises vouch'd,*
Wou'd seem but modest. SHAKESPEARE.

SPI'SSITUDE. *n.s.* [from *spissus*, Latin.] Grossness; thickness.

Drawing wine or beer from the lees, called racking, it will clarify the sooner; for though the lees keep the drink in heart, and make it lasting, yet they cast up some spissitude.
BACON.

Spissitude *is subdued by acrid things, and acrimony by inspissating.*
ARBUTHNOT ON ALIMENTS.

To **SPI'TCHCOCK.** *v.a.* To cut an eel in pieces and roast him. Of this word I find no good etymology.

No man lards salt pork with orange peel,
Or garnishes his lamb with spitchcockt *eel.* KING.

SPLE'NDENT. *adj.* [*splendens*, Latin.] Shining; glossy; having lustre.

They assigned them names from some remarkable qualities, that is very observable in their red and splendent *planets.*
BROWN.

Metallick substances may, by reason of their great density, reflect all the light incident upon them, and so be as opake and splendent *as it's possible for any body to be.* NEWTON.

SPONK. *n.s.* A word in Edinburgh which denotes a match, or any thing dipt in sulphur that takes fire: as, any *sponks* will ye buy? Touchwood.

SPO'NSION. *n.s.* [*sponsio*, Latin.] The act of becoming surety for another.

SPO'NSOR. *n.s.* [Latin.] A surety; one who makes a promise or gives security for another.

In the baptism of a male there ought to be two males and one woman, and in the baptism of a female child two women and one man; and these are called sponsors *or sureties for their education in the true Christian faith.* AYLIFFE'S PARERGON.

The sponsor *ought to be of the same station with the person to whom he becomes surety.* BROOME.

SPO'ONMEAT. *n.s.* [*spoon* and *meat.*] Liquid food; nourishment taken with a spoon.

We prescribed a slender diet, allowing only spoonmeats. WISEMAN.

Wretched
Are mortals born to sleep their lives away!
Go back to what thy infancy began,
Eat pap and spoonmeat; *for thy gugaws cry,*
Be sullen, and refuse the lullaby.
DRYDEN'S PERSIUS.

Diet most upon spoonmeats, *as veal, or cock-broths.* HARVEY.

SPO'RTULE. *n.s.* [*sportule*, French; *sportula*, Latin.] An alms; a dole.

The bishops, who consecrated the ground, had a spill or sportule *from the credulous laity.* AYLIFFE'S PARERGON.

SPRUCE. *adj.* [*Skinner* derives this word from *preux*, French; but he proposes it with hesitation: *Junius* thinks it comes from *sprout*; *Casaubon* trifles yet more contemptibly. I know not whence to deduce it, except from *pruce*. In ancient books we find furniture of *pruce* a thing costly and elegant, and thence probably came *spruce.*] Nice; trim; neat without elegance.

The tree
That wraps that crystal in a wooden tomb,
Shall be took up spruce, *fill'd with diamond.* DONNE.

Thou wilt not leave me in the middle street,
Tho' some more spruce *companion thou do'st meet.* DONNE.

Along the crisped shades and bow'rs
Revels the spruce *and jocund Spring;*
The graces, and the rosy-bosom'd hours,
Thither all their bounties bring.
MILTON.

I must not slip into too spruce *a style for serious matters; and yet I approve not that dull insipid way of writing practised by many chymists.* BOYLE.

He put his band and beard in order,
The sprucer *to accost and board her.*
HUDIBRAS.

He is so spruce, *that he can never be genteel.* TATLER.

This Tim makes a strange figure with that ragged coat under his livery: can't he go spruce *and clean?* ARBUTHNOT.

To **SPRUCE.** *v.n.* [from the noun.] To dress with affected neatness.

SPRU'CEBEER. *n.s.* [from *spruce*, a kind of fir.] Beer tinctured with branches of fir.

In ulcers of the kidneys sprucebeer *is a good balsamick.* ARBUTHNOT.

SPRUNT. *n.s.* Any thing that is short and will not easily bend.

SPUD. *n.s.* A short knife.

My love to Sheelah is more firmly fixt,
Than strongest weeds that grow these stones betwixt:
My spud *these nettles from the stones can part,*
No knife so keen to weed thee from my heart. SWIFT.

SPU'NGINGHOUSE. *n.s.* [*spunge* and *house.*] A house to which debtors are taken before commitment to prison, where the bailiffs sponge upon them, or riot at their cost.

A bailiff kept you the whole evening in a spunginghouse. SWIFT.

SPUNK. *n.s.* Rotten wood; touchwood. See **SPONK.**

To make white powder, the best way is by the powder of rotten willows: spunk, *or touchwood prepared, might perhaps make it russet.* BROWN'S VULGAR ERROURS.

SPU'RWAY. *n.s.* [*spur* and *way.*] A horseway; a bridle-road; distinct from a road for carriages.

To **SPU'TTER.** *v.n.* [*sputo*, Latin.]
1. To emit moisture in small flying drops.

If a manly drop or two fall down,
It scalds along my cheeks, like the green wood,
That, sputt'ring *in the flame, works outward into tears.* DRYDEN.

2. To fly out in small particles with some noise.

The nightly virgin, while her wheel she plies,
Foresees the storms impending in the skies,
When sparkling lamps their sputt'ring *light advance,*
And in the sockets oily bubbles dance. DRYDEN.

3. To speak hastily and obscurely, as with the mouth full; to throw out the spittle by hasty speech.

A pinking owl sat sputtering *at the sun, and asked him what he meant to stand staring her in the eyes.* L'ESTRANGE.

They could neither of them speak their rage; and so fell a sputtering *at one another, like two roasting apples.* CONGREVE.

Though he sputter *through a session,*
It never makes the least impression;
Whate'er he speaks for madness goes. SWIFT.

To **SPU'TTER.** *v.a.* To throw out with noise and hesitation.

Thou do'st with lies the throne invade,
Obtending heav'n for whate'er ills befall;
And sputt'ring *under specious names thy gall.* DRYDEN.

In the midst of caresses, and without the least pretended incitement, to sputter *out the basest accusations!* SWIFT.

SPU'TTERER. *n.s.* [from *sputter.*] One that sputters.

SPY'BOAT. *n.s.* [*spy* and *boat.*] A boat sent out for intelligence.

Giving the colour of the sea to their spyboats *to keep them from being discovered, came from the Veneti.* ARBUTHNOT.

SQUAB. *adj.* [I know not whence derived.]
1. Unfeathered; newly hatched.

Why must old pidgeons, and they stale, be drest,
When there's so many squab *ones in the nest.* KING.

2. Fat; thick and stout; awkwardly bulky.

The nappy ale goes round,
Nor the squab *daughter nor the wife were nice,*
Each health the youths began, Sim pledg'd it twice. BETTERTON.

SQUAB. *n.s.* A kind of sofa or couch; a stuffed cushion.

On her large squab *you find her spread,*
Like a fat corpse upon a bed. SWIFT.

SQUAB. *adv.* With a heavy sudden fall; plump and flat. A low word.

The eagle took the tortoise up into the air, and dropt him down, squab, *upon a rock, that dashed him to pieces.* L'ESTRANGE.

SQUA'BPIE. *n.s.* [*squab* and *pie.*] A pie made of many ingredients.

Cornwal squabpie, *and Devon whitepot brings,*
And Leister beans and bacon, food of kings. KING.

To **SQUAB.** *v.n.* To fall down plump or flat; to squelsh or squash.

SQUA'BBISH. *adj.* [from *squab.*] Thick; heavy; fleshy.

Diet renders them of a squabbish *or lardy habit of body.* HARVEY.

SQUA'DRON. *n.s.* [*escadron*, Fr. *squadrone*, Italian, from *quadratus*, Latin.]

1. A body of men drawn up square.

Those half rounding guards
Just met, and closing stood in squadron *join'd.* MILTON.

2. A part of an army; a troop.

Nothing the Moors were more afraid of, than in a set battle to fight with squadrons *coming orderly on.* KNOLLES.

Then beauteous Atys, with Iulus bred,
Of equal age, the second squadron *led.* DRYDEN.

3. Part of a fleet, a certain number of ships.

Rome could not maintain its dominion over so many provinces, without squadrons *ready equipt.* ARBUTHNOT.

To **SQUALL.** *v.n.* [*squala*, Swedish.] To scream out as a child or woman frighted.

In my neighbourhood, a very pretty prattling shoulder of veal squalls *out at the sight of a knife.* SPECTATOR.

I put five into my coat pocket, and as to the sixth I made a countenance as if I would eat him alive. The poor man squalled *terribly.* SWIFT.

Cornelius sunk back on a chair; the guests stood astonished; the infant squawl'd. ARBUTHNOT AND POPE.

SQUALL. *n.s.* [from the verb.]

1. Loud scream.

There oft are heard the notes of infant woe,
The short thick sob, loud scream, and shriller squall. SWIFT.

2. Sudden gust of wind. A sailor's word.

SQUA'LLER. *n.s.* [from *squall.*] Screamer; one that screams.

To **SQUEAK.** *v.n.* [*sqwaka*, Swedish.]

1. To set up a sudden dolorous cry; to cry out with pain.

2. To cry with a shrill acute tone.

The sheeted dead
Did squeak *and gibber in the Roman streets.* SHAKESPEARE.

Cart wheels squeak *not when they are liquored.* BACON.

I see the new Arion sail,
The lute still trembling underneath thy nail:
At thy well sharpen'd thumb from shore to shore,
The trebles squeak *for fear, the bases roar.* DRYDEN.

Blunderbusses planted in every loop-hole, go off constantly at the squeaking *of a fiddle and the thrumming of a guitar.* DRYDEN'S SPANISH FRIAR.

Who can endure to hear one of the rough old Romans squeaking *through the mouth of an eunuch?* ADDISON.

How like brutes organs are to ours;
They grant, if higher pow'rs think fit,
A bear might soon be made a wit;
And that for any thing in nature,
Pigs might squeak *love-odes, dogs bark satyr.* PRIOR.

In florid impotence he speaks,
And as the prompter breathes, the puppet squeaks. POPE.

Zoilus calls the companions of Ulysses the squeaking *pigs of Homer.* POPE'S ODYSSEY.

3. To break silence or secrecy for fear or pain.

If he be obstinate, put a civil question to

him upon the rack, and he squeaks, *I warrant him.*
DRYDEN'S DON SEBASTIAN.

SQUEAK. *n.s.* [from the verb.] A shrill quick cry; a cry of pain.

Ran cow and calf, and family of hogs,
In panick horrour of pursuing dogs:
With many a deadly grunt and doleful squeak,
Poor swine! as if their pretty hearts wou'd break. DRYDEN.

To **SQUEAL.** *v.n.* [*sqwala*, Swedish.] To cry with a shrill sharp voice; to cry with pain. *Squeak* seems a short sudden cry, and *squeal* a cry continued.

SQUIB. *n.s.* [*schiehen*, German, to push forward. This etymology, though the best that I have found, is not very probable.]

1. A small pipe of paper filled with wildfire. Used in sport.

The armada at Calais, sir Walter Raleigh was wont pretily to say, were suddenly driven away with squibs; *for it was no more than a stratagem of fire-boats manless, and sent upon them.*
BACON'S WAR WITH SPAIN.

The forest of the south, compareth the French valour to a squib, *or fire of flax, which burns and crackles for a time, but suddenly extinguishes.*
HOWEL'S VOCAL FOREST.

Lampoons, like squibs, *may make a present blaze;*
But time, and thunder, pay respect to bays. WALLER.

Furious he begins his march,
Drives rattling o'er a brazen arch;
With squibs *and crackers arm'd to throw*
Among the trembling crowd below.
SWIFT.

2. Any petty fellow.[203]

Asked for their pass by every squib,
That lift at will them to revile or snib.
SPENSER.

The squibs, *in the common phrase, are called libellers.*
TATLER.

STAFF. *n.s.* plur. *staves.* [*stæf*, Saxon; *staff*, Danish; *staff*, Dutch.]

1. A stick with which a man supports himself in walking.

It much would please him,
That of his fortunes you would make a staff
To lean upon.
SHAKESPEARE'S ANTONY AND CLEOPATRA.

Grant me and my people the benefit of thy chastisements, that thy rod as well as thy staff *may comfort us.* KING CHARLES.

Is it probable that he, who had met whole armies in battle, should now throw away his staff, *out of fear of a dog.* BROOME.

2. A prop; a support.

Hope is a lover's staff; *walk hence with that,*
And manage it against despairing thoughts. SHAKESPEARE.

The boy was the very staff *of my age, my very prop.* SHAKESPEARE.

3. A stick used as a weapon; a club; the handle of an edged or pointed weapon. A *club* properly includes the notion of weight, and the *staff* of length.

I cannot strike at wretched kernes, whose arms
Are hir'd to bear their staves.
SHAKESPEARE'S MACBETH.

He that bought the skin ran greater risque than t'other that sold it, and had the worse end of the staff. L'ESTRANGE.

With forks and staves *the felon they pursue.* DRYDEN.

4. Any long piece of wood.

He forthwith from the glitt'ring staff *unfurl'd*
Th' imperial ensign. MILTON.

To his single eye, that in his forehead glar'd
Like a full moon, or a broad burnish'd shield,
A forky staff *we dext'rously apply'd,*

Which, in the spacious socket turning round,
Scoopt out the big round gelly from its orb. ADDISON.

5.[204] An ensign of an office; a badge of authority.

Methought this staff, *mine office-badge in court,*
Was broke in twain.
SHAKESPEARE'S HENRY VI.

All his officers brake their staves; *but at their return new* staves *were delivered unto them.* HAYWARD ON EDWARD VI.

6. [*Stef*, Islandick] A stanza; a series of verses regularly disposed, so as that, when the stanza is concluded, the same order begins again.

Cowley found out that no kind of staff *is proper for an heroick poem, as being all too lyrical; yet though he wrote in couplets, where rhyme is freer from constraint, he affects half verses.* DRYDEN.

STAGE. *n.s.* [*estage*, French.]
1. A floor raised to view on which any show is exhibited.
2. The theatre; the place of scenick entertainments.

And much good do't you then,
Brave plush and velvet men:
Can feed on ort; and, safe in your stage *clothes,*
Dare quit, upon your oaths,
The stagers and the stage *wrights too.*
BEN JONSON.

Those two Mytilene brethren, basely born, crept out of a small galliot unto the majesty of great kings. Herein admire the wonderful changes and chances of these worldly things, now up, now down, as if the life of man were not of much more certainty than a stage *play.*
KNOLLES'S HISTORY OF THE TURKS.

I maintain, against the enemies of the stage, *that patterns of piety, decently represented, may second the precepts.*
DRYDEN.

One Livius Andronicus was the first stage *player in Rome.*
DRYDEN'S JUVENAL, DEDICATION.

Knights, squires, and steeds must enter on the stage. POPE.

Among slaves, who exercised polite arts, none sold so dear as stage *players or actors.* ARBUTHNOT ON COINS.

3. Any place where any thing is publickly transacted or performed.

When we are born, we cry that we are come
To this great stage *of fools.*
SHAKESPEARE'S KING LEAR.

4. A place in which rest is taken on a journey; as much of a journey as is performed without intermission. [*Statio*, Latin.]

I shall put you in mind where it was you promised to set out, or begin your first stage; *and beseech you to go before me my guide.*
HAMMOND'S PRACTICAL CATECHISM.

Our next stage *brought us to the mouth of the Tiber.* ADDISON.

From thence compell'd by craft and age,
She makes the head her latest stage.
PRIOR.

By opening a passage from Muscovy to China, and marking the several stages, *it was a journey of so many days.*
BAKER.

5. A single step of gradual process.

The changes and vicissitude in wars are many; but chiefly in the seats or stages *of the war, the weapons, and the manner of the conduct.* BACON'S ESSAYS.

We must not expect that our journey through the several stages *of this life should be all smooth and even.* ATTERBURY.

To prepare the soul to be a fit inhabitant of that holy place to which we aspire, is to be brought to perfection by gradual advances through several hard and laborious stages *of discipline.* ROGERS'S SERMONS.

The first stage *of healing, or the discharge of matter, is by surgeons called digestion.* SHARP'S SURGERY.

To **STAGE.** *v.a.* [from the noun.] To exhibit publickly. Out of use.

I love the people;
But do not like to stage *me to their eyes:*
Though it do well, I do not relish well
Their loud applause.
SHAKESPEARE'S MEASURE FOR MEASURE.

The quick comedians
Extemp'rally will stage *us, and present*
Our Alexandrian revels.
SHAKESPEARE'S ANTONY AND CLEOPATRA.

STA'GECOACH. *n.s.* [*stage* and *coach.*] A coach that keeps its stages; a coach that passes and repasses on certain days for the accommodation of passengers.

The story was told me by a priest, as we travelled in a stagecoach. ADDISON.

When late their miry sides stagecoaches *show,*
And their stiff horses through the town move slow,
Then let the prudent walker shoes provide.
GAY.

STA'GEPLAY. *n.s.* [*stage* and *play.*] Theatrical entertainment.

This rough-cast unhewn poetry was instead of stageplays *for one hundred and twenty years.*
DRYDEN'S JUVENAL, DEDICATION.

STA'GER. *n.s.* [from *stage.*]

1. A player.

You safe in your stage clothes,
Dare quit, upon your oaths,
The stagers *and the stage wrights too.*
BEN JONSON.

2. One who has long acted on the stage of life; a practitioner; a person of cunning.

I've heard old cunning stagers
Say, fools for argument use wagers.
HUDIBRAS.

One experienced stager, *that had baffled twenty traps and tricks before, discovered the plot.* L'ESTRANGE.

Some stagers *of the wiser sort*
Made all these idle wonderments their sport:
But he, who heard what ev'ry fool could say,
Would never fix his thought, but trim his time away. DRYDEN.

One cries out, these stagers
Come in good time to make more work for wagers. DRYDEN.

Be by a parson cheated!
Had you been cunning stagers,
You might yourselves be treated
By captains and by majors. SWIFT.

STALE. *n.s.* [from *stælan*, Saxon, to steal.]

1. Something exhibited or offered as an allurement to draw others to any place or purpose.

His heart being wholly delighted in deceiving us, we could never be warned; but rather one bird caught, served for a stale *to bring in more.* SIDNEY.

Still as he went he crafty stales *did lay,*
With cunning trains him to entrap unwares;
And privy spials plac'd in all his way,
To weet what course he takes, and how he fares. FAIRY QUEEN.

The trumpery in my house bring hither,
For stale *to catch these thieves.*
SHAKESPEARE'S TEMPEST.

Had he none else to make a stale *but me?*
I was the chief that rais'd him to the crown,
And I'll be chief to bring him down again.
SHAKESPEARE'S HENRY VI.

A pretence of kindness is the universal stale *to all base projects: by this men are robbed of their fortunes, and women of their honour.*
GOVERNMENT OF THE TONGUE.

It may be a vizor for the hypocrite, and a stale *for the ambitious.*
DECAY OF PIETY.

This easy fool must be my stale, *set up*
To catch the people's eyes: he's tame and merciful;
Him I can manage.
DRYDEN'S DON SEBASTIAN.

2. In *Shakespeare* it seems to signify a prostitute.

I stand dishonour'd, that have gone about
To link my dear friend to a common stale.
SHAKESPEARE.

3. [From *stale*, adj.] Urine; old urine.
4. Old beer; beer somewhat acidulated.
5. [*Stele*, Dutch, a stick.] A handle.

It hath a long stale *or handle, with a button at the end for one's hand.*
MORTIMER'S HUSBANDRY.

STA'LLION. *n.s.* [*ysdalwyn*, an old Welch word: the one is derived from the other; but which from which I cannot certainly tell. *Wotton. Estallion*, French; *stallone*, Italian; *stalhengst*, Dutch. *Junius* thinks it derived from *stælan*, to leap.] A horse kept for mares.

The present defects are breeding without choice of stallions *in shape or size.*
TEMPLE.

If fleet Dragon's progeny at last
Prove jaded, and in frequent matches cast,
No favour for the stallion *we retain,*
And no respect for the degen'rate strain.
DRYDEN.

I will not ask him one of his Egyptians;
No, let him keep 'em all for slaves and stallions. DRYDEN.

STA'MMEL. *n.s.* Of this word I know not the meaning.[205]

Reedhood, the first that doth appear
In stammel: *scarlet is too dear.*
BEN JONSON.

STA'NDISH. *n.s.* [*stand* and *dish.*] A case for pen and ink.

A grubstreet patriot does not write to secure, but get something: should the government be overturned he has nothing to lose but an old standish. ADDISON.

I bequeath to Dean Swift esq; my large silver standish, *consisting of a large silver plate, an ink-pot, and a sand-box.*
SWIFT.

STARGA'ZER. *n.s.* [*star* and *gaze.*] An astronomer, or astrologer. In contempt.

Let the astrologers, the stargazers, *and the monthly prognosticators, stand up and save thee.* BIBLE ISAIAH, XLVII. 13.

A stargazer, *in the height of his celestial observations, stumbled into a ditch.*
L'ESTRANGE.

STARK. *adv.* Is used to intend or augment the signification of a word: as *stark mad*, mad in the highest degree. It is now little used but in low language.

Then are the best but stark *naught; for open suspecting others, comes of secret condemning themselves.* SIDNEY.

The fruitful-headed beast, amaz'd
At flashing beams of that sun-shiny shield,
Became stark *blind, and all his senses doz'd,*
That down he tumbled. SPENSER.

Men and women go stark *naked.* ABBOT.

He is stark *mad, who ever says*
That he hath been in love an hour.
DONNE.

Those seditious, that seemed moderate before, became desperate, and those who were desperate seemed stark *mad; whence tumults, confused hollowings and howlings.* HAYWARD.

Who, by the most cogent arguments, will disrobe himself at once of all his old opinions, and turn himself out stark *naked in quest of new notions?* LOCKE.

In came squire South, all dressed up in feathers and ribbons, stark *staring mad, brandishing his sword.* ARBUTHNOT.

STA'RSHOOT. *n.s.* [*star* and *shoot.*] An emission from a star.

I have seen a good quantity of that jelly, by the vulgar called a starshoot, *as if it remained upon the extinction of a falling star.* BOYLE.

STA'RTUP. *n.s.* [*start* and *up.*] One that comes suddenly into notice.

That young startup *hath all the glory of my overthrow.* SHAKESPEARE.

STA'TESMAN. *n.s.* [*state* and *man.*]

1. A politician; one versed in the arts of government.

It looks grave enough
To seem a statesman.
BEN JONSON'S EPIGRAMS.

The corruption of a poet is the generation of a statesman. POPE.

2. One employed in publick affairs.

If such actions may have passage free,
Bond-slaves and pagans shall our statesmen *be.*
SHAKESPEARE'S OTHELLO.

It is a weakness which attends high and low; the statesman *who holds the helm, as well as the peasant who holds the plough.* SOUTH'S SERMONS.

A British minister must expect to see many friends fall off, whom he cannot gratify, since, to use the phrase of a late statesman, *the pasture is not large enough.* ADDISON.

Here Britain's statesmen *oft the fall foredoom*
Of foreign tyrants, and of nymphs at home. POPE.

STA'TESWOMAN. *n.s.* [*state* and *woman.*] A woman who meddles with publick affairs. In contempt.

How she was in debt, and where she meant
To raise fresh sums: she's a great stateswoman*!* BEN JONSON.

Several objects may innocently be ridiculed, as the passions of our stateswomen. ADDISON.

STA'TICAL, STATICK. *adj.* [from the noun.] Relating to the science of weighing.

A man weigheth some pounds less in the height of Winter, according to experience, and the statick *aphorisms of Sanctorius.* BROWN'S VULGAR ERROURS.

If one by a statical *engine could regulate his insensible perspiration, he might often, by restoring of that, foresee, prevent, or shorten a fit of the gout.* ARBUTHNOT ON DIET.

STA'TICKS. *n.s.* [στατική; *statique*, Fr.] The science which considers the weight of bodies.

This is a catholick rule of staticks, *that if any body be bulk for bulk heavier than a fluid, it will sink to the bottom; and if lighter, it will float upon it, having part extant, and part immersed, as that so much of the fluid as is equal in bulk to the immersed part be equal in gravity to the whole.* BENTLEY.

STA'TIONER. *n.s.* [from *station.*]

1. A bookseller.

Some modern tragedies are beautiful on the stage, and yet Tryphon the stationer *complains they are seldom asked for in his shop.* DRYDEN.

With authors, stationers *obey'd the call;*
Glory and gain th' industrious tribe provoke,
And gentle dulness ever loves a joke.
POPE'S DUNCIAD.

2. A seller of paper.

To **STAVE** *and Tail. v.a.* To part dogs by interposing a staff, and by pulling the tail.

The conquering foe they soon assail'd,
First Trulla stav'd, *and Cerdon* tail'd.
HUDIBRAS.

STA'YLACE. *n.s.* [*stay* and *lace.*] A lace with which women fasten their boddice.

A staylace *from England should become a topick for censure at visits.* SWIFT.

STEE'LYARD. *n.s.* [*steel* and *yard.*] A kind of balance, in which the weight is moved along an iron rod, and grows heavier as it is removed farther from the fulcrum.

STE'LLIONATE. *n.s.* [*stellionat,* French; *stellionatus,* Latin.] A kind of crime which is committed [in law] by a deceitful selling of a thing otherwise than it really is: as, if a man should sell that for his own estate which is actually another man's.

It discerneth of crimes of stellionate, *and the inchoations towards crimes capital, not actually committed.* BACON.

STENCH. *n.s.* [from *stencan,* Saxon.]
1. A stink; a bad smell.

Death, death; oh amiable and lovely death!
Thou odoriferous stench, *sound rottenness,*
Arise forth from thy couch of lasting night.
SHAKESPEARE'S KING JOHN.

So bees with smoke, and doves with noisome stench,
Are from their hives, and houses, driv'n away. SHAKESPEARE.

Physicians by the stench *of feathers cure the rising of the mother.*
BACON'S NATURAL HISTORY.

The ministry will be found the salt of the earth, the only thing that keeps societies of men from stench *and corruption.*
SOUTH'S SERMONS.

The hoary Nar,
Corrupted with the stench *of sulphur flows,*
And into Tiber's streams th' infected current throws. ADDISON.

2. I find it used once for a good smell.

Black bulls and bearded goats on altars lie,
And clouds of sav'ry stench *involve the sky.* DRYDEN.

STENTOROPHO'NICK. *adj.* [from *Stentor*, the Homerical herald, whose voice was as loud as that of fifty men, and φωνή, a voice.] Loudly speaking or sounding.

Of this stentorophonick *horn of Alexander there is a figure preserved in the Vatican.*
DERHAM'S PHYSICO-THEOLOGY.

STEP, in composition, signifies one who is related only by marriage. [*Steop*, Saxon, from *stepan*, to *deprive* or *make an orphan*: for the Saxons not only said a *step-mother*, but a *step-daughter*, or *step-son*; to which it indeed, according to this etymology, more properly belongs: but as it is now seldom applied but to the mother, it seems to mean, in the mind of those who use it, a woman who has *stepped* into the vacant place of the true mother.]

How should their minds chuse but misdoubt, lest this discipline, which always you match with divine doctrine as her natural and true sister, be found unto all kinds of knowledge a step-mother.
HOOKER.

His wanton step-dame *loved him the more;*
But when she saw her offered sweets refuse,
Her love she turn'd to hate.
FAIRY QUEEN.

You shall not find me, daughter,
After the slander of most step-mothers,
Ill-ey'd unto you.
SHAKESPEARE'S CYMBELINE.

A father cruel, and a step-dame *false.*
SHAKESPEARE.

Cato the elder, being aged, buried his wife, and married a young woman: his son came to him, and said, Sir, what have I offended, that you have brought a step-mother *into your house? The old man answered, Nay, quite the contrary, son; thou pleasest me so well, as I would be glad to have more such.* BACON.

The name of step-dame, *your practis'd art,*
By which you have estrang'd my father's heart,
All you have done against me, or design,

Shows your aversion, but begets not mine.
DRYDEN'S AURENGZEBE.

A step-dame *too I have, a cursed she,*
Who rules my hen-peck'd sire, and orders me. DRYDEN.

Any body would have guessed miss to have been bred up under the influence of a cruel step-dame, *and John to be the fondling of a tender mother.*
ARBUTHNOT HISTORY OF JOHN BULL.

STERCORA'TION. *n.s.* [from *stercora*, Latin.] The act of dunging; the act of manuring with dung.

The first help is stercoration*: the sheeps dung is one of the best, and next the dung of kine, and that of horses.* BACON.

Stercoration *is seasonable.*
EVELYN'S KALENDAR.

The exteriour pulp of the fruit serves not only for the security of the seed, whilst it hangs upon the plant, but, after it is fallen upon the earth, for the stercoration *of the soil, and promotion of the growth, though not the first germination of the seminal plant.* RAY ON THE CREATION.

STERNUTA'TION. *n.s.* [*sternutatio*, Latin.] The act of sneezing.

Sternutation *is a convulsive shaking of the nerves and muscles, first occasioned by an irritation of those in the nostrils.*
QUINCY.

Concerning sternutation, *or sneezing, and the custom of saluting upon that motion, it is generally believed to derive its original from a disease wherein* sternutation *proved mortal, and such as sneezed died.*
BROWN'S VULGAR ERROURS.

STE'VEN. *n.s.* [*stefen*, Saxon.] A cry, or loud clamour.

Ne sooner was out, but swifter than thought,
Fast by the hide, the wolf Lowder caught;
And had not Roffy renne to the steven,
Lowder had been slain thilke same even.
SPENSER.

To **STI'CKLE.** *v.n.* [from the practice of prizefighters, who placed seconds with staves or sticks to interpose occasionally.]

1. To take part with one side or other.

Fortune, as she's wont, turn'd fickle,
And for the foe began to stickle.
HUDIBRAS.

2. To contest; to altercate; to contend rather with obstinacy than vehemence.

Let them go to't, and stickle,
Whether a conclave, or a conventicle.
CLEAVELAND.

Heralds stickle, *who got who,*
So many hundred years ago. HUDIBRAS.

3. To trim; to play fast and loose; to act a part between opposites.

When he sees half of the Christians killed, and the rest in a fair way of being routed, he stickles *betwixt the remainder of God's host and the race of fiends.*
DRYDEN'S JUVENAL, DEDICATION.

STI'CKLER. *n.s.* [from *stickle.*]

1. A sidesman to fencers; a second to a duellist; one who stands to judge a combat.

Basilius came to part them, the stickler's *authority being unable to persuade cholerick hearers; and part them he did.*
SIDNEY.

Basilius, the judge, appointed sticklers *and trumpets, whom the others should obey.*
SIDNEY.

Our former chiefs, like sticklers *of the war,*
First fought t' inflame the parties, then to poise:
The quarrel lov'd, but did the cause abhor;
And did not strike to hurt, but made a noise. DRYDEN.

2. An obstinate contender about any thing.

Quercetanus, though the grand stickler *for the tria prima, has this concession of the irresolubleness of diamonds.* BOYLE.

The inferior tribe of common women have,

in most reigns, been the professed sticklers *for such as have acted against the true interest of the nation.* ADDISON'S FREEHOLDER.

The tory or high church clergy were the greatest sticklers *against the exorbitant proceedings of king James II.* SWIFT.

All place themselves in the list of the national church, though they are great sticklers *for liberty of conscience.* SWIFT.

STI'LLSTAND. *n.s.* [*still* and *stand.*] Absence of motion.

The tide swell'd up unto his height,
Then makes a stillstand, *running neither way.* SHAKESPEARE.

STI'NGO. *n.s.* [from the sharpness of the taste.] Old beer. A cant word.

STI'NGY. *adj.* [A low cant word. In this word, with its derivatives, the *g* is pronounced as in *gem.*] Covetous; niggardly; avaricious.

A stingy *narrow hearted fellow that had a deal of choice fruit, had not the heart to touch it till it began to be rotten.* L'ESTRANGE.

He relates it only by parcels, and wont give us the whole, which forces me to bespeak his friends to engage him to lay aside that stingy *humour, and gratify the publick at once.*
ARBUTHNOT'S HISTORY OF JOHN BULL.

STI'NKARD. *n.s.* [from *stink.*] A mean stinking paltry fellow.

STI'NKER. *n.s.* [from *stink.*] Something intended to offend by the smell.

The air may be purified by burning of stinkpots or stinkers *in contagious lanes.* HARVEY.

STI'NKPOT. *n.s.* [*stink* and *pot.*] An artificial composition offensive to the smell.

The air may be purified by fires of pitch-barrels, especially in close places, by burning of stinkpots. HARVEY.

STI'RIOUS. *adj.* [from *stiria*, Latin.] Resembling icicles.

Chrystal is found sometimes in rocks, and in some places not much unlike the stirious *or stillicidious dependencies of ice.* BROWN'S VULGAR ERROURS.

To **STIVE.** *v.a.* [Supposed of the same original with *stew.*]

1. To stuff up close.

You would admire, if you saw them stive *it in their ships.* SANDYS'S JOURNEY.

2. To make hot or sultry.

His chamber was commonly stived *with friends or suitors of one kind or other.* WOTTON.

STO'CAH. *n.s.* [Irish; *stochk*, Erse.] An attendant; a walletboy; one who runs at a horseman's foot; a horseboy.[206]

He holdeth himself a gentleman, and scorneth to work, which he saith is the life of a peasant; but thenceforth becometh an horseboy, or a stocah *to some kern, inuring himself to his sword, and the gentlemanly trade of stealing.* SPENSER.

STO'CKJOBBER. *n.s.* [*stock* and *job.*] A low wretch who gets money by buying and selling shares in the funds.

The stockjobber *thus from 'Change-alley goes down,*
And tips you the freeman a wink;
Let me have but your vote to serve for the town,
And here is a guinea to drink. SWIFT.

STO'OLBALL. *n.s.* [*stool* and *ball.*] A play where balls are driven from stool to stool.

While Betty dances on the green,
And Susan is at stoolball *seen.* PRIOR.

STO'RYTELLER. *n.s.* [*story* and *tell.*] One who relates tales; An historian. In contempt.

In such a satire all would seek a share,
And every fool will fancy he is there;
Old storytellers *too must pine and die,*
To see their antiquated wit laid by;
Like her, who miss'd her name in a lampoon,
And griev'd to find herself decay'd so soon. DRYDEN.

Company will be no longer pestered with dull, dry, tedious storytellers. SWIFT'S POLITE CONVERSATION.

STOUND. *n.s.* [from the verb.]

1. Sorrow; grief; mishap. Out of use. The Scots retain it.

Begin and end the bitter baleful stound,
If less than that I fear. FAIRY QUEEN.

The fox his copesmate found,
To whom complaining his unhappy stound,
He with him far'd some better chance to find. HUBBERD.

2. Astonishment; amazement.

Thus we stood as in a stound,
And wet with tears, like dew, the ground. GAY.

3. Hour; time; season. *Spenser.*

To **STRA'GGLE.** *v.a.* [Of this word no etymology is known; it is probably a frequentative of *stray*, from *stravviare*, Italian, of *extraviam*, Latin.]

1. To wander without any certain direction; to rove; to ramble.

But stay, like one that thinks to bring his friend
A mile or two, and sees the journey's end:
I straggle *on too far.* SUCKLING.

Having passed the Syrens, they came between Scylla and Charybdis, and the straggling *rocks, which seemed to cast out great store of flames and smoke.* RALEIGH.

A wolf spied out a straggling *kid, and pursued him.* L'ESTRANGE.

Children, even when they endeavour their utmost, cannot keep their minds from straggling. LOCKE.

2. To wander dispersedly.

He likewise enriched poor straggling *soldiers with great quantity.* SHAKESPEARE'S TIMON OF ATHENS.

They found in Burford some of the straggling *soldiers, who out of weariness stayed behind.* CLARENDON.

From straggling *mountaineers for publick good,*
To rank in tribes, and quit the savage wood;
Houses to build, and them contiguous make,
For cheerful neighbourhood and safety's sake. TATE.

3. To exuberate; to shoot too far.

Were they content to prune the lavish vine,
Of straggling *branches, and improve the wine.*

Trim off the small superfluous branches on each side of the hedge that straggle *too far out.* MORTIMER'S HUSBANDRY.

4. To be dispersed; to be apart from any main body; to stand single.

Wide was his parish, not contracted close
In streets, but here and there a straggling *house;*
Yet still he was at hand. DRYDEN.

STRA'PPING. *adj.* Vast; large; bulky. Used of large men or women in contempt.

To **STRA'TIFY.** *v.a.* [*stratifier*, Fr. from *stratum*, Lat.] To range in beds or layers. A chymical term.

STRA'TUM. *n.s.* [Latin.] A bed; a layer. A term of philosophy.

Another was found in a perpendicular fissure of a stratum *of stone in Langron iron-mine, Cumberland.* WOODWARD.

Drill'd through the sandy stratum, *every way*
The waters with the sandy stratum *rise.* THOMSON.

STRE'PEROUS. *adj.* [*strepo*, Latin.] Loud; noisy.

Porta conceives, because in a streperous *eruption it riseth against fire, it doth therefore resist lightning.* BROWN.

To **STREW.** *v.a.* [The orthography of this word is doubtful: it is generally written *strew*, and I have followed custom; but *Skinner* likewise proposes *strow*, and *Junius* writes *straw*. Their reasons will appear in the word from which it may be derived. *Strawan*, Gothick; *stroyen*, Dutch; *streawian*, Sax. *strawen*, German; *strôer*, Danish. Perhaps *strow* is best, being that which reconciles etymology with pronunciation.[207]]

1. To spread by being scattered.

The snow which does the top of Pindus strew,
Did never whiter shew. SPENSER.

Is thine alone the seed that strews *the pain?*
The birds of heav'n shall vindicate their grain. POPE.

2. To spread by scattering.

I thought thy bride-bed to have deck'd, sweet maid,
And not have strew'd *thy grave.*
SHAKESPEARE'S HAMLET.

Here be tears of perfect moan,
Wept for thee in Helicon;
And some flowers and some bays,
For thy herse, to strew *the ways.* MILTON.

3. To scatter loosely.

The calf he burnt in the fire, ground it to powder, and strawed *it upon the water, and made Israel drink of it.*
BIBLE EXODUS.

With furies and nocturnal orgies fir'd,
Whom ev'n the savage beasts had spar'd, they kill'd,
And strew'd *his mangled limbs about the field.* DRYDEN.

STRE'WMENT. *n.s.* [from *strew.*] Any thing scattered in decoration.

Her death was doubtful. — For charitable prayers,
Shards, flints, and pebbles should be thrown on her;
Yet here she is allow'd her virgin chants,
Her maiden strewments, *and the bringing home*
Of bell and burial.
SHAKESPEARE'S HAMLET.

STRI'GMENT. *n.s.* [*strigmentum*, from *stringo*, Lat. to scrape.] Scraping; recrement.

Many, besides the strigments *and sudorous adhesions from mens hands, acknowledge that nothing proceedeth from gold in its usual decoction.*
BROWN'S VULGAR ERROURS.

STRIPE. *n.s.* [*strepe*, Dutch.]

1. A lineary variation of colour. This seems to be the original notion of the word.

Gardeners may have three roots among an hundred that are rare, as purple and carnation of several stripes. BACON.

2. A shred of a different colour.

One of the most valuable trimmings of their cloaths was a long stripe *sowed upon the garment, called latus clavus.*
ARBUTHNOT.

3. A weal; or discolouration made by a lash or blow.

Cruelty marked him with inglorious stripes. THOMSON.

4. A blow; a lash.

A body cannot be so torn with stripes, *as a mind with remembrance of wicked actions.* HAYWARD.

To those that are yet within the reach of the stripes *and reproofs of their own conscience; I would address that they would not seek to remove themselves from that wholsome discipline.* DECAY OF PIETY.

To **STROLL.** *v.n.* To wander; to ramble; to rove; to be a vagrant.

She's mine, and thine, and strolling *up and down.* GRANVILLE.

Your wine lock'd up, your butler stroll'd *abroad.* POPE.

These mothers strole, *to beg sustenance for their helpless infants.* SWIFT.

STRO'LLER. *n.s.* [from *stroll.*] A vagrant; a wanderer; a vagabond.

Two brother-hermits, saints by trade,
Disguis'd in tatter'd habits, went
To a small village down in Kent;
Where, in the strollers *canting strain,*
They begg'd from door to door in vain.
SWIFT.

The men of pleasure, who never go to church, form their ideas of the clergy from a few poor strollers *they often observe in the streets.* SWIFT.

STRO'NGWATER. *n.s.* [*strong* and *water.*] Distilled spirits.

Metals receive in readily strongwaters; *and* strongwaters *do readily pierce into metals and stones: and some will touch upon gold, that will not touch upon silver.*
BACON'S NATURAL HISTORY.

To **STROUT.** *v.n.* [*strussen,* German.] To swell with an appearance of greatness; to walk with affected dignity; to strut. This is commonly written *strut,* which seems more proper.

To **STROUT.** *v.a.* To swell out; to puff out; to enlarge by affectation.

I will make a brief list of the particulars in an historical truth nowise strouted, *nor made greater by language.* BACON.

To **STROW.** *v.n.* [See to **STREW.**]

1. To spread by being scattered.

Angel forms lay entranc'd,
Thick as autumnal leaves that strow *the brooks*
In Valombrosa.
MILTON'S PARADISE LOST.

2. To spread by scattering; to besprinkle.

All the ground
With shiver'd armour strown.
MILTON'S PARADISE LOST.

Come, shepherds come, and strow *with leaves the plain;*
Such funeral rites your Daphnis did ordain. DRYDEN.

With osier floats the standing water strow,
With massy stones make bridges if it flow.
DRYDEN.

3. To spread.

There have been three years dearth of corn, and every place strow'd *with beggars.*
SWIFT.

4. To scatter; to throw at random.

Synah, can I tell thee more?
And of our ladies bowre;
But little need to strow *my store,*
Suffice this hill of our. SPENSER.

The tree in storms
The glad earth about her strows,
With treasure from her yielding boughs.
WALLER.

Possession kept the beaten road,
And gather'd all his brother strow'd.
SWIFT.

To **STROWL.** *v.n.* To range; to wander. [See **STROLL.**]

'Tis she who nightly strowls *with saunt'ring pace.* GAY.

STRU'CTURE. [*structure,* Fr. *structura,* from *structus,* Latin.]

1. Act of building; practice of building.

His son builds on, and never is content,
Till the last farthing is in structure *spent.*
DRYDEN.

2. Manner of building; form; make.

Several have gone about to inform them, but for want of insight into the structure

and constitution of the terraqueous globe, have not given satisfaction.
WOODWARD.

3. Edifice; building.

Ecbatana her structure *vast there shews,*
And Hecatompylos her hundred gates.
MILTON.

High on a rock of ice the structure *lay.*
POPE.

There stands a structure *of majestick frame.*
POPE.

To **STRUT.** *v.n.* [*strussen*, German.]
1. To walk with affected dignity; to swell with stateliness.

Adore our errours, laugh at's while we strut
To our confusion.
SHAKESPEARE'S ANTONY AND CLEOPATRA.

Does he not hold up his head and strut *in his gait?* SHAKESPEARE.

Though thou strut *and paint,*
Yet art thou both shrunk up and old.
BEN JONSON.

The false syren
Struts *on th' waves, and shews the brute below.* DRYDEN.

We will be with you ere the crowing cock
Salutes the light, and struts *before his feather'd flock.* DRYDEN.

2. To swell; to protuberate.

The goats with strutting *dugs shall homeward speed.* DRYDEN.

The pow'r appeas'd, with winds suffic'd the sail,
The bellying canvas strutted *with the gale.*
DRYDEN.

As thy strutting *bags with money rise,*
The love of gain is of an equal size.
DRYDEN.

STRUT. *n.s.* [from the verb.] An affectation of stateliness in the walk.

Certain gentlemen of the gown, by smirking countenances and an ungainly strut *in their walk, have got preferment.*
SWIFT.

STUD. *n.s.* [*studu*, Saxon.]
1. A post; a stake. In some such meaning perhaps it is to be taken in the following passage, which I do not understand.

A barn in the country, that hath one single stud, *or one height of* studs *to the roof, is two shillings a foot.*
MORTIMER.

2. A nail with a large head driven for ornament; any ornamental knob or protuberance.

Handles were to add,
For which he now was making studs.
CHAPMAN'S ILIAD.

A belt of straw, and ivy buds,
With coral clasps and amber studs.
RALEIGH.

Crystal and myrrhine cups emboss'd with gems,
And studs *of pearl.*
MILTON'S PARADISE REGAIN'D.

Upon a plane are several small oblong studs, *placed regularly in a quincunx order.* WOODWARD ON FOSSILS.

A desk he had of curious work,
With glitt'ring studs *about.* SWIFT.

3. [*Stode*, Saxon; *stod*, Islandick, is a stallion.] A collection of breeding horses and mares.

In the studs *of Ireland, where care is taken, we see horses bred of excellent shape, vigour, and size.*
TEMPLE.

STU'DENT. *n.s.* [*studens*, Latin.] A man given to books; a scholar; a bookish man.

Keep a gamester from dice, and a good student *from his book.*
SHAKESPEARE'S MERRY WIVES OF WINDSOR.

This grave advice some sober student *bears,*
And loudly rings it in his fellow's ears.
DRYDEN'S PERSIUS.

A student *shall do more in one hour, when all things concur to invite him to any special study, than in four at a dull season.* WATTS'S LOGICK.

I slightly touch the subject, and recommend it to some student *of the profession.* ARBUTHNOT ON COINS.

STULTI'LOQUENCE. *n.s.* [*stultus* and *loquentia*, Lat.] Foolish talk. *Dictionaries.*

STU'MBLINGBLOCK, STU'MBLINGSTONE. *n.s.* [from *stumble.*] Cause of stumbling; cause of errour; cause of offence.

We preach Christ crucified, unto the Jews a stumblingblock, *and unto the Greeks foolishness.*
BIBLE 1 CORINTHIANS, I. 23.

Shakespeare is a stumblingblock *to these rigid criticks.* SPECTATOR.

This stumbling stone *we hope to take away.* BURNET.

STUPE. *n.s.* [*stupa*, Latin.] Cloath or flax dipped in warm medicaments, and applied to a hurt or sore.

A fomentation was by some pretender to surgery applied with coarse woollen stupes, *one of which was bound upon his leg.* WISEMAN'S SURGERY.

STU'RDY. *adv.* [*estourdi*, French.]
1. Hardy; stout; brutal; obstinate. It is always used of men with some disagreeable idea of coarseness or rudeness.

This must be done, and I would fain see
Mortal so sturdy *as to gainsay.*
HUDIBRAS.

A sturdy *hardened sinner shall advance to the utmost pitch of impiety with less reluctance than he took the first steps, whilst his conscience was yet vigilant and tender.* ATTERBURY.

Aw'd by that house, accustom'd to command,
The sturdy *kerns in due subjection stand,*
Nor bear the reins in any foreign hand.
DRYDEN.

2. Strong; forcible.

The ill-apparelled knight now had gotten the reputation of some sturdy *lout, he had so well defended himself.* SIDNEY.

Ne ought his sturdy *strokes might stand before,*
That high trees overthrew, and rocks in pieces tore. FAIRY QUEEN.

3. Stiff; stout.

He was not of any delicate contexture, his limbs rather sturdy *than dainty.* WOTTON.

Sturdiest *oaks*
Bow'd their stiff necks, loaden with stormy blasts,
Or torn up sheer.
MILTON'S PARADISE REGAIN'D.

To **STUT,** To **STUTTER.** *v.n.* [*stutten*, to hinder, Dutch.] To speak with hesitation; to stammer.

Divers stut*: the cause is the refrigeration of the tongue, whereby it is less apt to move; and therefore naturals* stut. BACON.

STU'TTER, STUTTERER. *n.s.* [from *stut.*] One that speaks with hesitation; a stammerer.

Many stutters *are very cholerick, choler inducing a dryness in the tongue.*
BACON'S NATURAL HISTORY.

STYLE. *n.s.* [*stylus*, Latin.]
1. Manner of writing with regard to language.

Happy
That can translate the stubbornness of fortune
Into so quiet, and so sweet a style.
SHAKESPEARE.

Their beauty I will rather leave to poets, than venture upon so tender and nice a subject with my severer style. MORE.

Proper words in proper places, make the true definition of a stile. SWIFT.

Let some lord but own the happy lines,

How the wit brightens, and the style *refines.* POPE.

2. Manner of speaking appropriate to particular characters.

No style *is held for base, where love well named is.* SIDNEY.

There was never yet philosopher,
That could endure the toothach patiently,
However they have writ the style *of gods,*
And make a pish at chance and sufferance. SHAKESPEARE.

3. Title; appellation.

Ford's a knave, and I will aggravate his stile; *thou shalt know him for knave and cuckold.* SHAKESPEARE.

The king gave them in his commission the style *and appellation which belonged to them.* CLARENDON.

O virgin! or what other name you bear
Above that style; *O more than mortal fair!*
Let not an humble suppliant sue in vain.
DRYDEN'S ÆNEID.

Propitious hear our pray'r,
Whether the style *of Titan please thee more,*
Whose purple rays th' Achæmenes adore.
POPE'S STATIUS.

4.[208] Course of writing. Unusual.

While his thoughts the ling'ring day beguile,
To gentle Arcite let us turn our style.
DRYDEN.

5. A pointed iron used anciently in writing on tables of wax.
6. Any thing with a sharp point, as a graver; the pin of a dial.

Placing two stiles *or needles of the same steel, touched with the same loadstone, when the one is removed but half a span, the other would stand like Hercules's pillars.* BROWN.

7. The stalk which rises from amid the leaves of a flower.

Style *is the middle prominent part of the flower of a plant, which adheres to the fruit or seed: 'tis usually slender and long, whence it has its name.* QUINCY.

The figure of the flower-leaves, stamina, apices, stile, *and seed-vessel.* RAY.

8. STYLE *of Court*, is properly the practice observed by any court in its way of proceeding. *Ayliffe's Parergon.*

SUB, in composition, signifies a subordinate degree.

SUBBE'ADLE. *n.s.* [*sub* and *beadle.*] An under beadle.

They ought not to execute those precepts by simple messengers, or subbeadles, *but in their own persons.* AYLIFFE'S PARERGON.

SUBCELE'STIAL. *adj.* [*sub* and *celestial.*] Placed beneath the heavens.

The most refined glories of subcelestial *excellencies are but more faint resemblances of these.*
GLANVILLE SCEPSIS SCIENTIFICA.

SUBDERISO'RIOUS. *adj.* [*sub* and *derisor.*] Scoffing or ridiculing with tenderness and delicacy.

This subderisorious *mirth is far from giving any offence to us: it is rather a pleasant condiment of our conversation.* MORE.

SUBDITI'TIOUS. *adj.* [*subdititius*, Latin.] Put secretly in the place of something else.

SUBINGRE'SSION. *n.s.* [*sub* and *ingressus*, Latin.] Secret entrance.

The pressure of the ambient air is strengthened upon the accession of the air sucked out; which, forceth the neighbouring air to a violent subingression *of its parts.* BOYLE.

SUBLI'NGUAL. *adj.* [*sublingual*, French; *sub* and *lingua*, Lat.] Placed under the tongue.

Those subliming humours should be intercepted, before they mount to the head, by sublingual *pills.*
HARVEY ON CONSUMPTION.

SUBLU'NAR, SUBLUNARY. *adj.* [*sublunaire*, Fr. *sub* and *luna*, Latin.] Situated beneath the moon; earthly; terrestrial; of this world.

Dull sublunary *lovers, love,*
Whose soul is sense, cannot admit
Of absence, 'cause it doth remove
The thing which elemented it. DONNE.

Night measur'd, with her shadowy cone,
Half way up hill this vast sublunar *vault.*
MILTON.

Through seas of knowledge we our course advance,
Discov'ring still new worlds of ignorance;
And these discov'ries make us all confess
That sublunary *science is but guess.*
DENHAM.

The celestial bodies above the moon being not subject to chance, remained in perpetual order, while all things sublunary *are subject to change.*
DRYDEN'S DUFRESNOY.

Ovid had warn'd her to beware
Of strolling gods, whose usual trade is,
Under pretence of taking air,
To pick up sublunary *ladies.* SWIFT.

SUBO'RDINACY, SUBORDINANCY. *n.s.* [from *subordinate.*] *Subordinacy* is the proper and analogical word.
1. The state of being subject.

Pursuing the imagination through all its extravagancies, is no improper method of correcting, and bringing it to act in subordinacy *to reason.* SPECTATOR.

2. Series of subordination.

The subordinancy *of the government changing hands so often, makes an unsteddiness in the pursuit of the publick interests.*
TEMPLE.

SU'BSTANTIVE. *n.s.* [*substantif*, French; *substantivum*, Latin.] A noun betokening the thing, not a quality.

Claudian perpetually closes his sense at the end of a verse, commonly called golden, or two substantives *and two adjectives with a verb betwixt them.* DRYDEN.

SUBSTITU'TION. *n.s.* [*substitution*, Fr. from *substitute.*] The act of placing any person or thing in the room of another; the state of being placed in the room of another.

He did believe
He was the duke, from substitution,
And executing th' outward face of royalty,
With all prerogative.
SHAKESPEARE'S TEMPEST.

Nor sal, sulphur, or mercury can be separated from any perfect metals; for every part, so separated, may easily be reduced into perfect metal without substitution *of that which chymists imagine to be wanting.*
BACON.

To **SUBSTRA'CT.** *v.a.* [*subtraho*, Lat. *soustraction*, French.]
1. To take away part from the whole.
2. To take one number from another.

SUBSTRA'CTION. *n.s.* [*soubstraire, soubstraction*, French.]
1. The act of taking away part from the whole.

I cannot call this piece Tully's nor my own, being much altered not only by the change of the style, but by addition and substraction. DENHAM.

2. [In arithmetick.] The taking of a lesser number out of a greater of like kind, whereby to find out a third number, being or declaring the inequality, excess, or difference between the numbers given. *Cocker's Arithmetick.*

SUBSTRU'CTION. *n.s.* [*substructio*, from *sub* and *struo*, Latin.] Underbuilding.

To found our habitation firmly, examine the bed of earth upon which we build, and then the underfillings, or substruction, *as the ancients called it.*
WOTTON'S ARCHITECTURE.

SU'BTILE. *adj.* [*subtile*, Fr. *subtilis*, Lat. This word is often written *subtle.*]

1. Thin; not dense; not gross.

From his eyes the fleeting fair
Retir'd, like subtle *smoke dissolv'd in air.*
DRYDEN'S GEORGICKS.

Deny Des Cart his subtile *matter,*
You leave him neither fire nor water.
PRIOR.

Is not the heat conveyed through the vacuum by the vibrations of a much subtiler *medium than air, which, after the air was drawn out, remained in the vacuum?* NEWTON'S OPTICKS.

2. Nice; fine; delicate; not coarse.

But of the clock which in our breasts we bear,
The subtile *motions we forget the while.*
DAVIES.

Thou only know'st her nature, and her pow'rs;
Her subtile *form thou only can'st define.*
DAVIES.

I do distinguish plain
Each subtile *line of her immortal face.*
DAVIES.

3. Piercing; acute.

Pass we the slow disease and subtile *pain,*
Which our weak frame is destin'd to sustain;
The cruel stone, the cold catarrh.
PRIOR.

4. Cunning; artful; sly; subdolous. In this sense it is now commonly written *subtle.*[209]

Arrius, a priest in the church of Alexandria, a subtile *witted and a marvellous fair spoken man, was discontented that one should be placed before him in honour, whose superior he thought himself in desert, because through envy and stomach prone unto contradiction.* HOOKER.

Think you this York
Was not incensed by his subtle *mother,*
To taunt and scorn you?
SHAKESPEARE'S RICHARD III.

O subtile *love, a thousand wiles thou hast*
By humble suit, by service, or by hire,
To win a maiden's hold. FAIRFAX.

A woman, an harlot and subtile *of heart.*
BIBLE PROVERBS, VII. 10.

Nor thou his malice, and false guile, contemn:
Subtile *he needs must be, who could seduce*
Angels. MILTON'S PARADISE LOST.

5. Deceitful.

Like a bowl upon a subtle *ground,*
I've tumbled past the throw.
SHAKESPEARE'S CORIOLANUS.

6. Refined; acute beyond exactness.

Things remote from use, obscure and subtle. MILTON.

SU'BTILELY. *adv.* [from *subtile.*]

1.[210] Finely; not grossly.

The constitution of the air appeareth more subtilly *by worms in oak-apples than to the sense of man.* BACON.

In these plaisters the stone should not be too subtilely *powdered; for it will better manifest its attraction in more sensible dimensions.*
BROWN'S VULGAR ERROURS.

The opakest bodies, if subtilely *divided, as metals dissolved in acid menstruums, become perfectly transparent.* NEWTON.

2. Artfully; cunningly.

By granting this, add the reputation of loving the truth sincerely to that of having been able to oppose it subtilely. BOYLE.

Others have sought to ease themselves of affliction by disputing subtilly *against it, and pertinaciously maintaining that afflictions are no real evils.* TILLOTSON'S SERMONS.

SU'BTILENESS. *n.s.* [from *subtile.*]

1. Fineness; rareness.
2. Cunning; artfulness.

To **SUBTI'LIATE.** *v.a.* [from *subtile.*] To make thin.

A very dry and warm or subtiliating *air opens the surface of the earth.* HARVEY ON THE PLAGUE.

SU'BTILTY. *n.s.* [*subtilité*, French; from *subtile.*]

1. Thinness; fineness; exility of parts.

The subtilties *of particular sounds may pass through small crannies not confused, but its magnity not so well.* BACON.

How shall we this union well express?
Nought ties the soul, her subtilty *is such.*
DAVIES.

The corporeity of all bodies being the same, and subtilty *in all bodies being essentially the same thing, could any body by* subtilty *become vital, then any degree of* subtilty *would produce some degree of life.* GREW'S COSMOLOGIA SACRA.

Bodies the more of kin they are to spirit in subtilty *and refinement, the more spreading and self-diffusive are they.* NORRIS.

2. Nicety.[211]

Whatsoever is invisible, in respect of the fineness of the body, or subtilty *of the motion, is little enquired.* BACON.

3. Refinement; too much acuteness.

You prefer the reputation of candour before that of subtilty. BOYLE.

Intelligible discourses are spoiled by too much subtilty *in nice divisions.* LOCKE.

Greece did at length a learned race produce,
Who needful science mock'd, and arts of use;
Mankind with idle subtilties *embroil,*
And fashion systems with romantick toil.
BLACKMORE.

They give method, and shed subtilty *upon their author.* BAKER.

4. Cunning; artifice; slyness.

Finding force now faint to be,
He thought grey hairs afforded subtilty.
SIDNEY.

The rudeness and barbarity of savage Indians knows not so perfectly to hate all virtues as some mens subtilty. KING CHARLES.

Sleights proceeding
As from his wit and native subtlety.
MILTON.

To **SU'BTILIZE.** *v.a.* [*subtilizer*, French; from *subtile.*]

1. To make thin; to make less gross or coarse.

Chyle, being mixed with the choler and pancreatick juices, is further subtilized, *and rendered so fluid and penetrant, that the thinner and finer part easily finds way in at the streight orifices of the lacteous veins.* RAY ON THE CREATION.

Body cannot be vital; for if it be, then is it so either as subtilized *or organized, moved or endowed with life.* GREW.

2. To refine; to spin into useless niceties.

The most obvious verity is subtilized *into niceties, and spun into a thread indiscernible by common opticks.* GLANVILLE.

To **SUBTI'LIZE.** *v.n.* To talk with too much refinement.

Qualities and moods some modern philosophers have subtilized *on.* DIGBY ON BODIES.

SU'BTLE. *adj.* [Written often for *subtile*, especially in the sense of cunning.] Sly; artful; cunning.

Some subtle *headed fellow will put some quirk, or devise some evasion, whereof the rest will take hold.* SPENSER.

Shall we think the subtle *witted French*
Conj'rers and sorc'rers, that, afraid of him,
By magick verse have thus contriv'd his end? SHAKESPEARE'S HENRY VI.

The serpent, subtlest *beast of all the field.* MILTON.

The Arabians were men of a deep and subtle *wit.* SPRAT.

SU'BTLY. *adv.* [from *subtle.*]

1. Slily; artfully; cunningly.

Thou see'st how subtly *to detain thee I devise;*
Inviting thee to hear, while I relate.
MILTON'S PARADISE LOST.

2. Nicely; delicately.

In the nice bee, what sense so subtly *true,*
From pois'nous herbs extracts the healing dew! POPE.

To **SU'BTRACT.** *v.a.* [*subtractio*, Latin. They who derive it from the Latin write *subtract*; those who know the French original, write *substract*; which is the common word.] To withdraw part from the rest.

Reducing many things unto charge, which, by confusion, became concealed and subtracted *from the crown.* DAVIES.

What is subtracted *or subducted out of the extent of the divine perfection, leaves still a quotient infinite.* HALE.

The same swallow, by the subtracting *daily of her eggs, lay nineteen successively, and then gave over.* RAY.

SUBTRA'CTION. *n.s.* See **SUBSTRACTION.**

SUCCE'SSFUL. *adj.* [*success* and *full.*] Prosperous; happy; fortunate.

They were terrible alarms to persons grown wealthy by a long and successful *imposture, by persuading the world that men might be honest and happy, though they never mortified any corrupt appetites.* SOUTH'S SERMONS.

H' observ'd the illustrious throng,
Their names, their fates, their conduct and their care
In peaceful senates and successful *war.*
DRYDEN.

The early hunter
Blesses Diana's hand, who leads him safe
O'er hanging cliffs; who spreads his net successful,
And guides the arrow through the panther's heart. PRIOR.

SUCCE'SSLESS. *adj.* [from *success.*] Unlucky; unfortunate; failing of the event desired.

The hopes of thy successless *love resign.* DRYDEN.

The Bavarian duke,
Bold champion! brandishing his Noric blade,
Best temper'd steel, successless *prov'd in field.* PHILIPS.

Passion unpity'd, and successless *love,*
Plant daggers in my heart.
ADDISON'S CATO.

Successless *all her soft caresses prove,*
To banish from his breast his country's love. POPE.

SUCCI'NCT. *adj.* [*succinct*, French; *succinctus*, Latin.]

1. Tucked or girded up; having the cloaths drawn up to disengage the legs.

His habit fit for speed succinct.
MILTON'S PARADISE LOST.

His vest succinct *then girding round his waist,*
Forth rush'd the swain. POPE.

Four knaves in garbs succinct. POPE.

2. Short; concise; brief.

A strict and succinct *stile is that where you can take nothing away without loss, and that loss manifest.* BEN JONSON.

Let all your precepts be succinct *and clear,*
That ready wits may comprehend them soon. ROSCOMMON.

To **SUCCU'MB.** *v.n.* [*succumbo*, Latin; *succomber*, French.] To yield; to sink under any difficulty. Not in use, except among the Scotch.

To their wills we must succumb,
Quocunque trahunt, 'tis our doom.
HUDIBRAS.

SU'CKINGBOTTLE. *n.s.* [*suck* and *bottle.*] A bottle which to children supplies the want of a pap.

He that will say, children join these general abstract speculations with their sucking-bottles, *has more zeal for his opinion, but less sincerity.* LOCKE.

SUDA'TION. *n.s.* [*sudo*, Latin.] Sweat.

SUDS. *n.s.* [from *seodan*, to seeth; whence *sodden*, Saxon.]
1. A lixivium of soap and water.
2. *To be in the* SUDS. A familiar phrase for being in any difficulty.

To **SU'FFRAGATE.** *v.n.* [*suffragor*, Latin.] To vote with; to agree in voice with.

No tradition could universally prevail, unless there were some common congruity of somewhat inherent in nature, which suits and suffragates *with it, and closeth with it.* HALE.

To **SU'GGILATE.** *v.a.* [*suggillo*, Latin.] To beat black and blue; to make livid by a bruise.

The head of the os humeri was bruised, and remained suggilated *long after.*
WISEMAN'S SURGERY.

SUI'LLAGE. *n.s.* [*souillage*, French.] Drain of filth. Obsolete.

When they have chosen the plot, and laid out the limits of the work, some Italians dig wells and cisterns, and other conveyances for the suillage *of the house.* WOTTON.

SU'MMERSAULT, SUMMERSET. *n.s.* [*soubresault*, French. *Somerset* is a corruption.] A high leap in which the heels are thrown over the head.

Some do the summersault,
And o'er the bar like tumblers vault.
HUDIBRAS.

Frogs are observed to use divers summersaults. WALTON.

The treasurer cuts a caper on the strait rope: I have seen him do the summerset *upon a trencher fixed on the rope, which is no thicker than a common packthread.*
GULLIVER'S TRAVELS.

SU'MPTER. *n.s.* [*sommier*, French; *somaro*, Italian.] A horse that carries the cloaths or furniture.

Return with her!
Persuade me rather to be a slave and sumpter
To this detested groom.
SHAKESPEARE'S KING LEAR.

With full force his deadly bow he bent,
And feather'd fates among the mules and sumpters *sent.* DRYDEN.

Two sumpter *mules, bred of large Flanders mares.* MORTIMER'S HUSBANDRY.

SU'MPTUARY. *adj.* [*sumptuarius*, Latin.] Relating to expence; regulating the cost of life.

To remove that material cause of sedition, which is want and poverty in the estate, serveth the opening and well balancing of trade, the banishing of idleness, the repressing of waste and excess by sumptuary *laws.* BACON.

SUPER, in composition, notes either more than another, or more than enough, or on the top.

To **SUPERA'NNUATE.** *v.a.* [*super* and *annus*, Lat.] To impair or disqualify by age or length of life.

If such depravities be yet alive, deformity need not despair, nor will the eldest hopes be ever superannuated. BROWN.

When the sacramental test was put in execution, the justices of peace through Ireland, that had laid down their commissions, amounted only to a dozen, and those of the lowest fortune, and some of them superannuated. SWIFT.

SUPERCA'RGO. *n.s.* [*super* and *cargo.*] An officer in the ship whose business is to manage the trade.

I only wear it in a land of Hectors,
Thieves, supercargo's, *sharpers.* POPE.

SUPERCO'NSEQUENCE. *n.s.* [*super* and *consequence.*] Remote consequence.

Not attaining the deuteroscopy, and second intention of the words, they omit their superconsequences *and coherences.* BROWN.

SUPERE'XCELLENT. *adj.* [*super* and *excellent.*] Excellent beyond common degrees of excellence.

We discern not the abuse: suffer him to persuade us that we are as gods, something so superexcellent, *that all must reverence and adore.* DECAY OF PIETY.

SUPERLU'NAR. *adj.* [*super* and *luna.*] Not sublunary; placed above the moon; not of this world.

The mind, in metaphysicks, at a loss,
May wander in a wilderness of moss;
The head that turns at superlunar *things,*
Pois'd with a tail, may steer on Wilkins' wings. DUNCIAD.

SUPERSTI'TIOUS. *adj.* [*superstitieux,* Fr. *superstitiosus,* Latin.]
1. Addicted to superstition; full of idle fancies or scruples with regard to religion.

At the kindling of the fire, and lighting of candles, they say certain prayers, and use some other superstitious *rites, which shew that they honour the fire and the light.* SPENSER.

Have I
Been out of fondness superstitious *to him?*
And am I thus rewarded?
SHAKESPEARE'S HENRY VIII.

Nature's own work it seem'd, nature taught art,
And to a superstitious *eye the haunt*
Of wood-gods and wood-nymphs. MILTON.

A venerable wood,
Where rites divine were paid, whose holy hair
Was kept and cut with superstitious *care.* DRYDEN.

2. Over accurate; scrupulous beyond need.

To **SUPERVI'VE.** *v.n.* [*super* and *vivo,* Lat.] To overlive; to outlive.

Upon what principle can the soul be imagined to be naturally mortal, or what revolutions in nature will it not be able to resist and supervive. CLARKE.

SUPPEDA'NEOUS. *adj.* [*sub* and *pes,* Latin.] Placed under the feet.

He had slender legs, but encreased by riding after meals; that is, the humour descended upon their pendulosity, they having no support or suppedaneous *stability.* BROWN.

SUPPUTA'TION. *n.s.* [*supputation,* French; *supputo,* Latin.] Reckoning; account; calculation; computation.

From these differing properties of day and year arise difficulties in carrying on and reconciling the supputation *of time in long measures.* HOLDER ON TIME.

The Jews saw every day their Messiah still farther removed from them; that the promises of their doctors, about his speedy manifestations, were false; that the predictions of the prophets, whom they could now no longer understand, were covered with obscurity; that all the supputations *of time either terminated in Jesus Christ, or were without a period.* WEST.

To **SUPPU'TE.** *v.a.* [from *supputo*, Latin.] To reckon; to calculate.

To **SURBA'TE.** *v.a.* [*solbatir*, French.] To bruise and batter the feet with travel; to harrass; to fatigue.

Their march they continued all that night, the horsemen often alighting, that the foot might ride, and others taking many of them behind them; however they could not but be extremely weary and surbated. CLARENDON.

Chalky land surbates *and spoils oxens feet.* MORTIMER.

SU'RCOAT. *n.s.* [*surcot*, old French; *sur* and *coat*.] A short coat worn over the rest of the dress.

The honourable habiliments, as robes of state, parliament-robes, the surcoat, *and mantle.* CAMDEN.

The commons were besotted in excess of apparel, in wide surcoats *reaching to their loins.* CAMDEN.

That day in equal arms they fought for fame;
Their swords, their shields, their surcoats *were the same.* DRYDEN.

SU'RELY. *adv.* [from *sure*.]

1. Certainly; undoubtedly; without doubt. It is often used rather to intend and strengthen the meaning of the sentence, than with any distinct and explicable meaning.

In the day that thou eatest thereof thou shalt surely *die.* BIBLE GENESIS.

Thou surely *hadst not come sole fugitive.* MILTON.

He that created something out of nothing, surely *can raise great things out of small.* SOUTH.

The curious have thought the most minute affairs of Rome worth notice; and surely *the consideration of their wealth is at least of as great importance as grammatical criticisms.* ARBUTHNOT.

2. Firmly; without hazard.

He that walketh righteously, walketh surely.

SU'RFEIT. *n.s.* [from the verb.] Sickness or satiety caused by overfulness.

When we are sick in fortune, often the surfeits *of our own behaviour, we make guilty of our disasters the sun, the moon and stars.* SHAKESPEARE'S KING LEAR.

How ill white hairs become a fool and jester!
I have long dream'd of such a kind of man,
So surfeit *swell'd, so old, and so profane.* SHAKESPEARE'S HENRY IV.

Now comes the sick hour that his surfeit *made;*
Now shall he try his friends that flatter'd him. SHAKESPEARE'S RICHARD II.

Thou'st years upon thee, and thou art too full
Of the wars surfeits *to go rove with one*
That's yet unbruis'd. SHAKESPEARE'S CORIOLANUS.

Why, disease, do'st thou molest
Ladies, and of them the best?
Do not men grow sick of rites,
To thy altars, by their nights
Spent in surfeits? BEN JONSON.

Surfeits *many times turn to purges, both upwards and downwards.* BACON'S NATURAL HISTORY.

Peace, which he lov'd in life, did lend
Her hand to bring him to his end;
When age and death call'd for the score,
No surfeits *were to reckon for.* CRASHAW.

Our father
Has ta'en himself a surfeit *of the world,*
And cries, it is not safe that we should taste it. OTWAY.

SU'RFEITWATER. *n.s.* [*surfeit* and *water*.] Water that cures surfeits.

A little cold-distilled poppywater, which is the true surfeitwater, *with ease and abstinence, often ends distempers in the beginning.* LOCKE.

SU'RGEON. *n.s.* [Corrupted by conversation from *chirurgeon.*][212] One who cures by manual operation; one whose duty is to act in external maladies by the direction of the physician.

The wound was past the cure of a better surgeon *than myself, so as I could but receive some few of her dying words.* SIDNEY.

I meddle with no woman's matters; but withal, I am a surgeon *to old shoes.* SHAKESPEARE'S JULIUS CÆSAR.

He that hath wounded his neighbour, is tied to the expences of the surgeon, *and other incidences.* TAYLOR.

Though most were sorely wounded, none were slain:
The surgeons *soon despoil'd them of their arms,*
And some with salves they cure.
DRYDEN.

SU'RGEONRY, SU'RGERY. *n.s.* [for *chirurgery.*] The act of curing by manual operation.

It would seem very evil surgery *to cut off every unsound part of the body, which, being by other due means recovered, might afterwards do good service.* SPENSER.

But strangely visited people,
The mere despair of surgery, *he cures.*
SHAKESPEARE'S MACBETH.

They are often tarr'd over with the surgery *of our sheep, and would you have us kiss tar?* SHAKESPEARE.

SURPRI'SAL, SURPRISE. *n.s.* [*surprise*, French; from the verb.]

1. The act of taking unawares; the state of being taken unawares.

Parents should mark heedfully the witty excuses of their children, especially at suddains and surprisals; *but rather mark than pamper them.* WOTTON.

This let him know,
Lest, wilfully transgressing, he pretend
Suprisal, *unadmonish'd, unforewarn'd.*
MILTON'S PARADISE LOST.

I set aside the taking of St. Jago and St. Domingo in Hispaniola, as surprizes *rather than encounters.* BACON.

This strange surprisal *put the knight*
And wrathful squire into a fright.
HUDIBRAS.

There is a vast difference between them, as vast as between inadvertency and deliberation, between surprize *and set purpose.* SOUTH.

2. A dish, I suppose, which has nothing in it.

Few care for carving trifles in disguise,
Or that fantastick dish some call surprise.
KING'S COOKERY.

3. Sudden confusion or perplexity.

SURTOU'T. *n.s.* [French.] A large coat worn over all the rest.

The surtout *if abroad you wear,*
Repels the rigour of the air;
Would you be warmer, if at home
You had the fabrick, and the loom?
PRIOR.

Sir Roger she mortally hated, and used to hire fellows to squirt kennel-water upon him, so that he was forced to wear a surtout *of oiled cloth, by which means he came home pretty clean, except where the* surtout *was a little scanty.* ARBUTHNOT.

To **SU'SCITATE.** *v.n.* [*susciter*, French; *suscito*, Lat.] To rouse; to excite.

It concurreth but unto predisposed effects, and only suscitates *those forms whose determinations are seminal, and proceed from the idea of themselves.*
BROWN'S VULGAR ERROURS.

To **SUSPI'RE.** *v.n.* [*suspiro*, Latin.]
1. To sigh; to fetch the breath deep.
2. It seems in *Shakespeare* to mean only, to begin to breath; perhaps mistaken for *respire*.

Since the birth of Cain, the first male child,
To him that did but yesterday suspire,
There was not such a gracious creature born. SHAKESPEARE.

To **SWAG.** *v.n.* [*sigan*, Saxon; *sweigia*, Islandick.] To sink down by its weight; to lay heavy.

They are more apt, in swagging *down, to pierce with their points, than in the jacent posture, and crevice the wall.* WOTTON.

Being a tall fish, and with his sides much compressed, he hath a long fin upon his back, and another answering to it on his belly; by which he is the better kept upright, or from swagging *on his sides.* GREW.

To **SWAGE.** *v.a.* [from *asswage.*] To ease; to soften; to mitigate.

Apt words have pow'r to swage
The tumours of a troubled mind,
And are as balm to fester'd wounds.
MILTON.

Nor wanting pow'r to mitigate and swage,
With solemn touches, troubled thoughts, and chase
Anguish, and doubt, and fear from mortal minds. MILTON.

I will love thee,
Though my distracted senses should forsake me,
I'd find some intervals, when my poor heart
Should swage *itself, and be let loose to thine.* OTWAY.

To **SWALE,** To **SWEAL.** *v.a.* [*swelan*, Saxon, to kindle.] To waste or blaze away; to melt: as, the candle *swales*.

SWA'LLOW. *n.s.* [*swalewe*, Saxon.] A small bird of passage, or, as some say, a bird that lies hid and sleeps in the Winter.

The swallow *follows not Summer more willingly than we your lordship.*
SHAKESPEARE'S TIMON OF ATHENS.

Daffodils,
That come before the swallow *dares.*
SHAKESPEARE.

The swallows *make use of celandine, and the linnet of euphragia.* MORE.

When swallows *fleet soar high and sport in air,*
He told us that the welkin would be clear.
GAY.

The swallow *sweeps*
The slimy pool, to build his hanging house
Intent. THOMSON'S SPRING.

SWA'NSKIN. *n.s.* [*swan* and *skin.*] A kind of soft flannel, imitating for warmth the down of a swan.

SWEET. *n.s.*
1. Sweetness; something pleasing.

Pluck out
The multitudinous tongue, let them not lick
The sweet *which is their poison.*
SHAKESPEARE'S CORIOLANUS.

What softer sounds are these salute the ear,
From the large circle of the hemisphere,
As if the center of all sweets *met here!*
BEN JONSON.

Hail! wedded love,
Perpetual fountain of domestick sweets!
MILTON.

Taught to live
The easiest way; nor with perplexing thoughts
To interrupt the sweet *of life.*
MILTON'S PARADISE LOST.

Now since the Latian and the Trojan brood
Have tasted vengeance, and the sweets *of blood,*
Speak. DRYDEN'S ÆNEID.

Can Ceyx then sustain to leave his wife,
And unconcern'd forsake the sweets *of life?* DRYDEN.

We have so great an abhorrence of pain, that a little of it extinguishes all our pleasures; a little bitter mingled in our cup leaves no relish of the sweet. LOCKE.

Love had ordain'd that it was Abra's turn
To mix the sweets, *and minister the urn.*
PRIOR.

2. A word of endearment.

Sweet! *leave me here a while*
My spirits grow dull, and fain I would beguile
The tedious day with sleep.
SHAKESPEARE.

Wherefore frowns my sweet?
Have I too long been absent from these lips? BEN JONSON.

3. A perfume.

As in perfumes,
'Tis hard to say what scent is uppermost;
Nor this part musick or civet can we call,
Or amber, but a rich result of all:
So she was all a sweet. DRYDEN.

Flowers
Innumerable, by the soft south-west
Open'd, and gather'd by religious hands,
Rebound their sweets *from th' odoriferous pavement.* PRIOR.

To SWELL. *v.n.* Participle pass. *swollen.* [*swellan*, Sax. *swellen*, Dutch.]
1. To grow bigger; to grow turgid; to extend the parts.

Propitious Tyber smooth'd his wat'ry way,
He roll'd his river back, and pois'd he stood,
A gentle swelling *and a peaceful flood.*
DRYDEN'S ÆNEID.

2. To tumify by obstruction.

But strangely visited people,
All swol'n *and ulc'rous; pitiful to the eye,*
The meer despair of surgery he cures.
SHAKESPEARE'S MACBETH.

Forty years didst thou sustain them in the wilderness, so that their cloaths waxed not old, and their feet swelled *not.*
BIBLE NEHEMIAH, IX. 21.

Swol'n *is his breast; his inward pains encrease,*
All means are us'd, and all without success. DRYDEN.

3. To be exasperated.

My pity hath been balm to heal their wounds,
My mildness hath allay'd their swelling *griefs.* SHAKESPEARE.

4. To look big.

Here he comes, swelling *like a turkey-cock.* SHAKESPEARE.

Peleus and Telephus exil'd and poor,
Forget their swelling *and gigantick words.*
ROSCOMMON.

5.[213] To protuberate.

This iniquity shall be as a breach ready to fall, swelling *out in a high wall.*
BIBLE ISAIAH, XXX. 13.

6. To rise into arrogance; to be elated.

In all things else above our humble fate,
Your equal mind yet swells *not into state.*
DRYDEN.

7. To be inflated with anger.

I will help every one from him that swelleth *against him, and will set him at rest.*
BIBLE PSALMS, XII. 6.

We have made peace of enmity
Between these swelling *wrong incensed peers.* SHAKESPEARE.

The hearts of princes kiss obedience,
So much they love it; but to stubborn spirits
They swell *and grow as terrible as storms.*
SHAKESPEARE.

8. To grow upon the view.

O for a muse of fire, that would ascend
The brightest heaven of invention!
A kingdom for a stage, princes to act,
And monarchs to behold the swelling *scene.* SHAKESPEARE.

9. It implies commonly a notion of something wrong.

Your youth admires
The throws and swellings *of a Roman soul,*

Cato's bold flights, th' extravagance of virtue. ADDISON.

Immoderate valour swells *into a fault.* ADDISON'S CATO.

To **SWELL.** *v.a.*

1. To cause to rise or encrease; to make tumid.

Wind, blow the earth into the sea,
Or swell *the curled waters 'bove the main.* SHAKESPEARE.

You who supply the ground with seeds of grain,
And you who swell *those seeds with kindly rain.* DRYDEN.

2. To aggravate; to heighten.

It is low ebb with his accuser, when such peccadillos are put to swell *the charge.* ATTERBURY.

3. To raise to arrogance.

All these miseries proceed from the same natural causes, which have usually attended kingdoms swolen *with long plenty, pride, and excess.* CLARENDON.

To **SWIG.** *v.n.* [*swiga*, Islandick.] To drink by large draughts.

To **SWILL.** *v.a.* [*swilgan*, Saxon.]

1. To drink luxuriously and grossly.

The wretched, bloody, and usurping boar
That spoil'd your summer fields and fruitful vines,
Swills *your warm blood like wash, and makes his trough*
In your embowel'd bosoms.
SHAKESPEARE'S RICHARD III.

The most common of these causes are an hereditary disposition, swilling *down great quantities of cold watery liquors.* ARBUTHNOT ON DIET.

Such is the poet, fresh in pay,
The third night's profits of his play;
His morning draughts till noon can swill,
Among his brethren of the quill. SWIFT.

2. To wash; to drench.

As fearfully as doth a galled rock
O'erhang and jutty his confounded base,
Swill'd *with me the wild and wasteful ocean.* SHAKESPEARE.

With that a German oft has swill'd *his throat,*
Deluded, that imperial Rhine bestow'd
The generous rummer. PHILIPS.

3. To inebriate.[214]

I should be loth
To meet the rudeness and swill'd *insolence*
Of such late wassailers. MILTON.

He drinks a swilling *draught; and lin'd within,*
Will supple in the bath his outward skin.
DRYDEN.

SWILL. *n.s.* [from the verb.] Drink, luxuriously poured down.

Give swine such swill *as you have.* MORTIMER.

Thus as they swim, in mutual swill *the talk*
Reels fast from theme to theme.
THOMSON.

SWILLER. *n.s.* [from *swill.*] A luxurious drinker.

To **SWI'NGLE.** *v.n.* [from *swing.*]

1. To dangle; to wave hanging.
2. To swing in pleasure.

SWO'RDLAW. *n.s.* Violence; the law by which all is yielded to the stronger.

So violence
Proceeded, and oppression, and swordlaw,
Through all the plain, and refuge none was found.
MILTON.

SWO'RDMAN. *n.s.* [*sword* and *man.*] Soldier; fighting man.

Worthy fellows, and like to prove most sinewy swordmen.
SHAKESPEARE'S ALL'S WELL THAT ENDS WELL.

At Lecca's house,
Among your swordmen, *where so many associates*

Both of thy mischief and thy madness met. BEN JONSON.

Essex was made lieutenant-general of the army, the darling of the swordmen. CLARENDON.

SWO'RDPLAYER. *n.s.* [*sword* and *play.*] Gladiator; fencer; one who exhibits in publick his skill at the weapons by fighting prizes.

These they called swordplayers, *and this spectacle a swordfight.* HAKEWILL ON PROVIDENCE.

SYB. *adj.* [Properly *sib*; *sib*, Saxon.] Related by blood. The Scottish dialect still retains it.

If what my grandsire to me said be true,
Siker I am very syb *to you.*
SPENSER'S PASTORALS.

SY'CAMINE, SYCAMORE. *n.s.* A tree.[215]

Sycamore *is our acer majus, one of the kinds of maples: it is a quick grower.* MORTIMER'S HUSBANDRY.

Under the grove of sycamore
I saw your son.
SHAKESPEARE'S ROMEO AND JULIET.

If ye had faith as a grain of mustard-seed, ye might say unto this sycamine-*tree, be thou plucked up, and it should obey you.* BIBLE LUKE, XVII. 6.

I was no prophet, but an herdman, and a gatherer of sycamore *fruit.* BIBLE AMOS, VII. 14.

Go to yonder sycamore-*tree, and hide your bottle of drink under its hollow root.* WALTON'S ANGLER.

Sycamores *with eglantine were spread;*
A hedge about the sides, a covering over head. DRYDEN.

SY'LLABLE. *n.s.* [*συλλαβή*; *syllabe*, French.]

1. As much of a word as is uttered by the help of one vowel, or one articulation.

I heard
Each syllable *that breath made up between them.* SHAKESPEARE.

There is that property in all letters of aptness to be conjoined in syllables *and words, through the voluble motions of the organs from one stop or figure to another, that they modify and discriminate the voice without appearing to discontinue it.* HOLDER'S ELEMENTS OF SPEECH.

2. Any thing proverbially concise.

Abraham, Job, and the rest that lived before any syllable *of the law of God was written, did they not sin as much as we do in every action not commanded?* HOOKER.

To-morrow, and to-morrow, and to-morrow,
Creeps in this petty pace from day to day,
To the last syllable *of recorded time;*
And all our yesterdays have lighted fools
The way to dusty death.
SHAKESPEARE'S MACBETH.

He hath told so many melancholy stories, without one syllable *of truth, that he hath blunted the edge of my fears.* SWIFT.

SY'MBOL. *n.s.* [*symbole*, French; *σύμβολον*; *symbolum*, Latin.]

1. An abstract; a compendium; a comprehensive form.

Beginning with the symbol *of our faith, upon that the author of the gloss enquires into the nature of faith.* BAKER.

2. A type; that which comprehends in its figure a representation of something else.

Salt, as incorruptible, was the symbol *of friendship; which, if it casually fell, was accounted ominous, and their amity of no duration.* BROWN'S VULGAR ERROURS.

Words are the signs and symbols *of things; and as, in accounts, ciphers and figures pass for real sums, so words and names pass for things themselves.* SOUTH'S SERMONS.

The heathens made choice of these lights as apt symbols *of eternity, because, contrary*

to all sublunary beings, though they seem to perish every night, they renew themselves every morning.
ADDISON ON ANCIENT MEDALS.

SYMPHO'NIOUS. *adj.* [from *symphony.*] Harmonious; agreeing in sound.

Up he rode,
Follow'd with acclamation and the sound
Symphonious *of ten thousand harps, that tun'd*
Angelick harmonies. MILTON.

SY'MPHONY. *n.s.* [*symphonie*, French; *σύν* and *φωνή.*] Concert of instruments; harmony of mingled sounds.

A learned searcher from Pythagoras's school, where it was a maxim that the images of all things are latent in numbers, determines the comeliest proportion between breadths and heights, reducing symmetry to symphony, *and the harmony of sound to a kind of harmony in sight.* WOTTON.

Speak ye who best can tell, ye sons of light,
Angels! for ye behold him, and with songs
And choral symphonies, *day without night,*
Circle his throne rejoicing.
MILTON'S PARADISE LOST.

The trumpets sound,
And warlike symphony *is heard around;*
The marching troops through Athens take their way;
The great earl-marshal orders their array.
DRYDEN.

SYMPO'SIACK. *adj.* [*symposiaque*, French; *συμποσιακός.*] Relating to merry makings; happening where company is drinking together.

By desiring a secrecy to words spoke under the rose, we only mean in society and compotation, from the ancient custom of symposiack *meetings to wear chaplets of roses about their heads.*
BROWN'S VULGAR ERROURS.

In some of those symposiack *disputations amongst my acquaintance, I affirmed that the dietetick part of medicine depended upon scientifick principles.* ARBUTHNOT.

SY'NCOPE. *n.s.* [*syncope*, French; *συγκοπή.*]

1. Fainting fit.

The symptoms attending gunshot wounds are pain, fever, delirium, and syncope.
WISEMAN.

2. Contraction of a word by cutting off part.

SY'NCOPIST. *n.s.* [from *syncope.*] Contractor of words.

To outshine all the modern syncopists, *and thoroughly content my English readers, I intend to publish a Spectator that shall not have a single vowel in it.* SPECTATOR.

SY'NDROME. *n.s.* [*συνδρομή.*] Concurrent action; concurrence.

All things being linked together by an uninterrupted chain of causes, every single motion owns a dependance on such a syndrome *of prerequired motors.*
GLANVILLE'S SCEPSIS SCIENTIFICA.

SYNO'NYMA. *n.s.* [Latin; *συνώνυμος.*] Names which signify the same thing.

To **SYNO'NOMISE.** *v.a.* [from *synonyma.*] To express the same thing in different words.

This word fortis we may synonymise *after all these fashions, stout, hardy, valiant, doughty, couragious, adventurous, brave, bold, daring, intrepid.*
CAMDEN'S REMAINS.

SYNONYMO'US. *adj.* [*synonyme*, Fr. *συνώνυμος.*] Expressing the same thing by different words.

These words consist of two propositions which are not distinct in sense, but one and the same thing variously expressed; for wisdom and understanding are synonymous *words here.* TILLOTSON.

Fortune is but a synonymous *word for nature and necessity.*
BENTLEY'S SERMONS.

When two or more words signify the same thing, as wave and billow, mead and meadow, they are usually called synonymous *words.* WATTS'S LOGICK.

SYNO'NYMY. *n.s.* [*συνωνυμία.*] The quality of expressing by different words the same thing.

SYNTA'CTICAL. *adj.* [from *syntaxis*, Latin.]

1. Conjoined; fitted to each other.

2. Relating to the construction of speech.

SY'NTAX, SYNTAXIS. *n.s.* [*σύνταξις.*]

1. A system; a number of things joined together.

They owe no other dependance to the first than what is common to the whole syntax *of beings.* GLANVILLE.

2. That part of Grammar which teaches the construction of words.

I can produce a hundred instances to convince any reasonable man that they do not so much as understand common Grammar and syntax. SWIFT.

T

A consonant, which, at the beginning and end of words, has always the same sound nearly approaching to the *d*; but before an *i*, when followed by a vowel, has the sound of an obscure *s*: as, *nation*, *salvation*, except when *s* precedes *t*: as, *Christian*, *question*.

TA'BBY. *n.s.* [*tabi*, *tabino*, Italian; *tabis*, French.] A kind of waved silk.

> *Brocades, and* tabies, *and gauses.* SWIFT.

TA'BBY. *adj.* Brinded; brindled; varied with different colours.

> *A* tabby *cat sat in the chimney-corner.* ADDISON.
>
> *On her* tabby *rival's face,*
> *She deep will mark her new disgrace.*
> PRIOR.

TABEFA'CTION. *n.s.* [*tabefacio*, Latin.] The act of wasting away.

TA'BLEBEER. *n.s.* [*table* and *beer.*] Beer used at victuals; small beer.

TA'BLEMAN. *n.s.* A man at draughts.

> *In clericals the keys are lined, and in colleges they use to line the* tablemen. BACON'S NATURAL HISTORY.

TA'BLETALK. *n.s.* [*table* and *talk.*] Conversation at meals or entertainments; table discourse.

> *Let me praise you while I have a stomach.*
> *—— No, let it serve for* tabletalk.
> SHAKESPEARE'S MERCHANT OF VENICE.
>
> *His fate makes* tabletalk, *divulg'd with scorn,*
> *And he a jest into his grave is born.*
> DRYDEN'S JUVENAL.
>
> *He improves by the* tabletalk, *and repeats in the kitchen what he learns in the parlour.* GUARDIAN, NO. 165.
>
> *No fair adversary would urge loose* tabletalk *in controversy, and build serious inferences upon what was spoken but in jest.* ATTERBURY.

TA'BLET. *n.s.* [from *table.*]

1. A small level surface.

2. A medicine in a square form.

> *It hath been anciently in use to wear* tablets *of arsenick, or preservatives, against*

the plague; as they draw the venom to them from the spirits. BACON.

3. A surface written on or painted.

It was by the authority of Alexander, that through all Greece the young gentlemen learned, before all other things, to design upon tablets *of boxen wood.* DRYDEN.

The pillar'd marble, and the tablet *brass,*
Mould'ring, drop the victor's praise.
PRIOR.

To **TALK.** *v.n.* [*taelen*, Dutch.]

1. To speak in conversation; to speak fluently and familiarly; not in set speeches; to converse.

I will buy with you, sell with you, talk *with you; but I will not eat with you.* SHAKESPEARE.

Now is this vice's dagger become a squire, and talks *as familiarly of John of Gaunt as if he had been sworn brother to him; and he never saw him but once.* SHAKESPEARE'S HENRY IV.

The princes refrained talking*, and laid their hand on their mouth.* BIBLE JOB, XXIX. 9.

The children of thy people still talk *against thee.* BIBLE EZEKIEL.

If I talk *much, they shall lay their hands upon their mouth.* BIBLE WISDOM, VIII. 12.

Here free from court-compliances he walks,
And with himself, his best adviser, talks.
WALLER.

As God remembers that we are but flesh, unable to bear the nearer approaches of divinity, and so talks *with us as once with Moses through a cloud; so he forgets not that he breathed into us breath of life, a vital active spirit.* DECAY OF PIETY.

Mention the king of Spain, he talks *very notably; but if you go out of the Gazette you drop him.* ADDISON.

2. To prattle; to speak impertinently.

Hypocrites austerely talk
Of purity. MILTON.

My heedless tongue has talk'd *away this life.* ROWE.

3. To give account.

The crystalline sphere, whose balance weighs
The trepidation talk'd. MILTON.

The natural histories of Switzerland talk *much of the fall of these rocks, and the great damage done.* ADDISON.

We will consider whether Adam had any such heir as our author talks *of.* LOCKE.

4. To speak; to reason; to confer.

Let me talk *with thee of thy judgments.* BIBLE JEREMIAH, XII. 1.

Will ye speak wickedly for God, and talk *deceitfully for him?* BIBLE JOB, XIII. 7.

It is difficult task to talk *to the purpose, and to put life and perspicuity into our discourses.* COLLIER ON PRIDE.

Talking *over the things which you have read with your companions fixes them upon the mind.* WATTS.

TAME. *adj.* [*tame*, Saxon; *taem*, Dutch; *tam*, Danish.]

1. Not wild; domestick.

Thales the Milesian said, That of all wild beasts a tyrant is the worst, and of all tame *beasts a flatterer.* ADDISON.

2. Crushed; subdued; depressed; dejected; spiritless; heartless.

If you should need a pin,
You could not with more tame *a tongue desire it.* SHAKESPEARE.

And now their pride and mettle is asleep,
Their courage with hard labour tame *and dull.* SHAKESPEARE.

A most poor man made tame *to fortune's blows,*
Who by the art of known and feeling sorrows,
Am pregnant to good pity.
SHAKESPEARE'S KING LEAR.

Praise him each savage furious beast,
That on his stores do daily feast;

And you tame *slaves of the laborious plough,*
Your weary knees to your Creator bow.
ROSCOMMON.

3. Spiritless; unanimated: as, a *tame* poem. A low phrase.

TA'NKARD. *n.s.* [*tanquaerd*, French; *tankaerd*, Dutch; *tancaird*, Irish.] A large vessel with a cover, for strong drink.

Hath his tankard *touch'd your brain?*
Sure they're fall'n asleep again.
BEN JONSON.

Marius was the first who drank out of a silver tankard, *after the manner of Bacchus.* ARBUTHNOT ON COINS.

When any calls for ale, fill the largest tankard *cup top full.* SWIFT.

TA'NTIVY. *adv.* [from the note of a hunting horn, so expressed in articulate sounds; from *tantâ vi*, says *Skinner*.] To ride *tantivy* is to ride with great speed.

TA'PER. *n.s.* [*taper*, Saxon.] A wax candle; a light.

Get me a taper *in my study, Lucius:*
When it is lighted come and call me.
SHAKESPEARE.

My daughter and little son we'll dress
With rounds of waxen tapers *on their heads,*
And rattles in their hands.
SHAKESPEARE.

If any snatch the pure taper *from my hand, and hold it to the devil, he will only burn his own fingers, but shall not rob me of the reward of my good intention.* TAYLOR.

There the fair light,
Like hero's taper *in the window plac'd,*
Such fate from the malignant air did find,
As that exposed to the boist'rous wind.
WALLER.

To see this fleet
Heav'n, as if there wanted lights above,
For tapers *made two glaring comets rise.*
DRYDEN.

TA'PSTER. *n.s.* [from *tap*.] One whose business is to draw beer in an alehouse.

The oath of a lover is no stronger than the word of a tapster; *they are both the confirmers of false reckonings.* SHAKESPEARE.

Though you change your place, you need not change your trade: I'll be your tapster *still.* SHAKESPEARE.

The world is come now to that pass, that the vintner and tapster *may broach what religion they please; and the apothecary may mingle her as he pleases.* HOWEL.

Though the painting grows decay'd,
The house will never lose its trade;
Nay, though the treacherous tapster *Thomas*
Hangs a new angel two doors from us,
In hopes that strangers may mistake it.
SWIFT.

TARANTULA. *n.s.* [Italian; *tarentule*, French.] An insect whose bite is only cured by musick.

This word, lover, did no less pierce poor Pyrocles than the right tune of musick toucheth him that is sick of the tarantula. SIDNEY.

He that uses the word tarantula, *without having any idea of what it stands for, means nothing at all by it.* LOCKE.

TA'RDITY. *n.s.* [*tarditas* from *tardus*, Latin; *tardiveté*, Fr.] Slowness; want of velocity.

Suppose there may be some observable tardity *in the motion of light, and then ask how we should arrive to perceive it?* DIGBY.

Our explication includes time in the notions of velocity and tardity. DIGBY ON THE SOUL.

TA'RDINESS.[216] *n.s.* [from *tardy*.] Slowness; sluggishness; unwillingness to action or motion.

A tardiness in *nature,*
Which often leaves the history unspoke,
That it intends to do.
SHAKESPEARE'S KING LEAR.

TARPA'WLING. *n.s.* [from *tar.*]

1. Hempen cloath smeered with tar.

Some the gall'd ropes with dauby marling bind,
Or searcloth masts with strong tarpawling *coats.* DRYDEN.

2. A sailor in contempt.

Was any thing wanting to the extravagance of this age, but the making a living tarpawlin *and a swabber the hero of a tragedy.* DENNIS.

TA'SKER, TASKMASTER. *n.s.* [*task* and *master.*] One who imposes tasks.

All is, if I have grace to use it so,
As ever in my great taskmaster's *eye.*
MILTON.

The service of sin is perfect slavery; and he who will pay obedience to the commands of it, shall find it an unreasonable taskmaster, *and an unmeasurable exactor.* SOUTH.

Hear, ye sullen powers below;
Hear, ye taskers *of the dead.*
DRYDEN AND LEE.

To **TASTE.** *v.a.* [*taster,* to try, French.]

1. To perceive and distinguish by the palate.

The ruler of the feast tasted *the water made wine.* BIBLE JOHN, II.

2. To try by the mouth; to eat at least in a small quantity.

Bold deed to taste *it under ban to touch.*
MILTON.

3. To essay first.

Roscetes was seldom permitted to eat any other meat but such as the prince before tasted *of.* KNOLLES.

Thou and I marching before our troops May taste *fate to them, mow them out a passage.* DRYDEN.

4.[217] To feel; to have perception of.

He should taste *death for every man.*
BIBLE HEBREWS, II. 9.

To **TASTE.** *v.n.*

1. To try by the mouth to eat.

Of this tree we may not taste *nor touch.*
MILTON.

2. To have a smack; to produce on the palate a particular sensation.

When the mouth is out of taste, *it maketh things* taste *bitter and loathsome, but never sweet.* BACON'S NATURAL HISTORY.

When kine feed upon wild garlick, their milk tasteth *of it.* BACON.

If your butter tastes *of brass, it is your master's fault, who will not allow a silver saucepan.* SWIFT.

3. To distinguish intellectually.

Scholars when good sense describing,
Call it tasting *and imbibing.* SWIFT.

4. To relish intellectually; to approve.

Thou, Adam, wilt taste *no pleasure.*
MILTON.

5. To be tinctured, or receive some quality or character.

Ev'ry idle, nice, and wanton reason
Shall, to the king, taste *of this action.*
SHAKESPEARE.

6. To try the relish of any thing.

The body's life with meats and air is fed,
Therefore the soul doth use the tasting pow'r
In veins, which through the tongue and palate spread,
Distinguish ev'ry relish sweet and sour.
DAVIES.

7. To have perception of.

Cowards die many times before their deaths;
The valiant never taste *of death but once.*
SHAKESPEARE.

The tasting *of death touched the righteous*

also, and there was a destruction of the multitude in the wilderness. WISDOM.

8. To take enjoyment.

What hither brought us? not hope here to
taste
Of pleasure. MILTON.

Of nature's bounty men forbore to taste,
And the best portion of the earth lay
waste. WALLER.

9. To enjoy sparingly.

This fiery game your active youth
maintain'd,
Not yet by years extinguish'd, though
restrain'd;
You season still with sports your serious
hours,
For age but tastes *of pleasures, youth*
devours. DRYDEN.

TATTERDEMA'LION. *n.s.* [*tatter* and I know not what.] A ragged fellow.

As a poor fellow was trudging along in a bitter cold morning with never a rag, a spark that was warm clad called to this tatterdemalion, *how he could endure this weather?* L'ESTRANGE.

TA'VERNER, TAVERN-KEEPER, TA'VERNMAN. *n.s.* [from *tavern man* or *keep*; *tabernarius*, Latin; *tavernier*, French.] One who keeps a tavern.

After local names, the most in number have been derived from occupations; as tailor, archer, taverner. CAMDEN.

TAURICO'RNOUS. *adj.* [*taurus* and *cornu*, Latin.] Having horns like a bull.

Their descriptions must be relative, or the tauricornous *picture of the one the same with the other.* BROWN.

TEA. *n.s.* [a word, I suppose, Chinese; *thé*, Fr.] A Chinese plant, of which the infusion has lately been much drunk in Europe.

The muses friend, tea, *does our fancy aid,*
Repress those vapours which the head
invade. WALLER.

One has a design of keeping an open tea *table.* ADDISON.

I have filled a tea *pot, and received a dish of it.* ADDISON.

He swept down a dozen tea *dishes.* SPECTATOR.

Nor will you encourage the common tea *table talk.* SPECTATOR.

Green leaves of tea *contain a narcotick juice, which exudes by roasting: this is performed with great care before it is exposed to sale.* ARBUTHNOT ON ALIMENTS.

Here living tea *pot stands; one arm held*
out,
One bent; the handle this, and that the
spout. POPE.

The mistress of the tea *shop may give half an ounce.* SWIFT.

The fear of being thought pedants hath taken many young divines off from their severer studies, which they have exchanged for plays, in order to qualify them for tea *tables.* SWIFT.

When you sweep, never stay to pick up tea *spoons.* SWIFT.

TEAGUE. *n.s.* A name of contempt used for an Irishman.

TE'CHNICAL. *adj.* [τεχνικός; *technique*, Fr.] Belonging to arts; not in common or popular use.

In technical *words, or terms of art, they refrain not from calling the same substance sometimes the sulphur, and sometimes the mercury of a body.* LOCKE.

To **TED.** *v.a.* [*teadan*, Saxon, to prepare.] To lay grass newly mown in rows.

The smell of grain, or tedded *grass or kine,*
Or dairy, each rural sight, each rural
sound. MILTON.

Hay-makers following the mowers, and casting it abroad, they call tedding. MORTIMER'S HUSBANDRY.

Prudent his fall'n heaps
Collecting, cherish'd with the tepid wreaths
Of tedded *grass, and the suns' mellowing beams,*
Rivall'd with artful heats. PHILIPS.

TEENS. *n.s.* [from *teen* for *ten.*] The years reckoned by the termination *teen*; as, thirteen, fourteen.

Our author would excuse these youthful scenes,
Begotten at his entrance, in his teens;
Some childish fancies may approve the toy,
Some like the muse the more for being a boy. GRANVILLE.

To **TEH-HE.** *v.n.* [a cant word made from the sound.] To laugh with a loud and more insolent kind of cachinnation; to titter.

They laugh'd and teh-he'd *with derision,*
To see them take your deposition.
HUDIBRAS, P. III.

TE'MPERATURE. *n.s.* [*temperatura, tempero,* Latin; *temperature,* French.]

1. Constitution of nature; degree of any qualities.

It lieth in the same climate, and is of no other temperature *than Guinea.*
ABBOT'S DESCRIPTION OF THE WORLD.

Birds that change countries at certain seasons, if they come earlier, shew the temperature *of weather.* BACON.

Memory depends upon the consistence and the temperature *of the brain.* WATTS.

2. Mediocrity; due balance of contrarieties.

As the world's sun doth effects beget
Diff'rent, in divers places ev'ry day;
Here Autumn's temperature, *there Summer's heat,*
Here flow'ry Spring-tide, and there Winter gray. DAVIES.

If, instead of this variation of heat, we suppose an equality, or constant temperature *of it before the deluge, the case would be much altered.*
WOODWARD'S NATURAL HISTORY.

3. Moderation; freedom from predominant passion.

In that proud port which her so goodly graceth,
Most goodly temperature *you may descry.*
SPENSER.

TE'MPEST. *n.s.* [*tempeste,* Fr. *tempestas,* Lat.]

1. The utmost violence of the wind; the names by which the wind is called according to the gradual encrease of its force seems to be, a breeze; a gale; a gust; a storm; a tempest.

I have seen tempests, *when the scolding winds*
Have riv'd the knotty oaks.
SHAKESPEARE'S JULIUS CÆSAR.

Some have been driven by tempest *to the south.* ABBOT.

What at first was call'd a gust, the same
Hath now a storm's, anon a tempest's *name.* DONNE.

We, caught in a fiery tempest, *shall be hurl'd*
Each on his rock transfix'd. MILTON.

With clouds and storms
Around thee thrown, tempest *o'er* tempest *roll'd,*
Thou humblest nature with thy northern blast. THOMSON.

2. Any tumult; commotion; perturbation.

The tempest *in my mind*
Doth from my senses take all feeling else,
Save what beats there.
SHAKESPEARE'S KING LEAR.

TEMPESTI'VITY. *n.s.* [*tempestivus,* Lat.] Seasonableness.

Since their dispersion the constitutions of countries admit not such tempestivity *of harvest.* BROWN'S VULGAR ERROURS.

TE'MPLAR. *n.s.* [from the *Temple*, an house near the Thames, anciently belonging to the knights *templars*, originally from the temple of Jerusalem.] A student in the law.

Wits and templars *ev'ry sentence raise,*
And wonder with a foolish face of praise.
POPE'S EPISTLES.

TEMSE BREAD, TEMSED BREAD. *n.s.* [*temsen*, Dutch; *tamiser*, Fr. *tamesare*, Italian, to sift; *tems*, Dutch; *tamis*, French; *tamiso*, Italian, a sieve.] Bread made of flower better sifted than common.

TE'MULENT. *adj.* [*temulentus*, Lat.] Inebriated; intoxicated as with strong liquors.

TE'NSURE. *n.s.* [*tensus*, Lat.] The act of stretching, or state of being stretched; the contrary to laxation or laxity.

This motion upon pressure, and the reciprocal thereof, motion upon tensure, *we call motion of liberty, which is, when any body being forced to a preternatural extent, restoreth itself to the natural.* BACON.

TE'NTER. *n.s.* [*tendo*, *tentus*, Lat.]
1. A hook on which things are stretched.
2. *To be on the* TENTERS. To be on the stretch; to be in difficulties; to be in suspense.

In all my past adventures,
I ne'er was set so on the tenters;
Or taken tardy with dilemma,
That ev'ry way I turn does hem me.
HUDIBRAS, P. II.

TE'NUOUS. *adj.* [*tenuis*, Lat.] Thin; small; minute.

Another way of their attraction is by a tenuous *emanation, or continued effluvium, which after some distance retracteth unto itself.*
BROWN'S VULGAR ERROURS, B. II.

TEPEFA'CTION. *n.s.* [*tepefacio*, Latin.] The act of warming to a small degree.

To **TE'REBRATE.** *v.a.* [*terebro*, Latin.] To bore; to perforate; to pierce.

Consider the threefold effect of Jupiter's trisulk, to burn, discuss, and terebrate.
BROWN'S VULGAR ERROURS, B. II.

Earth-worms are completely adapted to their way of life, for terebrating *the earth, and creeping.* DERHAM.

TE'RRACE. *n.s.* [*terrace*, French; *terraccia*, Italian.] A small mount of earth covered with grass.

He made her gardens not only within the palaces, but upon terrasses *raised with earth over the arched roofs, planted with all sorts of fruits.* TEMPLE.

Fear broke my slumbers, I no longer stay,
But mount the terrace, *thence the town survey.* DRYDEN.[218]

To **TERRE'STRIFY.** *v.a.* [*terrestris* and *facio*, Latin.] To reduce to the state of earth.

Though we should affirm, that heaven were but earth celestified, and earth but heaven terrestrified; *or, that each part above had an influence on its divided affinity below; yet to single out these relations is a work to be effected by revelation.*
BROWN'S VULGAR ERROURS, B. IV.

TE'RRIBLE. *adj.* [*terrible*, Fr. from *terribilis*, Lat.]
1. Dreadful; formidable; causing fear.

Was this a face to be expos'd
In the most terrible *and nimble stroke*
Of quick, cross lightning.
SHAKESPEARE'S KING LEAR.

Fit love for gods
Not terrible, *though terrour be in love.*
MILTON.

Thy native Latium was thy darling care,
Prudent in peace, and terrible *in war.*
PRIOR.

2. Great so as to offend: a colloquial hyperbole.

Being indispos'd by the terrible *coldness of the season, he reposed himself till the weather should mend.* CLARENDON.

I began to be in a terrible *fear of him, and to look upon myself as a dead man.* TILLOTSON.

TERRI'FICK. *adj.* [*terrificus*, Latin.] Dreadful; causing terrour.

The serpent, subtlest beast of all the field,
Of huge extent sometimes, with brazen eyes
And hairy mane terrifick.
MILTON'S PARADISE LOST, B. VII.

The British navy through ocean vast
Shall wave her double cross, t' extremest climes
Terrifick. PHILIPS.

TE'RTIAN. *n.s.* [*tertiana*, Lat.] Is an ague intermitting but one day, so that there are two fits in three days.

Tertians *of a long continuance do most menace this symptom.*
HARVEY ON CONSUMPTIONS.

TE'STER. *n.s.* [*teste*, French, a head: this coin probably being distinguished by the head stamped upon it.]

1. A sixpence.

Come manage me your caliver: hold, there is a tester *for thee.*
SHAKESPEARE'S HENRY IV. P. II.

A crown goes for sixty pence, a shilling for twelve pence, and a tester *for sixpence.* LOCKE.

Those who bore bulwarks on their backs,
And guarded nations from attacks,
Now practise ev'ry pliant gesture,
Op'ning their trunk for ev'ry tester.
SWIFT'S MISCELLANIES.

Young man your days can ne'er be long,
In flow'r of age you perish for a song;
Plums and directors, Shylock and his wife,
Will club their testers *now to take thy life.*
POPE.

2. The cover of a bed.

TETE A TETE. *n.s.* [French.] Cheek by jowl.

Long before the squire and dame
Are tête à tête. PRIOR.

Deluded mortals, whom the great
Chuse for companions tête à tête;
Who at their dinners, en famille,
Get leave to sit whene'er you will.
SWIFT'S MISCELLANIES.

TE'TRICAL, TETRICOUS. *adj.* [*tetricus*, Latin; *tetrique*, Fr.] Froward; perverse; sour.

In this the tetrical *bassa finding him to excel, gave him as a rare gift to Solyman.*
KNOLLES'S HISTORY OF THE TURKS.

To **TEW.** *v.a.* [*tawian*, Saxon.] To work; to beat so as to soften.

To **TE'WTAW.** *v.a.* [formed from *tew* by reduplication.] To beat; to break.

The method and way of watering, pilling, breaking, and tewtawing, *of hemp and flax, is a particular business.* MORTIMER.

TEXT. *n.s.* [*texte*, Fr. *textus*, Lat.]

1. That on which a comment is written.

We expect your next
Shou'd be no comment but a text,
To tell how modern beasts are vext.
WALLER.

2. A sentence of scripture.

In religion
What errour but some sober brow
Will bless it, and approve it with a text.
SHAKESPEARE.

His mind he should fortify with some few texts, *which are home and apposite to his case.* SOUTH'S SERMONS.

TE'XTMAN. *n.s.* [*text* and *man.*] A man ready in quotation of texts.

Mens daily occasions require the doing of a thousand things, which it would puzzle the best textman *readily to bethink himself of a sentence in the Bible, clear enough to satisfy a scrupulous conscience of the lawfulness of.* SANDERSON.

TE'XTUARY. *adj.* [from *text.*]

1. Contained in the text.

He extends the exclusion unto twenty days, which in the textuary *sense is fully accomplished in one.* BROWN.

2. Serving as a text; authoritative.

I see no ground why his reason should be textuary *to ours, or that God intended him an universal headship.* GLANVILLE.

TE'XTUARIST, TEXTUARY. *n.s.* [*textuaire*, Fr. from *text.*] One ready in the text of scripture; a divine well versed in scripture.

THAT. *pronoun.* [*thata*, Gothick; *ðæt*, Saxon; *dat*, Dutch.]

1. Not this, but the other.

He wins me by that *means I told you.* SHAKESPEARE.

Octavia, not only that,
That *were excuseable,* that *and thousands more*
Of semblable import, but he hath wag'd
New wars against Pompey.
SHAKESPEARE.

2. Which; relating to an antecedent thing.

You'll rue the time
That *clogs me with this answer.*
SHAKESPEARE'S MACBETH.

Nothing they but dust can show,
Or bones that *hasten to be so.* COWLEY.

3. Who; relating to an antecedent person.

Saints that *taught and led the way to heav'n.* TICKELL.

4. It sometimes serves to save the repetition of a word or words foregoing.

I'll know your business, that *I will.*
SHAKESPEARE'S HENRY IV.

They said, what is that *to us? see thou to* that. BIBLE MATTHEW.

Ye defraud, and that *your brethren.*
BIBLE 1 CORINTHIANS, VI. 8.

Yet for all that, *when they be in the land of their enemies I will not cast them away.*
BIBLE LEVITICUS, XXVI. 44.

They weep as if they meant
That *way at least proud Nabas to prevent.*
COWLEY.

This runick subject will occur upon that *of poetry.* TEMPLE.

What is inviting in this sort of poetry proceeds not so much from the idea of a country life itself, as from that *of its tranquillity.* POPE.

5. Opposed to this as the other to one.

This is not fair; nor profitable that;
Nor t'other question proper for debate.
DRYDEN'S PERSIUS.

In this scale gold, in t' other fame does lie,
The weight of that *mounts this so high.*
COWLEY.

6. When *this* and *that* relate to foregoing words, *this* is referred like *hic* or *cecy* to the latter, and *that* like *ille* or *cela* to the former.

7. Such as.

By religion is meant a living up to those principles, that *is, to act conformably to our best reason, and to live as becomes those who believe a God and a future state.*
TILLOTSON.

8. That which; what.

Sir, I think the meat wants that *I have.*
—— Basting.
SHAKESPEARE'S COMEDY OF ERROURS.

9. The thing.

The Nazarite hath vowed, besides that *that his hand shall get.*
BIBLE NUMBERS, VI. 21.

He made that *art which was a rage.*
COWLEY.

10. The thing which then was.

Secure proud Nabas slept,
And dreamt, vain man, of that *day's barb'rous sport.* COWLEY.

11. By way of eminence.

This is that *Jonathan, the joy and grace,*
That *Jonathan in whom does mixt remain*
All that fond mothers wish. COWLEY.

Hence love himself, that *tyrant of my*
days. COWLEY.

12. *In* THAT. As being.

Things are preached not in that *they are taught, but* in that *they are published.* HOOKER, B. V.

THAT. *conjunction.*

1. Because.

It is not that *I love you less*
Than when before your feet I lay:
But to prevent the sad increase
Of hopeless love, I keep away. WALLER.

Forgive me that *I thus your patience*
wrong. COWLEY.

2. Noting a consequence.

That *he should dare to do me this disgrace,*
Is fool or coward writ upon my face?
DRYDEN.

The custom and familiarity of these tongues do sometimes so far influence the expressions in these epistles, that *one may observe the force of the Hebrew conjugations.* LOCKE.

3. Noting indication.

We answered, that *we held it so agreeable, as we both forgot dangers past and fears to come,* that *we thought an hour spent with him was worth years of our former life.* BACON'S NEW ATLANTIS.

4. Noting a final end.

Treat it kindly, that *it may*
Wish at least with us to stay. COWLEY.

THE. *article.* [*de*, Dutch.]

1. The article noting a particular thing.

Your son has paid a soldier's debt;
He only liv'd but till he was a man,
The *which no sooner had his prowess*
confirm'd,
In the *unshrinking station where he fought,*
But like a man he dy'd.
SHAKESPEARE'S MACBETH.

He put him in mind of the long pretence he had to be groom of the bed chamber, for the *which he could not chuse but say, that he had the queen's promise.*
CLARENDON, B. VIII.

Unhappy slave, and pupil to a bell,
Unhappy till the *last,* the *kind releasing*
knell. COWLEY.

I'll march the *muses Hannibal.*
COWLEY.

The *fair example of* the *heav'nly lark,*
Thy fellow poet, Cowley, mark;
Above the *stars let thy bold musick sound,*
Thy humble nest build on the *ground.*
COWLEY.

The fruit
Of that forbidden tree, whose mortal taste
Brought death into the *world.* MILTON.

Night shades the *groves, and all in silence*
lie,
All but the *mournful philomel and I.*
POPE.

2. Before a vowel *e* is commonly cut off in verse.

Who had th' *especial engines been to rear*
His fortunes up unto the *state they were.*
DANIEL.

Th' *adorning thee with so much art*
Is but a barb'rous skill,
'Tis like the pois'ning of a dart,
Too apt before to kill. COWLEY.

3. Sometimes *he* is cut off.

In this scale worth, in t'other *gold does*
lie. COWLEY.

4.[219] In the following passage *the* is used according to the French idiom.

As all the considerable governments among the Alps are commonwealths, so it is a constitution the *most adapted of any to the poverty of these countries.*
ADDISON ON ITALY.

THE'ORY. *n.s.* [*theorie*, Fr. *θεωρία*.]
Speculation; not practice; scheme; plan or system yet subsisting only in the mind.

If they had been themselves to execute their own theory *in this church, they would have seen being nearer at hand.* HOOKER, B. V.

In making gold, the means hitherto propounded to effect it are in the practice full of errour, and in the theory *full of unsound imagination.*
BACON'S NATURAL HISTORY, NO. 326.

Practice alone divides the world into virtuous and vicious; but as to the theory *and speculation of virtue and vice, mankind are much the same.*
SOUTH'S SERMONS.

THERAPE'UTICK. *adj.* [θεραπευτκός.] Curative; teaching or endeavouring the cure of diseases.

Therapeutick *or curative physick restoreth the patient into sanity, and taketh away diseases actually affecting.* BROWN.

The practice and therapeutick *is distributed into the conservative, preservative, and curative.* HARVEY.

Medicine is justly distributed into prophylactick, or the art of preserving health; and therapeutick, *or the art of restoring it.*
WATTS.

THERMO'METER. *n.s.* [*thermometre*, Fr. θερμός and μέτρον.] An instrument for measuring the heat of the air, or of any matter.

The greatest heat is about two in the afternoon, when the sun is past the meridian, as is evident from the thermometer, *or observations of the weather-glass.* BROWN.

THE'RMOSCOPE. *n.s.* [*thermoscope*, Fr. θερμός and σκοπέω.] An instrument by which the degrees of heat are discovered; a thermometer.

By the trial of the thermoscope, *fishes have more heat than the element which they swim in.* ARBUTHNOT ON ALIMENTS.

THI'CKSKIN. *n.s.* [*thick* and *skin.*] A coarse gross man; a numskul.

The shallow'st thickskin *of that barren sort,*
Who Pyramus presented in their sport,
Forsook his scene and enter'd in a brake.
SHAKESPEARE.

THIEF-CATCHER, THIEF-LEADER, THIEF-TAKER. *n.s.* [*thief* and *catch, lead, take.*] One whose business is to detect thieves, and bring them to justice.

A wolf passed by as the thief-leaders *were dragging a fox to execution.*
L'ESTRANGE.

My ev'nings all I would with sharpers spend,
And make the thief-catcher *my bosom friend.* BRAMSTON.

THILL. *n.s.* [*ðille*, Saxon, a piece of timber cut.] The shafts of a waggon; the arms of wood between which the last horse is placed.

More easily a waggon may be drawn in rough ways if the fore wheels were as high as the hinder wheels, and if the thills *were fixed under the axis.*
MORTIMER'S HUSBANDRY.

THING. *n.s.* [*ðing*, Saxon; *ding*, Dutch.]

1. Whatever is; not a person. A general word.

Do not you chide; I have a thing *for you.*
—— You have a thing *for me?*
It is a common thing ——
—— Ha?
—— To have a foolish wife.
SHAKESPEARE'S OTHELLO.

The great master he found busy in packing up his things *against his departure.*
KNOLLES'S HISTORY OF THE TURKS.

The remnant of the eat-offering is a thing *most holy.* BIBLE LEVITICUS, II. 3.

Says the master, you devour the same things *that they would have eaten, mice and all.* L'ESTRANGE.

A thing *by neither man or woman priz'd,*
And scarcely known enough to be despis'd.
DRYDEN.

I should blush to own so rude a thing,

As it is to shun the brother of my king. DRYDEN.

Wicked men, who understand any thing *of wisdom, may see the imprudence of worldly and irreligious courses.* TILLOTSON.

2. It is used in contempt.

I have a thing *in prose, begun above twenty-eight years ago, and almost finished: it will make a four shilling volume.* SWIFT.

3. It is used of persons in contempt, or sometimes with pity.

See, sons, what things *you are! how quickly nature*
Falls to revolt, when gold becomes her object?
For this the foolish over-careful fathers
Have broke their sleeps with thought, their brains with care.
SHAKESPEARE'S HENRY IV.

Never any thing *was so unbred as that odious man.* CONGREVE.

The poor thing *sighed, and with a blessing expressed with the utmost vehemence turned from me.* ADDISON.

I'll be this abject thing *no more.*
Love give me back my heart again.
GRANVILLE.

4. It is used by *Shakespeare* once in a sense of honour.

I lov'd the maid I married; never man
Sigh'd truer breath: but that I see thee here,
Thou noble thing*! more dances my wrapt heart.* SHAKESPEARE.

THIS. *pronoun.* [*ðis*, Saxon.]

1. That which is present; what is now mentioned.

Bardolph and Nim had more valour than this, *yet they were both hang'd; and so would* this *be, if he durst steal.* SHAKESPEARE.

Come a little nearer this *ways.* SHAKESPEARE.

Within this *three mile may you see it coming;*
I say a moving grove.
SHAKESPEARE'S MACBETH.

Must I endure all this*?*
SHAKESPEARE'S JULIUS CÆSAR.

This *same shall comfort us concerning our toil.* BIBLE GENESIS, V. 29.

This *is not the place for a large reduction.* HALE.

There is a very great inequality among men as to their internal endowments, and their external conditions, in this *life.* CALAMY'S SERMONS.

2. The next future.

Let not the Lord be angry, and I will speak yet but this *once: peradventure ten shall be found there.* BIBLE GENESIS, XVIII. 32.

3. *This* is used for *this time.*

By this *the vessel half her course had run.* DRYDEN.

4. The last past.

I have not wept this *forty years; but now*
My mother comes afresh into my eyes.
DRYDEN.

5. It is often opposed to *that.*

As when two winds with rival force contend,
This *way and that, the wav'ring sails they bend,*
While freezing Boreas and black Eurus blow,
Now here, now there, the reeling vessel throw. POPE.

According as the small parts of matter are connected together after this *or that determinate manner, a body of* this *or that denomination is produced.* BOYLE.

Do we not often hear of this *or that young heir? are not his riches and his lewdnesses talkt of together?* SOUTH'S SERMONS.

This *way and that the impatient captives tend,*
And pressing for release the mountains rend. DRYDEN.

6. When *this* and *that* respect a former sentence, *this* relates to the latter, *that* to the former member.

Their judgment in this *we may not, and in* that *we need not, follow.* HOOKER.

7. Sometimes it is opposed to *the other.*

Consider the arguments which the author had to write this, *or to design the other, before you arraign him.* DRYDEN.

With endless pain this *man persues*
What, if he gain'd, he could not use:
And t'other fondly hopes to see
What never was, nor e'er shall be.
PRIOR.

THRA'PPLE. *n.s.* The windpipe of any animal. They still retain it in the Scottish dialect.[220]

To **THREAP.** *v.a.* A country word denoting to argue much or contend. *Ainsworth.*

THRE'EPENCE. *n.s.* [*three* and *pence.*] A small silver coin valued at thrice a penny.

A threepence *bow'd would hire me,*
Old as I am to queen it.
SHAKESPEARE'S HENRY VIII.

Laying a caustick, I made an escar the compass of a threepence, *and gave vent to the matter.* WISEMAN'S SURGERY.

THRE'EPENNY. *adj.* [*triobolaris,* Lat.] Vulgar; mean.

THRO'ATPIPE. *n.s.* [*throat* and *pipe.*] The weason; the windpipe.

THRO'TTLE. *n.s.* [from *throat.*] The windpipe.

At the upper extreme it hath no larinx or throttle *to qualify the sound.*
BROWN'S VULGAR ERROURS.

THROUGHLI'GHTED. *adj.* [*through* and *light.*] Lighted on both sides.

That the best pieces be placed where are the fewest lights; therefore not only rooms windowed on both ends, called throughlighted, *but with two or more windows on the same side are enemies to this art.* WOTTON'S ARCHITECTURE.

THROUGHPA'CED. *adj.* [*through* and *pace.*] Perfect; complete.

He is very dextrous in puzzling others, if they be not throughpaced *speculators in those great theories.* MORE.

To **THRYFA'LLOW.** *v.a.* [*thrice* and *fallow.*] To give the third plowing in summer.

Thryfallow *betime for destroying of weed,*
Lest thistle and docke fal a blooming and
seed. TUSSER.

TICK. *n.s.* [This word seems contracted from *ticket*, a tally on which debts are scored.]

1. Score; trust.

If thou hast the heart to try't,
I'll lend thee back thyself awhile,
And once more for that carcase vile
Fight upon tick. HUDIBRAS, P. I.

When the money is got into hands that have bought all that they have need of, whoever needs any thing else must go on tick, *or barter for it.* LOCKE.

You would see him in the kitchen weighing the beef and butter, paying ready money, that the maids might not run a tick *at the market.*
ARBUTHNOT'S HISTORY OF JOHN BULL.

2. [*Tique*, Fr. *teke*, Dutch.] The louse of dogs or sheep.

Would the fountain of your mind were clear again, that I might water an ass at it! I had rather be a tick *in a sheep, than such a valiant ignorance.*
SHAKESPEARE'S TROILUS AND CRESSIDA.

3. The case which holds the feathers of a bed.

To **TI'CKLE.** *v.a.* [*titillo*, Lat.]

1. To affect with a prurient sensation by slight touches.

Dissembling courtesy! How fine this tyrant
Can tickle *where she wounds.*
SHAKESPEARE'S CYMBELINE.

The mind is moved in great vehemency only by tickling *some parts of the body.* BACON.

There is a sweetness in good verse, which tickles *even while it hurts; and no man can be heartily angry with him who pleases him against his will.* DRYDEN.

It is a good thing to laugh at any rate; and if a straw can tickle *a man, it is an instrument of happiness.* DRYDEN.

2. To please by slight gratifications.

Dametas, that of all manners of stile could best conceive of golden eloquence, being withal tickled *by Musidorus's praises, had his brain so turned, that he became slave to that which he that sued to be his servant offered to give him.* SIDNEY.

Expectation tickling *skittish spirits*
Sets all on hazard. SHAKESPEARE.

Such a nature
Tickled *with good success, disdains the shadow*
Which it treads on at noon.
SHAKESPEARE'S CORIOLANUS.

I cannot rule my spleen;
My scorn rebels, and tickles *me within.*
DRYDEN.

Dunce at the best; in streets but scarce allow'd
To tickle, *on thy straw, the stupid crowd.*
DRYDEN.

A drunkard, the habitual thirst after his cups, drives to the tavern, though he has in his view the loss of health, and perhaps of the joys of another life, the least of which is such a good as he confesses is far greater than the tickling *of his palate with a glass of wine.* LOCKE.

To **TI'CKLE.** *v.n.* To feel titillation.

He with secret joy therefore
Did tickle *inwardly in every vein,*
And his false heart, fraught with all treason's store,
Was fill'd with hope, his purpose to obtain. SPENSER.

To **TI'DDLE,** To **TIDDER.** *v.a.* [from *tid.*] To use tenderly; to fondle.

TI'DEWAITER. *n.s.* [*tide* and *wait.*] An officer who watches the landing of goods at the customhouse.

Employments will be in the hands of Englishmen; nothing left for Irishmen but vicarages and tidewaiters *places.* SWIFT.

TIFF. *n.s.* [A low word, I suppose without etymology.]

1. Liquor; drink.

I, whom griping penury surrounds,
And hunger, sure attendant upon want,
With scanty offals, and small acid tiff,
Wretched repast! my meagre corps sustain.
PHILLIPS.

2. A fit of peevishness or sullenness; a pet.

TI'MEFUL. *adj.* [*time* and *full.*] Seasonable; timely; early.

If this arch-politician find in his pupils any remorse, any feeling of God's future judgments, he persuades them that God hath so great need of mens souls, that he will accept them at any time, and upon any condition; interrupting, by his vigilant endeavours, all offer of timeful *return towards God.*
RALEIGH'S HISTORY OF THE WORLD, B. I.

TI'MELESS. *adj.* [from *time.*]

1. Unseasonable; done at an improper time.

Nor fits it to prolong the heav'nly feast
Timeless, *indecent, but retire to rest.*
POPE'S ODYSSEY.

2. Untimely; immature; done before the proper time.

A pack of sorrows, which would press you down,

If unprevented, to your timeless *grave.*
SHAKESPEARE.

Noble Gloster's death,
Who wrought it with the king, and who perform'd
The bloody office of his timeless *end.*
SHAKESPEARE'S RICHARD II.

TI'MEPLEASER. *n.s.* [*time* and *please.*] One who complies with prevailing notions whatever they be.

Scandal, the suppliants for the people, call them
Timepleasers, *flatterers, foes to nobleness.*
SHAKESPEARE.

TIN. *n.s.* [*ten*, Dutch.]
1. One of the primitive metals called by the chemists jupiter.

Quicksilver, lead, iron, and tin, *have opacity or blackness.*
PEACHAM ON BLAZONING.

Tin *ore sometimes holds about one-sixth of* tin. WOODWARD.

2. Thin plates of iron covered with tin.

To **TINK.** *v.n.* [*tinnio*, Latin; *tincian*, Welsh.] To make a sharp shrill noise.

TI'NY. *adj.* [*tint*, *tynd*, Danish.] Little; small; puny. A burlesque word.

Some pigeons, Davy, and any pretty little tiny *kickshaws.*
SHAKESPEARE'S HENRY IV.

When that I was a little tiny *boy,*
A foolish thing was but a toy.
SHAKESPEARE'S TWELFTH NIGHT.

But ah! I fear thy little fancy roves,
On little females and on little loves;
Thy pigmy children, and thy tiny *spouse,*
The baby playthings that adorn thy house.
SWIFT.

TI'REWOMAN. *n.s.* [*tire* and *woman.*] A woman whose business is to make dresses for the head.

Why should they not value themselves for this outside fashionableness of the tire-woman's *making, when their parents have so early instructed them to do so.*
LOCKE ON EDUCATION.

TI'THINGMAN. *n.s.* [*tithing* and *man.*] A petty peace officer; an under-constable.

His hundred is not at his command further than his prince's service; and also every tithingman *may control him.* SPENSER.

TITILLA'TION. *n.s.* [*titillation*, French; *titillatio*, Lat. from *titillate.*]
1. The act of tickling.

Tickling causeth laughter: the cause may be the emission of the spirits, and so of the breath, by a flight from titillation.
BACON.

2. The state of being tickled.

In sweets the acid particles seem so attenuated in the oil as only to produce a small and grateful titillation. ARBUTHNOT.

3. Any slight or petty pleasure.

The delights which result from these nobler entertainments our cool thoughts need not be ashamed of, and which are dogged by no such sad sequels as are the products of those titillations, *that reach no higher than the senses.* GLANVILLE.

TI'TTLE. *n.s.* [I suppose from *tit.*] A small particle; a point; a dot.

In the particular which concerned the church, the Scots would never depart from a tittle. CLARENDON, B. VIII.

Angels themselves disdaining
T' approach thy temple, give thee in command
What to the smallest tittle *thou shalt say*
To thy adorers.
PARADISE REGAIN'D, B. I.

They thought God and themselves linked together in so fast a covenant, that although they never performed their part, God was yet bound to make good every tittle *of his.*
SOUTH'S SERMONS.

Ned Fashion hath been bred about court,

and understands to a tittle *all the punctilios of a drawing-room.* SWIFT.

TI'TTLETATTLE. *n.s.* [A word formed from *tattle* by a ludicrous reduplication.] Idle talk; prattle; empty gabble.

As the foe drew near
With love, and joy, and life and dear,
Our don, who knew this tittletattle,
Did, sure as trumpet, call to battle.
PRIOR.

For every idle tittletattle *that went about, Jack was suspected for the author.*
ARBUTHNOT'S HISTORY OF JOHN BULL.

TOAD. *n.s.* [*taðe*, Saxon.] An animal resembling a frog; but the frog leaps, the toad crawls: the toad is accounted venomous, I believe truly.[221]

From th' extreamest upward of thy head,
To the descent and dust below thy foot,
A most toad-*spotted traitor.*
SHAKESPEARE'S KING LEAR.

I had rather be a toad,
And live upon the vapour of a dungeon,
Than keep a corner in the thing I love
For others use.
SHAKESPEARE'S OTHELLO.

In the great plague there were seen, in divers ditches about London, many toads *that had tails three inches long, whereas* toads *usually have no tails.*
BACON'S NATURAL HISTORY.

In hollow caverns vermin make abode,
The hissing serpent, and the swelling toad.
DRYDEN.

To **TOAST.** *v.a.* [*torreo*, *tostum*, Lat.]
1. To dry or heat at the fire.

Put up thy sword betime,
Or I'll so maul you and your toasting *iron.* SHAKESPEARE.

His breath stinks with eating toasted *cheese.* SHAKESPEARE.

The earth whereof the grass is soon parched with the sun, and toasted, *is commonly forced earth.* BACON'S NATURAL HISTORY.

To allure mice I find no other magick, than to draw out a piece of toasted *cheese.*
BROWN.

2. To name when a health is drunk. *To toast* is used commonly when women are named.

Several popish gentlemen toasted *many loyal healths.* ADDISON.

We'll try the empire you so long have boasted;
And if we are not prais'd, we'll not be toasted. PRIOR.

TOE. *n.s.* [*ta*, Saxon; *teen*, Dutch.] The divided extremities of the feet; the fingers of the feet.

Come all you spirits,
And fill me from the crown to th' toe, *topful*
Of direct cruelty.
SHAKESPEARE'S MACBETH.

Sport that wrinkled care derides,
And laughter holding both his sides;
Come and trip it as you go,
On the light fantastick toe. MILTON.

Last to enjoy her sense of feeling,
A thousand little nerves she sends
Quite to our toes, *and fingers ends.*
PRIOR.

TO'ILET. *n.s.* [*toilette*, Fr.] A dressing table.

The merchant from the exchange returns in peace,
And the long labours of the toilet *cease.*
POPE.

To **TOLE.** *v.a.* [This seems to be some barbarous provincial word.] To train; to draw by degrees.

Whatever you observe him to be more frighted at than he should, tole *him on to by insensible degrees, till at last he masters the difficulty.* LOCKE.

To **TOLL.** *v.a.* [*tollo*, Lat.]
1. To ring a bell.

When any one dies, then by tolling *or*

ringing of a bell the same is known to the searchers. GRAUNT.

2. To take away; to vacate; to annul. A term only used in the civil law: in this sense the *o* is short, in the former long.

An appeal from sentence of excommunication does not suspend it, but then devolves it to a superior judge, and tolls *the presumption in favour of a sentence.* AYLIFFE.

3. To take away.[222] Obsolete.

The adventitious moisture which hangeth loose in a body, betrayeth and tolleth *forth the innate and radical moisture along with it.* BACON'S NATURAL HISTORY, NO. 365.

TO'MBOY. *n.s.* [*Tom* a diminutive of *Thomas*, and *boy*.] A mean fellow; sometimes a wild coarse girl.

A lady
Fasten'd to an empery, to be partner'd
With tomboys, *hir'd with that self-exhibition*
Which your own coffers yield!
SHAKESPEARE'S CYMBELINE.

TONG. *n.s.* [See **TONGS**.] The catch of a buckle. This word is usually written *tongue*, but, as its office is to hold, it has probably the same original with *tongs*, and should therefore have the same orthography.

Their hilts were burnish'd gold, and handle strong
Of mother pearl, and buckled with a golden tong. FAIRY QUEEN.

TONGS. *n.s.* [*tang*, Saxon; *tang*, Dutch.] An instrument by which hold is taken of any thing: as of coals in the fire.

Another did the dying brands repair
With iron tongs, *and sprinkled oft the same*
With liquid waves. FAIRY QUEEN, B. II.

They turn the glowing mass with crooked tongs;
The fiery work proceeds.
DRYDEN'S ÆNEID.

Get a pair of tongs *like a smith's* tongs, *stronger and toothed.*
MORTIMER'S HUSBANDRY.

TONGUE. *n.s.* [*tung*, Saxon; *tonghe*, Dutch.]

1. The instrument of speech in human beings.

My conscience hath a thousand several tongue,
And ev'ry tongue *brings in a sev'ral tale,*
And ev'ry tale condemns me for a villain.
SHAKESPEARE.

Who with the tongue *of angels can relate.*
MILTON.

The terror of thy power or potent tongue.
MILTON.

They are tongue-*valiant, and as bold as Hercules where there's no danger.*
L'ESTRANGE'S FABLES.

My ears still ring with noise, I'm vext to death,
Tongue *kill'd, and have not yet recover'd breath.* DRYDEN.

Tongue-*valiant hero, vaunter of thy might,*
In threats the foremost; but the lag in fight. DRYDEN.

There have been female Pythagoreans, notwithstanding that philosophy consisted in keeping a secret, and the disciple was to hold her tongue *five years together.*
ADDISON'S GUARDIAN.

I should make but a poor pretence to true learning, if I had not clear ideas under the words my tongue *could pronounce.*
WATTS'S IMPROVEMENT OF THE MIND, P. I.

2. The organ by which animals lick.

Hiss for hiss returned with forked tongue
To forked tongue. MILTON.

3. Speech; fluency of words.

Tongue-*doughty giant, how dost thou prove?* MILTON.

Much tongue *and much judgment seldom*

go together; for talking and thinking are two quite differing faculties. L'ESTRANGE.

Parrots, imitating human tongue,
And singing-birds in silver cages hung. DRYDEN.

First in the council-hall to steer the state,
And ever foremost in a tongue *debate.* DRYDEN'S ÆNEID.

Though they have those sounds ready at their tongue's *end, yet there are no determined ideas.* LOCKE.

4.[223] Speech, as well or ill used.

Give me thy hand; I am sorry I beat thee: but, while thou liv'st, keep a good tongue *in thy head.* SHAKESPEARE.

On evil days though fallen and evil tongues. MILTON.

5. A language.

The Lord shall bring a nation against thee, whose tongue *thou shalt not understand.* BIBLE DEUTERONOMY, XXVII. 49.

With wond'rous gifts endu'd,
To speak all tongues *and do all miracles.* MILTON.

An acquaintance with the various tongues *is nothing but a relief against the mischiefs which the building of Babel introduced.* WATTS.

6. Speech as opposed to thoughts.

Let us not love in word, neither in tongue, *but in deed and in truth.* BIBLE 1 JOHN, III. 18.

7. A nation distinguished by their language. A scriptural term.

The Lord shall destroy the tongue *of the Egyptian sea.* BIBLE ISAIAH.

8. A small point: as, *the* tongue *of a balance.*

9. *To hold the* TONGUE. To be silent.

'Tis seldom seen that senators so young
Know when to speak, and when to hold their tongue. DRYDEN.

Whilst I live I must not hold my tongue,
And languish out old age in his displeasure. ADDISON.

TO'NGUEPAD. *n.s.* [*tongue* and *pad.*] A great talker.

She who was a celebrated wit at London is, in that dull part of the world, called a tonguepad. TATLER.

To **TOOT.** *v.n.* [Of this word, in this sense, I know not the derivation: perhaps *totan*, Saxon, contracted from *towetan*, to know or examine.] To pry; to peep; to search narrowly and slily. It is still used in the provinces, otherwise obsolete.

I cast to go a shooting,
Long wand'ring up and down the land,
With bow and bolts on either hand,
For birds and bushes tooting.
SPENSER'S PASTORALS.[224]

TO'OTHDRAWER. *n.s.* [*tooth* and *draw.*] One whose business is to extract painful teeth.

Nature with Scots, as toothdrawers, *hath dealt,*
Who use to string their teeth upon their belt. CLEAVELAND.

When the teeth are to be dislocated, a toothdrawer *is consulted.* WISEMAN'S SURGERY.

TO'PPING. *adj.* [from *top.*] Fine; noble; gallant. A low word.

The topping *fellow I take to be the ancestor of the fine fellow.* TATLER.

TOPSYTU'RVY. *adv.* [This *Skinner* fancies to *top* in *turf.*] With the bottom upward.

All suddenly was turned topsyturvy, *the noble lord eftsoons was blamed, the wretched people pitied, and new counsels plotted.* SPENSER ON IRELAND.

If we without his help can make a head
To push against the kingdom; with his help
We shall o'erturn it topsyturvy *down.*
SHAKESPEARE'S HENRY IV.

God told man what was good, but the devil surnamed it evil, and thereby turned the world topsy-turvy, *and brought a new chaos upon the whole creation.* SOUTH'S SERMONS.

Man is but a topsyturvy *creature; his head where his heels should be, grovelling on the earth.* SWIFT.

TORCH. *n.s.* [*torche*, French; *torcia*, Italian; *intortitium*, low Latin.] A wax light generally supposed to be bigger than a candle.

Basilius knew, by the wasting of the torches, *that the night also was far wasted.* SIDNEY.

Here lies the dusky torch *of Mortimer,*
Choak'd with ambition of the meaner sort. SHAKESPEARE.

They light the nuptial torch, *and bid invoke*
Hymen. MILTON.

Never was known a night of such distraction;
Noise so confus'd and dreadful: torches *gliding*
Like meteors, by each other in the streets.
DRYDEN.

I'm weary of my part;
My torch *is out; and the world stands before me*
Like a black desart at th' approach of night. DRYDEN.

TORE. *v.a.* [Of this word I cannot guess the meaning.][225]

Proportion according to rowen or tore *upon the ground; the more* tore *the less hay will do.* MORTIMER'S HUSBANDRY.

TORREFA'CTION. *n.s.* [*torrefaction*, Fr. *torrefacio*, Latin.] The act of drying by the fire.

When torrefied sulphur makes bodies black, why does torrefaction *make sulphur itself black.* BOYLE ON COLOURS.

If it have not a sufficient insolation it looketh pale; if it be sunned too long it suffereth torrefaction. BROWN.

TO'RSEL. *n.s.* [*torse*, Fr.] Any thing in a twisted form.

When you lay any timber on brickwork, as torsels *for mantle trees to lie on, or lintols over windows, lay them in loam.*
MOXON'S MECHANICAL EXERCISES.

TO'RTUOUS. *adj.* [*tortueux*, Fr. from *tortuosus*, *tortus*, Lat.]

1. Twisted; wreathed; winding.

So vary'd he, and of his tortuous *train*
Curl'd many a wanton wreath. MILTON.

Aqueous vapours, like a dry wind, pass through so long and tortuous *a pipe of lead.* BOYLE.

2. Mischievous. [Thus I explain it, on supposition that it is derived from *tort*, wrong; but it may mean *crooked*: as we say, *crooked* ways for *bad* practices, *crooked* being regularly enough opposite to *right*. This in some copies is *tortious*, and therefore from *tort*.]

Ne ought he car'd whom he endamaged
By tortuous *wrong, or whom bereav'd of right.* FAIRY QUEEN.

TO'RY. *n.s.* [A cant term, derived, I suppose, from an Irish word signifying a savage.] One who adheres to the antient constitution of the state, and the apostolical hierarchy of the church of England, opposed to a *whig*.

The knight is more a tory *in the country than the town, because it more advances his interest.* ADDISON.

To confound his hated coin, all parties and religions join whigs, tories. SWIFT.

TO'UCH-HOLE. *n.s.* [*touch* and *hole*.] The hole through which the fire is conveyed to the powder in the gun.

In a piece of ordnance, if you speak in the touch-hole, *and another lay his ear to the*

mouth of the piece, the sound is far better heard than in the open air.
BACON'S NATURAL HISTORY.

TOUPE'T. *n.s.* [Fr.] A curl; an artificial lock of hair.

Remember second-hand toupees *and repaired ruffles.* SWIFT.

To **TOUSE.** *v.a.* [probably of the same original with *taw, teize, tose.*] To pull; to tear; to haul; to drag: whence *touser* or *towzer*, the name of a mastiff.

As a bear whom angry curs have touz'd,
Having off shak'd them and escap'd their hands,
Becomes more fell, and all that him withstands
Treads down and overthrows. SPENSER.

Take him hence; to th' rack with him: we'll towze *you*
Joint by joint, but we will know his purpose. SHAKESPEARE.

To towze *such things as flutter*
To honest Bounce is bread and butter.
SWIFT.

TO'WARDLINESS. *n.s.* [from *towardly.*] Docility; compliance; readiness to do or to learn.

The beauty and towardliness *of these children moved her brethren to envy.*
RALEIGH'S HISTORY OF THE WORLD.

TO'WEL. *n.s.* [*touaille*, French; *touaglio*, Italian.] A cloath on which the hands are wiped.

His arm must be kept up with a napkin or towel. WISEMAN.

Th' attendants water for their hands supply,
And having wash'd, with silken towels *dry.* DRYDEN'S ÆNEID.

TO'WNTALK. *n.s.* [*town* and *talk.*] Common prattle of a place.

If you tell the secret, in twelve hours it shall be towntalk. L'ESTRANGE.

TRA'GEDY. *n.s.* [*tragedie*, Fr. *tragoedia*, Lat.]

1. A dramatick representation of a serious action.

Thousands more, that yet suspect no peril,
Will now conclude their plotted tragedy.
SHAKESPEARE.

All our tragedies *are of kings and princes; but you never see a poor man have a part unless it be as a chorus, or to fill up the scenes, to dance, or to be derided.*
TAYLOR'S HOLY LIVING.

Imitate the sister of painting, tragedy; *which employs the whole forces of her art in the main action.* DRYDEN.

An anthem to their god Dionysus, whilst the goat stood at his altar to be sacrificed, was called the goat-song or tragedy.
RYMER'S TRAGEDIES OF THE LAST AGE.

There to her heart sad tragedy *addrest*
The dagger, wont to pierce the tyrant's breast. POPE.

2. Any mournful or dreadful event.

I shall laugh at this,
That they, who brought me in my master's hate,
I live to look upon their tragedy.
SHAKESPEARE'S RICHARD III.

I look upon this now done in England as another act of the same tragedy *which was lately begun in Scotland.*
KING CHARLES.

TRAINBA'NDS. *n.s.* [*train* and *band*: I suppose for *trained band.*] The militia; the part of a community trained to martial exercise.

He directed the trainbands *of Westminster and Middlesex, which consisted of the most substantial housholders, to attend.*
CLARENDON.

Give commission
To some bold man, whose loyalty you trust,
And let him raise the trainbands *of the city.* DRYDEN.

A council of war was called, wherein we

agreed to retreat: but before we could give the word, the trainbands, *taking advantage of our delay, fled first.*
ADDISON'S FREEHOLDER.

To **TRAIPSE.** *v.a.* [A low word, I believe, without any etymology.] To walk in a careless or sluttish manner.

Two slip-shod muses traipse *along,*
In lofty madness, meditating song.
POPE.

TRAIT. *n.s.* [*trait*, Fr.] A stroke; a touch. Scarce English.

By this single trait *Homer marks an essential difference between the Iliad and Odyssey; that in the former the people perished by the folly of their kings; in this by their own folly.*
BROOME'S NOTES ON THE ODYSSEY.

TRALATI'TIOUS. *adj.* [from *translatus*, Lat.] Metaphorical; not literal.

TRA'NGRAM. *n.s.* [A cant word.] An odd intricately contrived thing.

What's the meaning of all these trangrams *and gimcracks? what are you going about, jumping over my master's hedges, and running your lines cross his grounds?*
ARBUTHNOT.

To **TRANSCU'R.** *v.n.* [*transcurro*, Lat.] To run or rove to and fro.

By fixing the mind on one object, it doth not spatiate and transcur. BACON.

TRANSFRETA'TION. *n.s.* [*trans* and *fretum*, Latin.] Passage over the sea.

Since the last transfretation *of king Richard the second, the crown of England never sent over numbers of men sufficient to defend the small territory.*
DAVIES ON IRELAND.

TRANSFU'SION. *n.s.* [*transfusion*, Fr. *transfusus*, Lat.] The act of pouring out of one into another.

The crooked part of the pipe was placed in a box, to prevent the loss of the quicksilver that might fall aside in the transfusion *from the vessel into the pipe.* BOYLE.

Poesy is of so subtile a spirit, that in the pouring out of one language into another it will all evaporate; and if a new spirit be not added in the transfusion, *there will remain nothing but a caput mortuum.*
DENHAM.

Something must be lost in all transfusion, *that is, in all translations, but the sense will remain.* DRYDEN.

What noise have we had about transplantation of diseases and transfusion *of blood.*
BAKER'S REFLECTIONS ON LEARNING.

TRANSLA'TION. *n.s.* [*translatio*, Lat. *translation*, Fr.]

1. Removal; act of removing.

His disease was an asthma; the cause a metastasis or translation *of humours from his joints to his lungs.* HARVEY.

Translations *of morbifick matter arise in acute distempers.* ARBUTHNOT.

2. The removal of a bishop to another see.

If part of the people be somewhat in the election, you cannot make them nulls or cyphers in the privation or translation.
BACON'S WAR WITH SPAIN.

The king, the next time the bishop of London came to him, entertained him with this compellation, my lord's grace of Canterbury, you are very welcome; and gave order for all the necessary forms for the translation. CLARENDON.

3. The act of turning into another language; interpretation.

A book of his travels hath been honoured with translation *into many languages.*
BROWN'S VULGAR ERROURS, B. I.

Nor ought a genius less than his that writ,
Attempt translation; *for transplanted wit,*
All the defects of air and soil doth share,
And colder brains like colder climates are.
DENHAM.

4. Something made by translation; version.

Of both translations, *the better I acknowledge that which cometh nearer to the very letter of the very original verity.* HOOKER, B. V.

TRA'NSMIGRANT. *adj.* [*transmigrans*, Lat.] Passing into another country or state.

Besides an union in sovereignty, or a conjunction in pacts, there are other implicit confederations, that of colonies or transmigrants *towards their mother nation.* BACON'S HOLY WAR.

To **TRANSPO'RT.** *v.a.* [*trans* and *porto*, Latin; *transporter*, French.]

1. To convey by carriage from place to place.

I came hither to transport *the tidings.* SHAKESPEARE.

Why should she write to Edmund! might not you
Transport *her purposes by word.* SHAKESPEARE.

Impose upon men the transportation of rivers from one end of the world to the other, which, among other uses, were made to transport *men.* RALEIGH'S HISTORY OF THE WORLD.

A subterranean wind transports *a hill*
Torn from Pilorus. MILTON.

In the disturbances of a state, the wise Pomponius transported *all the remaining wisdom and virtue of his country into the sanctuary of peace and learning.* DRYDEN.

2. To carry into banishment: as a felon.

We return after being transported, *and are ten times greater rogues than before.* SWIFT.

3. To sentence as a felon to banishment.

4. To hurry by violence of passion.

You are transported *by calamity*
Thither where more attends you, and you slander
The helms o' th' state. SHAKESPEARE.

They laugh as if transported *with some fit*
Of passion. MILTON.

I shew him once transported *by the violence of a sudden passion.* DRYDEN.

If an ally not immediately concerned contribute more than the principal party, he ought to have his share in what is conquered; or if his romantick disposition transport *him so far as to expect little or nothing, they should make it up in dignity.* SWIFT.

5. To put into ecstasy; to ravish with pleasure.

Here transported *I behold,* transported *touch.* MILTON.

Those on whom Christ bestowed miraculous cures were so transported *with them, that their gratitude supplanted their obedience.* DECAY OF PIETY.

To **TRAPE.** *v.a.* [commonly written *to traipse*: probably of the same original with *drab.*] To run idly and sluttishly about. It is used only of women.

TRA'PSTICK. *n.s.* [*trap* and *stick.*] A stick with which boys drive a wooden ball.

A foolish swoop between a couple of thick bandy legs and two long trapsticks *that had no calfs.* SPECTATOR, NO. 559.

To **TRA'VAIL.** *v.n.* [*travailler*, Fr.]

1. To labour; to toil.

2. To be in labour; to suffer the pains of childbirth.

I travail *not, nor bring forth children.* BIBLE ISAIAH, XXIII. 4.

She being with child cried, travailing *in birth, and pained to be delivered.* BIBLE REVELATIONS, XII. 2.

His heart is in continual labour; it travails *with the obligation, and is in pangs till it be delivered.* SOUTH'S SERMONS.

To **TRAVEL.** *v.n.* [This word is generally supposed originally the same with *travail*, and to differ only as particular from general: in some writers the word is written alike in all its senses; but it is more convenient to write *travail* for labour, and *travel* for journey.]

1. To make journeys: it is used for sea as well as land, though sometimes we distinguish it from voyage, a word appropriated to the sea.

In the forest shall ye lodge, O ye travelling *companies of Dedanim.*
BIBLE ISAIAH, XXI. 13.

Raphael deign'd to travel *with Tobias.*
MILTON.

Fain wou'd I travel *to some foreign shore,*
So might I to myself myself restore.
DRYDEN.

If others believed he was an Egyptian from his knowledge of their rites, it proves at least that he travelled *there.* POPE.

2. To pass; to go; to move.

By th' clock 'tis day;
And yet dark night strangles the travelling *lamp.* SHAKESPEARE.

Time travels *in divers paces, with divers persons; I'll tell you who time ambles withal, who time trots withal.*
SHAKESPEARE.

Thus flying East and West, and North and South,
News, travell'd *with increase from mouth to mouth.* POPE.

3. To make journeys of curiosity.

Nothing tends so much to enlarge the mind as travelling, *that is, making a visit to other towns, cities, or countries, beside those in which we were born and educated.*
WATTS.

4. To labour; to toil. This should be rather *travail.*

If we labour to maintain truth and reason, let not any think that we travel *about a matter not needful.* HOOKER.

I've watch'd and travell'd *hard;*
Some time I shall sleep out; the rest I'll whistle. SHAKESPEARE.

TRA'VELTAINTED. *adj.* [*travel* and *tainted.*] Harrassed; fatigued with travel.

I have foundered nine score and odd posts: and here, traveltainted *as I am, have, in my pure and immaculate valour, taken Sir John Coleville.*
SHAKESPEARE'S HENRY IV. P. II.

TRA'VESTY. *adj.* [*travesti*, Fr.] Dressed so as to be made ridiculous; burlesqued.

TRAY. *n.s.* [*tray*, Swedish.] A shallow wooden vessel in which meat or fish is carried.

Sift it into a tray, *or bole of wood.*
MOXON'S MECHANICAL EXERCISES.

No more her care shall fill the hollow tray,
To fat the guzzling hogs with floods of whey. GAY.

TRE'ACLE. *n.s.* [*triacle*, Fr. *triackle*, Dutch; *theriaca*, Lat.]

1. A medicine made up of many ingredients.

The physician that has observed the medicinal virtues of treacle, *without knowing the nature of each of the sixty odd ingredients, may cure many patients with it.* BOYLE.

Treacle *water has much of an acid in it.*
FLOYER.

2. Molosses; the spume of sugar.

TREME'NDOUS. *adj.* [*tremendus*, Latin.] Dreadful; horrible; astonishingly terrible.

There stands an altar where the priest celebrates some mysteries sacred and tremendous. TATLER, NO. 57.

In that portal shou'd the chief appear,

Each hand tremendous *with a brazen spear.* POPE'S ODYSSEY.

TRE'NCHER. *n.s.* [from *trench*; *trenchoir*, Fr.]

1. A piece of wood on which meat is cut at table.

No more
I'll scrape trencher, *nor wash dish.*
SHAKESPEARE'S TEMPEST.

My estate deserves an heir more rais'd,
Than one which holds a trencher.
SHAKESPEARE'S TIMON OF ATHENS.

When we find our dogs, we set the dish or trencher *on the ground.*
MORE'S ANTIDOTE AGAINST ATHEISM.

Their homely fare dispatch'd; the hungry band
Invade their trenchers *next, and soon devour.* DRYDEN.

Many a child may have the idea of a square trencher, *or round plate, before he has any idea of infinite.* LOCKE.

2. The table.

How often hast thou,
Fed from my trencher, *kneel'd down at the board,*
When I have feasted.
SHAKESPEARE'S HENRY VI.

3. Food; pleasures of the table.

It could be no ordinary declension of nature that could bring some men, after an ingenuous education, to place their summum bonum upon their trenchers, *and their utmost felicity in wine.*
SOUTH'S SERMONS.

TRE'NCHERFLY. *n.s.* [*trencher* and *fly.*] One that haunts tables; a parasite.

He found all people came to him promiscuously, and he tried which of them were friends, and which only trencherflies *and spungers.* L'ESTRANGE.

TRE'NCHERMATE. *n.s.* [*trencher* and *mate.*] A table companion; a parasite.

Because that judicious learning of the ancient sages doth not in this case serve the turn, these trenchermates *frame to themselves a way more pleasant; a new method they have of turning things that are serious into mockery, an art of contradiction by way of scorn.* HOOKER, B. V.

TRE'NDLE. *n.s.* [*trendel*, Saxon.] Any thing turned round. Now improperly written *trundle.*

TRICE. *n.s.* [I believe this word comes from *trait*, Fr. corrupted by pronunciation.] A short time; an instant; a stroke.

If they get never so great spoil at any time, the same they waste in a trice, *as naturally delighting in spoil, though it do themselves no good.* SPENSER.

Just in the nick the cook knock'd thrice,
And all the waiters in a trice
His summons did obey:
Each serving man with dish in hand,
March'd boldly up like our train'd band,
Presented, and away. SUCKLING.

He could raise scruples dark and nice,
And after solve them in a trice.
HUDIBRAS, P. I.

So when the war had rais'd a storm,
I've seen a snake in human form,
All stain'd with infamy and vice,
Leap from the dunghil in a trice.
SWIFT.

It seems incredible at first, that all the blood in our bodies should circulate in a trice, *in a very few minutes; but it would be more surprising if we knew the short periods of the great circulation of water.*
BENTLEY'S SERMONS.

TRI'CKER. *n.s.* [This is often written *trigger*; I know not which is right.] The catch which being pulled disengages the cock of the gun, that it may give fire.

Pulling aside the tricker *we observed, that*

the force of the spring of the lock was not sensibly abated by the absence of the air. BOYLE.

As a goose
In death contracts his talons close;
So did the knight, and with one claw
The tricker *of his pistol draw.*
HUDIBRAS, P. I.

TRI'CKISH. *adj.* [from *trick.*] Knavishly artful; fraudulently cunning; mischievously subtle.

All he says is in a loose, slippery, and trickish *way of reasoning.* POPE.

TRI'GGER. *n.s.* [derived by *Junius* from *trigue*, Fr. from *intricare*, Lat.]
1. A catch to hold the wheel on steep ground.
2. The catch that being pulled looses the cock of the gun.

The pulling the trigger *of the gun with which the murder is committed, has no natural connection with those ideas that make up the complex one, murder.* LOCKE.

TRI'MMER. *n.s.* [from *trim.*]
1. One who changes sides to balance parties; a turncoat.

The same bat taken after by a weazel begged for mercy: no, says the weazle, no mercy to a mouse: well, says t'other, but you may see by my wings that I am a bird; and so the bat 'scaped in both by playing the trimmer. L'ESTRANGE'S FABLES.

To confound his hated coin,
All parties and religions join,
Whigs, tories, trimmers. SWIFT.

2. A piece of wood inserted.

Before they pin up the frame of ground-plates, they must fit in the summer and the girders, and all the joists and the trimmers *for the stair-case.*
MOXON'S MECHANICAL EXERCISES.

TROCHI'LICKS. *n.s.* [*τροχίλιον*, *τροχός*, a wheel.] The science of rotatory motion.

There succeeded new inventions and horologies, composed by trochilicks, *or the artifice of wheels, whereof some are kept in motion by weight, others without.* BROWN.

It is requisite that we rightly understand some principles in trochilicks, *or the art of wheel instruments; as chiefly the relation betwixt the parts of a wheel and those of a balance, the several proportions in the semidiameter of a wheel being answerable to the sides of a balance.*
WILKINS'S DÆDALUS.

To **TROLL.** *v.a.* [*trollen*, to roll, Dutch; perhaps from *trochlea*, Lat. a thing to turn round.] To move circularly; to drive about.

With the phant'sies of hey troll,
Troll *about the bridal bowl,*
And divide the broad-bread cake,
Round about the bride's stake.
BEN JONSON'S UNDERWOODS.

To **TROLL.** *v.n.*
1. To roll; to run round.

How pleasant on the banks of Styx,
To troll *it in a coach and six.* SWIFT.

2. To fish for a pike with a rod which has a pulley towards the bottom, which I suppose gives occasion to the term.

Nor drain I ponds the golden carp to take,
Nor trowle *for pikes, dispeoplers of the lake.* GAY.

TRO'OPER. *n.s.* [from *troop.*] A horse soldier. A trooper fights only on horseback; a dragoon marches on horseback, but fights either as a horseman or footman.

Custom makes us think well of any thing: what can be more indecent now than for any to wear boots but troopers *and travellers? yet not many years since it was all the fashion.* GREW.

TRO'UBLE-STATE. *n.s.* [*trouble* and *state.*] Disturber of a community; publick makebate.

Those fair baits these trouble-states *still use,*
Pretence of common good, the king's ill course,
Must be cast forth.
DANIEL'S CIVIL WAR.

To **TROUL.** *v.n.* [*trollen*, to roll, Dutch.] See **TROLL.**

1. To move volubly.

Bred only, and completed, to the taste
Of lustful appetence; to sing, to dance,
To dress, and troul *the tongue, and roll the eye.* MILTON.

2. To utter volubly.

Let us be jocund. Will you troul *the catch*
You taught me while-ere.
SHAKESPEARE'S TEMPEST.

TRU'ANT. *n.s.* [*truand*, Old Fr. *treuwant*, Dutch, a vagabond.] An idler; one who wanders idly about, neglecting his duty or employment. To play the *truant* is, in schools, to stay from school without leave.

For my part I may speak it to my shame,
I have a truant *been to chivalry.*
SHAKESPEARE.

Though myself have been an idle truant,
Omitting the sweet benefit of time,
To cloath mine age with angel-like perfection;
Yet hath Sir Protheus made fair advantage of his days.
SHAKESPEARE'S TWO GENTLEMEN OF VERONA.

Providence would only initiate mankind into the knowledge of her treasures, leaving the rest to our industry, that we might not live like idle loiterers and truants.
MORE.

Our ships are laden with the Trojan store,
And you like truants *come too late ashore.*
DRYDEN'S ÆNEID.

To **TRUCK.** *v.a.* To give in exchange; to exchange.

The Indians truck *gold for glasses.*
L'ESTRANGE.

Go, miser! go; for lucre sell thy soul,
Truck *wares for wares, and trudge from pole to pole;*
That men may say, when thou art dead and gone,
See, what a vast estate he left his son.
DRYDEN.

I see nothing left us, but to truck *and barter our goods like the wild Indians, with each other.* SWIFT.

TRUCK. *n.s.* [from the verb.]

1. Exchange; traffick by exchange.

It is no less requisite to maintain a truck *in moral offices, than in the common business of commerce.* L'ESTRANGE.

Love is covetous; I must have all of you: heart for heart is an equal truck.
DRYDEN.

2. [*τϱοχός*] Wooden wheels for carriage of cannon. *Ainsworth.*

TRU'CKLEBED, or *Trundlebed.* *n.s.* [properly *troclebed*; from *trochlea*, Latin, or *τϱοχός*.] A bed that runs on wheels under a higher bed.

There's his chamber, his house, his castle, his standing bed and trucklebed.
SHAKESPEARE'S MERRY WIVES OF WINDSOR.

If he that is in battle slain,
Be in the bed of honour lain;
He that is beaten may be said,
To lie in honour's trucklebed.
HUDIBRAS, P. I.

To **TRU'CKLE.**[226] *v.n.* [This word is, I believe, derived from *trucklebed*, which is always under another bed.] To be in a state of subjection or inferiority; to yield; to creep.

Shall our nation be in bondage thus
Unto a land that truckles *under us.*
CLEAVELAND.

For which so many a legal cuckold

Has been run down in courts and
truckl'd. HUDIBRAS.

Men may be stiff and obstinate upon a wrong ground, and ply and truckle *too upon as false a foundation.* L'ESTRANGE.

Religion itself is forced to truckle *to worldly policy.* NORRIS.

His zeal was not to lash our crimes,
But discontent against the times:
For had we made him timely offers,
To raise his post or fill his coffers:
Perhaps he might have truckled *down,*
Like other brethren of his gown. SWIFT.

They were subdued and insulted by Alexander's captains, and continued under several revolutions, a small truckling *state, of no name till they fell under the Romans.* SWIFT.

To **TRU'NDLE.** *v.n.* [*trondeler*, Picard French; *trendl*, a bowl, Saxon.] To roll; to bowl along.

In the four first it is heaved up by several spondees intermixed with proper breathing places, and at last trundles *down in a continued line of dactyls.* ADDISON'S SPECTATOR, NO. 253.

TU'MBREL. *n.s.* [*tombereau*, French.] A dungcart.

Twifallow once ended, get tumbrel *and man,*
And compass that fallow as soon as ye can. TUSSER'S HUSBANDRY.

My corps is in a tumbril *laid, among*
The filth and ordure, and inclos'd with dung;
That cart arrest, and raise a common cry,
For sacred hunger of my gold I die.
DRYDEN.

What shall I do with this beastly tumbril? *go lie down and sleep, you sot.* CONGREVE.

To convince the present little race how unequal all their measures were to an antediluvian, in respect of the insects which now appear for men, he sometimes rode in an open tumbril. TATLER.

To **TUME'FY.** *v.a.* [*tumefacio*, Lat.] To swell; to make to swell.

I applied three small causticks triangular about the tumified *joint.* WISEMAN'S SURGERY.

A fleshy excrescence, exceeding hard and tumefied, *supposed to demand extirpation.* SHARP'S SURGERY.

TU'MOUR. *n.s.* [*tumor*, Latin.]

1. A morbid swelling.

Tumour *is a disease, in which the parts recede from their natural state by an undue encrease of their bigness.* WISEMAN.

Having dissected this swelling vice, and seen what it is that feeds the tumour, *if the disease be founded in pride, the abating that is the most natural remedy.* GOVERNMENT OF THE TONGUE.

2. Affected pomp; false magnificence; puffy grandeur; swelling mien; unsubstantial greatness.

His stile was rich of phrase, but seldom in bold metaphors; and so far from the tumour, *that it rather wants a little elevation.* WOTTON.

It is not the power of tumour *and bold looks upon the passions of the multitude.* L'ESTRANGE.

TU'MOROUS. *adj.* [from *tumour.*]

1. Swelling; protuberant.

Who ever saw any cypress or pine, small below and above, and tumorous *in the middle, unless some diseased plant.* WOTTON.

2. Fastuous; vainly pompous; falsely magnificent.

According to their subject, these stiles vary; for that which is high and lofty, declaring excellent matter, becomes vast and tumorous, *speaking of petty and inferior things.* BEN JONSON.

His limbs were rather sturdy than dainty,

sublime and almost tumorous *in his looks and gestures.* WOTTON.

TU'NNEL. *n.s.*

1. The shaft of a chimney; the passage for the smoke.

It was a vault ybuilt for great dispence,
With many ranges rear'd along the wall,
And one great chimney, whose long tunnel *thence*
The smoak forth threw. FAIRY QUEEN.

The water being rarified, and by rarification resolved into wind, will force up the smoke, which otherwise might linger in the tunnel, *and oftentimes reverse.* WOTTON'S ARCHITECTURE.

2. A funnel; a pipe by which liquor is poured into vessels.

For the help of the hearing, make an instrument like a tunnel, *the narrow part of the bigness of the hole of the ear, and the broader end much larger.* BACON.

3. A net wide at the mouth, and ending in a point, and so resembling a funnel or tunnel.

TU'RKOIS. *n.s.* [*turquoise*, French, from *turkey*.] A blue stone numbered among the meaner precious stones, now discovered to be a bone impregnated with cupreous particles.

Those bony bodies found among copper-ores are tinged with green or blue: the turcois *stone, as it is commonly stiled by lapidaries, is part of a bone so tinged.* WOODWARD.

TU'RNSICK. *adj.* [*turn* and *sick*.] Vertiginous; giddy.

If a man see another turn swiftly and long; or if he look upon wheels that turn, himself waxeth turnsick. BACON.

TU'RQUOISE. *n.s.* See **TURKOIS.**

One shew'd me a ring, he had of your daughter for a monkey. —— Out upon her! it was my turquoise, *I had it when I was a bachelor.* SHAKESPEARE'S MERCHANT OF VENICE.

TUSH. *interj.* [Of this word I can find no credible etymology.] An expression of contempt.

Tush, *say they, how should God perceive it: is there knowledge in the most high?* BIBLE PSALMS, LXXIII.

Sir Thomas Moor found fault with his lady's continual chiding, saying; the consideration of the time, for it was sent, should restrain her. Tush, tush, *my lord, said she, look, here is one step to heavenward, shewing him a friar's girdle. I fear me, quoth Sir Thomas, this one step will not bring you up a step higher.* CAMDEN'S REMAINS.

Tush *never tell me, I take it much unkindly*
That thou, Iago, who hast had my purse,
As if the strings were thine, should know of this. SHAKESPEARE.

TUT. *interj.* [This seems to be the same with *tush*.] A particle noting contempt.

Tut, tut*! grace me no grace, nor uncle me no uncle.* SHAKESPEARE.

Tut, tut*! here's a mannerly forbearance.* SHAKESPEARE.

TUZ. *n.s.* [I know not whether it is not a word merely of cant.] A lock or tuft of hair.

With odorous oil thy head and hair are sleek;
And then thou kemp'st the tuzzes *on thy cheek;*
Of these thy barbers take a costly care. DRYDEN.

To **TWANG.** *v.n.* [A word formed from the sound.] To sound with a quick sharp noise.

A thousand twanging *instruments*
Will hum about mine ears.
SHAKESPEARE'S TEMPEST.

His quiver o'er his shoulders Phœbus threw,
His bow twang'd, *and his arrows rattled as they flew.* DRYDEN.

With her thund'ring voice she menac'd high;
And every accent twang'd *with smarting sorrow.* DRYDEN.

The twanging *bows*
Send showers of shafts, that on their barbed points
Alternate ruin bear. PHILIPS.

Sounds the tough horn and twangs *the quiv'ring string.* POPE.

To **TWANG.** *v.a.* To make to sound sharply.

A swaggering accent sharply twang'd *off, gives manhood approbation.* SHAKESPEARE'S TWELFTH NIGHT.

To **TWA'TTLE.** *v.n.* [*schwatzen,* German.] To prate; to gabble; to chatter.

It is not for every twattling *gossip to undertake.* L'ESTRANGE.

TWI'STER. *n.s.* [from *twist.*] One who twists; a ropemaker. To this word I have annexed some remarkable lines, which explain twist in all its senses.

When a twister *a-twisting will twist him a twist,*
For the twisting of his twist, he three twines doth intwist;
But if one of the twines of the twist do untwist,
The twine that untwisteth untwisteth the twist.
Untwirling the twine that untwisteth between,
He twirls with his twister *the two in a twine;*
Then twice having twisted the twines of the twine,
He twitcheth the twine he had twined in twain.
The twain that in twining before in the twine,
As twins were intwisted, he now doth untwine,
'Twixt the twain intertwisting a twine more between,
He, twirling his twister, *makes a twist of the twine.* WALLIS.

TWITTLETWA'TTLE. *n.s.* [A ludicrous reduplication of *twattle.*] Tattle; gabble. A vile word.

Insipid twittletwatles, *frothy jests, and jingling witticisms, inure us to a misunderstanding of things.* L'ESTRANGE.

TYMBAL. *n.s.* [*tymbal,* French.] A kind of kettle-drum.

Yet gracious charity! indulgent guest!
Were not thy pow'r exerted in my breast;
My speeches would send up unheeded pray'r:
he scorn of life would be but wild despair:
A tymbal's *sound were better than my voice,*
My faith were form, my eloquence were noise. PRIOR.

TY'MPANY. *n.s.* [from *tympanum,* Lat.] A kind of obstructed flatulence that swells the body like a drum.[227]

Hope, the christian grace, must be proportioned and attemperate to the promise; if it exceed that temper and proportion, it becomes a tumour and tympany *of hope.* HAMMOND.

He does not shew us Rome great suddenly,
As if the empire were a tympany,
But gives it natural growth, tells how and why
The little body grew so large and high. SUCKLING.

Others that affect
A lofty stile, swell to a tympany.
ROSCOMMON.

Pride is no more than an unnatural tympany, *that rises in a bubble, and spends itself in a blast.* L'ESTRANGE.

Nor let thy mountain-belly make pretence
Of likeness; thine's a tympany *of sense.*
A tun of man in thy large bulk is writ,
But sure thou'rt but a kilderkin of wit.
DRYDEN.

The air is so rarified in this kind of dropsical tumour as makes it hard and tight like a drum, and from thence it is called a tympany.
ARBUTHNOT.

TYPO'GRAPHY. *n.s.* [*typographie*, Fr. *typographia*, Lat.]

1. Emblematical, figurative, or hieroglyphical representation.

Those diminutive and pamphlet treatises daily published amongst us, are pieces containing rather typography *than verity.*
BROWN'S VULGAR ERROURS.

2. The art of printing.

TYRO. *n.s.* [Properly *tiro*, as in the Latin.] One yet not master of his art; one in his rudiments.

There stands a structure on a rising hill,
Where tyro's *take their freedom out to kill.* GARTH'S DISPENSATORY.

V

Has two powers, expressed in modern English by two characters, *V* consonant and *U* vowel, which ought to be considered as two letters; but as they were long confounded while the two uses were annexed to one form, the old custom still continues to be followed.

U, the vowel, has two sounds; one clear, expressed at other times by *eu*, as *obtuse*; the other close, and approaching to the Italian *u*, or English *oo*, as *obtund*.

V, the consonant, has a sound nearly approaching to those of *b* and *f*. With *b* it is by the Spaniards and Gascons always confounded, and in the Runick alphabet is expressed by the same character with *f*, distinguished only by a diacritical point. Its sound in English is uniform. It is never mute.

VA'CUIST. *n.s.* [from *vacuum.*] A philosopher that holds a vacuum: opposed to a plenist.

> *Those spaces, which the* vacuists *would have to be empty, because they are manifestly devoid of air, the plenists do not prove replenished with subtle matter.* BOYLE.

VA'CUUM. *n.s.* [Latin.] Space unoccupied by matter.

> *Our enquiries about* vacuum, *or space and atoms, will shew us some good practical lessons.* WATTS.

VAIL. *n.s.* [*voile*, French. This word is now frequently written *veil*, from *velum*, Latin; and the verb *veil*, from the verb *velo*; but the old orthography commonly derived it, I believe rightly, from the French.]

1. A curtain; a cover thrown over any thing to be concealed.

> *While they supposed to lie hid in their secret sins, they were scattered under a dark* vail *of forgetfulness.* WISDOM.

2. A part of female dress, by which the face and part of the shape is concealed.

3. Money given to servants. It is commonly used in the plural. See **VALE.**

VALE. *n.s.* [*val*, Fr. *vallis*, Latin.]

1. A low ground; a valley; a place between two hills. *Vale* is a poetical word.

> *In Ida* vale*: who knows not Ida* vale?
> *An hundred shepherds woned.* SPENSER.

> *Met in the* vale *of Arde.*
> SHAKESPEARE'S HENRY VIII.

> *Anchises, in a flow'ry* vale,
> *Review'd his muster'd race, and took the tale.* DRYDEN.

2. [From *avail*, profit; or *vale*, farewell. If from *avail*, it must be written *vail*, as Dryden writes. If from *vale*, which I think is right, it must be *vale*.] Money given to servants.

Since our knights and senators account
To what their sordid, begging vails *amount;*
Judge what a wretched share the poor attends,
Whose whole subsistence on those alms depends. DRYDEN.

His revenue, besides vales, *amounted to thirty pounds.* SWIFT.

VA'LLANCY. *n.s.* [from *valance*.] A large wig that shades the face.

But you, loud Sirs, who through your curls look big,
Criticks in plume and white vallancy *wig.*
DRYDEN.

VA'LLEY. *n.s.* [*vallée*, Fr. *vallis*, Latin.] A low ground; a hollow between hills.

Live with me, and be my love,
And we will all the pleasure prove,
That hills and vallies *yield.* RALEIGH.

Vallies *are the intervals betwixt mountains.* WOODWARD.

Sweet interchange of hill and valley.
MILTON.

VA'LUE. *n.s.* [*value*, Fr. *valor*, Lat.]

1. Price; worth.

Ye are physicians of no value.
BIBLE JOB, XIII.

2. High rate.

Cæsar is well acquainted with your virtues,
And therefore sets this value *on your life:*
Let him but know the price of Cato's friendship,
And name your terms.
ADDISON'S CATO.

3. Rate; price equal to the worth of the thing bought.

He sent him money; it was with this obliging testimony, that his design was not to pay him the value *of his pictures, because they were above any price.*
DRYDEN.

VALVE. *n.s.* [*valva*, Latin.]

1. A folding door.

Swift through the valves *the visionary fair*
Repass'd. POPE'S ODYSSEY, B. IV.

2. Any thing that opens over the mouth of a vessel.

This air, by the opening of the valve, *and forcing up of the sucker, may be driven out.* BOYLE'S WORKS.

3. [In anatomy.] A kind of membrane, which opens in certain vessels to admit the blood, and shuts to prevent its regress.

The arteries, with a contractile force, drive the blood still forward; it being hindered from going backward by the valves *of the heart.* ARBUTHNOT ON ALIMENTS.

To **VAMP.** *v.a.* [This is supposed probably enough by *Skinner* to be derived from *avant*, Fr. before; and to mean laying on a new outside.] To piece an old thing with some new part.

You wish
To vamp *a body with a dangerous physick,*
That's sure of death without.
SHAKESPEARE'S CORIOLANUS.

This opinion hath been vamped *up by Cardan.* BENTLEY.

I had never much hopes of your vampt *play.* SWIFT.

VA'MPER. *n.s.* [from *vamp*.] One who pieces out an old thing with something new.

VA'PORER. *n.s.* [from *vapour*.] A boaster; a braggart.

This shews these vaporers, *to what scorn they expose themselves.*
GOVERNMENT OF THE TONGUE.

VA'SE. *n.s.* [*vase*, Fr. *vasa*, Latin.] A vessel; generally a vessel rather for show than use.

The toilet stands unveil'd,
Each silver vase *in mystick order laid.*
POPE.

VA'TICIDE. *n.s.* [*vates* and *cædo*, Latin.] A murderer of poets.

The caitiff vaticide *conceiv'd a prayer.*
POPE'S DUNCIAD.

VA'UDEVIL. *n.s.* [*vaudeville*, Fr.] A song common among the vulgar, and sung about the streets, *Trevoux.* A ballad; a trivial strain.

UBI'QUITARY. *adj.* [from *ubique*, Latin.] Existing every where.

For wealth and an ubiquitary *commerce, none can exceed her.* HOWEL.

VE'HICLE. *n.s.* [*vehiculum*, Latin.]

1. That in which any thing is carried.

Evil spirits might very properly appear in vehicles *of flame, to terrify and surprize.* ADDISON'S GUARDIAN.

2. That part of a medicine which serves to make the principal ingredient potable.

That the meat descends by one passage; the drink, or moistening vehicle *by another, is a popular tenent.* BROWN.

3. That by means of which any thing is conveyed.

The gaiety of a diverting word, serves as a vehicle *to convey the force and meaning of a thing.* L'ESTRANGE.

VEIL. *n.s.* [*velum*, Latin.]

1. A cover to conceal the face.

To feed his fiery lustful eye,
He snatch'd the veil *that hung her face before.* FAIRY QUEEN.

The Paphian queen from that fierce battle borne,
With gored hand, and veil *so rudely torn,*
Like terror did among the immortals breed. WALLER.

The famous painter cou'd allow no place
For private sorrow in a prince's face:
Yet, that his piece might not exceed belief,
He cast a veil *upon supposed grief.*
WALLER.

As veils *transparent cover, but not hide,*
Such metaphors appear when right apply'd.
When through the phrase we plainly see the sense,
Truth with such obvious meanings will dispense. GRANVILLE.

She accepts the hero, and the dame
Wraps in her vail, *and frees from sense of shame.* POPE.

2. A cover; a disguise.

I will pluck the borrow'd veil *of modesty from the so seeming Mrs. Page; divulge Page himself for a secure and wilful Acteon.* SHAKESPEARE'S MERRY WIVES OF WINDSOR.

Knock on my heart; for thou hast skill to find
If it sound solid, or be fill'd with wind;
And thro' the veil *of words thou view'st the naked mind.* DRYDEN.

The ill-natured man exposes those failings in human nature, which the other would cast a veil *over.* ADDISON.

VELLICA'TION. *n.s.* [*vellicatio*, Lat.] Twitching; stimulation.

All purgers have a kind of twitching and vellication, *besides the griping, which cometh of wind.* BACON.

There must be a particular motion and vellication *imprest upon the nerves, else the sensation of heat will not be produced.*
WATTS'S IMPROVEMENT OF THE MIND.

To **VEND.** *v.a.* [*vendre*, Fr. *vendo*, Lat.] To sell; to offer to sale.

He had a great parcel of glasses packed up, which not having the occasion he expected to vend, *and make use of, lay by him.*
BOYLE.

VENDEE. *n.s.* [from *vend.*] One to whom any thing is sold.

If a vicar sows his glebe, or if he sells his

corn, and the vendee *cuts it, he must pay the tithes to the parson.* AYLIFFE.

VE'NDER. *n.s.* [*vendeur*, Fr. from *vend.*] A seller.

Where the consumption of commodity is, the venders *seat themselves.* GRAUNT.

Those make the most noise who have the least to sell, which is very observable in the venders *of card-matches.* ADDISON.

VE'NDIBLE. *adj.* [*vendibilis*, Latin.] Saleable; marketable.

Silence only is commendable
In a neat's tongue dried, and a maid not
vendible. SHAKESPEARE.

This so profitable and vendible *a merchandize, riseth not to a proportionable enhancement with other less beneficial commodities.* CAREW.

The ignorant mine-man, aiming only at the obtaining a quantity of such a metal as may be vendible *under such a determinate name, has neither the design nor skill to make nice separations of the heterogeneous bodies.* BOYLE.

VE'NDIBLENESS. *n.s.* [from *vendible.*] The state of being saleable.

VE'NDIBLY.[228] *adv.* [from *vendible.*] In a saleable manner.

VENDITA'TION. *n.s.* [*venditatio*, from *vendito*, Latin.] Boastful display.

Some, by a cunning protestation against all reading, and venditation *of their own naturals, think to divert the sagacity of their readers from themselves, and cool the scent of their own fox-like thefts; when yet they are so rank as a man may find whole pages together usurped from one author.* BEN JONSON.

VENDI'TION. *n.s.* [*venditio*, Fr. *vendition*, Latin.] Sale; the act of selling.

VE'NEFICE. *n.s.* [*veneficium*, Latin.] The practice of poisoning.

VENE'REAL. *adj.* [*venereus*, Latin.]

1. Relating to love.

These are no venereal *signs;*
Vengeance is in my heart, death in my hand. SHAKESPEARE.

Then swol'n with pride, into the snare I fell,
Of fair fallacious looks, venereal *trains,*
Soften'd with pleasure and voluptuous life. MILTON.

They are averse to venereal *pleasure.* ADDISON.

2. Consisting of copper, called *venus* by chemists.

Blue vitriol, how venereal *and unsophisticated soever, rubbed upon the whetted blade of a knife, will not impart its latent colour.* BOYLE.

VENE'REOUS. *adj.* [from *venery.*] Libidinous; lustful.

The male is lesser than the female, and very venereous. DERHAM.

VE'NTIDUCT. *n.s.* [*ventus* and *ductus*, Latin.] A passage for the wind.

Having been informed of divers ventiducts, *I wish I had had the good fortune, when I was at Rome, to take notice of these organs.* BOYLE.

To **VE'NTILATE.** *v.a.* [*ventilo*, Latin.]

1. To fan with wind.

In close, low, and dirty alleys, the air is penn'd up, and obstructed from being ventilated *by the winds.* HARVEY.

Miners, by perflations with large bellows, letting down tubes, and sinking new shafts, give free passage to the air, which ventilates *and cools the mines.* WOODWARD.

2. To winnow; to fan.
3. To examine; to discuss.

Nor is the right of the party, nor the judicial process in right of that party so far perempted; but that the same may be begun again, and ventilated *de novo.* AYLIFFE.

VE'NTILATION. *n.s.* [*ventilatio*, Lat. from *ventilate.*]

1. The act of fanning; the state of being fanned.

The soul, worn with too frequent culture, must lie fallow, till it has recruited its exhausted salts, and again enriched itself by the ventilations *of the air.* ADDISON.

2. Vent; utterance. Not in use.

To his secretary Doctor Mason, whom he let lie in a pallet near him, for natural ventilation *of his thoughts, he would break out into bitter eruptions.* WOTTON'S BUCKINGHAM.

3. Refrigeration.

Procure the blood a free course, ventilation *and transpiration by suitable and ecphractic purges.* HARVEY.

VENTILA'TOR. *n.s.* [from *ventilate.*] An instrument contrived by Dr. *Hale* to supply close places with fresh air.

VENTRI'LOQUIST. *n.s.* [*ventriloque*, Fr. *venter* and *loquor*, Lat.] One who speaks in such a manner as that the sound seems to issue from his belly.

VERB. *n.s.* [*verbe*, Fr. *verbum*, Lat.] A part of speech signifying existence, or some modification thereof, as action, passion. And withal some disposition or intention of the mind relating thereto, as of affirming, denying, interrogating, commanding. *Clarke's Latin Grammar.*

Men usually talk of a noun and a verb. SHAKESPEARE.

VE'RBAL. *adj.* [*verbal*, Fr. *verbalis*, Latin.]

1. Spoken, not written.

2. Oral; uttered by mouth.

Made she no verbal *quest?* ——
—— *Yes; once or twice she heav'd the name of father*
Pantingly forth, as if it prest her heart. SHAKESPEARE.

3. Consisting in mere words.

If young African for fame,
His wasted country freed from Punick rage,
The deed becomes unprais'd, the man at least;
And loses, though but verbal, *his reward.* MILTON.

Being at first out of the way to science, in the progress of their inquiries they must lose themselves, and the truth, in a verbal *labyrinth.* GLANVILLE.

It was such a denial or confession of him as would appear in preaching: but this is managed in words and verbal *profession.* SOUTH.

4. Verbose; full of words. Out of use.

I am sorry
You put me to forget a lady's manners,
By being so verbal. SHAKESPEARE.

5. Minutely exact in words.

6. Literal; having word answering to word.

Neglect the rules each verbal *critick lays,*
For not to know some trifles is a praise. POPE.

Whosoever offers at verbal *translation, shall have the misfortune of that young traveller, who lost his own language abroad, and brought home no other instead of it.* DENHAM.

The verbal *copier is incumber'd with so many difficulties at once, that he can never disentangle himself from all.* DRYDEN.

7. [*verbal*, Fr. in grammar.] A verbal noun is a noun derived from a verb.

VERBA'LITY. *n.s.* [from *verbal.*] Mere bare words.

Sometimes he will seem to be charmed with words of holy scripture, and to fly from the letter and dead verbality, *who must only start at the life and animated materials thereof.* BROWN'S VULGAR ERROURS.

VE'RDANT. *n.s.* [*verdoiant*, Fr. *viridans*, Lat.] Green. This word is so lately naturalized, that *Skinner* could find it only in a dictionary.

Each odorous bushy shrub
Fenc'd up the verdant *wall.* MILTON.

VERSE. *n.s.* [*vers*, Fr. *versus*, Latin.]

1. A line consisting of a certain succession of sounds, and number of syllables.

Thou hast by moonlight at her window sung,
With feigning voice, verses *of feigning love.* SHAKESPEARE.

2. [*verset*, Fr.] A section or paragraph of a book.

Thus far the questions proceed upon the construction of the first earth; in the following verses *they proceed upon the demolition of that earth.* BURNET.

3. Poetry; lays; metrical language.

Verse *embalms virtue: and tombs and thrones of rhymes*
Preserve frail transitory fame as much
As spice doth body from air's corrupt touch. DONNE.

If envious eyes their hurtful rays have cast,
More pow'rful verse *shall free thee from the blast.* DRYDEN.

Whilst she did her various pow'r dispose;
Virtue was taught in verse, *and Athens' glory rose.* PRIOR.

You compose
In splay-foot verse, *or hobbling prose.* PRIOR.

4. A piece of poetry.

Let this verse, *my friend, be thine.* POPE.

VETERINARIAN. *n.s.* [*veterinarius*, Lat.] One skilled in the diseases of cattle.

That a horse has no gall, is not only swallowed by common farriers, but also receiv'd by good veterinarians, *and some who have laudably discoursed upon horses.* BROWN.

VICECHA'NCELLOR. *n.s.* [*vicecancellarius*, Latin.] The second magistrate of the universities.

VI'LLAIN. *n.s.* [*vilain*, Fr. *villanus*, low Latin.]

1. One who held by a base tenure.

The Irish inhabiting the lands fully conquered, being in condition of slaves and villains, *did render a greater revenue, than if they had been made the king's free subjects.* DAVIES.

2. A wicked wretch.

We were prevented by a dozen armed knights, or rather villains, *who, using this time of their extreme feebleness, all together set upon them.* SIDNEY.

O villain*!* villain*! his very opinion in the letter. Abhorred* villain*! unnatural, detested, brutish* villain*!* SHAKESPEARE.

What in the world,
That names me traitor, villain-*like he lies.* SHAKESPEARE.

He was stabbed to the heart by the hand of a villain, *upon the mere impious pretence of his being odious to the parliament.* CLARENDON.

Calm thinking villains, *whom no faith could fix;*
Of crooked counsels, and dark politicks. POPE.

VILLANY. *n.s.* [from *villain*; *villonnie*, old French.]

1. Wickedness; baseness; depravity.[229]

Trust not those cunning waters of his eyes;
For villainy *is not without such a rheum:*
And he, long traded in it, makes it seem
Like rivers of remorse and innocence. SHAKESPEARE.

He is the prince's jester; and the commendation is not in his wit, but in his villany. SHAKESPEARE.

2. A wicked action; a crime.

No villany, *or flagitious action was ever yet committed; but a lie was first or last the principal engine to effect it.* SOUTH.

Such villainies *rous'd Horace into wrath;*
And 'tis more noble to pursue his path,
Than an old tale. DRYDEN.

VIRTUO'SO. *n.s.* [Italian.] A man skilled in antique or natural curiosities; a man studious of painting, statuary, or architecture.

Methinks those generous virtuosi *dwell in a higher region than other mortals.*
GLANVILLE.

Virtuoso, *the Italians call a man who loves the noble arts, and is a critick in them. And amongst our French painters, the word vertueux is understood in the same signification.* DRYDEN.

This building was beheld with admiration by the virtuosi *of that time.*
TATLER, NO. 52.

Showers of rain are now met with in every water-work; and the virtuoso's *of France covered a little vault with artificial snow.*
ADDISON.

VI'SAGE. *n.s.* [*visage*, Fr. *visaggio*, Italian.] Face; countenance; look. It is now rarely used but with some ideas of dislike or horrour.

Phebe doth behold
Her silver visage *in the watry glass,*
Decking with liquid pearl the bladed grass.
SHAKESPEARE.

When she shall hear this of thee, with her nails
She'll flea thy wolfish visage.
SHAKESPEARE'S KING LEAR.

Whereto serves mercy,
But to confront the visage *of offence.*
SHAKESPEARE'S HAMLET.

With hostile frown,
And visage *all inflam'd, first thus began.*
MILTON.

By the rout, that made the hideous roar,
His goary visage *down the stream was sent;*
Down the swift Hebrus to the Lesbian shore. MILTON.

Love and beauty still that visage *grace;*
Death cannot fright 'em from their wonted place. WALLER.

VI'STA. *n.s.* [Italian.] View; prospect through an avenue.

In St. Peter's, when a man stands under the dome, if he looks upwards, he is astonished at the spacious hollow of the cupola, that makes one of the beautifullest vista's *that the eye can pass through.*
ADDISON'S REMARKS ON ITALY.

The finish'd garden to the view
Its vista's *opens, and its alleys green.*
THOMSON'S SPRING.

VITE'LLARY. *n.s.* [from *vitellus*, Latin.] The place where the yolk of the egg swims in the white.

A greater difficulty in the doctrine of eggs is, how the sperm of the cock attaineth into every egg; since the vitellary, *or place of the yolk, is very high.*
BROWN'S VULGAR ERROURS.

VI'TIOUS. *adj.* [*vicieux*, Fr. *vitiosus*, Latin.]

1. Corrupt; wicked; opposite to virtuous. It is rather applied to habitual faults, than criminal actions.[230]

Make known
It is no vitious *blot, murder, or foulness*
That hath depriv'd me of your grace.
SHAKESPEARE'S KING LEAR.

Witness th' irreverent son
Of him who built the ark; who, for the shame
Done to his father, heard his heavy curse,
'Servant of servants,' on his vitious *race.*
MILTON.

Wit's what the vitious *fear, the virtuous shun;*
By fools 'tis hated, and by knaves undone.
POPE.

No troops abroad are so ill disciplin'd as the English; which cannot well be otherwise, while the common soldiers have before their eyes the vitious *example of their leaders.* SWIFT.

2. Corrupt; having physical ill qualities.

When vitious *language contends to be high, it is full of rock, mountain, and pointedness.* BEN JONSON.

Here from the vicious *air and sickly skies,*
A plague did on the dumb creation rise. DRYDEN.

VIVE. *adj.* [*vif*, Fr. *vivus*, Latin.] Lively; forcible; pressing.

By a vive *and forcible perswasion, he mov'd him to a war upon Flanders.* BACON.

VIZ. *n.s.* [This word is *videlicet*, written with a contraction.] To wit; that is. A barbarous form of an unnecessary word.

That which so oft by sundry writers
Has been apply'd t' almost all fighters,
More justly may b' ascrib'd to this,
Than any other warrior, viz.
None ever acted both parts bolder,
Both of a chieftain and a soldier.
HUDIBRAS.

The chief of all signs which the Almighty endued man with, is humane voice, and the several modifications thereof by the organs of speech, viz. *the letters of the alphabet, form'd by the several motions of the mouth.* HOLDER.

Let this be done relatively, viz. *one thing greater or stronger, casting the rest behind, and rendering it less sensible by its opposition.*
DRYDEN'S DUFRESNOY.

U'MBREL, UMBRELLA. *n.s.* [from *umbra*, Lat.] A skreen used in hot countries to keep off the sun, and in others to bear off the rain.

I can carry your umbrella, *and fan your ladyship.* DRYDEN.

Good housewives
Defended by th' umbrella*'s oily shed,*
Safe through the wet on clinking pattens tread. GAY.

UN. A Saxon privative or negative particle answering to *in* of the Latins, and *a* of the Greeks, *on*, Dutch. It is placed almost at will before adjectives and adverbs. All instances of this kind of composition cannot therefore be inserted; but I have collected a number sufficient, perhaps more than sufficient, to explain it.[231]

The examples however, though numerous, might have easily been made more; for almost every adjective has a substantive and an adverb adhering to it, as *unfaithful*, *unfaithfulness*, *unfaithfully*. *Un* is prefixed to adjectives with their derivatives, as *unapt*, *unaptness*, *unaptly*; and to passive participles as *hurt*, *unhurt*; *favoured*, *unfavoured*: it is prefixed likewise to participial adjectives, as *pleasing*, *unpleasing*, but rarely in the verbal sense expressing action; we cannot say *the dart flew unwounding*, though we say *the man escaped unwounded*. *In* and *un* may be thus distinguished. To words merely English we prefix *un*, as *unfit*; to words borrowed in the positive sense, but made negative by ourselves, we prefix *un*, as *generous*, *ungenerous*. When we borrow both words we retain the Latin or French *in*, as *elegant*, *inelegant*; *politick*, *impolitick*. Before substantives if they have the English termination *ness*, as *unfitness*, *ungraciousness*; it is proper to prefix *un* if they have the Latin or French terminations in *tude*, *ice*, or *ence*; and for the most part if they end in *ty* the negative *in* is put before them, as *unapt*, *unaptness*, *inaptitude*; *unjust*, *injustice*;

imprudence; unfaithful, unfaithfulness, infidelity.

UNABA'SHED. *adj.* [from *abashed.*] Not shamed; not confused by modesty.

Earless on high, stood unabash'd *Defoe,*
And Tutchin flagrant from the scourge below. POPE.

UNA'CCURATE. *adj.* [from *accurate.*] Not exact.

Gallileo using an unaccurate *way, defined the air to be in weight to water but as one to four hundred.* BOYLE.

UNA'LTERABLE. *adj.* Unchangeable; immutable.

The law of nature, consisting in a fixed, unalterable *relation of one nature to another, is indispensable.* SOUTH.

They fixt unalterable *laws,*
Settling the same effect on the same cause. CREECH.

The truly upright man is inflexible in his uprightness, and unalterable *in his purpose.* ATTERBURY.

To UNBE'D. *v.a.* To raise from a bed.

Eels unbed *themselves, and stir at the noise of thunder.* WALTON'S ANGLER.

UNBOO'KISH. *adj.*

1. Not studious of books.
2. Not cultivated by erudition.

As he shall smile, Othello shall go mad;
And his unbookish *jealousy must construe*
Poor Cassio's smiles, gestures, and light behaviour,
Quite in the wrong.
SHAKESPEARE'S OTHELLO.

UNCA'PABLE. *adj.* [*incapable,* Fr. *incapax,* Lat.] Not capable; not susceptible.[232]

Thou art come to answer
A stony adversary, an inhuman wretch,
Uncapable *of pity, void and empty*
From any dram of mercy.
SHAKESPEARE'S MERCHANT OF VENICE.

He who believes himself uncapable *of pardon, goes on without any care of reforming.* HAMMOND.

This, whilst they are under the deceit of it, makes them uncapable *of conviction; and they applaud themselves as zealous champions for truth, when indeed they are contending for error.* LOCKE.

UNCI'VIL. *adj.* [*incivil,* Fr. *incivilis,* Lat.] Unpolite; not agreeable to rules of elegance, or complaisance.

Your undutiful, uncivil, *and uncharitable dealing in this your book, hath detected you.* WHITGIFT.

They love me well, yet I have much to do,
To keep me from uncivil *outrages.*
SHAKESPEARE.

My friends are so unreasonable, that they would have me be uncivil *to him.*
SPECTATOR, NO. 475.

UNCO'MEATABLE. *adj.* Inaccessible; unattainable. A low, corrupt word.

UNCONCE'IVABLE. *adj.* Not to be understood; not to be comprehended by the mind.

In the communication of motion by impulse, we can have no other conception, but of the passing of motion out of one body into another; which is as obscure and unconceivable, *as how our minds move or stop our bodies by thought.* LOCKE.

Those atoms wond'rous small must be,
Small to an unconceivable *degree;*
Since though these radiant spoils dispers'd in air,
Do ne'er return, and ne'er the sun repair.
BLACKMORE.

UNCRO'UDED. *adj.* Not straitened by want of room.

An amphitheatre,
On its publick shows, unpeopled Rome,

And held uncrouded *nations in its womb.* ADDISON.

UNDENI'ABLE. *adj.* Such as cannot be gainsaid.

That age which my grey hairs make seem more than it is, hath not diminished in me the power to protect an undeniable *verity.* SIDNEY.

Of those of the second class, we have a plain and undeniable *certainty.* WOODWARD'S NATURAL HISTORY.

UNDERBEA'RER. *n.s.* [*under* and *bearer.*] In funerals, those that sustain the weight of the body, distinct from those who are bearers of ceremony, and only hold up the pall.

UNDERFE'LLOW. *n.s.* [*under* and *fellow.*] A mean man; a sorry wretch.

They carried him to a house of a principal officer, who with no more civility, though with much more business than those underfellows *had shewed, in captious manner put interrogatories unto him.* SIDNEY.

U'NDERPLOT. *n.s.* [*under* and *plot.*]

1. A series of events proceeding collaterally with the main story of a play, and subservient to it.

In a tragi-comedy, there is to be but one main design; and though there be an underplot, *yet it is subservient to the chief fable.* DRYDEN'S DEDICATION TO JUVENAL.

2. A clandestine scheme.

The husband is so misled by tricks, and so lost in a crooked intrigue, that he still suspects an underplot. ADDISON.

UNDERSO'NG. *n.s.* [*under* and *song.*] Chorus; burthen of a song.

So ended she; and all the rest around
To her redoubled that her undersong.
SPENSER.

The challenge to Damætas shall belong;
Menalcas shall sustain his undersong;
Each in his turn your tuneful numbers bring. DRYDEN.

UNDERSTRA'PPER. *n.s.* [*under* and *strap.*] A petty fellow; an inferior agent.

Every understrapper *perk'd up, and expected a regiment, or his son must be a major.* SWIFT.

UNDERWRI'TER. *n.s.* [from *underwrite.*] An insurer; so called from writing his name under the conditions.

UNDETE'RMINATENESS, UNDETERMINATION. *n.s.* [from *undeterminate.*[233]]

1. Uncertainty; indecision.

He is not left barely to the undetermination, *incertainty and unsteadiness of the operation of his faculties, without a certain, secret, predisposition of them to what is right.* HALE.

2. The state of not being fixed, or invincibly directed.

The idea of a free agent is undeterminateness *to one part, before he has made choice.* MORE'S DIVINE DIALOGUES.

To **UNDRE'SS.** *v.a.* [from *dress.*]

1. To divest of cloaths; to strip.

Undress *you, and come now to bed.* SHAKESPEARE.

All were stol'n aside,
To counsel and undress *the bride.*
SUCKLING.

Her fellows press'd,
And the reluctant nymph by force undress'd. ADDISON'S OVID.

2. To divest of ornaments, or the attire of ostentation.

Undress'd *at evening, when she found*
Their odours lost, their colours past,
She chang'd her look. PRIOR.

U'NDRESS. *n.s.* A loose or negligent dress.

Reform her into ease,
And put her in undress *to make her please.* DRYDEN.

UNDRE'SSED. *adj.*

1. Not regulated.

Thy vineyard lies half prun'd, and half undress'd. DRYDEN.

2. Not prepared for use.

The common country people wore perones, shoes of undressed *leather.* ARBUTHNOT ON COINS.

UNE'QUITABLE. *adj.* Not impartial; not just.

We force him to stand to those measures which we think too unequitable *to press upon a murderer.* DECAY OF PIETY.

UNFI'NISHED. *adj.* Incomplete; not brought to an end; not brought to perfection; imperfect; wanting the last hand.

It is for that such outward ornament
Was lavish'd on their sex, that inward gifts
Were left for haste unfinish'd. MILTON.

I dedicate to you a very unfinished *piece.* DRYDEN.

His hasty hand left his pictures so unfinished, *that the beauty in the picture faded sooner than in the person after whom it was drawn.* SPECTATOR, NO. 83.

This collection contains not only such pieces as come under our review, but many others, even unfinished. SWIFT.

UNFRE'QUENT. *adj.* Uncommon; not happening often.

Part thereof is visible unto any situation; but being only discoverable in the night, and when the air is clear, it becomes unfrequent. BROWNE'S VULGAR ERROURS.

UNGE'NIAL. *adj.* Not kind or favourable to nature.

The northern shires have a more cloudy, ungenial *air, than any part of Ireland.* SWIFT TO POPE.

Sullen seas wash th' ungenial *pole.* THOMSON.

UNGRAMMA'TICAL.[234] *adj.* [from *un* and *grammatical.*] Not according to grammar.

UNINDI'FFERENT. *adj.* Partial; leaning to a side.

His opinion touching the catholick church was as unindifferent, *as, touching our church, the opinion of them that favour this pretended reformation is.* HOOKER, B. IV.

UNINTE'LLIGENT. *adj.* Not knowing; not skilful; not having any consciousness.

We will give you sleepy drinks, that your senses may be unintelligent *of our insufficience.* SHAKESPEARE'S WINTER TALE.

The visible creation is far otherwise apprehended by the philosophical enquirer, than the unintelligent *vulgar.* GLANVILLE.

This conclusion, if men allow'd of, they would not destroy ill-formed productions. Ay, but these monsters. Let them be so; what will your drivelling, unintelligent, *untractable changeling be?* LOCKE.

Why then to works of nature is assign'd
An author unintelligent *and blind;*
When ours proceed from choice? BLACKMORE.

The obvious products of unintelligent *nature.* BENTLEY.

U'NIVERSE. *n.s.* [*univers*, Fr. *universum*, Lat.] The general system of things.

Creeping murmur, and the poring dark,
Fills the wide vessel of the universe. SHAKESPEARE.

God here sums up all into man; the whole into a part; the universe *into an individual.* SOUTH'S SERMONS.

Father of heav'n!
Whose word call'd out this universe to birth. PRIOR.

UNIVE'RSITY. *n.s.* [*universitas*, Lat.] A school, where all the arts and faculties are taught and studied.

While I play the good husband at home, my son and servants spend all at the university. SHAKESPEARE'S TAMING OF THE SHREW.

The universities, *especially Aberdeen, flourished under many excellent scholars, and very learned men.* CLARENDON.

UNI'VOCAL. *adj.* [*univocus*, Lat.]

1. Having one meaning.

Univocal *words are such as signify but one idea, or but one sort of thing: equivocal words are such as signify two or more different ideas, or different sorts of objects.* WATTS.

2. Certain; regular; persuing always one tenour.

This conceit makes putrefactive generations correspondent unto seminal productions; and conceives inequivocal effects, and univocal *conformity unto the efficient.* BROWN.

To **UNLOO'SE.** *v.a.* To loose. A word perhaps barbarous and ungrammatical, the particle prefixed implying negation; so that to *unloose*, is properly *to bind.*

York, unloose *your long imprison'd thoughts,*
And let thy tongue be equal with thy heart. SHAKESPEARE.

The weak, wanton Cupid,
Shall from your neck unloose *his am'rous fold;*
And, like a dew-drop from the lion's mane,
Be shook to air. SHAKESPEARE'S TROILUS AND CRESSIDA.

Turn him to any cause of policy;
The gordian knot of it he will unloose,
Familiar as his garter. SHAKESPEARE'S HENRY V.

It rested in you,
T' unloose *this tied-up justice, when you pleas'd.* SHAKESPEARE.

The latchet of his shoes I am not worthy to stoop down and unloose. BIBLE MARK, I. 7.

He that should spend all his time in tying inextricable knots, only to baffle the industry of those that should attempt to unloose *them, would be thought not much to have served his generation.* DECAY OF PIETY.

UNME'RCHANTABLE. *adj.* Unsaleable; not vendible.

They feed on salt, unmerchantable *pilchard.* CAREW.

UNO'BVIOUS. *adj.* Not readily occurring.

Of all the metals, not any so constantly discloseth its unobvious *colour, as copper.* BOYLE ON COLOURS.

UNPE'NSIONED. *adj.* Not kept in dependance by a pension.

Could pension'd Boileau lash in honest strain
Flatt'rers and bigots, ev'n in Louis' reign;
And I not strip the gilding off a knave,
Unplac'd, unpension'd, *no man's heir or slave?* POPE.

UNPU'BLICK. *adj.* Private; not generally known.

Virgins must be retired and unpublick: *for all freedom of society is a violence done to virginity, not in its natural, but in its moral capacity; that is, it loses part of its severity and strictness, by publishing that person, whose work is religion, whose thoughts must dwell in heaven.* TAYLOR.

UNPU'BLISHED. *adj.*

1. Secret; unknown.

All blest secrets;
All you unpublish'd *virtues of the earth,*

Spring with my tears.
SHAKESPEARE'S KING LEAR.

2. Not given to the publick.

Apply your care wholly to those which are unpublish'd. POPE.

To **UNRI'DDLE.** *v.a.* To solve an enigma; to explain a problem.

Some kind power unriddle *where it lies,*
Whether my heart be faulty, or her eyes!
SUCKLING.

The Platonick principles will not unriddle *the doubt.* GLANVILLE.

A reverse often clears up the passage of an old poet, as the poet often serves to unriddle *the reverse.* ADDISON.

To **UNRI'P.** *v.a.* [This word is improper; there being no difference between *rip* and *unrip*; and the negative particle is therefore of no force; yet it is well authorised.] To cut open.

Like a traitor
Didst break that vow, and, with thy treach'rous blade,
Unrip'dst *the bowels of thy sov'reign's son.* SHAKESPEARE.

He could not now, with his honour, so unrip, *and put a lye upon all that he had said and done before, as to deliver him up.* BACON'S HENRY VII.

We are angry with searchers, when they break open trunks, and unrip *packs, and open sealed letters.* TAYLOR.

Cato well observes, that friendship ought not to be unripped, *but unstitched.* COLLIER.

UNSINCE'RE. *adj.* [*insincerus*, Lat.]

1. Not hearty; not faithful.
2. Not genuine; impure; adulterated.

I have so often met with chymical preparations, which I have found unsincere, *that I dare scarce trust any.* BOYLE.

3. Not sound; not solid.

Myrrha was joy'd the welcome news to hear;
But, clogg'd with guilt, the joy was unsincere. DRYDEN.

UNSOPHI'STICATED. *adj.* Not adulterated.[235]

The humour and tunicles are purely transparent, to let in light and colours, unfouled and unsophisticated *by any inward tincture.*
MORE'S ANTIDOTE AGAINST ATHEISM.

Blue vitriol, how venereal and unsophisticated *soever, rubb'd upon the whetted blade of a knife, will not impart its latent colour.* BOYLE.

If authors will not keep close to truth by unvaried terms, and plain, unsophisticated *arguments; yet it concerns readers not to be imposed on, by fallacies.* LOCKE.

UNTRO'LLED. *adj.* Not bowled; not rolled along.

Hard fate! untroll'd *is now the charming dye;*
The playhouse and the parks unvisited must lie. DRYDEN.

To **UNTWI'ST.** *v.a.* To separate any things involved in each other, or wrapped up on themselves.

Untwisting *his deceitful clew,*
He 'gan to weave a web of wicked guile.
FAIRY QUEEN.

The interest of prince and people is so enfolded in a mutual embrace, that they cannot be untwisted *without pulling a limb off.* TAYLOR'S RULE OF LIVING HOLY.

Untwisting *all the chains that tie*
The hidden soul of harmony. MILTON.

No, I'll untwist *you;*
I have occasion for your stay on earth.
DRYDEN.

Tarred hempen ropes cut small and untwisted, *are beneficial for lands.*
MORTIMER'S HUSBANDRY.

Untwist *a wire, and from her gums*
A set of teeth completely comes. SWIFT.

To **UNVA'IL.** *v.a.* To uncover; to strip of a veil. This word is *unvail*, or *unveil*, according to its etymology. See **VAIL**, and **VEIL**.

Troy reviv'd, her mourning face unvail'd. DENHAM.

Now unveil'd, *the toilet stands display'd,*
Each silver vase in mystick order laid.
POPE.

To **UNVE'IL.** *v.a.* [See **VEIL** and **VAIL**.]

1. To uncover; to divest of a veil.

The moon,
Apparent queen, unveil'd *her peerless light.* MILTON.

To the limpid stream direct thy way,
When the gay morn unveils *her smiling ray.* POPE.

2. To disclose; to show.

The providence, that's in a watchful state,
Knows almost every grain of Pluto's gold;
Does ev'n our thoughts unveil *in their dumb cradles.* SHAKESPEARE.

UNWA'RES. *adv.* Unexpectedly; before any caution, or expectation.

She, by her wicked arts,
Too false and strong for earthly skill or might,
Unwares *me wrought unto her wicked will.* FAIRY QUEEN.

His loving mother came upon a day
Unto the woods, to see her little son,
And chanc'd unwares *to meet him in the way,*
After his sports and cruel pastime done.
FAIRFAX, B. I.

Still we sail, while prosperous blows the wind,
Till on some secret rock unwares *we light.*
FAIRFAX.

UNWA'YED. *adj.* Not used to travel; not seasoned in the road.

Beasts, that have been rid off their legs, are as much for a man's use, as colts that are unwayed, *and will not go at all.*
SUCKLING.

UNWRI'TING. *adj.* Not assuming the character of an author.

The peace of the honest unwriting *subject was daily molested.* ARBUTHNOT.

VOCA'BULARY. *n.s.* [*vocabularium*, Lat. *vocabulaire*, Fr.] A dictionary; a lexicon; a word-book.

Some have delivered the polity of spirits, and that they stand in awe of conjurations, which signify nothing, not only in the dictionary of man, but in the subtiler vocabulary *of Satan.*
BROWN'S VULGAR ERROURS.

Among other books, we should be furnished with vocabularies *and dictionaries of several sorts.* WATTS.

VO'CATIVE. *n.s.* [*vocatif*, Fr. *vocativus*, Lat.] The grammatical case used in calling or speaking to.

VO'IDER. *n.s.* [from *void.*] A basket, in which broken meat is carried from the table.

A voider *for the nonce,*
I wrong the devil should I pick their bones.
CLEAVELAND.

VOLE. *n.s.* [*vole*, Fr.] A deal at cards, that draws the whole tricks.

Past six, and not a living soul!
I might by this have won a vole. SWIFT.

VOLCA'NO. *n.s.* [Italian, from *Vulcan.*] A burning mountain.

Navigators tell us there is a burning mountain in an island, and many volcano's *and fiery hills.*[236] BROWN.

When the Cyclops o'er their anvils sweat,
From the volcano's *gross eruptions rise,*
And curling sheets of smoke obscure the skies. GARTH.

Subterraneous minerals ferment, and cause

earthquakes, and cause furious eruptions of volcano's, *and tumble down broken rocks.* BENTLEY'S SERMONS.

VO'LERY. *n.s.* [*volerie*, Fr.] A flight of birds.

An old boy, at his first appearance, is sure to draw on him the eyes and chirping of the whole town volery; *amongst which, there will not be wanting some birds of prey, that will presently be on the wing for him.* LOCKE.

VO'LUBLE. *adj.* [*volubilis*, Lat.]

1. Formed so as to roll easily; formed so as to be easily put in motion.

Neither the weight of the matter of which a cylinder is made, nor its round voluble *form, which, meeting with a precipice, do necessarily continue the motion of it, are any more imputable to that dead, choiceless creature in its first motion.* HAMMOND.

The adventitious corpuscles may produce stability in the matter they pervade, by expelling thence those voluble *particles, which, whilst they continued, did by their shape unfit for cohesion, or, by their motion, oppose coalition.* BOYLE.

2. Rolling; having quick motion.

This less voluble *earth,*
By shorter flight to th' east, had left him there. MILTON.

Then voluble, *and bold; now hid, now seen,*
Among thick-woven arborets.
MILTON'S PARADISE LOST, B. IV.

3. Nimble; active. Applied to the tongue.

A friend promised to dissect a woman's tongue, and examine whether there may not be in it certain juices, which render it so wonderfully voluble *and flippant.* ADDISON.

These with a voluble *and flippant tongue, become mere echo's.*
WATTS'S IMPROVEMENT OF THE MIND.

4. Fluent of words. It is applied to the speech, or the speaker.

Cassio, a knave very voluble; *no further conscionable, than in putting on the meer form of civil and humane seeming, for the better compassing of his loose affection.* SHAKESPEARE.

If voluble *and sharp discourse be marr'd,*
Unkindness blunts it more than marble hard. SHAKESPEARE.

VO'LUME. *n.s.* [*volumen*, Lat.]

1. Something rolled, or convolved.

2. As much as seems convolved at once; as a fold of a serpent, a wave of water.

Threescore and ten I can remember well;
Within the volume *of which time I've seen*
Hours dreadful, and things strange.
SHAKESPEARE'S MACBETH.

Unoppos'd they either lose their force,
Or wind in volumes *to their former course.* DRYDEN.

Behind the gen'ral mends his weary pace,
And silently to his revenge he sails:
So glides some trodden serpent on the grass,
And long behind his wounded volume *trails.* DRYDEN.

Thames' fruitful tides,
Slow through the vale in silver volumes *play.* FENTON.

By the insinuations of these crystals, the volumes *of air are driven out of the watery particles, and many of them uniting, form larger* volumes, *which thereby have a greater force to expand themselves.* CHEYNE.

3. [*Volume*, Fr.] A book; so called, because books were antiently rolled upon a staff.

Guyon all this while his book did read,
Ne yet has ended; for it was a great
And ample volume, *that doth far exceed*
My leisure, so long leaves here to repeat.
FAIRY QUEEN.

Calmly, I do beseech you. ——
Aye, as an hostler, that for the poorest piece

Will bear the knave by th' volume. SHAKESPEARE.

I shall not now enlarge on the wrong judgments whereby men mislead themselves. This would make a volume. LOCKE.

If one short volume *cou'd comprize*
All that was witty, learn'd and wise:
How wou'd it be esteem'd and read?
SWIFT.

To **VOLUNTEE'R.** *v.n.* To go for a soldier. A cant word.

Leave off these wagers, for in conscience speaking,
The city needs not your new tricks for breaking:
And if you gallants lose, to all appearing,
You'll want an equipage for volunteering.
DRYDEN.

VO'WEL. *n.s.* [*voyelle*, Fr. *vocalis*, Lat.] A letter which can be uttered by itself.

I distinguish letters into vowels *and consonants, yet not wholly upon their reason, that a* vowel *may be sounded alone, a consonant not without a* vowel; *which will not be found all true; for many of the consonants may be sounded alone, and some joined together without a* vowel, *as bl. st. and as we pronounce the latter syllable of people, riffle.* HOLDER.

Virgil makes the two vowels *meet without an elision.* BROOME.

VOWFE'LLOW. *n.s.* [*vow* and *fellow.*] One bound by the same vow.

Who are the votaries,
That are vowfellows *with this virtuous king?* SHAKESPEARE.

UPHO'LDER. *n.s.* [from *uphold.*]

1. A supporter.

Suppose then Atlas ne'er so wise:
Yet when the weight of kingdom lies
Too long upon his single shoulders,
Sink down he must, or find upholders.
SWIFT.

2. A sustainer in being.

The knowledge thereof is so many manuductions to the knowledge and admiration of the infinite wisdom of the creator and upholder *of them.* HALE.

3. An undertaker; one who provides for funerals.

The company of upholders *have a right upon the bodies of the subjects.*
ARBUTHNOT.

Where the brass knocker wrapt in flannel band,
Forbids the thunder of the footman's hand;
Th' upholder, *rueful harbinger of death,*
Waits with impatience for the dying breath. GAY.

UPHO'LSTERER. *n.s.* [A corruption of *upholder.*] One who furnishes houses; one who fits up apartments with beds and furniture.

If a corner of the hanging wants a single nail, send for the upholsterer. SWIFT.

Mere wax as yet, you fashion him with ease,
Your barber, cook, upholsterer. POPE.

UPLA'NDISH. *adj.* [from *upland.*] Mountainous; inhabiting mountains.

Lion-like, uplandish, *and mere wild,*
Slave to his pride; and all his nerves being naturally compil'd
Of eminent strength; stalks out and preys upon a silly sheep.
CHAPMAN'S ILIADS.

U'PPISH. *adj.* [from *up.*] Proud; arrogant. A low word.

U'RINAL. *n.s.* [*urinal*, Fr. from *urine.*] A bottle, in which water is kept for inspection.

These follies shine through you, like the water in an urinal.
SHAKESPEARE'S TWO GENTLEMEN OF VERONA.

A candle out of a musket will pierce through an inch board, or an urinal *force a nail though a plank.* BROWN.

This hand, when glory calls,
Can brandish arms, as well as urinals.
GARTH.

Some with scymitars in their hands, and others with urinals, *ran to and fro.*
SPECTATOR, NO 159.

URINA'TOR. *n.s.* [*urinateur*, Fr. *urinator*, Lat.] A diver; one who searches under water.

The precious things that grow there, as pearl, may be much more easily fetched up by the help of this, than by any other way of the urinators.
WILKINS'S MATHEMATICAL MAGICK.

Those relations of urinators *belong only to those places where they have dived, which are always rocky.* RAY.

U'SHER. *n.s.* [*huissier*, Fr.]

1. One whose business is to introduce strangers, or walk before a person of high rank.

The wife of Antony
Should have an army for an usher, *and*
The neighs of horse to tell her approach
Long ere she did appear.
SHAKESPEARE'S ANTONY AND CLEOPATRA.

You make guards and ushers *march before, and then enters your prince.*
TATLER, NO 53.

Gay paid his courtship with the croud,
As far as modest pride allow'd;
Rejects a servile usher's *place,*
And leaves St. James's in disgrace.
SWIFT.

2. An under-teacher; one who introduces young scholars to higher learning.

Though grammar profits less than rhetorick's,
Yet ev'n in those his usher *claims a share.*
DRYDEN.

USQUEBA'UGH. *n.s.* [An Irish and Erse word, which signifies the water of life.] It is a compounded distilled spirit, being drawn on aromaticks; and the Irish sort is particularly distinguished for its pleasant and mild flavour. The Highland sort is somewhat hotter; and, by corruption, in Scottish they call it *whisky*.

USTO'RIOUS. *adj.* [*ustum*, Latin.] Having the quality of burning.

The power of a burning glass is by an ustorious *quality in the mirror or glass, arising from a certain unknown substantial form.* WATTS.

VU'LGAR. *n.s.* [*vulgaire*, Fr.] The common people.

I'll about;
Drive away the vulgar *from the streets.*
SHAKESPEARE.

Those men, and their adherents, were then looked upon by the affrighted vulgar, *as greater protectors of their laws and liberties than myself.* KING CHARLES.

The vulgar *imagine the pretender to have been a child imposed upon the nation by the fraudulent zeal of his parents, and their bigotted counsellors.* SWIFT.

W

Is a letter of which the form is not to be found in the alphabets of the learned languages; though it is not improbable that by our *w* is expressed the sound of the Roman *v*, and the Eolick *s*. Both the form and sound are excluded from the languages derived from the Latin. *W* is sometimes improperly used in diphthongs as a vowel, for *u*, *view*; *strew*: the sound of *w* consonant is uniform.

WAD. *n.s.* [*weod*, hay, Saxon.]
1. A bundle of straw thrust close together.
2. Wadd, or black lead, is a mineral of great use and value. *Woodward.*

WA'GGERY. *n.s.* [from *wag.*] Mischievous merriment; roguish trick; sarcastical gaiety.

> *'Tis not the* waggeries *or cheats practised among schoolboys, that make an able man; but the principles of justice, generosity, and sobriety.* LOCKE.

WA'ITER. *n.s.* [from *wait.*] An attendant; one who attends for the accommodation of others.

> *Let the drawers be ready with wine and fresh glasses;*
> *Let the* waiters *have eyes, though their tongues must be ty'd.*
> BEN JONSON'S TAVERN ACADEMY.

> *The least tart or pie,*
> *By any* waiter *there stolen and set by.*
> BISHOP CORBET.

> *A man of fire is a general enemy to all the* waiters *where you drink.*
> TATLER, NO. 61.

> *The* waiters *stand in ranks; the yeomen cry,*
> *Make room.* SWIFT.

WA'LKINGSTAFF. *n.s.* A stick which a man holds to support him in walking.

> *The club which a man of an ordinary size could not lift, was but a* walking staff *for Hercules.* GLANVILLE.

To **WA'MBLE.** *v.n.* [*wemmelen*, Dutch.] To roll with nausea and sickness. It is used of the stomach.

> *A covetous man deliberated betwixt the qualms of a* wambling *stomach, and an unsettled mind.* L'ESTRANGE.

WA'NTWIT. *n.s.* [*want* and *wit.*] A fool; an idiot.

> *Such a* wantwit *sadness makes of me,*

That I have much ado to know myself. SHAKESPEARE.

WA'RDROBE. *n.s.* [*garderobe*, French; *garderoba*, low Lat.] A room where cloaths are kept.

The third had of their wardrobe *custody,*
In which were not rich tires nor garments gay,
The plumes of pride, and wings of vanity,
But cloaths meet to keep keen cold away.
FAIRY QUEEN.

I will kill all his coats,
I'll murder all his wardrobe *piece by piece*
Until I meet the king.
SHAKESPEARE'S HENRY IV.

Behold!
What from his wardrobe *her belov'd allows,*
To deck the wedding day of his unspotted spouse. DRYDEN.

It would not be an impertinent design to make a kind of an old Roman wardrobe, *where you should see toga's and tunica's, the chlamys and trabea, and all the different vests and ornaments so often mentioned in the Greek and Roman authors.* ADDISON.

WA'REFUL. *adj.* [*ware* and *full.*] Cautious; timorously prudent.

WA'RELESS. *adj.* [from *ware.*] Uncautious; unwary. *Spenser.*

WA'RELY. *adv.* [from *ware.*] Warily; cautiously; timorously.

They bound him hand and foot with iron chains,
And with continual watch did warely *keep.* FAIRY QUEEN.

WA'RILY. *adv.* [from *wary.*] Cautiously; with timorous prudence; with wise forethought.

The charge thereof unto a courteous sp'rit
Commended was, who thereby did attend,
And warily *awaited day and night,*
From other covetous fiends it to defend.
FAIRY QUEEN.

The change of laws, especially concerning matters of religion, must be warily *proceeded in.* HOOKER.

It will concern a man to treat conscience awfully and warily, *by still observing what it commands, but especially what it forbids.* SOUTH'S SERMONS.

They searched diligently and concluded warily. SPRAT.

WA'RMINGPAN. *n.s.* [*warm* and *pan.*] A covered brass pan for warming a bed by means of hot coals.

WA'RREN. *n.s.* [*waerande*, Dutch; *guerenne*, French.] A kind of park for rabbits.

I found him here, as melancholy as a lodge in a warren.
SHAKESPEARE'S MUCH ADO ABOUT NOTHING.

The coney convenes a whole warren, *tells her story, and advises upon a revenge.*
L'ESTRANGE.

Men should set snares in their warrens *to catch polcats and foxes.*
DRYDEN'S SPANISH FRYAR.

WA'SHBALL. *n.s.* [*wash* and *ball.*] Ball made of soap.

I asked a poor man how he did; he said he was like a washball, *always in decay.*
SWIFT.

WA'TCHET. *adj.* [*wœced*, Saxon, weak. *Skinner.*] Blue; pale blue.

Whom 'midst the Alps do hanging throats surprise?
Who stares in Germany at watchet *eyes?*
DRYDEN'S JUVENAL.

WA'TCHWORD. *n.s.* [*watch* and *word.*] The word given to the centinels to know their friends.

All have their ears upright, waiting when the watchword *shall come, that they should all arise into rebellion.* SPENSER.

We have heard the chimes at midnight, master Shallow.

— *That we have, sir John: our* watchword, *hem, boys.* SHAKESPEARE.

A watchword *every minute of the night goeth about the walls, to testify their vigilancy.* SANDYS.

WATERGRU'EL. *n.s.* [*water* and *gruel.*] Food made with oatmeal and water.

For breakfast milk, milk-pottage, watergruel, *and flummery, are very fit to make for children.* LOCKE.

The aliment ought to be slender, as watergruel *acidulated.* ARBUTHNOT ON DIET.

WA'TERMAN. *n.s.* [*water* and *man.*] A ferryman; a boatman.

Having blocked up the passage to Greenwich, they ordered the watermen *to let fall their oars more gently.* DRYDEN.

Bubbles of air working upward from the very bottom of the lake, the watermen *told us that they are observed always to rise in the same places.* ADDISON ON ITALY.

The waterman *forlorn, along the shore,*
Pensive reclines upon his useless oar. GAY.

WA'TERWORK. *n.s.* [*water* and *work.*] Play of fountains; artificial spouts of water; any hydraulick performance.

Engines invented for mines and waterworks *often fail in the performance.* WILKINS'S MATHEMATICAL MAGICK.

The French took from the Italians the first plans of their gardens, as well as waterworks. ADDISON.

WEA'KSIDE. *n.s.* [*weak* and *side.*] Foible; deficience; infirmity.

This dog would have fought for his master in any other case; but the love of mutton was his weakside. L'ESTRANGE.

Their application to trade has increased their shipping, which they found to be their weakside *in their last attempts.* TEMPLE.

WEA'THER. *n.s.* [*weder*, Saxon.]

1. State of air, respecting either cold or heat, wet or driness.

Who's there, besides foul weather? —
One mended like the weather, *most unquietly.*
SHAKESPEARE'S KING LEAR.

I am far better born than is the king;
But I must make fair weather *yet a while,*
Till Henry be more weak and I more strong. SHAKESPEARE.

Men must content themselves to travel in all weathers, *and through all difficulties.* L'ESTRANGE.

The sun
Foretells the change of weather *in the skies,*
Through mists he shoots his sullen beams,
Suspect a drisling day. DRYDEN.

2. The change of the state of the air.

It is a reverend thing to see an ancient castle not in decay; how much more to behold an ancient family, which have stood against the waves and weathers *of time?* BACON.

3. Tempest; storm.

What gusts of weather *from that gath'ring cloud,*
My thoughts presage. DRYDEN'S VIRGIL.

To **WEA'THER.** *v.a.* [from the noun.]

1. To expose to the air.

He perch'd on some branch thereby,
To weather *him and his moist wings to dry.* SPENSER.

Mustard-seed gather for being too ripe,
And weather *it wel, yer ye give it a stripe.* TUSSER.

2. To pass with difficulty.

He weather'd *fell Charibdis; but ere long,*
The skies were darkened, and the tempests strong. GARTH.

Could they weather *and stand the shock of an eternal duration, and yet be at any time subject to a dissolution.* HALE.

3. *To* WEATHER *a point.* To gain a

point against the wind; to accomplish against opposition.

We have been tugging a great while against the stream, and have almost weather'd *our point; a stretch or two more will do the work.* ADDISON.

4. *To* WEATHER *out.* To endure.

When we have pass'd these gloomy hours,
And weather'd *out the storm that beats upon us.* ADDISON.

WEATHERGA'GE. *n.s.* [*weather* and *gage.*] Any thing that shews the weather.

To vere and tack, and steer a cause,
Against the weathergage *of laws.*
HUDIBRAS.

WEATHERSPY'. *n.s.* [*weather* and *spy.*] A star-gazer; an astrologer; one that foretels the weather.

And sooner may a gulling weatherspy,
By drawing forth heav'n's scheme tell certainly,
What fashion'd hats or ruffs, or suits next year,
Our giddy-headed antick youth will wear.
DONNE.

WEA'THERWISER. *n.s.* [*weather* and *wisen*, Dutch; to show.] Any thing that foreshows the weather.

Most vegetables expand their flowers and down in warm sun-shiny weather, and again close them toward the evening, or in rain, as is in the flowers of pimpernel, the opening and shutting of which are the countryman's weatherwiser.
DERHAM'S PHYSICO-THEOLOGY.

WELLDO'NE. *interject.* A word of praise.

Welldone, *thou good and faithful servant.*
BIBLE MATTHEW, XXV. 21.

WELLME'T. *interj.* [*well* and *meet.*] A term of salutation.

Once more to-day wellmet, *distemper'd lords;*
The king by me requests your presence straight. SHAKESPEARE.

WELLSPE'NT. *adj.* Passed with virtue.

They are to lie down without any thing to support them in their age, but the conscience of a wellspent *youth.*
L'ESTRANGE.

What a refreshment then will it be to look back upon a wellspent *life?*
CALAMY'S SERMONS.

The constant tenour of their wellspent *days,*
No less deserv'd a just return of praise.
POPE.

WE'NCHER. *n.s.* [from *wench.*] A fornicator.

He must be no great eater, drinker, or sleeper; no gamester, wencher, *or fop.*
GREW'S COSMOLOGY.

WHEE'LBARROW. *n.s.* [*wheel* and *barrow.*] A carriage driven forward on one wheel.

Carry bottles in a wheelbarrow *upon rough ground, but not filled full, but leave some air.* BACON.

Pippins did in wheelbarrows *abound.*
KING.

WHIFF. *n.s.* [*chwyth*, Welsh.] A blast; a puff of wind.

Pyrrhus at Priam drives, in rage strikes wide;
But with the whiff *and wind of his fell sword,*
Th' unnerved father falls.
SHAKESPEARE'S HAMLET.

Who,
If some unsav'ry whiff *betray the crime,*
Invents a quarrel straight. DRYDEN.

Three pipes after dinner he constantly smokes,
And seasons his whiffs *with impertinent jokes.* PRIOR.

Nick pulled out a boatswain's whistle: upon

the first whiff *the tradesmen came jumping in.* ARBUTHNOT.

WHIG. *n.s.* [*hwæg*, Saxon.]

1. Whey.
2. The name of a faction.

The southwest counties of Scotland have seldom corn enough to serve them round the year; and the northern parts producing more than they need, those in the west come in the Summer to buy at Leith the stores that come from the north; and from a word, whiggam, used in driving their horses, all that drove were called the whiggamors, and shorter the whiggs. *Now in that year before the news came down of duke Hamilton's defeat, the ministers animated their people to rise and march to Edinburgh; and they came up marching on the head of their parishes with an unheard-of fury, praying and preaching all the way as they came. The marquis of Argyle and his party came and headed them, they being about six thousand. This was called the whiggamor's inroad; and ever after that, all that opposed the court came in contempt to be called* whigs: *and from Scotland the word was brought into England, where it is now one of our unhappy terms of disunion.* BURNET.

Whoever has a true value for church and state, should avoid the extremes of whig *for the sake of the former, and the extremes of tory on the account of the latter.* SWIFT.

WHI'GGISH. *adj.* [from *whig.*] Relating to the whigs.

She'll prove herself a tory plain,
From principles the whigs maintain;
And, to defend the whiggish *cause,*
Her topicks from the tories draws.
SWIFT.

WHI'GGISM. *n.s.* [from *whig.*] The notions of a whig.

I could quote passages from fifty pamphlets, wholly made up of whiggism *and atheism.* SWIFT.

WHI'RLIGIG. *n.s.* [*whirl* and *gig.*] A toy which children spin round.

He found that marbles taught him percussion, and whirligigs *the axis in peritrochio.*
ARBUTHNOT AND POPE'S MARTIN SCRIBLERUS.

That since they gave things their beginning,
And set this whirligig *a spinning.*
PRIOR.

WHI'RLPIT, WHIRLPOOL. *n.s.* [*hwyrfpole*, Saxon.] A place where the water moves circularly, and draws whatever comes within the circle towards its center; a vortex.

Poor Tom! whom the foul fiend hath led through ford and whirlpool, *o'er bog and quagmire.*
SHAKESPEARE'S KING LEAR.

In the fathomless profound
Down sunk they, like a falling stone,
By raging whirlpits *overthrown.*
SANDYS.

This calm of heaven, this mermaid's melody,
Into an unseen whirlpool *draws you fast,*
And in a moment sinks you.
DRYDEN'S SPANISH FRYAR.

Send forth, ye wise! send forth your lab'ring thought:
Let it return with empty notions fraught,
Of airy columns every moment broke,
Of circling whirlpools, *and of spheres of smoke.* PRIOR.

There might arise some vertiginous motions or whirlpools *in the matter of the chaos, whereby the atoms must be thrust and crowded to the middle of those* whirlpools, *and there constipate one another into great solid bodies.* BENTLEY.

WHIST. [This word is called by *Skinner*, who seldom errs, an interjection commanding silence, and so it is commonly used; but *Shakespeare* uses it as a verb, and *Milton* as an adjective.]

1. Are silent.

Come unto these yellow sands,
And then take hands;
Curt'sied when you have, and kist,
The wild waves whist.
SHAKESPEARE'S TEMPEST.

2. Still; silent.[237]

The winds, with wonder whist,
Smoothly the waters kiss'd,
Whispering new joys to the mild ocean.
MILTON.

3. Be still.

WHIST. *n.s.* A game at cards, requiring close attention and silence.[238]

The clergyman used to play at whist *and swobbers.* SWIFT.

Whist *awhile*
Walks his grave round, beneath a cloud of smoke,
Wreath'd fragrant from the pipe.
THOMSON'S AUTUMN.

WHI'TEMEAT. *n.s.* [*white* and *meat.*] Food made of milk.

Much saltness in whitemeat *is ill for the stone.* TUSSER.

The Irish banished into the mountains, lived only upon whitemeats. SPENSER.

WHI'TEWINE. *n.s.* [*white* and *wine.*] A species of wine produced from the white grapes.

The seeds and roots are to be cut, beaten, and infused in whitewine.
WISEMAN'S SURGERY.

To **WHIZ.** *v.n.* [from the sound that it expresses.] To make a loud humming noise.

The exhalations, whizzing *in the air,*
Give so much light, that I may read by them. SHAKESPEARE.

Turn him about,
I know him, he'll but whiz, *and strait go out.* DRYDEN.

Soon all with vigour bend their trusty bows,
And from the quiver each his arrow chose:
Hippocoon's was the first; with forceful sway
It flew, and whizzing *cut the liquid way.*
DRYDEN.

WHYNO'T. *adv.* A cant word for violent or peremptory procedure.

Capoch'd your rabbins of the synod,
And snap'd their canons with a whynot.
HUDIBRAS.

WIDOWHU'NTER. *n.s.* [*widow* and *hunter.*] One who courts widows for a jointure.

The widowhunters *about town often afford them great diversion.*
ADDISON'S SPECTATOR.

WILDGO'OSECHASE. *n.s.* A pursuit of something as unlikely to be caught as the wildgoose.

If our wits run the wildgoosechace, *I have done; for thou hast more of the wildgoose in one of thy wits, than I have in my whole five.* SHAKESPEARE.

Let a man consider the time, money, and vexation, that this wildgoosechace *has cost him, and then say what have I gotten to answer all this expence, but loose, giddy frolick?* L'ESTRANGE.

To **WILL.** *v.a.* [*wilgan*, Gothick; *willan*, Saxon; *willen*, Dutch.]

1. To desire that any thing should be, or be done.[239]

To will, *is to bend our souls to the having or doing of that which they see to be good.*
HOOKER.

Let Richard be restored to his blood,
As will *the rest; so* willeth *Winchester.*
SHAKESPEARE.

I speak not of God's determining his own will, but his predetermining the acts of our will. There is as great difference betwixt these two, as betwixt my willing *a lawful thing myself, and my inducing another man to do that which is unlawful.*
HAMMOND ON FUNDAMENTALS.

Whosoever wills *the doing of a thing, if the*

doing of it be in his power, he will certainly do it; and whosoever does not do that thing, which he has in his power to do, does not properly will *it.* SOUTH.

A man that sits still, is said to be at liberty, because he can walk if he wills *it.* LOCKE.

2. To be inclined or resolved to have.

She's too rough for me;
There, there, Hortensio, will *you any wife?* SHAKESPEARE.

3. To command; to direct.

St. Paul did will *them of Corinth, every man to lay up somewhat on the Sunday, and to reserve it in store for the church of Jerusalem, for the relief of the poor there.* HOOKER.

How rarely does it meet with this time's guise,
When man was willed *to love his enemies.* SHAKESPEARE.

Our battle is more full of names than yours,
Our men more perfect in the use of arms,
Our armours all as strong, our cause the best;
Then reason wills *our hearts should be as good.* SHAKESPEARE.

He willed *him to be of good comfort, promising to bestow upon him whatsoever he should win.* KNOLLES.

If they had any business, his Majesty willed *that they should attend.* CLARENDON.

'Tis your's, O queen! to will
The work, which duty binds me to fulfil. DRYDEN.

4. It has a loose and slight signification.

Let the circumstances of life be what, or where they will, *a man should never neglect improvement.* WATTS.

5. It is one of the signs of the future tense; of which it is difficult to show or limit the signification.

I will come. I am determined to come; importing choice.

Thou wilt come. It must be so that thou must come; importing necessity.

Wilt thou come? Hast thou determined to come? importing choice.

He will come. He is resolved to come; or it must be that he must come, importing either choice or necessity.

It will come. It must so be that it must come; importing necessity.

The plural follows the analogy of the singular.

WI'MBLE. *n.s.* [*wimpel*, old Dutch, from *wemelen*, to bore.] An instrument with which holes are bored.

At harvest-home, trembling to approach
The little barrel, which he fears to broach:
He 'says the wimble, *often draws it back,*
And deals to thirsty servants but a smack. DRYDEN.

As when a shipwright stands his workmen o'er,
Who plye the wimble *some huge beam to bore;*
Urg'd on all hands it nimbly spins about,
The grain deep-piercing till it scoops it out. POPE.

The trepan is like a wimble, *used by joiners.* SHARP.

WI'NDEGG. *n.s.* An egg not impregnated; an egg that does not contain the principles of life.

Sound eggs sink, and such as are addled swim; as do also those termed hypenemia, or windeggs. BROWN'S VULGAR ERROURS.

To **WI'REDRAW.** *v.a.* [*wire* and *draw.*]

1. To spin into wire.
2. To draw out into length.

A fluid moving through a flexible canal, when small, by its friction will naturally lengthen, and wiredraw *the sides of the canal, according to the direction of its axis.* ARBUTHNOT.

3. To draw by art or violence.

I have been wrongfully accused, and my sense wiredrawn *into blasphemy.* DRYDEN.

WI'REDRAWER. *n.s.* [*wire* and *draw.*] One who spins wire.

Those who have need of unmixed silver, as gilders and wiredrawers, *must, besides an equal weight of silver mixed with other metals, give an overplus to reward the refiner's skill.* LOCKE.

WI'TCRACKER. *n.s.* [*wit* and *cracker.*] A joker; one who breaks a jest.

A college of witcrackers *cannot flout me out of my humour; dost thou think I care for a satire or an epigram?* SHAKESPEARE.

WI'TWORM. *n.s.* [*wit* and *worm.*] One that feeds on wit; a canker of wit.

Thus to come forth so suddenly a witworm. BEN JONSON.

WITHDRA'WINGROOM. *n.s.* [*withdraw* and *room.*] Room behind another room for retirement.

For an ordinary gentleman, a hall, a great parlour, with a withdrawingroom, *with a kitchen, butteries, and other conveniencies, is sufficient.* MORTIMER'S HUSBANDRY.

WI'TLING. *n.s.* [Diminutive of *wit.*] A pretender to wit; a man of petty smartness.

You have taken off the senseless ridicule, which for many years the witlings *of the town have turned upon their fathers and mothers.* ADDISON'S SPECTATOR.

Those half-learn'd witlings *num'rous in our isle,*
As half-form'd insects on the banks of Nile. POPE.

A beau and witling *perish'd in the throng,*
One dy'd in metaphor, and one in song. POPE.

WITSNA'PPER. *n.s.* [*wit* and *snap.*] One who affects repartee.

Go in, sirrah; bid them prepare for dinner. ——
—— *That is done, sir; they have all stomachs.* ——
—— *What a* witsnapper *are you!* SHAKESPEARE.

To **WOMANI'SE.** *v.a.* [from *woman.*] To emasculate; to effeminate; to soften. Proper, but not used.

This effeminate love of a woman doth womanize *a man.* SIDNEY.

WOO'DCOCK. *n.s.* [*woducoc,* Saxon.] A bird of passage with a long bill; his food is not known. It is a word ludicrously used for a dunce.

He hath bid me to a calve's head and a capon; shall I not find a woodcock *too.* SHAKESPEARE.

Soon as in doubtful day the woodcock *flies,*
Her cleanly pail the pretty housewife bears. GAY.

WOO'DHOLE. *n.s.* [*wood* and *hole.*] Place where wood is laid up.

What should I do? or whither turn? amaz'd,
Confounded to the dark recess I fly,
Of woodhole. PHILIPS.

WOO'DMONGER. *n.s.* [*wood* and *monger.*] A woodseller.

WORD. *n.s.* [*word,* Saxon; *woord,* Dutch.]

1. A single part of speech.

If you speak three words, *it will three times report you the three* words. BACON.

As conceptions are the images of things to the mind within itself, so are words *or names the marks of those conceptions to the minds of them we converse with.* SOUTH'S SERMONS.

Amongst men who confound their ideas with words, *there must be endless disputes, wrangling, and jargon.* LOCKE.

Each wight who reads not, and but scans and spells,
Each word *catcher that lives on syllables.* POPE.

2. A short discourse.

Shall I vouchsafe your worship a word *or two?*
—— *Two thousand, and I'll vouchsafe thee the hearing.* SHAKESPEARE.

A word, *Lucilius,*
How he receiv'd you.
SHAKESPEARE'S JULIUS CÆSAR.

A friend who shall own thee in thy lowest condition, answer all thy wants, and, in a word, *never leave thee.* SOUTH.

In a word, *the Gospel describes God to us in all respects such a one as we would wish him to be.* TILLOTSON.

3. Talk; discourse.

Why should calamity be full of words?
—— *Windy attorneys to their client woes!*
Let them have scope, though what they do impart
Help nothing else, yet they do ease the heart. SHAKESPEARE'S RICHARD III.

If you dislike the play,
Pray make no words *on't 'till the second day,*
Or third be past; for we would have you know it,
The loss will fall on us, not on the poet.
DENHAM.

Cease this contention: be thy words *severe,*
Sharp as he merits; but the sword forbear.
DRYDEN.

If words *are sometimes to be used, they ought to be grave, kind, and sober, representing the ill, or unbecomingness of the faults.* LOCKE.

If I appear a little word*-bound in my first solutions, I hope it will be imputed to the long disuse of speech.* SPECTATOR.

4. Dispute; verbal contention.

In argument upon a case,
Some words *there grew 'twixt Somerset and me.* SHAKESPEARE.

5. Language.[240]

Found you no displeasure by word *or countenance?* SHAKESPEARE.

I'll write thee a challenge, or I'll deliver thy indignation to him by word *of mouth.* SHAKESPEARE'S TWELFTH NIGHT.

He commanded the men to be ranged in battalions, and rid to every squadron, giving them such words *as were proper to the occasion.* CLARENDON.

An easy way, by word *of mouth communicated to me.* BOYLE.

6. Promise.

Obey thy parents, keep thy word *justly, swear not.* SHAKESPEARE.

I take your princely word *for these redresses.*
—— *I give it you, and will maintain my* word. SHAKESPEARE'S HENRY IV.

The duke shall wield his conqu'ring sword,
The king shall pass his honest word.
DRYDEN.

7. Signal; token.

Every soldier, kill his prisoners;
Give the word *through.*
SHAKESPEARE'S HENRY V.

8. Account; tydings; message.

Bring me word *thither*
How the world goes, that to the pace of it
I may spur on my journey.
SHAKESPEARE'S CORIOLANUS.

Why should she write to Edmund? Might not you
Transport her purposes by word?
SHAKESPEARE'S KING LEAR.

Two optick nerves she ties,
Like spectacles across the eyes;
By which the spirits bring her word,
Whene'er the balls are fix'd or stirr'd.
PRIOR.

9. Declaration.

I know you brave, and take you at your word;
That present service which you vaunt, afford. DRYDEN.

10. Affirmation.

Every person has enough to do to work out his own salvation; which, if we will take the apostle's word, *is to be done with fear and trembling.* DECAY OF PIETY.

I desire not the reader should take my word, *and therefore I will set two of their discourses in the same light for every man to judge.* DRYDEN.

11. Scripture; word of God.

They say this church of England neither hath the word *purely preached, nor the sacraments sincerely ministred.* WHITGIFT.

12. The second person of the ever adorable Trinity. A scripture term.

Thou my Word, *begotten son, by thee*
This I perform. MILTON.

To **WORD.** *v.n.* [from the noun.] To dispute.

He that descends not to word *it with a shrew, does worse than beat her.* L'ESTRANGE.

To **WORD.** *v.a.* To express in proper words.

Let us blacken him what we can, said Harrison of the blessed king, upon the wording *and drawing up his charge against approaching trial.* SOUTH'S SERMONS.

Whether I have improved these fables or no, in the wording *or meaning of them, the book must stand or fall to itself.* L'ESTRANGE.

The apology for the king is the same, but worded *with greater deference to that great prince.* ADDISON.

WO'RDY. *adj.* [from *word.*] Verbose; full of words.

Phocion, beholding a wordy *orator, while he was making a magnificent speech full of vain promises, said, I now fix my eyes upon a cypress-tree: it has all the pomp imaginable in its branches, leaves, and height; but it bears no fruit.* SPECTATOR.

We need not lavish hours in wordy *periods,*
As do the Romans, ere they dare to fight. PHILIPS'S BRITON.

Intemp'rate rage, a wordy *war, began.* POPE.

WO'RLDLING. *n.s.* [from *world.*] A mortal set upon profit.

Baseminded wretches! are your thoughts so deeply bemired in the trade of ordinary worldlings, *as for respect of gain to let so much time pass.* SIDNEY.

The one sort are nam'd the brethren, the godly; the other worldlings, *timeservers, and pleasers of men more than pleasers of God.* HOOKER.

God of the world and worldlings,
Great Mammon! greatest god below the sky. FAIRY QUEEN.

For his weeping in the needless stream;
Poor deer, quoth he, thou mak'st a testament
As worldlings *do, giving thy sum of more*
To that which had too much.
SHAKESPEARE'S AS YOU LIKE IT.

That other on his friends his thoughts bestows:
The covetous worldling, *in his anxious mind,*
Thinks only on the wealth he left behind.
DRYDEN.

If we consider the expectations of futurity, the worldling *gives up the argument.* ROGERS.

To **WO'RRY.** *v.a.* [*worigen*, Saxon: whence probably the word *warray.*]

1. To tear, or mangle, as a beast tears its prey.

If we with thrice such powers left at home,
Cannot defend our own doors from the dog,
Let us be worried.
SHAKESPEARE'S HENRY V.

The fury of the tumults might fly so high as to worry *and tear those in pieces, whom as yet they but play'd with in their paws.* KING CHARLES.

'Tis no new thing for the dogs that are to

keep the wolves from worrying *the sheep, to be deliver'd up to the enemy, for fear the sheep should* worry *the wolves.*
L'ESTRANGE.

This revives and imitates that inhuman barbarity of the old heathen persecutors, wrapping up christians in the skins of wild beasts, that so they might be worried *and torn in pieces by dogs.*
SOUTH'S SERMONS.

2. To harrass, or persecute brutally.

Then embraces his son-in-law; then again worries *he his daughter with clipping her.*
SHAKESPEARE'S WINTER'S TALE.

For want of words, or lack of breath,
Witness when I was worried *with thy peals.* MILTON.

It has pleased Providence at length to give us righteousness instead of exaction, and hopes of religion to a church worried *with reformation.* SOUTH'S SERMONS.

All his care
Was to preserve me from the barbarous rage,
Which worried *him only for being mine.*
SOUTHERN.

I shall not suffer him to worry *any man's reputation, nor indeed fall on any person whatsoever.* ADDISON.

Let them rail,
And then worry *one another at their pleasure.* ROWE.

Madam, contrive and invent,
And worry *him out, 'till he gives his consent.* SWIFT.

WOU'LDING. *n.s.* [from *would.*] Motion of desire; disposition to any thing; propension; inclination; incipient purpose.

It will be every man's interest to join good performances to spiritual purposes, to subdue the exorbitancies of the flesh, as well as to continue the wouldings *of the spirit.*
HAMMOND.

WREATH. *n.s.* [*wreoð*, Saxon.]

1. Any thing curled or twisted.

The wreath *of three was made a* wreath *of five: to these three first titles of the two houses, were added the authorities parliamentary and papal.*
BACON'S HENRY VII.

Clouds began
To darken all the hill, and smoke to roll
In dusky wreaths *reluctant flames.*
MILTON'S PARADISE LOST.

He of his tortuous train
Curl'd many a wanton wreath.
MILTON.

Let altars smoak,
And richest gums, and spice, and incense roll
Their fragrant wreaths *to heav'n.*
SMITH'S PHÆDRA AND HIPPOLITUS.

2. A garland; a chaplet.

Now are our brows bound with victorious wreaths,
Our bruised arms hung up for monuments.
SHAKESPEARE'S RICHARD III.

Dropp'd from his head, a wreath *lay on the ground.* ROSCOMMON.

The boughs of Lotos, form'd into a wreath,
This monument, thy maiden beauty's due,
High on a plane-tree shall be hung to view. DRYDEN.

When for thy head the garland I prepare,
A second wreath *shall bind Aminta's hair;*
And when my choicest songs thy worth proclaim,
Alternate verse shall bless Aminta's name.
PRIOR.

To prince Henry the laurels of his rival are transferred, with the additional wreath *of having conquered that rival.*
SHAKESPEARE ILLUSTRATED.

To **WREATH.** *v.a.* preterite *wreathed*; part. pass. *wreathed, wreathen.* [from the noun.]

1. To curl; to twist; to convolve.

Longaville
Did never sonnet for her sake compile,
Nor never laid his wreathed *arms athwart*

His loving bosom, to keep down his heart. SHAKESPEARE.

About his neck
A green and gilded snake had wreath'd *itself,*
Who, with her head, nimble in threats approach'd
The opening of his mouth; but suddenly,
Seeing Orlando, it unlink'd itself,
And with indented glides did slip away.
SHAKESPEARE'S AS YOU LIKE IT.

The beard of an oat is wreathed *at the bottom, and one smooth entire straw at the top: they take only the part that is* wreathed, *and cut off the other.* BACON.

2. It is here used for to writhe.

Impatient of the wound,
He rolls and wreaths *his shining body round;*
Then headlong shoots beneath the dashing tide. GAY.

3. To interweave; to entwine one in another.

Two chains of pure gold of wreathen *work shalt thou make them, and fasten the* wreathen *chains to the ouches.* BIBLE EXODUS, XXVIII.

As snakes breed in dunghills not singly, but in knots; so in such base noisome hearts you shall ever see pride and ingratitude indivisibly wreathed *and twisted together.* SOUTH.

Here, where the labourer's hands have form'd a bow'r
Of wreathing *trees, in singing waste an hour.* DRYDEN.

4. To encircle as a garland.

In the flow'rs that wreath *the sparkling bowl,*
Fell adders hiss, and pois'nous serpents rowl. PRIOR.

5. To encircle as with a garland.

For thee she feeds her hair,
And with thy winding ivy wreathes *her lance.* DRYDEN.

The soldier, from successful camps returning,
With laurel wreath'd, *and rich with hostile spoil,*
Severs the bull to Mars. PRIOR.

WRE'ATHY. *adj.* [from *wreath.*] Spiral; curled; twisted.

That which is preserved at St. Dennis, near Paris, hath wreathy *spires, and cochleary turnings about, which agreeth with the description of an unicorn's horn in Ælian.* BROWN.

WRETCH. *n.s.* [*wrecca*, Saxon.]

1. A miserable mortal.

When I loved, I was a wretch. ACCIDENCE.

She weeps, and says her Henry is depos'd;
He smiles, and says his Edward is install'd;
That she, poor wretch, *for grief can speak no more.* SHAKESPEARE.

The butcher takes away the calf,
And binds the wretch, *and beats it when it strives.* SHAKESPEARE.

Illustrious wretch! *repine not, nor reply:*
View not what heav'n ordains, with reason's eye;
For bright the object is, the distance is too high. PRIOR.

2. A worthless sorry creature.

Base-minded wretches, *are your thoughts so deeply bemired in the trade of ordinary worldlings, as for respect of gain some paultry wool may yield you, to let so much time pass without knowing perfectly her estate?* SIDNEY.

He now
Has these poor men in question: never saw I
Wretches *so quake; they kneel, they kiss the earth,*
Forswear themselves as often as they speak. SHAKESPEARE.

Title of honour, worth and virtue's right,
Should not be given to a wretch *so vile.* DANIEL'S CIVIL WAR.

When they are gone, a company of starved hungry wretches *shall take their places.* L'ESTRANGE.

3. It is used by way of slight, or ironical pity, or contempt.

When soon away the wasp doth go;
Poor wretch *was never frighted so:*
He thought his wings were much too slow,
O'erjoy'd they so were parted.
DRAYTON'S NYMPHID.

Then, if the spider find him fast beset,
She issues forth, and runs along her loom:
She joys to touch the captive in her net,
And drags the little wretch *in triumph home.* DRYDEN.

4. It is sometimes a word of tenderness, as we now say *poor thing.*

Chastened but thus, and thus his lesson taught,
The happy wretch *she put into her breast.*
SIDNEY.

To **WRITE.** *v.a.* preterite *writ* or *wrote*; part. pass. *written, writ,* or *wrote.* [*writan, awritan,* Saxon; *ad rita,* Islandick; *wreta,* a letter, Gothick.]

1. To express by means of letters.

I'll write *you down,*
The which shall point you forth, at every sitting,
What you must say. SHAKESPEARE.

Men's evil manners live in brass, their virtues.
We write *in water.*
SHAKESPEARE'S HENRY VIII.

When a man hath taken a wife, and she find no favour in his eyes, then let him write *her a bill of divorcement.* BIBLE DEUTERONOMY.

Write *ye this song for you, and teach it Israel.* BIBLE DEUTERONOMY, XXXI.

David wrote *a letter to Joab, and sent it by Uriah.* BIBLE 2 SAMUEL, XI.

The time, the place, the manner how to meet,
Were all in punctual order plainly writ.
DRYDEN.

2. To engrave; to impress.

Cain was so fully convinced that every one had a right to destroy such a criminal, that he cries out, every one that findeth me shall slay me; so plain was it writ *in the hearts of all mankind.* LOCKE.

3. To produce as an author.

When more indulgent to the writer's ease,
You are so good, to be so hard to please;
No such convulsive pangs it will require
To write —— *the pretty things that you admire.* GRANVILLE.

4. To tell by letter.

I chose to write *the thing I durst not speak*
To her I lov'd. PRIOR.

To **WRITE.** *v.n.*

1. To perform the act of writing.

I have seen her rise from her bed, take forth paper, fold it, and write *upon't.* SHAKESPEARE'S MACBETH.

Bassanio gave his ring away
Unto the judge that begg'd it; and his clerk,
That took some pains in writing, *he begg'd mine.* SHAKESPEARE.

2. To play the authour.

Hearts, tongues, figures, scribes, bards, poets, cannot
Think, speak, cast, write, *sing, number*
His love to Antony.
SHAKESPEARE'S ANTONY AND CLEOPATRA.

There is not a more melancholy object in the learned world than a man who has written *himself down.* ADDISON.

3. To tell in books.

I past the melancholy flood,
With that grim ferryman which poets write *of.* SHAKESPEARE'S RICHARD III.

4. To send letters.

He wrote *for all the Jews, concerning their freedom.* BIBLE 1 ESDRAS.

5. To call one's self; to be entitled; to use the stile of.

About it, and write *happy when thou'st done.* SHAKESPEARE.

Let it not your wonder move,
Less your laughter that I love;
Though I now write *fifty years,*
I have had, and have my peers.
BEN JONSON.

He writes *himself divina providentia, whereas other bishops only use divina permissione.* AYLIFFE.

6. To compose; to form compositions.

Chaste moral writing *we may learn from hence,*
Neglect of which no wit can recompence;
The fountain which from Helicon proceeds,
That sacred stream, should never water weeds. WALLER.

They can write *up to the dignity and character of their authors.*
FELTON ON THE CLASSICKS.

WRI'TER. *n.s.* [from *write.*]

1. One who practises the art of writing.

2. An authour.

All three were ruined by justice and sentence, as delinquents; and all three famous writers. BACON.

Peaceable times are the best to live in, though not so proper to furnish materials for a writer. ADDISON'S FREEHOLDER.

Writers *are often more influenced by a desire of fame, than a regard to the publick good.* ADDISON'S FREEHOLDER.

Would a writer *know how to behave himself with relation to posterity, let him consider in old books what he finds that he is glad to know, and what omissions he most laments.* SWIFT.

WRI'TINGMASTER. *n.s.* One who teaches to write.

The facility of which I spoke consists not in bold strokes, if it makes not a great effect at a distance: that sort of freedom belongs rather to a writingmaster *than a painter.* DRYDEN.

Is a letter, which, though found in Saxon words, begins no word in the English language.[241]

Y

At the beginning of words, is a consonant; at the end, and when it follows a consonant, is a vowel, and has the sound of *i*. It is used at the end of words, and whenever two *i i*'s would come together; and in words derived from the Greek, to express the *u*. *Y* was much used by the Saxons, whence *y* is found for *i* in the old English writers.

Y is in old English sometimes prefixed as an increasing syllable to preterites, and passive participles of verbs. It seems borrowed from *ge*, the Saxon *augmentum* of the preterite. It is sometimes put before present tenses, but, I think, erroneously.[242]

YACHT. *n.s.* A small ship for carrying passengers.

YELK. *n.s.* [from *gealewe*, yellow, Saxon.] The yellow part of the egg. It is commonly pronounced, and often written *yolk*.

> *The* yolk *of the egg conduceth little to the generation of the bird, but only to the nourishment of the same: for if a chicken be opened, when it is new hatched, you shall find much of the* yolk *remaining.*
> BACON'S NATURAL HISTORY.

> *That a chicken is formed out of the* yelk *of an egg, with some antient philosophers the people still opinion.* BROWN.

> *All the feather'd kind,*
> *From th' included* yolk, *not ambient white arose.* DRYDEN.

YE'LLOWBOY. *n.s.* A gold coin. A very low word.

> *John did not starve the cause; there wanted not* yellowboys *to see council.*
> ARBUTHNOT'S JOHN BULL.

YES. *adv.* [*gise*, Saxon.] A term of affirmation; the affirmative particle opposed to *no*.

> *This were a fit speech for a general in the head of an army, when going to battle:* yes, *and it is no less fit speech in the head of a council, upon a deliberation of entrance into a war.* BACON.

> Yes, *you despise the man to books confin'd,*
> *Who from his study rails at human kind,*
> *Though what he learns he speaks.*
> POPE.[243]

YEW. *n.s.* [*iw*, Saxon; *yw*, Welsh. This is often written *eugh*; but the former orthography is at once nearer to the sound and the derivation. See **EUGH.**] A tree of tough wood.[244]

It hath amentaceous flowers, which consist of many apices, for the most part shaped like a mushroom, and are barren; but the embryoes, which are produced at remote distances on the same tree, do afterward become hollow bell-shaped berries, which are full of juice, and include seeds somewhat like acorns, having, as it were, a little cup to each. *Miller*.

The shooter eugh, *the broad-leav'd sycamore,*
The barren plantane, and the walnut sound;
The myrrhe, that her soul sin doth still deplore,
Alder the owner of all waterish ground.
FAIRFAX.

Slips of yew,
Shiver'd in the moon's eclipse.
SHAKESPEARE'S MACBETH.

They would bind me here
Unto the body of a dismal yew.
SHAKESPEARE'S TITUS ANDRONICUS.

He drew,
And almost join'd the horns of the tough yew. DRYDEN.

The distinguish'd yew *is ever seen,*
Unchang'd his branch, and permanent his green. PRIOR.

YOLK. *n.s.* [See **YELK.**] The yellow part of an egg.

Nature hath provided a large yolk *in every egg, a great part whereof remaineth after the chicken is hatched; and, by a channel made on purpose, serves instead of milk to nourish the chick for a considerable time.* RAY ON THE CREATION.

YOU'THY. *adj.* [from *youth.*] Young; youthful. A bad word.

The scribler had not genius to turn my age, as indeed I am an old maid, into raillery, for affecting a youthier *turn than is consistent with my time of day.* SPECTATOR.

YUCK. *n.s.* [*jocken*, Dutch.] Itch.

YUX. *n.s.* [*yeox*, Saxon.] The hiccough.

Z

Is found in the Saxon alphabets, set down by Grammarians, but is read in no word originally Teutonick: its sound is uniformly that of an hard *S*. No word of English original begins with *Z*.[245]

ZA'NY. *n.s.* [Probably of *zanci*. The contraction of *Giovanni* or *sanna*, a scoff, according to *Skinner*.] One employed to raise laughter by his gestures, actions and speeches; a merry Andrew; a buffoon.

> *Some carrytale, some pleaseman, some slight* zany,
> *Some mumblenews, some trencher knight, some Dick,*
> *Told our intents before.* SHAKESPEARE.

> *Then write that I may follow, and so be*
> *Thy echo, thy debtor, thy foil, thy* zany,
> *I shall be thought, if mine like thine I shape,*
> *All the world's lion, though I be thy ape.*
> DONNE.

> *Oh, great restorer of the good old stage,*
> *Preacher at once, and* zany *of thy age.*
> POPE'S DUNCIAD.

ZE'CHIN. *n.s.* [So named from *zecha*, a place in Venice where the mint is settled for coinage.] A gold coin worth about nine shillings sterling.

ZEST. *n.s.*
1. The peel of an orange squeezed into wine.
2. A relish; a taste added.

ZOO'GRAPHER. *n.s.* [ζωή and γράφω.] One who describes the nature, properties, and forms of animals.

> *One kind of locust stands not prone, or a little inclining upward; but a large erectness, elevating the two fore legs, and sustaining itself in the middle of the other four, by* zoographers *called the prophet and praying locust.*
> BROWN'S VULGAR ERROURS.

ZOO'GRAPHY. *n.s.* [of ζωή and γράφω.] A description of the forms, natures, and properties of animals.

> *If we contemplate the end of the effect, its principal final cause being the glory of its*

maker, this leads us into divinity; and for its subordinate, as it is designed for alimental sustenance to living creatures, and medicinal uses to man, we are thereby conducted into zoography.
GLANVILLE SCEPSIS SCIENTIFICA.

ZOO'LOGY. *n.s.* [of *ζώον* and *λογος*.] A treatise concerning living creatures.

ZOO'TOMIST. *n.s.* [of *ζωοτομία*.] A dissector of the bodies of brute beasts.

ZOO'TOMY. *n.s.* [*ζωοτομία*, of *ζώον* and *τεμνω*.] Dissection of the bodies of beasts.

Notes

The notes below chiefly refer to the changes made in the fourth edition.

1. ABOVE-BOARD The second example is assigned to a separate sense 2: 'Without disguise or concealment'.

2. ACCOUPLE Added: 'We now use *couple*.'

3. ACE Added: 'a particle; an atom'.

4. ACQUIESCE Added: an extra illustrative quotation.

5. ACQUIESCENCE Added: a further synonym, 'confidence'.

6. ADOLESCENCY The entry for ADOLESCENCE is combined with that for ADOLESCENCY.

7. ADVENT This definition is turned into a quotation, and attributed to the Book of Common Prayer.

8. AFTER ALL Added: 'upon the whole; at the most.'

9. ALONE Added: 'forbidding' before 'to help'.

10. ALTER The definition is expanded: 'With *from* and *to*; as, her face is *altered from* pale *to* red.'

11. ANAGRAM See MOIL 'toil, drudge', but spelled with an *i*.

12. ANCIENT Added: 'but when *new* means *modern*'.

13. APPEAR Omitted: 'sometimes . . . *in*'.

14. APPOSE Added: a second definition, 'A latinism. To apply to', with an illustrative quotation from Harvey.

15. AQUA MIRABILIS Omitted: the last sentence.

16. ARCH Added: 'unless it be derived from *Archy*, the name of the jester to Charles I'.

17. ARMLET Added: a second illustration, from Dryden.

18. ARTICULATE The definition begins: 'Distinct; divided, as . . .'

19. ASPHALTOS The definition stops at this point.

20. ASSEMBLAGE This quotation is assigned to a separate sense 2: 'The state of being assembled'.

21. ASSHEAD An unusual error: the quotation is from *Twelfth Night*.

22. ASTROLOGY Replaced: 'without reason' by 'irrational and false'.

23. ATTRITION Added: a new sense 2, 'The state of being worn', and sense 2 becomes sense 3.

24. AUSPICE Omitted: the phrase 'by prosperous men'.

25. **AWARE** Added as the first definition: 'excited to caution'.

26. **AWFULNESS** Added: the comment 'little used'.

27. **AWLESS** Altered: 'without' to 'wanting', in both definitions. Added to the first definition: 'void of respectful fear'.

28. **BACHELOR** The word came immediately from Middle French *bacheler*, Middle Latin *baccalarius*, 'tenant farmer, squire, advanced student', but the early Latin and pre-Latin sources remain unclear. In the fourth edition, Johnson adds as a penultimate sentence to the etymological note: 'Dr. *Lawrence* observed, that *Menage*'s etymology is much confirmed by the practice in our universities of calling a Bachelor, Sir.'

29. **BALLIARDS** Compare the entry on **BILLIARDS**.

30. **BAMBOO** The definition is much reduced: 'An Indian plant of the reed kind. It has several shoots, much larger than our ordinary reeds, which are knotty, and separated from space to space by joints. The bamboo is much larger than the sugar-cane.'

31. **BARBARISM** Added: 'not in use'.

32. **BEAR-GARDEN** This quotation is moved to illustrate sense 2.

33. **BEGIN** Added: a quotation from Dryden.

34. **BEGIRD** This quotation is assigned to sense 2.

35. **BELOWT** Added: 'Obsolete'.

36. **BIBACIOUS** Lack of space in the line forces an unusual abbreviation in the original: *Dictionaries* to *D.*

37. **BLAME** Omitted in sense 1: the first use of 'fault'. Added in sense 3: 'Not now in use'. Added in sense 4: 'culpable; worthy of censure'.

38. **BLINDWORM** The definition is corrected: 'A small viper, called likewise a slow worm; believed not to be venemous'.

39. **BOB** Added: a fourth sense, 'A mode of ringing'.

40. **BOLD** Added to sense 5: 'or expression'. In sense 8, the example is replaced by: '*I was bold* to tell the house that scandalous livings make scandalous ministers. *Rudgerd.*'

41. **BOOTY** Note the use of *gotten*, here and in the L'Estrange quotation at sense 1, soon to disappear from standard British (but not American) English.

42. **BOPEEP** The definition begins: 'The act of looking out, and drawing back as if frighted . . .'

43. **BREAD-CHIPPER** Added: 'an under-butler'.

44. **BRISK** Added: 'this is not used'.

45. **BUMPKIN** Added: 'yet we use the word cabbage-head in the same sense'.

46. **BUREAU** Added: 'with a writing board'.

47. **CALMY** Added: 'Not used'.

48. **CAN** Johnson notes the overlap in meaning between *can* and *may*, which prescriptive grammarians later attempted to eliminate.

49. **CAR** Replaced: 'a chariot' by 'any vehicle of dignity or splendour'.

50. **CASTAWAY** 'Providence' is given an initial capital. Added: 'anything thrown away'.

51. **CAYMAN** This word is omitted in the fourth edition.

52. **CENSE** Altered: 'Public rate'.

53. **CERTAIN** Added three extra senses: 'Unfailing; which always produces the expected effect'; 'Constant; never failing to be'; 'Regular; settled; stated'.

54. **CIVILLY** Altered: 'not criminally' is made a separate sense 2, along with the quotation from Ayliffe. Omitted: 'not ecclesiastically'.

55. **CLEAR** This quotation is assigned to a new sense 2: 'Perspicacious; sharp'. Added: a new sense 3, 'Cheerful; not clouded with care or anger' and a new sense 9, 'Quick to understand; prompt; acute', making twenty senses differentiated in the later edition.

56. **CLINCH** Expanded: 'How it obtains this meaning is difficult to find. A nail caught on the *other side*, and *doubled*, is a nail clinched: a word taken in a *different meaning*, and *doubled* in sense, is likewise a *clinch*.'

57. **COLANDER** Added: 'a strainer'.

58. **COMEDIAN** Omitted: this unattributed couplet.

59. **COMEDY** Added: 'with an intention to make vice and folly ridiculous: opposed to *tragedy*'.

60. **COMPLIMENT** Added: 'this is properly *complement*, something superfluous, or more than enough'.

61. **CONCUSSION** Altered: this quotation is placed under a separate sense 2, 'The state of being shaken'.

62. **CONFORMATION** Added: 'With *to*'.

63. **CONSENT** A quotation from Milton illustrates this first sense: 'Though what thou tell'st some doubt within me move, / But more desire to hear, if thou consent, / The full relation'.

64. **CONSIDERATE** Added: 'Little used'.

65. **CONSOLATE** Added: 'Not much used'. The usage eventually lost out to *console* (next entry).

66. **CONTRISTATION** Added: 'Not used' (despite all these synonyms).

67. **CONVERSE** Added: 'action'.

68. **COQUET** Added: 'To entice by blandishments'.

69. **CORN-FLAG** This encyclopedic characterization is reduced to 'A plant' plus the penultimate sentence.

70. **CRACK** Sense split into two: the first quotation is assigned to 'Change of the voice in puberty' and the second to 'Breach of chastity'.

71. **CREEPLE** This is an example of a word added in the fourth edition.

72. **CRITIC** Added: a new sense 2, 'An examiner; a judge', illustrated by an additional quotation from Pope; a new sense 3, 'A snarler; a carper; a caviller', illustrated by the quotations here shown from Pope and Watts.

73. **CUTTER** Added: '[Incisores.]' before this definition.

74. **DADAL** The headword is spelled **DAEDAL**.

75. **DECLINATION** Added to sense 1: 'diminution of vigour'. Added: a new sense 4, 'Deviation from moral rectitude'.

76. **DEGREE** This definition begins 'The comparative state . . .'. Omitted in sense 5: 'of the angels'. In sense 11 the definition stops at 'quality'.

77. **DEPARTMENT** Added (rather redundantly, given the etymology): 'A French term'.

78. **DEPENDENT** Johnson's own uncertainty is illustrated by his change of mind between the first and the fourth editions. In the former, adjectival *dependent* in the sense of 'in the power of another' is spelled with *-ant*, and in its sense of 'hanging down' with *-ent*, as shown here; in the fourth edition the latter is a separate entry *dependant*.

79. **DESULTORY** Added: '*Desultorious* is not in use'.

80. **DETER** Altered: 'To discourage by terrour'.

81. **DETERMENT** Added: 'A good word, but not now used'.

82. **DEVIOUS** Added: a sense 4, 'It is used likewise of persons. Roving; idly vagrant; erring from the way'.

83. **DIAPER** Added: 'the finest species of figured linen after damask'.

84. **DIBSTONE** This entry is omitted.

85. **DIFFICILNESS** Added: 'A word not in use, but proper'.

86. **DIFFICULTY** The accent is represented as grave in the text.

87. **DISEMBITTER** Added: 'an unusual word'.

88. **DISPREAD** Added: 'This word is poetical'.

89. **DOLL** Added as an example: 'Doll Tearsheet' (from Shakespeare).

90. **DOSE** Added: new sense 2 ('Any thing nauseous') and sense 4 ('Quantity').

91. **DOUBLE-MINDED** Altered: 'Unsettled; undetermined'.

92. **EAST** Added: the antonym, 'opposite to the *West*'. An antonym is also added to the definition of **SOUTH**; but not for **NORTH** and **WEST**.

93. **ECONOMY** Added: a new sense 2, 'Distribution of expence'. Altered in sense 5 (sense 6 in the fourth edition), 'System of motions' to 'System of matter'.

94. **EFFUMABILITY** Added: 'An useful word but not adopted'.

95. **ESTABLISHMENT** Added: a sense 6, 'Settled or final rest'.

96. **EVESDROPPER** Johnson makes no reference to the spelling with **EA-**, which has its own entry.

97. **EXHIBITION** Added: 'it is much used for pensions allowed to scholars at the university'. Also added: a sense 3, 'Payment; recompence'.

98. **EXORBITANT** These two meanings are distinguished as separate senses, with the quotations assigned to sense 2.

99. **EXTREME** Added: a sense 5, 'Rigorous; strict'.

100. **FANGLED** Replaced: the second sentence by 'new fangled, is therefore new fashioned; dressed out in new decorations'.

101. **FEAGUE** Omitted: the Scottish allusion.

102. **FEMALE** Added: 'Not male'.

103. **FILE** Added: a new sense 3, 'To smooth; to polish'; sense 3 becomes sense 4.

104. **FIRECROSS** Omitted: 'like lightning'.

105. **FIT** Added: a sense 6, 'It was anciently used for any recommencement after intermission. The parts of a song, or cantos of a poem, were called *fits*'.

106. **FIZGIG** This quotation is added from the fourth edition.

107. **FLESH** Two stylistic comments are added: at sense 7, 'in theology'; at sense 8, 'a scriptural use'.

108. **FOOT** Added: an example, '*the* foot *of a table*'. Altered: senses 15 and 16 are presented in reverse order.

109. **FORE** Added: 'A vitious orthography has confounded *for* and *fore* in composition.'

110. **FRANKLIN** Added: 'Not in use' .

111. **FROG** Added: 'famous in Homer's poem'.

112. **FULSOME** Added: a new sense 3, 'Lustful'. The Shakespeare quotation from sense 1 is used to illustrate it.

113. **GAR** Added: 'Obsolete'.

114. **GAZETTEER** This sense ameliorates to: 'An officer appointed to publish news by authority, whom *Steele* calls the lowest minister of state.'

115. **GENTRY** Added: 'rank derived from inheritance'.

116. **GLASS** Added: a new sense 5, 'The destined time of man's life.'

117. **GOVERNANT** The spelling is changed to *governant.*

118. **GUTTLE** Added: 'A low word', corresponding to the other use of this verb.

119. **HA** Added: 'Used with reduplication'.

120. **HAGGLE** Added: 'always in a bad sense'.

121. **HALF-PENY** This quotation is placed under a separate sense 2: 'It has the force of an adjective conjoined with any thing of which it denotes the price'.

122. **HANDSEL** Added: 'It is now not used, except in the dialect of trade.'

123. **HAP-HAZARD** Added: 'perhaps originally *hap hazardè*'.

124. **HARNESS** Added: 'Somewhat antiquated'.

125. **HATCH** Added: 'perhaps from *hacher*, to cut, as a *hatch* is part of a door cut in two'.

126. **HAVER** Added: 'perhaps properly *aven*, from *avena*, Latin'.

127. **HEROESS** Added: 'Not in use'.

128. **HERSE** The duplication with **HEARSE** is noted: 'This is likewise written *hearse*; see **HEARSE**.'

129. **HIST** Added: 'but I have heard that it is an Irish verb commanding silence'.

130. **HITCH** Adding ruefully: 'nor here know well what it means'.

131. **HOSPITAL** Added: 'Obsolete'.

132. **HOUSEKEEPER** Added to sense 2, 'one that exercises hospitality'. Added to sense 5: 'not in use'.

133. **HUM** Added: a new sense 4, 'To make a dull heavy noise'.

134. **HUMANITY** Added: 'In Scotland, *humaniores literæ*.'

135. **HURLYBURLY** The speculation is rejected; the etymology reads simply, 'from the French; *hurlubrelu*, inconsiderately'.

136. **IMPERTINENT** Added: 'negligent of the present purpose'. The noun definition following also adds: 'one who enquires or interposes where he has no right or call'.

137. **IMPETRATION** Added: 'Not much used'.

138. **IMPLEX** Added: 'opposed to *simple*'.

139. **INCORRIGIBLE** A distinction is drawn between 'of persons', added to sense 1, and a new sense 2, 'of things': 'Not capable of amendment'. The first two quotations are assigned to this second sense.

140. **INDUSTRIOUS** Added: a new sense 2, 'Laborious to a particular end: opposite to *remiss*'.

141. **INDUSTRY** Added: 'habitual or actual laboriousness'.

142. **INJURY** Added: 'A French mode of speech, not now in use'.

143. **INSECTOLOGER** Added: 'A word, I believe, unauthorised'.

144. **INSTRUCTER**: Added: 'It is often written *instructor*'.

145. **INVENTION** Conflated: senses 1 and 4.

146. K Replaced: 'but is not much in use, except after' by 'It is used after'. The observation about the non-use of final *c* would soon prove to be out of date.

147. **LATTER** This quotation is from Horace's *Ars Poetica*: 'custom wills it, in whose power lie the arbitrament, the rule, and the standard of language'.

147. **LECTURER** The rest of this definition is separated as sense 2.

148. **LESS** Added: 'or to *so great*; not so much; not equal'.

150. **LESSER** Added: 'till it has all the authority which a mode originally erroneous can derive from custom'. See also note 147.

151. **LICH** 'Hail, great mother'. (Johnson was born in Lichfield.)

152. **LIFT** These two meanings are distinguished as senses 1 and 2, with the first

two quotations illustrating 'the manner of lifting' and the third illustrating 'the act of lifting'; sense 2 in the first edition then becomes sense 5.

153. LOUIS D'OR The value is raised to twenty shillings.

154. MACHINE Expanded: 'Any complicated work in which one part contributes to the motion of another.'

155. MAGAZINE Added: 'and published under the name of *Sylvanus* Urban'.

156. MANNER Added: 'distinct mode of person.' The quotation from Donne is used to substantiate a new sense 11: '*To take in the* MANNER: To catch in the actual commission of a crime.'

157. MECHANICK New ordering: sense 2 becomes sense 1, sense 3 becomes sense 2, and sense 1 becomes sense 3; also, sense 1 adds: 'bred to manual labour'.

158. MINNOCK Not surprisingly. *Minnock* (*A Midsummer Night's Dream*, III.ii.19) is a minim misreading in Q2 for *mimic*. For *minim*, see MINUM.

159. MISSIVE Added: 'Both obsolete'.

160. MISTRESS Replaced by: 'A woman who has something in possession.'

161. MITTENS Added: an etymological note, 'It is said that *mit* is the original word; whence *mitten*, the plural, and afterwards *mittens*, as in *chicken*.'

162. MORELAND Added (rather redundantly): 'from being hilly'.

163. NAPKIN *Georgics* IV: 'And they bring napkins of shorn pile'.

164. NATURE Added: a new sense 7, 'The constitution and appearances of things', with a quotation from Reynolds, and other senses renumbered. Added as a new sense 13: 'Of this word which occurs so frequently, with significations so various, and so difficultly defined, Boyle has given an explication, which deserves to be epitomised.' There then follows a long quotation from Boyle's 'Free Enquiry into the received Notion of Nature.'

165. NET Added: a more general sense 2, 'Any thing made with interstitial vacuities'.

166. NONSENSE Added: 'a low word'.

167. OBNOXIOUS Added: a new sense 3, 'Reprehensible; not of sound reputation', with this sense renumbered as 4.

168. OFF Replaced: 'On the opposite side of a question.' At the end of the entry, several idioms are added: *to be off*, *to come off*, *to get off*, *to go off*, *well/ill off*, along with a general observation: '*Off*, whether alone or in composition, means either literally or figuratively, disjunction, absence, privation, or distance.'

169. OVER-HEAD The 'i before e except after c' representation of this vowel sound was not yet standard. Earlier in the dictionary, Johnson locates the entry at CEILING, but also has a cross-reference from CIELING.

170. PET Added: a cross-reference to PEAT.

171. PIGMY Added: 'it should be written with a *y*, *pygmy*'.

172. PLUMP Added: 'I believe it is now corrupted to *clump*'.

173. **PROVERB** Added: 'a by-word'.

174. **PROVINCIAL** Added: 'belonging to a province'.

175. **PUDDING** Added: a sense 4, 'A proverbial name for victuals'.

176. **PYGMY** Added: 'Any thing little'.

177. **QUAFF** In fact, the etymology is obscure; the *Oxford English Dictionary* suggests it is onomatopoeic in origin.

178. **QUIRE** The singing senses are also listed earlier in the dictionary under the spelling **CHOIR**.

179. **RAGAMUFFIN** The definition is taken from the fourth edition.

180. **REAR** Added: sense 8, 'To raise; to breed'.

181. **REFINEMENT** This quotation is used to illustrate a new sense 2: 'The state of being pure'.

182. **REFORMATION** Added: '[By way of eminence]'.

183. **REREWARD** Omitted entry, presumably because of the fuller entry under the spelling **REARWARD**.

184. **RESORT** Added: 'a gallicism'.

185. **SAY** Added: 'by way of argument'. Also added, two new senses:

'4. To repeat; to rehearse: as, to *say* a part; to *say* a lesson.

5. To pronounce without singing.

Then shall be said *or sung as follows.* COMMON PRAYER.'

186. Added: 'to relate'.

187. **SCAVENGER** Added: 'more commonly the labourer employed in removing filth'.

188. **SCIOMACHY** The recommendation is changed to *sciamachy*.

189. **SCULK** There is a separate entry under **SKULK**, with a broadly similar definition. Similarly, there are separate entries for several other items, such as **SCULL** and **SKULL**, **SCREEN** and **SKREEN**.

190. **SENSUOUS** Added: 'not in use'.

191. **SHADE** Added to sense 9: 'the shadow'. Deleted from sense 10: 'A spirit; a ghost; manes.'

192. **SHALL** 'Using plain homespun wit.'

193. **SHAMBLING** In fact there is no entry **SCAMBLING**. The cross-reference has to be to the verb, **SCAMBLE**.

194. **SHARK** Added at the end of senses 2 and 3 of the noun, and of senses 1 and 2 of the *v.n.* entry: 'A low word.' The *v.n.* also adds a sense 3: 'To fawn upon for a dinner'.

195. **SHRUGG** Although the following verb and the associated noun both end in a single *G*, the double *G* is kept in the fourth edition, and continues to precede **SHRUG**.

196. **SIGN** Added: 'a prodigy'. At sense 6, definition replaced by 'Note or token

given without words.' At sense 7, definition replaced by 'Mark of distinction; cognizance.'

197. **SIGNATURE** Replaced by: 'Proof drawn from marks'.

198. **SIX** Added: 'A ludicrous expression that has been long in use'.

199. **SIZERS** There is no such entry: the correlative entry is **SCISSOR.**

200. **SLOP** Deleted: second sentence.

201. **SPARKISH** Added: 'It is commonly applied to men, rather than women'.

202. **SPEECH** Replaced by: 'Declaration of thoughts'

203. **SQUIB** Added: 'Not in use'.

204. **STAFF** Added: a new sense 5, 'Round or step of a ladder', with later senses renumbered.

205. **STAMMEL** Replaced by: 'A species of red colour.'

206. **STOCAH** Added: 'Not in use'.

207. **STREW** Added: 'See **STROW.**' The definitions in the two entries largely duplicate.

208. **STYLE** Added: a new sense 4, 'Style of painting', and sense 5, 'It is likewise applied to music', with subsequent senses renumbered. Sense 8 is relocated as sense 7.

209. **SUBTILE** Added to sense 4: 'Milton seems to have both. [See **SUBTLE.**]'. Replaced in sense 6: 'exactness' by 'necessity'.

210. **SUBTILELY** Added: a new sense 1, with subsequent senses renumbered: 'In a subtile manner; thinly; not densely.'

211. **SUBTILTY** Added: 'exility'.

212. **SURGEON** Johnson uses only *chirurgeon* in his definitions.

213. **SWELL** Added: a new sense 5, 'To be turgid. Used of style', with subsequent senses renumbered.

214. **SWILL** Added: 'to swell with plenitude'.

215. **SYCAMINE** Added: 'The sycamore of Scripture is not the same with ours'.

216. **TARDITY** and **TARDINESS** This is the order of entries in the dictionary, **TARDINESS** after **TARDITY.**

217. **TASTE** Added: a new sense 4, 'To obtain pleasure from', with the remaining sense renumbered. Also, in *v.n.*, sense 4 is deleted, and in sense 8 'enjoyment' is replaced by 'to be enjoyed'.

218. **TERRACE** Added: a sense 2, 'A balcony; an open gallery'.

219. **THE** Added: a new sense 4, with following sense renumbered: 'It is used by way of consequential reference'.

220. **THRAPPLE** Added: 'We say rather *throttle*'.

221. **TOAD** Added to the beginning of the definition: 'A paddock'. Replaced: 'I believe truly' by 'perhaps without reason'.

222. **TOLL** Added: 'or perhaps to invite'.

223. **TONGUE** Added: a new sense 4, 'Power of articulate utterance', with following senses renumbered. Sense 6 reads: 'Speech as opposed to thoughts or action.'

224. **TOOT** Added: a sense 2, 'It was used in a contemptuous sense, which I do not fully understand.' The illustrative quotation is from Howel: 'This writer should wear a tooting horn.'

225. **TORE** The *Oxford English Dictionary* defines as 'Long coarse grass remaining in the field in winter or spring', but offers no etymology.

226. **TRUCKLE** This ordering after **TRUCKLEBED** is as found in the dictionary.

227. **TYMPANY** Added: 'the wind dropsy'.

228. **VENDIBLY** Added as a new entry.

229. **VILLANY** Added: 'gross atrociousness'. Added to sense 2: 'In this sense it has a plural'.

230. **VITIOUS** Added: 'It is used of persons and practices'.

231. **UN** He is not exaggerating: the examples take up some 130 columns. The second paragraph has been taken from the fourth edition. Despite Johnson's attempt to distinguish *in-* and *un-*, several words later switched usage, as the selection of entries illustrates, and as he notices himself in such cases as **UNCAPABLE** and **UNDETERMINATENESS**.

232. **UNCAPABLE** Added: 'Now more frequently *incapable*'.

233. **UNDETERMINATENESS** Added: 'We say more regularly *indeterminateness* and *indetermination*'.

234. **UNGRAMMATICAL** Added as a new entry.

235. **UNSOPHISTICATED** Added: 'not counterfeit'.

236. **VOLCANO** Note the use of an apostrophe to mark plural, in a word ending in a vowel.

237. **WHIST** (interjection) Added: 'or, put to silence'.

238. **WHIST** (noun) Added: 'vulgarly pronounced *whisk*'. The definition shows the influence of the preceding entry.

239. **WILL** Added: 'or not be, or not be done'.

240. **WORD** Added to sense 5: 'oral expression; living speech'. Added to sense 7: 'order'. Added to sense 9: 'purpose expressed'.

241. **X** Johnson was wrong (see Introduction, n. 3).

242. **Y** This paragraph added from the fourth edition.

243. **YES** Added: a sense 2, 'It is a word of enforcement: even so; not only so, but more'.

244. **YEW** Added: 'used for bows, and therefore planted in churchyards'.

245. **Z** The last sentence is in the fourth edition only.